ENCYCLOPEDIA OF
JEWISH FOOD

GIL MARKS

Houghton Mifflin Harcourt
Boston   New York

To my parents, Beverly and Harold Marks for their love and support

Published by Houghton Mifflin Harcourt Publishing Company

Published simultaneously in Canada

For information about permission to reproduce selections from this book,
write to Permissions, Houghton Mifflin Harcourt Publishing Company,
215 Park Avenue South, New York, New York 10003.

www.hmhco.com

The information contained in this book is not intended to serve as a
replacement for professional medical advice. Any use of the information in this book
is at the reader's discretion. The author and the publisher specifically disclaim any
and all liability arising directly or indirectly from the use or application of any information
contained in this book. A health care professional should be consulted regarding
your specific situation.

Library of Congress Cataloging-in-Publication Data:

Marks, Gil.
Encyclopedia of Jewish food / Gil Marks.
    p. cm.
Includes bibliographical references and index.
ISBN 978-0-470-39130-3 (cloth)
1. Jewish cookery.   2. Cookery, International.   I. Title.
TX724.M31947 2010
641.5'676—dc22   2010000112

Printed in the United States of America

CRNC 10 9 8 7 6 5 4 3 2

4500564868

CONTENTS

ACKNOWLEDGMENTS

This book owes an enormous debt to many people, both in America and abroad. Among those who shared their recipes, ideas, comments, and time with me are Adam Anik and Annie Wright, Stephen Anchin, Dalia Carmel and Hebert Goldstein, Michelle Comet, Lillian Cooper, Rae Dayan, Louise Defez, Poopa Dweck, Diane Feldman, Sharon First, Israel Fridman, Julie Goell, Yochanan and Janet Gool, Liselotte Gorlin, Sheilah Kaufman, Sol Kirschenbaum, Phyllis Koegel, Emile de Vidas Levy, Lily Weiss Levinson, Barry List, Menachem Lubinsky, Paranavithana Ruwan Manjula, Faye Reichwald, Aaron and Laya Scholar, Stanley Allan Sherman, Mathilde Turiel, Eva Weiss, Stan Zimmerman, and David and Dr. Cynthia Zimm.

Very special thanks go to my family—Beverly and Harold Marks, Rabbi William and Sharon Altshul, Rabbi Elli and Dr. Efrat Zipporah Schorr, Moshe Raphael Schorr, Adira Tova Schorr, Meira Bracha Schorr, Nechemia Yitzchak Schorr, Penina Miriam Schorr, Rabbi Asher Yaakov and Anat Altshul, Shira Tifara Altshul, Talia Adi Altshul, Rabbi Naftali and Ora Rivka Derovan, Elchanan Matanya Derovan, Shiri Tehila Derovan, Esther Chana Altshul, Aryeh Dov and Zahava Altshul, Emunah Altshul, Merav Shalva Altshul, Adam and Eliana Bracha Pomerantz, Rabbi Jeffrey and Shari Marks, Shlomo Yosef Marks, Miriam Malka Marks, Efrayim Marks, Tehila Marks, Ashira Marks, Rivka Leah Marks, Rabbi Arthur and Aviva Marks, Rivka Marks, Moshe Marks, Leah Marks, Shmuel Marks, Ahron Marks, Yeshai Marks, Yakov Marks, Daniel Marks, Devora Marks, Rachel Marks, Rabbi Labby and Carol Vegh, Yosef and Chana Tzipora Steinberg, Dovid Steinberg, Menashe and Shifra Miriam Berger, Batsheva Bracha Berger, Avrohom Boruch Vegh, Elisheva Vegh, Yisroel Vegh, Adina Rivka Vegh, Moshe Yakov Vegh, Akiva Shabsi Vegh, and Menachem Meir Vegh—who bore the brunt of my culinary development and experimentation.

Very special thanks go to my dear friend and agent, Rita Rosenkranz, for her perseverance and counsel.

I want to express my gratitude to all the people at John Wiley & Sons involved in the production of this book. Most especially I want to thank my editor, Linda Ingroia, for her professionalism, enthusiasm, encouragement, insight, and advice; the *Encyclopedia of Jewish Food* sprang from Linda's vision and trust in me. I would like to thank Alda Trabucchi, the production editor for her attention to detail and care with keeping this book on schedule, Jeff Faust for his beautiful cover design, Deb Glasserman for an attractive interior design that makes so much information enjoyable to read, and Micaela Walker for her diligent photo research.

Miriam Rubin not only served as a skilled line editor, but also a confidant and counsel during the editing stage. My gratitude also goes to Carrie Bachman for handling the publicity with cheer and dedication.

I also want to acknowledge the hundreds of people I have interviewed and cooked with from Jewish communities around the world for their insights, recipes, and memories of Jewish food from their perspective. All these people were indispensable in transforming a two-decade dream into reality.

PHOTO CREDITS

INTRODUCTION

"But when from a long-distant past nothing subsists, after the people are dead, after the things are broken and scattered, taste and smell alone, more fragile but more enduring, more unsubstantial, more persistent, more faithful, remain poised a long time, like souls, remembering, waiting, hoping, amid the ruins of all the rest; and bear unflinchingly, in the tiny and almost impalpable drop of their essence, the vast structure of recollection."

—Marcel Proust, *Swann's Way* (1913)

To any individual or community, food is more than merely the fuel sustaining life and more than a matter of sensory stimulation. Culinary habits are an expression of a community's history and culture, an accumulation and expression of its environmental influences, experiences, conventions, beliefs, aspirations, and behavior. Food is an enduring element of individual and collective memory. Like its history and culture, each community's food is distinctive. It is a part of and a window to who a community is, how that community came to be, how it exists at a particular moment in time, and what it values in the present and hopes for in the future. No other aspect of existence more closely touches and reveals a community's life—both its everyday routines and its periods of celebration—than food. The contents of the dining table, engendered by a myriad of environmental, technological, demographic, and cultural influences, bespeak the experiences, capabilities, and sensibilities of the population. To know a community is to know its food.

Jewish life is a series of moments of ritual and tradition, bearing evocative symbolism and crucial life lessons; these experiences fill our existence with security, connection, continuity, and meaning. Associated with these Jewish rituals and traditions is food. Jewish food is a matter of affection, necessity, identity, and ritual. It is viewed as a source of both physical and spiritual sustenance. Food is essential to the observation of the Sabbath and Jewish festivals, establishing and enhancing the spirit of the day. Through food Jews internalize each holiday. For many assimilated Jews, food remains one of or sometimes the only anchor to Jewish culture. Food is an essential part of the collective memory that connects all Jews to their ancestors as well as to contemporary Jews. The accumulation as a whole of current Jewish culinary habits tells the story of the Jewish people over the past two and a half millennia, a tale of unique and influential culinary transformation and transmission.

DIFFERENCES AND DIVERSITY

What Jews eat today bears little or no relation to the food prepared in biblical Israel, for it was in the Diaspora that modern Jewish cooking came to be. The central feature of Jewish cooking in the Diaspora has been adaptation. In every location in which they settled, Jews adopted and modified local dishes, adapting foods to their dietary laws, lifestyle, and tastes—often improving them in the process—while symbiotically sharing their traditional dishes and culinary touches with their new neighbors. The dishes, ingredients, techniques, cooking utensils, and food rituals in the homes of Jews generally reflected their social and cultural milieu. When Jews fled an area due to persecution or poverty, they carried their foods to new homes, thereby repeating the process of gradually adopting new fare while spreading their own culinary wealth to many diverse locales. Thus historically the Jewish role in cuisine was never innovation per se, but rather transforming and transferring, processes occurring over and over throughout the past two millennia and continuing today.

American Jews, who are primarily descended from eastern European immigrants, generally associate only their ancestors' customs and foods with being Jewish. In a similar egocentric vein, Americans tend to divide the Jewish world between two European groups—Ashkenazim who originated in Franco-Germany and Sephardim who originated in Iberia—who were forced from their respective homelands and subsequently became the two largest and most widespread forms of Jewish culture. As a result, the sizable Jewish ethnic groups of Mizrachim (Easterners), such as Yemenites (Taimanim) and Persians, are frequently subsumed under the label of Sephardim, while Italians (Italkim) are often tagged as either Ashkenazim or Sephardim. Yet the Jewish communities of Persia, Yemen, and Italy predate those of Iberia and Franco-Germany, and all of these communities produced cultures different from those to which they are mistakenly ascribed. In actuality, a mosaic of enduring Jewish cultural communities of varying sizes and antiquity grew up across the globe—including in Afghanistan, Azerbaijan, Ethiopia, Georgia, Greece (Romaniotes), India (Calcutta, Cochin, and Mumbai), Iran (Persia), Iraq, Italy, Kurdistan, Tajikistan, Turkmenistan, Uzbekistan (Bukhara), and Yemen—based on neither the Ashkenazic nor Sephardic models, but on their own unique histories, customs, and cuisines.

Further complicating matters, even the two predominant forms of Jewish cuisine are far from monolithic. Among the areas in which refugees from Spain and Portugal settled were the Levant (Israel, Lebanon, Jordan, and Syria), the Maghreb (Algeria, Morocco, and Tunisia), Bulgaria, Egypt, Greece, Libya, Turkey, and western Europe (England, France, and Holland). Jews from Franco-Germany relocated to Alsace, Austria, the Baltic States (Latvia, Lithuania, and Estonia), Belarus, Bessarabia, the Czech Republic, Galicia (now southern Poland), Germany, Hungary, Poland, Romania, Slovakia, and Ukraine. In their various new homelands, Sephardic and Ashkenazic food developed differently.

Most of the Sephardim settled in the Mediterranean region and their food retained a commonality. Fifteenth-century Spanish Christian writers noted the distinctive marks of Jewish cooking—long-simmered stews, the pervasiveness of vegetables, the use of olive oil for frying, the frequent appearance of fish, and the prevalence of onions and garlic in meat dishes. Today, these culinary practices, now emblematic of the Mediterranean diet, remain the basis of Sephardic cookery. Yet Sephardic food from the Maghreb is quite different from that of western Europe, the Levant, the Balkans, or even northeastern Africa. Since it was primarily in the Ottoman Empire that the Spanish-Portuguese refugees found haven, the synthesis of Iberian and Ottoman cuisines emerged as the most conspicuous form of Sephardic cooking.

The areas in which the Ashkenazim settled had similar produce, or lack thereof, and there was constant interaction between these communities through expulsions, trade, rabbinic discourse, and marriages.

Jews living in the original home of the Ashkenazim in northern France and southwestern Germany demonstrated none of the Slavic influences of eastern Ashkenazim. Yet they shared many dishes, customs, and a rabbinic and cultural heritage. Since the ancestors of the majority of Ashkenazim came from the Slavic regions of eastern Europe (Poland, Latvia, Lithuania, Slovakia, and Ukraine), it is this form of Ashkenazic cooking that is most widespread and which most Americans associate with Jewish food.

There were once small Jewish communities in other countries, such as in Kaifeng and Canton in China, but the descendants of those Jews do not actively identify themselves as Jewish and do not participate in Jewish cultural life. Therefore, although American Jews demonstrate a pronounced love of Chinese food, Chinese dishes per se are not part of cultural Jewish food.

Consequently, defining Jewish cuisine is not a simple task. Borscht, brisket, buckwheat, and bagels comprised a prominent part of the Jewish diet in Poland; couscous, tagines, lamb, and salads dominated the menu in Morocco; and bulgur, *shorabit khodar* (vegetable and legume soups), and *kibbeh* (ground meat dishes) were basic in the Levant. The cooking fat of choice was schmaltz in northern Europe, olive oil in the Mediterranean region, and lamb's tail fat or sesame oil in central Asia. Even different parts of Poland developed quite distinct gastronomy, each affected by neighboring countries as well as local developments. In addition, the cuisine of urban areas inevitably differed greatly from the rustic dishes of even nearby rural sites, while typically the cookery of one village differed to varying degrees from that of another.

Jews may literally eat anything from the petite madeleines so cherished by Marcel Proust—his mother was a member of an Alsatian Jewish family—to the grilled organs so beloved by James Joyce's classic Irish Jewish character Leopold Bloom. Jewish food may be the meager fare of the impoverished masses that struggled to survive in the shtetlach of the Russian Pale (the only portion of czarist Russia in which Jews were permitted to live, stretching from the Baltic Sea to the Black Sea). Or it can be prepared by Marie-Antonine Carême, one of history's most important chefs—he was regarded as the founder of La Grand Cuisine and his last position was with Baron James de Rothschild in Paris. Some wealthy Jewish families even educated their chefs in the intricacies of kosher cooking and traditional Jewish dishes. After two thousand years of living in almost every country and culture, Jewish cuisine is the cuisine of the world.

IS THERE A JEWISH FOOD?

If food in general is basically fusion, and the foods Jews eat are adopted from their locales and constantly evolving and changing, is there actually such a thing as Jewish food?

Jewish comedians have long based a good deal of their material on food. Humorist Allan Sherman, in his 1962 parody "There Is Nothin' Like a Lox," sang, "We got herring sweet and sour. We got pickles old and young. We got corned beef and salami and a lot of tasty tongue. We got Philadelphia cream cheese in a little wooden box. What ain't we got? We ain't got lox! We got cole slaw, freshly made, and chopped liver, also fresh. And a lot of things to please a man whose name is Moish or Hesh. We got plenty pumpernickel. We got bagels hard as rocks. What ain't we got? We ain't got lox!"

Sherman touched on fare associated with and enjoyed by mid-twentieth-century Ashkenazim in the United States, none of which the Jews really invented or could claim to be exclusively theirs. Around the same time, comedian Lenny Bruce, in one of his better-known routines, ruminated on the contemporary nature of Jewish culture in 1960s America: "If you live in New York or any other big city, you are Jewish. It doesn't matter even if you're Catholic; if you live in New York, you're Jewish. If you live in Butte, Montana, you're going to be goyish even if you're Jewish. Kool-Aid is goyish. Evaporated milk is goyish even if the Jews invented it. Chocolate is Jewish and fudge is goyish. Fruit salad is Jewish. Lime Jell-O is goyish. Lime soda is very goyish. All Drake's cakes are goyish. Pumpernickel is Jewish and, as you know, white bread is very goyish. Instant potatoes, goyish. Black cherry soda's very Jewish, macaroons are very Jewish."

The items that Bruce identified as goyish had superficial style but were lacking in excitement, while the Jewish ones had less panache but more chutzpah. Bruce was taking aim at the Jewish propensity to see the world as starkly divided between Jews and non-Jews, as well as at Jews who were ashamed of their Jewishness in the face of Waspish society in general. Yet Sherman's and Bruce's lists could be revised

to reflect any place or time, past or present, because Jews have always gravitated to and accepted particular items. Certain things, certain foods, "feel" Jewish. Why? Certainly, because they are used by Jews. Yet more than that, particular foods become enmeshed in Jewish life, culture, and identity. Throughout most of history, Jews proved adept at adopting and Judaizing traditions from the non-Jewish societies in which they lived without assimilating into the wider culture.

In particular, over the many centuries, the dietary laws contributed to the survival of the Jewish people; they shaped and defined the Jewish identity and, in the process, helped to determine Jewish fare. Observant Jews could not simply adopt all of the dishes of their new homelands. The dietary laws exclude taboo foods—notably pork (and any mammals that are not ruminants), lard, and shellfish—as well as the mixing of milk and meat. Therefore, Jews replaced these items with others. The dietary laws produced a culinary commonality within each Jewish community, as well as social networks connecting diverse Jewish communities.

In addition, the Jewish lifestyle—shaped by Sabbath prohibitions, holiday traditions, Torah study, and life-cycle events—produced uniquely Jewish dishes that, although usually based on local foods, often manifested similarities to Jewish dishes and customs from other locales. Wine and bread are ubiquitous elements of Sabbath and holiday meals. Fish on the Sabbath is a tradition dating back to at least the time of the Talmud. Hot dishes slow-heated for many hours for Sabbath meals are found in all the Jewish communities. Since many other dishes were prepared ahead to be served cold on the Sabbath, in the days before the advent of artificial refrigeration, vinegar was commonly added as a preservative and often sweeteners and/or raisins were included to counter the acidity of the vinegar. As a result, cold and sweet-and-sour dishes proliferate in the Jewish culinary repertoire throughout the globe. The various Jewish communities incorporate items mentioned in the Bible or suggested by the Talmud—such as almonds, apples, dates, raisins, honey, and wine—as symbolic ingredients in assorted festival dishes. Thus the *plov* (rice pilaf) made by the Jews of Uzbekistan differed from that of their non-Jewish neighbors not only because the Jews omitted butter, but also because they included apples, quinces, and raisins.

Jewish food was all too often the product of poverty and scarcity—housewives endeavored to create filling and flavorful fare from meager supplies and from the least expensive items. Although pricey today, veal, brisket, and fish were once low-cost items and, consequently, emerged as prominent Jewish foods. Even in times of abundance, food retained its importance for Jews. Notably, for Conversos (forcibly converted Iberian Jews, also called Marrano-Anusim) living under threat of the Inquisition, Jewish food remained a socializing, unifying, spiritual, and comforting presence, for which it was worth risking their lives and well-being.

Jewish food is witness to the strength and management skills of untold generations of women who somehow managed to feed their families, frequently also while serving as the wage earner. Food is an expression of affection, a true and abiding gift savored in intimacy. Jewish mothers are legendary for using food as an expression of love. Much more important than the praise a meal may earn are the intangible dividends involved in the act of transforming and enhancing a simple meal or a major occasion through foods. Just as humor is a defense mechanism—surely the Jewish sense of humor emerged in part as a protective tactic—food can be a defense mechanism too, sheltering and investing the Jewish community. "*Ess, ess, mein kindt*" (eat, eat, my child) and "*ess a bisel eppis*" (eat a little something), two Yiddish directives repeated by Ashkenazic mothers for countless generations, were not only invitations to partake of physical nourishment, but also expressions of love, concern, fear, and a desire for survival. This behavior is certainly not limited to Ashkenazim; it is repeated in other languages, by Persian, Afghan, and Ethiopian Jewish mothers.

All the while, Jews maintained their historical role of transformation and transmission, a process continuing to this very day. By the end of the twentieth century, Ashkenazic favorites, not to mention the word nosh, had become a ubiquitous component of mainstream American gastronomy and parlance across the country. Meanwhile, American Jews ate standard American fare from hamburgers and hot dogs to salsa and sushi. Today, schmaltz is rarer in the average Ashkenazic kitchen than sushi. Jewish food has never been and is not now either monolithic or static.

Though varied and ever changing, there is a "Jewish food" beyond the generic fare consumed by a community at any one time or place. Jewish food evokes the spirit of a Jewish community as it celebrates the Sabbath, festivals, and life-cycle events. Jewish food is a dish that possesses the power to nostalgically conjure up the joy of millions of Sabbath dinners or resounds with the memory of the myriad of ghettos, shtetlach, and *mellahs* (Jewish quarters in Morocco) in which for millennia Jews struggled to eke out a living and raise their children as Jews. Jewish food is Ashkenazim serving honey-dipped apple slices, tzimmes, and *lekach* (honey cake) on Rosh Hashanah; stuffed cabbage, knishes, and strudel on Sukkot; potato latkes and jelly doughnuts on Hanukkah; kreplach and hamantaschen on Purim; matza balls and *chremslach* (matza pancakes) on Passover; and blintzes and cheesecake on Shavuot. It is Sephardim serving *keftes de espinaca* (spinach patties), *lubiya* (black-eyed peas), and *membrillo* (poached quinces) on Rosh Hashanah; *sakayu* (eggplant casserole) and *dolmas* (stuffed vegetables) on Sukkot; *shamlias* (fried pastry strips) and *bimuelos* (yeast doughnuts) on Hanukkah; *sambusak* (savory turnovers), *foulares* (hard-boiled eggs wrapped in pastry), and *oznei haman* (Haman's ear pastries) on Purim; *keftes de prasa* (leek patties), *minas* (matza pies), and *torta de las reyes* (flourless orange torte) on Passover; and *spanikopita* (spinach pie) and *sutlach* (rice-flour pudding) on Shavuot. It is food elevated to a special status, or perhaps sanctified, by its adoption into and enduring use in the cultural and/or religious life of a Jewish community. It is tradition.

WHY IS JEWISH FOOD IMPORTANT?

Rituals are reassuring—they tell people that things are the same as they always were, although different. The predictable presence of Jewish foods on the table, the clear-cut repetition from week to week and from holiday to holiday, provides a new generation with steady links to the past. It also provides links to the future, as well as a security blanket for the present, giving members of a new generation the sense of who they are and where they fit in a frequently unpredictable world. Cooking and eating together as a group, such as at celebratory feasts and synagogue community meals, allows for bonding, fellowship, building communal identity, and sharing knowledge.

There are some foods that each time we prepare or eat them we cannot help but think of our mother and perhaps grandmothers. A simple bite of matza at the Passover Seder transcends time, linking us through the generations back to the Israelites still struggling under Egyptian bondage and to the diverse Jewish communities of today. Even as we age, or perhaps especially then, we remember the smells of our mother's kitchen, the tastes of her table, the foods lovingly handed down from generation to generation. And even as Jewish foods are redefined and hybridized, the value and meanings invested in them endure, becoming relevant to the present generation as they are passed on to the next. Jewish foods remain an intrinsic part of our individual and communal identity, helping us deal with change and loss, and helping us to transmit our values and hopes to the future.

Unfortunately, the end of the second millennium proved devastating to many Jewish communities. Almost all of the ancient ones, some dating back two thousand to twenty-five hundred years, experienced decimation or outright destruction. The Nazi onslaught laid waste to the great Ashkenazic, Sephardic, and Italian centers of Europe and the subsequent Communist control of eastern Europe, for all practical purposes, finished off much of the remaining population. Most of the Jewish communities of the Muslim world were swept away in the face of the nationalism and hatred that emerged in response to the rise of Zionism and as a result of the spread of Nazi philosophy to some Arabs. Assimilation and emigration spelled the end of many other Jewish communities.

Today, once-vibrant Jewish communities exist only in the customs of their descendants living primarily in the two largest extant Jewish centers—Israel and America.

If Jewish communities no longer exist in their place of origin, why are their customs and foods important? Jews possess a sense of history and an intimate connection to that history as part of a diverse, scattered group. The constructive use of historical memory reverberates though the Bible and has directed Jewish life ever since. Judaism transforms historical events both advantageous and horrendous into a stimulus for future good—for personal growth, for family bonding, for community building, and for social justice. The identity and experience of any individual Jew is not based solely on a single family or local community, but rather on the entire Jewish history and people. The traditional Jewish term is *Clal Yisrael* (commu-

nity/entirety of Israel). And food is a major part of the Jewish historical memory.

The incomparable aggregation known as Jewish food inspires and shapes the communities that today eat, enjoy, and depend on these dishes, as it has for generations. Understanding what these foods are and how they came to be enables us to better comprehend and appreciate the collective Jewish past and present, while informing the future. Through understanding traditional dishes we can get a taste of the scattered Jewish communities, their nature, history, and customs. Those who cherish a culture, cherish its narratives, and thereby gain a sense of possession and inclusion by learning about its food. Sharing disparate dishes from different communities bolsters a sense of unity, understanding, and inspiration.

ABOUT THE ENCYCLOPEDIA OF JEWISH FOOD

The *Encyclopedia of Jewish Food* is a cultural odyssey of more than twenty-five hundred years, exploring and embracing traditional Jewish foods from across the globe—their history, etymology, cultural and religious significance, continuing usage in Jewish life, and relationship to the wider culture. It is a unique work in scope, content, and method, drawn from my diverse background and interests.

Regardless of the protests of some chauvinists, political opportunists, and fanatics, nothing in gastronomy is authentic, pure, or exclusive. Culture cannot be stolen nor does it develop in a vacuum. Rather, over the course of time, cultures continually and consistently borrow and learn from one another. Vibrant cultures have always adopted the best from others, including, of course, food. Cuisine has no political allegiance or fidelity. As always, Jews were frequently directly or indirectly involved in the spread and introduction of many foods and dishes.

We know much about Jewish dining habits and culinary customs over the past two millennia from numerous references in rabbinic literature and sometimes non-Jewish sources. Questions about kashrut and *halacha* (Jewish law) remain a constant. Throughout the ages, rabbis have dealt with dietary issues in great detail, so we can glean much of what Jews ate and how they prepared it by studying the Talmud, Midrash, rabbinic literature, and responsa.

Jews did not begin to record their recipes in books

until the nineteenth century and, therefore, the exact ingredients and techniques of Talmudic-era and medieval fare frequently remain unknown. Some insight can be garnered by comparisons with medieval non-Jewish cookery and with modern descendants of venerable dishes. Jewish cookbooks from the past two centuries open a window to that time. Even more so, home cooks willing to share the knowledge and experiences of their mothers and grandmothers—a chain of family transmission ensuring stability and authenticity—served as my primary resources for Jewish recipes and culinary habits. I relied on recipes provided by my own extended family as the basis for much of the traditional eastern European fare, then questioned friends, acquaintances, non-Ashkenazic in-laws, Israeli taxi drivers, and anyone who would share their culinary treasures and insights. I also pored over various sources, searching for any additional traditional recipes or variations and food history. Fortunately, the New York City metropolitan area and Israel serve as home to immigrant groups from across the globe and a wealth of culinary lore.

For the past twenty five years, I have amassed in my computer every relevant recipe—after trying them, typically several times, in my home kitchen—and bit of food information coming my way. I also researched various topics, exploring an array of Jewish foods and traditions. I had long wanted to use this data in a reference book on food, but was unsure of when or how. Then in 2007, my editor, Linda Ingroia, and I were discussing the follow-up to our previous successful collaboration, *Olive Trees and Honey*, and she suggested, "You're a walking encyclopedia of food, so how about an actual encyclopedia?" I certainly needed no convincing. This was a dream assignment.

I ambitiously wanted the *Encyclopedia of Jewish Food* to be both a detailed reference source as well as a practical cookbook. I began checking my information for accuracy and expanding and organizing it into an A-to-Z work exploring traditional foodstuffs and traditions from Jewish communities across the globe. The most difficult part was reducing it into a single manageable volume. The result is more than 650 entries of global scope. A few are only brief explanations,

most consist of about a page in length, while I devoted several pages to very important and international topics—including challah, matza, and Sabbath stews. I was able to include entries on various Jewish holidays and rituals and their related food traditions. I could not, of course, include every traditional Jewish recipe or foodstuff. I choose those things that I consider the most representative, meaningful, and pertinent. A particular dish is included for its historical or sociological relevance and a corresponding recipe is attached to illuminate the entry. I strove to provide adequate space for the mosaic of Jewish communities across the globe for which I have much respect and affection. I wanted these dishes to provide a sense of an individual Jewish community and its cuisine and mindset. I spent much time reading about and discussing with individuals from various communities their perspectives and tried to envision myself a member of those groups in order to include those items held dear and of particular cultural and culinary significance.

The *Encyclopedia of Jewish Food* is my individual voice and is based upon my erudition, experiences, and enthusiasm. I have intended it to be as comprehensive, accurate, and readable as possible. I trust that I was able to sufficiently and correctly reflect the life and history of Jewish food. However, one of the problems with food history is the number of misnomers and outright mistakes in documentation. If I have repeated any of them or made any omissions, please let me know in order that I can correct them at gil_marks@hotmail.com. This is a serious reference and recipe book, but is also intended as a smorgasbord (or *mezze*)—enough for everyone to enjoy.

The collection of information and traditional recipes in *Encyclopedia of Jewish Food*—the influential and integral parts of ancient and modern Jewish history and culture—tells the story of the past twenty-five hundred years of *Clal Yisrael*. In addition to testifying to the past and present, a community's food also influences what it will become. In the words of Jean Anthelme Brillat-Savarin in *The Physiology of Taste*, "The destiny of nations depends upon what and how they eat." By our food, we declare and affirm who we are and who we want to be.

TIMELINE OF JEWISH HISTORY

c. 1230 BCE The Merneptah Stele, a large black granite slab commemorating the victories of Pharaoh Merneptah, son of Ramses II, contains the earliest extra-biblical reference to Israel.

c. 1000 David captures Jerusalem and makes it the capital of his kingdom. The House of David will reign for about 424 years under twenty-one kings.

c. 1000 A 6-by-6½-inch pottery shard, discovered in 2008 in the remains of a fortified provincial Judean town (modern-day Khirbet Qeiyafa) near the Elah Valley and the site of David's battle with Goliath, bears the earliest extant Hebrew text (written in ink by a trained scribe in Proto-Canaanite script).

c. 960 The First Temple is built.

c. 925 Gezer northwest of Jerusalem, contains the second-earliest Hebrew inscription.

c. 922 The northern tribes, the Kingdom of Israel, secede from Judah.

722 The northern Kingdom of Israel is destroyed by the Assyrians.

597 Babylonians under Nebuchadnezzar capture Jerusalem and deport thousands of the upper class and craftsmen to Babylon, including the prophet Ezekiel, initiating the Iraqi Jewish community.

586 After King Zedekiah rebels against Nebuchadnezzar, and following a two-year siege, the Babylonians on the ninth day of Av destroy Jerusalem and the First Temple and more Jews are taken to Babylon.

586 or 582 Gedaliah, the governor of Judea appointed by the Babylonians and governing from Mitzpah, north of Jerusalem, is assassinated. In response, the bulk of the remaining Judeans, perhaps 150,0000, are exiled to Babylon, but a group escapes to Egypt, taking the prophet Jeremiah with them, starting the Egyptian Jewish community.

539 Cyrus the Great conquers Babylonia, engendering the Persian Jewish community.

538 Cyrus permits the Jews to return to Israel and rebuild the Temple, although only a small number accept his offer, resurrecting the Jewish community in Israel.

516 The Second Temple is completed.

c. 458 Ezra the Scribe leads a group of 5,000 Jews from Babylon to Israel. Ezra becomes spiritual leader of Judea and part of a new group of 120 sages known as the *Anshei Knesset ha-Gedolah* (Members of the Great Assembly), who strengthen Judaism in the wake of the return to Israel, including recording and sealing the biblical canon into twenty-four books (for some books, this process continues until 100 CE) and instituting formalized prayers and benedictions; this group functions until the death of Shimon ha-Tzaddik (c. 300).

332 Alexander the Great conquers the land of Israel on his way to Egypt. Alexander dies in 323 and in 312 his kingdom is divided among three generals, Israel coming under the control of Ptolemy, who reigns from Alexandria.

167 Antiochus IV Epiphanes outlaws the practice of Judaism and, at the beginning of the Saturnalia festival on the twenty-fifth of Kislev, desecrates the Temple.

164 Led by Mattathias and his five sons, known as the Hasmoneans or Maccabees, a revolt drives the Seleucids from Jerusalem and, exactly three years after its desecration, they rededicate the Temple (Hanukkah). The fight with the Seleucids continues for nearly a quarter of a century.

63 General Pompey intervenes in a Hasmonean civil war and annexes the land of Israel as part of the Roman Empire.

31 Hillel is appointed head (*nasi*) of the Sanhedrin. His descendants retain this position, as leaders of the Israeli Jewish community, for nearly four centuries.

66 The first revolt against Rome begins. At this time there are an estimated 8 million Jews in the world with about 2.5 million in Israel.

70 Following a lengthy siege, on the ninth day of Av, the Romans destroy Jerusalem and burn the wooden parts of the Second Temple. Large numbers of Jews are killed or sold into slavery.

70 Yochanah ben Zakkai reestablishes the Sanhedrin in the city of Yavneh, south of Jaffa. It will move several more times during the Roman period, until finally ending up in 193 in Tiberias, where it is disbanded by the Romans in 425.

73 Masada falls to the Roman army.

c. 130 Rabbi Yosi ha-Galili dies. Until this time, residents of his rabbinic district could eat fowl with dairy, but afterwards the rabbinic prohibition forbidding this practice, supported by Rabbi Akiva, comes into effect.

132–135 Bar Kokhba revolt. Again large numbers of Jews are killed or enslaved.

c. 140 The office of exilarch (Reish Galuta), leader of the Babylonian Jewish community, is established. It is a hereditary position among a lineage from King David.

c. 200 The Mishnah ("review/repetition" in Hebrew) is redacted by Rabbi Judah ha-Nasi, incorporating primary opinions as well as many dissenting opinions on the oral law of sages from the time of the destruction of the Temple; these sages are known as Tannaim (repeaters). The Mishnah is divided by topics into six *sederim* (sections), and each *seder* is subdivided into a total of sixty-three *masechtot* (literally "webs," called tractates).

219 Abba Areka, known as Rav, founds a Talmudic academy in the Babylonian city of Sura, located near a fork in the Euphrates River about forty miles south of modern Baghdad. For nearly eight centuries, the yeshiva will be a predominant spiritual and intellectual center of world Jewry.

259	Judah ben Ezekiel founds an academy in Pumbeditha (present-day Fallujah), along the Euphrates about forty-three miles west of modern Baghdad. It will rival and sometimes surpass Sura. The heads of Sura and Pumbeditha, initially elected by scholars of the academy, serve as the spiritual leaders of Babylonian-Persian Jewry and later, with the decimation of the Israeli Jewish community, of world Jewry.
326	Constantine, who converted to Christianity, moves the capital of the Roman Empire to Byzantium. Anti-Jewish policies accompany the ascendancy of Christianity, producing a dramatic decline in the Jewish community of Israel.
358	Hillel II institutes a set Jewish calendar, the final major act of the Sanhedrin.
c. 368	The discussions on the Mishnah and commentaries of Israeli rabbis after the Mishnah, known as Amoraim (speakers), are compiled in Tiberias. This collection, called the Gemara (Aramaic meaning "study"), together with the Mishnah, forms the Jerusalem Talmud (Hebrew meaning "learning").
425	The *nasi* Gamaliel VI is executed by the Byzantine emperor, who abolishes the position of *nasi* and disbands the Sanhedrin. The center of Jewish spiritual life shifts to Babylon.
450–470	The Sassanid persecution of Jews in Babylon includes shutting down Talmudic academies and the forced conversions of children to Zoroastrianism.
c. 475	The Babylonian Talmud is compiled, consisting of discussions and commentaries of Babylonian and some Israeli scholars after the Mishnah; the text is modified during the following century by rabbis called Savoraim (explainers).
476	The last Roman emperor is deposed. The ensuing five centuries in Europe are known as the Dark Ages. During much of this period, Jewish merchants control most of the international trade between the Christian and Muslim worlds, as well as the Silk Road to eastern Asia.
580	Sassanid repression resumes in Babylon and the academies are shut.
589	Sura and Pumbeditha reopen. The heads of the academies are subsequently appointed by the exilarch and known as *gaon* (from Psalms 47:4, *gaon Ya'akov*, "the pride of Jacob"). The *geonim* hold centralized spiritual authority over world Jewry for about 450 years.
638	Arabs under Omar I capture Jerusalem. The Arab conquest of the Middle East between 624 and 661 eliminates the anti-Jewish leaders of the Levant and Persia. By 650, the vast majority of world Jewry lives under Muslim rule. The Covenant of Omar establishes the Jews' status among Muslims as *dhimmi* (a protected subordinate community). In some areas and times, Jews are treated well, while in others they face severe repression and humiliations.
711	The Moors conquer Spain.
755	Umayyad rule in Spain produces the golden age of Spanish Jewry, a period of tolerance, economic prosperity, and intellectual and cultural achievement. This period comes to an end in 1146 when the fanatical Almohades, a Berber confederation from Morocco, conquer the country.
761	Anan ben David, disgruntled at being passed over for the exilarch, rejects rabbinic Judaism and founds what would become the Karaite sect, based on a literal interpretation of the Bible.
*800	Charlemagne is crowned emperor of the Holy Roman Empire, encompassing western Europe eastward to the Elbe River and southeastward to the Danube River. The initial growth of Ashkenazim begins.
857	Amram Gaon issues the first *siddur* (prayer book), including the first recorded Passover Haggadah.
934	The emergence of the fanatical Persian Buyid dynasty, which soon controls most of Persia and Babylon, oppresses the area's Jews. A series of events in the Islamic world produces a major shift in demographics and influence, as European Jewry begins to take precedence. Also at this time, taxation and denial of land in Muslim and Christian areas leads Jews to a shift from agriculture to urban locations and commerce and crafts.
1038	Hai Gaon of Pumbeditha dies, ending the Geonic period and centralized religious authority in Judaism and beginning the period of the Rishonim (early sages), in which local scholars serve as spiritual leaders.
1040	Rabbi Sholomo ben Yitzhak (Rashi), the essential Talmudic commentator, is born in Troyes, France.
c. 1080	Fanatical Almoravides outlaw Judaism in Spain. Jewish life in Iberia subsequently shifts to the Christian areas in the north, where Jews are tolerated and secure until 1390. During this time, Sephardim continue to develop a sophisticated cuisine.
1096–1099	During the First Crusades, Jews are massacred in the Rhine Valley and Germany and Israel. The Crusades end the dominant role of Jews in international trade.
1105	Following the death of Rashi, his sons-in-law, grandsons, and students, encompassing about two hundred rabbis in France and Germany, known as the Tosafists (additions), explain the Talmud and Rashi's commentary, forming the bedrock of future Ashkenazic scholarship.
1135	Rabbi Moses ben Maimon (Maimonides/Rambam) is born. His family flees Spain in 1148 due to the fanatical Almohade sect. His seminal work, *Mishneh Torah*, finished c. 1178 in Egypt, is the first compendium of the full range of Jewish law. Maimonides, in his role as physician, is the first Jewish source to mention chicken soup.
1144	The first known blood libel against Jews occurs in Norwich, England. Many more will follow in many parts of Europe.
1147–1149	The Second Crusade repeats violence against Jews and damages Ashkenazic life in France and Germany.
1187	Saladin captures Jerusalem from the Crusaders.
1189–1192	The Third Crusade fails to retake Jerusalem from Saladin, while the Jews of England suffer.
1215	The Fourth Council of the Lateran requires Jews to wear special clothing, most notably the Judenhut (a pointed hat or cloth hood) and yellow badge.

1240	Mongols and Tatars (Turkic peoples incorporated into the Mongols) invade Ukraine and, in the following year, southern Poland, Hungary, and Romania.
1254	Jews are expelled from France by Louis IX, ending the Tosafist era. Ashkenazic life shifts to central Europe and increasingly to eastern Europe. For the ensuing two centuries, Germany will be the predominant influence on Ashkenazic cookery, including gefilte fish, *gedempte fleisch* (pot roast), *klops* (meat loaf/meatballs), kugels, *knaidlach* (dumplings), tzimmes, *kichlach* (cookies), and *lekach* (honey cake).
c. 1286	Moses de Leon of Guadalajara, Spain, publishes the Zohar, which he attributes to the Tannanic rabbi Shimon bar Yochai. The Zohar, an immense commentary on the Bible in the Midrashic tradition, is the central work of Kabbalah (Jewish mysticism).
1290	The Jews are expelled from England.
1298	The Rindfleisch massacres begin in Germany, decimating its Jewish communities.
c. 1300	The first mention of pasta in a European Jewish source outside of Spain and Sicily appears in Italy in the writings of Kalonymous ben Kalonymous, who mentions "macaroni and tortelli" (filled pasta).
1333	Casimir the Great becomes king of Poland. During his reign, he invites Jews to settle in Poland and issues a series of charters protecting them.
1347	The Black Death begins in Europe as do attacks on Jews for poisoning wells. Subsequently, the center of Ashkenazic culture will be in eastern Europe and Ashkenazic foods will become increasingly Slavic, including borscht, blintzes, *chrain* (horseradish), pirogen, knishes, *kishke* (stuffed derma), and *kasha varnishkes* (buckwheat groats with noodles).
1453	Constantinople is conquered by the Ottoman Turks, ending the Byzantine Empire and bringing relief to the Jews from Byzantine oppression.
1475	The first printed Hebrew book to bear a date, the Bible with Rashi's commentary, is published in Reggio, Italy. This follows the world's first printed book, Johannes Gutenberg's Bible, published in 1452.
1480	The Spanish Inquisition is established.
1492	More than 200,000 Jews are expelled from Spain on the ninth day of Av (another 200,000 remain behind as Conversos and another 200,000 had been murdered in the preceding century). In the following year, 137,000 Jews are expelled from Sicily, which is under Spanish rule. Most Sephardim settle in the Ottoman Empire. Oppression of Sephardim and Mizrachim produces a major shift in demographics—before 1492, there were around 700,000 Mizrachim, 400,000 Sephardim, and 150,000 Ashkenazim. Within two centuries, there were about 1 million Jews in Muslim lands and 1 million Ashkenazim, and the Ashkenazic numbers would continue to grow.
1497	Portugal forces Jews to convert.
1506	Tatars from the Ural Mountains and Crimea begin a series of incursions into eastern Europe lasting for more than a century, killing and enslaving many people. Among the foods and techniques introduced by the Tatars during this time are stuffed cabbage, filled pasta (kreplach, *pelmeni*, and pirogen), buckwheat (*tatarki* in Yiddish), and lacto-fermentation (pickles, sauerkraut, and *rosl* beets), transforming eastern Ashkenazic cookery.
1516	Venice, Italy, establishes the first ghetto.
1516	The Ottomans defeat the Mamluks and take control of the land of Israel. Suleiman rebuilds the crumbling walls of Jerusalem, but the city inside declines under Ottoman neglect and misrule.
1520	The first printing of the Talmud is published by Daniel Bomberg of Venice, with a layout still generally used today featuring the commentaries of Rashi and the Tosafists.
1526	In the Battle of Mohács, the Ottoman Empire captures most of Hungary; the Ottomans retreat only in 1687. During this time, they introduce many cooking techniques, foods, and dishes to central Europe, including paprika, *pogácsa* (cookies/biscuits), *palacsinta* (crepes), and *yufka* (strudel dough).
1529	The siege of Vienna ends, halting the Ottoman advance into Europe at its farthest point.
1564	Rabbi Joseph Caro's *Shulchan Arukh*, a compendium of Jewish law from the Sephardic perspective, is published in Venice. In 1571, the glosses of Rabbi Moses Isserles of Kraków are appended to the *Shulchan Arukh*, making it the preeminent guide to Jewish law among both Sephardim and Ashkenazim. The *Shulchan Arukh* marks the end of the period of the Rishonim and beginning of the period of scholars of lesser authority, the Acharonim (later Sages).
1610	The first mention of bagels is found in the records of the Kraków Jewish community. In another four centuries, the bagel will become the most famous of Polish Jewish foods.
1648	The Chmelnitski pogroms devastate Polish and Ukrainian Jewry, killing about 100,000 Jews and uprooting hundreds of communities. Before the massacres, the Jewish population of Poland and the Baltic States was about 450,000.
1648	Shabbatai Tzvi declares himself the messiah and his followers spread through many Sephardic and Ashkenazic communities; in 1666, when threatened by the Ottoman sultan, he converts to Islam. In the wake of Chmelnitski and Shabbatai Tzvi, Ashkenazim experience a profound religious and spiritual collapse.
1654	Twenty-three Sephardic refugees from Recife, Brazil, arrive in New Amsterdam. In the following year, the Dutch West India Company permits them to settle in New Amsterdam and they become the first Jewish community in North America. For the following century and a half, Sephardim constitute the predominant force in the American Jewish community.
1655	Oliver Cromwell readmits Jews to England.
1683	The Battle of Vienna is the turning point in the Ottomans' 250-year advance into Europe. Crescent-shaped breads and pastries, connoting the symbol on the Ottoman flag, become widespread in Austria.
c. 1740	Israel ben Eliezer, the Baal Shem Tov, founds Chasidism. Within a few decades, his mystical movement is adopted

by two-thirds of eastern European Jews. Many other European Jews at this time, however, turn to the Haskalah (Enlightenment), which stresses rationality and a scientific approach to religion and engenders a wider engagement of Jews with the non-Jewish world. In the following decades, a number of Chasidim as well as their religious opponents (Mitnagdim) move to Israel to observe a more holy life.

1772	In the First Partition of Poland by Austria, Russia, and Prussia, more than 1,200,000 Jews are incorporated under Russian rule.
1790	Scottish explorer James Bruce reports the existence in Ethiopia of a group of black Jews known as Falashas and calling themselves Beta Israel (House of Israel).
1791	Russia establishes the Pale of Settlement, stretching from the Baltic Sea to the Black Sea, the only area of Russia open to Jews. At this time, there are about 1 million Jews in Muslim lands and 1.5 million Ashkenazim, most residing in the Pale.
1802	The first sugar beet–refining factory opens in Silesia, Germany (now southwestern, Poland). Soon sugar becomes, for the first time, an important component of Ashkenazic food, especially in Galicia (now southern Poland).
c. 1830	Political oppression and lack of economic opportunities lead to the large-scale immigration of German Jews to the United States. Germans remain the predominant force in the American Jewish community until overwhelmed by the arrival of millions of eastern Europeans in the early twentieth century.
1834	The Spanish Inquisition finally ends.
1838	Isaac Singer of Alsace introduces the first machine for rolling out matza dough.
1839	A two-year famine in Ukraine and Poland followed by a short cooling period in Europe lead to potatoes being widely planted and consumed in the area for the first time. Potatoes become the mainstay of the eastern Ashkenazic diet and contribute to the subsequent tremendous population growth. The potato kugel and latke soon become iconic Ashkenazic foods.
1840	The Ottomans retake Jerusalem. A census four years later shows 7,120 Jews in the city along with 5,760 Muslims and 3,390 Christians.
c. 1844	The Shamouti, a mutation of a native Israeli orange, appears. In three decades, this sweet, juicy fruit with extraordinary shipping abilities will become known as the Jaffa orange.
1860	Mishkenot Sha'ananim, funded by Moses Montefiore and Judah Touro, becomes the first Jerusalem Jewish neighborhood built outside of the city's walls.
1870	Israel Rokeach opens a kosher soap factory in Kovno, Lithuania, using the color blue for dairy and red for meat. He is the first person to use chemistry in the pursuit of kosher observance, and his soap becomes the first product under rabbinical certification.
1878	Petach Tikva, the first modern Jewish agricultural settlement in Israel, is founded northeast of Jaffa.
1881	The assassination of Czar Alexander II sparks government pogroms, killing tens of thousands and leading to a major

wave of Jewish immigration to America and Israel, the First Aliyah. Between 1881 and 1920, more than 2 million Jews flee the Russian Pale and Romania.

1883	Jacob Horowitz rents a bakery in New York City to make hand matzas. In 1888, he is able to purchase his own bakery.
1888	Dov Behr Manischewitz begins baking matzas in Cincinnati, Ohio. By 1900, he introduces a mechanized plant producing 50,000 tons of matza a day. The company becomes America's largest producer of kosher foods.
1888	Brothers Isaac and Joseph Breakstone open a shop in Manhattan to sell milk, butter, and traditional eastern European dairy products, helping to popularize sour cream and later cream cheese.
1889	Baron Edmond de Rothschild sends high-grade European grape vines to Israel. To process their yield he builds a large wine cellar in Rishon-le-Zion and, in 1892, a second one in Zichron Ya'akov.
1896	Theodor Herzl, an assimilated Austrian journalist shaken by the Dreyfus affair in France and unrelenting European anti-Semitism, publishes Der Judenstaat (The Jewish State), transforming Zionism into a political movement.
1899	Sam Schapiro begins selling Concord grape wine from his restaurant on the Lower East Side of Manhattan. He soon becoming the first kosher wine company in America.
1903	The Kishinev pogrom in Bessarabia and the prolonged Russian pogroms following Russia's defeat in the Russo-Japanese war in 1905 result in the Second Aliyah, lasting until the outbreak of World War I in 1914.
1903	Dov Behr Manischewitz, after observing his wife, Nesha, pound matzas in a cloth to make matza meal and farfel, introduces commercial versions. His matza meal revolutionizes Passover cooking, including transforming the matza ball from a seldom-made item into one common on Passover and also during the rest of the year.
1909	The first kibbutz (collective community), Degania, is founded on the shores of the Galilee.
1915	The New York State Legislature enacts the first kosher protection law.
1917	Britain takes Jerusalem from the Ottomans and issues the Balfour Declaration, stating that Britain would facilitate a Jewish state in Palestine.
1917	Russian Revolution. The Pale of Settlement is abolished, but thousands of Jews are murdered in numerous pogroms.
1920	Arab pogroms increasingly terrorize Jews in Israel. The Haganah (Jewish defense organization) is founded.
1921	The first moshav (cooperative settlement), Nahalal, is founded in the Jezreel Valley.
1922	The League of Nations gives Britain a Mandate for Palestine; Britain set up three-fourths of the area as Transjordan, excluding any Jews.
1923	The Union of Orthodox Jewish congregations, founded in 1898, introduces the OU symbol to use on the first kosher American national brand of food, Heinz Vegetarian Baked Beans.

1924	The United States passes the Immigration Restriction Act.
1929	*The Goldbergs*, a show about a Jewish family living in the Bronx with Molly Goldberg as the main character, becomes the first family-based situation comedy on the radio. The radio show ends in 1946, but in 1949, *The Goldbergs* becomes the first television sitcom featuring Jewish characters; it is finally canceled in 1956. During its quarter-century run, the proudly Jewish show introduces various Jewish customs and numerous Jewish foods to mainstream America.
1931	Maxwell House, America's largest coffee producer, publishes the first *Maxwell House Haggadah*; a later edition will be used at the 2009 Seder held by Barack Obama in the White House.
1935	The Nuremberg Laws revoke Jewish rights in Germany.
1935	Coca-Cola is certified kosher.
1936	Stalin institutes purges in Russia to destroy Jewish culture.
1938	Kristallnacht, a pogrom on November 9, begins Germany's persecution of Jews.
1939	The British White Paper prohibitively limits Jewish immigration to Mandatory Palestine. Britain maintains this restrictive policy through World War II and the remainder of its control of the area.
1939	Jewish demographics reach a high point—there are nearly 17 million Jews, with 9.5 million in Europe, 4.8 million in America, and 1 million in Muslim lands.
1941	The first record appears of the word rugelach, actually a synonym for the central European *kipfel* (crescent), which goes on to become one of America's favorite cookies.
1942	Nazi leaders formalize the Final Solution at the Wannsee Conference.
1945	World War II ends. There are about 11 million Jews worldwide with about 1 million Jews in the Muslim world: 265,000 in Morocco; 140,000 in Algeria; 135,000 in Iraq; 105,000 in Tunisia; 90,000 in Iran; 80,000 in Turkey; 75,000 in Egypt; 55,000 in Yemen; 50,000 in Kurdistan; 38,000 in Libya; 30,000 in Syria; 8,000 in Aden; 5,000 in Lebanon; 5,000 in Afghanistan; and 600 in Bahrain. Most will subsequently be forced to leave due to political instability, physical threats, and sometimes expulsion.
1947	The United Nations on November 29 votes to partition Palestine into two states.
1948	The state of Israel issues its Declaration of Independence on May 14. Arab armies immediately invade Israel.
1949	The Arab states agree to an armistice on April 3, ending Israel's War of Independence. Jews are prohibited from the Old City of Jerusalem and the Western Wall, which fall under Jordanian control.
1956	Sinai War.
1962	Daniel Thompson invents a bagel-making machine, which helps transform the then-obscure Polish bread into America's number-one fresh and frozen bakery product.
1967	Six-Day War. Jerusalem comes under Israeli rule.
1967	Several American companies begin to mass market traditional Jewish foods, such as Levy's rye bread and Hebrew National hot dogs, to appeal to non-Jews. By 2010, nearly 75 percent of Hebrew National's customers are not Jewish.
1973	Yom Kippur War.
1978	Israel and Egypt sign a peace treaty.
1993	Giant ConAgra Inc. acquires America's largest kosher meat processor, Hebrew National, while in the same year Sara Lee Corporation purchases the second-largest, Bessin, reflecting Jewish food's continuing acceptance by mainstream America.
2004	PepsiCo enters a joint venture with the Israeli company Strauss for Sabra brand, promoting hummus and other Israeli favorites in America. Osem, another Israeli company, also enters the American hummus market.
2010	There are an estimated 11 million kosher consumers in the United States, although only about 1 million are Jewish; the rest are Seventh-day Adventists, Muslims, and other religious groups (not to mention those with restrictive dietary needs, including vegetarians and lactose intolerants). Around 150,000 American packaged-goods items are certified kosher.
2010	There are about 14.5 million Jews worldwide: 6,452,000 in the United States; 5,550,000 in Israel; 491,500 in France; 375,000 in Canada; 297,000 in Britain; 228,000 in Russia; 184,500 in Argentina; 118,000 in Germany; 103,000 in Australia; 96,500 in Brazil; 80,000 in Ukraine; 72,000 in South Africa; 49,700 in Hungary; 39,800 in Mexico; 30,000 in the Netherlands; 28,600 in Italy; 18,200 in Belarus; 17,800 in Turkey; 10,800 in Iran; 10,000 in Romania; 9,800 in Latvia; 6,800 in Azerbaijan; 5,000 in Greece; 4,800 in Uzbekistan; 3,500 in Georgia; 3,500 in Morocco; 3,500 in Poland; 3,200 in Lithuania; 1,100 in Tunisia; 300 in Turkmenistan; 200 in Yemen; 100 in Egypt; 100 in Syria; 60 in Iraq; 50 in Lebanon; 1 in Afghanistan; and 0 in Aden, Algeria, Libya, and Jordan.

ADAFINA

Adafina is a Sephardic Sabbath stew in which the ingredients are typically cooked in layers and served in separate dishes.

Origin: Spain

Other names: Algeria: *t'fina*; central Morocco: *frackh, schena, shachina, skhina*; northern Morocco: *daf, dafina, d'fina*; Tangiers: *horisa, orissa*; Tunisia and Libya: *tafina, t'fina*.

The Register of Depositions before the Inquisitors in the Canary Islands on July 4, 1570, recorded, "Ana Goncales deposes that when she was in the service of Ana de Belmonte, she saw that her mistress cooked mutton with oil and onions, which she understands is the Jewish dish Adafina." During the Spanish Inquisition, the single most incriminating dish connoting a retention of Judaism was *adafina*. Even an accusation of preparing this stew led to Conversos being burned at the stake. Inquisition reports from the fifteenth century list ingredients for *adafinas*, including chickpeas, fava beans, fatty meat, onions, garlic, and cumin. The initial layer of flavor in any Sephardic stew is chopped onion sautéed in olive oil, and usually the meat is browned with the onions as well.

After the Sabbath stew developed and spread through medieval Spain, Sephardim from the north and center of the country generally adopted the Talmudic term *hamin* as the name of their Sabbath stew. However, an alternative nomenclature emerged in the south, *ad-dfina* or *adafina* (from the Arabic meaning "buried/covered"), corresponding to the Mishnaic phrase *"tomnin et ha'hamin"* (Aramaic meaning "cover/bury the warm dish"). In this vein, *al-kanz al-madfun* is Arabic for "buried treasure," once a Spanish sobriquet for the Sabbath stew. Pointedly, there is a homophone in Hebrew, *dafinah*, meaning "force into a groove" and "to press against a wall," either of which would be applicable to the medieval cooking methods of inserting the pot into a hole in the ground with embers or sealing it in an oven. Among the six Jewish dishes contained in an anonymous thirteenth-century Moorish cookbook from Andalusia was one for an antiquated "Adafina," which consisted of layers of spiced meatballs and spiced meat omelets. Following the expulsion, the name *adafina* or *d'fina* primarily survived across the Straits of Gibraltar in North Africa.

In addition to meat and onions, a basic *adafina* contains some sort of legume—Moroccans and Egyptians are partial to chickpeas, while white beans are more common among Tunisians and Algerians. For Passover, some cooks use fresh fava beans from the new crop. Vegetables differ regionally as well. Algerians typically add turnips, while Tunisians use a well-cooked leafy green (*sfanach*) or cardoons. After potatoes and sweet potatoes arrived in the region from South America, they eventually became familiar additions. Sephardic Sabbath stews are always seasoned with cumin and frequently with other spices as well. Some *adafinas* are slightly sweetened with dates or honey, while others possess a hint of fire with the addition of harissa (chili paste) or chilies. Some cooks add pieces of quince or dried apricots and plums. Ubiquitous to all Sephardic Sabbath stews are *haminados* (slow-cooked eggs). The key to what is used in the *adafina* is an ingredient's ability to stand up to the long cooking time.

Many *adafinas* are enriched with a calf's foot, a tongue, an ox tail, or a small meat loaf, providing another dish for Sabbath lunch. Once luxuries and generally the province of only the wealthy, these enhancements are common today. Moroccans generally include a *kouclas* (dumpling) wrapped in cheesecloth, typically consisting of any combination of rice, wheat berries, and ground meat, or separate bags for any or each of the three. Today, some cooks substitute ovenproof plastic bags for the cheesecloth, adding water and seasonings to each bag. Many Algerians, Tunisians, and Libyans make a *bobinet* (beef sausage) or *osbana/osban* (a sort of sausage made from the chopped entrails of a sheep mixed with eggs, rice or bread crumbs, sautéed onion, garlic, and spices and stuffed into a sheep's stomach). Egyptians tend to eschew dumplings, making just the basic stew. For the meal breaking the fast of Yom Kippur, some households make an *adafina* containing a whole chicken stuffed with ground beef, ground almonds, and cinnamon.

In North Africa, the stew was typically started over a fire on Friday, then set in the coals of a *kanoun* (brazier) and covered with special bulky blankets for insulation and left to simmer overnight. Families lacking a *kanoun* sealed the lid with a flour paste, then carried the pot on Friday afternoons to a large public oven in town. In most communities, a guard was hired to watch the oven all night to avoid any tampering.

The majority of Moroccan Sabbath stews are traditionally cooked in layers and separated into different dishes for serving. Consequently, Moroccan a*dafina* is technically a meal-in-one and not a blended stew. The *haminados*, usually peeled after cooking and put back in the pot for several minutes, are generally offered first as the appetizer. Diners can season their own eggs with salt and ground cumin. The remaining ingredients are then served in separate deep bowls. Presentation is important and fancier hosts line the dishes with lettuce leaves, which contrast with the intensely browned *adafina* ingredients. The legumes along with a little of the cooking liquid are sometimes spooned over couscous left over from Friday dinner. The remaining cooking liquid is presented as a warm soup, sometimes with thin noodles added. It is customary in many homes to follow the *adafina* with a glass of a digestif, such as fig liquor.

(See also Hamin, Haminado, Harisa, Kouclas, Sabbath, Shkanah, and T'fina)

ᘓ MOROCCAN SABBATH "STEW"
(*ADAFINA/DAFINA/SKHINA*)

6 TO 8 SERVINGS   [MEAT]

¼ cup olive or vegetable oil

2 large onions, chopped

3 to 6 cloves garlic, minced

8 ounces (1¼ cups) dried chickpeas, or 4 ounces chickpeas and 4 ounces dried white beans or dried baby lima beans, soaked in water to cover for 8 hours and drained

1 tablespoon paprika

1 to 2 teaspoons ground cumin

1 (3-inch) cinnamon stick, ½ teaspoon ground cinnamon, or 1 teaspoon ground coriander

½ teaspoon ground turmeric or ⅛ teaspoon ground saffron

About 2 teaspoons table salt or 4 teaspoons kosher salt

About ½ teaspoon ground black pepper

3 to 4 pounds boneless lamb shoulder or beef flanken, brisket, short ribs, or chuck, cut into 2-inch cubes

1 pound beef marrow or veal shin bones

1 chicken, cut into pieces, and/or 8 ounces garlic sausage, thickly sliced (optional)

1 pound (2¼ cups) wheat berries, soaked in water to cover overnight and drained, or 2 cups long-grain rice

1 recipe *kouklas* (Moroccan Rice and Meat Dumpling, page 328; optional)

8 medium (2 pounds) boiling or new potatoes

4 sweet potatoes or carrots, peeled and halved (optional)

1 to 2 tablespoons harissa (Northwest African Chili Paste, page 260), ½ to 1 cup pitted dates, or 3 to 4 tablespoons honey (optional)

About 7 cups water

6 to 8 eggs in shell

1. In a large, heavy pot or deep 10- to 12-quart ovenproof dish, heat the oil over medium heat. Add the onions and garlic and sauté until soft and translucent, 5 to 10 minutes. Add the chickpeas and stir to coat. Sprinkle with the paprika, cumin, cinnamon, turmeric, salt, and pepper.

2. In the order given, add to the pot (without stirring) the meat, bones, and optional chicken. Loosely tie the wheat berries in a large piece of cheesecloth and insert it into the center of the stew. Many cooks add a *kouclas* (dumpling). If using rice in the stew, use a meat and wheat berry dumpling; if using wheat berries in the stew, use a meat and rice dumpling. Surround with the potatoes and, if using, sweet potatoes and/or dates.

3. Add enough water to cover by more than 1 inch. Cover the pot and bring to a boil. Reduce the heat to medium-low and simmer for 2 hours. Add enough water to cover the stew. Arrange the eggs in the stew and press to submerge.

4. Tightly cover the pot. Place on a thin sheet of metal over a low heat or in a 225°F oven and cook overnight. Remove and peel the eggs, serving them separately. To serve, place the chickpeas, cooking liquid, meat, wheat berries, potatoes, and eggs in separate bowls.

ADZHAPSANDALI
Adzhapsandali is a vegetable stew, usually based on eggplant.
Origin: Georgia
Other names: *adzhapsandal.*

Until recently, most Georgian homes had a fire in the center of the large communal room with a *shwatzetzkhli* (large copper pot) hung by a chain from the ceiling, in which various stews were simmered, the main course of many meals. Outside was a clay oven, used to bake breads and casseroles. Vegetable dishes were either cooked in the pot or, less commonly, baked in the oven. The most popular of these stews is *adzhapsandali* (Adzha is a province on the Black Sea). Some versions are soupy, while others are dry. Eggplant, introduced by the Persians and subsequently becoming the Georgians' favorite vegetable, is commonly the heart of *adzhapsandali*; other produce is added depending on its availability and the discretion of the cook.

What distinguishes the stews of Georgian cookery from other vegetable stews is the large amount of fresh herbs and a kick from cayenne. Georgian Jews enjoy this lively stew hot on Sukkot and Friday night or at room temperataure for Sabbath lunch. *Adzhapsandali* is served as a main course or side dish, typically accompanied with *khachapuri* (filled pastries) or *mchadi* (corn cakes) and Georgian wine. At dairy meals, *adzhapsandali* is commonly accompanied with yogurt.

AFIKOMEN (TZAFUN)
Near the beginning of the Passover Seder, the middle of three matzas is broken in two and the larger section, called the *afikomen*, is wrapped and set aside to be eaten as the final item of food of the evening. This, however, was not the original usage of the word *afikomen*, but its modern convention, reflecting historical changes in Jewish ritual and lore.

The Mishnah states, "One may not add after the paschal offering an *afikomen*." This wording clearly indicates a forbidden activity. At the time that the Temple stood, the paschal offering (*korban pesach*) constituted the final part of the Passover Seder meal. Following the destruction of the Temple and the ces-

sation of the paschal offering, it was replaced with a portion of matza at the end of the meal, separate from the matza at the onset over which the Hamotzi (benediction over bread) is recited. This concluding piece of matza is not consumed because of hunger, but, according to some, for the fulfillment of the commandment of eating matza or, according to others, in memory of the Temple.

The formalized Passover-night liturgy was developed by Sages living in Israel two thousand years ago, at the time of the Roman occupation. They incorporated into the Seder not only the various biblical commandments but also many elements from the contemporary Greco-Roman *symposium* (Greek for "drinking together"). It was a ritualized upper class banquet and intellectual dialogue, including reclining on couches, eating from private small tables, ritual hand washing, dipping greens, consuming fruit-and-nut relishes, a series of ritual wine libations, a sumptuous meal, and a series of questions as a starting point for an intellectual discussion of a designated topic. These aspects of the *symposium* served as models of freedom and affluence, the ideals to which the Seder participants aspired.

At the end of the symposium, however, followed a *komos* (later *comissatio* in Rome), named after an intoxicated reveling group of satyrs who followed around the Greek god of wine and fertility, Dionysus. (The word comedy also comes from the *komos*.) The end of the symposium, living up to the namesake *komos*, consisted of a drinking party accompanied with revelry, music, and song. The host always provided various tidbits—most notably fruits, roasted grains, and nuts—similar to the modern beer nuts—to nosh on with the wine to induce the consumption of alcohol. (A *komos* also frequently featured masks and costumes, a practice, which around the seventeenth century, through the Italian commedia dell'arte, found its way into Purim festivities.) The *komos* served as a ritualistic transition from the intellectual and gastronomic parts of the symposium to its sensual, decadent side, inevitably and intentionally leading to lewdness. As part of the *komos*, the inebriated participants would then proceed (*komatsain*) from house to house, laughing and singing, to persuade others to join them in their drinking, carousing, and orgies. The Sages, not wanting the aftermath of the Seder to degenerate into the bawdy and lascivious behavior of the *komos*, realized that it was necessary to avoid the excesses of the symposium. Consequently, *afikomen* originally meant in Greek *epi komos/epikomion* (upon the revelry). The meaning of the Mishnah is that one may not add after the seder meal any of the activities associated with the *komos*.

Initially, the final matza had no specific name. Amram Gaon, author of the first recorded Haggadah (857 CE), simply states, "After eating [the meal], everyone eats an olive size portion of matza." Saadia Gaon (tenth century), in his *siddur* containing another early version of the Haggadah, refers to the final matza as *keenuach seudah* (wiping of the meal), a Talmudic euphemism for dessert. However, despite a common misconception, the word *afikomen* does not mean dessert in Greek or Aramaic. By at least the late twelfth century, the term *tzafun* (hidden) became prevalent among Ashkenazim for the final matza. The *Sefer ha-Rokeach* (c. 1200) proposed that the name of this custom derives from a verse in Psalms: "How abundant is Your goodness, which *tzafanta* [You have hidden away] for those who fear You."

Illustrations in early Ashkenazic Haggadahs reveal the practice of hiding the larger piece of the middle matza under or in a cloth, an act intended to peak the interest of the children. After dinner, the Seder leader redeems the matza in time to be consumed. Like other parts of the Seder, the acts of hiding and finding the matza developed various symbolic meanings, such as pointing to the unknown future redemption. Wrapping matza in a cloth is also reminiscent of the Israelites leaving Egypt. Although some Sephardim and Mizrachim have recently adopted the practice of *tzafun* (hiding the matza), it was not their tradition. Rather at a Sephardic and Mizrachi Seder, the final matza is wrapped in a special cloth bag, frequently embroidered, and the leader conducts a dramatic reenactment of the Exodus from Egypt.

The first record of the word *afikomen* employed in reference to the final matza, and no longer something forbidden, occurred in the *Responsa of Rashi*, a collection of Rashi's writings chronicled by his students (c. twelfth century). By the time of the *Shulchan Arukh* (c. 1555), the term *afikomen* was firmly entrenched among both Ashkenazim and Sephardim as the name of the final portion of matza at the Seder. The *Shulchan Arukh* also advised, "One should be careful to eat the Afikomen before midnight."

AGRAZ

Agraz refers to sour unripe grapes, the juice expressed from them (verjuice), and a sauce made from the grapes themselves.

Origin: Spain, Provence

Other names: Italian: *agresta*, *agresto*; Ladino: *agra*.

Verjuice or verjus (from the Old French *vertjus*, "green juice") is the light green unfermented juice of unripe grapes. The Spanish and Ladino equivalent is *agraz*. However, *agraz* also denotes the unripe grapes (*agraz entero*) as well as a sauce made from the grapes themselves (*salsa agraz*).

Verjuice is acidic and has a distinct grape flavor, but is less acidic tasting than lemon juice or vinegar, and grows milder as it ages. The grapes are picked before maturing at a period when they begin to change color and start to soften, around late July or August. Thinning grapes at this time is a natural aspect of viticulture and the immature portion are not wasted. As with wine, different varieties of grapes yield different qualities of verjuice. Salt is commonly added as a preservative and to prevent fermentation into vinegar, but preferably not enough to be detected. When the yearly stock of verjuice ran out, typically by spring, faux verjuices, with a much sharper taste, were made from sorrel, gooseberries, and crabapples until new sour grapes emerged each season.

The first recorded use of verjuice in cooking was by the ancient Romans, but it was most probably used in every ancient grape-growing society, as people were not wont to waste. During the medieval period, verjuice was the principal souring agent of the grape-growing regions of Europe—France, Italy, Spain, and Greece—as well as a common condiment in Turkey, Syria, and Persia. Throughout the medieval period, cooks used verjuice in a myriad of stews, sauces, pickles, condiments, and salad dressings, its intriguing flavor complementing wines served with foods and not overpowering or altering them as does vinegar. Taillevent in his influential late fourteenth-century cookbook, *Le Viander*, called for verjuice in more than 40 percent of the recipes. In Dijon, it was incorporated into the local mustard.

Verjuice was one of the paramount flavorings of early Ashkenazic cooking, but during the late medieval period, as most Ashkenazim relocated farther east from France and the Rhine River Valley and the grape-growing areas, they no longer had access to it.

Verjuice remained essential to Sephardim through the expulsion from Spain in 1492, and was subsequently used in the eastern Mediterranean. Then in the seventeenth century, with the popularization of the lemon and tomato, as well as the emergence of better-quality wines, verjuice increasingly fell into disfavor throughout most of Europe. Today, it is practically unknown to Ashkenazim, but still occasionally found among some Sephardim, Greeks, Lebanese, Syrians, Turks, and Persians. The classic Sephardic sauce *agristada* is now made principally with lemon juice rather than its namesake *agraz*.

Sephardim make a simple sauce called *salsa agraz* by simmering sour grapes with water and a little honey or sugar until the fruit breaks down. The sauce is served with roasted lamb, poultry, and fish to counteract their heat. Although many newer sauces now enjoy greater popularity, *salsa agraz*, sometimes now with a little tomato sauce added, is still beloved in some Greek, Turkish, and Levantine households.

For Sephardim, there was an added significance to *agraz*, for it sounds like the Hebrew word meaning reward, as in Ethics of the Fathers, "According to the effort is the *agra* [reward]."

❦ SEPHARDIC SOUR GRAPE SAUCE (AGRAZ)

ABOUT 1¼ CUPS [PAREVE]

  1 cup unripe grapes, seeded
  1 cup water
  ¼ cup tomato sauce
  1 to 2 tablespoons sugar or honey
  Salt to taste

In a medium saucepan, simmer all the ingredients over low heat, stirring occasionally, until the grapes break down into a sauce, about 1 hour.

AGRISTADA

Agristada is a thick, lemony, egg-based sauce served over vegetables and fish and used to thicken soups and stews.

Origin: Spain

Other names: Arabic: *beda b'lemune, tarbiya*; Greek: *avgolemono*; Italian: *bagna brusca, brodettato, brodo brusca*; Ladino: *salsa blanco*; Turkish: *terbiye*.

Among the foods prevalent with Sephardim in Iberia before the expulsion was the sauce *agristada*, which was used instead of cream and butter. Although sometimes described as "boiled mayonnaise," the emulsification does not derive by beating oil into eggs, but through cooking the egg yolks in a liquid. Originally, this sauce was flavored with *agraz* (verjuice), an acidic, fruity juice made from unripe grapes. Pomegranate juice or bitter orange juice was sometimes substituted, but vinegar was considered too sharp. After lemons became prevalent in the West during the late medieval period, they generally replaced *agraz* as the souring agent in this sauce, transforming it from a light grape flavor to citrus.

Since Sephardim were at the forefront of medieval citrus cultivation and growing citrons for the Sukkot festival, the practice of using lemons in sauces first became widespread among them. The cooking liquid from the respective vegetable, chicken, or fish with which the sauce is to be served is typically used to make the sauce, sometimes with the addition of dry white wine. Flour or matza meal is frequently added for extra thickening and to help prevent the sauce from separating. The color of the sauce depends on the intensity of the yellow of the yolks. For a brighter color, a pinch of turmeric may be added. Syrians frequently include a dash of cinnamon. In Modena, Italy, it is enhanced with garlic and anchovies. A related Greek soup known as *avgolemono* contains much more liquid.

In the Balkans and the Levant, *agristada* is used like mayonnaise is in the West, accompanying mild-flavored foods, such as fried or poached fish, veal, poached chicken, meatballs, rice, pasta, stuffed vegetables, artichokes, and fried cauliflower. Among some Greek Jews, fried fish with *agristada* is served cold after a bar mitzvah, as well as for Sabbath lunch. Romans like it with roast lamb. Artichokes or asparagus with *bagna brusca* is a traditional Italian Passover dish. In the ghetto of Pitigliano in southern Tuscany, established by Cosimo de' Medici in 1608, the sauce was commonly tossed with egg tagliatelle or drizzled over cooked vegetables. *Agristada* can be substituted for hollandaise sauce in most dishes.

❦ SEPHARDIC EGG-LEMON SAUCE (AGRISTADA)

ABOUT 1⅓ CUPS/3 TO 5 SERVINGS [PAREVE OR MEAT]

  2 large eggs, or 1 large egg and 2 large egg yolks
  1 cup vegetable, chicken, beef, or fish broth
  1 tablespoon all-purpose flour or matza cake meal
    or 1½ teaspoons cornstarch

About ⅓ cup fresh lemon juice or verjuice (unripe grape juice)

About ¼ teaspoon table salt or ½ teaspoon kosher salt

1. In a 1-quart saucepan, whisk the eggs until smooth. In a small bowl, gradually stir the broth into the flour to dissolve. Whisk the mixture into the eggs. Add the lemon juice and salt. The ingredients can also be mixed in a blender.

2. Cook over medium-low heat, stirring constantly with a wooden spoon or whisk, until smooth and thickened, about 3 minutes. Do not boil. Serve warm or pour into a bowl, press a piece of plastic wrap against the surface, and let cool. Store *agristada* in the refrigerator.

VARIATION

Mayonnaise-like Agristada: Reduce the flour to 2 teaspoons and add 2 tablespoons olive or vegetable oil.

AHILADO

Ahilado is a tomato sauce with onions, parsley, and olive oil in which fish is cooked.

Origin: Turkey

Other names: Greek: *salsa tomata, plaki.*

Ahilado, the past participle of the Ladino verb *ahilar* (to turn sour), technically refers to tart sauces. Cooking fish in a thick, tart sauce is an ancient method for producing a moist, flavorful dish. *Salsa agraz* (sour grape sauce), the most ancient of these sauces, is rarely used today. Plums are popular, coming into season in the fall, and rhubarb, appearing in the spring. The arrival of tomatoes from the New World brought an additional flavor dimension and became the most popular variation of this sauce.

Ahilado stands up to strong-flavored fish, such as carp, mackerel, and tuna, but does not overpower milder ones. Chicory or endive (*indivia*) is sometimes added to bring out the flavor of the fish, while fennel (*hinojo*) contributes a softer note. Fish with tomato sauce is traditional among Turkish and Greek Jews on Friday night, Rosh Hashanah, and festivals, and at the meal preceding the fast of Tisha b'Av. *Peshkado ahilado* is typically accompanied with rice.

AJADA

Ajada is Sephardic garlic mayonnaise and an earlier garlic sauce.

Origin: Greece

Other names: Greek: *skordalia, skorodalmi*; Italian: *agliata*; Turkish: *tarator.*

A popular condiment enjoyed in ancient Greece, *skordalia* consisted of raw garlic, vinegar, and salt; the name derived from the Greek word for garlic (*skorda*). The sauce was commonly served with fried and poached fish and meat. A medieval Mediterranean adaptation added a paste of bread, vinegar, and sometimes walnuts or almonds, and was called *ajada* by Sephardim, from the Ladino for garlic (*ajo*). Bartolomeo Scappi in *Dell'Arte Cucinare* (1570) included the Italian version, *agliata*, containing walnuts, almonds, and bread soaked in broth. The nuts produce a thicker, creamier texture.

In the late eighteenth century, after the invention of mayonnaise—a mixture of eggs emulsified with oil—*ajada* among Greek Jews evolved into a garlic mayonnaise, akin to the Provençal aioli. A modern Greek version containing bread or mashed potatoes is called *skordalia*. *Ajada* is served with fish, boiled potatoes, fried eggplant, cooked beets, and other vegetables and as a dip for crudités or bread. In some Greek households, fried fish with *ajada* is traditional for Hanukkah.

SEPHARDIC GARLIC MAYONNAISE (*AJADA*)

ABOUT 1¼ CUPS [PAREVE]

5 to 6 cloves garlic, minced

About ½ teaspoon table salt or 1 teaspoon kosher salt

1 large egg yolk

2 to 3 tablespoons fresh lemon juice or white or red wine vinegar

½ teaspoon Dijon mustard (optional)

About 1 cup vegetable oil, or ⅔ cup vegetable oil and ⅓ cup olive oil

1. Using a mortar and pestle, mash the garlic and salt. Or place the garlic on a cutting board, sprinkle with the salt, and, using the side of a knife blade, mash into a paste.

2. Transfer the garlic to a blender or food processor. Add the egg yolk and process until smooth. Add the lemon juice and, if using, mustard. With the machine on, gradually add the oil in a slow, steady stream. The *ajada* can be covered and stored in the refrigerator for up to 1 week.

AJIN (MIDDLE EASTERN DOUGH)

Ajin is the Arabic word for dough.

Origin: Middle East

Other names: *ajeen*, *agine*.

The Romans spread durum and common wheat throughout their Empire, the source of the famous "bread and circuses" that sustained their power, much of it grown in North Africa and Sicily. After the Romans, wheat remained the chief grain in medieval Arab lands, used to make a variety of breads and other baked goods. Middle Eastern Jews use a basic lean yeast *ajin* to make an array of flatbreads for both their weekday and Sabbath loaves. The most common *ajin* for making pastries is an unleavened one rich in butter or oil and made with part or all semolina (*smead*). Middle Eastern Jews enjoy these various pastries at all special occasions.

(See also Bread)

🍴 MIDDLE EASTERN YEAST DOUGH (*AJIN*)

ABOUT 50 LARGE RINGS OR TURNOVERS OR

2 MEDIUM LOAVES   [PAREVE]

- 1 package (2¼ teaspoons) active dry yeast or 1 (0.6-ounce) cake fresh yeast
- 1⅓ cups warm water (105 to 115°F for dry yeast; 80 to 85°F for fresh yeast)
- 1 teaspoon sugar or honey
- 2 teaspoons table salt or 3 teaspoons kosher salt
- 2 tablespoons olive or vegetable oil (optional)
- About 4 cups (20 ounces) bread or unbleached all-purpose flour, or 2 cups white flour and 2 cups whole-wheat flour

1. Dissolve the yeast in ¼ cup water. Stir in the sugar and let stand until foamy, 5 to 10 minutes. In a large bowl, combine the yeast mixture, remaining water, salt, optional oil, and 2 cups flour. Gradually add enough of the remaining flour to make a mixture that holds together. On a lightly floured surface, knead the dough until smooth and elastic, 5 to 10 minutes.

2. Place the dough in an oiled bowl and turn to coat. Cover loosely with plastic wrap or a kitchen towel and let rise in a warm, draft-free place until doubled in bulk, about 1½ hours. Punch down the dough.

🍴 MIDDLE EASTERN SEMOLINA DOUGH (*AJIN SMEAD*)

ABOUT 40 3-INCH TURNOVERS   [DAIRY OR PAREVE]

- ¾ teaspoon table salt or 1½ teaspoons kosher salt
- About ½ cup lukewarm water
- 2 cups (10 ounces) unbleached all-purpose flour
- 1 cup (6 ounces) fine semolina or farina
- 1 cup (2 sticks) unsalted butter or margarine, melted

In a small bowl, stir the salt into the water until it dissolves. In a large bowl, combine the flour and semolina. Stir the melted butter into the flour mixture until little clumps form. Add enough water to make a smooth, soft but not sticky dough. Cover with plastic wrap and let stand at room temperature for at least 1 hour or overnight. The dough firms as it rests.

AJIN TAIMANI

Ajin Taimani is an enriched, flaky dough, similar to puff pastry.

Origin: Yemen

Other names: *ajin*.

Taimani (Yemenite) Jewish cookery is remarkable as it developed in spite of a long history of oppression and poverty. Working with few resources, cooks had to be creative, developing an assortment of humble flatbreads that, along with various inexpensive legumes, formed the basis of almost every meal. For special occasions, notably the Sabbath, Taimanim prepare breads and pastries from an *ajin* enriched with clarified butter and made enticingly flaky by repeatedly folding and rolling in a manner similar to puff pastry.

Flaky *ajin* is very uncharacteristic of Yemenite food and was probably adapted from the similar Sephardic *ojaldre* (rudimentary puff pastry) after Iberian exiles arrived in the Ottoman Empire. It is not made by non-Jewish Yemenites. However it migrated into the cuisine, *ajin* became the pinnacle of Yemenite pastry. Thin dough rounds are cooked in a hot skillet to make a soft, flat bread (*melawah*), or the dough is rolled into cylinders (*jachnun*) or layered with a little egg (*subya*) and baked overnight for Sabbath lunch, the pastry caramelizing and crisping. These flaky pastries are commonly accompanied with *s'chug* (chili paste), *hilbeh* (fenugreek relish), cold chopped or pureed tomatoes, and baked eggs, or they are drizzled with a little honey.

Following the mass immigration of Yemenites to Israel beginning in 1949, this dough and pastries made from it became extremely popular among many non-Yemenites, and can be found frozen in every Israeli supermarket. Imports are also now available in America as well. Historically, Yemenite *ajin* was leavened by wild yeast as it stood, the rising always depending on chance. Most modern versions incorporate a little baking powder. In Yemen, the dough never contained sugar, but contemporary versions commonly add varying amounts. Too much sugar, however, will cause the dough to burn during an extended baking period.

(See also Jachnun, Melawah, and Subya)

YEMENITE FLAKY PASTRY (*AJIN*)

6 PIECES [DAIRY OR PAREVE]

4 cups (20 ounces) unbleached all-purpose flour
1 tablespoon sugar
½ teaspoon baking powder
¼ cup *samneh* (clarified butter), margarine, or vegetable oil
About 1¼ cups water
1½ teaspoons table salt or 1 tablespoon kosher salt
6 additional tablespoons *samneh* or margarine, softened, for spreading
Vegetable oil for rolling

1. In a large bowl, combine the flour, sugar, and baking powder. Cut in ¼ cup *samneh* to produce fine crumbs. Combine the water and salt. Add to the flour mixture and stir just until the dough holds together and cleans the sides of the bowl. Knead until smooth, about 3 minutes. Divide the dough into 6 equal pieces, form into balls, wrap in plastic wrap, and refrigerate for at least 30 minutes or overnight.

2. On a lightly oiled surface, press a dough ball into a square, then roll into a very thin square, about 9 inches in diameter. Spread each square with 1 tablespoon *samneh*. Fold down the top third of the dough over the center third, then fold up the bottom third to form a rectangle about 9 by 3 inches. Bring the short ends of the rectangle together to meet in the center to form a square about 3 inches. Repeat with the remaining dough. Cover with plastic wrap and refrigerate for 30 minutes.

3. Place each dough package seam side up on a lightly floured surface and roll into an 8-inch square. Fold the top third of the square over the center third, then fold the bottom third over. Wrap and refrigerate for 30 minutes. Repeat the process of rolling into 8-inch squares, folding in thirds, and refrigerating

twice more. At this point, the *ajin* can be wrapped in plastic wrap and frozen for up to 3 months, then thawed before using.

AJLOUK

Ajlouk is a spicy and chunky mashed-vegetable relish.
Origin: Maghreb
Other names: *ajlouke, zaalouk, zeilouk.*

Reminiscent of Indian chutney, *ajlouk* is a synthesis of Andalusian vegetable stews and Maghrebi flavors, typically quite fiery and spicy. It is intended to be eaten in small amounts as a condiment with bread or couscous.

The original relish was probably made with eggplant, which is still popular. However, a green summer squash similar to zucchini (*qura* in Arabic and *courgettes* in French) became a particular favorite of Tunisians. Other versions are made with pumpkin, winter squash, carrots, and a combination of eggplant and zucchini. Unlike most eggplant salads, the eggplant for *ajlouk* is always boiled or steamed, never grilled. Boiling the vegetables results in a texture many Westerners find off-putting, so many cooks now steam them so they absorb less water. The relish needs to stand for several hours for the vegetable to absorb the seasonings and for the flavors to meld.

These relishes are traditional on Sukkot as a symbol of the harvest and on other special occasions as part of a Tunisian *kemias* (appetizer assortment) along with various salads, pickles, other nibbles, and bread or crackers, or as an accompaniment to couscous.

TUNISIAN ZUCCHINI RELISH
(*AJLOUK DE COURGETTES*)

ABOUT 3½ CUPS/4 TO 5 SERVINGS [PAREVE]

1½ pounds small or medium zucchini, trimmed
Dressing:
3 to 4 cloves garlic
About 1 teaspoon table salt or 2 teaspoons kosher salt
2 teaspoons caraway seeds, freshly ground
1 to 2 teaspoons coriander seeds, freshly ground
About 3 tablespoons fresh lemon juice
1 to 4 teaspoons harissa (Northwest African Chili Paste, page 260) or ¾ to 1½ teaspoons cayenne
About 3 tablespoons extra-virgin olive oil or argan oil for drizzling

1. Bring a large pot of lightly salted water to a boil, add the zucchini, and boil until it is soft enough so that a knife pierces it easily, about 15 minutes. Or steam the zucchini over boiling water until tender. Drain, place in a colander, and gently press out the excess moisture. Many cooks save the cooking liquid for soup.

2. Transfer the zucchini to a bowl and, using a fork or potato masher, coarsely mash. Do not drain.

3. To make the dressing: Using a mortar and pestle, mash the garlic and salt. Or place the garlic on a cutting board, sprinkle with the salt, and, using the side of a knife blade, mash into a paste. Blend in the caraway and coriander. Stir in the lemon juice and harissa.

4. Stir the dressing into the zucchini. Cover and place in the refrigerator for at least 3 hours and up to 3 days. Spoon onto a serving platter and drizzle with the oil. Serve at room temperature, not chilled.

AJVAR

Ajvar is red pepper relish. Depending on the amount of medium-hot red peppers added, it can range in flavor from sweet to fiery hot.

Origin: Balkans

Other names: *aivar*, *ajwar*.

Wildly popular in Bosnia, Bulgaria, Croatia, Herzegovina, Kosovo, Macedonia, Serbia, and Slovenia, *ajvar* comes from the Turkish *khavyar* (salted roe/caviar), as the lumpy red relish resembles red fish eggs. The Turks, during centuries of control of the Balkans, introduced the main ingredient, peppers, as well as the cooking method and name. When eggplants are added, it becomes *pindzur*. Another variation, especially popular in Bulgaria, is *lyutenitsa*, containing a large proportion of tomatoes. Many people use the term *ajvar* for the variations too.

The principle feature of *ajvar* is the red bell pepper, called *paprika*. As peppers mature on the vine they turn from an intense green to an array of colors, including red, yellow, orange, brown, and black. The ingredients and amounts vary from country to country and town to town. When red peppers were unobtainable, tomatoes were used along with green peppers to produce a reddish hue and fruity flavor. Some versions are mild and sweet, especially those in Croatia and Slovenia. Adding various amounts of chilies can make the relish quite fiery, and this type is more common to the south in Kosovo. Adding eggplant makes

a less creamy and less red relish. The vegetables are roasted to impart a smoky undertone and create a silky texture in the peppers.

For generations, *ajvar* was traditionally made once a year in large batches in the early autumn from a plentiful harvest of red peppers. Making *ajvar* is a social event, binding family and friends. Today, the autumn air in the Balkans is still filled with the aroma of roasting peppers. After roasting, the relish is cooked outdoors in a large cauldron to remove excess liquid and increase the shelf life. Many locales banned *ajvar* making in public green spaces, due to the damage from the fires, and it must be done on private property. For long-term storage, *ajvar* is poured into jars and topped with a layer of oil or melted fat to last at least through the winter until fresh vegetables return in the spring. The fat is removed before eating. Gifts of homemade *ajvar* are only given to treasured friends and family.

In the Balkans, *ajvar* is daily winter fare served with black bread, pita bread, and crackers, as well as slices of feta cheese, or as a condiment for grilled meat. Today commercial *ajvar* is readily available in Israeli markets. Nevertheless, some families still insist on making their own and cook up a fresh supply whenever the mood or necessity strikes. There is even a quicker version, requiring only roasting and grinding the vegetables and omitting the reduction stage.

AJWAIN

Ajwain or ajowain, a member of the Apiaceae family, a native to the eastern Mediterranean. This spice is a tiny, greenish brown seed with a flavor and aroma similar to thyme and caraway, but a bit more pungent. Ajwain's assets are enhanced by frying or roasting. It is popular in Persian cuisine, most notably with fish and potatoes. In India around Mumbai, the Bene Israel use the seeds to flavor samosas and for bean and lentil dishes, because it purportedly counters the gaseous effects. Ethiopians include it as part of the spice mixture *berbere*.

ALBONDIGA

Albondiga is a meatball.

Origin: Spain

Other names: Maghreb: *boulette*; Portugal: *almondega*.

Meatballs were a staple of the medieval Persian and Arab world. In most areas, they were referred to by a variation of the Persian term *kufteh* (pounded) or *kubbeh* (dome). The Spanish and Ladino name derived from the Arabic *al-bunduqa*, meaning "hazelnut," denoting the small size and shape of the original meatballs as well as their Moorish heritage.

The word *albondiga* was first recorded in an anonymous thirteenth-century Moorish cookbook from Andalusia, which contained numerous recipes for meatballs. By that point, the characteristic Iberian method of preparing meatballs—pounding the meat into a smooth paste, binding the mixture with eggs, and frying the balls in oil before simmering—had already developed. In the recipe for meatballs, the author directs:

> "Take red, tender meat, free of tendons, and pound it as in what preceded about meatballs. Put the pounded meat on a platter and add a bit of the juice of a pounded onion, some oil, *murri naqî*, pepper, coriander, cumin, and saffron. Add enough egg to envelope the mixture, and knead until it is mixed, and make large meatballs like pieces of meat, then set it aside. Take a clean pot and put in it some oil, vinegar, a little bit of *murri*, garlic, and whatever quantity of spices is necessary, and put it on the fire. When it boils and you have cooked the meatballs in it, let it stand for a while."

Albondigas were enthusiastically adopted by Sephardim, becoming a long-standing mainstay of their cuisine. Meatballs stood alone as an entrée, as well as being served in vegetable dishes and stews. Sizes ranged from that of a hazelnut to "nearly the size of oranges," but walnut-sized meatballs, quicker and easier to prepare than tiny ones, eventually emerged as the most common. Whereas Middle Eastern *keftes* (patties) are typically oblong in shape, *albondigas* are round. Some were filled with an almond or hard-boiled egg. Sephardim prefer meatballs made of lamb. To achieve the desired smooth texture, the meat was traditionally pounded in a mortar or wooden bowl. Today, many Sephardic cooks grind it in a meat grinder at least two times, then knead it by hand for several minutes, or process it in a food processor. Although meatballs cooked with vegetables date back to early in Persian and Arabic history, the addition of vegetables to the meat mixture, most notably leeks and spinach, seems to have originated among the Sephardim.

After the Christian conquest of Spain, *albondigas* along with *adafina* were considered to be characteristic Jewish foods. During the Inquisition, the authorities would occasionally force Conversos to eat meatballs made with pork or stews containing pork to test if they were still keeping kosher. Refusal to eat the pork led to arrest, and often death.

After the expulsion from Spain in 1492 and the later forced conversion of the Jews of Portugal, Sephardim and Conversos introduced these meatball dishes to all their new lands, including Mexico and New Amsterdam. Gershom Mendes Seixas (1745–1816), the American-born *hazzan* (reader and spiritual leader) of Congregation Shearith Israel, the Spanish and Portuguese Synagogue in New York City, in describing his regular Sabbath dinner, wrote, "Nothing but Alibut [halibut] and Asparagus for Dinner and some Stew and Olmendigas [a misspelling of *almondegas*] for Shabbas-good appetite!" (Seixas was one of fourteen clergymen to officiate at George Washington's first presidential inauguration in 1789.) The first English language Jewish cookbook, *The Jewish Manual* by Judith Montefiore (London, 1846), a work reflecting a pronounced Sephardic influence, included recipes for meatballs made from meat, poultry, and fish and one for "Almondegos Soup" containing "balls of forced meat."

Albondigas were, throughout most of history, fare reserved for special occasions. They are typically served in a sauce or with just a squeeze of lemon juice, but are also added to soups, stews, and casseroles. Sephardim also cook meatballs with vegetables, such as cauliflower, celery, eggplant, and chard. During the nineteenth century, as tomato sauce grew popular, it commonly replaced the traditional souring agents of verjuice, lemon, pomegranate, and tamarind. Meatballs are often spooned over rice to catch the sauce. Fish *albondigas* are frequently served in a fish soup for Friday night dinner, while in the Maghreb they are ladled over couscous. In many Sephardic households, meatballs are ubiquitous on the Sabbath and festivals, particularly Passover, rather than the Ashkenazic matza ball.

(See also Kefta, Kubbeh, Kufta, and Meatball)

ALBORONIA

Alboronia is a chicken and eggplant casserole.
Origin: Morocco
Other names: *almoronia*, *barania*.

After the Persians brought eggplant west from India, it quickly became the favorite vegetable in Persia as well as subsequently the Arab world. A popular usage was in stews, often paired with lamb, one of which was called *buraniya*, possibly from the Hindi name for eggplant, *brinjal*, or, some contend, named after Queen Buran (c. 800), wife of the caliph of Baghdad. The earliest record of a dish with this name was "Stuffed *Buraniya*," in a collection of recipes by Ibrahim ibn al-Mahdi (779–839) of Baghdad, compiled in the cookbook *Kitab al-Tabikh* (Book of Dishes) by Muhammad ibn al-Hasan Al-Baghdadi, in Iraq in 1226.

In Andalusia, the dish was transformed into a Sephardic eggplant and lamb stew and sometimes a vegetarian eggplant stew, with the Arabic definite article *al*, becoming *alboronia*. In northern Morocco, *alboronia* eventually became a popular eggplant and chicken casserole. *Alboronia* is traditionally served by many Moroccans at the meal before Yom Kippur.

ALICHA
Alicha is a mildly spiced, thick vegetable- or legume-based stew.
Origin: Ethiopia
Other names: *alcha, aleecha.*

The two principal Ethiopian dishes, around which all meals revolve, are *injera* (pancake bread) and a vegetable- or legume-based stew. One version, called *wot,* is fiery hot, seasoned with *berbere* (chili-spice sauce) or *awaze* (chili sauce). The other stew, *alicha,* meaning "mild" in Amharic, is spicy but milder. In Ethiopia, the stews were generally cooked in earthenware pots over an open fire. The combination of spices in an *alicha,* influenced by centuries of trade with Arabia and India, has a flavor akin to an Indian curry. Except for the Sabbath and festivals, most Beta Israel (Ethiopian Jews) could not afford meat and, therefore, vegetarian stews were the most common.

(See also Injera and Wot)

ALLSPICE
When Christopher Columbus arrived in the West Indies looking for peppercorns (*pimiento* in Spanish), he found the natives using the dried brown berries of a local myrtle tree, which he misnamed pimento, a name it still has in the Caribbean. Actually, it was one of the few spices native to the Western Hemisphere—called allspice in America and England. Despite a confusing name, it is actually one spice, said to possess the flavor and scent of a combination of cinnamon, cloves, and nutmeg. Some also find a trace of pepper or ground ginger; others have trouble finding more than a note of cloves.

Allspice was among the New World produce, including cocoa and vanilla, for which Sephardim early on held a virtual monopoly on the production and trade. When the British finished their conquest of Jamaica, wresting it from the Spanish, in 1655—only a year after Jews were officially allowed to live in England—allspice was introduced into British and American cooking and quickly became popular. For the following century, Jews by and large maintained their role in the allspice trade. Today, most of the world's allspice is still grown in Jamaica, where it is used to season jerk and barbecue. Farmers collect the mature green berries and dry them in the sun. Oil from the leaves is used in processed foods and cosmetics. Jamaican allspice is noted for its high oil content.

Allspice (*tavalim m'oravim* or *pilpelet angli* in Hebrew) emerged as an important seasoning in certain Middle Eastern cuisines, most notably Syrian, becoming the country's favorite spice. Allspice is rather assertive, so use it sparingly. It has a special propensity for sweets and is used to flavor pickles, sauerkraut, chutneys, tomato sauces, and meat dishes.

ALMODROTE
Almodrote is a vegetable and cheese casserole, often featuring eggplant.
Origin: Spain, Turkey
Other names: *almatroc, almodroc, almodroti, cuajada, quajado.*

In Spain, vegetables, eggs, and cheese served as the basis of everyday Sephardic cookery. By the thirteenth century, Sephardim were preparing fried patties of eggplant, cheese, and eggs, the first known account of this combination, in which the eggplant and cheese complement and enhance each other. Shortly thereafter, as home ovens were disseminated amongst the generally well-to-do populace of Spain, baked vegetable, cheese, and, egg dishes appeared. This trio was so identified with the Sephardim that the Inquisition considered it as a sign of Jewish cooking. These casseroles were designated *kon queso* (with cheese) or *al horno* (literally "in the oven").

Almodrote (from the Arabic *al-matruq* "hammered"), originally the name of an early Sephardic olive oil, cheese, and garlic sauce commonly used with eggplant, became widespread in Turkey. The Iberian sauce traces back to the Roman *moretum*, a curd cheese, herb, and garlic paste (akin to pesto) crushed in a mortar. *Almodrotes* contain a smaller amount of eggs than *fritadas*, concentrating on the seasonal vegetables and including plenty of cheese, and have a more custard-like texture. Eggplant is the most common vegetable used in *almodrote*, but zucchini is also popular. The addition of bread crumbs or potatoes reflects a Turkish influence, resulting in a firmer texture that holds together better when the casserole is removed from the pan. In Spain, *almodrote* came to also mean "hodgepodge."

Almodrote is served at room temperature as part of a *desayuno* (brunch), as well as warm as an appetizer for dinner or a main course at various dairy meals. It is typically accompanied with a green salad and bread or, on Passover, matza.

SEPHARDIC EGGPLANT AND CHEESE CASSEROLE
(*ALMODROTE DE BERENGENA*)

6 TO 8 SERVINGS   [DAIRY]

3 medium (about 1¼ pounds each) eggplants
1 cup (5 ounces) crumbled creamy feta cheese, or 8 ounces farmer, ricotta, or cream cheese
1 cup (4 ounces) firmly packed grated kashkaval, Gouda, Gruyère, or yellow Cheddar cheese
3 large eggs, lightly beaten
¾ cup bread crumbs, matza cake meal, or mashed potatoes
1 to 2 cloves garlic, minced
3 tablespoons vegetable or olive oil
About ½ teaspoon table salt or 1 teaspoon kosher salt
Ground black pepper to taste
About 1 tablespoon olive oil or butter for drizzling

1. Cut several slits in the eggplants. Roast over hot coals or 5 inches under a broiler, turning occasionally, until charred and tender, about 40 minutes. Or place on a baking sheet and bake in a 400°F oven until tender, about 50 minutes. Peel the eggplants, being careful not to leave any skin. Place in a colander and let drain for about 30 minutes. Coarsely chop; do not puree.

2. Preheat the oven to 350°F. Oil an 11-by-7-inch or other shallow 2-quart baking dish.

3. In a large bowl, beat together the feta cheese, ¾ cup kashkaval cheese, eggs, bread crumbs, garlic, 3 tablespoons oil, salt, and pepper. Stir in the eggplants. Pour into the prepared dish and drizzle with 1 tablespoon oil.

4. Bake for 20 minutes. Sprinkle with the remaining ¼ cup kashkaval and bake until golden brown, about 25 minutes. Let stand for at least 5 minutes before serving. Serve warm or at room temperature.

ALMOND

On the surface, the almond tree, a member of the rose family, gives no indication of being special. This native of central Asia, among the earliest cultivated trees, is moderate in size. It has only a modest life expectancy of about fifty years, unlike the extended longevity of olives and figs. The bright green leaves are simple and its hard reddish wood is hardly exceptional. Almond-blossom honey is considered of poor quality and commonly left in the hives to feed the bees.

The almond's flesh, unlike that of its close relative the peach is of no gastronomic value. Nevertheless, the fruit of the almond tree is still of great worth and unique for what's inside. Unlike the peach and most other drupes, the kernel of the almond's fruit is edible and eminently delicious. Indeed, the seed of its fruit has from prehistoric times been the most widespread and important nut in the warm areas of both the ancient and modern Mediterranean and Middle East. Long before the advent of civilization, people discovered that the almond's kernels were tasty and nutritious. Eventually nomads and merchants spread this tree in all directions, especially along the trade routes of the Middle East and Mediterranean. By the fourth century BCE, the almond was already in the province of Granada, Spain.

The nature of the almond tree itself is unique, for it is the first tree to flower after the winter, sometimes as early as late January. The Hebrew word for almond, *shaked*, means "awakening one," because of its early blossoming, even before the appearance of its leaves. Thus the almond tree serves in Ecclesiastes as a symbol of the transitory nature of human life. Being a harbinger of spring, almonds also represent hope and renewal.

As the nut matures, it is enveloped in a leathery green case that looks like a slender unripe peach. When it ripens, the fruit splits, exposing a tough tan shell, rounded on one end and pointed on the other. Inside is the white kernel, surrounded by an edible brown skin that is frequently removed by blanching in boiling water.

There are two kinds of almonds—sweet and bitter. Sweet almonds are edible raw. There are around fifty varieties of almonds in Spain alone, each with a slightly different flavor and aroma. One sweet variety of almond is from Malaga, Spain; upon reaching France, it was called *jardin* (garden), denoting a cultivated nut. The name was later Anglicized to Jordan almonds. The bitter almond contains a poisonous chemical compound called amygdalin, which results in trace amounts of cyanide. When the bitter almond's harmful acid is removed, the remaining pulp is fermented and distilled to produce almond extract. It is illegal to sell bitter almonds in the United States, but they are sold in Europe for use in pastries, liqueur, and marzipan.

The almond was one of only two nuts mentioned in the Pentateuch (along with pistachios). Among the "choice fruits of the land [of Israel]," it was sent by Jacob as a gift to the Egyptian prime minister. The almond tree provided the rod of Aaron and the model for the menorah of the Temple. Since biblical times, the almond has been the most important nut among Jews, incorporated in a myriad of traditional dishes. Almonds are added to many versions of charoset. They are among the traditional fruits of Tu b'Shevat. Almond trees thrive in Iberia and early on became a characteristic component of Sephardic cuisine, ubiquitous on festivals and at life-cycle events, as well as in everyday fare. In the Mediterranean region and the Near East, almonds are incorporated into many dishes, including tagines, chicken dishes, soups, sauces, confections, and pastries.

Ashkenazim also used almonds, primarily imported from Italy and Provence, in festive fare, although much less frequently than Sephardim and Mizrachim. Among Ashkenazim, almonds are now primarily used for desserts, notably mandelbrot (almond bread). Almonds, along with raisins, have long been served at many Jewish celebrations as a symbol of good luck and fruitfulness. In the words of *"Ay-Lye, Lyu-Lye, Lyu-Lyee,"* an old Yiddish lullaby:

"Under the baby's cradle here, there's an all-white nanny goat, dear. Nanny's come to bring the baby, almond nuts and raisin candy. *Rozhinkes mit mandlen* [raisins with almonds] are a special treat. Baby will grow up healthy and sweet. Healthy is far better than wealthy. Baby will grow up a scholar. A scholar of the Torah will he be, a writer too, of holy works. A good man and a pious, God willing, that's what he will be."

ALMOND MILK

Almond milk is a milk substitute made from soaking finely ground sweet almonds in water and straining them.

Origin: Middle East

Other names: Arabic: *assir looz, harir, hariri, hlib b'looz*; German and Yiddish: *mandelmilch*; Italian: *latte di mandorle*; Spanish and Ladino: *leche de almendras*.

Until late in the nineteenth century, milk in urban areas was frequently dirty, spoiled, and unsafe and, therefore, typically avoided by those without direct access to a cow. Then the advent of refrigerated railroad cars in the 1880s led to a surfeit of fresh dairy products away from the farm and, beginning in the 1890s, widespread usage of pasteurization ensured a safe supply. Consequently, before that time, milk was seldom used in urban cooking, except in a fermented form, such as cheese, butter, buttermilk, and yogurt. Water generally was not much better, unless first boiled, a principle then not yet understood. Instead, most people relied on faux milk, most notably made from nuts, beans, or melon seeds. The most widespread of these in the Middle East and Europe was made from sweet almonds, with one or two bitter almonds typically added for a more pronounced almond flavor; this faux milk is now known as almond milk and amygdalate. Unlike animal milk, almond milk can be made fresh by any cook and be stored without refrigeration for a day or two.

Nuts contain a large amount of oil, stored in tiny compartments in the tissue surrounded by a layer of protein and lecithin. That is why the texture of nuts is dry when initially bitten, but grows creamier upon chewing and releasing the oil. Soaking the almonds in water before grinding is essential for separating the intact oil from the solid particles. After grinding the nuts with water and straining, the remaining oil- and protein-rich liquid provides a tasty and nutritious milk substitute. The leftover almond pulp can be used for puddings or cookies and other baked goods. Middle Easterners also mix strong almond milk with sugar syrup to create a refreshing drink.

Almond milk, like most culinary advances of the medieval period, arose in Islamic lands, and Sephardim adopted it early on. Europeans learned how to make nut milk from Arabs and Middle Eastern Jewish travelers, and subsequently almond milk was used in cooking and called for in recipes in most medieval cookbooks, both from Arabic and Christian lands. Columbus recorded cooking sweet potatoes in almond milk during one of his voyages. Medieval Jewish legal texts discuss how to substitute faux milk for animal milk at meat meals: almonds should be situated near the almond milk to signal that it is not animal milk.

Almonds can be expensive in Morocco and, as a result, almond milk, frequently accented with rose water or orange-blossom water, is considered a high-status beverage. Moroccans customarily serve a sweetened version called *sharbat bil looz* and *hlib b'looz* at weddings and other celebrations. In the Maghreb, almond milk is used to moisten and flavor sweetened couscous, also a prominent dish at celebrations. Syrians customarily serve glasses of it at engagement parties.

A particular favorite use of almond milk among Sephardim has been with rice. In this vein, Provençal poet and writer Frédéric Mistral, in *Lou Tresor Dóu Félibrige* (1880), noted the presence of *"Ris a l'amelo* [rice with almonds], the traditional dish eaten by Jews of Midl during their carnival, which they call Purim." In *The Jewish Manual* (London, 1846), the first Jewish cookbook in English, Judith Montefiore offered an updated British version of the dish, called "Almond Rice." Sephardim more generally made a pareve version, providing an ideal creamy dessert for eating at meat meals.

❧ ALMOND MILK (*LECHE DE ALMENDRAS*)

ABOUT 3 CUPS [PAREVE]

1 cup (4 ounces) whole almonds, blanched
3 cups water
Pinch of salt (optional)

1. Place the almonds in a large bowl and pour in enough water to cover them by 1 inch. Weigh down with a plate to completely submerge or you can wrap the almonds in cheesecloth. Place in the refrigerator and let soak for at least 12 hours. Drain and rinse the almonds.

2. In a blender, puree the almonds and 1 cup water. Gradually add the remaining 2 cups water and process until smooth, at least 3 minutes. If using, add the salt as a flavor enhancer. Strain through several layers of cheesecloth, squeezing out any liquid, or pour over a fine-mesh sieve set over a bowl and let drain. Store the almond milk, covered, in the refrigerator for up to 5 days. Shake before using.

ALMOND PASTE

For thousands of years, ground nuts have been used in the Middle East in cooking, initially, primarily as thickeners and flavorings in sauces and stews. In the fourth century BCE, Greeks were already mixing pulverized almonds with honey to make an early confection. When the Persians brought sugarcane westward from India around the sixth century CE, it soon led to sweetened nut pastes and their transformation into the basis of numerous beloved Persian treats.

Pastes were made from hazelnuts, pistachios, and walnuts, but blanched sweet almonds were by far the most widespread nut. Throughout much of history, a bitter almond or two were commonly added to intensify the flavor of the paste, but today, as they are illegal to purchase in many places, a little almond extract is used instead. Besides sugar, Persians began flavoring nut paste with rose water or orange-blossom water, a practice that endures in some communities. Later, in other locations, eggs—variously whole, whites, or yolks—were frequently substituted for the floral waters.

After the Arabs conquered Persia in 640, they began introducing sugar as well as these nut pastes westward, by the ninth century reaching Spain and Sicily and eventually extending into Byzantium and Renaissance Italy and subsequently into medieval Europe. The Moors, especially in Toledo, called almond paste *mazapán*, probably from the Arabic *mauthaban*, a small wooden box in which it was stored. At the time of the Spanish Inquisition, almond paste was viewed as a Jewish food.

Almond paste and marzipan are not the same, and

the two should not be used interchangeably in most recipes. Almond paste is an uncooked mixture consisting of nearly equal amounts by weight of finely ground blanched sweet almonds and sugar, along with a small amount of water or eggs to bind. Many American brands of commercial almond paste are one-third almonds and two-thirds sugar, while cheaper grades have an even higher proportion of sugar. Marzipan is a cooked almond paste with about twice the amount of sugar as almonds; the sugar is first boiled with water into a syrup, then blended with ground almonds and cooked until the mixture thickens. Almond paste, which has a more intense almond flavor than marzipan, is used primarily in baked goods. Marzipan, which is more malleable and less likely to become oily during handling, is generally used to make confections and shapes.

Well before the expulsion, Sephardim were sculpting almond paste into the form of fruits and other shapes. Some Sephardim call it *almendra* or *almendrada*, from the Ladino word for almond, while others refer to it interchangeably as *massapan*. In either case, historically Sephardim only prepared the raw paste, not the cooked dish now called marzipan. *Almendrada* is very versatile, forming the basis for a wide variety of Sephardic confections and pastries. It is ubiquitous at life-cycle celebrations honoring births, bar mitzvahs, and weddings and is frequently offered on Purim and especially on Passover. Almond paste is also used by Sephardim as the base for unbaked as well as baked treats, most notably *marunchinos*, akin to the Italian amaretti. Iraqis add a little cardamom for *hadgi badah*. Moroccans use almond paste to stuff dates and other dried fruit (*tmar b'looz et dates fourées*) and as the filling for a classic pastry, *kaab el gh'zal* (gazelle horn). Syrians form almond paste into rings calls *kaak loz*.

Italian Jews introduced almond paste to their brethren living along the Rhine River valley, and it entered the Ashkenazic culinary repertoire. Although sugar was the sweetener used in this treat in Iberia and the Middle East, early Ashkenazic versions were made with honey. Sugar gradually became more widespread in Europe, especially with the advent of the sugar beet in the eighteenth century. Subsequently, sugar-based almond paste became the norm in Europe too. Almond paste and marzipan were special treats among Ashkenazim in central Europe, but they were little known in northeastern Europe.

ALMONDS, CANDIED

Candied almonds are almonds that have been coated with a glaze of cooked sugar.

Origin: Middle East, Spain

Other names: Arabic: *lebas, m'lebass, melebes*; Italian: *confetti*; Yiddish: *gebrannte mandlen*.

After sugar arrived in the Middle East, cooks discovered how to caramelize the crystals and began cooking chopped nuts in it, such as the Persian *badam sukhte* (a sort of almond brittle), and whole nuts in it, resulting in a rough glaze of sugar. The Arabs gradually spread these candies westward, eventually reaching Spain. By the fifteenth century, sugar-coated almonds spread to France and Italy and eventually to Germany.

Cooks in Moorish Spain also developed a more sophisticated almond candy by adding repeated layers of water and fine sugar, resulting in almonds covered with a hard white candy coating. Later food dyes were added to create pastel-colored almonds. In English, they became known as candy-coated almonds and, more prominently, Jordan almonds, the Anglicized name of a cultivated—*jardin* (garden)—sweet variety of almond from Malaga, Spain.

Among Sephardim, Jordan almonds have long been a popular feature at life-cycle events, particularly weddings. At one time, family and friends used to throw Jordan almonds at the bride. At a Sephardic henna ceremony for an engaged couple, in which both future partners dye the palms of their hands, the bowl of henna is surrounded by Jordan almonds, wishing the newlyweds a sweet and fertile life together. In Syrian synagogues on Simchat Torah, after the children are called up for the mass reading of the Torah scroll, the congregants shower them with *m'lebass*.

At a special Sephardic rite, especially in Turkey, during the fifth month of pregnancy for a woman expecting for the first time, female relatives and friends traditionally gather for a rite called *Kortadura de Fashadura* (cutting of the swaddling cloth) in Ladino or *Tektiá el-G'daouere* in Arabic, at which the swaddling cloth for the new baby is ceremonially cut. Coinciding with the first cut, the expectant mother or all the women throw white Jordan almonds at the cloth, signifying a wish for a sweet life for the baby.

Additional sugared almonds are served with other treats to the guests.

ALOO MAKALLA

Aloo makalla are whole potatoes that are long-simmered in oil, allowing them to develop a tender interior and a crisp crust.

Origin: India

Other names: *alu makhala.*

Aloo makalla is the most famous Jewish dish in India. It is a nineteenth-century synthesis of Arabic and Indian cooking traditions, evolving as Middle Eastern Jews, called Baghdadis, relocated to Calcutta in the wake of the British Empire (*aloo* is Hindi for "potatoes," *makalla* is Arabic for "fried").

In Calcutta, the measure of a Jewish table was judged by the quality of its *aloo makalla.* Most of the Jews of Calcutta employed at least one person to do their cooking, although the woman of the household planned and supervised the menus. Thus many non-Jews learned how to prepare this classic Jewish dish and, even after most of Calcutta's Jewish community emigrated, *aloo makalla* remained popular in India.

The distinct cooking method results in potatoes with a moist interior and a very hard surface, so firm that they are a bit difficult to cut, requiring stealthy securing with a fork, which frequently causes the inside to "jump" out. Whence an Indian nickname for them—"jumping potatoes." Despite the long time in the oil, the potatoes do not become soggy or oily. *Aloo makalla* is traditionally served accompanied with green *methi* chutney (fenugreek chutney) every Friday night, on holidays, at weddings, and on other special occasions, along with *murgi* (spicy chicken), *bhaji* (curried potatoes and vegetables), *khutta* (vegetable dishes), and *pilau* (rice pilaf).

◌❈ CALCUTTA FRIED WHOLE POTATOES (*ALOO MAKALLA*)

4 TO 6 SERVINGS   [PAREVE]

    2 pounds (about 22) small boiling potatoes of
        uniform size, peeled
    1 teaspoon table salt or 2 teaspoons kosher salt
    ½ teaspoon ground turmeric
    About 3 cups vegetable, safflower, or peanut oil for
        frying

1. Place the potatoes in a large pot and add water to just cover. Add the salt and turmeric. Bring to a boil and parboil for 30 seconds. Drain. Let cool, then pat dry. Prick each potato once with the tines of a fork.

2. Place the potatoes in a *karahi* (Indian wok) or wide-bottomed pot and add enough oil to cover. Bring to a boil, without stirring, over medium-high heat, about 15 minutes.

3. Reduce the heat to low and simmer, shaking the pan occasionally, until the potatoes are crusty and lightly golden, about 1 hour. At this point, the potatoes can be removed from the heat and allowed to sit, in the oil, for up to 3 hours.

4. Shortly before serving, increase the heat to medium-high and fry until the crust is very hard and golden brown, about 10 minutes. Drain on paper towels. Serve warm.

AMBA

Amba is a condiment made from pickled ripe mango, seasoned with curry.

Origin: Iraq

Other names: *ambah.*

Aam ka achar is a venerable condiment from northern India consisting of pickled unripe mango, typically seasoned with roasted fenugreek, chili powder, turmeric, and mustard oil. Baghdadi Jews in India introduced Indian mango pickles to brethren in Iraq, where the dish, called *amba* (the Hindi and Arabic word for "mango"), spread throughout the country to become an integral part of Iraqi dining. *Amba* is made in a some homes and in numerous specialty stores. Unlike the original pickle, the Iraqi versions consist of ripe mangoes and usually no mustard oil. Mango slices are first cured in salt for several days, then seasoned with turmeric, chili powder, lemon salt, and spices. Today, Iraqis serve it, in both large pieces or small cubes, at most meals as a spread for bread and sandwiches and as a seasoning for salads, eggs, and kebabs. It is especially prevalent at breakfast, even on the Sabbath.

Beginning in the 1950s, Iraqi immigrants brought the condiment to Israel, where it initially found favor among Yemenites and other groups accustomed to hot and spicy fare. An acquired taste, *amba* was generally met with scorn by many Europeans. During the Gulf War in 1990, as Saddam Hussein's missiles rained down on Israel, a joke circulated that one fell in an Iraqi neighborhood because it smelled the *amba.* Eventually, even many Ashkenazim developed a taste for the spicy orange-brown mixture. In 2003, the band Teapacks had a hit song *"Rikudei Amba"* (Pickled Mango Dancing). *Amba* is now widely available in Israeli groceries, with some brands made in the country and others imported from India and Australia. It is commonly offered at stores selling *sabich* (Iraqi eggplant sandwich), *shawarmah* (roasted lamb and turkey), and falafel.

ANISE

Anise, also called aniseed, is indigenous to the eastern Mediterranean. It is not mentioned in the Bible and there is a question as to whether the Talmudic plant *shivta*, *shevet* in Hebrew, denotes anise or dill. Confusion between the two herbs was common in ancient times, as evidenced by the fact that the Greek name for the plant *anison* (anise) derived from *aneton* (dill). Romans greatly valued anise as a medicine and a seasoning, spreading it and its applications throughout the empire.

Anise contains anethol, an essential oil. The seeds resemble fennel, but anise seeds are smaller and slightly sweeter, and have a more pronounced licorice flavor. Fennel is typically used in savory foods, such as sausages, while anise is added to sweeter dishes. Star anise (Chinese anise), which also possesses a licorice-like flavor, is a different spice.

Today, anise is particularly popular in the Mediterranean area, where it is used, in both whole or ground form, in fish soups, pasta sauces, confections, cookies, puddings, and peach and plum desserts. Anise is added to various baked goods, such as the Moroccan Sabbath bread *khboz*, the Italian pre–Yom Kippur bread *il bollo*, Italian biscotti, and the German soft cookie *anisplätzchen*. Italians make anise-flavored yeast fritters for Hanukkah. Strong anise-flavored liquors abound in the Mediterranean, including Middle Eastern *arak*, Greek ouzo, Turkish *raki*, and French pastis, as well as the milder liqueur, anisette. Moroccans brew a homemade alcoholic drink from figs and anise called *mahia* (water of life).

(See also Arak)

ANISPLÄTZCHEN

Anisplätzchen are drop cookies strongly flavored with anise.

Origin: Germany

The German *plätzchen*, meaning "little place/spot," is a synonym for cookie, and is otherwise known as *keks* and *gebäck*. There are many varieties of *plätzchen*, but arguably the most well-known are these favorite anise drops, which are claimed to have originated in the city of Dresden. During baking, they form their own hard white icing on top. The soft yellow bottom part is known as *fuesschen* (little feet). Part of the cookies' appeal, besides the anise flavor, is that they can be prepared well ahead of a holiday. Those who prefer a less-pronounced anise taste add less seeds.

⟐ GERMAN ANISE DROP COOKIES (*ANISPLÄTZCHEN*)

ABOUT SIXTY 1-INCH COOKIES   [PAREVE]

1½ cups plus 2 tablespoons (8 ounces) all-purpose flour

½ teaspoon double-acting baking powder or ⅛ teaspoon ammonium carbonate (baker's ammonia)

½ teaspoon salt

3 large eggs

1 cup plus 2 tablespoons (8 ounces) sugar, preferably superfine

2 to 3 teaspoons anise seeds or 1 teaspoon anise extract

1. Grease and dust with flour 3 large baking sheets. Sift together the flour, baking powder, and salt. In a large bowl, beat the eggs until light and fluffy, 5 to 10 minutes. Gradually beat in the sugar, then continue beating for 20 minutes. Stir in the flour mixture and anise.

2. Drop the batter by heaping teaspoonfuls about ¾ inch in diameter onto the prepared baking sheets, leaving 2 inches between the cookies. Let stand at room temperature, uncovered, overnight or for up to 2 days. This step is critical for the icing to separate.

3. Preheat the oven to 325°F.

4. Bake until golden on the bottoms and creamy on the tops, about 10 minutes. Transfer the cookies to a wire rack and let cool completely. Store at room temperature in an airtight container with a large slice of apple.

APPAM

Appam are grain mixtures cooked as fritters, cakes, and bread puddings.

Origin: India

Other names: *aappam*, *apam*, *appadam*, hoppers, *paddu*.

Each of the three separate Indian Jewish communities—Cochin, Mumbai, and Calcutta—counts in its culinary repertoire grain dishes called *appam*. However, they are vastly different in each location, reflecting the distinctive history and milieu of these communities. The name *appam* derived either from the Sanskrit *apupa* (rice cake), mentioned in the oldest Sanskrit book, *Rig Veda*, or the Tamil *appa* ("father," *appam* plural).

The dish first emerged in the southern tip of India as pancakes, akin to a *dosa* (rice or lentil pancake), made from a batter of ground soaked rice and coconut milk and cooked on a *kal* (stone griddle). Basmati rice produces a rubbery texture, so Indians use other long-grain varieties, such as Sona Masori and Ponni. Savory versions sometimes contain fenugreek. On occasion, ground lentils are incorporated into the rice batter. A little *kall* (palm wine toddy) is frequently added and the batter is allowed to stand overnight to ferment; the resulting dish called *kallappam*. The basic bland rice batter is sometimes sweetened with varying amounts of jaggery—brownish unrefined raw sugar crystals extracted from sugarcane or certain palm trees—and spiced with cardamom. A variation of the cooking method emerged by deep-frying extruded strings of rice batter, reminiscent of noodles, called *idiyappam* or string hoppers.

The importation of two different specialized cooking vessels gave rise to massively popular variations of the basic *appam* recipe, both becoming prominent components of the southern Indian diet. The first was the wok, called *cheena chatti* (Chinese pot), originally brought from China. A smaller version of the wok, an *appachatti* or *appam-chatti*, is intended solely for making *appam*. A small amount of fermented batter is spread in the oiled *appachatti*, the lid is affixed, and the pancake is fried on one side. The result is a rather bland, thin, bowl-shaped pastry, with a soft, puffy interior and lacy, crisp edges.

Another *appam* variation followed the arrival of the *appakarai* or *neyyappa karal*, probably derived from the Scandinavian *aebleskiver*, which is a round pan with seven small curved compartments. A little ghee or oil is heated in each compartment and some sweetened and cardamom-spiced rice batter is poured in, then turned and cooked until golden brown, producing sweet, soft, spongy pancake balls, variously known as *neyyappam* (*neyy* means "ghee"), *kuzhi appam* (*kuzhi* means "small hole"), and *unniappam* (*unni* means "small"). These balls are frequently served along with coffee and tea as part of the daily evening snack, as well as for celebrations. For special occasions, the fritter batter is frequently enriched with bananas or mangoes. *Sooji* (semolina), rarer in the south than in the rest of the country, is sometimes substituted for some or all of the rice, a favorite variation of Cochini Jews.

Throughout southern India, *appam*, *appam chatti*, and *idiyappam* are typically served at breakfast and dinner, for both everyday and festival meals, accompanied by curried fish or chicken, a *dal* (legume dish), and some type of fresh chutney. Although semolina is forbidden on Passover, among Indian Jews rice is acceptable and, therefore, rice *appam*, commonly accompanied with date honey, constitute favorite Cohini Passover fare. The fried *neyyappam* are traditional Hanukkah treats.

Outside of southern India, *appam* took on different forms. Residents of the Konkan coast, including the Bene Israel, not only fried the semolina batter, but also baked it in a pan for a moist semolina cake, still known as *appam*. During their control of the subcontinent, the English introduced European foods, including bread puddings. The Baghdadis of Calcutta adopted a version substituting coconut milk for animal milk, also calling the pudding *appam*.

APIO
Apio is a cooked dish of celery served by many Sephardim at the Seder.
Origin: Spain

During the Passover Seder, Jews in Turkey, Greece, and the Balkans eat celery leaves as *karpas* (a green vegetable on the Seder plate, representing spring and renewal) and use the stalks in this dish. *Apio*, which means "celery" in Ladino, is made without any sugar, producing a piquant appetizer or side dish for fish and chicken. During the Renaissance, celeriac (celery root), which shares some of celery's flavor and aroma, was developed, and it became a frequent substitute in this dish for celery stalks.

Many families also make *apio* with carrots, *kon safanoria*, adding both flavor and color. Some Turkish Jews like to garnish *apio* with chopped fresh dill. If you prefer a more pronounced lemon flavor, increase the amount of juice, but in any case, insist on fresh lemon juice; it will make a major difference in taste. *Apio* is not intended to be a spicy or robust dish, but rather a refreshing start to the Passover feast.

(See also Celery)

❧ SEPHARDIC POACHED CELERY (*APIO*)
6 TO 8 SERVINGS   [PAREVE]

  1 cup water
  About ½ cup fresh lemon juice
  ¼ cup olive or vegetable oil
  1 to 3 tablespoons sugar
  About 1 teaspoon salt or 2 teaspoons kosher salt
  2 bunches celery, leaves removed and cut into
     1½-inch chunks

In a large saucepan, bring the water, lemon juice, oil, sugar, and salt to a boil over high heat. Add the celery, reduce the heat to low, cover, and simmer until tender, about 20 minutes. Serve warm as a side dish, or at room temperature or chilled as an appetizer.

APPLE

The apple, a member of the rose family, is currently the world's most widely cultivated temperate-zone fruit. Pliny the Elder (23–79 CE) listed three dozen different apples. Today, the apple has more than seven thousand horticultural forms, of which only about a dozen are grown commercially in the United States. Apples became a major crop in modern Israel, which produces more than sixty thousand tons annually.

The four primary American apple varieties are Red Delicious (originally Hawkeye), Golden Delicious, McIntosh, and Granny Smith, but, as with much of American produce, their popularity is based on such factors as appearance, resistance to disease, storage, and shipping rather than flavor. Apple coloring varies according to variety and maturity, ranging from shades of golden yellow to green to bright red. Flavors range from sugar-sweet to tart.

Among the cultivated fruits mentioned in the Bible was the *tapuach*, which in modern Hebrew means "apple." However, many authorities believe that the biblical *tapuach* was in fact a different fruit, perhaps the quince or a citrus fruit, because in the biblical period, the apple primarily grew wild and was not yet easily cultivated in tropical areas like Israel and Egypt. It would be centuries from the time of King Solomon before horticulture created an apple comparable to the exalted description in Song of Songs. In addi-

tion, in both the Bible and rabbinic literature, there is a strong emphasis on the aroma of the *tapuach*. Although the apple is delicious, scent is not among its main attributes. Pointedly, both the Greek term *mhlon* and the Latin *malum* originally encompassed any tree fruit, but eventually evolved (as the apple grew more widespread and popular) into the narrower meaning specifying an apple, contributing to the confusion in the translation of *tapuach* as apple. Note: In Jewish tradition, the apple is not the forbidden fruit of Eden. Rabbinic sources variously consider the forbidden fruit to be the fig, grape, wheat, or citron.

Nonetheless, in the popular imagination over the course of time, the apple became associated with the biblical *tapuach*, and it became an important element of Jewish ritual and cookery. Socialist Jews in Poland adapted the traditional Passover Seder song "*Chad Gadya*," which starts with a cat eating a goat, to become "The Apples Will Not Fall," beginning with a worker who refuses to pick apples for his boss, then progressing similarly to the original, but ending with the boss sending a cat to scratch the worker and the cat refusing.

Among Ashkenazim, who generally lived in areas where few biblical fruits were available, apples came into season in time for Rosh Hashanah and could then be stored in a cool place to last through the winter. As a result, apples became the basis for the Ashkenazic charoset of the Passover Seder. The most popular and widespread Rosh Hashanah tradition is the dipping of apple slices in honey while reciting the phrase, "May it be Your will to renew on us a good and sweet year." Hungarian Rosh Hashanah desserts generally continue the apple theme in the form of apple cake, strudel, tart, or compote. *Mansanada* (thick apple compote) is a traditional Sephardic Rosh Hashanah appetizer accompanied with a special benediction. Calcutta Jews serve apples cooked in honey and flavored with rose water for Rosh Hashanah.

Apples became familiar at other fall and winter celebrations as well. *Dolmeh sib* (stuffed apples) is a popular Sukkot appetizer among Persians, while apple strudel fills that role among Ashkenazim. Apples became the traditional Ashkenazic treat for children on Simchat Torah, customarily stuck on the top of paper flags. At a Tu b'Shevat Seder, the third cup of wine is followed by a completely edible fruit or those with very small seeds—notably apples.

Apples are also common to tzimmes, sweet kugels, and blintzes.

Greek Jews have a tradition that the Maccabees ate duck with apples at a feast in celebration of their victory. Some trace this to historian Josephus Falvius' description of huge banquets that followed the Maccabees' victory. Greek Jews further extended the theme of apples on Hanukkah by serving fried apple rings, apple fritters, and applesauce. Applesauce is star among Ashkenazim on Hanukkah as a topping for potato latkes; it was essential in those parts of eastern Europe where schmaltz was the only fat available for frying, ruling out the use of sour cream.

Beginning in the eighteenth century, the center of innovative cakes shifted to central Europe, where many professional bakers were Jewish; this region soon boasted an increasing variety of tortes and kuchens. These batters were frequently gilded with the addition of various seasonal fruits, most notably apples, which not only held up to the heat in the oven, but could be stored in cool places well into the spring. Apple cakes, such as *apfleschalet*, *apfelboyeleh*, and *apfelkuchen*, quickly became a part of Jewish cooking, emerging as favorite Sabbath and holiday fare. A feature of many Jewish apple cakes is the absence of dairy products, so they can be served at a meat meal.

(See also Charoset, Kuchen, Rosh Hashanah, and Schalet)

APRICOT

The apricot is a member of the rose family and a close relative of the plum. Apricots originated in Asia, probably in China, eventually traveling along the Silk Road to ancient Persia and Babylon. They do not seem to have moved farther west till much later, reaching the Mediterranean and Greece by way of Armenia around 100 BCE. The apricot is not mentioned in the Bible or Mishnah, but probably reached Judea by the end of the Second Temple period. The Arabs introduced the tree to Spain during the Middle Ages. Capable of withstanding some cold, apricots became a feature of central Europe. Leading contemporary apricot producers are Turkey, California, Iran, Italy, Pakistan, France, Spain, Hungary, and Israel.

The yellow-orange roundish fruit is sweet, but contains relatively little juice. Apricots are one of the few fruits that do not sweeten after harvesting, although they do soften, so for shipping purposes growers often pick them before they are completely ripe. The apricot season is rather short and they tend to become quickly infested with worms and insects, so much of the fruit is dried.

Turkey has long been the world's largest producer of apricots and this fruit found its way into many of the country's dishes and into cuisines throughout the former Ottoman Empire. Some Mizrachim, especially in Turkey, add apricots to their Passover charoset. Syrians incorporate them in numerous meat and vegetable dishes, such as stuffed grape leaves and meatballs, or make thin sheets of sun-dried apricot puree called *amradeen*. Moroccans cook them in stews, especially with lamb or chicken, and add them to sweetened couscous. Apricot kernels were sometimes substituted for almonds in marzipan. Apricots also became an important feature of Ashkenazic cooking in central Europe. Dried apricots added a special flavor to many dishes, including stews, tzimmes, fruit soups, compotes, jams, liqueur, and confections (such as *pletzlach*), and apricot lekvar became a popular hamantaschen filling. Hungarians make a special dumpling stuffed with an apricot and a sugar cube.

Apricot trees are quite common in parts of modern Israel and the fruit, fresh and dried, finds its way into many dishes. Since no ancient Hebrew word for apricot existed, modern Hebrew borrowed from the Arabic, technically *mishmesh*, but colloquially pronounced like the Arabic *mishmish*. A popular Israeli children's game is *gogo'im* (apricot pits), played by placing one *gogo* at a distance and attempting to hit it with another, akin to marbles.

ARAK

Today, throughout the Mediterranean region, the most popular liqueurs are licorice-flavored ones, called anisette and pastis in France, ouzo and *mastika* in Greece, *anesone* in Italy, *ojén* in Spain, *raki* in Turkey, and *arak* in Arabic.

A rudimentary process of distillation was invented in Persia more than twenty-five hundred years ago, an extremely difficult method resulting in rather rare, expensive, and often crude spirits. Many of the first liqueurs were made by steeping anise seeds, sometimes along with other spices and herbs, in a spirit. This process changed dramatically with the advent of the alembic still invented by the Arab scholar Jabir ibn Hayyn in 800 CE; his innovation produced plentiful, economical, and high-quality spirits. Since Islam forbids the consumption of alcohol, Arabs used the process primarily for floral waters. It was most probably Middle Eastern Jews who first developed liqueurs, most notably an anise-flavored distilled spirit called *arak* (originally the name of fermented date juice).

For most of history, *arak* was a homemade product, called *arak baladi*, often made from home-grown grapes or other fruit. Typically, distillers worked in the fall, making use of the seasonal grape crop. Today, some Jewish families continue to maintain a home still, distilling *arak* from either grapes or grain, sometimes because they prefer the quality of their own spirits and, in the case of those who keep kosher, because many commercial brands contain grape juice, which requires kosher supervision.

Arak is unsweetened and clear; the lack of coloring is because the essential oils in anise dissolve in alcohol, not in water. Consequently, when sufficient water is mixed into *arak*, some of the anise oils in the water transform into tiny white crystals, which turn the liqueur translucent white. If the water is not completely mixed in, the result will be layers of white and clear liquid. *Arak* is most commonly served with water and many like to add ice as well. The ice is always added after the water, as otherwise it creates a skin on the surface.

Today, *arak* remains a favorite spirit of Jews from the Mediterranean, an important part of *mezzes* (appetizer assortments), *desayunos* (brunches), and celebrations. *Arak* is typically consumed with food to curb its intoxicating effects.

ARANYGALUSKA
Aranygaluska is a cinnamon pull-apart coffee cake.
Origin: Hungary
Other names: golden dumpling cake, Hungarian coffee cake, monkey bread.

The name of this widely popular Hungarian coffee cake means "golden dumpling," reflecting that it is made out of small balls of yeast dough rolled in butter, coated with cinnamon-sugar and frequently chopped nuts, and stacked in a deep pan to bake. Diners pull individual balls of dough from the loaf or cut the cake into wedges. Some cooks make a double recipe of dough, using half for the cinnamon coffee cake and the other half for *kuchen-buchen* (cocoa-dipped coffee cake).

Throughout most of history, loaves or rolls of bread were baked free-form on the floor or walls of an oven. Consequently, the concept of rolling small pieces of bread dough in butter and baking them close together in a single pan goes back only to the nineteenth century. Some suggest this technique might have originated with those cooking in a Dutch oven, a covered pot with feet set over a fire with hot coals underneath and on top.

Aranygaluska was mentioned in Hungarian literature by the 1880s. By the mid-twentieth century, assorted Hungarian and Hungarian Jewish bakeries in America proudly featured *aranygaluska*. In 1972, a Betty Crocker cookbook included a recipe for "Hungarian Coffee Cake" consisting of balls of sweet dough rolled in cinnamon-sugar and baked in a tube pan. As the Hungarian coffee cake spread into mainstream America, it was confused with the similar monkey bread, in which the dough is not dipped into cinnamon or sugar, and the names became interchangeable, with monkey bread becoming the more common term.

ARGAN OIL
The thorny evergreen argan (*argania*) or ironwood tree, which is indigenous to southwestern Morocco and a small part of Algeria, bears almond-like nuts containing an oil rich in naturally occurring antioxidants and flavonoids; this oil is used in cosmetics, medicine, and cooking. The durable wood is resistant to termites and used for carved items and household utensils. The trees were nearly lost when an international monetary organization recommended cutting them down and replanting with citrus trees. However, during a prolonged drought in the Atlas Mountains in the 1990s, the argan trees were the only ones to survive.

In many parts of Morocco, argan oil plays a similar role to that of olive oil in much of the rest of the Mediterranean. The oil has a long shelf life and high smoking point. Its unique, subtle, nutty flavor and rich, velvety texture is traditional in many Moroccan salads (especially orange salads), soups, tagines, and various vegetable dishes; it is also used simply as a dip for bread. Argan oil is usually paired with lemon juice, which enhances its distinctive flavor. *Amelou* is a Moroccan mixture of ground almonds, argan oil, and honey served at breakfast as a dip for bread. Imported argan oil, unrefined and cold-pressed, is available

The oil pressed from the nuts of the argan tree has been used by Moroccan cooks for centuries.

from specialty stores and distributors. A mixture of half olive oil and half peanut oil can be substituted, although the taste is not exactly the same.

Previously, the argan tree would not grow outside of its home area. However, after twenty years of effort, Dr. Elaine Solowey of the Arava Institute, an expert on desert agriculture, finally adapted the tree to flourish in southern Israel. Argan oil is beginning to flow from Israel—good news for Moroccans in Israel who have for decades paid high prices for imported oil.

AROOK
Arook is a fried ball made of ground chicken, turkey, or fish mixed with cooked rice.
Origin: India
Other names: *arooq.*

Iraqis make little balls of ground lamb, pine nuts, scallions, cilantro, and parsley encased in a shell of ground rice, called *arooq bil riz*. The name may come from the Arabic word for the common plum, *al-barqooq* (also the source of the English word apricot), which these meatballs resemble. Jewish immigrants to Calcutta adapted the dish using chicken and fish and local seasonings, usually omitting the rice shell—including rice into the mixture. These balls are typically served as an appetizer or, with rice, lentils, and chutneys, as a main course, or in pita bread.

ARROPE
Arrope is a syrup made from raisins and water.
Origin: Spain
Other names: French: *sirop de raisin*; Spanish: *jarabe, jarope.*

When the Bible mentions *devash* (honey), it almost always refers to a dark, viscous liquid made by cooking down fruit juice, most notably dates, figs, and grapes. The Persians called these fruit honeys *robb/rubb*, later becoming *ar-rubb* in classic Arabic. *Robb* differs from another Persian fruit concentrate, *sharab* (the source of the English word syrup), which contains added sugar. The Moors brought *ar-rubb* to Iberia where it became a beloved component of the cooking, serving as a dip for bread and diluted in water for a refreshing beverage. Popular Spanish syrups include *arrope de meil* (honey syrup), *arrope de mora* (mulberry syrup), and *arrope de mosto* (grape must syrup). Grape syrup was traditionally made at harvest time, the juice cooked for hours until thick, dark, and about one-fourth the original volume. However, *pasa* (raisins) were more accessible in the spring, leading to the favorite Passover syrup, *arrope de pasa*.

On Passover, *arrope* is a popular Sephardic treat served with *bimuelos de massa* (matza pancakes) and *revanadas de parida* (fried matzas, literally "toast of the new mother"). Some Sephardim use *arrope* mixed with nuts for charoset.

SEPHARDIC RAISIN SYRUP (*ARROPE/ARROPE DE PASA*)
ABOUT 3 CUPS   [PAREVE]
    1 pound (3 cups) dark raisins
    6 cups water
    1 tablespoon fresh lemon juice
    1. In a large, heavy pot, soak the raisins in the water until plump, at least 15 minutes.

2. Bring to a boil, cover, reduce the heat to low, and simmer, stirring occasionally, until very soft, about 2 hours.

3. Strain the fruit and cooking liquid through a fine-mesh sieve or food mill, pushing through the pulp and discarding the skins. Add the lemon juice.

4. Simmer, uncovered, over low heat, stirring occasionally, until syrupy, about 30 minutes. Pour into a glass jar and store in the refrigerator.

ARROZ

Arroz, the Ladino word for rice, also designates a specific dish of rice with tomatoes.

Origin: Turkey, Greece
Other names: *arroz kon tomata.*

The Moors introduced rice to Spain in the eighth century and it quickly became an integral part of Sephardic cuisine. In the sixteenth century, Sephardim in Turkey, Greece, and Rhodes added the tomato, recently arrived from America, to their rice dishes. Whereas yellow rice (*arroz kon azafran* and *arroz de Sabato*) was customary for the Sabbath and special events, rice cooked with tomato sauce was found at many weekday meals as well as some special occasions, such as Rosh Hashanah dinner and during Passover. Every Turkish and Greek cook has a recipe for red rice, most preferring it to plain white rice, called *arroz blanco*. In some households, *arroz* is served at both lunch and dinner.

The widespread American dish called Spanish rice, reddened with tomatoes, was ironically completely unknown in Spain. It is actually akin to the classic Sephardic dish *arroz*. Sarah Rorer, the most famous American cooking teacher of her time, in *Mrs. Rorer's New Cook Book* (Philadelphia, 1902), included in her section "A Group of Jewish Recipes" a recipe for "Spanish Rice" made with tomatoes, chicken, onion, and red bell pepper.

(See also Rice and Rice Pudding)

SEPHARDIC RED RICE (*ARROZ/ARROZ CON TOMATA*)
6 TO 8 SERVINGS   [PAREVE]

3 tablespoons olive or vegetable oil
1 large onion, chopped (optional)
1 to 2 cloves garlic, minced (optional)
2 cups long-grain white rice, rinsed under cold water and drained
3 cups boiling water
1 cup tomato sauce, tomato puree, or tomato salsa
About 1½ teaspoons table salt or 2½ teaspoons kosher salt
About ¼ teaspoon ground black pepper
About 1 teaspoon sugar (optional)

1. In a large saucepan, heat the oil over medium-low heat. If using, add the onion and garlic and sauté until soft and translucent, 5 to 10 minutes. Add the rice and sauté until opaque, about 3 minutes.

2. Add the water, tomato sauce, salt, pepper, and, if using, sugar. Bring to a boil, cover, reduce the heat to low, and simmer until the rice is tender and the liquid is absorbed, 25 to 30 minutes. Or cover and bake in a 350°F oven for about 50 minutes. Remove from the heat and let stand, covered, for about 10 minutes. Fluff with a fork. Serve warm.

ARTICHOKE

The Levant is home to numerous wild thistles, most of which historically were considered a nuisance and set ablaze by farmers to open room for desirable plants. Among the few utile thistles were the cardoon and its close relative and probably descendant, the artichoke, the unopened flower bud of a tall, perennial eastern Mediterranean native. Unlike cardoons, which can still be found in the wild, artichokes are exclusively cultivated, leading many authorities to question their origins. They, however, certainly predate the Muslim period, as these vegetables are found throughout early rabbinic literature.

The Talmud and Midrash explain that the biblical *kotz v'dardar* (thorns and thistle) mentioned before Adam and Eve left Eden referred to cardoons and artichokes. Other rabbinical references also reflect the ancient Jewish culinary use of these plants. The Mishnah states that, unlike other thorny plants, *kinras* (artichokes) have gastronomic significance. The Talmud ruled that "one may trim the artichoke and *akaviyot* [cardoons] on a festival" for cooking, even though they require a significant amount of preparation. The Talmud even noted a special unit of measurement for artichokes, *kundasa*.

During the medieval period, the artichoke was held in particularly high esteem on the Arab side of the Mediterranean, where agronomists developed new and improved varieties. The Moors began cultivating this thistle in Spain, possibly as early as 800, but definitely by the eleventh century, and it subsequently became a much-beloved element of Sephardic cuisine, leading to the development of a sufficient number of recipes to fill a book unto itself. The English use of the Arabic-derived name artichoke from *al-kharshuf* (thorns of the ground), leading to the French *artichauts*, rather than the Latin *cynara* (certainly related to the Hebrew *kinras*), reflects the Arabic influence on the role of artichokes in medieval Europe.

Artichokes also became early on a favorite of Italian Jews. Non-Jewish Italians, at first, spoke disparagingly of the artichoke, referring to it as "the Jewish vegetable." Eventually, its regard spread from the Italian ghettos, particularly among the Medicis of Florence. It was Catherine de Médicis who popularized this vegetable in France following her marriage to Henry II. By the late sixteenth century, this once-reviled thistle constituted an important part of Mediterranean cuisine.

Almost all American-grown artichokes are of the Green Globe variety, an Italian cultivar. There are, however, more than fifty varieties, including *Provençal petit violet* and *verts de Florence*, both of which can be eaten untrimmed when young.

Sunchokes or Jerusalem artichokes are not artichokes and have nothing to do with the Holy Land. This native North American tuber, a member of the sunflower family, has lumpy knobs, a brownish skin, and a white, slightly sweet flavor. The name appears to be a mistranslation of the Italian word for sunflower, *girasole*, which sounds like *Gerusalemme* (Jerusalem).

Sephardim usually cook younger artichokes whole and use more mature globes, when the leaves are no longer edible, to make artichoke bottoms. Whole artichokes are commonly stuffed or fried. Artichoke bottoms and hearts are marinated, cooked with other vegetables, or added to salads, casseroles, omelets, and rice dishes. The two favorite Sephardic ways of preparing artichoke hearts are in lemon sauce and tomato sauce. Either dish, sometimes with fava beans or peas, is a common springtime Friday night favorite. Since artichokes make their first appearance of the year in the early spring, they are a common Passover food among Sephardim and Italians. Artichokes—either *keenras* or, from the Arabic, *charshof* in Hebrew—are very popular in modern Israel.

(See also Cardoon)

ARUGULA

A member of the mustard family, arugula was popular in salads as far back as ancient Rome where it was considered an aphrodisiac. Also called roquette and rocket, it has only been widely cultivated in the twentieth century. It is probably the wild plant *oroth* mentioned in the book of Kings. The Talmud recorded it as *gargir*, a food and medicine. Amram Gaon, in the original version of the Haggadah, recommended arugula as being among the five greens suitable for the *karpas* of the Seder.

ASABIA

Asabia is a tube-shaped phyllo pastry filled with nuts, meat, potatoes, or pudding.

Origin: Middle East

Other names: *asabia el aroos, assabih, assba;*
Maghrebi Arabic: *cigare, garro, sigare;* Spanish: *dedo.*

Asabia (akin to the Hebrew *etzba*) means "finger" in Arabic, here referring to crisp slender phyllo tubes. *Asabia* are particularly popular among Syrians, Egyptians, and Moroccans, who feature them at celebrations, notably those for soon-to-be brides. They are most commonly filled with ground almonds (*asabia bi loz*) and baked or deep fried, then dipped into sugar syrup or sprinkled with confectioners' sugar. These pastries, served warm or at room temperature, are considered a tasty alternative to baklava. For some dairy occasions, Syrians stuff the pastry layers with a rose water–accented Turkish rice-flour pudding, *sutlach.*

(See also Phyllo and Sutlach)

ASAFETIDA

Raw asafetida, the dried milky gum from the thick rhizomes of a perennial member of the Apiaceae family, has an unpleasant flavor and stinking, sulfurlike odor; cooked, it develops a garlicky flavor and truffle-like aroma that complements other foods. The name comes from the Farsi *aza* (resin) and Latin *foetida* (stinking). Ancient Persians, however, referred to it as "the food of the gods." It is mentioned in the Talmud as *chiltit* and is considered, along with the radish, an archetypical "sharp item." The Romans combined asafetida with vinegar as a salad dressing and used it to flavor sauces and wine. It also served as a medicine in ancient times.

Today, asafetida is primarily found in Indian cooking and, to a lesser extent, in Persian cooking. Indians believe that asafetida is good for the digestion and commonly add it in small amounts to legume, cabbage, and eggplant dishes to improve the digestibility of these foods. It is used in small amounts in curries, stews, and dried bean dishes.

ASH

Ash is a thick vegetable based soup that sometimes contains meatballs or a little meat.

Origin: Persia

Other names: *shorba*; Afghan: *aush*; Azeri: *aash*.

There are two basic traditional types of Persian soup, both thick like a stew: *ash* and *ab-gusht* or *ab-goosht*, a meat stew (literally "water of the meat"). A Persian synonym of *ash*, *shorba*, comes from the Arabic word for soup. The Farsi word for cook is *ash-paz* (soup maker), and for kitchen *ash-paz-khaneh* (room of the soup maker), reflecting the position of soup in Persian dining.

The ingredients of an *ash* vary among locations and depend on availability. Typical of Persian cuisine, soups are flavored with fresh herbs and greens. Although non-Jewish Persian soups commonly contain some form of yogurt, Jews rarely mix dairy ingredients into hot soups, even vegetarian soups. A simple, hearty *ash* serves as both everyday fare and comfort food, frequently functioning as a one-dish meal, accompanied with bread. These soups are also favored on special occasions. Persian Jews customarily serve some sort of *ghondi* (dumplings) or *reshteh* (noodles) in the soup for Friday night and festival dinners, and they may also accompany the soup with rice. Many Persians offer *ash* to break a fast.

ASHISHA

Ashisha is a lentil pancake.

Origin: Ancient Israel

In biblical times, lentils were the second-most-consumed food among the Jewish people, following only bread (barley and wheat). They were prepared primarily as a stew, but when sweetened with honey and fried, lentils were perhaps the earliest form of cake.

The Bible mentions numerous plants and animals, but very few actual dishes. One particular biblical food, *ashisha* (*ashishot* plural), is recorded in four locations, including the statement that King David "gave to every one of Israel, both man and woman, to every one a loaf of bread, and a cake [from grains] made in a pan, and an *ashisha*." Many classic English translations render the word "cake of pressed raisins." However, the prophet Hosea mentions "*ashishei anavim*" (cakes of grapes), which would make it redundant. The Jerusalem Talmud recorded "Rabbi Yosa went to Rabbi Yossi and brought him lentils that were roasted, ground, mixed with honey, and fried. He said, 'These are the *ashishim* mentioned by the Sages.'"

Song of Songs records: "Support me with *ashishot*, heal me with apples, for I am faint with love." Thus these pancakes developed a reputation as aphrodisiacs. Kabbalists recite this verse with Havdalah at the end of the Sabbath, as the word *ashishot* is akin to the term for "multiple fires." Lately in Israel, *ashishot* have become increasingly popular on Tu b'Av (the fifteenth of the month of Av), the traditional day of searching for romance and matchmaking.

(See also Lentil)

ASHURE

Ashure is a sweetened wheat berry pudding with nuts and dried fruit.

Origin: Turkey

Other names: Azeri: *gavurga*; Georgian: *korkoti*; Greek: *koliva*, *kolyva*; Turkish: *ashura*, *assuré*, *aşure*, *kofyas*, *trigo*.

Cooked grains were used as a holiday dish in many ancient Middle Eastern and Mediterranean cultures. The Greeks were the first known to sweeten the dish with honey. In the Middle East, wheat became the most common grain, particularly hulled durum wheat berries (also called shelled or peeled wheat), which are white in color, lack whole wheat's flavor, and are stickier and softer when cooked. Subsequently, Jews, Muslims, and Christians of the Ottoman Empire adopted versions with dried fruits, nuts, and cinnamon.

The name *ashure* comes from an Arabic word for ten, related to the Hebrew for ten (*ashurah*), as Moslems hold an informal fast day on the tenth day of the lunar month of Muharram (the first month of the Islamic calendar), derived from Yom Kippur, observed on the tenth of Tishri. This date is also the traditional anniversary of the assassination of Hussein, the first Shia imam and, therefore, all too frequently a time of violence. Turks have a legend that the pudding dates back to when Noah and his family left the ark in northeastern Turkey on the tenth of Muharram and celebrated by making a dish using the little food reserves left—some grain, dried fruit, and nuts. Many Sephardim arriving in the eastern Mediterranean adopted the pudding and the name *ashure*, while some Turkish Jews opted for *kofyas* (probably a mispronunciation of *kolva*, itself derived from halva, a different grain pudding). Whatever its name, this widespread dish represents abundance and diversity in connection with collectivity and solidarity, combining several staple ingredients to create a flavorful and rich treat intended to be shared with others.

Ashure is always made in a large quantity in order to share. Because of its name, many people add ten ingredients. Some people make it dry, by stirring the sugar into drained cooked wheat, while others prefer a more liquid dish containing a sugar syrup. Some versions are enhanced with other Middle Eastern standards, including chickpeas, rice, rose water, and orange-blossom water. Many versions are pareve, but some add milk for creaminess. A simpler pudding made with barley, bulgur, or wheat berries is known as *beleela* and *prehito*. Syrians enjoy an anise seed–flavored version called *sleehah*.

Ashure is traditionally enjoyed on Rosh Hashanah (usually made with honey), Sukkot (representing the harvest), and especially Tu b'Shevat (*Las Frutas*), the wheat, fruits, and nuts incorporating the essence of the day. Since wheat berries resemble teeth, Middle Easterners and Georgians customarily serve them at a party to honor a baby's first tooth. *Ashure* is very rich and, therefore, generally served in small portions, commonly garnished with pomegranate seeds or whole almonds.

(See also Beleela and Wheat)

⬥ NEAR EASTERN WHEAT BERRY PUDDING
(*ASHURE/KOFYAS*)

ABOUT 9 CUPS [PAREVE]

  1 pound (2¼ cups) wheat berries, soaked in water
    to cover overnight and drained
  8 cups water
  2 cups sugar or honey, or 1 cup sugar and ½ cup
    honey
Pinch of salt
  1½ to 2 cups coarsely chopped mixed almonds,
    hazelnuts, pine nuts, pistachios, and walnuts
    (use any combination)
  1½ cups raisins or dried currants, or ¾ cup each
  1 cup chopped dates or dried apricots, or ½ cup
    chopped dried apricots, ½ cup chopped dates,
    and ½ cup chopped dried figs
  1 to 2 teaspoons ground cinnamon, or 1 to
    2 tablespoons rose water or orange blossom
    water
Pomegranate seeds, or 1 cup white Jordan almonds
    or whole blanched almonds, for garnish
    (optional)

1. In a large pot, bring the wheat berries and 8 cups water to a boil. Reduce the heat to medium-low and simmer, stirring occasionally and adding more water if necessary, until tender but still slightly chewy, about 1 hour. Drain, reserving 2 cups of the cooking liquid.

2. In a medium saucepan, stir the reserved cooking liquid, sugar, and salt over low heat until the sugar dissolves, about 5 minutes. Increase the heat to medium and simmer until slightly syrupy, about 10 minutes. Pour over the wheat berries and toss to coat.

3. Add the nuts, raisins, dates, and cinnamon. Serve warm, at room temperature, or chilled. If desired, mound the *ashure* on a platter and garnish with pomegranate seeds.

ATAR

Atar is a sugar syrup.
Origin: Middle East
Other names: *attar, qater, sheerah, shira.*

Most Middle Eastern and Balkan pastries—such as baklava, *tishpishti* (semolina cake), *basboussa* (semolina cake), and *kanafeh/kadayif* (shredded wheat dough)—are not inherently sweet on their own. Perhaps this is the result of too much sugar in a dough causing the pastries to burn in the intense heat of the Persian oven. In addition, phyllo is best when baked unsweetened, married only with butter or oil. Rather, these pastries obtain sweetness and moistness from the liberal addition after baking of a simple sugar syrup. This concept dates back about fifteen hundred years to when sugar largely supplanted honey in Persian cooking and syrups. Greeks and others in the Balkans call these various syrup-soaked pastries and cakes *siropiasta*. Sugar syrup is also used to sweeten halvas.

Atar (from the Arabic *utur*, "aromas") is typically composed of two parts sugar to one part water and is often enhanced with rose water or orange-blossom water and/or lemon juice. A little honey produces a mellower syrup.

When pouring syrup over pastry, the rule is to use cold syrup and hot pastry or vice versa. The contrast in temperatures allows the cake to absorb the syrup, producing a moist rather than soggy result. If the pastry dries out while sitting, it can be remoistened with another drizzle of syrup.

❦ MIDDLE EASTERN SUGAR SYRUP (*ATAR/SHIRA*)

ABOUT 2 CUPS   [PAREVE]

- 2 cups (14 ounces) sugar, or 1 cup sugar and 1 cup honey
- 1 cup water
- 1 tablespoon lemon juice, rose water or orange water

In a medium, heavy saucepan, stir the sugar, water, and lemon juice over low heat until the sugar dissolves, about 5 minutes. Stop stirring. Increase the heat to medium, bring to a gentle boil, and cook until the mixture is slightly syrupy and reaches the thread stage or 225 degrees on a candy thermometer, about 10 minutes. If using rose water, stir it in now. The syrup keeps in the refrigerator for several months.

ATAYEF

Atayef is a small pancake filled with cheese or chopped nuts, deep-fried, and drizzled with sugar syrup.
Origin: Middle East
Other names: *ataif, gatayef, katayef.*

Pancakes are among the most ancient of dishes, the type of food popular among nomads cooking over a campfire. In the ninth century, cooks of the caliph of Baghdad were making an unleavened crepe-like pancake called *qata'if* or *qatayif* (from the Arabic for "velvet"), prepared by pouring a thin flour and water batter on a heated sheet of metal. The predominant early use of the *qata'if* was wrapping it around a filling, notably *lauzinaq* (almond paste), then frying it and topping it with honey. The name and concept traveled across the Islamic world, as an anonymous thirteenth-century Andalusian cookbook included a recipe for the dish and the Turkish version gave rise to the Ashkenazic *palacsinta* and blintz.

In the eastern Mediterranean, *qata'if* evolved into a deep-fried, filled, leavened pancake drenched in sugar syrup. The original Arabic dish *atayef,* was made with a yeast batter, but more recently baking powder versions have become very popular. *Atayef* are fried in a thin layer of oil on only one side. The uncooked surface is then stuffed, technically *atayef mehshi*, with ground nuts or soft cheese, then folded in half to enclose the filling. The filled pancakes are then deep-fried, scooped from the oil with a mesh utensil called an *apartand*, and finally doused with *atar* (sugar syrup) perfumed with rose water or orange-blossom water. The *atayef* are frequently made in teams of two: one person filling and folding and the second frying the pancakes. *Atayef* are sold at Middle Eastern bakeries, but many cooks still prefer to make them at home.

These pancakes were popular early on among Middle Eastern Jews, as Ibn al-Qata'if ("son of the pancake maker") became a Jewish family name in Egypt. Syrian and Lebanese Jews enjoy *atayef* on special occasions, sometimes topped with a thick cream called *ashta* or *kaymak*. These small sweet fritters, along with fried savory cheese or vegetable omelets called *edjeh*, are ubiquitous on Hanukkah. Cheese-filled *atayef* are traditional on Shavuot. *Atayef* are typically served with tea or coffee.

AUFLAUF

Auflauf is a baked layered casserole.
Origin: Southern Germany, Austria

An *auflauf* can be either sweet (technically a *suesser auflauf*) or savory; it is commonly made up of whatever leftovers are available, including noodles, vegetables, cheese, fish, and fruit. It can be a quickly assembled breakfast dish or dinner dessert. Most variations contain beaten egg whites, technically an *eierauflauf*, rendering it a soufflé or soufflé pancake. Jewish variations of *auflauf* tend toward sweet, the most common today containing apples. The "Auflauf" in *The International Jewish Cookbook* by Florence Kreisler Greenbaum (1919) is made from a soufflé batter, which is baked, then spread with jelly. The recipe for "Auf-lauf" in the initial edition of *The Settlement Cookbook* (1901), a book containing many Jewish recipes, consists of stale cake or macaroons covered with a sponge batter and baked. In the 1943 edition, in addition to the macaroon style, the author included a souffle version with apples, indicating its relatively late development.

AUFRUF/ARUS

On the Sabbath morning before his wedding (*Shabes oyfrufenish*), the groom in an Ashkenazic synagogue is summoned to the *bimah* (platform) to recite the blessing over the Torah reading. In egalitarian congregations, both the bride and groom may be so honored. This custom is known as an *aufruf* (from the German "up call") by Ashkenazim. Similar celebrations are called *Shabbat Haerusin* (Sabbath of Betrothal) by Moroccans and *arus* (betrothal) by Syrians.

The Talmud relates that King Solomon built a gate in the Temple where the citizens of Jerusalem would sit on the Sabbath to honor and perform kindnesses for imminent grooms, reciting the blessing, "May He whose Presence dwells in this house rejoice you with sons and daughters." The gate was destroyed with the First Temple, but the custom of honoring the groom before his wedding remains, although the honoring is now done in the synagogue.

In traditional communities, women did not publicly read from the Torah, but instead a custom among Ashkenazim emerged in which the bride was entertained with singing, dancing, and food in her parents' home on the Sabbath afternoon or night before the wedding, known as *forshpil* ("prelude," from the German *vorspiel*), *zmires* (religious songs), and *pikholts* ("a wooden cutting board," once hung near the front door of the house alerting passersby to the location of the party).

Many Sephardim and Mizrachim call the groom to the Torah reading on the Sabbath following the wedding (*Shabbat Chatan*). The congregation is customarily treated to a *mezze allegre* (sweet assortment) featuring almond foods, including almond paste, Jordan almonds, and baklava.

Tossing symbolic foods at the bride and groom is an ancient custom of fertility and good fortune. Thus in many congregations after the prospective groom finishes his *aliyah* (Torah reading), the congregation showers (*bevarfn*, literally "peltings" in Yiddish) the groom with nuts, dried fruit, and particularly candy, signifying that his married life should be sweet. Afterwards, children gather up and enjoy the treats. A kiddush customarily follows the services.

AUFSCHNITZ

Aufschnitz is an assortment of thinly sliced German cold cuts, some rather elaborate. Germans are quite proud of their favorite *aufschnitz* and serve them on the Sabbath and other special occasions.

AVGOLEMONO

Avgolemono is a rich, creamy soup, thickened with eggs and made tart with lemon.
Origin: Greece
Other names: Ladino: *sopa de huevo y limón.*

The popularization of the lemon in the Mediterranean around the tenth century sparked a culinary revolution, the juice serving as a bright essence in itself as well as a flavor enhancer for other foods. Vinegar is too harsh to be a surrogate in many dishes. In numerous venerable foods, such as *agristada*, lemon juice was substituted for verjuice (unripe grape juice).

In addition to the thick sauce, cooks in the Mediterranean developed a thinner soup version, *avgolemono* ("egg-lemon" in Greek), a rich, silken soup with a tangy but well-balanced lemony flavor. The eggs contribute both thickening, without dairy, and flavor. The rice or orzo, which imparts a little starch, also helps to thicken and stabilize the soup, as well as transform it into a more substantial dish. Some cooks add a pinch of saffron for a more intense color. Tunisians include a cinnamon stick and a touch of cayenne. Fresh lemon juice is a must, but do not overload it or the soup will be sour, not zesty, too much of a good thing.

In Greece, this mixture is one of the keystones of the cuisine and the ultimate comfort food, considered healthful and curative, in the manner of Ashkenazic chicken soup. Similarly, many Balkan and Turkish Jews eat *avgolemono* to break fasts. In some Mediterranean communities, the soup is part of the meal before and after Yom Kippur. It is also frequently served as the first course for Sabbath dinner and on Rosh Hashanah. *Avgolemono* is so beloved, that Greek Jews developed a Passover version incorporating matza, as well as pareve variations. *Avgolemono* is frequently accompanied with a Greek salad and phyllo pastries.

(See also Agraz and Agristada)

❦ **GREEK CHICKEN SOUP WITH EGG AND LEMON**
(*AVGOLEMONO*)

6 TO 8 SERVINGS   [MEAT OR PAREVE]

    8 cups chicken broth or vegetable broth, strained
    ¾ to 1 cup long-grain white rice, brown rice, orzo,
       or bulgur
    About 1 to 1½ teaspoons table salt or 2 teaspoons
       kosher salt
    Ground black pepper to taste
    1 bay leaf
    12 to 14 (3-by-½-inch) pieces lemon zest (optional)
    2 large eggs
    2 large egg yolks
    4 to 5 tablespoons fresh lemon juice

1. In a large pot, bring the broth to a boil. Add the rice, salt, pepper, bay leaf, and, if using, zest. Reduce the heat to medium-low and simmer until tender, about 7 minutes for orzo, 20 minutes for white rice, 40 minutes for brown rice, or 20 minutes for bulgur. Discard the bay leaf and zest.

2. In a medium bowl, lightly beat together the eggs and yolks. Gradually whisk in the lemon juice. Remove the soup from the heat and gradually beat 1½ cups of the hot soup into the egg mixture, beating continuously. Gradually stir the egg mixture back into the pot. Simmer over low heat, stirring constantly, until the soup thickens, about 5 minutes—do not boil or it will curdle. Serve hot or chilled.

AVICAS

Avicas is a stew or soup dish made of white beans simmered with tomatoes and onions.

Origin: Greece, Turkey

Other names: *avikas, fijones con carne, fijonicas.*

    Before Columbus' voyages to the New World, fava beans (*avas* in Ladino) were a staple of Sephardic cookery. Afterward, haricot beans, in particular, small dried white beans (*fijones* in Greek), quickly supplanted the fava, becoming commonplace both in everyday and festive Sephardic cooking. White beans are generally seasoned sparingly in order not to overpower the delicate flavor. They are used to make a simple yet filling salad common at weekday meals as well as a Sabbath *mezze* (appetizer assortment), and cooked with stuffed grape leaves (*yaprakes con avicas*).

    The most widespread and popular of these bean dishes are white bean and tomato stews and soups,

called *avicas*, a diminutive form of *avas* (as haricots are smaller than favas). Cooking legumes with tomatoes and onions or leeks is a signature of Sephardic cuisine in Turkey and the Balkans. Adding meat and more liquid results in a soup called *soupa de avicas* or simply *avicas*. To stretch the dish, potatoes may be included. On the other hand, reducing the amount of water produces a thicker *avicas*, usually vegetarian, which is served as a side dish over rice or couscous, or with bread to sop up the *caldo* (sauce). Unlike the sweet American style of baked beans, *avicas* is always savory.

    Arguably, no area relished *avicas* more than Salonika, where it was enjoyed as everyday food as well as Sabbath fare. The vegetarian version is served with rice at dairy meals, including during the ten days preceding the fast of Tisha b'Av and for Thursday night dinner. Bean stews proved particularly advantageous for the Sabbath, when no cooking was permitted, as they could stay on the fire for several hours or even overnight without drying out or losing texture. In some areas, they replaced the traditional Iberian *hamin* (Sabbath stew). *Soupa de avicas* with meat was a popular Friday night entrée, typically accompanied with *yaprakes finos* (stuffed grape leaves), *pastels* (meat pies), and spinach-filled *borekas* (turnovers) or *ojaldres* (phyllo triangles). Leftover soup was kept in the oven to simmer overnight, in the manner of a Sabbath stew, and then served for lunch with *arroz* (rice with tomatoes).

❦ **SEPHARDIC WHITE BEANS** (*AVICAS*)

5 TO 6 SERVINGS   [PAREVE]

    3 tablespoons olive or vegetable oil
    2 medium onions, chopped
    2 to 3 cloves garlic, minced
    About 2 quarts water (or 3 quarts for a soup)
    1 pound (2⅓ cups) dried navy, cannellini, or other
       white beans, picked over, washed well, and
       drained
    1 bay leaf
    2 cups tomato sauce, or 1 pound (2½ cups) peeled,
       seeded, and chopped plum tomatoes and
       1 tablespoon tomato paste
    About 1 teaspoon table salt or 2 teaspoons kosher
       salt
    Ground black pepper to taste
    ½ teaspoon ground cumin or pinch of sugar

Juice of 1 to 2 lemons (optional)

¼ cup chopped fresh flat-leaf parsley or cilantro

1. In a heavy 5- to 6-quart pot, heat the oil over medium heat. Add the onions and garlic and sauté until softened, 5 to 10 minutes. Add the water, beans, and bay leaf. Bring to a boil, partially cover, reduce the heat to medium-low, and simmer until the beans are tender, about 2 hours. Drain off most of the cooking liquid. (For a soup, do not drain.)

2. Add the tomato sauce, salt, pepper, cumin, and, if using, lemon juice. Simmer, stirring occasionally, until the flavors meld, about 20 minutes, or cover and bake in a 300-degree oven, without stirring, until most of the liquid is absorbed, about 2 hours. Discard the bay leaf and stir in the parsley.

AVOCADO

By the time the Spanish arrived in the New World, avocados (from the Aztec name, *ahuacatl*) were widely grown throughout Central America and the Caribbean. Montezuma introduced them to Hernando Cortés at a feast in 1519 and the conquistadors promptly shared this creamy fruit with the Spanish court. However, avocado was perhaps the last of the American produce brought by the conquistadors to find widespread acceptance in the Old World. In the United States, where they were known as alligator pears, avocados only gained importance following World War II.

There are about a dozen major varieties of avocado, possessing varying attributes. The most popular avocado in the United States and much of Europe is the Hass, introduced in 1926. The flesh is very rich, nutty, and creamy; the pebbly green skin turns black as it ripens. Hass, which softens evenly, is the preferred variety for guacamole, sauces, and soups. Fuerte, the most widely grown variety in the rest of the world, has a relatively smooth, bright green skin.

The avocado reached Israel in 1924; it was first planted at the Mikveh-Israel Agricultural School and was soon introduced to kibbutzim as well as home gardens. Commercial-scale production began in the early 1950s, and the avocado emerged as a national favorite and major export. In 1983, more than 2.5 million Israelis trees produced 7,200 tons of avocados and 80 percent of them were exported. Today, the world's leading avocado producers are Mexico, the United States, Chile, Spain, and Israel. Israelis adapted the fruit into various dishes, including *avakado eem tachina* (avocado dip) and *marak avakado* (avocado soup).

B

BABA GHANOUJ

Baba ghanouj is a salad made from mashed roasted or broiled eggplant, tahini (sesame seed paste), and lemon juice.

Origin: Lebanon

Other names: *baba ghanoush, badhinjin mutabbal, mutabbal, salat chatzilim.*

Mashed eggplant salads are popular from western Africa through Russia, but arguably the most famous variation is *baba ghanouj*, a Lebanese puree made with two other popular, inexpensive Levantine ingredients—tahini and lemon juice. The salad is also sometimes accented with other local favorites, including olive oil, garlic, chopped onions, parsley, cumin, sumac, and cayenne. *Baba* is the Arabic word for "father" as well as a term of endearment; *ghanouj* or *ghanoush* means "indulged/pampered." It is not known whether *baba* refers to an actual parent indulged by this special treat or to the eggplant, which is considered the most important (big daddy) of vegetables. The best *baba ghanouj* comes from young eggplants with a shiny skin, as they have fewer seeds. Roasting the eggplant imparts a characteristic pleasing smoky flavor. Good *baba ghanouj* should be smoky and creamy. It is a standard in a *mezze* (appetizer assortment) with warm pita, crackers, and crudités.

Israelis learned to make *baba ghanouj* from the Arabs, sometimes substituting mayonnaise or yogurt for the tahini. In the decade following the founding of the state in 1948, a period known as the *tzena* (austerity), eggplant in particular became widely used as a meat substitute and mashed eggplant salad emerged as a cultural icon. As a result, in contemporary Israel, *baba ghanouj* is commonplace at meals and as a starter in restaurants, and is usually kept in the refrigerator in prospect of unexpected guests or need for a snack. Due to the impact of Israelis in America in the late twentieth century, *baba ghanouj* is readily available in supermarkets there as well.

(See also Eggplant)

LEBANESE EGGPLANT SPREAD WITH TAHINI (*BABA GHANOUJ*)

ABOUT 3 CUPS/5 TO 6 SERVINGS [PAREVE]

2 medium (1¼ pounds each) eggplants
About ¼ cup tahini (sesame seed paste)
4 to 5 tablespoons fresh lemon juice
About 3 tablespoons olive oil
1 to 2 cloves garlic, minced
About ¾ teaspoon table salt or 1½ teaspoons kosher salt
Ground black pepper to taste
2 tablespoons chopped fresh flat-leaf parsley for garnish (optional)
2 tablespoons pine nuts for garnish (optional)

1. Cut several slits in the eggplants. Roast the eggplants over a flame, turning every 5 minutes, until charred and tender, 15 to 25 minutes. Or place on a baking sheet and bake in a 375°F oven until very tender, about 1 hour. Or roast over a flame until lightly charred, then transfer to a baking sheet and bake until tender and shriveled, about 30 minutes. Let cool until able to handle.

2. Peel the eggplants, being careful not to leave any skin, and let drain in a colander for about 5 minutes. Transfer the eggplants to a bowl, coarsely chop, then mash into a pulp. Mix in the tahini, lemon juice, oil, garlic, salt, and pepper. The mixture should have a soft, creamy consistency. If too thick, stir in a little water.

3. Spread the mixture on a plate and let stand at room temperature for 30 minutes. Sprinkle with the parsley and/or pine nuts. Baba ghanouj can be stored in the refrigerator for at least 3 days. Serve at room temperature.

BABANATZA

Babanatza is a dense semolina pudding, made with ground dried fruit, most often, raisins.

Origin: Greece

Semolina cakes and puddings, such as *revani* and *tishpishti*, are widespread throughout the Middle East and Balkans. What differentiates the Balkan *babanatza* is the ground dried fruit. Recipes vary from a rather simple batter without eggs to one with plenty of eggs that produces a lighter texture. In Greece, this semolina treat was often prepared on Friday and served for *shalosh seudot* (third meal) on the Sabbath afternoon or a *melava malcha* (post-Sabbath celebration) on Saturday night. A version using matza is very popular on Passover. A similar pudding made from cornmeal is called *bobota*; it emerged from the scarcity of World War II, when little was available except cornmeal, a grain the Greeks considered of poor quality. Some cooks like to moisten the pudding with *atar* (sugar syrup) in the Middle Eastern fashion, while others serve it with applesauce.

GREEK SEMOLINA AND RAISIN PUDDING
(*BABANATZA*)

9 TO 12 SERVINGS [PAREVE]

    2 cups raisins, or 1 cup raisins and 1 cup dried
        apricots or dried pitted plums
    Sweet wine or water
    6 large eggs
    1 cup sugar
    ¾ cup honey
    1½ cups (9 ounces) fine semolina (not semolina
        flour) or matza meal
    1 cup chopped almonds or walnuts
    2 to 3 medium green apples, peeled, cored, and
        chopped (optional)

1. Soak the raisins in wine to cover overnight. Drain. Grind or puree the raisins.

2. Preheat the oven to 350°F. Grease a 13-by-9-inch baking pan.

3. Beat the eggs until light, about 5 minutes. Add the sugar and honey and beat until thick and creamy, about 5 minutes. Stir in the raisins, semolina, nuts, and, if using, apples.

4. Pour into the prepared pan—the batter should be no more than 2 inches deep. Bake until golden brown, about 1 hour. Let cool. Cut into squares or diamonds.

BABKA

Babka is a cake of rich, yeast-raised dough, spread with a sweet filling, rolled up, and baked in a loaf pan.
Origin: Poland, Ukraine
Other names: *oogat kinamon,* Russian coffee cake.

The Germans and Austrians had their kuchen and the Hungarians their rolled cakes (*kakosh, makosh,* and *dios*) and *aranygaluska,* but in parts of Poland and Ukraine, it was babka. Babka takes its name from the endearment form of the Slavic *babcia* (grandmother), which is related to the Eastern Yiddish *bubbe,* thus literally meaning "grandma's cake." This name was derived because the cake's tall, stout, fluted sides, formed in a traditional Polish pan, were reminiscent of an old woman's skirt, and/or because grandmothers were the primary bakers of this treat. Those familiar with the contemporary Jewish loaf-like babka may be surprised by the tall cake, but that is because there are two styles of babka. The venerable non-Jewish version, baked in a "Turk's head pan" (a scalloped-edged tube pan that resembles a turban), is similar in texture (spongy) and shape (tall and cylindrical) to an Alsatian kugelhopf. Quite different is the more recent Jewish-style babka, a sweet bread made from a firm yeast dough, spread with a filling, and rolled up jelly-roll style.

Jewish babka evolved in early nineteenth-century Poland from the Sabbath egg challah when housewives prepared extra dough, spread it with a little jam or cinnamon, perhaps sprinkled some raisins over the top, rolled it up, and baked it alongside the bread, providing a delicious snack for hungry children on busy Friday afternoons or a special treat for the Sabbath. Unlike the butter-rich non-Jewish babka, Jewish versions were usually kept pareve by using oil. Since few eastern European Jewish households at that time had a Turk's head pan or other tube pan, the cake was typically baked as a loaf. The result is a light, eggy bread, which, when cut into slices, has generous alternate swirls of filling. Babka is firmer and slightly drier than a brioche, but makes up for its lack of richness with the delightful swirls; it should never be cloying or overwhelming. Part of babka's appeal is that it is fancier and more interesting than a typical coffee cake, yet it is not too gourmet or complex, so any home baker can easily replicate it. Besides Sabbath fare, a slice of babka with a glass of tea became a widespread way for some Poles to break the fast of Yom Kippur. Dairy babka filled with sweetened curd cheese might appear for Shavuot. Babka is also sliced and toasted for breakfast, as a sort of intense cinnamon bread. Besides the original cinnamon filling, numerous others emerged, including almond paste, apricot lekvar, cheese, chocolate, poppy seed, and walnut.

In the mid-twentieth century, some bakers began topping the loaf with streusel, which may or may not be gilding the lily. In addition, *shikkera babka* (literally "drunken grandma"), sometimes served during Purim, is an unfilled version drizzled with a syrup laced with whiskey or rum, akin to a French *savarin* and *baba au rhum* (technically *babka au rhum*).

Throughout much of the twentieth century, Jewish-style babka was little known outside of Polish Jewish homes. During the late 1950s, European-style bakeries in Israel began popularizing the cake there. Around the same time in America, Jewish babka began spreading outside Polish Jewish areas, gradually appearing in American sisterhood cookbooks and Jewish bakeries. Soon babka loaves could be found in Greek and other non-Jewish bakeries around New York City and other areas with a large Jewish population, and Americans came to associate the term babka with the Jewish version.

Babka achieved national fame in a 1994 episode of the sitcom *Seinfeld*; it served as the plot point as a gift for a dinner party, the character Elaine explaining, "You can't beat a babka."

❧ POLISH ROLLED YEAST CAKE (*BABKA*)

2 MEDIUM LOAVES   [PAREVE OR DAIRY]

Dough:

1 package (2¼ teaspoons) active dry yeast or
    1 (0.6-ounce) cake fresh yeast
½ cup warm water (105 to 115°F for dry yeast; 80 to
    85°F for fresh yeast), or ¼ cup warm water and
    ¼ cup warm milk
½ cup sugar
1 cup vegetable oil or unsalted butter
4 large eggs, or 2 large eggs and 2 large egg yolks
1 teaspoon table salt or 2 teaspoons kosher salt
About 4¼ cups (22 ounces) bread or unbleached
    all-purpose flour
Double recipe of 1 babka filling, or 1 recipe each of
    2 separate fillings (recipes follow)
½ to 1 cup raisins, dried currants, or coarsely
    chopped walnuts (optional)
Egg wash (1 large egg beaten with 1 teaspoon water)
    or egg white for brushing

1. Dissolve the yeast in ¼ cup water. Stir in 1 teaspoon sugar and let stand until foamy, 5 to 10 minutes. In a large bowl, combine the yeast mixture, remaining water, remaining sugar, butter, eggs, salt, and enough flour to make a dough that holds together. Knead until smooth and springy, about 5 minutes. Place in an oiled bowl and turn to coat. Cover with plastic wrap or a kitchen towel and let rise in a warm, draft-free place until doubled in bulk, 2 to 3 hours.

2. On a lightly floured surface or in an electric mixer with a dough hook, knead the dough, adding more flour as needed, until smooth and springy, about 5 minutes. Place in an oiled bowl and turn to coat. Cover loosely with plastic wrap or a kitchen towel and let rise in a warm, draft-free place until doubled in bulk, 2 to 3 hours, or cover with plastic wrap and refrigerate overnight. If refrigerating, let stand at room temperature for 30 minutes before using.

3. Punch down the dough and divide in half. Roll each piece into a 12-by-8-inch rectangle about ⅓ inch thick. Spread each with the same or different fillings, leaving a 1-inch border on all sides. If using, sprinkle with the raisins. Brush the edges with a little egg wash to help seal the babka. Starting from a narrow end, roll up jelly-roll style and pinch the seams to seal.

4. Place each babka, seam side down, in a greased 9-by-5-inch loaf pan, 9-inch tube pan, or 10-inch round cake pan; each pan should be no more than two-thirds full. Cover loosely with plastic wrap or a kitchen towel and let rise until nearly doubled in bulk, about 1 hour.

5. Preheat the oven to 350°F (325°F if using glass pans).

6. Brush each babka with the egg wash. Bake until the babkas are golden brown and hollow sounding when tapped, or until an instant-read thermometer inserted into the center registers 188°F, 35 to 45 minutes. Let stand in the pan for 10 minutes, then transfer to a wire rack and let cool. Wrap and store at room temperature for up to 2 days or in the freezer for up to 2 months.

Babka Fillings

❧ CINNAMON FILLING

ENOUGH FOR 1 MEDIUM LOAF

½ cup brown or granulated sugar, or ¼ cup each
1½ teaspoons ground cinnamon
2 tablespoons (¼ stick) unsalted margarine or
    butter, melted
1 tablespoon corn syrup or honey

In a medium bowl, combine the sugar and cinnamon. Stir in the margarine and corn syrup to make a smooth paste.

CHOCOLATE FILLING

ENOUGH FOR 1 MEDIUM LOAF

4 ounces bittersweet or semisweet chocolate, finely ground

¼ cup unsweetened cocoa powder

½ cup sugar, ¾ cup apricot jam, or ¼ cup almond paste

3 tablespoons unsalted butter or margarine, melted

1 teaspoon vanilla extract

½ teaspoon ground cinnamon (optional)

In a medium bowl, combine all the ingredients.

BACHSH

Bachsh is rice cooked with cubes of meat or liver and various fresh herbs that tint the rice green.

Origin: Uzbekistan

Most Bukharans associate the smell of rice cooking with their home and childhood. In many Bukharan households, no Friday night dinner or holiday meal would be considered complete without *bachsh*, a variation of the other major rice dish, *plov*. *Bachsh* is cooked in a cotton bag or a *lingharie*, which is a large oval ceramic dish, which helps to keep each grain of rice intact and separate. This dish is also traditional for Hanukkah. Another popular Friday night rice dish is *oshi piyozi* (rice-and-meat-stuffed onion shells). For Sabbath lunch there is *osh sevo*, rice with shin meat, dried plums, and cinnamon, which is baked overnight in a low oven.

(See also Plov)

BUKHARAN GREEN RICE (*BACHSH*)

5 TO 6 SERVINGS [MEAT]

3 tablespoons vegetable oil

1 medium onion, chopped

8 ounces lamb or beef chuck, cut into ½-inch pieces

Ground black pepper to taste

2 cups water

About 1 teaspoon table salt or 2 teaspoons kosher salt

⅛ teaspoon saffron strands (optional)

1 cup chopped fresh cilantro

1 cup chopped fresh flat-leaf parsley

½ cup chopped fresh dill

½ cup chopped fresh mint

1½ cups (10 ounces) basmati rice

1. In a large pot, heat the oil over medium heat. Add the onion and sauté until soft and translucent, 5 to 10 minutes. Add the meat and stir until it loses its red color, about 5 minutes. Add the pepper, cover, reduce the heat to low, and simmer, stirring occasionally, until tender, about 30 minutes.

2. Add the water, salt, and, if using, saffron, increase the heat, and bring to a boil. Add ¾ cup cilantro, all the parsley, all the dill, and ¼ cup mint. Cover, reduce the heat to low, and simmer for 10 minutes.

3. Meanwhile, place the rice in a bowl, add cold water to cover, swirl, and drain. Repeat rinsing the rice until no whiteness appears in the water. Drain. Add the rice to the meat and herb mixture and press the solids down—the water should cover the rice by about 1 inch.

4. Cover, bring to a boil, reduce the heat to low, and simmer until the liquid evaporates, about 20 minutes.

5. Using the handle of a wooden spoon, poke 7 holes in the rice, cover the pot with a kitchen towel, cover with the lid, and let stand for 15 minutes. Stir in the remaining herbs. Serve warm.

BAGALEH

Bagaleh is a soft ring-shaped bread that is coated with sesame seeds.

Origin: Israel

Other name: Jerusalem bagel.

Israelis love fresh baked breads, especially relatively smaller ones, perfect in size for a transportable breakfast or snack. Among the most prominent of contemporary Israeli breads, a common sight hanging at kiosks and markets, are *bagelach* (*bagaleh* singular), named after the similarly shaped Polish bagel.

The *bagaleh* seems to have originated among the Arabs of Jaffa around 1948, initially influenced by the European bagel (referred to as *bagaleh Amerikai*). *Bagaleh* gained widespread prominence among Jews after the Six-Day War, when Israelis noticed them in the *souk* (marketplace) of the Old City (Jerusalem).

Bagels are made from a lean dough (flour, water, yeast, and salt) and first boiled in water before baking, resulting in a very hard surface and chewy interior, while the larger *bagaleh* is made from a richer dough and merely baked, producing a softer bread. Each bakery's recipe is top secret, including the amount of oil and sugar, and some purportedly omit salt from the dough and others add dry milk powder.

The original *bagelach*, and still the most common, are rather skinny. More recently, larger and more hefty versions have become commonplace. Because of their size, shape, and sesame coating, *bagelach* are generally eaten plain or sometimes with butter, za'atar, or feta cheese, but they are not sliced and used for sandwiches. Many Israelis have one with their morning cup of coffee or merely nibble it on the way to work.

BAGEL

In light of the bagel's current ubiquity in America, it is often hard to imagine that a few decades ago this crusty, chewy, ring-shaped bread was basically unknown outside of Jewish circles. It only initially appeared in an English-language American newspaper in 1932. In 1951, during the intermission of the Broadway musical *Bagels and Yox,* bagels were distributed to the audience, many of whom were unfamiliar with them. As late as February 4, 1956, the *New York Times* tried to explain the bagel: "A form of Jewish baked goods sometimes described as a doughnut with rigor mortis, will not disappear from New York tables."

Ring-shaped pastries and breads are hardly unique, as examples in many cultures date back thousands of years. The bagel's distinction derives from being boiled in water before baking, a step that produces the characteristic crisp crust and moist, chewy interior. The bagel is related to the similar medieval pretzel, the soft kind. The scalding liquid kills any yeast on the surface, thereby restricting rising during baking and maintaining the shape, as well as contributing

The best bagels are still boiled then baked. The traditional crew: two people shape the bagels, one boils, and one bakes.

to the unique shiny surface. The bagel's ring shape had a practical purpose—the hole made the bagel easier to remove from the boiling water.

The *beigel* was first mentioned in 1610 in the records of the Kraków Jewish community, affirming that bagels were an appropriate gift for women about to give birth and for midwives. Jews from central Asia, where a similar type of ring bread still exists, might have brought the concept to eastern Europe during the Middle Ages. Or it may have come from the other direction, from Sephardim who prepared a boiled bread, *escaladadas*, a name derived from the Spanish *escalder* (to scald). The Yiddish name *beigel/beygel* may have derived from *bougal*, a Middle High German word for ring, or *beigen*, a Yiddish word for bend. It was later Americanized to bagel—this spelling appeared in print in September 14, 1930 *New York Times*.

By the seventeenth century, bagels had become a commonplace food among Jews in Poland and the Baltic States. Bagels did not, however, make much of an impact in the surrounding areas of Germany or Russia. The original bagel was smaller and much thinner (more hole, less bread) than the average modern bagel. There was little variation in Old World bagels, although eggs were occasionally added to the dough to make the finished product softer, as well as to lengthen the shelf life. Unlike most breads in Europe, such as rye and bialys, that were commonly produced in bakeries by professionals, bagels were typically prepared by women in modest home kitchens, then hawked from baskets or poles on street corners by the husband or children. Government officials occasionally aspired to license bagel selling, but most peddlers ignored this inconvenience, frequently at the risk of forfeiting their wares to hungry police.

The bagel's circular shape, with no beginning or end, led to its symbolic usage at various Jewish life-cycle events, including births, circumcisions, post-funeral gatherings, and meals before fast days. Nevertheless, it was primarily an everyday bread, not a beloved treat or icon. Following the impoverishment of Poland in the wake of the Cossack massacres in the mid-seventeenth century, bagels served as breakfast and lunch for the masses of Polish Jews, working men as well as school children, who ate them plain or with a schmear of butter or schmaltz.

Beginning in the 1880s, eastern European Jews

began to arrive in the United States in great numbers, bringing with them the bagel. Enough demand developed that there were three hundred bagel bakers in New York City in 1907, who banded together to form the International Beigel Baker's Union, Local #338. (After the advent of the bagel machine and the disappearance of unionized bagel makers, the union shifted to represent grocery workers and others.) This was a very restrictive group, with membership passed down from father to sons. Recipes and techniques were zealously guarded family secrets. For the following half century, bagels were all made by hand, customarily in groups of four—two men ambidextrously shaping the bagels, one boiling them, and one baking them. Workers, usually laboring in cramped cellars, were paid by the piece—constituting nineteen cents a box in 1910. An experienced team could churn out 6,400 bagels (that's 100 boxes) in a single overnight shift. As late as the 1950s, New York City still had more than thirty bagel teams practicing their craft in the traditional manner.

As the immigrants became more established and prosperous, the bagel became less of a staple, eventually ending up as a Sunday morning treat. Toppings expanded to include poppy seeds, sesame seeds, caraway seeds, dried onions, garlic, kosher salt, and "everything," a combination of all six. Whereas in Europe bagels were never used for sandwiches, in America they began to attract various fillings. When during the 1930s, many Jews abstained from eating the then-stylish but unkosher American Sunday brunch classic, eggs Benedict, they substituted lox slices for the ham, a schmear of cream cheese for the hollandaise sauce, and a bagel for the English muffin. Thus was born an American classic. Neither lox nor cream cheese had ever touched a bagel in Europe.

For decades, a number of people, hoping to expand production and break the union monopoly, struggled to invent a bagel-making machine. Among the most persistent of these was baker Meyer "Mickey" Thompson of Los Angeles. Finally in 1962, Thompson's son, Daniel, inventor of the first folded Ping-Pong table, fulfilled his father's quest, creating a machine that eliminated hand rolling and was capable of extruding up to four hundred bagels an hour; later large-scale commercial models could turn out nearly five thousand an hour. Ironically, the major American machine companies declined to produce the Thompson Bagel Machine, feeling that the bagel market would never be large enough to justify the expense of manufacturing the contraptions. Union protests managed to keep the new machine out of New York.

In 1927, Harry Lender emigrated from Lublin, Poland, ending up in New Haven, Connecticut, where he opened a bakery, which was eventually taken over by his sons, Murray and Marvin. They sold traditional Jewish breads and rolls and, on the weekends, bagels. In order to speed up production, the Lenders began feeding large chunks of dough into an Italian breadstick machine, allowing an individual to form six hundred bagels per hour. In 1955, Lender's began packaging its bagels in plastic bags for sale in local grocery stores. In August 1963, Thompson installed his first machine in the Lender's plant in New Haven. Within a few years, almost every major bagel baker in America was using Thompson's machine.

There was one problem with Lender's acquisition: The bakery was now producing more bagels than the geographic limitations of Connecticut could consume. To overcome the short shelf life, in 1965 Lender's began flash-freezing bagels, a step toward their eventual acceptance into the mainstream, although detrimental to their taste and texture. To further abet the bagel's acceptance, Lender's retooled its mass-produced bagel to be softer and sweeter than the traditional style. Lender's became and would remain the world's largest producer of bagels. A decade later, Lender's bagels were a common sight in supermarket freezers throughout the United States and ranked only behind frozen orange juice in frozen food purchases. By the late 1980s, the bagel emerged as America's most prevalent breakfast bread. The number of bagel stores nationwide jumped to 1,500 in 1994 and more than 9,000 in 1998. At the beginning of the twenty-first century, bagel shops ranked among the top chains for growth in units and bagel stores existed in most towns, even those with no Jewish population.

In Israel, as in early twentieth-century America, a few eastern European women boiled and baked bagels in their home kitchens. However, as these people died, so did the Israeli bagels. Then in 1994, Bonkers Bagels opened in Jerusalem, using a machine to produce American-style bagels. Other bagel stores soon followed and today in Israel bagels from plain to sun-dried tomato, with toppings from cream cheese to za'atar, are now commonplace.

BAHARAT

Baharat is an all-purpose spice blend.

Origin: The Levant

Other names: *bharat*; Farsi: *advieh*.

Baharat, a province in India and a name for non-Muslim southern India, gave rise to a generic Arabic word encompassing spices and herbs, as well as more specifically to a Levantine spice mixture akin to the Indian garam masala. The exact ingredients and proportions of *baharat* vary from region to region and cook to cook. It can be either a simple blend of a few basic spices or a more complicated production including any and all of black pepper, cardamom, cinnamon, cloves, coriander, cumin, ginger, nutmeg, paprika, and sumac. Since the arrival of the American allspice berry in the sixteenth century, allspice became a prominent feature of some versions, particularly in Syria, where the overall concept of *baharat* is equivalent to all spices. Turkish versions typically contain dried mint.

Baharat is used as a rub for grilled lamb, as well as a flavoring for beef, chicken, fish, *kibbeh* (a ground meat mixture), lentils, rice, eggplant, tomato sauces, and soups. In the Indian manner, it is generally first fried in fat to develop the flavor before it is added to a dish. The Iranian variation is added to Persian charoset (*advieh-e halegh*). *Baharat* is quite popular in Israel, readily available in groceries and spice shops.

❦ LEBANESE SPICE MIXTURE (*BAHARAT*)

ABOUT ½ CUP   [PAREVE]

  2 tablespoons ground black pepper

  2 tablespoons sweet paprika

  1 tablespoon ground cinnamon

  1 tablespoon ground coriander

  1 tablespoon ground cumin

  1½ teaspoons ground cloves

  1½ teaspoons ground nutmeg

  ½ teaspoon ground cardamom (4 green cardamom pods)

In a small bowl, combine all the ingredients. Adjust the proportions to personal preference. Store in an airtight container at room temperature for up to 3 months or in the freezer.

BAKLAVA

Baklava is a layered phyllo-dough pastry filled with ground nuts and spices and drenched in syrup.

Origin: Persia or Turkey

Other names: Afghan: *baghlawa*; Arabic: *baclawa*, *baqlawa*; Azeri: *paxlava*; Farsi: *baghlava*, *baqlava*; Georgian: *pakhlava*, *tapluna*; Greek: *baklavas*, *mpaklabas*; Kurdish: *baqlawa*; Romanian: *baclava*.

Baklava is the most popular and widespread pastry in the Middle East and the Balkans. Nut and honey confections date back early in history, but layering nuts between thin strips of pastry appears to have begun in the late medieval period. The cookbook *Kitab al-Tabikh* (Book of Dishes) by Muhammad ibn al-Hasan Al-Baghdadi, written in Iraq in 1226, but based on a collection of ninth-century Persian-inspired recipes, contained recipes for *lauzinaq*. These were small pieces of almond paste wrapped in very thin pastry and drenched in syrup. Eventually, Middle Eastern pastry makers devised the process of layering the ingredients; some scholars suggest they were influenced by the Mongols or Turks. Around

The crisp, layered baklava has for many generations been a favorite treat at Middle Eastern celebrations.

the fifteenth century, the Turks developed *yufka*, an extremely thin dough and the predecessor of phyllo, which was necessary for the invention of baklava.

The name baklava is probably derived from the Farsi word *balg/barg* (leaf) with the Persian suffix *va*, indicating a Persian origin. It was, however, the royal Ottoman bakers in the sultan's palace in Istanbul who, sometime after the sixteenth century, transformed the dish into its contemporary form of multiple layers of phyllo filled with nuts and spices and drenched in syrup. The Turks and Arabs eventually spread baklava throughout the Middle East and North Africa, as well as the Balkans, areas where it remains a beloved part of celebrations.

A common expression in Turkey was once, "I'm not rich enough to have baklava," as this dish was originally the sole province of the upper class. Because home horizontal ovens were until recently rare in many parts of the Middle East, baklava was primarily made by professional bakers. Then in the mid-nineteenth century, small pastry shops catering to the middle class appeared in large Ottoman cities, giving a large segment of society access to baklava. Around the same time, the popularization of the home oven led to baklava's increasing preparation by home cooks, making it a widespread indulgence. Baklava emerged as an important treat for Mizrachim and Sephardim from the former Ottoman Empire and Persia. Baklava became a common sight in Israeli groceries and bakeries. In the late twentieth century, it was popularized in America.

There are numerous variations of baklava, many a closely guarded secret passed down within families. Almond is the traditional nut used in Iran; pistachios or a mixture of the two nuts are occasionally substituted. Walnuts are most common in Turkey, the Balkans, and the Levant. In Iran, Iraq, and Syria, the sugar syrup is usually accented with rose water, while Greeks favor honey, lemon juice, and cinnamon in the syrup. Romanians prefer a plain sugar syrup. Although purists disdain anything except the classic nut filling, some cooks innovate by adding items such as dates and chocolate chips. Hungarians make an apricot version, developed after the Turks introduced the dish in the sixteenth century. Butter is used to brush the phyllo, but for meat occasions, Jews substitute oil or margarine.

Baklava is not everyday or even weekly fare, but generally reserved for special occasions, such as weddings and bar mitzvahs, as well as Rosh Hashanah and Purim. Sephardim refrain from serving dark-colored pastries, such as those made from walnuts, on Rosh Hashanah, which would portend a dark year. Therefore, blanched almonds or pistachios are traditional on Rosh Hashanah to produce a light color so that the year should be *dulce y aclarada* (sweet and bright). A Passover baklava is made by soaking matzas in wine or water to soften them and substituting these for the phyllo.

Traditionally, baklava was prepared in a *tifsin*, a deep round baking pan. Professional bakers cut the baklava into diamonds, but some home cooks opt for easier squares. This very rich treat is usually served in small portions and served with Turkish coffee.

BANANA

Today, more pounds of bananas, the fruit of a palm-like plant native to tropical Southeast Asia, are cultivated than any other fruit. Although the plant is called a tree, it is actually the world's largest herb. Each plant produces one bunch with three to twenty hands; each hand consists of ten to twenty bananas, called fingers. There are more than three hundred varieties, including some with large seeds, although only a very few are common in the West.

In 2008, India was the world's leading producer of bananas, most for domestic consumption. For generations, bananas have been a part of Indian cooking—fried, steamed with short-grain rice, and cooked in coconut milk. Carrots sweetened with bananas are a traditional Indian Rosh Hashanah dish.

Traders brought the fruit across the Indian Ocean to Africa and it subsequently followed the spread of Islam, appearing in Egypt by the tenth century and soon thereafter in Iberia. In 1516, the Spanish planted bananas in the West Indies.

The first known appearance of bananas in the mainland United States was a load that arrived in New York City in 1804. Bananas were initially popularized at the Philadelphia Centennial Exposition in 1876. Subsequently, Captain Lorenzo Baker established regular large-scale banana imports and founded the Boston Fruit Company, which in 1889, merged with another banana importer, giving rise to the United Fruit Company.

In 1885, fourteen-year-old Samuel Zemurray (originally Zmurri), born to a Jewish family in Kishinev, Russia, came in steerage to Selma, Alabama. He began working for an elderly fruit peddler to support himself. Four years after arriving in America, and after saving up $750, Zemurray purchased at a very low price a load of ripe bananas, the type of fruit that was usually thrown away. He sold the bananas, making a profit of $35. He continued successfully investing in banana transactions, buying carloads of "ripes" and becoming known as "Sam the Banana Man."

In 1906, Zemurray acquired part ownership in two steamers and full title to five thousand acres of prime banana-growing land in Honduras. Six years later, when a new Honduran government acted against his interests, Zemurray loaned the former president, General Manuel Bonilla, money to buy a yacht, arms, and ammunition, and provided him with mercenary soldiers. Six months later, the military coup swept into power, establishing a regime friendly to the planter and giving birth to the term "banana republic." When the United Fruit Company acquired Zemurray's Cuaymel Fruit in 1929, he became the largest shareholder in the world's largest banana company. In 1944, Zemurray took the then-extraordinary step of turning a type of generic fresh produce into a brand name by attaching the Chiquita label. By the time of Zemurray's death in 1961, at the age of eighty-four, the United Fruit Company possessed more than four hundred thousand acres of land in Latin America, a fleet of ships, more than one thousand miles of railroad tracks, and influence over several countries.

Beginning in the 1920s, Zemurray developed a friendship with future Israeli president Chaim Weizmann and supported Zionist causes. In 1946, Zemurray, through the Weston Trading Company (a front for the Haganah—a Jewish paramilitary group), purchased the recently decommissioned steamer USS *President Warfield*, named after the president of a shipping company, and having sway over the banana republic, registered it in Honduras. The ship became famous in 1947 when, under its new name, *Exodus*, it was manned by American volunteers and Haganah members who attempted to help settle 4,554 World War II refugees in Mandatory Palestine. A best-selling fictionalized account bearing the same name as the ship was written in 1959 by Leon Uris.

The British rammed the ship off the coast of Israel and in August forced the passengers to return to France, where they refused to disembark. For the ensuing month, the French authorities refused to force them. The British finally took the ship to Germany and forced the passengers, with tear gas and clubs, to disembark, cramming them into detention camps. The British actions in this incident helped lead on November 29, 1947, to the United Nations voting for the establishment of a Jewish state. The *Exodus*, however, met a sad ending, towed to Haifa harbor, where it languished before burning in 1952.

Meanwhile, in the early twentieth century, kibbutzim along the shores of the sea of Galilee began planting bananas and several decades later farmers in the coastal plains of Israel followed suit. A mysterious ailment threatened the industry until in 1956 it was discovered to be nematodes, insects that damage plants from the roots. Since 2006, after healthier plants were developed, bananas have been a major crop in Israel and are the top selling fruit in Israel. Today it is responsible for about 20 percent of all the West's bananas.

The fruit is primarily enjoyed fresh, but also in baking or as a crepe filling. Banana breads and cakes first appeared in America in the 1930s and soon became part of Ashkenazic baking. Among Yemenites, banana mashed with honey is a traditional remedy for swollen glands. On Passover, some variations of charoset incorporate bananas.

BARLEY

Coarsely ground barley grains have been found at excavations of prehistoric campsites throughout much of the Fertile Crescent. Initially, nomads followed the course of the maturing wild barley each spring, gathering as much of the grain as possible. Eventually, people learned to grow the plant and settled along the banks of the Tigris and Euphrates rivers and in the Levant to cultivate their annual barley crop, sparking the very nascence of civilization. Barley, possibly a native of the Levant, is arguably the world's most ancient cultivated plant and, for a long time, was the most widely grown one, and the most important food. Before the advent of money, barley or barley products served as the predominant form of currency in both Egypt and Sumer.

Among the reasons for barley's early widespread usage were its high yield potential, its drought and heat tolerance, its remarkable resistance to insect infestation, and its ability to thrive in poor soil. As a result, it could be cultivated even on the edges of a desert and even in times of minor drought. Barley, unlike many grains, can be planted without plowing and, therefore, can be grown on small parcels of land, as well as on property inaccessible to oxen and donkeys, and without the necessity of irrigation. Barley ripens a full month earlier than wheat and other important grains, even when planted simultaneously, furnishing a much needed replacement for supplies depleted during the winter, as well as providing insurance in case that year's vulnerable wheat crop failed. The maturation of barley to the point of being ripe enough to eat gave rise to the Hebrew word for spring, *aviv*.

As the Ice Age ended and the Mesolithic period commenced nomads in Asia Minor discovered how to boil wild barley into porridges. When barley gruel was left off the fire for a period wild yeast frequently found their way into the mixture, transforming it into beer. When some barley gruel accidentally dropped into the coals of ancient campfires, the first rudimentary breads emerged from the ashes, proving tastier and more portable than gruel. In the Neolithic age, the very first farmers probably settled down in order to ensure sufficient and consistent amounts of cultivated barley to maintain a stable supply of beer. Also during this time, after someone figured out how to grind grains into flour, barley bread became the most common form of food throughout much of Asia, North Africa, and Europe, a position it retained for many millennia. In biblical times, bread, unless otherwise specified, meant bread made from barley. Ancient barley bread was nothing like a loaf of modern wheat bread, but rather a scone-like product or a thick pancake. There was little variety in these loaves beyond the occasional addition of a spice, such as coriander or cumin. The dough was generally a simple mixture of barley flour and water, typically divided into small pieces and clapped into thin cakes between the palms of the hands, then baked on a griddle or, in the archaic method, directly on the coals of a fire.

In ancient Israel, there were two cultivated varieties of barley, the two most widely grown plants at that time: two-rowed barley, which was the older form, and six-rowed barley. These two types are observably different: the awns on six-rowed barley are long and come to a point, while the hairs on two-rowed barley are tiny and, from a small distance, impercep-

tible. The head of six-rowed barley appears fatter and rounded. Two-rowed barley is hulled, while six-rowed barley is sometimes naked—and therefore much easier to thresh and, since the kernels remain intact, capable of being stored for a much longer period. Today, two-rowed barley, generally considered the best type for malting as it contains a higher enzyme content, predominates in Europe and Canada. The six-rowed variety, the coarser of the two but hardier and with a higher protein content, is more widespread in the United States. Today, barley ranks fourth among grains in worldwide production.

Mature barley kernels are enclosed in two inedible protective hulls (the lemma and palea), which in primitive varieties adhere to the seeds even after threshing. Removing the two outer hulls produces hulled barley, also called whole barley, which must be soaked before stewing. Hulled barley, the prevalent type in biblical times, is brownish gray in color and has a chewy texture. Gruels made from it tend to have a somewhat gritty taste due to the outer layers. Rubbing off those layers—the entire hull, the edible aleurone (the thin coating that protects the endosperm), and the endosperm—and, along with them, much of the nutrition, yields pearl barley. Pot barley, also called Scotch barley, is scoured less than pearl barley, leaving part of the endosperm intact.

Barley, mentioned by name thirty-two times in the Pentateuch, was one of the Seven Species with which the land of Israel was praised. The importance of barley in ancient Israel can be seen from an injunction stating that the valuation of a field was to be determined according to the measurement of the barley—not wheat—that could be sown in it. The Omer offering on the second day of Passover consisted of barley flour made from the new crop.

Shortly after the Greek conquest of Israel, wheat—by that time modern bread wheat had reached the area—became the primary grain of the land, and recently arrived rice emerged as a favorite grain. The Romans, in particular, favored wheat and promoted it throughout their domains. Barley provided the diet of the Roman gladiators, who were called *hordearii* (barley eaters), but Roman citizens preferred wheat, a component of the famous "bread and circuses" that maintained the empire. Barley was thereafter reduced to being poor person's food, going from the staple during the Biblical period to a disparaged, generally avoided substance by the end of the Second Temple period. Hence the statement of Rabban Gamliel in the Talmud that barley was animal fodder.

After the collapse of the Roman Empire, wheat remained the predominant grain in the Arab world, while barley made a comeback in some locales. For the masses of southern Europe, barley served as the primary source of gruel and bread until at least the sixteenth century.

Today, barley is generally overlooked in much of the world as a food and primarily utilized to make beer and whiskey. Sephardim and western Europeans rarely use it in their cooking, while eastern Europeans reserve it for hearty fare, such as winter soups and cholent (Sabbath stew).

(See also Beer, Beleela, Bread, Cholent, and Krupnik)

BAR MITZVAH/BAT MITZVAH

In Judaism, a child is not held personally responsible for his or her religious acts until reaching puberty, which is determined to be twelve years and one day for a female and thirteen and one day for a male. This transition is automatic with no ritual required. By the fourteenth century, this change in status was formalized in Germany with a ceremony in which a young man was called up to the reading of the Torah to publicly demonstrate his new role in the community. If the bar mitzvah boy is capable, he reads from the Torah scroll, then recites the haftorah (reading from the Prophets); otherwise he only recites the blessing. Afterward, it is customary in many congregations to shower the bar mitzvah with candy, frequently tied in small sacks. Some parents employ a little creativity in preparing for this custom by decorating the bags; they paint black lines on a white bag, then tie strings on the four corners to resemble a tallit (prayer shawl).

The concept of the bar mitzvah (meaning both "son of the commandment" as well as "subject to the law") ceremony eventually spread to other parts of the Ashkenazic community, as well as to various non-European Jewish communities. Today, it is among the most well-known of all Jewish rituals. However, since women historically played no role in the synagogue, a girl's maturation was observed quietly or not at all. Eventually, however, the recognition of the need for religious instruction for females, as well as the value of a ceremony to mark the emergence of their religious obligations, increased. Jacob Ettlinger (1798–1871), a German rabbi, approved such an observance for females in order to combat assimilation. The first record of the term bat mitzvah was in the book *Ben Ish Chai* (1898) by Joseph Chaim ben Elijah of Baghdad. The actual observance of a bat mitzvah ceremony similar to one for males did not occur until 1922, when Judith Kaplan, the oldest daughter of Reconstructionist founder Mordechai Kaplan, was called to the Torah at the Society for the Advancement for Judaism in New York City. Today, traditionalists who observe a bat mitzvah generally do so after the synagogue service or at home or school, while egalitarian congregations encourage girls to perform the same rituals as boys.

The custom among many Sephardim has been to celebrate a bar or bat mitzvah with a *mezze allegre* (sweet assortment), a symbolic way of wishing a sweet life. In central Europe, the bar mitzvah was generally held on Saturdays, followed by a buffet and sometimes a banquet. Eastern Europeans, on the other hand, historically downplayed what they considered a minor event, usually holding it on Mondays or Thursdays (two other times when the Torah scroll is publicly read) with little or no fanfare.

However, as the bar mitzvah grew in importance in affluent post–World War II America, the accompanying meal did so as well, all too often turning into an excessive and pretentious affair, stereotyped in popular culture by chopped liver sculptures, exotic dancers, and marching bands. More recently, in place of an elaborate catered affair, an increasing number of parents are using the money to take the immediate family to Israel. Others make a point of establishing a family program of performing traditional acts of kindness, such as visiting the elderly and helping the poor. Some celebrants donate part of their gift money to *tzedakah* (charity).

BAZARGAN

Bazargan is a tangy relish consisting of bulgur, onion, tamarind, lemon juice, and parsley.
Origin: Syria

The name of this bulgur relish means "of the bazaar" in Arabic, denoting the commonness of its ingredients in the local market. In the West, of course, many of these items are still quite exotic. Tamarind, an acidic tropical fruit, is available as a sauce or concentrate at stores specializing in Middle Eastern fare.

Pomegranate molasses, also found in those stores, is sometimes substituted for the tamarind. Either one gives the bulgur its characteristic sour-sweet flavor. Some cooks like to mix in some chopped nuts or toasted pine nuts and a little fresh mint. *Bazargan* can be transformed into a salad by adding chopped bell peppers or dried fruit.

Syrians typically feature *bazargan,* along with several other dips and salads, at a *mezze* (appetizer assortment) served with pita bread to start an important meal. It is frequently offered for Sabbath lunch alongside poultry or meat.

❦ SYRIAN BULGUR RELISH (*BAZARGAN*)
ABOUT 2 CUPS/4 TO 6 SERVINGS [PAREVE]
1 cup (6 ounces) fine-grain bulgur
2 cups cold water
Dressing:
3 tablespoons tamarhindi (tamarind sauce), or
 2 tablespoons pomegranate molasses
2 tablespoons tomato paste or ½ cup tomato purée
3 tablespoons extra-virgin olive oil
2 tablespoons fresh lemon juice
1 to 2 teaspoons ground cumin
About ½ teaspoon table salt or 1 teaspoon kosher
 salt
About ¼ teaspoon ground black pepper
¼ to ½ teaspoon cayenne (optional)
½ cup finely chopped walnuts or pistachio nuts
¼ cup chopped fresh flat-leaf parsley

1. Place the bulgur in a bowl, pour in the water, and let stand until tender, about 30 minutes. Drain in a sieve, pressing out any excess water. Transfer the bulgur to a medium bowl.

2. To make the dressing: Whisk together the tamarhindi, tomato paste, and oil. Whisk in the lemon juice, cumin, salt, pepper, and, if using, cayenne. Add the nuts and parsley.

3. Pour the dressing over the bulgur and toss to coat. Cover and refrigerate for at least 2 hours to let the flavors meld. Store in the refrigerator for up to 5 days.

BAZHA
Bazha is a walnut sauce.
Origin: Georgia

Arguably no group loves walnuts (*nigozee*, related to the Hebrew *egoz*) more than Georgians, who add them to almost any dish. This ardor manifests itself in dozens of *satsebeli* (sauces), originally adapted from Persian cuisine, which are served with almost everything. The most versatile of these sauces is *satsebeli bazha*, based on a smooth walnut paste. The name probably derived from the Turkic and Uygur word meaning "market/fair," the place one would acquire its sundry spices. Typical of Georgia, this uncooked sauce is slightly tart, with a hint of wine vinegar and/or pomegranate juice, since sweeteners are not used in savory dishes. Marigold petals or turmeric give it a yellowish hue. The thickness of *bazha* varies according to the nature of the dish it will be served with: a thicker sauce is used for flavoring *pkhali* (salads) and a thinner one for topping fish and poultry. The key is allowing the sauce sufficient time to stand for the flavors to meld. Georgian Jews feature *bazha* on the Sabbath, festivals, and other special occasions.

❦ GEORGIAN WALNUT SAUCE (*BAZHA*)
ABOUT 1 CUP [PAREVE]
1 cup (4 ounces) walnut pieces
1 small onion, chopped
3 to 5 cloves garlic, minced
About ½ teaspoon table salt or 1 teaspoon kosher
 salt
About ¼ cup red wine vinegar or pomegranate juice
3 to 4 tablespoons chopped fresh cilantro
¼ to 1 teaspoon ground coriander
¼ to ½ teaspoon cayenne or hot paprika
¼ teaspoon ground turmeric or ½ teaspoon ground
 dried marigold petals
½ teaspoon ground fenugreek or 1 seeded and
 minced jalapeño chili (optional)
About ¼ cup water

Using a mortar and pestle or in a food processor, grind the walnuts, onion, garlic, and salt into a paste. Stir in the vinegar, cilantro, coriander, cayenne, turmeric, and fenugreek. Add water to make a sauce with the consistency of heavy cream. Let stand at room temperature for at least 1 hour. The sauce thickens as it stands. Cover and refrigerate for up to 3 days.

BEANS
The fava bean (*pol*), along with lentils (*adashim*), and chickpeas (*chamitz*), are the only three legumes mentioned in the Bible. *Pol* were among a number of staples sent to King David when he was hiding from

the rebellion of Absalom, while Ezekiel included it in a set of ingredients in a poverty bread before the destruction of Jerusalem. The Talmud expanded the use of *pol* with the attachment of a denominative to other members of the Fabaceae family once grown for consumption. The term *pol* itself, however, denotes a specific plant from the genus *Vicia*, the fava bean.

Most of the beans consumed today, except for soy beans, are members of the genus *Phaseolus*; they are known as haricot beans and come in more than four thousand varieties (e.g., black, cannellini, cranberry, kidney, marrow, navy, and pinto). Haricot beans originated somewhere in Central or South America. Thousands of years before the arrival of Columbus, they were already being cultivated. The Spanish brought American beans back to Europe and, unlike most other American imports, haricot beans gained immediate acceptance among sixteenth-century Europeans, who were generally averse to adopting any new foods. In a relatively short time, the American beans supplanted the Old World bean, the fava. Subsequently, in parts of Europe and the Near East, haricot beans have for centuries served as one of the main sources, if not the major source, of protein, effectively complementing the nutrition in grains.

The original haricot beans were used in South America for their seeds, then, more than twenty-two hundred years ago, varieties were developed so that the immature pods along with the seeds could be eaten fresh; these became known as string, snap, or green beans. Although the string has long since been cultivated out of most green beans, the name lingers. Snap refers to the sound made when fresh beans are broken. Today, there are more than five hundred green bean cultivars, differing in size, shape, texture, and color. Green beans are most tender when picked before the seeds can be seen through the pods.

Following his second voyage, Columbus introduced the green bean to Europe in 1493. By the beginning of the seventeenth century, green beans had spread throughout the Mediterranean. The favorite Sephardic way of preparing green beans is in tomato sauce, sometimes with other favorite vegetables, such as spinach and leeks. In Turkey and Greece, they are liberally doused in olive oil. Persians cook them with rice or smother them in yogurt. Arguably, no group loved green beans as much as Georgians, who flavor them in numerous ways.

Much of the world's supply of legumes comes in a dried form. Beans consist of layers of starch granules and require liquid to replace the moisture in the starch lost during drying. Dried beans are commonly used to make a wide variety of salads, spreads, soups, and stews. In many Jewish communities, dried haricot beans were used in Sabbath stews and other traditional dishes. Purportedly, the favorite food of the Baal Shem Tov, Israel ben Eliezer, founder of Chasidism, was black bean soup. Georgians have a penchant for red beans. The longstanding significance of beans to Sephardim may be seen from their Spanish name, *judia*, which is also the Spanish word for Jewess. White beans became particularly important in the Balkans, where *avicas/fijones*, a thick bean soup, was once a ubiquitous Friday night entrée and left to simmer overnight, in the manner of a Sabbath stew, for Sabbath lunch.

On the other hand, the Jews of northeastern Europe rarely ate beans, except in cholent (Sabbath stew). The consumption of legumes, which were even less expensive than potatoes, was generally limited to periods of famine, when Ashkenazic rabbis even permitted their use during Passover. Hungarians and Romanians, however, influenced by the lengthy Ottoman occupation of their countries and by contact with Sephardim, absorbed numerous Middle Eastern proclivities, including an affection for beans, both dried and fresh. As a result, Hungarian and Romanian cuisines contain a number of legume dishes. The more vegetable-accepting Ukrainians, especially those in the south, adopted a bit of the neighboring Romanian fare and even some Polish Jews eventually succumbed to the bean's charms. Nevertheless, most Jews in Poland and the Baltic States steadfastly refused to eat most green vegetables or legumes. Indeed, *bubkes* (little beans) became the Yiddish term for "insignificant" and "nothing of value."

In 1923, the H. J. Heinz Company, at the time generally known for their pickles, decided to do something totally unprecedented—offer a kosher version of a national brand of food. At the time, it was a revolutionary idea. The only kosher foods in the United States were produced at home or by a few small local Jewish companies and stores. But America's Jewish community was growing (more than 3.6 million in 1920, 4.2 million in 1930), and Heinz saw an interesting opportunity to reach this untapped market. There was one important obstacle to overcome—certifying that the product was kosher. Because this was an untested notion, Heinz was reluctant to carry the word "kosher" on its label. The company agreed to use something recognizable yet not overtly Jewish. The supervising agency, the Union of Orthodox Jewish Congregations of America, and the advertising agency devised the first and still most-recognized symbol of kosher supervision, the OU. Thus were born both Heinz Vegetarian Baked Beans and a new industry—kosher supervision. Other national companies eventually followed suit and by the year 2010, nearly half of all national brands in the United States were under kosher supervision, certainly not *bubkes*.

(See also Avicas, Fava Bean, Lobio, and Shkanah)

BEEF

Beef refers to the meat of cattle over the age of nine months. Meat from younger animals is called veal. Beef as a major component of the diet, except among the very wealthy, is a relatively recent phenomenon, engendered by the transformation from animal power to machines with the Industrial Revolution and late nineteenth-century cattle raising in the American West. Throughout most of history, with a few exceptions, cows were more valuable while alive, serving as the predominant draft animal rather than as food. Oxen not only plowed the fields, but also turned the wheels that drew water from canals and wells, hauled the harvest in carts from the field, carried items on their backs, and provided fertilizer for the crops. In essence, cows provided a low-maintenance as well as self-perpetuating tractor, truck, pump, soil revitalizer, and currency. If the modern world operates on horsepower, the ancient one ran on ox power.

Thus the Bible established that if someone stole an ox, thereby seriously affecting the owner's livelihood, he must pay back "five oxen for an ox," a fine levied exclusively for this particular animal. Cows, along with the other ancient beast of burden, the donkey, are singled out in the Bible to be allowed to rest on the Sabbath. Cattle, unlike sheep, were rarely raised in large herds, but most families owned one or a few for work animals and progenitors.

During the medieval period, as laws emerged in many parts of Europe forbidding Jews from owning land, some turned to raising and selling cattle, ensuring a steady supply of beef in the Jewish community. Still, most Ashkenazim could at best afford the organs and the tougher cuts of meat—brisket, plate, and flanken—so these emerged as the focus of many traditional dishes. Many households could only manage to purchase some bones or scraps for the Sabbath cholent.

One of the few historical exceptions to the limited consumption of meat occurred in western Europe during the two centuries following the Black Death (approximately 1350–1550), which saw the loss of 30 to 60 percent of Europe's population. Due to a big decline in farming and corresponding increase in pastureland, a previously unparalleled meat surplus emerged in western and central Europe. Cattle were also raised in eastern Europe and driven on foot to the west.

It was during this state of plenty that many of the Ashkenazic customs relating to meat and slaughter developed. As there was more than enough kosher meat available from the front half of the cow, Ashkenazim began avoiding the entire problematic hindquarter, which includes the tenderloin and porterhouse steaks, containing forbidden sinews and fats. Sephardim, who neither experienced this period of meat profusion nor were particularly bothered by the effort and expertise involved in these rituals, continued to utilize cuts from the hindquarter. Also at that time in Franco-Germany, the position of *shochet* (ritual slaughterer) was institutionalized; previously any Jew versed in the ritual could slaughter an animal. Suddenly, dairy products were to a much greater degree incorporated into various Ashkenazic dishes and serving large roasts and beef stews on a regular basis became commonplace. Whereas previously goose had been the preferred Ashkenazic festival dish, beef emerged as the prevalent Sabbath and holiday food. It was also at this time that the Yiddish words *milchig* (dairy) and *fleishig* (meat) first appeared, terms unnecessary among Jews in the contemporary Islamic world, where other than cheese, dairy products were still rarely used in cooking. In addition, in the Middle East and southern Europe, most milk came from goats and most meat from sheep. Beef was a rare sight on the Sephardic table and when used in cooking was primarily a flavoring ingredient.

Subsequently, toward the end of the sixteenth century, when much of the fallow land had been transferred back to agriculture, Europe faced an extended meat shortage and beef again became extremely expensive. Yet the Ashkenazic preference for beef remained. Rabbi Yair Chaim Bacharach (1638–1702) of Germany wistfully noted, "The taste of poultry does not awaken the joy of a festival as does the taste of beef."

Until the late nineteenth and into the twentieth century, beef remained a rare part of the Ashkenazic diet. When Ashkenazic immigrants in America began achieving a degree of financial success, their traditional preference for beef returned, as did its regular, if not daily, presence in the diet. Sabbath meals in America featured huge briskets and roasts, the tzimmes often became more meat than vegetables, and the cholent was typically packed with chunks of beef. During the latter part of the twentieth century, although growing health consciousness in the United States led to the decline of red meat consumption beef remained a popular part of hearty Ashkenazic dinners and festive occasions. Meanwhile, beef plays a much smaller role among Ashkenazim in Israel, where poultry fills more of both the everyday and festive roles in cooking. The vast majority of beef in Israel is imported, already slaughtered, primarily from South America.

Today, Ashkenazic butchers use only the five cuts of the forequarter of the animal—rib, chuck, brisket, plate, and shank. Beef terminology can be a bit confusing, since names of cuts differ from region to region and often from butcher to butcher. And American butchers generally cut across muscle and bone, unlike the European style of separating the muscle sections. In Israel, cuts are connoted by numbers.

The more tender cuts of the meat come from the sections of the animal that are not used for movement and therefore develop little connective tissue. As the muscles on the back of the animal involve the least amount of motion, the rib and the loin areas are the most tender parts. Ironically, the very factors that toughen beef—exercise and age—produce more flavorful meat. Cuts from tender sections are generally cooked by dry heat (broiling and roasting) or fast cooking (stir-frying). Moist-heat cooking (braising and stewing) is better for the leaner, more sinewy cuts.

(See also Brisket, Cheilev, Cholent, Corned Beef, Delicatessen, Flanken, Fleishig, Glatt, Kishke, Kolichel, Kosher, Liver, Lungen, Meatball, Miltz, Pastrami, Sausage, Shank, Shechita, Sweetbread, Tongue, Treibern, Treif, and Udder)

BEER

Beer, from the Latin *bibere* (to drink), is a low-alcohol beverage made from fermented grain, most commonly barley. Beer is divided into two categories: top-fermented (ales) and bottom-fermented (lagers). Lagers, from the German *lagern* (to store), are generally aged longer and tend to be lighter, clearer, drier, maltier, and lower in alcohol than ales. Lager beers have long been the favorite of Germanic countries, while the British traditionally prefer ales. Today, almost all beers receive their tangy-bitter flavor and aroma from hops, a relative of mulberry, or, more likely, a blend of hops, which are added to balance the sweetness of the malt. The taste, strength, and color of the beer are determined by the variety of barley, the malting process, the water, the varieties and amount of hops, the type of yeast, the added ingredients, the brewing process, and the type of bottling. The biblical term *shechar* probably included several non-grape alcoholic beverages, such as beer and date wine.

People early on discerned that brewed beverages were safer to drink than water, which was all too often tainted; they also noticed that these drinks provided an enjoyable buzz. And when food was scarce, primitive beer provided an important source of nutrition. The earliest Mesopotamian tablets mentioned beer. Hammurabi's Code dictates laws concerning its sale. Egyptian tomb illustrations depict the brewing process. In ancient Egypt and Mesopotamia, barley beer served as the common beverage of the entire population, drunk throughout the day by rich and poor, young and old. From their contact with Egypt, the Greeks learned the techniques of brewing barley and spread this information to the rest of Europe.

Early in history, a dichotomy developed between areas conducive to viticulture and areas where conditions were unfavorable to grape production. Along the Mediterranean, the ancient Israelites, Phoenicians, Greeks, and Romans maintained a preference for wine and generally viewed beer with little enthusiasm. After the Babylonian Exile in 586 BCE, the Jews living there adopted their new country's fondness for beer. Several Babylonian rabbis earned considerable fortunes from brewing. The Talmud permits beer as a substitute for wine in Havdalah, (the ceremony performed at the end of Sabbath encompassing all the senses—reciting and hearing the benedictions, tasting wine or beer, smelling the spices, seeing the flames, and feeling the fire's heat) in countries where it is a national drink.

While wine was favored by the early Ashkenazim in France and Alsace, and later in Hungary and Romania, beer became common among the Jews of Germany, Austria, and Czech Republic. Eastern Europeans, however, rarely had barley beer. Instead, the predominant beer was *kvas* (from the Slavic meaning "sour"), an acidic, slightly sweet, lightly alcoholic beverage made from malted rye grains or rye bread, for all levels of society. *Kvas* was even used to make a soup.

Early central European settlers in Israel relied on beer imported from Europe or, without the benefit of hops, homemade brews. The first commercial Israeli brewery, the Palestine Brewery Ltd, also known as Nesher Brewery, opened in 1934, a joint French-Israeli venture. The brewery produced a light lager and Nesher Malt, a very slightly alcoholic malt "beer," referred to as *bira shechora* (black beer), with a dark color and noticeably sweet taste, more akin to root beer than European brews. In 1950, Cabeer Breweries, using old facilities at Rishon LeZion, introduced Goldstar, a Munich-style pale lager, with an amber color and malty aroma. The main rival to Goldstar, Maccabee, appeared in 1968; this yellow Pilsner lager quickly became the country's best-selling beer and a symbol of young Israel.

Then in the 1970s, Israel's breweries, using outdated equipment that too frequently turned out undrinkable beer, and subjected to the Israeli socialist economic practices, were driven into receivership and the government was forced to search for an investor. Filling that role was Murray Goldman, a Toronto real estate developer, who, in conjunction with John Labatt Ltd. Brewery, purchased Goldstar and Maccabee in 1975, forming the National Brewery. Acquiring new equipment and establishing new production and marketing practices based upon the Canadian model, Goldman revived the brands, which he sold in 1986 to the country's largest soft drink manufacturer, Tempo. Also in 1986, Tempo Beer Industries Ltd. purchased Nesher, becoming Israel's largest brewer. Goldstar grew into Israel's favorite local brew, while Maccabee, which had once dominated the country's beer market, by 2007 had shrunk to only 10 percent of the market, with much of that being consumed by tourists.

(See also Barley, Bread, and Wine)

BEET

The modern world knows the beet, a native of the eastern Mediterranean region, primarily for its sweet red root. The original vegetable, however, possessed thin, fibrous white roots and large stalks and leaves, similar to those of its close relative or progenitor, chard. The Talmudic term *silka* denotes both what we now call chard as well as the beet green. Early sources refer only to the consumption of the beet greens, although the root was used occasionally for medicinal purposes. An autumn and spring vegetable that does not fare well in hot weather, the beet was so highly regarded in ancient Israel, as well as Greece and Rome, that methods were found to produce it during the summer. The Talmud made note of the beet green's nutritional and health benefits. In response to the question, "Wherewith does one show delight in the Sabbath?" the Talmud responded, "With beets [greens], a large fish, and garlic." Besides being favorite foods, all three of these items were considered to be aphrodisiacs.

The fleshy red beet root was developed either in Italy or Germany and first recorded in 1542; initially it was elongated like a parsnip, but it transformed into the modern swollen root by the end of the century. The red root quickly became the most widespread type, yet failed to make a culinary impact on most of the world for another two centuries. It was in northeastern Europe that the beetroot emerged as a staple of the diet, as it was among the few vegetables available throughout the winter. Eastern Ashkenazim feature beets in borscht, salads, pickles, preserves, and confections, as well as mixing them with ground horseradish. Ashkenazim also make a simple salad from the greens or add them to various soups.

The beet eventually became popular in the Middle East as well, most notably in salads, relishes, and soups; a slice was typically added to Middle Eastern turnip pickles called *turshi* to produce a pink hue. The beet's root and greens are commonly made into separate salads, or the greens are cooked with chickpeas. Beets particularly complement the slight tang of goat cheese and sour cream. Beets have long been a traditional Rosh Hashanah food.

In 1747, the Berlin chemist Andreas Marggraf discovered the process of producing sucrose from sugar beets. A half century later, in 1806, one of his students capitalized on this process to open the first sugar beet factory in Kunem, Germany, now western Poland. Today, almost half of the world's sugar comes from the long, white roots of sugar beets.

(See also Borscht, Chard, Kubbeh, Rosl, and Sugar)

BELEELA

Beleela is a grain pudding made from barley, wheat berries, or bulgur.

Origin: Middle East

Other names: Lebanon: *belila, qamhiyya*; Syria: *belila*; Turkey: *moostrahana, prehito*.

Cooked whole grains sweetened with honey date back at least to ancient Greece. In the Middle East, whole grains are considered to be healthy, as it takes the body a long time to break them down. In this vein, Middle Easterners have long prepared puddings from whole pearl barley, wheat berries, and bulgur. Plain porridge provides everyday fare for breakfast and sometimes dinner, especially during the cold months of winter, Puddings enhanced with honey or sugar, nuts, and sometimes dried fruits are offered on special occasions. A medieval European version made from wheat berries was frumenty.

Beleela is a term dating back at least to the Mishnah, a *beleela avah* denoting a thick mixture and a *beleela rakhah* a thin one. The term *prehito* may be derived from the Hebrew *pri hita* (fruit of wheat) or may be from a Ladino barley pudding. During the medieval period in the eastern Mediterranean, *beleela* came to denote wheat and barley porridges, the grain differing from place to place. Puddings made from bulgur, quicker and easier to prepare, became especially popular. Turkish and Syrian cooks tend to use bulgur for *beleela*, while Egyptians more frequently opt for wheat berries or barley.

Grain pudding is a traditional Turkish Sukkot dish, because it symbolizes the harvest. *Beleela* is popular for Tu b'Shevat and some Sephardim serve it during a *Frutikas* Seder on the evening of Tu b'Shevat, during which ten items are presented, each with an appropriate blessing. Since whole grains resemble teeth, Middle Easterners customarily serve *beleela* at a party to honor a baby's first tooth.

(See also Ashure)

BERBERE

Berbere is a spice mixture with at least six and up to sixteen ingredients, especially chilies.

Origin: Ethiopia

The most fiery cuisine on the African continent comes from Ethiopia, due primarily to *berbere*. This complex seasoning takes its name from the Amharic *beri-beri*, in turn derived from the Portuguese *piri-piri*, denoting an African bird's-eye chili. This small red variety, also aptly called African devil, is extremely hot. In Ethiopia, the chilies are dried in the sun, then toasted, combined with at least a half dozen spices, and all finely ground. Cardamom, cinnamon, nutmeg, and allspice contribute a sweet counterbalance to the chilies and peppercorns. Many versions contain *ajwain*, a spice that has a flavor and aroma similar to thyme. *Mitmita*, a hotter Ethiopian spice mixture also based on the bird's-eye chili, is less vibrant in color and flavor and primarily used in *kitfo* (a form of steak tartare).

Berbere, reminiscent of Indian curry powders, reflects the Arabic and Indian influences on Ethiopian culture. Essential for Ethiopian cookery, it is added in conjunction with onions and water to *wots* (stews); without *berbere*, a stew is an *alicha*. Mixing the powder with a little oil and *tej* (honey wine) and allowing the mixture to ferment produces a hot sauce called *awaze*, used as a condiment. Every Ethiopian household maintains a jar of *berbere* and/or *awaze*, often homemade from a time-honored recipe. Marketplaces in Ethiopia have at least one and frequently several spice stalls featuring huge sacks of dried chilies as well as tubs of premade *berbere*. Although some cooks use it judiciously, many typically add prodigious amounts, resulting in very fiery dishes. When done correctly, a dish should have a combination of heat and subtlety. *Injera* (pancake bread) always accompanies these chili dishes to somewhat mute the potency.

ETHIOPIAN CHILI POWDER (*BERBERE*)

ABOUT ¾ CUP   [PAREVE]

7 to 8 small dried red chilies, 7 to 8 dried pequín chilies, or 3 ounces dried New Mexican chilies, or any combination (or 2 tablespoons cayenne and 3 tablespoons sweet paprika)

1 tablespoon whole black peppercorns

1 teaspoon green cardamom pods or ½ teaspoon ground cardamom

1 teaspoon coriander seeds or ½ teaspoon ground coriander

1 teaspoon cumin seeds or ½ teaspoon ground cumin (optional)

1 teaspoon fenugreek seeds or ½ teaspoon ground
   fenugreek
1 teaspoon ground ginger
½ teaspoon ground cinnamon
½ teaspoon ground nutmeg
¼ teaspoon ground allspice
¼ teaspoon ground cloves
⅛ teaspoon ground turmeric

1. If using whole chilies, stir them in a dry skillet over medium heat until they darken and feel warm but are not burnt. Let cool. Remove and discard the stems. For a milder powder, also discard the seeds. Grind the chilies. If using cayenne, combine with all the other ingredients in step 3.

2. In a dry large skillet, toast the peppercorns and seeds (cardamom, coriander, optional cumin, and fenugreek) over medium heat, stirring constantly, until lightly browned, about 3 minutes, or toast the ground cardamom, coriander, optional cumin, and fenugreek for about 1 minute. Let cool.

3. In a spice grinder, coffee mill, or blender, process the chilies, toasted spices, ginger, cinnamon, nutmeg, allspice, cloves, and turmeric until smooth and powdery. Store in an airtight container in the refrigerator for up to 6 months.

VARIATIONS

Mock Ethiopian Hot Sauce (Awaze): Combine 2 tablespoons berbere, 2 tablespoons tej (Ethiopian honey wine), and 2 tablespoons olive oil. To make an equivalent of tej, combine 2 tablespoons dry white wine without oak barreling, 2 tablespoons water, and 1 tablespoon honey. Today some Ethiopians substitute red wine, Scotch, or other alcohol for the tej. Awaze is used as an all-purpose condiment.

BHAJI

Bhaji is a curried vegetable dish, first sautéed, and then cooked in its own juices without added liquid.
Origin: India
Other names: *bhaaji, subji, takari.*

During the week, most Indians prepare one or two vegetables for lunch and dinner, while on the Sabbath and holidays there will likely be at least three or four besides the ubiquitous *dal* (legumes). Indians make two primary types of stir-fried vegetables—*gobi*, containing a liquid, and a dry version called *bhaji.* Consequently, Indian cooks using basically the same ingredients create rather different dishes. *Bahji* can

be prepared with any vegetable, but most variations contain potatoes, which absorb the flavors of the other ingredients and make the dish more substantial. In India, curried dishes prepared in Jewish households tend to be less spicy and oily than those of their neighbors. In Calcutta, a Friday night dinner typically features a *bhaji* along with *murgi kari* (pot-roasted chicken), *aloo makalla* (fried potatoes), and *pilau* (rice pilaf).

◆ CALCUTTA CURRIED VEGETABLES (*BHAJI*)

3 TO 4 SERVINGS   [PAREVE]

   4 large (2 pounds) potatoes
   3 tablespoons vegetable oil
   ½ teaspoon mustard seeds (optional)
   1 medium onion, sliced
   1 teaspoon minced fresh ginger
   1 large clove garlic, minced
   2 to 3 small green chilies, minced, or ¼ teaspoon
      cayenne or ground black pepper
   2 to 4 curry leaves or 1 to 2 bay leaves
   ½ teaspoon ground turmeric
   2 whole cloves or cardamom pods
   Pinch of ground asafetida (*hing*) (optional)
   About 1 teaspoon table salt or 2 teaspoons kosher
      salt
   2 pounds sliced green beans, 1 pound (½ head)
      thinly sliced cabbage, 1 medium head
      cauliflower cut into florets, 1 pound okra
      sliced lengthwise into quarters, 2 cups green
      peas, 2 bunches coarsely chopped spinach,
      or 2 pounds thinly sliced zucchini or any
      combination of vegetables
   2 tablespoons chopped fresh cilantro
   1 to 2 tablespoons fresh lemon juice (optional)

1. In a large pot, boil the potatoes in water to cover until semi-tender but not mushy, about 20 minutes. Drain. When cool enough to handle, peel and cut into chunks.

2. In a large pot, heat the oil over medium heat. If using, add the mustard seeds and sauté until they begin to pop, 2 to 3 minutes. Add the onion and sauté until soft and translucent, 5 to 10 minutes. Add the ginger, garlic, chilies, curry leaves, turmeric, cloves, and, if using, asafetida and sauté for 2 to 3 minutes. Add the salt.

3. Add the potatoes and sauté until well coated, about 2 minutes. Stir in the green beans. Cover, reduce the heat to low, and cook, stirring occasionally, or bake in a 425°F oven until the vegetables are tender, 10 to 25 minutes. If the potatoes are not cooked sufficiently, add 2 tablespoons water and cook until tender.

4. Stir in the cilantro and, if using, lemon juice and cook until most of the liquid has evaporated. Serve warm, if desired, accompanied with rice or bread, or at room temperature.

BIALY

Residents of the northeastern Polish town of Bialystock (literally "white slope"), which at its height before World War II boasted a Jewish community of more than fifty thousand, enjoyed an onion-topped roll with an indentation in the center that they referred to as kuchen. Outsiders commonly called the roll after its home, a *Bialystoker kuchen* or simply bialy. *Bialystoker kuchen* is a variation of the widespread Ashkenazic onion flatbread *tzibele pletzl*, originating in the early nineteenth century with the emergence in Europe of the technological and agricultural methods needed to produce inexpensive white flour. Uniquely, the lean dough is shaped by hand into small dough balls (*tagelach*), flattened, and left to rise slightly; then a distinctive large indent is pressed into the center of each *tagel*. The indent is spread with grated onion, both flavoring the bread and helping to preserve the depression. The result is a delicious roll—crisp on the bottom, fluffy in the center of the ridges, and oniony on top. Bialys are made without an egg wash glaze and turn out paler than most breads.

By the end of the century, nearly every street in the Jewish sections of Bialystock contained a small kuchen bakery. These breads were once part of every weekday meal and sometimes constituted the entire meal; they complemented both dairy (delicious with a schmear of butter) and meat. In the late nineteenth century, immigrants from Bialystock brought their favorite roll to America and eventually old-fashioned bialy bakeries dotted the Lower East Side of Manhattan, later appearing in other large Jewish communities, such as Chicago and Los Angeles.

New York City had enough bakeries for the owners to form an alliance, the Bialy Bakers Association. Bialys became a mainstay of Jewish dairy restaurants. In 1927, Morris Kossar immigrated from Bialystock to New York, and in 1936, he founded with Isadore Mirsky what is now the world's oldest extant bialy bakery, Kossar's Bialystocker Kuchenon on the Lower East Side. After the original location was destroyed by an explosion and fire, the result of a union dispute, in the early hours of February 20, 1958, the Kossar family reopened on Grand Street. At its peak, Kossar's turned out twenty-seven thousand bialys daily, or nearly ten million a year.

During World War II, the once dynamic Jewish community of Bialystock was liquidated by the Nazis; subsequently, Jews as well as bialys actually disappeared from the city. Today, residents of Bialystock no longer have any recognition of the kuchen or the role it once played in their city. Around the same time that the bialy disappeared from its birthplace, the masses of Jews relocated from the Lower East Side and other poorer urban American areas, and the bialy's star faded. Even the restaurants once featuring bialys, such as Ratner's, Dubrow's, and Famous Dairy, closed their doors. By the 1970s, only one bialy bakery remained in New York, Kossar's.

In a twist of history, although bialys arrived in America at the same time as bagels, the latter went on to achieve unparalleled popularity throughout mainstream America, while the bialy remained primarily a Jewish–New York specialty food. Among the principle reasons for this disparity is that bagels can be made from a machine, while bialys still need a human touch. Bialys also have a relatively short shelf life of only about six hours, which is not conducive to shipping. In addition, the bagel lends itself to variety. Historically, there has been little variation in the nature of bialys, although poppy seeds were an accepted American adaptation. Finally, bagels excel at being halved for sandwiches, while bialys are not sliced, but spread on the top or bottom with butter or cream cheese.

Toward the end of the twentieth century, an increasing number of bagel stores in America, many owned by non-Jews, began offering bialys as well, although these tend to be inauthentic and inferior. At the end of the 1990s, an entrepreneur opened a shop in Bialystock, ironically named New York Bagels, which also offered bialys, reclaiming part of the city's heritage. *New York Times* food critic Mimi Sheraton devoted a 2002 book to the bialy and its lore, *The Bialy Eaters: The Story of a Bread and a Lost World*. The bialy endures as an image of nostalgia.

POLISH ONION ROLLS (*BIALYS*)

12 SMALL ROLLS [PAREVE]

Dough:

1 package (2¼ teaspoons) active dry yeast or
   1 (0.6-ounce) cake fresh yeast
1¼ cups warm water (105 to 115°F for dry yeast;
   80 to 85°F for fresh yeast)
2 tablespoons sugar
2 teaspoons table salt or 4 teaspoons kosher salt
About 4 cups (20 ounces) bread flour
Rye flour, cornmeal, or semolina for dusting

Topping:

½ cup minced onion
1 tablespoon vegetable oil
1½ to 2 teaspoons poppy seeds (optional)
½ teaspoon kosher salt

1. Dissolve the yeast in ¼ cup water. Stir in 1 teaspoon sugar and let stand until foamy, 5 to 10 minutes. In a large bowl, combine the yeast mixture, remaining water, remaining sugar, and salt, and 2 cups flour. Gradually add enough of the remaining flour to make a mixture that holds together.

2. On a lightly floured surface, knead until smooth and elastic, about 10 minutes. Place in an oiled bowl and turn to coat. Cover and let rise until doubled in bulk, about 1½ hours.

3. Punch down the dough and knead briefly. Return to the bowl, cover, and let rise a second time until doubled in bulk, about 1 hour.

4. Punch down the dough and knead briefly. Divide into 12 equal pieces, roll into balls, cover, and let stand for 10 minutes. Dust 2 large ungreased baking sheets with rye flour. On a lightly floured surface, roll each ball into a 3½-inch round about ½-inch thick. Place on the prepared baking sheets, cover, and let rise until puffy and increased in size by about half in bulk, about 30 minutes.

5. To make the topping: Combine the onion, oil, optional poppy seeds, and salt.

6. Using your thumb or the bottom of a small glass (about 1½ inches in diameter), press down the center of the dough rounds, leaving at least a 1-inch rim. Sprinkle about 1 teaspoon onion topping mixture into each indentation. Cover and let rise until puffy, about 15 minutes.

7. Preheat the oven to 425°F.

8. Bake the bialys until lightly browned, switching the pans halfway through baking, about 12 minutes.

If the onions are not browned, place under a broiler for about 1 minute. Transfer to wire racks and let cool slightly or completely. For softer rolls, place cooled bialys in a plastic bag.

BICHAK

Bichak are yeast turnovers.
Origin: Uzbekistan, Afghanistan
Other names: *bishak*; Hebrew: *bitzak*.

   Bichak, a favorite comfort food, are common at most Bukharan and Afghan celebrations. Filled with pumpkin or meat, the turnovers are traditional on Rosh Hashanah and Sukkot. At dairy meals, pumpkin or cheese *bichak* are frequently served with yogurt or sour cream.

BUKHARAN TURNOVERS (*BICHAK*)

ABOUT 20 TURNOVERS [PAREVE OR MEAT]

1 recipe ajin (Middle Eastern Yeast Dough,
   page 7)
About 2 cups *bichak* filling (recipes follow)
Egg wash (1 large egg beaten with 1 teaspoon
   water)
Poppy seeds or nigella seeds for sprinkling
   (optional)

1. Preheat the oven to 375°F. Line 2 large baking sheets with parchment paper or lightly grease.

2. Divide the dough into 1½-inch balls (about 2 ounces). On an oiled surface, roll each ball into a 4-inch round about ⅛ inch thick. Or roll out the dough ⅛ inch thick and cut out 4-inch rounds. Place a heaping tablespoonful of filling in the center of each round. Gather the edges from 3 sides and bring together toward the center to form a triangle, pinching the edges to seal. Place 2 inches apart on the prepared sheets. Brush with the egg wash and, if using, sprinkle with the poppy seeds. Prick with the tines of a fork to vent the steam.

3. Bake until golden brown, about 20 minutes. Serve warm or at room temperature. To reheat, place in a 350°F oven until heated through, about 10 minutes.

Bichak Fillings

PUMPKIN FILLING (*KADOO*)

¼ cup vegetable oil
2 medium yellow onions, halved and sliced
1½ pounds pumpkin or winter squash, peeled and
   chopped

½ cup water

2 to 3 tablespoons cumin seeds, 2 tablespoons sugar, or ¼ teaspoon red chili flakes

About ¼ teaspoon table salt or ½ teaspoon kosher salt

In a large pot, heat the oil over medium heat. Add the onions and sauté until golden, about 20 minutes. Add the pumpkin, water, cumin, and salt. Bring to a boil, cover, reduce the heat, and simmer until the pumpkin is very tender, about 20 minutes. Uncover and cook until the liquid evaporates and the mixture thickens. Let cool. This is not a smooth mixture.

❧ CHEESE FILLING (*PANEER*)

1 pound pot or farmer cheese

1 large egg yolk

Salt to taste

In a medium bowl, combine all the ingredients.

BIMUELO

Bimuelo refers to a variety of small fried foods, sweet or savory, including doughnuts, fritters, and pancakes.

Origin: Spain

Other names: Arabic: *awamee*; Greek: *loukoumas*; Romaniote Greeks: *zvingous*; Ladino: *bimuelo, bimwelo, bumwelo, burmuelo*; Spanish: *bunuelo*.

Frying dough in fat is an ancient method of pastry making, dating back to at least the invention of pottery. During the early medieval period, residents of Iberia began deep-frying loose yeast-leavened batters. Later, European sources referred to similar rudimentary doughnuts as "Spanish fritters," connoting an Iberian origin. By at least the thirteenth century, a singular Sephardic term emerged to encompass various Iberian fried doughs, *bimuelos* (lumps). Rabbi Jacob Culi of Istanbul in his Ladino biblical commentary *Me'am Loez* (1730), in explaining the biblical description of the taste of manna as being "like dough in honey," uses the term *bilmuelos*. When used alone, the term *bimuelos* generally refers to small yeast-dough fritters. Pancakes usually have an adjunctive phrase attached, for example, *bimuelos de massa* (matza pancakes) and *bimuelos de kezo* (cheese pancakes).

The doughnut version emerged as the preeminent Sephardic Hanukkah treat (*bimuelos de hanuka*) and for generations, most households enjoyed homemade fritters at least once or, not infrequently, daily during the holiday. Unlike round European donuts, when

spoonfuls of the loose dough hit the hot oil, they puff up into various asymmetrical shapes. Although Sephardim originally sweetened their fritters with a dusting of sugar, after the expulsion many adopted the Middle Eastern manner of drenching them in syrup. Those from Greece typically use a honey syrup, accented with lemon juice or cinnamon. In Spain, these puffs were fried in olive oil and considered by Christians to be a sign of Jewish and Moorish cooking. Indeed, many Converso families, most not even realizing their Jewish roots and having lost the connection to Hanukkah, traditionally prepared fritters each December.

Traditional Passover *bimuelos* are made with either crumbled whole matza or less frequently matza meal. They can be deep-fried in oil or dropped on a griddle as pancakes. Greeks sometimes refer to matza pancakes as *masa tiganitas*, taking the name of a special Greek skillet. *Bimuelos de massa*, typical Passover breakfast fare, are commonly served with *arrope* (raisin syrup), *dulce* (fruit preserves), a sprinkling of sugar, or a dollop of yogurt. Today in Israel, date honey is also a popular topping. More recently, pancakes made from mashed potatoes (*bimuelos de patata*) have also become widespread as Passover fare.

Bimuelos emerged as a Sephardic cultural icon. A very popular modern Hanukkah song from Israel is the Ladino "*Vayehi Miketz Burmuelos con Miel*," a parody from a woman's point of view of the biblical tale of Joseph interpreting the dreams of Pharaoh, which is read in the synagogue on the Sabbath of Hanukkah: " 'And it was at the end'; *Burmuelos* with honey; Pharaoh made them, and Joseph ate them, Pharaoh fell into the river, and Joseph went to the bath, Pharaoh went to the cemetery, and Joseph went to the wedding."

(See also Bola, Doughnut, Fritter, and Lokma)

BIRD

There are more than ten thousand extant species of birds, warm-blooded vertebrates bearing feathers, laying hard-shelled eggs, and ranging in size from the hummingbird to the ostrich. Accounts, depictions, and parables of birds occur throughout the Bible and Talmud, but birds primarily became a regular element of Jewish cooking during the medieval period. In biblical times, most birds were caught wild, many of those in Israel being migratory. The generic Hebrew word for bird is *tzipor*, derived from the root "to turn/flee," connoting avian tendencies. The Hebrew term *oaf*, from the root "to cover," encompasses not only flying fowl, but also winged mammals (bats) and flightless birds (for example, ostriches). In modern Hebrew, *oaf*, following the Yiddish usage, implies specifically a chicken.

Unlike mammals and fish, for which the Bible provided precise anatomical *simanim* (signs) to determine their kosher status, in regard to fowl, the majority of which are kosher, the text listed the forbidden bird species without any mention of empirical signs. The Sages, however, by observing doves, which could be offered in the Temple, and contrasting them to known nonkosher species, distinguished four characteristics possessed by kosher birds: "Any fowl that *ha-dorais* [seizes with its claws] are unkosher; all that have an *etzbah yetairah* [extra toe], *zefek* [crop], and *korkebano neeklaf* [peelable gizzard] are kosher."

It is generally accepted that unfit fowl are birds of prey, but the exact identity of some of the forbidden birds cannot be determined. Therefore, the custom developed, which became the standard Ashkenazic and Sephardic practice, that in order for any fowl to be considered kosher, it must have a *mesorah* (oral tradition). This means that penguins and cockatoos, which have no *mesorah*, cannot be part of a kosher meal. To further complicate matters, the presence of a *mesorah* varies among the various different Jewish communities. Iraqi Jews never had a *mesorah* for ducks. In the 1960s, a disagreement arose between the Ashkenazic and Sephardic chief rabbis of Israel concerning the status of pheasant, the latter group possessing a *mesorah* for it. On the other hand, some Ashkenazim lack a *mesorah* for quail.

Eventually, other birds, notably geese, ducks, and chickens, were domesticated and fowl correspondingly attained a wider role in the Jewish diet. Among Jews, fowl possessed an additional attribute—while mammals were generally too complicated for most people to ritually slaughter, birds proved sufficiently easy for many individuals to handle themselves. In addition, until the Mishnaic period, when domesticated fowl other than pigeons were initially becoming common in Israel, fowl could be eaten with dairy. However, a rabbinic enactment forbade cooking and eating poultry with dairy as with meat.

The permissibility of other birds proved particularly important by the late Roman period as the predominant position of pigeons on the Jewish table began to diminish. Other birds, most notably chicken and turkey, gradually supplanted it. Records from the Spanish Inquisition reveal that Sephardim of the fifteenth and sixteenth centuries ate chicken, pigeon, duck, partridge, peacock, swallow, and thrush. In the Mediterranean and Middle East, poultry, generally more expensive than lamb and beef, was rarely consumed during the week, except among the very wealthy. Birds were regarded as special items, reserved for the holidays and sometimes the Sabbath.

(See also Chicken, Duck, Egg, Goose, Pigeon, Quail, and Turkey)

BIRKHAT HAMAZON (GRACE AFTER MEALS)

The Bible, in the section of the Seven Species with which the land of Israel is praised, mandates, "And you shall eat, *ve'savata* [and you shall be satisfied], *u'verachta* [and you shall acknowledge] the Lord your God for the good land which he has given you." This verse is the source of the obligation to thank and praise God after eating, *Birkhat Hamazon* ("Benediction of the Sustenance," commonly referred to as Grace after Meals), which serves as the archetype of other *berakhot* (benedictions) and all Jewish liturgy. In Yiddish, this prayer is known as *benschen*, ultimately from the Latin *benedicere* (also the source of the English word benediction) with the suffix *en*. Similarly, Friday night candle lighting is *licht benschen*, while a *benscher* refers to the booklet containing the Grace after Meals.

According to the prevailing opinion, the Bible directed a benediction only after eating bread made from the two grains included in the Seven Species, wheat and barley. The Sages instituted an abridged version of the Grace after Meals, the *Al-ha'Michya* (on the sustenance), recited after eating any of the Seven Species. In addition to the benedictions recited after eating, the Sages instituted benedictions to be recited before eating, as well as before all the commandments; these benedictions are attributed to the *Anshei Knesset ha-Gadolah* (Members of the Great Assembly). Each of these benedictions commences with the same terminology, "Blessed are You,

O Eternal our God, Ruler of the Universe, Who . . ." Before eating any of the Five Species of grain, such as a dish of bulgur wheat or barley, a person recites *"borei menay mezonot"* (creates the types of grains). Fruit from trees and plain grapes require the generic *"borei peri ha-eitz"* (creates the fruit of the tree). Vegetables require the blessing *"borei peri ha-adamah"* (creates the fruit of the earth). Any other food that does not fall into a specific category, such as meat, eggs, and processed foods such as juice, requires the less specific blessing of *"shehakol nehyah bidvaro"* (that all things came to be by His word). However, both bread and wine, the two most processed biblical foods, have special benedictions. Before drinking wine, one recites the more specific *"borei peri ha-gafen"* (creates the fruit of the vine). Bread, including matza, calls for the higher form of blessing, which when recited subsumes all other foods at the meal: *"ha-motzi lechem min ha-arertz"* (brings forth bread from the earth).

Today, *Birkhat Hamazon* consists of four benedictions, the first three of much greater antiquity, and various adjuncts. According to tradition, Moses instituted the first benediction while in the wilderness, instructing the Israelites to thank God for their sustenance, and Joshua added a second paragraph after he led the people into the land of Israel.

The Grace after Meals is generally sung or at least major parts of it are, rendering the prayer easier to remember and elevating it to a more mystical and emotional experience. The most widespread of the contemporary tunes was composed in the 1940s by Cantor Moshe Nathanson (also the author of the words to Hava Nagila).

BIRYANI

Biryani is a baked dish consisting of rice layered with meat, poultry, and/or vegetables.
Origin: India
Other names: *biriani.*

Biryani derives from the Farsi word *biryan* (fried/roasted), denoting a Persian dish of raw rice sautéed in fat before cooking, resulting in separate grains with a nutty flavor. Originally, the rice was fried, then parboiled with water, mixed with spices and minced roasted lamb, and steamed in a pan over a fire. This rice was flavored throughout with the meat and spices.

Biryani spread throughout central and eastern Asia, coming to encompass a variety of rice dishes, many no longer fried and mixed. A method was developed, some contend by nomads, of layering the rice and meat, rice always constituting the bottom and top layers, in an earthenware pot, which was then sealed and placed on hot embers to cook. The Mughals popularized this type of *biryani* in India, where it was typically made from goat or lamb and baked (*dum*) over coals in an earthenware pot known as a *handi*. Initially, *biryani* was a royal dish, but eventually Hindu employees developed vegetarian (*tahiri*) versions, which became far and away the most widespread. In 1856, after the British conquered Calcutta, *biryani* reached that region, with a widespread innovation—it was baked as a casserole in an oven. Chicken emerged as a popular substitute for meat. Potatoes were a common addition to the vegetable layer in Calcutta. Long-grain white or brown rice (*chaval*) was customary in northern and central India, while short-grain (*jeera samba*) was typically used in the south of the country.

The Jewish vegetarian version, *tahiri biryani*, is a synthesis of Middle Eastern and Indian heritages. Since the dish does require a bit of work, it is generally reserved for special occasions. In particular, Indian Jews serve this casserole and another rice dish, *pilau* (pilaf), on holidays, especially Sukkot and Passover (Sephardim and Mizrachim eat rice on that festival), and for celebrations. *Biryani* is accompanied with a curry or, on dairy occasions, with *raita* (yogurt salad) or plain yogurt.

BISCOCHO

Biscocho is both the generic Ladino word for cookie as well as a term denoting a ring-shaped cookie baked at a high temperature until firm, then baked a second time at a lower temperature until crisp and dry.
Origin: Spain
Other names: *biscotcho, biskotcho, bizcocho, panezico.*

The concept of twice baking bread to greatly increase its shelf life dates back at least to the ancient Romans, who included such bread in army rations. Ring-shaped *biscochos* are based on one of the most ancient of pastries, already mentioned in the Talmud, and still popular in the Middle East, small savory bread rings called *kaak* and, by Sephardim, *biscochos de levadura* (yeast biscuits). Where the evolutionary step of adding sugar—technically creating a *biscocho dulce*—first occurred remains a matter of question. Medieval Iberia seems an appropriate location, as the dish was widespread well before the expulsion and Spain had a plentiful supply of sugar. The Spanish cookbook *Libro del Arte de Cozina* (1599) by Diego Granado, much of whose contents are borrowed from earlier Spanish and Italian cookbooks, contains two *biszocho* recipes as well as one for a *rosquillas*, akin to a sweet bagel.

Although the Sephardic *biscocho* is similar in name and nature to the Italian biscotti, there were two major differences in the earliest forms of these cookies—biscotti were slices from a larger loaf and originally lacked any fat, while *biscochos* were ring-shaped and, from the onset, contained oil. Early Sephardim rarely baked with butter and cookies instead contained oil, creating an elastic dough that is easy to shape and a tender cookie. Sweet bread sticks are called *biscochatha* and *parmak* ("finger" in Turkish). Cookie versions containing egg are also known as *biscochos de huevo* (egg cookies).

Biscochos are typically not overly sweet. Most contemporary Sephardic cooks enhance their cookies with vanilla, but some still add flavorings prominent before the advent of that extract, notably orange-blossom water, cinnamon, and anise. Some cookies are coated with sesame seeds or ground nuts, a widespread Turkish and Greek practice.

These rings are ubiquitous at a Sabbath *desayuno* (brunch) and on Rosh Hashanah, as a symbol of the sweet year to come. Sesame-topped rings, variously called *biscochos de susam, kaak ib sumsum,* and *taraleekoos,* or the pretzel-shaped *reshicas,* are customarily served to break the fast of Yom Kippur. On Sukkot, some families hang *biscochos* from the branches of the sukkah as decorations. At a Sephardic Tu b'Shevat seder, the second item in order is a *biscocho* made from wheat flour. Turkish and Greek Jews use strips of the dough on Purim to encase hard-boiled eggs, symbolizing Haman's bars or a part of his anatomy; the dish is called *foulares* in Turkey and *folarikos* in Greece. A special mounded cookie, *biscochos Har Sinai,* representing Mount Sinai, is enjoyed on Shavuot. Matza meal is substituted for the flour for Passover *biscochos.*

(See also Kaak and Rosca)

SEPHARDIC COOKIE RINGS
(BISCOCHOS DULCES/BISCOCHOS DE HUEVO/KAAK)
ABOUT FORTY-EIGHT 2-INCH COOKIES   [PAREVE]

About 4 cups (20 ounces) all-purpose flour
5 teaspoons cornstarch or potato starch (optional)
1 tablespoon baking powder
¼ teaspoon salt
4 large eggs, lightly beaten (1 cup)
1 cup sugar
1 cup vegetable or olive oil
1 teaspoon vanilla extract, 1 tablespoon orange-blossom water, 2 tablespoons anise seeds, or ¼ cup ground cinnamon
1 cup sesame seeds or ½ cup coarse sugar (optional)

1. Preheat the oven to 350°F. Line 2 large baking sheets with parchment paper or grease the sheets.

2. Sift together the flour, cornstarch, baking powder, and salt. In a large bowl, beat together the eggs and sugar until thick. Beat in the oil and vanilla. Stir in the flour mixture to make a soft, shiny dough. Cover and refrigerate for at least 8 hours.

3. Take 1 tablespoon of the dough, roll into a 4-inch long rope, and bring the edges together to form a ring. If desired, cut gashes on the outer edges every ¼ to ½ inch or, before sealing, twist the strip several times to coil. If using, dip 1 side into the sesame seeds and place, seed side up, onto the prepared sheets, leaving 1 inch between the rings. Repeat with the rest of the dough.

4. Bake until the rings are firm but not browned, about 15 minutes. Remove the cookies from the oven and repeat with the next batch.

5. When all the cookies are firm, place them close together on the baking sheets, reduce the heat to 250°F, return the cookies to the oven, and bake until crisp and golden, about 20 minutes. Transfer to wire racks and let cool completely. Store in an airtight container for up to 1 month or in the freezer for up to 6 months.

VARIATIONS
Greek Pretzel-Shaped Cookies (Reshicas): Loop the ends of the dough ropes over the middle to produce a pretzel shape.

BLACK-EYED PEA
There are a number of Asian and African legumes subsumed under the category of field beans, the most

well-known in the West being the mung bean and its close relative, the black-eyed pea. Despite its common name, it is actually a bean, not a pea.

Black-eyed peas have been cultivated for more than five millennia in eastern Africa, India, and southern China. By biblical times, they emerged as an important crop in Africa and were commonly identified with that continent; they were known as *pol ha-mitzri* (Egyptian bean) in the Talmud. Widely grown in Israel in Talmudic times and common among Sephardim before the expulsion from Spain, they remain popular in only a few Jewish communities, particularly those from the Balkans, Turkey, Syria, northern Iraq, southern India, and the southeastern United States.

Black-eyed peas are a late-harvest bean, typically planted in June. Differing from most Old World legumes, black-eyed peas are eaten both fresh and dried. Fresh seeds are pale green with a nutty-earthy, somewhat sweet flavor. When young, the pods can also be boiled and eaten. Similar to other legumes, black-eyed peas have an amino acid profile that complements grains. In Africa, black-eyed peas are commonly eaten with millet. In the eastern Mediterranean, they are typically partnered with rice. Middle Eastern Jews prepare a black-eyed pea salad or, for a favorite Friday night dish, cook them with tomatoes and onions, a common practice among Jews from the domains of the former Ottoman Empire; tomato, onion, and garlic all enhance the bean's flavor. Black-eyed peas are generally served as a side dish or for breakfast.

Sephardim have lived on the Caribbean island of Curaçao for more than three and a half centuries. One of their classic dishes is *tutu* (black-eyed peas with cornmeal mush), a synthesis of Iberian and Caribbean influences, which has been widely adopted by non-Jews there.

During the medieval period, the black-eyed pea's Arabic name—*lubiya* (derived either from *Luv,* "Libya," or the Greek *lobos,* "pod")—was mistakenly confused with the Talmudic *rubiya* ("fenugreek" in Aramaic), the latter a traditional Rosh Hashanah food because its name sounds similar to the Hebrew word for multiply/increase (*yirbu*). Thus black-eyed peas, fresh ones coming into season just before the holiday, became a symbol of fertility and prosperity and a popular Sephardic Rosh Hashanah food. Many families, especially those from Egypt, serve fresh black-eyed peas at Rosh Hashanah dinner as the sixth item among seven *simanim* (symbolic foods) consumed in a Seder-like ceremony of a series of blessings known as *Yehi Ratzones,* "May it be Your will, Lord our God and God of our Fathers *sheh'yirbu zachi'yoteinu* [that our merits may multiply]." During the meal, Egyptians also use fresh or dried black-eyed peas in a stew with lamb or veal or a salad (*lubiya*). In other Sephardic communities, Rosh Hashanah dinner usually contains a black-eyed pea dish, typically served over rice or cooked with rice, such as the Greek and Turkish black-eyed peas in tomato sauce (*fijones frescos*) and Syrian black-eyed peas with veal (*lubiya m'sallat*). The Sephardic custom of eating black-eyed peas on Rosh Hashanah was continued by those living in the southeastern United States and, around the time of the Civil War, widely adopted by non-Jews there, black-eyed peas becoming a traditional Southern New Year's Day food in dishes like hoppin' John (black-eyed peas with rice).

BLEHAT

Blehat is a meat loaf, typically with whole hard-boiled eggs arranged in the center before baking.

Origin: Egypt

Other names: *blehat lahme bi beid.*

The Jews of Spain more frequently possessed a home oven than members of most other communities, and they often baked dishes, such as *carne al horno* (meat of the oven). Because of the home oven's rather late arrival in North Africa and the Middle East, the predominant way of cooking ground meat was in small portions over a flame, such as stuffed into vegetables or as meatballs. In the Maghreb, small meat loaves were cooked in a Sabbath stew or in a pot over a flame. In Egypt, these meat loaves typically contained hard-boiled eggs, akin to the Anglo Scotch eggs. After Sephardim introduced *carne al horno* to Middle Eastern communities, some cooks also began baking the loaf inside an oven, preparing loaves such as the Egyptian *belehat,* a traditional Sabbath dish served warm at night or cold for lunch.

Whether cooked on the stovetop or baked, the ground meat must, in the Middle Eastern manner, have a smooth texture, not be coarse in the European fashion. For generations, the meat was customarily pounded with a mortar and pestle, but today a food processor is more common. Some versions mix in chopped dried apricots and pine nuts. Middle Eastern meat loaves, especially those topped with tahini (sesame seed paste), became immensely popular in modern Israel.

BLINI

Blini are yeast- or baking powder–leavened pancakes, traditionally made with buckwheat flour.
Origin: Eastern Europe
Other names: Russian: *blinchiki*; Ukrainian: *blyntsi*, *mlynets*.

Blini (*blin* singular) is the generic Slavic word for pancakes, derived from the Slavic *mlin/mlyn* (to mill). The difference between a blini and a blintz is that the former is usually thicker and often contains some form of leavening, while the latter, like a crepe, does not. Pancakes made from various grains, especially barley, have been prepared in the Slavic areas of eastern Europe for thousands of years, a round shape being the natural form of a pancake on a griddle. To the Slavs, this shape became symbolic of the sun. Thus around the spring equinox, Slavs celebrated Maslenitsa ("Pancake Week," but also called Butter Week), and cooked pancakes to honor the return of the sun.

The most famous type of blini is made from buckwheat (*grechnevoy* in Slavic), technically a fruit, not a grain. When buckwheat, which thrives in poor soil and weather extremes, arrived in western Russia and Ukraine around the early fourteenth century, it quickly emerged as a staple of the diet and subsequently was adopted by Jews to make some traditional fare, notably Hanukkah latkes. Buckwheat flour (*tattarijauho* in Slavic) imparts a distinctive hearty, earthy, slightly nutty flavor. Dark buckwheat flour, a gray color with black specks, is made from unroasted, unhulled groats and sometimes extra hulls are added. Light buckwheat flour, also called white buckwheat flour, has most of the hulls removed. The dark type has a more intense flavor and produces a grayish purple color in baked goods.

Blini are traditionally about four inches in diameter and thin, only slightly higher than a standard blintz. As a result of the yeast sponge, there should be numerous little holes dotting the surface. Miniature blini made from a thicker batter, the type common at the modern cocktail party, are called *oladyi*. Some batters may also contain raisins or grated apple. Slavic cooks traditionally grease the skillet or griddle by dipping the cut side of half a potato into oil (holding it with a fork), then rubbing it on the hot surface. Like crepes, the first thin pancake usually does not turn out well, leading to the Russian saying "The first *blin* is always a lump."

(See also Blintz and Kasha)

BLINTZ

Blintzes are thin, unleaved pancakes, cooked only on one side, then folded to enclose a filling and pan-fried.
Origin: Eastern Europe
Other names: *blintze*.

Tevye the Milkman, in Sholem Aleichem's tales, was quite proud of his wife's blintzes. In one passage, he basks in glory as they are served to guests on the holiday of Shavuot: "And very soon Golda appeared with the blintzes, piping hot, right from the frying pan, plump and tasty! My visitors couldn't praise them enough."

In the fourteenth century, the Turks conquered the Balkans, where they introduced very thin wheat pancakes that were cooked in a shallow pan, then filled and rolled up. The Romanians called these *clătită* or *plăcintă*, the Romanian pronunciation of the word for the ancient Roman flat cheesecake, *placenta*. In the sixteenth century, the thin pancake spread from Romania to Ukraine, with the name changing to the Slavic *blintze*. From Ukraine, the *blintze* continued into Poland and Lithuania. The term *blintze*—blintz is the Americanized Yiddish—can denote both a plain as well as a filled pancake, but among some Yiddish speakers unfilled blintz pancakes are also referred to as *bletlach* (leaves). In France, they became *crêpes* from the Latin *crispus* (curly/wrinkled), supplanting the previous medieval thicker pancakes of the same name.

The blintz is not exactly a crepe, being somewhat sturdier and less fussy, partially due to the larger proportion of eggs and, sometimes, absence of milk. For dairy meals the batter can contain milk, but for meat it is made with water. Similarly, dairy blintzes can be fried in butter, while those intended for a meat meal are fried in oil or schmaltz. Crepes are cooked on both sides, while *bletlach* only on one. A blintz is typically folded and rolled up into a package to enclose the filling like an envelope, all the better for frying.

Until relatively recently, buckwheat *bletlach* provided an inexpensive base for common use, while more delicate ones made from luxurious white flour were typically reserved for special occasions. It was only in the nineteenth century, with the increased availability and affordability of fine wheat flour in Europe, that wheat *bletlach* became widespread in the general population. Still, since blintzes are rather labor-intensive, they were hardly everyday fare in most households. Many a Jewish cook, when they could afford it, had two frying pans to speed the process, handily churning out blintz after blintz, as it was the rare person who could eat only one.

Traditional blintz fillings include curd cheese, mashed potatoes, kasha, chopped cooked beef, chopped liver, and fruit, or a combination of cheese and fruit. Lekvar blintzes were common in Poland. Hungarians created a "blintz soufflé," which become popular in late twentieth century America.

Cheese fillings, both savory and sweet, have long been the most prevalent. European curd cheeses were drier and more intensely flavored than today's cottage cheese. At present, farmer and/or pot cheese provide more texture, generally mixed with a little cream cheese or sour cream for creaminess and a slight tang. There should be just a bare hint of salt and only a little sugar should be added to sweetened versions, as the delicate flavor of the cheese should be pronounced. Hot cheese blintzes are typically topped with a dollop of cool sour cream or fruit sauce (not too sweet) to contrast and complement the hot creamy filling.

Ashkenazic immigrants brought the blintz to America, and it was already common on the Lower East Side of Manhattan by the end of the nineteenth century. Perhaps the word's first appearance and explanation in America was in the November 7, 1900, edition of the *Duluth News Tribune* in an article entitled "Jewish Coffee and Tea Houses." The reporter wrote, "One of the distinguishing features of the East Side [of Manhattan] . . . is found in the tea and coffee houses kept by Hebrews . . . The glory of these establishments, however, is the blintz, which is a sort of pancake rolled up and inclosing curds made savory. The Jews seem fond of the blintz which is cooked upon gas stoves just like buckwheat cakes, and is eaten as hot as the customer's mouth can endure."

Blintzes were soon popular fare at Jewish dairy restaurants and Catskills hotels. A manager at Ratner's, a famous Lower East Side restaurant founded in 1905

and closed in 2002, revealed that 75 percent of the hundreds of blintzes sold on a daily basis were cheese, followed far behind by cherry, and then blueberry (they also offered potato, dried plum, and apple). Cheese blintzes were the favorite dish of gangster Meyer Lansky, once a regular Ratner's patron.

As with other Ashkenazic foods that entered the American mainstream, blintzes began appearing in popular culture. In origami, the term "blintz fold" denotes a maneuver in which all four corners are folded to the center. It was coined by Gershon Legman, who associated the fold with the image from his mother's Hungarian cooking. Later, Legman's mother informed him that technically it should have been a "knish fold," which actually is folded to the center, while the blintz is folded over and rolled. By then, the term had stuck and blintz remains part of origami-folding lore.

Ashkenazim traditionally serve cheese blintzes on Shavuot, during the week before Tisha b'Av, and on other occasions when it is customary to eat dairy dishes. Blintzes have two additional symbolic rationales for Shavuot: two blintzes placed side by side resemble the two tablets that Moses received on Mount Sinai, as well as the two leavened loaves waved by the high priest in the Temple on Shavuot. Since they are fried, blintzes became traditional Hanukkah fare, a cheese filling encompassing the festival's dairy symbolism as well. A special Passover blintz uses matza meal or potato starch for the flour.

(See also Atayef, Blini, and Palacsinta)

EASTERN EUROPEAN THIN PANCAKES (*BLINTZES*)

ABOUT TWELVE 6-INCH OR EIGHTEEN 5-INCH PANCAKES

[DAIRY OR PAREVE]

1 cup milk, soy milk, seltzer, or water

4 large eggs, lightly beaten

2 tablespoons vegetable oil or unsalted butter or margarine, melted

2 tablespoons sugar (optional)

¼ teaspoon table salt or ½ teaspoon kosher salt

1 cup (5 ounces) pastry or all-purpose flour

Butter or vegetable oil for frying

1 recipe Ashkenazic filling (pages 197–198)

1. In a medium bowl, whisk together the milk, eggs, oil, sugar, and salt. Gradually add the flour to make a smooth, thin batter. Strain if there are any lumps. Or process all the ingredients in a blender or food processor. Cover and refrigerate for at least 2 hours or overnight. Stir to recombine.

2. Heat a 6-inch heavy skillet over medium heat until a few drops of water sprinkled on the surface scatter and evaporate, 3 to 5 minutes. Add about 1½ teaspoons butter to thinly coat the pan; if too thick, lightly wipe off the excess. Pour in about 2 tablespoons batter, tilting the pan until the batter coats the bottom. Do not add too much batter. Cook until the blintz is dry on the top and the bottom edges begin to brown, about 1 minute.

3. Remove the pan from the heat. Using a spatula or blunt knife, loosen the pancake's edges. Flip the pancake onto a plate. To stack, place a piece of wax paper, foil, or dampened paper towel between each blintz. It is best to regrease the pan after every 2 or 3 blintzes. The blintzes can be stored in the refrigerator for up to 4 days or in the freezer for up to 1 month. Return to room temperature.

4. Arrange a blintz on a flat surface, cooked side up, and place 2 to 3 tablespoons filling just below the center. Fold the bottom of the blintz over the filling, then fold the sides over and roll up, enclosing the filling completely. The blintzes can be refrigerated overnight or stored in the freezer for up to 1 month. Do not thaw before cooking.

5. In a large skillet, heat a little butter over medium heat. Add the blintzes, seam side down, and fry, turning once, until browned on both sides, about 5 minutes per side for fresh. For frozen blintzes, cover the pan for the first 5 minutes.

BODEK

A *bodek* ("examiner" in Hebrew) is a person specially trained to examine the insides of an animal following slaughter to determine if it was healthy and, therefore, kosher. Since the lungs are most commonly affected by defects, they must be inspected before a cow can be certified as kosher. The act of examination is called *bedikah*.

(See also Glatt and Kosher)

BOLA

Bola refers to various Sephardic cakes and pastries.
Origin: Spain, Portugal
Other names: *bolo*, *booler*, *boyo*.

Bola, the Ladino word for ball, has two denotations in Sephardic cooking, which can be a little confus-ing. The more widespread usage encompasses various Iberian cakes and pastries, while the lesser-used meaning is a globular cut of beef shoulder. Thus when Esther Levy, in *Jewish Cookery* (Philadelphia, 1871), in a recipe for "Coogle, or Pudding, and Peas and Beans" (cholent with kugel), calls for "a shin bone and a piece of bola, about three pounds" she intended a piece of meat, not cake.

The original medieval pastry *bola* consisted of croquettes of yeast dough or mashed soaked bread deep-fried in oil, the round shape providing its Ladino name. Over the centuries, the simple fritters developed into an assortment of both fried and baked cakes and pastries, including the more modern *bola de ovo* (egg cake), *bola de chocolate* (chocolate cake), and *bola de coco* (coconut cake). Unquestionably, the most popular form of *bola* before the expulsion from Spain was a large, soft, rich yeast-raised cake studded with raisins and candied citron, akin to the Teutonic kugelhopf and Italian panettone, which it may have inspired. These yeast-raised dishes were never used by Sephardim to commence the meal in the manner of the Ashkenazic challah, but were always offered as a treat at *desayuno* (brunch) or on a holiday afternoon.

Following the expulsion, the Iberian term *bola* persevered mostly among those Sephardim, predominantly Portuguese, who settled in western Europe. Those who relocated to the east eventually adopted local names for cakes, relegating this ancient term primarily to an anise sweet bread and to a variety of cheese pastries called *boyo*. In Tunisia, the *bolo* gave rise to the orange-flavored doughnut, *yoyo*. Sephardic exiles also introduced the now popular *il bollo* to Italian Jews.

The classic Portuguese-inspired work *The Jewish Manual* (London, 1846) by Judith Montefiore included recipes for four types of *bolas*, which she described as "a kind of rich cake or pudding" (referring to English cake-like steamed puddings). Three of her *bolas* consisted of yeast-raised cakes: "Bola Toliedo," "A Bola D'Hispaniola," and "A Plain Bola." The fourth, "Bola D'Amor," was a type of confection. Montefiore's "Plain Bola" follows the manner of a classic Iberian *bola*: "Take three quarters of a pound of white sugar, three quarters of a pound of fresh butter, two eggs, one pound and a half of flour, three spoonsful of yeast, a little milk, and two ounces of citron cut thin, and mix into a light paste; bake in a tin, and strew powdered sugar and cinnamon over it before baking. The above ingredients are often baked in small tins or cups."

At the time of the expulsion from Spain and subsequent forced conversion of Portugal's Jews, the Netherlands was under Spanish control and, therefore, many Conversos moved there in the hopes of escaping the Inquisition and reclaiming their religion. In Holland, the plain *bola*, a yeast cake shaped like a scone, became known as *bolussen*. It was probably in dairy-rich Holland that butter was initially substituted for the traditional olive oil of Iberia. Other newer forms of *bola* emerged in the Netherlands as well, referred to by the Dutch as *Joodse keuken* (Jewish cakes). Among the most prominent Dutch *bola* are *gember bolussen* (ginger cakes) and *orgeade bolussen* (with bitter and sweet almonds), made by rolling out a rich yeast dough on a bed of cinnamon-sugar, sprinkling it with citron and jam or *calder* (a Portuguese syrup), rolling it up, cutting the roll into slices, and baking. This led to one of the most popular Dutch pastries, *Zeeuwse bolussen* (Zeeland-style cakes), described by a Dutch dictionary as "flat, round cakes made of flour, milk, citron, cinnamon, and syrup."

Dutch Jews later brought classic *bolas,* as well as the spiral versions, to England, where they became known in the nineteenth century as "stuffed monkeys." The name may be a whimsical corruption of the Arabic word for stuffed, *mashi*. *Bolas* and stuffed monkeys became popular English holiday fare, especially on Purim.

Israel Zangwill, in his novel *Children of the Ghetto: A Study of a Peculiar People* (London, 1892), offered a vivid description of Purim in Victorian London: "At Purim a gaiety, as of the Roman carnival, enlivened the swampy Wentworth Street, and brought a smile into the unwashed face of the pavement. The confectioners' shops, crammed with 'stuffed monkeys' and 'bolas,' were besieged by hilarious crowds of handsome girls and their young men, fat women and their children, all washing down the luscious spicy compounds with cups of chocolate; temporarily erected swinging cradles bore a vociferous many-colored burden to the skies; cardboard noses, grotesque in their departure from truth, abounded."

Later, in discussing Passover, Zangwill noted, "Now the confectioner exchanges his stuffed monkeys, and his bolas and his jam-puffs, and his cheese-cakes

for unleavened 'palavas,' (sponge cakes) and worsted balls and almond cakes."

(See also Bimuelo and Boyo)

SEPHARDIC SOFT CHEESE FRITTERS (*BOLOS DE QUESO*)

ABOUT 48 FRITTERS   [DAIRY]

1¼ cups (6.25 ounces) all-purpose flour
½ teaspoon ground cinnamon
⅛ teaspoon baking powder
⅛ teaspoon salt
1 pound (2 cups) farmer cheese or mild soft goat cheese
4 large eggs, lightly beaten
3 tablespoons sugar
1 tablespoon unsalted butter, melted
½ teaspoon brandy
½ teaspoon grated lemon zest
Vegetable or peanut oil for deep-frying
Confectioner's sugar or sugar syrup (*Atar*, page 26) (optional)

1. Sift together the flour, cinnamon, baking powder, and salt. In a large bowl, combine the cheese, eggs, sugar, butter, brandy, and zest. Stir in the flour mixture.

2. In a deep, heavy skillet or saucepan, heat at least 1 inch oil over medium heat to 375°F.

3. In batches, drop the batter by tablespoonfuls into the oil and fry, turning, until golden brown on all sides, about 2 minutes. Drain on paper towels. If desired, sprinkle with confectioners' sugar or dip in syrup.

BOLLO

Bollo is a round, anise-flavored, slightly sweet bread or bun.

Origin: Portugal, Spain
Other names: French: *pain à l'anis*; Ladino: *bolo, boyo.*

Sephardim historically used unembellished pita-like bread as their Sabbath loaves, sometimes adding anise. Breads flavored with anise seeds, such as the Moroccan *khboz*, are still common among Mediterranean Jewish communities. Sephardim did not recite Hamotzi on enriched breads containing eggs and sweeteners, which they considered to be cakes, rejecting the use of the Ashkenazic egg challah for their Sabbath and festival loaves. Some Sephardim made round loaves—symbolizing a coin—or intricate shapes, ranging from spirals to flowers, but only using lean dough. Moroccan Sabbath loaves tend to be round and raised, frequently with a fluted edge.

What differentiated the Iberian round loaf *bollo* from other anise breads was the addition of eggs, olive oil, and sugar or honey. *Bollo*, the name coming from its ball-like shape, was among the myriad of advanced baked goods common to the medieval Sephardic kitchen. Sweet breads might be offered as a treat at a *desayuno* (brunch) or as a holiday afternoon snack, especially on Rosh Hashanah, as sign of a sweet year to come. For Sukkot, *bollos* are frequently studded with dried and candied fruits and nuts, symbolic of the harvest. *Bollo* is also traditional at the meal to break the fast of Yom Kippur. For Sukkot, Moroccans prepare raised, sesame-seed-sprinkled loaves laden with eggs, sugar, and anise, called *pain petri*.

After the expulsion from Spain in 1492, Sephardim introduced *bollo* to locations around the Mediterranean, where several communities adopted it, notably Italians as *il bollo*. Italian versions tend to be richer with larger amounts of eggs, sugar, and oil. Italians customarily serve *bollo* throughout Sukkot and to break the fast of Yom Kippur. During Sukkot, Venetian Jews laid out a ritual "Table of the Angel," always featuring *il bollo*.

(See also Bola, Bread, Challah, and Fritter)

⚜ SEPHARDIC SWEET ANISE BREAD (*BOLLO*)

2 MEDIUM LOAVES OR ABOUT 26 ROLLS   [PAREVE]

 1 package (2¼ teaspoons) active dry yeast or
  1 (0.6-ounce) cake fresh yeast
 1½ cups warm water (105 to 115°F for dry yeast;
  80 to 85°F for fresh yeast)
 ⅓ cup sugar or honey
 2 large eggs
 ¼ cup olive, peanut, or vegetable oil
 About 2 tablespoons anise seeds or ½ teaspoon
  ground anise
 1½ teaspoons table salt or 1 tablespoon kosher salt
 About 4 cups (20 ounces) bread or unbleached all-
  purpose flour
 Egg wash (1 large egg beaten with 1 teaspoon water)

1. Dissolve the yeast in ¼ cup water. Stir in 1 teaspoon sugar and let stand until foamy, 5 to 10 minutes. In a large bowl, combine the yeast mixture, remaining water, remaining sugar, eggs, oil, anise, salt, and

2 cups flour. Gradually add enough of the remaining flour to make a mixture that holds together.

2. On a lightly floured surface, knead the dough until smooth and elastic, 10 to 15 minutes. Place in an oiled bowl and turn to coat. Cover loosely with plastic wrap or a kitchen towel and let rise until doubled in bulk, about 2 hours.

3. Punch down the dough, knead briefly, cover, and let rest for about 15 minutes. Divide in half or 26 equal pieces. Shape each piece into a ball, cover, and let rest for about 10 minutes.

4. Line a large baking sheet with parchment paper or grease and flour the sheet. Shape each dough half into a flat 6-inch round or 8-inch-long oval. For the small pieces, shape into balls. Place on the prepared baking sheet, cover, and let rise until doubled in bulk, about 1½ hours.

5. Preheat the oven to 375°F.

6. Brush the loaves or rolls with the egg wash. Bake until golden brown and hollow sounding when tapped on the bottom, 30 to 40 minutes for a large loaf or about 20 minutes for rolls. Transfer to a wire rack and let cool. Store wrapped in plastic wrap at room temperature for up to 4 days.

BOMBA

Bomba is a baked, molded rice cake. It is made with the varieties of rice used in risotto, but is not cooked in the same manner as risotto.

Origin: Italy

Other names: *bomba al salto, bomba di riso.*

The Arabs introduced rice to Sicily during their control of that island. Later, in the sixteenth century, this grain became widely planted in northern Italy and the people became avid rice consumers. Risotto originated in Lombardy and, by the nineteenth century, had spread throughout Italy, with every northern part of the country developing its own version. Tuscan housewives tended to cook large batches of risotto for the Sabbath and holidays and then used the leftovers to make assorted dishes, most notably the large *bomba di riso* and stuffed croquettes variously called *suppli di riso* and *arancini di riso* (literally "little oranges of rice"). Later, as these dishes gained in popularity, people began making them in their own right, not merely to repurpose leftovers.

The name *bomba* derives from the Italian word for swelling, referring to the action of the pancake while frying, the original method of preparation. As the home oven became more prominent in the late nineteenth century, cooks began baking the *bomba* as a casserole rather than frying it in a skillet. Thus today *bomba* is typically a molded form of risotto. The same rice mixture can also be used to make the more tedious fried *bomba al salto* (large rice pancakes) as well as the smaller *suppli* and *arancini*. A more elaborate version, *con piccione* (with pigeon), is made with poultry. *Bomba* is served as a main course with a vegetable stew or green salad, or as a side.

ITALIAN BAKED RICE CAKE (*BOMBA*)

6 TO 8 SERVINGS   [DAIRY]

- 5 cups vegetable broth or water (or 4½ cups broth and ½ cup dry white wine)
- 2½ cups (16 ounces) risotto rice, such as Arborio, Carnaroli, Vialone, or other short- or medium-grain varieties
- About 2 teaspoons table salt or 4 teaspoons kosher salt
- ¼ teaspoon ground turmeric or saffron threads (optional)
- 4 large eggs, slightly beaten
- ⅓ cup grated Parmesan cheese
- 2 tablespoons (¼ stick) unsalted butter
- About ½ teaspoon freshly grated nutmeg (optional)
- 1 pound (4 cups) mozzarella cheese, shredded, or 12 ounces (3 cups) mozzarella and 12 ounces (1½ cups) ricotta cheese

1. In a large saucepan, place the broth, rice, salt, and, for a yellow color, turmeric. Cover and bring to a boil, about 5 minutes. Reduce the heat to low and simmer, without removing the lid, until the rice is tender, about 15 minutes. The cooking time depends on the age and type of rice. Spread over a flat tray and let cool.

2. Preheat the oven to 350°F. Grease a 2-quart baking dish or 9-by-2¼-inch ring mold.

3. In a large bowl, combine the rice, eggs, Parmesan, butter, and, if using, nutmeg. Spread half of the rice mixture into the prepared dish, scatter with the cheese, and top with the remaining rice mixture. Alternately, mix the mozzarella and ricotta into the rice mixture instead of layering it.

4. Place the dish into a large baking pan and add about 1 inch of boiling water to the pan. Bake until set and golden, about 25 minutes. Run a knife along the

inside of the dish to loosen the rice. Place a large serving platter over the top, invert, and remove the dish. Serve warm, if desired, accompanied with a tomato sauce or vegetable stew.

BONDA

Bonda is a vegan fritter coated with *besan* (chickpea flour) and fried.
Origin: India
Other names: *mysore bonda.*

Snacks are a beloved part of southern Indian culture and among the most popular is the *bonda*, meaning "naked," which is strange since these vegan fritters from Mysore are actually encased in a crisp shell. Chickpea flour produces a crisp, nongreasy crust that contrasts with the smooth interior. The most popular *bonda* is made from mashed potatoes (*aloo bondas*), but others include hard-boiled eggs (*mutta bondas*), manioc (*tapioca bondas*), or curd cheese mixed with soaked bread (*panir bondas*).

Besides loving the taste of potatoes (*aloo*), Indians consider them to be an aphrodisiac. There are two predominant types of *aloo bondas*, of which Cochinis generally prefer the slightly sweet variety made with raisins and coconut, while northerners typically opt for a spicy one (also called *batata varda*). Westerners generally tone down the chilies. The filling can be solely potatoes or potato with various chopped or mashed vegetables. They are eaten as a snack accompanied with chutneys, or as part of a lunch, and are popular as Hanukkah treats.

COCHINI POTATO FRITTERS (*ALOO BONDAS*)

ABOUT 30 CROQUETTES   [PAREVE]

Filling:

- 3 pounds (6 large) baking (russet) potatoes, peeled
- 2½ teaspoons table salt or 5 teaspoons kosher salt
- 2 tablespoons fresh lime or lemon juice
- 3 to 6 fresh small green or serrano chilies, minced
- ½ cup minced fresh cilantro
- 2 teaspoons ground turmeric
- 1 to 2 teaspoons minced fresh ginger

Coating:

- 1½ cups (5.25 ounces) chickpea flour (*besan*) or lentil flour (*gram dal*)
- 1 cup (5 ounces) all-purpose flour (*maida*), or ½ cup rice flour and 2 tablespoons cornstarch
- 1 teaspoon table salt or 2 teaspoons kosher salt

¼ teaspoon baking soda

½ teaspoon ground turmeric, 1 teaspoon garam
masala, or ¼ teaspoon asafetida (*hing*)

¼ to 1 teaspoon cayenne

About ¾ cup water

Vegetable or peanut oil for deep-frying

1. To make the filling: Place the peeled potatoes in a bowl of cold water until ready to use. (Do not cut the potatoes as this lets in excess water.) Rinse the potatoes under cold running water. Place in a large pot, add cold water to cover by 1 inch, then add 1 teaspoon salt. Bring to a low boil, reduce the heat to medium-low, and simmer until fork-tender, about 25 minutes. Drain.

2. While still warm, run the potatoes through a food mill or ricer. Or return the potatoes to the warm cooking pot and mash with a potato masher, heavy whisk, or pastry blender over medium-low heat. You should have about 6 cups.

3. Combine the potatoes, lime juice, chilies, cilantro, turmeric, remaining 1½ teaspoons salt, and ginger.

4. To make the coating: In a large bowl, combine the flours, salt, baking soda, turmeric, and cayenne. Stir in enough of the water to form a medium-thick batter.

5. In a wok or deep saucepan, heat at least 1 inch oil to 350°F over medium-high heat.

6. Form the potato filling into 1½-inch balls (the size of a small lemon). Dip into the coating, letting the excess drip off. In batches, fry the balls, turning, until golden brown, about 2 minutes. Remove with a slotted spoon and drain on paper towels. Serve hot or at room temperature with a slightly sweet chutney, such as coconut, mint, and tamarind.

BORANI

Borani is a cold yogurt and vegetable salad and dip.
Origin: Persia
Other names: *buranee, burani, mast-e esfanaj.*

No Persian dairy meal, including Shavuot, Passover, and Hanukkah, would be considered complete without a *borani*, a dish quite refreshing in hot weather. The name derives from the first woman to rule Persia thirteen hundred years ago—a queen named *Poorandokht* (or Pouran), who purportedly had a particular fondness for yogurt. Over the centuries, the pronunciation of *pouran* evolved into *boran/buran*. (The suffix *i* or *e* means "with".) By the thirteenth century, spinach *borani* was already recorded in Damascus. Each type of *borani* consists of a garlic-enhanced yogurt sauce with a single vegetable, including spinach, eggplant, beet, cardoon, celery, and cucumber, with mint as a common flavoring. *Borani* can be rather plain, with only a hint of garlic, or vibrant with caramelized onions and spices or mint. If the vegetables are chopped coarsely, the *borani* is served as a salad or side dish; if chopped finely, it becomes a dip for bread.

Borani is popular in neighboring countries as well, especially Afghanistan and Georgia. It also most certainly inspired the Turkish yogurt-cucumber *cacik*, called *tzatziki* by the Greeks, as well as Indian raitas.

✂ PERSIAN SPINACH AND YOGURT SALAD
(*BORANI ESFANAJ*)

ABOUT 5 CUPS/6 TO 8 SERVINGS   [DAIRY]

¼ cup (½ stick) butter or vegetable oil

2 large onions, chopped or thinly sliced

4 to 5 cloves garlic, minced

2 pounds fresh spinach, destemmed, washed, and
chopped; or 20 ounces frozen spinach, thawed
and squeezed dry

2 cups strained plain yogurt

About 1 teaspoon table salt or 2 teaspoons kosher
salt

¼ to ½ teaspoon ground black pepper,
2 tablespoons chopped fresh mint, or
2 tablespoons fresh dill

1. In a large saucepan, melt the butter over medium heat. Add the onions and sauté until golden, about 20 minutes. Stir in the garlic and sauté for 1 minute. Add the spinach and sauté until wilted, 5 to 10 minutes. Let cool.

2. In a medium bowl, combine the yogurt, salt, and pepper. Stir in the spinach. The mixture should be rather thick. Refrigerate for at least 1 hour and up to 1 day to let the flavors meld. Serve chilled or at room temperature as an appetizer, side dish, or dip.

BOREKA

Boreka is a pastry turnover.
Origin: Turkey
Other names: Greek: *bourekakia, pastelle*; Hebrew: *borekas*; Italian: *burriche*; Ladino: *empanada, empanda*; Turkish: *boureka, bureka.*

Borekas, along with *boyos* and *bulemas,* form the trio of preeminent Ottoman Jewish pastries. Among these Sephardim, *borekas* have long been a sign of hospitality, comfort, and culinary capability. As with

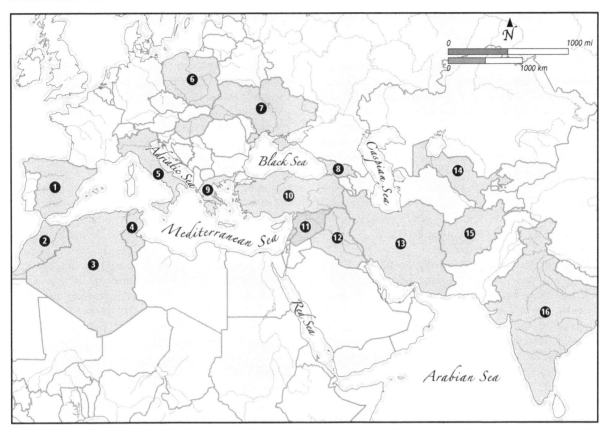

Turnovers and Filled Pastries Cooks discovered an efficient and tasty way to use up leftovers or stretch meager resources—wrapping them in dough. *1* **Spain**—*empanada, pastelito;* *2* **Morocco**—*breewat;* *3* **Algeria**—*bourak;* *4* **Tunisia**—*brik;* *5* **Italy**—*buricche;* *6* **Poland**—*knish;* *7* **Ukraine**—*piroshke;* *8* **Georgia**—*khachapuri;* *9* **Greece**—*boreka, pasteliko;* *10* **Turkey**—*börek, boreka, borekita, pogaca, sambusak, samsa;* *11* **Syria, Lebanon**—*sambusak;* *12* **Iraq**—*burag, sambusak;* *13* **Persia**—*sanbusaj;* *14* **Uzbekistan**—*bichak, samsa;* *15* **Afghanistan**—*sambosa;* *16* **India**—*samosa*

most Jewish foods, *borekas* are a synthesis of cultures and styles; over the course of history, they have been transformed and transferred, on their way to becoming a ubiquitous treat in modern Israel.

When the Turks relocated from central Asia to the area that now bears their name, among the foods they brought with them was a deep-fried filled dumpling, *burga.* According to some, the name derived from the Turkic *bur* (to twist). By the fifteenth century, this simple fritter evolved into a myriad of Ottoman filled and layered pastries—baked and fried, large and small, sweet and savory—collectively known as *börek* or *burek.* *Börek* are the cornerstone of Turkish cuisine; the classic pastries are so highly regarded that the head *börek* baker held one of the most important

positions in the Ottoman imperial household. The common denominator among *börek* is a pastry and filling. Authentic *börek* are made from *yufka,* which by the fifteenth century had evolved into a sophisticated, very thin dough; at around the same time, the modern Turkish *börek* were developing. Due to their numbers and diversity, *börek* must be identified by cooking style or region. The Turks spread the *börek* throughout their empire and variations are still found in those areas.

Among the foods the Sephardim brought with them when they arrived in the realm of the sultan, at the same time *börek* were developing, were half-moon-shaped turnovers called *empanadas,* made from an oil pastry and a rudimentary puff pastry. The newcomers, proudly clinging to their traditional foods and language, did not immediately adopt Turkish foods, but by the eighteenth century, Sephardim in Turkey and Greece merged the Iberian *empanada* with the *börek* (adding the Spanish feminine ending *a*) to create one of the favorite Ottoman Jewish pastries, the *boreka*.

Many cooks retained a traditional Iberian dough for their homemade *borekas*, while others opted for the Ottoman *yufka*. In any case, *borekas* generally call for a slightly heavier, thicker dough than the Turkish *börek*. In texture, the *boreka* is somewhat thicker than both the *boyo* and the very thin, very crisp *bulema*. Many Sephardim reserve the term *boreka* for the *empanada*-type pastries and called the triangular phyllo-type by the Ladino term *ojaldres*. Today, however, these terms are frequently used interchangeably, at least by the general public.

Borekas can be large or small, the fillings either sweet or savory—cheese, eggplant, potato, and spinach have long been the most traditional and more recently mushroom and pizza have become popular. So as not to use a dairy *boreka* at a meat meal, Jewish cooks developed several means of differentiating among the various fillings, including diverse toppings, such as grated cheese, sesame seeds, and plain; varied shapes; and different border designs.

Homemade turnovers are rather labor-intensive and, therefore, in most instances in most cultures, were reserved primarily for special occasions or for the very wealthy. Not totally so *borekas*, which were sometimes eaten throughout the day as well as to celebrate life-cycle events and holidays. In nineteenth-century Turkey and Greece, breakfast often meant a *boreka* or two with yogurt, while in modern Israel, it is frequently *borekas* and coffee.

Turnovers with cheese or cheese and vegetable fillings, sometimes called *borekitas*, are ubiquitous at *desayuno* (brunch), Shavuot, and other dairy meals. At Sabbath dinner and other meat meals, the *borekas* might be meat, fish, or pareve. In Salonika, spinach-filled borekas or the phyllo version, *ojaldres*, were the traditional Friday night pastry, accompanying the main dish of *avicas* (bean stew). Pumpkin and winter squash fillings are traditional on Rosh Hashanah and Sukkot. Purim pastries contain a nut paste filling, *borekas de muez* (walnut) or *borekas de almendra* (almond). So beloved were these pastries that cooks invented a Passover version utilizing soaked matzas. It is not uncommon for hosts to offer several or even five different varieties of *borekas* at a single meal.

In modern Israel, *borekas* (the Ladino plural form is used as singular in Israel) follows only falafel in popularity as a street snack food and rank among the favorite home treats for the Sabbath or a simple weekday nosh. They are also common appetizers at weddings, bar mitzvahs, *brits*, and almost any buffet. Commercial brands, generally made from puff pastry or phyllo, are found frozen (baked and ready-to-be-baked) in Israeli grocery freezers and fresh in most bakeries. Some locales, such as parts of Tel Aviv, have so many *borekas* outlets in close proximity, aficionados argue over who bakes the better *borekas*. Many, of course, insist that honor belongs to *borekasim ema* (my mother's).

By the end of the twentieth century, *borekas* were finally beginning to impact America, influenced by Israeli immigrants and American visitors to Israel; they have gradually appeared in kosher pizza shops and bakeries, and as frozen imports in Jewish markets.

(See also Empanada, Pastelito, and Phyllo)

BORSCHT

Borscht is a soup made with beets. It may be hot or cold and it may contain meat or be vegetarian.
Origin: Ukraine
Other names: Polish: *barszcz*; Russian: *borshch*;
    Ukranian: *borshch*; Yiddish: *borsht*.

Northern Poland and the Baltic States are rather far north, lying in a region with long dark winters, a relatively short growing season, and a limited number of (as well as sometimes an aversion to) available vegetables. During the early medieval period, eastern Europeans began making a chunky soup from a wild whitish root related to carrots, called *brsh* in Old Slavonic and cow parsnip in English. Possibly originating in Lithuania, the soup spread throughout the Slavic regions of Europe to become, along with *shchi* (cabbage soup), the predominant dish, each area giving the name its local slightly different pronunciation. In May, peasants would pick the tender leaves of the *brsh* to cook as greens, then gather and store the roots to last as a staple through the fall and winter. Typically, a huge pot of *brsh* stew was prepared, using whatever meat and bones one could afford and variously adding other root vegetables, beans, cabbage, mushrooms, or whatever was on hand. This fed the family for a week or more and was sporadically refreshed with more of the ingredients or what was found. The root's somewhat acrid flavor hardly made the most flavorsome of soups, even with the addition of meat, but the wild roots were free to foragers; *brsh* was one of the few vegetables available to peasants during the winter and provided a flavor variation essential to the Slavic culture. The mainstays of the eastern European medieval diet were bland starches—black bread and gruels—and, to provide an essential sensory offset, eastern Europeans would always accompany them with acidic foods, which Ashkenazim called *zoyers* (sours), notably sauerkraut, pickles, sorrel, rhubarb, sour cream, and *brsh*. Augmenting the tartness of the cow parsnip, as well as contributing essential nutrition and helping to slightly thicken the broth, peasants commonly topped the soup with tangy sour cream (*smetana*), which was always added individually at the table to achieve the desired texture and flavor, and never stirred into the pot.

In the mid-sixteenth century, the modern-day beetroot—fat, red (but paler than modern varieties), inexpensive, and easily grown—was developed in Italy or Germany, and initially received with little enthusiasm. However, eastern Europeans soon began adding beetroots, which grew well in much of the region, to their classic soup. Increasingly, beets supplanted the cow parsnip entirely, although the soup retained the meat and other root vegetables, as well as the name, *borshch*. Since the erstwhile Russian name for beet soup was *borshch malorossisky* (the former name for Ukraine), it is probable that the development of beet *borshch* happened in Ukraine.

In any case, beet soup quickly spread throughout much of eastern Europe to become the quintessential Slavic dish; as with the original *borshch*, it was commonly accompanied with sour cream. (Borscht was predominant in Ukraine, while cabbage soup held sway in Russia.) In keeping with the eastern European passion for acidity to compensate for the bland starches, cooks induced a mildly tart flavor to the sweeter beet soups with vinegar or fermented beet juice. Lemons were rare in northern Europe and vinegar often expensive, and people commonly made their own beet vinegar, called *rosl* in Yiddish. *Borshch* also contained the basic Slavic seasoning combination of chopped onions and carrots. In Ukraine, the predominant beet-growing region of eastern Europe,

borshch was everyday fare. Much farther north, where beets were less accessible, it was generally reserved for special occasions.

Beetroot soup (*boreke borsht*) first appeared in Jewish sources, pronounced *borscht* or *borsht* in Yiddish, toward the end of the 1500s in eastern Europe, corresponding to its initial usage in the region. Soup was also made with the beet greens, known as *botvenye borsht*, but this was generally considered a dish for the poor. Borscht was most fundamental among Jews in Ukraine and southeastern Poland. The farther west and north one traveled, the lesser the amount and frequency of borscht consumed. Germans tended to sneer at the red soup, as well as at most eastern fare.

Jews imitated the Slavic practice of adding meat and bones to borscht, yielding a hearty, sustaining dish. However, in order to enjoy the soup with sour cream, another practice Jews absorbed from the Slavic culture, they also developed a vegetarian version. This borsht, typically containing only beets and the Jewish favorite, onion, produces a translucent, bright red liquid, which turns pink when blended with sour cream. In the Slavic vein, Jews added tartness with vinegar or the less-expensive *rosl*. Following the establishment of the first sugar beet refineries in the early 1800s, which resulted in inexpensive sugar becoming accessible in the region, many Jews in those areas started adding sugar, turning Jewish vegetarian borscht into a distinctive sweet-and-sour dish. Galician Jews tended to add a large—some might say copious—amount of sugar, while most Ukrainians preferred more vinegar. In the mid-nineteenth century, after the potato became accepted in eastern Europe, it became a ubiquitous accompaniment to Jewish borscht, along with the sour cream.

When eastern European Jews immigrated in huge numbers to America beginning in the 1880s, they brought both their meat and vegetarian versions of borscht with them. Thus the original edition of *The Settlement Cookbook* (1901), a work primarily aimed at eastern European immigrants, included both a "Beet Soup Russian Style (Fleischik)," consisting of beets, brisket, onions, sugar, and citric acid, and a "Beet Soup Russian Style (Milchik)," made with beets, citric acid, sugar, and either sour cream or milk thickened with egg yolks. Within decades of *The Settlement Cookbook*, Jewish companies, notably Rokeach and Gold's, began producing borscht in jars. As the

Jewish simple sweet-and-sour borscht appeared on American grocery shelves, it became associated with the name. And since Jewish immigrants initially popularized this soup in America, it took on the Yiddish terminology, borscht, rather than the Russian or other Slavic names.

For many centuries, beets, along with cabbages (frequently added to meat borscht) and potatoes, were among the few produce items in eastern Europe capable of storage through the winter. Thus at the end of the winter enough beets remained, as well as remnants in the barrel once full of fermented *rosl,* to provide a *peysakhdiker borsht,* a note of brightness and sweetness for the Passover holiday. This season, corresponding to the birth of new calves, also meant a renewed supply of fresh sour cream. The classic combo of borscht, boiled potatoes, and sour cream emerged toward the end of the nineteenth century as a quintessential Ashkenazic comfort food. Today, in most eastern European households, no Passover would seem complete without borscht. Many mothers, like their mother before them, each year order a case or more of the red liquid, using any leftovers for the following months, though rarely having enough to last till the next Passover. Some people, however, find commercial brands too sweet and prepare their own.

Beginning on Passover eve, when the household is busy with preparations for the Seder, and continuing for much of the ensuing week, many lunches and dinners consist of ice-cold borscht paired with soft, hot, boiled potatoes and creamy, cool sour cream. Borscht is the lifeblood of Ashkenazic Passover cuisine. Borscht emerged not only as traditional fare among eastern Europeans on Passover, but also seven weeks later on Shavuot, on the third meal of the Sabbath, and at the festivities immediately following the Sabbath.

EASTERN EUROPEAN BEET SOUP WITH MEAT (*FLEISHIDIK BORSCHT*)

6 TO 8 SERVINGS   [MEAT]

- 2 pounds beef brisket, flanken, or stewing meat, cubed
- 2 beef marrow bones
- 8 cups water
- 2 pounds (8 medium) beets, peeled and diced
- 2 medium yellow onions, chopped

- 1 to 2 cloves garlic, minced
- 2 tablespoons tomato paste or ¼ cup tomato puree
- 3 to 6 tablespoons cider vinegar, red wine vinegar, or fresh lemon juice
- 1 to 3 tablespoons granulated or brown sugar
- About 2 teaspoons table salt or 4 teaspoons kosher salt
- Ground black pepper to taste
- 2 bay leaves
- 12 ounces (4 large) carrots, peeled and sliced or coarsely grated (optional)
- 1 cup shredded turnips or rutabagas (optional)

1. Place the meat, bones, and water in a large, heavy pot. Bring to a boil, cover, reduce the heat to low, and simmer, skimming the foam from the surface occasionally, for 1 hour.

2. Add the beets, onions, and garlic. Cover and simmer for an additional 1 hour.

3. Stir in the tomato paste, vinegar, sugar, salt, pepper, bay leaves, and, if using, carrots and/or turnips. Simmer until the meat is tender, about 30 minutes. Serve hot with boiled potatoes.

BORSCHT BELT

As early as the 1820s, the Jewish Agricultural Society settled new Jewish immigrants as farmers in Sullivan and Ulster counties in the Catskill Mountain region of eastern New York, about one hundred miles from New York City. Some of these settlers in this 250-square-mile area joined together to form agricultural communities akin to a kibbutz, while others went it alone. By the 1870s, the wealthier residents of New York City began escaping the summer heat by heading to resorts in the Pocono and Catskill mountains. At that time and for the following century, however, Jews were excluded from most American hotels, especially resorts, due to open and unabashed discrimination, as dramatized in the precedent-breaking 1947 film *Gentleman's Agreement.* Seeing a lucrative situation, beginning in the late 1890s, some Jewish farmers in the Catskills divided their homes into boarding houses, while others built small bungalows on their land to house wealthy Jewish guests. Some of these evolved into small hotels, *kuchaleyns* (self-catered boarding houses), or large bungalow colonies.

Beginning in the 1930s, the popularization of the automobile led to an annual mass exodus of New

York City Jews to the Catskills. As housing guests proved much more profitable than tilling the land, many of the farmers gave up agriculture for hospitality. As disposable income grew following World War II, so did the demand for summertime in the country. Typically, the women and children stayed in the bungalow or *kuchaleyn* throughout the week, while the husbands spent only the weekend, returning to the city early Monday morning in a commute called "the bull run." Jewish summer camps tended to the children. Large resorts emerged to cater to the growing crowds by hiring numerous Jewish entertainers and musicians, as well as providing jobs for college students, all of whom were excluded from similar opportunities elsewhere due to anti-Semitism. The Catskills emerged as a center of Jewish entertainment and culture, which, as these entertainers were increasingly accepted into mainstream America, became part of American culture.

Eastern European Jewish fare was prominent in the area's resorts, many offering all-you-can-eat kosher (or kosher-style) fare. Non-Jewish cooks and bakers learned traditional Jewish dishes in the kitchens of the Catskills' resorts and subsequently spread this cuisine throughout the country. Dairy meals were popular in the morning and at lunch; dining rooms offered classics such as blintzes, kugels, gefilte fish, and borscht. At Grossinger's, borscht was served all day long, 365 days a year, giving rise to the region's nickname, attributed to Abel Green, longtime editor of *Variety*—the Borscht Belt. The term was originally intended at least partly in derision, but eventually emerged as one of affection.

At its heyday in the 1950s, more than a million people spent their summers in the Catskills in more than three hundred hotels and another couple hundred boarding houses. Then in the late 1960s, changing holiday norms, the accessibility of airplane travel, the increasing number of women entering the workplace, and a major lessening in discrimination in the hotel and travel industry led to a quick and dramatic decline of the Borscht Belt, as portrayed in the popular 1987 movie *Dirty Dancing*. By the turn of the twenty-first century, less than a dozen old-time Jewish resorts remained and all the great ones had disappeared. Nevertheless, the impact of the Borscht Belt on American culture and cuisine endures.

BOTERKOEKE

Boterkoeke is a mildly sweet butter cookie.
Origin: Holland
Other names: Danish: *Jodekager*; Dutch: *bolusse, Joodse boterkoeke.*

Historically, few Dutch houses had an oven. Most home baking was done in a Dutch oven, a raised cast-iron pot set over coals, which was not exactly conducive to sophisticated pastries. Instead, the populace relied on high-quality neighborhood bakeries for its breads and pastries. Consequently, there were few home-baking experiments.

In the years following the expulsion from Spain and forced conversion of Portuguese Jews, the Netherlands became a haven for beset Sephardim and Conversos. Sephardim in Holland more commonly baked at home, merging their Moorish-influenced Iberian fare with the local Scandinavian cuisine. Instead of olive oil, they used the butter found in great quantity in Dutch cookery to create small rich morsels, still called *Joodse boterkoeke* (Jewish butter cookie) in Holland. The addition of egg makes butter cookies less crisp and more fragile than the English shortbread. Because the dough contains no leavening, the cookies hold their basic shape during baking. The Dutch, through their vast shipping enterprises to the Far East and Caribbean, had access to fresh ginger and its various offshoots, such as preserved and candied ginger, and these were frequently added to butter cookies. Later, Sephardic culture and cuisine in Holland were overwhelmed by Ashkenazim. However, several Dutch Sephardic innovations, notably these cookies, remain ubiquitous in Dutch bakeries and culture. Dutch Jews serve butter cookies on Hanukkah and Shavuot, and at other dairy meals.

Jewish butter cookies spread to other parts of Scandinavia. In Denmark, round or scalloped butter cookies sprinkled with cinnamon and chopped almonds or hazelnuts are called *Jodekager* (Jewish cookies); these are firmer and crisper than the Dutch version, a longtime traditional Danish pre-Christmas treat. Dutch Sephardim also brought *boterkoeke* to England, as evidenced by the "Butter Cakes" Judith Montefiore included in *The Jewish Manual* (London, 1846), a synthesis of Portuguese Sephardic and contemporary English cuisines. Tellingly, in 2005, a group of Danish Muslims demanded that the traditional name be changed from *Jodekager*, as they found it offensive. Certain Danish officials, fearful it could hurt sales, were inclined to go along with this intolerance. Nevertheless, most Danes continued to refer to them as *Jodekager*.

DANISH JEWISH COOKIES (*JODEKAGER*)

ABOUT THIRTY 3-INCH COOKIES   [DAIRY OR PAREVE]

2½ cups (12.5 ounces) all-purpose flour

1 teaspoon ammonium carbonate, or ½ teaspoon baking powder and ½ teaspoon baking soda

½ teaspoon salt

1 cup (2 sticks) unsalted butter or margarine, softened

¾ cup granulated sugar, 1 cup confectioners' sugar, or ⅔ cup confectioners' sugar and ¼ cup granulated sugar

1 large egg

1 teaspoon vanilla extract (optional)

About 1 cup finely chopped almonds or hazelnuts

Cinnamon-sugar (¼ cup ground cinnamon mixed with ¼ cup pearl sugar or crystal sugar) or ¼ cup granulated sugar

1 large egg white, lightly beaten

1. Sift together the flour, ammonium carbonate, and salt. In a large bowl, beat the butter until smooth, about 1 minute. Gradually add the sugar and beat until light and fluffy, about 4 minutes. Beat in the egg. Add the vanilla. Stir in the flour mixture.

2. Preheat the oven to 375°F.

3. Combine the nuts and cinnamon-sugar. On a lightly floured surface, roll out the dough ⅛ inch thick (the "thickness of a straw"). Cut into 3-inch rounds or rounds with scalloped edges. Place close together on ungreased baking sheets. Brush the tops lightly with the egg white and sprinkle with the nut mixture.

4. Bake until lightly browned, 8 to 10 minutes. Let the cookies stand until firm, about 1 minute, then transfer to a wire rack and let cool completely. Store in an airtight container at room temperature for up to 1 week or in the freezer for up to 6 months.

BOUGATSA

Bougatsa is a phyllo-dough pie with a creamy, savory or sweet, cheese filling.

Origin: Greece

Other names: Bulgaria: *banitsa*; Greece: *staka*; Syria: *bugacho*.

With the spread of the Ottoman Empire into North Africa and southeastern Europe came its Middle Eastern foods, including *pogaca/bogaca*, a category of savory and sweet yeast breads, many with a filling. In Greece, phyllo dough was substituted for the bread dough while retaining the filling, giving rise to the very popular treat *bougatsa*, a large pie akin to the semolina-custard-filled Turkish *galactoboureko*. *Bougatsa* seems to have originated among the Sephardim of Thessaloniki. It originally featured a cheese filling, the type predominant in the Turkish *pogaca*. Today, custard fillings are the most popular type in the specialty shops of Thessaloniki found on nearly every street. An almond-paste-filled version is known as Copenhagen. *Bugacho*, a savory Syrian variation of the Greek *bougatsa*, is a traditional Shavuot dish.

Sephardic *bougatsa* features a creamy cheese filling wedged between crispy phyllo, served fresh and cut into hefty slices. The Greek version was originally made from water buffalo or sheep cheese or fresh mitzithra (a Greek cheese made from feta and kefalotyri byproducts). Modern Western versions use cow's milk cheese. The filling can be savory, even combining feta and spinach, but the sweetened type is far and away more popular. Occasionally, *bougatsa* is drenched in sugar syrup in the Middle Eastern manner, but most shops and home cooks simply sprinkle it with a little confectioners' sugar, sometimes mixed with cinnamon. Some also like the filling with a hint of cinnamon or nutmeg, while many prefer a purer cheese flavor.

After finishing the large pie, any leftover filling and phyllo are customarily mixed together, rolled into ropes, formed into rings, and baked to make cookies called *bougatsokouloura*.

In Greece, *bougatsa* are popular breakfast pastries typically consumed with coffee. Among Sephardim from Salonika, they are a traditional Shavuot dessert or part of the *desayuno* (brunch).

(See also Galaktoboureko and Pogaca)

BOYO

Boyos are an assortment of fried and baked cheese pastries, made from either flour or bread.

Origin: Spain and Portugal

Other names: *boyiko, prenesa*.

Sephardim generally made bread—for much of

history an arduous, time-consuming process—only twice a week, on Mondays and Fridays. After a few days, the bread would become stale and innovative cooks would seek ways to utilize it, as nothing was wasted. A favorite of these methods was to soak dry bread in water or milk, season the mixture with cheese and spices, then fry dollops of the batter in hot olive oil, producing a dish called *bollos de pan* (balls of bread). Judith Montefiore, in the first Jewish cookbook in English, *The Jewish Manual* (1846), containing numerous Portuguese Jewish dishes, provides a recipe for fritters called *"Prenesas,"* which is another type of *boyo*: "Take one pint of milk, stir in as much flour as will bring it to the consistency of hasty pudding; boil it till it becomes thick, let it cool, and beat it up with ten eggs; when smooth, take a spoonful at a time, and drop it into a frying-pan, in which there is a good quantity of boiling clarified butter, fry of a light brown, and serve with clarified sugar, flavored with lemon essence."

After the Sephardim arrived in Turkey and the Balkans, they slightly changed the pronunciation to *boyos de pan* or simply *boyos*. Over the centuries, more sophisticated variations of *boyo* developed, including different fried and baked pastries, the common denominators being a bread or flour base.

Boyos, along with *borekas* and *bulemas*, comprise "the three Bs," the most characteristic and popular of Sephardic baked goods in the eastern Mediterranean. They are an integral part of Sephardic *desayuno* (brunch), accompanied with *haminados* (long-cooked eggs) and olives. *Boyos* are also served during the period before Tisha b'Av and on other dairy occasions. In Salonika, a leftover *boyo*, along with a hot cup of *salep/sachlav* (orchid drink), constituted a comforting winter breakfast.

(See also Bola, Boreka, and Bulema)

SEPHARDIC CHEESE-FILLED SQUARES IN YEAST DOUGH (*BOYOS DE QUESO*)

ABOUT 12 PASTRIES   [DAIRY]

Pastry:
- 1¼ teaspoons active dry yeast or ½ (0.6-ounce) cake fresh yeast
- 1¼ cups warm water (105 to 115°F for dry yeast; 80 to 85°F for fresh yeast)
- 1 teaspoon sugar
- 1 teaspoon table salt or 2 teaspoons kosher salt
- About 3 cups (15 ounces) bread or unbleached all-purpose flour

Vegetable oil

Filling:
- 1 cup (3 ounces) grated Parmesan, Romano, or hard cheese
- ½ cup all-purpose flour
- Additional grated cheese for sprinkling (optional)
- About 3 cups Sephardic pastry filling, such as cheese, potato, eggplant, leek, onion, or spinach (pages 230–232)

Additional grated cheese and/or sesame seeds for sprinkling

1. To make the pastry: Dissolve the yeast in ¼ cup water. Add the sugar and let stand until foamy, 5 to 10 minutes. In a large bowl, combine the yeast mixture, remaining water, salt, and 1 cup flour. Gradually stir in enough of the remaining flour to make a soft dough. Knead until smooth and elastic, 10 to 15 minutes. Place in an oiled bowl, cover, and let rest for about 30 minutes.

2. Place about ½ inch oil in a shallow medium pan. Divide the dough into thirds and knead each third until smooth. Form into balls, place in the pan, and turn to coat in the oil. Let stand for about 20 minutes.

3. Preheat the oven to 400°F. Grease a large baking sheet.

4. On a lightly oiled surface, roll out each dough third into a thin square about 12 inches in diameter. Rub the dough with oil.

5. To make the filling: Combine the cheese and flour. Sprinkle one-third of the cheese mixture over each dough square. Roll up jelly-roll style. Cut the rolls into four 2½-inch lengths. Place the pieces, uncut side down, on the lightly oiled surface, flatten, and roll into thin 5-inch squares. (This step creates a flakier pastry.)

6. Rub each square with oil and, if desired, sprinkle with additional cheese. Spoon 1 tablespoon Sephardic pastry filling in the center. Using oiled hands, bring the four corners together in the center, slightly overlapping, and press the edges together to seal in the filling.

7. Place the boyos, folded side down, on the prepared baking sheet. Brush the tops with oil and sprinkle with cheese and/or sesame seeds.

8. Bake until golden brown, about 25 minutes. Serve warm or at room temperature.

BRAIN

Brains—*moach* in Hebrew, *n'khaat* or *mokh* in Arabic, *meyoyo* or *meollo* in Ladino, *cervello* in Italian, and *moi'ech* or *gehrin* in Yiddish—were once a popular treat, but are now rarely eaten. Lamb and veal are the most common type. Brains must be very fresh to have the appropriate texture. A sign that the brains are not fresh is that the outer membrane will be difficult to remove. Before cooking, they must be washed and cleaned of the membranes and veins. In most recipes, they are first poached until firm, cooled, and then sliced. The slices are pan-fried, deep-fried, or cooked with scrambled eggs or soufflés, resulting in a creamy texture, similar to sweetbreads, which people either love or hate. Brains in tomato sauce are found in both Sephardic and Ashkenazic communities. Brains should not be partnered with strong ingredients that would overwhelm their delicate flavor. Brains are a traditional appetizer for Rosh Hashanah, reflecting the biblical directive that one should "be like the head and not the tail."

BREAD

In ancient Israel, bread was part of every meal, constituting at least 50 percent and frequently up to 70 percent of the diet. The generic Hebrew term for bread, *lechem*, also used as a synecdoche for food in general, is found seventy-five times in the Pentateuch alone. (Contrast this to the comparable Arabic *lahum*, which possesses the specific denotation of meat.) Reflecting the importance of *lechem*, it is related to the word *milchamah* (war), as the cultivation of grain led to both trade and war. Barley bread was the predominant form in biblical Israel, while wheat assumed that position during the Second Temple period.

By applying the Sapir-Whorf hypothesis, which states that the importance of an item to a society is reflected in the number of variations developed in the language, we can see the special place held by bread in ancient Jewish life. The Bible contains about a dozen names for various shapes and types of bread, including *lechem*, matza, *paht* (a piece of bread), *kikkar* ("circuit/round shape," hence a large round loaf

akin to pita), *oogah* (round), *rakik* (thin wafers), challah ("perforated" thick loaves), *revuchah* (a dough made with hot water and oil), *levivah* (pancake bread), *nikkudim* ("spotted/pierced," generally translated as "biscuits"), and *tzelil* (from "circle/rotate"). The Talmud records even more types of bread.

Consequently, it is hardly surprising that bread found its way into Jewish ritual. The Bible mandates the various Temple flour offerings baked as bread, *lechem ha'panim* (the showbread of the Temple, a fresh set of twelve changed every Sabbath), *shtei ha'lechem* (two leavened wheat loaves waved in the Temple on Shavuot), and the Passover matza. Following the destruction of the Temple, the home table symbolically replaced the altar and the Sabbath loaves the showbread. Thus every Sabbath and festival meal commences with bread. Most communities used their regular loaves for the Sabbath, but Ashkenazim developed special ones known as challah. Bread is served with a sprinkling of salt, an allusion to the altar, where salt was a mandatory component of the offerings. In addition, the Talmud directed serving salt and relishes with bread, as throughout most of history, loaves were frequently coarse and dry, and required condiments to make them palatable.

The Daily Grind

Among the personal effects the Israelites took with them from Egypt were the three necessities of bread making: wooden kneading troughs, mortars, and the two-piece heavy grindstones; the latter were certainly transported on wagons. In order to make its daily bread, every home in the ancient Middle East had to have some form of grinding device, its indispensability recognized in the biblical law forbidding the use of either the top or bottom part as collateral for a loan. Without access to a quern, a family would literally starve to death.

For millennia, every household ground its own flour fresh daily from stored grains. Ingenuity led to a more efficient way of milling the kernels: the saddle quern, which is called *raichayim* in the Bible, from the root *rachah* (to rub), the plural form denoting a pair of stones. The larger lower part of this duo is the quern/metate. This large stone, either rectangular or oval in shape, has a shallow depression chiseled out in the center (hence it looks like a saddle). It generally weighed at least twenty pounds and up to one hundred pounds.

The second part of this device is the handstone/mano. It is a smaller cylindrical stone (akin to a stone rolling pin). The upper stone, sufficiently heavy to crush the grains, but not too cumbersome to move, typically weighed about four and a half pounds, but could weigh as much as twenty-seven pounds. The heaviness of a handstone is vividly illustrated in the Prophets: "And a certain woman threw a handstone on Abimelech's head, and broke his skull."

Until the advent of commercial mills, the daily grinding of grain, a task relegated to women (threshing and winnowing were men's work), was the most labor-intensive activity of every household; the work began many hours before breakfast. Thus the line in Proverbs: "She gets up while still night and provides food to her household." The Mishnah, in listing the seven minimum domestic responsibilities of a housewife, counts flour preparation first and baking second: "She grinds, bakes, launders, cooks, nurses her children, makes the bed [literally "stuffing mattresses"], and makes [spins] wool."

The heavy quern was positioned on the floor, requiring the woman operating the device to kneel. A small amount of grain was placed in the center of the quern and, using both hands, the grinder pushed the handstone forward to the end of the quern, her shoulders and nose nearly parallel to the ground, then sharply drew back to her original position. This movement was repeated for hours on end, until enough flour was produced for the family's daily needs, inflicting great pressures and frequently pains on the knees, toes, hips, and lower back. An hour of grinding would typically produce about one and three-quarters pounds (about six cups) of flour, less than enough for two people, if each one consumed the typical eighteen ounces a day. Thus a family of five required at least three hours of grinding every morning.

A major innovation in milling occurred about three thousand years ago with the development of the rotary millstone. Large versions, generally turned by cattle, donkeys, or slaves—such as the millstone that the Philistines forced Samson to push—consisted of a pair of flat, circular stones, the bottom one remaining stationary while the top one turned. The use of animal power and later water resulted in greater speed and efficiency, producing a sudden abundance of flour and leading to large-scale commercial milling. Smaller versions for the home, called the rotary quern or beehive

quern, also appeared, but were not widespread in the Middle East until some six hundred to eight hundred years thereafter, during the early Persian period.

After grinding, the baker placed the flour, usually coarse, in a large wooden kneading trough and mixed it with water and, for wheat dough, a reserved starter (*seor*). After a lengthy, strenuous kneading, often by foot, the dough was left to rise (occasionally it failed to live up to expectations) for hours or overnight. Barley dough, lacking gluten, did not require rising.

Into the Oven

Initially, bread dough was baked directly on the coals of a campfire, a method some Bedouin in the Middle East still use during their roaming. Later, cooks discovered the effectiveness of a heated stone and then primitive clay ovens. In the time of the First Temple, there were two types of rudimentary ovens in Israel employed for bread baking: the jar-oven and pit-oven. The jar-oven consists of a large, thick-walled earthenware vessel, narrowing into an opening toward the top. It was heated from the inside by burning wood and dung; the dough was then pressed against the outside to cook. The pit-oven was a clay-lined excavation in the ground. When sufficiently hot, the fuel was swept off and the loaves were baked directly on the heated surface. At some point, people also began placing a convex dome (thirteen to twenty inches in diameter and about three inches high), initially earthenware and later metal, over the pit-oven and cooking the flatbreads on the dome instead of on the ash-covered surface; this type of oven was known as a *sajj/sag* and is probably what was meant by the biblical *machabat*, one of the methods of baking in the Temple frequently translated as "griddle." The only types of bread able to be cooked on all these devices were rather thin loaves.

Later, the Persians introduced a newfangled clay *tanur* (the same as the contemporary Indian tandoor), in which the bread was baked on the inner wall of the upper chamber, allowing for slightly thicker loaves. Akin to the *tanur* was the *tabun*, a terra-cotta beehive-shaped oven heated by placing the fuel underneath. Many families had their own *tanur* or *tabun*.

A major advance in bread and pastry baking, possibly introduced by the Romans, came when a bottom was added to the oven, resulting in the *furn*. It is a large stationary stone-lined oven in which the wood is burned inside; the ashes are then raked out or to the side, and the dough or baking sheet is set directly on the floor of the oven or against the walls. The *furn* allowed for much thicker loaves. Few homes possessed their own *furn*, so housewives prepared the loaves at home, then carried them to the community *furn* for baking.

Black and White

The medieval European masses primarily subsisted on gruels, stews, occasional fish, and simple, coarse rye or black breads of varying quality. During a medieval European meal, meat and broth were commonly poured onto a large piece of bread, called a sop (from the Old English sopp). Hence the origin of the various European words for soup. The British took it a step further: Since the combination of bread and broth often served as the mainstay of the evening meal, one was said to sup, thus supper.

Wheat was the predominant grain in the Muslim world. In much of northern Europe, wild rye commonly made its way into wheat fields, blown by the wind, resulting in the two grains being harvested, planted, and milled together. This combination flour, known as maslin, remained the primary form of flour in northern Europe well into the seventeenth century. White bread was usually reserved for the Sabbath and festivals. Only in the mid-nineteenth century did white flour become predictably and widely accessible in most of Europe. In eastern Europe, various types of black bread remained the norm well into the twentieth century.

In modern Israel, there are two predominant breads: the Middle Eastern pita and the European loaf known as *lechem achid* (standard bread) subsidized by the government. The latter emerged with the founding of the state, the government setting the price and compensating the large bakeries, which also produce a variety of nonsubsidized loaves. This is a basic unbleached white bread with a rather firm texture and wheaty flavor. However, every ethnic group arriving in the Promised Land eventually opened and patronized bakeries offering traditional breads. As a result, Israeli bakeries and groceries now offer a vast array of breads in every shape and size.

(See also Bagaleh, Bagel, Barley, Bialy, Birkhat Hamazon, Bollo, Challah, Fattot, Injera, Khachapuri, Khboz, Kimochdun, Kubaneh, Laffa, Lahuh, Lángos, Lavash, Malai, Matza, Melawah, Naan, Nan, Non, Pandericas, Pita, Pletzl, Potatonik, Puri, Rye, Sabbath, Seor, Semolina, Wheat, Yeast, and Zemmel)

BRIK

Brik is a turnover made from a flaky, crisp dough with a variety of fillings, and often a whole egg.

Origin: Tunisia

Other names: Algeria: *bourak, burak*; Libya: *bureka*; Morocco: *biouat, briate, briwat*; Tunisia: *breek*.

When the Turkish *börek* reached the Maghreb, the residents readily adapted it. Since home ovens were rare, they deep-fried the filled packages. *Brik* emerged as the Tunisian national snack food, commonly sold by stands at the *souk* (marketplace) and street vendors throughout the country. Tunisians pack *briks* with a wide array of fillings, including minced lamb, beef, or tuna, but Jewish versions tend to favor mashed potatoes. There is even a distinctly Jewish dessert variation with almond paste, *briks au meil*. Some Tunisian Jews earned a meager living vending *briks* in a town market. *Brik* has become a popular snack food in modern Israel as well.

In Tunisia, *briks* are made with a dough called *malsuqa/malsouka* ("to adhere" in Arabic), also called *feuilles de brick* in French and *warka* (leaf) in Morocco; it is the Tunisian semolina-based form of phyllo dough. Many Israelis, however, substitute standard phyllo or, more recently, Chinese egg roll wrappers or, preferably since they are thinner, Filipino spring roll wrappers called *lumpia*. However, since the substitutes are all made from bread flour rather than semolina, there will be a little difference. Square sheets of dough are folded into rectangular packages or triangles, while rounds become a half moon. In any case, the pastry must be thin to ensure an appropriately crisp and delicate *brik*.

In Tunisia, *brik* makers customarily break an uncooked egg into the filling, the egg becoming soft-boiled, but still runny, during frying. These are called *brik bil adma* in Arabic or *brik à l'oeuf* in French. The light, crisp pastry contrasts with the soft, somewhat viscous egg. People customarily eat a *brik* with their fingers, aiming to capture the egg yolk in the middle with the first bite and avoid having it run down their chin.

TUNISIAN POTATO-FILLED PASTRY (*BRIK BIL BATATA*)

6 PASTRIES   [PAREVE]

Filling:

3 tablespoons olive or vegetable oil

1 large onion, chopped

2 to 3 cloves garlic, minced, or ½ cup chopped scallions

⅓ cup chopped fresh flat-leaf parsley
1½ cups mashed potatoes
1 large egg, lightly beaten
About ¼ teaspoon table salt or ½ teaspoon kosher
   salt
Ground black pepper to taste

6 (6- to 8-inch) square or round *brik (warka)* sheets,
   lumpia (Filipino spring roll wrappers), or large
   thin Chinese egg roll wrappers
6 very fresh small eggs (optional)
2 tablespoons harissa (Northwest African Chili
   Paste, page 260) or 6 pinches of *tabil* (Tunisian
   Spice Mixture, page 572)
1 large egg white, lightly beaten
Vegetable oil for deep-frying
Lemon wedges (optional)

1. To make the filling: In a large skillet or wok, heat the oil over medium heat. Add the onion and sauté until golden, about 20 minutes. Add the garlic and sauté for 1 minute. Add the parsley and sauté for 1 minute. Let cool. Stir in the potatoes, egg, salt, and pepper.

2. To assemble the *brik* packages, place each dough sheet on a flat surface and spoon a heaping tablespoon of the potato filling in the center. If using the eggs, press an indentation into the filling on each dough sheet and break an egg into the indentation. Top each *brik* with 1 teaspoon harissa or a pinch of *tabil*. Fold the two sides over the filling, slightly overlapping, then fold over the top and bottom. Brush the inside edges with a little egg white and press to seal. The rolls can be prepared up to 2 hours ahead to this point before frying.

3. In a large skillet, heat at least 1 inch oil to 375°F.

4. In batches, add the *briks* and fry, spooning some of the oil over the top of the pastry, until the bottom is golden brown, about 1 minute. Using a large metal spatula, turn and fry until the other side is golden brown, about 1 minute. Be careful of spattering the hot oil. Remove with a slotted spoon, drain on a wire rack for 1 minute, then serve immediately. If using, serve the lemon wedges on the side. Squirt a little lemon juice over the filling before each bite.

BRINZA

Brinza is a brined, white, semisoft, curd cheese made from sheep's or goat's milk.
Origin: Romania

Other names: Bulgaria: *sirene*; Hungary: *brynza*; Israel: *bulgarit*; Romania: *brânza telemea*; Slovakia: *bryndza*.

"One drinks wine everywhere, one eats with kashkaval. Oy vey, I am *meshige* [crazy]! I love only *brinza mamaliga*." (From "Romania, Romania," a famous Yiddish folk song by Aaron Lebedeff.)

Mamaliga (cornmeal mush) is the national dish of Romania, and one of the favorite ways of enjoying it is with slices of cheese, either hard kashkaval or soft *brinza*. *Brinza* is made from sheep's or goat's milk, but the latter is more of a delicacy. It is similar to but milder, creamier, and less salty than the Greek feta. When young, it is soft and creamy; as it matures in the brine, it becomes semidry, slightly grainy, and crumbly, with an appealing earthy flavor.

Due to its mostly mountainous terrain, Romania historically relied on sheep and goats, and rarely cows, for milk. Medieval Balkan shepherds or the nomadic Vlach of Romania devised a cheese preserved in brine, allowing it to be stored through the winter without a loss of quality. By the sixteenth century, the Vlach, offering their cheese as barter for salt and other goods during their travels, spread it throughout the Balkans, Caucasus, and Slavic regions. *Brinza* derives its name from the Romanian word for cheese (*brânza*); it is the primary cheese in Romania as well as neighboring Slovakia. In Romania, to differentiate it from other cheeses, it is officially called *brânza telemea*. It is also common, with slight variations, in Bulgaria, Georgia, Hungary, Macedonia, southern Poland, Russia, and Ukraine.

Until relatively, recently *brinza* was a homemade item. Artisan cheeses still endure, but today much of the yearly output, generally pasteurized, is the product of industrialization. The characteristics vary depending on the breed of goat or sheep, pasturage, and age of the cheese.

Until recently in modern Israel, sheep and goat cheeses were very limited due to governmental quotas and corporate indifference and, therefore, primarily only a basic firm feta was available. Then, with a relaxing of laws against sheep and goat milk production (before becoming prime minister, Ariel Sharon was a sheep raiser and active member of the Israel Sheepbreeders Association), small companies across the country began making high-quality sheep and goat cheeses, including traditional *brinza*, known as *bulgarit* (Bulgarian cheese). It is now an integral part of Israeli cuisine.

Brinza is commonly sliced or coarsely crumbled and added to a myriad of salads (greens, lentils, etc.), drizzled with an herb vinaigrette, incorporated into dumplings, stuffed into roasted peppers and pastries (such as strudel and *borekas*), and added to omelets. A popular Israeli summertime treat is eating cubes of *bulgarit* with cubes of watermelon.

(See also Cheese, Feta, and Watermelon)

BRISKET

The often-impoverished Jews of eastern Europe could rarely afford to "live high on the cow"—to buy the more tender cuts from the rib and chuck. With great ingenuity they learned how to make do with the cheaper, less desirable parts of the cow, such as the brisket, plank, shank, and offal. Not coincidentally, Ashkenazic Sabbath and holiday fare tended to feature these cheaper cuts. Other Jewish communities made use of brisket sliced into smaller pieces, and also used the rear of the cow, but among Ashkenazim brisket was one of the few available cuts; it was frequently cooked in a large portion. These dishes became a memorable part of Jewish lore.

Brisket is the meat covering the cow's breastbone, situated between the foreleg and below the short ribs (flanken), another popular eastern European cut. A whole, untrimmed brisket can weigh more than fourteen pounds; trimming will reduce the weight to ten to twelve pounds. In America, brisket is generally sold in halves, cut at the place where a thick layer of fat runs diagonally through the center. The squarish-shaped first cut roast (also called flat cut) is leaner and thinner, generally weighing four to five pounds. The second cut (also called point cut) contains more interior fat and is coarser—the extra fat carries flavor in preparations such as corned beef and barbecue, producing more succulent meat. The top section of the second cut, between the main muscle of the brisket and the bone, is called a deckel. Some aficionados insist that a whole brisket actually cooks up moister and tastier than only the first cut. Talented cooks discovered ways to convert brisket from a less desirable object into a juicy, tender, incredibly flavorful piece of meat.

Brisket did not become an Ashkenazic classic simply because it tastes delicious. The source for various holiday dishes, besides any biblical or historical origins, often lay in seasonal surpluses. Domesticated animals were inexpensive to raise from spring to fall, when they could freely feed on wild grains and grasses. Winter, however, meant purchasing food for the livestock. Therefore, animals not intended for propagation or work purposes were slaughtered at the onset of freezing weather, around Hanukkah time. This seasonal surfeit led to roast goose becoming the most popular Hanukkah dish among Alsatians and western Germans. However, as Ashkenazim relocated eastward, chickens replaced geese as the standard fowl. And, since chickens were utilized for continued egg laying, even during the winter, a mass slaughter of hens was ill-advised. Cows, however, were costly to keep through the winter. Therefore, those unnecessary for reproduction, milk, or hauling were commonly slaughtered around Hanukkah, resulting in a sudden temporary surplus of meat. Even those who raised their own cows would sell the preferred sections as a source of income. For the generally impoverished eastern European Jews, if they could afford even this, it typically meant the less desirable parts, with the brisket becoming the most widespread eastern European Hanukkah entrée. Once again, necessity proved the Jewish mother's source of invention.

Alsatians add brisket to their favorite Sabbath lunch dish, *choucroute garnie*. In Slavic areas, brisket is often added to meat borscht. More common is the simple pot-roasted brisket, sometimes referred to as *gedempte brustfleisch* (boiled breast meat), although it is actually slow-simmered in plenty of liquid for hours to achieve the desired tenderness. Ashkenazic brisket is always made with onions, and plenty of them. After the mid-nineteenth century, potatoes and carrots were frequently added to provide more sustenance. *Gedempte brustfleisch* is a soul-and-body-satisfying meal-in-one dish: the cooking liquid as soup, and the meat as the entrée, accompanied by the various vegetables. Eastern Europeans also use brisket as a base for cholent (Sabbath stew) and tzimmes, which may appear as a Rosh Hashanah or Sukkot entrée.

In early twentieth-century America, as eastern European immigrants began rising up the socioeconomic ladder, they started to serve their favorite foods more frequently. Brisket would often appear for Sabbath dinner and other special occasions, including the Passover Seder (although seasonal veal breast was historically more traditional), converting a rare treat into regular Sabbath and holiday fare. Sarah Rorer, in *Mrs. Rorer's New Cook Book* (Philadelphia, 1902), in a section called "A Group of Jewish Recipes," included "Stewed Beef and Beans (Sweet and Sour)," beginning with "Two pounds of brisket, or any part that is fat." In addition, brisket was transformed, by soaking in brine and slow-cooking the meat, into a mainstay of the Jewish deli, corned beef. Delis also served hot brisket sandwiches, but they are far less popular than corned beef and pastrami. Since brisket is a boneless cut, it is perfect for slicing for sandwiches.

Aunt Babette's (Cincinnati, 1889), the author from a German background where brisket was of minor importance, provided a single basic "Brisket of Beef" recipe, cooked on a bed of sauerkraut with some grated raw potato, "a little brown sugar," and "a few caraway seeds added," along with the suggestion that "you may prepare it with horseradish sauce, garlic sauce, onion sauce, etc." Slightly later, the original edition of *The Settlement Cook Book* (1901), intended for eastern European immigrants, included six recipes for brisket of beef, generally reflecting Old World preferences: "Brisket of Beef with Celery Sauce," "Brisket of Beef with Carrots," "Brisket of Beef with Beans," "Brisket of Beef with Cabbage," "Sweet and Sour Brisket of Beef," and "Sauerkraut with Brisket of Beef" as well as used in a dozen other recipes.

Soon American Jews began adapting brisket to contemporary tastes and using new commercial condiments, for example, glazing the meat or adding canned cranberry sauce, onion soup mix, and/or chili sauce. There is now even a version of brisket from Atlanta, Georgia, made with Coca-Cola, purportedly the inspiration of a Jewish family's black cook. Southerners also serve slices of brisket on a biscuit. More modern variations featured brisket with sun-dried tomatoes or rice wine.

Ashkenazic brisket did not readily translate to the Middle East and is rarely seen in Israeli restaurants. This is partially cultural, but also attributable to the nature of Israeli brisket, labeled cut "number 3," which encompasses both the first and second cuts and tends to be much tougher than in America. Consequently, when Israelis do make brisket, it typically contains a large amount of acid, such as wine and citrus juice, to help tenderize the meat.

Similarly, among non-Jews in America, brisket was for a long time a disregarded cut of meat, practically given away or utilized for ground beef, except in Texas. Barbecue has been a longtime political food in the Lone Star State where barbecue still means succulent brisket. At his ranch along the Pedernales River, Lyndon Johnson frequently held barbecues, as senator, vice president, and president, tapping into a mythical America, one that impressed foreign notables while appealing and connecting to the people. During the five years of the Johnson presidency alone, the LBJ Ranch was the site of more than a hundred of these convivial barbecues, representing a unique style of statesmanship referred to as "barbecue diplomacy." Johnson entertained foreign dignitaries and hundreds of guests at a time at these events. In a few short years, Texas-style barbecue became a national food and brisket was no longer an undesirable, inexpensive cut of the meat.

As a result, toward the end of the century, as the price of brisket skyrocketed and cultural norms looked askance at fatty red meat, Jewish brisket once again became a rare indulgence. Nevertheless, brisket still maintains a major presence in the Jewish culture of America, counted among Ashkenazic comfort foods.

(See also Corned Beef, Pastrami, and Tzimmes)

BRIT MILAH

The Hebrew word *brit* means "covenant," referring originally to God's pledge to Abraham that his descendants would inherit the Land of Canaan, which was sealed by the act of *milah* (circumcision). Thus *brit milah* endures as one of the integral symbols of Judaism.

Historically, prohibitions against *brit milah* by Antiochus Epiphanes and later the Roman emperor Hadrian helped lead respectively to the Maccabean and Bar Kokhba rebellions.

On the night preceding the *brit*, many Jewish communities hold a gathering, called *vakhnacht* (watch night) by Ashkenazim. Some believe that this custom developed from a practice of the *mohel*, who was accompanied by anxious family and friends as he examined the baby before his *brit*. Eventually, it became customary to surround the baby's crib to recite various psalms and study Torah. Folklore suggests that this vigil was once thought to be a way of protecting the uncircumcised baby from Lilith, the legendary first wife of Adam, or other demons. Ashkenazim light candles, have school children visit the baby to recite the Shema, and serve honey cakes, poppy seed cakes, and sometimes a meal featuring bean dishes, a symbol of fertility.

Among Sephardim, the ritual of protecting the newborn is variously known by the Talmudic terms *yeshua haben* (protect the boy), *brit Yizchak* (circumcision of Isaac), *leil hazohar* (eve of the splendor), and, in Salonika, *veula* (from the Ladino and Latin *vigilia*, "wakefulness/watch"). On the night preceding the *brit*, family and friends gather at the newborn's home and read about topics concerning the *brit* of the patriarchs from Midrashim and the Zohar. The new father reads the final portion. Afterwards, anything from a simple table to a large festive meal is held, accompanied with singing and dancing.

Syrians hold a gathering called a *shadd-il-asse* (Arabic for "pulling of the branches") or *akad-al-asse* (binding of the branches). The name derives from a custom in accordance with the Zohar of bringing to the home the "chair of Elijah" that will be used at the *brit* and tying myrtle branches to it. Family and friends, hold a *limud* (learning session), including excerpts from the Zohar, to protect the baby. Following the *limud*, the assembly chants *pizmonim* (liturgical poems) and partakes of special foods, especially traditional sweets and soft drinks.

Moroccans hold a *Tachdid* ceremony each night from birth until the *brit* to protect the baby. Amulets— including Psalms 121 and 126, the names of three angels, and the phrase *Adam, Chava, chutz Lilit* (Adam and Eve, get out Lilith)—are dispersed throughout the baby's room, excerpts from the Zohar are read, and *piyutim* (liturgical poems) are sung. On the evening prior to the *brit*, female relatives and friends spend the night, offering the wisdom of their experience and protecting the mother and child from harm.

The *brit* is held on the baby's eighth day and is of such importance that it takes place even if the day falls on the Sabbath or Yom Kippur. Indeed, tradition recounts that Abraham's *brit* occurred on Yom Kippur. If the baby suffers from any ill health, however, it is postponed until there is no longer any threat of danger to the child. That day is considered as if it is his new birthday and the *brit* is performed seven days later. In this instance, however, it is not performed on the Sabbath or Yom Kippur.

It is the father's obligation to circumcise his son, a duty usually fulfilled through a specially trained agent known as a *mohel*. In the tenth century, the custom arose among Ashkenazim of honoring a relative or friend with the role of *sandek* (from the Greek *synteknos* meaning "with the child," but assuming the sense of "godfather"). The *sandek* is seated in a special chair and holds the child on his lap during the ceremony. In addition, Ashkenazim created the roles of *kvater* (from the German for "godfather," *gottvater*) and *kvaterin* (godmother), usually fulfilled by a wife and husband team who relay the child from the mother to the *sandek* and back. Among Sephardim, the *madrino* (godmother) and *padrino* (godfather) fulfill this role. It is customary to place another chair next to that of the *sandek* called the Chair of Elijah, in honor of the prophet considered to be the protector of children and "the angel of the covenant" and "the herald of the covenant."

There is a longstanding custom of not directly inviting people to a *brit*, since refusing such an honor would be improper. Therefore, desired attendees are simply informed of the time and place of the ceremony.

In the Middle Ages, the custom arose among Ashkenazim and some Sephardim of performing the circumcision in the synagogue. Today, some have reverted to the earlier practice of holding the ceremony at home. Following the actual circumcision, the *mohel* recites the blessing over a glass of wine, then a prayer praising God for establishing the covenant. The *mohel* then names the baby and gives him a few drops of wine to drink.

The *brit* and baby naming are usually performed in the morning, emulating Abraham who arose early in his eagerness to perform the divine command. Thus the accompanying *seudat mitzvah*, generally a sit-down brunch, tends to be dairy and relatively simple. Sephardim traditionally serve filled foods, including *borekas* (small turnovers), *bulemas* (pastry coils), and stuffed vegetables, symbolizing a rich and full life. Typical Ashkenazic fare includes bagels, lox, herring, cheese platters, honey cake, Danishes, rugelach, and *branfen* (whiskey). If the meal is served for lunch or later in the day, deli meats, tuna salad, and egg salad frequently replace the brunch fare.

BUDINO
Budino is a baked pudding, both sweet and savory.
Origin: Italy
Other names: *budino alle uova, pudino.*

The Italian *budino*, a source of the English word pudding, originally referred to a type of medieval sausage, which, similar to the English pudding, gradually evolved into a sweet dish, commonly rich and creamy. In the sixteenth century, Sephardic exiles arrived in Italy, merging their Iberian cuisine—notably baked custards—with Italian cuisines, including the new-fangled baked pudding. By the eighteenth century, both Jewish and non-Jewish Italians, borrowing the name and some ideas from the English, were calling their baked puddings *budino*. Classic Jewish *budinos* are basically variations of the Iberian baked custard, based upon milk and eggs, with various thickening agents and flavorings. For meals containing meat, another liquid, notably wine or dried mushroom-soaking water, was substituted for the milk.

In Italy, baked puddings were initially served warm as a side dish; however, as their sweetness increased, *budinos* primarily became desserts. A few savory *budinos* endure, notably *budino di pollo* (chicken pudding), but most are sweet, including *budino di arancia* (orange), *budino di cioccolata* (chocolate), *budino di ricotta* (cheese), *budino di ris* (rice), and *budino di farina di riso* (rice flour). *Budinos* tend not to be too elaborate or time-consuming, although they can be rich.

ROMAN CHICKEN PUDDING (*BUDINO DI POLLO*)

6 TO 8 SERVINGS   [MEAT]

½ cup (0.5 ounce) dried porcini mushrooms
1 cup hot water
2 pounds (4 cups) boneless chicken breasts, ground
3 large eggs
2 large egg whites
2 tablespoons all-purpose flour
1 medium shallot, 5 to 6 scallions (white part only), or 1 medium yellow onion, minced
About 1½ teaspoons table salt or 1 tablespoon kosher salt
About ½ teaspoon ground white or black pepper

1. In a small bowl, soak the mushrooms in the water until softened, about 20 minutes. Drain, straining the soaking liquid and reserving ½ cup. Chop the mushrooms.

2. Preheat the oven to 350°F. Grease a 2-quart soufflé dish or 9-by-5-inch loaf pan, line the bottom with wax paper, and grease again.

3. In a food processor or blender, process the chicken, reserved mushroom soaking liquid, eggs, egg whites, and flour until smooth. Stir in the mushrooms, shallot, salt, and pepper.

4. Spoon the mixture into the prepared dish and cover with a piece of greased wax paper. Place the dish in a larger pan and add boiling water to reach halfway up the dish. Bake until the pudding is firm and the liquid and fat are clear, about 1½ hours. Serve warm or chilled. If serving warm, let stand for 15 minutes before unmolding onto a larger platter. If serving chilled, weigh down the pudding and set in the refrigerator overnight. Cut the *budino* into slices.

BULEMA

Bulema is a coiled filled pastry made with a very thin dough.

Origin: Spain

Other names: *bolema, boulema, rodancha, rollito.*

The Ladino *bimuelo* (fritter) gave rise to an array of pastries, including a filled spiral bun known as *bulema*. In the Ottoman Empire, Sephardim combined their bun with the Turkish coiled pastry *kol boregi* ("branch/arm *börek*," as it is long and bent), a name some Turkish Jews still call it, into *bulema*. In Greece, the coils are also known as *rodanchas* ("roses" akin to the island of Rhodes), probably because they resemble not a flower, but rather the spiral shape of Greek architectural and artistic rosettes. Today, some people call these pastries snails, a less lyrical but perhaps more accurate description. Whatever the name, the formation entails spreading a filling on an extremely thin sheet of dough, rolling it jelly-roll style into a long tube, then coiling the tube around itself into a chubby spiral. In Ladino, to call someone "*esta entero una bulema*" is a derogatory way of saying "he is plump."

Traditional *bulemas* use a thinly stretched homemade yeast dough. The dough is shaped into balls, then coated with oil and left to briefly rest before being rolled out. As commercial phyllo became widely accessible, many substituted it for an easier version. Others, however, insist on using the traditional yeast dough, as it coils easier and tears less than phyllo. Spinach-cheese, eggplant-cheese, and plain cheese are the most common fillings. Sweet versions are called *bulemas dulces*.

Bulemas, along with *borekas* and *boyos*, constitute the triumvirate of Sephardic pastries, served at a *desa-*

yuno (brunch) and other important Sephardic dairy occasions. However, unlike *borekas*, which became ubiquitous in modern Israel, the *bulema* remains largely obscure beyond the Sephardic community. According to Sephardic lore, the spiral shape of the *bulema* symbolizes the life cycle and the ascent of the soul to Eden.

A sweet pumpkin filling (*kalavasa*) is traditional on Rosh Hashanah and Sukkot. Cheese filling is customary on Hanukkah and spinach filling, utilizing the new crop, is eaten on Purim. Eggplant filling is enjoyed throughout the summer. Moroccans feature almond-filled coils (*rose aux amandes*) at weddings and other special occasions. *Bulemas* are typically accompanied with a glass of *arak*.

ᆗ SEPHARDIC CHEESE COILS (*BULEMAS*)

ABOUT 12 LARGE OR 18 MEDIUM PASTRIES [DAIRY]

Dough:

1 teaspoon active dry yeast or ½ (0.6-ounce) cake fresh yeast
1 cup warm water (105 to 115°F for dry yeast; 80 to 85°F for fresh yeast)
Pinch of sugar
1¼ teaspoons table salt or 2½ teaspoons kosher salt
1 tablespoon vegetable oil or melted butter
About 3 cups (15 ounces) bread or unbleached all-purpose flour

½ cup vegetable oil
About 2 cups Sephardic pastry filling (pages 230–232)
1.5 ounces (½ cup) grated Parmesan, Romano, or kefalotiri cheese, or any combination, for sprinkling (optional)

1. Preheat the oven to 375°F. Grease 2 large baking sheets.

2. To make the dough: Dissolve the yeast in ¼ cup water. Stir in the sugar and let stand until foamy, 5 to 10 minutes. In a large bowl, combine the yeast mixture, remaining water, salt, 1 tablespoon oil, and 2 cups flour. Gradually add enough of the remaining flour to make a mixture that holds together. The dough can also be blended in an electric mixer fitted with a dough hook or a food processor. Knead until smooth and elastic.

3. Pour the ½ cup oil into a large shallow pan. Divide the dough into eighteen 1-inch balls or twelve larger

balls. Place the balls in the oil and turn to coat all over. Cover the pan with plastic wrap and let stand for about 30 minutes to allow the gluten to relax.

4. Working with one dough ball at a time, place each ball on an oiled surface (use any remaining oil from the shallow pan) and flatten. Roll and stretch the smaller balls into rounds about 7 inches in diameter or the large balls into very thin rounds about 10 inches in diameter. Brush with oil. Spread a generous tablespoon of filling in a thin line along one edge of the dough. From the filling side, roll up jelly-roll style into a long tube. Starting from one end of the roll, curl up into a coil, seam side in.

5. Place the coils on the prepared baking sheets, leaving a little space between the coils for rising. Brush with oil and, if using, sprinkle with the cheese.

6. Bake until golden brown, about 30 to 40 minutes. Serve warm or at room temperature.

BULGUR

Six millennia ago, people in the Middle East and eastern Mediterranean, after discovering beer and bread, developed a combination process for preparing whole grains by parboiling them, then drying them in the sun; thus bulgur was one of the first processed foods, if not the first. By far the favorite of these sun-dried grains was durum wheat groats, now commonly known as bulgur; the Turkish pronunciation of the Arabic *burghul*, which comes itself from the Farsi *barghul*. It is mentioned twice in the Bible as *rifot*, including an instance of a woman hiding two allies of King David from the forces of the rebellious Absalom by spreading a cloth over a well and scattering bulgur over the top, a natural way of drying the grain and, therefore, unsuspicious. It is most commonly referred to as *burghul* in modern Israel.

For millennia and even today in many rural areas, families prepared their own bulgur each summer, typically as part of a communal effort. After removing the chaff, the kernels were boiled in a large open kettle for about two and a half hours until nearly tender, then drained and sun-dried on the flat roofs of the houses for at least a week, occasionally being turned and separated by hand. After drying, the kernels were typically rubbed to remove some or all of the outer bran layers. The more layers of bran removed, the less nutty the flavor. The dried kernels were usually cracked in a mortar or by stone, thus the statement in Book of Proverbs: "Even if you pound a fool in a mortar with a pestle along with bulgur, his foolishness will not depart from him."

Today, bulgur is generally taken to a nearby mill for crushing. Finally, it is sieved to separate various degrees of fineness, then stored to feed the family for much of the year. In Turkey, Kurdistan, and some other parts of the Middle East, after parboiling, part of the wheat is dried as bulgur, while the remainder is fermented with the whey drained from yogurt and then sun-dried, creating an ancient processed food called *tarhana* in Turkey, *kutach* in the Talmud, and *kashk* in Persia.

The bulgur form of wheat allows for easy preparation (soaking in liquid or quick simmering), as well as a long storage period of at least eight months, even in humid conditions. The heat kills any insect eggs and mold in the wheat, while its new hard nature hinders insect attacks from outside. The partial processing of the wheat berries imparts a nutty flavor as well as gelatinizing the starch, while removing very little of the kernel's protein, vitamins, and minerals. Another attribute of bulgur is that it can be prepared well after the wheat harvest and, therefore, is not a distraction.

Sun-dried grains were a staple of ancient Mesopotamia and have been found in early Egyptian tombs. For millennia, bulgur along with *kashk* provided the principal winter meals throughout much of the Middle East and eastern Mediterranean. Turks remain the predominant producers and consumers of bulgur. The average rural family in Turkey and Kurdistan still purchases, toward the end of the summer, about fifty kilos of wheat to prepare their own bulgur and *kashk*.

The situation was quite different in America, where bulgur was practically unknown until well into the twentieth century. Commercial bulgur was first introduced in 1945 as a means of utilizing part of the country's wheat surplus, although little was consumed domestically. To support declining farm prices, the U.S. Congress enacted the Agricultural Act of 1948, making surplus foods available to the needy abroad through registered volunteer agencies (RVA). Although the food supplies were free, the voluntary agency had to bear all shipping and distribution costs. In order to arrange for surplus American foods to go to the young state of Israel, undergoing its rationing period known as the *tzena* (austerity), Hadassah and

its medical organization, known for its humanitarian activities, registered in 1950 as an RVA with the State Department, which attempted at every turn to prevent this development.

Nevertheless, after several months of wrangling, Hadassah won approval and, in the years until 1955, boxes of dried skim milk, dried eggs, cheese, butter, and potatoes—the shipping costs covered by the Jewish Agency for Israel—arrived in Israel marked "Donated by the People of the United States" and "Not for Resale." After the first year, other goods were added, including rice, corn, and bulgur. The latter was primarily due to the efforts of Senator Hubert Humphrey of Minnesota, who even read a statement on the Senate floor calling attention to the nutritional and economic advantages of bulgur. When the *Congressional Record* recorded the article, it did so in Hebrew, certainly the first and possibly only instance of Hebrew in the official record of Congress, as well as the first time bulgur was mentioned in the *Congressional Record*. Subsequently, bulgur remained a common food in Israel, found packaged in supermarkets along with unprocessed wheat berries.

The rise of the health food movement led to an increased American interest in bulgur. Correspondingly, the sudden popularity in America of the Lebanese herb salad tabbouleh led to the widespread discovery of bulgur.

Bulgur served as a staple "poor person's dish" among Middle Eastern Jews, especially the very impoverished communities of Kurdistan and Yemen. It was paired with other inexpensive items, such as lentils, in dishes similar to the more upscale *mengedarrah* (rice with lentils). Fine bulgur is generally utilized for cooked cereals, breads, and some salads. Medium can be used for anything and is preferred for *kibbeh* (ground meat dishes), tabbouleh, salads, and soups. Fine- and medium-grain bulgur can generally be substituted for each other and prepared by simply soaking in liquid, although a little cooking improves the texture. In Israel, a little soaked bulgur is sometimes added to falafel and meat loaf for texture and binding. The coarse type of bulgur, requiring a brief cooking period, is commonly used for pilafs, cooked salads, casseroles, stuffings, and stews. Bulgur can be substituted for rice in most recipes.

(See also Bazargan, Beleela, Kashk, Kibbeh, Kibbeh Mahshi, Kubbeh, and Tabbouleh)

BUNDT CAKE

Bundt cakes are coffee cakes baked in round, high, scalloped pans with a hole in the center. Firm, yet moist, they are most often served without a frosting.

Origin: Germany, central Europe

Other names: *bundkuchen.*

For generations, central Europeans baked butter- and egg-rich yeast doughs in ceramic bowls, calling the cakes kugelhopfs (*gugelhopf* in Austria and southern Germany). However, the centers of those dense cakes tended to turn out doughy. Then centuries ago, someone came up with the idea of constructing a hole in the center of the mold, guaranteeing uniform cooking. In addition, a scalloped surface was added, exposing more of the batter to the heat and giving a cake or bread baked in the pan the appearance of a wound turban. The fluted pan, a large, glazed, bowl-shaped terra-cotta mold with a central tube, became known as a Turk's Cap or Turk's Head.

In the mid-nineteenth century, craftsmen began producing a fluted cast-iron version of the Turk's Cap, the first metal tube pan; this heavy pan was necessary for the dense, Teutonic butter cakes and was less fragile than pottery. Around the same time, cooks in northern Germany began referring to it as a *bund* pan and to coffee cakes baked in it as *bundkuchen.* The name *bund* (German for "bundle/band") probably connoted the banded appearance of the flutes, which resembled a bundle of straw or twigs, but as the word also came to mean a "gathering of people," a deeper meaning was added: a large baked good shared by many.

The first American records of *bund* and Bundt cakes were all in Jewish sources. Bertha F. Kramer, the German Jewish author of *Aunt Babette's* (Cincinnati, 1889), included a recipe, immediately following "*Abgeruehrter Gugelhopf*," for "Plain Bund, or *Napf Kuchen*," a butter-and egg-rich yeast cake akin to the kugelhopf but without the traditional raisins and candied citron. Kramer provided no explanation of the type of pan used, stating only "Butter the form well that the cake is to be baked in," presuming that her readers would know the appropriate baking vessel.

Shortly thereafter, the original edition of *The Settlement Cook Book* (1901) by another Midwestern German Jew, Lizzie Kander, contained three recipes for "Bundt Kuchen," all made from a butter-and-egg-rich yeast dough. The "Spice Bundt Kuchen" simply called for adding cinnamon and raisins to "Bundt Kuchen No. 1." The directions in "Bundt Kuchen No. 2," somewhat richer than No. 1, direct "Grease Bundt form (a heavy round fluted pan with tube in center) well, and flour lightly." This was the first description of the pan and first record of the word Bundt with the *t* suffix. All of Kander's Bundt cakes were yeast-raised. On the other hand, *The Neighborhood Cook Book* by the Council of Jewish Women (Portland, Oregon, 1912) offered a recipe for a yeast-raised, kugelhopf-like "Rum Bund," as well as a "Plain Bund Kuchen," made from a pound cake–like batter without any yeast baked in a "bund form."

As acculturation led to the adoption of American layer cakes, Bundt cakes began disappearing from Jewish cookbooks and kitchens. Bundt forms were all manufactured in Europe and, as the twentieth century progressed, were unobtainable in America. Yet a few children of immigrants grew nostalgic for the dense, moist, and flavorful Teutonic butter cakes their mothers and grandmothers lovingly produced. Thus in 1950, when a Hadassah chapter in Minneapolis, Minnesota, wanted to experiment with some Old World *bundkuchen*, they could not find any appropriate pans. Undeterred, the women forwarded a request to nearby Northland Aluminum Products, then a small struggling firm manufacturing Scandinavian pastry molds and bakeware under the Nordic Ware trademark, asking if the company could create a pan similar to the *bund* but using lighter-weight aluminum.

H. David Dalquist, who had purchased the company two years before, was mystified until one of the Hadassah members, Rose Joshua, brought over her grandmother's German kugelhopf pan. Using Joshua's mold as a prototype, Dalquist added folds to the flutes and trademarked the name Bundt, as well as patenting the pan's design. Thus was born, or more precisely reborn, the now classic American Bundt pan.

Initially, the Bundt pan attracted little attention and most of them were purchased by Hadassah women. In the 1960 edition of the *Good Housekeeping Cookbook*, a picture of a pound cake baked in a Bundt pan sparked somewhat wider interest. Then a popular entry in the 1966 Pillsbury Bake-Off, the Tunnel of Fudge Cake, which required a Bundt pan, suddenly ignited a Bundt craze. Ironically, the Tunnel of Fudge Cake only earned second prize, losing to the now-disregarded Golden Gate Snack Bread. Within a few weeks, Pillsbury received more than two hundred thousand requests from people trying to locate the then relatively unknown Bundt pan. Northland went into twenty-four-hour production to meet the demand and, within a year, was churning out thirty thousand pans a day. By the beginning of the twenty-first century, the Bundt pan had become the top-selling cake pan in the world and a standard piece of equipment in American kitchens.

In gratitude for its input, Northland for many years afterward donated the Bundt pan seconds to Hadassah, which sold them at fundraisers and donated much of the proceeds to Hadassah Medical Center in Jerusalem and other charitable projects.

Technically, anything baked in a Bundt pan is considered a Bundt cake. However, by its nature, the pan lends itself to a particular type of cake, one that stands high and erect. Bundt cakes, partway between a pound cake and American butter cake, contain less butter and sugar than pound cakes and more than layer cakes. They are firm, yet moist, and rich enough to not require a frosting. Therefore, Bundt cakes are best when focusing on simple flavors, such as vanilla, chocolate, and citrus. Buttermilk or sour cream is commonly used as the liquid, the acid producing a pleasant tang and tender texture. Bundt cakes are now universal and a recognized American comfort food, yet they remain an important part of American Jewish cuisine, not only served at Hadassah meetings but at Sabbath meals and various life-cycle events.

BURAG

Burag is a fried or baked square or roll of phyllo dough filled with mildly spiced meat or vegetables.

Origin: Iraq

Other names: *bourag.*

When the Turks relocated from central Asia to the area that now bears their name, among the foods they brought with them was a deep-fried filled dumpling called *bugra*, which, by the fifteenth century had evolved into a large number of filled pastries collectively known as *börek* or *burek*. The standard pastry for these dishes was *yufka*, called *fila* by the Arabs and phyllo by the Greeks. After Iraq was absorbed into the Ottoman Empire, a form of *börek* emerged there, filled phyllo squares or cylinders called *burag*, which became some of Iraq's most popular pastries.

The most common fillings are ground meat, ground chicken, potatoes, and cheese. Like most Iraqi appetizers, *burag* were originally deep-fried, but today baked versions are also common. Iraqi Jews typically commence meals for special occasions with *burag* and several other appetizers. *Burag* is typically accompanied with *turshi* (pickles) and *amba* (curried mango condiment).

(See also Boreka)

BURICCHE

Buricche are turnovers made with puff pastry and filled with vegetables or meat.

Origin: Italy

Other names: *burchita, burriche.*

Pasta sfoglia (puff pastry) originated in Florence, Italy, during the Renaissance, as ingenious bakers, using techniques from Iberia, found a way to produce layered pastry as with phyllo dough but without the necessity of the time-consuming and skilled art of rolling each piece paper-thin. The water and butter embedded in the dough steam and puff up during baking, resulting in numerous flaky layers. Sephardic exiles introduced Italian Jews to Iberian turnovers, such as *empanadas*, and their various fillings, especially seasonal vegetables—spinach, eggplant, and pumpkin. Other popular Italian fillings included meat, liver, chicken, anchovy, tuna, and almond. Eventually, the concept of the *boreka* (filled pastries) arrived from Turkey, giving rise to the Italian *buricche*, utilizing the Italian Jewish version of puff pastry and distinctively Italian fillings to make small turnovers. For meat meals, goose or veal fat was substituted for the butter in the dough, although today margarine is more prominent. You can use store-bought puff pastry or standard flaky pie pastry. *Buricche* are among the favorite Italian Purim foods.

🍧 ITALIAN TURNOVERS (*BURICCHE*)

ABOUT 20 PASTRIES   [PAREVE OR DAIRY]

Pastry:

½ cup olive or vegetable oil

½ cup lukewarm water (80 to 90°F)

½ teaspoon table salt or 1 teaspoon kosher salt

About 2½ cups (12.5 ounces) pastry or all-purpose flour, sifted

About ½ cup plus 2 tablespoons (1¼ sticks) unsalted butter or margarine, softened

Additional flour for sprinkling

1 recipe spinach filling (recipe follows) or
  Sephardic pastry filling (pages 230–232)

Egg wash (1 large egg beaten with 1 tablespoon
  water)

1. To make the pastry: In a medium bowl, combine the oil, water, and salt. Stir in 1 cup flour. Gradually stir in enough of the remaining flour to make a soft dough that comes away from the sides of the bowl. Cover with plastic wrap and let stand at room temperature for 30 minutes.

2. On a lightly floured surface, roll out the dough into a ⅓-inch-thick rectangle, about 9 by 6 inches. Spread with 2 tablespoons butter and lightly sprinkle with flour. With the narrow end facing you, fold over the top third of the dough, then fold over the uncovered bottom third, forming about a 6-by-3-inch rectangle. Wrap in plastic wrap and refrigerate for about 30 minutes.

3. Place the dough, seam side up, on a lightly floured surface and roll into a ¼-inch-thick rectangle. Spread with 2 tablespoons butter, lightly sprinkle with flour, and fold in thirds as in the previous step. Repeat rolling, spreading, and folding 3 more times. Refrigerate the dough for at least 2 hours or overnight. Let stand at room temperature for about 15 minutes before rolling.

4. Preheat the oven to 400°F.

5. On a lightly floured surface, roll out the dough ⅛ inch thick. Cut into 3-inch rounds or squares. Spoon 1 tablespoon filling in the center, fold over to form a half-moon or triangle, and press the edges to seal. Place on an ungreased baking sheet, 1 inch apart, and brush with the egg wash.

6. Bake until golden brown, 15 to 20 minutes. Serve warm or at room temperature. Store in an airtight container at room temperature for up to 3 days or in the freezer for up to 6 months.

SPINACH FILLING

2 tablespoons olive or vegetable oil

1 medium onion or 6 scallions, chopped

2 cups (1 pound fresh or 10 ounces frozen) cooked, squeezed, and chopped spinach

1 large egg, lightly beaten

½ to ¾ cup grated provolone, kashkaval, Muenster, Monterey Jack, or Swiss cheese

About ½ teaspoon table salt or 1 teaspoon kosher salt

Dash of ground black pepper

Dash of ground nutmeg or cayenne (optional)

In a large skillet, heat the oil over medium heat. Add the onion and sauté until soft and translucent, 5 to 10 minutes. Stir in the spinach. Let cool. Add the remaining ingredients.

BUTTER

When raw cow's milk is left to stand, due to the presence of an agglutinating protein, the fat globules cluster and rise to the top. Two gallons of milk yield about six cups of cream, a mixture of suspended fat globules and water. When beaten, the globules bump into each other, which causes the fat to cling together. The more the cream is beaten, the larger the fat clumps grow, producing what we call whipped cream. Churning cream further transforms the mixture from pockets of fat suspended in water into an emulsion consisting of fat, water, proteins, and carbohydrates, what we call butter. The liquid left from making butter is buttermilk.

Butter was discovered in prehistoric times, probably when nomads or herdsmen placed milk into leak-proof bags made from animal skins and hung the sacks onto their animals, and the movement as they traveled then "squeezed" the cream until butter formed. Much later, tools were invented to facilitate the process, such as the ancient *machbetzot* (wooden churns) found in several locations in Israel. After the cream was skimmed off the milk, the cream was allowed to ripen briefly in order for bacteria to ferment the lactose in it, transforming it into the lactic acid that is necessary for the separation of the butterfat during churning. The actions of these bacteria also give butter its characteristic flavor and aroma. When ready, the cream was placed in a churn and the blades of a wooden dasher worked until the liquid firmed.

Until the advent of refrigeration, butter was generally only used when it was relatively fresh or plenty of salt was added as a preservative. Eventually, people discovered a method to increase its shelf life without salt—by clarifying it. As butter melts, the water gradually evaporates and the remainder separates into three layers: foam consisting of trapped proteins and carbohydrates on the surface, fat (pure liquid butter) in the center, and a whitish layer of proteins and carbohydrates (whey) along with water on the bottom. It is the milk solids that turn rancid, spoiling the butter,

as well as burn easily. When most of the milk solids are removed, the remaining yellow liquid is called
clarified butter. Clarified butter, however, lacks regular butter's rich flavor.

European-style clarified butter, also called drawn
butter, is only melted for about two minutes, then
strained without any cooking, leaving some water. *Sam-
neh/samna/smen*, the Middle Eastern form of clarified
butter, historically made from sheep or goat butter, is
generally cooked to eliminate more of the solids and
water, thereby greatly extending the amount of time it
can be stored even without refrigeration. The Indian
ghee, frequently made from water buffalo butter, is
typically cooked for a lengthy period, during which
time the milk solids brown and the sugar caramelizes,
imparting a slightly nutty flavor. Ghee is an essential
element of northern and central Indian cuisine; coconut or vegetable oil serves that role in the south.

In post-Biblical Hebrew, *chemah* means butter,
which seems appropriate as the word is derived from
the root meaning "fury" or "disturbed," reflecting the
agitation necessary to make it. Proverbs appears to
support this intent as well: "For squeezing milk brings
forth *chemah*, and squeezing the nose brings forth
blood; so the squeezing of anger brings forth strife."
However, the biblical use of *chemah* most likely
encompassed both butter and buttermilk. When
Abraham served his three parched guests *chemah* and
Yael gave *chemah* to the exhausted general Sisera, it
was probably the refreshing buttermilk.

In biblical Israel, a land rich in olive oil, butter
was a luxury and minor fat. On the other hand, butter
was a mainstay in northern Europe, an area with very
limited amounts of oil. In any case, since the time
of Abraham, butter and buttermilk have remained an
important part of Jewish dining.

C

CABBAGE

Cabbage, one of the oldest cultivated vegetables, has been the most widely eaten vegetable in history, a food of the poor and, in some areas, among the few types of produce available. The cabbage's short growing time of about three months allows for several plantings a year and, therefore, yields more of it than any other vegetable. It has also been revered for thousands of years for medicinal purposes, such as for treating coughs and bronchitis. Today, cabbage remains among the world's top ten most widely grown plants.

The original wild cabbage—actually a colewort, as the term cabbage technically refers only to a headed variety—was a loose bunch of leaves attached to a main stalk, similar to its close relative kale, and also very bitter, because it contained a significant amount of mustard oil. Initially, both the leaves and stalk were consumed, but they required pickling or boiling to be palatable. From the wild ancestor, horticulturists over the millennia developed nearly five hundred varieties of cabbage, as well as flowering cabbages (all the same species), including broccoli and cauliflower.

Around the first century BCE, the first head cabbage evolved, possibly in northern Europe; however, it was not widely used until the medieval period, and colewort remained the most important green for European peasants until the seventeenth century. The now-familiar green cabbage, also called white cabbage, with a firm, light green head and mild-flavored smooth leaves, first appeared in Germany around the middle of the twelfth century. The two other main types of head cabbages are the crinkle-leaf savoy, with a milder flavor and softer texture, dating to the middle of the sixteenth century, and the smooth-leaf red (actually more purple). Red cabbage was first mentioned in Germany in 1150, but as a green cabbage with red veins and edges, and it only evolved into the version with the solid purple color on the exterior (the inside of the leaves is white) in the sixteenth century. Chinese cabbages belong to a different species.

The cabbage/colewort is never mentioned in the Bible, but recorded in the Mishnah. It entered Jewish cooking relatively late in history, probably reaching the Levant around 275 BCE by way of the Greeks. The cabbage's Hebrew name, *kruv*, derives from the Greek *krambe/krámvi*, and only came into usage during the late Second Temple Period. It is probable that the Celts, who called the plant *bresic*, which gave rise to the Latin term *Brassica*, spread the colewort to the eastern Mediterranean around 600 to 300 BCE, where it was adopted by the Romans, Egyptians, and Greeks, strengthening the theory of a western European origin. Another sign of Celtic influence on cabbage is the relationship of the Celtic *caul/crl* (stalk) to the Greek *kaulion*, the source of many words for cabbage. The Greeks and Romans introduced colewort to northeastern Europe, where the Slavs were growing it by the ninth century. Since headed cabbage grows best in cooler climates, northern Europe emerged as the early center of this form of cabbage, which eventually became a mainstay of the diet.

In any case, around two thousand years ago, colewort first emerged as one of the most important plants in the Jewish diet. A Talmudic saying, "Together with the thorn the cabbage is smitten," connotes the importance of the edible colewort in contrast to the problematical thorn. The Talmud considers the colewort as being healthful and sustaining, noting the benefits of "cabbage for sustenance" and including it among "the six things that heal a sick person."

In a listing of chores that noted rabbis performed to help their wives in the preparation for the Sabbath, the Talmud recorded, "Rav Chisda cut cabbage." Cabbage remains festive as well as everyday fare. Since the Teutonic name for cabbage, *kohl,* sounds like the prominent Hoshanah Rabbah prayer *kol mevaser* (a voice announcing), Germans traditionally serve cabbage soup (*kohl mit vasser*) on Hoshanah Rabbah at the end of Sukkot. Some Germans offer a sweetened dish of red cabbage with apples on Rosh Hashanah. Cabbage is among the traditional vegetables in the

Rosh Hashanah stew served atop couscous by Moroccans. Around the sixteenth century, the arrival of the concept of stuffed vegetables led to one of the favorite eastern European holiday dishes, stuffed cabbage. Stuffed cabbage and cabbage strudel are served by many Ashkenazic households on Sukkot, while Russians offer a cabbage and meat soup. Cabbage is traditional on Simchat Torah as well, partially because its Hebrew name (*kruv*) is a homonym for cherub, and a pair of cherubs hovered over the Ark of the Covenant bearing the tablets of the Ten Commandments. Raw cabbage salads entered the Jewish repertoire rather late, as Ashkenazim rarely ate uncooked vegetables; however, these salads subsequently became common and widespread among Ashkenazim for Sabbath lunch.

Colewort and, even more importantly, the headed cabbage, served as northern Ashkenazim's predominant vegetable until the acceptance of the potato in the mid-1800s. For a millennia, cabbage was the most common cooking odor of the *shtetlach*. Cabbage was boiled, braised, stewed, and pickled for sauerkraut. It also served as the basis for numerous soups and fillings for savory pastries, including strudel, blintzes, *piroshki*, and knishes. Cabbage was typically paired with another Ashkenazic standard, the onion. A common central European and Ukrainian way of preparing cooked cabbage was to mix it with noodles; this dish was frequently flavored with caraway.

Although less vital to other Jewish communities, cabbage has also been important, especially in Ethiopia and India, where it goes into intensely spiced salads and braises. However, residents of the Mediterranean and Mesopotamia, having numerous other vegetables at their disposal, relied much less on cabbage, although they pickled it, stuffed it, and used it in stews.

(See also Cabbage, Stuffed; Choucroute Garni; and Sauerkraut)

CABBAGE, STUFFED
Origin: Turkey or Persia
Other names: cabbage roll; Arabic: *mahshi malfuf*; Azeri: *dolma*; Belorussia: *halubsy*; Bessarabia: *prake*; Bulgarian: *zelevi sarma*; Farsi: *dolmeh kalam, tolma*; Galicia: *holeptshe, tabelakh, teibelekh*; Georgian: *kombostos tolma*; German: *gefulte kroyt, gevikelte kroyt, kohlrouladen*; Greek: *dolma de kol, dolma kalam, samas de kol, yemista*

me lahano; Hebrew: *kruv memulah*; Hungarian: *töltött káposzta, sorma*; Italian: *cavoli ripieni*; Ladino: *samas de kol*; Lithuania: *goluptshe*; Poland: *galloptchy, geluptze, golomke, goluptshe, holishike, holoptsche, holubtshe*; Romanian: *sarmale*; northern Russia: *goluptsi*; Serbia: *sarma*; Slovakia: *holupki, kapusta*; Turkish: *käbestä dolmasi, lahana dolmasi, lahana sarma, yaprak dolmasi*; northern Ukraine: *halupki, holubtsi*; southern Ukraine: *prake*.

Already two millennia ago, stewed cabbage was a winter staple in Europe and the Middle East. During the medieval period, peasants in either Turkey or Persia began stewing cabbage leaves wrapped around grains and pounded meat as a way of producing a more substantial dish and stretching limited

Cabbage leaves, ground beef, and chopped onions are transformed into the Ashkenazic beloved stuffed cabbage.

resources. Eventually, the notion of stuffing cabbage leaves spread throughout much of western Asia and Europe, where it became known by an assortment of names and, as with other well-traveled dishes, developed numerous variations. Middle Easterners and residents of the Balkans generally preferred stuffing grape leaves. It was in eastern and central Europe, the cooler climates there not conducive to growing grapes, where stuffed cabbage emerged as one of the most beloved of festive dishes and comfort foods.

The Tatars overran Ukraine and Poland throughout the sixteenth century, and probably introduced the concept of stuffed vegetables to those countries at that time. The most available leaf for stuffing in that area was cabbage. It soon became popular peasant fare and was whimsically named after local Slavic words for dove—*golub* in Russian, *holub* in Ukrainian, *golab* in Polish, and *teibel* or *tabel* in Yiddish—with a diminutive suffix. Perhaps the stuffed cabbage rolls reminded them of little birds in a nest or in a pot.

While stuffed cabbage arrived in Russia by way of the Tatars, Turks and Middle Eastern Jews introduced the dish to the Balkans and Hungary, then under the control of the Ottoman Empire. There it took names from the Turkish *sarma* (to wrap) or *yaprak* (leaf) as well as *dolma* (stuffed). The term *prakes* penetrated far enough north as to be common around the city of Lodz in central Poland and in parts of Ukraine. Most of central Europe adopted literal rather than whimsical terms for stuffed cabbage. By following the name, one can identify the direction from which a community's stuffed cabbage entered Europe. The Yiddish name in many American cities or neighborhoods was commonly determined by the dominant immigrant group, until the English "stuffed cabbage" generally supplanted most of the Old World terms.

Today, stuffed cabbage filling consists primarily of ground meat, but throughout much of history, meat was a minor element or even absent. In a time when meat was expensive, mixing a little meat with a lot of filler—besides stretching resources, the filler lightens the texture and binds the meat—and wrapping the mixture with readily available cabbage leaves, usually the less desirable outer ones, proved an ideal and practical way of making something special for a festival or the Sabbath. Middle Easterners and Romanians typically added rice in the stuffing, while Jews

from northeast Europe used bread or barley. Among the very poor, sauerkraut, barley, or buckwheat was all too frequently used to stuff the leaves in place of meat.

European-style ground meat tends to be coarser than the smooth Middle Eastern type. Middle Easterners tend to sauté the onions and meat for the filling, while Ashkenazim usually use raw meat and onions, along with an egg to bind. Hungarians add sweet paprika or marjoram, Syrians allspice and cinnamon, Persians dill or mint, and Romanians paprika, savory, and plenty of garlic.

Jews from Hungary, Italy, Romania, and northern Poland prefer a savory sauce, Sephardim enjoy a tart sauce made by adding a little lemon juice, and those from Galicia and Ukraine favor a sweet-and-sour sauce. Greeks also make a version *kon huevos y limon*, with an egg-lemon sauce poured over the top afterwards. In order to thicken the sauce, Poles added *einbren* (browned flour) or a *zaprashka* (roux). In the nineteenth century, tomatoes became a common addition to the sauce, negating the need for a flour thickener. Some eastern European cooks traditionally use sour salt (citric acid) in the tomato sauce, because, unlike lemon juice and vinegar, its flavor does not diminish during the long cooking time, which is needed to develop the flavor and properly tenderize the cabbage. In America, many Ashkenazim adopted the sweet-and-sour version, commonly adding raisins. Also in America, the proportion of meat dramatically increased and rice became the common grain.

Stuffed cabbage is a beloved Ashkenazic dish, favored as an entrée or appetizer at festive occasions, including the Sabbath, Passover, and weddings, or as just a comfort food. Stuffed cabbage became traditional Ashkenazic fare for Sukkot because cabbage was abundant in eastern Europe at that time of the year. In addition, filled foods symbolize abundance. On Simchat Torah the shape of the cabbage roll resembles a Torah scroll.

(See also Dolma and Grape Leaves, Stuffed)

❦ ASHKENAZIC STUFFED CABBAGE (*HOLISHIKES/PRAKES*)

16 TO 18 SERVINGS   [MEAT]

White or cider vinegar

1 large head (about 3 pounds) green or savoy cabbage, cored

1 medium onion, sliced

Stuffing:

1½ pounds ground beef

About ½ cup raw rice, dry bread crumbs, or matza meal

1 large egg

½ cup water

1 medium yellow onion, chopped

About ¾ teaspoon table salt or 1½ teaspoons kosher salt

About ½ teaspoon ground black pepper

Sauce:

2 cups crushed tomatoes or tomato sauce, or 1 cup each

3 tablespoons tomato paste

1 cup water

2 bay leaves

1 to 8 tablespoons sugar

About ½ teaspoon table salt or 1 teaspoon kosher salt

Ground black pepper to taste

2 to 4 tablespoons lemon juice or cider vinegar, or ¼ teaspoon sour salt

1. Fill a large pot about three-fourths full with water, add a little vinegar, and bring to a rapid boil. Carefully place the cabbage in the boiling water and cook until the outer leaves are pliable enough to roll easily, about 5 minutes. Using a pair of tongs, pull off the supple leaves. Repeat the process until you have 16 to 18 untorn large leaves. Trim the tough center rib of each leaf. Shred any extra cabbage leaves and place in the bottom of a deep heavy pot or baking dish. Scatter the onion over the top.

2. To make the stuffing: Combine all the stuffing ingredients.

3. Place about ¼ cup stuffing on each large cabbage leaf, arranging it a little off center. Use 1 to 2 table-spoons for smaller leaves. Fold the sides of the leaf over the stuffing, fold over the rib end, and roll up. Arrange the cabbage rolls, seam side down, in the prepared pot.

4. To make the sauce: Combine all the sauce ingredients. Pour over the cabbage rolls. If the sauce does not cover the cabbage rolls, add enough water to cover.

5. Cover and simmer over low heat until tender, about 1½ hours. Or bake, covered, in a 350°F oven for about 1½ hours, then uncover and bake until the sauce is thickened and the cabbage rolls are lightly browned, 30 to 60 minutes. Serve warm. Stuffed cabbage is tasty reheated and freezes well too.

CALSONES

Calsones is a filled egg pasta frequently served mixed with noodles.

Origin: Syria

Other names: *calsones b'rishta, kalsonnes, kelsonnes.*

Calsones is the Syrian version of stuffed pasta. It can be formed into rounds, half-moons, or triangles, and is typically thicker and chewier than Italian ravioli. Cheese is the most common filling, but sometimes spinach is substituted.

The dish and its name resulted from the arrival in Syria of refugees from the kingdom of Naples in southern Italy, then under Spanish rule, after their expulsion in 1533. The original dish in Naples consisted of a slice of sausage enwrapped in lean yeast dough and deep-fried. The fritters were served warm or cooled. For a dairy version, Jews substituted cheese for the meat. Italians named the ragged fried pastries after the baggy long underpants (*calzones*) worn by the men of Naples. In Crete, another area where olive oil was plentiful and inexpensive, Jews continued to deep-fry *calsones*. In Syria, however, oil was less abundant and deep-frying less common. Consequently, Syrians transformed *calsones* into boiled pasta.

In Syria, *calsones* became primarily dairy fare. After boiling, the *calsones* were fried in a little butter or simply tossed with butter and baked. In Aleppo, cooks took any leftover dough from making the filled pasta, cut out wide noodles, and mixed them with the filled pasta (*calsones b'rishta*) for a more substantial dish. With the advent of kosher commercial cheese tortellini and egg noodles, some cooks cheat and use the store-brought products.

In Syrian households, the standard Thursday dinner is a dairy meal before the Sabbath. For generations, *calsones b'rishta* with a cheese filling provided the main course, typically accompanied with yogurt and a green salad. A cheese filling also became a popular Shavuot treat, while spinach is traditional for Purim. Some cooks insist that the best filling is made with *miz-ithra/anthotiro* (fresh sheep's milk cheese), imparting a slightly nutty flavor, while others maintain that mild Muenster, is more appropriate. Today, a combination of Parmesan and ricotta or farmer cheese has become common. *Calsones* remains a Syrian comfort food.

CAPER

The caper is a perennial shrub that grows wild throughout the mountainous areas of the eastern Mediterranean. Its long roots draw nourishment from poor soil, arid land, or even cracks in a rock. In July and August, the plant produces tiny buds also known as capers. The buds blossom in the morning when exposed to light and last for only a few hours before wilting. Each day, during this period, new buds appear. They range in size from that of a green peppercorn (called nonpareil) to slightly larger than half an inch (known as capote), and the larger buds are softer and more intensely flavored. Some buds are allowed to blossom and grow into a succulent, teardrop-shaped, semimature fruit called caperberries. The flavor is similar to that of the buds, but more intense and sour.

Remains of wild caperberries and seeds have been found in prehistoric sites in Iraq, while the first record of capers was in the forty-seven-hundred-year-old Sumerian Epic of Gilgamesh. Capers were used as a condiment and medicine in ancient Greece and Rome.

Capers have a long standing in Jewish tradition. The caper is one of the few plants found in the Judean Desert between the Judean Hills and south to Masada and the Dead Sea, the lowest spot on earth. Because the caper tenaciously regenerates after being cut back or burned, and so determinedly thrives in difficult locales—even growing on the Western Wall in Jerusalem—the Talmud compares it to "Israel among the nations." The name of the biblical figure Tzlafchad means "sharp caper." The Mishnah considered capers, known as *kahfars* and *tzalaf*, as a type of "budding fruit" and tithable crop, connoting its usage as an important cultivated food in Judea two thousand years ago. In Talmudic times, caperberries were also fermented into a wine (*yein kafrisin*), the strongest fruit wine, which was used to soak one of the ingredients incorporated into the Temple incense. In Ecclesiastes, the caperberry symbolizes the brevity of human life, "and the *ahvi'onah* [caperberry] shall fail."

Since they grow wild, capers were used throughout history by the poor and wealthy alike. While very occasionally used fresh, capers are more often pickled in vinegar or salt. Caperberries are also pickled and used to add piquancy to various dishes. Capers have a spicy aroma and a slightly bitter flavor—a combination of mustard and black pepper—that complements other Mediterranean seasonings, most notably basil, chervil, oregano, garlic, and olives. The acidic, salty caper provides flavor and textural contrast. Capers are used with fish and poultry and in a number of salads

(e.g., the Middle Eastern cucumber and feta salad, *michoteta*), dips, relishes (such as caponata), stews, and sauces (most notably lemon-wine sauces and tartar sauce). Since intense heat destroys their aroma, capers are generally added to sauces near the end of cooking. Among Ashkenazim, more recently, capers are paired with lox and cream cheese.

CAPONATA

Caponata is a cooked sweet-and-sour eggplant relish.
Origin: Sicily

Sicilian Jews, who lived on the island since Roman times, developed various salads that could be prepared a day or more ahead of the Sabbath and, before the advent of refrigeration, be served at room temperature for Sabbath lunch. Vinegar was added as a preservative and sugar or honey to tame the potency of the acid. Thus *cappone*, a venerable Latin term for sweet-and-sour dishes—related to the similar term in Catalan, *caponada*, from a word meaning "tied together"—became an integral component of Sicilian Jewish cookery.

In addition to vinegar and sugar, these dishes commonly contained other local favorites—capers, olives, and raisins or dried plums. The Arabs controlled parts or all of Sicily from 827 to 1061 and during this time they introduced their favorite foods, including the eggplant. Except for Arabs and Jews, most Europeans ignored eggplant, a member of the nightshade family, until well into the sixteenth century. Sicilian Jews, on the other hand, quickly embraced eggplant, developing various dishes featuring it, including caponata.

Sicily fell under the rule of Spain in 1377. In 1493, the Spanish edict of expulsion was applied to the nearly forty thousand Jews of Sicily. Although this ancient Jewish community disappeared from the island of Sicily, they left behind one of the area's most famous dishes. Most Sicilian Jews resettled in central and northern Italy or the Ottoman Empire, bringing with them their foods, including caponata.

In Italy, caponata is commonly designated *alla giudia* (the name of the Roman Ghetto), denoting its longtime ubiquity among Italian Jews. Eventually, it was further refined with the addition of another questionable member of the nightshade family, tomatoes. Today, there are almost as many versions of caponta in Italy as there are cooks who make it. Caponata is served as an appetizer, side dish, and a pasta topping, as well as a bed for chicken or fish.

CARAWAY

Caraway is a small, brown, ridged, crescent-shaped fruit that is used as a spice, most often whole. Caraway, a close relative of parsley, is one of the oldest known spices. It imparts a slightly bitter anise-like flavor with a trace of lemon. It is often confused with the similar-looking cumin seed, although the two spices possess very different flavors. Jews were highly involved in the spice business, as Kemmoun and Kemoun (Arabic for caraway) became a Jewish surname in the Arab world, while Kimmel (Yiddish for caraway) and Kimmelman paralleled it among Ashkenazim.

Caraway is one of the primary seasonings of central Europe and Scandinavia and it is occasionally used in Yemen and the Maghreb. Its assertive flavor does not blend well with most other spices and it is typically featured solo, along with garlic and onion. It is used to make *kummelsuppe* (caraway soup), a Jewish mother's traditional remedy for an upset stomach. Caraway is added to vegetable dishes, especially sauerkraut, coleslaw, and braised cabbage. It flavors cheese as well as dishes made with cheese and is used in potato soups, stews, roasts, meat loaf, savory dumplings, and in "Jewish" rye breads.

CARDAMOM

Cardamom, a member of the ginger family, is the most fragrant of spices. Inside the brittle oblate pods are clusters of intensely flavored tiny black seeds. The pods are green or, after bleaching, white. Both pods and seeds (whole or ground together) are used in cooking. Cardamom's distinctive aroma fades rather quickly, so Indians primarily purchase it in pod form. The pods are usually bruised or steeped in liquid first to release their flavor. Green pods are preferred in India and the Middle East. They have more flavor and aroma—with notes of black pepper, eucalyptus, lemon, and mint—than the white pods. Cardamom follows only saffron and vanilla among spices in expense, but a little goes a long way.

Black cardamom, also called brown cardamom, is not a true cardamom. It has larger, darker pods, a smoky, nut-like flavor, and a more pronounced camphor odor. Black pods are a staple of African cooking, but are rarely used among the Jews of India or in Middle Eastern cooking. However, these wild and cultivated relatives of cardamom are sometimes used to adulterate ground forms of the real thing. Green and white pods can usually be substituted for each other, but never black ones.

Cardamom is an essential spice not only in Southeast Asia, but also in the Middle East, North Africa, and Scandinavia. Indians add whole pods to stews, vegetable dishes, puddings, and rice dishes, and use ground cardamom in curries and confections. In Scandinavia, ground white pods are used to flavor baked goods. In the Middle East, cardamom provides flavor in fruit compotes, pilafs, rice puddings, and a coffee drink called *gahwa*, and sometimes it is brewed in tea. Iraqis add it to numerous dishes, including an apple compote for Rosh Hashanah and cookies called *hadgi badah*. Many Middle Eastern spice mixtures contain this spice, including the Turkish *baharat*, Ethiopian *berbere*, Libyan *bzar*, Moroccan *ras-el-hanout*, and Yemenite *hawaij*.

CARDOON

The cardoon is a relative of and possibily the ancestor of the globe artichoke. Unlike artichokes, which are prized for the flower buds, cardoons are raised for their edible succulent petioles (leafstalks), which reach two feet or more in length upon maturity. The name cardoon comes from the French *chardon* ("thistle," from the Latin *carduus,* "thistle"). This member of the thistle family grows in bunches somewhat like ridged celery, the ridges housing razor-sharp spines. The cardoon is little known in much of the world, which is a shame. It is a tasty and interesting vegetable with a long history.

The Talmud reveals that although the plant referred to as *akavit* (from *akav,* meaning "hooked" and "to be curved"), the Talmudic-era name for cardoon, was a wild vegetable, it was for human consumption. Jewish tradition relates the cardoon to the biblical *kotz* (thorn) of post-Eden, with cardoons and artichokes—and grain (bread)—exemplifying tasty plants that require preparation, and thus human creativity, to be edible.

The Greek philosopher Theophrastus (372–287 BCE) mentioned that cardoon was a great delicacy. The cardoon, imported from Sicily and North Africa, was much beloved in ancient Rome and, according to Pliny, it commanded a higher price than any other vegetable. Medieval Arabs spread cultivated cardoons and artichokes throughout North Africa and into Spain. During his visit to Egypt around 1170, Benjamin of Tudela observed that cardoons were among the vegetables used by Egyptian Jews.

Cardoons grow aggressively and a single plant can spread over an area six feet in diameter, dominating other vegetation and basically spreading like weeds. Animals will not eat them, due to their bitterness and prickles, so they were once commonly used as borders in vegetable and ornamental gardens. More than two millennia ago, someone discovered that cooking this tough, monstrous-looking plant for an extended time tenderized it, yielding an intriguing and complex bittersweet flavor reminiscent of artichoke hearts. The flavor, however, is more subtle and the texture firmer than those of artichokes.

Cardoons are a cold-weather crop; the height of their season is during the autumn and winter, and they turn very bitter and woody as the weather warms. There are two types of cardoon, growing differently depending on the cultivation practices: lunghi and gobbi. Lungi is the natural form with straight stalks. Gobbi (hunchback) has curved stalks produced by bending the plants when very young and covering them with dirt, yielding a curved, lighter-colored, more tender, and less bitter stalk. Wild cardoons and lungi have to be cooked to be edible, but some cultivated gobbi types can be enjoyed raw when young and tender.

Cardoon stalks vary greatly in flavor and texture, even within a single plant—the inner stalks are generally more tender than the outer ones, which are typically discarded. The flower heads produce an extract used as a vegetable substitute for rennet in cheese making, yielding a creamier texture and a slight tang, once important for kosher cheese.

Italians have a particular fondness for the vegetable, preparing it stewed, baked, and fried. In northern Italy, cardoon soup is claimed to keep away colds in the winter. Tunisians and Moroccans make a beloved Passover soup with a mixture of cardoons, carrots, and kohlrabi combined with crumbled matza, and use cardoons in stews to top couscous. Persians, among the world's staunchest cardoon lovers, smother the stalks in a garlicky yogurt sauce and cook it in soups.

(See also Artichoke)

CAROB

Carob, a legume, is the pod of a large evergreen shrub indigenous to the eastern Mediterranean. Carob trees take longer than most trees to bear, and only the females produce pods, but by the twelfth year a single tree can yield one hundred pounds of fruit and is capable of producing for more than a century. Each pod encases a sweet pale brown pulp and ten to twelve very hard seeds. The carob is a hardy tree, resistant to disease and insects. Thus in Jewish tradition, it represents tenacity, long-term success, delayed gratification, and fertility. After the founding of the state of Israel, the government planted carobs near many settlements to provide a source of income and fodder for animals.

Carob cultivation is quite ancient; the seeds have been found in Egyptian tombs dating from the Twelfth Dynasty (c. 1970 BCE). The ancient Egyptians used the image of a carob pod as the hieroglyph for "sweet."

Carob is never mentioned in the Bible, an absence particularly mysterious as many people believe the carob, which grows wild in Israel, may be a native of the Levant. Carob seeds dating from the Neolithic period have been found in archeological sites from Jericho and Haifa. In addition, other languages took their name for carob from the Hebrew name *charuv*. Some contend that the Hebrew name comes from carob's similarity in shape to a sword (*cherev*), while others theorize it derives from the way the fruit becomes dry (*cherev*).

Although the carob is not mentioned in the Bible, its seeds are. In the book of Exodus, they serve as a measure of weight—a shekel is said to weigh twenty *gera* (*gerot* plural). *Gerot* was later pronounced *kirat* in Arabic, which became the Greek *keration*, ultimately the source of the English measure of gemstone weight and gold purity, karat.

Although the carob was overshadowed by the fruit of other Israeli trees, especially dates and figs, and relegated to a minor status among Jews, it does play an important role in subsequent Jewish tradition, as recorded in numerous Talmudic incidents. Among Ashkenazim, carob, *bokser* in Yiddish, is the fruit most associated with the arbor holiday of Tu b'Shevat. In the days before quick transport and refrigeration, the carob's hard, dry texture made it one of the few fruits grown in the land of Israel capable of withstanding long-distance shipping without spoilage and, therefore, was available to Ashkenazim. Unfortunately, often it was too hard and dry. Carob is also traditional on the minor holiday of Lag b'Omer, purported to be the anniversary of the death of Rabbi Shimon ben

Yochai, a central figure in Jewish mysticism. Rabbi Shimon, who along with his son spent much of his career in hiding in a cave from the Roman authorities, were said to have subsisted on carob.

For millennia, carob was an important food in the Middle East consumed in pod form and, when ground and boiled with water, a source of fruit honey (*dibs kharoob* in Arabic) After the advent of sugarcane in the region, however, the importance of carob faded and it was subsequently called upon primarily in times of famine. Today, many of the world's carob pods are given to animals for fodder or found in a powder, which is substituted for cocoa powder. The tastes are not the same, although carob powder imparts a sweet flavor, brown color, and velvety texture to baked goods. It is available both raw (actually it is cooked for a short time) and roasted; the roasted type possesses more intensity. The seeds yield locust bean gum, used as a stabilizer and thickener in commercial baked goods, ice cream, and liquids. In parts of the Middle East, people enjoy fresh carob as a snack, spitting out the seeds in between chewing. *Dibs kharoob* is still used—mixed with cold water it becomes a refreshing beverage. A tasty dip for bread, *dibs wa taniha*, is made by mixing the syrup with sesame paste. The syrup is sometimes used in pastries, such as a variation of the Lebanese *sfoff* (semolina cake).

CARP

Carp refers to a number of species of large freshwater fish native to China and, in particular, to the common carp, which was cultivated there more than twenty-five hundred years ago. Because they can survive for extended periods in small crowded containers, domesticated carp could be transported throughout Asia and Europe. By the eleventh century, and perhaps as early as the seventh century, Jewish merchants conducting trade along the Silk Road had brought carp—probably several times—by way of Turkey, to southern Europe, where Ashkenazim by and large took over its cultivation.

In medieval Europe, anti-Semitism excluded Jews from the guilds and frequently from agriculture. Therefore, they were generally in the forefront of establishing new ventures and promoting new products, including carp. Ashkenazim emerged as leading pisciculturists, operating fish farms in various lakes and artificial ponds. The other leading medieval

fish farmers were monks. Carp cultivation reached Austria in the early thirteenth century and followed three decades later in southern Germany and France. Bohemia (now in the Czech Republic) and southern Germany emerged as the center of European carp cultivation with thousands of little ponds. Carp was mentioned in 1420 in *Du Fait de Cuisine* by Amiczo Chiquart, chef for the Duke of Savoy (now southeastern France), which indicated that it was used by the upper class. Today, carp remains the most widely cultivated fish in the world.

Carp also spread wildly though Europe. This large, hardy (it can withstand a wide range of temperatures and will eat almost anything), very prolific (a single female can lay up to three million eggs in one season) fish does well in brackish water, and it quickly adapted itself to different environments. Consequently, carp was relatively inexpensive and available everywhere—it could be found near almost any source of fresh water.

The carp's lean, firm, meaty flesh make it a favorite for cooking, although the many small bones do present a problem. Carp drawn from fresh water during the fall and winter (November to April) generally have a firm texture and pleasant flavor, while those taken from mucky water and during warmer temperatures tend to be softer and possess a somewhat muddy flavor.

Because of the instrumental role of Jews in spreading and breeding this European newcomer, carp became associated with Jewish cuisine. Carp emerged as the predominant Ashkenazic Sabbath fish, supplanting pike and sometimes appearing for both Sabbath dinner and lunch. The favorite Jewish method of cooking carp, probably based on the Italian *pesce in bianco* or Sephardic *jelatine di pescado*, was to poach steaks with sliced onion in water, boil down the cooking liquid, then let the cooked fish cool in the broth. Due to the large amount of gelatin in the bones, the broth would transform into aspic, creating *fish gelee* (jellied fish).

As sugar began to become less expensive in Europe in the sixteenth century, and continued to grow cheaper in the ensuing centuries, cooks began to make variations adding sugar. The first record of Jewish-style carp was in Germany in 1758 in the non-Jewish *Nieder-Sächsisches Koch-Buch* (Example Cook Book of Lower Saxony) by Marcus Looft, published in Altona and Lubeck. *Larousse Gastronomique* (1938), the compendium of French haute cuisine, included three Alsatian variations of jellied carp that had become part of the

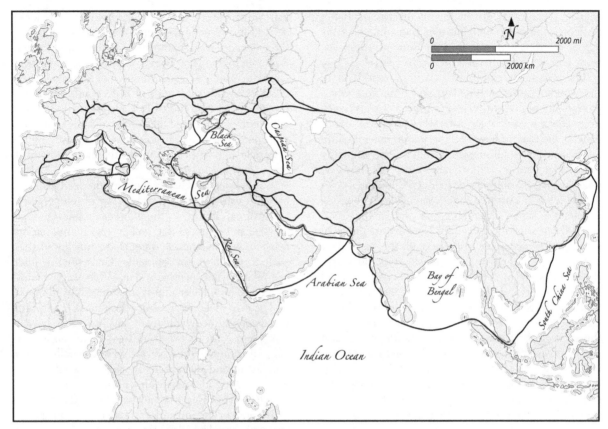

Radhanite Routes *From about 600 CE (following the fall of Rome) to 1000 (before the Crusades), Jewish merchants called Radhanites controlled the East-West trade, including the Silk Road. Among the items they introduced to Europe was carp from China, which Ash-kerazim then helped cultivate and spread.*

cooking repertoire of the non-Jews of the area: "*Carpe à la Juive au Persil*" (Jewish Carp with Green Sauce), "*Carpe à la Juive aux Raisins*" (Jewish Sweet-and-Sour Carp), and "*Carpe à la Juive à l'Orientale*" (Jewish Carp with Almonds). A similar dish made with pike is called "*Brochet à la Juive.*" Even today, Alsatians serve a version of jellied carp with sugar and raisins for Rosh Hashanah, symbolizing a sweet and fruitful year, while jellied carp with green sauce, making use of new spring herbs, is traditional at Alsatian Passover Seders.

Carp became the predominant Ashkenazic Sabbath fish in central and then eastern Europe as well. However, some Jews opted to use carp in a different form—gefilte fish. In Germany, carp replaced or joined pike as the primary ingredient of these ground fish quenelles; cooks initially stuffed the mixture into the skinned fish and baked or poached it. There also emerged versions combining the two dishes—jellied carp stuffed with gefilte fish. Since many carp were too big to cook whole, typically only individual steaks were stuffed. When housewives began cooking the chopped fish mixture as dumplings rather than in the skin, they also began using combinations of fish, especially carp in accompaniment with pike and/or whitefish. Although gefilte fish is now far and away the most well-known Jewish fish dish, actually the most widespread form of Sabbath fish among Ashkenazim before the advent of commercial gefilte fish in the mid-twentieth century was *fish gelee*, which was much easier to make and, according to many, much tastier, despite the bones.

Although Poland's Jews vanished during World War II, as in Spain, France, and other areas from which thriving Jewish communities were removed, Jewish food remained. Consequently, today, gefilte fish and jellied carp are featured in restaurants and fancy Polish hotels, while "carp Jewish-style" (*kap po zydowsku*), poached carp in fish aspic with blanched almonds and raisins, has become a traditional Christmas Eve dish in parts of the country.

Carp also became popular, although not the most important fish, among those Sephardim who moved to the Balkans and Turkey. Greek Jews prepare *sazan* (carp with greengage plums) or *peshe en salsa* (carp in walnut sauce). In Salonika, a whole carp on the table became a tradition for Rosh Hashanah. Carp roe is commonly used to make the Greek dip *taramasalata*.

Carp was only imported into the United States in 1877, and subsequently was generally disregarded in North America, except among Jews and Chinese. *"Carpe à la Juive"* was the first known Jewish recipe to appear in the *New York Times*, in an 1879 article discussing the preparation of carp, then practically unknown in America. Well into the twentieth century, many Ashkenazic families kept a live carp in cold water in the bathtub, sometimes weekly before each Sabbath, or only before Passover and Rosh Hashanah, to be transformed into jellied fish or gefilte fish. Jewish cooks customarily insisted on live carp, because the flavor greatly deteriorates the longer the fish is dead and, in addition, the changes of cold water in the tub purged any potential muddy flavor. Yet as the twentieth century progressed, jellied fish and carp in general continued to lose popularity among American Ashkenazim.

In 1983, there was a temporary panic in the weeks before Passover when high levels of the dioxin were discovered in Michigan's Lake Huron near one of America's major centers of carp raising. Gefilte fish producers were forced to quickly find alternative sources, and some worried consumers opted to avoid gefilte fish containing carp that year. Normality returned the following spring. However, American commercial brands of gefilte fish increasingly emphasized milder white fish and pike, while diminishing the traditional role of carp.

Carp was initially imported to Israel from eastern Europe in 1927, and the first experimental aquaculture farm was established seven years later south of the city of Acre. By 1939, carp farming was extensive throughout the Bet Shean Valley. By the time the state of Israel was established in 1948, farmed fish accounted for more than 70 percent of all fish consumed in the country, with carp being the predominant one.

(See also Fish, Gefilte Fish, and Taramasalata)

CARROT

The original wild carrot, a member of the Apiaceae family, was quite different from its contemporary sweet, elegant, orange descendant. This native of southern Afghanistan was originally small, fibrous, woody, and not particularly tasty, and had a purple coloring. A wild carrot still around today, called Queen Anne's lace, gives a sense of what early carrots looked like. The roots were used primarily as medicine, while the parsley-like leaves were picked as an herb, and the seeds were treated as a spice, used similarly to the seeds of its relatives—anise, caraway, coriander, and cumin. The wild carrot's belated emergence as a food crop may have been due in part to physical similarities to a relative, the poisonous hemlock.

The carrot, never mentioned in the Talmud or Midrash, was a rather late arrival to the Middle East and Jewish cookery. It was first recorded as being cultivated for its root around 600 CE in Afghanistan. Traders along the Silk Road brought seeds of the purple carrot westward, where the Persians, Arabs, Dutch, and French successively developed longer, straighter, and more succulent varieties. Horticulturists in western Asia bred out the anthocyanin pigment that gave early carrots their purple coloring. The results were yellow and whitish roots, considered preferable because they no longer colored soups and stews. The carrot's taste and texture also improved, although they were certainly not up to modern standards. Subsequently, the carrot and its close relative the parsnip were frequently confused with each other, although the parsnip was at the time more common and popular.

Yellow carrots were first recorded in Anatolia in a tenth-century Arab text and, shortly thereafter, carrots made their initial appearance in Jewish sources, in the writings of medieval Persian rabbis. The Hebrew name of the previously unknown vegetable became *gezer*, from either the Farsi *gazar* or Arabic *jazar*, reflecting the route of the root. The Moors introduced yellow carrots to Spain, where they entered Sephardic cookery. Nevertheless, carrots never became a major player in the cooking of most Sephardim and Mizrachim.

The Spanish eventually brought these new varieties to their territories in Holland, where they spread eastward. By the thirteenth century, yellow carrots were being planted in France and Germany. The now-common orange variety, colored by high levels of carotene, emerged in Holland in the sixteenth century, and was first recorded in a painting by the Flemish artist Joachim Beuckelaer. Orange carrots had already made their way to Spain by 1600, when they appeared in a painting by Juan Sanchez. This new color was particularly attractive to the Dutch ruling family, the House of Orange, then in a heated struggle for independence from Spain. The carrot's now-familiar pronounced sweetness, too, was developed in Holland at that time; the root by that time ranking second only to beets in the amount of sugar it contained. In the seventeenth through nineteenth centuries, the French developed new elongated varieties that found commercial success in western Europe and America.

Initially, carrots were a rarity and luxury item in much of Europe. However, they thrive even in poor soil and can be left in the ground or a root cellar through the winter. Therefore, around the early fifteenth century, cultivation grew widespread and carrots became a significant European food. At this time, the carrot emerged as one of the foremost vegetables in the cookery of central European Jews, a position it would shortly achieve in eastern Europe as well.

In the Middle East, carrots are added to soups, stews, pickles, and omelets. Persians add them to a sweet rice dish (*shirin polow*). Bukharans typically use it in their rice dish *palov*. Among Syrians, fat carrots are hollowed out, stuffed, and braised for holiday meals. Indians make spicy glazed carrots sweetened with raisins and bananas, as well as carrot halva. For Passover, Jews in the Balkans and Turkey sometimes add carrots to a sweet-and-sour celery dish called *apio*.

It was in northwestern Africa that carrots, both cooked and raw (*gezer chai*), became the featured component of salads, typically served as an accompaniment to couscous or offered in an assortment with other salads. Moroccans brought carrot salads to Israel in the 1940s and they quickly emerged as a ubiquitous part of the country's cookery. At many Israeli restaurants, carrot salads automatically appear on the table with the bread, pickles, and hummus. The carrots are usually flavored with *charmoula*, a Moroccan marinade of oil, lemon juice, garlic, and cumin. Most cooks add heat, sometimes in dangerous proportions, with varying amounts of chilies.

Eastern Europeans viewed raw carrots as unhealthy and only ate them cooked, reciting the benediction for vegetables only when eating a cooked carrot. Ashkenazim commonly exploited and complemented the carrot's sweetness by cooking it with honey in stews, preserves, puddings, and candy. It is also a frequent sight and flavor in soups, especially traditional golden Jewish chicken soup. German Jews adopted the Teutonic dish of carrots glazed with sugar, which eventually spread eastward to Poland. Also at that time in Germany, a soon-to-be-widespread vegetable and meat stew, tzimmes, emerged incorporating various root vegetables.

As the carrot developed into an important European crop, it also became a notable part of the Ashkenazic Rosh Hashanah tradition, supplanting the longstanding role of turnips as the standard symbolic food. The carrot's sweetness fits the theme of the holiday and slices of the yellow carrots of that time resembled gold coins, an omen of future wealth and success. The carrot also befitted the ancient Rosh Hashanah custom of eating foods with symbolic names—carrot in Yiddish is *mehren/merren*, a homonym of the Yiddish word *merin* (multiply/increase), an auspicious wish for fertility and prosperity, and the Hebrew name for carrot (*gezer*) is the same as the Hebrew word for tear, indicating that any unfavorable heavenly decrees should be torn up. A favorite Ashkenazic Rosh Hashanah dish, incorporating slices of carrot, is *mehren tzimmes*, a long way from its tough purple ancestor.

The term carrot cake made its first appearance in an American source in *The Neighborhood Cook Book* by the Council of Jewish Women (Portland, Oregon, 1912), along with a Jewish-style carrot pudding. Baked carrot puddings and cakes made with carrots became a staple of Jewish sisterhood cookbooks. Nevertheless, carrot cake caught on rather slowly in mainstream America until, in the 1960s, it was topped with a cream cheese frosting. The carrot cake's popularity increased dramatically and it became one of America's favorite treats.

(See also Pletzlach and Tzimmes)

CAULIFLOWER

The cauliflower's name, derived from the Italian *caulis floris* (cabbage flower), indicates that it evolved from a colewort, a primitive cabbage. Instead of the stalk or leaves, the prefered part of cauliflower is the mass of immature flower stalks that form its compact head. Cauliflower appeared relatively late in history; it was first recorded in Asia Minor in the twelfth century and soon found its way to Moorish Spain, where it was originally called "Syrian cabbage." It was introduced to Italy only in 1490 and to the rest of Europe in the sixteenth century. During the ensuing two centuries, cauliflower became the rage of western Europe, favored on the tables of royalty and incorporated into a wide array of dishes. Its popularity, however, waned, except in a few areas, most notably China, India, Italy, Scandinavia, and Spain. Today, cauliflower is all too often relegated to the role of a plain side dish.

Sephardim, in particular, retain a fondness for *kulupidya* ("cauliflower," from the Ladino for cabbage, *kol*), preparing it in numerous ways, including fried, pickled, drizzled with a little olive oil and lemon juice, and stewed with other vegetables; they also serve it with potatoes in cheese sauce, in stews, in *fritadas* (omelets), in *keftes* (patties), and in tomato sauce. Middle Easterners use cauliflower, variously called *zahra* and *karnabeet*, among other vegetables to make pickles called *turshi*, typically tinted yellow with turmeric or pink with beets. They also enjoy it topped with tahini (sesame seed paste). Although not historically Ashkenazic fare, except among Hungarians and Romanians, cauliflower kugels and latkes have recently gained popularity.

In Israel, cauliflower—*kruvit* in modern Hebrew, derived from *kruv* (cabbage)—has become extremely popular, particularly during the autumn and winter; it is used in an array of salads, soups, patties, and casseroles.

CELERY

Celery originated in marshy areas along the shore of the eastern Mediterranean, where uncultivated rudimentary celery, also called smallage or water parsley, can still be found. Wild celery, inedible raw, was valued primarily for its flavorful seeds and leaves. Celery seeds, possessing a warm, pungent flavor, were used medicinally for a variety of ailments, including colds, indigestion, hangovers, arthritis, gout, and liver problems. The leaves, similar in appearance to those of its relative flat-leaf parsley, were utilized as an herb, sometimes eaten raw but primarily consumed cooked.

Celery was probably first cultivated more than two thousand years ago by the Romans, but remained rather bitter and intensely flavored. Romans incorporated the leaves, stalks, or seeds in everything from appetizers to desserts, adding it profusely to nearly every salad and sauce. The familiar contemporary celery—crisp, sweet, and succulent, with overlapping stalks relatively free of strings—was developed in Italy in the late seventeenth century and barely resembles its wild ancestor. To this day, Italians still grow two types of celery: a mild one for eating fresh and a sharper one for cooking. Most American celery is the Pascal type, a bright green, crisp, sweet variety introduced in Kalamazoo, Michigan, in 1874. Pascal is sometimes grown with the stalks shielded from direct sunlight, producing a white, softer stalk.

Celeriac, also known as celery root and knob celery and called *cavessas de apio* and *apio nabo* in Ladino, is a variety of celery cultivated for its thickened edible root. Celeriac was developed in Italy from a variety of celery during the Renaissance. The ivory flesh of the knobby roots is crisp and juicy, but larger roots tend to be woody. Although celeriac is sometimes served raw, it is most often cooked and can be substituted for potatoes in mashing and, in most recipes, for cauliflower and cardoons.

Celery and parsley were commonly confused in ancient writings, as they are botanically close, to the point that their leaves are similar and their seeds are nearly indistinguishable. Early Greeks referred to both of these close relatives as *selinon*—celery was called *heleioselinon* (*selinon* of the marshes) to distinguish it from parsley, which was called *oreoselinon* (*selinon* of the mountains) or the synonym *petroselinum* (*selinon* of the rocks). Similarly, the Mishnah noted that *karpas she'baneharot* (green of the rivers), meaning wild celery, was not cultivated in Israel, while *karpas she'baharot* (green of the mountains), regarded as parsley, was a cultivated plant in Israel. Many families adopted celery (some the leaves, others the stalks) or parsley for the *karpas*, a fresh green herb eaten at the start of the Passover Seder.

In Western cooking, celery is primarily used as a flavoring component for other items, including soups, stews, stuffings, and salads. In the Middle East, celery is sometimes allowed to stand as the central ingredient; it is served stuffed, pickled, and cooked in a vinaigrette. A venerable Sephardic dish features stewed celery in a cumin-accented chickpea sauce. Persians combine the stalks with a few seasonings to create a tasty stew for topping rice. *Apio* (sweet-and-sour celery) is a popular Passover dish among Jews from Turkey and parts of the Balkans. For the meal before Yom Kippur, Italians make a version of *pinzette* (veal or chicken patties) in a celery sauce. However, because Middle Eastern celery is usually the harder, more flavorful type, it is rarely used raw in salads.

One of the world's first flavored seltzers was Dr. Brown's Cel-Ray Tonic. Infused with celery seeds and sugar, this drink is said to have been invented in 1869 by a doctor on New York's Lower East Side. This mildly sweetened carbonated beverage with an acquired tart taste became popular with New York Jews in the 1930s; it shares the nickname "Jewish champagne" with plain seltzer. Cel-Ray Tonic became ubiquitous at New York delicatessens, where it provided a better counterpoint to the heavy, briny meats than sweeter, fruit-flavored sodas. Still a common beverage in delis today, Dr. Brown's sells about one million cans a year.

(See also Apio, Karpas, Parsley, and Seder)

CHALLAH

Challah (*challot* plural) is a much-misunderstood biblical term whose meaning has changed greatly over the centuries. Most contemporary American references describe it as "a braided egg loaf." This, however, was a notion completely unknown in biblical or even Talmudic times. Even many knowledgeable sources call it "a small portion removed from bread dough to be burned," which was also not the original intent. Nor, as described in various translations, did it mean "round," "rolled," or "cake." Rather, the word challah is derived from the root *chalal* (to pierce/to be hollow), indicating something perforated or poked full of holes, similar to *chalil* (flute), *chalon* (window), and *challal* (a hollow space/hole).

Abraham Ibn Ezra noted that challah was "thick" and the commentator Rashi translated challah into Old French as *tourte*, which in his time had also developed the connotation of thick. The various breads in the ancient world were typically cooked on hot coals, griddles, or in rudimentary ovens, and thinness was essential in order for them to cook evenly all the way through. Any bread more than about a quarter of an inch or so thick required special baking techniques to allow the center to cook before the exterior burned. Thicker breads needed to be baked in spiked containers that transmitted heat into the loaves in order to properly cook them all the way through before the exterior burned. All of the biblical instances of challah indicate thickness.

The Priestly Portion

One of the three biblical references to challah pertains to the portion of bread given to a Kohain (priest, Kohanim plural): "Of the first of your kneading-troughs, you shall set apart a challah as a gift." This reference to challah was not as an offering in the Temple, but rather as one of the twenty-four perquisites of the Kohanim. Certain of these perquisites were only applicable in the Temple, while challah was given to any Kohain anywhere in the land of Israel.

It is a misconception to suppose that Kohanim went from house to house collecting chunks of raw dough or that housewives had to drop everything in the middle of baking, in those days a very strenuous and time-consuming activity, to run off and find a Kohain to which to give a piece of raw dough. Rather, the commandment involved giving a loaf of baked bread. And not just any old bread, but one baked into a loaf befitting presentation to a Kohain, a superior loaf.

The biblical obligation to give challah to the Kohanim applies only to the land of Israel when the majority of Jews are living there. After the destruction of the Temple, the Sages, in order that "the obligation of challah will not be forgotten," instituted a substitute for giving a baked loaf of bread to the Kohain. Instead, a one-ounce piece of dough, subsequently called challah, is customarily removed and burned in its place. This is called in Hebrew *hafrashat challah* (removal of challah) or in Yiddish *nemn khale*. Throughout most of history, and until relatively recently, bread making at home was relegated to women, so beginning in Talmudic times, baking bread for the Sabbath and taking the portion of challah dough became a woman's religious obligation.

There are several opinions as to the minimum amount of flour necessary in a batch of dough for removing this substitute "challah" and for making a benediction over that act. The predominant decision is: If the amount of flour weighs less than 2 pounds and 11 ounces (approximately 9⅛ cups unsifted), no challah is taken. If the flour weighs more than 2 pounds and 11 ounces, but less than 3 pounds and 11 ounces (about 12 cups unsifted), challah is taken, but without a blessing. A blessing is only recited on the removal of challah when the dough is made from at least 3 pounds and 11 ounces of flour (about 12 cups unsifted).

For the past two millennia, the term challah referred to the small portion of dough removed from each batch and burned. Only much later and initially only among some Ashkenazim did that name become attached to the Sabbath loaves themselves.

The Sabbath Loaves

Following the destruction of the Temple, the altar was symbolically replaced by the home dining table, considered a *Mikdash Ma'at* (a miniature Sanctuary), and the showbread by the Sabbath loaves. The showbread were twelve special unleavened wheat loaves—which were called challah in the Bible—that were continually on view in the Temple, arranged on a golden table located across the room from the menorah and changed every Sabbath day.

In the early medieval period, a custom developed in Babylonia of reciting the benediction of Hamotzi on the Sabbath and festivals over two loaves of bread (*lechem mishneh*), representing the double portion of manna gathered on Fridays for the Sabbath during the forty years the Israelites were in the wilderness after leaving Egypt. Some Mizrachim, Kabbalists, and Chasidim use twelve small loaves, representing the number of showbreads. Subsequently, some embellishments to the Sabbath bread became symbolic of the manna.

A tradition common to every Jewish community is to place the Sabbath loaves on a cloth or board and cover them with a cloth (*dekel* or *mapah*), usually a specially embroidered one, in recognition of the manna, which was protected by layers of dew. Ashkenazim typically slice the challahs with a knife, while most Sephardim favor breaking the bread with their hands, as a knife is also an object of violence and war and not allowed on the altar of God. In certain Sephardic communities, especially among Syrians, pieces of the Sabbath bread are tossed to the various diners, reflecting the concept that food actually comes from the Lord, not the host.

Historically, Sephardim and Mizrachim used their regular weekday loaves, (generally round flatbreads) for the Sabbath and festivals, and they had no special

name for the Sabbath bread. Since one of the most prominent symbols for the Sabbath is that of queen, it was only appropriate that the Sabbath bread would be bread fit for royalty—loaves made from white flour, the type usually reserved for the upper class. Therefore, during the early medieval period, Sephardim and Ashkenazim began to use only white flour, whenever possible, for the Sabbath loaves. This was much more of a problem for Ashkenazim, who generally did not live in areas that grew wheat, while wheat was the predominant grain in the medieval Muslim world. Some communities, however, especially many Persians, used whole-wheat flour for their Sabbath loaves. Some Sephardim and Mizrachim did make one change from their regular bread to their Sabbath loaves—they sprinkled seeds, primarily sesame, over the dough rounds, an allusion to the manna that fell in the form of coriander seeds.

Yemenites still use pita-like loaves called *salufe* and thin breads called *lahuh* for the Sabbath. Indian Jews use local flatbreads, such as *naan* or *chapatis*, traditionally baked on the sides of a tandoor, a clay oven. The Bene Israel of Mumbai add coconut milk and sugar to their *chapatis* for the Sabbath.

On the other hand, among the Ashkenazim of northern Europe, most families ate black bread—round loaves of dark rye flour or maslin—throughout the week. For the Sabbath, however, even the poorest of families would make certain to have loaves, even a very small one, made from white flour. If a family was too poor to obtain the more expensive flour themselves, the Jewish community would provide the necessary funds. Whereas Ashkenazim generally purchased their weekday breads, such as rye loaves and bagels, housewives made their Sabbath loaves at home, providing the opportunity to remove the portion of challah.

Ashkenazic Braided Loaves

Initially, Ashkenazim too had no special shape or name for their Sabbath loaves, simply using any type of white bread and calling it either the Yiddish *broyt* or Hebrew *lechem*. Then in the fifteenth century, Jews in Austria and southern Germany adopted a new form of Sabbath bread—an oval, braided loaf, modeled on a popular Teutonic bread, which was called *berchisbrod* or *perchisbrod* in southern Germany.

In honor of the winter solstice, ancient German tribes prepared special breads, some shaped in the form of animals. After adopting Christianity, many Germans continued the custom, creating new shapes. *Berchta* or *Perchta* was another name of the malevolent demon/witch *Holle*, an ugly Teutonic crone with long, matted hair. Germans twisted dough to resemble hair and offered the loaves to *Holle* to escape her punishment. Although European Jews certainly did not worship or even to a large extent know anything about *Berchta* or *Holle*, they assimilated the attractive bread. Medieval German Jews also adopted a baby-naming ceremony called *Hollekreisch*, "*Holle's* cry," in which the cradle and baby were lifted up before confirming the infant's German name.

So a braided lean loaf, suggestive of a special occasion, soon became the most popular form of Ashkenazic Sabbath bread. Braiding (*flekhtn* in Yiddish), besides adding an attractive appearance, has a practical usage, keeping bread fresh for slightly longer. Many families developed a unique braid in order to tell their loaves apart from their neighbors' at the bakery or communal oven. Three-strand braids are perhaps the most popular among home bakers, as they are rather easy and uncomplicated. Six-strand braided loaves also became commonplace, two of them together representing the twelve showbreads, as well as being a bit fancier than three- or four-strand braids. Braided loaves sometimes contain two rows of six bumps, a clear allusion to the showbread. There are also challahs with ten or twelve braids in a single loaf.

At this point, Ashkenazic Sabbath bread grew increasingly enriched and embellished. The use of oil replicated the ingredients of the breads prepared in the Temple. Eggs and, less frequently, a pinch of saffron added to the dough simulated the yellow color of cooked manna. Not coincidentally, the large amount of oil and eggs produced a softer texture and richer flavor, as well as serving to keep the loaves fresher for a longer period. A coating of egg wash imparted a glossy sheen. By the end of the fifteenth century, challah was commonly sprinkled with seeds, primarily poppy and sesame.

The original enriched Sabbath braids were not sweetened. With the spread of sugar beet–refining factories in parts of eastern Europe beginning in 1806, the price of sugar in those areas plummeted as its availability rose. Soon Ashkenazim living in sugar beet–producing regions developed a preference for sweeter

dishes and began adding sugar to their challahs, sometimes in prodigious amounts. Sweeteners are symbolic of the taste of manna, which, when pounded into cakes, tasted like honey. Many Sephardic authorities, however, disputed whether the Hamotzi (benediction over bread) could properly be recited over enriched loaves, since adding large amounts of eggs or sweetener actually transformed the finished product into a cake, like the Sephardic *bollo*. This notion was not so farfetched, for some eastern Europeans used part of the sweet egg challah dough to make babka and other yeast cakes.

A Challah by Any Other Name

The usage of the biblical word challah to colloquially refer to the Sabbath bread was first recorded in 1488 in the work *Leket Yosher* by Joseph ben Moses of Austria. He described the Sabbath loaves served by his teacher, Israel Isserlein, who was born in Regensburg, Germany, and forced to relocate to Austria. It is probable that the braided German *Holle* bread sounded like the biblical challah.

It would be more than a century before the term challah for the Sabbath breads made its way eastward to Poland and the Baltic region. Rabbi Moshe Isserles (1525–1572) of Cracow, the preeminent Ashkenazic authority of his time, in his glosses on the *Shulchan Arukh* still referred to the Sabbath loaves by the generic *lachamim*. However, by the seventeenth century, both the braided loaf (*geflokhtene khale*) and the name *khale*, as it is typically pronounced in Eastern Yiddish—challah is the early twentieth century Anglicized version—had spread eastward to become the predominant Sabbath bread in eastern Europe. Challah rolls are commonly called *bulke* and *bilke* (*bulkalach* or *bilkelekh* plural) in Eastern Yiddish. Toronto, Canada, has a unique Polish-inspired Sabbath bread called *bulke challah*, consisting of three medium or twelve smaller rolls baked together in a large rectangular loaf pan.

However, challah was far from the only name for the new Ashkenazic braided loaf. In southern Germany, it became known as *barches* or *berches*—possibly a corruption of the Yiddish word *broches* (blessing), but more likely from the German *bercht* (braid) or the name *Berchta*, sounding like *birkat* (blessing). Like most Sabbath loaves, these braided ones were made using the best available white flour. Unlike Austrian and Polish challah, German *barches* were made from a lean dough containing no oil or eggs and possessed a distinct sourdough flavor. This lean loaf also became known as *vasser challah* (water bread) in contradistinction to the richer eastern *eier challah* (egg bread).

Within a short time, the braided *barches* spread westward to Alsace and south to parts of Hungary—the braids sprinkled with poppy seeds were called *barhesz* or *szombati kalács*—to become the prevailing form and name of Sabbath bread in those areas. Today in Austria, bakeries sell braided sweetened loaves sprinkled with poppy seeds called *barches*, without being aware of the bread's Jewish heritage.

In addition to the braided loaf, some German Jews began making a lean oblong *vasser challah* with a dough strip running down its center, symbolizing the ascent to heaven. Each center strip also represented the Hebrew letter *vav*, which has a numerical value of six. Since two loaves are used at each Sabbath meal, the two loaves together equal twelve, the number of tribes of Israel as well as the number showbreads.

Several other lesser-known names emerged for the braided Sabbath loaf as well. In part of western Germany, it became known as *datsher* or *dacher*, from the verse in Proverbs "the blessings of the Lord, it *ta'ashir* [makes rich]." (In that area, *d* was sometimes substituted for *t*, as in the prayer shawl being referred to as *dallis.*)

In Lithuania and Latvia, a braided Sabbath bread or sometimes the braid on top of a regular loaf was called *kitke* (possibly meaning "weave"). Today in South Africa, where much of the original Jewish population is from Lithuania, *kitke* is the prevailing term for braided sweet egg bread, while the word challah is completely foreign. The Sabbath bread cover there is called a "*kitke* cloth." The most widespread form of *kitke* features a braided large loaf with a second smaller strand of braids arranged over top.

Ashkenazic Festival Loaves

Holiday loaves, many originating in Ukraine in the eighteenth century, possess their own special characteristics. Round thick white loaves seem to have emerged among Ashkenazim during the late medieval period when some began making breads with milk for the festival of Shavuot. To distinguish them as dairy, these loaves were formed into rounds rather than the Sabbath ovals and braids. Afterwards, cooks began making nondairy rounds for Rosh Hashanah, representing the continuity of the year and life, and other shapes, includ-

ing spirals (*faiglan*), symbolizing the ascent to heaven; crowns (*keter*), symbolizing divine majesty; and birds (*faigele*), an allusion to the verse in Isaiah, "As hovering birds, so will the Lord of hosts shield Jerusalem." Challah for Rosh Hashanah and Sukkot is traditionally kneaded with raisins or various chopped dried fruits, a symbol of sweetness and the harvest.

Ukrainian Jews developed the custom of shaping challahs for the meal before the Yom Kippur fast into images of ascension: birds, symbolizing that all sins should fly away and that our prayers soar to the heavens, or ladders, reminiscent of Jacob's dream and the ascent to heaven. The form of a hand is sometimes placed on the bread for Hoshanah Rabbah, the last day of Sukkot, connoting that the verdict of Yom Kippur is signed on that day. The hand decoration was common in Lithuanian for the meal before Yom Kippur, as it was customary to shake hands while asking forgiveness from others. A *schlissel* ("key" in Yiddish) shape became traditional for the Sabbath following Passover, the first Sabbath that the manna no longer fell. For Shavuot, a five- or seven-rung ladder was sometimes formed on the challah, because the numerical value of ladder (*sulam*) is the same as that of Sinai and symbolizes the ascent of Moses to receive the Torah.

A Polish synonym for a very large braided oval challah of more than one and a half feet is variously spelled *koyletsh, keylitsh, keylitch, koilitch,* and *koylatsh*. It is served at festive occasions, notably weddings and the Purim feast. At Polish weddings, a woman holding the *koyletsh,* sometimes with lit candles set into it, would dance (*koyletsh tanz*) solo in front of the seated bride and groom, conveying a wish that they might always have bread. In the classic 1936 Yiddish movie *Yidl mitn Fidl* (Yiddle with a Fiddle), which featured Molly Picon in her most famous role and was the first Yiddish movie to play large American theater chains, a klezmer band helps a perspective bride escape an arranged marriage with a much older rich man after her grandmother performs the *koyletsh tanz*.

Coming to America

Since most of the Ashkenazic immigrants to America in the nineteenth century came from Germany, not surprisingly they did not call their Sabbath bread challah. In the early American cookbook, *Aunt Babette's* (1889), the author, who was from a German background, provides recipes for "Butterbarches," consisting of a large braided oval topped by a smaller braided oval and sprinkled with "(mohn) poppy seed all over the top," as well as "Twisted Bread (Barches)," directing for the latter: "This is to be used with meat and made in the same manner, omitting the milk and butter; use water, and a little shortening of nice drippings or rendered suet."

It was only slightly later in America and England, as eastern European culture overwhelmed that of the Germans and Sephardim, that challah emerged as the predominant English term for the Sabbath bread. One of the first appearances of the word challah, spelled "Chollas," in English was in *Dainty Dinners and Dishes for Jewish Families* (London, 1907) by May Henry and Kate Halford. Within a decade, the spelling of the name began to formalize. An article in the *Jewish Guardian* (London, October 31, 1919) described the bread: "Challa. The twisted Sabbath loaf, [is] very often baked at home. It is of finer and whiter flour than the ordinary bread. The word has been adopted by English bakers, and the 'challas' are often seen advertised in provincial shops as 'Jews' Collars.'"

The first record of the word in America seems to be in the self-published *Glimpses of a Strange World* by Henry S. Stollnitz (Cambridge, Mass., 1908), who noted, "He spoke the prayer over the 'Chalos' (show-bread), and the repast progressed amid joy of mind, grasped the '*gefillte kishke*' (filled intestine) and thrust it into the throat of her beloved Chatskel, which process would surely have suffocated the agonized man had it not been for Esther's presence of mind quickly to pull it out again. Once more happiness reigned and Chatskel turned his voice for 'Zemiros' (the table hymns)." Although most Jewish immigrants in America continued to pronounce the word as *khale*, by the late 1920s, native English speakers had largely adopted the more biblical pronunciation and spelling of challah, challa, or hallah.

The use of challah as the name for Sabbath bread was widely adopted in Israel as well. Braided challah loaves are sold at every Israeli market, large or small, and most bakeries. The Linder bakery in the Mea Shearim section of Jerusalem, dating back to the late nineteenth century, is devoted solely to making challah; each Thursday and Friday it turns out batch after batch of golden braided egg loaves and rolls. Israeli challah tends to be less sweet than American versions, as it is eaten with an array of savory spreads.

In America, the sweet, rich egg challah or the rather redundant "challah bread," has become well-known in non-Jewish circles. It is sold at many mainstream bakeries and supermarkets. Many recipes for French toast and bread pudding call for challah as the bread of choice. Non-Jewish cookbooks and magazines offer recipes for these braided loaves; some chefs, like Julia Child, add the unorthodox milk and butter, and some even offer vegan versions. Martha Stewart published a recipe for pumpkin challah, without any butter or milk, but plenty of eggs. Today, there are even recipes for chocolate challah containing cocoa powder and chocolate chips.

Although in mainstream America, the term challah specifically denotes a braided loaf, among many Jews, the meaning subsumes any special Sabbath bread, whether braided or not.

(See also Bollo, Bread, Khboz, and Sabbath)

ASHKENAZIC EGG BREAD (*EIER CHALLAH*)

1 VERY LARGE, 2 LARGE, OR 3 MEDIUM LOAVES   [PAREVE]

> 2 packages (4½ teaspoons) active dry yeast or 1 (1-ounce) cake fresh yeast
>
> 2 cups warm water (105 to 115°F for dry yeast; 80 to 85°F for fresh yeast)
>
> About ⅔ cup sugar or honey
>
> 4 large eggs
>
> ½ cup vegetable oil
>
> 1 tablespoon table salt or 5 teaspoons kosher salt
>
> About 8 cups (2½ pounds) bread or unbleached all-purpose flour
>
> Egg wash (1 large egg beaten with 1 tablespoon water)
>
> About 3 tablespoons poppy or sesame seeds for sprinkling (optional)

1. Dissolve the yeast in ¼ cup water. Stir in 1 teaspoon sugar or honey and let stand until foamy, 5 to 10 minutes. In a large bowl, combine the yeast mixture, remaining water, remaining sugar or honey, eggs, oil, salt, and 3 cups flour. Gradually add enough of the remaining flour to make a mixture that holds together. Place on a lightly floured surface and knead until smooth and elastic, about 10 minutes. Place in an oiled large bowl and turn to coat. Cover loosely with plastic wrap or a kitchen towel and let rise in a warm, draft-free place until doubled in bulk, about 1½ hours, or in the refrigerator overnight.

2. Punch down the dough and let rest for 10 minutes. Shape the challah into three-strand braids, six-strand braids, or spirals (recipes follow). Place the shaped loaves on a greased large baking sheet or in greased loaf pans, cover with a kitchen towel, and let rise in a warm, draft-free place until doubled in bulk, about 45 minutes.

3. Preheat the oven to 350°F.

4. Brush the challah with the egg wash, being careful not to drip any onto the baking sheet, and sprinkle with the optional poppy seeds. Bake until golden brown and hollow sounding when tapped on the bottom, about 35 minutes for medium challahs and 45 minutes for large ones. Transfer to a wire rack and let cool.

Challah Shapes

THREE-STRAND BRAIDED CHALLAH

3 MEDIUM LOAVES

1 recipe Ashkenazic Egg Bread dough (page 100)

1. Divide the dough into 3 equal pieces, then divide each piece into 3 equal pieces. Roll into ropes with the middle slightly thicker than the ends.

2. Working with 3 ropes at a time, place them parallel to each other, then pinch together one end. Number the ropes from right to left #1 through #3. With the pinched side away from you, place the right-hand rope #1 over the center rope #2 and bring the left-hand rope #3 over rope #1. Bring rope #2 over rope #3. At this point, rope #1 is now on the left-hand side and rope #3 is on the right side. Bring rope #1 over rope #2, then #3 over #1.

3. Continue this pattern until reaching the ends of the ropes, then pinch the ends together to seal. Repeat in the same fashion with the remaining ropes.

SIX-STRAND BRAIDED CHALLAH

2 LARGE LOAVES

1 recipe Ashkenazic Egg Bread dough

1. Divide the dough in half, then divide each piece into 6 equal pieces. Roll into 12-inch-long ropes with the middle slightly thicker than the ends.

2. Arrange 6 of the ropes parallel to each other, numbering the ropes from left to right #1 through #6. Starting from the right side, place the ends of the ropes on top of each other, then pinch to seal.

3. With the pinched side away from you, move #1 on the far left over the other pieces to be on the far right side, perpendicular to the others, then move #6 from the far right over the other pieces to be on the far left

side, perpendicular to the others. Now bring #1 over to be in the middle of the central four ropes between #3 and #4.

4. Bring #2 to the far right to be perpendicular to the others, then bring #6 from the far left down the middle between #1 and #4.

5. Continue in this pattern of alternately bringing what had previously been the far right rope to the other side, then bringing the far left-hand rope into the middle. Upon reaching the ends of the rope, place one on top of the others and press to seal. Repeat in the same fashion with the remaining ropes.

SPIRAL CHALLAHS (*FAIGLAN*)

3 MEDIUM LOAVES

1 recipe Ashkenazic Egg Bread dough

1. Divide the dough into 3 equal pieces. Roll each piece into a 3-inch-thick rope with one end tapered.

2. Place the thicker end in the center of a greased baking sheet and coil the dough around it in a spiral fashion, tucking the tapered end into the center or under the bottom. Repeat in the same fashion with the remaining ropes.

CHAMBALIYA

Chambaliya is a medieval honey cake.

Origin: Italy

Other names: *dolce di miele; torta di miele.*

The fall of Rome and advent of the Dark Ages led to a dramatic decline in European agriculture and food. Medieval European baked goods were crude, heavy concoctions, typically made from bread crumbs. Later even with the addition of flour, most traditional Italian honey cakes remained more of a confection, like the *panforte*. On Purim, Italian Jews eat this cake, which is drizzled with syrup in the Middle Eastern manner.

CHAMETZ

The word *chametz*, which can serve as a noun or as an adjective, derives from *chamas* (to do violence/oppress). Some people mistakenly translate *chametz* as "soured," partially because it is related to the word for vinegar (*chometz*), which is neither the source nor intent of the word. In addition, *chametz*—although frequently mistranslated as "leavened bread," "fermented," "fermentation," and "yeast"—means none of these things.

According to Maimonides, there are three positive biblical commandments and five prohibitions applicable on Passover if you are Jewish. The three positive commandments are to dispose of all *seor* (inedible starter dough) on the fourteenth day of the month of Nisan, to eat matza on the first night of Passover (the fifteenth), and to relate the events of the Exodus from Egypt on the first night of Passover.

The five Biblical prohibitions are not to eat *chametz* from noon on the fourteenth day of Nisan, not to eat *chametz* all seven days of Passover (eight outside Israel), not to eat food mixtures containing *chametz* throughout the seven days of Passover, not to own *chametz* or *seor* during Passover, and not to have *chametz* or *seor* found in your possession during Passover. In addition, the Bible forbade the presence of *chametz* on the altar of the Temple. Entirely unique about *chametz* is that it is the only substance prohibited for a limited time span—the seven days of Passover.

The Talmud makes clear that only five particular grains and their subvarieties, collectively known as the *Chamesha Minim* (Five Species), are capable of becoming *chametz* when exposed to water, as well as being appropriate to use for making matza. The Five Species are *chittim, se'orim, kusmin, shippon,* and *shibbolet shi'al,* which probably refer, respectively, to naked wheat varieties (the husks are loosely attached to the seed), including durum and bread wheat, six-rowed barley, emmer, einkorn, and two-rowed barley. According to the Talmud, any similar physical processes in grains other than the Five Species, such as "rice and millet," are the result of *sirachon* (decay/rotting). In any case, the wheat and barley families definitely share a special and unique attribute that enables them, unlike other grains, to become *chametz.*

Chametz is the result of enzymatic activity. Certain enzymes specialize in breaking down starch in the presence of water into complex sugars and simple sugars; this process is called degradation. Only degraded grain items, *chametz,* are prohibited by the Bible during Passover. The Bible does not prohibit plain yeast (yeast is necessary to make wine), other leavening agents (such as baking soda and baking powder), or other grains (besides the Five Species). *Seor* (starter dough) is prohibited.

Although all leavened bread is *chametz,* not all *chametz* is leavened bread. Pasta, generally a simple mixture of durum wheat and water, is neither leavened nor fermented, but is definitely *chametz.* So is beer. Pointedly, degradation occurs whether yeast is present or not (as does *chimutz*) and, thus *chametz* is neither equivalent to nor dependent on yeast or fermentation. Consequently, kosher wine and hard cheese, both created by fermentation (wine from yeast and cheese from bacteria and not from grain degradation), are permissible on Passover, as is a matza meal cake containing baking soda or kosher-for-Passover baking powder (both forms of leavening).

(See also Kitniyot, Matza, Passover, and Seor)

CHARD

Chard, a member of the Chenopodiaceae (goosefoot) family, is so closely related and linked to the beet, both being subspecies of the same plant, that they share the same name in ancient Aramaic (*silka*). The English word chard derives from the French name for cardoon (*carde*), to which it is not related. To distinguish it from cardoons, in the nineteenth century, some people took to calling it Swiss chard, although it is neither native to nor popular in Switzerland. Unlike the beet, chard never developed a large edible root, so its culinary usage remains limited to its leaves.

Chard grows best in coastal areas with plentiful rainfall and it is in those countries around the Mediterranean where this plant is primarily used. It tolerates both heat and cold, and was historically among the few greens available in winter, as the leaves grow back after trimming. Chard served as a replacement for spinach during the heat of the summer when many greens turn exceedingly bitter and go to seed.

The large, crinkled chard leaves range in color from dark green to red; the stalks are white or red. Some plants have striking vivid red stems running like veins through bright green leaves. Young leaves can be used raw in salads. Older leaves are used like spinach and the tougher stalks are cooked like asparagus and celery or pureed. The stems are usually detached and cooked separately. Unlike collard and other tough greens, chard cooks quickly, yet can be simmered for a long time without falling apart like most greens do.

Chard is popular in France, Italy, Syria, the Maghreb, and Israel. In Israel, it is more widely available fresh than spinach, which is not commonly grown commercially there. Chard is generally prepared simply and rounded out by a basic olive oil dressing. It is also added to lentils and stews, used as a filling for pastry or pasta, or stuffed like grape leaves. Italians add chard to winter lentil and white bean soups and, along with chicken meatballs, to their *hammin* (Sabbath stew). Syrians use it in pancakes, omelets, dips, and stews. Turks stuff it (*pazi sarmasi*) as well as add it to a casserole with mashed potatoes, feta, and kashkaval cheese. Kurds enjoy chard in a variety of soups with *kubbeh* (dumplings), including *chamutzta*, a sour green soup, and *marak kubbeh adom*, a red soup with chard, beets, tomato paste, and paprika, which are traditional Friday night dishes.

Chard is a traditional Rosh Hashanah food, as its Aramaic name *silka* is similar to the Aramaic word for "to remove/disappear," as in *sheyistalek oyvenu* (may our enemies be removed). Thus for Rosh Hashanah dinner, Sephardim from Turkey might serve *keftes de silka* (chard patties), while Syrian meals would typically feature chard with meat.

CHAROSET

Charoset is a fruit mixture used at the Passover Seder for dipping *maror* (bitter herbs). The charoset also accompanies the bitter herbs, along with matza, in the *koraik* (Hillel sandwich).

Interestingly, most of the early rabbinic sources in all Jewish communities also required the *karpas* (the first dipping of the Seder) be immersed into charoset, and Maimonides instructed that all ritual foods of the Seder, including the matza, be dipped into it. Many Yemenites, who generally follow Maimonides, maintain the custom of dipping the *karpas* into charoset. On the other hand, today Ashkenazim and most Sephardim dip the *karpas* into salt water or wine vinegar, reserving charoset exclusively for the bitter herbs.

Charoset, already in widespread use by the time of the Mishnah (c. 200 CE), is unquestionably the most flavorful and arguably everyone's favorite of the Seder foods. The institution of charoset, as with much of the Seder not mandated by the Bible, derived from Greco-Roman practices two thousand years ago. Attendees at the Seder were expected, for that evening, to emulate the practices of nobility and free people and, at the table of the Roman elite, greens were always accompanied with a dressing or condiment. The emergence of charoset was also probably influenced by the fruit relishes served at the Roman symposium, although the ingredients of the original charoset were based upon Middle Eastern produce. In effect, the use of charoset has the same effect as the customs of dipping the *karpas* at the onset of the

Seder and reclining during the Seder—these practices are all intended to produce an overall sense of affluence, aristocracy, and atypicality for the Seder. The Talmudic discussion emphasizes that the more symbolism we can impart to the charoset (and other items), the richer the experience will be. Thus the Sages constructed (and deconstructed) charoset, instilling it with a multitude of symbolic meanings, to help convey the Egyptian experience and create a special atmosphere and enriched ceremony for the participants of the Seder.

The Talmud presented three different outlooks on the symbolism of charoset: "Rabbi Levi said: In memory of the *tapuchim* [a fruit tree]. Rabbi Yochanan said: In memory of the *tit* [mud]. Abaye observed [combining the two]: Therefore one must *l'kahavyhu* [make it acrid] and thicken it: make it acrid in memory of the *tapuchim* and thicken it in memory of the *cheres* [clay]."

The opinion of Rabbi Yochanan that the origins of charoset lay in Nile mud is the most obvious one, reflected in its very name, derived from the later preferred term *cheres*. According to this view, charoset, like the bitter herbs dipped into it, serves as a reminder of the slavery and oppression of Egypt and the mud the Israelites used to make bricks. Mashed dried fruits, particularly dates, evoke this symbolic meaning, as they resemble mud. The more obscure assertion of Rabbi Levi—"in memory of the *tapuachim*"—refers to Songs of Songs: "Under the *tapuach* I raised you up [awakened you], there your mother was in travail with you, there she was in travail and gave birth to you." Tradition explains that the Israelite women in Egypt would give birth in *tapuach* orchards, away from prying eyes, so that the Egyptians would be unable to discover that a male was born; this pratice served to perpetuate the Israelites. In Kabbalah, a *tapuach* orchard is frequently pictured as a symbol of the divine presence. Thus *tapuchim* denotes hope and redemption even in the muck and mire of extreme oppression and suffering. The symbolism of *tapuchim* is the reason for using various fresh fruits and acidic elements in charoset.

Exactly which tree is the *tapuach* and which fruit should be used in the charoset are matters of contention. The word *tapuach*, from the root *napach* ("to exhale/exude," i.e., a sweet scent), was not mentioned in the Pentateuch, but the fruit it names was certainly an important Israeli crop by the end of the

First Temple period more than twenty-five hundred years ago. As its name and other citations indicate, the fruit has a pronounced fragrance. In addition, the Talmud directed that the charoset "be acidic/acrid in memory of the *tapuach*." Thus this fruit must have been extraordinarily fragrant, yet sharp and bitter.

In modern Hebrew as well as in many Talmudic references, *tapuach* has the meaning of "apple," a fruit that was perhaps native to the Caucasus region. Many authorities, however, believe that the biblical *tapuach* was in fact a different fruit, for in the biblical period apples only grew wild and they were not easily cultivated in tropical areas like Israel and Egypt. The apple is also neither fragrant nor acrid.

A clue to the *tapuach*'s identity may come from a biblical mention in Proverbs of "golden *tapuchim*," indicating a yellowish tint. One candidate that meets all the qualifications for the *tapuach* is the quince, a relative of apples and pears that was already cultivated in biblical times and called *chavushim* in the Talmud. As it matures, the quince's greenish skin turns a dark yellow color and the fruit, shaped like an elongated apple, develops an intense musky aroma. The quince's fragrance is highly regarded and the quince and the etrog (citron) are the only fruits that require a special blessing to be recited over their aroma. Thus some Mizrachim, especially Kurds, and Sephardim incorporate raw quince (peeled, cored, and grated) into their charoset.

Other authorities consider the biblical *tapuach* to be a citrus fruit, which is certainly acidic. The orange has been proposed for this role. Indeed, some Sephardic versions of charoset contain a chopped raw orange (including the peel). However, although the original orange, a native of India, was exceedingly acidic like the contemporary bitter orange, this plant probably only first reached the land of Israel during medieval times.

The Targum (Aramaic translation) of Song of Songs renders *tapuach* as the other notably fragrant fruit—the etrog. Similarly, the Talmud, in its exposition of the biblical passage "like the smell of the field which the Lord has blessed," notes that the reference is to a field of "*tapuchim*"; Tosafot, in its commentary on the Talmud, contends that the smell was that of the etrog. Consequently, some Sephardim use an etrog (or the grated rind of an etrog soaked overnight) in their charoset.

The Sages did not direct that charoset actually contain any *tapuach*, just as there is no instruction to include actual mud, only that it have an acidic component in memory of the *tapuach*, which in many communities was fulfilled by adding a little wine vinegar or pomegranate juice. In this vein, the Jerusalem Talmud notes "charoset [with the addition of a red liquid] also serves as a reminder of the blood in Egypt." This does not mean that charoset should be pungent. As the Talmud notes, "A person must not keep the bitter herbs [an extended time] in the charoset lest the sweetness of its ingredients neutralize the bitterness [of the *maror*]." The tart ingredient is intended to be only a minor component of the charoset, with sweet fruit constituting the bulk of the relish.

In addition, the custom arose of incorporating various produce besides the *tapuach* mentioned in Song of Songs—dates, figs, pomegranates, and nuts. The most common nuts are among the few mentioned in the Bible, almonds and walnuts. Most Italians and some Sephardim and Mizrachim apply both verses from the Song of Songs and use both dried biblical fruits, such as dates, figs, and raisins, and fresh fruits, particularly apples and quinces.

The Talmud's final touch to charoset is the addition of long-shaped spices "as a remembrance of the straw" with which the Israelites made mud bricks in Egypt. In Temple times, in the days preceding Passover, street peddlers could be heard throughout Jerusalem calling out, "Come and get your spices for the commandment" (of charoset). In the Roman period, these spices, primarily ginger brought by traders from the Orient and *Kinamon* (see Cinnamon) from Israel, were often freshly chopped. Many Yemenites uniquely call charoset by the name *doukeh* or *dukah*, from the instructions in the Jerusalem Talmud: "Why is it called *doukeh*, because *docheh iman* ["grinds with them" spices]."

The basis for the charoset of Mizrachim and Sephardim, and most certainly for the earliest versions from Talmudic times, was dates, either boiled into a honey (*devash*) or crushed. On a symbolic level, the palm is a metaphor for a lofty stature and the righteous. The reddish brown color of the date honey serves to emphasize its connection to mud. In those areas not conducive to date production, dried figs and raisins provided an acceptable alternative or addition.

The first known charoset recipe, which was included in the *siddur* (prayer book) of Saadia Gaon (882–942 CE), head of the academy of Sura in Babylonia, instructs, "Make a moist sauce from dates, walnuts, and sesame [the spice] and knead it in red wine vinegar [the acidic element], and that is called *halek.*" Note the absence of apples or any fresh fruit. Saadia also used the term *halek/haleq*, a still common central Asian synonym for charoset, which is purportedly the name of a type of walnut added to the date honey to transform it into charoset. Iraqis, many Syrians, and Baghdadis of India still refer to charoset as *halek.*

Charoset from Crete by at least the eighteenth century, was zesty, consisting of mashed raisins, ground almonds, wine vinegar, black pepper, and sometimes a little ground brick, the latter based on a misreading of Rabbi Samuel ben Meir (Rashbam); the use of actual brick was greatly disapproved of by rabbinic authorities.

Rabbi Eleazar ben Judah (c. 1165–1230) of Worms, France, in *Sefer ha-Rokeach*, reflecting an Ashkenazic position shortly after the disasters of the First Crusade, instructed, "Charoset is made from *tapuchim*, into which is added a little of the fruits from Song of Songs—walnuts, figs, and pomegranates—and pepper, ginger, cumin, horseradish [yes, in charoset for pungency and as a spice; it was not yet used as *maror*], and black radish." Today, the basic Ashkenazic charoset recipe, consisting of apples, honey, wine, cinnamon, and walnuts or almonds, is virtually identical in communities from Alsace to the Ukraine. For many generations, charoset was traditionally made in a wooden bowl using a *hackmesser/mezzaluna* (half-moon chopper).

Until relatively recently, in much of northern Europe, even apples could be sparse, especially in the springtime, not to mention grape wine and imported spices. Thus in numerous eastern European communities, many individuals could not make their own charoset. Rather, the local wine merchant, vintner, distiller, or one of the wealthiest members of the community made a large batch of charoset with whatever apples and other ingredients could be obtained and doled out small portions to the townsfolk.

(See also Date and Honey)

AFGHAN CHAROSET

ABOUT 6 CUPS [PAREVE]

½ cup almonds
½ cup walnuts
½ cup dried apricots
½ cup dried figs
½ cup raisins
1 pomegranate, peeled and seeded
1 medium apple, peeled, cored, and chopped
1 medium ripe banana, peeled
1 medium pear, peeled, cored, and chopped
1 cup strawberries, hulled
1 cup fruity dry red wine
2 tablespoons fresh lemon juice
About 1 tablespoon red wine vinegar
About 1½ teaspoons ground cinnamon
About ½ teaspoon ground ginger
About ½ teaspoon ground black pepper

1. Place the almonds, walnuts, apricots, figs, and raisins in a large bowl. Cover with cold water, and let soak for at least 2 hours. Drain.

2. Place the pomegranate seeds in a food processor fitted with a metal blade and pulse several times. Add the soaked ingredients, apple, banana, pear, and strawberries and process into a paste. Blend in the wine. Add the lemon juice, vinegar, cinnamon, ginger, and pepper, adjusting the seasoning to taste.

ASHKENAZIC CHAROSET

ABOUT 4 CUPS [PAREVE]

3 medium apples, cored and chopped
½ to 1 cup chopped almonds or walnuts
About 2 tablespoons honey
About 1 teaspoon ground cinnamon, or 1 (3-inch) cinnamon stick, shaved or slivered
¼ teaspoon ground ginger (optional)
About ¼ cup sweet red wine or grape juice

In a medium bowl, combine the apples, nuts, honey, cinnamon, and, if using, ginger. Stir in enough wine to make a paste that holds together.

CURAÇAO CHAROSET (*GAROZA*)

ABOUT 6 CUPS/36 BALLS [PAREVE]

3¼ cups (1 pound) unsalted peanuts
1 cup unsalted cashews
¾ cup dried figs, stems removed
¾ cup pitted dried plums

¾ cup dark raisins
⅔ cup pitted dates or candied fruit
1 cup dark brown sugar
¼ cup honey
About 3 tablespoons sweet red wine
2 tablespoons orange juice
1 tablespoon fresh lime or lemon juice
About 2 tablespoons ground cinnamon

In a food processor or meat grinder, grind the peanuts, cashews, figs, plums, raisins, and dates. Mix in the sugar, honey, wine, and juices. Using wet hands, shape into 1-inch balls. Roll in the cinnamon to coat. Arrange in a single layer and cover with plastic wrap.

GEORGIAN *HALEK*

ABOUT 8 CUPS [PAREVE]

¼ cup whole cloves
¼ cup boiling water
¼ cup almonds
¼ cup hazelnuts
¼ cup walnuts
4 medium apples, cored and finely chopped
4 medium pears, cored and finely chopped
About ⅓ cup honey

1. Place the cloves in a small bowl, pour in the boiling water, and let stand for 15 minutes. Strain, reserving the liquid.

2. In a food processor, nut grinder, or meat grinder, grind the almonds, hazelnuts, and walnuts until smooth.

3. In a medium bowl, combine the nuts, clove water, apples, pears, and honey.

ISRAELI CHAROSET

ABOUT 5 CUPS [PAREVE]

2 medium apples, peeled, cored, and grated
2 medium bananas, mashed
14 pitted dates, chopped
⅓ cup blanched almonds, ground
¼ cup matza meal
Juice and zest of ½ lemon
Juice and zest of ½ orange
1 teaspoon ground cinnamon
Sugar or honey to taste
¼ cup sweet red wine

In a medium bowl, combine all the ingredients, adding enough wine to make a paste.

ITALIAN CHESTNUT CHAROSET

ABOUT 7 CUPS [PAREVE]

Only the chestnuts are cooked in this version, but there are other versions from Padua in which all the ingredients are cooked, and still others from Veneto in which chestnut puree is substituted for the whole chestnuts.

1¼ cups (6 ounces) dried chestnuts
2 medium apples, or 1 apple and 1 pear, cored and peeled
1¼ cups pitted dates
1¼ cups dried figs or pitted dried plums
1 cup raisins
1 cup blanched almonds, finely chopped
About 1 teaspoon ground cinnamon
About 3 tablespoons orange juice
About 3 tablespoons fruity dry red wine

1. Place the chestnuts in a medium saucepan and add water to cover. Bring to a boil, reduce the heat to low, and simmer until tender, about 1½ hours. Drain and pat dry.

2. In a food processor or meat grinder, chop the chestnuts, apples, dates, figs, and raisins. Mix in the almonds, cinnamon, orange juice, and wine.

PERSIAN CHAROSET

ABOUT 5 CUPS [PAREVE]

½ to 1 teaspoon ground cinnamon
¼ to ½ teaspoon ground ginger or 1 to 2 teaspoons grated fresh ginger
¼ teaspoon ground cardamom or to taste
¼ teaspoon ground coriander or to taste
⅛ teaspoon ground cloves or to taste
⅔ cup pomegranate juice
2 medium apples, or 1 medium apple and 1 medium pear, cored and grated
1 cup pitted dates, ground
½ to 1 cup raisins
½ cup ground almonds
½ cup ground pistachios
½ cup ground walnuts
Juice and zest of ½ lemon, or 2 tablespoons red wine or cider vinegar
About ⅔ cup sweet red wine

In a medium bowl, combine the cinnamon, ginger, cardamom, coriander, and cloves, then stir in the pomegranate juice to dissolve the spices. Mix in the remaining ingredients.

SEPHARDIC CHAROSET

ABOUT 4 CUPS   [PAREVE]

  1 pound (2⅔ cups) pitted dates
  About 1¼ cups water
  ½ to 1 cup chopped almonds or walnuts, or ½ cup
    each
  ½ to 1 teaspoon ground cinnamon
  About 3 tablespoons fruity dry red wine

1. Place the dates in a medium saucepan and add water to cover. Let soak for at least 2 hours.

2. Bring to a boil, reduce the heat to low, and simmer, stirring frequently with a wooden spoon, until soft and thick, about 40 minutes. Let cool. The date syrup can be prepared ahead and stored in the refrigerator for up to 1 month.

3. Stir in the nuts, cinnamon, and enough wine to make a paste.

SURINAM CHAROSET

ABOUT 10 CUPS   [PAREVE]

  3¼ cups (8 ounces) unsweetened grated coconut
  2 cups ground almonds or walnuts
  2⅔ cups dried apples, coarsely chopped
  1⅓ cups dried apricots, coarsely chopped
  2 cups dried pears, coarsely chopped
  1⅓ cups dried plums, coarsely chopped
  1½ cups raisins
  ¼ cup sugar
  2 to 3 teaspoons ground cinnamon
  1 to 2 teaspoons grated fresh ginger (optional)
  About 3 cups water
  ½ cup cherry preserves
  About ⅔ cup sweet red wine

In a large, heavy pot, combine the coconut, nuts, apples, apricots, pears, plums, raisins, sugar, cinnamon, and, if using, ginger. Add the water to cover. Bring to a boil, reduce the heat to medium-low, and simmer, stirring frequently and adding more water if necessary, until the coconut and fruits soften and the mixture thickens, about 1½ hours. Stir in the preserves. Let cool for about 15 minutes, then stir in the wine to moisten. Let cool completely. The mixture should be moist, so if it looks dry, stir in a little additional wine.

YEMENITE CHAROSET (*DOUKEH*)

ABOUT 10 CUPS   [PAREVE]

  1¾ cups sesame seeds

  3 cups pitted dates, chopped
  3 cups raisins, chopped
  1 cup almonds, chopped
  1 cup walnuts, chopped
  4 teaspoons ground cinnamon
  ½ teaspoon ground cardamom
  ½ teaspoon ground cloves
  ½ teaspoon ground ginger
  ½ teaspoon salt
  Water

1. In a dry, large, heavy skillet, stir the sesame seeds over medium heat until lightly browned. Remove from the skillet and let cool.

2. In a large saucepan, combine all the ingredients and enough water to make a mixture that resembles preserves. Simmer over medium-low heat, stirring frequently, until the mixture thickens, about 15 minutes. Let cool.

CHEESE

According to legend, a Middle Eastern herdsman nearly six thousand years ago stored some milk in a sack made from a calf's or lamb's stomach, waterproof animal organs then providing the best portable containers for liquid, only to discover later that the milk had separated. Sampling the coagulated curds, which we now call cheese, he realized that it was not only tasty but longer lasting than the very perishable milk from which it was made. By 2000 BCE, fresh cheese was a common food throughout the area as demonstrated by the discovery in Middle Eastern digs of numerous small cheese molds replete with holes for draining the whey. In the Bible, as soon as David is crowned king of Israel, his father, Jesse, sends him to bring food to his brothers fighting in the army against the Philistines, and also directs him to give their commander a gift of ten cheeses (called *charitzei ha'chalav,* "cuttings of the milk"). Later the Romans discovered that cooking the milk to produce curds, pressing the curds, soaking the cheese in salt, and aging it for several months produced hard cheeses with a much longer shelf life and much more diversity. Pliny the Elder (c. 77 CE) described many of the cheeses favored by Roman gourmands, including ones similar to Swiss and blue. While the basics of cheese making remain relatively unchanged from Roman times, there are now more than two thousand basic varieties around the globe.

Cheese is the solid portion of the milk of a few cloven-hoofed, cud-chewing animals separated from a liquid called whey. Goat and sheep cheeses are most prevalent in the Middle East and Mediterranean. When the Bible spoke of "a land flowing with milk and honey," it was referring to goat's milk. The amazing aspect of cheese making is how small differences—including variations in milk, amount of salt and other flavorings, temperature, pressing, and length of aging—result in major changes in flavor, color, texture, and aroma. Raw milk from the cheese-producing animals differs little in taste and color, yet the cheeses made from their milk come in a wide range of flavors, colors, and aromas. Goat's milk cheese has a more piquant flavor and a whiter color than cow's milk cheese. Sheep's milk cheese is also white but carries a distinctly sharp flavor.

Curd cheeses (fresh cheeses)—including cottage, ricotta, and chèvre—have a high moisture content and are unripened or only slightly ripened, resulting in a soft texture and a mild, sometimes slightly acidic flavor. The younger the cheese, the less flavor it has. An array of fresh cheeses were originally made from sour milk or buttermilk, which contained sufficient lactic acid bacteria to coagulate the curds, in a process that remains widespread in Europe. The curds are then heated, drained, and salted. Middle Easterners eventually learned how to acidify fresh milk by adding a little lemon juice, vinegar, or rennet; the acid in the lemon juice or vinegar yielded a softer, more fragile texture than rennet. Today, a bacterial culture is usually added to fresh milk to convert the lactose into lactic acid, equalizing the pH level, and then either a rennet or an acid is added to coagulate the milk, separating the curds from the whey. Kosher cooks could not use animal-based rennet from nonkosher sources and, therefore, historically relied on acid until a practical vegetable-based rennet was developed.

Fresh cheese can be eaten immediately and only lasts for a rather short time. Salt is usually added, not only for flavor but also as a preservative. Soaking or boiling a drained soft cheese, such as feta, in salt brine, stops the ripening process, which allows for longer storage as well as a saltier flavor. Hard cheeses are pressed into molds and left to ripen by microorganisms; the range of possibilities is much greater for these than for fresh cheeses.

Around the time of the destruction of the Second Temple, due to the expansion of the types of cheeses available and their role, the Sanhedrin enacted a law against eating non-Jewish cheese (*gevinat akum*) to prevent people from eating various unkosher ingredients (i.e., animal-based rennet, enzymes, and milk) and perhaps also to create a social barrier. A disagreement exists as to whether supervision (occasional visits) or constant participation of a *mashgiach* is necessary to permit *gevinat akum* to be considered kosher. Most kosher supervising agencies are strict in regard to hard cheeses, but lenient with soft cheeses. Consequently, most kosher hard cheeses today are made by small Jewish companies (typically renting the facilities of a large producer), while soft cheeses, such as cottage cheese and cream cheese, are widely available from large manufacturers with kosher certification. It is also the reason why today Israelis can enjoy a wide range of kosher native hard cheeses, while the selection in America is generally quite limited.

Sephardim, Italians, and other Mediterranean Jews have long enjoyed both fresh and hard cheeses variously made from cow's, sheep's, and goat's milk. For millennia, many Mediterranean and Asian housewives weekly made their own soft, white, fresh cheese, called *keso blanco* by Sephardim and *jiben beida* in Arabic, the most common type used in cooking. In the Roman manner, the curds were frequently placed in a breadbasket to drain. Typically, cheese was made once or twice a week; it was a part of most meals and, when lightly salted, it lasted for a few days.

The variety of cheeses in the generally mountainous Balkans of the Ottoman Empire—Greece, Romania, Bulgaria, and Slovakia—was more expansive than in eastern Europe. These cheeses were made mostly from goat's milk and sometimes from sheep's milk. The intense flavor of goat cheese marries well with many other Middle Eastern favorites, especially eggplant, olives, tomatoes, and bell peppers, and makes it a perfect complement to bread, as well as an important ingredient in vegetable dishes and pastry fillings.

Jiben halloum in Arabic, or *halloumi* in Greek, is a white, mild, semihard sheep's milk cheese (or a mixture of sheep's and goat's milk), made by boiling the pressed curd and then brining it, resulting in a layered and somewhat rubbery, chewy texture; it is firmer and milder than feta. *Halloumi* has a high melting point and, therefore, is frequently used for frying and grilling.

The Romanian kashkaval, based on the Italian caciocavallo, a Provolone type cheese is made from sheep's milk or a combination of sheep and cow's milk. When aged for two to three months, kashkaval is mild with a slightly nutty flavor and used for the table; more mature cheeses, with the color of straw, are stronger and used for grating and may be substituted for Parmesan. It is known as kasseri in Greece and kaser in Turkey.

In 1840, Meir Arzoni, a jeweler from Persia, moved to the city of Safed (north of the Sea of Galilee), Israel, three years after a major earthquake devastated the town and its Jewish population. Unable to practice his trade in his new location, Arzoni turned to producing kosher cheese made from sheep's and goat's milk from local shepherds. His venture was successful and Arzoni established Israel's first commercial dairy, Hameiri. More than a century and a half and six generations later, the original four-story factory shop and former family home are still operating, and still family owned. The signature cheese of the Hameiri Dairy is Safed cheese (*gevinat Tzfatit*). Among the few native Israeli cheeses, it is a white semisoft cheese formed in a round block with distinctive ridges derived from encasing in salt aging in large wicker breadbaskets. Young Safed cheese is soft, smooth, and lightly flavored, but as it ages, the texture hardens to that of a grating cheese.

In the 1930s, nearly a century after Meir Arzoni opened his cheese factory, the Israeli agricultural cooperative Tnuva (Hebrew for "produce"), which had been founded in 1929 to represent kibbutzim and *moshavim*, expanded to include dairy products. It became and it remains the country's largest producer of dairy products and cheese. Most Israeli cheeses were divided into three basic types: *gevina levana* (white cheese), *gevina tzehuba* ("yellow cheese," including various mild-flavored hard and semisoft cheeses), and *gevina melucha* ("salty cheese," meaning feta types). Today Israel has more than seventy large and boutique dairies producing an increasing variety of cheeses.

Historically, all the Jewish cheeses in northeastern Europe were the curd type, almost always made from cow's milk. On the other hand, Ashkenazim in Romania and parts of Ukraine also had various soft and hard goat's and sheep's cheeses; these were frequently brined and the most notable were *brinza/bryndza* (a creamy, less salty type of feta) and kashkaval.

For centuries, many eastern European meals consisted solely of potatoes or black bread and curd cheese. Ashkenazim, many of whom owned their own cow or goat for homemade cheese and sour cream, ate curd cheese on a regular basis. It was commonly mixed with chopped cucumbers and radishes, mixed into noodles, and used as a filling for various pastries, including kreplach, blintzes, knishes, and strudels. The original Hanukkah latke was made from curd cheese. In a more elaborate dish, curd cheese was sweetened, fruit was sometimes added, and then the mixture was baked. In Romania, Galicia, and the Ukraine, curd cheese was frequently added to or layered with *mamaliga* (cornmeal mush) for dairy meals.

A grainy European version of dry curd made from cow's milk is variously called pot cheese (from the Dutch *pot kees*), baker's cheese, and hoop cheese; it is similar to dry-curd cottage cheese, except that not all the whey is pressed out. Farmer cheese can be a synonym of pot cheese or, typical of the Jewish style, refer to pot cheese with a little cream added. The American cottage cheese, first recorded in 1848, is usually made by adding a bacterial culture to cow's milk to produce lactic acid, which coagulates the protein, separating the curds and whey.

Ricotta (Italian for "cooked again") is a creamy, fine-grained curd cheese produced from the whey that results as a by-product of making cheese, especially mozzarella. The whey is heated, then mixed with acid to curdle the remaining protein. Ricotta is sweeter, grainer, and has a finer curd than cottage cheese. The ricotta is also pressed, salted, and dried, resulting in a hard white cheese called ricotta salata. Some authorities believe that ricotta originated among the Jews of Rome or Sicily, but in any case, Sicilian Jews were long prominent in ricotta production; much of it was exported to mainland Italy, until they were expelled by the Spanish in 1493.

(See also Brinza, Feta, Gevina Levana, Labaneh, and Panir)

CHEESE, CREAM

In 1872, William A. Lawrence, a dairyman from Chester, New York (in Monroe County), attempted to make a batch of Neufchâtel, a soft, fresh cow's milk cheese from France. Instead, by adding too much heavy cream, he accidentally created an even richer, silkier cheese, which he called "cream cheese." Any citations of "cream cheese" in books before that time referred to heavy cream strained through muslin, then left to dry for several days. Today's cream cheese is a fresh cheese with a mild flavor and a slight tang. Most brands, and those best for cheesecakes, contain emulsifiers to enhance the firmness and lengthen shelf life.

Other dairies in Upstate New York soon began manufacturing their own cream cheese. In 1880, C. D. Reynolds purchased the Empire Cheese Company in South Edmeston, New York, a new village near Chester, and launched production of cream cheese under the brand name Philadelphia. Some say the name came from Philadelphia, New York, a tiny town near the St. Lawrence River, while others contend the name came from the Pennsylvanian city, known for the high-quality of its produce. To protect the fresh cheese, Reynolds began to package his cream cheese in tin foil wrappers. In 1902, Philadelphia was acquired by the Phoenix Cheese Company, which in turn merged with the Kraft Cheese Company in 1928.

Meanwhile in 1907, the Breakstone Brothers (originally Isaac and Joseph Bregstein of Panemune, Lithuania) began manufacturing cream cheese in a small plant in Brooklyn. Then in 1920, they opened a larger facility in Downsville, New York, and began mass marketing cream cheese. Breakstone was purchased by National Dairy Products in 1928, which in turn merged with Kraft in 1930.

Cream cheese, known as *schmear kaez in* Yiddish, early on became popular among New York's Jews, who began schmearing it on bagels and, since it was kosher for Passover, matza. The combo of bagels and cream cheese would eventually conquer mainstream America as well. In the 1930s, central and eastern European Jews in New York City substituted cream cheese and sour cream for curd cheese, creating the Jewish cheesecake, also called New York cheesecake. Cream cheese was also incorporated into central European Jewish pastries, such as rugelach, in place of *quark* and *topfen*. In the early 1960s, cream cheese emerged as the preferred frosting for carrot cake, transforming this dessert's status from practically unknown to an American favorite.

CHEESECAKE

Cheesecake is a thick, baked custard made with soft cheese, usually with a bottom crust.

Origin: Ancient Greece, New York City
Other names: Austria: *topfenkuchen*; German: *kaesekuchen*; Hebrew: *oogat gevina*; Hungarian: *túrós pile*; Italian: *torta al formaggio*; Latin: *placenta*; Romanian: *placinta*; Russian and Ukranian: *Yatrushka*; Yiddish: *gomolkhes kaesekuchen*.

Cheesecake is basically a thick, baked (and sometimes unbaked) cheese custard, usually with a bottom crust, and sometimes with a crust that comes partway or all the way up the sides.

By the fourth century BCE, Greeks were preparing several types of griddle cakes incorporating curd cheese, flour, and sometimes honey. Subsequently, Romans made cheesecakes that were cooked on a griddle and some types that were baked in a crust.

In late medieval Italy, cakes were made from curd cheese, milk, eggs, sugar, butter, and ginger. From the onset, medieval cheesecakes were actually more of a cheese tart, with a crust providing a sturdy base and baking container for the soft custardy filling. Cheese-filled pastry, called *fluden*, was widespread among Franco-German Jews by at least 1000 CE, and eventually it became popular in Germany and eastern Europe, with the filling becoming deeper and the top crust omitted. Cheesecake, made from curd cheese, became a popular Ashkenazic dessert, leading to the Yiddish expression, *"Mit shney ken men nit makhn gomolkes"* (From snow you can't make cheesecakes).

In the mid-nineteenth century, immigrants brought the German *kaesekuchen* (cheese cake) to America.

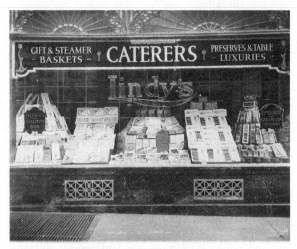

Lindy's helped make New York cheesecake famous.

Reflecting the nineteenth century German and Jewish styles of cheesecake, the original edition of *The Settlement Cook Book* (1901) contained four versions of cheese kuchen, all made from cottage cheese, calling for pastry or kuchen pastry as the crust.

Until the early twentieth century, cheesecakes had a somewhat coarse, heavy texture. This would change due to a new product, cream cheese, created in 1872. In the 1930s, Jews in New York City substituted cream cheese and sour cream for the curd cheese, creating the Jewish or New York cheesecake, which soon became ubiquitous in New York delis and America's favorite type of cheesecake. Originally, New York cheesecake was made with a pastry crust, akin to that of the medieval versions. Soon a simpler crust made from crushed zwieback became popular. By the late 1930s, crushed zwieback was supplanted by another American innovation, graham cracker crumbs.

In the 1943 revision of *The Settlement Cook Book*, one of the cheese pies included a "Graham Cracker Shell," although all the fillings still called for cottage cheese. In the 1965 revision, three of the cheese cakes used cottage cheese and one was "Cream Cheese Cake."

Among those claiming credit for the creation of New York cheesecake was Arnold Reuben (1883–1970), a German Jewish immigrant who became the owner of a succession of Manhattan restaurants. In 1928, he opened Reuben's Restaurant and Delicatessen on East 58th Street. In 1942, he launched the Turf restaurant in the Brill Building (a longtime center of American songwriting) at Broadway and 49th Street. Reuben recounted how, after sampling a cheese pie at a dinner party in 1929, he asked the hostess for the recipe and proceeded to play with the ingredients, substituting cream cheese for the cottage cheese. If this story is true, Reuben is truly a major contributor to gastronomy, as he is also credited with creating the famous Reuben sandwich, consisting of sour rye bread (or pumpernickel) spread with Russian dressing and topped with sauerkraut and slices of corned beef and Swiss cheese, then grilled on both sides.

When Reuben's cheesecake was served in the 1940s to a high-profile clientele at the Turf restaurant, it earned such high praise it was copied by other restaurants. New York bakers began experimenting with cream cheese in their cheesecakes and found that it produced the creamiest texture and a slightly piquant flavor.

If Reuben created the New York cheesecake, Lindy's Restaurant put it in the limelight. In August 1921, eight years after Leo "Lindy" Lindemann arrived in Manhattan from Berlin, Germany, he and his wife, Clara, opened a deli on Broadway near 50th Street in Manhattan, the heart of the Theater District. Lindy's featured standard, kosher-style Ashkenazic fare, including super-sized sandwiches, blintzes, gefilte fish, and especially their creamy cheesecake, topped with strawberries in a gel. Rumor claims that Lindy hired Reuben's baker, thereby, procuring the famous recipe, although the two cakes were not identical. Damon Runyon frequented Lindy's and incorporated it into some of his stories, renaming Lindy's "Mindy's." In 1950, when Runyon's short story "The Idyll of Miss Sarah Brown" was transformed by Frank Loesser, Abe Burrows, and Jo Swerling into the musical *Guys and Dolls*, Lindy's cheesecake was immortalized in the scene where Nathan Detroit attempts to entice Sky Masterson to wager on whether Mindy's sold more cheesecake or apple strudel on a single day.

In 1949, Charles W. Lubin (1903–1988), a Jewish baker from Chicago, left a small baking business owned with his brother-in-law and founded his own company, named after his then eight-year-old daughter, Sara Lee. His first product was a Jewish-style cheesecake, sold fresh to local supermarkets. Five years later, after discovering a way to quick-freeze his product, the company went national, as did the concept of New York cheesecake.

A genuine New York cheesecake is firm, yet so sensually creamy that it melts in the mouth; it has a slightly tangy flavor derived from cream cheese, lemon juice, sour cream, and vanilla. The basis of a classic creamy cheesecake is cream cheese. Cheesecake is a traditional Ashkenazic dessert for Shavuot and Hanukkah and a favorite comfort food.

(See also Pite)

❧ NEW YORK CHEESECAKE

ONE 9-INCH CAKE   [DAIRY]

Crust:

1½ cups (ounces) graham cracker crumbs

3 tablespoons granulated or packed brown sugar

6 tablespoons (¾ stick) unsalted butter, melted

Cake:

24 ounces (3 cups) cream cheese, softened

1½ cups sugar

2 cups sour cream

About 2 tablespoons fresh lemon juice

2 teaspoons vanilla extract

¼ teaspoon salt

4 large eggs

1. To make the crust: In a medium bowl, combine the crumbs and sugar. Stir in the butter. Press onto the bottom of a 9-inch springform pan. Chill while preparing the filling.

2. Preheat the oven to 325°F. Wrap the outside of the springform pan with heavy-duty foil. Place a large pan of water on the bottom shelf of the oven and pour in 1 inch boiling water.

3. To make the cake: In a large bowl, beat the cream cheese until smooth. Gradually beat in the sugar. Blend in the sour cream, lemon juice, vanilla, and salt. Beat in the eggs.

4. Pour into the prepared pan. Set in the water bath. Bake until the cake is firm around the edges (2 inches in the center will jiggle slightly, but will firm during cooling) and lightly browned, or until an instant-read thermometer inserted into the center registers about 150°F, about 1½ hours. Run a sharp, thin knife around the outside of the cake to loosen from the pan.

5. Turn off the oven, open the door, and let cool in the oven for 30 minutes. Immediately move to the refrigerator and let cool uncovered. Cover with plastic wrap or an inverted bowl and chill overnight or for up to 4 days. Or freeze for up to 2 months. Let stand at room temperature for at least 30 minutes before serving.

CHEILEV (FORBIDDEN FAT)

1. The blood and certain fats of kosher animals are forbidden for consumption by Jews.

2. Their function and what they represent are significant.

3. Blood is the immediate and constant provider of nutrients, while fat is stored energy.

4. Blood represents life and fat represents luxury.

5. Blood is the present and fat is potential for the future. Blood is movement and action, while fat is indolence and complacency. Blood (red) is associated with sin and *cheilev* (white) with purity and forgiveness. These two extremes of an animal's body were both given as an offering on the great altar in the outer courtyard of the Temple, and they still play a major role today in the Jewish dietary laws. All kosher meat must be soaked and salted in order to extract the forbidden blood and all *cheilev* must be removed.

The Bible directs, "It is an eternal statute for your generations in all your dwelling places; you may not consume any *cheilev* [forbidden fat/suet] or any blood." Later the text adds, "All *cheilev* of ox and sheep and goat [although the front and the rest of the rear of the animal is kosher] you shall not eat. And the *cheilev* of *neveilah* [a carcass not properly slaughtered] and *cheilev* of *treifa* [torn/mangled] may be used for any other purpose; but you must surely not eat it. For anyone who eats *cheilev* from the beast [cows, sheep, and goats] that is offered from it as a fire-offering to the Lord, the soul that eats it shall be cut off from his people. And all blood you shall not eat, in all your dwellings, of fowl or beast. Anyone who eats any blood, that soul shall be cut off from his people."

The upshot is that *cheilev* of any cow, sheep, or goat is prohibited from consumption. The word *cheilev* does not mean fat in the generic sense, because that would effectively forbid the eating of nearly every part of a cow, sheep, or goat, as the meat is marbled with fat and impossible to disentangle. In addition, the Bible neither forbade all fat nor all the animal parts offered on the altar, but specifically proscribed only *cheilev*. Permitted fat is called *shuman*. (A major issue between the rabbis and Karaites was whether the tail fat of sheep, an important culinary element in the Middle East, was included in the category of *cheilev*—rabbinic authorities permitted its consumption.)

Cheilev, suet in English, refers to certain adipose tissue. The Talmud defined the biblical references as *cheilev ha-mecasheh et ha-kerev* (the layer of fat that stretches over the abdomen), *cheilev asher al ha-kerev* (fat draped over compartments of the stomach and part of the intestines), *shtei ha-calayot v'et hacheilev asher allayhem asher al ha-kesaleem* (fat connected to the kidneys and over the loins), and *yoteret al ha-kavaid* (fat adjoining the liver and diaphragm, and fat separating the heart and lungs from the rear digestive system).

The Talmud also explained how to differentiate *shuman* from *cheilev*. *Cheilev* are fats that are not intertwined with the meat of the animal but peel away as a solid layer. Nachmanides expanded on the differences: "The nature of *shuman* found in the ribs, sides, and tail, which is not separate from the meat, is warm and moist, while the fat which can be separated from the meat, such as that which is on the kidneys, is cold and moist, thick and coarse."

The prohibition against consuming *cheilev* applies only to a trio of domesticated ruminants which could be an offering in the Temple—cows, sheep, and goats. All other kosher animals, including deer and birds, are not subject to this taboo. The status of buffalo and bison is uncertain, and, therefore, requires the removal of *cheilev*.

Only the ingestion of *cheilev* is forbidden. It can be used for other purposes. In many cultures, suet, which is not the same as lard (rendered pork fat), was a prized resource. Suet is solid at room temperature and below seventy degrees. The fat is usually rendered by melting, then it is strained, which removes impurities and allows it to be stored without refrigeration for an extended period. Suet is used for frying various foods and incorporated into many dishes, imparting a richness unobtainable from other sources. It is also used to make tallow for candles, soap, and lubricants. The first product to receive rabbinical supervision was a precedent-setting pareve soap without suet created by Israel Rokeach in Kovno, Lithuania, in 1870.

Suet was especially important in English cookery, where it was integral to many traditional recipes, including steamed pudding, stuffing, mincemeat, and various pastries. In baked goods, the tiny pockets of suet melt and steam, providing a flaky or fluffy texture, depending on the type of dough, and a resonant taste. In the modern fast-food industry, suet was commonly used for deep-frying, especially for potatoes and doughnuts. Thus of all the fat of a cow, suet was the most flavorful and useful and, therefore, the most valuable.

For traditional Jews, however, even a trace of *cheilev* in food was unacceptable and all of it had to be carefully removed from the meat and organs. The process of extricating the forbidden fats, as well as the large arteries and veins, where blood coagulates after slaughter, and the forbidden sciatic nerve (a process called *nikkur* in Hebrew and *treibor* in Yiddish), which is primarily located in the hindquarter of an animal, is extremely complicated and time-consuming. There is a little *cheilev* in the front section, located on the diaphragm, liver, and the ribs closest to the hindquarter, which must also be removed. Following the Black Death (about 1350 to 1550), a decline in farming and increase in cattle raising in western and central Europe led to an unprecedented meat surplus. As a result, Ashkenazim stopped

consuming the rear portion of these animals. However, Sephardim and Mizarchim had less access to meat and thought the efforts were worthwhile and continued to permit the rear cuts.

CHELOW/POLOW
Chelow is rice cooked by a special two-part method. First it is parboiled and then steamed for an extended period.
Origin: Persia
Other names: *chelou.*

Rice probably first reached Persia and was cultivated in the plains of the Caspian area in the fourth century BCE; the highest-quality rice in the country still comes from that region in what is now Iran. Rice, called *berenj* in Farsi from the Sanskrit *vrjana* (enclosed settlement/community), did not make an immediate impact on the Persians. Eventually, however, it became the country's favorite grain. Persians created special cooking methods for rice and numerous rice dishes. They incorporated it into stews, soups, casseroles, stuffed vegetables, and puddings. Rice was ground into a flour used to make various cookies and confections. Simple cooked rice is called *kateh* and this dish was most prominent in northern Iran. Much more important and intricate is *chelow*, a dish served at all important occasions.

Chelow, which might be a word of Indian origin, was first mentioned in the fourteenth century, and the dish was subsequently refined and expanded over the centuries. Before cooking, the rice is carefully inspected to remove any grit and small particles. It is washed in lukewarm water in a large bowl or pot, stirred gently with the hand, then drained. The washing is repeated about five more times, until the water remains clear. The rice is then soaked in cold water to cover for at least two hours or overnight. After draining, the kernels are parboiled in plenty of water over medium heat for about ten minutes, then drained and rinsed again. Saffron or turmeric is sometimes used to tint the rice a bright yellow, the color of good fortune. Finally, the partially cooked rice is steamed in a covered pot until it is tender and the bottom forms a golden and crisp crust known as a *tahdiq/tah-dig* (literally "bottom of the pan"), the favorite part of the dish for many Persians. When the rice is ready, a cloud of steam emerges when the lid is lifted.

Rinsing the rice before and after parboiling removes any surface starch, which means that each grain remains whole and separate after cooking. In addition, well-washed rice emits a pronounced fragrance during cooking. Soaking and parboiling in plenty of water infuses the rice with moisture; this is necessary for the final step of steaming, which is done without any additional water, and ensures that each kernel will turn out firm, long, succulent, and fluffy. The quality of the rice and particularly the *tahdiq* is a sign of any Persian cook's ability. Every aspect of the dish—the quality, length, and age of the rice; the amount of soaking and steaming time; the fluffiness, separateness, and color of the finished rice; and the crispness and golden color of the crust (it should never be burned or dark brown)—is a matter considered and judged.

Plain *chelow* is usually served in three ways: with a *khoresh* (stew-like gravy) in a dish referred to as *chelow-khoresh*; with kebabs in *chelow-kebab*, which is considered the Iranian national dish; or with a stew, such as *fesenjan* (chicken with pomegranates and walnuts). *Chelow* is typically accompanied with the ubiquitous *turshi* (pickles) and, for a vegetarian version, with *mast* (yogurt) on the side.

Besides serving plain *chelow* with various stews, Persians synthesized it with the Indian *pulavu* (pilau). This variation of *chelow* was first recorded in Persian texts in the sixteenth century, reflecting the culinary advances of the new Safavid Dynasty. In the dish called *polow*, rice is cooked using the same method used for *chelow*, but the rice is layered or mixed with various ingredients and then steamed. During steaming, the added ingredients, including precooked meat and vegetables as well as spices, impart flavor and sometimes color into the rice. Some cooks add herbs or tiny green peas, producing a green tint. The number of variations of *polow* is limited only by the imagination. The more types of *polow* a cook masters, the higher her or his standing.

The preferred types of rice for making *chelow* in Persian cooking are a long-grain variety called *domsiah* (black-tailed), which comes from a rather low-yielding plant, and two lesser varieties, *sadri* and *champa*. *Domsiah* rice grains more than double in length during cooking. In Israel, brands labeled "Persian rice" are commonplace, but in America, basmati makes an acceptable substitute, although the taste and aroma are somewhat different.

Persians feature plain *chelow* or a *polow* (usually three or more types of *polow*) on all special occasions,

including the Passover Seder. Carrot and chicken *polows* are traditionally offered on Rosh Hashanah; the carrots are frequently cut into round slices to resemble coins, which represent prosperity. *Shirin polow* (sweet rice), also called *morasah polow* (jeweled rice), is usually served at weddings. *Sabzi polow* (rice with herbs) is another popular version featured at most occasions. The rice is typically mounded on a large tray and topped with various garnishes and the *tahdiq*, although this treasured element is sometimes offered on its own platter.

(See also Pilau, Plov, Rice, and Tachin)

PERSIAN CRUSTY RICE (*CHELOW*)

6 TO 8 SERVINGS [PAREVE OR DAIRY]

3 cups long-grain rice, such as *domsiah* or basmati
8 cups water
2 tablespoons table salt or ¼ cup kosher salt

Crust (*Tahdiq*):
¼ cup vegetable oil or clarified butter
¼ teaspoon ground turmeric or pinch of (about 20) saffron strands
2 tablespoons water
½ teaspoon ground white pepper (optional)

1. Wash the rice in lukewarm water several times, then soak in cold water to cover for at least 2 hours or overnight. Drain, rinse under cold running water, and drain again.

2. In a large pot, bring the 8 cups water and salt to a boil over medium heat. Add the rice and cook, uncovered, stirring occasionally to prevent sticking, until barely cooked at the core, 7 to 10 minutes. Drain, gently rinse under cold running water, and drain again.

3. To make the crust: In a large, heavy saucepan, heat 2 tablespoons oil over high heat. Stir in the turmeric, water, and, if using, pepper. Spoon the rice over top.

4. Using the handle of a wooden spoon, poke 7 deep scattered holes into the rice. Drizzle with the remaining 2 tablespoons oil.

5. Place a kitchen towel or several layers of paper towels over the top of the pan. Cover tightly with the lid and cook over medium heat until steam appears, about 10 minutes. Reduce the heat to low and simmer until the rice is tender and the bottom is crisp, about 30 minutes.

6. For easier removal of the crust, place the pot in a sink filled with 2 inches cold water and let stand for

10 minutes. Other people prefer to line the bottom of the pot with aluminum foil.

7. Be careful. A cloud of steam will be released when you lift the lid. Run a spatula around the sides of the pot to loosen the rice. Gently stir the rice to fluff. Invert onto a large serving platter. Break the *tahdiq* into large pieces and scatter over the top.

CHERMOULA

Chermoula is a relish with a base of parsley or cilantro used as a marinade for fish and chicken, and as a sauce and dip.

Origin: Morocco, Algeria, Tunisia

Other names: *charmoula, sharmoula, shermula.*

Chermoula is a versatile staple of North African kitchens and a relatively inexpensive way to add plenty of flavor to food. *Chermoula* is commonly added to tagines near the end of cooking to brighten the flavors. All variations contain a basic four ingredients: parsley and/or cilantro, olive oil, lemon juice, and garlic. The Jews of Fez sometimes substitute wine vinegar, an ingredient forbidding to their Moslem neighbors, for the lemon juice. Various versions include assorted spices, chilies, and shallots. Most are finely chopped, with a texture similar to that of Italian pesto, but some are smoother and formed into an emulsion. Although *chermoula* was originally pounded in a mortar, most cooks today use a blender or food processor. Moroccan Jews enjoy it for weekday fare and on holidays, such as Rosh Hashanah and Passover. *Chermoula* has become very popular in Israel.

✣ MOROCCAN PARSLEY-LEMON CONDIMENT (*CHERMOULA*)

ABOUT 2 CUPS   [PAREVE]

1 generous cup finely chopped fresh flat-leaf Italian parsley, or 1 large bunch parsley and 1 large bunch cilantro

6 to 8 cloves garlic, minced

2 teaspoons finely grated lemon zest

1 cup extra-virgin olive oil

⅔ cup fresh lemon juice

1 tablespoon sweet paprika

About 1½ teaspoons ground cumin, or 2 teaspoons cumin seeds, toasted and ground

About 1½ teaspoons table salt or 1 tablespoon kosher salt

About 1½ teaspoons ground coriander (optional)

1 to 2 small red chilies, 1 teaspoon harissa (Northwest African Chili Paste, page 260), or a pinch of cayenne (optional)

Using a mortar and pestle, food processor, or blender, process all the ingredients to form a coarse paste. Chermoula is best fresh. To store, drizzle a thin layer of olive oil over the top of the chermoula to stop the discoloration, and store in the refrigerator for up to 3 days.

CHERRY

Cherry pits have been discovered in prehistoric sites in western Asia, yet there are no references to this fruit in ancient literature. The cherry, a member of the Rosaceae family, is not mentioned in the Bible or Talmud, although its modern Hebrew name, *duvdevan*, which is of unknown entomology, is used in the Mishnah for a bunch of grapes. Some contend that the cherry tree originated in Asia Minor near the Black Sea. The Greeks and later the Romans, purportedly in 72 or 79 BCE, brought the cultivated cherry westward from the northeastern Turkish port of Kerasous (modern Giresun), the source of its Greek name, *kerasion*, which became *cerasum* in Latin and cherry in English. In Europe, the fruit was grown from Iberia to the Baltic States, becoming a favorite fruit in any place it arrived.

There are two principle types of domesticated cherries, which do not cross-pollinate with each other: sweet cherries and sour cherries (Morello). Sweet cherries are primarily eaten fresh, while sour cherries, which are smaller and paler, are most often used in cooking, baking, and liqueurs. Different varieties of sour cherries range in color from yellow to bright red to dark purple. But cherries are a fragile fruit, with most varieties too delicate for shipping, so only a few varieties show up in the market.

Cherries are part of the cuisine of nearly every Jewish community. Persians use cherries in rice dishes and various sweets. Persians also grind the soft, bitter interior of the pit of the mahlab cherry to make a spice called mahlab. Syrians find cherries complementary to meat dishes, including meatballs and lamb roasts. Cherries are also popular in Europe and used in jams, soups, sauces, strudels, cakes, and liqueurs. The French serve cherries with duckling and other poultry and in desserts. Italians (for *crostata*), Sephardim (for *inchusa*), and Georgians (for *kada*) use the fruit to fill double-crusted tarts.

In Alsace, sour cherries are used to make the well-known cherry brandy called kirsch. In eastern Europe, they are macerated with sugar and vodka for *vishniak*. Since cherries make their appearance in early summer, which means that every so often they arrive in time for Shavuot, cherry dishes became traditional for that holiday, including cherry soup, compote, preserves, blintzes, kreplach (filled pasta), coffee cakes, and strudel.

The cherry may have only reached Israel during the Crusader period and it then disappeared toward the end of the Mamluk period. It was later reintroduced with the growth of Israeli agriculture in the early twentieth century primarily in the mountainous regions of the Golan and the Judean Hills. Today, many Israelis in cooler areas also plant cherries trees in their gardens. The annual early-summer surplus inspires many cooks.

(See also Mahlab and Vishniak)

CHESTNUT

Chestnut varieties are native to temperate regions of northern Europe, Asia, and America. Of the ten species of chestnut, it is primarily the sweet chestnut, also called the European chestnut and Spanish chestnut, that has served as a staple European food for at least three thousand years; the tree can live up to five hundred years.

Chestnuts grow in burs (casings with fine spines) that contain one to seven nuts and split open when ripe. The creamy yellowish or beige nuts are covered with a bitter, dark reddish brown pellicle (skin) and encased in a hard brown shell. The variety that produces only one large chestnut per bur, called *marrone* in Italian and *marron* in French, yields nuts with a high sugar content that are vastly superior to nuts from varieties that produce several nuts per bur. The latter nuts are typically dried and ground into chestnut flour, which, since at least the time of the ancient Romans, has been used to make breads and sweets.

Chestnut shells—along with wild date seeds, pine nuts, and walnuts—have been found in one of the earliest sites of human activity, the Shanidar Cave of northern Iraq. The Greeks brought the chestnut to Europe from Asia Minor. The English word chestnut derives from the Greek *kastanea*, possibly itself from an old Farsi word *kasutah* (dry fruit). The chestnut tree is not native to the Levant, nor does it grow well in Israel or Syria, and, therefore, it is not mentioned in the Bible or Talmud. The modern Hebrew name for chestnut, *armon*, is the result of a misidentification of it as the biblical "plane tree" (*armon* meaning "naked"), which denoted the oriental plane tree. This confusion may be based on the similarity of the Hebrew *armon* to the French *marron*. Consequently, chestnuts are absent from most Middle Eastern cuisines, except that of northern Iran. Rather, it is in the Caucasus and southern Europe that the chestnut initially entered Jewish cooking and remains important to this day.

When cooked and husked, chestnuts are the sweetest of all nuts. Although today chestnuts are generally regarded as a luxury item, for much of European history they served as poor person's food and were boiled, roasted, or ground into flour. This role only changed in the eighteenth century with the spread of the potato. Chestnuts remain a favorite ingredient in Italian, French, and central European cooking, where they are added to vegetables or used in desserts. Whole cooked chestnuts are often paired with Brussels sprouts and red cabbage. Cooked and chopped, they are added to poultry stuffings and rice pilafs. Pureed, they are used for soups or a garnish, and sweetened to make puddings. Hungarian chestnut puree (*gesztenyepure*), less sweet than those from Italy and France, is served as a rich dessert accompanied with sweetened whipped cream. It is also used as a spread for toast or crepes, beaten with butter, eggs, chocolate, and rum for a cake filling (*gesztenyetorte*), and stirred into hot milk or cocoa. Turks and Bukharans cook chestnuts in a lamb stew. The French soak them in a sugar syrup to produce a translucent confection called marrons glacés. Many versions of charoset in northern Italy are based on chestnuts.

Chestnuts are also available dried. As with dried fruit, dried chestnuts are sweeter than fresh. Dried chestnuts are ground to make a sweet golden flour used in breads, pastas, and desserts.

CHICKEN

The numerous varieties of chickens (males a year or older are called roosters and females are called hens), the world's most populous bird, are all descended from the Southeast Asian red jungle fowl, a bird with a patchwork of reddish, brown, and black feathers that was domesticated more than forty-five hundred years

A depiction of a rooster on the sixth century BCE onyx seal of Jaazaniah (right; the impression of the seal is on the left). It is among the earliest representations of a chicken.

ago in India. A major reason for the chicken's early domestication and subsequent dissemination was that it is a less skillful flyer than any other small bird—it is able to fly for no longer than thirteen seconds—rendering it relatively easy to catch and keep corralled. The fact that the hen can lay eggs on a daily basis for many years also contributed to its desirability. The chicken's move westward was slow. The birds may have arrived in Ur in Sumeria by 2100 BCE (the Third Dynasty), but seem to have taken another millennia to travel much farther west. The Persians, in particular, spread this bird throughout their empire and introduced it to the Greeks. Aristophanes, in his play The Birds (414 BCE), called the chicken "the Median [Persian] bird," indicating the area from which the Greeks had somewhat recently been introduced to it. Chicken bones found in Egypt only date to the Greek period, when the chicken came into widespread usage.

The reason for the chicken's initial sudden popularity about twenty-five hundred years ago and its successive spread throughout the Persian, Greek, and Roman empires had little to do with the tastiness or utility of its flesh or its prolific egg laying, but rather with the aggressive rooster's ability to fight. Cockfighting was among man's earliest entertainments and forms of gambling. Jewish law forbade the practice of cockfighting, not to mention gambling, and the practice never caught on among Jews. In many cultures of the ancient world, especially Rome, chickens were also used for auguries and sacrifices in temples and

in folk medicine. Few people in ancient times ate chicken, unless it had lost in the cockfight or the hen had passed its egg-laying days.

The first depiction of the chicken in Israel was a seventh century BCE red jasper seal with the inscription "Jehoahaz, son of the king" above the image of a rooster. This motif occurred again on a small round seal stamped with the Hebrew for "Jaazaniah, the Servant of the King" and decorated with the image of a rooster in fighting stance. The artifact, found at Tel Mizpah (8 miles north of Jerusalem, near Ramallah), probably dates from the time of Gedaliah, who in 586 BCE, after the destruction of Jerusalem, was appointed governor of Judah by the Babylonians and, according to the biblical account, made his capital at Mizpah (a name meaning "lookout/watchtower"), along with an officer named Jaazaniah. The images were most certainly intended to emphasize his ferocity. (Chickens did not become associated with cowardice until much later.) This does not mean that the domestic chicken had actually reached Israel at this point, just that important officials inscribed their seals with it. It is also possible that for many centuries roosters had been in Israel and Egypt, but only as an exotic showcase indulgence of monarchs; they may have been sent as a diplomatic gift from a Mesopotamian king, but they were certainly not widespread among the populace. Chickens only became prevalent in Israel around the second century BCE; they were subsequently called in Hebrew *tarnegol,* from the Sumerian *tarlugal/darlugallu* (king's bird).

The Romans, though, loved the taste of chicken and, of course, its fighting ability, and introduced it throughout their domains, where it very gradually supplanted the pigeon. During the Roman period, chicken emerged as a prominent feature of Jewish cooking, the Talmud considering it "the choicest of birds." (This is one of the many disagreements with the Karaites, who hold that chickens and their eggs are not kosher.) In the Talmud, the chicken egg (beitzah), which is larger and more useful in cooking that of the less prolific pigeon, is referred to as a basic unit of volume measurement.

Nevertheless, the Sages, at the time of the Second Temple, instituted a regulation that no chickens could be raised in Jerusalem or by Kohanim, as they were quite messy and tended to wander into places they were not wanted. Throughout most of history, anyone in poultry production faced the problem that birds living in large flocks tend to contract and spread various diseases, wiping out most of or all the animals. Therefore, individual farmers tended to raise chickens in small groups of generally fifteen to thirty or, for a major producer, perhaps risk a large flock of two hundred birds. Consequently, chickens were always relatively rare and rather expensive. The French king, Henry IV, on the occasion of his coronation in 1589, famously declared, "I want there to be no peasant in my realm so poor that he will not have a chicken in his pot every Sunday." Although typical of a politician's bluster in any age, his declaration of the prevalence of chickens was a pipe dream in the sixteenth century.

Until well into the twentieth century, because of the chicken's expense and inaccessibility, many urban Europeans and Americans rarely, if ever, ate chicken. Among Sephardim and Mizrachim throughout the medieval and much of the modern periods, chicken, more expensive then beef or lamb, remained a popular but rare treat.

In Europe, chickens practically disappeared following the fall of Rome, except for their limited use in cockfighting, and only began to make a comeback with the revival of European cuisine and agronomy that followed the First Crusade. It was only in the face of a meat shortage in Europe in the fifteenth century that the widespread raising of chickens flourished, although Ashkenazim in western and central Europe favored geese and beef. A seventeenth century German rabbi wistfully noted that "chicken does not awaken the joy of the festival as does beef."

A different mentality emerged in eastern Europe in the fifteenth century, where beef and geese were always less common than in the west. Among eastern Ashkenazim, chicken served as the most important food animal and many Jewish families, urban as well as rural, kept at least a few hens, frequently along with a goose or two, in their yards or in coops. Even then, only the wealthy or those who raised chickens ate them. For much of the year, the birds fended for themselves through foraging and generally required little attention, care, or expense.

The Yiddish word for chicken, *hindel* (also *hendel*), was also a woman's name. Since most eastern Ashkenazim ate only a single species of bird, in Eastern Yiddish the generic Hebrew word for a kosher or nonkosher fowl, *oafot* (*oyfes, oyf* singular, in Yiddish),

became a narrower synonym for chicken, an application that transferred to modern Hebrew as well. Even so, for the majority of eastern Ashkenazim, chicken was a luxury reserved for the Sabbath or, for those with less access, only special occasions. The hen's primary role was laying eggs, a major source of protein or added income. Hens were generally kept until their egg-laying days had passed. In the words of author Bernard Malamud, the child of Russian Jewish immigrants who spent his childhood in Brooklyn during the Depression, "We didn't starve, but we didn't eat chicken unless we were sick, or the chicken was." The housewife would defeather, kasher, and cook the chicken in honor of the Sabbath. Experienced housewives knew that as the newly slaughtered chicken cooled, the feathers would become harder to remove, so they would begin plucking as soon as possible. However, the chicken could not be subjected to heat before it was soaked and salted to remove the blood, so the feathers could only be plucked using cold water. To kasher the chicken, the housewives soaked it in cold water for thirty minutes, covered it on all sides with kosher salt, set it to drain on an inclining surface for an hour, then washed it in cold water three times to get rid of the salt and blood.

Among Ashkenazim, no part of the bird was wasted. The feet (*hun fus*) replete with nails, along with the head, neck (*helzel*), wing tips (wings are called fliegel), and gizzards (*pupiks*), went into the soup pot with onions and some root vegetables to be transformed into a rich broth or braised with onions to make a fricassee. The fat was rendered into schmaltz; the skin was cooked to make *gribenes* (cracklings). The liver was grilled, chopped with a little schmaltz and hard-boiled eggs, and used to fill doughs to make knishes and kreplach, mixed into a kugel, or simply spread over bread and sprinkled with some grated black radish. The neck skin was filled with bread crumbs or flour (*helzel*) and roasted or cooked in the cholent (Sabbath stew). The carcass served as the main course for Sabbath or holiday meals. The feathers became stuffing for pillows, mattresses, and quilts. Under extremely desperate circumstances, which too frequently befell eastern Europena Jews after the seventeen century, even the bones were ground up, fried, and eaten.

Various communities developed chicken dishes that could slow-cook for a long time, providing a warm and flavorful meal on Friday night. Since few homes had an oven, many of these dishes were cooked in a liquid over a fire or charcoal. Hungarians prefer chicken paprikash. Some Greek and Turkish Sephardim prepare *gayina con tomat* (chicken with tomato sauce) or *gayina con vinagreta* (chicken with vinegar sauce). Syrians feature *dajaaj al riz* (chicken with rice), in which pieces of roasted chicken are buried in cooked rice for a long, slow baking, or a variation with potatoes, pasta, or eggplant. In Calcutta, the favorite for Friday night is *murgi* (chicken stew). Ethiopians frequently prepare a chicken *wot* for the Sabbath. Yemenites use chicken in a soup or stew. Persians frequently make a slow-cooked *morgh e tu pur* (chicken in the pot). Georgians have *kotmis* (pot—roasted stuffed chicken in pomegranate juice) or *chakhokhbili* (chicken fricassee), while for Sabbath lunch they enjoy *satsivi* (cold poached chicken in walnut sauce). Italians make a chicken *hamin* for Sabbath lunch.

In Jewish tradition, chickens are the epitome of procreation and prolificacy, the Talmud declaring, "Be fruitful and multiply like chickens." Consequently, they are ubiquitous at Jewish weddings. Ashkenazim traditionally serve chicken soup and roast chicken. Persians add chicken to a sweetened rice *polow*. Moroccans might offer chicken with couscous. Moroccans also feature chicken in honor of an engagement and upon entering one's new home. In Israel, chicken schnitzel and *pargiyot* (grilled deboned chicken thighs) are now common.

Toward the end of the nineteenth century, the advent of the incubator led to chickens becoming more commonplace. Still, raising chickens for meat was primarily a by-product of egg production and merely a source of economic diversity on farms or in urban households, not a pursuit unto itself. This situation dramatically changed during the twentieth century. In 1930, the U.S. Department of Agriculture developed broilers, young tender birds bred specifically for their meat. Broilers are easy and relatively inexpensive to raise and mature rapidly with little care or equipment. This new breed, along with revamped raising procedures, reduced the time required to reach market to only forty-two days. Beginning in 1956, vaccines added to chicken feed became available to prevent common poultry illnesses. This allowed producers to raise massive numbers of chickens, including three-story poultry coops, each floor housing tens of thousands of birds.

In 1938, Joseph Katz, an immigrant from Austria, realized that kosher chickens were inaccessible to the masses of Jews moving to the suburbs and rural areas far from a neighborhood kosher butcher. Whereas in Europe, almost every Jewish settlement large or small had someone qualified to slaughter chickens, in America only the larger urban areas with a sizable Jewish population hosted a shochet and the facilities to process chickens in any number. Katz founded in a garage in Liberty, New York, what would soon become one of the world's largest processors of kosher poultry, Empire.

In the 1950s, Katz took advantage of emerging innovations in freezing and vacuum wrapping to offer frozen kosher chickens to markets across the country, forever changing the nature of kosher chickens. Previously, chickens were inspected, soaked, salted, and kashered at home or, much less frequently, by butchers. Today in America, kosher chickens, requiring no further preparation beyond cooking, are readily available not only from kosher butchers, but also from most mainstream supermarkets. In blind taste tests, kosher chickens consistently score at the top and are frequently purchased by non-Jews as well.

(See also Bird, Chicken Soup, Egg, Falsche Fish, Paprikás, Pigeon, Schmaltz, Schnitzel, Tabyeet, Wot, and Yom Kippur)

CHICKEN SOUP

Poultry has been added to stews since humans started making them. A relatively recent innovation, although dating back several thousand years, is simmering only chicken in water with a few complementary vegetables and herbs to produce a transparent, flavorful broth. Initially, the institution of chicken soup seems to have emerged for its medicinal value, a notion that became widespread in a number of diverse locales millennia before Jewish comedians of the 1960s popularized the now-common epithet for chicken soup—Jewish penicillin. Indeed, components of the soup aid in anti-inflammatory activity, while the warm liquid soothes the throat. Of course, it does not hurt that the sight and taste transports us back to childhood and the sense of security and well-being our mothers gave us.

The Babylonian Talmud mentions "the chicken of Rabbi Abba," wherein the chicken was cooked in water, then left to soak in hot water for a few days until the chicken meat dissolved. Regardless of its effectiveness as a remedy, another rabbi found this particular medicine so revolting that even the very memory of tasting it made him want to wretch. Chicken soup, on the other hand, has the exact opposite effect; it is a delicious comfort food evoking pleasant memories of childhood and nurturing.

The first record of chicken soup, as well as of its curative role, was in *Huang Di Nei Jing*, the classic book of traditional Chinese medicine written around the second century BCE, which includes chicken soup among the yang (warming foods) and states that the broth also serves as a base for delivering the essence of various therapeutic herbs. Drawing on his medical training, Moses Maimonides (1135–1204), the Spanish philosopher, codifier, and physician to the vizier of Egypt, recommended poultry soup for the weak and sick. Traditionally, Sephardim prepared *caldo de gayina vieja* (old-hen chicken broth) for anyone ill and for women who had recently given birth. From this emerged the Sephardic custom of serving *soupa de gayina* with rice or orzo, sometimes called *soupa de kippur*, at the meal preceding the fast of Yom Kippur.

Although chicken soup has been a part of the Mizrachi and Sephardic culinary repertoires since at least early medieval times, long before it entered Ashkenazic cookery, it was among Ashkenazim that chicken soup found its greatest appreciation. Indeed, chicken soup, variously called *goldene yoykh*, *gilderne*, and *goldzup* (the gold refers to the globules of fat floating on top of the soup), is arguably the most identifiable Ashkenazic dish in America. It is a constant in Ashkenazic culture. In Yiddish, a schlemiel is someone who spills his chicken soup, while the schlimazel is the one on whom the soup is spilled.

This soup first came to prominence in Ashkenazic circles in the fifteenth century, after the revival of chicken raising in Europe that surged in the wake of a meat shortage. Soon chicken soup with noodles became the common first course for Ashkenazic Friday evening dinners. Ever since, in many Ashkenazic households, no Friday night, holiday, or wedding meal can begin without a bowl of golden chicken soup. It is also traditional at special anniversaries, such as the twenty-fifth and fiftieth, where the floating bubbles of fat represent happiness and contentment for the couple. In twentieth-century America, chicken soup was still associated with Jewish cooking; humorist Sam Levenson referred to it as "oil on troubled waters."

Chicken soup is rather easy to make. All that it requires is the time needed to slowly simmer the bird; too high a heat results in bitterness. A good chicken soup is characterized by a rich golden color, pronounced chicken flavor, and full-bodied mouthfeel. Historically, a rich broth was created by cooking parts of the chicken—especially the feet, gizzards, neck, wings, and bones—along with a few large pieces of vegetables. Soup provided an ideal way to use a tough aging hen that was no longer capable of laying eggs; an older bird produced a much more flavorful broth. Since chicken feet are nearly impossible to procure these days, wings are added for extra flavor and body.

Most soups also contain onions, carrots, and celery, and only a few herbs, notably parsley, celery leaves, and dill. Ashkenazim distinctively add parsnips for a sweet, earthy flavor. Turnips are common in the Middle East. Some cooks use the brown onion skins to impart extra color. The soup reduces as it simmers, intensifying the flavors, so it is best to add the salt near the end of the cooking time.

In addition to enjoying chicken soup with noodles, Ashkenazim typically serve it with *mandlen* (soup nuts) or rice. Matza balls (*knaidlach*) are traditional at the Passover Seder and, more recently, at other times of the year. Any unlaid eggs (*ayeleh*) found in the hen, considered by the Sages to be meat, were generally poached for a few minutes or hard-boiled in the soup and served as a special addition. Romanians sometimes garnish the soup with a little ground hazelnuts.

Chicken soup with kreplach (filled pasta) is customary among eastern Ashkenazim for three meals during the year. Mystics compared the wrapping of dough with the divine envelopment of mercy and kindness demonstrated on Yom Kippur and, therefore, kreplach are featured in the soup at the meal before the fast. Hoshanah Rabbah (the seventh day of Sukkot) is regarded as the day on which the verdicts of judgment that were decided on Yom Kippur are sealed and, consequently, traditional Yom Kippur eve foods are served on this day. Besides a similarity in names, in kabbalistic tradition, Yom Kippur is compared with Purim; a parallel is drawn between the physical lots of Purim cast by Haman and the metaphysical lots of Yom Kippur. As a result, chicken soup with kreplach also became commonplace at many eastern European Purim feasts.

(See also Avgolemono, Gundi, and Mandlen)

⬩❦ ASHKENAZIC CHICKEN SOUP (*GOLDENE YOYKH*)

ABOUT 2 QUARTS   [MEAT]

1 (4- to 5-pound) chicken, quartered, or 3 pounds chicken thighs
1 to 2 pounds chicken bones and parts, such as trimmings, frames, backs, and wings
3 quarts cold water
2 medium yellow onions, quartered
4 medium carrots, cut into 3- to 4-inch lengths
2 to 3 stalks celery, cut into 3- to 4-inch lengths
1 to 2 medium parsnips, cut into 3- to 4-inch lengths
6 sprigs fresh flat-leaf parsley
8 to 10 whole black peppercorns or about ¼ teaspoon ground black pepper
1 bay leaf
About 2 teaspoons table salt or 4 teaspoons kosher salt
3 to 5 sprigs fresh dill

1. Place the chicken, chicken bones, and cold water to cover in a large pot. Bring to a boil, reduce the heat to medium, and simmer, occasionally skimming the scum from the surface, for about 15 minutes. Add the onions, reduce the heat to medium-low, and simmer for 1 hour.

2. Add the carrots, celery, parsnips, parsley, pepper, and bay leaf, and simmer for another 1½ to 2 hours.

3. Gradually add the salt, tasting to determine when the flavor matches your preference. Add the dill and simmer for 10 minutes.

4. Discard the bones. Debone and shred the chicken, then return the flesh to the soup or serve separately. The broth can be cooled, covered, and stored in the refrigerator for up to 2 days or frozen. Skim any fat that accumulates on top of the soup as it cools.

CHICKPEA

The chickpea is actually not a pea, but a legume that grows two to a short pod. Around six thousand years ago, it was already cultivated in southeastern Turkey, where wild plants still grow. Its exact origins cannot be definitely ascertained, since the chickpea, which is among the first domesticated plants, was already widespread long before recorded history. By the early Bronze Age, chickpeas were common as far east as India, and they have been found in Neolithic burial mounds in Switzerland. Chickpeas thrive in tropical and subtropical climates with plenty of water, so the Mediterranean, central Asia, and India have naturally emerged as the centers of chickpea consumption.

The nutty-flavored, nourishing chickpea has long been a staple throughout much of the world. Fresh green chickpeas in their pods are occasionally available and, when shelled, are quite tasty, even raw, although most people find them tedious to prepare. The vast majority of chickpeas are used in dried form. There are two primary types (of the same species): *desi* and *kabuli*. *Desi* (a Hindi term meaning "local/in country"), popular in India and Iran for flour, are smaller with a thick seed coat and a color ranging from light brown to black. The more common *kabuli* (referring to the capital of Afghanistan, which it passed on its way to India) is larger, has a thin seed coat, and ranges in color from white to tan.

The chickpea remains India's predominant legume, and India is the world's top chickpea producer by far. They are prepared boiled, roasted, or fried. *Chole* is the Indian word for the *kabuli* type of chickpea and *chana* or *chana dal* denotes the *desi* type, but they are commonly used interchangeably. Thus the popular dish of curried chickpeas is known as both *chole* and *chana masala*. A ritual for naming a girl, usually on the twelfth day after birth, developed among the Bene Israel of Mumbai. Female relatives and friends, along with children, gather in the home and decorate the crib with flowers. On the inner edges of the crib, they arrange cookies, pieces of coconut, and cooked chickpeas to signify a sweet, prosperous, and happy life.

People have been grinding dried chickpeas into a flour since at least the time of ancient Rome, where it was simmered into a mush. Subsequently, it was used by the poor of southern Europe as a substitute for wheat. Italians used it for a porridge called *panissa*, the forerunner of cornmeal polenta. Chickpea flour is called *ard-e nokhodchi* in Iran and in India it is variously known as *besan*, *chana atta*, and *gram* flour. There are two types of chickpea flour, one made from raw chickpeas and the other from roasted ones. The roasted is more flavorful, while the unroasted tends to be slightly bitter. Indians use chickpea flour in fritters, pancakes, crackers, confections, and even sherbets. Persians make chickpea flour meatballs, called *koofteh nokhodchi* and *gondi*, and cookies.

The chickpea is mentioned only once in the Bible in Isaiah: "And the oxen and the young asses that till the ground shall eat salted *chamitz* [chickpeas] that have been winnowed with shovel and with fan." The chickpea's Hebrew name is *chamitz* or *chimtza* (sour), the cognate of the Arabic *hummus*. The Talmud mentions various species of chickpeas: light and dark, as well as large and small. In ancient Israel, chickpeas and fava beans trailed lentils in importance among legumes, although chickpeas were favored as an important animal fodder.

The opposite is the case in modern Israel, where chickpeas are the most popular legume. It is the main ingredient in two of the most well-known contemporary Middle Eastern dishes: hummus (chickpea puree) and falafel. Hummus, technically *hummus bi tahini*, denotes both the chickpea as well as the puree made from it.

Mizrachim add chickpeas to numerous stews, soups, salads, and pilafs and mash it into a savory pastry filling. Chickpeas (*garvansos*) were such prevalent fare among Sephardim that the authorities of the Spanish Inquisition considered them a Jewish food and people making chickpea stews were subject to arrest. Sephardim use chickpeas in *hamin/adafina* (Sabbath stew) and salads and mix them with rice, bulgur, pasta, and various vegetables. Moroccans add them to *harira* (soup) and tagines. More than half a millennium after the expulsion from Spain, Sephardim continue to make chickpea stews and soups nearly identical to those of their Iberian ancestors. Even among the "Hidden Jews" of the American Southwest, descendants of Conversos fleeing to Mexico and then migrating to areas above the Rio Grande, chickpeas remain ubiquitous.

Chickpeas are a traditional Rosh Hashanah food, a symbol of fertility, abundance, and a wish for a well-rounded year to come. In the Maghreb, Jews carry this circular theme further, cooking chickpeas with meatballs and serving the dish with couscous and round pastries. Although most Sephardim eat the chickpea on Passover, there is a small group who abstain, as its Hebrew and Arabic names are so similar to the forbidden *chametz*.

Northeastern Ashkenazim rarely ate legumes unless forced to by famine, but among the few exceptions were beans in cholent (Sabbath stew) and, for certain occasions, boiled chickpeas. The eastern Yiddish word for chickpeas is *nahit*, derived from the Turkish *nohut*, from the Farsi *nokhod*, showing the linguistic and geographic path of these ancient legumes. They are also called *arbes* ("peas" in Yiddish from the German *erbse*).

Among Ashkenazim, *nahit* are traditional on Purim, alluding to a legend that Esther maintained a vegetarian diet while living in the palace of the king. *Nahit* can sometimes be found in the synagogue at a Saturday morning kiddush. They are prominent at a *shalom zachar* ("welcoming the male," a celebration held at home on the first Friday evening following birth), *brit milah* (circumcision), and *Seudat Havra'ah* ("meal of consolation" following a burial), because circular foods symbolize the life cycle and fertility. When Ashkenazim eat chickpeas, they are generally served simply boiled and tossed with salt and pepper.

Isaac Bashevis Singer, in his short story *Gimpel the Fool* (1957), describes a *brit* in nineteenth-century Poland: "Women brought peppered chickpeas, and there was a keg of beer from the tavern."

(See also Falafel, Harira, Hummus, and Lablabi)

CHICORY/ENDIVE

Chicory refers to two varieties of a cultivated herb: one variety is grown for its leaves (leaf chicory), which are used in salads and cooked, and the other for its fleshy root (root chicory), which is roasted, ground, and added to coffee blends or used as a coffee substitute.

Wild chicory, also called blue succory, was consumed in the Mediterranean region for many millennia and still grows in parts of Israel. It is much like wild lettuce in appearance, with long, narrow, serrated bitter leaves growing close to the ground and spreading out into a rosette. The leaves and stems of wild chicory contain a milky sap, also a trait found in wild lettuce. The ancient Romans, and possibly also the Egyptians before them, cultivated chicory. In the sixteenth century, chicory was developed into larger and less bitter leaves. Modern leaf chicory forms loose heads of bitter, narrow, ragged-edged, light green leaves that are white nearer the heart and milder near the center.

Chicory has long been confused with its close relative, endive. Endive is possibly a hybrid of chicory and dwarf chicory—which grows wild throughout much of Israel. In any case, endive had already developed into a distinct species from chicory in prehistoric times, although as late as the Talmudic era, endive and chicory looked rather similar to each other. The Roman naturalist Pliny the Elder noted that chicory was darker and more bitter than endive. Not surprisingly, the ancients preferred the milder endive to chicory.

Endive now consists of two cultivated subspecies: escarole and curly endive. Escarole—also called scarole, broadleaf endive, and Batavian endive—is the more ancient subspecies. It has flat, murky green leaves that are broader and less curly than those of its relatives and form a loose head. It is the least bitter member of the chicory family. Curly endive, also called frisée (French for "curly"), was first recorded in 1586.

Belgian endive, or more properly witloof chicory, is not a separate species, but the same plant as leaf chicory that has been treated in a special manner. Introduced in Brussels in 1850, the plant was, according to legend, discovered when a Belgian farmer threw some leaf chicory roots into a shed and, in the spring, noticed that the roots, in the absence of sunlight, had grown yellow-tipped white shoots. Radicchio (red chicory) is another relatively recent form of leaf chicory.

Leaf chicory, escarole, and curly endive are primarily used raw in salads, but Europeans also cook them, especially in soups. Both chicory and endive were part of the diet of ancient Israel. The Talmud uses the terms "garden [cultivated] *ulshin*" and "*ulshin* of the field [wild]" to distinguish between the two. The Talmud also uses a synonym for *ulshin, hindvei,* which is obviously the root for endive. In modern Hebrew, endive is variously called *ahntubin, tzeekoreem, hindvei,* and *olesh selet,* while chicory is called *olesh.*

Ulshin is among the five leafy greens that the Talmud recommends for the bitter herbs of the Passover Seder. Similar to lettuce, chicory and endive both are milder when young, in the early spring corresponding to Passover, and grow increasingly bitter with age. Today, some Sephardim and Mizrachim use chicory or escarole for the bitter herb as well as make a salad for Passover, *salata de maror,* containing escarole, chicory, arugula, and romaine lettuce.

(See also Maror)

CHILI

Chili, a capsicum pepper, is a relative of the potato and tomato. By the time Columbus stumbled onto the New World, varieties of capsicum—which the Nahutals of the Caribbean called *chilli*—had already spread throughout most of Central and South America. On sampling the fiery pods, Columbus, who thought he was in the Spice Islands of India, assumed capsicum to be the source of peppercorns or, at least, a possible cheap substitute and called them *pimienta* (Spanish for "pepper"); this name was combined with the Nahutal name to form the misleading but enduring name chili pepper.

In 1493, the Spanish brought these fruits—peppers contain seeds meant for dispersal—to the Old World and began growing and crushing the dried chilies in the same way they prepared peppercorns. Only the hot chilies existed at that time and they were first used as a substitute for the extremely expensive Indian spice. Portuguese merchants also attempted to capitalize on them, taking them to Africa and India. Chilies, however, were virtually ignored in most of Europe, although Hungary was a notable exception. The Ottomans, who probably first discovered the crushed form of chili pods around 1513 in their dealings with the Portuguese or Italians, quickly took a liking to the zest it added to foods. The chili's fiery charms were also warmly appreciated in areas with hot climates, notably the Maghreb, Ethiopia, Yemen, and southeastern Asia.

Capsicums interbreed with relative ease, producing an ever-increasing array of chili varieties. In 1680, there were thirty-three species listed by Europeans and by 2000 there were more than two hundred. All capsicums start out green, then, as they mature on the vine, turn into an array of colors, including red, yellow, orange, brown, and black. Chili flavors range from mild to fire-alarm hot. Determining a chili's piquancy is no easy matter, since even chilies of the same variety can differ in intensity.

For the past several centuries, the favored type of crushed chili in the Levant and the Maghreb has been the Aleppo pepper, also known as the Halaby pepper and Near East pepper. This cultivar with a detectable but mild amount of heat is grown in northwestern Syria near the Turkish border, around the city of Halab (formerly Aleppo), once an important Jewish center. The coarsely ground pepper has a deep red color and a robust, sweet, smoky ancho-like flavor with a mod-

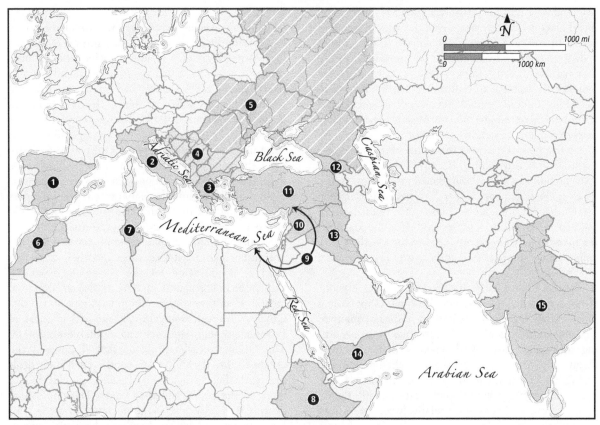

Relishes and Sauces *Condiments are relishes, sauces, and other flavorings added to or served with prepared foods to enhance their taste and aroma. Some condiments based on vinegar are enjoyed by cultures across the globe. Others are common only in a specific area. Condiments based on chilies became popular in warmer climates.* ***1 Spain***—*agraz;* ***2 Italy***—*caponata;* ***3 Greece***—*agristada, ajada;* ***4 Balkans***—*ajvar;* ***5 Eastern Europe***—*chrain, kissel;* ***6 Morocco***—*chermoula, kahrmus, zeilouk;* ***7 Tunisia***—*ajlouk, harissa;* ***8 Ethiopia***—*awaze, berbere;* ***9 Levant***—*tahini;* ***10 Syria***—*bazargan, hamud, tamarhindi;* ***11 Turkey***—*ahilado, muhammara;* ***12 Georgia***—*bazha, tkemali;* ***13 Iraq***—*amba;* ***14 Yemen***—*hilbeh, s'chug;* ***15 India***—*chutney, halba*

erate heat that becomes more fiery when cooked. It became an important element in many Jewish dishes in Syria and Lebanon. Another pepper belonging to the same variety as the Aleppo pepper is the Maras pepper, named after a Turkish province near Syria and also known as the Maras biber and Turkish pepper. Although related, Aleppo and Maras peppers possess noticeable differences in color, flavor, and aroma. The Maras pepper is the most prevalent chili in Turkish cuisine and it is an essential ingredient in popular fare such as Syrian *muhammara* (red pepper relish), kebabs, and scrambled eggs.

In a slightly different league is cayenne. Technically, cayenne is a powder made by grinding the small, deep red, pungent cayenne chili; however, the term frequently encompasses any ground tabasco chili, such as the African bird pepper. Cayenne, which has little flavor in itself, is typically used in a dish when heat is required without affecting the flavor. Georgians have access to the fiery Abkhazia red pepper from the Black Sea region. Paprika, ground from dried sweet and hot peppers, is a key to Hungarian cooking.

Chilies are an important ingredient in spice mixture and sauces which are essential to certain Jewish cuisines, including the Maghrebi harissa, Ethiopian *berbere*, and Yemenite *s'chug*.

(See also Berbere; Harrisa; Paprika; Pepper, Sweet; and S'chug)

CHIZHIPIZHI

Chizhipizhi is an omelet.

Origin: Georgia

Other names: *erbokvertskhi.*

This name of this omelet comes from the Georgian word for eggs, *kvertskhi*. *Erbo* means butter. The dish is derived from the Persian *kuku*, but features typical Georgian flavors, such as walnuts and peppers. *Chizhipizhi* is most often served with yogurt.

CHOCOLATE

The evergreen cacao tree, a native of Central America, bears fruit in the form of a pod growing up to a foot in length and containing twenty to forty seeds, called beans. The tree grows in moist tropical climates near the equator (twenty degrees north or south), and most contemporary cacao grows in Java, Indonesia, Ghana, the Ivory Coast, Madagascar, Brazil, Colombia, Ecuador, Venezuela, and Hawaii. The cacao seeds were being processed by at least 700 BCE, probably first by the Olmec Indians of southeastern Mexico. The Aztecs processed cocoa beans, called *kakaw*, and used them to make an unsweetened beverage called *xocolatl* (bitter water), which later gave rise to the European term chocolate. This drink, considered an aphrodisiac, was seasoned with red chilies and vanilla, the latter perhaps originating on the eastern coast of Mexico. Aztec warriors drank the beverage before military campaigns. During the fifteenth century, the Aztecs even used cocoa beans as currency. Chocolate is made by fermenting, drying, and roasting the beans.

Columbus introduced cocoa beans to Spain after his fourth voyage, but it was not until Hernando Cortés brought back the knowledge of how to use them, around 1528, that chocolate's popularity began to spread to the Old World. Cortés first tasted this "food of the gods" at a feast with the emperor Montezuma, who reportedly drank more than fifty cups a day. The Spaniards were intrigued by chocolate, but found it too bitter for their tastes. Soon someone added sugar, a remnant of the long Moorish control of the Iberian Peninsula, and the new drink immediately became the rage of the Spanish royal court. Along with vanilla, Spaniards commonly flavored the drink with cinnamon.

The Spanish kept the process for chocolate secret through the sixteenth century, as the Indians were unwilling to share it with other Europeans. Finally, the Florentine traveler Francesco Carletti, who described in his journals how the Aztecs roasted the beans and made the chocolate paste during a trip to Central America, introduced chocolate to Italy by 1606. Soon Sephardim associated with the Dutch supplanted the Spanish in the chocolate trade. Sephardim and Conversos living in Central America learned the secrets of chocolate as well as vanilla from friendly Indians. As a result, Jews entered the then-exotic chocolate business early on, both as producers and middlemen. Many of the latter were from the Portuguese Jewish centers of Amsterdam; Bayonne and Bordeaux in France; Hamburg, Germany; and Livorno, Italy. In addition, Jewish merchants maintained a monopoly on the vanilla business for several centuries by keeping the vanilla drying and extraction process a secret.

Benjamin d'Acosta de Andrade, a Portuguese Converso and translator, reached Dutch Brazil and returned to Judaism, only to be expelled after the Portuguese recapture of the area in 1654. He arrived in French Martinique and established two large sugar plantations, as well as, with knowledge obtained from Indians, the world's first modernized cacao-processing plant. Using his family and other Sephardic connections in Amsterdam and other parts of Europe, he began exporting cacao. Other Sephardim soon followed suit, and chocolate for beverages became the island's most important export. After the enactment of the Black Code in 1685, engendered by resentful competitors, the French restricted all business in Martinique to French citizens and expelled all the Jews. Subsequently, d'Acosta and the other Jewish owners of cocoa and vanilla enterprises shifted to Dutch Curaçao and English Jamaica. Jewish control of the European chocolate trade declined in the eighteenth century as cocoa production in Africa increased and Central American cocoa grew prohibitively expensive.

Although condemned in the seventeenth century by the church as "the beverage of Satan," chocolate's popularity continued to grow. In the early seventeenth century, chocolate drinks were already popular in the Jewish ghetto of Bayonne, St. Esprit. In 1691, French authorities banned the sale of chocolate to those outside the ghetto. Later in the eighteenth century, St. Esprit emerged as an early center of chocolate making. Subsequently, Jews have been in the forefront of chocolate manufacturing from San Francisco to

Melbourne, Australia. Chocolate houses soon began appearing in the rest of Europe, where the beverage was viewed as an aphrodisiac and fatigue reliever. By 1657, chocolate houses began springing up in England, offering the beverage at a steep price.

Meanwhile, because of the Jewish familiarity with chocolate and vanilla, these items entered Jewish cuisines before most others. In the seventeenth century, professional bakers in Bayonne and Italy, many of them Jews, introduced chocolate fillings and later chocolate cakes. Hungarian housewives became fond of a chocolate filling in cake rolls, naming it *kakosh*, while Polish cooks later did the same in babkas. In 1832, a Jewish apprentice baker in Vienna by the name of Franz Sacher—at the time, many central European pastry bakers were Jewish—created a dense, dry chocolate cake with a thin layer of apricot jam in the middle, the famous Sachertorte. Later his son Eduard Sacher opened the Sacher Hotel, where he served and further popularized his father's famous creation.

The first eating chocolate appeared in London in 1674. This confection, however, consisted of grated chocolate paste, sugar, and plant gums, and was rather different from contemporary chocolate bars. Until 1828, chocolate was primarily consumed as a drink or in cakes. Then Conrad J. van Houten of Holland invented a method of extracting cocoa butter from the chocolate liquor (ground cocoa beans in liquid form) through a hydraulic press, leading to a revolution in the candy industry. The extruded chocolate butter enabled chocolate makers to reinforce the chocolate liquor, allowing them to produce a chocolate hard enough to form into bars and candy. In 1847, capitalizing on van Houten's innovations, the English company of Fry and Sons introduced the first "eating chocolate" recognizable to modern chocolate lovers.

In 1876, Rudolph Lindt of Switzerland discovered a process known as conching, which produced a smoother chocolate. In Europe, chocolate making became a fine art. Skill and craftsmanship went into the production, whether of simple candies or elaborate confections, with American chocolate falling well below European standards.

Van Houten's method for extracting cocoa butter from the chocolate liquor led to another by-product, cocoa powder. Cocoa powder is produced by extracting at least half of the cocoa butter from the chocolate liquor, leaving a dry cake that is ground into a powder.

In 1933, Eliyahu Fromenchenko, a Jewish chocolate maker from Russia, opened the Elite candy factory in Ramat Gan, Israel. It became the country's largest producer of chocolate.

In 1938, Stephen Klein, a Jewish master candy maker, arrived in New York City from Vienna, Austria, and began producing chocolates in the Old World style from his home kitchen. Soon he established his first Bartons Salon de Chocolat shop. By 1950, the number of shops grew to fifty. At its height, nationwide, Bartons consisted of about two hundred company-owned or franchised boutiques offering a wide range of exclusive confections as well as prepackaged items. Boxes of Bartons were also sold at retail stores across the country.

What made Bartons candies unique, besides the high quality and elegant presentation, was that they were all strictly kosher, from the Seder Mints and Almond Kisses to the chocolate Easter bunnies and Santas. At a time long before the American mainstream discovered kosher—when Jews were streaming into the middle class and acculturating, although some refused to give up their religious values—Bartons represented the emerging religious materialism and marketing potential of kosher supervision. Under Klein's direction, Bartons not only introduced the concept of gourmet candy to America, but also grew into an important part of American Jewish life. For half a century, no Hanukkah or Passover in America was complete without a box or more of Bartons chocolates, often purchased through synagogue or day-school fundraisers. As a result, every Jewish child was familiar with Bartons and many Jewish institutions relied on the extra income from its fundraisers. Jewish guests and businessmen could give or receive a box of Bartons with no embarrassment over quality or qualms about kashrut.

After Klein's death, however, his sons, occupied in real estate, sold Bartons in 1981. The new owner, American Safety Razor Company, which had also recently acquired Schrafft's Candy Company, closed most of the Bartons stores, ignored Klein's standards of quality, and neglected the synagogue fundraisers. On the verge of bankruptcy, American Safety Razor

Company passed through several hands before Bartons was revived, albeit as a much smaller presence and with the loss of its former role and status in the American Jewish culture. However, by this time, American business had discovered the marketing importance of kosher and many of America's best chocolates had acquired kosher supervision.

CHOLENT/SCHALET

Cholent is a slow-simmered stew, often based on beans, that is served hot for Sabbath lunch.

Origin: France

Other names: Alsace and southern Germany: *schalet*; Austria: *scholet*; Hungary: *sholet*, *sólet*; Lithuania: *chulent*; Poland: *cholent*, *tsholnt*.

In the eleventh century, as Christians gradually conquered Spain, the scientific knowledge and culinary techniques of the Moors from Toledo and other Spanish intellectual centers increasingly flowed into Provence and from there transformed the rest of Europe. These ideas and methods were largely transmitted through Jewish translators. Sometime after the First Crusade, around the late twelfth or early thirteenth century, the Sephardic Sabbath stew, *hamin/ adafina*, probably traveling by way of Provence, eventually reached the Jews of France to become an indelible part of their Sabbath. Certain medieval French bishops, distressed at the good relations between Christians and Jews in their region, issued a series of edicts forbidding various practices, including eating long-simmered bean stews. From France, the stew moved eastward to southern Germany and later to eastern Europe.

Among the French Ashkenazim, the stew received a new name, spelled *schalet* in Western Yiddish and *tsholnt* in Eastern Yiddish, probably from the Old French word for warm, *chald/chalt* (*chaud* in modern French), or, some contend, from *chald-de-lit* (warmth of the bed). Alternatively, some insist that the dish flowed to France directly from Spain, the name emerging from the Spanish *escallento* (warm). The widespread modern American notion that the name of the stew derived from the Yiddish *shul ende*, reflecting the time of day when the dish was eaten, is obviously mistaken, as the name emerged in France among French speakers before the development of Old Yiddish (c. 1250).

For generations, the family's cholent pot was carried to the baker's oven (here in Bialystok, Poland, 1931) on Friday to cook overnight for Sabbath lunch.

The first known use of the term *tsholnt* was in the *Or Zarua* (Light Is Sown), written by Rabbi Isaac ben Moses of Vienna (c. 1200–1260), who was raised in Bohemia and went to Paris in 1217 to study under Rabbi Judah ben Isaac Messer Leon, one of the Tosafot. By this time, the stew had already become commonplace in Bohemia and southern Germany. The *Or Zarua* describes the way the stew was cooked at the home of Messer Leon: "I saw in the home of my teacher that sometimes their *tsholnt* which was covered, was cooling on the Sabbath close to the time of eating the food, the [non-Jewish] servants lit fires close to the pots, in order that they should be heated or moved them closer to the fire." At this point, the French rabbis permitted the cooking of the Sabbath stew on the home hearth and allowed non-Jews to adjust the heat on the Sabbath according to the need of the dish, practices the authorities farther east in Germany forbade. As a consequence, German rabbis required the stew pots to be sealed in an oven or cooked over a nonadjustable heat source (i.e., a thin sheet of metal). According to Jewish law, cholent should be at least half-cooked before the Sabbath begins; then it was usually left at a low heat to cook overnight. Since in Europe few private homes had an oven, particularly one large enough to maintain its heat overnight, cholent was typically left in the stone oven of the town bakery or in a large private oven.

On Friday afternoons in the large urban centers and villages of Europe, after the last loaves of fragrant golden challah were pulled from the stone ovens and put aside to cool, housewives or children would haul the family's blackened cholent pot to the bakery. The women took the opportunity to socialize before heading home to continue their weekly preparations for the Sabbath. The lids of the pots were traditionally sealed with a flour paste, preventing the contents from drying out while safeguarding that nothing untoward could make its way inside. When all the pots were assembled, the oven door would be sealed with clay where the entire collection would remain undisturbed overnight. Although the fire would eventually go out, the heat would abide well into the following day, slowly cooking the stews inside and melding the various flavors. Late on Saturday morning, following synagogue services, the oven would be unsealed and the pots eagerly reclaimed by their owners or representatives. The treasure was hurried home and placed in the center of the Sabbath table or insulated in the bed under down quilts until the appropriate time. When the seal on the pot was broken, a unique yet familiar aroma would waft through the house, setting mouths to watering as the diners anticipated the first bite. The potatoes had turned a translucent golden brown and the cooking liquid had become rich and viscous from the gelatinous meat and bones.

Ashkenazim tweaked cholent to more readily fit their environment and tastes. The only known ingredient of the early French cholents was fava beans, although it can be assumed they also contained meat, some sort of grain, and a Jewish standard, onions. However, the arrival of the more versatile dried haricot beans from America in the sixteenth century quickly led to their substitution for fava beans. White beans, red kidneys, pintos, and dried limas, closely resembling the former fava bean, are the most common. Most cooks use a combination and some American Jewish companies began selling a commercial "cholent mix." Some Romanians add chickpeas, a remnant of Sephardic influence due to the Ottoman control of the area.

Since the French grew bread wheat rather than the firmer durum wheat, and rice was quite rare, some substituting was necessary for the grain component. An early surrogate may have been spelt (*dinkel* in German) or the roasted immature spelt kernels (*gruenkern*), which are still used in German Sabbath soups. Barley became the standard grain in eastern Europe.

The usual meat of choice is beef, such as flanken and brisket, which benefits from the long slow-cooking. The amount of meat largely depended on the tastes of the community and economic condition of the household. In western and central Europe, goose and occasionally duck were also added. Some poor eastern European families used chicken, as it was much cheaper than beef. Other poor families might simply add a bone or two. Today, vegetarian cholents are in vogue in some circles.

In the mid-nineteenth century, Polish cholents always featured plenty of *bulbes* (potatoes), while most Hungarians would never allow one near their cholent. Germans tend to add various root vegetables. Some cooks fry the onions in schmaltz, while others add them raw to the pot. The stew may be sweetened with honey, caramelized sugar, or fruit, or spiced with cloves or paprika and a bay leaf. The old Jewish favorite, garlic, is found in many variations.

A cholent may be dry or watery, but most fall somewhere in between. Hungarian cholent leans toward the soupy side, while Polish and German cholents tend to be thicker. Some add a little semolina to thicken it. Actually, cholent never comes out the exact same way twice in a row. Consequently, sometimes the amount of moisture is the result of a mistake rather than intent. Thus when Ashkenazim began cooking cholents in home ovens, more than a few anxious housewives kept an eye peeled on the level of the cooking liquid, even in the middle of the night. If it fell below an acceptable amount and the heat source was covered by a piece of metal, they removed the pot from the direct heat and added a ladle of water kept very hot. Today, slow cookers are often used. Although cholent can be served as a meal in itself, it is commonly accompanied with a kugel, dill pickles or cucumber salad, and sometimes coleslaw or pickled beets.

Today among Alsatian Jews, *schalet* competes with another hot dish for Sabbath lunch, *choucroute garnie*, consisting of cured meats, sausages, and sauerkraut. On the other hand, some non-Jewish Alsatians cook a stew overnight on Saturday to serve after Sunday mass, a dish they call *schalet*. Although the French are loath to admit it, the classic southern French dish cassoulet is most certainly a descendant of the Jewish *schalet*, as the injunction of those medieval French bishops against eating slow-cooked bean stews was largely ignored. Similarly, the related Hungarian *sholet/sólet* has been widely adopted by non-Jews, practically becoming a national dish of Hungary. The common denominator remains the slow-simmered beans.

People are not nonchalant about cholent—they seem to feel passionate about it one way or another. This reaction is not only about taste, but also about mindset: Cholent is either viewed as a delicious and integral component of religious devotion and Jewish culture or as an old-fashioned remnant of a disregarded ethnic background and a time when poor nutrition was common. But many would agree with the German poet Heinrich Heine, who immortalized the stew in his poem "*Prinzessin Sabbat.*" He wrote, "*Schalet* is the food of heaven . . . *Schalet* is the kosher ambrosia."

(See also Hamin, Harisa, Helzel, Kishke, Kugel, and Schalet)

ASHKENAZIC SABBATH STEW (*CHOLENT*)

6 TO 8 SERVINGS [MEAT]

    1½ pounds beef or veal marrow bones
    About 2 cups any combination mixed dried navy,
        lima, pink, pinto, and kidney beans
    3 medium yellow onions, sliced
    2 to 3 cloves garlic, whole or minced
    6 medium potatoes, peeled and quartered
    3 pounds beef flanken, brisket, or chuck roast
    ¾ to 1 cup pearl barley
    2 to 3 bay leaves
    About 2 teaspoons table salt or 4 teaspoons kosher
        salt
    About 1 teaspoon ground black pepper
    About 2 quarts water

1. In the order given, place the bones, beans, onions, garlic, potatoes, beef, barley, bay leaves, salt, and pepper in a large, heavy pot. Add enough water to cover.

2. Bring to a boil, cover, reduce the heat to medium-low, and simmer, skimming the froth from the surface, until the beans are nearly soft, about 1 hour.

3. Add more water if necessary. Tightly cover, place on a *blech* (a thin sheet of metal placed over the range top and knobs) over low heat, or in a 225°F oven, and cook overnight. Serve warm.

CHOLENT KUGEL (SHABBOS GANIF)

Cholent kugel is a dumpling cooked in the Sabbath stew.
Origin: Germany
Other names: *cholent knaidel, Shabbos ganif.*

With the spread of dumplings into central Europe by the twelfth century, housewives began to add them to the Sabbath stew, making it more substantial and stretching resources. In western Europe, these dumplings were originally called by the same name as the stew, *schalet*. In Germany, they became known as cholent kugel. (The dumpling eventually emerged from the stew to be cooked on their own, giving rise to the world of baked kugels.) In eastern Europe, they were whimsically called *Shabbos ganif* (Sabbath thief), since the dumplings stole flavor from the liquid of the stews in which they were cooked. The dumpling absorbs liquid while cooking, so it is necessary to add more water to the cholent. Cholent kugels originated as poverty food because they could be made from very inexpensive ingredients, but they became a beloved component of Jewish cookery. Today, many cooks still add a dumpling to their kugel, variously made from bread, flour, or matza.

(See also Dumpling and Kugel)

CHOLENT KUGEL

4 TO 6 SERVINGS [PAREVE OR MEAT]

    5 thick slices challah or 2 large rolls, torn into small
        pieces
    1½ cups (7.5 ounces) all-purpose flour
    ¼ cup vegetable oil or schmaltz
    1 large egg, lightly beaten
    1 to 3 teaspoons paprika
    About 1 teaspoon table salt or 2 teaspoons kosher
        salt
    ½ teaspoon ground white or black pepper

In a medium bowl, soak the challah in water until soft but not mushy, about 2 minutes. Drain and squeeze out the excess moisture. Place in a medium bowl and mash until smooth. Add the flour, oil, egg, paprika, salt, and pepper, adding more flour if too loose; the mixture should be able to hold its shape. Form into a log and place it on top of hot cholent.

CHOUCROUTE GARNIE

Choucroute garnie is a dish of sauerkraut baked slowly with cured meats and sausage.
Origin: Alsace

For centuries, the residents of Alsace in early fall after the cabbage harvest would fill at least one barrel in the cellar with shredded cabbages tossed with salt and weigh it down with a large stone. Salt is the oldest and still most widely used preservative—it discourages the growth of harmful bacteria, while allowing the survival of the flavor-producing acidifying bacteria that are responsible for the fermentation and tangy flavor of pickled cabbage, cucumbers, and olives. As the shredded cabbages sat in the barrel, the salt extracted much of its juices, forming a flavorful brine. Today, when few homes still pickle their own cabbage, signs across Alsace announce each fall the arrival of *nouvelle choucroute* (new sauerkraut).

In Alsation cooking, the use of sauerkraut, which is more common in German cookery than in French, reflects the area's Teutonic roots. The favorite Alsatian way of using sauerkraut is in one of the region's great dishes, simply referred to as *choucroute*. This dish originated as fall and winter peasant fare because it made use of inexpensive sauerkraut and preserved meats; it was simmered for an extensive period to tenderize the meat, mellow the cabbage, and enhance the flavors. As the dish gained prominence, wealthier people added higher-quality meats and sausages.

Among the prominent professions of medieval Alsatian Jews was charcuterie, the preparation of meat products, which included curing, brining, smoking, and poaching. Using their skill at sausage making, cooks added kosher meats and sausages to sauerkraut to create their own version of *choucroute*, referred to as *choucroute garnie à la Juive*. Although the classic recipe uses an assortment of pork cuts and lard, Alsatian Jews substitute kosher meats and goose fat. Jewish-style *choucroute* is accepted in Alsace as an authentic variation and can sometimes be found in non-kosher restaurants offering a selection of *choucroutes*.

There is no official recipe for this dish other than the inclusion of sauerkraut. The amount and types of meat used (cured cuts and fresh and cured sausages) is a matter of personal preference and availability. However, there are certain guidelines and standards. Traditional recipes call for goose fat, cloves, juniper berries, and bay leaves. Alsatians insist on using naturally fermented sauerkraut made without vinegar—the vinegar cannot be removed by washing, while the excess salt can. Fresh sauerkraut remains somewhat crisp and slightly acidic, properties that fade as the cabbage ages. The sauerkraut is then heated in some goose schmaltz or oil and then moistened with Riesling or other dry white wine. *Choucroute* usually contains potatoes, making it a one-dish meal. A good *choucroute* is a balance—never too fatty, acidic, dry, or watery.

Choucroute garnie is cooked overnight over a very low heat as a popular Alsatian Sabbath lunch. Although now served year-round, it remains most prominent in the fall and winter. *Choucroute garnie* is commonly accompanied with a lentil salad and mustard or horseradish sauce.

⟡ ALSATIAN SAUERKRAUT WITH CURED MEATS
(*CHOUCROUTE GARNIE À LA JUIVE*)

8 TO 10 SERVINGS [MEAT]

3 pounds raw cured corned beef
2 pounds pastrami or smoked goose breast
6 pounds sauerkraut

Spice Bag:
2 cloves garlic, smashed
8 whole black peppercorns
2 whole cloves or 1 teaspoon caraway seeds
2 bay leaves
10 juniper berries (optional)

3 tablespoons schmaltz or vegetable oil
2 medium yellow onions, coarsely chopped
4 cups Riesling or other dry white wine
1 cup chicken broth or water
1 pound beef knackwurst or knoblewurst (garlic sausage)
6 to 10 beef frankfurters (optional)
16 to 24 small new potatoes

1. In a large pot, simmer the corned beef and pastrami in water to cover for about 1 hour. Drain.

2. If the sauerkraut is very salty, wash it in cold water to remove most of the salt. Drain and press out the liquid.

3. Place the garlic, peppercorns, cloves, bay leaves, and, if using, juniper berries on a piece of cheesecloth. Fold the cheesecloth into a bundle and tie.

4. In a large pot, heat the schmaltz over medium heat. Add the onions and sauté until soft and translucent, 5 to 10 minutes. Add the sauerkraut, wine, broth, and cheesecloth bag and bring to a low boil.

5. Arrange the corned beef, pastrami, sausages, and, if using, frankfurters on top of the sauerkraut. Add the potatoes, cover the pot, and simmer over low heat or bake in a 325°F oven for at least 3 hours or overnight. *Choucroute garnie* can be prepared a day ahead as it tastes even better reheated.

6. Slice the corned beef and pastrami against the grain. Place the sauerkraut on a serving platter and arrange the meats, sausages, and potatoes on top.

CHREMSEL

Chremsel is a pancake, primarily for Passover, made from matza meal or mashed potatoes. It can be plain, stuffed, or dipped in honey.

Origin: Southwestern Germany

Other names: *bubeleh, chremzel, fasputshes, grimsel, khremzl, pfannkuchen, pontshkes.*

Two thousand years ago, a very popular dish among Romans was *vermiculos* (Latin for "little worms"), known in the Jerusalem Talmud as *iytree* (strings). The Roman epicure Apicius, in his work *De Re Conquinaria Libri Decem* (Cuisine in Ten Books), compiled around 400 CE, included a recipe for *vermiculos*—thin strips of dough fried in oil then coated with honey. *Vermiculos* would, in the course of time, lead to a beloved Ashkenazic pancake, *chremslach.*

During the Middle Ages, the original dish disappeared from Italian kitchens. After the concept of boiling dough in water reached the Mediterranean in the thirteenth century, *vermiculos* became the source of the Italian vermicelli, long, thin threads of pasta.

Meanwhile, Italian Jewish merchants and immigrants brought *vermiculos* to the Rhineland, the seat of early Ashkenazim. By the twelfth century, numerous Franco-German rabbis mentioned the practice of starting the Friday evening meal with an appetizer of fried strips of dough in honey called *vermesel* or *verimslish.* This tradition remained in the area for more than three centuries, until it was eventually replaced at Friday night dinner with noodles in chicken soup. Then in the fifteenth century, the term *vermesel* evolved into *frimsel*, the Western Yiddish word for noodles. It also became *grimsel*, denoting various fritters and pancakes. The first Jewish cookbook in America, *Jewish Cookery* (1871) by Esther Levy, who was of German heritage, includes "Grimslechs (for Passover)." Shortly thereafter, *Aunt Babette's* (1889), another cookbook by an author from a German background, calls the pancakes "Grimslich"; the pancakes in this recipe are made with bread.

When the dish reached eastern Europe, it became *chremsel.* The Yiddish diminutive suffix *lach* was added to denote the plural. The most widespread version of *chremslach* are small matza meal pancakes topped with preserves or, like the *vermiculos*, soaked in honey. The first edition of *The Settlement Cook Book* (1901) offered five recipes for "Matzos Crimsel." Noble laureate Saul Bellow, in a 1983 *New York Times* interview by Mimi Sheraton, reminisced about the dishes made by his mother from Riga, Latvia: "My mother made some wonderful dishes that I can still taste, especially her turnip dishes and chremslach, the pancakes of nuts and vegetables that we ate with conserves."

(See also Latke, Lokshen, and Matza Brei)

ASHKENAZIC MATZA MEAL PANCAKES (*CHREMSLACH*)

ABOUT THIRTY-SIX 1-INCH OR SIXTEEN 3-INCH PANCAKES

[PAREVE OR MEAT]

1 cup matza meal

About ⅓ cup finely chopped almonds, hazelnuts, or walnuts

About 2 tablespoons sugar

1 teaspoon ground cinnamon

About ½ teaspoon table salt or 1 teaspoon kosher salt

Pinch of ground ginger (optional)

4 large eggs, lightly beaten

1 cup sweet wine or water

Vegetable oil or schmaltz for frying

1 pound (1⅓ cups) honey

1. In a medium bowl, combine the matza meal, nuts, sugar, cinnamon, salt, and, if using, ginger. Combine the eggs and wine. Stir into the matza meal mixture and let stand for at least 30 minutes.

2. In a large skillet, heat about ⅛ inch oil over medium heat. Drop the batter by teaspoonfuls or tablespoonfuls and fry until lightly browned on the bottom, about 1 minute. Turn and fry until browned on the other side, about 30 seconds. Drain on paper towels.

3. Pour off most of the oil and add the honey to the skillet. Bring to a boil, stirring frequently (the honey may boil up). Add the pancakes and toss to coat. Store the *chremslach* in the honey at room temperature, tossing occasionally to recoat.

CILANTRO

Fresh coriander, a member of the Apiaceae family, is commonly called cilantro, which is the Spanish name for the plant. It is also known as Chinese parsley and Mexican parsley. A native of Israel, it is called *kuzbara* in both Arabic and Hebrew. The leaves, seeds (fruits), and roots are all used in cooking; each of them has a very different flavor and should not be substituted for another. Cilantro is among the fresh herbs recommended for the *karpas* of the Passover Seder.

Cilantro has long been one of the world's most widely used herbs and is a popular component of the cuisines of Asia, Mexico, the Middle East, Georgia, and the Caribbean. It adds an herbal note to the essential Yemenite chili paste, *s'chug*. Although cilantro looks like its relative flat-leaf parsley, the leaves are thinner and lighter green and the flavor (slightly musty-peppery-citrusy) is more pungent. Cilantro complements both cool and hot foods, including citrus, mint, ginger, and chilies. Heat dissipates cilantro's flavor and turns it bitter, so it is usually added near the end of cooking.

(See also Coriander)

CINNAMON/CASSIA

Cinnamon is the inner bark of a tropical evergreen tree of the laurel family that is native to Sri Lanka (Ceylon). Cinnamon has a pleasing fragrance, and a sweet-pungent flavor with a hint of citrus and cloves. It contains eugenol, which also gives cloves their characteristic flavor. So cherished was cinnamon, that its source was hidden for centuries and legends were created to deter the curious from searching for it.

Today, cinnamon is one of the world's favorite spices—at least we might think the spice we enjoy is cinnamon. In the early twentieth century, the price of true cinnamon skyrocketed and American spice companies began to frequently substitute the inexpensive bark of a laurel tree native to Myanmar (Burma) and Assam (northeastern India); this spice is called cassia and Chinese cinnamon. In the United States and France, the terms cinnamon and cassia can legally be used interchangeably, although this is not permitted in England, Australia, and many other countries. True cinnamon has a pale tan color and a sweeter and more delicate flavor than the dark reddish brown, almost coppery, pungent cassia. Cassia sticks are hollow, while cinnamon sticks are filled with thin layers. Although there is only one true cinnamon, there are several types of cassia

primarily grown in China, Vietnam, and Indonesia. Each type of cassia has a slightly different flavor. The now-more-prevalent Indonesian cassia tends to be the most complex with a combination of sweetness, sharpness, and bitterness. Chinese cassia is generally stronger (with a note of heat) and sweeter than the other types. Vietnamese cassia tends to be subtler and more balanced with plenty of sweetness and sharpness and only a note of spice.

Neither the biblical *kinamon* nor *ketziah/keydah* is, in all likelihood, identical to what we today call cinnamon and cassia. Nachmanides, relying on the Midrash, noted that "*kinamon* grew in the land of Israel"—and cinnamon never did. The Midrash is in accord with statements in the Jerusalem Talmud that "the kindling of Jerusalem were of cinnamon . . . but when Jerusalem was destroyed, they [the cinnamon] were hidden" and "goats in Israel fed on cinnamon and Jews once grew it there." In addition, Nachmanides insisted that *kinamon* was not a tree, but rather "an aromatic grass, called *adbar* in Arabic, *ascinant* in Latin, and *saika domika* in Old French." Nachmanides, noting its original use in charoset in memory of the straw, continued, "such as *kinamon* and *sanbal*, which are similar to straw." Similarly, some Sephardim consider the biblical *kinamon* to be *paja de Mecca* (Mecca straw), an aromatic red herb, which is called *kyabi shamani* in Turkish.

Ancient non-Jewish sources also point to a Middle Eastern origin for ancient cinnamon and cassia. The Greek writers Herodotus and Theophrastus both recorded that they grew in Arabia. Pliny contended that they came from Ethiopia. The descriptions of these plants by Theophrastus as well as Pliny do not at all reflect contemporary forms of cinnamon and cassia. Apicius never mentioned cinnamon or cassia in his cookbook, so it was certainly absent from imperial Rome.

No record of what we currently call cinnamon appeared in its homeland of Sri Lanka—where it is called *kurundu*—before the thirteenth century CE, when it was first noted in Arabic sources.

In the two centuries after the disappearance around 1000 CE of the Radhanites, an enigmatic group of Jewish merchants, Asian spices disappeared from Europe. Meanwhile, the Middle Eastern spices *kinamon* and *ketziah* lost favor. When Asian spices began to again flow into Europe in the twelfth century,

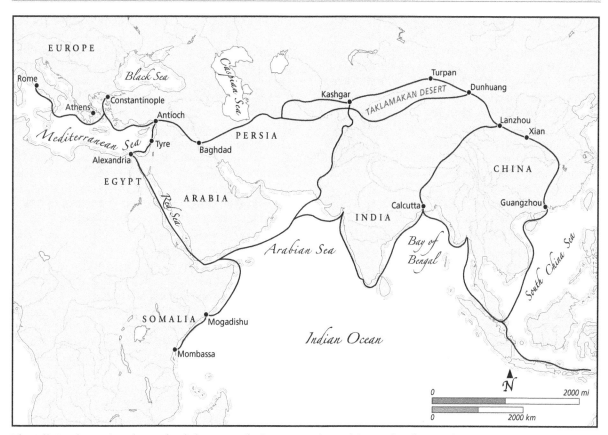

The Silk Road *was a four-thousand-mile-long network of contiguous thoroughfares and trails proceeding from numerous Chinese cities and villages into a few westward passages. The most important segments of the Silk Road consisted of two major courses running north and south of the Taklamakan Desert, dreaded for its fierce heat and dangerous winds. Caravans once passed through the area bearing the riches of the Orient to Europe, ranging from cinnamon to carp.*

two newer arrivals from the Far East subsumed the names of their faded predecessors, probably sparked by a medieval marketing ploy. (It only took a few years in America for cassia to subsume the name of cinnamon.) It was around this time in the twelfth century that cassia and cinnamon first began to proliferate in Arabic cuisine. *Kitab al-Tabikh* (Book of Dishes) by Muhammad ibn al-Hasan Al-Baghdadi, compiled in Iraq in 1226, referred to both cinnamon and Chinese cinnamon. By this point, the terms cinnamon and cassia had taken on their contemporary meanings.

It was not until the Portuguese sailed by ship around the southern tip of Africa to Sri Lanka in the fifteenth century, soon followed by the Dutch in 1640 and then the English in 1796, that cinnamon became a common item in Europe. Cinnamon emerged as the most popular central European spice for baking, including any number of cakes, tarts, and cookies.

Cinnamon is used in every Jewish community, complementing a myriad of dishes, including stews, Moroccan tagines, soups, pilafs, chutneys, beverages, spiced wines, fruits, and most baked goods. Cinnamon is essential to Indian curries. Ashkenazim use it in tzimmes, babka, and cake rolls. Cinnamon is also incorporated into many variations of charoset.

(See also Spice and Zimtsternen)

CITRUS

Citrus (from the Greek *kedros,* "cedar") are evergreen plants of the Rutaceae family with shiny leaves and brightly colored fruit. They originated in eastern Asia and are probably all descended from the citron (etrog). Over the centuries, through continuous crossing, citrus has developed into one of the largest of fruit families. In 1178 CE, Han Yen-Chih in the oldest known treatise on citrus fruits, described the twenty-seven varieties of citrus then in existence, including citrons, kumquats, lemons, mandarins, and oranges. Today, there are thousands of varieties of which only several hundred are grown in any number. Individual citrus varieties vary in flavor and color depending on soil and climate.

Lemon is a high-acid citrus fruit native to eastern Asia. Lemons appear to be depicted in Italian mosaics beginning toward the end of the first century CE. Initially, the Romans treated lemons like the citron, as a garden decoration.

Lime, the fruit of an evergreen shrub probably native to Malaysia, is the most acidic of all citrus fruits. Limes thrive in tropical climates, where they are the predominant souring agent, a role played by lemons in the subtropics. Limes contain more citric acid and essential oils than lemons and, therefore, cannot always be substituted in equal amounts.

What most of the rest of the world refers to as a lime is not the same as the characteristic American fruit by that name. The most common type in America is the Persian lime—also called Bearss lime and Tahitian lime—which is not considered a true lime, but is a hybrid between the lime and citron. The true lime and the most widespread outside of the U.S. is the Key or Mexican lime. Key limes are smaller, thinner-skinned, more yellow, more acidic, more flavorful, and more aromatic than Persian limes. Key limes, however, do not fare as well as Persian limes in milder climates and have a shorter shelf life.

Limes play a particularly important role in the cuisines of central Asia, where they are used fresh and dried, the latter called *limoo omani* or *loomi* in Iran and *noumi basra* in Iraq. Loomi are made by blanching fresh Key limes in salted water, then sun-drying them. The fruit turns hard, hollow, and brown or black; the darker the color, the more pungent the fruit. They are sold in Middle Eastern and specialty stores, whole or finely ground. Dried limes contribute a distinctive sweet-tart flavor and musty aroma to stews, fish dishes, and rice.

Following the Lombard invasions of 568 CE, citrus disappeared from Europe and much of the Mediterranean, except among the Jews, who continued to cultivate etrogim for the Sukkot ritual, as well as other citrus trees. As pointed out by Erich Isaac in his article "Influence of Religion on the Spread of Citrus: The Religious Practices of the Jews Helped Effect the Introduction of Citrus to Mediterranean Lands" (*Science*, 1959), "that it is the antiquity of citrus culture, originally introduced to these regions [Spain, the Maghreb, Sicily, southern Italy, and Egypt, all of which correspond to the large Jewish centers of the Mediterranean] by Jews, for whom the cultivation of other citrus species was a by-product of citron cultivation which explains the persistence of this horticultural speciality." The first reference in Arabic sources to limes as well as lemons appeared in the tenth century. Subsequently, Arabs spread the lemon and lime west to North Africa and Spain, while Crusaders brought the lemon back to Italy.

Beginning in the eighth century, Jewish traders began selling citrons and later lemons and oranges to eastern and northern Europe and these traders continued to serve as the primary source of citrus for these regions until the late nineteenth century. Citrus fruit's importance increased as people discovered that it was a cure for scurvy, and the fruit's effect gave rise to the term limey for British sailors. In modern Israel, citrus production, including that of the famous Jaffa orange, provided a vital early source of income for the fledgling economy.

(See also Etrog, "Lemon, Preserved," and Orange)

COCONUT

Coconuts are the large fruits of a tropical palm tree, which, throughout much of the Pacific, provides food, clothing, shelter, and more. Some say the Spanish named it after a popular clown of the sixteenth century, Coco, while others contend the name belonged to a legendary Portuguese goblin, the three "eyes" of the coconut reminding them of a clown's or demon's face. The coconut's place of origin is unknown, but it was widely used in India more than twenty-five hundred years ago. Nautical trade between Rome and India brought coconuts to Egypt and remains of coconuts dating to the first century CE have been discovered there. By the sixth century, Arab traders had spread the coconut through Egypt and parts of the Middle East. Thus some medieval sources, such as Marco Polo, called it "Pharaoh's nut."

Meanwhile, Arab traders were selling the shells to Europeans; the shells had reached Italy by 1250 and had traveled as far as England and King Edward III by 1337. The shells were so rare, however, that they were formed into gold or silver cups or fancy decorations in castles and cathedrals. It is doubtful whether the actual coconut flesh ever reached medieval Europe. In 1498, Vasco da Gama, in his accounts of sailing to India, mentioned seeing coconuts after reaching the Indian Ocean, and Portuguese traders soon introduced them to Europe. It was not, however, until around 1840 that trading schooners on a regular basis brought coconuts from the Pacific to Europe and North America. The flesh soon appeared in a few dishes, and coconut became more than a rarity for the wealthy. Coconut was first mentioned in print in America in 1834, when they had to be peeled and grated by hand at home.

The first Jewish cookbook in English, *The Jewish Manual* (London, 1846), provides three recipes incorporating "cocoa nut": "Cocoa Nut Pudding," "Cocoa Nut Doce," and "Chejados," the latter a sort of coconut tart. The first American Jewish cookbook, *Jewish Cookery* (1871) also offers three coconut recipes: "Cocoanut Cheesecakes," Cocoanut Tarts," and, for the first time, "Cocoanut Macaroons." Another early American Jewish cookbook, *Aunt Babette's* (1889), contains several recipes with this still-exotic ingredient: "Loaf Cocoanut Cake," "Cocoanut Cake," "Cocoanut Icing," "Cocoanut Caramels," "Cocoanut Cones," "Cocoanut Drops," and "Cocoanut Pie."

In 1895, when a Cuban merchant lacked the cash to pay Franklin Baker, a Philadelphia miller, for a shipment of flour, Baker accepted a load of coconuts instead. Unable to sell enough of the fresh coconuts, Baker developed a method of uniformly shredding the meat. This innovation proved so popular that within two years Baker sold his flour mill to concentrate solely on shredded coconut. With Baker's innovation, cooks were no longer required to peel and grate their own coconut, and coconut soon became a standard in American baked goods and other desserts.

In the Pacific, coconuts are utilized in an incredible number of ways. They are essential in cooking and are also made into an oil and used for utensils and fibers. Many Indians have a special grater to pre-

pare fresh coconut. Westerners primarily use coconut in grated or shredded form in desserts, such as macaroons, cakes, pastries, cookies, and candy. In central Europe in the nineteenth century, hydrogenated coconut fat (*kokosfett*), called *Palmin* in Germany, replaced schmaltz and butter for pareve dishes and baking. It was also around this point that coconut became associated with Passover macaroons, a cookie previously made from ground almonds; coconut was also sometimes added to mandelbrot, *fluden*, and other Ashkenazic baked goods.

Coconut water, also called coconut juice, is the liquid found inside fresh coconuts. More important to cooking is coconut milk, a thicker emulsion made by steeping grated coconut flesh in hot water to extract oils and aromatic compounds. When the mixture is left standing in the refrigerator, a thick, sweet coconut cream (with a strong coconut flavor) separates and rises to the top. The thinner liquid left on the bottom is coconut milk, the thicker part is coconut cream. It is not the same as canned sweetened coconut cream, a very thick, sugary liquid used in cocktails. Coconut milk, now available in cans but also homemade, is essential to many Far Eastern cuisines. For observant Jews, it provides an excellent dairy substitute.

(See also Macaroon)

COD

Cod is the largest member (weighing up to one hundred pounds) of an extensive family that includes haddock, hake, pollack, and whiting. This native of the north Atlantic has firm, white flesh suited for grilling, poaching, and frying. Since it is so large, cod is generally available only in steaks or fillets. Cod and the other members of the family are interchangeable in recipes with flounder, halibut, and sea bass. Scrod is not a species of the fish, but rather a term for a young cod or other member of the cod family.

As a way to preserve vital resources, various countries of the eastern Mediterranean have long prepared cod and some other white fish by salting and drying, producing a firm, yellowish-colored fish with an assertive flavor. Beginning in the eleventh century, this abundant fish primarily in its salted form—called *bacalao* and *bakala* in Spanish, *baccalà* in Italian, and *morue* in French—became the staple of much of western Europe, including Sephardim. This was not so in Arabic countries, where people never developed a taste for it. In the fifteenth century, cod was discovered in the Grand Banks off of Newfoundland and salt cod became an important component of European commerce.

Salt cod is soaked in water to rehydrate the fish, as well as to remove the excess salt. Soaking time varies according to thickness. When rehydrated cod is ready to eat, it will swell and the white color will return. Salt cod differs in flavor and texture from fresh cod, so they should not be substituted for each other. Among Sephardim, salt cod is used to make stews, fish balls, fritters, purees, and fillings for *empanadas*.

COFFEE

The coffee tree, an evergreen shrub bearing two-seeded fruit, is indigenous to Ethiopia, where the berries and leaves were chewed for their stimulating effects. Ethiopians may have brought coffee to Yemen during occasional forays across the narrow Gulf of Aden, and around 1000 CE in Yemen, coffee first emerged as a hot beverage, a Sufi Muslim substitute for the forbidden alcohol. In 1511, coffee made its initial appearance in Mecca; by this point the beans were roasted, ground, and infused in the manner of the modern beverage.

Although briefly forbidden by the Meccan authorities, by 1524 coffee was accepted and it subsequently became a prominent feature of hospitality in the Muslim world. The Ottomans captured Yemen in 1536 and took control of the coffee trade emanating from the port of Mocha. Because coffee tended to be rather bitter, not to mention strong, residents of the Ottoman Empire developed the practice of adding sugar, a custom that would forever after affect the world through international commerce and conquest.

It seems to have been in Istanbul, around 1550, where coffee was first consumed in a social setting, the coffeehouse. In these shops, which quickly spread throughout the Ottoman Empire, the beverage that would become known as Turkish coffee was consumed on a daily basis by both rich and poor, literati and illiterates, Moslem and Jew, although only men were then allowed in these establishments. Around 1553, David ibn Abi Zimra, a rabbi in Cairo, initially addressed the situation of Jews and coffeehouses, stating, "There is no problem with the beverage being prepared by a non-Jew." However, the rabbi was against Jews patronizing coffeehouses and urged that

the beverage "be delivered home." In these shops, patrons conversed, played backgammon and chess, smoked (beginning in the early seventeenth century, coffee and tobacco commonly went hand in hand), and frequently listened to music, as well as drinking cup after cup of the relatively inexpensive intense black beverage. In the days before the modern modes of entertainment, the coffeehouse was a primary form of and forum for arts and entertainment, occupying a role these establishments would soon play in Europe as well.

Middle Easterners use green Arabica coffee beans and a generous amount of cardamom, sometimes including more spice than coffee. Arabs never add sugar to coffee, serving it *murra* (bitter) and generally accompanied with dates, but Middle Eastern Jews in Israel prefer it *mazboota* (medium) or *hilwe* (sweet).

Turkish coffee is variously served *hilwe*, *mazboota*, or *murra*, but always black. The coffee is poured, about halfway, into *fincan/finjan*, tiny porcelain cups with no handles. Refusing a cup is considered impolite. A host customarily refills the cup up to three times; more than three cups is considered greedy, while less than two impolite. The scalding-hot coffee is meant to be sipped slowly.

By the end of the sixteenth century, coffee had become and would remain an integral part of daily life throughout the Middle East. During this time, the Ottomans, particularly the merchants of Cairo, kept the Arabian coffee plant a carefully guarded monopoly, resulting in its extremely high price outside the Ottoman Empire. Indeed, coffee temporarily filled the trade vacuum created by the loss of the spice trade after Columbus and Vasco da Gama.

For nearly a century after its introduction to Europe, coffee was the exclusive province of the aristocrats and bourgeoisie; it was highly priced due to the Ottoman monopoly and accumulated import tariffs. Then in the mid-1600s, Dutch smugglers managed to sneak some fresh coffee beans out of the region. They were planted in Ceylon in 1658 and Java in 1699, and then in other Dutch colonies. For decades, the Dutch controlled the world coffee market. Coffee cultivation was brought by the French to Martinique in 1723, beginning with a single plant, and then surreptitiously by the Portuguese to Brazil four years later, further expanding the production and reducing the price.

Today, coffee is grown in temperate climates with

sufficient rainfall across the globe, with Brazil producing nearly half of the world's output. Around the same time that coffee cultivation was spreading wider, the cost of sugar in much of Europe plummeted due to the influx of Caribbean cane and subsequently European sugar beets. By the end of the eighteenth century, the masses of central Europe could also partake of *kaffee* with kuchen on a daily basis. Coffee replaced beer as the most widely consumed beverage, creating a much more alert population.

Coffee was first introduced to Europe by way of Venice in 1615; merchants and travelers had taken note of it during visits to the Ottoman Empire, and to England in 1630, several years before the arrival of tea there. As with many other new ventures (e.g., soap, sugar refining, and paper), Jews, excluded from guilds and frequently from owning farmland, were typically in the forefront of promoting coffee. In 1632 Jews in Livorno, Italy, a center of Tuscan trade, opened the first coffeehouses in Europe. In the Netherlands, Sephardim along with Armenians and Greeks established the early Dutch coffeehouses, before the Sephardim in the late seventeenth century turned more of their efforts to the chocolate business. Coffee reached France in 1646 and, after becoming fashionable in the court of Louis IV, cafés (named after the French word for coffee) began to spring up throughout Paris. Jews along with various Turks and Armenians were responsible for opening most of the French coffeehouses.

The first coffeehouse in England was opened at the Angel Inn in Oxford in 1650 by a Lebanese referred to as "Jacob the Jew." He later moved to London to open a similar establishment there. In 1654, a Jew named Cirques Jobson (who many believe was none other than the aforementioned Jacob) opened the Queen's Lane Coffee House in Oxford, the oldest extant coffeehouse in the world. By 1715, there were more than two thousand coffeehouses in the London area.

The *kaffeehaus* was introduced to Germany by the Dutch in the mid-1660s, and it was in central Europe that coffee and coffeehouses were most appreciated. These were male bastions and women were relegated to private forums called *kaffeekränzchen* (coffee clubs) and *kaffeeklatsche* (coffee chat). Coffeehouses emerged as a social milieu and center of intellectual discourse. By the nineteenth century, coffeehouses became a vehicle by which Jews and non-Jews could emulate and enter the emerging bourgeois society.

Jews discovered and developed intellectual ideas and also refined the Jewish comic culture. In particular, Vienna, Prague, Berlin, and Budapest became renowned for these establishments, as well as the pastries sold in many of them.

Eating a piece of cake with a hot beverage provides textural and flavor differences that enhance each item, making for a more pleasurable experience. Throw in caffeine, and a nosh becomes downright uplifting. Thus during the early seventeenth century, coffee drinkers in central Europe commonly accompanied their morning and afternoon fixes with various sweet yeast pastries. Germans referred to these generic baked goods as *kaffeekuchen* (coffee cakes), small coffee cakes as *kleina kaffeekuchen*, those covered with a crumb topping as *streuselkuchen* and *krum kuchen*, and those baked in a tube pan or as a ring as *gugelhopf* (this pan was the forerunner of the modern Bundt pan).

Jewish emigrants would help spread central European coffee styles and cakes to much of the world. In America, by the end of the nineteenth century, the term coffee cake supplanted the British tea cake.

Edna Ferber (1885–1958), noted author of, among other works, *Giant* and *Show Boat*, underscored the Teutonic and Jewish heritage of coffee and cake in her novel *Dawn O'Hara, the Girl Who Laughed* (1911), in a chapter entitled "Kaffee and Kaffeekuchen.":

I have visited Baumbach's. I have heard Milwaukee drinking its afternoon Kaffee.

O Baumbach's, with your deliciously crumbling butter cookies and your kaffee kuchen, and your thick cream, and your thicker waitresses and your cockroaches, and your dinginess and your dowdy German ladies and your black, black Kaffee, where in this country is there another like you!

As early as 1900, some American commercial manufacturers had taken note of the growing Jewish population and, for the first time, began to directly market to the Jewish community, using techniques such as targeted advertising. Among these pioneers was the Maxwell House Coffee Company, which from the early 1900s until the 1980s sold the most coffee in the United States. However, a particular problem emerged in regard to coffee. For following World War I, some Jewish consumers mistook the term "coffee bean" for some sort of legume rather than a berry, which led them to believe that it was in the prohibited Passover category of *kitniyot*. To clarify the situation, Maxwell House launched an unprecedented publicity campaign replete with, in 1931, the first *Maxwell House Haggadah*, which was an advertisement in the form of a religious book. Maxwell House was perhaps the first national brand to identify its products as being kosher for Passover and was certainly the first, of what is now a legion of institutions, to offer its own Haggadah. The approach worked and coffee remained a permitted and well-selling item for Passover, while Maxwell House went on over the decades to print millions of Haggadahs, which became a fixture in many American homes.

In the early twentieth century, central Europeans and Middle Eastern Jews brought their love of coffee to Israel, and coffeehouses became the favorite meeting places of German Jews there. After the British left the region and immigrants from other Western areas grew in influence, coffee soon overshadowed tea, becoming the top hot beverage in Israel.

COLLARD

Collard, also called collard greens or collards, and its close relative kale are both primitive nonheading cabbages native to the eastern Mediterranean or Asia Minor, and have been cultivated since prehistoric times. The English name collard is a corruption of the Old English coleworts (nonheading cabbage). It consists of a large stalk and broad, loose, oval leaves similar to those of the original wild cabbage. It is milder than the crinkled, bitter kale. In many early cultures, the collard stalk was the preferred part of the plant to eat. Both the Greeks and Romans consumed a good deal of collard (and kale; the two were rarely distinguished), as it was an extremely easy plant to grow. However, as milder varieties of headed cabbage emerged during the Middle Ages, the use of collard increasingly declined, and today it is best known as an African food or American soul food; in America, it is traditionally accompanied with hot sauce and vinegar. When Southern Jews cook collard greens, they usually do so without the regional staple ham; sometimes turkey or schmaltz is used. Collard greens (*gomen*) remain part of Jewish tradition in contemporary Ethiopian cuisine, following only cabbage (*tikil gomen*) and onions in importance among vegetables.

Unlike the western African style of slow-cooking greens "down to a low gravy," Ethiopians first boil the greens in salted water to remove excess bitterness; then, after draining the collards, they stew, cream, or puree them, cooking them in the same way that primitive cabbages were prepared in the ancient Middle East. The cooked collard greens have a slightly bitter, vaguely cabbage-like flavor. Ethiopians usually add plenty of spices, particularly chilies, or *iab* (curd cheese). The greens are commonly mixed with white beans or black-eyed peas. Ethiopians often serve collard greens warm or at room temperature with a *wot* (stew) and *injera* (pancake bread).

COMPOTE
Compote is a dish of stewed fresh or dried fruit.
Origin: France

The name compote comes from the Old French *composte* and Latin *compositum* (mixture). During the early Middle Ages, the term *compositum* was used for various dishes containing a number of ingredients, including vegetables and even meat; frequently the ingredients were layered. Among the first records of this dish was an early fourteenth-century French manuscript containing a recipe for "Confectio Compositi," consisting of an unsweetened dish of layered parsley root, celery root, cabbage, vinegar, and meat baked in an earthenware vessel.

Shortly after the advent of sugar in the Islamic world, cooks developed simple and sophisticated dishes of cooked fruit in a sugar syrup. Middle Easterners generally did not serve these dishes during or after a meal, but rather in the afternoon or evening as a treat with coffee. In any case, these fruit dishes probably influenced later Europeans. The French, in accord with the medieval notion that cooked fruits help to rebalance the humors, developed a particular predilection for sweetened fruit compotes. Following the Renaissance, compotes evolved to a form closer to the modern version; they were generally sweetened with sugar and increasingly offered for dessert at the end of a banquet. This idea spread throughout the continent, becoming particularly popular among Germans. A form of the word and of the dish is common to almost every European country. With the popularization of the sugar beet in the nineteenth century, compotes became a typical Ashkenazic dessert.

Compote differs from fruit soups, which are basically composed of the same ingredients, in that the latter contain a large amount of thin liquid, while compotes feature the fruit in a small amount of syrup. Historically, fresh fruit was commonplace in compotes in the summer and fall, making use of seasonal abundance, while dried fruit was used during the winter and early spring. A compote can be made from a single fruit, notably apples, berries, pears, or rhubarb, but the most common type lives up to its name and contains a mixture.

Romanians, Hungarians, and Alsatians commonly added some wine for extra flavor, but Poles, who rarely had access to wine, cooked the fruit in only sugar water. Although compote is primarily thought of as a dessert, it also serves as an accompaniment to grilled or roasted meat or poultry. Ashkenazim commonly serve compote on Passover, accompanied with macaroons or other cookies, as a light course at the end of the Seder meal, but in some homes it also makes an appearance on Rosh Hashanah (signifying a wish for a sweet and fruitful year), Sukkot (representing the harvest), and the Sabbath.

❦ ASHKENAZIC POACHED DRIED FRUIT
(*FRUCHT KOMPOT*)

ABOUT 8 CUPS/6 TO 8 SERVINGS   [PAREVE]

 2 pounds (about 7 cups) mixed dried fruit, any
     combination of apples, apricots, cherries, figs,
     peaches, pears, pineapple, plums, and raisins
 8 cups water, or 4 cups dry white wine (such as
     Riesling or Chenin Blanc) and 4 cups water
 1 cup sugar or honey
 6 thin orange slices
 6 thin lemon slices
 2 (3-inch) cinnamon sticks or 3 whole cloves

1. In a large, heavy pot, bring all the ingredients to a boil over medium heat. Reduce the heat to low and simmer, stirring occasionally, until just tender, about 20 minutes.

2. Remove and reserve the fruit. Increase the heat to high and boil until the cooking liquid is reduced to about 3 cups, about 10 minutes. Remove from the heat and return the fruit. Serve warm or chilled. Store in the refrigerator for up to 4 weeks.

COOKBOOK

Throughout most of history, books were handwritten and prohibitively expensive and, consequently, Jews never devoted any to gastronomy. The Talmud and subsequent rabbinic literature may be filled with the names of numerous dishes, foods, and even occasionally ingredients, but they do not contain actual recipes. If recipes were not transmitted from mother to daughter, they were lost. The earliest surviving Jewish recipes are six preparations—four poultry concoctions and "A Jewish Dish of Eggplants Stuffed with Meat" and "A Jewish Buried Stuffing"—included in an anonymous Andalusian handwritten cookbook of the thirteenth century. Even after the advent of movable type, printing remained relatively costly and typically was devoted to "serious" subjects. Some Jewish recipes appeared in the 1796 edition of Hannah Glasse's *The Art of Cookery*, the best-selling English cookbook of the eighteenth century.

Following the industrialization of printing and the development of pulp paper in the 1800s, books for the first time became much cheaper, leading to the appearance and increasing proliferation of Jewish

The 24th edition (1941) of the most successful American charity cookbook. It began in 1901 as a fund-raiser for the Jewish Settlement House in Milwaukee.

cookbooks. The earliest Jewish cookbooks emerged in the homeland of printing, Germany, perhaps the first of these being *Kochbuch fur Israeliten* (Carlsruhe, 1815) by Josef Stolz. Ten more German Jewish cookbooks followed during the nineteenth century, the most impactful being *Kochbuch fur Israelitischen Frauen* (Berlin, 1856) by Rebekka Wolf, itself inspired by contemporary non-Jewish works. Wolf emphasized thrift, while presenting a variety of German and international recipes. Wolf was reprinted many times through the early 1940s and translated into Dutch in 1881 and Polish in 1904. These volumes, all in accordance with the dietary laws and containing varying numbers of holiday dishes, reflect the continuity and changes in Jewish cuisine in Germany. Pointedly, as the nineteenth century progressed, the fare in Jewish cookbooks changed from thrifty to bourgeois.

The first Jewish cookbook in English was *The Jewish Manual* (London, 1846) written by Lady Judith Cohen Montefiore, wife of Sir Moses Montefiore, the most famous Jew of his time. The author begins her preface with these words: "Among the numerous works on Culinary Science already in circulation, there have been none which afford the slightest insight to the Cookery of the Hebrew kitchen." This work was meant to appeal to the growing Jewish middle class, offering, in the author's words, dishes that are "sophisticated" and "elegant." The recipes represent a mixture of English and Portuguese Sephardic cuisine.

Other early Anglo-Jewish cookbooks were *Aunt Sarah's Cookery Book for a Jewish Kitchen* (Liverpool, 1872) and the 188-page *An Easy and Economical Book of Jewish Cookery: Upon Strictly Orthodox Principles* (London, 1874) by Mrs. Estella Atrutel, cook to the family of Lionel de Rothschild.

In mid-nineteenth century Germany, the arduous economic and social conditions and a new wave of anti-Semitism induced many of its Jews to immigrate to America. While most of these newcomers settled in Manhattan, others scattered throughout the country. By the time of the Civil War, the American Jewish population had grown to about one hundred fifty thousand, the bulk coming from Germany. Quite a few of these German Jews obtained the success that had so long been withheld from them in their homeland. By force of their numbers and affluence, German Jews dominated the American Jewish scene until the early twentieth century.

In the manner of Monterfiore's book, the first American Jewish cookbook, *Jewish Cookery Book on Principles of Economy Adapted for Jewish Housekeepers* (Philadelphia, 1871) by Esther Jacobs Levy, also offered food for the refined palate; it included primarily contemporary middle-class American and English dishes with a spattering of traditional German Jewish dishes. Levy's book emphasized the kosher kitchen, while reflecting the growing influence of Reform Judaism in the United States. She notes, "Without violating the precepts of our religion, a table can be spread, which will satisfy the appetites of the most fastidious. Some have, from ignorance, been led to believe that a repast, to be sumptuous, must unavoidably admit of forbidden food. We do not venture too much when we assert that our writing clearly refutes that false notion."

As the German Jews assimilated, their cookbooks mirrored this change. Typical was *Aunt Babette's* by Bertha F. Kramer (Cincinnati, 1889). Unlike Levy's book, this work not only contained middle-class American fare and some German Jewish dishes, but many of the recipes utilized unkosher ingredients or combinations. The book also presented advice on holding the theme parties so widely popular in the 1890s.

The first Yiddish cookbook was *Kokhbuch far Yudishe Froyen* (Vilna, 1896) by Ozer Bloshsteyn, which was reprinted in New York two years later. Clearly inspired by Wolf's German *Kochbuch fur Israelitischen Frauen*, this work too featured only kosher foods.

One of America's great contributions to cuisine is the fund-raising community cookbook. It first emerged during the Civil War as a way to raise money for soldiers and their families. Today, these books have become an American institution, with a wide variety of nonprofit organizations offering a staggering array of cookbooks: Some are spiral-bound works, others are beautiful hard-cover volumes; some contain standard American fare, others are a valuable source of ethnic and regional food and culture.

Jewish women's groups early on recognized the potential for fund-raising cookbooks to support their various programs. Most of these initial works were published in the smaller Jewish communities in the South and West, where participation in Jewish organizations was necessary to maintain Jewish identity and philanthropy was a major component of organizational life. Sometimes cookbooks were published to raise money for the building fund. Although most of these early books contained a few traditional Jewish dishes, few were kosher—almost all featured recipes calling for shrimp and bacon.

Typical of these early Jewish organizational cookbooks is *The Settlement Cook Book*, unquestionably the most successful of the genre. First published in 1901, *The Settlement Cook Book* was meant to introduce eastern European immigrants to the American middle-class milieu. The book was the brainchild of Lizzie Black Kander (1858–1940). Born in Wisconsin to German Jewish immigrants, Kander was one of the founders of the "The Settlement," a neighborhood house in Milwaukee where recent immigrants took classes in English language, citizenship, sewing, and cooking. Kander, who also supervised the cooking classes, wanted to eliminate the laborious process of students copying recipes from the blackboard. Although the men on the house's board refused to fund the project, the women raised the necessary money and set about collecting recipes from members of high society and noted chefs, and from their students. The book's contents reflect the varied sources; it includes many unkosher dishes as well as traditional Jewish fare, such as kugels, gefilte fish, and matza balls. This dichotomy is particularly apparent in the holiday menu section.

The Settlement Cook Book has gone through thirty-three editions—Kander continued to revise the book until her death—has sold nearly two million copies, and has grown from 174 pages to 563 pages, with more than 3,000 recipes. The many revisions over the years have so totally altered the book that it no longer resembles the very Jewish nature of the original volume. However, the effort has been so successful at raising funds that the Settlement Cook Book Company continues to disperse proceeds to educational and recreational projects.

In the same year that *The Settlement Cook Book* first came out, so did one of the first Yiddish cookbooks in America, the self-published *Ler-bukh vi Azoy tsu Kokhn un* (Book for How to Cook and Bake) by Hinde Amkhanitski. Unlike the earlier German-based volumes, this was unabashedly kosher and eastern European, featuring "*Kneydlekh* [dumplings]," "*Khremzlekh* [matza meal pancakes]," and "*Teyglekh* [baked dough balls in honey]." However, for the next couple of decades, the typical American Jewish cook-book tended to be in English, unkosher, and with a tone conveying authors somewhat embarrassed by or even vehemently opposed to traditional Ashkenazic cooking.

Meanwhile, after the Civil War, Jews started to impact mainstream American cooking. The first generic cookbook to feature a section of "Jewish Receipts" was *Jennie June's American Cookery Book* (New York, 1866) by Jane Cunningham Croly. The author notes, "These are all original and reliable, the contribution of a superior Jewish housekeeper in New York." This unnamed source was probably Croly's good friend Genie H. Rosenfeld, wife of the dramatist and first editor of *Puck*, Sydney Rosenfeld. Among the twenty-five recipes in the chapter, reflecting an Americanized German milieu, are "White Stewed Fish," "Brown Fricassee Chicken," "Purim Fritters," "Meringues," and "Pickled Cucumbers." The Purim fritters are an early appearance of what would become known as French toast.

Sarah Rorer was the grand dame of early twentieth-century American cookery, the head of a Philadelphia cooking school for eighteen years, the domestic editor of the *Ladies' Home Journal* for fourteen years, and the author of more than seventy-five books and pamphlets. In *Mrs. Rorer's New Cook Book* (Philadelphia, 1902), considered her magnum opus, she included a section called "A Group of Jewish Recipes." Four of the nineteen Jewish recipes are attributed to a Mrs. Henry Cohen and her daughter Katherine and many have a Sephardic accent, including "Spanish Rice," "Okra Soup," and some of the fish dishes. Six of the recipes are Passover related: "Matzot Balls for Soup," "Hot Stewed Fish" (made with "3 matzoth"), "Matzoth Pudding," "Soup Balls" (based on soaking "six matzoths in cold water"), "Passover Raisin Wine," and "Matzoth Sponge Cake."

Following World War I, Jewish cookbooks began appearing with several notable differences from their predecessors. Like earlier organizational cookbooks, they were developed to raise funds for various causes; unlike those earlier efforts, not only were the contents strictly kosher, but they often stressed other traditional aspects of Jewish home and family life. Some of these volumes contain lengthy sections on Jewish law, holidays, and history meant to transmit Jewish heritage to future generations.

The first Israeli cookbook, published by WIZO (Women's International Zionist Organization) in Hebrew, German, and English, *Wie Kocht man in Erez Israel? (How to Cook in Palestine?)* by Dr. Erna Meyer, published in Tel Aviv in 1936, recommends, "We housewives must make an attempt to free our kitchens from European customs, which are not appropriate to Palestine." Meyer, an immigrant from Germany, directed her efforts to helping Europeans adapt to Middle Eastern ingredients and equipment, such as a primus stove.

The first complete cookbook in modern Hebrew, published in 1948, was *Ani Mevashelet* (I Am Cooking) by *Jerusalem Post* columnist Lilian Cornfeld. She had earlier an English book, *What and How to Cook in Wartime* (Tel Aviv, 1943). During the *tzena* (austerity), the period of rationing following the founding of the state, she provided recipes for eggless cakes and other dishes with simple ingredients in the 1949 work, *Ma Avashel Mimanot Tzena* (What to Cook with the Austerity Portions). Cornfeld, born in Montreal and educated at McGill University and Columbia University as a teacher and dietician, immigrated to Israel in the 1920s. She was one of the most popular and influential figures in Israeli food, eventually writing a dozen books emphasizing the emerging Israeli cuisine from a synthesis of the nation's ethnic communities.

In America, Jewish cookbooks, now issued by major publishing houses, number in the hundreds and can be most easily classified as traditional Ashkenazic, ethnic, or contemporary. Beginning in the 1980s, several food columnists for Jewish newspapers compiled excellent texts with a wealth of valuable information, notably *The Jewish Holiday Cookbook* (1985) by Gloria Kaufer Greene, *Sephardic Holiday Cooking* (1986) by Gilda Angel, and *International Jewish Cookbook* (1991) by Faye Levy. Also at that time, another interesting development in cookbook publishing was the exploration of recipes from a specific ethnic group that put food in a social and cultural context, including *The Classic Cuisine of Italian Jews* (1981) by Edda Servi Machlin, *Sephardic Cookery* (1983) by Emile de Vidas Levy, and *Cookbook of the Jews of Greece* (1986) by Nicholas Stavroulakis.

Jewish cookbooks now span the culinary spectrum from international to gourmet to healthy. They are self-published or issued from the major publishing houses. They reflect current social trends or traditional fare. The best ones are genuinely informative, evocative of a time and place, and make for great reading.

CORIANDER

The Bible describes manna as follows: "And the house of Israel called its name manna; and it was like *zera gad* [coriander seed]." A coriander seed is about three millimeters in diameter. Thus it required quite a number of manna to constitute the *omer* (9.4 cups) designated to feed each person daily.

Coriander, a relative of parsley, is native to the Levant. Every part of the coriander plant is edible and each contributes a different flavor—the dark green leaves (commonly called cilantro), thin off-white roots, pale pink flowers, and the ridged, globular tan seeds. The plant's English name was derived from the Greek *koris* (bedbug), either referring to the tiny leg-like sprouts on the husk or to the malodorous smell of immature seeds. Unripe seeds are extremely bitter. Upon ripening, the seeds are dried and threshed in a process similar to that used for grain—a reason why some Ashkenazim abstain from using coriander seeds on Passover. The brittle seeds are ground into an aromatic powder possessing a nutty-peppery-orange flavor quite different from the musty-peppery flavor of the leaves.

In the ancient Middle East, the coriander seed was far from being merely another spice, as it followed only salt and cumin as the most important and widespread seasoning. The earliest known examples of coriander seeds, dating to prehistoric times, were discovered among human artifacts in the Nahal Hemat cave in Israel. Coriander was among the ingredients in the world's first recorded recipes, which were found on four-thousand-year-old Sumerian tablets. Documents discussing the cultivation of coriander were among those in the library of the Assyrian king Ashurbanipal (seventh century BCE).

Unlike the expensive imported spices, commonplace coriander was grown locally in the Levant and in Egypt and was accessible to every level of society. The seeds were used in both savory and sweet dishes, as well as added to many varieties of wine and beer. In addition, coriander was valued for its medicinal properties and its essential oil has long been considered a digestive stimulant. In Egypt, coriander was also used in perfume and as an aphrodisiac. Egypt had a long history with this plant; the Roman naturalist Pliny praised Egyptian coriander for its quality. Its prominence in Egypt also contributes to its usage in describing the manna.

Whole seeds are relatively mild; ground coriander has a much more pronounced flavor. Toasting or exposing the seeds to acid (as in a brine) brings out the flavor. Coriander is used in foods cooked for a long time, such as roasts, or in foods cooked over a high heat, such as grilled meats. In Indian cooking, coriander is often combined with cumin and turmeric, and is an essential ingredient in curry powder. Middle Easterners add ground coriander to meatballs and stews, Moroccans to roast lamb, Germans to sausages, and Americans to hot dogs. Coriander is also used in pickles, marinades, liquors, fritters, and a variety of baked goods.

(See also Cilantro)

CORN/CORNMEAL

Corn, in England a generic term for any small, hard particle, including grains, refers in North America more specifically to Indian corn, which the English named maize. This native of southern Mexico descended from a thin wild grass called *teosinte*, which has been cultivated and modified since the late Neolithic Age. Rudimentary corn, after generations of breeding, was still only about three inches long with eight rows of tiny kernels. Nevertheless, when very fresh, the kernels were sweet, a rarity at that time and place and, therefore, of appeal to ancient farmers. Long before Columbus arrived in the Caribbean, corn had spread from Canada to the tip of South America. It had been cultivated to increase dramatically in size and utilization and had become the most essential New World food. Hundreds of varieties had been developed—some to eat fresh, others to dry for popping, but most were intended for grinding. Cornmeal was transformed into fundamental dishes, such as tortillas, cakes, tamales, stews, and porridges.

Corn, beans, and squash were designated by Native Americans as the "Three Sisters of Life" and formed the staples of the diet, together providing the essential amino acids for complete protein. This trio provided all the necessary nutrients and foods were combined together in various dishes, such as the corn, bean, and vegetable stew called succotash, or corn tortillas served with cooked beans. Moreover, the Aztecs of Mexico learned to boil dried corn kernels in a wood ash solution; the highly alkaline material softens the kernels and loosens the hulls, which slip off during processing. Corn treated with wood ash is easier to grind, cooks up softer, and holds together better for tortillas. As an incredibly beneficial side effect, the alkaline also converts various vitamins, such as niacin, calcium, and potassium, into a form capable of being absorbed by humans.

Shortly after Columbus' first voyage, Spanish explorers introduced corn to the Old World and Portuguese ships began shipping it from the Americas. Corn initially achieved popularity in North Africa. It was recorded in Egypt by at least 1530. In 1650, the Ottoman Turks, who preferred wheat and contemptuously rejected eating the new grain, introduced the less expensive corn to territories in the Balkans as well as to Italy. Always on the lookout for a good deal, Venetian and Dutch merchants grasped the commercial potential of this American import and began peddling it, mainly in cornmeal form, throughout Europe.

As usual with a new item, Jews, who were generally excluded from trade guilds and owning land, frequently served as the middlemen. Corn had a short growing season and a high yield, and it did not need to be threshed and winnowed. This made it much less expensive and problematic to grow than wheat or even barley. Corn was also tastier and more versatile than barley. In addition, corn matches well with wheat in crop rotation. Although corn did not fare very well in the cooler climes of northern Europe, the milder conditions in the south proved ideal. In particular, Europe had entered a cold period from the middle of the sixteenth century until the eighteenth century, during which corn cultivation suffered.

However, there emerged an even more serious problem than weather conditions. The Old World areas that shifted to cornmeal were unaware of the Native American practices of treating the grain with wood ash or of eating it with beans. People soon found themselves plagued with pellagra (skin lesions, inflammation, and mental disorders) and other diseases caused by vitamin deficiency. As a result, most populations quickly switched back to Old World grains and corn was mainly grown as animal fodder.

On the other hand, in some areas, most notably the part of the Roman Empire accustomed to subsisting on *pulmentum* (grain porridges) and also to consuming legumes and dairy products that supplemented the nutrition in corn—northern Italy, Bulgaria, southern Ukraine, southern Hungary, western Georgia, and especially Romania—unprocessed cornmeal emerged as the most important component of the diet, much as potatoes, another American import, did in Poland and Ireland. Today, corn is the most planted field crop globally.

Only a very small percent of corn is consumed fresh; most of it is used for animal feed and processed into oil, syrup, starch, cold cereals, cornmeal, and various other edible and inedible items. Cornmeal can be adapted in numerous ways, including porridges, gnocchi (Italian dumplings), breads, soufflés, and desserts. Romanians even make a spirit from it.

The primary difference between yellow and white cornmeal is the color—the yellow variety contains a larger amount of beta-carotene. Otherwise, there is no perceptible difference in taste or texture between dishes made from either color meal.

(See also Malai and Mamaliga)

CORNED BEEF

Two weeks after the historic 2008 election, President-elect Barack Obama, accompanied by a throng of Secret Service agents, visited a local Chicago deli and purchased three corned beef sandwiches to go, explaining, "I have to get corned beef for Rahm [Emanuel, his new chief of staff]." The American public needed no explanation of corned beef on rye, understanding full well this iconic Jewish food. Jewish corned beef, called salt beef in England and *pickelfleisch* in Yiddish, is beef brisket that is cured with a brine of salt, sugar, and spices, and then cooked.

Although early humans did not understand the chemistry involved in salting and curing meat, they recognized the empirical effects, thereby stretching a limited and expensive resource. The typical time to slaughter cattle was in the late fall, to avoid the necessity of feeding any unwanted animals for the winter. At this time, much of the meat was dry-salted—coated with coarse grains of salt and air dried—to preserve it at least until spring. Cool weather also helped prevent the meat from spoiling.

During the medieval period, the English began referring to the dry-salted type of preserved meat as cured beef, salt beef, and corned beef, the latter term first appearing in 1621 in the medical text *Anatomy of Melancholy* by Robert Burton. The name has nothing to do with what Americans call corn (maize in Britain). In England, corn is a term used for any small, hard particle, such as a grain of coarse salt. The medieval English concept of corned beef, referring to dry-salted meat, is rather different from the contemporary item in Jewish delis bearing that name. The English dry-cured meat was so excessively salty and hard, akin to salt cod (*bacalao*), it had to be soaked in water and boiled for hours in order to be palatable.

Beginning in the sixteenth century, another salt, potassium nitrate (saltpeter) was commonly added by Europeans to maintain the meat's color and improve the flavor, texture, and shelf life. In the eighteenth century, as the availability of sugar rose and its price dramatically fell, sugar, also a preservative, was frequently mixed with the two salts. The advent of saltpeter eventually led to a different wet method for curing meat. It was still called cured or corned beef, but it was preserved in a concentrated salt solution (pickle)—the source of the German and Yiddish term *pickelfleisch*. This method was most popular in cooler climates, notably Alsace, Holland, Germany, and Austria. Beef tongue was also commonly pickled as was fish, such as herring. Pickled meat did not become as salty and hard as dry-cured meat and was also much cheaper than fresh. It therefore became the most common type of meat consumed in parts of eighteenth-century Europe and America.

In America, pickled beef first appeared in print in the recipe "A Good Pickle for Beef and Pork, Called the 'Knickerbocker Pickle' " in the anonymous twelve-page pamphlet *The Family Receipt Book, Containing Thirty Valuable and Simple Receipts* by "A Long-Island Farmer" (1825). Earlier American cookbooks only recorded the dry-cured method for meat.

Mrs. E. A. Howland, in *The New England Economical Housekeeper* (1844), provided the two mid-nineteenth-century American methods of curing meat. The dry-curing entailed sprinkling one hundred pounds of beef with "four pounds brown sugar, four ounces saltpetre, and four quarts fine Liverpool salt," with no added liquid, only "the juice of the meat." The other method was to sprinkle the meat lightly with salt and place it in barrels, then "cover the meat with a pickle made by boiling together, in four gallons of water, eight pounds of salt, three pounds of brown sugar, three ounces saltpetre, one ounce saleratus [sodium bicarbonate], for one hundred pounds of meat . . . beef packed in this manner will keep a year." The classic New England boiled dinner was originally made from this type of salted beef.

Meanwhile, the term corned beef took on a different meaning in the mid-nineteenth century after the German organic chemist Justus von Liebig invented meat extract in an attempt to develop an inexpensive meat substitute. In 1866, Liebig opened a factory to manufacture the meat extract in Uruguay, in the heart of gaucho country, to make use of the meat from animals primarily slaughtered for their hides. Seven years later, as the company was slaughtering about one hundred fifty thousand head of cattle a year, he mixed the boiled meat left over from the meat extract process with sodium nitrite, canned it, and sold it as corned beef, which the English also referred to as bully beef (from the French *bouilli* "boiled"). William Vestey, son of a Liverpool meatpacking family, began to precook and can vast amounts of trimmings from the Chicago stockyards, also calling it corned beef and popularizing the term in America. In 1920, the Vesteys bought Liebig's plant and merged the operations.

In the mid-nineteenth century, artificial refrigeration allowed the substitution of a much weaker saltwater brine, which also contained less sugar, that could be used for curing meat any time of the year and produced milder and more tender meat. The first known to use this process were German who called it *pickelfleisch*. Toward the end of the nineteenth century, central European immigrants in America, including Germen Jews, popularized *pickelfleisch* made from brisket. It was typically flavored with peppercorns and bay leaves, and was cured using the lighter brine and the refrigeration method available in America. Jews in lower Manhattan, who had long enjoyed the economical brisket as traditional fare, found pickled beef and tongue intriguing, as well as less expensive than fresh cuts, and began preparing it for special occasions, usually with potatoes and other vegetables. This is where Irish neighbors picked up the idea for their corned beef and cabbage, which became a substitute for Irish bacon—back home in Ireland, they had no history of pickled beef.

Home kitchens and small stores, some called delicatessens, began selling food catering to Jewish immigrants, many of them males who were either single or attempting to save up enough money to bring over their families from Europe. These eateries commonly served the less expensive pickled and cured meats, all of it beef and much of it kosher, between slices of rye bread—the simple dish was a filling meal. Sandwiches were also more portable than plain meat and could be taken home or to work. The patrons took a liking to these deli sandwiches, when done well. Pickled beef soon became known by the same name as the popular canned meat, corned beef. In England, American-style pickled corned beef, called salt beef in London, is still relatively rare; it is available primarily in a few Jewish-style delis.

In delis, the meat is still always served on rye bread and it is offered cold as well as hot (steamed); the hot corned beef sandwich was also born in New York City. The rainbow specter that sometimes appears on corned beef and other slices of deli meat is merely an optical illusion created by the thin slicing process; the bundles of myofibrils are cut at an angle that refracts a spectrum of light. In some establishments, patrons are asked if they want the meat "lean" or "juicy" (with fat). Mustard or occasionally horseradish is the proper condiment and sour dill pickles and "half sours" the ubiquitous accompaniments.

It was in Manhattan's "kosher style" delis in the 1930s and 40s, a time when there were more than five thousand delis in the New York metropolitan area, that overstuffed sandwiches, filled with inches of sliced meat and available in a multitude of combinations, emerged. The concept spread to other cities with sizable Jewish populations. A strip of East Lombard Street in downtown Baltimore, once the center of the city's Jewish life and dotted with delis, was nicknamed "Corned Beef Row." In the 1920s, Toronto became a Canadian center of Jewish delicatessens.

In 1893, two Jewish immigrants, Emil Reichel of Austria and Sam Ladany of Hungary, opened a small store on the West Side of Chicago, the Vienna Sausage Company, which was subsequently responsible for turning Chicago into a hot dog town. The partners, whose business grew into the multi-million-dollar Vienna Beef Company, also introduced other central European meats, including a sideline of corned beef, which they marketed as *pickelfleisch*. Although Jewish-style, these products were not kosher, but targeted to the general market. Within a few years, Vienna Sausage began selling items to stores and restaurants in the area and, by the 1940s, many delicatessens in the Midwest were featuring Vienna's products.

By the 1960s, Jewish corned beef had spread to the American mainstream. In a *Gemini 3* flight in 1965, astronaut John Young as a practical joke smuggled onboard a corned beef sandwich from a Jewish deli near Cape Canaveral to give to Virgil (Gus) Grissom who did not want to eat the NASA food during the nearly five-hour flight. Because crumbs from the sandwich posed a potential safety hazard, this became, so far, the one and only corned beef sandwich in space.

(See also Brisket, Choucroute Garnie, and Delicatessen)

COUSCOUS

Couscous is rolled pasta granules made from crushed and ground semolina, bound with water. In addition, the term means the various stews (*marga*) that are served with or on top of the couscous.

Origin: Maghreb

Other names: Arabic: *kouskous, mugrabieh*; Berber: *k'seksu*; Lebanon: *maftoul*; Turkish: *kuskus*.

An ancient African cooking technique consisted of steaming foods in woven baskets. Among the aftereffects of the Arab conquest of northwestern Africa at the end of the seventh century was the widespread cultivation of durum wheat in the Maghreb. By the eleventh century, the Berbers, pre-Arab northwest African tribes, utilized the venerable African steaming practice to develop a process of steaming semolina granules made from the durum endosperm called couscous. The name possibly came from the Arabic *kaskasa* (to pound/make small). Others contend the word is an onomatopoeia derived from the sound of the semolina granules being stirred to form the couscous.

The first recorded recipe and one of the earliest references to couscous was the term *kuskusu*, the Arabic cognate of the Berber *seksu*, in an anonymous Moorish Andalusian thirteenth-century cookbook, where a dish attributed to Marrakesh called "*Kuskusu Titian*" (Soldiers' Couscous) was described as "famous all over the world." Also in the thirteenth century, references to couscous begin appearing in Tunisia. It was in the Maghreb that couscous was created and found its greatest popularity. Couscous-like dishes in other parts of the Arab world are commonly called *maghribiyya* (from the Maghreb). Couscous—simply topped with sour milk and butter or with an elaborate stew—has long served as daily fare throughout the Maghreb.

In some areas, couscous was made from other hard grain pellets, such as millet, sorghum, and barley, but versatile semolina remains the standard. Historically, couscous in the Maghreb was made at home by hand. Husbands would purchase a large sack of durum wheat berries, usually in August when there was plenty of sun for drying. Then the women, usually in a group of family and friends, gathered to form the pellets, a time-consuming process requiring much skill. Wealthier families would hire a Berber woman to prepare their supply.

Unlike pasta, couscous is not flour kneaded into a dough, but instead the *smeed* (finely crushed semolina) is placed in a large shallow earthenware or wooden bowl—called a *qasa* in Morocco and an *iyan* in Algeria—gradually sprinkled with salty water and one part semolina flour, and stirred in a circular motion or rubbed with the right hand; the starch accumulates around the semolina granules to form progressively larger bits. The couscous must be sifted through several progressively smaller sieves to achieve a uniform grain; fine pellets, in some areas reserved for sweetened couscous, are called *seffa* in Morocco and *masfuf/masfouf* in Tunisia, and very large ones are called *berkukes* or *mhammsa*.

The couscous is then steamed, spread out on a mat or cloth to dry in the sun for several days, and placed in airtight containers for storage. Moroccans and Tunisians prefer medium-sized grains, while Algerians generally opt for finer granules. Large-grain granules, which have to be steamed five times or cooked in a liquid, are popular in southern Morocco.

In the Maghreb, both the grains and the stew are traditionally made in a *couscousière*, a two-compartment barrel-shaped vessel with a stewing pot on the bottom—called a *qidra* in Morocco and Algeria, an *ikineksu* by Berbers, and a *makful* in Tunisia—and an uncovered perforated steamer (*kiskis*) on top. As the couscous granules cook and soften, they absorb the flavors of the stew. A flour and water paste or dough rope is commonly wrapped around the juncture of the top and bottom parts of the *couscousière* to prevent the steam from escaping. Berbers traditionally used *couscousières* of unglazed earthenware, while many Arabs and Jews preferred ones consisting of copper lined with tin.

After steaming, the granules are customarily fluffed up and heaped onto a deep-sided serving platter. Moroccans typically arrange the meat and/or vegetables on top of the couscous and pour the broth over the top to moisten the grains. Algerians generally present the couscous, meat and vegetables, and broth in separate serving dishes. In the Maghreb, for a feast, couscous with stew is rarely served as a main course, but in accord with the Middle Eastern style of hospitality, hosts offer the couscous as a finale to a number of courses to produce *shaban* (complete satisfaction).

Couscous can be fiery or sweet; it can contain an assortment of meats, poultry, or fish or be vegetarian. Tunisians prefer more robust stews with plenty of fire, while Moroccans use a subtle combination of spices. Algerians typically add tomatoes. Savory stews are generally accompanied by a fiery chili paste called harissa. Although Westerners find it more comfortable to eat couscous with a spoon, the more traditional and sensual method is to use your right hand to scoop up some of the granules and stew, form into a small ball, and pop it into your mouth.

Jews, who have been a major presence in the Maghreb since at least Roman times, have been making couscous for nearly a thousand years. Moroccan, Tunisian, and Algerian Jews serve couscous accompanied with several salads every Friday night, on the festivals, and at special occasions, including a *brit*, bar mitzvah, and wedding. Most cooks make an extra-large quantity on Friday night so that they can serve the leftover grains with the following day's *hamin/adafina* (Sabbath stew). The Moroccan couscous stew for Rosh Hashanah, called *couscous aux sept legumes*, customarily contains seven symbolic vegetables; seven is considered a fortuitous number as Rosh Hashanah falls on the first day of the seventh month and the world was created in seven days. The dessert couscous for Rosh Hashanah is sprinkled with pomegranate seeds or small grapes. On Sukkot, a large assortment of vegetables, especially sweet potatoes and carrots, are added to the stew as a sign of the harvest.

When *seffa* (fine couscous) is mixed with chopped dried fruits and nuts, and typically moistened with almond milk, it is known as *couscous hillo* (sweet). For grand public affairs, such as weddings and bar mitzvahs, sweetened *seffa* is mounded into a large pyramid, sprinkled with ground cinnamon, and garnished with *datils rellenos* (stuffed dates); the sweetness of the dish denotes happiness. Moroccans prefer their desserts rich and sugary, and their *seffa hillo* is generally sweeter than Tunisian versions.

Although some Mahgrebi cooks still insist on making their own couscous from scratch, considering it a disgrace to buy it in a store, convenient machine-made couscous grains are found at Middle Eastern markets. Most of the couscous available in the West consists of finer grains processed through steaming under tremendous pressure, thereby transforming it into "instant" couscous; this product requires no additional steaming or lengthy cooking, just a soak in hot water.

Following the establishment of the state of Israel in 1948, the government imposed a period of national belt-tightening and rationing, known as the *tzena* (austerity). Because rice was still prohibitively expensive in the early 1950s, Prime Minister David Ben-Gurion asked the Osem company to devise a carbohydrate food that would be filling and inexpensive. The company responded with *petitim* (from the Hebrew root *petat*, "to break into pieces/to crumble"). In America, it became known as Israeli couscous. *Petitim* are made from a wheat paste extruded into small balls about ten times larger than Maghrebi couscous, then toasted. Israeli couscous must be cooked like pasta in plenty of boiling water. It has a chewier texture and a slightly nutty flavor, which is made more pronounced if it is first browned in hot fat. Israeli couscous cannot be substituted in recipes for standard couscous.

CROSTATA

Crostata is a tart, usually covered with a top crust.
Origin: Italy

Italian tarts, called *crostate* (*crostata* singular) are a specialty of Rome and Tuscany and are generally made with a thicker crust than the French type. This sweet, rich crust is made from a dough called *pasta frolla* (fragile pastry). It was developed during the Renaissance and has been the basic pastry of Italy ever since.

Crostate were originally rustic free-form pastries.

The cook filled the pastry with jam, folded the sides over, and baked the pastry directly on the floor of the oven. However, after the advent of baking pans, the pastries were more commonly rolled out and shaped in molds. Besides jam, seasonal fruits and nuts serve as the basis for most fillings. The pastries were also filled with ricotta cheese, pastry cream, and lemon curd. Many of the fillings were brought to Italy by Sephardim following the expulsion from Spain. Meat and vegetable pies are known as *pasticcio*.

A small bakery, Boccione, dating back to 1555, in the old Roman Jewish ghetto continues to produce *crostate*, which are sold by the tart or slice, and other handmade traditional Jewish pastries. Among its specialties is *crostata di ricotta e cioccolato* (ricotta and chocolate), which originated in the ghetto and is now common throughout the country. Some of the other traditional Jewish fillings include *mandorla e visciole* (almond paste and sour cherries) and *ricotta e visciole* (ricotta and sour cherries).

CSIPETKE

Csipetke is a cross between a dumpling and noodle.
Origin: Hungary

Csipetke, meaning "pinched" in Hungarian, is an evolutionary link between dumplings (like *galuska*) and egg noodles (*metelt*), not quite one or the other. It serves as a garnish for many Hungarian soups and stews (such as goulash) or, with gravy, as a side dish or even as a main course.

(See also Galuska)

❧ HUNGARIAN PINCHED DUMPLINGS (*CSIPETKE*)

5 TO 6 SERVINGS   [PAREVE]

2 cups (10 ounces) all-purpose flour
1 teaspoon salt
4 large eggs

1. In a large bowl, combine the flour and salt. Make a well in the center and drop in the eggs. Using a fork, lightly beat the eggs, then gradually stir in the flour to make a firm dough. On a lightly floured surface, knead until smooth. Cover with a kitchen towel or plastic wrap and let rest at room temperature for at least 30 minutes.

2. Bring a large pot of salted water to a boil. Flatten the dough with your hands or roll out the dough to a ½-inch thickness. Cut into ½-inch-thick strips. Pinch off small pieces of the dough.

3. In batches, add the dumplings to the boiling water and simmer until they float to the surface, about 5 minutes. Remove with a slotted spoon and drain. The *csipetke* can also be cooked directly in soup or goulash. Add to a soup or toss with about 2 tablespoons vegetable oil to prevent sticking until ready to use. Store covered in the refrigerator for up to 2 days.

CUCUMBER

Melons, gourds, and cucumbers all belong to the Cucurbitaceae family; these plants grow on trailing, tendril-bearing vines. There exists, however, much confusion over the names and identities of melons and cucumbers throughout history.

The common translation of the *kishuim* mentioned in the Bible is cucumbers. It was among the Egyptian foods the Israelites waxed nostalgic over in the wilderness. However, this is a misnomer. Seeds found in Egyptian tombs, as well as images in ancient illustrations, point to chate melons and possibly also snake melons, both common in ancient Egypt, as the biblical *kishuim* and not cucumbers.

The chate melon (from the Arabic *qatta* or *qitha*, a cognate of *kishuim*)—also variously called chate cucumber, hairy melon, and cucumber melon—was probably the first cultivated melon in Africa; it was commonly being grown in the Bronze Age. Already four thousand years ago, residents of Egypt and Mesopotamia preserved them in salt, somewhat like the modern pickle.

The snake melon—also variously called vegetable melon and Armenian cucumber—is an elongated fruit that grows up to three feet in length, is heavily ribbed lengthwise, and reaches one to three inches in thickness. Grown on the ground, it typically coils like a snake, while those grown on a trellis tend to be straight. When young and unripe, snake melons can be eaten raw, cooked, or pickled; the crisp, mild, white flesh has somewhat of a cucumber-like taste. In Lebanon and Afghanistan today, pickled young snake melons are sold bottled under the name "pickled wild cucumbers."

The vegetables (*cucumis* and *sikyos hemeros*) mentioned by Pliny and other Roman writers and in the Talmud were most certainly the chate and snake melons.

In the wake of the fall of the Roman Empire, melon cultivation disappeared in most of Europe. With the spread of the hardy Indian cucumber and its gradual improvement, the popularity of any remaining chate melons and snake melons further declined.

The cucumbers common today—the intensely succulent, dark-green-skinned, cylindrical fruit-vegetables—are descendants of an annual native to a region in northwestern India near the Himalayas, where their ancestor was cultivated more than three thousand years ago. When cucumbers initially reached western Asia and the Mediterranean, they were confused with the African melons they resembled and called by their names. The modern Hebrew word for cucumber, *melafefon*, a contraction of the Greek words *melo* (apple) and *pepon* (watermelon), referred in the Talmud to a rudimentary muskmelon, not the modern cucumber. In addition to the confusion over linguistics, there is a lack of archaeological evidence because the cucumber's soft seeds have not been preserved at ancient sites. Consequently, we do not know when cucumbers actually arrived in Europe. It may have been as late as the thirteenth century. The cucumber only reached England in the fourteenth century.

The original Indian cucumber that arrived in western Asia was small, curved, prickly, and bitter. Nevertheless, the Arabs developed a fondness for it and spread the vegetable westward; the Moors probably introduced it to Spain during the early Middle Ages. In Europe, because the same compounds that caused cucumbers to be bitter also made them hard to digest, they were considered an unhealthy food. The British

The Beit Alpha originated in the late 1940s on a kibbutz of that name in the Jezreel Valley, and is now Israel's—and Europe's—predominant cucumber, but mysteriously often called Persian cucumber in America.

initially used the vegetables for animal feed, calling them cowcumbers. Over the centuries, however, gardeners bred much of the bitterness and "burps" out of them.

Around the middle of the sixteenth century, about a century after the cucumber arrived in northeastern Europe, nomadic Tatars and Turks brought the Chinese method of lacto-fermentation to eastern Europe. This pickling technique was more advanced than earlier European methods and led to the advent of pickled cucumbers. Soon the cucumber emerged as the predominant European pickled vegetable; in English, pickled cucumbers even became known simply as "pickles." As a result, cucumbers were among the few vegetables eaten by northeastern Ashkenazim; however, they were only eaten in pickled or marinated form, never raw.

Today, cucumbers constitute the fourth-most-cultivated "vegetable" crop. Gherkin (a diminutive of *gurk*, the Dutch word for a small cucumber) refers to any immature cucumber or small variety used for pickling. There are four basic types of cucumbers: the smooth-skinned garden cucumbers most common in America; the small Kirby; the very long, seedless hothouse, also known as Dutch and English cucumbers; and the Beit Alpha, also called the Middle Eastern cucumber. The Beit Alpha, originated in the late 1940s on a kibbutz of that name in the Jezreel Valley, and is now Israel's as well as Europe's predominant cucumber.

In modern Israel, cucumbers emerged as one of the most important vegetables; along with tomatoes, they constitute the ubiquitous Israeli salad. Israelis are passionate about their small, thin *melafefonim* and enjoy them in salads, pickled, marinated, and added to cold yogurt soups.

A favorite way of preparing cucumbers in most Jewish communities is marinated in a salad. Salting the cucumbers keeps them crunchy, while removing the excess water. Vinegar acts as a preservative, making the salad ideal for Sabbath lunch in the era before refrigeration. To counteract the pungency of the vinegar, a little sugar was sometimes added. For dairy meals, sour cream was mixed in for the tang. Dill was a favorite flavoring in the Baltic States, while mint served that role in the Middle East. Cucumber salad goes well with roasted chicken, chicken paprikash, or salmon. It is popular in modern Israel with schnitzel.

(See also Melon, Pickle, and Tarator)

CUMIN

Cumin, a member of the Apiaceae family, is a small yellow fruit (called a seed) with an acrid fragrance and warm, bitter-nutty, earthy flavor. Cumin resembles caraway seeds but it is longer, lighter in color, and straighter.

Cumin, perhaps native to the Levant or the Nile Valley, is one of the most ancient and important of Middle Eastern spices. It was the most common spice in biblical Israel and, along with nigella and coriander, one of the few cultivated spices at that time. The prophet Isaiah observed, "For *ketzach* [nigella] is not threshed with a threshing sledge, nor is the wheel of a threshing sledge rolled over *kammon* [cumin], but *ketzach* is beaten out with a stick, and *kammon* with a rod."

In the Far East, cumin is among the preferred warming spices (yang), along with cinnamon, coriander, ginger, and nutmeg. During the medieval period, cumin lost favor in most of Europe, except those areas with a pronounced Arab influence. It is largely nonexistent in the kitchens of most Ashkenazim, who favor caraway, and Italians. The exceptions, due to the long Ottoman domination, are Romanians and Hungarians. Cumin was subsumed by Ashkenazim under the category of *kiyniyot* and prohibited on Passover, which, considering that in Europe it was rarely if ever used, was not much of an imposition.

In contrast, cumin is essential to Sephardim and Mizrachim, who permit it on Passover. It is used alone, whole or ground, and paired with other spices, notably cinnamon, coriander, and especially turmeric. Cumin contributes a gentle pungency and warmth to foods and adds a base note that complements more assertive spices, so it is frequently used in spice mixtures, such as Indian curries, Egyptian *dukkah*, Moroccan *ras el hanout*, Turkish *baharat*, Yemenite *hawaij*, and American chili powder.

Cumin is the prominent spice in falafel, hummus, kebabs, *shawarma*, Sephardic Sabbath stews, *kamounia* (cumin stew), and Yemenite *s'chug* (chil paste). Moroccans add cumin and garlic to carrot salads, fish and *merguez* (sausages). Tunisians flavor grilled fish with cumin and cilantro. Syrians use it in red lentil soup and potato salad. The Arabic word for the spice, *kemoun*, meaning "grocer," was used by Middle Eastern Jews as a surname.

Black cumin (*Bunium persicum*), distantly related to cumin, is native to Kashmir and Pakistan. It is darker, smaller, and more intense than the more common cumin. Black cumin is not the same as the biblical *ketzach* (nigella).

D

DABO

Dabo is a soft, spiced honey-wheat bread, made in both a large loaf and smaller buns, that is eaten during the Sabbath and festivals.

Origin: Ethiopia

Other names: *ambasha, dabbo, yemarina, yewotet dabo.*

During the week, the mainstay of the Ethiopian diet is *injera*, a very thin, spongy, sour bread made from a grain called teff. On the Sabbath, however, spiced honey-wheat breads called *dabo* are also customary. Technically, these tender, lightly sweetened breads are called *ambasha*, but since in Ethiopia the Jews rarely ate any other wheat bread other than this type, it is simply referred to as *dabo* (Amharic for "bread"). *Dabos* are used to commence the meal or served as a dessert, or enjoyed as a snack throughout the day, while *injeras* are eaten during the meal.

This sourdough bread was originally made from semolina flour, formed into a substantial slab of dough, and wrapped in banana or kabo leaves (*defo dabo*). It was steamed in a covered circular clay pot over a fire, then cut into pieces, either squares or slices, before serving. In the contemporary method, the dough is placed into a large circular pan or shaped into rolls and baked. In either case, the dough is lightly sweetened with honey, which was rather abundant in Ethiopia, and lightly spiced with coriander and sometimes cardamom, cinnamon, cloves, or fenugreek.

Typically, Ethiopian housewives would start getting ready for the Sabbath on Wednesday, including preparing *dabo* dough. It was left to rise overnight and cooked on Thursday to be enjoyed during the Sabbath. After Saturday morning prayers, the women would bring a *dabo* to the village *kes* (priest), who would communally bless the breads, calling them *misvaot* (akin to the Hebrew word for commandments). Before eating, *Yitbarek*, a special Amharic benediction replete with a traditional melody, is recited over the Sabbath bread. The ensuing Sabbath meal would typically feature *doro wot* (chicken stew

with hard-boiled eggs) served on a bed of *injera*, and *gomen* (collard greens). Many Ethiopians enjoy the sweet *dabo* warm as a snack with *shai* (spiced tea), *tallah* (beer), or *agwat* (curd cheese).

Dabo kolo (the latter word means "roasted") are small pieces of fried spicy bread dough. They are enjoyed as a crunchy snack and as fare for travelers. In Israel, *dabo kolo* are popular opening tidbits at Ethiopian weddings.

DAL

Dal is a stew-like dish made from legumes.

Origin: India

Few Indian meals would be considered complete without some type of legume. Peas and beans are vital in this frequently vegetarian land and are usually served as an accompaniment to a curry or spiced rice dish. Indeed, many Indian meals consist wholly of *dal* and rice. *Dal* is the Hindi world for a split lentil, but it also refers to the different dried beans and peas that are cooked by Indians.

Chana dal or *chuna dal* are small deep-yellow Indian split peas. They have a nutty taste when fried and are also used as a spice. *Chowli dal* are split black-eyed peas. *Sabut massor dal* are brown lentils and *massor dal* (also *masore dal* or *masar dal*) are red lentils. Red lentils were popularized in India by Jews who used them in a variety of dishes, such as *piaju* (lentil fritters). *Toovar dal* (also *toor dal*, *arhar dal*, or yellow lentils) are kidney-shaped yellowish brown pigeon peas. These are the primary *dal* of southern India and have an earthy flavor. *Urad dal* (black lentils, beluga lentils), actually a pea and not a lentil, have a dark skin and a nutty flavor. When split and hulled, they reveal an ivory-colored interior and are sold as "white lentils." *Moong dal* (*mung dal*) are yellow mung beans and *rajma* refers to red kidney beans.

Rice and *dal* serve as the basis for both meat or dairy meals for weekdays, Sabbath, and holidays. Thin *dal* is served as a soup, medium-thin *dal* as a dip, and thick *dal* as a side dish. Indian food is always zestfully seasoned. For holidays, some cooks prepare a colorful dish using five different legumes, each added separately to the pot according to its cooking time.

(See also Black-Eyed Peas and Lentil)

DANDELION

The dandelion has long grown wild throughout much of Asia and Europe. The name is derived from the Latin *dens leonis* (lion's teeth), referring to the jagged edges of its leaves. Fresh dandelion leaves are crisp and slightly bitter as well as nutritious. The ancient Romans used them stewed or raw in salads, while the roots were cooked or transformed into a tea and the flowers into a wine. Some scholars believe dandelion was one of the five bitter herbs appropriate for the Passover Seder. Due to their diuretic properties, dandelion leaves were employed by medieval Middle Eastern and European healers as medicine and brought by early English settlers to America, where they, of course, spread like weeds. The cultivated Italian variety of dandelion has a milder flavor and lighter green color than the wild kind. Organic wild dandelion leaves are edible if they are picked before the flowers develop. Thus dandelion was a seasonal green, prominent in the spring. In parts of the Mediterranean and Middle East, the leaves are still used to make salads and soups (they can be substituted for spinach).

DANISH

Danish is a buttery yeast pastry filled with almond paste, cheese, or fruit.

Origin: Austria

Other names: Austria and southern Germany: *Kopenhagener*; Scandanavia and northern Germany: *wienerbrod, wienbrod*.

In his 1955 novel *Marjorie Morningstar* (née Morgenstern), a commentary on Jewish assimilation in America in the mid-twentieth century, Herman Wouk described the foods at a typical Jewish brunch, almost none of which were ever consumed by Jews in eastern Europe: "Platters of smoked salmon, smoked whitefish, kippered herrings, lettuce and tomatoes, scrambled eggs, French-fried potatoes, rolls, toast, Danish pastry, and coffee cake covered the table."

Danish pastry, a cross between sweet yeast dough and puff pastry, is ubiquitous to Ashkenazic bakeries and morning celebrations. Typical Danish dough contains about half as much fat in weight as flour.

During baking, the fat particles in Danish melt and steam, producing flaky layers in the rich dough. The classic filling is butter beaten with sugar and ground almonds or almond paste. Other popular fillings include cheese, prune, and apricot.

Despite its English name, Danish pastry, or more simply Danish, was actually created in Austria, where the dough is known as *germbutterteig* (yeast butter dough) and *plunderteig*. In fact, residents of Denmark, as well as most of Europe, call it *wienerbrod* or *wienbrod* (Vienna bread). This dough, related to croissant dough, was brought to Denmark in the early nineteenth century by an Austrian baker whose skills were so superior to those of his Danish counterparts that they were soon imitating his techniques. According to a legend, a strike by Austrian bakers around 1840 induced some to immigrate to Denmark with its better working conditions. Another version places the strike in Denmark, and the Danish owners importing Austrian bakers. Danes and Scandinavians used this rich dough to create small pastries, such as *kringler* (braids/pretzels), *kammer* (combs), and *spandauer* (squares with the corners folded in the center).

The terms Danish pastry and Danish both seem to have originated in New York City around 1915, where the pastry as well as the name was popularized by Jews. An earlier citation attributed to a 1907 book was an appendix added in 1920.

Toward the end of 1915, L. C. Klitteng, a baker from Denmark, arrived in New York City. According to his claims, he had just prepared pastries for the wedding of President Woodrow Wilson to Edith Bolling Galt, on December 18, 1915. He approached Herman Gertner (1872–1962), a German Jew who at the time owned five restaurants in Manhattan along Broadway from 38th Street to 97th Street. Klitteng arranged to teach Gertner's pastry chefs the secrets of rich, flaky *wienerbrod*, which Gertner called Danish. Theatergoers would commonly stop at one of Gertner's establishments after a show for coffee and pastries; during the day people came by for coffee breaks and a Danish. Meanwhile, Klitteng worked to popularize Danish pastry throughout America, traveling to some thirty states to teach the baking techniques.

Danish pastry immediately proved a big hit with Gertner's patrons and began spreading to other New York restaurants and delis. One of Gertner's busboys and later managers, Leo Lindemann, himself a Jewish immigrant from Berlin, married Gertner's sister Clara. In 1921, Lindemann started his own famous deli, Lindy's, which also featured Danish. Gertner hired additional bakers and began selling his Danish wholesale. By the time Gertner retired in 1939, Danish had become ubiquitous in New York delis, coffee shops, and bakeries and at Jewish morning celebrations, especially *brit milah*.

DATE

The date palm is a towering, slender evergreen tree, hence its Hebrew name *tamar*, from the root "to be lofty." The date palm was most probably the first cultivated tree. The earliest evidence of its domestication was found in the city of Eridu in Lower Mesopotamia and dates back more than five thousand years, about a millennium before the initial cultivation of grapes. Date seeds from the third millennia BCE were found in the Royal Cemetery at Ur of Chaldeas, twenty-five miles northeast of Eridu, so this fruit was certainly a conspicuous part of the diet of Abraham and his family.

Since the date palm's nearest relative and possible ancestor, the sugar date palm/toddy palm, still grows wild in northern India, the Indus Valley may very well be its home. In any case, long before the advent of the first civilization, nomads spread dates westward, especially at oases and wells. Most of these early plantings occurred accidentally as travelers pausing to rest at water holes spit out the seeds

Dates are one of, if not the oldest, cultivated fruit. They are still a beloved part of Jewish cuisine.

from dried dates, one of the few portable and nonperishable foods of the ancient Middle East. Later, various traders, particularly those from Israel's northern neighbor Phoenicia, whose name means "land of the palms" in Greek, intentionally sowed the date palm throughout much of the Mediterranean region. The Talmud frequently employed a synonym for the date palm—*dekel*, related to the Greek *dactylon* (finger/toe), which is a reference to the fruit's shape and is also the source of the English word date.

Palms do not have branches like most trees, but rather leaf-like expansions similar to a fern called fronds, *kapot* in Hebrew. A *lulav* is a closed frond. The feather-like fronds consist of a thick midrib (*shedrah* in Hebrew) covered with long, slender leaves (*aileem*) that are folded in half lengthwise. The gray-green palm fronds sprout in a group from a spot at the center of the top of the tree, called the *lev* (heart), from which they draw their sustenance. *Lev* is the source of the word *lulav*. To the Kabbalists, the *lulav* is viewed as an instrument for channeling spiritual energy into our hearts. Thus the *lulav* represents the Torah, the *lev* of Israel. The mature fronds form a crown on the top of the palm tree; the arching configuration of this canopy is called a *kippah*, and this is the source of the modern Hebrew word for a skullcap.

Green buds begin to appear on date palms in March and shortly thereafter the flowers emerge. Pollination occurs in a brief interval between mid-March and April, around the month of Nisan (Aviv), and the dates then take about two hundred days to reach full maturation. About a month after pollination, small green berries begin to develop in clusters on stalks. They mature in August or early September. Dates, which contain a single slender pit, vary in size, texture, color, and sweetness depending on the variety and environmental conditions.

In the ancient Middle East, fresh dates were strung on lines made from goat's hair and hung to individually dry in the sun. In addition, like figs and raisins, they were pressed into blocks in baskets to completely dry, then the tough fruit was used throughout the year, especially in cooking and as food for travelers. Much of the date harvest was boiled into a thick, long-lasting syrup called *devash* (honey) in the Bible. When the Bible talks about "a land flowing with milk and honey," it is referring to dates.

In the arid, nonhumid sections of the Middle East,

where it grew best, the date was sometimes the only plant-based food available and, therefore, a primary component of the diet. Dates were commonly eaten with dairy products or, when available, fish or lamb. In Sumeria as well as Egypt, dates were also used to flavor beer, the primary beverage. The original *arak*, now an anise-flavored liquor, was made from fermented date juice and is considered by some to be the Biblical *shekar* (strong drink). Lesser-quality dates along with the husks were fed to animals. In addition to food, date palms provided shade, fuel, roofing material, utensils, mats, baskets, and ropes. The palm's lumber was of particular importance in Egypt, which, due to a scarcity of rainfall, lacked forests and timber trees. An ancient Babylonian poem claimed that there were 360 uses for this invaluable tree.

Of all the plants mentioned in the Bible, only the date palm is included in both the *Sheva Minim* (Seven Species) with which the land was praised, and the *Arbah Minim* (Four Species) constituting the Sukkot ritual. Nonetheless, the date palm, despite its obvious attributes, was less important to the diet and economy of ancient Israel than the other six members of the Seven Species because those plants thrived in almost every part of the country and most farmers could grow their own.

Palms, on the other hand, require specialized conditions to bear fruit in general and high-quality dates in particular. The area suitable for growing dates in Israel lies primarily in the Rift Valley running from Jericho (called "the city of date palms") north to the Sea of Galilee and to Lake Hula in the north; this stretch of land two thousand years ago was carpeted with palms. In Roman times, Jericho dates were considered the best in the world. Palm trees grow well in the coastal areas of Israel too, although the humidity there tends to hinder fruit production. Date palms can grow in Jerusalem, although these trees generally produce poor-quality fruit or no fruit.

The Romans during their Judean wars in 135 CE intentionally destroyed the Judean date cultivars of Jerusalem and other Israeli locales, and the unique Judean palm went extinct. For the ensuing two thousand years, few date trees grew in the country. In 1909, Kibbutz Degania, on the south shore of the Galilee, reintroduced the date palm to that region and today these graceful trees once again thrive in the land. Pop-

ular Israeli lyric poet Rachel Bluwstein (1890–1931), who lived in Kvutzat Kinneret on the Sea of Galilee, wrote in her 1926 poem *"Kinneret"*:

> There on the shore of the sea is a low-hanging palm [*dekel*],
> Disheveled is the palm's hair like that of a mischievous child,
> Who has slid down and in the waters of the Kinneret,
> Splashes his feet.

In the 1970s, an excavation at Herod's palace on Masada unearthed a jar containing some two-thousand-year-old Judean palm seeds. The seeds sat for four decades until Dr. Elaine Solowey of the Arava Institute treated and planted three of them on the festival of Tu b'Shevat in January 2005. One of them sprouted, making it the oldest known seed to germinate. As of 2010, the tree was nearly six feet tall with ten fronds. If it turns out to be female, the tree, nicknamed Methuselah, could bear the first Judean dates in nearly two millennia, resurrecting an extinct species.

The date palm and fruit naturally play a prominent role in Jewish lore and ritual. The palm tree is the backbone of the Sukkot ritual of the Four Species. It was under a date palm that Deborah judged the nation. Psalms declares, "The righteous person will flourish like a date palm." The motif of the beautiful palm has long been popular in Jewish art and eventually emerged as a national emblem of the state of Israel. Notably, images of date palms adorned the walls of the Temple. The Maccabees used the tree as a symbol of their military success, its towering stature and sword-shaped fronds connoting victory. Several bronze and silver coins minted by Bar Kokhba in 132 CE bear a picture of the date palm, as do Roman coins issued by Vespasian celebrating the fall of Jerusalem, which depict a weeping woman sitting beneath a date palm. The Talmud noted that "seeing a *lulav* in one's dream connotes that a person is serving God wholeheartedly." Hence the palm is a symbol of Israel's devotion to God.

In Talmudic times, some people saved the *lulav* after Sukkot and used the dried leaves for searching for the *chametz* before Passover (later a feather took on this role), then burned it with the *chametz*. The fruit of the date palm also served as the basis for the original form of charoset at the Passover Seder, a role

it retains in many communities. Dates are also traditionally served at holidys such as Rosh Hashanah and
Tu b'Shevat.

(See also Charoset and Date Honey)

DATE HONEY (DEVASH)

Date Honey is a syrup made from dates.
Origin: Middle East
Other names: Arabic: *dibs*; Hebrew: *silan;* Iraq:
halek, hullake.

Throughout most of history, much of the Middle Eastern date harvest was boiled into a thick,
long-lasting syrup called *devash* (honey) in Hebrew.
Date honey could be stored for much longer than other
forms of date and was more useful, imparting a touch
of sweetness to everything from stews to desserts. It
was also more plentiful and safer to collect than bee
honey. A large apparatus dating back twenty-five hundred years for boiling fruit into honey was uncovered
in excavations at Lachish (thirty miles southwest of
Jerusalem). Among the ruins of Qumran, best known
for its Dead Sea scrolls, was a two-thousand-year-old
date-honey press. The descriptive biblical denotation of the Promised Land as "flowing with milk and
honey" referred to date syrup.

Unlike bee honey, which requires relatively little
effort beyond risking a few stings and perhaps climbing a tree, date honey entails a labor-intensive process. Unlike most fruits, the solids in dates are too
concentrated for the juice to be pressed out in any
sizable amount. Therefore, water is necessary to dissolve the soluble solids before the nonsoluble solids can be removed. First the dates are crushed or
chopped. Then the pulp is mixed with cold water,
usually in a one-to-one ratio, and allowed to stand for
several hours or overnight. Afterwards, it is boiled for
about an hour and a half. The juice is then strained
through a basket or pressed through filter bags into
containers. The material in the basket is reboiled several more times to extract as much juice as possible.
Any remnants of pulp are fed to the animals. The
combined juice is filtered again, then boiled down,
the amount of time depending on the desired degree
of thickness and intensity of flavor, into a thick
honey-like syrup.

Traditionally, a piece of the date stalk was placed
in the pot to prevent the syrupy mixture from burning.
The long-established test of the syrup's readiness was
to sprinkle a few drops onto sand; if they formed tiny
balls, the honey was done. The final honey output was
about half the weight of the dates used. The entire
process took about a total of twelve hours divided over
two days.

Since date honey lasts for several years, this laborious task was generally performed only once a year,
shortly after the harvest. Iraqi Jews, as well as their
descendants in India, still prepare date honey. Eventually, commercial enterprises began producing it.
Today date honey is common on the shelves of Israeli
groceries.

Although today fruit honeys are little known outside of the Middle East, they were once an essential
component of cooking and remained a principal food
in Judea throughout the First and Second Commonwealth. Date honey is spread on bread, pancakes,
and, on Passover, matza. It is mixed with tahini (sesame seed paste) for a breakfast dip for bread. It is also
stirred into water or goat yogurt for a beverage and
used to flavor beer and wine. Mixed with chopped
walnuts or almonds, date honey yields the original
form of charoset, which is still popular in some Middle Eastern communities.

(See also Charoset and Honey)

DECKEL

The German word *deckel*, meaning "little covering/
lid," is confusingly used to denote four distinct cuts
of beef. One of these cuts is from the shoulder blade
near the neck (technically the chuck deckel). Some
delis use this cut to make pastrami, which is more
usually made from the plate. Another deckel (rib-eye
deckel) is a highly marbled strip of muscle from the
top of the ribs, which is also called the calotte or cap.
Deckel can also refer to the muscle and fat, weighing
about two pounds, between the bones of the rib cage
and the main muscle and flat section of the brisket
(on the opposite side from the point cut). In addition, the word deckel (technically the breast deckel)
is also used for the top section of a second-cut brisket; this is a triangular three-inch-thick piece of meat
covered with a cap of fat, which is also called the
point cut. Good Jewish delis include the point cut in
their corned beef as part of the whole brisket, while in
homes it is also a favorite for cholent (Sabbath stew)
and tzimmes.

DELICATESSEN

The 1962 play *A Thousand Clowns* by Herb Gardner contains the memorable line, "People fall into two distinct categories, Miss Markowitz; people who like delicatessen, and people who don't like delicatessen. A man who is not touched by the earthy lyricism of hot pastrami, the pungent fantasy of corned-beef, pickles, frankfurters, the great lusty impertinence of good mustard—is a man of stone and without heart."

The Jewish delicatessen is a uniquely American innovation. Its roots come from medieval French cheese making and Alsatian charcuterie—the preparation of meat products, including curing, brining, smoking, and poaching. Centuries ago, the French created an adjective to encompass these cold meats, cheeses, and other choice prepared foods—*délicatesse* (delicious things). In Germany, shops selling these prepared foods, many of them imports, became known by the German plural of the French word, *Delikatessen*. (The word was not, contrary to a widespread misconception, connected to the German word *essen*, "to eat.")

German immigrants in America, who arrived in a great wave beginning in the 1840s, opened similar small grocery stores offering canned goods along with homemade prepared foods. Many of the then-alien foods offered by the German shops eventually became standards of American cuisine, including Frankfurt sausages (hot dogs), Hamburg steaks (hamburgers), cold cuts, potato salad, Muenster cheese, pumpernickel bread, and kaiser rolls. Later from the American German delicatessen also came commercial mayonnaise.

Jews were among the millions of German immigrants seeking economic prospects and religious freedom. Around the same time the Germans were opening the first American *delikatessens*, some German Jewish immigrants in the New York area began offering prepared foods and canned goods, initially selling them from their tenement apartments, to other recent Jewish arrivals, many of them homesick and culinarily inept single men. Later, some of the more successful operations moved to commercial spaces outside of the home; a typical shop was a narrow storefront with room for a long counter and perhaps a very few small tables and chairs.

In 1872, shortly after the Civil War, Isaac Gellis (d. 1906) transferred his kosher sausage business from Berlin to Essex Street on New York's Lower East Side.

He found a strong market for his kosher delicatessen meats among the shops catering to the growing number of Jewish immigrants. Gellis initially offered a selection of German wursts, but eventually added emerging American favorites, including salami and hot dogs. In the nineteenth century, preserved meats and fish—such as corned beef, pickled tongue, pickled herring, and, with the advent of the mechanical meat grinder in the 1860s, sausages—were much cheaper than fresh meat and, therefore, it became the norm for shops to sell these items sliced by the pound. To further stretch resources, the proprietors served the thinly carved meat on thick slices of Jewish rye bread, which also acted to soak up excess fat and render the dish more transportable. The inevitable accompaniment was Jewish dill pickles provided by the numerous neighborhood pickle makers. The Jewish market owners used an Americanized Yiddish version of the German name for their meat-centered businesses—delicatessen. The term was first recorded in the United States around 1889, using the American Yiddish and not the German spelling.

Like the German establishments, the Jewish shops were at first typical nineteenth century groceries, offering an array of canned goods as well as pickled and smoked meats and fish and some prepared salads. Unlike German *delikatessens*, Jewish ones, even the few nonkosher ones, rarely sold pork products, but rather concentrated on beef. By the time masses of eastern European Jews began flooding into New York City toward the end of the nineteenth century, German Jews and a few earlier-arriving eastern Europeans had already established a number of kosher delicatessens, as well as a few nonkosher Jewish-style delicatessens. Many individual stores began to cater to specific Jewish communities beyond the Germans, some stressing Romanian fare, and others Polish or Russian; the result was an array of diverse shops. Much of the merchandise offered by these delicatessens was not the food the immigrants had consumed in their home countries, but rather a synthesis of old and new; this fare was a step toward assimilating into the wider American society.

The patrons developed a liking and in some instances a passion for this hearty, flavorful fare. For the millions of bewildered and sometimes overwhelmed immigrants, however, Jewish delicatessens proved more than a place to purchase some kosher and filling foods. Patrons not only came for takeout, but also stayed to schmooze. Delicatessens were akin to the country store in rural America—they were a place where people could socialize and connect in a welcoming, familiar atmosphere. Besides the synagogue, these stores offered a singular haven where one could feel a sense of community and connection. Consequently, the fare offered in the delicatessens became comfort foods, producing a sense of security and well-being. It became the American Jewish soul food.

Through the early twentieth century, delicatessens were an intrinsic part of the fabric of life in New York City and increasingly in other American cities with any sizable Jewish community. At that time, delicatessens were still primarily small grocery stores. Then the nature of American food and its distribution radically changed and, in response, so did the delicatessen. After World War I, the concept of the American large self-service supermarket began to spread and the rudimentary Jewish delicatessens either went out of business or evolved. A few of these establishments survived as larger versions of delicatessens. These neighborhood markets differentiated themselves from the huge chains by offering some of the old-fashioned Jewish fare along with other desirable items; one such store is Manhattan's Zabar's, which started in 1934 with Louis Zabar selling smoked fish and now advertises itself as a "gourmet epicurean emporium."

However, most delicatessens changed from grocery stores to homey (*heimish*) restaurants offering some takeout foods. The Jewish deli—the shortened name was first recorded in 1954—is the accumulation of a large variety of culinary innovations arising from the mingling masses of immigrants in Manhattan in the late nineteenth and early twentieth centuries.

Some delicatessens specialized in fish or dairy fare, such as Ratner's Delicatessen on Delancey Street, which closed its doors in 2002 after ninety-seven years in business, and two years after it first sold nonkosher food. Most, however, focused on meat. A sort of uniformity increasingly developed as well, with many competing delis offering nearly the same core menu, a conglomeration of foods from various ethnic groups. The superstars of any true deli are corned beef and pastrami. Slicing is a special and necessary talent—too thick and the meat is chewy, too thin and it crumbles. Mustard, of course, was the predominant condiment. As the hot dog grew popular, and

then French fries, they became mainstays as well. Delis also adopted the Italian beef salami; during the decades before World War II, many posted a sign stating, "a nickel a shtickel," meaning that the ends of salamis were available for five cents each.

American turkey eventually joined the ranks of meats. Various Ashkenazic standards, based on poverty food, also emerged as ubiquitous deli fare, including chopped liver, brisket, tongue, roast chicken, gefilte fish, stuffed cabbage, *kishke* (stuffed derma), matza ball soup, kugels, massive knishes, and potato pancakes. Among the other contributions of New York delis were the Reuben sandwich, celery soda, and New York cheesecake.

Pickles maintain their popularity in America partially because of the deli. After all, what would a pastrami or corn beef sandwich be without a pickle? Yet even more important then the flavor of the pickle is something that ancient cultures understood—the pickle's ability to clear the palate. With each successive bite of fatty and zesty meat, the flavors begin to dull and eventually we hardly taste anything as the taste buds get coated with fat or zapped with spices. A pickle cuts through the residue in the mouth, restoring the taste buds to their original state and allowing the diner to once again savor the food.

The twentieth-century proliferation of Jewish entertainers and artists maintaining an affiliation to their ethnic gastronomy helped to bring Jewish food and delicatessens into the mainstream American consciousness. Singer Eddie Cantor's first job was as a delivery boy for Isaac Gellis Wurst Works, and he remained a lifelong devotee of Jewish deli. Besides the food and homey ethnic milieu, Jewish delis became known for their character wisecracking owners, surly waiters, sandwiches named after celebrities, and walls lined with photographs of celebrities. Among the New York theater crowd, it became common to frequent a midtown deli before or after a show.

Indeed, a deli, Lindy's (it was called Mindy's in the show) was one of the stars of the 1950 Broadway musical *Guys and Dolls*, a show filled with Yinglish phrases and New York Jewish cadences and ambiance. The Works Progress Administration (WPA) estimated that in 1936, at the height of the deli's heyday, there were about five thousand Jewish-style delicatessens in the New York metropolitan area. There was even a Greater New York Delicatessen Dealers' Association.

As New York Jews moved throughout the country, they not only took their love for deli with them, but they took the business concept, opening restaurants in various cities. The Jewish deli emerged as one of America's most relished culinary traditions.

For more than a century, Americans frequented traditional delicatessens. Then toward the end of the twentieth century, in the era of fat-fear, carb-consciousness, and Atkins dieting, many people objected to the hearty, old-fashioned fare of the traditional delicatessen. In addition, high food and labor costs, along with rising rents, particularly affected the delis that cooked, cured, and sliced their meats.

The Jewish population of New York City fell from 2.1 million in 1950 to 1 million by 1990. Meanwhile, Jews' education levels and income rose, and their living styles changed. Plus, the quality of the products in many delicatessens declined, resulting in humdrum meats and breads. Consequently, in the United States toward the end of the twentieth century, individual delicatessens tended to suffer, and many even went under. In the 1960s, there were still more than three hundred Jewish-style delis in the New York metropolitan area. By 2000, however, only about thirty-five remained, about a dozen survivors in Manhattan, most of them not kosher.

Fortunately, in the twenty-first century, the obsession with no-fat and no-carb eased, while interest in comfort food and ethnic fare returned. People once again began frequenting delicatessens. The seventy-five-year-old Canter's Deli from Los Angeles opened a branch in Las Vegas, while New York's Stage Deli aligned with Trump Taj Mahal in Atlantic City. Junior's from Brooklyn opened a second location in midtown Manhattan. The Second Avenue Deli returned from oblivion, though it is no longer on Second Avenue. Like the Jewish people, the deli endures. Only "a man of stone and without heart" could not appreciate the delicatessen and its place in American Jewish life.

(See also Corned Beef, Hot Dog, Mustard, Pastrami, Pickle, Rye, and Salami)

DELKEL

Delkel is a version of cheese Danish.
Origin: Hungary
Other names: *delkelekh, delkli, túrós delkli, túrós táska.*

Delkel, probably from the Turkish adjective *deliki* (holey/hollowed out), is a delicate filled yeast pastry that gets its flakiness from layers of butter that are rolled into the dough. Like Danish, it is based on techniques that originated in Austria. There are also several easier versions that incorporate the butter in pieces into the dough and substitute baking powder for yeast. Some cooks even make these from commercial puff pastry. The filling was originally made with *túró*, the thicker Hungarian version of the Teutonic *quark*, but farmer and pot cheese are commonly substituted. Many versions also contain a sprinkling of golden raisins. *Delkel* is a popular Hanukkah and Shavuot treat, but also a favorite morning bun.

HUNGARIAN CHEESE BUNS (*DELKELEKH/DELKLI*)

10 BUNS [DAIRY]

Dough:
½ package (1⅛ teaspoons) active dry yeast or
    ½ (0.6-ounce) cake fresh yeast
6 tablespoons warm milk (105 to 115°F for dry yeast;
    80 to 85°F for fresh yeast), or ¼ cup milk and
    2 tablespoons sour cream
¼ cup sugar
¼ cup (½ stick) unsalted butter, softened
1 large egg
¾ teaspoon table salt or 1½ teaspoons kosher salt
About 2¼ cups (11.25 ounces) unbleached all-
    purpose flour

6 tablespoons (¾ stick) unsalted butter, softened
Filling:
2 cups (16 ounces) farmer, pot, or cream cheese
2 tablespoons sour cream or *gevina levana* (Israeli
    white cheese)
¼ to ½ cup sugar or prune lekvar
2 large egg yolks
1 teaspoon vanilla extract
Pinch of salt
1 to 2 tablespoons all-purpose flour or bread
    crumbs (optional)

Egg wash (1 large egg beaten with 1 teaspoon
    cream, milk, or water)
Confectioners' sugar for sprinkling (optional)

1. To make the dough: Dissolve the yeast in the milk and let stand until foamy, 5 to 10 minutes. In a large bowl, combine the yeast mixture, sugar, butter, egg, and salt, and 1 cup flour. Add enough of the remaining flour, ½ cup at a time, to make a mixture that holds together.

2. On a lightly floured surface or in an electric mixer with a dough hook, knead the dough, adding more flour as needed to prevent sticking, until smooth and springy, about 5 minutes. Place in an oiled bowl and turn to coat. Cover loosely with plastic wrap or a kitchen towel and let rise in a warm, draft-free place until nearly doubled in bulk, 1½ to 2 hours, or cover with plastic wrap and refrigerate overnight.

3. Punch down the dough. Fold over and press together several times. Let stand for 10 minutes.

4. On a lightly floured surface, roll the dough into a 20-by-10-inch rectangle about ¼ inch thick. Spread with the butter. Bring the right and left sides of the dough together to meet in the center, then bring the top and bottom together to meet in the center. Wrap in plastic wrap and let stand in the refrigerator for 20 minutes, then roll out and fold twice more, making sure the seam is on the top, and allowing the dough to rest for 20 minutes between each rolling.

5. Preheat the oven to 350°F. Line a large baking sheet with parchment paper or grease the sheet.

6. To make the filling: In a medium bowl, combine all the filling ingredients. Add the flour or bread crumbs if the mixture is too loose.

7. Roll the dough into a 25-by-10-inch rectangle about ⅛ inch thick. Cut into ten 5-inch squares. Spoon about 2 tablespoons filling in the center of each dough square. Bring the 4 corners together in the center over the filling and pinch to seal.

8. Place the filled dough pieces, seam side up, on the prepared baking sheet, about 1½ inches apart. Brush with the egg wash. Bake until golden brown, about 20 minutes. Transfer to a wire rack and let cool. If desired, sprinkle with confectioners' sugar. Store, wrapped in plastic wrap, at room temperature for up to 1 day or in the freezer for up to 2 months.

DESAYUNO

The Spanish noun *ayuno* means a "fast." By adding the prefix *des*, which indicates the opposite meaning of the word it modifies, the combination literally becomes "un-fast" or, more precisely, "breakfast." However, in the Sephardic sense, *desayuno* connotes a special "brunch."

Historically, morning prayer services were conducted very early in the day, even on the Sabbath and holidays. And since it is traditional not to eat before services, the first meal of the day is truly a break-the-fast. However, when worshippers returned home from synagogue, it was generally too early for lunch—typically the heaviest meal of the day—yet too late for a usual breakfast.

Instead, following Sabbath and festival morning synagogue services and also on Sundays, particularly in summer, Sephardim enjoy a *desayuno*, a casual dairy meal consisting primarily of finger foods, including cheeses (kashkaval and feta), yogurt, *fritadas* (vegetable omelets), rice pudding, olives, jams, fresh fruit, and *raki* (anise liqueur). Some serve the classic Sephardi dish *peshkado frito* (fried fish). Ubiquitous to the *desayunos* of Turkish and Balkan Sephardim are a trio of pastries, "the three Bs"—*borekas*, *boyos*, and *bulemas*. Since these pastries require assembly, what Ashkenazim call *potchke* (fuss or a slow, time-consuming handmade process), they are typically prepared by a group of relatives or friends on Thursday, during which time there is much socializing and the young learn and practice venerable culinary techniques.

Among the other popular foods at a contemporary *desayuno* are *huevos haminados* (long-cooked eggs), *ful medames* (Egyptian slow-simmered fava beans), *melitzanes tiganites* (Greek marinated fried eggplant), *almodrote de berengena* (Turkish eggplant and cheese casserole), *yaprakes finos* (stuffed grape leaves), hummus, *pastelitos* (miniature pies), *quesadas* (small cheese pies), and *biscochos e huevo* (egg cookies).

DILL

Dill is an aromatic relative of parsley. It is grown for its feathery green leaves (sometimes called dill weed), flowers (dill heads), and seeds. The plant has a flavor akin to anise, but with a subtler, fresher taste and notes of celery and parsley. The word dill comes from the Norse word *dilla* (to lull/calm), referring to this herb's purported power to sooth stomach problems and headaches and lull babies to sleep. An Egyptian papyrus dating back more than three thousand years testifies to similar properties.

From the Talmud we understand that dill (*shevet*) was cultivated in Judea two millennia ago; its seeds, leaves, and heads were used as a spice; in modern Hebrew dill is commonly called *shamir*.

Dill is among the few fresh herbs available in much of northern Europe and appears in signature Ashkenazic items, including chicken soup, potato salad, and Jewish pickles. It is much appreciated in Russia, Poland, Scandinavia, and throughout the Middle East for soups, stews, fish, vegetables, savory pastry fillings, and cucumber dishes. Persians add it to salads, rice, and omelets. Turks and Greeks add dill to cooked and stuffed vegetables, yogurt salads, and sauces. Georgians use it in combination with other fresh herbs, including the classic spice mixture *khmeli-suneli*. Indians use dill to flavor bean and lentil dishes and give coconut milk with dill seed to nursing mothers.

DIMLAMA

Dimlama is a stew based on vegetables, although it may also include meat.

Origin: Uzbekistan

Other names: *bosma.*

Hearty stews and soups are a mainstay of the diet throughout central Asia, and Uzbekistan boasts several important ones. *Dimlama* is popular during the late spring through early fall, when there are plenty of fresh vegetables. Traditionally, *dimlama* is prepared in a large clay pot. The lid is sealed to the pot with a strip of dough and the stew is slowly simmered over a low fire. The name and the concept may have derived from a Persian cooking method for meat and vegetables called *dum pukht* (literally "choke off the steam"). Some *dimlama* variations include chunks of mutton, sheep bones, or beef. The vegetarian version is called *sabzavotli dimlama*. Bukharan Jews prepare a special autumn version incorporating quinces and apples. Some cooks layer and steam the vegetables, while others prefer mixing them. *Dimlama* is usually served with flatbread.

✦ BUKHARAN VEGETABLE STEW (*SABZAVOTLI DIMLAMA*)

5 TO 6 SERVINGS   [PAREVE]

¼ cup vegetable oil

2 large onions, chopped

2 medium carrots, thickly sliced

2 medium potatoes, peeled, and diced

2 yellow summer squash, chopped, or ½ head green cabbage, shredded

1 small eggplant, peeled and chopped

1 medium turnip, peeled and diced

1 red or yellow bell pepper, seeded and chopped

3 to 4 cloves garlic

2 large tomatoes, coarsely chopped

¼ cup chopped fresh flat-leaf parsley

¼ cup chopped fresh cilantro

Salt to taste

1 teaspoon ground cumin (optional)

About 2 cups water

2 tablespoons each additional chopped parsley and cilantro for garnish

1. In a large pot, heat the oil oven medium heat. Add the onions and sauté until soft and translucent, 5 to 10 minutes. Add the carrots, potatoes, squash, eggplant, turnip, bell pepper, and garlic and sauté until well coated, about 5 minutes.

2. Stir in the tomatoes, parsley, cilantro, salt, and, if using, cumin. Add enough water to cover the mixture. Bring to a boil, cover, reduce the heat to low, and simmer until tender, about 45 minutes. Serve with rice or noodles. Sprinkle with the additional parsley.

DOBOS TORTE

Dobos torte is a cake consisting of thin layers sandwiched with chocolate buttercream.

Origin: Hungary

Other names: Dobosh torte, seven-layer cake.

The idea of cake layers sandwiched with alternating thin layers of creamy cooked buttercream emerged in southeastern Europe, possibly inspired by Turkish layered pastries, such as baklava. Dobos torte is arguably the most famous of these layer cakes. In 1885, it was created by and named after pastry maker József Dobos of Budapest, Hungary.

This famous seven-layer cake was filled with chocolate buttercream and topped with a caramelized sugar glaze. The Dobos torte's fame spread worldwide when its creator found a way to package it for shipment to other countries. In 1906, Dobos donated the original recipe to the Budapest Pastry and Honey Bread Makers' Guild. Subsequently, seven-layer cakes became a regular component of Hungarian Jewish baking and a Sabbath treat. They later became ubiquitous in American Jewish bakeries, although usually without the caramel topping.

DOLMA

Dolma is an array of stuffed vegetables.

Origin: Turkey

Other names: Arabic: *mahshi, mehshi*; Georgia: *tolma*; Greek: *yemista*; Hebrew: *memulah*; Ladino: *rellenada*; Persia: *dolmeh.*

Medieval Middle Eastern cooks expanded the concept of stuffing grape and cabbage leaves to hollowing out and filling nearly any type of vegetable and even fruit. Stewing was the usual method of preparing stuffed vegetables before home ovens became available, and baked versions relatively recently became widespread.

Many credit the Ottoman Turks with this innovation; they may have picked up the idea in central Asia, inspired by the Chinese *mantou* (stuffed pasta). The Turks, who called stuffed vegetables dolma (from the Turkish verb *dolmak*, "to get filled/to be stuffed"), certainly transformed them from peasant food to a dish befitting upper-class tables, and also developed diverse versions. Technically, the term dolma encompasses hollowed-out vegetables and *sarma* ("wrap" in Turkish) designates only those leaves filled and rolled, but colloquially dolma is used for both. Turks spread the concept and term *dolma* throughout the northern part of their empire and to the Persians. The Arabs became fervent stuffed vegetable lovers as well and spread the concept from the Levant through North Africa.

Sephardim developed an array of stuffed vegetables which they called *medias* (halves), as cooks typically cut their vegetables in half to be stuffed. Consequently, indigenous Syrian Jews derisively referred to the Sephardic exiles settling in Syria as *medias*, a reference to their way of preparing stuffed vegetables instead of using the Middle Eastern technique of hollowing out whole vegetables. A distinctive Sephardic practice was to dip the tops of the stuffed vegetables in eggs and flour, then fry them, open side down, before simmering them in a sauce.

Many communities hollow out beets, carrots, onions, and turnips. Eggplant is a longstanding favorite. Mediterranean Jews also stuff artichokes and artichoke hearts, which come into season in early spring in time for Passover. Even celery and chard stems are stuffed in some places. Following their arrival from America, tomatoes, summer squash, pumpkins, and potatoes emerged as popular items to stuff as well; peppers became especially popular, partially because they do not require any tedious hollowing. Persians developed a particular fondness for stuffed fruit, notably quinces, apples, and melons. Romanians and Hungarians, due to their prolonged contact with Sephardim and the Turks, adopted several types of stuffed vegetables, including tomatoes and mushrooms, but particularly favor peppers.

As with other well-traveled dishes, stuffed vegetables developed numerous variations. Stuffings can include primarily meat or eschew it entirely. All-meat fillings are called *sheikh mahshi*. Turks refer to vegetarian dolmas as *zeytinyagli dolma* (olive oil dolma) and *yalanci dolma* (the former word meaning "false/liar"). Turks tend to use more meat, while Persians generally favor more rice and also add yellow split peas. Sephardim in the Balkans tend to use raw meat in the filling and mix in some egg as a binder. Middle Easterners typically sauté the ground meat with onions and omit any egg. Many Middle Eastern fillings contain pine nuts and currants or raisins. Indians use chopped chicken instead of meat, or use all rice. Bulgur is sometimes substituted in the Levant.

Meat or cheese dolmas are customarily served hot, while vegetarian rice ones are appropriate hot or at room temperature. Served together on a platter with other vegetables, dolmas are a colorful part of a *mezze* (appetizer assortment). Vegetarian versions were especially popular among Jews for dairy meals, which in many households were served every day except the Sabbath and holidays.

The sauce for most Middle Eastern stuffed vegetables tends to be on the tart side. In the nineteenth century, tomatoes became a common addition. Jews from Hungary, Italy, Romania, and northern Poland prefer a savory sauce; Sephardim prefer a sauce made tart with lemon juice; and those from Galicia and Ukraine favor a sweet-and-sour sauce.

Stuffed vegetables became an important dish in nearly every Jewish community. Sephardim and Mizrachim do not limit themselves to a few types, but stuff any number of vegetables including artichokes, beets, carrots, celery, onions, potatoes, radishes, and turnips. Sephardim, however, typically prepare one or more types of stuffed vegetables in separate vessels, preferring the taste of each one to stand alone. Middle Easterners favor a medley of stuffed vegetables in the same pot and each vegetable imparts some of its flavor to the filling and sauce. The vegetable assortment usually consists of a trio of American imports—bell peppers, zucchini, and tomatoes—and sometimes eggplant. For large crowds, the vegetables are stacked in the pot, firm ones below and more delicate items on top. A cook's culinary skill and degree of hospitality were once measured by her dolmas. Since preparing a variety of stuffed vegetables was somewhat time-consuming, they were typically reserved for holidays and other special occasions, especially bar mitzvahs and weddings. Stuffed foods, symbolizing the harvest and abundance, are particularly prominent during the holidays of Sukkot and Purim. Kurds bake various stuffed vegetables, including peppers, eggplants, and zucchini, in their version of Sabbath stew (*matphoni*). The women of the household traditionally gathered with relatives and friends to prepare the vegetables, chatting and joking as they turned a tedious chore into good-spirited fun and a social event. Such gatherings have grown rare of late, as caterers and store-bought versions became commonplace.

(See also Cabbage, Stuffed; Grape Leaves, Stuffed)

❦ MIDDLE EASTERN STUFFED VEGETABLE MEDLEY
(*DOLMAS/MAHASHA*)

12 STUFFED PIECES   [MEAT]

3 medium bell peppers
3 large yellow onions, peeled
3 large, firm tomatoes
3 medium zucchini

Stuffing:

2 tablespoons olive or vegetable oil
1½ pounds ground beef or lamb
½ cup raw rice, soaked in cold water for 30 minutes and drained, or ½ to 1 cup matza meal or dry bread crumbs
¼ cup chopped fresh parsley
About 1 teaspoon salt
About ¼ teaspoon ground black pepper

Sauce:

3 tablespoons olive or vegetable oil
2 cups tomato juice, chicken broth, or water (or 1 cup tomato sauce and 1 cup water, or 1½ cups water and 6 ounces tomato paste)
2 to 4 tablespoons fresh lemon juice
1 to 8 tablespoons sugar or honey
Salt and ground black pepper to taste

1. Slice the tops from the bell peppers. Remove and discard the seeds and the core. Slice the tops from the onions, tomatoes, and zucchini. Remove or scoop out the inside parts, leaving a ¼-inch-thick shell. Set aside the vegetable shells.

2. Chop the inside part of the onion and reserve for the stuffing and sauce. Chop the inside parts of the tomato and zucchini and reserve for the sauce.

3. To make the stuffing: In a large skillet, heat the oil over medium heat. Add half of the onions and sauté until soft and translucent, 5 to 10 minutes. Add the meat and sauté until it loses its red color, about 5 minutes. Stir in the rice. Remove from the heat and stir in the parsley, salt, and pepper.

4. To make the sauce: In a large pot, heat the oil over medium heat. Add the remaining onions and sauté until soft and translucent, 5 to 10 minutes. Add the reserved chopped tomato and zucchini and sauté until slightly softened, about 5 minutes. Add the tomato juice, lemon juice, sugar, salt, and pepper.

5. Spoon the stuffing into the vegetable cavities, leaving room for expansion. Any extra stuffing can be shaped into balls and cooked with the vegetables. Arrange the stuffed vegetables upright on top of the sautéed vegetables in the pot.

6. Cover and simmer over low heat or bake in a 350°F oven until tender, about 1 hour. Serve warm. Store in the refrigerator for up to 1 week.

DOUGHNUT

Doughnut is a deep-fried ball or ring of dough leavened with either yeast or chemicals.

Origin: The Netherlands or western Germany

Other names: Dutch: *oliebollen, oliekoeken*; German: *krabbl, krapfen, krapffen, krapfl, fettkrapfen, pfannkuchen*; Hebrew: *sufganit*; Hungarian: *fank*; Ladino: *bimuelo*: Turkish: *lokma*; Ukrainian: *pampushky*; Yiddish: *krapfen, ponchik*.

Fried doughs have several advantages over sophisticated pastries—they are rather easy to make, for even relatively inexperienced cooks, and they do not require an oven or much equipment, only a frying pot. Before the spread of the home oven in the late nineteenth century, fried doughs were the most common form of homemade pastry. The ancient Greeks and Romans fried strips of pastry dough in olive oil, afterwards coating them with honey or *garum* (pungent fish sauce). During the early medieval period, cooks in Arab lands began deep-frying blobs of loose plain yeast dough, dropping them from a hand or a spoon into hot oil. Yeast doughs cannot contain too much sugar—it impairs or even kills the yeast, and causes the fritter's surface to burn before the interior cooks through. Because these fritters were not inherently sweet, residents of the Muslim world began to drench their fritters with sugar syrup.

Medieval Moslem armies advancing into Spain, Sicily, and the Balkans introduced fried yeast dough to those areas. Among Mizrachim and Sephardim, these deep-fried yeast dough balls are prepared today much as they were more than a thousand years ago, served on festive occasions, especially Hanukkah.

Yeast fritters eventually spread north through Europe. The Harleian Manuscript 279 (c. 1430), from a collection in the British Museum, contains an early English recipe for "Cryspes," exemplifying the nature of fried yeast dough at the end of the Middle Ages. A thin batter of egg whites, milk, flour, sugar, salt, and barm (ale vat foam) was fried by placing one's hand in the batter and letting it run down the fingers into a pot of hot oil. The fritters were sprinkled with sugar.

The modern doughnut probably emerged in the early fifteenth century somewhere in northwestern Europe—the Dutch and Germans each claim credit. Rudimentary doughnuts had one major drawback—they did not contain egg yolks and therefore absorbed an unpleasant amount of grease. Only with the popularization of the chicken in Europe during the late medieval period and the ready supply of inexpensive eggs, did eggs become added to doughs. This meant less greasy fritters, greater versatility, and the widespread popularity of what would become the doughnut.

The use of egg yolks also led to firmer doughs, which were generally shaped in the hands rather than dropped from a spoon, resulting in firmer, larger, tastier fritters. But this created a new problem—relatively large doughnuts made from a firm dough may end up with a bit of raw dough at the center. Some cooks tried to solve this problem by placing a raisin or nut in the center, while others were content with frying small or thin doughnuts. It would be another several centuries before the center dilemma would be resolved with the American innovation of a hole (attributed by some to Captain Hanson Gregory in 1847).

As was common at that time, the dough was heavily spiced and usually contained raisins or dried currants. On occasion, cooks tied the dough into decorative knots (*knoten* in German and *knopen* in Dutch) or rolled it out and cut it into diamond shapes. In the fifteenth century, an inspired central European baker added filling and the jelly doughnut was born.

However, not all early filled doughnuts were sweet, as sugar was then still a rarity in Germany, and many of the original ones were stuffed with savory mixtures, such as meat, fish, and mushroom. Subsequently, the doughnut's rise to prominence coincided with—the increasing popularity of coffee, which became a frequent accompaniment. Although Jews did not invent the doughnut, they played key roles in transmitting and transforming it.

The Dutch introduced doughnuts to the New World. The Pilgrims also brought the practice of doughnut making with them to America. Eventually, Americans began to reduce or eliminate the spices as well as braiding the dough and, in the mid-1800s, they introduced the hole in the center. It was only following World War I, however, that the doughnut gained mass popularity in the United States. During the war, Red Cross and Salvation Army workers treated soldiers to doughnuts, exposing many Americans to this treat for the first time. The servicemen returned home with a passion for doughnuts and many bakeries responded. At that time, most doughnut makers offered only the few basic varieties.

It was automation that would transform the doughnut from an exotic inconsistent treat into standardized everyday fare. Adolph Levitt of New York, a Jewish refugee from the pogroms of czarist Russia, sold handmade doughnuts that he fried up in a large pot in his store in Harlem. In 1920, working with engineers, he developed the first automated doughnut machine and founded Display Doughnut Machine Corp, which later became the Doughnut Corporation of America. Five years later, he released a standardized mix to use in his machines, creating a near monopoly through the 1940s. At the 1934 World's Fair in Chicago, machine-produced doughnuts were billed as "the food hit of the Century of Progress." In 1931, making use of his machines and mixes, Levitt launched the first doughnut shop chain, Mayflower Donuts. The chain eventually had eighteen locations nationwide, before disappearing in the 1970s. Within fifteen years, Levitt was annually selling more than twenty-five million dollars' worth of machines. Around that time, the appearance of doughnuts in assorted diners and cafeterias, as well as the spread of doughnut chains, led to the doughnut becoming America's favorite cake.

Emerging local fire safety laws in the United States in the middle of the twentieth century severely restricted the ability of most bakeries to continue making doughnuts, as they were unable to purchase and maintain the special equipment and environment for frying. Therefore, today most American bakeries offering doughnuts do not make them in-house, but contract for them from a wholesaler. In place of part-time doughnut makers, there emerged stores specializing in them, a few spawning large franchises.

William Rosenberg (1916–2002), the son of immigrant Jewish parents, was operating an industrial catering business in which he sold snacks in converted secondhand trucks near factories around his native Dorchester, Massachusetts. He noticed that doughnuts and coffee accounted for 40 percent of his sales and in 1948 launched a doughnut shop called the Open Kettle in Quincy, Massachusetts, the heart of America's original doughnut country, aiming for a blue-collar clientele. Among Rosenberg's innovations was offering fifty-two varieties of doughnuts, one for every week of the year. This unassuming store would eventually become, in Rosenberg's words, "the world's largest coffee and baked goods chain."

Two years after opening, Rosenberg changed the store's name to Dunkin' Donuts and five years after that, arranged the first franchise in nearby Worcester. When his skeptical business partner and brother-in-law, Harry Winokur, protested this move, Rosenberg bought him out. By 1963, there were 100 Dunkin' Donuts shops, and by 1979, there were 1,000. In 1988, England's Allied-Lyons, in a friendly takeover, purchased Dunkin' Donuts, then consisting of 1,850 locations.

In 1956, Harry Winokur started a competing franchise chain, Mister Donut. The upstart went national and soon became Dunkin' Donuts' major competitor. Mister Donut was also the first doughnut chain to receive kosher supervision for some of the franchises.

By the time of Rosenberg's death, there were more than 5,000 Dunkin' Donut shops, including about 40 outlets under kosher supervision, in nearly 40 countries, and serving nearly 2 million customers per day.

(See also Bimuelo, Fritter, Lokma, Pampushka, Sfenj, Sufganiyah, Yoyo, Zalabia, and Zvingous)

DUCK

Ducks, smaller relatives of geese, are mostly aquatic birds found wild as well as domesticated throughout much of the world. All contemporary domesticated ducks, except the Muscovy, are descended from the wild mallard. There are seven subspecies of the mallard, the most prominent today being the Pekin. The other common domesticated duck is the Muscovy, a South American species. Most of the domesticated ducks in North America today are mixed breeds between the Pekin and Muscovy, sometimes called a Moulard. Because of the American Muscovy's ability to breed with Old World ducks, the Israeli chief rabbinate pronounced them kosher.

Duck is particularly prized in China, France, Poland, and central Europe but is generally overlooked farther south toward the Mediterranean and in much of the Middle East. Unlike geese and chicken, ducks were rarely raised by Jews. It is uncommon among Sephardim and most Mizrachim and in some Middle Eastern communities duck is considered unkosher.

On the other hand, in parts of central and eastern Europe, duck was considered festive fare. In this vein, the standard Yiddish word for female duck, *katshke*, derives from the Slavic word, reflecting the principal area of its popularity among Ashkenazim.

Duck meat is darker and richer than that of the chicken and turkey and possesses less flesh in proportion to bone than most other birds. The favorite dish of duck cooked with sauerkraut be found from Germany to Bulgaria. All commercially available kosher duck is domesticated and usually comes frozen. The majority of the world's contemporary foie gras comes from Moulards.

(See also Bird)

DUKKAH

Dukkah is a spice and nut mixture.
Origin: Egypt

Dukkah (from the Arabic meaning "to pound"), a staple among Egyptians, is a spice blend containing toasted nuts, seeds, and sometimes pepper, mint, za'atar, or thyme. Most Egyptian Jews would not purchase *dukkah* from street vendors, for reasons of kashrut, but would prepare their own at home. The most popular and traditional way to consume this is to dip bread into olive oil, then into the *dukkah*. It is also used as a coating for pan-fried fish and poultry, in lamb stews, and over salads and pasta.

❧ EGYPTIAN NUT AND SPICE MIXTURE (*DUKKAH*)

ABOUT ¾ CUP [PAREVE]

½ cup hazelnuts, pine nuts, pistachios, or peanuts
¼ cup sesame seeds
3 tablespoons coriander seeds
2 tablespoons cumin seeds
About ¾ teaspoon salt
1 teaspoon dried mint or thyme (optional)

In a dry medium skillet, stir the nuts over medium-high heat until golden brown, about 5 minutes. If using hazelnuts, place on a towel and rub to remove the skins. Let cool. Add the sesame seeds to the skillet and stir over medium-high heat until lightly browned, 2 to 3 minutes. Let cool. Add the coriander and cumin to the skillet and and stir over medium-high heat until lightly browned, 1 to 3 minutes. Let cool. In a mortar and pestle or food processor, coarsely grind the nuts and seeds. Stir in the salt and, if using, mint. Store in an airtight container in the refrigerator for up to 1 month.

DULCE

Dulce refers to an array of sugar confections, candied fruits, jellied candies, and preserves.

Origin: Spain

Other names: Arabic: *helou*; Greek: *glyko*; Hebrew: *matok*.

After the Arabs conquered Persia in the seventh century, they began introducing sugar cane throughout the Arab world and cooks began to experiment with it. By the tenth century, they had created rudimentary confections—called *halwa* (literally "sweet" in Arabic)—based on sugar syrup. By the thirteenth century, recipes for pulled sugar and marzipan (called *faludhaj*) appeared in Baghdad. Building on these advances, Sephardim developed an array of confections, especially candied fruits and jellied candies, called *dulces* or *dulses*. Sephardim enjoy these fruit confections on special occasions, especially Rosh Hashanah and Passover.

Fruit cooked in sugar syrup until soft, *dulce de fruta*, has been popular among Sephardim since well before the expulsion from Spain. Sugar contributes additional sweetness and also intensifies the flavors; it contributes body so that the paste can be cut into shapes. Many early Sephardic *dulces* were based on ground nuts and oranges and featured the profusion of spices typical of fourteenth-century European cookery. More recently, the spices have been toned down or eliminated, focusing instead on the fruit flavors. Almost any fruit can be used in this process, but hard ones require cooking and dried ones soaking. Favorite *dulces* are made from high-pectin fruits that gel, notably *bimbriyo* (quince) and *mansana* (apple). Sephardim in India use mangoes. Conversos in Central America and the Caribbean inspired New World versions, such as *dulce de guayaba* (from guava paste). In the sixteenth century, *dulces* appeared in England, where the Iberian quince paste (*marmelo* in Spanish) eventually became the English marmalade.

Dulce blanco (white sweet), also known as *sharope* (Ladino for "syrup"), is a thick, creamy sugar paste that is akin to fondant, but softer. In the traditional method, *dulce blanco* is prepared by beating it with a wooden spoon, always stirring in the same direction, for at least twenty minutes. When food coloring is added, it becomes *sharope kolorado*. *Dulce blanco* is used as a spread for sweet breads and, on Passover, for matza. Some hosts serve *dulce blanco* with apples slices to dip into it. *Dulce blanco* is also a coating for nuts, such as Jordan almonds, as well as the base for a variety of confections.

Sephardic hospitality is offered on diverse occasions, such as Saturday evening following the Sabbath (starting the new week on a sweet note) or the initial meeting of prospective in-laws. Sephardic hosts customarily offer their guests *la tavla de dulce* (a silver "tray of sweets") featuring *dulce blanco*, assorted confections, and homemade fruit preserves, which are presented in glass bowls with small silver spoons arranged on a silver tray. The *dulces* were typically accompanied with a glass of water (*dulce con aqua*) to clean the palate. Customarily following the *tavla* is Turkish coffee, often served with pastries.

In her 2006 book, *The Fortune Teller's Kiss*, Brenda Serotte portrayed her bout with polio in 1954 in the Sephardic subculture of New York City, describing hospitality in a Turkish home: "Either the host or a girl of marriageable age brought out the tray with the good demitasse cups, glasses of water, Jordan almonds, Turkish Delights candies, or a rare delicious treat: a white-jelly fondant called *sharope*."

SEPHARDIC FRUIT PASTE CANDIES (*DULCE DE FRUTA*)

ABOUT TWENTY-FIVE 1-INCH CANDIES   [PAREVE]

About 4 cups fruit pulp from peeled, cored,
   chopped, and cooked until soft apples, apricots,
   berries, mangoes, peaches, pears, or quinces
About 4 cups (28 ounces) sugar
2 tablespoons fresh lemon juice
Confectioners' or granulated sugar for coating
   (optional)

1. In a medium bowl combine the fruit pulp and
sugar and stir until well blended. Cover with plastic
wrap and let stand overnight.

2. Stir in the lemon juice. Transfer the fruit mixture
to a large nonreactive pot (do not use iron, copper, or
brass) and bring to a boil. Reduce the heat to low and
simmer, stirring frequently and toward the end stirring constantly, until the mixture thickens and sput-
ters, 30 to 50 minutes.

3. Remove from the heat, cover, and let stand for
about 10 minutes. Mash the fruit until smooth.

4. Spread the warm fruit paste to a 1-inch thickness
on a greased 13-by-9-inch baking pan or a greased
baking sheet. Let cool, then cut into squares or diamonds. Or form the warm fruit paste into 1-inch balls.

5. Cover loosely with wax paper and let stand at
room temperature in a dry place for 12 hours. Turn
the candies over and let stand for another 12 hours. At
this point, if desired, dredge the candies in the sugar
to coat. This helps to keep the candies from sticking
together. Store between sheets of wax paper in an airtight container at room temperature.

DUMPLING

Dumpling is a piece of dough boiled or steamed.
Origin: Probably China
Other names: Czech: *knedliky*; French: *quenelle*;
   German: *kleise, klopse, kloss, knödel*; Hungarian:
   gomboc; Italian: gnocchi; Polish: *kluski*; Romanian:
   papanush; Slavic: *halushky*; Slovakian: *knedlicky*;
   Yiddish: *halkes, kloese, klopse, knaidel, knedlicky*.

A Yiddish proverb advises, "Dumplings in a dream
are not dumplings but a dream."

The English term dumplings (most sources indicate it came from "dump lump"), initially appearing
around 1600, denotes balls of dough simmered or
steamed; the primary starch varies from region to
region. In related but separate categories are pasta,
filled pasta dough, and rudimentary puddings, all
containing similar ingredients but prepared in dis-
similar ways. European noodles and filled pasta are
made from a firm dough made of egg and wheat flour.
Medieval puddings, containing varying amounts of
chopped meat and frequently omitting any eggs, were
simmered or steamed, like sausages, inside of animal
intestines and stomachs.

Among Mizrachim, dumplings were popular with
Persians, Kurds, and Georgians and were primarily
reserved for special occasions. Dumplings historically
were rarely, if ever, found among Sephardim, who had
access to durum wheat and olive oil and preferred
pasta and fried doughs, such as *boyos* and *bimuelos*.
Sephardim even fry some noodles before boiling. On
the other hand, dumplings formed an important part
of the cooking of every Ashkenazic community, but
particularly those from central Europe, where they
served as both weekday and festive fare.

Although the concept of boiling clumps and strips
of dough in water may seem obvious, the method actually developed relatively late in European history. One
reason is that grain pastes, except those made from
durum wheat, do not hold together in boiling water
without the addition of eggs. Since durum was rare
in most of Europe, cooks had to wait for the spread
of chicken raising in the twelfth century following the
First Crusade and the arrival of the concept of adding
eggs to the dough. Once those elements converged,
dumplings quickly became a widespread element of
late medieval European cookery, especially among
peasants. Meanwhile, the forests that then blanketed
much of Europe provided plenty of free fuel for extensive boiling. Since much of medieval European food
consisted of stews and soups, these dishes proved the
ideal environment for dumplings and a tasty way to
stretch and enliven a meal.

As with many medieval European cooking innovations, dumplings first emerged in Italy, probably
through contacts with Middle Easterners. The basis
for the earliest European dumplings was a basic bread
mixture—later in the sixteenth century called a *panada* (from the Spanish for "boiled bread")—which was
a way to utilize stale bread. The earliest Italian records
of "macaroni"—either from the Greek *makaria* (food
made from barley) or the Italian *maccare* (bruise/
crush)—in the early thirteenth century referred not
to pasta, but rather to dumplings made from "bread
paste" and boiled in stews and soups. Shortly there-

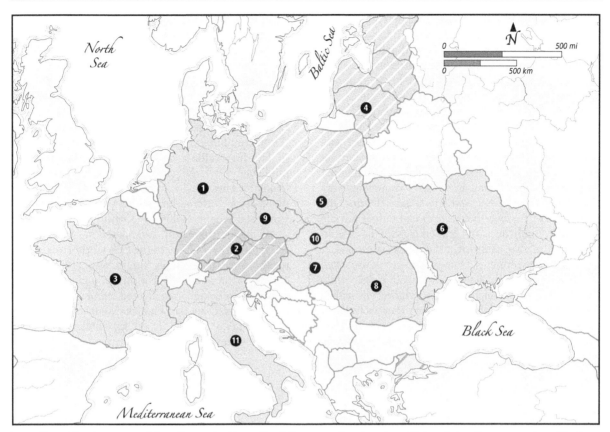

Dumplings *After the concept of dumplings arrived in medieval Europe, each region adopted it into their culinary repertoire. 1 **Northern Germany, Bavaria**—kloes, kleis; 2 **Southern Germany, Austria**—knodel; 3 **France**—quenelle, boulette; 4 **Central and northern Poland, Baltic States**—knaidel (kneydl); 5 **Southern Poland**—halke; 6 **Ukraine**—galushki; 7 **Hungary**—gombóc, galuska; 8 **Romania**—papanash, galusca; 9 **Czech**—knedliky; 10 **Slovakia**—knedlicky; 11 **Italy**—gnocchi*

after, in other parts of Italy, rudimentary bread dumplings acquired the name gnocchi (Italian for "lumps").

By the thirteenth century, dumplings had spread to southern Germany, where they were called *knödel* (akin to the Old High German *knoto*, meaning "knot") in the south and Austria. Later in Bavaria, Rabbi Meir ben Baruch of Rothenburg (1215–1293), the supreme Ashkenazic rabbinical authority of his time, mentioned the consumption of dumplings, so they were ensconced in the southern German Jewish kitchen by that time. Today, central Europeans remain the world's most fanatical and prodigious dumpling consumers. Before the popularization of the potato in northern Europe in the nineteenth century, Ashkenazim relied on dumplings for much of their diet.

Beginning in the fourteenth century, as Italy and then other parts of Europe began moving out of the medieval period, flour and sometimes semolina were increasingly substituted for the bread in dumplings. Initially, most of these new dishes consisted of loose rudimentary batters, such as the German *einlauf* (run in) and *ribbles* (to rub), the Austrian *nockerl/nockerlach* (perhaps from the Italian gnocchi), the Bavarian and southern German *spätzle* (little sparrow), and the Hungarian *galuska*. Unlike the preparation of egg noodles, the rolling and drying stages were omitted and the thick gruel was dropped, cut, or squeezed directly into boiling broth or water. Soon large flour dumplings grew increasingly widespread. To stretch limited resources or use up leftovers, they were sometimes filled (*gefullte kloese*) with chopped cooked vegetables, chopped meat, or pieces of fruit. Sometimes soft cheese was incorporated into dumplings, both savory and sweet. In the eighteenth century, cornmeal became a popular dumpling ingredient, and in the nineteenth century, potatoes followed suit.

For weekday meals, Ashkenazim, particularly those from central Europe, might simmer dumplings in stews, cover them with a sauce, or cook them with sauerkraut. They were also considered proper fare for the Sabbath and holidays, some holidays earning their own special type of dumpling. Cheese dumplings were traditional on Shavuot and Hanukkah. During the eight days of Passover, housewives had to find ways to feed their family using the limited ingredients permitted and available, and matza dumplings were one of their crowning triumphs. Dumplings were slow-cooked in cholent (Sabbath stew), which would evolve into kugels, and the dumplings were whimsically called *Shabbos ganif* (Sabbath thief), since they stole flavor from the medium in which they were cooked. They were also cooked separately with fruits for the Sabbath.

In the nineteenth century, Ashkenazic immigrants brought their Jewish-style dumplings to America. Initially, various German terms predominated, but as the twentieth century progressed, eastern European counterparts supplanted them. *Jewish Cookery* by Esther Levy (1871), reflective of her German heritage, contains five dumplings: "Dampfnudeln, or German Dumplings," "Suet Dumplings," "Yeast Dumplings," "Drop Dumplings for Soup," and "Matzo Cleis Soup."

The first Yiddish cookbook in America, the self-published *Ler-bukh vi Azoy tsu Kokhn un Bakhn* (Book for How to Cook and Bake) by Hinde Amkhanitski (1901), offered fare with a pronounced eastern European accent, including "*Kneydlekh.*"

As many Ashkenazim assimilated in America, they frequently lost touch with the Old World names, calling the dough balls simply "dumplings," and many lost a taste for them as well. For others, a cheese *gombóc* or potato *halke* remain a favored comfort food.

(See also Csipetke, Galuska, Gnocchi, Gombóc, Gundi, Halke, Knaidel, Knedliky, Kubbeh, Papanash, and Shlishkes)

E

EGG

Humans have been eating eggs since the days of aboriginal hunter-gatherers, but in most areas eggs only gained a prominent role in cooking relatively late in history. Even after people learned how to farm various fowl, domesticated eggs, primarily from geese and ducks, were first and foremost conserved to produce future animals and, therefore, only occasionally eaten. Only with the popularization of the prolific chicken could a sizable number of the eggs be consumed without threatening the reproductive cycle.

Eggs were rarely mentioned in the Bible and then only in reference to being gathered from the wild. The most common fowl and among the few domesticated species in ancient Israel were turtledoves and their close relative, pigeons, both of which were raised for their flesh and offspring, not for their small eggs. By Talmudic times, chickens were so prominent in Jewish life that the *beitzah* (egg) was used as a Talmudic standard measure of volume. *Beitzah* is even the name of one of the Talmudic tractates, which deals with the generic laws of the biblical holidays. Eggs from kosher fowl, except those found inside a slaughtered bird (the latter considered meat), are pareve and, therefore, particularly versatile in Jewish cooking.

Egyptians were the most prolific consumers of eggs in the ancient world; they even developed a method of incubation. However, eggs were very seldom called for in ancient Greek recipes, and in Rome, even among the wealthy, they were used sparingly and generally reserved for special occasions. In the upper-class Roman cookbook of Apicius (c. 400 CE), eggs are called for in only a few of the work's five hundred recipes. Apicius served hard-boiled eggs (*ova elixa*) with *liquamen* (fermented fish sauce), oil, and honey, and prepared fried eggs (*ova frixa*) in wine sauce. Unlike the Egyptians, who enjoyed any type of eggs, Romans favored those from chickens and pheasants. After the fall of the Roman Empire, however, chickens fell into general disuse, except for their limited use in cock-fighting, in much of Europe for nearly a millennium.

On the other hand, in Arab Spain and on the southern side of the Mediterranean, chickens maintained their widespread popularity during the early medieval period. Newer chicken breeds provided more meat and eggs, leading to increased utilization. Sephardim had a plentiful and relatively inexpensive supply of chicken eggs; even the poor ate them on a regular basis. Every market had at least one *huevera* (egg dealer) peddling fresh eggs. The Spanish painter Diego Velázquez, a descendant of Portuguese Conversos, in his 1618 painting *Old Woman Cooking Eggs*, now hanging in the National Gallery of Scotland, depicted a woman frying eggs in hot olive oil in a small *cazuela* (cooking pot) set over a brazier. The woman is holding a wooden spoon to flick olive oil around the edges of the eggs to create crisp, lacey edges (*sin puntilla*).

Medieval Sephardim used eggs (*huevos* in Ladino) in prodigious amounts and typically in complex and varied ways. A cook's egg dishes were a demonstration of culinary ability and those who executed them well were praised and told that they had *manos del oro* (hands of gold). Sephardim developed a highly advanced egg cookery, including *huevos haminados* (long-cooked eggs), *fritadas* (omelets), *agristada* (egg-lemon sauce), *huevos de Haman* (Purim pastry with hard-boiled eggs), *pan esponjado* (sponge cake), egg matzas, and a host of casseroles and baked goods. Egg dishes could be eaten at breakfast, at dinner, or as part of a light lunch, accompanied by salads. Following the expulsion in 1492, Sephardim spread these dishes throughout the Mediterranean, where subsequently each area added local touches.

In the Middle East, where eggs were scarcer than in Iberia and generally reserved for special occasions, the egg dishes were simpler and less varied than Sephardic fare. Eggs, primarily paired with various tart items, were hard-cooked and served whole. They were also fried on a bed of greens, cooked as small fritter-like omelets, or scrambled and combined with a few basic ingredients. Mediterranean and Middle

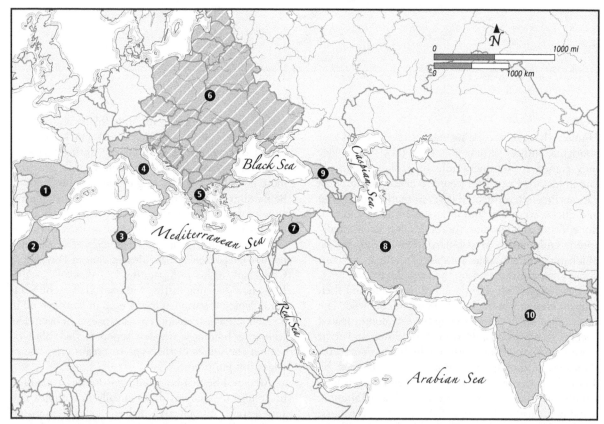

Egg Dishes *Of the basic methods of preparing eggs—skillet-sized omelets, small egg patties, casseroles, scrambled eggs, and hard-boiled eggs—Jewish communities developed a diverse array of dishes.* **1 Spain**—*fritada, haminados, quajado, tortilla de huevos;* **2 Morocco**—*dajada milina, eggah;* **3 Tunisia**—*aijjah, maquda, shakshuka;* **4 Italy**—*fritatta;* **5 Greece**—*sfoungato, avgolemono;* **6 Eastern Europe**—*gehakte eier, gogol mogol;* **7 Syria**—*ijeh (edjeh);* **8 Iran**—*kuku, nargesi, edjeh;* **9 Georgia**—*chizhipizhi;* **10 India**—*mahmoosa*

Eastern omelets (from the Latin *lamella* "thin plate"), in contrast to the French type, tend to emphasize the flavorings more than the eggs, using eggs more as a binder. These omelets come in a myriad of variations, generally making use of seasonal produce or leftovers. The Maghrebi *shakshuka* (tomato stew with eggs) has become a modern Israeli staple. Eggs were particularly prevalent on Passover, which the Arabs nicknamed *Id-al-Beid* (the egg holiday).

Chickens began to make a comeback in Europe with the revival of cuisine and agronomy in the twelfth century, following the First Crusade. The Responsa of Rashi (c. 1100) reveals that one of his favorite foods was *abbstr* (omelets sweetened with honey), which he ate as an appetizer before making the benediction over bread, in order to be able to first recite a benediction "with what I love." Hard-boiled eggs, then considered a luxury, were an early Ashkenazic Sabbath delicacy and among the special treats given to a young boy on his first day of school. By the late fourteenth century, eggs were the primary or secondary ingredients in more than 50 percent of the recipes in European cookbooks.

The fowl of choice for early Ashkenazim was the goose, a bird that lacked the chicken's egg-laying capacity. Goose eggs are also larger than chicken eggs, and their shells are much harder; if they are boiled for too long or at too high a temperature, they tend to be inedible. In central and eastern Europe in the fifteenth century, chickens emerged as the most important food animal for Ashkenazim; most families keeping at least a few in their yard or in coops to provide a regular supply of eggs. At that time, eggs began appearing in Ashkenazic Sabbath loaves (*eier challah*). Subsequently, eggs provided much of the protein in Ashkenazic cookery, ranging from simple Polish *eier mit tzibbeles* (scrambled eggs with onions) to the more sophisticated Alsatian *tarte aux oignons* (creamy onion tarts). Eggs were essential for classic Ashkenazic fare, such as kugels, *knaidlach* (dumplings), *triflach* (egg drops for soup), *lokshen* (noodles), blintzes, latkes, *matza brie* (fried matza), and *eier kichlach* (egg cookies). The unhatched eggs in a properly slaughtered bird, called *eierlach* or *ayelach* (little eggs) in Yiddish, are considered meat and typically poached in chicken soup.

By the eleventh century, Franco-German Jews had developed the Sabbath custom of eating hard-boiled eggs and salted raw onions, but separately. At some point, the two items came together in the form of an egg salad. This dish, variously called *gehakte eier* (chopped eggs) and *eier un schmaltz* (eggs with poultry fat), remains popular among Ashkenazim for light meals, such as a kiddush (Sabbath morning buffet) or *shalosh seudot* (Sabbath afternoon meal), and at many life-cycle events. Raw onions are most frequently added, producing a sharper flavor, but some people prefer the caramelized taste of browned onions. Schmaltz was originally added to bind, moisten, and flavor the ingredients, but in the twentieth century pareve mayonnaise became a common substitute. The duo of hard-boiled eggs and raw onions was also mixed with other favorite items to form popular Ashkenazic appetizers, including *gehakte leber* (chopped liver) and *gehakte hirring* (chopped herring).

During the Middle Ages, as eggs gained wider convention in the Ashkenazic kitchen, they also took on various symbolic meanings and usages. In Jewish tradition, eggs are cited as the only food that becomes harder as it is cooked, while the eggshell is noted as being, paradoxically, both resilient and fragile. Thus eggs are symbolic of Jewish history, as well as of fertility and life and death. Hard-boiled eggs are customarily served at all somber occasions, including the meals preceding major fasts and a *Seudat Havra'ah* (the meal following a funeral). A roasted hard-boiled egg is used on the Passover Seder plate to commemorate the *Chagigah* (festival offering) that was presented in the Temple. Many Ashkenazim also traditionally start the Seder meal with hard-boiled eggs in salt water, while Sephardim feature the ubiquitous *huevos haminados*; these customs probably derived from the Roman practice of starting feasts with eggs.

(See also Bird, Chicken, Chizhipizhi, Fritada, Goose, Haminado, Ijeh, and Kuku)

EGG CREAM

In 1996, Brooklyn-born musician Lou Reed, reminiscing about the 1950s New York of his childhood, wrote a song entitled "Egg Cream," which begins with these lines:

When I was a young man, no bigger than this
A chocolate egg cream was not to be missed
Some U-Bet's chocolate syrup, seltzer water
  mixed with milk
You stir it up into a heady fro, tasted just like
  silk.

In 1890, a little more than a century before this song was written, Louis Auster, a young Jewish recent immigrant, was experimenting at the soda fountain in his tiny candy store on the Lower East Side when he mixed a few ingredients and concocted what would become New York's iconic drink. Despite its name, there is neither egg nor cream in an egg cream. The term was first used by Lettice Bryan in *The Kentucky Housewife* (1839) for a custard and later appeared in the *Modern Guide for Soda Dispensers* (1896) for a syrup made from eggs and cream, but no chocolate.

The New York term most probably came from the egg-white-like foam that rose to the top in a properly-prepared drink when the spritz of carbonated water met the velvety-textured brown liquid below. Auster kept his recipe secret and clandestinely concocted his own chocolate syrup, which, until his death, he made in a room in his store with darkened windows to prevent observation. One of Auster's sons later revealed that among the egg cream's original ingredients were seltzer, cocoa, sugar, and milk. Auster began selling his new drink for three cents and was soon averaging three thousand sales on a hot day, with customers frequently lined up around the block. He eventually added four other locations in Brooklyn and Manhattan, which were run by his children.

Competitors began offering their own versions of the drink, some even containing eggs and/or cream.

Did you see what was said in one of New York's leading newspapers about **FOX's U-BET?**

It says that

"For a delicious Egg Cream*
(without eggs or cream)
the finest Chocolate Syrup is
FOX's u-bet

✱ Use FOX's U-BET Syrup, with **Good Health Seltzer** and a dash of Milk.

When Fox's U-Bet syrup—a staple for classic egg creams—introduced a kosher-for-Passover version, egg creams suddenly became a widespread Passover treat.

Eventually, a somewhat uniform recipe evolved, made with Fox's U-Bet Chocolate Syrup, created by Herman and Ida Fox in Brooklyn in 1895. (Today, there is even a kosher-for-Passover version of Fox's chocolate syrup.) By the 1920s, the egg cream was standard at all soda fountains throughout New York City.

None of Auster's grandchildren went into the family business and the stores closed following the founder's death in 1955. Around this time, soda fountains began disappearing and by the end of the 1960s few of the surviving stores knew how to make a proper egg cream. In addition, a classic egg cream contains no additional sugar than that in the syrup and, as the twentieth century progressed, America's tastes tended toward sweeter beverages. Consequently, by the end of the twentieth century, the egg cream had lost much of its stature. To New Yorkers born before that time, however, it remains an integral nostalgic component of their childhood.

EGG CREAM

1 SERVING   [DAIRY]

To produce a proper egg cream with a 2-inch head of thick white foam, you need a siphon bottle. Do not sip an egg cream through a straw—as you will miss the texture of the foam—but directly from the glass.

2 tablespoons Fox's chocolate syrup
⅓ cup whole milk, chilled
⅔ to 1 cup seltzer (from a pressurized bottle),
    slightly chilled

Pour the chocolate syrup into a chilled 12-ounce glass. Do not use a paper cup. Slowly add the milk, but do not stir. Spritz in enough seltzer down the center of the glass to form a foamy head that nearly reaches the top of the glass. Using a long spoon, stir with an up-and-down motion to blend without deflating the foam.

EGGPLANT

"My food [the eggplant] is the most praised, better than the tomato!" (From a popular Ladino folksong, "*Si Savesh la Buena Djente*" [Dear People, Do You Know of the Battle of the Vegetables?], depicting a dispute between the two favorite vegetables of the Sephardim, an eggplant and a tomato.)

The eggplant is actually a large berry, although usually it is consumed as a vegetable. The original European eggplant cultivar was small, white (sometimes with purple streaks), and ovate—hence the American name, which was only first recorded in England in the seventeenth century. Another early English name for the eggplant was Jew's apple, denoting its usage among Sephardim. In the eighteenth century, the French word for eggplant, *aubergine*, supplanted the name eggplant in Britain. Since the white type bruised easily, the purple hybrid became the most widespread, although white eggplants are still very popular in India and are available in some Western markets.

The eggplant is a native of southeast Asia and it has been cultivated in India for more than four thousand years. The plant's path can be traced backward through its French name, *aubergine*, derived from the Catalan *alberginia*, which comes from the Arabic *al-batinjan* by way of the Persian *badenjan*, which itself comes from the Sanskrit *vatin-ganah* (antiflatulence vegetable). By the fourth century CE, the eggplant had arrived in Persia, where it was initially disregarded, but eventually became a favorite vegetable. In the eighth or ninth century, the Arabs began spreading the plant westward. Eggplant was among the dishes served at the wedding of Buran, daughter of Al-Mamun, the caliph of Baghdad; this reflected its acceptance by the upper class. It probably reached Spain in the late ninth century, where it was enthusiastically received and soon appeared in numerous Moorish and Sephardic recipes. In the fifteenth century, during the Spanish Inquisition, a sign of "eating Jewish" was a preference for eggplants.

The attitude was very different, however, in the rest of Europe, where eggplant was considered poisonous and utilized only as a garden ornament. Indeed, the Italian name for eggplant, *melanzana*, and the Greek, *melitzane*, came from its sixteenth-century scientific classification as *mala insana* (mad apple), an identity derived from its membership in the nightshade family. Jewish exiles fleeing southern Spain in 1146, and again fleeing from Spain and Spanish-controlled Sicily and southern Italy in 1492, helped to popularize the eggplant, bringing it and numerous eggplant dishes to northern Italy and much of the Mediterranean. This strikingly beautiful vegetable became a staple of the lighter and more varied cookery of the Mediterranean, where it is beloved today by every level of society. The few areas in which Ashkenazim developed a fondness for eggplant were under Turkish control notably Romania, or areas nearby, such as Ukraine.

The rich texture of the versatile eggplant makes it an ideal meat substitute. Cooked eggplant has a subtle flavor that is deliciously complemented by a large variety of assertive seasonings, including lemon, vinegar, garlic, goat cheese, yogurt, and tahini (sesame seed paste). Eggplant can be prepared in an extensive variety of ways—Turks claim more than thirty different basic methods—including fried, roasted, baked, grilled, boiled, stuffed, marinated, pickled, simmered, and stewed. Today, Turkey produces more eggplants than all of Europe.

Eggplant is certainly the most popular vegetable in its native India, where numerous varieties, in an array of shapes and colors, are sold at almost every market. It has also long been a mainstay from central Asia through North Africa. Georgians incorporate it into a myriad of stews, salads, and relishes. Syrians love stuffed eggplants, pickled baby eggplants, and even candied eggplant. Iraqis use grilled slices for a

sandwich called *sabich*. Moroccans serve it in tagines with couscous and make it into a slightly sweet eggplant jam.

From Turkey came eggplant-based vegetables stews—generally incorporating several American natives, notably peppers, tomatoes, and zucchini—including the Turkish and Romanian *guvetch* and Provençal ratatouille. Sephardim serve plain or marinated fried eggplant slices cold as part of a Sabbath lunch and *mezze* (appetizer assortment) or warm as a side dish, usually accompanied with a tomato sauce or *labni* (yogurt cheese). They also use it in casseroles (such as *alboronia*), stews, salads, omelets, and pickles; as a pastry filling; and even for confections.

Middle Easterners have long made mashed salads from various cooked vegetables, but following the introduction of the Indian eggplant by the Persians, it became the most popular base. Versions of *salata batinjan* (eggplant salad), also called *caviare d'aubergines* (eggplant caviar) in the Maghreb, are common from India to Morocco. The most famous one, made with tahini (sesame seed paste), is probably the Lebanese *baba ghanouj*. The Ottomans, during their occupation of the Balkans and Hungary, introduced eggplant, which eventually spread to Ukraine and parts of Russia, emerging as the favorite type of *ikra* (vegetable "caviar").

Today, there are many versions of stuffed eggplant, and numerous names for it, including the Sephardic *berengena rellenas* and *medias de berengena*, Turkish *patlican dolmasi*, Bulgarian *merendjen a inchidos*, Greek *dolmas de melitzanes*, Arabic *batinjan mahshi*, and Hebrew *chatzilim memulim*. Meat fillings are generally reserved for special occasions, while cheese is more common during the week. Meat-stuffed eggplant is a Sabbath and special-occasion dish, particularly prominent on Sukkot as stuffed foods symbolize abundance.

There were numerous eggplant casseroles, including the Turkish *sakayu/saqu*, Romanian *musaca de vinete*, and Greek moussaka. Greeks, as a result of French influences, began adding a layer of milk-based béchamel sauce to their moussaka, but traditional Jews continued to make it the old-fashioned and kosher way with just eggplant and ground meat. Many Middle Easterners prefer a sweet-and-sour eggplant casserole (*ingria* or *engreyee*), with lemon juice or tamarind. Tomatoes were a relatively late, but very popular, addition. Sweet-and-sour eggplant casseroles became a favorite festival fare in Iran, Iraq, Syria, and Mumbai. Eggplant casseroles are particularly prevalent on Sukkot, but they are also popular as Sabbath fare.

The early Zionist settlers discovered the eggplant in Ottoman-controlled Palestine and soon adopted some of the Turkish eggplant dishes. During the period of *tzena* (austerity) following the founding of Israel in 1948, *chatzilim* (eggplant) was one of the few plants grown in any quantity. Government sources and newspapers promoted eggplant recipes, so it became commonplace and some of the dishes emerged as iconic. Today, eggplant remains a prominent feature of Israeli cuisine. Israelis regard eggplant as Polish Jews once did the potato: as an essential food that can be prepared in a myriad of ways.

EINBREN

Einbren is browned flour, used to thicken sauces, gravies, soups, and stews.
Origin: Germany

A mark of medieval cooking was the use of pieces of bread to thicken sauces, gravies, soups, and stews, resulting in rather crude and coarse dishes. Although flour thickens the liquids better than bread, it also imparts a disagreeable raw flour taste and tends to form lumps. Then in the seventeenth century cooks discovered that they could remove the raw taste and preserve the flour's thickening capability by mixing it with a fat and then cooking the mixture until it turned golden or reddish. The invention of this flour and fat mixture—called *balsamella* in Italy, *mehlschwitze* in Germany, *zaprashka* in Polish, and roux in France—proved a milestone in culinary history, marking the transition point between medieval and modern cooking. With the advent of roux in place of bread as a thickener, sauces—the glory of haute cuisine—and soups entered a new, more refined era in which they were capable of achieving a lusciously smooth texture. Using a roux, cooks could obtain the maximum thickening capacity with a minimum amount of flour and no detrimental effects on the flavor.

An alternative was simply browning the flour in a dry pan, a process called *einbren* in Yiddish (*ein* means "a/one" and *brenn* "burn" in German); this removes the raw flour taste as well as creates a nutty flavor.

Until well into the twentieth century, Ashkenazic housewives browned one to two cups of flour at once and stored it in a jar in a cool place and, when needed, added a little to dishes such as *gedempte fleisch* (pot roast), tzimmes, and carp in brown sauce to thicken and flavor the dish.

Cooking flour in a dry skillet, however, has its drawbacks, as it tends to smoke after about five minutes and requires at least twenty to thirty minutes, and nearly constant stirring to reach a light brown shade; the long cooking time reduces the flour's thickening ability to half that of white flour. In addition, the nutty flavor is undesirable in some dishes.

EINGEMACHT

Eingemacht is a jam and preserve, made from fruit or root vegetables, such as beets and black radishes.
Origin: Germany
Other names: *ayngemachts*.

Among the verses in a nineteenth-century eastern European Yiddish folk song about a couple marrying off their youngest child is "This is how, this is how, we marry off our children, *mit a sloy ayngemachts* [with a jar of preserves], witness the Lord's miracles." The last line of the song is "I am marrying off my youngest now, and am through with poverty."

The Yiddish word *eingemacht* comes from the German *eingemachtes* (from *einmachen*, "to preserve"). These preserves and jams (preserves have large pieces of produce) consist of chunks of fruits and vegetables cooked in honey or sugar. Those made with fruit, such as raspberries or cherries, are called *frucht eingemachts*. Following Sukkot, citrons were cooked into an *esrig eingemachts*.

More commonly, *eingemachts* were made with root vegetables. In northern Europe, little produce was available in the winter through early spring, except the various root vegetables stored over the winter in cellars or mounds of dirt. Consequently, for generations, in the days preceding Passover, eastern Ashkenazic housewives would chop or grate the roots—notably beets, black radishes, carrots, and turnips—and cook them with honey and a touch of vinegar (in America, lemon juice) into *eingemachts*. With the popularization of the sugar beet—the first sugar beet factory was established in Kunem, Germany, now western Poland, in 1806—*eingemachts* became very inexpensive and subsequently housewives would typically cook up a huge pot of beet or other *eingemachts* for Passover use.

As the song reflects, *eingemachts* appeared at special occasions like wedding feasts, but in the nineteenth century, with affordable sugar, it became more commonplace as well. It was spread on bread and incorporated into various baked goods. Many people simply nibbled spoonfuls of *eingemachts* while sipping hot tea. In some communities, the *rebbitzen* (rabbi's wife) prepared a pot of *frucht eingemachts* and distributed some to the sick of the shtetl. A jar of *eingemachts* made a much-appreciated gift, akin to the contemporary practice of bringing a bottle of wine for future in-laws, a rebbe, or anyone you wanted to impress. Nevertheless, *eingemachts* played its most important role on Passover, when little else was available. A jar of *eingemachts* was once a common, if not a constant, sight on Ashkenazic Passover tables; it was spread on matza, matza pancakes, and matza brei; stuffed inside dumplings; and served as a relish with meat and chicken.

Eingemachts was also transformed into a traditional confection called *pletzlach* ("board" in Yiddish). The preserves were cooked a little longer, spread on a moistened marble slab or baking sheet, and set aside until firm. Then they were cut into diamond shapes and rolled in sugar. Those who could afford it, seasoned these confections with ground ginger, which was among the few spices common in northern Europe; these treats were called *ingberlach* (literally "little gingers").

The first edition of *The Settlement Cookbook* (Milwaukee, 1901) contains a recipe for "Radish or Beet Preserves (Russian Style)." Although in Europe *eingemachts* were eaten throughout the year, immigrants in America typically reserved them for Passover.

After World War II, as more and more commercial kosher-for-Passover foods became available, including fruit preserves, and many Old World items were deemed old-fashioned, *eingemachts* became a rarity in most homes. Still, a few people did maintain the practice of bringing a jar of homemade *eingemachts* to a host when visiting, as well as offering some to guests. Variations of this venerable dish have recently appeared, under the name beet marmalade, in some trendy American restaurants and gourmet food magazines.

(See also Etrog, Ingberlach, and Pletzl)

❦ EASTERN EUROPEAN BEET PRESERVES
(*BURIK EINGEMACHTS*)

ABOUT 5 CUPS [PAREVE]

4 cups (28 ounces) sugar, or 3 cups sugar and 1 cup honey
¾ cup water
2 pounds (eight 2-inch) fresh beets or *rosl* beets, weighed without the greens, peeled and coarsely shredded (4 cups)
6 tablespoons fresh lemon juice
2 teaspoons grated lemon zest
1 cup chopped blanched almonds, or ½ cup chopped blanched almonds and ½ cup chopped walnuts
1 to 3 teaspoons ground ginger or 1 tablespoon grated fresh ginger

1. In a large pot, using a long-handled wooden spoon, stir the sugar and water over low heat until the sugar dissolves. Increase the heat to medium and bring to a boil. Add the beets and reduce the heat to medium-low. Simmer, uncovered, stirring occasionally, for 1 hour.

2. Add the lemon juice and zest and simmer for 15 minutes. Add the nuts and ginger and simmer, stirring occasionally to make sure the beets don't stick, until the syrup is thickened and the beets are translucent and reach a temperature of 220°F, about 15 minutes. The traditional method of testing doneness was to drop a little of the eingemachts on a chilled plate; if it sets up but moves slightly when the plate is tipped within a few minutes, it is done. If underdone, it will run; if overcooked it will be too thick to move.

3. Pour the hot preserves into glass jars. Store the preserves in the refrigerator for up to 1 month.

EINLAUF
Einlauf are drop dumplings.
Origin: Germany
Other names: Alsace: *noques*; Austria: *nockerln*; Germany: *triflach*.

The first Jewish American Cookbook, *Jewish Cookery* (1871), contained a recipe for "Drop Dumplings for Soup," which the first edition of *The Settlement Cook Book* (1901) called "Ein Lauf." One of the favorite and easiest of European dumplings, *einlauf* are made from a simple, loose egg batter. The name comes from the German for "to come in/to flow," from *lauf*, which means "run/course." Unfortunately, in modern German *einlauf* means "enema" and in sports also denotes "finish" or "placing."

This dumpling contains nearly equal amounts of egg and water, bound with a little flour, making it light and fragile. The batter must be thin enough to drop into boiling soup, stew, or water, but not too thin. To achieve a long noodle-like shape, the batter is slowly drizzled from a height. A matza meal variation developed for Passover tastes like *knaidlach*. The batter can be cooked in any soup or stew, but a clear broth is the most common. With the advent in the mid-twentieth century of commercial packaged noodles, *einlauf* and other traditional homemade soup garnishes lost much of their popularity.

(See also Dumpling)

ASHKENAZIC EGG DROP DUMPLINGS (*EINLAUF*)

4 TO 5 SERVINGS   [PAREVE]

    1 large egg, lightly beaten
    ¼ cup water
    About 5 tablespoons all-purpose flour or ⅓ cup
        matza meal
    2 teaspoons chopped fresh flat-leaf parsley
        (optional)
    About ⅛ teaspoon salt
    Pinch of ground black or white pepper (optional)

In a medium bowl, beat together all the ingredients until smooth. Using a large spoon and from a height, in a slow, steady stream let the batter drop into a pot of boiling soup or stew. Or for more distinct dumplings, drop the batter by teaspoonfuls, one at a time. Cover and simmer for 3 to 5 minutes. Serve in the hot soup or stew.

EMMER

At some point in prehistory, in the Fertile Crescent, *Triticum urartu*, a close relative of einkom, crossbred with another wild grass, yielding wild emmer, which, like durum, is considered a subspecies of tetraploid wheats. Wild emmer, nicknamed in Hebrew *em ha'chitah* (mother wheat), still grows in parts of northern Israel. Emmer, einkorn, and two-row barley were the first domesticated crops; they were possibly initially domesticated in southeastern Turkey, just east of the Euphrates River. Emmer was initially boiled to make porridges. When some of the gruel fell into the fire, the first breads were created. Eventually, wild yeast found its way into some of the emmer porridges, giving rise to the first yeast breads.

Emmer is a hulled wheat. Typically, kernels of hulled wheat were pounded or roasted to remove the husks, requiring a large amount of labor and, due to breakage of the kernels, significantly decreasing its shelf life. Despite any drawbacks, farmers continued to cultivate emmer, as it grows well in warmer climates, resists fungal rot, and is high yielding, with large grains and a relatively high amount of protein (gluten). Breads made from emmer are fairly light in texture and flavorful, although they are heavier than those made from contemporary common (bread) wheat. Consequently, in the late Mesolithic Age, emmer became the most prominent grain throughout the Near East, North Africa, and much of Europe, and this popularity lasted until Roman times.

Emmer and barley were the main crops of biblical Egypt and Israel; emmer was the source of the bread of the Egyptian upper class and was probably used in the original matzas of the Exodus. Although durum wheat emerged in Israel as the favorite grain—it was used for the *solet* (fine flour) required in the Temple offerings—emmer remained the most widely grown wheat, while barley was the most common grain. Emmer (*kusmin*) was among the five grains detailed by the Talmud as being forbidden during Passover.

Beginning at the end of the Iron Age (c. 900 BCE), naked wheats (the chaff does not cling to the kernels), in particular durum and modern bread wheat (descendants of emmer), gradually supplanted emmer, and its usage all but disappeared in most locales. It does remain a relic crop in parts of the Mediterranean. One of the few areas where emmer retains a degree of popularity is in Tuscany, where it is called *farro* and used to make breads, pasta, and especially soups.

(See also Grain and Wheat)

EMPANADA

Empanada is a folded half-moon-shaped turnover that is either deep fried or baked.
Origin: Iberia
Other names: Ladino: *boreka*; Farsi: *sanbusak*;
    Portuguese: *empada*.

Turnovers are one of the most widespread foods—enwrapping meat, vegetables, fruit, or cheese in thin layers of bread or pastry dough is an ideal and portable way to extend limited resources. The first record of a turnover was the *sanbusak*, a Farsi word indicating it originated in Persia, initially a fried triangular filled pastry, which was first recorded in Iraq in the early ninth century. It arrived in Iberia by at least the early thirteenth century and probably became a popular Sephardic dish even earlier. In parts of Spain, however, particularly Galicia (in the northwest, abutting Portugal), these pastries eventually became known as *empanadas*, from the Spanish *empanar* (to cover with bread); this name is now found in most Spanish-speaking countries, each of which has its own variation.

Rabbi Joseph Caro (1488–1575), part of a family from Toledo, Spain, that settled in Turkey following the expulsion, in his work *Shulchan Arukh*, still the preeminent code of Jewish law, states: "It is permissible [on the Sabbath] to place an [already cooked] empanada near the fire in a place that is hot enough to scathe the hand even though the fat in the empanada melts." (By the way, Ashkenazim tended not to allow this leniency for warming cooked food unless "absolutely required.") Pointedly, at this time, Sephardim still referred to their turnovers as *empanadas* and some of those who settled in western Europe after the expulsion of 1492 continued to use this term.

The sizable number of Conversos who settled in Brazil, Mexico, and what would later be the American Southwest brought their versions of *empanadas* with them; many cooks retained the use of chopped beef rather than the Spanish pork. Sweet potato became another popular filling. However, as Sephardim in the Ottoman Empire gradually merged their food with the local cuisine, the name *empanada* eventually became *boreka*, the term for a Ladino-inspired version of the Turkish *börek*.

The classic *empanada* evolved from its original triangular shape to the easier-to-form half-moon; smaller ones are sometimes called *empanadillas* or *empanaditas*. Large *empanadas* are served as an entrée or side dish, while small versions are offered as an appetizer or dessert. The original *empanada* was made from bread dough, but later an oil-based pastry was developed, and still later a flaky pastry. Initially, they were fried, but eventually baking became the predominant means of preparation. Traditional fillings included meat, fish, and vegetables, and dessert *empanadas* became a later variation. A favorite remains *empanadas de pishkado*, a Turkish version filled with mackerel. *Empanadas* (or *borekas*) filled with meat or vegetables are longstanding Sephardic Sabbath fare; they are served cold or reheated for Sabbath lunch. *Empanadas* fried in oil are traditional on Hanukkah.

(See also Boreka, Pastelito, and Sambusak)

ESSIG FLEISCH

Essig fleish is a sweet-and-sour pot roast.
Origin: Germany
Other names: *sauer fleisch.*

Sweet-and-sour is a popular flavoring in much of Jewish cookery; the prominence of the flavor combination developed because vinegar (*essig* in Yiddish) was added to foods as a preservative and tenderizer, and honey or sugar was then used to temper and complement the vinegar's sharpness. Ashkenazim of northern Europe, who had few fresh herbs or inexpensive spices at their disposal, relied very heavily on sweet-and-sour flavors, especially in dishes based on fish or meat, such as meatballs, stuffed cabbage, tongue, borscht, and pot roast. Plain pot roast is called *gedempte fleisch* (well-stewed meat). As the name *essig fleisch* denotes, the sour of the pot roast originally came from vinegar. Ukrainians use *rosl* (fermented beet vinegar) for the cooking liquid. However, more recently lemon juice and sour salt have become the preferred acid among many cooks. With the spread of sugar beet factories in parts of Europe in the mid-nineteenth century, and the arrival of inexpensive sugar in those areas, sweet-and-sour dishes became even more prominent. Germans add gingersnaps and some others use tomato paste or flour as another element of flavor and as a thickener for the cooking liquid.

ASHKENAZIC SWEET-AND-SOUR POT ROAST (*ESSIG FLEISCH*)

6 TO 8 SERVINGS   [MEAT]

- 1 (3½- to 5-pound) boneless beef chuck, shoulder roast, or plate
- 3 tablespoons vegetable oil or schmaltz
- 3 medium yellow onions, sliced
- 1 cup chopped carrots
- 1 cup chopped celery
- 1 to 2 cloves garlic, minced
- 1 teaspoon paprika (optional)
- 2 to 3 tablespoons tomato paste or 2 tablespoons all-purpose flour

2 cups chicken broth or water, or 1 cup broth and
  1 cup dry red or white wine
2 bay leaves or ½ teaspoon ground cinnamon
About 1 teaspoon table salt or 2 teaspoons kosher
  salt
Ground black pepper to taste
⅓ to ½ cup fresh lemon juice or cider vinegar
¼ to ½ cup brown sugar or honey

1. Pat the beef dry. In a large pot or roaster with a tight-fighting lid, heat the oil over medium-high heat. Place the beef in the pot and cook, turning frequently, until it is brown—but not blackened—on all sides, about 20 minutes. Remove the roast from the pot.

2. Reduce the heat to medium, add the onions, carrots, and celery, and sauté until softened and lightly browned, about 15 minutes. Add the garlic and paprika and stir briefly. Add the tomato paste and stir until slightly darkened, or add the flour and stir until bubbly, 2 to 3 minutes.

3. Add the broth and stir to remove any browned particles from the bottom. Add the bay leaves, salt, and pepper. Return the beef and any accumulated juices. Cover and bring to a simmer on top of the stove.

4. Bake in a 325°F oven or simmer over a low heat, turning occasionally, until almost tender, about 2 hours. The roast may be prepared up to this point up to 2 days in advance, cooled, covered, and stored in the refrigerator before reheating.

5. Add the lemon juice and sugar and cook, uncovered, until the meat is fork-tender, about 30 minutes. Remove from the heat and let stand for 20 minutes before carving. Meanwhile, strain the cooking liquid, pressing out the solids. Slice the meat against the grain and serve with the cooking liquid.

ETROG (CITRON)

The citron, the earliest cultivated citrus tree, probably originated in northern India or southwestern China. The subtropical tree bears large bright yellow fruit that have a very thick skin and a sparse pulp. Until the popularization of sugar in the late medieval period, its fruit was rarely consumed, although in Talmudic times the rind was occasionally pickled or cooked into a paste. The citron's fragrance has long been highly regarded, and Talmud related that the citron and quince were the only fruits that require a special blessing to be recited over their aromas.

The first written record of this fruit was *jambila*, the Sanskrit word for citron and later lemon, in the Vajasaneyi Samhita around 800 BCE. The first European record of the citron was around 310 BCE by the Greek philosopher Theophrastus, who called it *malus medica* (Median fruit), as he believed the plant originated in Media or Persia. The word *citron* in modern French refers to what Americans call a lemon; what Americans know as a citron (often candied) is called *cédrat* in French (from the Latin *cedrus* "cedar"). Because of its association with Jews, the citron is also called *citronnier des juifs* in French and *Judenapfel* in German. The Hebrew word for citron is etrog, a word not contained in the Bible, but which was derived via the Persian *torong* from the Sanskrit *suranga* (beautifully colored).

The citron is unique in that it is the only tree that can flower and bear fruit throughout the year under proper conditions; it can also distinctively retain the fruit from one year to the next. Thus the citron is the only tree that can have buds, blossoms, and mature fruit at the same time. When citrons are left on the tree for more than one growing season and up to several years, they can reach a foot or more in length and can weigh more than ten pounds. The size of the citron explains the Talmudic incident, "It happened that Rabbi Akiva entered the synagogue carrying his etrog on his shoulder." Another feature of the citron fruit is its *pitom* (carpel), a small knob on the tip consisting of the pistils and stigma. Some citron varieties retain their *pitom* into maturity, while other varieties lose it naturally during development.

The scrawny citron tree, which is really more of a thorny shrub, has a weak root system, requires intense irrigation, is vulnerable to disease and cold temperatures, and has a relatively short life span of about fifteen years. Grafting branches from a citron tree onto a heartier lemon tree enables the citron to produce more fruit and for much longer. The fruit from a citron tree grafted onto a lemon tree is identical to that of a natural one. However, the Torah forbids mingling two different species. Consequently, grafting branches from one citron variety to another citron variety is acceptable, while grafting branches from a citron onto a lemon tree is unacceptable and its fruit may not be used for the Sukkot ritual.

Historically, the citron, to put it mildly, was not a very useful plant. The citron is far from the most beautiful or hardy tree. Its wood is not prized as lumber. Nor could its fruit even be considered a luxury food, like cherries or kumquats. The ancient Chinese and Indians employed citron for certain medical purposes, while the Talmud mentioned its effectiveness in countering snake venom. In ancient Greece and Rome, the fruit was primarily used as an insect repellent, stored with clothing similar to mothballs. In effect, the citron was completely unnecessary for survival, sustenance, or even shade; this was an important consideration in decisions about plant cultivation in the days when every scrap of food, clothing, and shelter tended to be of critical concern.

Despite its deficiencies, the citron eventually moved westward from its birthplace through Persia and into the Levant. By the Hasmonean period, it had become one of the most popular Jewish symbols, commonly appearing on mosaics, tombstones, coins, and monuments. Precisely when the citron arrived in the Holy Land is a matter of contention. Many claim that the citron did not reach Israel until the era of Alexander the Great because there was no specific mention of it in the near East before this time. Other scholars insist that the Jews brought the citron back from Persia in the sixth century, after returning from the Babylonian exile. However, even in the centuries after Alexander citrons were of such insignificant commercial and dietary value that they were rarely, if ever, cultivated or recorded in the Middle East, with the noted exception of Israel, where they were used for Sukkot. Thus this ancient fruit surely could have arrived on the shores of the eastern Mediterranean before the Israelite conquest of Canaan around the thirteenth century BCE. The Israelites may even have become familiar with the citron during their stay in Egypt, because it may have been used in the Egyptian embalming process.

Following the fall of the Roman Empire, citrus fruits disappeared from Italy and much of the Mediterranean, except among the Jews who continued to cultivate the etrog for the Sukkot ritual. As new varieties of citrus arrived from the East, notably the lemon and bitter orange, Jews began to cultivate these citrus trees alongside the citron. By the ninth century, Jewish traders re-introduced citrus fruit to much of the Mediterranean. Eventually, non-Jews began to raise various citrus trees as well.

The Fruit of the Goodly Tree

For the festival of Sukkot, the Bible instructs each person to "take for yourself" four agricultural items—*peri eitz hadar* (fruit of the goodly tree), palm fronds (*lulav*), myrtle branches (*hadasim*), and willows of the brook (*aravot*). The Four Species (Arbeh Minim) are shaken together while reciting the verse "Save us now O Lord, cause us to prosper now O Lord." Jewish tradition posits that the biblical *peri eitz hadar* is the etrog.

There are several requirements to qualify an etrog for use in the Sukkot ritual. It should be at least twice the size of a chicken egg. The peel can have no black spots, scratches, or blemishes. To produce a kosher etrog, the fruit has to be protected from wind, sand,

The etrog or citron, top, has been an essential part of Jewish tradition and culture, for millenia, as depicted in this "Four Species of Sukkot" mosaic floor in Hamat Tiberius, one of the earliest synagogues ever discovered.

sunburn, and insects. An etrog must have an *ukatz* (stem from where it was attached to the tree). If the *pitom* is broken off of an etrog after maturation, it is not acceptable; if the etrog variety is one that naturally grows without a *pitom*, it is permissible. Hybrids, such as a cross between an etrog and lemon, are forbidden for the Sukkot ritual. Any etrog from a tree grafted onto a lemon tree or even an etrog from a tree grown from a seed of a grafted fruit, is unsuitable for the Jewish ritual.

For medieval Sephardim and Mizrachim, most of whom lived near areas of citron cultivation, etrogim were relatively inexpensive and most families procured their own fruit each year. On the other hand, among Ashkenazim, who had to import etrogim at great expense, few individuals historically could afford to purchase their own, except perhaps a small number of the wealthier Jews. Instead, a single etrog would typically be obtained by the town and shared by all. In the sixteenth century, after lemon cultivation became widespread in the Mediterranean, acquiring an etrog became more problematic, as the practice of grafting citron branches onto lemon trees and crossing the fruit with lemons became prevalent.

Etrog Variety

There are a dozen or more distinct varieties and their cultivars of etrogim acceptable for the Sukkot ritual; different ones are preferred by various communities.

Citron varieties differ greatly in shape, the thickness and bumpiness of the peel, acidity of the pulp proportion of pulp to peel, texture of the albedo (the fluffy white inner part of the peel), acidity of the pulp, and number of seeds. The pulp of most varieties is highly acidic, but there are a few low-acid varieties, called sweet, that are edible raw. There are also pulpless varieties.

The shape of the etrog variety favored for the Sukkot ritual is a matter of tradition. Some prefer a *migdal* ("tower" in Hebrew), narrower on the top than the bottom. Others look for the *lev* (heart), wider on the top than the bottom. Some Chasidim opt for a variety slightly indented around the middle alluding to the *gartel* ("belt" in Yiddish) they wear. Besides the original oblong citron, there is the fingered citron (also called Buddha's hand), a pulpless variety that is unsuitable for Sukkot, named after the deep finger-shaped grooves along its length.

A very ancient variety, perhaps the original one brought from India to Persia, is the Cedruna. Its fruit is roundish or obovoid in shape, furrowed, and a dark yellow in color. The Cedruna was once widely grown in the Mediterranean, especially Calabria and Campania, but was supplanted by Greek and Italian varieties.

A unique variety is the Yemen (Temoni or Taimani) citron, which is completely pulpless and juiceless, with the seeds resting in a strip in the core of the albedo. According to Yemenites, the lack of any pulp is proof that it is not a hybrid with a lemon. It is also edible raw. Yemenites prefer etrogim rather large, the result of having remained on the tree for more than one season. In the late nineteenth century, Yemenites arriving in Israel planted this variety of etrog.

A sweet citron is the Moroccan, which retains its *pitom*. The very elongated Assads cultivar has deep ribs and narrows slightly in the center, a feature than some Chasidim find appealing. It is frequently seedless.

The predominant variety in medieval Greece and Turkey was the Greek variety (botanically classified as "Etrog"), which is ellipsoid with a prominent tip and bumpy, ribbed peel and looks somewhat like a large lemon. The Greek variety of citron is sometimes called *Pitima* because of the fruit's tendency to retain its *pitom*. The Romaniotes (Jews who have lived in Greece since before the destruction of the Second Temple and once had large communities on the Ionian Islands) claim that they have used this variety since the time of the Second Temple. After the expulsion of 1493, Sephardim who settled in Italy and the eastern Mediterranean generally adopted the Greek etrog. The Greek citron is the typical variety used today by many Ashkenazim.

The most popular citron in the early medieval period among Ashkenazim was the Diamante from Calabria on the southwestern tip of Italy, which was called Yanover or Yanova (meaning "Genoa," the northern Italian port from which it was shipped). The elongated Diamante is elliptical with square shoulders and the peel is rather smooth and only faintly ribbed. The pulp is very sparse and the albedo quite thick. Most Diamante lack a *pitom*, as it tends to dry up and fall off during the initial few weeks of growth. The Italian citron is similar to the Diamante, but slightly bumpier, with more pulp and a thinner albedo.

The Yanover has long been particularly prized by eastern Ashkenazim, especially members of the Lubavitch sect of Chasidim. Rabbi Schneer Zalman of Ladi (1745–1812), founder of the Lubavitch movement, even claimed that Moses, after the Exodus from Egypt, used the Yanover etrog from Calabria for the first Sukkot. Lubavitchers contend that the Yanover etrog has been protected from grafting, although actual inspections have revealed that many of the citron trees of Calabria had been grafted.

When grafting became a common practice in Italy and Greece in the sixteenth and seventeenth centuries Ashkenazim looked for alternative sources of etrogim. Beginning in the eighteenth century, the island of Corsica was the most sought after, by both Jews and bakers (by this point, candied citron had become widely popular in Europe and America, and citron crops were the major source of income for several Mediterranean locales). The Corsican citron is among the sweet varieties. The large fruit is ovoid and quite lumpy. The pulp is substantial, although not very juicy.

However, in the early nineteenth century, the political instability engendered by the Napoleonic wars led to the stifling of the Corsican etrog market. In its place, the Greek island of Corfu and nearby Ionian Islands, such as Naxos, which were then part of the Ottoman Empire, which grew the Greek citron, emerged as the foremost etrog producers. In 1785, when Corfu began shipping to eastern Europe, Ashkenazim, accustomed to the Yanover etrog, were initially extremely suspicious of the newcomer from Corfu. However, within a few decades, the Yanover became unavailable and Corfu subsequently dominated the European etrog market. Consequently, Sephardim and Ashkenazim became accustomed to etrogim with an attached *pitom* and balked at those without. In addition, etrogim were thereafter sold with rabbinic identification, stating "kosher with no concern of being grafted."

Sholem Aleichem, in his short story "The Esrog," wrote a tale of a boy whose father waited year after year to purchase his own etrog. Here is the exchange between the father and the seller:

"But is it from the island of Corfu?" My father asked, examining the esrog from every angle as one does a diamond, his hands trembling with excitement.

"What do *you* think?" the cap [the seller] replied, shaking with laughter. "Nowhere else *but* from Corfu!"

The boy, overwhelmed by temptation, takes a bite of the expensive fruit, rendering it unfit for the upcoming Sukkot holiday.

As the Jewish population of eastern Europe exploded in the eighteenth and nineteenth century, the etrog trade became a large, lucrative business. Throughout the nineteenth century, controversy repeatedly sprang up, usually engendered by a merchant insisting that only his source was kosher. In 1845, a merchant representing Parga, in the northwest along the Ionian Sea, claimed that Corfu etrogim came from grafted trees. Various Sephardic rabbis testified to the validity of some or all of the Greek etrogim, while some Ashkenazic authorities banned them all and others accepted them all. These disputes came to a head after 1875, when the Corfu growers banded together, dumping thousands of their citrons into the sea and dramatically escalated the cost of the remainder. In an attempt to undercut the monopoly and the exorbitant prices, Rabbi Yitzchak Elchanan Spektor of the Volozhin Yeshiva banned all Corfu etrogim. Then in 1891, a ritual murder accusation against the Jews of Corfu led to the massacre there of 139 Jews; in protest, Ashkenazim and Sephardim boycotted the Corfu etrogim. Today, citrons are no longer grown commercially on Corfu.

In the 1950s, a Satmar rabbi visited orchards in Calabria, where he was freely allowed to inspect the trees and fruit, and orchards in Greece, where he was denied entry. Consequently, most Satmars and some other Chasidim switched back to the Yanover citron from the Greek citron, but they use only citrons picked under the supervision of representatives who ensure that they come from trees that have not been grafted.

Around 1850, Moses Montefiore sent seeds from Corfu citrons to settlers in Israel; they were planted by Sephardim along the central coastal region, especially near Jaffa. However, these newcomers did not fare well in Israel and required widespread grafting for survival. Consequently, many growers began grafting Greek branches onto Israeli Balady citron rootstock, which was permissible. Within a short time, Israeli etrogim emerged as the predominant choice for much of the world. In the twentieth century, the person most influential on which etrog varieties were used by many Jews was Rabbi Avrohom Yeshaya Karelitz, known as the Chazon Ish. After arriving in Israel from Lithuania in 1933, he searched until finding a Balady tree near Safed. Karelitz gave etrogim from that tree to associates to grow acceptable trees. Two of these emerged as important cultivars: Chazon Ish-Halperin and Chazon Ish-Lefkowitz.

Today, about 70 percent of all Israeli etrogim are grown by the Central Israel Etrog Company, owned by the Ludmir family, on a seventy-four-acre spread outside Bnei Brak. During the *shemitah* year (seventh year when agriculture in Israel is forbidden), however, the company ceases operations, with Italy, Greece, and California taking up the slack. Before the onset of the *shemitah* year, green etrogim can be picked and sent, but none can be harvested for another year after Rosh Hashanah.

The citron tree only arrived in the United States in the middle of the nineteenth century. For nearly four decades, California's citron production thrived, until a severe frost in 1913 decimated the state's citron orchards. Today, there is only one large commercial grower in America, John Kirkpatrick of Lindcove, Cal-

ifornia, who has 250 trees from five varieties Braverman, Kivelvitz, Chazon Ish-Lefkowitz, Halperin and Yemenite. Kirkpatrick's orchards annually produce about 3,000 etrogim acceptable for the Jewish ritual; some 9,000 remainders are sold to processors.

The popularization of sugar in the medieval Arab world led to an increased culinary use of the etrog, most notably in jelly, candy, and candied rinds. The thick rind of citron is suitable for candying, and candied citron is typically found in fruitcakes. There are also several brands of citron liqueur. Among Jews, these treats usually appear following Sukkot and are made from the etrogim used to celebrate the holiday. Some people have the custom of saving a jar of etrog preserves (*dulce de etrog* and *esrig eingemanchts*) or candy to serve at the Tu b'Shevat meal. There is also a custom in some households of sticking whole cloves all over an etrog and using it for the spice for the Havdalah ceremony.

(See also Citrus, Date, and Eingemacht)

F

FALAFEL

Falafel is a deep-fried croquette of ground, raw chickpeas and/or fava beans.

Origin: Probably Egypt

Fava beans and chickpeas have been cultivated in southwest Asia since at least the onset of the Neolithic Age. At some unknown point and location much later, cooks began deep-frying croquettes of ground raw dried legumes, transforming a common, long-keeping protein source into a quick-cooking, tasty, nutritious foodstuff. The first known presence of legume fritters in the Middle East appears to be in medieval Egypt, where they were made from dried white fava beans (*ful nabed*) and called *tamiya/ta'amia* (from the Arabic for "nourishment"); these fritters were a light green color inside. Many attribute *tamiya* to the Copts of Egypt, who practiced one of the earliest forms of Christianity. They believed that the original state of humankind was vegetarian and, therefore, mandated numerous days of eating only vegan food, including *tamiya*.

Others believe legume fritters originated on the Indian subcontinent, a region where deep-frying was more common than in Egypt, and were brought westward by Arabs or Turks. Still others contend they came from Yemen. In the Levant and Yemen, chickpeas were substituted for some or all of the fava beans in the fritters, and they became known as falafel, the plural of the Arabic word for pepper, as well as an adjective denoting something fluffy, *filfil*. Initially, the raw legumes were mashed in a mortar and pestle, a time-consuming and strenuous effort. The advent of the mechanical meat grinder in the 1860s eliminated the tedious process of preparing the legumes by hand, transforming falafel into an easier, more common food.

Middle Eastern Jews have been eating falafel for centuries, the pareve fritter being ideal in a kosher diet. However, many Jews inherited G6PD deficiency or its more severe form, favism; these hereditary enzymatic deficiencies are triggered by items like fava beans and can prove fatal. Accordingly, Middle Eastern Jews overwhelmingly favored chickpeas solo in their falafel. Falafel was enjoyed in salads as part of a *mezze* (appetizer assortment) or as a snack by itself. An early Middle Eastern fast food, falafel was commonly sold wrapped in paper, but not served in the familiar pita sandwich until Yemenites in Israel introduced the concept.

The ideal falafel is extremely crisp on the outside and moist and airy inside. To make classic falafel, the raw chickpeas are soaked, never cooked; this technique produces the proper crunchy texture and leaves the fritters relatively dry, which allows them to hold together during frying without the addition of eggs. The fritters are frequently bound by adding a little flour, bread, or bulgur. The amount of cumin and the inclusion of other spices varies. Green falafel contains a large amount of parsley and/or cilantro. Some mix in a little baking soda to help lighten the texture. Many professional falafel and *tamiya* makers, as well as some home cooks, use an *aleb falafel*, a special brass scooping device with a plunger down the middle, to mold flat disks and propel them into hot oil. Some cooks make variations, typically torpedo-shaped, by inserting cooked fava beans or a hard-boiled egg inside the falafel.

In the late nineteenth century, Ashkenazic immigrants in Israel found many of the foods from their homelands inappropriate in their new environs. In addition, many of these Zionists were socialists who stridently rejected their European traditions, including foods, and looked toward the regional fare of the Levant for inspiration. Among the items that fit the bill were two inexpensive chickpea dishes, hummus and falafel. Yemenite immigrants in Israel, who had made a chickpea version in Yemen, took up falafel making as a business and transformed this ancient treat into the Israeli iconic national food. Most importantly, Israelis wanted a portable fast food and began eating the falafel tucked into a pita topped with the ubiquitous Israeli salad (cucumber-and-tomato salad). Lilian Cornfeld, food columnist for the *Pal-*

Fried chickpea croquettes, top, with all the fixings, are Israel's favorite fast food.

ished young country. As contact with Arabs in Israel decreased in the face of growing hostilities, many Israelis lost track of falafel's origins and began thinking of it as Israel's alone.

Falafel is now peddled by street vendors and sold at kiosks and small shops throughout Israel. Typically the vendor inserts a number of hot falafel balls in each pita, then allows the patron to select from various toppings, most popularly Israeli salad and sour pickles, and a sauce: diluted tahini (sesame seed paste), Maghrebi harissa (red chili paste), or Yemenite s'chug (green chili paste). Other options include grilled eggplant, grilled bell peppers, sliced onions, shredded pickled beets, pickled turnips, and whole pickled green chilies. The condiment choices vary among consumers, with Europeans typically preferring mild toppings and Middle Easterners favoring *harief* (fiery). Some vendors add French fries to the falafel, calling it *chipsalat*. A whole pita, the top slit off and containing five to six falafel, is the most common version, but the sandwich is also offered as a *chatzi-manah* (half portion), with less room for toppings. Besides pita, many consumers wrap the falafel and condiments in *laffa*, the round flatbread introduced by Iraqi Jews, although the pocket pita version remains more common.

Since falafel is so inexpensive to buy few cooks make it at home. Most Israelis purchase their falafel in stores or stands, and many have a favorite. Some Israelis maintain fierce loyalty to a specific shop and argue vehemently over which vendor makes the best falafel.

The first known record of the word in an American source was in the December 16, 1949 issue of *The Jewish Criterion* (Pittsburgh). It said: "Falafel, most nearly described as an 'everything but the kitchen sink plus red pepper' sandwich." In the early 1950s, the English spelling crystallized as falafel. In *Israel Diary* in 1950, Bernard Bloomfield wrote, "I must make some notations on the falafel which, to Israel, is what the hot dog is to us. This creation is really something. We first discovered falafel while waiting for a bus outside a little street kiosk on a corner in Haifa."

In the 1960s, Israelis and Jews who had visited Israel began spreading the chickpea version of this Middle Eastern dish to Europe and America, and falafel in pita emerged as an international food. Kosher pizza stores began selling falafel as a standard item, while a few Israelis in New York City peddled

estine *Post*, a Jerusalem English-language newspaper, wrote several articles about the food in 1939, including one entitled "Filafel Comes into Its Own," noting its transformation from "Oriental" fare to a common Israeli food and quick meal. An article from October 19, 1939 concluded with a description of the common preparation style of the most popular street food, "There is first half a pita (Arab loaf), slit open and filled with five filafels, a few fried chips and sometimes even a little salad," the first written record of serving falafel in pita.

During World War II, when chickpeas were scarce in Israel, white beans were sometimes substituted. However, as soon as possible, Israelis switched back to chickpeas. The quality and variety of Israeli falafel increased with the mass arrival of Middle Eastern Jews in the wake of the founding of the state in 1948. Falafel proved the ideal street food for an impover-

the cumin-accented chickpea ball sandwiches from pushcarts on street corners; some initially gave away free samples to introduce the new food to potential customers. Eventually, mainstream American supermarkets stocked packaged falafel mix and tahini. Consequently, in much of the West, falafel became associated with Israeli cuisine. In response, some Palestinians created a controversy, accusing the Jews of "stealing their culture." In 2002, a pro-Palestinian group at Montreal's Concordia University accused the Hillel organization of "cultural theft" for serving falafel at its table during orientation week. Of course, food and culture cannot be stolen—they have been borrowed and shared throughout history. (Besides, falafel was probably initially an Egyptian Coptic or Indian innovation.) Thus falafel is another classic instance of Jews transforming and transmitting a food.

❧ MIDDLE EASTERN CHICKPEA CROQUETTES (*FALAFEL*)

MAKES ABOUT 24 SMALL BALLS   [PAREVE]

8 ounces (1¼ cups) dried chickpeas, soaked in
    water to cover in the refrigerator for 12 hours
    and drained
1 medium yellow onion or 4 scallions, chopped
2 to 3 large cloves garlic
About 2 tablespoons all-purpose flour, 1 slice white
    bread soaked in water and squeezed, or
    6 tablespoons fresh bread crumbs
2 to 3 tablespoons chopped fresh flat-leaf parsley or
    cilantro
About 1 teaspoon ground cumin
1 teaspoon salt
¼ teaspoon ground black pepper
⅛ to ¼ teaspoon cayenne (optional)
1 teaspoon baking powder or ½ teaspoon baking
    soda (optional)
Vegetable oil for deep-frying

1. In a meat grinder or food processor fitted with a metal blade, grind together the chickpeas, onion, and garlic. The chickpeas should not be totally smooth, but have a slightly coarse consistency. Stir in the flour, parsley, cumin, salt, pepper, and, if using, the optional cayenne, and/or baking powder. The mixture should be moist enough to just hold together. Chill for at least 1 hour.

2. In a deep pot, preheat at least 2 inches oil to 365°F. Shape the chickpea mixture into 1-inch balls. Leave

round or flatten slightly. In batches, fry the falafel, turning occasionally, until evenly golden brown on all sides, about 5 minutes. Remove with a slotted spoon and drain on paper towels.

FALSCHE FISH

Falsche fish are poached balls of ground chicken or veal, served in place of gefilte fish.

Origin: Eastern Europe

Other names: *bailik fish*, *falshe fish*, gefilte chicken.

Carp, pike, whitefish, and other freshwater fish swarmed in abundance in the rivers and streams that flowed through central and eastern Europe. For Jews, this inexpensive source of protein was particularly auspicious, because fish was considered an essential part of Sabbath and holiday meals, and this aquatic plenty could be used to make a beloved fish dish, gefilte fish. However, in the nineteenth century, some Chasidim proscribed fish on Passover, contending that in areas far from large bodies of water—Romania, Hungary, and much of Poland—fish transporters stored fish in alcohol distilled from grains to preserve them during the journey inland. In place of their favorite fish dish, Chasidic cooks developed a substitute and formed ground chicken or occasionally veal into balls to create a mock gefilte fish called *falsche fish*. A synonym for the dish is *bailik fish*, probably from the Yiddish *bilik* (cheap).

Like gefilte fish, this dish is commonly served cold accompanied with a slice of poached carrot and horseradish. Some people liked this innovation so much that they began making it during the rest of the year as well, serving it for the Sabbath, Rosh Hashanah, and the meal before Yom Kippur.

❧ ASHKENAZIC MOCK GEFILTE FISH (*FALSCHE FISH*)

ABOUT 8 SMALL OR 5 LARGE MEATBALLS   [MEAT]

Meatballs:

1 pound boneless chicken or turkey breast, ground
¼ cup matza meal, 1 cup mashed potatoes, or
    ⅔ cup fresh bread crumbs
¼ cup chicken broth
1 large onion, grated, or 5 scallions (white part
    only), chopped
1 clove garlic, mashed (optional)
1 large egg
About 1 teaspoon salt
About ½ teaspoon ground white or black pepper

Broth:
Chicken breast bones (from which the chicken was removed)
3 carrots, sliced
2 stalks celery, sliced
2 medium yellow onions, sliced
2 quarts water
2 teaspoons salt
Dash of ground white or black pepper
1 tablespoon sugar

1. To make the meatballs: Combine all the meatball ingredients. The mixture should be very soft; if too loose to form into the desired shape, refrigerate until firm, about 1 hour.

2. To make the broth: In a large pot, bring all the broth ingredients to a boil, reduce the heat, and simmer for 30 minutes. Strain and discard the solids. Return the broth to the pot and bring to a boil.

3. Using wet hands, form the meatball mixture into 1-inch balls or 3-inch long and 1-inch thick dumplings. Drop into the boiling stock in a single layer. Return the stock to a boil, reduce the heat, cover partially, and simmer, shaking the pot occasionally, until the meatballs are white or an instant read thermometer inserted in the center registers at least 165°F, 30 to 40 minutes. Transfer the cooking liquid and meatballs to a large storage container and let cool, then refrigerate until chilled.

FALUDEH

Faludeh refers to thin rice noodles as well as a bright white sorbet made from the noodles and shaved sweetened ice, rose water, and lime juice.

Origin: Persia
Other names: Farsi: *faloda, faloodeh*; India: *falooda*.

A *yakhchal* (ice storage) was an ancient Persian freezer. By at least 400 BCE, Persians had developed techniques for storing ice, which was gathered during the winter or carried from the tops of mountains, in large insulated underground chambers topped by domed structures. This innovation allowed ice to be available throughout the summer, even in the desert. A favorite use of this stored ice was in one of the earliest frozen desserts; the forerunner of all ice creams and sorbets, this ancient Persian mixture included ice, honey, and various flavors, notably saffron and fruits. Later, as distillation techniques developed, rose water was added, and as sugar cane was introduced, it was substituted for the honey. Today, sugar syrup is mixed with water and frozen, then the sweetened ice is shaved.

At some point, Persians began mixing *faludeh*, which are homemade noodles, into the ice. *Faludeh* are made from a thin rice batter, which is pressed through a sieve to produce delicate strings that look like grated coconut. Today, most people use rice sticks, very thin off-white rice-flour noodles, which are also called rice vermicelli and, in Chinese, *mei fun*. When cooked, the noodles turn bright white. The noodles are stirred into sweetened shaved ice, where they create a textural contrast while retaining their white color. A little lime juice counteracts any soapy flavor from the rose water. The version from the city of Shiraz, *faludeh shirazi*, which is the most famous, contains more lime juice for a rather tart flavor. In Israel, where limes are generally unavailable, lemon juice is typically substituted. Sour cherry syrup is frequently drizzled over the sorbet to temper the sweetness or mixed in to create a pink color. *Faludeh* is usually sprinkled with chopped pistachios.

Faludeh, also long popular in Afghanistan, is ubiquitous at Persian parties and as a treat throughout the summer. Being nondairy, it is common at barbecues and other meat meals. Occasionally, *faludeh* is *makhlut* (mixed) with *bastani* (ice cream). The Indian version consists of *kulfi* (ice cream), translucent wheat-starch noodles, and pink or yellow syrup; in Mumbai, it is served like a milk shake. Today, there are also versions made without the noodles and blended with fruit, such as melons. *Faludeh sib* is a variation substituting grated apples for the noodles; it is customarily served to break the fast of Yom Kippur.

In Iran, *faludeh* is sold at *bastani* (ice-cream stores) as well as shops specializing only in this treat. In modern commercial renderings, available at Persian markets in America, the syrup and noodles are frozen in an ice-cream maker rather than mixed with crushed ice. However, *faludeh* is intended to be slushy, not solid like an Italian ice or velvety like ice cream.

PERSIAN ROSE SORBET WITH RICE NOODLES
(*FALUDEH*)
6 TO 8 SERVINGS   [PAREVE]
 4 cups water
 1½ cups sugar
 2 tablespoons rose water

About 2 tablespoons fresh lime or lemon juice

8 ounces thin rice noodles or Chinese rice sticks, broken into 1-inch pieces

About ½ cup *sharbat-e albaloo* (cherry syrup; optional)

1. In a medium saucepan, stir the water and sugar over low heat until the sugar dissolves, about 5 minutes. Increase the heat to medium and bring to a boil. Let cool. Stir in the rose water and lime juice. Pour into ice cube trays and freeze.

2. Soak the noodles in cold water to cover for 1 hour. Drain. Bring a large pot of water to a boil. Add the noodles and cook until tender but not mushy, 3 to 5 minutes. Drain, rinse with cold water, and drain again. Refrigerate until chilled.

3. Crush the frozen sugar syrup cubes or pulse in a food processor. Energetically stir together the noodles with the crushed ice until well mixed. Transfer to servings bowls and serve immediately or freeze. If frozen, let stand at room temperature for 5 to 10 minutes to slightly soften, then crush with a spoon. If using, drizzle the cherry syrup over the top.

FARFEL

Farfel is a small barley-shaped egg noodle, as well as any small irregularly shaped food bit.

Origin: Germany

Other names: egg barley; German: *eiergraupen, farfl, pfarvel.*

By the early fourteenth century, after the concept of noodles had reached central Europe, Germans were making a soup, called in the Middle High German *varvelen*, containing small clumps of rudimentary noodles. German Jews began using the term, spelling it "farfel" in Yiddish, to denote small pellets of dough. The name is not related to the Italian bowtie pasta, *farfalle* (butterflies).

Early northern European pastas were made from barley, rye, and sometimes legumes, or from a combination of grains, but eventually wheat became the standard. Originally, the pasta pellets were formed by repeatedly hacking the flour-and-egg dough with a knife, but later two less precarious ways became prominent. In some areas, the dough was formed into a log or large balls, allowed to firm, then run along the coarse holes of a grater. Another method was to thinly roll out the dough, cut it into strips, and chop the strips into small bits; this produced pellets that were

more uniform. In any case, the pellets were spread out in a single layer and completely dried.

The shape of the small rough noodles resembled barley grains (*graupen* in German), giving rise to the German name *eiergraupen*. The first record of the word in English was in Israel Zangwill's tale of Jewish life in late nineteenth-century London, *Children of the Ghetto* (1892), in which he mentioned "*ferfel*, which are *lockshen* in an atomic state."

Over the course of time, the term farfel was also applied to other irregular food bits, including the Ashkenazic version of streusel and especially to crumbled matza. To differentiate them, Americans sometimes refer to the noodles as barley farfel. *Farfelach* is a name of a traditional Ashkenazic Passover candy made from matza farfel and honey, a treat also known as *farfel ingberlach*, as it was generally seasoned with ground ginger.

As refined egg noodles proliferated in Germany, farfel became predominantly a Polish and Ukrainian standard; it was typically made in bulk during warm weather, dried thoroughly in the sun, then stored for use over the year. Thus farfel was a staple throughout the autumn and winter, when fresh produce was scarce, and served as an essential food before the popularization of the potato in the mid-nineteenth century. Farfel appeared at both Sabbath and weekday meals.

According to a Chasidic legend, the founder of Chasidism, the Baal Shem Tov, regularly ate egg farfel on Friday night because the word sounds similar to the Yiddish word *farfellen*, meaning "done/finished." Thus these noodle pellets connote that with the onset of the Sabbath all the occurrences of the past week are finished. Many Chasidim still emulate the practice of serving farfel at the Friday night meal.

The Yiddish word *farfellen* also means "thwarted/doomed/fallen away," making farfel a befitting dish for Rosh Hashanah, when we express the wish that our misdeeds should "fall away" and those who wish us ill should be "thwarted." Round farfel is traditionally served on Rosh Hashanah as an accompaniment for chicken soup or in a kugel. The round shape symbolizes the hope that the coming year will be well-rounded, as well as the circular nature of life; the numerous pellets symbolize fertility and abundance. Some families, before eating their Rosh Hashanah farfel, recite the benediction, "May it be Your will,

Lord our God, God of our fathers, that all our enemies be thwarted."

Egg farfel was among the first Jewish foods to be mass-produced in early twentieth-century America. When manufacturers fabricated machine-made farfel, its shape commonly became uniformly round. In modern Israel, a type of round farfel (*petitim*) is marketed under the name couscous, and can be substituted for farfel (but not for Moroccan couscous).

Farfel is prepared both plain or, for a nutty flavor, toasted (*geroestete fervelchen*). Farfel is cooked in boiling water like other pasta, but can also be simmered in a smaller amount of liquid like a pilaf. Besides being added to soups, farfel is commonly served as a side dish with stews and pot roasts, cooked in tzimmes, and used as the base for kugels.

In America, farfel (especially with mushrooms) became standard at Jewish delis and Catskills resorts. In 1950, while performing at one of these resorts, ventriloquist Jimmy Nelson was first exposed to various Jewish foods. Shortly thereafter, Nelson introduced a new figure to his act, a brown floppy-eared dog who he whimsically named Farfel after one of those Jewish foods. Nelson and his sidekicks soon gained national prominence as regulars on Milton Berle's *Texaco Star Theater*. Farfel then became one of the best known and longest-running product "spokespersons"; each Nestlé's Quik television commercial from 1955 to 1965 ended with Farfel saying "chawwwwk-lit" (chocolate) and snapping his mouth shut. As a result, farfel became part of the wider American lexicon, as well as a popular name for dogs.

EGG BARLEY WITH MUSHROOMS
(FARFEL MIT SHVEML)

6 TO 8 SERVINGS [PAREVE OR MEAT]

3 tablespoons vegetable oil or schmaltz

2 large onions, chopped or sliced

2 cups (10 ounces) uncooked farfel or Israeli couscous, plain or toasted

12 ounces mushrooms, sliced

4 cups chicken broth, vegetable broth, or water

About 1 teaspoon table salt or 2 teaspoons kosher salt

About ¼ teaspoon ground black pepper

1. In a large skillet, heat 2 tablespoons oil over medium heat. Add the onions and sauté until soft and translucent, about 10 minutes, or golden, about 20 min-

utes. Stir in the farfel and stir until well coated, about 2 minutes. Transfer the farfel mixture to a large saucepan or 2-quart ovenproof dish.

2. Add the remaining 1 tablespoon oil to the skillet. Add the mushrooms and sauté until tender, about 8 minutes. Add to the farfel mixture.

3. In a separate medium saucepan, bring the broth, salt, and pepper to a boil. Add to the farfel mixture. Cover and simmer over a low heat, stirring occasionally, until the farfel is tender but not mushy and the liquid is absorbed, about 30 minutes; if the farfel is still too hard, add a little more water and continue to cook. Alternatively, place the farfel mixture in an ovenproof dish, cover, and bake in a 325°F oven for 30 minutes, then uncover and bake, stirring occasionally, until the liquid is absorbed, about 30 minutes more.

FASÍROZOTT

Fasírozott is a meatball or meatloaf.

Origin: Hungary

Other names: *fasírt, húsgombóc.*

Chopped meat dishes have been prominent in Europe since at least the time of ancient Rome, more than two thousand years ago; they were once time-consuming and expensive fare, reserved for special occasions. Hungarians enjoy a variety of meatball dishes; they frequently use both beef and veal to produce a dish called *fasírozott*, whose name may derive from an Austrian word for chopped meat, *faschierte*.

Hungarians insist that *fasírozott* should neither be bland nor contain too much bread, and that you should be able to taste the meat. Some cooks shape the meat mixture into balls, while others make small flat patties. Ground meat filled with whole boiled eggs is called *töltött* (stuffed). As a main dish, *fasírozott* is typically accompanied with noodles or boiled potatoes, or served in soups (*leves*) for the Sabbath and other special occasions.

FASOULIA

Fasoulia is a stew of green beans, tomatoes, onions, and olive oil.

Origin: Turkey

Other names: Balkans: *yachni di fijon verde*; Greek: *fasolia yiahni, fijolettes*; Ladino: *fasooleeye, fijon verde kon tomat*; Turkish: *fasoulia.*

Both green beans and tomatoes were brought from South America to Europe by the Spanish. Beans found immediate acceptance; they became a common component of many favorite stews and were also enjoyed solo. Tomatoes, on the other hand, were considered poisonous by Europeans and would not make their way into most European cooking for many centuries.

Traders brought American produce eastward through the African stretches of the Ottoman Empire into Egypt, Turkey, and the Balkans. The vegetable-loving Sephardim in the eastern Mediterranean adopted both green beans and tomatoes relatively quickly. One of their favorite dishes combined both of these, and sometimes included other favorite vegetables, such as spinach and leeks.

Cooking vegetables with tomatoes, onions, and olive oil is a characteristic technique of Turkish Jewish cuisine. Stewed vegetables in Greece are also called *yahni* or *yachni*, the name of the covered earthenware vessel in which it was originally cooked. The Middle Eastern predilection is for green beans that are cooked until mushy and served at room temperature, a taste that is perhaps attributable to the arid climate. The relatively long cooking time helps to develop the flavor. *Fasoulia* is a common sight on the Sabbath table and in the Sukkah in eastern Mediterranean Sephardic communities.

❦ SEPHARDIC GREEN BEANS WITH TOMATOES (*FASOULIA*)

6 TO 8 SERVINGS [PAREVE]

¼ cup olive or vegetable oil

2 large yellow onions, chopped

2 large carrots, sliced (optional)

2 to 3 cloves garlic, minced (optional)

2 pounds green beans, tips trimmed

2 cups (12 ounces) peeled, seeded, and chopped tomatoes

¼ cup water

1 to 3 teaspoons sugar

About 1 teaspoon table salt or 2 teaspoons kosher salt

Ground black pepper to taste

½ cup chopped fennel or 1 to 2 small chilies (optional)

1 tablespoon fresh lemon juice (optional)

1. In a large pot, heat the oil over medium heat. Add the onions and, if using, carrots and/or garlic and sauté until softened, about 10 minutes. Add the green beans and stir until well coated, 3 to 4 minutes.

2. Add the tomatoes, water, sugar, salt, pepper, and, if using, fennel and/or lemon juice and cook until the mixture simmers. Cover, reduce the heat to low, and simmer until the beans are tender and the sauce is reduced, 20 to 30 minutes. Or cover and bake in a 300°F oven for 30 minutes. Serve warm or at room temperature accompanied with bread or rice and, if desired, plain yogurt.

FATOOT/FTUT

Fatoot refers to a group of dishes made with crumbled bread. Among Yemenites, it is most often a meat soup containing or served with small pieces of bread.

Origin: Middle East

Other names: *fatta, ftut*.

Bread, particularly lean flatbread, without modern preservatives tends to become stale relatively quickly. Throughout most of history, instead of wasting this precious resource, cooks found ways to transform these dried loaves into practical and tasty fare, including puddings and stuffings. In the Middle East, many of these bread dishes are designated *fatoot* (*fatta* singular), an Arabic word denoting "anything crumbled," and a cognate of the Hebrew root *pattat* meaning "to break into pieces/to crumble." Certainly, the best known of these dishes in the West is a bread salad called *fattoush* or *fettoush*. Another *fatoot* was a simple bowl of bread soaked in sour milk and oil. The Levant is home to a group of crumbled bread casseroles collectively known as *fattat*, such as *fattat al-hummus* (bread and chickpea casserole), *fattat al-batijan* (bread and eggplant casserole), and *fattat al-dajaj* (bread and chicken casserole).

There are also several popular Yemenite bread dishes bearing the name *fatoot*. Among Yemenites, Friday was a unique transitional day, as people prepared for the oncoming Sabbath. Many tried not to perform their regular jobs on Friday or at least stopped working at some time in the morning. Even the clothing worn on Friday was generally different from that of either the weekday or Sabbath. In addition, Friday food was also distinctive. One of these special Friday morning dishes, *fatoot,* technically *fatoot samneh* (crumbled bread with clarified butter), consists of pieces of *saluf* (pita-like flatbread) or *melawah* (Yemenite puff pastry) fried with beaten eggs and, in Israel, sometimes honey.

The most widespread and important form of Yemenite *fatoot* is a hearty and spicy soup, technically *fatoot marak* or *fatoot wa hilbeh* (with fenugreek relish), containing or accompanied with plenty of crumbled bread. In Yemen, meat is generally prepared in the form of thin stews and soups that were, until recently, left to simmer much of the day. Yemenites usually serve meat only for lunch, as it is considered unhealthy to eat meat late in the day. The exception is on the Sabbath and festivals, when meat soup is served as the main course for dinner, and no Yemenite Sabbath or festival meal would be considered complete without it. *Fatoot* is also ubiquitous at Yemenite weddings.

Lamb has long been the predominant meat in *fatoot*. In Israel, however, beef has gained in popularity. In Yemen, *fatoot* was made with either meat or chicken, and never the two together, but some Israeli *marak taimani* (Yemenite soup) recipes call for both. Also in Yemen, the only vegetables used were onions and frequently potatoes (typically one each per person), while in Israel a variety of vegetables are sometimes added to *marak taimani*, including carrots, celery, pumpkin, tomatoes, turnips, and zucchini. Many Yemenites, however, vehemently object to these untraditional additions, insisting that they jarringly alter the taste. Some even object to the presence of parsley, while others add both parsley and cilantro. The soup is always left to simmer for at least three hours. In Israel, this was traditionally done on a small kerosene single-burner cooker (*ptiliya*, from *ptil*, "wick"). Today, Yemenite restaurants in Israel typically feature a row of five or more cookers, each topped with a pot bearing a different type of traditional soup.

There are several ways of adding bread to the soup. Just before eating, some households sprinkle pieces of *saluf* (flatbread) over the soup, letting it soften, but not turn mushy. Others remove some of the broth, add some boiling water along with several tablespoons of *hilbeh* and/or *s'chug* (chili paste), stir in the torn bread, let the mixture boil for several minutes, and then remove it from the heat and let it stand. This method produces two dishes: the remaining meat broth and the slightly thick, but liquidy, *fatoot*. Other families place the communal soup pot in the center of the table and diners dip pieces of *saluf*, *melawah*, or *lachuach* (Yemenite unleavened flatbread)—Yemenites consider biting from a large piece of bread animallike—into the soup; the bread is frequently first dipped into some *hilbeh*, a spicy relish. On Passover, soft Yemenite matza is

substituted. Instead of bread, some add bulgur, letting the kernels soften in the soup. When wheat berries are used instead of bread and the soup is cooked overnight for Sabbath lunch, this dish is called *harisa*, the forerunner of Sabbath stews.

Yemenites prefer a spicy soup, so they stir in a spoonful or several of *hawaij* (a spice blend of cardamom, cumin, turmeric, and black pepper), which produces a curry flavor and yellowish tint; they also add *hilbeh* and/or *s'chug*. Some stir in fresh lemon or lime juice just before serving. *Fatoot* is typically accompanied with hard-boiled eggs, which are also dipped into the *hilbeh*. After the broth is finished, the meat and potatoes in the pot are divided among the diners.

❦ YEMENITE MEAT SOUP (*FATOOT/FTUT*)

6 TO 8 SERVINGS   [MEAT]

   2 pounds lamb shoulder, beef chuck, or brisket, cut into 2-inch pieces
   2 to 3 marrow bones
   8 cups cold water
   2 large yellow onions, quartered
   6 to 8 cloves garlic, unpeeled
   1 to 4 tablespoons *hawaij* (Yemenite Spice Mixture, page 260), or 2 tablespoons ground cumin, 2 teaspoons ground turmeric, 1 teaspoon ground black pepper, and ⅛ teaspoon ground cardamom
   6 to 8 medium potatoes, peeled
   About 1½ teaspoons table salt or 1 tablespoon kosher salt
   6 to 10 sprigs fresh flat-leaf parsley or cilantro (optional)
   6 to 8 (5- to 6-inch) *salufe* (Yemenite flatbread) or pita bread, torn into pieces
   Hilbeh (Yemenite Fenugreek Relish, page 263)
   S'chug (Yemenite Chili Paste, page 538)

1. In a large pot, combine the meat, bones, and cold water. Bring to a boil, reduce the heat to low, and simmer, occasionally skimming the scum from the surface, for about 10 minutes. Add the onions, garlic, and *hawaij*, cover, and simmer, occasionally skimming the scum from the surface, for about 2 hours.

2. Add the potatoes and salt, reduce the heat to low, and simmer until the meat and potatoes are tender, about 1 hour. If using the parsley, add about 15 minutes before the soup is done. Discard the onions and garlic. Scrape any marrow from the bones into the soup, then discard the bones.

3. Place a torn bread in the bottom of each soup bowl and top with plenty of soup, a potato, and some of the meat, or serve with the bread pieces and let each person add or dip their own. Pass the *hilbeh* and *s'chug*, and let each person stir them into their soup.

FAVA BEAN

Fava beans are the seeds of a herbaceous plant with coarse hollow stems. It is a mysterious crop, as the fava cannot hybridize with any of its relatives. Its point of origin has not been determined nor have wild fava or any intermediate types ever been found. The earliest evidence of fava's use by humans was a cache of about 2,600 dried wild beans discovered in a late Neolithic site near Nazareth. Around the third millennium BCE, fava beans suddenly were cultivated from Persia to Iberia and North Africa. They were generally a peasant food, but were staples in ancient Egypt and Greece. Greeks and later Romans used the bean seeds for voting—white indicated "yes" and black indicated "no." Fava beans (*pol*) were mentioned twice in the Bible, both references denoting an item that was stored and useful in times of emergency.

Even before Columbus brought unknown beans from America, the fava bean was less than universally beloved. Around 450 BCE, Pythagoras described fava beans as unwholesome and forbade people to eat them, while Herodotus noted that Egyptian priests "never sow or eat fava beans and, even if any grow wild, they will not even endure to look at them, since they consider it an unclean type of legume." Although favas were consumed in ancient Israel, it was not a favorite food. The ambiguous sentiments may be due to the lack of a blood enzyme (G6PD deficiency) among some people, especially males, of Mediterranean, African, and south central Asian ancestry. For those who inherit this genetic condition, eating fava beans produces deleterious or even lethal effects.

The three most prominent contemporary fava bean varieties are the large, whitish, kidney-shaped Greek or European fava (*ful rumi* in Arabic; broad or Windsor bean in England), which is most commonly served in a *mezze* (appetizer assortment) and found fresh in Western markets; the medium-sized whitish Upper Egyptian bean (*ful baladi*, literally "local/country beans" in Arabic; horse bean in England); and the small, nearly round, dark brown pigeon bean, which is not the same as the pigeon pea. In Egypt, pigeon beans are called *ful hamam* (bathhouse fava), because they were cooked over the fires of Egyptian public bathhouses. These require a long cooking time and are often used for stews and the classic Egyptian dish *ful medames* (stewed dried fava beans).

Soft, young fava bean pods, with a velvety exterior and very small beans, can be cooked and eaten without shelling. Once the beans have developed, but the pods are still young and soft, the pods can still be eaten, but the pale green beans must be shelled first. Fresh favas—*avas frescas* in Ladino and *ful akhdar* in Arabic—are sometimes served raw, but are more often cooked. The skin of fresh favas is tough and is frequently removed after blanching. When making a batch of *ful*, the children in the family are frequently drafted for the tedious but necessary step of removing the skins. A common way to eat fresh fava beans in Italy and the Middle East is lightly cooked, then drizzled with olive oil, salt, and pepper. Europeans like flavoring fava beans with summer savory and the two plants are often grown together.

Dried fava beans (*ful nabed*) and canned beans—rehydrated and cooked dried fava beans—can be found in specialty markets. Both of these have a very different flavor than fresh fava beans and are generally not interchangeable. The dried beans are used like chickpeas. Egyptians have a special copper or clay pot called a *qidra*, with a narrow base and neck and large center, for cooking dried fava beans.

For centuries, fava beans constituted the principal ingredient of the Sabbath stews of Sephardim and Ashkenazim. Ashkenazim traditionally featured fava beans (*bub*), at *shalom zachor*, a celebration held on the Friday night following the birth of a son. In recognition of Esther, who maintained a vegetarian diet while living in the king's palace, fava was a traditional Ashkenazic Purim food. However, since the popularization of the American haricot beans, the fava virtually disappeared from the dishes of most Ashkenazim. In America, the fava bean was, with the exception of a few ethnic enclaves, practically nonexistent. However, recently, it has become trendy and can be found in vegetable markets and fashionable restaurants.

The fava remains an important food in a few parts of Europe, China, and the Middle East. In Egypt, cooked beans are mashed into a puree akin to hummus and soaked raw beans are ground and fried to produce *tamiya*, which are similar to falafel. Ethiopians commonly add fava beans to stews. The long-standing significance of these beans to Sephardim may be seen in the bean's old Spanish name, *judia*, which is also the Spanish word for Jewess. Some Sephardim still use fava beans to make *hamin/adafina* and other Sabbath dishes. Jews in Mediterranean regions—recalling that fava beans were a staple of the Israelites' diet in Egypt, and also wanting to make use of the first of the winter bean crop—include bean dishes in their Passover fare, most notably soups (called *bissara* in the Maghreb), rice with fresh fava beans, and *kubba* (filled dumplings) cooked with fresh favas and artichoke hearts. Fava beans with artichokes are a popular Friday night side dish during the spring. In the Maghreb, fresh fava beans are served over buttery couscous on Shavuot. Bean soups and stews are common during the Nine Days before the fast of Tisha b'Av, providing a source of protein during this meatless period. Since the Hebrew name for fava beans (*pol*) sounds like the Hebrew verb *pahl* (fall), some families from the Maghreb eat them during Rosh Hashanah dinner as a sign of the hope that "those who hate us may fall."

FENNEL

Fennel, a member of the Apiaceae family, has been cultivated since at least the time of ancient Rome. The recent cultivar of that ancient plant is a version that has an enlarged leaf base and resembles celery with a bulbous bottom; it goes by the names finocchio, Florence fennel, bulbing fennel, sweet fennel, and, sometimes mistakenly, anise. Bulb fennel may have been developed in Sicily or southern Italy.

The original fennel still grows wild through much of the Mediterranean. The Greeks called it *marathon* (from *maraino*, "to grow thin"), referring to its use in weight loss—the seeds were believed to be an appetite suppressant and aide to the digestion of fat. The Romans knew it as *foeniculum* (fragrant hay) and spread the plant to all parts of the empire. Some scholars contend it is the *ketzach* mentioned by Isaiah. The Mishnah called fennel *gufnan*, while the Jerusalem Talmud referred to it as *shumar* and explained that the residents of Judah, who cultivated it, considered fennel to be a spice, but those in the Galilee did not. Its name in modern Hebrew is also *shumar*, which should not be confused with the modern Hebrew word for dill, *shamir*.

In the ancient world, the feathery green or bronze fennel leaves were used raw in salads, the young succulent shoots were eaten fresh and cooked, and the thin carrot-like roots were brewed into a remedy for indigestion. However, it was the plant's fruits, called seeds, that were of primary importance; they were utilized as both a spice and a medicine. Pliny recorded twenty-two medical remedies obtained from the plant. In herbal healing, fennel was widely used to drive away evil spirits. The yellowish-green seeds contain anethol, an essential oil with a licorice flavor that is somewhat milder and less sweet than that of anise. The seeds are particularly popular in central Europe, where they are used to flavor rye breads, sausages, liqueurs, and pickles. Italians add them to pasta sauces, marinades, and fish.

Sociologists coined the term "conservatism of cuisine," reflecting the observation that few people are adventurous when it comes to foreign food, preferring to rely on fare to which they are accustomed. Historically, an alien dish or vegetable generally took many years to seep into a country, if it did at all, even when the newcomer was delicious or superior to native food. Bulb fennel exemplifies this fact. In the sixteenth century, Jews from Sicily and southern Italy popularized bulb fennel among Jews in the middle and northern sections of Italy, and subsequently they incorporated it into numerous dishes. The favorite Italian way of enjoying fennel is baked. Meanwhile, bulb fennel was largely ignored by many non-Jewish Italians. In 1891, the Florentine cookbook writer Pellegrino Artusi, in *La Scienza in Cucina e L'Arte di Mangiare Bene*, observed that forty years earlier bulb fennel and eggplant "were considered to be vile because they were food eaten by Jews." Only in the late nineteenth century did Italians at large come to adore what Italian Jews had loved for centuries.

Bulb fennel is popular among other Mediterranean Jewish communities as well, especially in the Maghreb. Raw fennel with oranges and olives is a classic dish. Fennel salad (*salata bisbas*) with olives and harissa (chili paste) is a specialty of the island of Djerba. Egyptians make a cooked salad of fennel and celeriac.

Some Ashkenazim call three spices that resemble each other—fennel, caraway, and cumin—by the name of *kimmel* (from the German word for caraway, *echter kümmel* and for cumin *kreuzkümmel*) and forbid them on Passover because they can become contaminated with wheat. The fennel bulb, however, is permitted. There is a long-standing custom in some Mediterranean communities of eating fennel seeds or bulb fennel during the Passover Seder, as the plant's Hebrew name is reminiscent of the biblical phrase for Passover night, *lail shimurim* (night of watching).

FENUGREEK

Both the leaves and seeds of fenugreek, a relative of the pea, have long been used in Asian and North African cooking. The plant bears light green, obovate (egg-shaped) leaves and small, flat pods, each containing ten to twenty aromatic yellowish seeds. Fenugreek seeds have been discovered at several Bronze Age sites in the Near East. When the leaves are dried, they emit a hay-like scent. The Ebers papyrus (c. 1500 BCE), reveals that the Egyptians utilized the seeds in medicines, as a skin softener, and in the mummification process.

Fenugreek is among the foods recommended by the Talmud for Rosh Hashanah, as its Aramaic name (*rubia*) is similar to the wish *sheh-yirbu* (may our merits increase). The name may come from an ancient practice of giving fenugreek to nursing mothers to increase milk production. Fenugreek comes from the Latin term for Greek hay, a reference to the use of its leaves as animal fodder, perhaps due to its purported ability to enhance milk production. Its Arabic name, *hilbeh*, and modern Hebrew name, *chilbeh*, derived from the Semitic root for milk. Later, Sephardim confused the term *rubia* with the Arabic name for fresh black-eyed peas (*lubia*), a mistaken identity they passed on to Ashkenazim.

Raw fenugreek seeds are very astringent. Lightly heating the seeds brings out a celery-like aroma and mellow, slightly bitter flavor similar to that of caramelized sugar. Fenugreek has a particular affinity for beef, bread, and potatoes. Several cultures cherish its earthy, bitter flavor and musky aroma, and cooks find it especially useful for adding accents to vegetarian fare. Fenugreek seeds are essential to the Yemenite relish *hilbeh;* Indian curry powders, chutneys, pickles, and *dosas* (rice or lentil pancake); Georgian sauces (such as *bazha*); and the Ethiopian spice mixture *berbere*. The seed's principal use in America is in imitation maple syrup. Dried fenugreek leaves, although rarer than seeds, are also used to add bitter notes to foods,

including the Persian *ghorme sabzi* (meat sauce with herbs) and the Georgian spice mixture *khmeli-suneli.*

FESENJAN

Fesenjan is a stew consisting of chicken, duck, or meatballs, along with pomegranates and walnuts.
Origin: Persia
Other names: *khoresh-e fesenjan.*

Fesenjan is the jewel of Persian stews. It originated in the province of Gilan on the banks of the Caspian Sea, where wild ducks were in abundance. Chicken is now more commonly used than duck. The purplish *khoresh* (the thick sauce in which it cooks) must simmer long enough for the oil in the walnuts to exude and the flavors to fuse. The result is a thick, tangy, complex dish with a hint of sweetness that contrasts with the intense poultry flavor. The dish was most prominent in the fall, when pomegranates matured, and emerged as a popular Persian Rosh Hashanah recipe. *Fesenjan* is accompanied by *chelow* (crusty rice).

PERSIAN CHICKEN WITH POMEGRANATES AND WALNUTS (*FESENJAN*)

4 TO 6 SERVINGS   [MEAT]

  1 (3- to 4-pound) chicken or duckling, cut into 8 pieces, or 8 chicken thighs or 6 duck breasts, bone-in and with skin on
  3 tablespoons vegetable or olive oil
  1 large yellow onion or 3 shallots, chopped
  ½ teaspoon ground cinnamon or cardamom
  2 cups (8 ounces) finely ground walnuts
  ½ cup chicken broth or water
  2 cups pomegranate juice, or ½ cup pomegranate syrup and 2 cups chicken broth or water
  ¼ cup fresh lemon juice or tomato sauce
  1 to 2 tablespoons sugar or molasses
  ½ teaspoon ground turmeric or pinch of saffron
  About 1 teaspoon table salt or 2 teaspoons kosher salt
  Ground black pepper to taste

1. Rinse the chicken well and pat dry. In a large, heavy pot, heat the oil over medium-high heat. Add the chicken—do not crowd the pan—and brown on both sides, about 5 minutes per side. Remove the chicken.

2. Drain off all but 3 tablespoons fat from the pot. Add the onion and sauté until soft and translucent,

5 to 10 minutes. Add the cinnamon and sauté for 1 minute. Stir in the walnuts and sauté, being careful not to burn the nuts, for about 5 minutes. Stir in the broth, pomegranate juice, lemon juice, sugar, turmeric, salt, and pepper. Return the chicken to the pot.

3. Cover and simmer over a low heat or bake in a preheated 375°F oven until tender, about 1 hour. If the sauce becomes too thick, stir in a little water.

FETA

Cheese was historically produced from March through October, during the animal's grazing season. Sprinkling a soft cheese with coarse salt and letting it stand for a minimum of two months, or soaking it in salt brine as is done with feta, stops the ripening process, allowing for longer storage through the winter without a loss of quality as well as a brinier flavor. The saltiness, firmness, and creaminess of the cheese depend on the maker's style and the types of milk used.

Brined cheese appears to have originated during the early medieval period among the nomadic Vlach of Romania and eventually spread throughout the Balkans. It may have only reached Greece in the seventeenth century. Today, the most well-known brined cheese in America is the Greek feta. It was originally called *tyripheta*, from the Italian *fette* (slice), as the ten- to thirty-pound blocks of cheese are cut into wedges before being brined. This crumbly cheese is primarily made from sheep's milk, but occasionally it contains up to 30 percent goat's milk, and poorer-quality types are made from cow's milk. Sheep's milk feta has a slightly nutty flavor and a texture that ranges from creamy to dry. Feta made from goat's milk has a tangier flavor, denser texture, and whiter color than feta drawing on sheep's milk. Most feta in the West is imported and the type of milk and brining should be indicated on the label.

Feta cheese is an integral part of Jewish cookery in the Balkans, Turkey, and the Levant, where it is ubiquitous at most dairy meals. Besides its saltiness, feta has an acidic, earthy flavor. When cooked, the flavors mellow and become more complex. The simplicity of feta's flavor makes it a perfect complement to bread and olives, as well as an important ingredient in salads, vegetable dishes, and pastry fillings. In fillings, feta is frequently combined with a mild cheese, such as farmer or pot, for balance, and mashed potatoes are sometimes added for fluffiness.

(See also Brinza)

FIDELLO

Fidello is a thin noodle, often shaped into coils.
Origin: Spain
Other names: Arabic: *sheriya*; Greek: *fideiko*;
Ladino: *fideo, fideyo*.

By at least the tenth century, the Arabs had introduced pasta as well as the cultivation of durum wheat to Spain. Semolina is necessary for pasta to dry without cracking and to hold together during cooking without the addition of eggs. By the fourteenth century, Sephardim applied the term *fila* to fresh egg noodles made from common wheat and *macaron* to all dried durum pasta. Traditional types of Sephardic pasta included *alatria* (vermicelli, from the Semitic *itriya*), *escolacha* (pressed through a strainer), and *fidellos*, which beginning in the fourteenth century, were the prevailing Sephardic form of pasta. The Ladino term *fidello* was derived from the Arabic word for noodle, *fidawsh/fidaush* (meaning "to swell/grow"), as noodles expand in boiling water.

Maimonides, in his medical treatise *Regimen of Health* (c. 1172), warned against eating noodles and dumplings, although he ate plain chicken soup on a regular basis. The vast majority of Sephardim, however, rejected Maimonides' advice and pasta became an integral element of Sephardic cuisine.

For generations, groups of women would sit and chat while churning out an enormous batch of durum pasta to be dried and stored for an extended period. In some locations, this was done on the fast day of Tisha b'Av, as the preparation was a productive way to pass the time and make use of the warm weather for drying the pasta. For *fidellos*, each person would roll small pieces of dough between her thumb and forefinger, creating very thin, inch-long, tear-shaped durum noodles. The pasta was sun-dried on large metal sheets, then stored in containers to avoid bug infestation. Today, oven drying typically replaces the sun.

Following the advent of mechanized pasta production, commercial *fidellos* took on a new shape—coils of very fine noodles—that was slightly different from that of the venerable homemade type. Since few people still make homemade *fidellos*, the term now generally denotes these coils as well as manufactured vermicelli. The thinnest coils, akin to angel's hair pasta, are generally used in soups, while slightly thicker ones are reserved for sauces and casseroles (which were once cooked in an earthenware pot called a *cazuela*). Most Sephardic cooks insist on using semolina pasta and not egg noodles for dishes containing *fidellos*.

The typical Spanish method of preparing pasta was not to dress it with a sauce after cooking, but rather to simmer it in a meat sauce until the liquid was absorbed and the noodles were well coated with the sauce, but not soupy. Spanish pasta is customarily cooked until completely soft; it is not made al dente in the Italian manner. This method allows the pasta to impart starch into the sauce and soak up the sauce's flavor. In addition to being added to sauces, noodles were added to soups (*sopa de fidello*), a role they continue to play. Many Moroccans stir cooked *fidellos* into the liquid of their Sabbath stew (unlike the Ashkenazic cholent, it is very liquidy), enjoying this combination as a soup separate from the other ingredients. *Fidellos* are also served as a side dish for stews, baked with cheese, topped with various sauces, or simply tossed with a little butter, salt, and pepper.

A distinctive Sephardic way to prepare this pasta is *fidellos tostados*; the noodles are first fried in oil until golden brown, imparting a nutty flavor, and then added to the cooking liquid. In the Iberian manner, the noodles are then simmered in a small amount of sauce or broth until the liquid is absorbed. Browned noodles are sometimes cooked with rice (*arroz kon fidellos*). On Purim, boiled *fidellos* tossed with a simple dressing of lemon juice and olive oil is called *kaveyos di Haman* (Haman's hair).

Although *fidellos tostados* is a Sephardic dish dating back to well before the expulsion from Spain in 1492, the addition of tomatoes happened afterwards. This eastern Mediterranean variation, technically called *fidellos kon domates*, became so popular that it is typically referred to as simply *fidellos*. Many cooks make a basic, mild tomato sauce; others add a little sautéed onion and/or spices (such as a dash of cinnamon) or herbs, although not enough to make it a spicy dish. The noodles are sometimes served loose and soft, but they are also allowed to solidify into a cake and then cut into wedges. An advantage of the tomato ver-

sion is it tastes as good, or to some even better, when prepared a day ahead and reheated. Although *fidellos tostados* is a common everyday dish, it also appears at the meal before Yom Kippur accompanying *armico* (chicken in tomato sauce), and on Sukkot tables.

(See also Pasta)

SEPHARDIC TOASTED NOODLES
(*FIDELLOS TOSTADOS*)

5 TO 6 SERVINGS   [MEAT OR PAREVE]

> 6 tablespoons olive or vegetable oil
> 1 (12-ounce) package fidellos (fine coiled noodles; do not break apart) or 12 ounces angel hair pasta or semolina vermicelli, broken into 2-inch pieces
> 1 medium onion, chopped (optional)
> 3 cups chicken broth, vegetable broth, or water
> 2 cups (12 ounces) peeled, seeded, and chopped tomatoes, or strained stewed tomatoes, or ½ cup tomato sauce
> About ¾ teaspoon table salt or 1½ teaspoons kosher salt
> Ground black pepper to taste

1. In a large, heavy pot, heat the oil over medium heat. Add the fidellos coils (do not break apart yet) and sauté until light golden, but not burned, about 5 minutes. Using a slotted spoon, remove the fidellos. Or, instead of frying the fidello, spread over a baking sheet and toast in a 350°F oven until lightly browned.

2. If using, add the onion and sauté until soft and translucent, 5 to 10 minutes. Add the broth, tomatoes, salt, and pepper and bring to a boil.

3. Return the noodles, cover tightly, reduce the heat to very low, and simmer, stirring occasionally and breaking up the coils, until the pasta is tender, about 10 to 12 minutes.

4. Remove from the heat and let stand, covered, until the noodles absorb all the liquid and the flavors meld, about 10 minutes. Stir. Serve warm or at room temperature.

FIG

The fig is the first fruit specifically mentioned in the Bible—its leaves provided Adam and Eve with their original clothing. Among the suggestions for the identity of the tree of knowledge of good and evil in Eden, the fig is mentioned by Jewish commentators more often than any other tree. In the words of the Tal-

Fig harvests in Israel signal the beginning and end of summer.

mud, "By the thing which they were corrupted were they redressed." The fig is represented prominently in Jewish literature and tradition; only the grape is mentioned more often in the Bible or Talmud. Figs are among the Seven Species with which the land of Israel is praised. The biblical term "under his fig tree" has become a symbol of peace and prosperity.

The common fig is native to the eastern Mediterranean. Remains of dried figs from the Neolithic Age were uncovered in Gezer, near present-day Ramla. The average fig tree lives fifty to ninety years, but can survive for more than two centuries. The fig's multibranched, dense summer foliage provides more shade than that of other trees of comparable size. The fig tree's bark is smooth and grayish. Its wood is unexceptional; it is relatively soft and subject to decay and, therefore, of little use in building. The wood was, however, the type preferred in the Temple for fueling the altar and making charcoal for the incense. Rashi explained that just as the fig's leaves were the very first items employed by humans for self-improvement, so should the wood be used by Adam's descendants to achieve self-improvement.

Female fig trees of older varieties generally produce two crops every year. The two fig harvests not only mark the summer season in Israel, but also give the season its Hebrew name, *kayitz*; summer begins with the arrival of the first figs and ends with the arrival of the second harvest. Breba, the lesser early crop, which is called *bakkurot* in Hebrew, begins appearing

on the trees even before the yearly leaves, around the vernal equinox (March 21), and ripens around Shavuot (June). One of the signs of spring recounted in Song of Songs is "The fig tree has formed her *paggim* [green figs]." Late figs, which are the main crop and are called *te'enim* in Hebrew, ripen around the month of Elul (August to September), at about the same time as the date harvest. Each season, weather conditions, such as a cool summer or a prolonged drought, affect the maturation of figs, as well as the amount and size of the fruit. Hence even on the same tree, the harvest differs from year to year. A mature tree yields forty to fifty pounds of fruit annually for about fifty years.

Immature figs are hard, smooth, and flavorless. Figs must be fully ripened on the tree to possess the appropriate sweetness and flavor. Ripeness cannot be judged by color or size. There are several indications of ripeness: when they smell mildly sweet, soften slightly when they are touched, and start to bend at the neck. Some varieties exude a single drop of syrup from the bottom. Very mature figs tend to exhibit cracks in the skin and bruise easily; ironically, perfect-looking fruits tend to lack flavor. Rain during ripening can cause the fruit to split, so an early arrival of the rains in Israel can prove disastrous for the crop.

In biblical times, figs were cultivated throughout the land of Israel and fresh or dried figs were part of the daily diet. A common way of preparing dried figs for storage was to chop them and then press them into a mass; the resulting fruit cake was called *develah* (pressed together). Fresh figs were also squeezed and the pulp was boiled down to make a thick honey-like syrup, although that role was more commonly filled by dates. Today, Sephardim and Mizrachim use fresh and dried figs in salads, jams, and pastries, but the favorite way to eat them is simply plain. Among Jews in the Maghreb, fig brandy is sometimes used instead of wine for reciting the Kiddush on the Sabbath. This spirit is known in Morocco as *mahia* (water of life).

FILLING/FULLUNG (ASHKENAZIC PASTRY FILLINGS)

Since ancient times, filled pastries have served as a way to mark the significance of an occasion or, in more mundane uses, have helped to uplift leftovers or efficiently exploit scarce foods to make a tasty and hardy meal. For much of history, delicate pastry, which requires finely milled flour, was generally the province of the wealthy, or reserved for special occasions. Traditional Ashkenazic fillings typically included the most common and inexpensive ingredients, such as mashed potatoes, kasha, curd cheese, and cabbage, with few or no added spices. Occasionally, fillings were a way to stretch more costly fare, notably meat and liver, and make use of seasonal produce, including cherries, plums, and apples. In America, as income levels rose, these ingredients grew to be more commonplace and filled pastries and pastas became widespread comfort foods; however, they also remain traditional fare for various holidays and other special occasions.

Use the fillings on the following pages for blintzes, Danishes, hamantaschen, knishes, *kolache*, kreplach, pirogen, and *varenikis*, as well as other dumplings, turnovers, and pastries. Four cups is enough to fill twenty-four medium knishes, sixty-four 3-inch kreplach, or twelve 6-inch blintzes.

Savory Fillings

ASHKENAZIC CABBAGE FILLING (*KRAUTFULLUNG*)

ABOUT 4 CUPS [PAREVE OR MEAT]

1 medium-small (1½ pounds/9 cups) cabbage, coarsely shredded
¼ cup vegetable oil or schmaltz
1 large onion, chopped
2 tablespoons granulated or brown sugar or chopped fresh dill
Salt and ground black pepper to taste

1. Bring a large pot of water to a boil, add the cabbage, return to a boil, and parboil for 3 minutes. Drain, squeezing out the excess moisture.

2. In a large skillet, heat the oil over medium heat. Add the onion and sauté until soft and translucent, 5 to 10 minutes. Add the cabbage, reduce the heat to low, and cook, stirring occasionally, until soft, about 15 minutes. Stir in the sugar, salt, and pepper. Let cool.

ASHKENAZIC SAVORY CHEESE FILLING (*KAESEFULLUNG*)

ABOUT 4 CUPS [DAIRY]

2 tablespoons (¼ stick) unsalted butter
2 medium onions, 4 large leeks, or 12 scallions, chopped
2 to 3 cloves garlic, minced (optional)

2 pounds pot or farmer cheese
2 tablespoons sour cream or ¼ cup cream cheese
2 tablespoons all-purpose flour or matza cake meal
2 large egg yolks or 1 large egg, lightly beaten
About ½ teaspoon salt
About ¼ teaspoon ground white or black pepper

In a large skillet, heat the butter over medium heat. Add the onions and sauté until soft and translucent, 5 to 10 minutes. If using, add the garlic and sauté for 2 minutes. Remove from the heat. In a large bowl, combine the cheese, sour cream, flour, egg yolks, salt, and pepper. Stir in the onions.

ASHKENAZIC KASHA FILLING (*KASHAFULLUNG*)

ABOUT 3 CUPS [PAREVE]

3 tablespoons vegetable oil
1 large onion, chopped
1 cup (5.75 ounces) kasha, medium granulation
3 cups boiling water
About ½ teaspoon table salt or 1 teaspoon kosher salt
Ground black pepper to taste
1 large egg, lightly beaten (optional)

In a large saucepan, heat the oil over medium heat. Add the onion and sauté until soft and translucent, 10 to 15 minutes. Stir in the kasha and cook until well coated, 2 to 3 minutes. Add the water, salt, and pepper. Cover, reduce the heat to low, and simmer until tender and the liquid is absorbed, about 15 minutes. Remove from the heat and let cool. If using, stir in the egg.

ASHKENAZIC POTATO FILLING (*KARTOFFELFULLUNG*)

ABOUT 4 CUPS [PAREVE OR MEAT]

3 tablespoons vegetable oil or schmaltz
2 medium yellow onions, chopped
About 3½ cup mashed potatoes
About 1 teaspoon table salt or 2 teaspoons kosher salt
Ground black pepper to taste
1 large egg, lightly beaten

In a large skillet, heat the oil over medium heat. Add the onions and sauté until golden brown, 20 to 30 minutes. Remove from the heat and stir into the potatoes. Add the salt and pepper. Let cool. Stir in the egg.

VARIATIONS

Mit Neshamos (with Souls): With the egg, add ¼ to ⅓ cup coarsely chopped gribenes (cracklings).

Sweet Fillings

ASHKENAZIC SWEET CHEESE FILLING
(ZEESIH KAESEFULLUNG)

ABOUT 2 CUPS   [DAIRY]

12 ounces (1½ cups) farmer or pot cheese
4 ounces cream cheese, softened
1 large egg yolk or ½ large egg, lightly beaten
2 to 4 tablespoons granulated or confectioners'
    sugar
¾ teaspoon vanilla extract
Pinch of salt
1 teaspoon grated lemon zest (optional)

In a medium bowl, beat together all the ingredients until smooth.

ASHKENAZIC POPPY SEED FILLING (MOHNFULLUNG)

ABOUT 2½ CUPS   [PAREVE OR DAIRY]

2 cups (about 10 ounces) poppy seeds
1 cup water or milk
1 cup sugar or honey, or ⅔ cup honey and ¼ cup
    light corn syrup
About 2 tablespoons fresh lemon or orange juice
Pinch of salt
2 teaspoons grated lemon or orange zest
    (optional)
½ to 1 cup golden raisins or chopped dried
    apricots (optional)
½ to 1 cup finely chopped almonds or walnuts
    (optional)

1. In a nut grinder, coffee grinder, food processor, or blender, grind the poppy seeds. Or seal the poppy seeds in a plastic bag and crush using a rolling pin.

2. In a small saucepan, combine the poppy seeds, water, sugar, lemon juice, salt, and, if using, zest and simmer over medium-low heat, stirring frequently, until the mixture thickens, about 12 minutes. Remove from the heat and, if using, add the raisins and/or nuts. Let cool. Store in the refrigerator for up to 1 week.

ASHKENAZIC PRUNE FILLING (FLOHMENFULLUNG)

ABOUT 2 CUPS   [PAREVE]

1½ cups (9 ounces) pitted dried plums, or 1 cup
    pitted dried plums and ½ cup raisins
½ cup ground walnuts or fresh bread crumbs
¼ cup honey or 2 tablespoons sugar
1 teaspoon grated lemon zest (optional)
1 teaspoon grated orange zest (optional)

In a medium saucepan, simmer the prunes in water to cover until soft, about 30 minutes. Drain. Grind or mash the prunes. Stir in the walnuts, honey, and, if using, zests.

FISH

There are more than thirty thousand types of fish worldwide, of which only those that possess fins and cycloid (round) or ctenoid (comblike) scales are deemed kosher. These species of fish have been an integral part of Jewish cookery from the onset and they are enjoyed in a wide variety of forms. Until relatively recently, fish provided an inexpensive source of protein in many locales, and was a necessity in some places, or in times of poverty. As the Israelites complained to Moses in the wilderness, "We remember the fish that we ate in Egypt for nothing," referring to the more than two hundred species native to the Nile. Over the succeeding generations, the species of fish favored by Jews and the ways in which fish was popularly prepared became dependent upon where people lived. Certain species of fish and certain ways to prepare fish became particularly associated with Jewish cookery.

During the First and Second Temple periods, the Sea of Galilee (Yam Kinneret in Hebrew, Israel's only freshwater lake and the lowest freshwater lake on earth), the Mediterranean Sea, and the Jordan River provided a plentiful supply of fish. Anyone who could travel to any body of water was free to fish there. The prominence of aquatic creatures is confirmed by the large number of fish bones that have been unearthed in various Jerusalem archeological sites. One of the gates of Jerusalem was called the Fish Gate in reference to the adjoining fish market. The profusion of references to fish and fishermen in both the Jerusalem and Babylonian Talmud reflect the continuing importance of fish. The abundance of fish in the rivers and canals of Babylon made them a valuable source of protein, which was available to even the very poor.

Those living close to the Mediterranean and Arabian seas made use of saltwater fish, such as anchovies, bass, cod, flounder, haddock, halibut, mackerel, red mullet, sardines, smelts, and sole. Sea bass, which can grow up to twenty pounds and is delicately flavored and firm fleshed, is particularly beloved by Mediterranean Jews. Favorite ways of preparing fish in the eastern Mediterranean include stewed, grilled, baked (such as the Greek *Plaki*) and poached (especially in lemon-dill sauce).

German, Baltic, and Polish Jews enjoyed a plentiful supply of herring from the brackish waters of the Baltic Sea. Land-locked parts of northern Europe relied on freshwater species, most notably carp, perch, pike, smelts, and whitefish. Herring, tench, and chub were the fish of the poor; they were served along with black bread as everyday fare.

Raising fish in artificial ponds, including rock-hewn pools in Caesarea and Rosh Hanikra, has been a Jewish practice for more than two thousand years. In medieval Europe, Ashkenazim emerged as leading pisciculturists, operating fish farms in various lakes and the Black, Caspian, and Azov seas. In 1939, Kibbutz Nir-David in the Jezreel Valley introduced the first artificial fish ponds in Israel, primarily raising carp, and the country soon became the world leader in fish farming. Due to the dramatic decrease in Mediterranean fish toward the end of the twentieth century, farm-raised fish became all the more important. Besides carp, Israelis produce barramundi, rock bass, sea bass, sea bream, gray mullet, salmon, tilapia, and trout. As the amount of fresh fish increased, fish became a growing part of the Israeli diet.

In Jewish tradition, more symbolism has become attached to fish, the creatures of the hidden world (water), than almost any other food besides bread. Fish were not destroyed with the land animals during the Flood at the time of Noah and, therefore, are considered to be lacking in sin. Appended to the biblical account of the creation of the denizens of the deep was a special blessing, "Be fruitful and multiply," and fish consequently serve as a Jewish symbol of fertility and prosperity. Hence fish are common on illustrated *ketubot* (marriage documents), as well as on Middle Eastern amulets for barren women. Among Moroccans, the seventh day of *Sheva Berachot* (the seven feast days following a wedding) is called "the day of the fish"; on this occasion, the groom takes a bite from a fish, then gives the remainder to his bride, as a symbol of prospective fertility.

During the Babylonian exile, fish also became a symbol of good fortune because Pisces is the *mazel* (zodiac sign) of the month of Adar, an auspicious month for the Jews due to the events of Purim. The Talmud noted that water protected fish from the evil eye, so fish became popular for good luck charms in the Middle East. In eastern Europe, the word fish even became a name, Fishel, reflecting an optimistic belief that the boy bearing it would be lucky and protected.

Fish are not only connected to creation in the Jewish tradition, but also to the ultimate destiny as well. According to legend, the Leviathan is a giant fish that rules over all the creatures of the sea. From the beautiful skin of the Leviathan, God will, at the onset of the messianic age, construct a canopy called "the Succah of the Leviathan" to shelter the righteous from the sun. The righteous will then eat the flesh of the Leviathan in a feast amidst great joy. In this allegory, written under Roman oppression, the Leviathan symbolizes chaos, destruction, and the historical empires of Egypt, Assyria, and Rome. The myth therefore represents the ultimate destruction of despotism and evil.

As a result of the fish's accrued mystical dimensions, for millennia no Sabbath has been considered complete without it. Friday night encompasses the theme of creation and *shalosh seudot* (the third meal) at the end of the Sabbath is devoted to the subject of the messianic age, and fish as a thematic symbol appears on both occasions. A passage in the Talmud refers to fish contributing to the ambiance of the Sabbath: "Wherewith does one show delight in the Sabbath? Rav Judah the son of Samuel ben Shilath said in the name of Rav, 'With beet greens, a large fish, and garlic.' Even a trifle, if it is prepared in honor of Shabbat, is a delight. What is it [a trifle]? Rav Papa said, 'A chopped fish casserole.'" Some commentators posit that the three items mentioned by Rav Judah are aphrodisiacs, echoing the fertility aspect of fish.

Israel Zangwill, in his tale of Jewish life in London, *Children of the Ghetto* (1892), described Jewish cookery: "Fish was indeed the staple of the meal. Fried fish, and such fried fish! With the audacity of true culinary genius, Jewish fried fish is always served cold. The skin is a beautiful brown, the substance firm and succulent . . . and there is even gefullte Fisch, which is stuffed fish without bones—but fried fish reigns above all in cold, unquestioned superiority."

On Rosh Hashanah, fish contains a multiplicity of symbolic meanings, including creation and the hope for a fruitful future. Among the most well-known Rosh

Hashanah traditions is the presence of a fish head on the table to indicate that one should be "a head rather than a tail" during the coming year. Moroccans poach or bake a whole white-fleshed fish with the head attached for the occasion. Italians eat sweet-and-sour fish on the New Year, while Alsatians offer a version with carp and raisins. Greeks start their year with *plaki* (baked fish with tomatoes). Indian Jews serve fish rubbed with masala (curry) and baked in a tandoor oven, or fillets poached in romaine lettuce leaves. Iraqi Jews, however, avoid fish on Rosh Hashanah altogether, since its Hebrew name, *dag*, is similar to *da'ag* (to worry).

Fish is also traditional among many communities for breaking the fast of Yom Kippur: cold fried fish for some Sephardim, poached fish seasoned with lemon among Greeks and Turks, herring and potato salad among the Dutch, and pickled fish for many Ashkenazim. Some communities follow an ancient custom of placing cooked fish on the Passover table during the Seder in honor of Miriam, who supported her brother Moses alongside two bodies of waters—the Nile and the Red Sea—and through whose merit the Jews received water during their forty-year stay in the wilderness. Fish is common on Shavuot, as the meals are frequently dairy.

Sephardim also usually serve fish, notably fried flounder (*peshkado frito*), for Thursday night dinner, which was customarily a meatless meal before the Sabbath. Weekday fish dishes tend to be warm, while those meant for the Sabbath are generally cold. In modern Israel, the fried fish served for Thursday dinner became known as *dag Moshe rabbeinu* (fish of Moses, our teacher).

In addition to its various mystical meanings, fish offers several practical elements for the Jewish home, most notably that it is pareve and it does not require ritual slaughter or preparation, such as soaking and salting. Reflecting the relative simplicity of the kosher status of fish, the *Shulchan Arukh* (the codification of Jewish laws par excellence written by Joseph Caro c. 1565) devoted only a single chapter to it, while the various issues surrounding meat and poultry required nearly a hundred chapters.

FLAMMEKUECHE
Flammekueche is a thin tart with cheese filling.
Origin: Alsace, France
Other names: *tarte flambée.*

Flammekueche, which literally means "flamed cake" or "cooked in flames," is an Alsatian classic born of frugality and expediency in the nineteenth century among the peasants of Bas Rhin. Housewives typically baked bread once a week; in Jewish households, the bread was baked on Thursday or Friday for the Sabbath. The women, their time otherwise occupied with numerous tasks, would use a little of the dough along with a few other handy pantry items to make a quick and filling lunch or dinner for the family, while testing the heat of the wood-fired oven. After the logs had been burning in the oven, the embers would be brushed aside and a thin tart would be placed on the oven floor in order to judge the temperature before inserting the precious loaves of bread. If the oven was hot enough, within a minute or two, the thin crust would be baked and the edges would be nearly blackened—hence the name of the tart. After the loaves of bread were baked and pulled from the oven, the heat would gradually fade and various treats for the family would be baked, such as a kugelhopf or *zimtkuchen* (cinnamon cookies).

Flammekueche became so beloved that it was prepared in its own right in homes throughout the week, as well as offered on the menu of restaurants; some cooks made versions without yeast and others substituted puff pastry for the bread dough. The dough is stretched thin, like a pizza, then spread with fromage blanc (similar to the German *quark*) and cream and sometimes sprinkled with a bit of pepper or nutmeg. Today, some cooks substitute the French crème fraîche for some or all of the Teutonic fromage blanc. Whereas non-Jews topped their versions with smoked bacon, Jews always whipped up a *vegetarienne* (vegetarian) version by substituting mushrooms. *Flammekueche* is still baked at a very hot temperature, ensuring crispy edges, then cut into serving slices akin to a pizza. Some people roll a wedge from the crust end to the point, then eat the roll from end to end.

❦ ALSATIAN CHEESE TART (*FLAMMEKUECHE*)
8 SERVINGS AS AN APPETIZER OR 4 AS A MAIN COURSE [DAIRY]
Dough:
  1 package (2¼ teaspoons) active dry yeast or
    1 (0.6-ounce) cake fresh yeast
  ¾ cup plus 2 tablespoons warm water (105°F to
    115°F for dry yeast; 80°F to 85°F for fresh yeast);
    or ½ cup plus 2 tablespoons water and ¼ cup

beer; or ¼ cup water, ¼ cup beer, and
6 tablespoons milk
1 teaspoon sugar
1 large egg
2 tablespoons vegetable oil or shortening
1 teaspoon table salt or 2 teaspoons kosher salt
About 2¼ cups (11.25 ounces) bread or unbleached
all-purpose flour

Topping:
2 tablespoons vegetable oil
1 medium onion, chopped
1 pound mushrooms, sliced
½ cup plus 2 tablespoons (5 ounces) crème fraîche
or sour cream
½ cup (4 ounces) fromage blanc, *quark*, *gevina
levana* (Israeli white cheese), or farmer cheese
About ½ teaspoon table salt or 1 teaspoon kosher
salt
About ¼ teaspoon ground white or black pepper
and/or 4 pinches of ground nutmeg

1. To make the dough: Dissolve the yeast in ¼ cup
water. Stir in the sugar and let stand until foamy, 5 to
10 minutes. In a large bowl, combine the yeast mixture, remaining water, egg, oil, salt, and 1 cup flour.
Gradually add enough of the remaining flour to make
a mixture that holds together.

2. On a lightly floured surface, knead the dough
until smooth and elastic, about 10 minutes. Place in
an oiled bowl and turn to coat. Cover loosely with
plastic wrap or a kitchen towel and let rise in a warm,
draft-free place until doubled in bulk, about 1½ hours.

3. To make the topping: In a large skillet, heat the
oil over medium heat. Add the onion and sauté until
slightly golden, about 15 minutes. Add the mushrooms
and sauté until tender, about 7 minutes. Let cool.

4. Preheat the oven to 450°F.

5. Line a 15½-by-10½-by-1-inch or 12-inch square
baking sheet with parchment paper or grease the
sheet. Or use a large baking stone. Punch down the
dough and knead briefly. Let stand for 10 minutes,
then on a lightly floured surface, roll out to fit the baking sheet. Or divide the dough in half and roll each
into a 9½-inch round. Transfer the dough to the baking sheet.

6. Combine the crème fraîche, cheese, salt, and
pepper. Spread evenly over the dough, leaving a rim
around the outside. Sprinkle the mushrooms and
onions over the top.

7. Bake until the edges are browned and the topping
is bubbly, about 20 minutes on a baking sheet and
about 12 minutes on a baking stone. Cut into wedges
and serve hot.

FLAN

Flan is a baked custard which sometimes features a
caramelized sugar base. When the custard is inverted
to serve, the caramel becomes a sauce.

Origin: Spain

Other names: French: crème caramel, *crème ren-
versée*: Spanish: *flan de huevo, leche flan*.

The ancient Romans understood the binding
capacity of eggs; they were the first known to cook
them with milk and honey into various custard-like
dishes. The Roman writer Apicius included in his
cookbook (compiled c. 400 CE) one sweet custard,
tiropatinam. He directed, "Take enough milk for the
baking dish, mix the milk with honey like for a milk
dish, add five eggs for a *sextarius* [about 2.4 cups],
three for a half *sextarius*, mix until fully integrated,
strain through a clay vessel and cook gently; when
firm sprinkle with pepper and serve." Most of Apicius'
rudimentary custards, however, were savory. In addition, most of the Roman egg dishes were made with
wine, fruit purees, or other various liquids, rather
than milk, and contained poultry, seafood, or other
proteins.

After the fall of Rome, many of its foods and cooking
techniques vanished from Europe and, subsequently,
soft cheese was commonly paired with eggs in creamy
cooked dishes instead of milk. Medieval cheese "custards" were typically baked in open pastry shells,
such as the Italian *crostata* and fourteenth-century
Anglo-French *crustade*, which around the beginning
of the eighteenth century became the source of the
English word custard. Another western European
cheese tart, the *flaon*, gave rise to the Spanish word
for custard, flan.

Meanwhile, in the medieval Arab world, probably
Spain, cooks discovered how to make a more delicate
and subtly sweet custard by blending eggs, cream, and
sugar, and baking it in an earthenware dish instead of
pastry; this custard was called *leche flan* (milk custard). By the end of the sixteenth century, the English followed suit, using milk and sugar and baking
the custard without a crust. Unlike the English, who

used the word custard, most other Europeans never developed a specific word for the dish. Early sweet custards were typically flavored with wine, brandy, or spices (vanilla only emerged in European cooking in the mid-nineteenth century). In addition to sweetening the custard, Moorish cooks also lined the baking dish with a thin covering of caramelized sugar. Many cooks prepare flan in a special round metal mold with a lid; this mold can be used in the oven or in a double boiler on the stovetop.

Sephardim enjoyed various *leche flans* at dairy occasions and pareve flans at either meat or milk meals; modern cooks sometimes replace cow's milk with soy milk. In *flan de naranjas*, the favorite Sephardic type of sweet custard, orange juice is substituted for the milk. Orange flan remains a popular dessert, especially on Passover. The custard is frequently made with the remaining egg yolks after the egg whites go into a sponge cake.

SEPHARDIC BAKED MATZA CUSTARD
(*FLAN DE PESSAH/PEETE DE CHE*)

6 TO 8 SERVINGS   [DAIRY]

5 large eggs, 7 large egg yolks, or 2 large eggs and
    4 large egg yolks
3 cups whole milk or half-and-half, or 1½ cups
    heavy cream and 1½ cups whole milk
½ cup sugar
1½ teaspoons vanilla extract
⅛ teaspoon table salt or ¼ teaspoon kosher salt
About 1 cup crushed matza
¾ teaspoon ground cinnamon or ¼ teaspoon
    ground nutmeg (optional)

1. Preheat the oven to 325°F. Place a kitchen towel in the bottom of a large baking pan. Grease a 1½-quart baking dish or six ¾-cup or eight ½-cup custard cups or ramekins.

2. In a large bowl, beat the eggs. Blend in the milk, sugar, vanilla, and salt. Pour into the prepared dish or cups. Sprinkle with the matza and, if using, cinnamon.

3. Set the baking dish or cups in the baking pan, add hot water to reach halfway up the sides, and cover loosely with aluminum foil.

4. Bake until the custard is set but the center trembles, about 50 minutes for cups or about 1¼ hours for a baking dish. The custard firms more as it chills. Remove the baking dish or cups from the water. Let cool for 1 hour, then cover and refrigerate for at least

4 hours. The custard can be prepared up to 2 days ahead.

FLANKEN

Flanken, from the German word meaning "side/flank," is used in Yiddish for the short ribs, the lower section (sixth, seventh, and eighth ribs) of the chuck ribs. The upper part surrounds the rib eye; the scrap bones from trimming rib-eye steaks are called beef back ribs. The chuck short ribs are leaner but less tender than those from the plate, which is below the rib section. Short ribs that are cut across the bone and grain into strips about two inches thick are called flanken, brust flanken, and cross-cut short ribs. When cut with the grain and parallel to the bone, they are called English short ribs. In the 1950s, the term flanken—first mentioned in 1951 in both *Commentary* ("How can a Jew be expected to carry on without boiled beef flanken and chopped chicken liver?") and the *New York Times*—entered American English and became common among non-Jewish butchers and cookbook writers as well.

Flanken is a fatty cut and contains a large amount of connective tissue, making it a very flavorful cut when braised or slow-simmered. Browning the meat imparts additional flavor as well as color. The ribs are usually cooked with aromatic vegetables (onions, garlic, carrots, and celery) to round out the flavors.

In Europe, flanken was among the cheapest and least desirable cuts; consequently, it became popular holiday and Sabbath fare. In America, it became a mainstay of the deli and for many it was a favorite comfort food. Ashkenazim cook flanken plain, which is called *gedempte flanken* (boiled beef), or in soups (barley, borscht, cabbage, and split pea), cholent (Sabbath stew), and tzimmes. For very special occasions, flanken was sometimes cooked topped with stuffed cabbage and meatballs, then boned, cut into pieces, and served with the cabbage and meatballs. Many people serve flanken with horseradish as a condiment and kasha varnishkes, farfel, or potatoes as a side dish.

FLEISHIG

The Yiddish adjective *fleishig* or *fleyshik* is derived from the Middle High German word for meat (*fleish/fleysh*). It denotes food that contains kosher meat, including ruminants and poultry, or utensils with which hot meat or poultry have come into contact (the heat causes absorption of the meat). The equivalent term in Hebrew is *basari*. Any dish that contains meat items is a *fleishig* dish and any meal that contains any meat foods is a *fleishig* meal. Eggs found inside a slaughtered chicken are called *fleishig* eggs and considered to be a meat food. Homes that maintain the dietary laws typically have a separate set of dishes on which to serve *fleishig* foods and set of utensils with which to cook them. Since the late nineteenth century, the color red has typically been used to designate *fleishig* soap, utensils, and sometimes kitchen towels.

FLUDEN

Fluden is a layered pastry with a filling.
Origin: France
Other names: Hungarian: *flodni*; Romanian: *flandi*.

Ancient Romans enjoyed a variety of savory and sweet curd cheese dishes cooked in dough casings—including *tracta*, a dough rolled out to make pastries. Both the Jerusalem Talmud and Babylonian Talmud mention *t'rahkta* and *troknin* (*tracta*), although the Babylonians were unfamiliar with the exact nature of the dish. In Judea, which was under Roman domination, a pastry with an upper and lower crust of *tracta* became traditional Sabbath fare. The Talmud fails to mention the nature of the fillings. These outer dough layers came to represent the double portion of manna collected for the Sabbath, as well as the lower and upper layers of dew that protected the manna. The culinary practice of preparing covered pastries for the Sabbath was adopted by Italians, Sephardim, and later Franco-Germans, most notably in the Ashkenazic *pashtida* (meat-filled pies) and the favorite dessert of the early Ashkenazim, *fluden*, which originated amond the Jews of France.

Fluden initially consisted of layers of dough sandwiching a honey-sweetened cheese filling. The name derived from the Late Latin *fladon* (flat cake), itself from the Old High German word *flado* (flat cake), which is also the source of the name of the French flan (an open-faced tart) and Spanish flan (baked custard). The medieval Ashkenazic *fluden*, however, was quite different than the Teutonic *flado*. A hard, thick, pastry evolved into one with thinner layers of buttery pastry (*muerberteig*) or rich yeast dough (*heifeteig*), the pastry cut into sections to serve.

The earliest record of *fluden* occurred in the writings of Rabbi Gershom ben Judah of Mainz (a city on the Rhine River) around the year 1000 CE, in which he discussed an argument between his teacher Rabbi Judah Hacohain ben Meir Leontin (from Lyons, France) and Rabbi Eleazar ben Gilo over whether it was permitted "to eat bread with meat if it [the bread] was baked in an oven with a cheese dish called fluden," and rendering the bread *milchig*. Since this disagreement persisted for centuries, similar references appear in rabbinic writings on a frequent basis throughout the period. In any case, by the year 1000, cheese *fluden* was already widespread throughout the Jews of France and western Germany.

The original cheese version became a traditional Sabbath and Rosh Hashanah treat. Until the sixteenth century, Ashkenazim did not wait between eating meat and dairy, but merely cleared the table and rinsed out their mouths, so a cheese *fluden* could be served as dessert soon after a meat meal. On Shavuot, a large cheese *fluden*, sometimes called Mount Sinai cake, was traditionally garnished with white flowers as a symbol of purity and of the blossoms that flourished on the mountain during the giving of the Torah. Cooks eventually developed several other fillings besides cheese, as it was not always available or affordable. Apples or raisins, sometimes combined with cheese, became traditional on Sukkot and Simchat Torah. Jam, nut, fig, and poppy seed fillings were used on other festivals. All these variations were also commonplace on the Sabbath. For Purim, some people cut the *fluden* into triangles.

Alsatians prepare a dish, called *schalet à la Juive* in the *Larousse Gastronomique*, that is similar to the original apple *fluden*. It is a sort of deep-dish apple pie made with layers of flaky pastry; they also make a variation, called *apfelschalet* or *apfelbuwele* (apple boy), consisting of the apple filling rolled up in the dough.

With the destruction of the Franco-German Jewish communities—precipitated by the massacres in the wake of the Black Death (1348–1350) and the expulsion of the remaining Jews from France in 1394—the popularity of *fluden*, particularly cheese *fluden*, declined. One reason for this change was when the eastern Ashkenazim began upholding the tradition of waiting six hours after eating meat before eating dairy, and by German Jews of the custom of waiting three hours; these stringencies effectively ended the use of dairy desserts on the Sabbath and festivals. Some eastern Europeans even transferred the term *fluden* to a beef stew containing fruit. However, descendants of cheese *fluden* are still served by some Ashkenazim with a revamped pastry and filling. In parts of Galicia (now southern Poland) and Ukraine, apple *fluden* remained a traditional Simchat Torah treat; pieces were presented to the children in the synagogue after the en masse Torah reading.

It was primarily among Hungarians and Romanians that *fluden* continued to flourish. Romanians serve *flandi* on Rosh Hashanah and Purim. Passover versions are made by soaking whole matzas until softened and layering them with fillings or different-colored almond pastes. Some Romanians and Hungarians began referring to a strudel made from *muerberteig* as a *fluden*. In addition, some Hungarians use the word *fluden* to refer to a version of *farfel torten*—a cookie bar consisting of a pastry base topped by layers of jam, ground nuts, and meringue. All Hungarians enjoy what they call *flodni*, a dessert typically consisting of three to five pastry layers. When topped with chocolate icing, it is known as *zserbo* or *jerbeau*, after the Emile Gerbeaud pastry shop in Budapest. A Budapest specialty is a *flodni* with a diverse trio of fillings, one for each layer—apples, ground nuts, and poppy seeds. Of the scores of kosher bakeries and cafés that once flourished in Budapest, today only the small Fröhlich Cukrászda, which opened in 1954, survives; it sells traditional Hungarian Jewish baked goods, notably *flodni*. In Hungary, this type of *fluden* remains ubiquitous at weddings and other special occasions.

In general, *fluden* failed to make any significant impact in America, perhaps because it was replaced with the similar but easier apple pie. Early American Jewish cookbooks omit any reference to *fluden*, but around the mid-twentieth century, the dish began to make an appearance in America, reflecting a growing Hungarian presence. The *fluden* in *The Jewish Examiner Prize Kosher Recipe Book* (Brooklyn, 1937) consisted of eighteen thin pastry layers and was filled with raisins and ground walnuts. A 2005 article in the *New York Times* featured a Passover "Cashew Nut Strudel with Guava and Lime (Fluden de Pasach)" from Brazil, which was made from matza meal and ground roasted cashews and filled with guava paste.

ASHKENAZIC LAYERED CHEESE PASTRY
(KAESE FLUDEN)

12 TO 24 SERVINGS [DAIRY]

Dough:

4½ cups (22.5 ounces) all-purpose flour

2¼ teaspoons double-acting baking powder

¾ teaspoon salt

½ cup sugar

1½ cups shortening, or 1 cup shortening and ½ cup chilled butter

4 large egg yolks, or 2 large egg yolks and 1 large egg

About 6 tablespoons water, or 3 tablespoons water and 3 tablespoons milk, sour cream, orange juice, or sweet wine

2 teaspoons white wine vinegar, mild cider vinegar, or lemon juice

Filling:

4 cups (2 pounds) pot, farmer, or drained ricotta cheese, or 1 cup sour cream, quark, or gevina levana

4 large egg yolks

About 1 cup sugar

¼ cup all-purpose flour or ½ cup fine semolina or farina

2 teaspoons vanilla extract or 1 tablespoon grated lemon zest

Pinch of salt

½ to 1 cup (3 to 5 ounces) golden raisins (optional)

Egg wash (1 large egg beaten with 1 tablespoon water)

About ⅓ cup sugar, or ⅓ cup sugar mixed with 1 teaspoon ground cinnamon, for sprinkling

1. To make the dough: In a large bowl, sift together the flour, baking powder, and salt. Mix in the sugar. Cut in the butter to resemble coarse crumbs. Combine the egg yolks, water, and vinegar. Stir into the flour mixture until the dough just holds together. Form into a ball. On a lightly floured surface, roll the dough into a rectangle with the narrow end facing you. Fold the top third of the dough toward you, then fold the bottom third upward. Turn the dough 90 degrees so that a narrow end faces front and, using a rolling pin, roll into a rectangle. Fold in thirds again. Press to hold together. Wrap in plastic wrap and refrigerate for at least 4 hours or up to 4 days, or store in the freezer for up to 2 months. Let stand at room temperature until malleable but not soft, about 30 minutes.

2. Preheat the oven to 350°F (325°F if using a glass pan). Grease a 13-by-9-inch baking pan.

3. To make the filling: In a large bowl, combine all the filling ingredients.

4. Cut the dough rectangle into four equal pieces. Place the dough pieces on a lightly floured surface and, using a floured rolling pin, roll out each piece into a 13-by-9-inch rectangle. Fit a dough rectangle into the prepared pan and spread with one-third of the filling. Repeat the layering with the remaining dough and filling, ending with a layer of dough. Brush the top with the egg wash and lightly sprinkle with the sugar. Using the tines of a fork, prick the top repeatedly to vent the steam.

5. Bake until golden brown, about 45 minutes. Place the pan on a wire rack and let cool for at least 1 hour. Cover and store at room temperature for up to 1 day or in the refrigerator for up to 5 days.

VARIATIONS

Ashkenazic Layered Apple Pastry (Apfel Fluden): Combine 10 peeled, cored, and grated large apples, 16 ounces apricot preserves or orange marmalade (or ½ cup honey), ½ cup cake, cookie, or bread crumbs, 1 cup chopped walnuts or almonds, and, if desired, 1 cup raisins and/or 2 teaspoons grated lemon zest, and substitute for the cheese filling.

FORSHMAK

Forshmak is salt-cured herring that is soaked, chopped, and mixed with other ingredients. It is served hot and cold.

Origin: Ukraine

Herring became an important part of Ashkenazic cookery, although it was almost never found fresh. By the time the herring, pulled from the distant Baltic Sea or the Atlantic Ocean, reached the Jewish cook in eastern Europe, it had been cured with salt to extract the moisture, in a preserving process akin to that utilized for preparing the Mediterranean *bacalao/bakala* (salt cod). Before they could be used, the cured fillets had to be soaked to remove the excess salt, then flavored in some way. To make the well-known dish pickled herring, cooks marinated the refreshed fish in a vinegar-sugar bath, to which they typically also added sliced raw onions, bay leaves, and peppercorns. An alternative to pickling was to chop the refreshed fillets with various ingredients; in the Ukraine, this dish was called *forshmak* (literally "foretaste," from

the archaic German *Vorschmack*), reflecting a Teutonic origin and possibly indicating that Jews were the source of its transmission eastward.

Unlike Polish and Lithuanian *gehakte herring* (chopped herring), which was always served cold and accented with raw onions, Ukrainians served their versions either cold or hot. Hot *forshmak* was typically enhanced with sautéed onions and sometimes tart apple, bread, and/or hard-boiled eggs were mixed in. Potatoes became a common addition in the late nineteenth century. Due to a medieval Sephardic and Ashkenazic tradition of not eating meat and fish together, Jews did not emulate the widespread Russian manner of combining chopped herring with chopped meat in their *forshmak*. *Forshmak* is eaten either as an appetizer or, accompanied with boiled potatoes, as a main course. Cold *forshmak* was a typical Sabbath appetizer and it was once common at the Saturday morning kiddush after synagogue services; it is eaten with crackers or lightly sugared *kichlach* (egg cookies).

🦢 UKRAINIAN CHOPPED SALT HERRING (*FORSHMAK*)

4 TO 6 SERVINGS [DAIRY]

4 salt herring fillets
4 slices white bread, crusts trimmed
⅔ cup milk or water
¼ cup (½ stick) unsalted butter
2 medium onions, chopped
1 large tart apple, peeled and cored
1 cup sour cream

1. Soak the herring in water to cover, changing the water twice, for 12 hours. Drain.

2. Soak the bread in the milk for about 5 minutes, then squeeze dry.

3. Preheat the oven to 375°F. Grease a 2-quart baking dish.

4. In a large skillet, heat the butter over medium heat. Add the onions and sauté until soft and translucent, 5 to 10 minutes. Remove from the heat.

5. Using a knife, meat grinder, or a food processor fitted with a metal blade, finely chop the herring. Add the onions, bread, and apple and finely chop. Stir in the sour cream. Transfer to the prepared dish.

6. Bake until golden, about 25 minutes. Serve hot.

FORSPEIS/FORSPEIZEN

Forspeis, from the German *vorspeisen* (before food), is the Yiddish term for appetizer. Unlike a Middle

Eastern *mezze* (appetizer assortment) or Sephardic *desayuno* (brunch) with its many small foods, the *forspeis* served by Ashkenazic Jews reflects the Teutonic practice of serving one large first course to inaugurate the *seudah* (meal).

The typical Ashkenazic Sabbath and festival meal begins with a *forspeis*, which may be a specially created pastry, such as a knish or *piroshki*; a chopped bread spread, such as liver, egg salad, black radish, or herring; a fish appetizer, such as gefilte fish or jellied fish; or a smaller portion of a main course, such as offal or stuffed cabbage. The soup and then the main course are served after the *forspeis*.

FOULARE/FOLAR

Foulare is a sweet pastry enwrapping a hard-boiled egg or a Sephardic long-cooked egg.

Origin: Iberia

Other names: Greek: *folariko*; Italian: *scalera*.

For a special treat, Sephardim enwrap *huevos haminados* (long-cooked eggs) or plain hard-boiled eggs in sweet yeast dough; as the pastries bake, the eggs bake into the dough. The dish is called *foulare*, which is Ladino for "scarf/enwrapping." Cooks take great pride in the artistry of these pastries, frequently creating a different design for every family member. Each person removes the egg from the pastry, then peels and eats it as well as the sweet bread.

The name of the eggs, *haminados*, sounds similar to that of the evil Persian prime minister, Haman, in the Purim story and—analogous to the Ashkenazic hamantaschen—eggs are referred to as *huevos de Haman* (Haman's eggs). The pastry-wrapped eggs are traditionally served on Purim as well as the Sabbath preceding it, *Shabbat Zakhor*, when the weekly Torah portion mentions Haman's ancestor, Amalek. Consequently, *Shabbat Zakhor* is referred to as *Shabbat de Foulares*. For Purim, the shape of the pastry is meant to symbolize either Haman's prison bars (a basket with strips over the top of the egg) and/or parts of his anatomy (Haman's foot and Haman's ear). The pastries are first displayed on fancy plates before being consumed by children and adults, usually for Purim breakfast, as few can wait. *Foulares* may also be included among the food gifts in a Sephardic Purim *misholach manot* (sent portions).

It is also customary to serve *foulares* to honor a newborn child; different shapes are prepared for males and females.

TURKISH "HAMAN'S EGG" YEAST PASTRIES

(*FOULARES/HUEVOS DE HAMAN*)

12 PASTRIES   [PAREVE]

1¼ teaspoons active dry yeast or ½ (0.6-ounce) cake fresh yeast

½ cup warm water (105°F to 115°F for dry yeast; 80°F to 85°F for fresh yeast)

3 tablespoons sugar

¼ cup vegetable, olive, or peanut oil

1 large egg

½ teaspoon table salt or 1 teaspoon kosher salt

About 2 cups (10 ounces) bread or unbleached all-purpose flour

12 *huevos haminados* (Sephardic Long-Cooked Eggs, page 253) or hard-boiled eggs in their shells

Egg wash (1 large egg beaten with 1 teaspoon water)

1. Dissolve the yeast in ¼ cup water. Stir in 1 teaspoon sugar and let stand until foamy, 5 to 10 minutes. In a large bowl, combine the yeast mixture, remaining water, remaining sugar, oil, egg, and salt. Blend in 1 cup flour. Gradually add enough of the remaining flour to make a mixture that holds together.

2. On a lightly floured surface or in an electric mixer with a dough hook, knead the dough until smooth and springy, about 5 minutes. Place in an oiled bowl and turn to coat. Cover loosely with plastic wrap or a kitchen towel and let rise in a warm, draft-free place until nearly doubled in bulk, about 2 hours.

3. Line a large baking sheet with parchment paper or grease the sheet. Punch down the dough. On a lightly floured surface, roll out the dough ¼ inch thick. Cut out 3-inch rounds. Cut the remaining dough into thin strips. Place 1 egg, large end down, on each round and bring up the edges of the base to form a cup. Use several dough strips to secure the eggs to the bases. Place the pastries on the baking sheet. cover with a kitchen towel, and let rise until doubled in bulk, about 1 hour.

4. Preheat the oven to 350°F.

5. Brush the dough with the egg wash. Bake until golden brown, about 35 minutes. Transfer the foulares to a wire rack and let cool.

FOURMA

Fourma is a meat pie or omelet.

Origin: Tunisia

Meat omelets and casseroles are a prominent component of Sephardic cuisine. The name of this large Tunisian dish is derived from the French *forme* (shape/form). It is either cooked in a skillet over a brazier or flame, or baked in a ovenproof dish in the oven. A version with rice is a traditional Passover dish; it is served as a main course accompanied with salads and matza (or bread during the rest of the year) or as an appetizer.

ᙎ TUNISIAN MEAT OMELET-PIE (*FOURMA À LA VIANDE*)

6 TO 8 SERVINGS [MEAT]

3 tablespoons vegetable oil
8 ounces ground lamb, beef, or veal
1 small onion, chopped
1 clove garlic, minced
2 cups cooked long-grain rice or tagliatelle
10 large eggs, lightly beaten
About 1 teaspoon table salt or 2 teaspoons kosher salt
Ground black pepper to taste
¼ cup chopped fresh flat-leaf parsley (optional)
2 hard-boiled eggs, chopped

1. In a large skillet, heat 2 tablespoons oil over medium heat. Add the beef, onion, and garlic and sauté until the meat loses its red color, about 5 minutes. Stir in the rice and let cool. Add the raw eggs, salt, pepper, and, if using, parsley. Gently stir in the hard-boiled eggs.

2. In a large skillet, heat the remaining 1 tablespoon oil over low heat. Add the egg mixture, cover, and cook until the top firms, about 25 minutes.

3. Loosen the sides, slide onto a large plate, and invert back into the skillet, browned side up. Cover and cook until set, about 10 minutes. Serve hot or at room temperature.

FRESS

Fress, from the German *fress* (devour), is the Yiddish word for "eat a lot." A *fresser* is a person who eats a lot.

FRICASSEE

Fricassee refers to a dish in which bone-in meat (usually chicken) is cut into chunks, browned in fat with onions, and then slowly simmered in a small amount of liquid. As a verb, to fricassee means to prepare meat in a fricassee.
Origin: Spain, France
Other names: Ladino: *armico de pollo, pollo sofrito*; Morocco: *fricassada*.

In *Everything But Money* (1966), humorist Sam Levenson reminisced about his childhood in 1920s Brooklyn, noting, "There was also fricassee of chicken livers, fricassee of hearts, fricassee of necks, fricassee of chicken feet, fricassee of fricassee."

A popular dish in medieval Spain was *olla poderida* (powerful pot), an intensely flavored stew derived from the Sephardic Sabbath stew. Using a technique typical of Moorish and Sephardic cuisine, the cook browned the meat and poultry along with onions in olive oil, added water and flavorings, and then simmered the stew. The French adapted the dish, calling it *potpourri*. A particular form of the braised stew featured pieces of one type of either meat or poultry, and was referred to as *fricassée*, from the Old French *frire* (to fry) and *casser* (to break). The French term *friquassée* was originally recorded in 1485 in the first printed edition of *Le Viandier* (this was an altered version of a French manuscript from around 1300). The recipe in this book called for a cut-up chicken and chopped onion fried in lard; these were simmered in beef stock with ginger and verjuice (juice of unripe grapes).

Chicken fricassees along with the name became common in many cuisines, as they were an ideal way to tenderize older birds and produce a richer sauce; they could also be cooked over a fire, which was an advantage because few families possessed a home oven. The famous French dish coq au vin is simply a fricassee with red wine. In many countries, the term fricassee came to refer specifically to braised chicken with mushrooms in a white sauce made from cream. Since at least the sixteenth century, Germans have prepared a dish called *hühnerfrikassee*, which makes use of chicken giblets (*hühnerklein*) and other small pieces and is simmered in a cream sauce. This concept was foreign to European Jews, who used schmaltz instead of lard and thickened the sauce with only flour and no cream. Italian Jews created a form of fricassee called *ngozzamodi di pollo con polpotte*, consisting of odds and ends of chicken along with chicken meatballs and minus any cream.

The term fricassee probably entered Ashkenazic cookery in western Germany shortly after the Peace of Westphalia (1648), which increased contacts with the French, and then spread eastward, where it also became known as *gehahkteh hindel*. Ashkenazim, who utilized every part of the chicken, simmered the odds and ends—*pupiks* (gizzards), *gorglach* (necks), *fliege-*

lach (wing tips), and *fisselach* (feet)—into a hearty dish for Friday night dinner, at which it was served as either an appetizer or a main course. Cooks were able to stretch the dish by using the unattractive and less fleshy parts of the bird; as a result, a single chicken or even a few parts of one, along with a starch, could easily and amply feed a large family. Less frequently, fricassees were made from goose and veal. Chicken fricassee remains a standard Alsatian Sabbath dinner. Moroccans make a version introduced during the French colonization of the Maghreb, which is accented with cinnamon and turmeric.

In the first Jewish cookbook in English, *The Jewish Manual* (1846), the author's husband from a Sephardic background, offered an expanded definition of fricassee: "This is a name used for delicate stews, when the articles are cut in pieces." Braised versions are referred to in *The Jewish Manual* as "brown fricassee," while any foregoing this step are called "white fricassee." The author's fricassees are made from veal and not poultry. Already found in this work was the addition of meatballs, in this case encasing a hard-boiled egg.

The first American record of this term associated with Jews was in *Jennie June's American Cookery Book* (1866) by Jane Cunningham Croly in a section of "Jewish Receipts." Her recipe for "Brown Fricassee Chicken" directed: "Take a chicken, cut it up in pieces and fry them brown, either in the best sweet oil or rendered fat. Then take six onions, slice them and cover them in frying-pan with enough oil or fat to fry them; when soft take the cover off, so as to let them brown, then scald and peal two tomatoes, cut them up and put them in the pan with the onions to simmer a little. Put the fried chicken into a saucepan with the onions etc., add a little thyme, pepper, salt and a few grams of allspice, and enough hot water to make a rich gravy; cover it up and let it cook for half an hour or an hour, according to the tenderness of the chicken; a very small piece of garlic and mace can be added when cooking, if liked." Tomatoes would become a common addition to fricassees in America. Soon thereafter, the first Jewish cookbook in America, *Jewish Cookery* (1871) by Esther Levy, offered a recipe "To Fricassee Chicken," which was a white fricassee, in which readers were instructed: "Cut the chicken up, and lay the pieces in a saucepan, with enough water to cover them; season it well; after it has boiled a few minutes, skim the surface, and add pepper. When the chicken is boiled tender, take the pieces out, and pour off the water, if there is too much for gravy. When the chickens are fat, they require no suet. Lay the chicken back in the saucepan, and thicken with flour, and see it is seasoned sufficient."

The first edition of *The Settlement Cookbook* (1901) contained recipes for "Ganseklein or Fricasseed Goose," "Veal Fricassee," and "Chicken Fricassee"; the latter, similar to the version in *Jewish Cookery*, was a basic boiled chicken dish (not braised), which called for a little celery and carrots, and was flavored with a little ground ginger and thickened with flour.

In America, until after World War II, chicken was relatively expensive and, therefore, poorer families continued to make fricassee using the odds and ends. A distinctive twentieth-century American augmentation by Ashkenazim, possibly adopted from the Italians in America, was the addition of small beef meatballs (*mit klops*) to further enhance the fricassee, because ground beef was then much cheaper than chicken. As Jews moved up the economic ladder, the amount of thigh and breast meat in the fricassee increased, but for the most part, the meatballs stayed. As certain chicken parts, notably the feet and beaks, became difficult or impossible to obtain, the main parts of the bird became necessary. In many Ashkenazic homes, housewives served the dish at special occasions. Chicken fricassee became a favorite comfort food, conjuring up images of a mother or grandmother holding sway over the stove. The ingredients and amounts in a fricassee are very informal and can be adjusted according to availability and taste—for example, adding fewer or more meatballs, using tomatoes instead of flour, adding peppers and other vegetables, adding rice, and so on. The essence of any fricassee remains the gravy, which should be rich, flavorful, and relatively thick. Fricassee is typically served with rice, noodles, barley farfel, or dumplings.

FRIMSEL

Frimsel is an egg noodle.
Origin: Western Germany, Alsace
Other names: Eastern Yiddish: *lokshen*.

By the twelfth century, a popular treat among Franco-German Jews was *vermesel* or *verimslish*, fried strips of dough in honey. This was originally an ancient Roman dish known as *vermiculos* (Latin for "little worms"), which the Talmud called *iytree* from a Persian word for string, the source of the modern Hebrew word for noodles. Shortly thereafter, the name of this fried pastry, *vermesel*, was adopted for the recently introduced boiled strips of egg dough, which are now known as noodles. Around the fourteenth century, egg noodles had become *frimsels* in Western Yiddish. The use of a Jewish term *frimsel* rather than a contemporary Teutonic one indicates that noodles probably initially reached western and central Ashkenazim via Italian Jews rather than from non-Jewish Germans.

Initially, the predominant use of noodles by Ashkenazim was in soups. By the late fifteenth century, chicken soup with noodles was replacing the fried dough *vermesel* as the first course for Ashkenazic Friday evening dinners. The first American Jewish cookbook, *Jewish Cookery* by Esther Levy (1871), provided a recipe "To Make a Good Frimsel (Or Noodle) Soup." The author suggests "frimsel soup, as that will keep best over night," as the first course for Saturday dinner (then meaning lunch). Almost the exact recipe for "Frimsel Soup" appeared, along with other Ashkenazic recipes, in a February 23, 1896, article in the *New York Times* entitled "The Shoket, and Kosher and Trefa Dishes—Where to Buy Meats," discussing Jewish food practices. The introductory sentence to the recipes read, "As our Christian readers may like to try some genuine Hebrew cookery, we give a seasonable menu, which is both economical and savory."

Eventually, the pasta came out of the soup and was transformed into a variety of noodle dishes. Alsatians love noodles, which they generally serve rather simply. A prevalent Friday night food is called *frimsels* and *spätzles*, which consists of cooking noodles, then heating two-thirds of them with butter or schmaltz, frying the remaining noodles in oil until crisp and golden, then mixing the plain and fried noodles; this dish is unknown among eastern Europeans and reflects the German influence on the culture.

Montague Glass, a lawyer and writer noted for his humorous depictions of early twentieth-century American Jewish life, in his novel *Elkan Lubliner: American* (New York, 1912), included this exchange:

"There's some dessert coming," Mrs. Lesengeld said.

"Dessert after this, Mrs. Lesengeld," he replied, through clouds of contented smoke, "would be sacrilege, ain't it?"

"That's something I couldn't make at all," Mrs. Lesengeld admitted. "All I got it here is some frimsel kugel."

"Frimsel kugel!" Scharley exclaimed, laying down his cigar. "Why ain't you told me that before?"

A quarter of an hour later he again lighted his cigar, and this time he settled back in his campstool for conversation, while Mrs. Lesengeld busied herself about the oil stove.

(See also Chremsel, Lokshen, and Pasta)

FRITADA

Fritada is a flat, thick, vegetable-laden omelet.
Origin: Spain
Other names: *cuajadas, quajados, tortilla de hueveos.*

In ancient Rome, some egg dishes were cooked in a skillet over a fire, as recorded by Apicius. One of these dishes, *ova spongia* ("sponge egg," denoting its texture), was an omelet consisting of eggs, milk, and olive oil. By the twelfth century, Sephardim would call similar omelets *tortilla de huevos* (little round of eggs), a name still common in Mexico. Later, under the influence of the Italian frittata (fried egg pie), the name changed, as there is no double *t* in Spanish, to *fritada.*

By the thirteenth century, egg and vegetable dishes were so identified with Sephardim that the Spanish Inquisition considered them a sign of Jewish cooking, which could lead to arrest. Until relatively recently, few people had a home oven, so in order to bake, most people had to use the local baker's oven. However, schlepping the dish across town or farther, and only when the baker was off duty, tended to be a major bother. Therefore, most housewives preferred cooking the egg mixture in a large skillet over a brazier, the omelet was either cooked covered or inverted after the bottom set. *Fritadas* were cut into wedges for a warm side dish or entrée, or divided into smaller squares to serve at room temperature as an appetizer.

In the nineteenth century, as the home oven became more commonplace, many cooks began to bake these large omelets like a casserole, eliminating the frying and saving a lot of bother. Initially, baking the omelets was a less common practice than frying, but today baking is the more widespread method. When the same ingredients are baked, the dish is technically a *quajado* (coagulated) or, in the Balkans, a *sfongo*. However, these terms became interchangeable in many Sephardic communities. As a result of baking, *fritadas* went from being round to frequently being square or rectangular. When made with only cheese and no vegetables, the dish is called *huevos kon keso*.

Unlike the ancient Roman *ova spongia*, *fritadas* are not so much about the eggs—which generally are used only to hold the other ingredients together—but rather a means of showcasing vegetables, and a way to use and enhance leftovers. Most also contain cheese. *Fritadas* are similar to the Persian *kuku*, although the latter are generally pareve. The Italian frittata tends to have a little more egg than the *fritada* and the French omelet has a lot more egg.

At least one, if not several, *fritadas* are commonplace at almost any Sephardic family get-together. Spinach, a favorite Passover vegetable, is the most popular *fritada* flavoring, but *fritadas* include vegetables of all sorts, notably eggplant, leeks, potatoes, tomatoes, and zucchini. The addition of bread, matza, or mashed potatoes reflects a Turkish influence. Meat omelets are popular on Passover and may also be served as a side dish at Sabbath dinner. At the Sabbath *desayuno* (brunch), cheese and vegetable *fritadas* are served at room temperature.

SEPHARDIC VEGETABLE OMELET
(*FRITADA DE VERDURAS*)

4 TO 6 SERVINGS   [DAIRY OR PAREVE]

4 large eggs, lightly beaten

½ cup dry bread crumbs, matza meal, or mashed potatoes; or 2 matzas or 2 to 3 slices white bread, soaked in water until soft but not mushy and squeezed dry

3 cups cooked cauliflower florets; 3 cups chopped cooked leeks; 1 pound boiled, peeled, and thickly sliced russet potatoes; 1 pound chopped fresh spinach or 10 ounces thawed frozen chopped spinach; 3 cups peeled, seeded, and chopped tomatoes; or 3 cups cooked coarsely grated zucchini

1 cup (4 ounces) grated kashkaval, mozzarella, Cheddar, Gouda, Muenster, or Swiss cheese, or pot cheese (optional)

About ½ teaspoon table salt or 1 teaspoon kosher salt

Ground black pepper to taste

1 tablespoon olive or vegetable oil

Yogurt for garnish (optional)

1. In a large bowl, combine the eggs, bread crumbs, vegetable of choice, optional cheese, salt, and pepper. The mixture should be slightly loose and lumpy, and not overly liquidy or smooth.

2. In a 9- to 10-inch skillet, heat the oil over medium-low. Add the egg mixture and cook, puncturing the bottom in several places to allow the liquid to seep through and lifting the sides to allow the liquid to seep under, until the eggs are set but still wet, about 4 minutes.

3. Loosen the sides, slide the *fritada* onto a large plate, and invert back into the skillet, browned side up. (Proficient cooks flip the *fritada* in the pan.) Cook the second side until set, about 3 minutes. Alternatively, for a casserole, spread the oil in an 8-inch square baking pan, place in a 375°F oven to heat for about 2 minutes, add the egg mixture, and bake until golden brown and firm, about 30 minutes.

4. Let stand at least 10 minutes. Serve warm or at room temperature. Cut into large squares or wedges. If desired, serve with dollops of yogurt.

FRITTER

A fritter is a small deep-fried cake, made from either a thick batter or from pieces of food dipped into a batter. It may be sweet or savory.

Other names: Austria: *plinz*; French: *beignet*; German: *krapfen, kuchel, pfannkuchen, puffer*; Hebrew: *mahahfay zeeloof*; Italian: *frictelle, frittelle*; Ladino: *birmuelo, frita*; Yiddish: *fritlach, fritteln*.

Frying pieces of dough in fat is an ancient method of pastry making, dating back at least 4,500 years, perhaps to the Egyptians; when the dough is fried, the moisture inside the dough puffs up the pastry and lightens it without the use of modern leavenings. Among the various types of flour offerings for the Temple, the Bible records a bread that was made by mixing fine semolina flour with olive oil, kneading the mixture with lukewarm water to make a soft unleav-

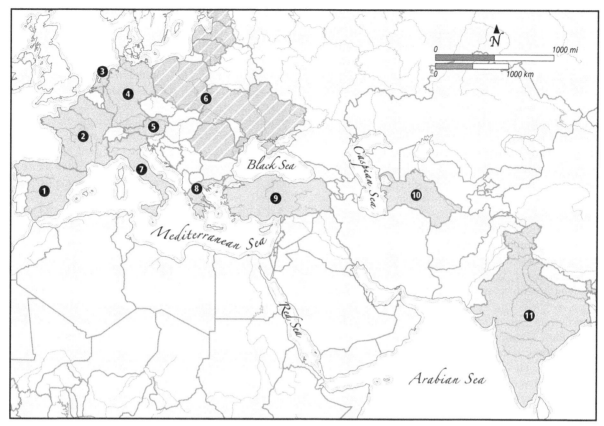

Fritters Areas with plentiful supplies of inexpensive fat deep-fry small masses of food. The names and ingredients vary from place to place.
1 **Spain**—*bimuelos, bolos, fritas*; 2 **France**—*beignet*; 3 **Netherlands**—*beignet, grimsel*; 4 **Germany**—*fritlach, pfannkuchen, krapfen*; 5 **Austria**—*plinz*; 6 **Poland, Baltic States, Ukraine, Romania**—*crimsel*; 7 **Italy**—*frittella, pizzarelle*; 8 **Greece**—*loukoumades, zvingous*; 9 **Turkey**—*lokmas*; 10 **Uzbekistan**—*samsa*; 11 **India**—*samosa, bonda, gulab jamun, malpuah*

ened dough, coating the thin loaf with additional olive oil, then frying it in a *marcheshet* (deep pan). According to commentators, this pan received its name because the dough vibrates or sizzles (*rachash*) as it cooks, making movement and sounds indicative of the frying action. An inscription from the time of Rameses III (c. 1200 BCE) depicts two cooks deep-frying strips of dough in a pot over an open fire.

Deep-fried dough was popular among Romans, who called it *globi/globuli* (balls). Cato the Elder (c. 160 BCE) recorded the method for making this dish: "Mix the [soft white] cheese and spelt flour in equal parts, sufficient to make the number desired. Pour fat into a hot copper vessel, and fry one or two at a time, turning them frequently with two spoons.

Remove when done, coat them with honey, and sprinkle poppy seeds on it. They are ready to serve." Later, the Roman cookbook author Apicius (c. 400 CE) described the making of *vermiculos* (Latin for "little worms"), deep-fried strips of dough bathed in either honey or the ubiquitous pungent Roman condiment *liquamen* (fermented fish sauce). After the fall of the Roman Empire, however, these fried doughs disappeared from much of Europe.

Meanwhile, Arabs during the early medieval period continued to fry unleavened strips of dough, and also used yeast to leaven loose doughs (creating rudimentary doughnuts). The Arabs in the seventh century also brought sugarcane westward from Persia to Egypt; sugar refining was soon mastered in Egypt, leading to an increase in sweet pastries. These techniques eventually spread to Europe. For centuries after the First Crusade (1095), Spain (under the enlightened Moors) and Italy served as the epicenters of European culinary advances, with many of these innovations gradually making their way northward. These new dishes and techniques were primarily transmitted by Jews, who traded or relocated throughout Europe, and by the Catholic clergy—many monasteries and convents retained Roman culinary techniques, as well as adopted the new ones and developed their own. Commonly, a new item would appear in an Italian source, then show up in Germany about a century or so later.

In early fourteenth-century Italy, a new technique for cooking dumplings, either sweet or savory—deep-frying—and a new term for them—*fritelle*—appeared. *Fritelle de pome* (apple fritters) were recorded in the fourteenth century, as were *fritelle* made from slices of fresh cheese and pine nuts; ones from ground elderflowers (*fiore de sambugho*); and dumplings from a dough of almond milk, flour, and starter dough. In France, these deep-fried dumplings became known as *en friture*. This led to the English word frytour and, by the seventeenth century, fritter. The Yiddish name, *fritlach*, is very different from other central European names, which suggests that this dish reached the Ashkenazim from Italy and not central Europe.

Since few households except those of the upper class possessed an oven, until relatively recently most homemade pastry tended to be fried. Along the Mediterranean and in Romania and parts of Hungary, there was an abundance of oil and, consequently, even peasants could enjoy fritters; cooks were able to transform a few inexpensive ingredients into tasty treats for both everyday and holiday fare. However, there was generally a dearth of oil in most of northern Europe, where doughs were more commonly boiled as dumplings and noodles. Therefore, among most Ashkenazim, deep-frying was rather rare, and fried pastries were generally reserved for special occasions. Many Ashkenazic fried pastries were associated with a specific holiday, in particular Passover and Hanukkah.

A fritter batter can be fried solo in lumps, mixed with various chopped ingredients, or used for coating large pieces of vegetables or fruit (*frucht fritlach*). The consistency must be thick enough so that the batter adheres to the food. The addition to the dough of olive oil and anise are a mark of a fritter's Mediterranean origins. For the fillings in coated fritters, Ashkenazim were generally limited to a few types of fruit, notably apples and cherries, while Italians enjoyed more exotic fare, such as figs, pumpkin, ricotta cheese, and rice. Sephardim use a wide range of ingredients to make various fritters, including *bolos de keso* (soft cheese fritters), *tulumbas* (boiled dough), and *bolos de pan* (bread fritters). Deep-frying is an ancient technique in India, where the Bene Israel of Mumbai make a number of fritters, including *malpuah* (banana fritters), *kaftas* (grated vegetable-and-chickpea flour fritters), and *vadas* (lentil fritters).

A widespread form of Passover fritters and pancakes is made from crumbled matza. These fritters are known as *knopfle* in parts of southern Germany and Austria, *matza crimsel* in eastern Europe, and *gremsel* or *gremselish* in western Europe. *Jewish Cookery* by Esther Levy (1871) offered recipes for both a sweet fritter called "Grimslechs for Passover" and a savory version titled "Matzo Fritters." Sephardim refer to matza fritters as *bimuelos del pesaj* and dip them in *arrope* (raisin syrup). Romans add raisins, pine nuts, and orange zest to the matza batter and dip the fritters in honey to make *pizzarele con giulebbe* and *pizzarele col miele*. In Ferrara, Italy, matza fritters are made with honey, candied etrog, raisins, pine nuts, and cinnamon.

The advent of baking powder in 1835 and its popularization in the 1880s led to a revolution in pastry making and frying, allowing cooks to produce light fritters without the need for yeast. Although fruit fritters found some popularity in Israel, the country's favorite fritter is far and away the savory falafel.

(See also Bimuelo, Bonda, Doughnut, Haman's Ear, Kefte, Lokma, Malpuah, and Zalabia)

ITALIAN RICE FRITTERS
(*FRITTELLE DE RISO PER HANUKKAH*)

ABOUT 24 FRITTERS   [PAREVE]

3 cups water
About 1 teaspoon salt
1½ cups Arborio, Carnaroli, or Vialone Nano rice
¾ to 1 cup raisins
6 large eggs, lightly beaten
¾ cup pine nuts or chopped almonds
2 teaspoons grated lemon zest
1 teaspoon vanilla extract

Olive or vegetable oil for deep-frying

Sugar or cinnamon-sugar for sprinkling

1. In a medium saucepan, bring the water and salt to a boil. Add the rice, cover, reduce the heat to low, and simmer until the rice is tender and has absorbed all the water, about 25 minutes. Let cool.

2. While the rice cools, soak the raisins in warm water to cover. Drain.

3. Transfer the rice to a medium bowl and stir in the eggs, raisins, nuts, zest, and vanilla.

4. In a deep, heavy skillet or saucepan, heat at least 1 inch oil over medium heat to 375°F.

5. In batches, drop the batter by tablespoonfuls into the oil. Fry, turning once, until golden brown on all sides, 2 to 3 minutes per side. Using a slotted spoon, remove the fritters and drain on paper towels. Sprinkle with the sugar. The fritters can be kept warm in a 250°F oven while preparing the remaining fritters.

FUL MEDAMES

Ful medames is a vegetarian dish of slow-cooked fava beans.

Origin: Egypt

Other names: *ful mudammas, ful.*

The Talmud mentions a practice in the town of Sepphoris of slow-cooking *shachalayim* (fava beans with vinegar) in the hot springs and furnaces of Roman baths for the Sabbath. This dish resembles the later Sephardic *hamin/adafina* (Sabbath stew). In some other areas, notably Egypt, the ashes of the public baths, which were used to heat the water, proved an ideal medium for cooking the hard beans for Sabbath lunch.

The Coptic Orthodox of Egypt, who practiced one of the earliest forms of Christianity, believed that the original state of humankind was vegetarian and, therefore, mandated numerous days of eating only vegitarian food, including two well-known Coptic vegetarian dishes, *tamiya* (fava bean falafel) and *ful medames.* The Copts slow-cooked fava beans in the local Cairo bathhouses, probably imitating their Jewish neighbors, who cooked their Sabbath stews there. Even the dish's name reflects a similarity with *adafina*—*medames* comes from the Coptic word for buried, reflecting the linguistic and cooking method's similarity to the ancient Jewish practice of *tomnin et ha'hamin* (burying the warm dishes).

In Egypt, *ful medames,* practically the national dish, is enjoyed daily by rich and poor alike. It can be found everywhere at any time of the day—it is sold at fancy restaurants, special *ful* stores, and by street vendors. Even today, many Egyptians do not make *ful* at home, but rather rely on vendors. After slow-simmering, the soupy fava beans are typically mashed and then served with fresh bread, which is used to scoop up the beans. People flavor their own servings with their choice of olive oil, garlic, lemon juice, yogurt, fresh mint, cilantro, and chopped onions. For breakfast, *ful* is frequently topped with a fried egg.

Ful medames is served by Egyptian Jews as a breakfast dish, commonly accompanied by tomato and cucumber salads, black olives, and plenty of pita bread to sop up the sauce. It is also served as a side dish at lunch and dinner, as part of a *mezze* (appetizer assortment), and for Sabbath lunch. Hard-boiled eggs are a distinctive Jewish touch.

EGYPTIAN SLOW-SIMMERED FAVA BEANS
(*FUL MEDAMES*)

4 TO 5 SERVINGS   [PAREVE]

3 quarts water

1 pound (about 2 cups) dried fava beans, preferably the small, round variety called pigeon bean (*ful hammam*); dried white beans; or large dried lima beans; soaked in water to cover for 8 hours and drained

About ⅓ cup olive or vegetable oil

5 to 6 cloves garlic, minced, or 1 medium onion, chopped

About ¾ teaspoon ground black pepper or ½ teaspoon ground cumin

6 to 8 eggs in shell, washed well

⅓ cup chopped fresh flat-leaf parsley or cilantro

About ¼ cup fresh lemon juice

About 1½ teaspoons table salt or 2½ teaspoons kosher salt

Mashed garlic, ground cumin, *samna* (clarified butter), and/or olive oil (optional)

1. In a large pot, bring the water to a boil. Add the beans, return to a boil, cover, reduce the heat to medium-low, and simmer, stirring occasionally, for 30 minutes.

2. Stir in the oil, garlic, and pepper. Add the eggs in their shells. Reduce the heat to low and simmer, stirring occasionally and adding more water if necessary, until the beans are very soft, at least 2 hours or even overnight. The cooking time varies according to the size and variety of the bean. Drain.

3. Remove the eggs. Peel, then quarter or chop. Set aside.

4. Some people prefer the beans whole, while others prefer them slightly or completely mashed. If desired, mash one-third of the beans, then stir in the remaining beans. Add the parsley, lemon juice, and salt to the beans and toss to coat. (Egyptians commonly let individual diners add their own salt at the table.) Taste the beans and adjust the seasonings if necessary. To further flavor the *ful*, mix in a little garlic, cumin, and *samna* or olive oil. Divide the beans between serving bowls and top with the eggs. Serve warm or at room temperature accompanied with pita bread.

G

GALAKTOBOUREKO

Galaktoboureko is phyllo dough layered with a semolina custard (*galakto*) and drizzled with a sugar syrup or sprinkled with confectioners' sugar.

Origin: Greece

Other names: *galakto bouriko, galaktopita, galatopita.*

Centuries of Persian control over western Asia, central Asia, and India left its imprint on the cuisine of those areas. In turn, the Turks absorbed Persian fare and spread it to the regions under their control. Therefore, many of the dishes enjoyed throughout the Middle East, as well as in Greece, the Balkans, and Italy, can be directly traced to the Persians and Turks. Among the foods that the Turks brought with them from central Asia was a dumpling called *bugra*, which by the fifteenth century had evolved into a myriad of filled and layered pastries—baked and fried, large and small, sweet and savory—collectively known as *börek*.

Until the eighteenth century, the bulk of the southern European diet consisted of porridges, called *sitos* in Greek, *puls* in Latin, and *dysah* in Hebrew. These gruels were usually served plain or flavored with onions, garlic, and herbs. For a special treat, they were cooked with milk instead of water and sweetened with a touch of honey. Over the years, *börek* was combined with a semolina *sitos* and refined with milk (*gala*), butter, eggs, and sugar, giving rise to a popular Turkish and Greek phyllo-layered treat, *galaktoboureko*. The phyllo and filling are formed into large pies as well as small individual rolls. Semolina pudding is also baked without the phyllo, a particularly Jewish practice; this version is known as *galaktopita zarka*, the latter word meaning "naked." These pastries are made at home as well as sold in sweet shops called *zacharoplasteion* (*zacharo* means "sugar") and *galaktozacharoplasteion*.

The semolina pudding has a creamy, though slightly grainy texture similar to that of curd cheesecake. The pudding should not be too thick, but rather custardy. The proportion of semolina and eggs varies. Adding a little orange juice and zest to the filling and soaking syrup produces a *galaktoboureko portokali*. Some people like pieces of dried fruits and nuts in their filling, while others insist on enjoying the custard pure and plain. A *galaktoboureko* filled with an almond custard is called a Copenhagen. Versions are also made with a rice-flour pudding. The pastry was typically enriched with and drizzled with sugar syrup in the Middle Eastern manner, although today many people prefer it simply sprinkled with confectioners' sugar.

Galakto pastries make a tasty breakfast treat, but are also served by Greek Jews after special dairy meals, such as on Shavuot, when the rectangular shape of individual small pies resembles the stone tablets of the law that Moses formed on Mount Sinai. They are also popular at the meal following Yom Kippur.

(See also Boreka)

GREEK SEMOLINA CUSTARD PIE (*GALAKTOBOUREKO*)

12 TO 16 SERVINGS   [DAIRY]

Galakto:

¼ cup (½ stick) unsalted butter

¾ cup (4.5 ounces) fine semolina or farina (not semolina flour)

4 cups milk

1 cup sugar, or ½ cup sugar and ½ cup honey

¼ teaspoon table salt or ½ teaspoon kosher salt

4 large eggs, lightly beaten

2 teaspoons vanilla extract, grated lemon zest, or grated orange zest

½ to 1 cup finely chopped dried apricots, golden raisins, finely chopped blanched almonds, or finely chopped walnuts (optional)

1 teaspoon grated orange or lemon zest, or ¾ teaspoon ground cinnamon (optional)

16 sheets phyllo dough

About ½ cup (1 stick) unsalted butter or margarine, melted and preferably clarified

2 cups cooled atar (Middle Eastern Sugar Syrup, page 27) or 1 cup confectioners' sugar

1. To make the galakto: In a large saucepan, melt the butter over medium heat. Stir in the semolina. Gradually stir in the milk. Add the sugar and salt. Reduce the heat to medium-low and simmer, stirring frequently, until the mixture thickens, about 10 minutes. Remove from the heat and gradually beat in the eggs. Stir in the vanilla. If using, add the dried fruit and/or zest. Pour the pudding into a medium bowl, press a piece of plastic wrap against the surface, and let cool. The pudding can be stored in the refrigerator for up to 2 days.

2. Preheat the oven to 350°F (325°F if using a glass pan). Grease a 13-by-9-inch baking pan.

3. Place a sheet of phyllo in the prepared pan, letting the edges drape over the sides, and lightly brush with butter. Repeat with 7 more sheets. Spread with the cooled galakto and turn the overhanging sides of the pastry over the filling.

4. Cut the remaining 8 phyllo sheets into 13-by-9-inch rectangles and arrange on top of the filling, brushing each with butter. Using a sharp knife, carefully cut crosswise through the top sheets of phyllo into serving size diamonds or squares.

5. Bake until the pastry is golden brown, about 40 minutes. Cut into squares. Drizzle with the cooled atar or sprinkle with confectioners' sugar. Serve warm or at room temperature. Store at room temperature for up to 1 day.

GALUSKA

Galuska is a small flour-based dumpling.

Origin: Hungary

Other names: Hungarian: *galushka, nokedli*; Slavic: *halushki, halusky*; Ukrainian: *galushki*.

Galuska (the plural is technically *galuskák*, but *galuska* is used colloquially for the plural also) is elemental to the Hungarian kitchen—certain Hungarians insist that anyone who cannot cook *galuska*, cannot cook Hungarian. *Galuska*, which is economical and easy to prepare, is the most widespread form of Hungarian dumplings or pasta.

When dumplings and pasta reached eastern Europe, Slavs began making small irregularly shaped loose egg batters called *halushki* (meaning "little ears," as they were originally triangular), akin to the German spaetzle (little sparrows) and *ribbles* (little rubs) and Ashkenazic *triflach* (little trifles). Ukrainians called them *galushki*, which the Hungarians adapted as *galuska*. It was in Hungary that these simple dump-lings, sometimes referred to as a "pasta dumpling," achieved their widest popularity.

Most of Europe did not grow durum wheat, which is necessary to make Italian-style pasta, so cooks needed to add eggs to their dough of common wheat flour to enable it to hold up during boiling. *Galuska* dough also contains about an equal amount of water as it does eggs, and is a somewhat loose mixture, making it more of a dumpling than a pasta. *Csipetke* (literally "pinched") are Hungarian soft egg noodles pinched or dropped from a dough firmer than *galuska* and looser than egg noodles, a culinary link between *galuska* (dumplings) and *metelt* (noodles). When made with semolina, these dumplings are known as *daragaluska*. Unlike some versions, Jewish *galuska* does not include milk or lard. Cooked *galuska* are soft and tender.

In the nineteenth century, Hungarians invented precedent-setting milling techniques, producing finer white flour and, consequently, higher-quality dumplings and noodles. Around the same time, some cooks began adding mashed potatoes to the *galuska* dough, forming a dough (*krumpli galuska*) similar to that of Italian gnocchi, although most continued to use the original pure flour version. *Somloi galuska* is an unrelated dessert of sponge cake pieces with vanilla cream, chocolate sauce, raisins, and walnuts.

Recently, manufacturers created a *galuskaszaggató*, a simple utensil with holes through which the batter is pressed that is similar to the rotary spaetzle machine. However, many cooks insist on making *galuska* in the old-fashioned manner by cutting strips of the dough and pushing them off of a board or plate into a pot of boiling water. *Galuska* should all be bite-sized. Forming the irregularly shaped dumplings is a matter of speed, not uniformity or fastidiousness. It does take a bit of practice to get the rhythm and wrist action down to cut each batch. *Galuska* are served with soups and any dish that is creamy or has a rich gravy, notably goulash, chicken paprikash, cooked cabbage, and soft cheese (*túrós galuska*).

(See also Csipetke, Halke, and Paprikás)

⚜ HUNGARIAN DUMPLINGS (*GALUSKA*)

5 TO 6 SERVINGS/ABOUT SEVENTY-FIVE 3-INCH-LONG
DUMPLINGS   [PAREVE, DAIRY, OR MEAT]

  3 cups (15 ounces) all-purpose flour
  1½ teaspoons salt
  3 large eggs, lightly beaten

About ½ cup cold water

2 tablespoons vegetable oil, butter, or schmaltz for tossing

1. In a large bowl, combine the flour and salt, make a well in the center, and pour in the eggs. Using a large wooden spoon, stir in the eggs. Gradually stir in enough water to form a dough that is sticky but holds together; a fork should just stand upright in it. (If there is too much flour, the dumplings will turn out dense and chewy.) Using a wooden spoon, beat until the dough slips off the spoon and comes away from the sides of the bowl, about 10 minutes. Cover with a kitchen towel and let stand for at least 30 minutes.

2. Bring a large pot of salted water to a boil—use 1 tablespoon salt for 2 quarts water. Wet a cutting board or flat dish and spoon some of the dough on top. Using a large knife, spread the dough to a thickness of ⅛ inch. Holding the board over the pot, cut off a small slice of the dough (1 to 3 inches long and ¼ inch wide) and flick it into the boiling liquid. If the knife becomes clogged with batter and difficult to cut with, dip it in the boiling water.

3. In batches, boil until the dumplings rise to the surface, 3 to 5 minutes. Galuska swell as they cook. Continue cooking until firm and tender in the center, an additional 1 to 2 minutes. Overcooking results in mushy dumplings. Using a wire-mesh skimmer or slotted spoon, remove the dumplings and drain. Toss with the oil. Serve immediately.

GARLIC

After escaping bondage in Egypt, the Israelites in the wilderness waxed nostalgic over six common foods, including *shummim* (garlic), an integral element of Jewish cookery from the onset.

This native of central Asia has been part of humankind's cooking from before recorded history. Garlic, along with onions and leeks, played an important role in the Sumerian and Egyptian diet five-thousand years ago. The Egyptians valued garlic so highly that they buried it in the pyramids for use in the afterlife. To be sure, some cultures, especially in America, disparaged garlic. Jewish tradition, on the other hand, maintained an exceedingly positive view of the pungent bulb. According to the Jerusalem Talmud, Ezra the Scribe decreed that garlic should be eaten on Friday night as an aphrodisiac. A passage in the Babylonian Talmud notes, "Our Rabbis taught: Five things were said

of garlic: It satiates, it warms the body, it brightens one's face, it increases semen, and it kills intestinal parasites. Some say that it fosters love and removes jealousy." In addition, the Talmud relates: "Wherewith does one show delight in the Sabbath? With beets [the greens], a large fish, and garlic." All three of these items were considered to be aphrodisiacs, and Friday night a traditional time of sexual relations.

Nevertheless, garlic's basic importance to Jews was as a seasoning. Historically, the addition of garlic was among the typical Jewish touches that enhanced local dishes. In many cultures, the presence of garlic marked a dish as Jewish. Europeans frequently used garlic in anti-Semitic caricatures, a practice dating back to the time when some ancient Romans contemptuously referred to Jews as "garlic eaters," a term the Talmud conversely took as a compliment. Ashkenazim added garlic to everything from sausages (e.g., knobelwurst) to dill pickles. As Sholem Aleichem described in his tale "What Kind of Rabbi We Have" (1915), "You could smell the roast all over the house, it had so much garlic in it. A roast like that, with fresh warm [challah] braid, is a delicacy from heaven."

The poor, unable to afford imported spices, relied on this pungent bulb to break the monotony of food, while those better off understood its role in contributing layers of flavor in dishes with other seasonings. Romanians, in particular, are renowned for their profuse use of garlic in a wide variety of dishes. Garlic is essential for a vast array of Mediterranean sauces, soups, and salads. However, many Sephardim who settled in Asia adopted the local Muslim aversion to garlic, so it was less popular in Turkey and widely disregarded in Persia.

Historically, garlic was considered a health food and associated with medicine as well as gastronomy—before the twentieth century, there was a fine line dividing the two. Hippocrates as well as the Talmud recommended it as a cure for a variety of ailments. In 1858, Louis Pasteur proved that garlic could kill bacteria in laboratory dishes. Among garlic's principal assets are sulfur compounds that act as antibiotics and antifungal agents. Today, research has begun to justify its status, including its role as a possible antioxidant. The only side effect of this bulb is a garlicky odor in breath and sweat.

A medieval Sephardic folk belief was that garlic protected against the evil eye (*ojo kui/mal ojo*); this superstition may be based on garlic's antibacterial properties, as well as the similarity of the Ladino word for garlic (*ajo*) to eye. Because of this belief, garlic was placed under a pillow or in a child's pocket to ward off the spirits. After complimenting a child or commenting on another's good fortune, a person would ward off the evil eye by saying, "*Al ajo ke se le vaiga.*" (Let it go to [be absorbed by] the garlic). Some Ashkenazim also viewed garlic (*knobel* in Yiddish) as a defense against the evil eye; accordingly, bulbs sometimes appeared on a tray alongside the infant at a *brit* or *Pidyon HaBen* (redemption of the first born son).

GEBROCHTS

According to the Talmud and all early rabbinic sources, matza that comes into contact or is saturated with any liquid, known as *matza sheruyah* (soaked matza), is permitted for consumption during Passover. Nevertheless, in the late eighteenth century, Chasidim began to use the Yiddish term *gebrochts* (broken) as a synonym for matza that has come into contact with a liquid and to forbid its consumption during Passover, except on the eighth day. This precluded many iconic Ashkenazic dishes, including *matza knaidlach* (dumplings), *matza chremslach* (pancakes), and matza kugel. Some Chasidic groups even eat matza in such a manner as to avoid dropping any crumbs on the table or the floor lest they come into contact with a liquid. These stringencies are not followed by Sephardim, Mizrachim, or most non-Chasidic Ashkenazim. Indeed, many Lithuanian rabbis at the time of the emergence of this custom ate matza ball soup on Passover to demonstrate that there is no restriction. Chasidic Passover recipes are non-*gebrochts*, (made without matza) frequently necessitating the substitution of potato starch for matza.

GEDEMPTE FLEISCH

Gedempte fleisch is pot-roasted beef.
Origin: Germany
Other names: *gedempte brust.*

In the several centuries following the Black Death (1348–1350), including the demise of more than a third of the farmers, western and central Europe experienced an unprecedented meat surplus, as much of the farmland lay fallow and was turned to grazing. Ashkenazim in Germany and Aus-

tria became accustomed to celebrating the Sabbath and festivals with beef. Unlike Sephardim and Mizrachim, who typically cooked meat as small pieces as a flavoring agent in a larger dish, Ashkenazim more frequently followed the European manner of cooking large, whole cuts of meat. This unusual situation of plentiful, relatively inexpensive meat ended around 1550, yet afterwards, the Ashkenazic predilection for beef remained. In addition, in eastern Europe, meat was usually an extravagance and large cuts were primarily enjoyed only by the wealthy or on special occasions.

The favorite Ashkenazic way of preparing a chuck roast or brisket was slow-simmering it in a covered pot set over a fire, creating the Yiddish equivalent of pot roast. In Yiddish and German, *gedempte fleisch* translates as "steamed meat," and *gedempte brust* as "steamed brisket." Sweet-and-sour versions are known as *essig fleisch*. A version made with beet vinegar is *rosl fleisch*. Germans, to forestall rotting or salvage minimally spoiled meat, occasionally pickled roasts in vinegar, making a dish called sauerbraten. The flavorful cooking liquid, which was frequently served with noodles as a first course, is known as *yoykh* (broth) or *rosl*, the same name used for beet vinegar.

Although the concept of browning a large piece of meat then slowly simmering it in a relatively small amount of liquid in a covered vessel dates back to antiquity, the term "pot roast" was first recorded in 1881, in *All Around the House, or, How to Make Home Happy* by Mrs. H. W. Beecher. Shortly thereafter, it first appeared in a Jewish source, *Aunt Babette's* (1889). Around that time in America, large cuts of beef, especially the tasty and economical chuck roast, became a regular Sabbath dish and, in some households, were commonly eaten during the week; the meat was typically served with potatoes or kasha and pickles.

Gedempte fleisch was traditionally cooked with onions, garlic, and sometimes potatoes and carrots. *The Sinatra Celebrity Cookbook: Barbara, Frank & Friends* (1996) included singer Neil Diamond's recipe for his mother Rose's "Gedempte Fleish," seasoned with packaged onion soup mix (instead of fresh onions) and ketchup, which were common additions beginning in the mid-twentieth century (turning the dish into sort of a mock *rosl fleisch*). Sometimes cooks flavored the meat with other American ingredients, including cranberries or cola. Many, however, prefer the simplicity of old-fashioned *gedempte fleisch*, an enduring comfort food.

(See also Beef, Brisket, and Sauerbraten)

⚜ ASHKENAZIC POT ROAST (*GEDEMPTE FLEISCH*)

6 TO 8 SERVINGS   [MEAT]

1 (3½- to 5-pound) boneless beef chuck, chuck-eye, or shoulder roast
3 tablespoons vegetable oil or schmaltz
2 medium yellow onions, sliced
1 cup chopped carrots
1 cup chopped celery
1 to 2 cloves garlic, minced
1 teaspoon paprika
1 sprig fresh thyme or 1 teaspoon dried thyme, marjoram, or basil
2 tablespoons tomato paste or 2 teaspoons sugar (optional)
2 cups chicken broth or water, or 1 cup chicken broth and 1 cup beef broth or dry red wine
1 bay leaf
About 1½ teaspoons table salt or 1 tablespoon kosher salt
About ¼ teaspoon ground black pepper

1. Pat the roast dry with paper towels. In a large pot or roaster with a tight-fighting lid, heat the oil over medium-high heat. Place the roast in the pot and cook, turning frequently, until it is browned—but not blackened—on all sides, about 20 minutes. Remove the roast from the pot.

2. Reduce the heat to medium, add the onions, carrots, and celery, and sauté until softened and lightly colored, about 15 minutes. Add the garlic, paprika, and thyme and stir until fragrant, about 30 seconds. If using, stir in the tomato paste and cook until slightly darkened, 2 to 3 minutes.

3. Add the broth and stir to remove any browned particles from the bottom of the pot. Add the bay leaf. Return the beef and any accumulated juices. If necessary, add enough water to reach halfway up the sides of the roast. Cover and bring to a simmer on top of the stove.

4. Place in a 325°F oven or simmer over a low heat, turning every 30 minutes, until fork-tender, 3½ to 4 hours. The roast may be prepared up to 2 days in advance, cooled, covered, and stored in the refrigerator before reheating.

5. Remove from the heat and let stand for 20 minutes. Meanwhile, strain the cooking liquid, pressing out the solids. Boil the liquid in the pot over high heat until reduced to about 1½ cups, about 10 minutes. Season with the salt and pepper.

6. Slice the meat against the grain and transfer to a warmed serving platter. Serve with the cooking liquid.

GEFILTE FISH

Gefilte fish is ground, boned fish that is stuffed back into the fish skin or formed into quenelles or a loaf, then poached and served cold.

Origin: Germany

Other names: filled fish; Hebrew: *dag memula*.

"The old woman was meek and timorous. And quiet as a mouse. But in her gefilte fish (and in her fingers that prepared the samovar) lay (the history of the Jewish people), a true history with a hefty dash of peppery passion." (From an essay in *Reports from Petersburg, 1918* by Ukrainian journalist and author Isaac Babel)

Fish, a symbol of fertility and blessing, has been traditional Sabbath and festival fare since at least Talmudic times. However, among the prohibited forms of creative work on the Sabbath is *borer* (to select/sort), meaning to separate undesirable items from desirable ones. Therefore a person can remove the edible flesh from the bones on the Sabbath, but may not pick the inedible bones from the flesh. Since much of the fish in the Middle East was particularly bony, removing the flesh from the bones before the Sabbath was a practical way of preparing it. Fish forcemeat dishes continued in numerous forms in many Jewish communities, including the Sephardic *albondigas de pescado* (fish balls in a savory sauce) and *empanadas de pescado* (fish turnovers), and the Italian *polpettine* (fish balls). Beginning in the fourteenth century, Franco-German rabbis discussed the permissibility of adding vinegar—which cooks the flesh—to chopped-up fish on the Sabbath.

Ancient Romans loved to skin animals, chop the flesh, and stuff it into the skin before cooking. Medieval German and French cooks in upper-class households retained this practice with pike, perch, and other large freshwater fish. The first medieval record of this fish dish, *gefuelten hechden* (stuffed pike), was in a non-Jewish source in southern Germany around 1350, in the oldest German cookbook, *Daz Buoch von Guoter Spise* (The Book of Good Food). The dish was

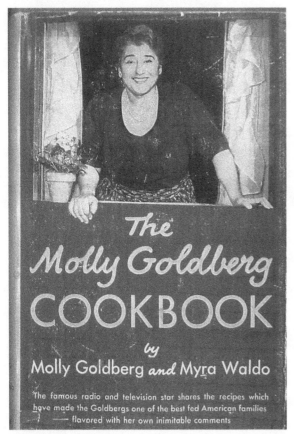

Forty million Americans first learned about gefilte fish and many other Ashkenazic foods from The Goldbergs *TV show and the companion cookbook.*

stretching the dish) and onions (as both a flavoring and preservative), seasoned, and stuffed into the skin; the fish was then sewn up and roasted. Eventually, cooks began to poach the stuffed fish. In this way, a small fish or even just the stuffed skin could feed a large family.

By the sixteenth century, the process was simplified by some Ashkenazic cooks in Germany who eliminated the tedious stuffing step and, instead, poached the fish mixture as quenelles in a fish broth, called *fish yukh* or *yoykh* in Yiddish, which was made from the head and bones. The result was a light, flavorful fish dumpling far different from the heavy, rather tasteless commercial kind prevalent today. The stock was either served warm as a soup or cooled and jellied and offered with the fish. However, the stuffed-skin version remained commonplace in many households well into the twentieth century.

In western and central Europe, gefilte fish was never the most popular Sabbath fish. That position was long held by the various types of *fish gelee* (jellied fish), including *suz-und-sauer fish* (sweet-and-sour fish) and *scharfe fish* (poached fish in egg-lemon sauce). On the other hand, after gefilte fish, both stuffed and quenelles, reached eastern Europe by at least the seventeenth century, shortly after the popularization of the imported carp, these preparations soon emerged as the most widespread forms of Sabbath fish in much of Poland, the Baltic States, Hungary, and Ukraine. The success of gefilte fish was partially because the added onions and other fillers stretched limited resources. In addition, the predominant fish used, carp, is filled with numerous tiny bones, and gefilte fish eliminated the potential of the forbidden *borer* (separating the bones from poached carp steaks) on the Sabbath. Impoverished families that could not afford a fish would obtain fish skins and perhaps some bones given away free by fishmongers, then stuff the skins with bread crumbs and whatever else was available, sometimes without even a little fish flesh. Using a skin also meant that the dish could be held together in the poaching liquid without adding any eggs, another expense. The head of the household, the grandfather or in his place, the father, along with a slice of fish, was customarily served the fish head, which was considered the tastiest part of the fish, as a symbol of his status.

The term gefilte fish seems not to have been applied to fish quenelles in Germany, where it denoted only

popular among upper-class Catholics during Lent and other days when meat was forbidden. The stuffing consisted of poached and mashed fish flavored with sage, caraway seeds, saffron, salt, and pepper. After being stuffed, the fish was set on a wooden grill and roasted. Shortly thereafter, recipes for stuffed fish, in which the flesh was typically mixed with ground almonds and saffron, appeared in French manuscripts of recipes for the gentry.

Stuffed whole fish eventually emerged in medieval German-Jewish cookery and was known in Yiddish as *gefilte fish*, meaning "filled/stuffed." Originally, the bones were discarded and the flesh was carefully removed from the fish, chopped, mixed with matza meal or bread (which acted as a binder as well as

the actual stuffed skins, but rather to have been picked up as a term for quenelles in eastern Europe and then in America, as masses of eastern European Jews immigrated toward the end of the nineteenth century. Consequently, early Jewish mentions of poached fish forcemeat in English, almost all from German roots, never mention the term gefilte fish. Poached fish patties were called "Stewed-Fish Balls" in the first American Jewish cookbook, *Jewish Cookery* (1871) by Esther Levy, who was of German heritage. In the British cookbook *An Easy and Economical Book of Jewish Cookery* (1874) by Mrs. Estella Atrutel, cook to the Lionel Rothschild family, they were called "Stewed Fish Balls with Egg Sauce." The term "gefullte fisch" first appeared in print in English in 1892 in a description of Jewish cookery in *Children of the Ghetto*, a tale of Jewish life in London by Israel Zangwill, the son of Russian immigrants.

The initial edition of *The Settlement Cook Book* (1901), the classic American cookbook by Lizzie Kander, also from a German background, offered only generic poached "Filled Fish" and "Fish Balls." By the 1943 edition, the work contained "Filled Fish (Gefüllte Fish)." Directions were provided for both a poached and baked filled whole fish and, in addition, a recipe was given for poached quenelles called "Lincoln House Fish Balls", which the 1965 edition admits are "Gefillte Fish." Another early twentieth-century American cookbook, *The Neighborhood Cook Book* (1912) by the Council of Jewish Women in Portland, Oregon, called poached quenelles "Gefullte Fish." But soon, the spelling "gefilte" was widespread.

Since most central and eastern European Jewish communities were located a distance from the seas, and the Baltic Sea was too brackish to support more than herring, most of the fish available were freshwater varieties. Pike was the prevalent freshwater fish in Germany and it was commonly used in central Europe for gefilte fish. In Poland, the more common carp or, when available, whitefish was generally substituted or, when possible, the two or three were used in combination. This fish trio remains the favorites for this classic dish. Cooks who makes gefilte fish have their own preferences in the varieties and proportion of fish: Using more carp renders a stronger, richer flavor, while adding a larger portion of whitefish and pike creates a more delicate one.

English Jews typically use saltwater fish, particularly a combination of cod and either haddock or hake and, in addition, prefer to pan-fry small gefilte fish patties rather than poach them. In the American Northwest, the unorthodox salmon has become commonplace, producing pink-colored quenelles. In the nineteenth century, some Chasidim who had developed a custom of not eating fish during Passover, but so loved gefilte fish, created a mock form from chicken called *falsche fish*.

Various other differences in the dish developed over time. Raising the most passion is the amount of added sugar or pepper, which depends on personal preference and heritage. In general, those from Galicia (now southern Poland and northern Ukraine), the location of the first sugar beet factories in the early nineteenth century, developed a preference for a very sweet fish, while Hungarians and Ukrainians continued to make it savory, and Lithuanians added a pronounced amount of ground black pepper. This heated debate endures after two centuries. Some Ukrainians add ground bitter almonds or a dash of almond extract to the fish, while others mix in grated carrot and parsnip. Some Polish Jews put a few onion skins in the cooking liquid to produce a light brown fish. In Germany, gefilte fish was originally accompanied with vinegar and later mayonnaise, but in eastern Europe *chrain* (horseradish) became the principal and much-beloved condiment.

Originally, the fish was chopped by hand in a wooden bowl using a curved blade, called a *hackmesser* in Yiddish. The advent of the mechanical grinder in the 1860s made the job of preparing the fish easier—whether it was done at home or by the fishmonger—and led to a smoother, denser texture. Still, many grandmothers insisted on chopping the fish by hand, adamant that it was the only way to incorporate enough air for a proper fluffy texture. Yet shortly thereafter, as the twentieth century progressed and Jews experienced increasing economic growth as well as access to a wide assortment of prepared food, gefilte fish began disappearing from many tables. To be sure, in America, some housewives continued the Old World practice of making gefilte fish at home; they kept a carp alive in the bathtub to remove any muddy taste and killed it on Friday for that evening's gefilte fish. However, since the preparation of gefilte fish was too laborious for most and uninteresting to those less connected with their roots, for a while it seemed that gefilte fish would become the exotic province of delicatessens and Catskill resorts and a rarity in homes. Then the nature and fate of gefilte fish was altered with the emergence of mass-produced versions.

In 1883, Nathan Leibner (1843–1929), a clothing peddler, immigrated from Zmigrod, Galicia (now southern Poland), to New York City and within three years he had earned enough money to bring over his wife and their children. Around this time, eastern Europeans began popularizing gefilte fish in the New World. In 1910, Leibner began selling live carp, a standard food for the masses of eastern European immigrants, and eventually he opened a fish store on the Lower East Side. Nathan's youngest son, Sidney, later took over the business. Then, shortly before World War II, several small manufacturers began offering commercial gefilte fish in cans, products with poor flavor and quality. Leibner decided to offer a more palatable canned gefilte fish, in the sweet Galician style of his family, and called his business Mother's Fish Products. After the war, Mother's switched to glass bottles, which would quickly become the predominant form of container for American gefilte fish. In Israel, on the other hand, canned *dagim memula'im*, sometimes consisting of slices of fish with their cavity filled with gefilte fish, endured for many more decades.

In 1954, Manischewitz, then known for its matza, opened a processing plant in Vineland, New Jersey, and began producing its own gefilte fish in jars. Soon other Jewish food producers, notably Mrs. Adler's and Rokeach, began offering bottled gefilte fish. Since the equipment for making and bottling gefilte fish was specialized and expensive, initially only the early two companies possessed it; all other brands rented their facilities for production, although each brand used a slightly different recipe. To suit blander tastes, carp was reduced or eliminated in many versions. The fish typically contained matza meal year-round so as to be kosher for Passover. As a result of mass-production, shoppers in America could easily find gefilte fish on grocery shelves and this availability made it typical Sabbath and holiday fare.

Around the time that gefilte fish appeared in bottles, forty million Americans were introduced to the dish on the first Jewish television sitcom, *The Goldbergs* (1949–1956), a highly popular show derived from an earlier radio program. The particular episode revolved around Molly Goldberg's inability to provide exact measurements to a large food manufacturer for her homemade gefilte fish. A recipe for gefilte fish did, however, appear in the bestselling *Molly Goldberg Jewish Cookbook* (1955). Thus this classic and distinctive Ashkenazic food became a well-known, but still recognizably Jewish, dish. As noted by American humorist Calvin Trillin in his collection of essays, *Feeding a Yen* (2004), "Roughly corresponding to the time it took our girls to grow up and move to California, bagels had become assimilated. Gefilte fish was still Jewish food, but not bagels."

Indeed, gefilte fish was subjected to deprecation and mockery. Some of this resentment was a result of discomfort with some elements of their Jewish identity, but for others it was due to the inferior quality of commercial products. The patties of early canned and bottled gefilte fish tended to crumble, discolor, and undergo a loss of flavor during storage, while the broth was thin, liquefying at room temperature. To help mask the flavor deficiencies and to appeal to the sweet-loving American palate, producers began adding more sugar, sometimes in copious amounts.

The appearance and flavor situation was improved, when on October 29, 1963, Monroe Nash (yes, he was Jewish) was granted a U.S. patent for preparing gefilte fish with jellied broth that included carrageen, which allowed the gel to remain stable on store shelves. The jarred fish torpedoes were improved, but still a pale imitation of homemade gefilte fish.

Beginning around 1977, kosher fish stores in the New York metropolitan area and manufacturers introduced a more old-fashioned product that could be cooked at home—raw ground fish, without the chemicals and preservatives, that had been formed into logs and frozen. Although the product is an improvement, the texture of the commercial frozen logs is smoother and still more rubbery than that of the old-fashioned hand-chopped type. In addition, the original stuffed skin version unexpectedly made a small comeback in America toward the end of the twentieth century, spread by immigrants from the former Soviet Union, who had grown up on it. Russians also preferred a higher proportion of carp to whitefish for a more robust flavor. Still, bottled gefilte fish maintained its domination on the American table. At the onset of the twenty-first century,

Manischewitz offered about thirty different types of gefilte fish products and sold more than 1.5 million jars of gefilte fish annually.

After centuries, gefilte fish, arguably the most representative of Ashkenazic dishes, not only endures but continues to change. Recently, unorthodox flavor variations were introduced, including jalapeño, Cajun, almond-raisin, and lemon-dill. Vegetarians even prepare a version made from mashed potatoes and eggplant. Gefilte fish is even on the menu of many non-Jewish restaurants in Poland, even though very few Jews now live in that country. Whatever its form, gefilte fish remains the quintessential Ashkenazic Sabbath and holiday appetizer—it is still a favorite at Passover Seders, Rosh Hashanah dinners, and Sabbath meals and kiddushes.

(See also Carp, Fish, Horseradish, and Whitefish)

ASHKENAZIC FISH QUENELLES (*GEFILTE FISH*)

ABOUT 24 MEDIUM FISH PATTIES   [PAREVE]

3 pounds fish fillets (whitefish, carp, or yellow pike, or any combination)
3 to 5 medium yellow onions
½ to 1 cup ice water
3 to 4 large eggs, lightly beaten
2 to 6 tablespoons sugar
About 1½ teaspoons table salt or 1 tablespoon kosher salt
½ to 1½ teaspoons ground white or black pepper
About ¼ cup matza meal or cracker crumbs (optional)

Fish Broth:

3 pounds fish bones, heads, and tails
3 to 4 medium carrots, sliced
2 stalks celery, sliced
2 medium yellow onions, sliced
2 quarts cold water
2 to 3 bay leaves
About 1 tablespoon table salt or 2 tablespoons kosher salt
Dash of ground white pepper or ½ teaspoon whole white peppercorns
1 to 4 tablespoons sugar (optional)

1. With a hackmesser (curved blade) in a wooden bowl or in a food grinder or a food processor fitted with a metal blade, finely grind the fish fillets and onions, but do not puree. With the hand chopper or in the food processor, gradually mix in the water. For a soft consistency, use more water; for a firmer consistency, decrease the amount of water.

2. Add the eggs. Use more egg for fluffier gefilte fish, less for firmer. Stir in the sugar, salt, pepper, then matza meal. Too much matza meal produces a heavy texture. Cover the mixture and refrigerate for 1 hour while preparing the broth.

3. To make the fish broth: Place all the broth ingredients except the sugar in a large pot. Bring to a boil and simmer for 20 to 30 minutes. Strain and discard the solids.

4. For easier handling, wet your hands often while shaping the fish. For each patty, form about ⅓ cup fish mixture into a 3-inch-long oval patty.

5. Drop the fish patties into the boiling broth. Return the broth to a boil, reduce the heat, cover partially, and simmer, shaking the pot occasionally, for 1½ hours. Remove the cover, add the optional sugar, and simmer for 30 minutes. Let cool in the broth.

GEVINA LEVANA

Israeli recording artist Noa (Achinoam Nini), in her 2001 song *"Nanua,"* intoned (in Hebrew), "Come my love, to the old kitchen, the fridge has been humming to us for four years now. It's his own little tune about *gevina levana*. You know, he's not out of order. Like us, he's just stuck." To Israelis, *gevina levana* (white cheese) is not an obscure reference, but a ubiquitous and usually uncontemplated element of modern Israeli life.

The Roman historian Tacitus mentioned that Germanic tribes ate *lac concretum* (thick milk), implying that these "barbarians" did not understand the art of making hard cheese. Instead, they consumed a fresh white cheese made without rennet by adding buttermilk to heated milk and letting it stand for several days to ferment. Similar fresh cheese is still prepared today by central Europeans, called *fromage blanc* in Alsace, *topfen* in Austria, *tvaroh* (from the Slavic *tvarog* "curd") in the Czech Republic, *quark* or *qvarg* in northern Germany, *weisskase* in southern Germany, and *túró* in Hungary. In Israel, it is known as *gevina levana*.

Gevina levana is an unripened cheese made from cow's milk curdled with lactic acid bacteria. It may be based on whole milk, skim milk, or nonfat milk, and a higher-fat version is produced with added cream. Although the European versions were traditionally made with raw milk, *gevina levana* uses pasteurized milk. It is somewhat similar to the Sephardic queso blanco and Middle Eastern *jiben bayda*, although those are typically made from sheep's or goat's milk and are firmer. It is less acidic and looser than *labaneh* (yogurt cheese). *Gevina levana* is lower in fat, drier in texture, and less tart than sour cream, which is prepared by adding a bacterial culture to cream.

In central Europe, this type of fresh white cheese is spread plain on bread or used in a wide variety of both savory and sweet dishes, including sauces, dressings, dips, Liptauer (spicy cheese spread), dumplings, pies, crepes, strudels, and cheesecakes. Because it was originally made without rennet, it proved ideal for kosher cooks. On the other hand, Polish and other eastern European versions tended to use rennet for a denser cheese and, consequently, this cheese never made an impact on eastern Ashkenazim, who instead relied on sour cream and curd cheese.

Quark never developed a noticeable following in mainstream America, primarily because eastern Europeans popularized commercial sour cream in the United States during the late nineteenth and early twentieth centuries before the central European white cheese had a chance to gain a strong foothold. The contrary occurred in Israel, where *quark/gevina levana*, holds a much higher degree of popularity than sour cream. This now most consummate of Israeli cheeses was introduced by, of all people, the Christian members of the German-based Temple Society. In 1868, members began immigrating to Israel, then part of the Ottoman Empire, where they established the famous Germany Colony in Jerusalem, as well as several agricultural societies, including Sarona, in the Sharon Plain.

Among the Templers' agricultural ventures was cow dairy farming, unlike the local husbandry of sheep and goats. In particular, the Templers made a form of the German *quark*—which they called *weisskase* (white cheese), and Israelis translated the name into Hebrew as *gevina levana*. For eastern Europeans in Israel longing for sour cream, *gevina levana* proved an acceptable substitute; for central Europeans, it was a taste of the old homeland. When Jews began establishing their own dairies in the 1930s, most produced *gevina levana*. During World War II, the German Templers, quite a few of whom were Nazi sympathizers, were interned by the British authorities in Australia and their presence disappeared from Israel.

Gevina levana, however, remained and during the decade of *tzena* (austerity) following the founding of the state in 1948, it emerged among the few widely available foodstuffs to become a mainstay of Israeli dairies and tables. In 2005, Israel's large dairy producer Tnuva introduced its brand of *gevina levana* to America.

Today, inexpensive brands of commercial *gevina levana* are sold at every Israeli grocery, and a few people still make it at home. *Gevina levana* is commonplace at Israeli breakfasts and dinners. It is used in baked goods, as the base for most dairy *pashtidas* (kugels and casseroles), in dumplings, with vegetables, as a topping for potato latkes, and as a standard bread spread. It serves as a substitute for mayonnaise and sour cream in many salads, sauces, and dips. Most Israeli cheesecakes are made from *gevina levana*; typically cooks use a special thicker version *genna levan l'afiya* (for baking).

(See also Cheese, Flammekueche, and Gombóc)

GHRAYBEH
Ghraybeh is a tender butter cookie.
Origin: Middle East
Other names: *ghorayebah, gourabia, ghorayebah*;
Greece: *kourabiedes, kourabiethes, kurabie*;
Morocco: *ghouribi, ghribi*.

Versions of delicate butter cookies called *ghraybeh* (from the Arabic for "swoon") are found in most parts of the former Ottoman Empire with slight differences in pronunciation or spelling. The classic *ghraybeh* is made from *samneh* (clarified butter), and the absence of any water or egg results in a very white, fragile cookie. For meat meals, Jewish cooks substitute oil or tahini (sesame seed paste) for the butter. The original cookie also contained semolina, resulting in a distinctive crunch, but many modern recipes call for only white flour, producing a slightly less flavorful cookie. *Ghraybeh* are not as sweet as the typical Western cookie. They are frequently flavored with orange-flower water or almond extract.

Housewives commonly keep a container filled with these tender cookies as well as *ma'amoul* (filled cookies) to serve to guests with tea or coffee. They are typically shaped like little balls, diamonds, or rings (sometimes called bracelets); the latter style is more fragile than the solid cookies. On Purim, the ring cookies, with a single-skinned whole pistachio or almond as a gem, represent Queen Esther's jewelry. Ball- and diamond-shaped cookies are sometimes topped with a whole almond, which is frequently blanched to keep the cookie entirely white to represent purity. Moroccans serve these cookies at nearly every celebration.

❧ MIDDLE EASTERN BUTTER COOKIES (*GHRAYBEH*)

ABOUT 36 COOKIES   [DAIRY]

  1 cup samneh (Middle Eastern clarified butter), cooled, or 1 cup (2 sticks) unsalted butter, softened

  ⅔ cup superfine sugar, 1 cup confectioners' sugar, or ½ cup granulated sugar and ½ cup confectioners' sugar

  2 teaspoons vanilla extract, 1 teaspoon orange-blossom water, or ½ teaspoon almond extract

  ¼ teaspoon salt

  About 2⅔ cups (13.5 ounces) unbleached all-purpose flour, or 1⅓ cups unbleached all-purpose flour and 1⅓ cups semolina flour

  About 36 blanched whole almonds or pistachios (optional)

  Confectioners' sugar for sprinkling (optional)

1. In a medium bowl, beat the butter until smooth, about 1 minute. Gradually add the sugar and beat until light and fluffy, about 10 minutes. Beat in the vanilla and salt. Gradually stir in the flour to form a smooth dough that holds together. Cover with plastic wrap and refrigerate for at least 1 hour.

2. Preheat the oven to 300°F.

3. For rounds: Form the dough into 1-inch balls, place 2 inches apart on ungreased baking sheets, and flatten slightly. For diamonds: On a lightly floured surface, roll out the dough ¼ inch thick and cut into 1-inch-long diamonds. If using, press a nut in the center of each cookie. For rings/bracelets: Roll 1½-inch balls of dough into thin ropes, 3½ or 4 inches long and ½ inch wide. Place the ropes 2 inches apart on ungreased baking sheets, bring the ends together, and press one end slightly over the other end. If desired, press a nut at the conjunction point.

4. Bake until set but not browned, about 12 minutes. Let the cookies cool on the sheets set on a wire rack. If desired, sprinkle with confectioners' sugar. Store in an airtight container at room temperature for up to 1 week or in the freezer for up to 6 months.

GINGER

Ginger is the knotty rhizome of an orchidlike plant grown in tropical climates. A native of east Asia, possibly southern China, it spread throughout much of the Orient before recorded history. As international trade expanded, ginger's pungency became an integral part of cuisine and medicine throughout most of the ancient world. Traders brought ginger to the Greeks and Romans, who in turn spread it throughout Europe. However, with the breakdown of trade during the medieval period, ginger and other Eastern spices frequently became scarce commodities in the West. On his return from China, in 1295, Marco Polo created a renaissance for ginger in Europe, and with the resumption of trade its availability returned. However, ginger only regained its former popularity in northern Europe, where it was used in the dried and ground form, as southerners had developed a taste for more delicate flavors.

Fresh ginger grows in the shape of a hand. There are two types—gray (sometimes called green) and white. The exact flavor of each variety depends on the locale in which it was grown. Gray ginger, grown primarily in India, is slightly lemony and camphoric and the more pungent variety. White ginger, common in Jamaica, is more delicate and aromatic. The larger the hand, the more piquant the flavor.

Besides fresh, ginger is available in a variety of forms: ground, crystallized, and pickled. Ground ginger, which is dried and powdered, has a different flavor from fresh and the two do not generally serve as substitutes for each other in most dishes.

Ginger is one the principal spices of Indian Jews, who primarily enjoy it fresh. Sephardim and Mizrachim occasionally include it among the numerous spices in their pantry, most often dried and in combination with other spices. The ground form of ginger (*ingber*) was one of the few spices used by eastern Ashkenazim, who commonly and pronouncedly added it to tzimmes, *lebkuchen* (gingerbread), *lekakh* (honey cake), and *ingberlach* (confections).

GLATT

The Bible states: "Meat from an animal that *treifah* (has been torn) in the field you shall not eat."

The Sages interpreted this verse to mean that to be kosher an animal must be free of any mortal injury, even if that animal was ritually slaughtered before death. Thus after slaughter, the animal is examined to determine if it was healthy and, therefore, kosher. Most major organs—including the heart, brain, liver, spleen, kidneys, intestines, and stomach—rarely evidence diseases or injuries and do not require any special scrutiny, unless there is some indication of a problem. Lungs, on the other hand, are commonly affected by defects and must be carefully examined (*bedikah*) before an animal can be certified as kosher. Glatt ("smooth" in Yiddish) refers to an animal that upon examination is determined to have no perforations or other defects in its lungs.

When cattle graze, they commonly swallow other objects besides grass; as the food descends the esophagus into the upper stomach, these objects tend to puncture a lung. Therefore, more often than not, the lungs of even domesticated animals bear patches of body tissues united by fibrous tissues called adhesions (*sircha*), which are indicative of a puncture in the lung. Unless this wound heals, the animal is not kosher. The Talmud permits an animal with damaged lungs as long as any puncture is covered with a scab, indicating that it has healed. After slaughter but before the removal of the organs from the chest cavity, the examiner (*bodek*) runs his hands over the lobes of the lungs to determine if they are properly formed and free of any tangible adhesions. If he discovers any lesions, the lungs are removed and visually examined for defects. Those lungs determined to be free of any perforations or other defects are called *chalak* (literally "smooth" in Hebrew) or glatt, the more commonly used Yiddish equivalent. Nonetheless, even lungs with an adhesion can be kosher. To determine if a lung is punctured or not, the lung is inflated with air, then the questionable section is submerged under water. If no air bubbles appear on the surface, the animal is perfectly acceptable, although not glatt. Only a relatively small percentage of cattle prove to be glatt, generally one in twenty.

Since such a small percentage of cattle turn out to be glatt, meeting this demanding qualification is a major hardship. Thus the practice among Ashkenazim, as codified by Rabbi Moses Isserles (1525–1572) of Kraków, Poland, was that if small adhesions can be peeled from the surface of a cow's lung without per-

forating it and the lung remains airtight, the animal is deemed kosher although not glatt. Most Sephardim and Chasidim, on the other hand, only accepted glatt meat as kosher. Even among European Jews, the leniency of adhesion removal only applies to large cattle and buffalo, not to small herd animals. Therefore, lambs, goats, and deer must have smooth lungs. In any case, for the vast majority of European Jews, the acceptability of cattle with permissible lesions on the lungs remained the rule, a practice that their descendants later brought to America.

At the beginning of the twentieth century, agents of the nascent Chasidic communities in New York would once or twice a week travel to a New Jersey slaughterhouse to butcher glatt beef for their fellow Chasidim, barely producing enough to meet even this limited demand. Then in the 1950s, after the influx of Hungarians and Chasidim in the wake of World War II, the demand for glatt meat began to increase and spread outside of its traditional strongholds. At that time, there were more than thirty-five hundred kosher butcher shops in the New York metropolitan area, none of them offering exclusively glatt meat. As the attention to kosher food in general increased in the 1960s and 1970s and community standards frequently grew more rigid, so too did the interest in glatt meat. Because kosher meat production and distribution in America was rife with problems, including no way to ensure kashrut standards, many kosher consumers turned to glatt as a means of ensuring that the meat was kosher. The Orthodox Union (OU) only adopted a policy of requiring exclusively glatt meat in the late 1970s. Ultimately, glatt became the predominant standard for kosher meat in America.

As the popularity of glatt kosher meat increased, however, so did the misuse of the term. It is all too common for the term glatt to be applied to chickens, although it is impossible to check their tiny lungs, or fish, which do not even have lungs. Even dairy products have been promoted as glatt, a completely absurd development. Indeed, today the label "glatt kosher" does not even ensure that the lungs of a cow were actually free of all adhesions; many authorities agree that small adhesions that come off easily without leaving a perforation are not considered a problematic *sircha* and the meat, therefore, is still considered glatt. Indeed, beef labeled simply as "kosher" can actually have fewer adhesions than some meat sold as "glatt."

In order to indicate genuinely "glatt" meat—meat that is free of all adhesions—a new term has emerged in some circles: "glatt Beit Yosef," referring to the teachings of the Sephardic scholar Rabbi Joseph Caro. Thus today glatt is generally a marketing tool and frequently not a sign of a smooth lung or even a higher degree of kashrut standards.

GNOCCHI

Gnocchi are dumplings, often made with mashed potatoes or ricotta cheese.

Origin: Italy

As with many medieval European culinary innovations, dumplings first emerged in Italy, probably through contacts with Middle Easterners around the thirteenth century. Dumplings were a flavorful, filling, easy to make, and versatile way to use up leftovers. A basic bread mixture was the foundation for the earliest European dumpling—later in the sixteenth century called a *panada* (from the Spanish for "boiled bread")—which provided a way to utilize stale bread and extend stews and soups. The earliest Italian records of "macaroni" (from the Italian for "paste") in the thirteenth century referred not to pasta but rather to rudimentary dumplings made from "bread paste" and boiled in stews and soups. In the Renaissance, as modern cooking began to develop, semolina and other cereals were substituted for the bread in dumplings and the term macaroni came to mean only pasta.

In Tuscany by the fourteenth century, dumplings had already acquired the name gnocchi (Italian for "lumps"). Shortly thereafter, versions of dumplings were made—many originating with Italian Jewish communities—with ricotta, spinach, and chard, and, with the arrival of American foods in the sixteenth century, cornmeal, winter squash, and pumpkin. These types of gnocchi probably emerged as a way to use leftover ravioli filling, but eventually became a beloved dish on their own. After the popularization of the potato in Italy in the nineteenth century, cooked and mashed potato became the most popular base for gnocchi. Also around this time, tomato sauce became a widespread topping for gnocchi, joining cream, browned butter, and butter-sage sauces.

The sizes, shapes, and flavorings of Italian dumplings vary from region to region. However, typically ridges are imprinted on one side of each *gnocco* (singular), creating a surface to catch the sauce, and an indentation is made on the other side to help the center to cook through. Most gnocchi are cooked like pasta in lightly salted boiling water, although gnocchi cook more quickly, and there are also versions calling for baking. Once cooked, they are simply tossed with butter and grated cheese or topped with a sauce. Ricotta dumplings are also served plain, called *gnocchi gnudi* (naked dumplings). Thursday emerged in Rome as the traditional day to serve gnocchi, as it was customary to serve a dairy meal before the Sabbath, but they are popular anytime, usually as a *primo piatto* (first course).

(See also Dumpling)

ITALIAN CHEESE DUMPLINGS (*GNOCCHI DI RICOTTA*)
ABOUT 36 DUMPLINGS/6 TO 8 SERVINGS   [DAIRY]

2 cups (1 pound) whole-milk ricotta cheese
½ cup (1.5 ounces) grated Parmesan cheese
¾ cup (3 ounces) grated mozzarella or Swiss cheese (optional)
2 large eggs, lightly beaten
1 large egg yolk
½ teaspoon table salt or 1 teaspoon kosher salt
Ground white pepper to taste
1 cup cooked, squeezed, and chopped spinach (optional)
¼ to ½ teaspoon ground nutmeg
About ¼ cup all-purpose flour
½ cup (1 stick) unsalted butter

1. Line a sieve or colander with cheesecloth, place over a large bowl, spoon the ricotta in the center, place in the refrigerator, and let drain overnight. You will have about 1¼ cups ricotta.

2. In a large bowl, combine the cheeses, eggs, egg yolk, salt, pepper, optional spinach, and nutmeg. Stir in enough flour to bind. Cover with plastic wrap and refrigerate until firm, about 1 hour.

3. Flour your hands and form the cheese mixture into walnut-size balls. Flatten slightly and place on floured parchment paper or wax paper.

4. Bring a large pot of salted water to a simmer. In several batches, add the gnocchi, stirring to prevent sticking. Simmer until they rise to the surface, about 10 minutes. Remove with a slotted spoon and drain.

5. Preheat the oven to 375°F. Heat a large overproof dish.

6. Place the butter and gnocchi in the heated dish and toss to coat. Bake until heated through but not dry, about 15 minutes. If desired, top with additional Parmesan cheese, tomato sauce, or cream sauce.

GOAT

Goats—the word refers to any of the eight species belonging to the genus *Capra*—were originally nomadic residents of cliffs and arid climates throughout much of Asia, Africa, and Europe. Goats were among the earliest domesticated animals; they were probably first tamed in the highlands of western Iran and became an essential element of human life well before sheep and cattle came into the picture. The generic Hebrew term for a goat is *eiz* (*ezzim* is the plural and the name of the species), which is derived from the root "strength" and is utilized for both female and male goats. Most of the various breeds of domesticated goats are descended from the Near Eastern bezoar goat (*Capra aegagrus*, probably the biblical *akko*), except for the Angora (source of mohair) and Kashmir (source of cashmere), which are descended

Goats, a familiar sight in Marc Chagall's depictions of the shtetl, such as Man and Goat, 1925, were kept by many Ashkenazic families to provide milk, and when too old, meat.

from the Markhor (*Capra falconeri*). The predominant breed in the ancient Middle East was the Syrian mountain goat or Mamber (*Capra hircus mambrica*), which sports longer hair than most other domesticated breeds. Its predominantly black hair is occasionally streaked, speckled, and spotted with white and brown. Today, there are more than eighty thousand Mamber goats in Israel, primarily in Bedouin flocks in the Negev, which are tended as in the days of the patriarchs. Also in Israel are crossbreeds of Mambers with Saanen goats imported from Europe; the Saanens have a higher milk yield than the Mambers.

Goats and sheep are close relatives and share many characteristics. But the goat's hollow horns arch backward and outward, while sheep horns twist spirally. Since humans first domesticated them, both goats and sheep have been raised for their wool, milk, skins, and flesh. However, the sheep's principal asset has been its wool, while the goat's has been its milk. The biblical phrase "a land flowing with milk and honey" refers to goat's milk.

Goat meat tends to be very lean and, as a result, it is frequently less tender than other red meats. The meat of kids, which are usually slaughtered between three and six months, is more tender and delicate than meat from older goats, and not as strongly flavored as lamb.

Considering the goat's importance in ancient Israel, it is hardly surprising to find it utilized in various Jewish rituals. Goat hair was employed to make the curtains used to cover the portable Tabernacle (*Mishkan*) that accompanied the Israelites until the construction of the Temple in Jerusalem. The goat is one of the animals suitable to be an offering in the Temple; it was sometimes optional—as in the paschal offering and a sin-offering of an individual—and sometimes mandatory. Noting the utilization of goats for the various public sin-offerings, Maimonides in *Guide to the Perplexed* explained that this was to compensate for the actions of the sons of Jacob, who dipped Joseph's cloak into the blood of a goat.

Goats, which had been indispensable in biblical times and the predominant form of meat and milk, by the Talmudic period were viewed in Israel with more ambiguity. The Mishnah states: "Sheep and goats are not to be raised in the land of Israel but may be raised in Syria and the [uncultivated] wilderness of Israel." Although there was a dissenting opinion that a goat was permitted if it was tied up, most of the Israeli rabbis forbade goats even under that circumstance. This negative attitude probably arose in the wake of the massive ecological devastation wreaked by the Roman army in the wake of the first rebellion (67–70 CE); as large swaths of the land of Israel were left a wasteland, which sparked hostility toward flocks of goats that further threatened agriculture. The Babylonian rabbis never developed the aversion to goats and sheep of their Israeli counterparts.

Despite these negative attitudes toward goats, most of the milk, cheese, and meat consumed in the Middle East during the Talmudic period through the early twentieth century was still from goats. Goat was the primary meat of Ethiopians, reserved for special occasions. Goat is traditional Passover fare in Italy. Many Ashkenazic households owned a goat to maintain a regular supply of milk for the family, which explains the goat's common reoccurrence in artist Marc Chagall's depictions of Jewish life in eastern Europe. Today, goat remains the principal source of meat in much of North Africa and parts of the Middle East, but goat meat is a rarity in America, Europe, and Israel.

GOGOL MOGOL

Gogol mogol is a drink containing raw egg yolks, which serves as a remedy for sore throats and colds.
Origin: Ukraine
Other names: *gogl-mogl.*

Gogol is Ukrainian for "wild duck," a source of eggs in that region. Beginning in the seventeenth century, among Jews in Ukraine, Byelorussia, Russia, Romania, and some parts of Poland, the rhyming nonsense phrase *gogol mogol* referred to a familiar home remedy for sore throats and colds. The name may have been inspired by its similarity to the names of a well-known biblical pair of kings, Gog and Magog, who will wage the final war before the onset of the messianic age. The Jewish drinkable version is different from the more complex non-Jewish Russian *gogol mogol*, which is a mousse-like dessert.

The simplest form of *gogol mogol* consisted of raw egg yolks beaten with a little honey or sugar until nearly white in color. Some cooks added warm milk to the sweetened egg yolks, rendering it similar to eggnog, while others mixed in some whiskey, to help the sick person sleep, or a little lemon juice. Others stirred in a little schmaltz or butter. In a 2009 interview

in the *New York Times*, Barbra Streisand recalled that during her Brooklyn childhood her mother gave the future singer what she pronounced "guggle muggle", which contained hot milk, to soothe and strengthen her voice. The research of Dr. Shmuel Givon of the Israel General Medical Service revealed that a *gogol mogol* widens the blood vessels in the throat, thereby allowing the flow of more blood, and stimulates an immune response that eases the inflammation. Some children looked forward to a *gogol mogol*, while others had to have it poured down their throats. With the development of commercial cold medicines and fears concerning raw eggs, the use of *gogol mogols* dramatically decreased.

ASHKENAZIC RAW EGG DRINK (*GOGOL MOGOL*)
1 SERVING   [PAREVE]

2 large egg yolks
2 to 3 tablespoons brown sugar, granulated sugar, or honey
Dash of vanilla extract, lemon juice, whiskey, or rum
1 cup warm milk (optional)

In a small bowl, beat together the egg yolks, sugar, and vanilla until thick and creamy and the sugar dissolves. If using, add the milk.

GOMBÓC

Gombóc is a large dumpling, either sweet or savory. Some are stuffed with various fruit and vegetable fillings.
Origin: Hungary

Hungarians, influenced by Austrians, northern Italians, and Ukrainians, prepare a variety of dumplings, notably *galuska* (rudimentary dumplings), *csipetke* (pasta-like dumplings), and the larger *gombóc* (from the Hungarian *gömb*, "ball/sphere"). (*Gombócok* is technically the plural, but colloquially *gombóc* is also used for the plural.) Hungarian dumplings, like other central European versions, originated in the medieval period as bread dumplings. Inspired by changes in Italian Renaissance cuisine, Hungarians began substituting semolina and flour for the bread. For dessert, sugar was added. Matza balls are called *macesz gombóc*. In the mid-nineteenth century, mashed potatoes (*krumplis gombóc*) also became common dumpling bases.

To further stretch and enhance dumplings, fillings were frequently inserted, such as sautéed cabbage (*káposztás gombóc*). The most popular Hungarian filled dumpling contains a whole Italian prune plum (*szilvás gombóc*), featuring a fresh fruit that is widespread in the early fall during plum season, while pitted dried plums and lekvar are sometimes substituted at other times of the year. *Gombóc*, after cooking, are commonly rolled in browned bread crumbs.

Dumplings made from a creamy fresh cheese are popular throughout central and eastern Europe—called *túrós gombóc* in Hungary, *topfenknodel* in Austria and Germany, *tvarohovo-sýrové knedliky* in the Czech Republic, *sirni halushki* in Russia, and *kluski z bryndza* in Poland. *Topfen* and *túrós* are made with less whey than the similar German quark, making it drier and appropriate for dumplings. Since *topfen* and *túrós* are unavailable in America, you can add a little cream cheese to the firmer farmer cheese to approximate it. The dumplings themselves are not inherently sweet, but are flavored by topping with sweetened whipped cream, sour cream, browned bread crumbs, cinnamon-sugar, or jam. Cheese dumplings are an everyday dish as a main course or side, but in many central European households also traditional on Shavuot and Hanukkah.

(See also Dumpling, Gevina Levana, and Shlishkes)

❧ HUNGARIAN SWEET CHEESE DUMPLINGS (*TÚRÓS GOMBÓC*)

ABOUT 24 DUMPLINGS   [DAIRY]

   1 pound (2 cups) *túrós* or *gevina levana* (Israeli white cheese) for baking, or 14 ounces (1¾ cups) pot or farmer cheese and ¼ cup cream cheese or mascarpone, softened
   1 to 5 tablespoons sugar
   ½ teaspoon table salt or 1 teaspoon kosher salt
   2 large eggs, lightly beaten
   2 tablespoons (¼ stick) butter, softened
   About ¾ cup semolina, farina, or matza meal

   1. In a food processor, blender, or electric mixer, combine the cheese, sugar, and salt. Add the eggs and beat until smooth. Beat in the butter. Stir in enough semolina to produce a soft, but manageable dough. Cover and place in the refrigerator for at least 2 hours.

   2. Bring a large pot of lightly salted water to a low boil. Using moistened hands, form the batter into 1½-inch balls.

   3. Drop the dumplings in the water, stirring gently to prevent sticking. Reduce the heat and simmer, uncov-

ered, until they rise to the surface, 10 to 15 minutes. Remove the dumplings with a slotted spoon. Keep warm in a 200°F oven. If desired, serve with sweetened whipped cream, sour cream, cinnamon-sugar, or jam.

GOMO (SEPHARDIC PASTRY FILLINGS)

From early in their history, Sephardim prepared various filled pies and pastries for the Sabbath and other special occasions. Almost anything can be used as a filling, but vegetable-cheese mixtures are the most prevalent, particularly during the spring and summer. Cheese fillings are popular treats at dairy meals, including Saturday and Sunday morning *desayuno* (brunch) and Hanukkah. Meat fillings are widespread for Friday night dinner and during the winter. Spinach, pumpkin, and winter squash fillings are traditional for Rosh Hashanah and sweet nut for Purim. During Passover, pieces of moistened matza are substituted for the pastry.

(See also Ajin, Almond Paste, Boreka, Boyo, Bulema, Empanada, Masa, Mina, Pastida, Pastelito, Phyllo, Sambusak, and Travado)

❧ SEPHARDIC CHEESE FILLING (*GOMO DE QUESO*)

ABOUT 4 CUPS; ENOUGH FOR FORTY-EIGHT 3-INCH TURNOVERS OR SEVENTY-TWO PHYLLO TRIANGLES   [DAIRY]

   8 ounces (1½ cups) crumbled feta or pot cheese
   8 ounces (2 cups) shredded Muenster, Cheddar, or Gruyère cheese
   2 large egg yolks or 1 large egg, lightly beaten
   1 tablespoon cornstarch or all-purpose flour
   About ½ teaspoon table salt or 1 teaspoon kosher salt
   Ground black pepper to taste
   In a medium bowl, combine all the ingredients.

❧ SEPHARDIC CHICKPEA FILLING (*GOMO DE GARVANSOS*)

ABOUT 4 CUPS; ENOUGH FOR FORTY-EIGHT 3-INCH TURNOVERS OR SEVENTY-TWO PHYLLO TRIANGLES   [PAREVE]

   3 tablespoons sesame or vegetable oil
   2 medium onions, chopped
   1½ to 2 teaspoons ground cumin
   ½ teaspoon ground turmeric
   4 cups cooked chickpeas, mashed
   About ¾ teaspoon table salt or 1½ teaspoons kosher salt

Ground black pepper to taste

⅓ cup chopped fresh cilantro or flat-leaf parsley (optional)

In a large skillet, heat the oil over medium heat. Add the onions and sauté until soft and translucent, 5 to 10 minutes. Stir in the cumin and turmeric. Add the chickpeas, salt, and pepper and cook until dry. If using, stir in the cilantro.

SEPHARDIC EGGPLANT FILLING
(*GOMO DE BERENJENA*)

ABOUT 4 CUPS; ENOUGH FOR FORTY-EIGHT 3-INCH

TURNOVERS OR SEVENTY-TWO PHYLLO TRIANGLES   [PAREVE]

3 medium (1 pound each) eggplants

2 large eggs, lightly beaten

3 tablespoons olive or vegetable oil

About 1 teaspoon table salt or 2 teaspoons kosher salt

Ground black pepper to taste

About ½ cup matza meal or bread crumbs, or 1½ cups mashed potatoes

Cut several slits in the eggplants. Roast over hot coals or broil 3 to 4 inches from the heat source under a broiler, turning occasionally, until charred and tender, about 20 minutes. Or place on a baking sheet and bake in a 400°F oven until very tender, about 50 minutes. Let stand until cool enough to handle. Peel the eggplants, place in a colander, and let drain for about 30 minutes. In a large bowl, mash the eggplants into a pulp. There should be about 3¼ cups. Add the eggs, oil, salt, and pepper. Stir in enough matza meal to make a thick filling.

TURKISH EGGPLANT AND TOMATO FILLING (*GOMO DE HANDRAJO*)

ABOUT 4 CUPS; ENOUGH FOR FORTY-EIGHT 3-INCH

TURNOVERS OR SEVENTY-TWO PHYLLO TRIANGLES   [PAREVE]

Handrajo means "rags" in Ladino. This is a specialty of Turkey's third largest city, Izmir, (once known as Smyrna), which lies 210 miles southeast of Istanbul on the Aegean Sea. The filling is primarily used in *borekas* (*borekas de handrajo*).

2 medium (about 1 pound each) eggplants, peeled and cut into ½-inch cubes

About 1 tablespoon table salt or 2 tablespoons kosher salt

¼ cup vegetable oil

2 medium onions, chopped

1 cup (8 ounces) peeled, seeded, and chopped plum tomatoes

Ground black pepper to taste

1. Place the eggplant pieces in a colander or on a wire rack, lightly sprinkle with the salt, and let stand for about 1 hour. Rinse the eggplant under cold water, then press repeatedly between several layers of paper towels until it feels firm and dry.

2. In a large pot, heat the oil over medium heat. Add the onions and sauté until golden, about 15 minutes. Add the eggplants, tomatoes, and pepper and cook, stirring frequently, until the eggplant is soft and the liquid evaporates, about 15 minutes. Mash, then let cool.

SEPHARDIC LEEK FILLING (*GOMO DE PRASSA*)

ABOUT 4 CUPS; ENOUGH FOR FORTY-EIGHT 3-INCH

TURNOVERS OR SEVENTY-TWO PHYLLO TRIANGLES   [PAREVE]

3 tablespoons olive oil

3 pounds (8 large) leeks (white and light green part only), chopped

1 medium onion, chopped (optional)

¼ cup water

3 large eggs, lightly beaten

About ½ teaspoon table salt or 1 teaspoon kosher salt

Ground black pepper to taste

¾ cup matza meal or bread crumbs

In a large skillet or pot, heat the oil over medium heat. Add the leeks and, if using, onion and sauté until slightly softened, about 3 minutes. Add the water, cover, and cook until the leeks are tender, about 5 minutes. Uncover and cook, stirring frequently, until the liquid evaporates. Let cool, then stir in the eggs, salt, pepper, and enough matza meal to make a thick filling.

SEPHARDIC MEAT FILLING (*GOMO DE CARNE*)

ABOUT 4 CUPS; ENOUGH FOR FORTY-EIGHT 3-INCH

TURNOVERS OR SEVENTY-TWO PHYLLO TRIANGLES   [MEAT]

3 tablespoons olive or vegetable oil

2 medium onions, chopped

24 ounces lean ground beef or lamb

About 1 teaspoon salt

Ground black pepper to taste

1 teaspoon ground cinnamon or ½ teaspoon ground allspice (optional)

1 cup mashed potatoes or about ¼ cup matza meal

¼ to ½ cup chopped fresh flat-leaf parsley

1 large egg, lightly beaten

2 to 3 *huevos haminados* (Sephardic Long-Cooked Eggs, page 253), finely chopped (optional)

¼ to ⅓ cup pine nuts (optional)

In a large skillet, heat the oil over medium heat. Add the onions and sauté until soft and translucent, 5 to 10 minutes. Add the meat and cook until it loses its red color, about 5 minutes. Pour off the excess fat. Add the salt, pepper, and, if using, cinnamon. Let cool. Stir in the potatoes, parsley, and egg. If using, add the *haminados* and/or pine nuts.

SEPHARDIC POTATO FILLING (*GOMO DE PATATA*)

ABOUT 4 CUPS; ENOUGH FOR FORTY-EIGHT 3-INCH TURNOVERS OR SEVENTY-TWO PHYLLO TRIANGLES   [PAREVE]

1½ pounds (3 large) baking (russet) potatoes, peeled and cut into chunks

2 cloves garlic, mashed (optional)

3 tablespoons olive or vegetable oil

2 medium onions, chopped

About ½ teaspoon table salt or 1 teaspoon kosher salt

Ground white or black pepper to taste

2 large eggs, lightly beaten

½ cup chopped fresh flat-leaf parsley or cilantro (optional)

1. Place the potatoes and, if using, garlic in a large pot and add cold water to cover. Bring to a boil, reduce the heat to low, and simmer until tender, 15 to 20 minutes. Drain and mash in a large bowl. You should have about 3 cups.

2. In a large skillet, heat the oil over medium heat. Add the onions and sauté until golden, about 15 minutes. Stir the onions into the potatoes and add the salt and pepper. Let cool. Stir in the eggs and, if using, parsley.

SEPHARDIC SPINACH FILLING (*GOMO DE ESPINACA*)

ABOUT 4 CUPS; ENOUGH FOR FORTY-EIGHT 3-INCH TURNOVERS OR SEVENTY-TWO PHYLLO TRIANGLES   [PAREVE]

2 pounds (about 8 cups packed) stemmed fresh spinach or chard, rinsed but not dried; or 30 ounces thawed chopped frozen spinach, squeezed dry

3 tablespoons olive or vegetable oil

1 medium onion or 8 scallions, chopped

1 to 1⅓ cups mashed potatoes

2 large eggs, lightly beaten

About ½ teaspoon table salt or 1 teaspoon kosher salt

Ground black pepper to taste

About ⅛ teaspoon ground nutmeg, ground cumin, or paprika; or 1 teaspoon dried dill

1. If using fresh spinach, place it, with the water clinging to the leaves, in a large pot over medium heat, cover, and cook until wilted, about 5 minutes. Drain and chop.

2. In a large skillet, heat the oil over medium heat. Add the onion and sauté until soft and translucent, 5 to 10 minutes. Add the spinach and stir until the liquid evaporates. Let cool. Stir in the potatoes, eggs, salt, pepper, and nutmeg.

GOOSE

Geese, part of the family of birds including swans and ducks, are among the kosher animals. The most important goose species for consumption is the migratory greylag, domesticated by the Egyptians around forty-five hundred years ago. As the name reflects, the wild greylag has gray-brown plumage, but some domesticated descendants were bred to have white feathers. As geese mature and become heavier, flying grows more difficult, and geese are therefore easily domesticated and maintained in yards and fields. Since at least ancient Roman times, domesticated geese were frequently force-fed in order to fatten them, a process probably originating as a means of making them too heavy to fly. Domesticated geese were prominent more than three thousand years ago in Israel. Scholars have identified the fatted fowl on King Solomon's table as geese, and later the Mishnah discussed goose breeding in Israel. Geese were well regarded among Jews, as is reflected in a comment in the Talmud: "One who sees a goose in a dream should expect wisdom." However in Talmudic times, pigeons and chickens were the principal poultry in the Roman Empire.

During the Middle Ages, geese lost significance in most of the Middle East, except primarily in Persia. Many Persians served roasted goose (*duaz fenjo*) as a traditional Rosh Hashanah main course. Sephardim tended not to favor the more intensely flavored goose flesh and, therefore, it never developed a substantial place in their culinary repertoire.

It was during the early medieval period that geese first attained widespread popularity in Europe, spreading northward through the continent to become the predominant fowl, particularly in urban areas. The Jews of the Rhineland, faced with exclusion from the trade guilds and from various traditional occupations, found raising geese an important source of income. Subsequently, geese (*ganz* or *gandz* in Yiddish; *gendzl*, a gosling) replaced pigeons in the Ashkenazic diet. Gregarious fattened geese, while not producing many eggs, offered a number of advantages over the more prolific chicken for early Ashkenazim: They flourish on lower-quality feed (grazing in fields), can live and reproduce for up to fifty years, form more cohesive family and group units, can be herded rather than carried, are less prone to diseases, and provide more fat for schmaltz. In addition, geese honk loudly and persistently when strangers approach or when frightened, so historically they have guarded themselves as well as their owners' property. In many areas, goose eggs were the predominant types consumed, while the feathers provided down—which was stuffed into mattresses and pillows for softness, and into quilts and clothes as insulation—as well as quills for writing.

In Franco-German Jewish communities, beef was the common Sabbath entrée, while goose was generally reserved for festivals, weddings, and other special occasions. Most Ashkenazic housewives kept at least a few geese in a pen to provide for the family, while some raised large flocks. Geese were also essential for their ample fat, as goose schmaltz served as the predominant cooking fat. Schmaltz was a necessity because oils were rare and expensive, while butter was unacceptable with meat foods. In the seventeenth century, chef Jean-Pierre Clause of Strasbourg used goose liver raised by Alsatian Jews to create the classic pâté de foie gras.

Only centuries later, with the movement of most of the Ashkenazim to eastern Europe, did the chicken emerge there as the principal fowl. Yet even in eastern Europe, many families raised a goose or two. Sholem Aleichem, in his short story "Geese," describes the manner of a woman fattening a flock of thirty geese in a shtetl. The old woman explains, "Geese is my business . . . but you think it's as easy as all that? The first thing you got to do is this: you start buying geese right after Sukkot [from peasants], in the autumn. You throw them into a coop and keep them there all winter, until December. You feed them and take good care of them. Comes Hanukkah, you start killing them, and you turn geese into cash."

Geese were fattened through the autumn. Then as free grazing material decreased at the end of the summer, around Rosh Hashanah, or disappeared before the onset of winter and the winter migration, around Hanukkah, most of them were slaughtered. Another goose or two might be purchased in January to serve as a Passover delicacy in March or April. In eastern Europe, where geese were rarer then western Europe, veal breast was frequently the traditional Rosh Hashanah and/or Sukkot entrée and brisket was the most traditional Hanukkah dish. But in Alsace, Germany, the Czech Republic, and Hungary, those roles were played by roast goose. Younger geese were served on Rosh Hashanah and Sukkot, and more mature, fatter geese were enjoyed on Hanukkah—besides serving as the traditional holiday main course, the larger bird supplied more schmaltz to last through the winter, and a separate crock of schmaltz was set aside for Passover cooking. However, in eastern Europe, chickens provided most of the fat for schmaltz.

For a special Sabbath treat, the goose's long neck was stuffed and roasted to make a dish called *helzel*. In Alsace, Jews cut up and salted geese, then simmered them in goose fat for hours to make *confit d'oie*; the pieces were stored in crocks, then added to Sabbath stews and the Sabbath *choucroute garnie*. The favorite Ashkenazic ways to prepare goose were roasted (*gebratene*) whole—the dish was called *liba pecsenye* by Hungarians—and braised in pieces (*ganseklein*) and, frequently, cooked along with sauerkraut or cabbage. Stuffings of fruit or potatoes perfectly complemented the rich, fatty meat of geese. Europeans traditionally served roast goose with braised cabbage or Brussels sprouts. Italian Jews prepared various goose dishes and have long used goose flesh in place of pork to make sausages, notably *salame d'oca* (goose salami). Braised duck (*yiaourtli*) was a traditional Sabbath lunch in central Greece.

The American turkey, arriving in Europe in the sixteenth century, gradually supplanted the goose, even in western Europe. Consequently, most modern foie gras comes from duck liver rather than goose liver. Still, goose remains a beloved holiday dish in Alsace, southwestern Germany, and Hungary. However, geese are infrequent at best in most modern kosher butcher shops and markets in America and Israel, even on Hanukkah.

(See also Bird, Gribenes, Hanukkah, Helzel, Liver, and Schmaltz)

GOULASH

Goulash is a meat stew or soup simmered with lots of onions and seasoned with paprika.

Origin: Hungary

Other names: Czech: *gulás*; German: *gulasch*; Hungarian: *gulyás*; Polish: *gulasz*; Romanian: *gulas, tocanita de carne*.

Goulash is arguably the most famous of all Hungarian dishes. It is certainly among the earliest, dating back to the Magyars' nomadic days before the ninth century, when they cooked stews over campfires in easily transportable cauldrons called *bogrács*. At that time, Magyar shepherds made similar stews in which they cooked onions and rehydrated pieces of dried meat; the stew is called *gulyás* (literally "herdsmen") after its originators. Eventually, peasants adopted the term for the soupy stews that became the mainstay of their diet; these stews were prepared with any available meat, but preferably with beef (*marha gulyás*). After the Turks introduced paprika to the Balkans in the late sixteenth century, it made its way to Hungary, where peasants began seasoning their stews with this inexpensive spice and sometimes also caraway. The addition of paprika led to the emergence of the modern form of *gulyás*.

For a related stew called *pörkölt* (literally meaning "roasted")—Jews call it *paprikás*—the meat is cut into larger pieces than in a *gulyás* and simmered in much less liquid; instead, it is braised in onions and its own fat. To non-Jewish Hungarians, *paprikás*, known as paprikash in America, is the same as a *pörkölt*, but with sour cream added. For goulash soup, called *gulyásleves*, the amount of liquid is increased.

As is typical of Hungarian cooking, the meat is not browned, but only simmered until meltingly tender. Real goulash is never thickened with flour, but rather with the onions that break down during cooking. Goulash contains a large proportion of onions; according to some Hungarians, the weight of the onions should equal that of the meat. Following the arrival of tomatoes, many cooks began adding them to goulash, while others find their presence inappropriate. Hungarians never add bell pepper, although some do use fresh Hungarian paprika peppers, in addition to the ground paprika. The popularization of the potato in

the nineteenth century led to its inclusion in some versions, while other cooks insisted on a pure-meat *gulyás*. Traditional *gulyás* never contained sour cream, which was added to many American versions. Consequently, Hungarian Jews could readily adopt *gulyás* into their repertoire and it became a popular Friday night and holiday dish.

In the nineteenth century, the Hungarian upper class finally embraced *gulyás*. At this time, Hungarians were attempting to distinguish and separate themselves from the Austrians by stressing their culture and language, and *gulyás* emerged as a symbol of the country and a national dish. Nevertheless, neighboring countries soon discovered *gulyás* as well. The Viennese version tends to be much thicker, more like an American stew. Czechs serve it with steamed bread dumplings. Romanians omit the paprika punch, but typically season it with garlic, green peppers, and sometimes horseradish.

The word goulash only appeared in English in 1866 and was subsequently brought to America by Hungarian immigrants. The early American Jewish cookbook *Aunt Babette's* (1889) offered a recipe akin to goulash entitled "Paprica (Hungarian Hash)." It was among the first American cookbooks to include paprika, let alone a Hungarian stew. The first edition of *The Settlement Cook Book* (1901) provided a recipe for "Hungarian Gulash." The directions said, "Veal and beef mixed. Cut into one-inch squares and brown in hot fat with one onion, salt, and paprika. When the meat is brown, add the tomatoes, and one-half hour before serving, add some small potatoes." By the 1943 edition of *The Settlement Cook Book*, the title was spelled "Hungarian Goulash."

By the onset of the twentieth century, goulash had become a standard dish among many American Jews from non-Hungarian roots. During the Depression, goulash emerged as one of America's most famous dishes, although many American versions are actually *pörkölt*, made with less liquid.

(See also Paprika and Paprikás)

ᨆ HUNGARIAN BEEF GOULASH (*MARHA GULYÁS*)

6 TO 8 SERVINGS [MEAT]

¼ cup schmaltz, vegetable oil, or shortening
2 large yellow onions, halved and thinly sliced
2 to 4 cloves garlic, minced
2 to 3 tablespoons sweet paprika

¼ teaspoon hot paprika or cayenne (optional)

3 pounds boneless beef chuck or shoulder, cut into 1- to 1½-inch cubes

1 cup (6 ounces) peeled, seeded, and chopped plum tomatoes

2 medium green bell peppers, seeded and sliced (optional)

About 4 cups beef broth, chicken broth, or water

About ½ teaspoon table salt or 1 teaspoon kosher salt

Ground black pepper to taste

1 teaspoon caraway seeds (optional)

2 pounds baking (russet) potatoes, peeled and cut into ½-inch cubes (optional)

1. In a large, heavy pot, heat the schmaltz over medium heat. Add the onions and sauté until soft and translucent, about 10 minutes. Add the garlic and stir for 2 minutes. Remove from the heat and stir in the paprika(s) until the onions are well coated.

2. Place the pot over low heat, add the beef, and stir to coat. Add the tomatoes and, if using, bell peppers. Add enough broth to almost cover the beef. Add the salt, pepper, and, if using, caraway. Bring to a boil, cover, and simmer over low heat, stirring occasionally, until the meat is nearly tender, about 1½ hours.

3. If using, add the potatoes, cover, and simmer until the meat and potatoes are tender, about 30 minutes. Skim any fat from the surface and check the seasonings. *Gulyás* is even better if allowed to cool, refrigerated overnight, and reheated. Serve with *csipetke* (noodle pellets), *galuska* (dumplings), or wide noodles.

VARIATIONS

Hungarian Veal Goulash (Borjú Gulyás): Substitute 3 pounds boneless veal shoulder for the beef and reduce the cooking time to about 1¼ hours.

GOZINAKI

Gozinaki is a walnut and honey candy.

Origin: Georgia

Other names: *gozinaqi.*

Georgians historically did not eat many confections and pastries, primarily reserving them for special banquets and weddings. Instead, they preferred fresh and dried fruit and preserves. However, the walnut-loving Georgians boiled their favorite nut in honey to create a popular confection, *gozinaki*. These are traditional on Rosh Hashanah, to start the new year on a sweet note.

GEORGIAN WALNUT AND HONEY CANDY (GOZINAKI)

ABOUT 48 PIECES [PAREVE]

2 cups (24 ounces) honey

½ cup sugar

1 pound (4 cups) walnuts, toasted and finely chopped (not ground)

1. In a heavy medium saucepan, stir the honey and sugar over medium-low heat until the sugar dissolves, about 5 minutes. Stop stirring, increase the heat to medium, and boil until the syrup reaches the thread stage or 230°F on a candy thermometer, about 8 minutes.

2. Reduce the heat to low and add the walnuts. Cook, stirring, until golden and reaches the soft-ball stage or 240°F, about 10 minutes. Do not burn.

3. Pour the syrup onto a moistened cutting board or oiled marble slab. Using a moistened spatula or rolling pin, spread into ½-inch thickness and smooth the surface. Let stand until firm but not solid, about 15 minutes, then cut into 2-inch diamond shapes or squares. Let cool completely, at least 2 hours. If desired, wrap individually in pieces of cellophane. Store in an airtight container at room temperature for up to 1 week.

GRAIN

The grass family, consisting of more than eight thousand species, is the third-largest family of flowering plants. Nevertheless, it has long been the single most important food source for humans, providing the bulk of the diet in the form of cereal grains: rice and millet in eastern Asia; sorghum and millet in Africa; teff, wheat, and millet in Ethiopia; corn in South America; rye, wheat, barley, and oats in Europe; and wheat and barley in western Asia. These seeds possess certain important attributes accounting for their long-standing importance to humans: They are versatile (they are the basis for bread and many other foods); they do not spoil as quickly as other sources of protein; they are rich in carbohydrates, the major source of calories in the human diet since the advent of civilization; they provide fodder for domesticated animals; and, not coincidentally, they can also be transformed into alcoholic beverages. Grains, at least a few of them, are also the only substances that can become either *chametz* or Passover matza.

Well before humanity discovered agriculture, hunter-gatherers picked and amassed primitive barley and wheat, which was spread by the wind and sprouted wild throughout much of the Fertile Crescent. At first, kernels were roasted in campfires, which not only cooked them but simultaneously removed the inedible husks. Later, people began boiling the grains in the cavities of concave rocks beside the campfire and then in woven baskets. After the invention of earthenware during the Neolithic period, people boiled them in clay pots, to create what we call porridge or gruel—the Greeks knew it as *sitos*, the Romans as *puls,* and the Jews as *dysah*. Early meals consisted primarily of these stewed cereals, which were sometimes served plain and at other times flavored with onions, garlic, and herbs, or perhaps sweetened with honey. When some mush was left standing too long, it fermented, creating rudimentary beer, which in itself probably convinced the first farmers of the advantage of settling in one spot: If they could raise enough barley, they would be guaranteed a large, steady supply of fermented gruel. When people accidentally dropped some of the porridge into campfires—they were certainly not intentionally wasting a scarce resource—they discovered that the baked mishaps were tastier, more portable, and more useful than the gruel, and created the first rudimentary breads. In due course, cooks realized that finely crushed kernels cooked more quickly than whole ones and also gave the gruel a smoother texture—this discovery led to the development of flour.

In the late Neolithic period, rudimentary farmers near the Euphrates River discovered how to plant barley and wheat seeds to propagate a more-or-less stable supply, requiring them to settle in a permanent location and thus marking the very inception of civilization. In that vein, all the earliest records of writing have to do with grain transactions. Barley and wheat thrive throughout most of the Middle East, while most other grains fare poorly in much of the region. Therefore, bread from those two grains has long been more important in the Middle East than in any other area. In the earliest levels at digs in Jericho, one of the oldest continuously inhabited cities in the world, archeologists found carbonized seeds of two primitive varieties of wheat—einkorn and emmer—as well as two-rowed barley. In the Seven Species with which the land of Israel is praised, the Bible lists two grains first—*chitah* (wheat) and *se'orah* (*barley*).

The Fertile Crescent was not only home to these important grains, but also to three of the most useful animals capable of being domesticated—cattle, sheep, and goats. Cows became an important part of agriculture with the advent of the iron plow in the Near East around 2500 BCE. This instrument was generally pulled by cattle, allowing for deeper burrowing and engendering a revolution in agriculture, especially for wheat. Barley can be planted without plowing, but wheat benefits from it.

Eventually, people discovered that they could thresh grain (remove it from the stalks) without roasting by beating the wheat or other grain with sticks or by having oxen repeatedly tread on the stalks. Yet all these methods generally resulted in most of the grains being broken, thereby allowing rancidity and limiting storage. Later, a threshing sledge (tribulum), a large board with spikes on the underside, was pulled over the stalks by oxen, leaving more unbroken kernels. In archeological sites of biblical Israel, numerous threshing floors and sledges have been discovered; these were needed for processing hulled grains like emmer, einkorn, and two-rowed barley.

The Romans preferred common wheat and distributed it throughout their domains. Around two millennia ago, common wheat in the Near East and, along with durum, constituted the bulk of the cereal crop, with barley increasingly relegated to animal fodder. Later, the Arabs spread rice west from Persia to Iberia. After the arrival of American corn, this new grain eventually became important in parts of the Old World. Beginning in the nineteenth century, corn, rice, and wheat would increasingly account among them for the vast majority of all grains produced worldwide, reaching nearly 90% in 2009.

In 2010, corn leads among all grains in worldwide production by weight, although a significant portion of the corn crop is used in industrial processes and for animal feed. In second place in production is rice, which is the predominant grain in tropical and semi-tropical areas, and only barely surpasses wheat (including common wheat and durum), the principal grain of temperate lands. Barley, the fourth most widely grown grain, remains important for malting and livestock, while sorghum (fifth) and millet (sixth) endure as staples of the human diet in parts of Africa and eastern Asia. Seventh in worldwide production is oats, its primary area still in northern Europe and North America. The last of the eight major contemporary grain crops (buckwheat, amaranth, and quinoa are pseudocereals and not members of the grass family) is rye, a grain increasingly over the past two decades decreasing in popularity and still most appreciated in the colder regions of Europe. There are also a few grains enduring as local favorites, such teff in Ethiopia, spelt (*dinkel*) in Germany, and emmer (*faro*) in Italy.

(See Barley, Bread, Emmer, Millet, Rye, Semolina, and Wheat)

GRAPE

Grapes are small, firm berries with a semitranslucent flesh enclosed within a smooth skin that grow in bunches on a perennial woody vine. Colors include green, red, purple, and blue-black. When mature, grapes contain about 75 to 80 percent water and 14 to 25 percent sugar. The vine is one of the most versatile plants, with most parts being used in cooking—whole berries with poultry, fish, salads, soups, and desserts; the pulp for juice and preserves; grape sugar as a sweetener; grape seeds for oil; and tender, young leaves for stuffing and cooking. The juice of unripe grapes is squeezed to make verjuice.

Today, there are more than eight thousand varieties of grapes and three types—wine, raisin, and table grapes. All grapes are descended from two diverse lines—labrusca (American) and vinifera (Asian and European). Labrusca, also called slip-skin, have skins that separate easily from the pulp and seeds. On the contrary, the skin of vinifera grapes adheres to the pulp, while the seeds are easily removed, or occasionally they are seedless. A single vinifera parent resulted in the many varieties of vines that produce all the world's premium wines and most of the world's table grapes. Among the earliest grapes, and possibly the original vinifera, was the Muscat, which still produces a fruity, perfumed wine. Crossing European and American grapes has produced varieties such as Concord and Catawba. Most labrusca grapes are used in commercial processing for juice, preserves, and sacramental (Kiddush) wine. Much more important to the world are the vinifera species.

From its home in southern Transcaucasia or southwest Asia, not far from Mount Ararat, the vinifera grape, initially cultivated around 3000 BCE, spread across the ancient world. Grape seeds have been found in many of the earliest archaeological excavations. Paintings on the walls of Egyptian tombs depict

viticulture, and grapes have long been prominent fixtures of Judaism. Noah's first act following the Flood was to plant a vineyard (*kerem*). The Bible recounts that the Israelites' first exposure to the Promised Land was a grape cluster (*eshkol*) of legendary proportions brought back by the spies sent by Moses. The vine (*gefen*) is listed in the Bible among the Seven Species with which the Land of Israel is praised. The people of Israel were compared to grapes and God to the owner of a vineyard. Wine—symbolizing joy and fruitfulness ("wine that cheers man's heart")—is an integral element of many Jewish rituals, including Kiddush, Havdalah, *brit milah*, the marriage ceremony, and the Passover Seder. According to a Midrash, grapes were the forbidden fruit in Eden.

In the ancient world, grapes were eaten fresh, but only sparingly and for the very brief period when they came into season. Some of the crop was spread over flat wicker baskets and set in the sun to dry, becoming raisins, or pressed into clusters and dried as cakes. The bulk of the grape harvest was crushed for its juice, specifically, fermented juice. Hence the Bible repeatedly reiterates the trio of agricultural blessings: "of your grain, *tiroshcha* [your partially fermented grape juice], and your olive oil." (The word *tirosh* refers to grape juice that is not mature enough to be considered *yayin*, "wine.") The predominant form in which the fruit of the vine was used was in the liquid form and not as *anavim* (grapes), the actual fruit.

(See also Agraz, Raisin, Vinegar, and Wine)

GRAPE LEAVES, STUFFED

Origin: Probably Turkey

Other names: Arabic: *mehshi wara ainub*; Azeri: *yarpag dolmasi*; Bulgaria: *lozova surma*; Croatia: *sarma*; Georgia: *tolma*; Greece: *dolmades, yaprakes dolmas*; Kurdistan: *yaprach*; Ladino: *yaprakes finos*; Persian: *dolma bargh*; Romania: *sarmale in foi de vita*; Turkey: *yaprak dolmasi*.

Throughout most of history, resources were never wasted, but some vegetation proved more difficult to utilize than others. Perhaps the first culinary usage for otherwise inedible grape leaves was enwrapping fish to insulate the tender flesh while roasting. During the early medieval period, someone in the Caucasus region (the home of the grape vine), Sasanian Persia, or possibly Byzantium figured out that grape leaves could be filled with various leftover grains or meat, then simmered in a pot until tender. In the late medieval period, the Arabs spread the concept westward. The Ottoman Turks, for the five centuries following their ascension in the fourteenth century, honed and refined the art of making stuffed vegetables, generically known as dolma or *dolmasi*, thus transforming peasant fare into sophisticated food.

Consequently, the concept was most popular in the Ottoman Empire and adjacent areas. Three Turkish words—*yaprak* (leaf), *sarma* (wrap), and *dolmak* (to get filled/to be stuffed)—are used by various communities to specify stuffed vine leaves. In northern Europe, where vineyards did not thrive, the ubiquitous cabbage provided the principal leaves for stuffing, while in western and central Asia and the Balkans, grape leaves were far and away the most popular, with each country developing a slight flavoring variation.

There are two basic categories of stuffed grape leaves: ones containing meat and ones without meat. Grape leaves made without meat are sometimes called *yalanci*, from the Turkish meaning "false/liar." According to the Turks, meat-stuffed *etli yaprak dolma* should be served warm, while rice-stuffed *yalanci dolma* should be served at room temperature. Rice dolmas are particularly popular among Jews, as they can be eaten at both dairy or meat meals. Rice-stuffed grape leaves are frequently served with yogurt. Meat grape leaves are typically offered as a main course accompanied with rice and salads, while rice versions are usually appetizers, providing wonderful finger food on the Sabbath for *mezzes* (appetizer assortments) and lunches. Stuffed grape leaves were regular Friday evening fare in Salonika.

(See also Cabbage, Stuffed; and Dolma)

❧ SEPHARDIC STUFFED GRAPE LEAVES

(*YAPRAKES FINOS*)

ABOUT 40 ROLLS   [MEAT OR PAREVE]

Stuffing:

  1 cup raw Baldo or long-grain rice
  ¼ cup olive oil
  1 large yellow onion, chopped
  2 cups water
  About 1 teaspoon table salt or 2 teaspoons kosher salt
  About ¼ teaspoon ground black pepper
  ¼ cup chopped fresh flat-leaf parsley or mint (optional)

¼ cup dried currants (optional)
¼ cup pine nuts (optional)
1 (1-pound) jar grape leaves (about 60 small or 40 medium leaves) or 40 medium fresh leaves
About 1½ cups chicken broth or water
4 to 6 tablespoons fresh lemon juice
2 tablespoons extra-virgin olive oil
About 1 teaspoon table salt or 2 teaspoons kosher salt
2 to 8 whole cloves garlic or 1 teaspoon sugar (optional)

1. To make the stuffing: Soak the rice in cold water to cover for 30 minutes, then drain, rinse under cold water, and drain again. In a large saucepan, heat the oil over medium heat. Add the onion and sauté until soft and translucent, 5 to 10 minutes. Add the rice and sauté until well coated, 3 to 5 minutes. Add the water, salt, pepper, and, if using, parsley, currants, and/or nuts. Bring the mixture to a boil, cover, reduce the heat to low, and simmer until the liquid is absorbed, about 15 minutes. Let cool.

2. If using preserved leaves, unroll, rinse under cold water, then soak in cold water to cover for 15 minutes. If using fresh grape leaves, blanch in boiling lightly salted water for about 5 minutes. Drain and pat dry. Carefully cut off the stems.

3. Place the leaves on a flat surface, shiny side down and vein side up. On the small leaves, place 1 heaping teaspoon stuffing near the stem end; on the larger leaves, place about 2 teaspoons. Carefully fold each leaf from the stem end to cover the stuffing. Fold the sides over, then roll up the leaf to make a neat package.

4. Cover the bottom of a large, heavy pot or 3-quart baking dish with several leaves. Arrange the rolls, seam side down, in layers in the prepared pot.

5. In a small bowl, combine the broth, lemon juice, oil, salt, and, if using, garlic. Pour over the stuffed grape leaves to cover, if necessary adding more broth. Weigh down the rolls with a heavy plate.

6. Bring to a boil, cover, reduce the heat to low, and simmer until the filling is tender but not mushy, 45 to 60 minutes. Stuffed grape leaves keep in the refrigerator for up to 1 week. Serve at room temperature or chilled.

GRIBENES

Gribenes are golden brown curly, crispy poultry skin cracklings left over during the process of rendering schmaltz.

Origin: Germany

Other names: Yiddish: *grieven, grivalach, griven, shkvarkes*; Hungarian: *libapertõ, töpörtyû*.

Schmaltz was essential to the Jewish communities of northern Europe, an area lacking in cooking oils. It served as the predominant frying medium and food moistener. Since much fat adheres to the goose and chicken skin, the skin was prudently cut up and rendered with the larger clumps of fat, not only resulting in a more substantial amount of schmaltz, but also transforming the poultry skin into cracklings called *gribenes*, meaning "ripped apart" and "scraps," as they were never evenly cut into pieces. To be crisp enough, the bits of skin must be fried for an extended period. Unlike schmaltz, which can keep for months, *gribenes* are best eaten on the day they are made or at least within a few days.

In wealthier eastern Europe homes, these crispy browned bits were a popular *forspeis* (appetizer), while in poorer households *gribenes* was the meat main course. *Gribenes* were eaten alone with a little salt as a Sabbath snack or they were stirred into chopped liver, egg salad, or mashed potatoes; sprinkled over a green salad or chicken soup; spread over a thick slice of rye bread; or mixed into a potato kugel or *knaidlach* (matza ball) batter. The better delis once offered a small bowl of *gribenes* as an *amuse bouche*. A whimsical Yiddish adjunct for dishes containing *gribenes* is *mit neshamos* (with souls).

Since schmaltz was historically prepared in a big batch just before the onset of winter, *gribenes* was prevalent as Hanukkah fare. Some families also traditionally eat *gribenes* on Rosh Hashanah and during the preceding month of Elul (in accord with the statement in the Jerusalem Talmud that a person is held accountable for not enjoying this world—and to eastern Ashkenazim, very little was more enjoyable than *gribenes*.) For those households rendering fresh schmaltz for Passover, *gribenes* was a special treat for that holiday as well. The dish gave rise to a popular Yiddish saying, *"meshugeneh ganz, meshugeneh gribenes"* (crazy goose [i.e., parents], crazy children).

In mid-twentieth-century America, *gribenes* became more commonplace fare as Jews ascended the economic ladder and could afford chicken on a more frequent basis. Some Jews in Louisiana add it to Creole Jambalaya instead of shrimp. However, by the 1960s, as fewer cooks rendered their own schmaltz and America entered a cholesterol-watching era, *gribenes* all but disappeared from many Ashkenazic kitchens. *Gribenes* went from being perhaps the most beloved Ashkenazic treat to being a forbidden food or a guilty pleasure.

(See Schmaltz)

GRUENKERN (GREEN KERN)

Gruenkern is dried, slightly immature spelt. Spelt, *dinkel* in German and Yiddish, is a hybrid of emmer and a wild goat grass native to the Near East. The kernels are slightly longer and more pointed than those of wheat and somewhat resemble barley in appearance. Spelt contains a lower amount of gluten than common wheat and, therefore, can sometimes be tolerated by those with wheat allergies; however, spelt's protein, fat, and amino acid content are similar to that of common wheat. Spelt grows well in poor soil, but it is a hulled grain (the husks tightly adhere to the kernels, making it much more difficult to thresh) and relatively low yielding. Spelt found its greatest popularity in the Bronze and Iron ages in Europe, becoming the main wheat species of Germany. Later Ashkenazim in the area mistakenly confused spelt, which was not grown in biblical Israel, with its ancestor emmer, which is one of the Five Species of grain forbidden on Passover. In the late medieval period, as new species of naked wheat (the husks easily come away from the kernels) became prevalent in central Europe, spelt fell out of favor, although it stayed popular in parts of southern Germany and southwestern Poland.

In Germany, spelt is most often available as a product called *gruenkern* ("green kernels"); the grain is harvested slightly immature, husked, and kiln-dried. Harvesting green grains, such as barley for the biblical Omer offering and the Middle Eastern *ferik* (green wheat), is an ancient practice devised to collect a small part of a springtime crop while still immature, thereby salvaging at least that portion in case heavy storms damage or rot the entire yield before maturation. If the green grain is harvested before it has developed sufficient starch, however, it will shrivel up and be wasted. The slightly immature kernels still contain too much moisture to store and could rot relatively quickly, so for long-term storage, the immature kernels are dried (akin to the biblical *kali*, which are immature grains roasted in fire in order to be processed for making flour for the Omer offering.) For centuries, farmers in parts of Germany and Poland have collected part of the spelt crop at the point when the grains had developed sufficient starch; this stage is called *Milchreife* in Germany and is akin to the biblical *aviv* (which was the stage at which the barley was harvested each year for the Omer offering on the second day of Passover, giving rise to the Hebrew name for spring.)

Primarily produced in parts of southern Germany and southwestern Poland, *gruenkern* is rare in America, but found in some specialty food stores. *Gruenkern* is primarily used to make soups. Many German Jews enjoy it in a Sabbath soup. The first edition of *The Settlement Cook Book* (1901), written by an author from a German Jewish heritage, included a recipe for "Green Kern Soup." Germans also use the kernels in stews, puddings, cereals, breads (the kernels are mixed with wheat flour), and fritters.

Today, many German families, instead of preparing cholent (Sabbath stew), will slow-simmer a *gruenkernsuppe*, flavored with beef and *mach beyn* (marrow bones), overnight to commence Sabbath lunch. Some cooks use whole grains, while others insist on ground. It is flavored with a *suppengrün* (soup greens), a vegetable mixture consisting of a bundle of a leek, carrot, a slice of celeriac, parsley root, and some fresh herbs (such as parsley, celery leaves, or thyme). Historically, in order to prevent any tampering with the fire over the Sabbath, the pots were sealed in a communal oven to be collected by each family following the morning services. Today, a thick, flavorful *gruenkernsuppe* is cooked at home over low heat or in an oven. For many German families, Sabbath lunch is associated with *gruenkern*.

❧ GERMAN GREEN KERN SOUP (*GRUENKERNSUPPE*)

6 TO 8 SERVINGS   [MEAT]

- 1 cup roasted green kern (gruenkern), soaked in water to cover for 8 hours and drained
- 2 pounds boneless beef chuck, brisket, or flanken, cubed
- 1½ to 2 pounds soup marrow bones
- 2 cups suppengrün (soup greens), including diced carrots and/or celeriac, leeks, and fresh flat-leaf parsley
- 2 tablespoons oatmeal
- About 2 teaspoons table salt or 4 teaspoons kosher salt

Ground black pepper to taste

10 cups water

In a large, heavy pot, combine all the ingredients. Bring to a boil, place on a blech (a thin sheet of metal placed over the range top and knobs) over very low heat, or place in a 225°F oven, and cook for at least 6 hours or overnight. Serve warm.

GULAB JAMUN

Gulab jamun are small sweet fritters made from milk. They are soaked in a sugar syrup, which was originally flavored with rose water.

Origin: India

Other names: *gulam jamun, panthu.*

Most Indian confections are milk based, including *gulab jamun*. The fritters resemble a native Indian fruit called *jamun*—hence their name. Although *gulab* means "rose water" in Hindi, some people now omit it from the ingredients in this recipe, as the flavor can be somewhat soapy.

Originally, these soft and sweet fritters were made by cooking fresh milk over low heat for an extended period to reduce the water content by around 85%, the thickened milk known as *khoya*. Because this was time-consuming, the fritters were primarily purchased from the local *mishti dokan* (sweet shop). The invention of dry milk powder led to an easier version, making it less complicated to make at home. Flour holds the balls together, but too much causes them to crack during frying. After cooling, the balls are soaked in a *chini pani* (sugar syrup) accented with cardamom, a

Gulab jamun, *cake-like fritters made from milk, are one of the popular sweets in India, and are enjoyed by the Bene Israel of Mumbai on many occasions including Hanukkah.*

favorite Indian spice. Recently, vanilla ice cream has become a popular accompaniment to these fritters. *Gulab jamun* is a traditional Hanukkah treat among the Bene Israel of Mumbai, as it combines the two primary holiday foods—dairy and fried.

MUMBAI MILK FRITTERS (*GULAB JAMUN*)

ABOUT 20 FRITTERS   [DAIRY]

Pastry:
- 1 cup (5.45 ounces) nonfat dry milk powder
- ¼ cup (1.25 ounces) unbleached all-purpose flour
- ¼ teaspoon baking soda
- Pinch of salt
- 3 tablespoons ghee (clarified butter) or unsalted butter, melted and cooled
- 3 to 4 tablespoons milk

Vegetable or peanut oil for deep-frying

Syrup:
- 2 cups granulated or brown sugar
- 2 cups water
- 4 to 5 cardamom pods or ¼ to ½ teaspoon ground cardamom
- 1 teaspoon rose water (optional)

1. To make the pastry: In a medium bowl, combine the milk powder, flour, baking soda, and salt. Drizzle with the butter and rub between your fingers until the mixture resembles fine crumbs. Gradually stir in enough milk to form a dough that just holds together. Knead briefly until smooth. Cover with plastic wrap and let stand for 30 minutes.

2. In a large saucepan, heat at least 1 inch oil over medium heat to 350°F.

3. Lightly coat your fingers with a little ghee or oil and divide the dough into 20 equal balls, each about 1½ teaspoons. In batches, fry the balls, turning frequently, until golden brown on all sides, about 4 minutes. Remove with a wire-mesh skimmer and place on a wire rack to drain. Let cool.

4. To make the syrup: In a medium saucepan, stir the sugar and water over low heat until the sugar dissolves, about 5 minutes. Stop stirring, increase the heat to medium, and cook until the mixture is slightly thickened and registers 225°F on a candy thermometer, about 5 minutes. Meanwhile, discard the outer shells of the cardamom pods and crush the seeds. Stir the cardamom and, if using, rose water into the syrup.

5. Transfer the cooled fritters to a casserole dish or other container. Drizzle the warm syrup over the fritters, place in the refrigerator, and let soak for at least 3 hours or overnight. The fritters can be covered and stored in the syrup in the refrigerator for up to 1 month. Serve the fritters chilled, at room temperature, or reheated, in a little syrup.

GUNDI

Gundi is a cross between a dumpling and meatball. The most popular type is made from chicken and roasted chickpea flour.

Origin: Persia

Other names: *gondi, gundi nokhochi, kufteh-e ard-nokhochi.*

The most beloved, and arguably the most distinctive, food in Persian Jewish cuisine is *gundi* (Farsi for "testicles of"), a variation of the Persian *kufteh* (meatball). By far, the favorite version is made with ground chicken and roasted chickpea flour, which provides a nutty taste and also transforms it from a meatball into a dumpling.

Chicken in Persia was historically more expensive than meat and reserved for special occasions. Turkey has become a more recent substitute, but, when necessary, veal or even beef is used. Although similar in appearance to an Ashkenazic matza ball, *gundi* taste very different. The proportion of chickpea to chicken, as well as the types and amount of spices, vary from home to home, although cardamom and turmeric are constants. Turmeric imparts a yellow color as well as an interesting aroma. Some cooks prefer a prodigious amount of ground pepper. Many versions are akin to large curried meatballs. Some recipes direct cooks to shape the balls into the size of "a small lime," while others specify the size of "an apricot."

Gundi may be featured alone as an appetizer, typically with fresh herbs and wrapped in flatbread, or served in a soup or sauce. Lamb and beef *gundi* are more commonly cooked in a sauce, while chicken and veal *gundi* are usually simmered in soup (*abgush-e-gundi*). They are traditional in chicken soup (*morgh-gushe gundi nokhochi*) for Sabbath dinner, Rosh Hashanah dinner, and the Passover Seder. Persians do not generally add carrots and celery to chicken soup, but Ashkenazim in Israel typically do when making this dish. Some cooked chickpeas are generally added to the soup for garnish and textural contrast. Any leftover dumplings are eaten with bread and *sabzi* (chopped mixed fresh herbs) at Sabbath lunch. *Gundi* also appear at the meal before the fast of Yom Kippur; for that occasion, the balls and soup contain less spice and salt, to prevent thirst.

Sabbath night *gundi* in chicken soup is usually served with *chelow* (steamed rice). A large spoonful of rice is placed in the bottom of each bowl and topped with a ladle of chicken soup and several cubes of potatoes, pieces of chicken, and chickpeas, then a few *gundi* are added, then the dish is sprinkled with a little *sabzi* and, for a more intensely sour flavor, *limoo omani* (ground dried limes).

❧ **PERSIAN CHICKEN AND CHICKPEA BALLS (*GUNDI*)**
ABOUT 18 MEDIUM MEATBALLS   [MEAT]

Meatballs:

1 pound ground chicken, turkey, lamb, or lean veal; or 8 ounce ground chicken and 8 ounces ground beef or veal

2 cups (6.5 ounces) roasted chickpea flour (*ard-e nokhochi*)

2 medium yellow onions, grated

3 tablespoons vegetable oil or 1 large egg, lightly beaten

1 teaspoon ground cardamom

1 teaspoon ground turmeric

½ to 1 teaspoon ground cumin or ¼ teaspoon ground cinnamon

About 1 teaspoon table salt or 2 teaspoons kosher salt

About ½ teaspoon ground black pepper

¼ cup chopped fresh flat-leaf parsley (optional)

About 2 tablespoons water

1½ to 2 quarts chicken soup

1 pound (4 medium) boiling potatoes, peeled and cubed

1 tablespoon lemon juice or tomato paste

1 teaspoon ground tumeric

Salt to taste

1 to 2 cups cooked chickpeas (optional)

1. In a medium bowl, combine all the meatball ingredients, adding enough water to form a mixture that is smooth but not sticky. Refrigerate until firm, at least 3 hours. Using moistened hands, shape into smooth 1-inch balls.

2. In a large pot, bring the chicken soup to a boil. Add the potatoes, lemon juice, turmeric, and salt and simmer for 30 minutes. Add the gundi and, if using, chickpeas, cover, and simmer until the gundi are tender, about 40 minutes.

GUTMAN

Gutman is a type of Sabbath porridge, unique to the Polish town of Slonim, made from buckwheat flour and browned onions.

GUVETCH/GHIVECI

Guvetch is a slow-cooked vegetable ragout. The most well-known version is based on eggplant.

Origin: Romania, Turkey

Other names: France: ratatouille; Greece: *briami*; Romania: *ghiveci, ghivech, guvech, yuvetch*; Ladino: *khandrajo*; Turkey: *kapama, turlu*.

When the Turks arrived in Asia Minor, they adopted various earthenware pots, which were typically used in ancient Mediterranean cooking, to slow-cook pieces of meat, onions, and vegetables, either over a fire or in a pit oven (*tandir*). This became a preferred method of Ottoman cuisine. Among these vessels was the *güveç*, a wide-mouthed earthenware stewing pot that was a descendant of the ancient Roman *olla*. When the stew is baked uncovered in an oven, it is called a *guvetch*. A covered baked stew is technically a *turlu*, Turkish for "diverse" and "varied," or *kapama*, from the Turkish *kapamak* (to cover). For covered stews, the lid of the pot was sealed with a strip of dough to keep in the moisture and flavors. A *yahni*, named after a Persian earthenware vessel, is a stew cooked covered over a fire. Nevertheless, many people use these terms interchangeably. Sephardim in Turkey typically cooked *turlu* in an *oya*, a Spanish squat, rounded, wide-mouth earthenware pot also descended from the Roman *olla*. Although an earthenware pot enhances and contributes to the flavor of the stew, it can be cooked in any ovenproof vessel.

After the Turks introduced these stews to the Balkans, *guvetch* quickly became a staple in Romania and Bulgaria, ranking among the most popular of foods. As with most plebeian dishes, there is no definitive recipe. However, to be authentic, *guvetch* must contain a selection of vegetables—just a few or more than twenty—and be slow-cooked. A little water is added to uncovered stews, while no water is used when the stew is cooked covered. The contents are based upon preference, habit, and availability. Stews containing summer vegetables—eggplants, green beans, okra, peppers, tomatoes, and zucchini—are called *guvetch yaz* (summer stew). Those predominantly made with winter squash and root vegetables—carrots, celeriac, potatoes, and turnips—are called *guvetch kis*. *Guvetch de riz* is cooked with rice.

Eggplant stews were already mentioned in Turkey in the fourteenth century and stews based on eggplant are common throughout the former Ottoman Empire and adjacent areas. As new produce arrived in the Near East, such as the American tomatoes, zucchini, peppers, and green beans, cooks readily included them in their stews. Other commonly added items include cabbage, leeks, lima beans, mushrooms, and even unripe grapes. Frequently, leftovers are added to stretch resources. Turks often first fry the onions and garlic in olive oil, while Romanians and Greeks usually add them raw. Many Turks, in the manner of ratatouille, also sauté each vegetable separately before combining them in the pot, while in the Balkans most cooks simmer the raw vegetables together to mellow and blend the flavors. Middle Eastern vegetable stews tend to be cooked until all the ingredients are very soft; any crispness is a sign of a bad cook.

The stews originally included meat and the Turkish *güveç* still contains some lamb or beef. Sephardim in Bulgaria make a *guvetch kon karne* (with meat). Some Turks insist a *turlu* should have pieces of mutton, while others contend it should never contain eggplant. However, Romanian Jews typically make vegetarian versions (*ghiveci din legume*). A freshwater fish, such as carp or trout, is sometimes cooked in *guvetch*.

Seasonings in these hearty stews are generally rather mild; the essential flavor is derived from the combination of vegetables and the cooking process. For Romanians, as is characteristic of their cookery, there must be garlic and plenty of it, frequently both minced and whole. Turks generally add a little lemon juice. In some areas, a chili is included for a little heat. *Guvetch* is served hot or cold. Romanians frequently spoon *guvetch* over *mamaliga* (cornmeal mush), while Turks prefer rice. At dairy meals, summer *guvetch* is usually accompanied with yogurt or sour cream.

Romanians brought *guvetch* to Israel, where it is now commonly sold in containers in most supermarkets.

(See also Yakhna)

ROMANIAN VEGETABLE STEW (*GUVETCH/GHIVECI*)

6 TO 8 SERVINGS AS A SIDE DISH   [PAREVE]

1½ pounds (1 large) eggplant, peeled and cut into 1-inch-thick slices

About 2 tablespoons kosher salt or 1 tablespoon table salt for sprinkling

4 cups (28 ounces) peeled, seeded, and coarsely chopped plum tomatoes

1 cup extra-virgin olive oil

4 medium onions, sliced

2 to 4 cloves garlic, minced

1 pound green beans or okra, trimmed

4 small zucchini or yellow squash or any combination, cut into chunks

2 medium green bell peppers, seeded and sliced

2 medium red bell peppers, seeded and sliced

1 to 2 large carrots, sliced (optional)

4 to 8 whole cloves garlic

About 1 teaspoon salt

Ground black pepper to taste

Pinch of sugar

1 cup vegetable broth or water

1. Place the eggplant slices in a colander or on a wire rack, lightly sprinkle with the 2 tablespoons kosher salt, and let stand for about 1 hour. Rinse the eggplant under cold water, then press repeatedly between several layers of paper towels until it feels firm and dry. Cut into 1-inch cubes.

2. Preheat the oven to 350°F. Oil a 4-quart ovenproof dish or pot. Spread half of the tomatoes in the dish.

3. In a large skillet, heat ½ cup oil over medium-high heat. Add the eggplant and sauté until lightly browned, about 8 minutes. Transfer the eggplant to the prepared dish.

4. Drain off any oil from the pan, add ¼ cup oil, and heat over medium heat. Add the onions and minced garlic and sauté until soft and translucent, 5 to 10 minutes. Spread half of the onions over the eggplant.

5. Combine the green beans, zucchini, bell peppers, carrots, and whole garlic cloves. Transfer the vegetable mixture to the dish. Top with the remaining onions, then the remaining tomatoes. Sprinkle with the salt, pepper, and sugar. Drizzle with the broth, then the remaining ¼ cup oil.

6. Bake, uncovered, until the vegetables are tender, about 1½ to 2 hours. Serve warm, at room temperature, or slightly chilled.

HADGI BADAH

Hadgi badah are round almond cookies lightly flavored with cardamom.

Origin: Iraq

Other names: hadji bada, hajji bada.

These cardamom-accented cookies, a favorite of Iraqi Jews, are traditionally served on Purim and at the meal following Yom Kippur. There is also a flourless meringue version popular on Passover.

(See also Macaroon)

 IRAQI CARDAMOM-ALMOND COOKIES (*HADGI BADAH*)

ABOUT 48 COOKIES   [PAREVE]

  2¼ cups (11.25 ounces) all-purpose flour

  1 teaspoon ground cardamom

  ½ teaspoon salt

  ¼ teaspoon double-acting baking powder

  1⅓ cups (9.25 ounces) sugar

  4 large eggs

  2 cups (10 ounces) ground blanched almonds

  Rose water or orange-blossom water for moistening hands (optional)

  About 48 whole almonds or pistachios (optional)

1. Preheat the oven to 350°F. Line 2 large baking sheets with parchment paper or grease the sheets.

2. Sift together the flour, cardamom, salt, and baking powder. In a large bowl, beat together the sugar and eggs until light and creamy, about 10 minutes. Stir in the flour mixture, then the ground almonds.

3. Moisten your hands with rose water, if desired, and form the dough into 1-inch balls. Place on the prepared baking sheets and flatten slightly. If using, press a whole almond into the center of each cookie.

4. Bake until lightly browned, about 12 minutes. Let the cookies stand until firm, about 1 minute, then transfer to a wire rack and let cool completely. Store in an airtight container at room temperature for up to 1 week or in the freezer for up to 6 months.

HAIMISH

The Yiddish adjective *haimish* (from the Old High German *heim*, "home"), also spelled *heimish*, means "homey/plain/cozy/informal"; the male adjective is *haimisher* and the female *haimisheh*. In Arabic it is *baladi* (country-style). Much of Ashkenazic cooking and many of the dishes, being relatively simple comfort foods, are described as *haimisheh*.

HALKE

Halke is the Yiddish name for dumpling in some Slavic areas of northeastern Europe. They are frequently potato based and can be plain or filled.

Origin: Galicia (southern Poland)

Other names: Hungary: *galuska, haluska*; Poland: *haluski*; Russia: *galushki*; Slovakia: *halusky*; Ukraine: *halushki*.

By the twelfth century, dumplings, initially made from bread, had become a staple of the central European diet and were known by different names in different places. Shortly afterward, the Slavs of eastern Europe began making small, irregularly shaped, pasta-like dumplings named *halushki* (meaning "little ears," as they were originally triangular). Among segments of Jews in eastern Europe, especially in Galicia, flour dumplings were called *halkes* in Yiddish.

In the mid-nineteenth century, as potatoes were accepted in central Europe, versions of *halkes*—made from either mashed or grated raw potatoes—became the most popular types. Potato dumplings are called *krumpli galuska* in Hungary, *kartoffel kloese* in northern Germany, and *kartoffel knaidel* in southern Germany. *Halkes*, which sometimes feature a savory or sweet filling, tend to be firmer and heavier than the Italian potato gnocchi. Plain potato dumplings are traditionally served with sauerbraten, *gedempte fleisch* (pot roast), or soup. They are also sometimes cooked in a tzimmes (*tzimmes mit halkes*) or sprinkled with cinnamon-sugar and bread crumbs.

(See also Dumpling and Knaidel)

◆ ASHKENAZIC MASHED POTATO DUMPLINGS
(*HALKES*)

16 TO 18 DUMPLINGS   [MEAT OR PAREVE]

2 pounds (5 to 6 medium) baking (russet) potatoes
About 1¼ cups (6.25 ounces) all-purpose flour or
    matza meal, or ¾ cup flour and ½ cup semolina
    or farina
2 large eggs, lightly beaten
About 1½ teaspoons table salt or 1 tablespoon
    kosher salt
About ¼ teaspoon ground pepper
2 teaspoons grated yellow onion or leek, white part
    only (optional)
Schmaltz or margarine (optional)

1. Bring a large pot of lightly salted water to a low boil over high heat. Add the potatoes, reduce the heat to medium-low, and simmer until fork-tender in the center, about 25 minutes. Drain the potatoes, rinse with cold water, and peel. While still warm, run the potatoes through a food mill or ricer into the warm cooking pot. Or return the potatoes to the warm pot and mash with a potato masher, heavy whisk, or pastry blender over medium-low heat. You should have about 4 cups. Let cool.

2. In a large bowl, combine the potatoes, flour, eggs, salt, pepper, and, if using, onion. For heavier dumplings, add additional flour. On a lightly floured surface, knead until smooth. Dust your hands with flour and form into 1- or 1½-inch balls.

3. Bring a large pot of lightly salted water to a boil. In batches of 4 to 5, add the dumplings to the pot, stirring to prevent sticking. Return to a boil and cook until the dumplings rise to the top, 10 to 15 minutes. Remove with a slotted spoon.

4. Brush the dumplings with schmaltz and keep warm in the oven while preparing the remaining dumplings. Serve warm.

HALVA/HALVAH

Halva is a dense confection. The original type is grain based, typically made from semolina, and another kind is seed based, notably made from sesame seeds.
Origin: Persia
Other names: Arabic: *halwa*; India: *halwa*; Syria:
    mamounie, ma'mounia; Turkish: *helva*.

When the conquering Arabs arrived in Persia in 642, they discovered sugar as well as a highly sophis-

ticated and diversified cuisine, including a vast range of confections, puddings, and pastries, which they adopted and spread westward. The Arabs referred to certain confections as *halwa* from the Arabic root *hilwa* (sweet), which the Persians pronounced halva. Later the Ottoman Turks introduced these confections to their domain. Consequently, halva, evolving into an array of versions, became popular from India to the Balkans and North Africa.

Over the course of centuries, various terms and identifications changed as well. When the word *halwa* first appeared in the seventh century, it referred to a mixture of mashed dates with milk. By the time of the *Kitab al-Tabikh* (Book of Dishes)—compiled in Baghdad in 1226 but based on a collection of ninth-century Persian-inspired recipes—there were so many versions of the confection that the chapter on *"halwa* and its varieties" entailed nine recipes, including *barad* (Arabic and Hebrew meaning "hail," a confection of yeast fritters encased in a boiled honey and rose water candy), *mukaffan* (Arabic for "shrouded," a confection wrapped in thin pastry), *makshüfa* (Arabic for "uncovered," a boiled confection of ground nuts, sesame oil, and saffron), and several types of almond paste sweets. The book also contained an entire chapter devoted to *judhab/gudab*, sweetened grain dishes dating back to at least the ninth century.

An anonymous thirteenth-century cookbook from Moorish Spain contained a recipe for *halwa al* (excellent confection), consisting of sheets of boiled sugar, honey, sesame oil, and flour that were rolled out; spread with ground pistachios, sugar, and rose water;

An array of flavored sesame-based halva entices shoppers at the Carmel Market in Tel Aviv, Israel.

topped with a second candy sheet; and cut into triangles. Sephardim enjoyed similar confections, including *turron* (a nougat lightened with egg whites) and *azuqaques* (from "sugar," an almond confection).

Shortly thereafter in central Asia, the term halva was applied to a newfangled type of *judhab*, entailing a flour (usually semolina, wheat, or rice) toasted in fat, then sweetened and thickened with a sugar syrup or fruit honey. It was frequently enhanced with the addition of spices, chopped nuts, dried fruit, and coconut. These grain puddings—semolina (*halva aurd-e sujee* and *halva di gris*), wheat (*halva khoshk*), and ground rice (*halva aurd-e birinj*)—soon became the most widespread form of halva, eaten straight as a sweet, but also spread on flatbreads.

The *Kitab al-Tabikh* was a major influence on the Turks, who pronounced the term *helva*, and these sweets became an integral component of Ottoman cuisine. During the reign of Suleiman the Magnificent (1520–1566), the height of Ottoman power, the kitchens of his Topkapi Palace in Istanbul were rebuilt and a separate kitchen, called the Helvahane (house of halva), was devoted solely to sweets. The Turks honed and enhanced *helva*, expanding it to thirty basic types, and spread it into their territories in southeast Europe. The most common type in Turkey is semolina (*irmik helvasi*), sometimes made with *pekmez* (grape honey) or bee honey.

The addition of sesame seeds to confections was an ancient practice, but the Ottomans developed a sweetened sesame confection with a flaky consistency made from tahini (*tahin helvasi*). During the Ottoman domination of Romania, the country's Jews adopted the sesame confection, also calling it *halavah* or halva in Yiddish, then spread the dish and name to some fellow Ashkenazim. Romanian Jews also introduced the Yiddish name halva to America, where it entered the English language in 1846. Although of less importance in Asia and the Balkans, the sesame type of halva became common in American Jewish markets and delicatessens, emerging as the most well-known version in the West.

Grain halva remains extremely important in much of Asia. More than just a simple treat, it is the foremost comfort food and a cultural and sociological expression of life. Halva is frequently eaten on occasions of both happiness and sorrow, particularly at weddings, in a house of mourning, during recuperation from a serious illness, on a return from a long trip, at *brit milahs*, at Sabbath lunch, on Hanukkah, and especially on Purim. Following the Megillah reading to break the Fast of Esther, many Persian synagogues serve halva decorated with scenes from the Purim story. Halva is also a common component of Persian *mishloach manot* (gifts of foods) on Purim day. In Aleppo, Syria, it is served at breakfast and brunch, as well as given to nursing mothers.

The Baghdadis of Calcutta traditionally serve semolina halva as a sweet on Hanukkah, as the grain is cooked in oil. The Bene Israel of Mumbai enjoy a rice-flour halva on Rosh Hashanah, weddings, and other special occasions. However, the most widespread forms of halvas among Indians are made from fruit and vegetables, carrots being the most popular.

(See also Tahini)

◖ PERSIAN SEMOLINA PUDDING (*HALVA AURD-E SUJEE*)

6 TO 8 SERVINGS   [DAIRY OR PAREVE]

> 3 cups water, or 1½ cups water and 1½ cups milk
> 1½ cups sugar
> 1 cup unsalted butter or vegetable oil
> 1½ cups (9 ounces) fine semolina (*smead*) or farina
>   (not semolina flour)
> ¾ to 1 cup chopped blanched almonds, pistachios,
>   toasted hazelnuts, or walnuts, or any
>   combination (optional)
> 1 teaspoon ground turmeric (optional)
> 1 to 2 teaspoons rose water or 1 teaspoon vanilla
>   extract
> 1 teaspoon ground cinnamon or ½ teaspoon ground
>   cardamom

1. In a medium saucepan, bring the water and sugar to a boil and stir until melted. Cover, reduce the heat to very low, and let the syrup stand until ready to use.

2. In another medium saucepan, melt the butter over low heat. Stir in the semolina and, if using, nuts and/or turmeric, and cook, stirring constantly, until golden brown, about 15 minutes. For darker-colored halva, continue toasting until the grains are dark brown.

3. Return the syrup to a boil, then slowly stir into the semolina. Cook over low heat, stirring constantly, until the liquid evaporates and the mixture comes away easily from the sides of the pan, about 5 minutes. Stir in the rose water and cinnamon.

4. Remove from the heat, cover with a damp kitchen

towel, replace the lid, and let stand for at least 10 minutes. Serve warm or at room temperature.

HAMAN'S EAR (OZNEI HAMAN)

Haman's ear is a pastry of fried strips of dough in honey or sugar syrup.

Origin: Spain or Italy

Other names: Alsace: *schunzuchen*; Austria: *heizenblauszen*; Dutch: *hamansooren*; Farsi: *gushfil*; Georgia: *burbushella*; German: *hamanmuetzen*; Greek: *aftia tou Amman*; Hebrew: *oznei Haman*; Hungary: *fritteln*; Italian: *orecchi de Aman*; Ladino: *hojuelos de haman, orejas de Haman*.

In contemplating Purim, the Mishnah, Midrash, and Jerusalem Talmud, all composed in Israel and not the Diaspora, focused on the intricacies of reading the Megillah. The Babylonian Talmud, on the other hand, compiled in the very area in which the Purim story unfolded, also delved into the ramifications of Jewish life in the Diaspora. According to the Talmud, Haman, the villain of the Purim story, is the eternal personification of Jewish vulnerability in exile. As a result of the Babylonian Talmud's perspective, Purim uniquely became a holiday of parody and pleasure, partially accomplished through plenty of food and drink. A whimsical expression of the holiday was through an early Ashkenazic custom of making Purim pastries in the shape of animals, soldiers, and other forms. In other Jewish communities, the preeminent Purim pastry consisted of fried strips of dough in honey or sugar syrup, most commonly known as *oznei Haman* (Haman's ears).

Among the recipes in an anonymous thirteenth-century Moorish cookbook from Andalusia was a deep-fried pastry called *udhun* (Arabic meaning "ear"), so named because the dish resembled that part of the human anatomy. The fried pastry was typically filled with ground pistachios or almonds mixed with sugar and rose water. The concept of deep-fried dough was adopted by Sephardim, who sometimes called strips by the name *shamlias* (Ladino for "frills") and *hojuelos* (leaflets/flakes). In this vein, Isaac Abarbanel (1437–1508), in his Biblical commentary on the manna, notes, "The wafers are a flour food cooked in oil in the form of a water flask that are eaten with honey and it is like the wafers that they make from dough like the shape of ears, cooked in oil and dipped into honey, and we called them *ozneim* [ears]."

There exists a longtime Jewish custom of responding to a particularly evil person by uttering the phrase *y'mahk shemo* (Hebrew meaning "may his name be erased"). However, singular scorn and derision was directed toward Haman, perhaps because Jews in the Diaspora identified him with their contemporary problems and oppressors. In one of the oldest Purim customs, the Jews of Persia and Babylonia burned Haman in effigy in bonfires. In medieval Europe, the custom developed of blotting out Haman's name. During the Megillah reading, some people wrote Haman on the soles of their shoes and stomped, while others wrote his name on an object and bashed it against another. The most widespread Ashkenazic custom became, upon hearing Haman's name during the Megillah reading, to good-naturedly stomp one's feet and sound *groggers* (noisemakers). So eating a pastry bearing the name of the archfiend or formed to represent part of Haman's clothing or anatomy—most notably his pocket, hat, foot, or ear—thereby symbolically eliminating some part of Haman and erasing his name, contributed to the enjoyment and theme of the holiday.

When the name of the Spanish dish evolved from "ears" to "Haman's ears" for Purim is uncertain. The first record of the term *oznei Haman* was in 1550 in an Italian Jewish comedy *Tzachut Bedichuta de-Kiddushin* (An Eloquent Marriage Farce) written in Hebrew by Judah Leone Ben Isaac Sommo (1527–1592) of Mantua. It is the oldest extant Jewish play, drawing from the Midrash and Italian comedy, and was originally produced for a Purim carnival. In an exchange between two characters, one man asks, "Behold it is written in the Scroll of Purim 'and they hung Haman,' and in the portion of Balak it is written in explanation 'and the Children of Israel ate *ha'mahn* [the manna].' How could the Jews, who keep themselves from every wicked thing [Deuteronomy 23:10], eat the carcass of the one that was hung, but to the dog you shall cast it?"

His friend provides an answer: "For what the Torah says 'and they ate *ha'mahn*' it is a warning and commandment to us that we eat during these days of Purim from *oznei Haman* [Haman's ears]—they are the thin wafers made from fine semolina flour mingled with olive oil [based on Exodus 29:2], and thus it says afterward 'and their taste was like wafers with honey [Exodus 16:31].'"

This custom of enjoying *oznei Haman*, fried strips of dough in honey, soon spread throughout the Mediterranean and Europe. As with many Jewish food traditions and names, after Haman's ears pastries appeared, reasons were retroactively attached to them. A Midrash related that the ears of Haman were "*oznayim mekutafot.*" The Roman scholar and poet Immanuel ben Solomon (c. 1261–1328) translated this phrase as "clipped ears," contending that Haman's ears were cut off after his hanging, a misinterpretation arising from the medieval Italian custom of cutting off a criminal's ear before execution. The phrase more precisely means "twisted ears," denoting either that someone wrenched his ears or they were deformed or twisted or triangular in shape, like those of a donkey.

The characteristic Jewish way to deal with the precarious nature of life in the Diaspora was by fasting in the face of potential danger, then feasting and reveling in response to a positive outcome, a philosophy evidenced in the modern Jewish joke, "They tried to kill us, we survived, let's eat." The Jewish sense of humor, forged by life in exile and a vital element in dealing with it, particularly manifests itself on Purim, a time when joking and frivolity are encouraged.

✿ HAMAN'S EARS (*OZNEI HAMAN*)

ABOUT 36 PASTRIES   [PAREVE]

3 large eggs, or 2 large eggs and 2 large egg yolks, lightly beaten
3 tablespoons olive or vegetable oil
3 tablespoons sugar
2 tablespoons brandy, rum, orange juice, orange-blossom water, or water
½ teaspoon salt
2 teaspoons finely grated lemon zest or orange zest, or 1 teaspoon ground cinnamon (optional)
¼ cup finely ground blanched almonds or walnuts (optional)
About 2½ cups (12.5 ounces) all-purpose flour, or 1½ cups flour and 1 cup fine semolina
Vegetable, sunflower, or peanut oil for deep-frying
About 1 cup confectioners' sugar or cinnamon-sugar for dusting or 2 cups warm *atar* (Middle Eastern Sugar Syrup, page 27)

1. In a large bowl, blend together the eggs, oil, sugar, brandy, salt, and, if using, zest and/or nuts. Gradually stir in enough of the flour to make a soft dough. On a lightly floured surface, knead until

smooth, 5 to 10 minutes. Cover with plastic wrap or a kitchen towel and let stand at room temperature for at least 30 minutes.

2. Divide the dough in half. On a lightly floured surface, roll out each piece of dough into a ⅛-inch-thick rectangle. With a pastry cutter or sharp knife, cut into strips 1 inch wide and 4 to 6 inches long. Pinch each strip in the center and twist the ends.

3. In a deep pot, heat at least 2 inches oil over medium heat to 375°F.

4. In batches, fry the strips, turning once, until golden brown on both sides, about 1 minute per side. Remove with a wire-mesh skimmer or tongs and drain on a wire rack. Sprinkle generously with confectioners' sugar or dip the cooled pastries into the *atar*. Store in an airtight container at room temperature for up to 2 weeks.

HAMANTASCH

Hamantasch is a filled pastry shaped in a triangle.
Origin: Germany

Among the medieval Teutonic pastries was a triangular-shaped treat filled with jam, curd cheese, and various sweets called *maultasche* (mouth pocket/pouch) and, when stuffed with poppy seeds, *mohntasche* (poppy seed pocket). The Middle High German word *tasche*—which also gives rise to the English words task and tax, where the money was put—means "pocket" or "pouch." Around the late sixteenth century, influenced by an Italian custom and by the similarity of the word *mohn* to Haman (his name is *Hamohn* in Hebrew), German Jews renamed this Teutonic cookie as hamantasch or hamantash (hamantaschen plural), meaning "Haman's pocket."

Subsequently, various symbolic meanings were ascribed to the hamantasch. The triangular shape came to represent either Haman's pockets, alluding to the bribes the prime minister took, or his tricornered hat, connoting his execution. Persians, however, never wore tricornered hats; such headwear and subsequently this symbolism became popular in Europe around 1690. According to the mystics, the three corners symbolize the three patriarchs—Abraham, Isaac, and Jacob—whose merit saved their descendants from Haman's plot. The filling veiled inside the dough alludes to the hidden presence of God in the Purim story; God is never mentioned in the Megillah. The poppy seeds symbolize the vegetarian diet maintained by Queen Esther while living in the palace.

Beginning in the fourteenth century, when masses of Jews from the Rhineland and western Germany moved eastward, they brought the *mohntasche* with them and it became the preeminent Ashkenazic Purim pastry in eastern Europe. In Poland, some people began calling these pastries *pireshkes*, from the Slavic word for "feast," when they were made at times other than Purim. However, the pastries lost favor among German, Alsatian, and Dutch Jews, who favored gingerbread men for Purim, as eating them was a way of hanging Haman in effigy. Nevertheless, by force of sheer numbers, in the nineteenth century

The tri-cornered hamantasch literally means "Haman's pouch," but to Ashkenazim it is the iconic Purim food.

eastern Europeans and their foods came to dominate the Ashkenazic world and hamantaschen emerged as the quintessential Ashkenazic Purim treat.

The original hamantaschen were made from pieces of kuchen, a rich yeast dough. In the twentieth century, cookie doughs, due to their ease of preparation and keeping abilities, became more widespread. Yeast dough hamantaschen tend to be larger than the cookie dough types. Over the course of centuries, fillings changed as well. In eastern Europe, ground nuts, which were relatively inexpensive and plentiful, became a common substitute for poppy seeds. Almonds paste and dates were also popular fillings in some areas.

Prune and plum jams emerged as a traditional hamantaschen filling in 1731 when a Bohemian merchant, David Brandeis, was accused of selling poisoned *povidl*, prune and plum preserves, which Americans now call lekvar. After the charge was proven false, he was freed from prison four days before the holiday of Purim. The entire city of Jungbunzlau, Bohemia, celebrated his release and, from that day forward, his family honored that day as a special holiday, the *Povidl* Purim. Historically, prunes ranked second in popularity to poppy seeds as a hamantaschen filling. However, these original fillings have recently lost favor, and are being replaced by apricot, cherry, raspberry, strawberry, caramel, chocolate, and even s'mores (chocolate chips, chopped nuts, and marshmallows).

Hamantaschen were unknown in America until the arrival of eastern Europeans toward the end of the nineteenth century. The word was first recorded in America in *The Jewish Encyclopedia* (New York, 1903): "The Haman Tash, a kind of a turnover filled with honey and black poppy-seed, is eaten on the Feast of Purim, but probably has no special meaning." It took seven decades, however, for hamantaschen to spread beyond the Jewish community and nearby environs. Ranking behind only rugelach and perhaps mandelbrot among Ashkenazic pastries known to mainstream Americans, this venerable Purim treat can now be found year-round on the shelves of many non-Jewish American bakeries and gourmet stores. In New England, hamantaschen are sometimes renamed "patriot hats" in some non-Jewish bakeries. In modern Israel, some people, particularly Sephardim and Mizrachim, refer to hamantaschen as *oznei Haman* (Haman's ears), an inappropriate usage it never held previously.

(See also Haman's Ear and Purim)

HAMANTASCHEN

ABOUT 42 SMALL PASTRIES [DAIRY OR PAREVE]

11 tablespoons (1 stick plus 3 tablespoons) unsalted butter or margarine, softened

½ cup sugar

1 large egg or 3 large egg yolks

3 tablespoons orange juice, sour cream, milk, white wine, or water; or 2 tablespoons water and 1 tablespoon lemon juice or cognac

1 teaspoon vanilla extract

¼ teaspoon salt

About 2¾ cups (13.75 ounces) all-purpose flour

About 2 cups mohnfullung (Ashkenazic Poppy Seed Filling, page 198), lekvar (prune jam), or any Ashkenazic sweet filling (page 198)

1. In a large bowl, beat the butter until smooth. Gradually add the sugar and beat until light and fluffy, 5 to 10 minutes. Beat in the egg. Blend in the orange juice, vanilla, and salt. Stir in enough flour to make a soft dough. Wrap with plastic wrap and refrigerate until firm, at least 2 hours. Let stand at room temperature for several minutes until malleable but not soft.

2. Preheat the oven to 375°F. Have 2 large baking sheets ready. Do not grease the baking sheets, but it's preferable to line them with parchment paper.

3. For easy handling, divide the dough into 2 to 4 pieces. On a lightly floured surface, roll out each piece ⅛ inch thick. Using a 3-inch cookie cutter or drinking glass, cut out rounds. Reroll and cut out the scraps until all the dough is used.

4. Place 1 teaspoon filling in the center of each round. Bring the edge of the lower section of the dough round up and pinch the 2 sides together at the corner where they meet. Press together the other 2 sides to form a triangle, leaving some filling exposed in the center.

5. Place the hamantaschen 1 inch apart on the baking sheets. Bake until golden, about 13 minutes. Transfer the hamantaschen to a wire rack and let cool.

VARIATIONS

Yeast Dough Hamantaschen: Substitute Ashkenazic Yeast Pastry (page 582) for the cookie dough. Cut out 3- to 4-inch rounds and place 1 tablespoon filling in the center. Bake at 350°F until golden brown, 25 to 30 minutes.

HAMIN

Hamin is a stew cooked over a low heat or in a low oven to serve hot for Sabbath lunch.

Origin: Spain

Other names: Algeria and Tunisia: *dfina, tfina*; Italian: *hamin, hammin*; Kurdistan: *matphoni*; Morocco: *adafina, dafina, skhina, shachina*; Persian: *chalebibi*.

Among the early Middle Eastern Sabbath dishes was *harisa*, cracked durum wheat berries, lamb, and some chopped onion slow-simmered overnight in a sealed earthenware pot. Some Sephardim, principally in northern Spain, began referring to *harisa* by the Mishnaic name *hamin di trigo* (warm of grain) or simply *hamin*. Around this time, many cooks, perhaps first in Iberia, began adding chickpeas or fava beans and more water to *harisa* and creating a more liquidy Sabbath stew. People eventually began to differentiate the Sabbath bean stews from the *harisa*. The bean stew made its way to France and Germany, becoming the Ashkenazic cholent.

Whatever the name, the basic ingredients of Sephardic Sabbath stews consisted of a whole grain, chickpeas or beans, cubes of meat, onion, and cumin although the exact recipe varied from place to place and even according to the season of the year. Following the expulsion, *hamin* sometimes took on new qualities when adapted to local ingredients, cooking styles, and popular local seasonings and spice combinations, including cinnamon, paprika, saffron, and turmeric. The arrival of South American produce in the sixteenth century led to white beans becoming a prominent substitute for fava beans; white potatoes, sweet potatoes, pumpkin, and red chilies were sometimes added, contributing new notes of texture and flavor.

During the Spanish Inquisition, the most incriminating dish connoting a retention of Judaism was *hamin/adafina*. Some Conversos, who wanted to enjoy their Sabbath stew without risking arrest and even death, replaced the customary mutton with pork. Thus were born two of Spain's classic dishes: a slow-simmered chickpea and meat stew called *cocida madrileno* (literally "boiled from Madrid"), now the national dish of Spain; and *olla poderida* (powerful pot).

Syrians, as well as those who later went to India, retained the name *hamin*, while many Sephardim in the Balkans and Turkey adopted newer terminology. Italians generally made *hamin* with fava beans, meat (beef brisket, flank steaks, or breast of lamb), meatballs (from chicken or beef), and frequently beet greens or chard. Italians might enhance their stew with a little sage. Romaniote Greeks made a simple *hamin* using large cuts of beef, onions, and *pligouri* (a type of cracked wheat). In Jerusalem, cooks typically added potatoes and rice to the beans. Indians developed a rice *hamin* seasoned with garam masala and fresh ginger. When the Sephardim arrived in northwest Africa, they merged their Sabbath stew with the native tagines to create a host of variations—most containing a calf's foot or a *kouclas* (dumpling)—that were commonly served for Sabbath lunch with couscous left over from Friday dinner. Cinnamon and nutmeg or ground ginger were common in many Moroccan versions, in which dates, honey, or quince preserves imparted an interesting depth of flavor. In the Sephardic tradition, all these stews contained that distinctive Sephardic food, *huevos haminados*, whole eggs in the shell simmered in the stew to develop a brown color and creamy consistency during the extended cooking.

On *Shabbat Beraisheet* (the Sabbath after Sukkot), some communities prepare a special seven-layered *hamin*, one layer for each day of Creation, with rice in between each layer. For the Sabbath before Tu b'Shevat, quinces, dates, prunes, and raisins may be added. In the early fall, *hamin* was sometimes made with little pumpkins, while spinach and grape leaves were popular additions in the spring.

For more than a millennium in Spain, on Friday afternoons, the husband, an older child, a maid, or an errand boy would haul the family's special earthenware *olla* (stew pot), the lid secured with wire latches or a flour and water paste, to the massive public oven. When all the pots were assembled, the oven door was closed and sealed with clay, and the collection was left undisturbed overnight in the fading heat. During the long, slow cooking process, the ingredients melded and permeated the dish, developing a distinctive complex flavor and a rich, creamy texture. On Saturday morning following synagogue services, the oven would be unlocked, the pots would be reclaimed by their owners, and the cherished stew would be rushed home for the Sabbath table. Similar scenes were played out in the Islamic world where *hamin*

pots were crowded into the town's public bakery or sometimes into the furnaces of the *hammam* (public steam baths). Later, with the advent of the *kanoun* (brazier) in the Middle East, an increasing number of Jews cooked their *hamin* at home over coals and covered the pots with special bulky blankets for insulation. For the masses, however, the bakery oven prevailed well into the twentieth century.

Today, the pots are no longer "buried" in ashes or baked in public facilities, but instead commonly placed in a home oven set to low or on a thin sheet of metal placed over the range top over very low heat, to cook overnight. In Israel, *hamin* is generally left on a large hot plate called a *platta* and covered with an insulating cloth. Otherwise, these stews are nearly identical to those prepared weekly for centuries by almost every Jewish community from the large cities of Istanbul and Cairo to the secluded mountain towns of the Maghreb.

At present, in parts of Spain as well as parts of Central and South America and the American Southwest, places where there were no overt Jews, some home cooks, many of them practicing Catholics, still prepare a bean and meat stew on Friday and let the dish cook overnight, a residual effect of the Inquisition's pursuit of Conversos into the New World. It is probable that the classic Tex-Mex chili con carne, which developed in the hinterlands north of the Rio Grande (away from the Inquisition) and contained the basic ingredients of *hamin*—slow-simmered meat cubes, beans, onions, and cumin—with the addition of American chilies, derived from the Sabbath stews of Conversos.

(See also Adafina, Cholent, Haminado, Sabbath, Shkanah, Tabyeet, and T'fina)

🕯 SEPHARDIC SABBATH STEW (*HAMIN*)

5 TO 6 SERVINGS   [MEAT]

  ¼ cup olive or vegetable oil

  4 to 5 pounds (5 to 6 small) lamb shanks, lamb neck with bone, or beef short ribs (or 2 pounds beef brisket cut into 2-inch cubes and 2 pounds lamb or beef bones)

  3 medium yellow onions, sliced

  3 to 6 cloves garlic, minced

  1½ to 2 cups dried fava, navy, or lima beans, or any combination, soaked in water to cover for 8 hours and drained

6 to 8 medium (2 to 2½ pounds) potatoes, peeled and halved or quartered

1 cup (6.75 ounces) wheat berries or long-grain rice

About 2 teaspoons table salt or 4 teaspoons kosher salt

About ½ teaspoon ground black pepper

1 teaspoon ground cumin

¼ teaspoon ground cinnamon (optional)

About 2 quarts water

5 to 6 eggs in shell

1. In a large pot, heat the oil over medium-high heat. Add the meat and brown on all sides, about 10 minutes. Remove the meat. Add the onions and sauté until lightly golden, about 15 minutes. Add the garlic and sauté for 1 minute.

2. Return the meat and add the beans, potatoes, wheat berries, salt, pepper, cumin, optional cinnamon, and enough water to cover. Bring to a boil. Cover, reduce the heat to medium-low, and simmer until the beans are nearly soft, about 1 hour.

3. Add more water if necessary. Place the eggs on top and push into the liquid. Cover tightly, place on a thin sheet of metal placed over the range top and knobs over low heat or in a 200°F oven, and cook overnight.

⊰ ITALIAN SABBATH STEW (*HAMIN*)

6 TO 8 SERVINGS   [MEAT]

Meatballs:

  1 pound ground chicken breast

  ½ cup fresh bread crumbs or matza meal

  1 large egg

  About ¾ teaspoon salt

  About ½ teaspoon ground white or black pepper

  1 clove garlic, mashed, or pinch of ground nutmeg (optional)

Greens:

  2 pounds fresh chard or spinach

  3 tablespoons olive or vegetable oil

  1 medium onion, chopped

  1 clove garlic, minced

Hamin:

  3 tablespoons olive or vegetable oil

  3 medium yellow onions, sliced

  4 fresh sage leaves or 1 teaspoon dried sage

  1½ pounds beef or veal marrow or neck bones

  2 to 3 pounds beef chuck, whole or cut into 2-inch cubes

  2 cups dried white beans

2 to 3 cloves garlic, minced

About 2 teaspoons table salt or 4 teaspoons kosher salt

About ½ teaspoon ground black pepper

About 2 quarts water

1. To make the meatballs: Combine all the meatball ingredients and form into ½-inch balls.

2. To make the greens: Separate the chard leaves from the stems. Cut the tender stems into ½-inch-wide pieces and the leaves into 1-inch pieces. In a large saucepan, heat the oil over medium heat. Add the onion and garlic and sauté until soft and translucent, about 5 minutes. Add the chard and sauté until wilted. Top with the meatballs, cover, reduce the heat to low, and simmer until the chard is tender and the meatballs are cooked, about 20 minutes. Let cool, then refrigerate until shortly before using.

3. To make the *hamin*: In a large, heavy pot, heat the oil over medium heat. Add the onions and sage and sauté until golden, about 15 minutes. In the order given, add the bones, beef, beans, salt, pepper, and enough water to cover. Bring to a boil, cover, and simmer over a medium-low heat or bake in a 375°F oven until the beans are nearly soft, about 1½ hours.

4. Add more water if necessary. Cover the pot tightly. Place on a *blech* (a thin sheet of metal placed over the range top and knobs) over low heat or in a 200°F oven and cook for at least 6 hours or overnight.

5. Shortly before serving, stir the meatballs and chard into the *hamin* and let stand until heated through.

HAMINADO/HUEVOS HAMINADOS

Haminado is a long-cooked whole egg.

Origin: Spain

Other names: Arabic: *beid hamine*; Greek: *Selanlik yamurta, Yahudi yamurta*; Ladino: *guevos haminados, ouevos haminados*; Uzbeki: *tchumi osh sevo*.

The Talmud, in a discussion of vows, mentions the inclusion of whole eggs in meat stews and, in a different location in a discussion of cooking on the Sabbath, mentions the roasting of eggs in warm ashes and in sand heated by the sun. These ancient methods gave rise to one of the most distinctive Sephardic dishes, long-cooked whole eggs, *huevos haminados*.

Originally, these eggs, known as *huevos asados* (roasted eggs), were buried in the hot ashes of an open hearth, commonly near the pot of Sabbath stew, and left to bake overnight Friday for Sabbath lunch. In the morning, the shell had turned a caramel color as had the egg inside, which also had shrunk to about half its size. Some North African and Calcutta Jews still prepare the eggs in this way, covering them in sand and/or ashes or the more modern aluminum foil and baking in a low oven overnight. A few Ashkenazim, particularly from parts of Austria and southern Germany, adopted the Sephardic manner, layering the whole eggs with ashes in a simple earthenware pot, sealing the lid with a soft dough, and baking them alongside the cholent (Sabbath stew) pot in the oven; the resulting *cholent eiers* (the Yiddish word for "eggs") were offered as the appetizer for Sabbath lunch.

At some point, possibly when the place for cooking the Sabbath stew moved from the home hearth to the local large commercial oven, probably after the thirteenth century, eggs were also added directly to the *hamin* (Sabbath stew) to slow-cook overnight, becoming *huevos haminados*. The word *huevos* is Ladino for eggs and the adjective *haminado* means "warmed," from the Aramaic *hamin* (warmed) as well as from the most common name of the Sephardic Sabbath stew in which they were cooked. Because of the moisture in the pot, the eggs did not shrink like those baked in ashes and sand, and *huevos haminados* quickly grew more common than *huevos asados*. Eggs cooked for an extremely long time in the *hamin* have a softer texture and richer flavor than regular hard-boiled eggs, and their shells are transformed to a light brown hue. The secret is to keep the temperature below the boiling point, as too high a heat will dry out the eggs.

However, eggs cooked in a meat stew cannot be eaten with dairy. Therefore, dating back at least to the early fifteenth century, in order to have pareve eggs, Sephardim developed an easier technique of simmering them in water along with onion skins (thought from Talmudic times to relieve pain), usually saved from the previous week's cooking. The combination of a long cooking time and onion skins gives these eggs a brown color, creamy texture, and rich flavor. Red onion skins yield a vermillion hue. The onion skins, besides creating a color on the shell reminiscent of roasting, also cradle and protect the eggs during cooking and impart a somewhat smoky-nutty flavor. According to the Spanish Inquisition, one of the signs of Jewish food was slow-cooking whole eggs with onion skins. Sephardim in Greece sometimes add a little coffee or a few tea leaves for extra flavor

and color. A little oil in the cooking water helps to remove the shells from the eggs. Later, Ashkenazim in a few parts of Poland and Byelorussia developed a custom of dying eggs for Passover, using onion skins for brown eggs and leaves for green eggs; these eggs were called *valetshovnes*.

Haminados, usually served warm, are ubiquitous at Sephardic celebrations and life-cycle events. These include the meal following Yom Kippur, birth commemorations, and a *Seudat Havra'ah* (the meal of consolation that follows a burial). There is a tradition that these eggs symbolize mourning for the Temple. On the Sabbath, *haminados* cooked with onion skins are served at *desayuno* (brunch) with cheese pastries, feta, and ouzo. These eggs are also the first course of the Passover Seder and are served throughout the holiday. Because of the similarity of the word *hamin* to Haman, the villain of the Scroll of Esther, *haminados* became a traditional Purim food and many Sephardim prepare pastries encasing the eggs, representing Haman in jail, called *foulares*.

Haminados are typically served as an appetizer along with salt or a dipping sauce. In modern Israel, they are sometimes accompanied with hummus. Yemenites typically eat them with *hilbeh* (fenugreek relish). Egyptians chop the eggs and sprinkle them over *ful medames* (fava beans) for breakfast. Bukharans typically serve them with and sometimes cook them in the classic Bukharan Sabbath lunch rice dish, *osh sevo*. Cooks usually make a large batch of *haminados* before the Sabbath, ensuring leftovers to add to salads and vegetable stews during the following week. They are also baked in meat loaf and meatballs, minus the shell.

SEPHARDIC LONG-COOKED EGGS
(*HUEVOS HAMINADOS*)

12 SERVINGS [PAREVE]

Brown or red outer skins from 10 to 12 onions, rinsed if dirty (about 4 cups)

12 eggs in shell, at room temperature

About 3 tablespoons olive or vegetable oil (optional)

In the bottom of a large pot or ovenproof casserole dish, arrange the onion skins. Place the eggs on top and pour in enough water to cover by at least 2 inches. Bring to a boil and, if using, drizzle with the oil. Cover the pot with a lid or foil. Simmer over very low heat or bake in a 200°F oven for at least 8 hours and preferably 12 hours. Remove the eggs from the cooking liquid, rinse, and pat dry. Serve warm or at room temperature. Store in cold water in the refrigerator for up to 4 days.

VARIATIONS

Omit the onion skins and oil and add ½ cup strong brewed coffee. Some cooks use both the onion skins and 2 tablespoons ground coffee.

HAMOTZI

Before eating bread, including matza, a person recites the benediction Hamotzi. The Sages used the terminology of Psalms, *"ha-motzi lechem min ha-arertz"* (Who brings forth bread from the earth), in the formulation of this benediction. Strictly speaking, it is the farmer and baker who create bread. Judaism, however, views the benediction over bread as thanking God for creating nature and human intelligence, by which a farmer grew and harvested seeds, and a miller ground the grain into flour, and a baker mixed the flour with water, kneaded it, and baked it. This is part of *Tikkun Olam* (mending the world), the principle that God created the world incomplete so humanity could serve as partners in finishing the job of Creation, thereby transforming the world for good. *Tikkun Olam* is why medicine is encouraged in Judaism and not considered an affront to God. Human creativity is part of the human endeavor toward perfection, as manifested by reciting Hamotzi. Ritual hand washing is performed before reciting Hamotzi. Following the meal, *Birkhat Hamazon* (grace after meals) is recited.

(See also Birkhat Hamazon and Bread)

HAMUD

Hamud is a tart sauce or a soup consisting of vegetables, in particular celery, and redolent with lemon and garlic.

Origin: Syria

Hamud is Arabic for sour. Syrians and Iraqis serve *hamud* as a sauce over rice for the Sabbath and holidays. Some cooks transform the same ingredients into a soup, typically served with rice, by increasing the amount of water. In Egypt, a chicken carcass is simmered in the liquid, yielding a lemony chicken soup. Syrians add veal and sometimes also *kibbeh mahsi*

(Middle Eastern fried stuffed dumplings) or meatballs for a more substantial dish. A more elaborate version with lamb is a popular Iraqi Rosh Hashanah dish. Some housewives serve both the soup and sauce versions at the same meal.

Potatoes help to thicken the liquid. Syrians and Egyptians enjoy the straight sour flavor from the lemon juice, but it tends to be too sour for most Westerners, who like to add a little sugar. Many Iraqis also favor a little sugar. Syrians commonly add a touch of mint. The dish is still called *hamud* when sweet-and-sour, but if all the lemon is omitted, the dish is referred to as *helou* (sweet), even if it contains no sugar.

❧ SYRIAN SOUR SAUCE WITH MINT (*HAMUD*)

6 TO 8 SERVINGS   [PAREVE]

    2 to 3 large cloves garlic
    ½ teaspoon kosher salt
    4 cups water
    3 stalks celery, diced
    2 medium boiling potatoes, peeled and diced
    2 to 3 medium leeks or 6 to 8 scallions (white and
        light green part only), sliced
    3 to 6 tablespoons fresh lemon juice
    1 tablespoon chopped fresh spearmint leaves or
        2 tablespoons dried spearmint
    1 to 3 teaspoons sugar (optional)

Using a mortar and pestle or the flat blade of a large knife, mash the garlic with the salt. In a large saucepan, combine the garlic with the remaining ingredients and simmer until the vegetables are tender, about 35 minutes. Serve over rice.

HANUKKAH

The Emperor Antiochus IV Epiphanes, who ascended to the Seleucid throne in 175 BCE, sought to replace Judaism with Hellenism and in 168, looted the Second Temple and outlawed the practice of Judaism. Then on the twenty-fifth day of the month of Kislev in 167 BCE, the day of the winter solstice and beginning of the Saturnalia festival, his Syrian forces desecrated the Temple. Long before Antiochus, the twenty-fifth of Kislev was the traditional date in Israel for the end of the olive oil harvest, as well as the last day on which that year's *bikkurim* (first fruits) could be brought to the Temple, engendering an ancient Hebrew celebration. The Hasmonean patriarch Mattathias and his five sons (Yochanan, Judah, Eleazar, Jonathan, and Simon), from a priestly family and better known as the Maccabees (*Makabim* in Hebrew), launched a revolt against Antiochus, the first known war fought for religious freedom. Three years later, after numerous battles, the Jews chased their oppressors out of Jerusalem. The Temple, however, lay in a state of physical and spiritual disarray. After rededicating the Temple on the twenty-fifth day of the month of Kislev in 164 BCE (some scholars say 165), the people replicated the eight-day holiday of Sukkot and Shemini Atzeret, which they had been unable to observe a few months before, and celebrated with the recitation of *Hallel* (psalms of praise) and the waving of palm branches.

Afterwards, the surviving Hasmoneans seized power and became a corrupt dynasty, and their machinations eventually led to the tragic entry of Rome into Judea in 63 BCE. Five centuries after the Maccabees, while compiling the Talmud, the Sages ignored the military angle of the episode as well as the then-despised Hasmoneans. Instead, they related another tale: The priests found only a single small vial of ritually untainted olive oil, enough to burn in the Temple's seven-branched candelabra for barely one day, but the flame lasted for eight days.

The menorah in the Sanctuary was not perpetually burning, but rather was lit every evening shortly before sunset, then after the flames died out the following morning, the cups were cleaned and fresh wicks and oil were added. The Talmud estimated the amount of pure olive oil needed to burn through the longest night of the year, about fifteen hours in the month of Tevet, to be half a *log*, measuring about six tablespoons; therefore, a half a *log* of oil was daily poured into each cup, no matter the time of year, and left to burn out.

Hanukkah ("dedication" in Hebrew) commemorates the rededication of the Temple by the Hasmoneans. Light is the preeminent theme of this eight-day festival, one that is particularly apropos at the time of the year when daylight once again begins to increase. Despite Hanukkah's prominent position in American Jewish life, before the twentieth century, it was a rather minor winter festival with no rituals in the synagogue and only a few prayers added to the services. The central ritual of Hanukkah is the kindling after sunset each evening of an eight-branched candelabra containing oil or candles with a ninth higher or lower branch for the *shamash* ("servant/caretaker" used to light the others). A single candle is lit on the first evening and an additional candle is added on each successive night reaching a total of eight for the final day. The candelabra is called a *hanukkiyah* by Sephardim and a menorah by Ashkenazim.

A popular Ashkenazic custom is the spinning of a four-sided top—called a dreidel/*dreydl* (a diminutive of the German word *dreyen*, "to turn") in eastern Europe, *trendl* and *kreisel* (to spin) in Western Yiddish, *verfl* (a word for "dice") in Northeastern Yiddish, and *sevivon* in modern Hebrew—derived around the seventeenth century from a German gambling game. This was followed in the eighteenth century by the custom of giving teachers and children Hanukkah gelt (Yiddish for "money"), typically a few small coins used to wager in games, which in the mid-twentieth century was largely replaced with chocolate coins.

Daniel Moritz Oppenheim, one of the premier Jewish painters of the modern era, commemorates Hanukkah in Germany, circa 1880. The holiday would include roast goose, apfelmus (applesauce), and, for a special treat, some families enjoyed fritlach *(fruit fritters).*

Another modern American culinary custom is baking sugar cookies in the shape of menorahs, dreidels, stars of David, and other holiday-related symbols. The practice of giving Hanukkah presents is also a modern American phenomenon derived from the Christmas celebrations.

Moroccans had a custom on the day following Hanukkah, called the "day of the *shamash*," the ninth day corresponding to the ninth candle, for the children to collect any leftover Hanukkah candles in the neighborhood and burn them in a bonfire as they danced, sang, and ate leftover pastries.

Because it formerly held a minor status and had not been ordained a day of feasting like other Jewish holidays, Hanukkah initially failed to inspire any specific festival dishes. Indeed, until around the fourteenth century, there were no records of any traditional Hanukkah fare. Then two types of foods became popular symbols— dairy foods and fried foods.

The tradition of dairy products, particularly cheese, was first mentioned in the fourteenth century by the Spanish rabbi Nissim ben Reuben Gerondi (known as the Ran). This custom grew out of a misunderstanding of one of the books of the Apocrypha, Judith, composed around 115 BCE. There are actually four different extant manuscript versions of Judith, none surviving in the original Hebrew. The narrative, replete with anachronisms and misnomers, tells of Nebuchadnezzar (who reigned from 605 to 561 BCE), sending his Assyrian general, Holofernes, to conquer Judea and laying siege to Bethulia (perhaps Meselieh), a fortified town on the outskirts of Jerusalem. Judith, a young righteous widow from the town, infiltrated the enemy camp, fed Holofernes salty cheese or milk (in those days probably indicating a form of loose yogurt) to induce thirst, plied him with wine to slack his thirst until the general fell into a drunken stupor, then cut off his head with his own sword. In response to the loss of its leader, the enemy army panicked and fled. The timing of this story actually predates the Greek period by four centuries, but during the Middle Ages, when Jews no longer possessed the original text of Judith, the oral tale became associated with the Hasmonean revolution and Judith became variously the aunt or daughter of Judah Maccabee.

There is no mention of Judith in the Talmud or Midrash. Indeed, there are very few references to Hanukkah in the Talmud, all subsumed in a small section in the tractate Sabbath, as both are occasions entailing candle lighting. Purim, on the other hand, has an entire tractate.

The first record of the name Judith in association with Hanukkah was in the *Kol Bo*—either an abridgment of or precursor to the early fourteenth-century work *Orchot Chaim* (Paths of Life) by Aaron ben Jacob Ha-Koheni from Narbonne—which explained, "Women are obligated to light the Hanukkah candles because they too were in the miracle: The enemy came to destroy everyone—men, women, and children. Some explain it was through a woman that the great miracle occurred and her name was Judith, as it is explained in the *Agaddah*: There was a daughter of Yochanan the High Priest, and she was very beautiful, and the king of the Greeks said that she should lie with him. She fed him a food of cheese so that he would become very thirsty and drink a lot, and become drunk and fall deep asleep. This happened, and she took his sword and cut off his head and brought it to Jerusalem, and when the army saw that their leader was dead, they fled."

The *Shulchan Arukh* makes no mention of the custom of dairy foods, but Rabbi Moses Isserles (c. 1520–1572) in his glosses notes, "There are those who say to eat cheese on Hanukkah because the miracle was done through milk, which Judith fed the enemy."

Fried foods became a Hanukkah tradition in recognition of the miracle of oil. Sephardim and Mizrachim typically prepare various fried pastries or doughnuts (*bimuelos* and *lokmas*). In many Sephardic communities, members of wealthier families bring trays of sweets to less fortunate ones. In Morocco and Egypt these trays include *zangula*, deep-fried batter poured into hot oil in a thin spiral, similar to Amish funnel cakes, and coated with a combination of either cinnamon and sugar or honey. Algerians fry various doughs called *sefengor kindel*, some filled with plums. North African Jews prepare *debla*, a dough rolled to resemble a rose, which is deep-fried and dipped in sugar syrup or honey. Turkish families serve a dessert similar to a doughnut called *burmuelos*. The Bene Israel in India prepare a milk-based fried pastry called *gulab jamun*. Italians make *frittelle*, deep-fried diamond-shaped pieces of dough that are dipped in honey. Yemenites serve a carrot sauté called *lachis djezar*.

Ashkenazim fry latkes ("pancakes," *levivot* in modern Hebrew), blintzes, and doughnuts. A less well-known eastern European dish is *ritachlich*, a salad of radishes fried in schmaltz. In the twentieth century, the Polish jelly doughnut *ponchik* made its way to Israel, taking on the Hebrew name *sufganiyot*, and subsequently emerged as the most popular Israeli Hanukkah food, sold throughout the eight-day festival at almost every bakery and market.

In the early fourteenth century, Kalonymus ben Kalonymus, a Provençal native who spent many years in Rome, wrote about frying pancakes in oil for Hanukkah. The original latkes were cheese pancakes, fulfilling the two predominant Hanukkah culinary customs in one dish. Later, dairy noodle kugels, cheese dumplings, cheesecakes, and rugelach also became common Ashkenazic foods for the festival. Russian Jews serve barley soup with sour cream, while Hungarians might offer some *delkelekh* (cheese buns).

In the Maghreb, in commemoration of Judith and Hannah (who lost her seven sons to the Syrians), a special celebration was established on the seventh day of Hanukkah corresponding to the new moon of the month of Tevet, called *Chag ha'Banot* (Festival of the Daughters). On this occasion, women gather together to sing and dance, eat dairy foods and sweetened couscous, and drink buttermilk.

Meat also became traditional Hanukkah fare in some areas. Often a fried or baked pastry will have a meat filling resembling foods said to be served at the Maccabean victory banquet. In Uzbekistan and Syria, meat was covered with a matza-like dough. Some eastern Europeans added meat fillings to their *punichkes* (doughnuts). Algerians eat *khosekham*, a dish with meat and wine. Some Greek Jews prepare a meat-filled baked pastry called *pastilicos de carne* as well as fried apple rings, apple fritters, and applesauce.

Abraham Ibn Ezra (1089–1164), in his hymn *"Zemer Naeh,"* sung by some families on the Sabbath of Hanukkah, lists items for the Hanukkah feast, including wine, fine flour, doves, ducks, and fatted geese. Roast goose was traditional Hanukkah fare among Ashkenazim, a role sometimes filled by brisket in eastern Europe. Historically, all unnecessary domesticated animals, generally males and older females past their reproductive period, were slaughtered before the onset of the winter and the consequent need to expend vital resources to feed them. Since this season corresponded to Hanukkah, there was much more meat available at holiday time. Geese were the predominant fowl of western Ashkenazim, with many families keeping at least a small flock to provide eggs and occasional meat, which was generally eaten only at special occasions or at Hanukkah.

On the final day of Hanukkah, many Turkish Jews hold a *merenda* (snack/party), a festive potluck meal in which family and friends all contribute dishes, providing the opportunity for guests to show off a specialty or use up leftovers. This custom is the subject of a short Ladino folk song covered by Theodore Bikel, *"Hazermos una Merenda"* (Let's Make a Party), which begins, "Let's make a *merenda*. What time? You decide."

(See also Bimuelo, Goose, Kefte, Latke, Lokma, Olive Oil, Schmaltz, and Sufganiyah)

HARIRA
Harira is a thick, hearty legume soup.
Origin: Morocco

There are as many versions of *harira*, from the Farsi and Arabic word meaning "silk," as there are cooks. It can be vegetarian or include plenty of meat. Most versions contain lentils and chickpeas. Moroccan Arabs serve it during the month of Ramadan to end the daily fast and Moroccan Jews serve it to break the Yom Kippur fast, as well as throughout the winter. *Harira* frequently constitutes a meal in itself. It is traditionally accompanied with dried figs, dates, flatbreads, and harissa (chili paste).

MOROCCAN CHICKPEA AND LENTIL SOUP (*HARIRA*)
8 TO 10 SERVINGS [MEAT]

- 3 tablespoons olive or vegetable oil
- 2 medium yellow onions, chopped
- 1 cup chopped celery
- 1 to 2 cloves garlic, minced
- 1 to 1¼ pounds boneless lamb or beef shoulder or neck, cut into 1-inch cubes
- 1 tablespoon sweet paprika or 2 teaspoons ground cumin
- 2 teaspoons ground black pepper
- 1 teaspoon ground turmeric or ¼ teaspoon crumbled saffron strands
- 1 (3-inch) stick cinnamon or 1 teaspoon ground cinnamon
- 1 teaspoon ground coriander (optional)
- ¼ to ½ teaspoon ground ginger (optional)
- ¼ teaspoon cayenne (optional)

1 tablespoon tomato paste
5 cups (2 pounds) peeled, seeded, and chopped
tomatoes
7 cups water
2 cups (14 ounces) dried chickpeas, soaked in water
to cover for 8 hours and drained
¾ to 1 cup brown lentils
⅓ cup all-purpose flour
1 cup water
About 1 teaspoon table salt or 2 teaspoons kosher salt
Ground black pepper to taste
½ cup chopped fresh cilantro
½ cup chopped fresh flat-leaf parsley
Juice of 2 lemons

1. In a large, heavy pot, heat the oil over medium
heat. Add the onions, celery, and garlic and sauté until
softened, about 10 minutes. Add the meat, paprika,
pepper, turmeric, cinnamon, and, if using, coriander,
ginger, and/or cayenne and stir for 5 minutes. Add the
tomato paste and stir for 2 minutes.

2. Drain the tomatoes and add the pieces, reserving
the liquid, and cook, stirring occasionally, for 10 minutes. Add the reserved tomato liquid, 7 cups water,
and chickpeas. Bring to a boil, cover, reduce the heat
to low, and simmer for 1½ hours.

3. Add the lentils, cover, and simmer, stirring occasionally, until the meat, chickpeas, and lentils are
tender, about 35 minutes. The soup may be cooled,
covered, and refrigerated for up to 4 days, then
reheated.

4. About 15 minutes before serving, dissolve the
flour in 1 cup water. In a slow, steady stream, stir into
the soup. Add the salt and pepper. Simmer, stirring
frequently, until the soup is slightly thickened and the
raw flour taste disappears, about 15 minutes. Add the
cilantro, parsley, and lemon juice.

HARISA

Harisa is a wheat berry or bulgur porridge, generally
cooked overnight and served for Sabbath lunch.
Origin: Middle East
Other names: Arabic: *haresa*; Farsi: *haleeme gusht,
keshkek*; Morocco: *horisa, orissa*.

Since the advent of civilization, the diet of most
residents of the Middle East and Mediterranean overwhelmingly consisted of grains, primarily in the form
of porridges, breads, and beer. Barley was the predominant grain originally used, but by the Roman period
various species of wheat supplanted it in breads and
porridges. Plain gruel, rather boring day in and day
out, could be enhanced with the addition of herbs,
spices, sweeteners, or meat, as in two widespread
Arabic dishes included in an anonymous thirteenth-
century Moorish cookbook from Andalusia—*asida*
(dairy porridge) and *harisa* (meat porridge). Both of
these porridges were popular throughout much of the
medieval Arab world. In thirteenth-century Spain,
Jewish vendors commonly sold *harisa* from street corners on Fridays.

Asida was a thick semolina porridge. Some versions
were enriched with butter and sweetened with honey,
sorghum, or date honey. In the Maghreb, it was also
flavored with a hot chili sauce. Initially, sweet *asida*
was primarily a festive dish, but in some locations it
became a regular breakfast cereal.

The Arabic word *harisa* or *haris*, from the Semitic
haras (to break), refers to the method of pounding the
cooked grains into a smooth porridge. It is not related
in content or history to the Maghrebi chili paste of the
same name. When the term *harisa* initially appeared
in Mesopotamia nearly two millennia ago, it referred
to a dish of any cooked cracked cereal, particularly
barley but wheat eventually emerged as the preferred
grain.

When a group of Yemenite Jews visited the
Umayyad Caliph Mu'awiya (founder of the first Arabic
Islamic dynasty in 661 CE) in his capital of Damascus,
the first question the ruler asked was whether they
knew how to prepare the Jewish *harisa*, which he had
sampled during a visit to Arabia. The visitors obliged
by whipping up a batch of this Jewish specialty for the
grateful ruler.

Middle Eastern Jews devised their own distinctive form of *harisa* in conjunction with the Sabbath
by slow-simmering cracked durum wheat berries or
bulgur with lamb or, less frequently, beef, goose, or
chicken—generally in a proportion of two-thirds
wheat to one-third meat—along with some optional
chopped onion, overnight in a sealed earthenware
pot. Muslim *harisa*, on the other hand, was cooked
relatively quickly and, therefore, the ingredients did
not meld and infuse the dish. Just before serving, the
bones were removed, the mixture was pounded into
a creamy consistency by a non-Jewish maid or neigh-

bor, and the final dish was sprinkled with ground cinnamon. There is also a vegetarian version served with *samneh* (clarified butter) and honey. Mizrachim compared *harisa* or *al-harissa* to the manna, which was pounded in a mortar and baked or stewed, and the dish therefore became symbolic for the Sabbath. Jewish-style *harisa* soon spread to many parts of the Islamic world. The Andalusian cookbook explains that there are a variety of *harisa* made from fatty veal, sheep, goose breasts or legs, or chicken, noting, "All these have a flavor and taste that is not like the others and have an attribute that the others do not have." The book also contains recipes for both a rice and bread crumb *harisa*. The recipe for wheat *harisa* directs, "Take good wheat and soak it in water. Then pound it in a wooden or stone mortar until it is free from husks. Then shake it and put the clean wheat in a pot with red meat and cover it with plenty of fresh water. Put it on a strong fire until it falls apart. Then beat it with the mallet very forcefully until it becomes blended and one part blends together with the other. Then pour on enough melted fresh fat to cover it and beat them together until they are mixed. When it seems that the fat begins to separate and remain on top, turn it onto a platter and recover it with salted fat. Dust it with ground cinnamon and use it as you please."

In medieval Arabic markets, vendors (*haraisiyyun*) commonly sold bowls of steaming *harisa* boiled up in large cauldrons; home cooks reserved it for special occasions. When the dish reached England in the fourteenth century, it was renamed frumenty, from a Middle French word meaning "grain," and for the ensuing several centuries the porridge remained an important English food.

Although the Jewish *harisa* has become less prominent in recent years, supplanted by the Sabbath *hamin/adafina*, many Middle Eastern Jews, especially Yemenites and Iraqis, still prepare various Saturday breakfast whole-wheat dishes called *harisa*; some are mashed, while others are vegetarian versions that leave the grains whole. In some instances, sugar is added at the table. Spinach or other seasonal greens might be mixed in. Potatoes are a relatively recent innovation. Indians garnish *harisa* with minced fresh ginger, green chilies, and cilantro. Many Moroccans from Spanish descent and those from Tangiers make

a zesty Sabbath porridge from crushed durum wheat berries and red chilies. Non-Jewish cooks customarily still do the mashing, only now they usually use a food processor to achieve a creamy consistency. Kurds traditionally serve *harisa* on the Sabbath when the Torah portion of *Beshalach*, which contains the crossing of the Reed Sea during the exodus from Egypt, is read, due to the Hebrew phrase *"b'Shabbat Shira lechem chitah* (on the Sabbath of Song wheat bread)," the initials of which spell *beshalach*.

(See also Hamin and Sabbath)

MIDDLE EASTERN SABBATH PORRIDGE (*HARISA*)

6 TO 8 SERVINGS   [MEAT OR PAREVE]

- 3 tablespoons vegetable oil
- 3 large yellow onions, chopped
- 1 to 2 cloves garlic
- 1 tablespoon paprika or 1½ to 3 teaspoons cayenne
- 1 tablespoon granulated or brown sugar
- About 1¼ teaspoons table salt or 2½ teaspoons kosher salt
- About ½ teaspoon ground black pepper
- 1½ to 2 pounds boneless lamb or beef chuck, cut into cubes (optional)
- 1 pound lamb or beef marrow bones (optional)
- 2¼ cups (1 pound) wheat berries, soaked in water to cover overnight and drained, or coarse bulgur
- About 2 quarts water

1. In a large pot, heat the oil over medium heat. Add the onions and sauté until lightly golden, about 15 minutes. Stir in the garlic, paprika, sugar, salt, and pepper and stir for 1 minute. If using, stir in the meat and/or bones. Add the wheat berries and water to cover.

2. Cover and cook over medium-low heat or in a 350°F oven for 1 hour.

3. If necessary, add more water to cover. Tightly cover the pot. Place on a *blech* (a thin sheet of metal placed over the range top and knobs) over very low heat or in 225°F oven and cook overnight. Serve warm.

HARISSA

Harissa is a spice paste based on chilies.

Origin: Tunisia

The Spanish occupied part of Tunisia from 1535 until the Turks conquered the region in 1574, introducing various New World produce, including chilies. During that time, harissa (from the Arabic "to break"), a scorching chili paste, originated in Tunisia, then subsequently spread throughout the Maghreb. A mixture of chilies is the predominant base. Caraway is commonly added in Tunisia, while cumin is preferred in Morocco. It is traditionally drizzled over a host of Tunisian and Moroccan dishes, including couscous, soups, vegetables, and salads. In Israel, *harissa*, called *charif* (fiery), became a common topping for falafel. Harissa should be used sparingly by the fainthearted.

(See also Chili)

❧ NORTHWEST AFRICAN CHILI PASTE (*HARISSA*)

ABOUT 1⅓ CUPS [PAREVE]

5 ounces (about 18) assorted dried hot red chilies, such as 12 New Mexico/Anaheim chilies, 3 ancho or pasilla chilies, and 1 arbol, cayenne, cascabel, guajillo, or pequin chili; for more heat, increase the amount of the latter chilies

4 to 5 cloves garlic, chopped

About 1 teaspoon kosher salt or ½ teaspoon table salt

2 to 3 tablespoons olive oil

Additional olive oil for covering the paste

1. Remove and discard the seeds and stems from the chilies. Cover the chilies with hot water and let soak until softened, about 30 minutes. Drain.

2. In a blender or a food processor fitted with a metal blade, or using a mortar and pestle, puree the chilies, garlic, and salt. Add enough oil to make a smooth, thick paste. Transfer to a jar and cover with a thin layer of additional oil. Harissa keeps in the refrigerator for up to 1 month.

HAWAIJ

Hawaij is a spice blend.

Origin: Yemen

The signature note to the cooking of Yemenite Jews is *hawaij* (Arabic meaning "what is needed" in the plural), a spice blend similar to the Indian garam masala across the Arabian Sea. As with other classic spice blends, there is no single recipe, but each family creates a unique combination. The predominant flavors are cumin and black pepper, while turmeric imparts a bright yellow color. Many versions also contain cardamom and coriander. Yemenites popularized *hawaij*

in Israel, where it is widely available in stores and still made at home. In America, it is sometimes labeled "Israeli rub" or "Israeli seasoning spice mix." *Hawaij* is used as a dry rub for grilled chicken, fish, lamb, beef, and eggplant. It is added to tomato sauces, stews, and soups, such as *fatoot* (beef soup) or *marak regel* (foot soup), and *harisa* (Sabbath porridge).

❧ YEMENITE SPICE MIXTURE (*HAWAIJ*)

ABOUT ¾ CUP [PAREVE]

¼ cup cumin seeds

2 tablespoons coriander seeds

4 teaspoons green cardamom pods

¼ cup whole black peppercorns

3 tablespoons ground turmeric

Heat a dry, large, cast-iron or other heavy skillet over medium-low heat. Add the cumin, coriander, and cardamom and toast, stirring constantly, until the spices are fragrant and begin to color, about 3 minutes. Transfer to a bowl and let cool. Add the pepper. In a mortar or spice grinder, grind into a powder. Add the turmeric. Store in an airtight container in a cool, dark place for up to 1 month.

HEART

The first American Jewish cookbook, *Jewish Cookery* (Philadelphia, 1871), included a recipe "to cook the lights [soft parts, e.g., pancreas, head, and lungs] and heart of a calf," with these directions: "The heart must be made cosher, then well washed. Season it with some sage and onions, and make a stuffing in the following manner: chop some sage, well dried, and onion, bread crumbs, and suet, some salt and pepper, rub some flour and salt outside the heart, and roast with plenty of fat. When it is done, dip it in a pan of boiling water, or pour boiling water over it, to make the gravy. Be careful to have the dish and plates made very hot, as the fat is apt to stick to the roof of the mouth, but dipping it in water will prevent that."

Today, in animal-rich America, most organs are ignored with the occasional exception of liver and sweetbreads. In previous times and poorer cultures, however, waste was considered a sin and people used every part of the animal, including every part of the innards.

Since organs contain little or no fat, there is almost no trimming. Veal and lamb hearts are tender with a delicate flavor and can be grilled or braised. A beef heart, weighing about three pounds, requires simmering in water to tenderize.

HELZEL

Helzel is poultry neck skin, often from a goose, that is stuffed with bread crumbs or flour, then cooked.

Origin: Germany

Other names: England: *magel*; Hungary: *halsli*; Yiddish: *falsa kishke*, *gefillte helzel*, *gorgle*.

Before the development in 1925 of a casing made from cellulose, sausages required some animal part for stuffing, notably the intestines and stomach. Economical cooks could feed the family using these less desirable items by filling them with inexpensive starches. The skin from around a goose's neck also proved ideal for stuffing; much of a goose's fat is attached to the skin, so the fatty skin provided extra moisture and flavor for the stuffing. The Yiddish word for neck, *helzel*, from the German *hals*, gave rise to the name. Stuffed poultry neck certainly was not unique to Ashkenazim and may well have been introduced to Europe during the Ottoman control of the Balkans and Hungary. Turkish Jews enjoyed a version with a little chopped walnuts added to a flour mixture.

Throughout most of history, particularly among the poor, sausages contained very little or no meat. Medieval Ashkenazim began filling the neck skin, as well as the intestines, with any combination of bread, flour, matza meal, or buckwheat groats enriched with schmaltz. Potato kugel batter was also substituted for the classic stuffing. Stuffed intestines are known as *kishke*.

Until well into the twentieth century, Ashkenazic families for a special occasion or from time to time either brought one of their home-raised geese to a kosher butcher to be slaughtered or purchased a freshly killed bird, and used every part. The neck itself often went into a soup or fricassee. In Alsace and central Europe, where geese were the longstanding principal poultry and cattle and sheep intestines were scarcer, cooks used the skin surrounding the elongated goose neck and sometimes a duck neck as a casing. In eastern Europe, where geese were rarer, the smaller chicken neck skin from a mature bird was substituted and, later, with the introduction of the larger American turkey, its neck skin was also used. The filled neck was sewn up on both ends and typi-

cally roasted alongside the poultry or by itself with plenty of schmaltz, or simmered in a cholent (Sabbath stew). Goose, due to the extra fat, yields a more flavorful dish than chicken and turkey. To serve, the *helzel* is cut into thin slices.

Among Ashkenazim, *helzel* was a comfort food reserved for the Sabbath or other special occasions, in many homes rivaling *kishke* (stuffed derma) as a favorite dish. However, after the popularity of geese declined among Ashkenazim and butchers started selling dressed and koshered chickens without the head and feet, the absence of neck skins as well as changing tastes in twentieth-century America, led to the decline of *helzel*.

(See also Goose, Kishke, Liver, and Schmaltz)

ASHKENAZIC STUFFED POULTRY NECK (*HELZEL*)

6 TO 8 SERVINGS　　　　　　　　　　[MEAT]

Skin of 1 goose or turkey neck or 2 large chicken necks

2 to 3 large yellow onions, sliced

1½ cups (7.5 ounces) all-purpose flour, or ¾ cup flour and ¾ cup matza meal, bread crumbs, semolina, or mashed potatoes

2 to 4 tablespoons schmaltz, vegetable oil, or shortening, melted

1 small yellow onion, grated or minced

1 clove garlic, crushed

1 small carrot, grated (optional)

¾ teaspoon paprika

About ½ teaspoon salt

About ¼ teaspoon ground black pepper

About ¾ teaspoon ground ginger, ¼ teaspoon cayenne, or dash of ground nutmeg (optional)

1. Using plain white cotton thread, sew up or tie the narrower end of the neck.

2. Preheat the oven to 325°F. Scatter the sliced onions in a shallow roasting pan.

3. In a medium bowl, combine the flour, schmaltz, grated onion, garlic, optional carrot, paprika, salt, pepper, and, if using, ginger. Loosely stuff the mixture into the poultry neck, filling it about three-fourths of the way. Sew up or tie the open end. Pour boiling water over the neck in a large pot or place in a pot of boiling water and let sit for 10 minutes.

4. Place the *helzel* on the bed of onions in the roasting pan. Roast, basting occasionally with the cooking liquid, until golden brown, at least 1½ hours. Or roast the *helzel* in the same pan as the poultry from which it came or along with a pot roast (*gedempte fleisch*). Or cook overnight on top of a cholent (Sabbath stew).

HERRING

Herring, a relative of shad and sardines, has long been the world's most important food fish. Herring travel in immense schools in cold waters and spawn near the surface around March, making these silvery fish easy to net, as they have been for millennia. Atlantic herring can grow up to eighteen inches and one and a half pounds, but they are usually captured small, at three to twelve ounces, and sometimes packaged as sardines.

As one of the few fish capable of surviving in the brackish waters of the Baltic Sea, herring became the primary form of protein for many people in the bordering lands. Herring, however, is a very fatty fish and turns rancid relatively quickly. As a result, throughout much of history, herring was eaten soon after capture, primarily in the spring, and typically nearer the coast.

There were many fishing boats trawling the Baltic. Always enterprising, the Dutch sailed far from home in search of the fish, discovering a location in the North Sea where herring (*baring*) swam in abundance. However, the sailors needed a means of preserving the fish on these lengthy voyages. In the fifteenth century, the Dutch devised a process called *gibbling*, whereby the herring, immediately upon being caught, were scaled and gutted, the gills were removed, and the herring were then butterflied and layered in airtight barrels with coarse salt. Subsequently, salted herring became the primary form in which herring was available, and cooks usually needed to soak it in water to remove the excess salt. (When this process later was applied to salmon, the result was lox.)

Herring's importance to Dutch, German, and eastern European Jews after the fifteenth century, both financially and gastronomically, cannot be over-emphasized. After barrels of salt herring arrived in ports in Holland, Britain, or Scandinavia, Jews were prominent in trading the fish through central and eastern Europe. The artist Marc Chagall occasionally depicted a flying fish in his pictures in memory of his father, a herring merchant in the Byelorussian village of Vitebsk. Even in early twentieth-century America,

fish markets and general stores in large Jewish centers featured a large barrel of schmaltz herring for sale.

In the sixteenth century, the European appetite for herring led to three major wars between the Dutch and the English, off whose coast the Dutch were fishing. The English also loved herring, and won out, resulting in a decline in Dutch sea power and trade and the supremacy of the British. The Dutch were forced to search elsewhere for their herring, but for the next three centuries, the schools of the North Sea continued to provide a livelihood to British fishermen and, along with the Baltic, provide plenty of Europe's dry-salt herring. Today, herring is typically chilled on ice, then salted after reaching port.

Salt herring is ready to eat once soaked, with a firmer texture and more intense flavor than fresh. Most cooks, however, further prepare it. The most popular way is in a marinade of vinegar, sugar, and frequently raw onions, known as pickled herring and marinated herring. Pickled unskinned fillets are known as Bismarck herring. After pickling, the fish pieces can be repackaged with fresh ingredients, sour cream, or a wine sauce.

Schmaltz herring refers to a mature fresh herring, with at least 18 percent fat. It comes with the head off but the insides intact. Matjes herring, Dutch for "maiden," refers to a young herring from the first catch of the year, which has been mildly salted. Milch (*milt* or *miltz*) herring are adult male fish containing a long pinkish gray organ filled with sperm and seminal fluid. Many connoisseurs consider these best for pickling, as the milky sacs impart a creaminess to the brine. A male fish at breeding time is called a milter.

Kipper, probably from the Dutch *koper* (copper), refers to a split, gutted, dry-salted, and cold-smoked herring. It is golden red in color, the intensity of the hue depending on the amount of curing. A bloater is similar to a kipper, except it is left whole with the insides intact. A buckling is also salted and left whole, but is hot-smoked, making it milder flavored and more perishable. In England, hunters would commonly lay a copper-colored bloater across a fox trail to throw the hounds off the animal's scent, thereby making the hunt more challenging and giving rise to the term "red herring" as a device used to divert attention.

Herring was a mainstay of the diet of Jews in Poland, Ukraine, and the Baltic States, where it was commonly eaten with black bread and/or boiled potatoes. Herring not only served as everyday fare, but was frequently present on the Sabbath and other special occasions. Some housewives even made gefilte fish from schmaltz herring. Pickled herring was traditionally served by Ashkenazim at a Sabbath kiddush, accompanied with *kichel* (egg cookies), and at a meal to break a fast. Among Chasidim, pickled herring became a traditional Hanukkah dish. A favorite Ashkenazic cold salad consisted of finely chopped herring mixed with onions, hard-boiled eggs, and sometimes apples—this dish was called *gehakte herring* (chopped herring) and, by Russians, *forshmak* (foretaste). When liver was unavailable, *gehakte herring* provided a substitute for chopped liver. *Gehakte herring* might be featured at a *shalosh seudot* (the third meal of Sabbath), the meal following the fast of Yom Kippur, and dairy brunches. Although herring grew less important as the twentieth century progressed, various forms of pickled herring as well as *gehakte herring* remain important in Jewish appetizing stores and delis.

(See also Fish, Forshmak, and Kichel)

❦ EASTERN EUROPEAN CHOPPED HERRING (*GEHAKTE HERRING*)

6 TO 8 SERVINGS   [PAREVE]

2 slices challah or white bread, trimmed of crusts, or 2 crumbled matzas
¼ cup cider vinegar or white vinegar
2 cups (16-ounce jar) pickled herring; or 2 schmaltz herrings, soaked for 1 day, and 1 pickled herring
2 to 3 hard-boiled eggs
1 medium yellow onion, chopped
1 to 3 teaspoons sugar or sweet red wine

Soak the bread in the vinegar for 5 minutes. Drain the herring and discard the onions and liquid from the jar. In a chopping bowl, grinder, or food processor fitted with a metal blade, chop the herring, bread mixture, eggs, onion, and 1 teaspoon sugar until almost pureed. Check the seasoning and add more sugar to taste, if necessary.

HILBEH

Hilbeh is a relish made from fenugreek seeds and chilies.

Origin: Yemen
Other names: India: *halba*.

The fenugreek seed, called *hilbeh* in southern Yemen and *hulbah* in the northern part of the country, probably from the Semitic root *hlb* (milk), has long been a traditional lactation aide. Fenugreek also serves as the basis for a spicy Yemenite relish, functioning as an all-purpose spread and condiment, much in the manner that Americans use ketchup and salsa.

In Yemen, Jews lived in extreme poverty and, consequently, *hilbeh* typically consisted of only the basic ingredients. To make *hilbeh*, the raw fenugreek is first soaked in water, giving it a gelatinous texture and spicy, balsamic vinegar-like bitter flavor. Then *s'chug* (chili paste) or chilies and sometimes tomatoes are added: chili for its bite and tomatoes to mellow the flavor. For a special occasion, various imported spices may also be added. Contact between the Jewish communities of Yemen and southern India introduced the latter to the beloved Yemenite condiment. Indian Jews augmented *halba* with their own special touches, such as fresh ginger.

During the week, *hilbeh* is used as a dip for breads, a condiment for soups at lunch, and a seasoning for various dishes. Breakfast, even on the Sabbath, commonly consists of a hard-boiled egg with *hilbeh*. Bread with *hilbeh* is eaten at the end of the meal before the fast of Tisha b'Av, as the uncooked *hilbeh* is permitted at an occasion when only a single cooked food is allowed. In Israel, *hilbeh*, sold in containers in markets, also doubles as a spicy topping for falafel; this addition is beloved by many Mizrachim, but generally avoided by most Ashkenazim.

(See also Fatoot, Fenugreek, and Regel)

❦ YEMENITE FENUGREEK RELISH (*HILBEH*)

ABOUT ⅔ CUP   [PAREVE]

3 tablespoons fenugreek seeds or 2 tablespoons ground fenugreek
2 cups cold water, plus more if needed
1 to 2 teaspoons *s'chug* (Yemenite Chili Paste, page 538), 1 to 3 small hot green chilies, or ½ teaspoon cayenne
About ½ teaspoon table salt or 1 teaspoon kosher salt
2 to 4 tablespoons fresh lemon juice
About ¼ cup water

1. If using fenugreek seeds, grind them to a fine powder in a mortar. Put the ground fenugreek in a medium bowl, add the 2 cups water, stir well, and let soak for at least 4 or preferably 12 hours. Carefully pour off the water.

2. With a mortar and pestle or in a blender or food processor fitted with a metal blade, process the fenugreek, *s'chug*, and salt into a paste. Transfer to a medium bowl and, using a wooden spoon, gradually beat in the lemon juice and enough water to produce a smooth mixture with the consistency of mayonnaise, 5 to 10 minutes. Or in the food processor with the machine running, gradually add the juice and water. Cover and store in the refrigerator for up to 1 week. If it becomes too firm, beat in a little more water.

VARIATIONS

Indian Fenugreek Relish (Halba): Add ¼ to ½ cup chopped fresh cilantro, 1 teaspoon grated fresh ginger, and 2 to 3 minced garlic cloves.

HILU

A vast array of candied fruits and vegetables—called *hilu/hellou*, from the Arabic word for sweet (*helwa*), and akin to the Sephardic *dulce* (fruit preserves)—are popular throughout the Middle East and North Africa. Syrians are arguably the most prolific *hilu* makers. The most prevalent of these treats, and perhaps the most popular Rosh Hashanah *hilu*, is made from quince (*membrillo*). Other common types are coconut (*joz hindi hilu*), citrus peel (*brit'an hilu*), baby eggplant (*batijan hilu*), and figs (*teen hilu*). Some variations, such as fresh green walnuts, are rather rare. The fruit and vegetables in *hilu* can be served in relatively large chunks or cut small like the fruit pieces in marmalade. Sweet-and-sour candies are known as *hamud-u-hilu*.

Hilu of pumpkin (*yatkeen fijil*), spaghetti squash (*cheveux d' ange*), and trumpet squash (*urigh*) are traditional Rosh Hashanah fare in Turkey, Syria, and the Maghreb, the many seeds of these squash representing fruitfulness and the golden color symbolizing prosperity. In the Maghreb, *hilu* is sometimes served over couscous. Among Jews from the eastern Mediterranean, *hilu* is commonly offered to guests in glass or silver dishes arranged on a silver tray, and accompanied with sweetened Arabic coffee.

HONEY

According to the Talmud, "Honey (*devash*) and sweet food enlighten the eyes of man."

The world's first sweetener was honey, a supersaturated solution produced by certain types of bees from the nectar of blossoms. In many cultures, honey, which comes ready-made from nature and does not spoil, symbolizes immortality and truth. This was the reason many ancient people embalmed or buried their great leaders with honey. Honey was used to make mead (*yayin devash* in Hebrew), one of the earliest alcoholic beverages; it was probably created accidentally when some wild yeasts settled into a container of diluted honey and fermented. The Ethiopian form of mead (*tej*) remains important to Ethiopian culture. To this day, the quality of honey's sweetness stands it in high regard, and it is valued for its supposed therapeutic attributes as well as for its flavor.

Honey is the only food widely used by humans that is manufactured by animals. It takes up to two million flowers (or 556 bees) to make one pound of honey and each beehive produces between sixty and one hundred pounds of honey a year. Thus honeybees can only thrive in areas with plenty of blossoms. More than a third of the fruits and vegetables eaten by humans depend on bees for pollination.

Ancient Israelites viewed honey with high regard. The Hebrew word for bee, *devorah*, was the name of two female biblical figures.

In 2007, the earliest intact beehives in the Middle East, dating to the middle to the end of the tenth century BCE (about the time of the biblical split between the northern and southern tribes), were discovered at Tel Rehov in Israel's Beit Shaean Valley. This apiary consisted of three rows containing more than thirty and perhaps a hundred hives, which would have yielded perhaps a half a ton of honey annually. It is the first evidence of large-scale honey production in "the land of milk and honey" or anywhere in the Middle East before the Greek period.

Nevertheless, the honey made by the region's fierce Syrian bees was rather difficult to obtain. Only with the introduction of the more docile European species of bee by the Greeks, did bee honey become common in the Near East. In addition to bee honey, people early on learned how to boil certain high-sugar fruits, most notably dates, grapes, pomegranates, and figs, into long-lasting honey-like syrups, which in ancient Hebrew were also called *devash*, and in Arabic, *dibs*. (When the Bible refers to "a land of milk and honey," it is referring to date honey.) In an era long before the advent of cane sugar, fruit honey served as the primary sweetener of the ancient Middle East and Mediterranean. In biblical Israel, the most common *devash* was made from dates. By Talmudic times, the Hebrew word *devash* generally meant bee honey, while fruit honey became less common.

Beginning in the seventh century, after the Arabs discovered sugar cane during their conquest of Persia and subsequently spread it through the Muslim world, the position of honey largely dwindled in that region. Honey, however, remained the predominant sweetener of Europe for nearly another millennium. Then, with the growth of sugar plantations in the Caribbean in the seventeenth century and the advent of sugar beet factories in the nineteenth century, the use of honey in Europe markedly declined as well. Nevertheless, it maintains a traditional place in most forms of Jewish cooking.

Among Ashkenazim, honey adds a touch of sweetness to everything from stews (such as tzimmes) to desserts. Honey, representing a wish for a sweet year to come, is traditional on Rosh Hashanah, including the enduring Ashkenazic *lekach* (honey cake) and *teiglach* (honey-cooked balls of dough) and the Middle Eastern honey-soaked *tishpishti* (semolina cake). The most popular and widespread Rosh Hashanah tradition is the dipping of apple slices in honey while reciting the phrase, "May it be Your will to renew on us a good and sweet year." In addition, from Rosh Hashanah until after Sukkot, many households dip the first piece of challah into honey instead of the customary salt. Honey is also found in various traditional Passover foods, such as *chremslach* (pancakes), and in food for Shavuot, a holiday of "milk and honey." At the beginning of the twenty-first century, apiculturists in Israel produced more than thirty-five hundred tons of honey a year from ninety thousand hives.

(See also Date Honey and Rosh Hashanah)

HORSERADISH

"Horseradish that does not bring a pious tear to the eye is not God's horseradish." (From *Tevye the Dairyman* by Sholem Aleichem.)

Horseradish, a member of the Brassicaceae family (and not a radish), is a native of eastern Europe, the area where it is still most appreciated. The fleshy white tapered root, which can reach depths of two feet, grows best in cool climates and marshy land. Its roots and leaves have long been used as medicine. The white root only becomes aromatic and fiery when cut, releasing the volatile oils in its cells. After grating,

the oils and the bite, if not preserved with vinegar, noticeably fade within ten minutes and practically disappear after less than half an hour. The plant is propagated by root cuttings and even a small part of the root will grow. In some cool, moist areas, the plant is treated as a troublesome weed. However, there are more than enough horseradish lovers to make it a profitable crop.

In northern Germany, horseradish was called *meerrettich* (more radish), meaning larger and more intense, while in the south of the country and Austria it was known as *kren*, a word of Slavic origin and the source of the Yiddish name *chrain*, also spelled *khrain* and *khreyn*. A misinterpretation of the German *meerrettich* as "mare radish" gave rise to the English name horseradish. The first mention of *chrain* in a Jewish source was in a list of ingredients used to make charoset (horseradish was not yet considered appropriate as *maror*, bitter herbs) by Eliezer ben Nathan of Mainz (c. 1090–1170), who spent several years living in Slavic lands. Similarly, Rabbi Eleazar ben Judah of Worms in *Sefer ha-Rokeach* (c. 1200) included it in his charoset ingredients.

Today, horseradish is widely identified by many Ashkenazim as the *maror* of the Passover Seder, but this is actually a rather late development. Horseradish was unknown in Israel in Talmudic times and was not among the five vegetables cited by the Talmud as acceptable for *maror*. The first recorded source in which permission was given to use horseradish for *maror*, but only when the preferable lettuce was unavailable, was written in the fourteenth century by Israel ben Joel Susslin of Erfurt. Subsequently, as Jews moved farther north and greens on Passover became impractical, horseradish root became a norm. The practice developed among Germans of using whole pieces of horseradish, while eastern Europeans generally insisted on grating it. Among the first to misidentify horseradish as one the Talmudic vegetables for *maror* was Rabbi Yom Tov Lipman Ben Nathan Heller (1579–1654) of Moravia, in his commentary on the Mishnah, *Tosfot Yom Tov*, who considered it to be the Talmudic *tamchah*. (Rashi identifies *tamchah* as horehound and Maimonides as a type of chicory.) This mistake subsequently became widespread among Ashkenazim. To further complicate matters, in modern Hebrew, horseradish is called *chazeret*, another item in the Talmudic list of acceptable *maror*, although in ancient times the word *chazeret* meant lettuce.

Horseradish root seems a most unlikely candidate for a "bitter herb," being neither bitter nor an herb. It is pungent and fiery, not bitter (harsh and acrid), a completely different sensation. Even the leaves of the horseradish possess a sharp, somewhat mustard-like taste and not a bitterness. The requirement for *maror* is only leaves or stalks, but, for culinary purposes, horseradish is a root. Although the top of the mature root may protrude above the ground, that does not make it a stalk. Horseradish also lacks the other characteristics for *maror* prescribed by the Talmud—latex sap and dull green foliage—as its leaves are dark green and contain no white sap. Moreover, the consumption of an amount of raw unprocessed horseradish, whether whole or ground, equal to a *kazayit* (olive) would generally prove impractical if not dangerous.

In any case, Passover was only one aspect of horseradish, for this root was an integral element in eastern European life and culture. It even turned up in a proverb about the nature of existence: "A worm living in horseradish thinks his life is sweet."

In eastern Europe, horseradish went hand in hand with gefilte fish. According to a Yiddish saying, "Gefilte fish without *chrain* is punishment enough." Horseradish served as a condiment for cold meats, poultry, and fish and was mixed into salads, vegetables, potatoes (boiled, mashed, and salads), sauces, kugels, and pickles. Hungarians used it to make a sauce for poached carp. Beets, beet juice, or *rosl* (fermented beet juice) were occasionally added to the horseradish (*chrain mit burik*) to mellow the taste and create a red hue. In America, some people added grated carrot instead of beets to the horseradish, producing an orange hue.

Eastern and central European immigrants brought their fondness for horseradish with them to America. The first American Jewish cookbook, *Jewish Cookery* (Philadelphia, 1871), included a recipe for "Horseradish Stew," which directed, "Stew three pounds of meat in a pint of water; grate one large horseradish, add it to the gravy and some fine bread crumbs, a little pepper, ginger and salt, with a cupful of the best vinegar. It is very highly recommended by all who have tasted it." Horseradish's principal use, though, was in sauces and relishes. The first edition of *The Settlement Cook Book* (Milwaukee, 1901) provided two recipes for "Horseradish Sauce" and two for "Beet and Horseradish Relish"—one with vinegar and a little sugar and the other with chopped raw cabbage and lots of sugar—as well as directions for adding it to herring salad and several types of pickles.

Anyone wanting to use horseradish had to grate it themselves, a tear-inducing task much worse than chopping onions. In 1869, H. J. Heinz, the son of German immigrants, started a new business outside of Pittsburgh, Pennsylvania, processing and bottling horseradish. Heinz, however, soon began to concentrate on ketchup and other condiments rather than horseradish. Then in 1932 during the Depression, well before the era of the food processor, Hyman Gold, a Polish Jewish immigrant, received a vegetable-grating machine from a cousin. His wife, Tillie, presuming that there were people willing to pay not to have to grate horseradish, decided to help support her struggling family by preparing horseradish in their Brooklyn apartment. Tillie cleaned, ground, and mixed the horseradish with vinegar and salt. Her three young sons helped with filling the bottles, pasting on the labels, and screwing on the lids by hand, while Hyman peddled the bottles from store to store and by pushcart. The family of Polish immigrants sold only a few dozen jars in the first batch. Today, the company run by Tillie and Hyman's grandsons is the world's largest producer of horseradish, turning out more than ninety thousand bottles a day under the Gold's brand as well as under dozens of private labels.

Twice a year, before Passover and Rosh Hashanah, the pace of horseradish production at Gold's quickens to meet increased demand. Passover requires special changes. About ten weeks before Passover, all the machinery is kashered. Afterwards, a *mashgiach* (kosher supervisor) is on the premises during all working hours. Cider vinegar is delivered in tank trucks to substitute for grain-based vinegar. The enormous root cellar is crammed with high stacks of horseradish roots. For most of the day, the plant is abuzz, producing narrow bottles that are a familiar sight at Seder tables across America. The intense fumes around the plant can even water the eyes of passersby. Other horseradish producers emerged in Baltimore and several other locales with large Jewish populations. As a result, today few consumers see horseradish in its fresh form.

Gold's still makes only classic horseradish, both plain and with grated beets, without sugar. Many later brands, both in America and Israel, began adding increasingly larger proportions of beets and sugar, to the point that the horseradish was completely overwhelmed. In some, the root is actually a minor ingredient with nary a hint of horseradish flavor. As a result, much American and Israeli horseradish has lost its potency and personality.

Fresh or preserved, the pungent, sinus-clearing horseradish has earned its place in Jewish cuisine and is still featured today on most Ashkenazic Seder plates and as a topping for gefilte fish.

HOSHANAH RABBAH

The seventh and last day of Sukkot (the twenty-first of Tishrei) is regarded as the day on which the verdicts of judgment decided on Yom Kippur, ten days earlier, are sealed. Accordingly, special prayers of redemption called *Hoshanot* (Help us O God) are recited during the morning service, engendering the name of the day, Hoshanah Rabbah. It is also the last day for the Four Species (lulav, etrog, myrtle, and willow). The congregation, carrying the Four Species, encircles a Torah scroll held on the center dais of the sanctuary seven times. At the conclusion, it is a very old custom to beat a bunch of five willow branches (*aravot*) and recite a special hymn, "*Kol Mevasser*" (A Voice Brings News), conveying messianic hopes. Afterwards, it is traditional to eat a festive meal in the sukkah, the last such repast of the holiday, without saying Kiddush. As an extension of Yom Kippur, Ashkenazim serve foods traditional for the meal before the fast, notably kreplach in chicken soup. Alluding to the "*Kol Mevasser*" hymn, German Jews traditionally include a dish of braised cabbage or cabbage soup, in Yiddish *kohl mit vasser* (cabbage with water). In some eastern European households, the challah for Hoshanah Rabbah is shaped like a hand, connoting the final judgment of Yom Kippur being handed down on this day.

HOSKA

Czech Jews adapted a local Bohemian sweet bread, called *hoska* or *houska* (braid or roll) and *vanochka*, into a holiday braided challah accented with lemon and nutmeg. The dough can also be shaped into a simpler regular braid.

HOT DOG

Among the most ardent devotees of sausages were the Germans, who devised a myriad of wursts. During the mid-nineteenth century, Frankfurt sausages, also called dachshund sausages and, in Yiddish, *vurshtlekh* (small wursts), began appearing in those areas of America with large pockets of German immigrants, most notably New York City. The advent of the mechanical meat grinder in the 1860s greatly reduced the effort and cost of making sausages and spurred their presence in America. Pushcart venders peddling various prepared foods, including cooked sausages, were a common sight in nineteenth-century New York.

In 1871, German immigrant Charles Feltman had a small charcoal stove installed in his cart, on which he set a kettle to boil Frankfurt sausages, and began selling them on Brooklyn's Coney Island, a peninsula on the Atlantic Ocean and popular holiday destination. For neater and easier handling for his genteel customers, he served the warm sausages in a slit roll, which he kept warm in a special tin box in the cart, in essence transforming the Frankfurt sausage into the portable American frankfurter, also known as the hot dog. The earliest known mention of the term hot dog was in the October 19, 1895, issue of the *Yale Record*, which in a piece of fiction about an actual local lunch wagon nicknamed "the Kennel Club," noted that students "contentedly munched hot dogs." In the Teutonic style, Feltman topped his hot dogs with mustard and sauerkraut. Feltman's sausage sandwiches proved so popular and profitable that, in only three years, he had enough money to purchase a parcel of beachfront land and build a restaurant.

By the end of the nineteenth century, frankfurters, originally made in the German manner from pork, had been embraced by the wealthy and the poor, but not by most of those in between. The mass popularization of the hot dog and its switch to beef was due to another hardworking immigrant, a young Polish Jew named Nathan Handwerker who arrived in New York City in 1902. One day in 1915 while visiting Coney Island, Handwerker noticed a "help wanted" sign in Feltman's window and took a job hand slicing buns at a salary of eleven dollars a week. Handwerker proved both adept at his craft and popular with the patrons, among whom were two struggling vaudeville performers, Eddie Cantor and Jimmy Durante. When Feltman raised the cost of his frankfurters from five to ten cents, Cantor and Durante, fearing that they and other performers would starve, encouraged Handwerker to start his own store selling the sandwiches at the five-cent price.

In 1916, having saved three hundred dollars, purportedly by eating only the hot dogs at work, Handwerker established his own stand at the corner of Stillwell and Surf Avenues, down the street from Feltman's. Handwerker, using a recipe created by his nineteen-year-old bride, Ida, introduced a spicier frankfurter, and, in the Jewish tradition, used pure beef and incorporated garlic and more pepper. Handwerker bought from two different spice suppliers in order to keep the exact recipe secret. Handwerker's initial location (called simply Nathan's) was little more than a shack of weathered clapboard and a twenty-foot-long counter. The franks were cooked on an extremely hot grill that burst the casings as they cooked, resulting in an alluring aroma that wafted through the air. Unlike Feltman's, Nathan's did not offer sauerkraut as a topping.

Although Nathan's charged half the price of Feltman's, people were wary about franks that cost so little. Even promotions of free pickles and root beer failed to convince most potential customers to patronize his shop. Eventually, Handwerker came up with another promotional stunt, offering free hot dogs to doctors and nurses at Coney Island Hospital, as long as they wore their white lab coats. When few accepted the offer, Handwerker dressed some freshly shaved vagrants in doctor's whites borrowed from a theatrical costume business and had them hang around his stand. He even posted a sign: "If doctors eat our hot dogs, you know they're great." As another promotion, Handwerker created a hot dog–eating contest on the Fourth of July in 1916, which became an annual event and led to the activity of competitive eating events. According to members of the Handwerker family, at the time that Nathan's was struggling to survive, vaudeville star Sophie Tucker, the "last of the red hot mamas" (in her case, "red hot" did not refer to frankfurters), had a popular song containing the line, "Nathan, Nathan, why are you waitin'?" When someone joked to Handwerker that he was becoming famous, he renamed his stand, "Nathan's Famous," which, as things turned out, proved quite fitting.

With any health concerns about his franks eliminated, people began buying Nathan's hot dogs. Business proved so good that Handwerker was forced to hire helpers, including a vivacious redhead named Clara Gordon Bow. In 1921, after winning a national Fame and Fortune Contest sponsored by Brewster Publications, Bow left Nathan's to pursue a more glorious occupation as a silent movie star and America's first sex symbol. (Stories that Bow was discovered by a talent agent while working at Nathan's were not true.)

Cantor and Durante both eventually became major stars and subsequently rewarded Handwerker by recommending his franks to their friends and occasionally returning to give Nathan's additional publicity. Numerous celebrities—such as Lucille Ball and Desi Arnaz, Jackie Gleason, Grace Kelly, and the Marx Brothers—were pictured munching on hot dogs, contributing an element of glamour and, in the process, creating a true food icon. Nathan's dogs were reportedly gangster Al Capone's favorite food. Whereas Feltman may have been the inventor of the hot dog, Handwerker was the one who brought it to the masses.

Nathan's dogs were all-beef, but not kosher. By the end of the nineteenth century, various kosher butchers and small factories began producing kosher versions. In 1905, Romanian Jewish immigrant Isadore Pinckowitz (who later changed his name to Pines) began making kosher sausages and frankfurters from his apartment in a walk-up on the Lower East Side, which became the Hebrew National Kosher Sausage Factory. Beef hot dogs became a fixture of delicatessens, ballparks, and family barbecues. Besides going into a bun, hot dogs commonly went into split pea soup, baked beans, sauerkraut, and even cholent (Sabbath stew). In modern Hebrew, sausage is *naknik* and hot dog *naknikiya*.

H'RAIMI
H'raimi is fish cooked in a spiced, chili-spiked tomato sauce.
Origin: Libya
Other names: *chreime, hamraya, haraymi, hraimeh, h'reimi.*
Beginning in the sixteenth century, the arrival in North Africa of American produce, particularly chilies and tomatoes, dramatically transformed the cuisines of that area. *H'raimi* means "hot" in some Maghrebi

Arabic dialects, as the fish is cooked in a *pilpelchuma*, a chili-enhanced tomato sauce spiced with Libya's favorite seasoning combination—garlic, caraway, cayenne, cumin, and paprika. The fish itself is typically mild flavored. The seasonings vary slightly from region to region and home to home, including the amount of cumin and the addition of coriander or allspice. Moroccans either increase the amount of cumin and add some chopped cilantro or use a wider assortment of spices.

This stewed fish is a typical Sabbath eve dish, particularly among Libyans, but also among Algerians, Moroccans, and Tunisians. The fish course usually begins the Sabbath meal, followed by soup, then couscous and an assortment of cooked vegetable salads. *H'raimi* is also popular as the opening course of the Passover Seder in many Maghrebi homes, with fava bean soup being served as the next course. *H'raimi* is typically accompanied with plenty of bread or, on Passover, matza.

In the 1950s, North African Jews brought *h'raimi* to Israel, where it is now found in many restaurants and even Ashkenazic homes. This dish is also popular in Rome, where it was introduced by the three thousand Libyan Jews who fled to Italy in 1967.

LIBYAN RED FISH (*H'RAIMI*)

5 TO 6 SERVINGS   [PAREVE]

¼ cup vegetable or olive oil

1 large yellow onion, chopped

6 to 8 large cloves garlic, minced

1 to 3 teaspoons seeded and minced fresh hot red chilies, such as serrano; 1 to 2 teaspoons harissa (Northwest African Chili Paste, page 260); 1 to 2 tablespoons red chili flakes; or 1 to 3 teaspoons hot paprika or cayenne

1 teaspoon ground caraway or a pinch of ground coriander

About 1 teaspoon ground cumin

About ½ teaspoon table salt or 1 teaspoon kosher salt

¼ teaspoon ground black pepper

¼ cup tomato paste

¼ cup fresh lemon juice

1 tablespoon paprika

2 cups water

2 to 2½ pounds fillets or 5 to 6 (1-inch) steaks mild-flavored firm-fleshed fish, such as sea bass, sea bream, cod, grouper, haddock, halibut, gray mullet, pike, red snapper, sole, tuna, or whitefish

¼ cup chopped fresh flat-leaf parsley or cilantro

1. In a large skillet or pot, heat the oil over medium heat. Add the onion, garlic, and chili (if using harissa or dried or ground chili, add them later) and sauté until softened, 5 to 10 minutes.

2. Add the caraway, dried or ground chili, cumin, salt, and pepper and stir until fragrant, about 1 minute. Add the tomato paste, lemon juice, paprika, and, if using, harissa and stir for 2 minutes. Add the water, bring to a boil, reduce the heat to medium-low, and simmer for 10 minutes.

3. Carefully place the fish in the sauce. Return to a boil, cover, reduce the heat to low, and simmer until the fish is tender and loses its translucency, 10 to 15 minutes for fillets and tuna, or about 20 minutes for thick, fatty steaks. Transfer the fish to a storage container or serving dish.

4. Increase the heat to medium-high and boil until the cooking liquid is reduced by half, about 15 minutes. Stir in the parsley. Pour over the fish. Serve warm, at room temperature, or chilled. Store in the refrigerator for up to 3 days.

HUMMUS

Hummus is a thick dip made from chickpeas and sesame seed paste.

Origin: Near East

Other names: *hoummus, hummus bi tahini*.

Legumes have long been a staple of the Middle East, where they are often boiled, mashed into a smooth consistency, and served as a dip for bread. Unquestionably, the most popular and famous of these legume dishes is a thick protein-rich chickpea and sesame paste puree called *hummus bi tahini* (Arabic for "chickpeas with sesame seed paste") or, more informally, hummus. Among some Arabs, hummus is primarily a breakfast food, while others consider it necessary for a proper *mezze* (appetizer assortment). In the Levant, there have long been numerous *hummusia*, small restaurants devoted solely to hummus, which is made fresh daily, and its accompaniments, notably pita, pickles, onion, hard-boiled eggs, and coffee.

Hummus primarily consists of four basic ingredients—cooked chickpeas, tahini (sesame seed paste), lemon juice, and garlic. Families in the Levant have secret techniques and flavorings, passed from father to son, for creating prized tastes and textures. A little baking soda is frequently added to the soaking liquid to help soften the chickpeas. Good hummus contains a hint of cumin. Aficionados reject canned chickpeas, insisting on soaking and cooking dried ones, as the flavor is far superior. Some, especially in the Galilee, like little chunks of chickpea in the hummus, best obtained by mashing with a spoon, while most prefer it pureed into a smooth, creamy paste. For serving, the puree is typically spread over a plate or a widemouthed bowl, then drizzled with olive oil and lightly sprinkled with some sumac, sweet paprika, or even cayenne. Some people scatter pine nuts, whole chickpeas, chopped parsley, or minced garlic over the top as well. A popular Arab breakfast version is *hummus bi ful*, in which the hummus is topped with a heaping spoonful of cooked fava beans. Hummus is usually eaten with warm pita bread and sometimes crudités.

The same ingredients in *hummus bi tahini* can also be used to make *masabacha*, also called *hummus masabacha* and, in the Galilee, *mashausha*. *Masabacha* is a chunky, warm mixture made with hummus mingled with whole chickpeas and sometimes hard-boiled egg—eating it is an experience in contrast—while hummus is a smoother, cool puree. As with hummus, *masabacha* is eaten with fresh pita.

The exact history of hummus is unclear, as this dish, once peasant food, was unmentioned in most medieval Persian or Arabic texts. The earliest record of a related chickpea dish was a recipe for "*Hummus Kasa*" (*kasa* means a "coarse woolen cloth") in the anonymous thirteenth-century Cairo cookbook *Kitab Wasf al-Atima al-Mutada*. The recipe directed, "Take chickpeas and pound them fine after boiling them. Take vinegar [rather than lemon juice], oil, tahina, pepper, *atraf tib* [mixed spices], mint, parsley, dry thyme, [ground] walnuts, hazelnuts, almonds, and pistachios, cinnamon, toasted caraway, dry coriander, salt, salted lemons, and olives. Stir it and roll it out flat and leave it overnight and serve it." Some people trace the contemporary simpler chickpea and tahini version to the Ottoman Empire.

A number of the European Jews arriving in Israel in the nineteenth century, especially kibbutzniks, were ardent socialists. Rejecting the culture and foods of Europe, they attempted to replace them with idealized local Levantine fare, in particular hummus, along with another widespread chickpea dish, falafel. These new culinary habits were further reinforced by the arrival of Jews from Near Eastern countries, who had long enjoyed hummus.

Initially, hummus was not everyday fare among Israelis. To make it at home required time and effort to cook and smash the chickpeas, while the hummus sold in restaurants, at numerous hummus stores, and by street vendors was expensive for the average person. Then in 1994, the Strauss Group introduced to Israel prepackaged refrigerated salads, including hummus, sold under the brand name Achla (from the Arabic meaning "awesome/great"). Strauss launched a simple ad campaign focusing on hummus at home, hummus at school, hummus on family outings, and hummus for soldiers. In 1999, the Osem Company began competing with the Strauss group by offering its own hummus and salads under the Tzabar label. To be sure, some families still insist on fresh homemade versions, often adding their own special touches, because hummus is so easy to prepare with a food processor. Also, making their own hummus allows them to control the flavor. However, most Israelis, including Arabs, now purchase their hummus in markets. The industrialization of hummus transformed it from a beloved Israeli food into a ubiquitous one.

More recently various exotic seasonings have been incorporated, including za'atar, red bell pepper, roasted garlic, olives, spinach, and sun-dried tomatoes. Some find these additions heretical, feeling that they overwhelm the basic ingredients.

The word hummus first appeared in English in the December 16, 1949 issue of the Pittsburg newspaper *The Jewish Criterion*. In "A Guide for Tourists," the paper refered to "the bland succulence of 'tehina and chumus,' eaten with hunks of the platter-shaped bread peeta." By the end of the twentieth century, hummus had also emerged as part of the American culinary fabric. England adopted hummus (where it is typically spelled houmous) even more eagerly; in 2008, more than eight million Brits ate hummus on a regular basis as compared to fifteen million in the United States, although the U.S. has five times the population. As with many standard Middle Eastern foods, it was Jews returning from visiting Israel, along with wandering Israelis, who initially popularized hummus in the West. Beginning in the 1980s, regional commercial brands of hummus became commonplace in American markets. In addition, in the early twenty-first century, Israeli expatriates increasingly opened hummus restaurants across New York City and other large urban areas, further popularizing it in the American mainstream.

The gastronomic and cultural significance of hummus in modern Israel cannot be overstated. The 2008 Adam Sandler movie *You Don't Mess with the Zohan* poked fun at the Israeli passion for hummus—characters even brushed their teeth with it and used it to put out fires. Hummus has become more than a mere food; it is now ubiquitous at every celebration and *mezze* and is on the table at most weddings and bar mitzvahs. Israelis typically keep an extra container on hand in the refrigerator for a quick meal or to offer to unexpected guests. Many Israelis consume hummus on a daily basis and almost all enjoy it on a weekly basis; hummus is eaten at any time of the day, and can be either an appetizer or the focus of a meal.

(See also Chickpea and Tahini)

I

IAB

Iab is a slightly tangy, soft white curd cheese made from buttermilk and flavored with fresh herbs or spices.

Origin: Ethiopia

Other names: *aiyb, ayib.*

Iab, a by-product of making butter, is the most popular cheese in Ethiopia. The Beta Israel there only use cow's milk for dairy products. The buttermilk is heated in a clay pot over a low fire until the curds and whey separate; the mixture is allowed to cool, then drained through a muslin cloth. Readily available soft curd cheeses mixed with *ergo* (Ethiopian fermented milk, which is similar to yogurt) or *gevina levana* (Israeli white cheese), and a little lemon can be substituted for the original.

Iab accompanies *injera* (Ethiopian pancake bread) or various other breads and vegetarian *wots* (fiery stews). It is spooned over the top of or mixed into *gomen* (collard greens). *Iab* is also frequently offered at the end of a meal to cleanse and soothe the palette.

❧ ETHIOPIAN CURD CHEESE (*IAB*)

ABOUT 2 CUPS   [DAIRY]

6 cups buttermilk (if making your own iab), or
    1 pound fresh goat cheese, sheep cheese, farmer
    cheese, or pot cheese mixed with ¼ cup gevina
    levana (Israeli white cheese), quark, or plain
    yogurt
3 tablespoons chopped fresh flat-leaf parsley or
    cilantro
1 tablespoon chopped fresh basil or ½ teaspoon
    dried basil
1 tablespoon chopped fresh oregano or chives, or
    1 teaspoon dried oregano
1 to 3 teaspoons grated lemon zest or 2 tablespoons
    fresh lemon juice
About 1 teaspoon table salt or 2 teaspoons kosher
    salt
About ¼ teaspoon ground black pepper

1. To make your own iab: In a large saucepan, heat the buttermilk over medium-low heat until the curds and whey separate, about 25 minutes. Drain through cheesecloth, press to extract the liquid, and let the solids stand in the cloth and drain until thick, at least 30 minutes. Or use the packaged cheese mixed with the gevina levana.

2. In a large bowl, combine the iab or packaged cheese with the remaining ingredients. Cover and let stand in the refrigerator for several hours for the flavors to meld.

IJEH

Ijeh is a small fritter-like omelet.

Origin: Middle East

Other names: Egypt: *eggah*; Iran and Iraq: *edjeh*;
    Levant: *iijjeh, ijjet, ujja*; Maghreb: *aijjah, eggah.*

A beloved Middle Eastern specialty is *ijeh*, a small omelet pan-fried in enough oil to produce a fritter-like exterior. The *ijeh* mixture can also be cooked en masse as a large omelet and cut into bite-sized pieces like the Persian *kuku.*

Whether the idea of the large and small omelets originated in Moorish Spain, where eggs were plentiful, and spread to the rest of the Arab world, or whether it came from Persia and spread westward is unknown, but the concept is found throughout the Mediterranean and central Asia. Arabic-style omelets are firmer and contain more vegetables, cheese, or meat than the fluffy French types, the eggs basically serving as a binder for the filling. No variation contains more than a few ingredients. A favorite simple flavoring is made by adding chopped parsley and scallions. Mixing in a little bread crumbs, matza meal, or flour produces a pancake-like texture; omitting the yields for a more custardy texture. Various vegetables or bits of meat are generally mixed in, a tasty way to use up leftovers and produce a more substantial dish.

Jews in central Asia serve *edjeh bi jiben* (cheese omelets) on Hanukkah, during the week before Tisha b'Av, and for other dairy meals. For meat occasions, parsley, cooked vegetables (such as artichokes, cauliflower, spinach, and squash), or ground meat are substituted for the cheese. *Ijeh* are featured on their own with jam or yogurt, as a side dish, as part of a *mezze* (appetizer assortment), or, with pickles and tomato slices, in pita bread.

Among many Syrians, both children and adults, *ijeh* is a favorite food. On special occasions, such as a bar mitzvah, *ijeh* are frequently featured as appetizers, sometimes packed into pita bread as sandwiches. Because *ijeh* can be served hot or cold, they are also common on the Sabbath and at picnics. In many Syrian households, *ijeh* are served, generally accompanied with a salad, any time there are a lot of leftovers, especially on Sundays, when the remains of the Sabbath meals need to be used up.

SYRIAN OMELETS (*IJEH*)

ABOUT 12 SMALL OMELETS   [PAREVE, DAIRY, OR MEAT]

4 large eggs, lightly beaten
1 small onion or 2 to 3 scallions (white and light green part), minced
1 to 2 tablespoons fine bread crumbs, matza meal, or all-purpose flour
About ½ teaspoon table salt or 1 teaspoon kosher salt
¼ to ½ teaspoon ground allspice or nutmeg (optional)
4 cooked and chopped artichoke hearts; 2 cups cooked and chopped cauliflower; 8 ounces chopped mushrooms; 3 peeled and grated medium potatoes; 1 pound cooked and chopped fresh spinach or 10 ounces thawed and squeezed frozen spinach; 2 peeled, seeded, and diced medium zucchinis; ¼ cup chopped fresh mint; ½ to 1 cup chopped fresh flat-leaf parsley; 1½ cups (6 ounces) grated white cheese or Parmesan cheese; or 6 ounces chopped beef, lamb, or veal
About ½ cup vegetable oil for frying
Plain yogurt or harissa (Northwest African Chili Paste, page 260) as a condiment
Salad or pita (optional)

1. In a medium bowl, combine the eggs, onion, bread crumbs, salt, and, if using, allspice. Stir in the artichokes or flavoring of choice.

2. In a large skillet, heat about ¼ inch oil over medium heat. In batches of 4 to 5, drop the mixture by heaping tablespoonfuls and slightly flatten with the back of the spoon or a metal spatula to form 3-inch patties about ¼ inch thick. Fry until the edges turn golden brown, about 2 minutes. Turn and fry until golden brown, about 1½ minutes. Drain on paper towels. Serve warm or at room temperature. If desired, accompany with yogurt (except for the meat ijeh) or harissa and a salad, or serve in a pita.

IKRE

Ikre is the Slavic word for fish roe. In Ukraine and Romania, besides meaning caviar, it refers to various finely chopped cooked vegetable salads. These are made with many different vegetables, including beans, beets, mushrooms, zucchini, and especially eggplant, whose seeds resemble fish eggs. Ukranian and Romanian Jews typically serve seasonal *ikres* with bread for the Sabbath and holidays.

(See also Eggplant)

IMPADE

Impade is an S-shaped cookies filled with almond paste.

Origin: Venice

Jewish life in Venice centers around Campo di Ghetto Vecchio and Campo di Ghetto Nuovo (the latter was the first ghetto in Europe, established in 1516 and abolished by Napolean in 1797)—which contain five sixteenth century synagogues, a handful of kosher restaurants, and two kosher bakeries including Vople, in the Ghetto Vecchio. The small store's assortment of traditional Jewish baked goods includes *bollo* (sweet breads popular for Rosh Hashanah), *orecchietta di Aman* (triangular cookies filled with plum or poppy seeds), amaretti (macaroons), *bissa* ("viper," referring to a snake-shaped cookie), and its signature cookie *impade* (the name of an Italian lamp). *Impade* are a traditional Purim *dolci* (sweet), but are also enjoyed at other times of the year.

VENETIAN ALMOND-FILLED COOKIES (*IMPADE*)

ABOUT 42 COOKIES   [PAREVE]

Pastry:
3 large eggs
½ cup vegetable oil

1¼ cups plus 2 tablespoons (9.5 ounces) sugar
Pinch of salt
3½ cups (17.5 ounces) all-purpose flour
Filling:
9 ounces blanched almonds (2½ cups finely
   ground)
1 cup (7 ounces) sugar
2 large eggs
1 teaspoon grated lemon zest
Confectioners' sugar for dusting

1. To make the pastry: In a large bowl, combine the eggs and oil. Stir in the sugar and salt. Stir in the flour to form a soft dough that holds together. Wrap in plastic wrap and let stand for 30 minutes.

2. To make the filling: In a food processor fitted with a metal blade or a nut grinder, process the almonds into a powder. Add the sugar, eggs, and zest and process into a paste.

3. Preheat the oven to 375°F. Line 2 large baking sheets with parchment paper or lightly grease the sheets.

4. Divide the dough in half. Roll each half into a ¾-inch-thick rope, then cut the ropes into 2-inch-long pieces. Flatten each piece and roll into a thin rectangle. Spread a heaping teaspoon of the almond filling along the center of each rectangle, leaving the edges uncovered, then bring the long sides of the rectangle over the filling and press to seal. Bend the cookie into an S shape and place on the prepared baking sheets.

5. Bake until golden brown, about 20 minutes. Immediately roll in the confectioners' sugar, then place on a wire rack and let cool.

INCHUSA

Inchusa is a tart containing a sweet or savory filling.
Origin: Spain

Vegetable custards, varying in the amounts of eggs, cheese, and other ingredients, are ancient and important components of Sephardic cuisine, including *enchusa*, which evolved into a tart called *inchusa*. The original dish incorporated *enchusa*, an herb from the borage family, but that was soon replaced with spinach, after its arrival in Spain.

The custard was originally baked without a crust. To prevent it from sticking to the baking pan, some flour was mixed with oil and the thick spinach and egg mixture gratin was spread over the top and baked. The flour mixture eventually evolved into a tart crust

and the savory custard filling into a sweetened custard (*inchusa de leche*). Some versions have a single crust, while others have an upper and lower crust.

Pareve fillings appropriate for a meat meal also emerged, notably fruit (*inchusa de fruta*), especially apricots, sour cherries, and grapes.

INJERA

Injera is a soft, chewy, very thin, sourdough pancake bread made from the grain teff.
Origin: Ethiopia
Other names: *engera*.

The most common grain in the Ethiopian highlands is the indigenous teff, literally "lost" in Amharic, referring to the tiny size of the grains, the smallest in the world and all too easily lost. For more than three thousand years, Ethiopians have ground teff to make various porridges, *kita* (unleavened pancakes), and especially *injera*, their main bread.

Teff or tef, also called lovegrass in English and *tahf* in Arabic, is an ancient annual summer cereal grass native to Ethiopia, where it has long been the staple and still accounts for about 31 percent of the country's farmland. Today, the grain is also grown in India, Australia, and Canada, and since the 1980s, a small amount has been produced in the United States. There are around 250 species of teff with three main types: ivory, brown, and dark red. The brown has slightly more flavor than the ivory, but ivory is the most difficult to grow and has become the preferred and most expensive type. Red teff, on the other hand, is the least desirable and least expensive, although it has the highest level of iron and white the lowest. Teff and teff flour are available at Ethiopian markets and health food stores, but are frequently adulterated with other grains.

Teff is the only grain that, like grapes, has symbiotic yeast. Thus water is mixed into the ground teff (with no added yeast) and the batter is left standing for two to four days until naturally fermented, a method that imparts a sour flavor and also leads to the formation of holes on the top of the bread during cooking. To help speed up the fermentation process, Ethiopians sometimes add a small amount of reserved *ersho*, the clear yellow liquid that accumulates on the surface of fermented teff dough, but not yeast, which changes the flavor. In Israel and America, however, many Ethiopians have adapted the recipe to use yeast and some or all wheat flour. Ethiopians consider *injera* made without teff to be merely a pancake.

Injera, never eaten without other foods, has long served as the bulk of the Ethiopian diet and a major part of every meal. The thin *injera* batter is poured in a circular motion from the outside to the center onto a round clay griddle (*meted*) and then a lid is set over the top to produce a spongy bread, thicker than a typical crepe, but thinner than an American griddle cake. A little ground fenugreek is typically added to the batter for a softer texture and shinier appearance. In a cooking process similar to that of griddle cakes, tiny bubbles produced by carbon dioxide appear on the top as the batter cooks, indicating the degree of doneness. *Injera* are only cooked on the bottom, never inverted; the spongy top cooked by indirect heat and not browned or crisped. They are usually made in large batches and stored in a woven basket (*messob*) for up to three days.

When served, several *injera* are stacked on a communal plate and the meat or legume stew (*wot* or *alicha*) is then spooned on top of it. Each person pulls off pieces of the *injera* to scoop up some of the *wot*, then folds the bread around the filling to eat it. Flatware is unnecessary. The tangy flavor of the *injera* complements and enhances the spicy stew. After all the *wot* is finished, the remainder of the stack of *injera*, now soaked with gravy, is eaten. At the end of vegetarian meals, some *injera* is usually served with *iab* (soft cheese).

(See also Alicha, Iab, and Wot)

🦑 ETHIOPIAN PANCAKE BREAD (*INJERA*)

ABOUT 14 BREADS   [PAREVE]

You will need to let the batter sit for 2 to 3 days before using. Have the utensils ready and clean to avoid adding bacteria.

About 4½ cups lukewarm water (80° to 90°F)
3 cups (13 ounces) organic teff flour, preferably freshly ground
About 1 teaspoon table salt or 2 teaspoons kosher salt (optional)

1. In at least a 3-quart ceramic or glass bowl or container and using a large wooden spoon or your hand, stir the water into the teff flour to produce a smooth consistency like that of pancake batter. Make sure the utensils are very clean to avoid adding any unwanted bacteria. Cover with a kitchen towel and let stand at room temperature until the batter bubbles and emits a sour odor, 48 to 72 hours. When the batter is ready, if not using immediately, stir in ½ teaspoon salt and store in the refrigerator for up to 1 day, then return to room temperature before cooking. Carefully pour off any dark liquid that rises to the surface. If using, stir in the remaining ½ teaspoon salt.

2. Heat a 10- to 12-inch skillet, preferably one with a nonstick surface, over medium-low heat. If your skillet does not have a nonstick surface, lightly oil it.

3. Using a 4-ounce ladle, pour ½ cup batter into one side of the skillet and quickly rotate the pan so the batter covers the surface in a layer about ⅛ inch thick. For smaller *injera,* use about ¼ cup batter in an 8-inch skillet or ⅓ cup in a 9-inch skillet.

4. Cover and cook until the top is spongy and dotted with tiny air bubbles and the edges just begin to curl, about 1½ to 2 minutes. The bottom will be firm but not browned. Do not turn over, as *injera* is only cooked on one side.

5. Using a spatula or your fingers, carefully lift the *injera* out of the pan. Place the bread on a kitchen towel or plate and let cool. Repeat the process with the remaining batter, stacking the cooled *injera*.

ISRAEL

By the beginning of the first millennium CE, Jews constitiuted 10% of the entire population of the Roman Empire, most of them in Israel. After several revolts, particularly 132–135 CE, masses were killed and an expulsion of Jews followed. Only a small group of Jews remained in the land that the Romans renamed Palestine.

Israel in the late nineteenth century was a neglected backwater of the Ottoman Empire, a harsh landscape part of it arid and much of it consisting of swamps ridden with malaria-spreading mosquitoes. When Mark Twain toured the Holy Land, as recorded in *Innocents Abroad* (1869), he noted his movement through the north: "We traversed some miles of desolate country whose soil is rich enough but is given over wholly to weeds—a silent, mournful expanse, wherein we saw only three persons."

Under the Ottoman Empire, Israel consisted of five *sanjaks* (subdivisions): Acco, Nablus, Jerusalem, Maan, and Hauran. The latter two, on the east bank of the Jordan River, were given by the British in 1946 to Abdullah, who became king, and his new

Machaneh Yehudah Market in Jerusalem began in the 1870s as a gathering place for cart vendors and continues to thrive.

country was renamed Jordan. Parts of the remaining area to the west were gradually transformed by the cooperative efforts of scattered Jewish communities, kibbutzim (collective communities), and *moshavim* (cooperative settlements).

Before the late nineteenth century, most of the area's Jews were Mizrachim and Sephardim. Then between 1882 and 1903, the existing Jewish communities were overwhelmed by about thirty thousand eastern Europeans escaping oppression and pogroms, known as the First Aliyah. Most of these early European arrivals were socialists who rejected traditional Jewish and European practices. Also arriving at that time were five thousand Jews from Yemen, thousands from Uzbekistan and Iraq (including Kurds), and smaller numbers from other Asian locales most of whom maintained their religious practices. The Second Aliyah, between 1904 and 1914, brought forty thousand eastern Europeans, and another forty thousand Europeans Jews arrived between 1919 and 1923 in the Third Aliyah. The 1930s saw a quarter of a million Jews arrive. Beginning in 1939 and through World War II, the British prohibited Jewish immigration to Mandatory Palestine, although thousands of Jews managed to sneak into the country. When independence was claimed on May 14, 1948, Holocaust survivors could seek refuge in Israel. After 1948, as Arab nationalism devastated many of the Jewish communities of Asia and North Africa, exiles from those far-flung Jewish communities streamed to the new Jewish state. The new state was a blend of citizens from nearly every country in the world and from every stripe of religosity and politics. Some Israelis rejected anything smacking of religion, however, most non-religious Israelis maintained a respect and affection for Jewish traditions.

Ethnic groups tend to cling to their traditional foods, one of the last remaining vestiges of their former life and identity, but over time, and due to necessity, they begin to adapt, their children even more so. For Middle Eastern Jews in Israel, the process was relatively easy, as the ingredients and dishes in the Levant were similar to those of their native lands, although they did have to endure the patronizing attitude of Europeans to their food. Ashkenazim, on the other hand, as they flowed into the land from which their ancestors had been ejected two millennia ago, had to adjust to a very different climate and food culture, one emphasizing vegetables, legumes, fresh herbs, spices, and olive oil. Few aspects of Israeli society have changed more in the country's history than its food, at least for a sizable segment of the population.

Some Yemenites found a livelihood selling a local food, falafel, which they stuffed into a local bread, pita, with a salad of cucumbers and tomatoes, a combination that went on to become the Israeli national food. From the communal dining halls of the early kibbutzim emerged a new way of eating and thinking about food, one inspired by biblical Israel and based on the modern Levant. The usually spartan kibbutz, where work started at daybreak or earlier, was the source of the archetypical Israeli breakfast and dinner. Famished, the kibbutzniks swarmed into the communal dining room at seven in the morning and then again later at night, piling their plates from a buffet of fresh bread, cucumber and tomato salads, assorted produce, eggs, cheese, *leben* (coagulated low-fat milk), and olives. Soon Israeli homes across the country imitated this menu. Later, the Israeli hotel breakfast emerged as a lavish expansion of the basic kibbutz fare.

Kibbutzim and *moshavim* marketed the fruits of their labor through the cooperative Tnuva, which soon had so much produce, it began exporting and canning some of it. Farmers raised turkeys and chicken instead of cattle, and Israelis substituted these for traditional meats, such as the veal in schnitzel. The first Israeli cookbook, *How to Cook in Palestine*, was published by WIZO (Women's International Zionist Organization) in Hebrew, German, and English in 1936. The author, Dr. Erna Meyer, told her readers, "We housewives must make an attempt to free our kitchens from European customs, which are not appropriate to Palestine." Meyer appealed to westerners to adopt into their diet local foods available in abundance such as zucchini, eggplant, okra, and olives, and, eventually, most did. However, due to the sheer number of Ashkenazim in Israel, some of their food traditions endured. Consequently, a typical Israeli Sabbath dinner now consists of foods from numerous cultures: to start, perhaps a Moroccan fish dish, which is followed by an Ashkenazic or Kurdish chicken soup along with Middle Eastern hummus and eggplant salad, then possibly a main dish of chicken schnitzel or even Moroccan couscous.

Shopping was originally done only in a *souk* (Arabic for marketplace), such as Jerusalem's still-thriving Machaneh Yehudah. Initially consisting of vendors selling produce from carts, this market was formed in the 1870s to meet the needs of the increasing number of Jews residing outside Jerusalem's Old City. The first stalls arrived in 1908 when the adjacent new *Etz Chaim* yeshiva built some stands to provide income for the organization. The stalls and small stores of Machaneh Yehudah quickly expanded, stretching for several blocks, as Jerusalemites from a multitude of ethnic backgrounds, in particular Kurds, opened shops. In 1920, Tel Aviv's Souk Hacarmel opened to allow families to sell their produce in the new city. Machaneh Yehudah was renovated toward the end of the twentieth century and Souk Hacarmel as well. Today, both still consist of small shops, some now upscale, offering a vast array of fresh produce, meats, fish, cheeses, baked goods, spices, nuts, and confections, as well as coffee shops.

The late 1940s to late 1950s, when the population of Israel more than tripled with the arrival of refugees from Europe and Arab countries, was a period of *tzena* (austerity), with scarcity and government regulations. People made do with limited food choices, among them bread, pasta, eggplant (as a meat substitute), and *leben*. The new Ministry of Absorption taught the diverse housewives from across the globe to prepare new, simple, and healthy recipes, including hummus, eggplant salad, chicken schnitzel, and salads made from cucumbers and tomatoes, which were plentiful. Although many Israelis did not eat kosher, David Ben-Gurion agreed, for a sense of unity and accessibility, to place all public food, including that served by government organizations, hospitals, and the army, under rabbinical supervision. There were few ethnic restaurants in which to experience other culinary cultures and those restaurants that did exist were principally patronized by tourists. At that time, for Israelis eating out meant grabbing an inexpensive and filling falafel or perhaps *shawarma*.

Integral to Israeli cuisine are an array of Middle Eastern dips and spreads, including *baba ghanouj* (Lebanese eggplant with tahini), *matbucha* (Moroccan stewed tomato and pepper salad), *muhammara* (Turkish red pepper relish), and, most important of all, hummus (mashed chickpeas with tahini). All of these as well as several other types of dips are sold in every grocery store, large or small. Typical Israelis keep at least one container of a dip/spread in their refrigerator at all times for guests or a snack, which is always accompanied by pita and perhaps some more exotic types of breads and crackers.

By the early 1960s, the economy had grown and the range of foods along with it. Israeli food still consisted primarily of a simple selection of local commercial packaged goods and produce sold from a cramped *mahkolet* (small market). The late 1960s and early 1970s was a turning point in the Israeli culture and economy, as foreign influences began to seep in and incomes began to rise. In the course of only a decade, the country evolved from an underdeveloped nation to a marketing-oriented economy. Israel's first supermarket and currently the largest chain, Shufrasol (later Supersol), opened in 1958. After the 1967 war, the concept of supermarkets began to spread and in many areas, they largely replaced the neighborhood *mahkolet*. Today, customers can choose from a vast assortment of goods, both foreign and domestic, in massive supermarkets, and even many *mahkolets* offer a selection of upscale imports.

Not only did eating-in change, so too did dining out, perhaps even more dramatically. In the early 1970s, dining out in Israel all too frequently meant grills called *steakiya*; these eateries selling very tough meat at budget prices were a synthesis of Middle

Eastern and European influences. Israel grills cooking up tough meat continued, meat quality improved and there was soon an array of high-quality restaurants and ethnic eateries as well.

In the 1980s, some Israeli chefs began merging haute cuisine with local ingredients, while others began fusing Mediterranean and Middle Eastern cuisine with international influences, attempting to create a genuine Israeli cuisine. After experimenting with butter and cream, many chefs found they preferred olive oil, lemon juice, and native ingredients. Instead of the French tarragon and lavender, they preferred the local za'atar and cumin. At the same time, high-quality wines began flowing from the Golan Heights Winery, while small producers introduced boutique cheeses. With the general rise in income and lifting of travel taxes, many Israelis traveled abroad, while many soldiers, following their mandatory two-year service, took a long trek through the exotic locales of Asia and South America. These travelers returned with an expanded culinary vocabulary, and some became chefs or opened restaurants. By the end of the twentieth century, Israeli cooking had evolved, becoming more cosmopolitan while also embracing a seemingly paradoxical emphasis on traditional ethnic cuisines.

Unfortunately, not all of these changes were for the best. Health and, all too often, flavor seemed to be lost in much of contemporary Israeli dining. At home, most Israelis, who no longer put in long hours in the fields but led increasingly busy lives, increasingly substituted corn flakes and coffee for breakfast. The environment was all too often neglected by farming and food processing practices.

Now in the new millenium, a growing number of Israeli boutique food businesses stress quality and craftsmanship over quantity and expediency. Individuals, communities, and organizations across the country have begun to emphasize sustainable food production and consumption. They are leading the call for using the freshest and most flavorful natural ingredients possible, with the maximum regard for the environment, local economy, and health. An increasing number of Israelis support organic agriculture, the slow food and artisanal food movements, CSAs (community-supported agriculture), and food co-ops; there are also trends toward permaculture and eco-living. In addition, Israeli food companies have progressed significantly in the past few years, turning out products capable of attracting American and European taste buds, along with those seeking exotic fare.

Over the decades, immigrants came to Israel from as far away as India and Ethiopia (the biblical *"Hodu ahd Kush"*). As a result, the Israeli population hails from more than seventy countries and, not surprisingly, has a diverse and constantly changing cuisine. As Jews have done since the onset of the Diaspora more than twenty-five hundred years ago, Israelis have transformed the fare at hand to their tastes and circumstances, creating the ultimate fusion cuisine.

ISRAELI SALAD (SALAT KATZUTZ)

Israeli salad is a mixture of finely chopped tomatoes and cucumbers, and sometimes other vegetables, dressed with olive oil and lemon juice.

Origin: Middle East
Other names: *salat aravi, salat chai, salat katzutz, salat turka, salat yerakot.*

The arrival in the Mediterranean of the Indian cucumber and much later the South American tomato completely transformed the fresh salad from a dish consisting principally of leafy greens to a mixture that frequently did not include any herbage. In the late nineteenth century, Jewish immigrants to the Levant found locally grown Kirby cucumbers and tomatoes in popular salads, such as the Turkish *coban salatsi* (shepherd's salad), a tasty combination dressed with olive oil, fresh lemon juice, and a touch of salt. It soon became a ubiquitous dish in the communal dining halls of kibbutzim. During the decade-long period of the *tzena* (austerity) following independence in 1948, the salad made from the plentiful cucumbers and tomatoes became a staple of the diet throughout the country.

Today, Israeli salad, a name primarily used outside of the country, is a standard side dish at most Israeli meals, both dairy and meat. At breakfast and dinner, it is traditionally accompanied with eggs, cheeses, yogurt, and olives. A spoonful or more is added to falafel and other pita sandwiches and it is a favorite accompaniment to grilled meats and schnitzel. Israeli salad is made at home, as well as found in restaurants, hotels, and kiosks.

The key to Israeli salad is ripe, fresh vegetables. The vegetables are cut into small, uniformly sized pieces, but the size of the dice is a matter of preference and much contention; some favor *katan* ("small," about a quarter inch) and others insist on *dak* (very fine). Many people prefer eating the salad soon after mixing for the crispest texture, while others let the dressed salad sit for a couple of hours until the vegetables begin to marinate and the mixture turns soupy.

Today in Israel, this salad is almost always made with unpeeled Beit Alpha cucumbers—the crisp, sweet, thin-skinned, slender four- to six-inch long seedless Israeli variety—and usually with plum tomatoes. Bell peppers and green onions are commonly added and sometimes fresh herbs, notably parsley, cilantro, chives, and dill. Bukharans make a version that is chopped very fine and enhanced with fresh cilantro and parsley. Occasionally, the basic ingredients are augmented with radishes, chickpeas, olives, feta cheese, and even croutons; the elaborate version is called, in the Hebrew vernacular, *hakol salat* (everything salad). Some modern versions even include unorthodox items, such as jicama. Lettuce, however, is never part of a real Israeli salad.

(See also Cucumber and Tomato)

ISRAELI SALAD (*SALAT KATZUTZ*)

4 TO 5 SERVINGS [PAREVE]

5 to 6 Beit Alpha or Kirby cucumbers, or 2 medium long cucumbers, diced

4 to 8 plum tomatoes, diced

2 medium green bell peppers, or 1 green bell pepper and 1 red or yellow bell pepper, seeded and diced (optional)

1 medium red onion or 4 to 8 scallions, diced (optional)

Dressing:

¼ cup extra-virgin olive oil or vegetable oil

2 to 4 tablespoons fresh lemon juice or red wine vinegar

2 to 3 tablespoons chopped fresh flat-leaf parsley

About ½ teaspoon table salt or 1 teaspoon kosher salt

Ground black pepper to taste

In a medium bowl, combine the cucumbers, tomatoes, and, if using, bell peppers and onion. Whisk together all the dressing ingredients, drizzle over the salad, and toss to coat. Serve at room temperature.

J

JAALEH

The ancient Greeks believed that eating fruit at the beginning of a meal prepares the stomach to absorb heavier foods, a practice acknowledged in the Jerusalem Talmud. In this vein, Moses Maimonides offered the medical advice of eating lighter foods and fruit at the beginning of a meal. In accordance, many early medieval Jewish communities practiced the custom on Friday evening of reciting Kiddush over wine, then—before reciting Hamotzi over the bread—eating some fruit. This custom was still observed in Iraq and some other Middle Eastern communities as late as the end of the eighteenth century. However, a question arose as to whether a person needed to recite a final benediction over the fruit before reciting Hamotzi over the bread. To avoid this dilemma, many Sephardic sages forbade the practice, and it disappeared from most communities. The tradition was also known among medieval Ashkenazim, as Rashi noted a practice of eating fruit before all large meals. Later, Rabbi Moses Isserles required people to proceed directly from reciting Kiddush to the Hamotzi; therefore, Ashkenazim no longer enjoyed fruit at the beginning of their Sabbath meal.

Yemenites, on the contrary, continued the venerable tradition of eating fruit after Kiddush and before Hamotzi, customarily commencing all three Sabbath meals as well as any *Seudat Mitzvah*, such as weddings and *brits*, by nibbling on various goodies subsumed under the general term *jaaleh*, which is Arabic for "gratification" and "live in abundance." *Jaaleh* always begins with dried fruit and nuts, or, when in season, fresh fruit, over which people recite the Hebrew benediction *"borei peri ha-eitz"* (Who creates the fruit of the tree). Also commonly served are roasted fava beans or other legumes, over which is pronounced *"borei peri ha-adamah"* (Who creates the fruits of the earth), and finally small pieces of pepper-spiced roasted meat (*shawiyeh*) or spicy fish, over which is recited the generic *"shehakol nehyah bidvaro"* (that all

things came to be by His word). Each person in turn, from older to younger, expresses the various benedictions before eating. These appetizers are accompanied with traditional songs and words of Torah before the recital of Hamotzi. Besides any health benefits, the various morsels that constitute *jaaleh* help the Yemenites to achieve the total of one hundred blessings traditionally recited every day, as they say a benediction over each item from a different category of food before eating it. When performing these various benedictions before doing the Hamotzi, Yemenites have in mind that the *Birkhat Hamazon* at the end of the meal will include the foods served before the bread. In Israel, some Yemenite families abandoned the practice of *jaaleh* at the onset of the meal and only eat it after the bread, while others serve it both at the beginning and end, accompanying the final *jaaleh* with spiced tea and more singing and conversation.

(See also Hamotzi and Birkhat Hamazon)

JACHNUN

Jachnun is a flaky pastry cylinder baked overnight in a covered pot, sometimes alongside whole eggs.

Origin: Yemen

Other names: *jahnoon, jihnun.*

Yemenites, for special occasions, prepare breads and pastries from an unleavened *ajin* (dough) enriched with clarified butter and made enticingly flaky by repeated folding and rolling, in a manner similar to the preparation of puff pastry. Individual dough cylinders called *jachnun* (a diminutive form of *ajin*) are traditionally cooked overnight in a low oven and served warm after the morning synagogue service for Sabbath dairy breakfast. Yemenites typically bake the cylinders in a special covered aluminum *jachnun* pot, widely available in Israel, but any pot or casserole dish works. The layers of the cylinders should be separate as well as dense, moist, and soft inside. *Jachnun* is usually accompanied with *s'chug* (chili paste), *hilbeh* (fenugreek relish), *resek agvaniyot* (cold finely chopped tomatoes), and with the eggs that baked alongside it. The pastries are also drizzled with a little honey.

Jachnun is different from another slow-cooked Yemenite Sabbath bread, *kubaneh*, which is made with yeast and baked in large balls. *Melawah* is made from the same dough as *jachnun*, but is pan-fried, not baked.

Yemenites brought *jachnun* to Israel, where today it is much beloved well beyond the Yemenite community; it can be found at many restaurants, hotel breakfasts, and bakeries, as well as in frozen packages at most groceries. Israelis enjoy *jachnun* not only on the Sabbath but also at any time during the week, especially as breakfast fare. Israelis, in turn, brought *jachnun* to America, where it is now common in many Middle Eastern restaurants.

YEMENITE FLAKY ROLLS (*JACHNUN*)

6 LARGE ROLLS   [DAIRY OR PAREVE]

1 recipe ajin taimani (Yemenite Flaky Pastry, page 8), divided into 6 portions

6 to 8 eggs in shells (optional)

1. Preheat the oven to 200°F. Grease an ovenproof pot or 8-inch square baking pan.

2. Roll the square *ajin* pieces into cylinders, but do not flatten. Place the dough cylinders in the prepared pan. If using, arrange the eggs in between. Cover with a piece of parchment paper or greased heavy-duty aluminum foil, then a tight-fitting lid. Bake for about 10 to 12 hours. Serve warm or at room temperature. For a slightly quicker version, bake at 250°F for about 6 hours.

K

KAAB EL GHAZAL

Kaab el ghazal is a crescent-shaped cookie with an almond-paste filling.

Origin: Maghreb

Other names: Algeria: *cherek, tcharak msekker, tcherek, tcherek msekker*; France: *cornes de gazelles*; Libya: *kaak halkoom*; Morocco: *kabuzel*.

These cookies, a Moroccan Algerian and Libyan favorite, are a sweet variation of the widespread Middle Eastern turnover *sambusak*. The name *kaab el ghazal* is commonly mistranslated into English as the fanciful "gazelle horn," purportedly because the crescent shape of the cookie resembles this animal's long, curved horns. Incidentally, gazelles are now nearly extinct in Morocco. Actually, *kaab el ghazal* means "gazelle heel." The Arabic word *kaab*, a cognate of the Hebrew *ahkaiv*, (the source of the name Yakov/Jacob, who was born holding onto the heel of his twin brother) besides referring to a heel, denotes anything bulging or protruding; in the instance of this cookie, it describes the bulging filling.

The *kaab* dough was traditionally made with *smen*, clarified butter, but more recently fresh butter has become commonplace, while oil is substituted for meat occasions. The dough is flavored with orange-blossom water and frequently cinnamon. The filling is a mildly sweet almond paste (*mazhar*), which some cooks like to dye with a little green, or other-hued, food coloring. The traditional manner of forming the cookies was rolling out individual balls and folding the sides over to completely enclose the filling, then bending the cookie into a crescent. A more recent and easier version calls for rolling out the dough in a sheet, cutting out triangles, and rolling them in such a way as to partially expose some of the filling. In Fez, the cookies are dipped into sugar syrup flavored with orange-blossom water. Algerians dip their version into sugar syrup and then roll it in chop toasted almonds or sprinkle it with confectioners' sugar; when left uncoated, they are *tcherek el-aryan* (naked).

Kaab el ghazal appear at Moroccan celebrations, notably weddings and the minor spring holiday of Lag b'Omer. Similarly, Algerian Jews serve *tcherek* and Libyan's *kaak halkoom* for special occasions. They are usually served with *naa-naa* (mint tea).

MOROCCAN ALMOND-FILLED CRESCENTS
(*KAAB EL GHAZAL*)

ABOUT FORTY 3-INCH COOKIES   [DAIRY OR PAREVE]

Filling:

2 cups (7.5 ounces) blanched almonds, lightly toasted

1 cup confectioners' sugar or ¾ cup granulated sugar

Pinch of salt

1 teaspoon ground cinnamon (optional)

1 tablespoon egg white

About 2 tablespoons orange-blossom water

Several drops green food coloring (optional)

Pastry:

3 cups (15 ounces) all-purpose flour

¼ teaspoon salt

1 cup clarified butter, unsalted butter, or margarine, chilled

About ½ cup orange-blossom water, or 3 tablespoons orange-blossom water and 5 tablespoons water

Orange blossom-water-flavored Atar (Middle Eastern Sugar Syrup, see page 27) or confectioners' sugar for dipping

1. To make the filling: In a food processor fitted with a metal blade, finely grind the almonds, sugar, salt, and, if using, cinnamon. Add the egg white and enough orange-blossom water to make a firm, cohesive paste. If using, add enough food coloring to produce the desired green hue. Cover and refrigerate overnight or for up to 2 weeks.

2. To make the pastry: In a large bowl, combine the flour and salt. Cut in the butter to make a mixture that resembles coarse crumbs. Gradually stir in enough orange-blossom water to make a mixture that holds together. Knead briefly to form a soft, pliable dough. Cover with plastic wrap and refrigerate for at least 1 hour.

3. Preheat the oven to 375°F. Line 2 large baking sheets with parchment paper or lightly grease the sheets.

4. On a lightly floured surface, roll 1-inch balls of dough into thin rounds about 3 inches in diameter. For each cookie, roll a heaping teaspoon of the almond filling into a 2-inch-long crescent shape and place on top of a dough round, near the lower edge. Fold the upper half of the dough over the filling and pinch to seal. Using a fluted pastry wheel, trim the curved edge. (For large cookies, form into 6-inch rounds and fill with 1 heaping tablespoon filling.) Bend the cookies into a crescent shape and prick with the tines of a fork to vent the steam.

5. Place the cookies, 1 inch apart, on the prepared baking sheets. Bake until just lightly colored but not browned, about 12 minutes. Let the cookies stand until firm, about 3 minutes, then dip in the syrup to cover. Transfer to a wire rack and let cool completely. Store in an airtight container at room temperature for up to 1 week.

KAAK

Kaak is a ring-shaped pastry or bread, sometimes sweet and sometimes savory.

Origin: Iraq

Other names: Hebrew and Arabic: *kahk, kaik*;
   Ladino: *biscotcho, biscocho de huevo, biscotcho dulce, roskita.*

The Babylonian Talmud, on several occasions, mentions a special ancient Middle Eastern bread, *kaak*; the name presumably derived from an Aramaic term for teeth, *kaka*, as the tenacious cakes certainly required plenty of molar grinding to eat. In one instance, the Talmudic discussion specifies that the *kaak* was shaped, although the exact form is not recorded, before the bread was baked. In another place, *kaak* are described as small loaves that do not "bite" one another, meaning they do not touch and attach to each other during baking, connoting their independent formations. The spread of sugar in the medieval Arabic world led to a sweetened form of this venerable pastry. Recipes for several types of *kaak* appeared in the cookbook *Kitab al-Tabikh* (Baghdad, 1226); the shape of those small ancient breads was in a ring.

Today, ring-shaped pastries are enjoyed by Jewish communities from the Maghreb to Calcutta; the pastry was introduced by Iraqis to India in the nineteenth century. There are three predominant extant Jewish forms of these ancient pastries: hard yeast-bread rings, in the original savory and later sweetened versions; a flourless nut-paste type (*kaak bi loz*), ideal for Passover; and the more recent savory and sweetened cookie variations leavened with baking powder. In the Levant, Arabs use *kaak* to denote large soft bread rings coated with sesame seeds akin to *bagaleh*. Lebanese Arabs use *kaak* to refer to round flatbreads with a handle-like hole, which is typically split open and spread with cheese. In modern Iraq, the term *kaak* has also taken on the meaning of "valve" and "faucet."

Before a holiday or celebration, typically the women of the family as well as female friends gathered to turn out large batches of *kaak*, in what was as much a social event as a culinary occasion. Until the advent of the home oven, these cookies were prepared at home and arranged on metal sheets, then carried to the closest local bakery to cook. Unlike the dairy *graybeh* (Middle Eastern butter cookies), Jewish *kaak* are always pareve, made with oil. Originally, *kaak* were eggless, but many modern versions include eggs, as well as more fat, for a richer and lighter pastry. The dough is usually flavored with anise and sometimes other spices, including a standard Turkish

References to a bread called KAAK *in the Middle East date back to the Babylonian Talmud and have long referred more specifically to a savory or sweet pastry or bread ring. Bakers pride themselves on making perfectly uniform shapes. These are the cookie version coated in confectioners' sugar.*

spice blend called *rihat el kaak*, consisting of equal parts toasted and finely ground anise (*yansoon*), fennel (*shammar*), and mahlab (ground sour cherry kernels). Iraqis sometimes add raisins to the dough (*kaak eem tzmukim*). Many recipes are closely guarded family secrets passed on from mother to daughter. Some people prefer unadorned cookies, while others coat the rings with sesame seeds, making a version technically called *kaak sumsum*. Proficient home bakers pride themselves on being able to produce batch after batch of uniform shapes; a few experienced cooks are able to determine by eye precisely the number of *kaak* that can be made from any batch of dough. Today, *kaak* are sold at numerous Israeli bakeries, as well as those in America near large Middle Eastern communities, and consequently many people now buy these pastries. Still, there remain cooks who insist on homemade.

Like their ancient namesake, contemporary Jewish *kaak* are always quite hard, which makes them ideal for dunking into tea, coffee, and anise liqueur. Among the advantages of dry, very hard cookies is that they can be stored for a rather long time without refrigeration or freezing, if they are not consumed first. So for millennia, housewives have kept a container on hand in case of unexpected guests. These cookies are customarily served on the Sabbath at a *desayuno* (brunch) or as part of a *mezze* (appetizer assortment). They are also common at all festivals, except Passover (when flourless almond versions are enjoyed), and at weddings, *brits*, and bar mitzvahs. Salty ones are offered to break the fast of Yom Kippur. On Rosh Hashanah, they represent the circular nature of life, while the anise and sesame seeds symbolize fertility, plenty, and a multitude of good deeds in the year to come.

(See also Biscocho and Rosca)

MIDDLE EASTERN BREAD RINGS (*KAAK*)

ABOUT 48 MEDIUM RINGS   [PAREVE]

1 package (2¼ teaspoons) active dry yeast or 1 (0.6-ounce) cake fresh yeast
1⅓ cups warm water (105°F to 115°F for dry yeast; 80°F to 85°F for fresh yeast)
1 teaspoon sugar or honey
½ cup vegetable oil or shortening
1½ teaspoons table salt or 1 tablespoon kosher salt

3 to 4 tablespoons anise seeds or 1 tablespoon ground anise, or 2 tablespoons anise seeds and 1 tablespoon ground anise
Pinch of mahlab (optional)
About 4 cups (20 ounces) bread or unbleached all-purpose flour, or 3½ cups flour and ½ cup semolina flour or fine semolina
Egg wash (1 large egg beaten with 1 tablespoon water) for brushing
About ½ cup sesame seeds (optional)

1. Dissolve the yeast in ¼ cup water. Stir in the sugar and let stand until foamy, 5 to 10 minutes. In a large bowl, combine the yeast mixture, remaining water, oil, salt, anise, optional mahlab, and 2 cups flour. Gradually add enough of the remaining flour to make a mixture that holds together.

2. On a lightly floured surface, knead the dough until smooth and elastic, 10 to 15 minutes. Place in an oiled bowl and turn to coat. Cover loosely with plastic wrap or a kitchen towel and let rise in a warm, draft-free place until doubled in bulk, about 2 hours.

3. Line 2 large baking sheets with parchment paper or lightly grease the sheets. Punch down the dough and divide into 1-inch balls. On a flat surface, roll the balls, from the center out, into ½-inch-thick ropes about 5 inches long. Bring the ends together to form a ring and pinch to seal. Dip the top of the rings into the egg wash, then, if using, into the sesame seeds. Place, sesame side up, on the prepared baking sheets, leaving about 1½ inches between the rings. Cover and let rise for 20 minutes.

4. Preheat the oven to 375°F.

5. Bake until lightly golden, about 20 minutes.

6. After all the kaak are golden, reduce the heat to 225°F. Return the kaak to the oven and bake until crisp, but not excessively hard, about 20 minutes. Transfer to a wire rack and let cool completely. Store in an airtight container at room temperature or in the freezer.

VARIATIONS
Sweet Kaak (Biscotchos Dulces): Add ½ cup sugar.

KADA

Kada refers to several types of pastries made from sweet bread dough with a sweet filling.
Origin: Georgia

Georgians are not ardent consumers of sweets and

have few pastries; dessert typically consists of fresh fruit or cheese. Most Georgian sweets reflect a Persian or Ottoman heritage in the form of phyllo pastries, nut confections, and halva. *Kada*, a celebration food, probably derived from the Turkish sweet bread *çörek* (rounded), which in turn may have been introduced to the Ottoman Empire in the sixteenth century by Sephardic refugees. There are several types of *kada*. Some versions consist of a sweetened bread dough, while others evolved into a sort of a cross between a tart and a coffee cake. A third version is sort of strudel-type pastry with the dough stretched very thin, spread with sweetened butter, rolled up, then coiled and baked. For a flavor variation, some cooks toast the flour in the filling in a dry skillet until lightly browned. In the tart-like version, besides the original butter filling, Georgian Jews also enjoy a cherry filling for meat meals, such as at a traditional *supra* (feast).

GEORGIAN BUTTER PASTRY (*KADA*)

ONE 10-INCH CAKE/8 TO 10 SERVINGS   [DAIRY]

Pastry:

1¾ cups (8.75 ounces) unbleached all-purpose flour
1 teaspoon baking soda
½ teaspoon salt
½ cup (1 stick) unsalted butter, softened
½ cup sugar
2 large eggs
¾ cup sour cream or plain yogurt
1 teaspoon vanilla extract

Filling:

6 tablespoons (¾ stick) unsalted butter, softened
1 cup (5 ounces) all-purpose flour
1 cup sugar
1 teaspoon vanilla extract
Pinch of salt

1. To make the pastry: Sift together the flour, baking soda, and salt. In a large bowl, beat the butter until smooth, about 1 minute. Gradually add the sugar and beat until light and fluffy, about 4 minutes. Beat in the eggs, one at a time. Add the sour cream and vanilla. Blend in the flour mixture to make a smooth dough. Divide the dough in half. Wrap in plastic wrap and refrigerate until firm, at least 30 minutes.

2. Preheat the oven to 375°F. Grease a 10-inch springform pan and dust with flour.

3. To make the filling: In a medium bowl, beat together all the filling ingredients until smooth.

4. Place one half of the dough in the pan and press it to cover the bottom and reach 1 inch up the sides. Spread the filling over the dough.

5. On a lightly floured surface, roll out the remaining piece of dough into a 10-inch round. Place over the filling and press down on the edges.

6. Bake until golden brown and a tester inserted in the center comes out clean, about 45 minutes. Remove the *kada* from the pan, place on a wire rack, and let cool.

VARIATIONS

Georgian Cherry Pastry: Combine 1 pound (3 cups) pitted sour cherries, ½ cup sugar, ¼ cup cherry preserves, ½ cup toasted slivered almonds, and 1 teaspoon grated lemon zest and substitute for the butter filling.

KALETZIN

Kaletzin are cheese-filled pastries made by Russian Jews. Many prepared these pastries only once a year—for the meal following Yom Kippur. They are also ideal for Shavuot.

RUSSIAN CHEESE ROUNDS (*KALETZIN*)

12 PASTRIES   [DAIRY]

Dough:

1 package (2¼ teaspoons) active dry yeast or
    1 (0.6-ounce) cake fresh yeast
¼ cup warm water (105°F to 115°F for dry yeast;
    80°F to 85°F for fresh yeast)
½ cup sugar
¾ cup warm milk, or ¾ cup warm water and ¼ cup
    nonfat dry milk
6 tablespoons (¾ stick) unsalted butter or
    shortening, softened
2 large eggs
1 teaspoon table salt or 2 teaspoons kosher salt
About 4 cups (20 ounces) bread or unbleached all-
    purpose flour

Filling:

2 pounds (4 cups) pot or farmer cheese
1 cup (2 sticks) unsalted butter

1. To make the dough: Dissolve the yeast in ¼ cup water. Stir in 1 teaspoon sugar and let stand until foamy, 5 to 10 minutes. In a large bowl, combine the yeast mixture, milk, remaining sugar, butter, eggs, and salt. Blend in 1½ cups flour. Gradually add enough of the remaining flour to make a mixture that holds together.

2. On a lightly floured surface or in an electric mixer with a dough hook, knead the dough, adding more flour as needed, until smooth and springy, about 5 minutes. Place in an oiled bowl and turn to coat. Cover loosely with plastic wrap or a kitchen towel and let rise in a warm, draft-free place until doubled in bulk, 2 to 3 hours, or cover with plastic wrap and refrigerate overnight.

3. Punch down the dough, knead briefly, divide into 24 equal pieces, form into balls, and let stand for 10 minutes.

4. Preheat the oven to 400°F. Line a large baking sheet with parchment paper or lightly grease the sheet.

5. Roll each dough piece into a 2-inch round about ¼ inch thick.

6. To make the filling: Place a spoonful of pot cheese and several dots of butter in the center of half the rounds.

7. Top with the remaining 12 rounds and press the edges to seal. Prick the tops with the tines of a fork.

8. Place the dough rounds on the prepared baking sheet, leaving 1½ inches between each pastry. Bake until golden brown, about 20 minutes. Transfer the pastries to a wire rack and let cool completely.

KANAFEH/KADAYIF

Kanafeh is a very fine semolina dough that is shredded and made into pastries. The dough is usually coated with butter and baked or fried.

Origin: Levant or Egypt

Other names: Arabic: *knafeh*; Egyptian: *konafa*, *kunafa*; Greek: *kadaifi*, *kataifi*; Persian: *ghaatayef*; Turkish: *kadayif*, *kiinefe*.

In the ninth century, cooks of the caliph of Baghdad made a simple crepe-like pancake called *qata'if* (from the Arabic for "velvet"), prepared by pouring a thin flour and water batter on a heated sheet of metal and cooking the batter on one side. The predominant early use of the *qata'if* was wrapping it around a filling, notably a piece of *lauzinaq* (almond paste), then frying it and topping it with honey. In Syria and the Levant *qata'if* evolved into a deep-fried filled leavened pancake drenched in sugar syrup, colloquially called by Syrians *atayef*.

In addition, Arabic cookbooks of the thirteenth century reveal that Middle Eastern cooks thinly sliced the *qata'if* and tossed the shreds with honey. Soon, instead of cutting up the cooked pancakes, they began to drizzle the batter into thin lines onto the metal sheet. This unique dough, as well as pastries made from it, became known as a variation of the word *qata'if*, called *kadayif* or *knafeh*.

A Jewish marriage document found in the Cairo *Geniza* (synagogue archives) dating from around 1010 CE included among the witnesses "ben Isaac ha-Levi known as al-Qata'if [a nickname meaning maker of *qata'if* pastry], witness," while about a century later

A vendor in Acre's Old City making kanafeh, *a shredded dough, the old-fashioned way—on a heated metal sheet.*

a Jewish document from Alexandria mentioned "the scribe Ibn al-Qata'if [in this instance, a family name]," reflecting the early adoption and production of this pastry by the Jewish community.

Kanafeh batter, composed of only semolina flour and water, comes in two types: *knishneh* (Arabic meaning "rough"), long, thin threads looking something like shredded wheat; and *na'ama* (Arabic for "fine"), small pellets formed by coarsely grinding the threads. When the two types of pastry are mixed together, it is known as *mhayara*. Historically, *kanafeh* dough, much easier to make than phyllo, was relatively inexpensive and, therefore, accessible for home cooks as well as professional vendors. Today, frozen *kanafeh* dough can be found in many Israeli supermarkets, as well as in America at a few specialty stores.

Some small Middle Eastern bakeries still make fresh *knishneh* in the traditional manner by drizzling the batter by hand on a heated stationary metal sheet. However, many bakeries have adopted a slightly mechanized approach: They use a heated revolving circular turntable (*furn*) about four to five feet in diameter. A *juzza*, a movable container with a six-inch-long bottom plate with a row of twelve tiny perforations, is positioned above the turntable and, while the heated table is rotated, the batter is slowly squeezed out to gradually cover the entire surface of the table. The batter dries nearly upon contact with the heated surface, then is quickly gathered, wound into skeins, and piled in boxes.

The uniqueness of *kanafeh* lies in the amount of surface area on the dough, which becomes crisp during baking or frying. The common practice is to first separate the threads, which exposes more area, then coat the dough with melted butter or oil. *Kanafeh* is crisper than any other pastry, yet light and delicate. The hard *kanafeh* pastry is frequently complemented with a filling of a soft, creamy texture. Crumbled shredded wheat can be substituted for the *kanafeh*, but the texture will be much coarser.

Initially, cooks began to use the *kanafeh* by filling a bundle of dough threads with chopped nuts, then deep-frying the pastry. In Lebanon, the dough is also toasted in clarified butter, then mixed with cheese, sugar, and orange-blossom or rose water, to make a popular breakfast dish called *kanafeh bil jiben*. Eventually, a method emerged of preparing a large pastry without deep-frying, by pressing a layer of *kanafeh* dough into the bottom of a large flat-bottomed pan, then lightly and evenly browning it over a flame while frequently moving the pan. The dough was topped with a layer of filling (nuts, cream, or cheese), then a top layer of dough, and the pastry was inverted and cooked over the burner until the other side was browned. The large fried pastry was then cut into individual servings, called *tel kadayif* (string) in Turkey. Later, as the *furn* (flat-bottomed oven) supplanted the *tandor* (vertical oven), cooks began to bake small individual pastries as well as a large round pastry similar to baklava, as these were much easier to prepare than the pastries made using the old-fashioned stovetop method.

Typical of Middle Eastern cuisine, the pastries are drenched in sugar syrup, sometimes accented with orange-blossom water or rose water, and garnished with chopped nuts. Some color the syrup with a special reddish orange dye. Turks frequently top the pastries with a spoonful of a rich cream called *kaymak*.

Levantine Arabs prefer a filling with *jiben nabulsi*, also called *ackawi* (a semihard cheese akin to mozzarella), or *jiben hulwa* (unsalted fresh cheese); Turks favor *peyniri* (a cheese akin to clotted cream); and Syrian Jews tend to use *bil crema* (cream mixtures). Syrians also have a pareve filling made from mashed bananas (*bil moz*). Some of the cheese fillings have a slightly salty note that contrasts with the syrup. Pastries that have long been particularly renowned are the *kanafeh* of Aleppo, Syria, called *kanafeh halabi* (of Aleppo); the pistachio-sprinkled pastries from Gaziantep, Turkey; and the cheese version of Nablus (*Nabulsiyye*).

Although unknown to most Westerners and only first mentioned in English in 1950, *kanafeh* is extremely popular in the eastern Mediterranean. *Kanafeh* is important not only among Mizrachim, but also among Sephardim, who arrived in the Ottoman Empire and adopted the pastry as well. Among Jews from the eastern Mediterranean, *kanafeh* is widespread at life cycle events, especially weddings, *brit milahs*, and bar mitzvahs. Nut-filled *kanafeh* (*bil joz*) is a beloved Purim treat; in some Sephardic communities, it is called *kaveyos di Haman* (Haman's hair) on this holiday. *Kanafeh* is typically served with Turkish coffee or tea.

(See also Atayef)

⋇ MIDDLE EASTERN SHREDDED WHEAT PASTRY
(KANAFEH/KADAYIF)

ABOUT 24 PASTRIES   [DAIRY OR PAREVE]

Filling:

2 cups (about 8 ounces) finely chopped blanched almonds, pistachios, or walnuts, or any combination

¼ cup sugar

1 tablespoon water or orange juice

1 teaspoon ground cinnamon, rose water, or orange-blossom water

¼ teaspoon ground cloves or ½ teaspoon grated lemon zest (optional)

1 pound kanafeh/kadayif dough (found in Middle Eastern specialty stores)

¾ cup (1½ sticks) unsalted butter or margarine, melted and cooled

3 cups Atar (Middle Eastern Sugar Syrup, page 000)

1. Preheat the oven to 350°F. Grease a 13-by-9-inch baking pan or 10-inch round springform pan.

2. To make the filling: In a medium bowl, combine all the filling ingredients.

3. In a large bowl, shred the kanafeh, prying apart the strands. Drizzle with the butter and toss to coat and fluff. Evenly spread slightly more than half of the kanafeh in the prepared pan and press gently to flatten. Spread with the filling, leaving a ½-inch border on all sides. Top with the remaining kanafeh and press gently to flatten. Sprinkle with a few drops of water.

4. Bake until golden brown, 35 to 45 minutes.

5. Drizzle half of the cooled syrup over the hot pastry, wait 10 minutes until the syrup is absorbed, then drizzle with the remaining syrup and let stand until absorbed. For a smooth top surface, invert the kanafeh onto a tray. While still warm, cut into 1- to 2-inch squares. Serve warm or at room temperature. Kanafeh tastes best on the day it is made.

KÁPOSZTA

Káposzta is braised cabbage.

Origin: Central Europe

Other names: Czech: dusené zelí; German: gedunstetes kraut; Hungarian: párolt káposzta.

While cabbage was a staple among all central European countries, none developed as many variations as Hungary. Cabbage stars in several beloved Hungarian

celebratory dishes, such as töltött káposzta (stuffed cabbage) and káposztás rétes (cabbage-stuffed strudel), and it also constitutes everyday fare.

Káposzta is the Hungarian word for cabbage, that country's king of vegetables, as well as the common vernacular for a favorite central European method for cooking cabbage—braising (párolt káposzta). The cabbage is first cooked in fat, producing extra flavor and a firmer texture. Then as the cabbage cooks over a low heat in its own juices, its sweetness emerges. When cabbage was out of season, cooks frequently substituted sauerkraut for fresh cabbage. Sometimes braised cabbage was mixed with sour cream (tejfolos káposzta), simmered in a tomato sauce (paradicsomos káposzta), or sautéed with apples (almaval párolt káposzta). Basic braised cabbage is typically served with roast meat and dumplings,

Unquestionably, the favorite Hungarian variation of braised cabbage—and for many the ultimate comfort food—is cabbage with noodles (káposztás teszta), a dish in which pasta is infused with a hint of cabbage flavor and seasoned with plenty of pepper. Káposztás teszta is served as both a side dish and a main course. Cabbage with noodles was typically prepared in a large batch to fill a family's stomachs. The leftovers, considered just as good if not tastier, are reheated and enjoyed the following day. In some Hungarian households, cabbage with noodles is traditional Purim fare, typically sprinkled with poppy seeds.

(See also Cabbage)

⋇ HUNGARIAN BRAISED GREEN CABBAGE
(PÁROLT KÁPOSZTA)

6 TO 8 SERVINGS   [DAIRY, MEAT, OR PAREVE]

2 pounds (1 medium head) green or savoy cabbage, cored and coarsely shredded

1 teaspoon salt

¼ cup butter, schmaltz, or vegetable oil

1 large yellow onion, chopped

About 1 cup water or broth, or ½ cup light dry white wine and ½ cup water

Salt and ground black pepper to taste

1 pound cooked pasta squares or wide egg noodles (optional)

1. Sprinkle the cabbage with the salt. Let stand for about 1 hour. Drain and squeeze out the excess liquid.

2. In a large skillet or pot, heat the butter over medium heat. Add the onion and sauté until soft and translucent, 5 to 10 minutes. Add the cabbage (if using a skillet, you might have to add it in batches, waiting for each portion to shrink) and sauté until reduced and slightly wilted, about 3 minutes.

3. Add enough water to prevent the cabbage from sticking. Add the salt and pepper. Bring to a boil, cover, reduce the heat to medium-low, and simmer until tender but still slightly crunchy, about 20 minutes. For káposztás teszta (braised cabbage with noodles), add the noodles and heat through, about 5 minutes. Serve warm. Braised cabbage can be stored in the refrigerator for up to 3 days and reheated.

KARNATZEL/KARNATZLACH

Karnatzel is a garlicky meat patty.
Origin: Romania
Other names: *carnatzel.*

"There to live is a pleasure; what your heart desires, that you can receive: A mamaliga, a pastrami, a karnatzele, and a glass of wine!" (From "Roumania, Roumania," a famous Yiddish folk song by Aaron Lebedeff.)

The Romanian word for fresh sausage, *cârnat,* from the word for meat, *carne,* gave rise to the name of a much-beloved meat patty, a foremost Romanian comfort food, in Yiddish *karnatzel* or *karnatzlach.* (It is not the same as the *karnatzel* from Montreal, Canada, a thin, long, dry beef sausages with a texture akin to pepperoni.) The non-Jewish version of this patty is called *mititei* (miniature), a term Jews sometimes also use for a diminutive *karnatzlach,* the size of a thumb.

Karnatzlach reflect the more than three-hundred-year Ottoman domination of Romania, from the early sixteenth to nineteenth century. During that time, many Ottoman foods arrived, as did some Sephardim and their fare. Similar to the Sephardic *kefte* and Ottoman *kofte,* the Romanian offshoot *karnatzlach* are shaped like torpedoes and grilled. However, displaying its European side, Romanian cookery never absorbed the frills of the Middle Eastern influences, and the dishes tend to be simpler and less spicy. The primary flavoring is garlic, and plenty of it. Some people prefer the pure flavor of meat and garlic, while others favor a little spice in the patties. Herbs, such as parsley and savory, are acceptable, as is a little cumin or allspice, reflecting the Middle Eastern influence.

Well-made *karnatzlach* are juicy and tender. Lean cuts of meat turn out dry, so medium-fat meat is used. These patties are nearly pure meat, containing no binders or fillers, such as eggs or bread crumbs. Because they are made without bread or grains, *karnatzlach* are popular on Passover as well. Perhaps the most unique feature of traditional *karnatzlach* is the addition of soda—baking soda or soda water—which makes the patties springy and keeps them juicy.

In Romania, *karnatzlach* were almost always grilled over charcoal, imparting a smoky accent, or on a grill pan, but some people now fry them. Due to the many Romanian restaurants in Israel, including more than a dozen in Jerusalem alone, Israelis experience the genuine article, properly cooked over an open grill. However, in Israel, during the period of *tzena* (austerity) from 1950 to 1955, when meat was strictly rationed, Romanians were forced to do the unthinkable—add bread crumbs as filler to *karnatzlach.*

Karnatzlach are commonly served with slices of *mamaliga* (corn meal mush) or black bread, assorted salads, sauerkraut, plenty of sour kosher pickles, mustard, and perhaps some well-chilled vodka or "*a glezele vayn*"—"a glass of wine," an accompaniment Lebedeff celebrated in his song.

ROMANIAN MEAT PATTIES (*KARNATZLACH*)

MAKES 30 TO 32 PATTIES [MEAT]

3 pounds beef neck meat or lamb chuck, or
   1½ pounds beef and 1½ pounds veal
6 to 12 cloves garlic (2 to 4 tablespoons chopped)
About 1 tablespoon kosher salt or 1½ teaspoons
   table salt
1 cup water
1 tablespoon baking soda

1. Process the meat through a meat grinder 3 times or in a food processor fitted with a metal blade. Or have your butcher do this. The texture of the meat should be almost a paste, in the Middle Eastern style.

2. Using the flat side of a large knife or cleaver, or in a mortar, mash and schmear the garlic with the salt until smooth. Or puree the garlic and salt with 1 tablespoon water in a blender.

3. Using your hand or a wooden spoon, mix the garlic into the meat, gradually adding the 1 cup water as you mix, about 5 minutes. Cover and refrigerate overnight. This allows the garlic to permeate the meat. Let stand at room temperature for 1 hour before cooking.

4. Stir the baking soda into the meat. Wetting your hands to ensure a smooth surface, shape the meat into patties about 3 inches long and 1 inch wide with tapered ends. Wetting your hands ensures a smooth surface.

5. Grill or broil the patties about 4 inches from the heat source, turning once, until browned, about 4 minutes per side for rare, 5 minutes per side for medium-rare, or 6 minutes per side for medium. Using a pair of tongs, remove the karnatzlach from the grill; do not use a fork, which releases the juices. Let rest for at least 1 minute to allow the juices to stabilize.

VARIATIONS

Spicier Meat Patties: In Step 3, add ¾ cup chopped flat-leaf parsley, about 1½ teaspoons ground black pepper, and 1½ teaspoons ground cumin or ¾ teaspoon ground allspice. Or add 2 teaspoons dried marjoram, 2 teaspoons dried sage, 2 teaspoons dried savory, 1 teaspoon ground black pepper, and 1 teaspoon paprika.

KARPAS

During the Passover Seder, two ritual "dippings" occur at different times. The first dipping, commonly referred to as *karpas*, usually consists of immersing a piece of raw vegetable less than the size of a large olive into either salt water or vinegar. The second dipping, performed after eating the matza, is the *maror* (bitter herb) dunked into charoset. The ritual of *karpas* occurs near the very beginning of the Seder, immediately after the Kiddush over the first cup of wine and a ritual washing of the hands, the first of two washings. After dipping and before eating the *karpas*, the benediction *"borei peri ha'adamah"* (Who creates the fruit of the earth) is recited, the intent being that it also applies to the *maror* to be eaten later. Most people do not recline while eating the *karpas*.

The word *karpas* is borrowed from the Persian, meaning "fine cotton," which in turn derived from the Sanskrit *karpasa* (cotton). The first appearance of *karpas* in a Jewish source was, appropriately, in the Persian-era Scroll of Esther: "There were hangings [in the court of the gardens of the king's palace] of white linen, *karpas*, and blue [wool or linen]." Most Jewish translations of Esther render *karpas* in its original sense as "fine white cotton," but in the biblical context, it may actually indicate a color, thus meaning a green fabric, reflecting the cotton plant's original hue. In addition, Persians began to use an unrelated word, *karafs*, to denote celery and parsley, the two close relatives typically confused in the ancient world, which

probably led to *karpas* denoting both celery and parsley in Talmudic Hebrew. (In modern Farsi, celery is still *karafs*, while parsley is *ja'fari*; in modern Hebrew, celery is *sehlehri* or *karpas* and parsley is *petrozillah*.)

However, nowhere in the Talmud or even Geonic literature (the time from about 700 to 1000 CE when the *geonim*, the heads of two major Talmudic academies in Persia and Babylonia, served as the principal authorities of Jewish law and tradition) is this initial Seder vegetable ever referred to as *karpas*, although the word is used elsewhere in the Talmud as the name of specific vegetables. Indeed, well through the Middle Ages, the first dipping had no formal name and was simply called *tibul rishon* (first dipping), the act of dunking being the primary point. In addition, there is confusion over what vegetables are used for the first dipping. To further complicate the situation, the Talmud does not mention the name of the liquid in which the first vegetable is dipped.

To avoid any confusion or controversy, the Sages suggested that for the first dipping, any vegetable other than those customary for *maror* would be preferable. The Babylonian Talmud never mentions any specific vegetables, although the Jerusalem Talmud records that Rav used raw beet greens for the first dipping (certainly tender young leaves). Amram Gaon (857 CE), compiler of the first *siddur* (prayer book) and Haggadah, rules that if there are two types of vegetables available, different ones are used for the two dippings, but in a situation in which only *maror* is obtainable, it is used for both dippings. Rav Amram also lists examples of those vegetables recommended for the first dipping: *chamah* (radish leaves), *chasah* (lettuce), *gargira* (arugula), *karpasa* (parsley), and *kusbarta* (cilantro). Moses Maimonides (c. 1170) referred to the object used for the first dipping as *yerek ahchair* (another green vegetable) and all the other early commentators also employed the generic *yerek* for the first dipping. By the time of the *Shulchan Arukh* (c. 1565) by Rabbi Joseph Caro, however, the first dipping had officially acquired the designation of *karpas*, because celery and parsley leaves were the predominant vegetables used for the ritual.

Interestingly, the special coat that Jacob gave to Joseph is described in the Bible as *passim*, generally translated as "many colored." Rashi points out that this word "denotes a cloak of *karpas* [green] and blue," a clear reference to the phrase in Esther.

Rashi emphasizes that the green and blue hangings of King Ahasuerus reflect the disharmony and animosity of the Jewish community of Persia, which nearly led to its destruction before the community was saved through unity and common concern. Similarly, Joseph's brothers were green with envy, leading directly to the descent to Egypt and centuries of pain and suffering. Consequently, the green *karpas* (to use a redundant phrase) of the Seder reminds us of the enmity of Joseph's brothers, who dipped the green and blue garment into goat's blood, engendering the descent to Egypt. Only through harmony, and through the inclusion and care of the outsider, the poor, and the helpless, can redemption be achieved.

The intent of the term *karpas*, in terms of the Seder, is not to prescribe a specific vegetable, but rather to indicate any green-colored vegetable, the two most prevalent at the Seder being celery and parsley. The leaves of both plants are also natural antispasmodics and aids to digestion and were, therefore, common at Greek and Roman feasts. However, in sections of northern Europe, where fresh greens were unavailable in the early spring, white radishes, turnips, or, beginning in the mid-nineteenth century, raw white potatoes stored over the winter were substituted under the rationalization that the leaves, although not eaten, were green. (Whether the benediction "Who creates the fruit of the earth" can be recited over a raw potato, which is not in the form in which it is normally consumed, is another matter.)

As to what liquid the first vegetable is dipped in, the early sources—Amram Gaon, Saadia Gaon, Maimonides, Rabbenu Tam, *Machzor Vitry* (c. 1105 by Simcha ben Shumuel, a student of Rashi, of Vitry-en-Perthois in Northern France), and the Sarajevo Haggadah (c. 1350)—all state that the first dipping is, like the second dipping, into charoset. According to Maimonides, all the symbols of the Seder—*maror*, *koraik* ("wrap" of matza and *maror*), *karpas*, and even the matza—are dipped into charoset. Many Yemenites (*Baladi* and *Dardei*), who generally follow Maimonides, still dip the *karpas*, usually parsley, into charoset; the *Shami* (followers of the Ari, a tradition brought to Yemen by Syrian Sephardim) use vinegar. Some Iraqis and Indians use lemon juice. The *Shulchan Arukh* ruled that one should dip the *karpas* into wine vinegar. Tosafot, reflecting the custom of medieval Ashkenazim, directed that one should dip the first vegetable into wine vinegar or salt water; however, if no other vegetable is available and *chazeret* (lettuce) must be used for the first dipping, then it should be immersed into charoset for the first dipping. This opinion differs from that of Rashbam, who held that charoset should never be used for the first dipping, and is only appropriate for *maror*.

Today, some families continue to dip the *karpas* into vinegar, while many others, particularly Ashkenazim, opt for salt water. The dipping of a green vegetable into red charoset or red wine vinegar at the onset of the Seder was probably inspired by the biblical account of the hyssop leaves that were dipped into blood and spread on the doorposts in Egypt. On the other hand, salt water is symbolic of the tears shed by the Israelites in Egypt, as well as of the liberating waters of the Sea of Reeds. Birth and rebirth inevitably entail pain. Because the tears and moans of the Israelites sparked the redemption from Egypt, the dipping of *karpas*, representative of renewal and springtime, was appropriately placed at the beginning of the Seder.

Besides contributing to the sense of freedom of the evening, the two hand washings and two dippings were intended to arouse the curiosity of the children, as this was an otherwise unusual practice in Jewish households two thousand years ago. Even today, Sabbath and festival meals commence with Kiddush, which is followed immediately by the washing of the hands with a benediction, then Hamotzi (the benediction over bread). The incongruity of placing *karpas* and hand washing without a benediction in between Kiddush and Hamotzi was intended to be different and unsettling, thereby immediately sparking questions. Adults tend to be socialized against making public remarks, but children are more observant and more honest, and therefore more likely to cut though the pretense when they see things out of kilter.

(See also Celery, Charoset, Parsley, Passover, and Seder)

KASHA

Cooked cereals subsumed under the term kasha were once served at all Slavic feasts and important occasions, including the signing of peace treaties. This practice was the source of an ancient Russian adage describing an implacable enemy: "You can't make kasha with him."

By the second century CE, a standard Persian dish was *kashk* (*kutach* in the Talmud and later *kishk* in Arabic), originally denoting a porridge made from cracked grains fermented with whey, then dried. Later, some Middle Easterners began using *keshkek* or *kishk* to denote any type of cooked cereal. The Persian name eventually traveled to eastern Europe, becoming the Slavic kasha and encompassing all grain porridges—fine and coarse, thick and thin, sweet and savory. Incidentally, when leftover *kashk* was stuffed into animal intestines, the dish became *kishke* (stuffed derma).

Later, around the early fourteenth century, in the wake of the Tatar invasions, buckwheat, a native of northern China first cultivated about one thousand years ago, arrived in Russia and Ukraine. It quickly emerged as a staple of the diet. Buckwheat, a relative of rhubarb and sorrel, is neither a grass nor a wheat, but botanically a fruit seed. However, since it shares most of a grain's properties, possesses the general nutritional breakdown of a grain, and is cooked like one, buckwheat is usually categorized as a pseudo-cereal. Buckwheat, a sturdy plant that grows well in cooler climates and even in poor soil, reaches maturity in only sixty to seventy days, generates two crops every year, and is very nutritious.

The Slavic word for buckwheat became *grechka* or *grecha*, from the Slavic term for "a Greek," either in association with Greek monks in Orthodox monasteries who cultivated it or Greek merchants who traded it. Consequently, buckwheat porridge is *grechnevaya kasha*. Buckwheat also was associated with the Tatars and Saracens (some say because of its dark complexion), a term used during the medieval period to denote Arabs and Turks. Among eastern Ashkenazim, who were not prone to making hot cooked cereals, *kashe* or kasha in Yiddish took on the meaning of "husked and toasted buckwheat groats."

By the end of the fifteenth century, buckwheat had spread to western Europe, where it was most commonly ground into a flour. The Dutch introduced buckwheat to America by planting it in New Amsterdam in the seventeenth century. The English name for the plant came from the Dutch *boekweit* (beech wheat), as the groats resemble the triangular beechnut.

In early America, almost all the buckwheat sold was in the form of flour. Then beginning in the late nineteenth century, eastern European Jews began to popularize the toasted groats in America. Most Ashkenazic households had a box of Wolff's kasha in the cupboard. Today, the vast majority of buckwheat groats sold in America is still purchased in areas with large Jewish populations, notably New York City, Los Angeles, and southern Florida. As a result, the English word kasha reflects the circumscribed Jewish connotation and not the Slavic.

Buckwheat is ideally suited for Russia, Ukraine, and the Baltic region, where for centuries, along with dark bread, barley, and cabbage, it constituted the daily fare. It is still in those areas that much of buckwheat's popularity lies. Buckwheat is available in flour form as well as in cone-shaped groats (kasha), which are sold both whole and ground into coarse, medium, and fine granulations. Commercial kasha comes plain or toasted, although most brands are now, in the Jewish style, toasted.

Kasha's assertive nutty flavor complements bland foods, such as noodles, and also pairs well with hearty fare, including cabbage and root vegetables. Coating the kasha with a little egg before cooking is a characteristic Jewish practice; it keeps the groats separate and prevents them from becoming mushy. The four favorite Jewish ways of using kasha are with sautéed onions (sometimes along with mushrooms or shredded cabbage), with noodles (*kasha varnishkes*), in chicken soup, and as a filling for knishes, pirogen, blintzes, strudels, cabbage, and bell peppers. Until relatively recently, filling for a knish was either potato or kasha. In addition to traditional Old World additions to kasha, Americans also mix in some green peas, green beans, chickpeas, carrots, or toasted almonds.

The emergence of the potato in the mid-nineteenth century led to a diminution in the importance of buckwheat on the Ashkenazic table in eastern Europe, a decrease which further continued in America. Kasha was also brought to Israel, where it is called *kusemet* in modern Hebrew, although some non-Ashkenazim disparagingly refer to it by a similar-sounding generic Arabic expletive. However, to some Ashkenazim, kasha remains a beloved comfort food.

(See also Blini, Kasha Varnishkes, and Kashk/Kutach)

KASHA VARNISHKES

Kasha varnishkes is buckwheat groats mixed with noodles, most often small bow-tie noodles.

Origin: Eastern Europe

Other names: *kasha mit varnishkes*, *kashe un varnishkes*, *kashe varnishkes*.

In the early Yiddish play *Die Mumeh Soseh* (Aunt Sosya) by Avrom Goldfaden, written in Odessa in 1869, the title character's sister, Khantshe, misinterprets her cousin's question about *tsivilizatsye* (Russian for "civilization") as *tsibilis* (Yiddish for "onions"). She proceeds to describe how she fries them and puts them into her "*kashe un varnishkes*," providing the first record of this now-classic dish of buckwheat groats and noodles. At this early stage of his career, Goldfaden, the father of the Yiddish theater and a native of Starokostiantyniv, Ukraine, was still influenced by the zealously antitraditional elements of the *Haskalah* (Enlightenment), and may have chosen *kashe un varnishkes* as a pejorative fare of "the shtetl." Nevertheless, just as Goldfaden soon came to view Jewish traditions with more nostalgia and warmth, eastern Ashkenazim in America began to consider *kashe un varnishkes* as an enduring eastern Ashkenazic icon.

Around the sixteenth century, shortly after buckwheat arrived in Russia and Ukraine, eastern Europeans began making meat- or cheese-filled pasta; these dishes may have been a by-product of Tatar incursions from Asia or may have been introduced from Italy, or both. Ukrainians took to calling these filled pasta *vareniki* (little boiled things), from the Slavic *var* meaning "to boil." In due course, the inexpensive kasha became one of the prevalent fillings; it was typically enhanced by Jews in the Ashkenazic manner with sautéed onions and sometimes *gribenes* (cracklings). The nutty, earthy flavor of buckwheat groats contrasts with the sweetness of soft, caramelized onions and toothsome pasta. Mushrooms are occasionally added as another counterpoint. It is preferable to sauté the onions and mushrooms separately and then add them to the hot kasha, as their flavors tend to become muted when cooked with the kasha. Pasta stuffed with this filling was known as *kashe vareniki*. Eventually, cooks figured out that it was easier to simply mix the kasha with some cooked noodles than to go through the tedious process of filling the pasta; the resulting dish was called *kasha varnishkes*.

The traditional Ukrainian way to shape noodles was to roll out the pasta sheets and cut them into squares or rectangles about one and a half inches wide. Among Ukrainian Jews, the plain noodles typically mixed with kasha became known by the name *varnishkes*, called *plaetschen* in Poland. Eastern Europeans brought *kasha varnishkes* to America, where it became a popular comfort food as well as holiday fare. "In the mid-1800s, Augustus Goodman immigrated from Posen, Poland (then part of Prussia) and ended up in Washington, D.C., where he went into his family's business, baking hand matzas. During the Civil War, Goodman became a baker for the Union Army, making a different form of unleavened bread, hardtack. Following the War in 1865, he moved to Philadelphia and launched a matza bakery; in 1881, he relocated to New York City and, with his brother Isaac, opened another matza bakery. By 1888, the business had expanded and shortly thereafter, with the company renamed A. Goodman & Sons, Augustus branched out into making kosher egg noodles. Over the years, Goodman's repertoire of noodle products increased. During the early 1900s, probably influenced by the farfalle (butterflies) pasta of Italian immigrants, Goodman's began pinching the top and bottom edges of dough rectangles inward to the center, which Americans called bow-ties. These soon became the favorite form for eastern European Jews in America for making kasha varnishkes."

Kasha varnishkes was once served for Sabbath dinner, Hanukkah, Purim, and other special occasions, usually as an accompaniment to roast chicken and brisket; brisket and *kasha varnishkes* the traditional Hanukkah duo in some households. For years, *kasha varnishkes* was a standard at Jewish delis and dairy restaurants, like the now extinct Garden Cafeteria, Ratner's, and, another block south on the Lower East Side, Rapoport's. In Europe, the dish consisted predominantly of inexpensive kasha with a few noodles, while in America the opposite was generally true.

Although the passion for *kasha varnishkes* faded somewhat in the American Jewish community, through popular culture, it was introduced to the American mainstream. In a 1995 episode of the sitcom *Seinfeld*, Elaine is asked by a rabbi in her building, "Can I offer you some *kasha varnishkes*?" Although absent from earlier versions, the 1997 edition of the classic American cookbook *The Joy of Cooking* offered a recipe for "Bowties with Kasha (Kasha Varnishkes)." *The Star Trek Cookbook* (1999) included a recipe from the mother of actor Leonard Nimoy entitled "Kasha Varnishkas à la Vulcan," which noted, "This dish is particularly delicious when served with pot roast gravy. If you want to stay traditionally Vulcan vegetarian, you can make a brown mushroom gravy and use that instead."

(See also Kasha, Lokshen, and Varenik/Varenikes)

UKRAINIAN BUCKWHEAT AND NOODLES
(*KASHA VARNISHKES*)

6 TO 8 SERVINGS [PAREVE OR MEAT]

    2 cups water, or 1 cup chicken broth and 1 cup
        water
    About 1 teaspoon table salt or 2 teaspoons kosher
        salt
    About ¼ teaspoon ground black pepper
    5 tablespoons schmaltz or vegetable oil
    1 large egg or 1 large egg white, lightly beaten
    1 cup (5.75 ounces) kasha (roasted buckwheat
        kernels), medium or coarse granulation
    1 large onion, sliced or chopped
    8 ounces bow-tie noodles, *plaetschen* (noodle
        squares), or wide egg noodles

1. Bring the water, salt, pepper, and 2 tablespoons schmaltz to a boil.

2. Meanwhile, in a small bowl, stir the egg into the kasha to coat the kernels. Transfer to an ungreased medium saucepan, place over medium heat, and stir until each grain is dry and separated, about 3 minutes. Remove from the heat and gradually stir in the boiling water. It will sputter. Cover, place over a low heat, and simmer until the kasha is tender and the liquid is absorbed, about 12 minutes. Remove the kasha from the heat and let stand covered to firm and absorb any excess moisture, about 10 minutes.

3. Meanwhile, in a large skillet, heat the remaining 3 tablespoons schmaltz over medium heat. Add the onion and sauté until soft and translucent, 5 to 10 minutes, or until golden, about 20 minutes. Set aside.

4. Meanwhile, cook the noodles in a large pot of lightly salted boiling water according to the package directions and drain.

5. Fluff the kasha and add the sautéed onions, then stir in the hot noodles. Serve warm. If you like the top lightly browned, bake in a 350°F oven for about 15 minutes. If it is dry, stir in a little chicken broth.

KASHK/KUTACH

Kashk are dried balls of fermented cracked wheat or barley and yogurt whey that are usually simmered with water into a thick soup.

Origin: Persia

Other names: Arabic: *kishk;* Greek: *trahana;* Hebrew: *kutach;* Iraq: *kushuk;* Turkish: *tarhana, tarhina.*

Kashk is a fermented product encompassing the two enduring staples of the Middle East, grains and dairy. In the Middle East, a combination of agricultural and pastoral cultures, grains (primarily varieties of barley and wheat) and dairy products each provide nutritional elements lacking in the other. Much of ancient food technology was devoted to preserving scarce resources for as long as possible, and not necessarily to creating the most sophisticated and flavorful fare. Although whole grains could be stored for many months, if they were fractured—a common occurrence during threshing—the oil inside became prone to spoilage. Fermentation could extend the shelf life of dairy products, such as yogurt, cheese, and buttermilk, for a few days or so, but additional processing was necessary for longer storage.

Kashk was typically prepared during the summer, after the grain harvest, but while there was still a surplus of milk, as well as heat from the sun for aiding both fermentation and drying. Families set aside part of their harvest or purchased large amounts of wheat or barley, then coarsely cracked some of it between two rotating stones. The crushed grain was slowly stirred into warmed acidified whey drained from sheep or goat yogurt or cheesemaking, and the doughy mixture was salted and transferred to porous clay vessels to ferment for at least two or three days and sometimes up to two weeks. After it was properly fermented, the thick mixture was formed into coarse lumps and spread out to dry in the sun—a slow, thorough drying of at least a week or more. Finally, the *kashk* was crumbled into smaller balls and stored in clay vessels until needed. *Kashk* was reconstituted in water, then simmered into a thick, lumpy porridge, or simmered with available vegetables into a soup. When added to a liquid, the brownish lumps whiten somewhat and crumble easily, remaining relatively intact when cooked for a short period. Some people, unfamiliar with the process for making *kashk*, have mistaken the small *kashk* lumps for crusts of bread.

Throughout most of history, *kashk* was a home production run by women and children, although in the later twentieth century, commercial manufacturers, primarily in Turkey and Greece, emerged. Nevertheless, in many rural areas in the Middle East, this process continues annually to this very day. In Iran, *kashk* has taken on the meaning of dried whey or dried yogurt (without any grain), while *kateh* is now the Persian name of basic cooked rice.

The acid in *kashk* produced during fermentation, along with the salt and low-moisture content, acts to suppress spoilage. As a result, *kashk* can be stored for up to two years. The acid and fermentation also give the *kashk* its distinctive sour, nutty, yeasty flavor and smell, which vary according to the types of lactic acid bacteria used. Although members of one culture become accustomed to or even grow to love the flavor of a particular fermented item, that food is all too often offensive to other communities.

The Talmud relates that Rabbi Yochanan "would spit [in disgust] every time he was reminded of *kutach ha'Bavli* [*Bavli* means "Babylonian"]." The Israeli rabbis claimed three things about *kutach ha'Bavli*, the Talmudic term for the Persian *kashk*, in the process revealing its ingredients: "it clogs the heart, on account of the whey [*nisyube de chalba*, Aramaic meaning "separated from milk"]; it blinds the eyes, on account of the salt; and weakens the body, on account of the fermentation of the flour."

Kutach ha'Bavli is among the most commonly mentioned foods in the Talmud. Although it was a much-beloved dish among Jews in central Asia, *kutach* merited extreme scorn among the residents of Israel. Persian Jews commonly ate *kutach* with bread, which the Israelis, who stressed fresh vegetables and legumes in their diet, found the practice of "eating flour with flour" in a meal at best puzzling. However, the principal problem with *kutach* for most Israelis was its taste.

The citation of *kutach* in the Mishnah, at least four centuries before the earliest record of *kashk* in a non-Jewish source, reveals that it was well established by at least 200 CE, around the time the Mishnah was compiled and, for the next several centuries, remained primarily a central Asian food. *Kashk*, along with other fermented dairy products that provided much-needed nutrition and protein, was an everyday food in the Middle East, as well as an essential part of the cached winter food supply and a vital resource in times of famine. The porridge was principally breakfast food but, depending on necessity and preference, often served as part of a meal or the entirety of a meal, especially during the winter. *Kashk* was ideal for soldiers, shepherds, nomads, and travelers of all sorts, requiring just a small vessel, a fire, and some water to produce a filling repast.

In addition, the porridge, considered by its proponents to be very healthy and nutritious, was commonly served any time of the year to nursing mothers, infants, the sick, and the elderly. Rav Gaza, a Babylonian, rebutted the Talmud's criticism of *kutach*, explaining, "I was in the West [Israel] at one time and made that same dish [*kutach*], and all the sick of Israel begged me for it." Maimonides, while a physician in Egypt, in an official medical letter written to the son of Saladin, prescribed *kashk* to be drunk and included his recipe, made primarily with barley, vinegar, and salt.

In the ninth century, the word first appeared in Arabic, pronounced *kishk*, while the Turks called it *tarhana* (from the Persian *tar* "soaked" and *khan* "food") and sometimes added chopped vegetables, such as onions and chickpeas, and spices, including dill and mint, to the dough. During the Ottoman domination of the Balkans, the Turks introduced the dish to that area, where it was adopted as everyday food and the Greeks pronounced it *trahana*. *Trahana* soups are still widespread in the Balkans and packaged dried *trahana* is commonly available in markets. Medieval Hungarian *tarhonya* was identical to *kashk*, but after the concept of pasta arrived in central Europe, *tarhonya* evolved into a basic egg noodle dough.

This ancient dish had an impact on Ashkenazim as well, although not as *kutach*. When *kashk* made its way to eastern Europe, it became kasha, a word used in Slavic languages for any type of cooked grain porridge (with or without the dairy); in Yiddish, kasha came to mean only toasted buckwheat groats. When *kishk* was stuffed into intestines, it became *kishke*.

🎜 GREEK WHEAT SOUP (*TRAHANAS*)

6 TO 8 SERVINGS   [DAIRY]

    1½ cups (9 ounces) trahana (kashk)

    1½ cups water

    5½ to 7½ cups vegetable broth or water

    ¼ cup vegetable oil, olive oil, or clarified butter

Salt and ground black pepper to taste

¼ cup chopped fresh flat-leaf parsley or 1 cup feta cheese (optional)

1. In a medium bowl, soak the *trahana* in 1½ cups water for at least 30 minutes.

2. In a large, heavy pot, heat the oil over medium-low heat. Add the trahana and stir to coat. Add the broth, salt, and pepper and bring to a boil, stirring constantly. Simmer, stirring occasionally, until the trahana is tender and the soup slightly thickened, 10 to 15 minutes. If using, stir in the parsley.

KEBAB

Kebab denotes an array of Middle Eastern grilled or broiled meat dishes; in America, it typically refers to shish kebab, while in Europe it more commonly indicates *doner kebab* (*shawarma*) and in Israel kebab means skewers of ground meat patties.

Origin: Persia, Turkey

Other names: Farsi: *kabab*; Turkey: *kebap*.

The Persian poem *The Rubáiyát of Umar Khayyám* (c. 1100 CE) contains a famous quatrain, usually mistranslated, but actually reading, "Here with a loaf of bread beneath the bough, a flask of wine, a *kabab* [not *kitab*, which means "book"], and thou."

In medieval Persia, *kabab* (pronounced *kebab* in Arabic) denoted chunks of meat that were variously roasted, baked, fried, or stewed. The Persian term *kabab* probably derived from the Aramaic word *kabbaba* (burning/charring). The term was used in the Babylonian Talmud in discussions of Temple animal offerings that they not be *kabbaba* (burned). The Persian term was adopted by medieval Arabs and Turks as kebab, and has come to mean different things in different places. The Iraqi cookbook *Kitab al-Tabikh* (Book of Dishes) by Muhammad ibn al-Hasan Al-Baghdadi, written in 1226 but based on a collection of ninth-century Persian-inspired recipes, contained recipes using meatballs called kebab. Among the book's medieval Arabic meatball dishes were *mudaqqaqat hamida* ("sour meatballs," flavored with verjuice), *raihaniya* (meatballs with spinach), *buraniya* (meatballs with eggplant), and *naranjiya* (orange stew with both meat chunks and meatballs).

Roasting small chunks of meat is a process dating back into antiquity. Middle Eastern nomads and later soldiers cooked meat over an open fire. Smaller pieces of meat need less fuel than large cuts, so cooking these chunks was practical in an area where wood and even brambles were in limited quantity; this cooking technique was also valuable when time was of the essence. It was the Turks around the sixteenth century who popularized the usage of kebab to refer to grilled and broiled meat. In the Ottoman Empire, the Turkish term *sis* (sword/skewer) was attached to the Persian term for roasted pieces of meat, called *sis kebab*. In the late nineteenth century *doner kebab* became a synonym for shawarma.

Today, shish kebab a term adopted in English around 1913—known as *shashlik* in the Caucasus, *basturma* in Georgia, and *frigarui* in Romania—refers to any type of meat cut into cubes of one inch or slightly larger in size, including lamb, beef, and chicken, and grilled on skewers. In parts of the Arab world, roasted pieces of meat are called *lahm mishwi*, although in Iraq, they are known as *tikka*. Some of the most widespread modern Persian *kababs* are *kabab-e barg*, strips of marinated lamb threaded on skewers and grilled; *kabab-e koobideh*, ground beef, chopped onions, and parsley pressed around a skewer and grilled; *joojeh kabab*, grilled chicken chunks; and *mahi kabab*—*samek kebab* in Arabic—grilled fish chunks. In Persian restaurants, grilled meat, or a combination of *kababs*, served on a bed of fluffy saffron rice and usually accompanied with grilled tomatoes is called *chelow kabab*.

Whatever the terminology, roasted skewered pieces of meat are ubiquitous from India to the Caucasus and Balkans. Many versions call for marinating the meat and also helps keep it moist during grilling. Turkish kebabs tend to be spiced with cumin, while Persians typically favor cardamom and turmeric. Many Greeks like a little marjoram.

Oval ground meat patties on skewers are called *kufta kebab/kefte kebab* in Arabic, kebab in Iraq (*kubbeh* are Iraqi ground meat dumplings), *köfte kebab* in Turkish, and *luleh kabab* (*tube*) in Persian, the latter sometimes containing toasted chickpea flour. The most common Iraqi way to eat the grilled elongated ground beef patties is as *laffat kebab*, wrapped in flatbread and sprinkled with sumac and sliced onions.

Kebabs, whether chunks or ground meat, are particularly important among Persian, Kurdish, and Turkish Jews, many of whom enjoy them on a weekly basis as well as at celebrations, such as an engagement party or *Shevah Berachot* (festive meals in the week following the wedding). Middle Eastern Jews popularized their native kebabs in Israel, where they became integral to the cuisine and culture. On Israel Independence Day and during the week of Sukkot, as well as on other days when Israelis typically enjoy grilling and picnics, some type of kebab is always on the menu. Kebabs are also ubiquitous in Middle Eastern restaurants in Israel and Israeli restaurants in the West. Kebabs are usually served with rice and/or flat bread, although Kurds frequently enjoy ground meat kebabs with bulgur.

(See also Kefte, Kufta, and Me'orav Yerushalmi)

MIDDLE EASTERN GROUND MEAT ON SKEWERS
(KUFTA KEBAB)

8 SERVINGS   [MEAT]

2 pounds ground lamb or beef chuck
½ to 1 cup chopped fresh flat-leaf parsley
6 scallions or 1 medium yellow onion, chopped
1 to 4 cloves garlic mashed with about 1 teaspoon salt
About ¾ teaspoon ground black pepper
1 teaspoon ground cumin, 1 teaspoon ground cinnamon, ½ teaspoon cayenne, or 2 tablespoons dried mint
Vegetable or olive oil

1. In a large bowl, combine the meat, parsley, scallions, garlic, pepper, and cumin.

2. Prepare a charcoal fire by heating coals until they reach medium heat and are covered in a light gray ash, about 20 minutes. Set the grill rack about 5 inches over the coals.

3. Divide the meat mixture into 8 equal portions. Shape each portion around a flat or two-pronged skewer into 1½-inch-thick ovals about 4 to 6 inches long. Brush with the oil. Or divide the meat mixture into 16 or 24 portions and shape each portion into a 2-inch oval, using 2 to 3 ovals per skewer.

4. Grill or broil the kebabs, turning occasionally, until browned on all sides, about 15 minutes.

KEFIR

Kefir is a fermented, effervescent milk product produced from a complex mixture of bacteria and yeast.

The first kefir was produced by letting milk sour naturally, resulting in the generation of carbon dioxide, alcohol, and the aromatic compounds that set kefir apart from other cultured milk products. The various microorganisms and casein are symbiotically grown together in colonies called grains. This makes kefir unique, as no other milk culture forms grains. These grains contain the bacteria and yeast mixture clumped together with casein (milk proteins) and complex sugars. They look like pieces of coral or small clumps of cauliflower and range from the size of a kernel of wheat to that of a hazelnut. The grains ferment the milk, incorporating their friendly organisms to create the cultured product. The grains are typically left in the milk for six hours to a day. Before kefir is drunk, the grains are removed with a strainer—never a metal one, which can kill them—and they are added to a new batch of milk.

To make kefir, the Caucasians historically placed milk and some kefir grains in a sack made from animal hide and usually hung it near the door, so that anyone entering, or leaving, the house would remember to prod the sack to mix the contents. As the kefir was removed from its container, fresh milk was added, and so the process of kefir making continued. If left for too long, the kefir turned too lumpy and sour. Kefir grains were regarded as part of the family's assets and passed on from one generation to the next.

Kefir has a refreshing, mild, slightly tart flavor reminiscent of buttermilk; the flavor varies according to the type of milk used, the grains, and the incubation period. Because the curd size of kefir is smaller than that of yogurt, it is easier to digest. Kefir is a thin, drinkable product, and is not congealed like yogurt. In America, kefir is commonly flavored with sugar and fruit in a manner similar to yogurt. In Azerbayan, kefir is used along with fresh greens to make a favorite soup called *dovga*.

The massive Russian migration to Israel following the end of the Soviet Union led to the popularization of kefir in Israel. Ready-cultured kefir is now found in many stores, but quite a few Russian and Caucasian Jews make their own kefir at home. A number of Israelis even readily give away free kefir grains, encouraging recipients to share the grains with others, as kefir's popularity continues to grow in the country.

KEFTAJI

Keftaji is a stew of fresh vegetables in a tomato sauce, typically with a fried egg on top.
Origin: Tunisia

Keftaji, a Tunisian comfort food, reflects definite Ottoman and Sephardic influences. The vegetables are cooked separately, then married with a tomato sauce. The last Sephardic touch is a sunny-side-up fried egg. In Tunisia, *keftaji* is served as a main course, making use of high-quality homegrown produce. The mixture is also spooned over a Tunisian sausage called *merguez*, and over meatballs called *kefta*, which may be the source of its name. *Keftaji* is typically served with bread.

❦ TUNISIAN SAUTÉED VEGETABLES (*KEFTAJI*)

4 SERVINGS [DAIRY OR PAREVE]

Tomato Sauce:

½ cup water

3 tablespoons tomato paste

½ teaspoon ground coriander or cumin

About ½ teaspoon table salt or 1 teaspoon kosher salt

About ¼ teaspoon ground black pepper

1 tablespoon red wine vinegar

About 1½ teaspoons harissa (Northwest African Chili Paste, page 260; optional)

Vegetables:

1 pound (5 small) potatoes, cut into ¼-inch-thick slices

Salt

5 tablespoons olive or vegetable oil

1 large red or yellow onion, halved and sliced

1 pound (3 medium) zucchini, sliced

10 ounces (2 medium) red or green bell peppers, seeded and sliced

Fried Eggs:

4 large eggs

1 tablespoon unsalted butter or margarine

2 teaspoons water

Pinch of salt

1. To make the tomato sauce: In a medium saucepan, combine the water, tomato paste, coriander, salt, and pepper. Simmer, stirring occasionally, until slightly thickened, about 10 minutes. Remove from the heat and stir in the vinegar and, for a more fiery dish, the optional harissa.

2. To make the vegetables: Place the potatoes in a large saucepan and add water to cover. Add 1¼ teaspoons salt for every quart of water. Bring to a boil, cover, reduce the heat to medium-low, and cook gently until tender but not mushy, about 20 minutes. Drain.

3. In a large skillet, heat 3 tablespoons oil over medium heat. Add the onion and sauté until soft and

translucent, 5 to 10 minutes. Transfer the onion to a heated bowl and keep warm.

4. Add the remaining 2 tablespoons oil to the skillet, then add the zucchini and sauté until tender, about 4 minutes. Remove the zucchini and add to the onion.

5. Add the bell peppers to the skillet and sauté until tender, about 5 minutes. Remove the peppers and add to the zucchini and onion.

6. Add the potatoes to the skillet and cook, stirring occasionally, until lightly golden, about 8 minutes. Combine the potatoes with the zucchini, bell peppers, and onion; pour the tomato sauce over the top, and toss to coat. Keep warm.

7. To make the fried eggs: Crack the eggs into a small bowl. Heat a large skillet over low heat, about 5 minutes. Add the butter and wait until the foam subsides, about 1 minute, then swirl to coat the skillet. Gently slide the eggs into the pan. Drizzle the water around the outside edges of the eggs. Sprinkle with the salt. Cover and cook until the whites are set, about 2½ minutes for runny yolks, and 3½ minutes for firm yolks.

8. Serve immediately, topping each serving of vegetable stew with a fried egg.

KEFTE

Kefte is a fried patty made from ground meat, chicken, fish, or vegetables, and sometimes simmered in a sauce.

Origin: Turkey

Other names: Balkans: *kiofte*; Greek: *keftede*, *keftike*; Hebrew: *kefeftah*; Romanian: *chiftele*, *kiftaln*.

Before the expulsion from Spain, Sephardim commonly prepared ground meat in the form of *albondigas* (meatballs) and *rollos* (meat loaves). Upon arriving in the Ottoman Empire, they adapted the concept and name of the Middle Eastern *kufta* (meatballs and patties), but added their own special touches, resulting in *keftes*. Typical of Sephardic cuisine, they can be all meat (*keftes de carne*) or, more frequently, favorite vegetables are commonly mixed with the meat. The patties can also consist entirely of vegetables, such as spinach (*keftes de espinaca*) and leeks (*keftes de prasa*). Ground poultry (*keftes de gallina*) or fish (*keftes de peshkado*) is also frequently substituted for the meat. Unlike round meatballs, the ingredients for *keftes* are formed into small, oval patties with tapered ends—they are essentially oval burgers or flattened meatballs. *Kefte kebabs* are ground meat on a skewer.

Keftes are often a tasty excuse to use up leftovers, such as cooked fish or mashed potatoes (*keftes de patata*). These patties, after browning, are frequently simmered in a lemon or tomato sauce, a practical way of preparing *keftes* well in advance, then rewarming them to serve. They are also dished up straight with lemon wedges or *techina* (sesame seed sauce) or as a sandwich in pita bread.

Sephardim serve *keftes* as an appetizer, side dish, or main course as both weekday fare and holiday food. *Keftes*, being fried, make an ideal Hanukkah food. Leek or spinach *keftes*, making use of seasonal produce, are traditional on Rosh Hashanah and Passover.

(See also Kebab and Kufta)

SEPHARDIC LEEK PATTIES (*KEFTES DE PRASA*)

ABOUT 16 PATTIES   [PAREVE OR MEAT]

2 pounds (6 medium) leeks (white and light green parts only), halved lengthwise, thinly sliced and rinsed

1 cup mashed potatoes, 1 pound ground lamb, or ⅓ cup ground walnuts

About ½ cup matza cake meal or bread crumbs

2 large eggs, lightly beaten

1 tablespoon olive or vegetable oil

2 to 4 cloves garlic, mashed

About 1 teaspoon salt

About ½ teaspoon ground black pepper

¼ to ½ teaspoon ground nutmeg, chili flakes, or cayenne (optional)

About 2 cups olive or vegetable oil for frying

Lemon wedges (optional)

1. Bring a large pot of lightly salted water to a boil. Add the leeks, cover, reduce the heat to low, and simmer until very tender, about 20 minutes. Drain and let cool. Squeeze out the excess liquid.

2. In a large bowl, combine the leeks, potatoes, and matza meal. Add the eggs, 1 tablespoon oil, garlic, salt, pepper, and, if using, nutmeg. If the mixture is too soft to form into patties, add a little more matza meal or form the loose mixture into clumps and dredge them in matza meal or bread crumbs and flatten. For each patty, shape about ⅓ cup leek mixture into an oval 2½ inches long, 1 inch-wide, and ½ inch thick, with tapered ends.

3. In a large skillet, heat about ½ inch oil over medium-high heat. In batches, fry the patties, turning once, until golden brown on both sides, about

3 minutes per side. Drain on paper towels. Serve hot or at room temperature, accompanied, if desired, with the lemon wedges.

KESKASUNE

Keskasune is a couscous-shaped pasta.

Origin: Syria

Other names: *keskasoon*, pearl pasta.

The Turks and Arabs never developed the art of pasta shaping or saucing of the Italians. Their pasta generally came in only a few basic shapes, including the Syrian *keskasune* (from couscous), which is the equivalent of acini de pepe, the Italian pasta whose name means "peppercorn," connoting the shape of the small pasta pellets. Syrians serve pasta without a sauce; it is generally simply flavored with a little salt and maybe pepper or mixed with cheese, a vegetable, or meat. Browning the pasta pellets in oil before cooking helps to keep them firm and separate.

Keskasune with chickpeas is one of the most ancient of Middle Eastern pasta dishes, combining pasta pellets with the area's favorite legume—chickpeas. The result is filling, hearty fare that provides complementary nutrition. It is a traditional Rosh Hashanah dish, the round pasta and chickpeas representing life, fertility, and prosperity. A version topped with cheese, usually accompanied with yogurt, is popular for Thursday night dinner as well as for Saturday night dinner after the Sabbath, both of which are typically dairy meals.

KHACHAPURI

Khachapuri is a savory filled bread or pastry.

Origin: Georgia

The Persians, arriving from the East, introduced to Georgia various flatbreads as well as their clay oven (akin to the Indian tandoor) called a *tone*. For centuries, a favorite Georgian treat was to take plain flatbread (*puri*) hot from the oven and wrap it around a chunk of cheese, the combination of fresh bread and melting cheese proving irresistible. At some point, an inspired cook took this union a step further, baking the cheese inside the bread, thereby producing the Georgian national dish, *khachapuri* (*khacho* is a word for fresh cheese). Originally, *khachapuri* were baked on the inner walls of a *tone* or in an earthenware dish called a *ketsi* placed over coals in a fireplace. With the advent of the flat-bottomed oven, an array of thicker, larger, and more sophisticated versions developed.

The Georgian feast bread or pastry, khachapuri *comes in several varieties—here, the square, layered* achma. *It is usally filled with cheese, but for meat meals, a bean or potato filling is substituted.*

Various regions of the country also created different *khachapuri* pastries. There are now nearly a dozen different types, including round with cheese inside (*imeruli*), rectangular or square with layers (*achma*), diamond shaped with an egg floating in the center (*acharuli*), and even a version resembling a small pizza. The original *khachapuri* were made from bread dough, but other doughs, such as phyllo, puff pastry, and flaky pastry, were adapted to this dish.

The combination of Georgian cheeses most commonly used in khachapuri is *suluguni* (a slightly tangy string cheese, similar to mozzarella), *imeruli* (a slightly sour fresh cheese), and *bryndza* (similar to mild feta; it needs to be soaked in water first). Georgian Jews, unable to eat cheese breads at meat meals, introduced bean (*lobiani*) and potato (*kartopiliani*) fillings, which were adopted by their non-Jewish neighbors, although cheese remains the favorite *khachapuri* filling.

Today, *khachapuri* are sold at special cafés throughout Georgia and proficient home cooks prepare their own pastries for special occasions. No Georgian *supra* (feast) would be considered complete without *khachapuri*; smaller ones are perfect for hors d'oeuvres, larger ones for dinner. *Khachapuri* is typically served with local Georgian wine, which at feasts is traditionally offered in a horn rather than a glass—the horn cannot be set on a table and therefore must be drunk.

(See also Mchadi and Puri)

„ GEORGIAN CHEESE BREAD (*IMERULI KHACHAPURI*)

4 TO 6 SERVINGS   [DAIRY]

Pastry:

½ cup plain yogurt
1 tablespoon sunflower or vegetable oil
½ teaspoon baking soda
⅛ teaspoon salt
1 cup (5 ounces) all-purpose flour

Filling:

5 ounces (1¼ cups) mozzarella, Gruyère, or Havarti cheese, grated
4 ounces (¾ cup) mild feta cheese, crumbled
3 ounces (6 tablespoons) farmer or pot cheese
2 tablespoons unsalted butter, softened
½ large egg, lightly beaten
About ⅛ teaspoon table salt or ¼ teaspoon kosher salt
Egg wash (½ large egg beaten with ½ teaspoon water)

1. To make the pastry: In a medium bowl, combine the yogurt, oil, baking soda, and salt. Stir in the flour, then knead until smooth, adding more flour if the dough is too sticky, 5 to 8 minutes. Cover and let stand for about 30 minutes.

2. Preheat the oven to 400°F. Line a large baking sheet with parchment paper or lightly grease the sheet.

3. To make the filling: Combine all the filling ingredients.

4. On a lightly floured surface, roll out the dough into a 13-inch round, ¼ inch thick. Spread the filling over the dough, leaving a 2-inch border all around. Gather the edges together to meet in the center, then press down to expel any air. Pinch the edges to seal. Place, seam side down, on the prepared baking sheet. Brush with the egg wash and poke a hole in the center to vent the steam.

5. Bake for 5 minutes. Reduce the heat to 350°F and bake until golden brown, about 20 minutes. Cut into wedges and serve warm.

KHALIA

Khalia is a beef soup and sauce with a tart and spicy flavor.

Origin: Georgia

Meat soups and stews constitute a major component of Georgian cuisine, including *kaurma* (spicy lamb), *chanahi* (lamb and eggplant cooked in pottery), *kharcho* (meat soup), and *khalia* (spicy beef). *Khalia,* inspired by the Persian palate, is prepared both as a thick sauce and as a soup. Its tartness comes from sour plums, tamarind, or pomegranates. *Khalia* with pomegranates is popular Rosh Hashanah fare. Some versions are thickened with ground walnuts.

GEORGIAN BEEF SOUP WITH POMEGRANATE (*KHALIA*)

5 TO 6 SERVINGS   [MEAT]

2½ pounds beef chuck, brisket, or flanken, cut into 1-inch cubes

¼ cup sunflower or vegetable oil

3 medium yellow onions, chopped

1 red bell pepper or Italian frying pepper, seeded and chopped

3 to 4 cloves garlic, minced

2 teaspoons ground coriander

1 teaspoon hot or sweet paprika

½ teaspoon dried oregano or 1 teaspoon dried tarragon

½ teaspoon ground fenugreek

2 tablespoons tomato paste

8 cups water, or 4 cups beef broth and 4 cups water

2 bay leaves

About 1½ teaspoons table salt or 1 tablespoon kosher salt

About ½ teaspoon ground black pepper

½ cup pomegranate juice

Pinch of sugar or honey, or to taste

Seeds of 1 pomegranate

½ cup chopped fresh cilantro (optional)

½ cup chopped fresh flat-leaf parsley (optional)

1. Pat the beef dry with paper towels. In a large pot, heat 2 tablespoons oil over medium-high heat. In several batches, add the beef and brown on all sides, 5 to 8 minutes per batch. Do not overcrowd the pan. Remove the beef.

2. Reduce the heat to medium and add the remaining 2 tablespoons oil. Add the onions and sauté until soft and translucent, 10 to 15 minutes. Add the bell pepper, garlic, coriander, paprika, oregano, and fenugreek and stir for 1 minute. Add the tomato paste and stir until it darkens, 2 to 3 minutes.

3. Add the water and stir to release any browned particles from the bottom. Return the beef and add the bay leaves, salt, and pepper. Bring to a boil, reduce the heat to low, and simmer, occasionally skimming the scum from the surface, until the meat is tender, about 1½ hours for chuck, or about 2 hours for brisket or flanken.

4. Add the pomegranate juice and sugar and simmer for 15 minutes. The soup may be prepared up to this point, cooled, covered, refrigerated for up to 3 days, and reheated before serving.

5. Add the pomegranate seeds and, if using, cilantro and/or parsley, and simmer for 10 minutes.

KHARCHO

Kharcho is a rustic meat soup.

Origin: Georgia

The Georgian word *kharch*, from the verb *kharen* (to eat), encompasses nearly all articles of food, especially meat, but excluding bread. Thus *kharchevnia* is a place for eating (e.g. a restaurant) and *kharcho* a much-loved meat soup. *Kharcho* is to Georgia what borscht is across the Black Sea in Ukraine, the favorite soup and a mainstay of the diet.

Considered to be reinvigorating, *kharcho* is served to someone after an arduous undertaking as well as at celebrations. Typical of Georgian cuisine, *kharcho* is tangy and slightly spicy, with a pronounced fresh-herb flavor, although each region of the country has a different variation of seasonings. Beef is the predominant meat for this soup—the version with beef is technically called *dzrokhie kharcho*—but lamb is occasionally used (*myasnoya kharcho*). Some cooks add a little ground walnuts as a thickener, while others insist the soup should be light and delicate. Although Georgians generally use *tklapi tkhlopi* (sour plum leather—dried sheets of sour plum puree) as the souring agent, the more readily available tamarind concentrate or lemon juice may be substituted.

GEORGIAN BEEF SOUP (*KHARCHO*)

6 TO 8 SERVINGS   [MEAT]

2 pounds beef or veal marrow bones, cut into 2-inch pieces

9 cups cold water

1½ pounds beef brisket or flanken or 3½ pounds beef short ribs, cut into 1-inch pieces

3 tablespoons sunflower or vegetable oil

2 large yellow onions, chopped

3 to 4 cloves garlic, mashed

3 tablespoons tomato paste

2 cups (16 ounces) seeded and chopped tomatoes

¾ cup long-grain rice

1 sheet *tkhlopi* (sour plum leather), 3 tablespoons *tkemali* (plum sauce), 1 tablespoon tamarind concentrate, or ¼ cup fresh lemon juice

1 whole fresh small hot chili or ½ to ¾ teaspoon red chili flakes

1 to 2 teaspoons ground coriander

½ teaspoon paprika

¼ teaspoon ground fenugreek

2 bay leaves

About 1 teaspoon table salt or 2 teaspoons kosher salt

Ground black pepper to taste

¼ to ½ cup ground walnuts (optional)

¼ cup chopped fresh cilantro, plus additional for garnish

¼ cup chopped fresh flat-leaf parsley, plus additional for garnish

¼ cup chopped fresh dill or basil, plus additional for garnish

1. In a large pot, bring the bones and water to a boil, reduce the heat to low, and simmer, occasionally skimming the scum from the surface, for 4 hours. Discard the bones.

2. Add the beef pieces and simmer until nearly tender, about 2 hours.

3. In a large skillet, heat the oil over medium heat. Add the onions and sauté until golden, about 15 minutes. Stir in the garlic, then the tomato paste, and sauté until the paste begins to darken, 2 to 3 minutes.

4. Stir the onion mixture into the soup. Add the tomatoes and rice, cover, and simmer for 15 minutes.

5. Add the *tkhlopi*, chili, coriander, paprika, fenugreek, bay leaves, salt, pepper, and, if using, walnuts. Simmer, uncovered, until the rice is nearly tender, about 18 minutes.

6. Add the cilantro, parsley, and dill and simmer for 5 minutes. Ladle into serving bowls and garnish with additional chopped fresh herbs. Serve with *deda puri* (Georgian flatbread) or pita bread.

KHOBZ

Khobz is the Arabic word for bread. The standard *khobz* is a round, somewhat flat, slightly coarse and dense, and rather plain loaf.

Origin: Middle East

Other names: Arabic: *khobez, khubz*; Berber: *kisra, ksra.*

In Morocco, bread is a staple, served at every meal. Those who work away from home typically take a loaf with them for lunch. Moroccans by and large disparage those who buy bread and insist on home-made; these breads are generally prepared on a daily basis, sometimes twice a day. *Khobz el-dâr* (bread of the house) is typically leavened with a starter dough and kneaded in a *gsaa* (massive unglazed earthen-ware bowl) or a bowl carved from wood. Although the French introduced the baguette to the Maghreb, most people favor the standard *khobz*. Many Moroc-cans find pure white bread too bland and fluffy and, instead, prefer partially whole wheat loaves or partially semolina loaves (*khobz dyal smida*). The larger the proportion of semolina flour, the yellower the color and the chewier the texture. For variety and special occasions, the breads are flavored with anise seeds.

The shape of *khobz* produces plenty of crust, which is handy for dipping and scooping. Pieces of the absorbent bread are torn off and dipped into tagines or salads or used to transport a piece of stew to the mouth. For breakfast, *khobz* is sometimes served with *amalou*, a spread made by browning ground almonds in a little oil, then pounding them with honey until smooth.

In the past, most Moroccan kitchens contained only a *kanoun* (an earthenware brazier) on which to cook. As a result, there were generally two types of bread. For *khobz al-tajin*, the dough was pressed into very thin loaves and cooked on a *mikla* (earthenware

Moroccan Jews use their thick, round everyday breads for Sabbath and holidays, too, although seasonings like anise seeds may be added.

griddle) set over the *kanoun*, and turned to brown on both sides. For thicker breads, generally about an inch thick in the center, the loaves were prepared and left to rise at home, then sent to the communal oven for baking, each family's bread identified by a special stamp. Even today, a number of commercial Moroccan bakeries do not sell bread, but rather sell space in their wood-fired ovens for homemade loaves.

Historically, Moroccans did not prepare special or enriched loaves for the Sabbath and festivals, but rather used their everyday *khobz*, although usually flavored with anise seeds for the occasion (*pain de Shabbat*). A pattern is sometimes made in the bread by pricking the risen loaf around the outside at three-quarter-inch intervals. A thicker, anise-flavored loaf is traditional on Rosh Hashanah—the rounded shape representing the cycle of the year. Almonds and rose water are sometimes added for Shavuot and Sukkot.

(See also Bread and Pita)

MOROCCAN ANISE BREAD (*KHOBZ*)

2 MEDIUM LOAVES [PAREVE]

1 package (2¼ teaspoons) active dry yeast or
   1 (0.6-ounce) cake fresh yeast
1½ cups warm water (105°F to 115°F for dry yeast;
   80°F to 85°F for fresh yeast)
1 teaspoon sugar or honey
1 tablespoon anise seeds, crushed
½ teaspoon caraway seeds (optional)
2 teaspoons table salt or 4 teaspoons kosher salt
1 to 3 tablespoons vegetable oil (optional)
About 4 cups (20 ounces) bread or unbleached
   all-purpose flour; or 3 cups unbleached all-
   purpose flour and 1 cup whole-wheat flour or
   fine semolina; or 2 cups whole-wheat flour,
   ½ cup fine semolina, and about 1 cup
   unbleached all-purpose flour
Cornmeal or semolina for dusting
1 large egg white, lightly beaten
3 tablespoons sesame seeds (optional)

1. Dissolve the yeast in ¼ cup water. Stir in the sugar and let stand until foamy, 5 to 10 minutes. In a large bowl, combine the yeast mixture, remaining water, anise, optional caraway, salt, optional oil, and 2 cups flour. Gradually add enough of the remaining flour to make a mixture that holds together.

2. On a lightly floured surface, knead the dough until smooth and elastic, 10 to 15 minutes. Place in

an oiled bowl and turn to coat. Cover loosely with plastic wrap or a kitchen towel and let rise in a warm, draft-free place until doubled in bulk, about 2 hours.

3. Punch down the dough, knead briefly, divide in half, and shape each piece into a ball. Cover and let rest for at least 15 minutes.

4. Sprinkle a large baking sheet with cornmeal, or line the sheet with parchment paper. Shape each dough ball into a flat 6-inch round and place on the prepared sheet. Cover and let rise until almost doubled in bulk, about 1½ hours.

5. Preheat the oven to 375°F.

6. With the tines of a fork or a toothpick, prick the dough around the sides at ¾-inch intervals. Brush with the egg white and, if using, sprinkle with the sesame seeds.

7. Bake for 15 minutes. Reduce the heat to 300°F and bake until golden brown and hollow sounding when tapped on the bottom, about 30 minutes. Transfer the loaves to a wire rack and let cool.

KHEER

Kheer is a creamy cardamom-flavored rice pudding.
Origin: India
Other names: Southern India: *payasam*.

Kheer, from the Sanskrit word *ksheer* (milk), is a rice pudding from northern India. Records of *kheer* date back at least two thousand years. Milk is actually the predominant element, and instead of rice, some versions are made with barley and semolina. A version made with coconut milk, common in the south, is prepared for kosher meat meals. Neither eggs nor additional starch are added. Instead, the pudding is thickened by cooking the rice or other grain until it breaks down to a creamy consistency of a porridge. The preferred rice is basmati (literally "queen of fragrance"), which is aromatic and flavorful.

Kheer is a favorite treat among the Bene Israel of Mumbai, who commonly serve it at special occasions and to break a fast.

INDIAN RICE PUDDING (*KHEER*)

5 TO 6 SERVINGS [DAIRY]

3 quarts milk
½ cup basmati rice or other long- or medium-grain
   rice
3 to 5 green cardamom pods, bruised, or ¼ to
   1 teaspoon ground cardamom

½ to ¾ cup jaggery or sugar

Pinch of salt

½ cup raisins (optional)

About ¼ teaspoon saffron strands (optional)

1 teaspoon vanilla extract or 2 to 3 teaspoons rose
water

½ cup chopped almonds and/or pistachios for
garnish

1. In a large, heavy saucepan, bring the milk to a low
boil over medium heat. Add the rice and cardamom,
reduce the heat to medium-low, and cook, uncovered,
stirring frequently to prevent sticking, until reduced
by about half and thickened, about 1¼ hours. If using
cardamom pods, remove them.

2. Add the sugar, salt, and, if using, raisins and/
or saffron. Cook, stirring constantly, until the sugar
dissolves and the flavors meld, about 10 minutes.
Remove from the heat and stir in the vanilla. Serve
warm or chilled. Cover with a piece of plastic wrap to
prevent a skin from forming. Garnish with the nuts.

KHENAGHI

These dumplings—incorporating the Georgian favorite,
walnuts—are popular Passover fare. They are served
warm in chicken or lamb soup, or cool with a pomegranate sauce (*narsharab*) or walnut sauce (*bazha*).

❧ GEORGIAN WALNUT MATZA BALLS (*KHENAGHI*)

ABOUT 18 DUMPLINGS [PAREVE]

2 cups finely ground walnuts

½ cup matza meal

4 large eggs, lightly beaten

½ cup minced yellow onion

2 tablespoons chopped fresh oregano or flat-leaf
parsley

About 1 teaspoon salt

Ground black pepper to taste

2 large egg whites

1. In a large bowl, combine the walnuts, matza meal,
eggs, onion, oregano, salt, and pepper. In a medium
bowl, beat the egg whites until stiff but not dry and
fold into the walnut mixture.

2. Bring a large pot of lightly salted water to a boil.
Using moistened hands, shape the batter into 1½-inch
balls. Drop the khenaghi into the boiling water and
cook until tender, about 15 minutes. Remove with a
slotted spoon. Serve hot or cold with a savory sauce or
in chicken soup.

KHORESH

Khoresh is a sauce-stew of meat and seasonings that
is slow-cooked.

Origin: Persia

Other names: *horisht, khoresht.*

Before the advent of refrigeration, inspired cooks
had to find ways to preserve foods. In Persia, meat
was cut into one-inch cubes and sautéed in fat with
favorite spices. These meat cubes, called *gheimeh*,
were then stored in crocks in a cool place and, when
needed, cooked in a small amount of water to produce a sauce-stew known as *khoresh* (derived from
the Persian word *khordan*, "to eat"). The basic meat is
usually stretched and complemented with the addition of seasonal produce, fruit, and herbs to create
a vast array of stews that serve as regular fare. Jews,
unlike Muslims, do not use butter in their stews.
The combination of *khoresh* over *chelow* (rice), called
chelow khoresh, constitutes the essence of Persian
cuisine.

Today, *khoresh* is generally made fresh and not
from stored cooked meat, but the process and seasonings remain the same. Versions are also made
with chicken and fish, but those are usually reserved
for special occasions. The meat is simmered for an
extended time over low heat to build and meld the
flavors and tenderize the meat. These sauces, reflecting the Persian tradition of balancing hot and cold,
tend toward the tart side, are subtly spiced, and frequently contain fresh herbs. Tartness is typically produced by adding ground dried limes. Two of the most
popular dishes are *khoresh-e sabzi* (with fresh herbs)
and *khoresh-e geimeh lapeh* (with split peas); often
served for the Sabbath holidays, and other special
occasions. Khoresh-e bay (with quince) is served for
Rosh Hashanah. Spring variations typically contain
spinach, eggplant, cardoon, celery, or rhubarb; fresh
cherries, plums, peaches, tangerines, and okra are
popular during the summer. Autumn versions feature
apples, pomegranates, quinces, and pumpkins; dried
fruits replace fresh ones during the winter.

(See also Chelow and Fesenjan)

❧ PERSIAN MEAT SAUCE-STEW (KHORESH)

3 TO 4 SERVINGS [MEAT]

2 tablespoons vegetable oil

1 pound boneless lamb shoulder or beef chuck, cut
into 1-inch cubes

1 leek (white part only) or 1 large yellow onion, thinly sliced

½ teaspoon ground cinnamon or ¼ teaspoon ground cloves

½ teaspoon ground turmeric

¼ teaspoon ground nutmeg

About 2 cups water

2 to 3 tablespoons fresh lime or lemon juice, or 1 tablespoon dried lime powder (*limuomani*; see Citrus)

About ¾ teaspoon table salt or 1½ teaspoons kosher salt

About ¼ teaspoon ground black pepper

1. In a large, heavy pot, heat the oil over medium heat. Add the meat, leek, cinnamon, turmeric, and nutmeg and sauté until the meat is browned, about 10 minutes.

2. Add the water, lime juice, salt, and pepper. Bring to a boil, reduce the heat to low, and simmer—adding a little more water if too much liquid evaporates—until the meat is tender and the sauce is thick, about 2 hours. The *khoresh* can be prepared 1 or 2 days ahead and reheated. Serve with rice.

VARIATIONS

Persian Beef Stew with Herbs (Khoresh-e Sabzi):
With the water, add 1 pound finely chopped fresh spinach or 20 ounces frozen spinach, 1 cup finely chopped fresh flat-leaf parsley (or ½ cup parsley and ½ cup cilantro), and ½ cup chopped scallions.

Persian Beef and Quince Stew (Khoresh-e Bay):
With the water, add 1 tablespoon sugar. After simmering the stew for 1 hour, add ⅓ cup yellow split peas and simmer for 15 minutes. Meanwhile, in a large skillet, heat 2 tablespoons oil over medium heat; add 2 large peeled, cored, and sliced quinces; and sauté for 2 to 3 minutes. Add to the stew, cover, and cook for another 15 minutes.

KIBBEH

Kibbeh refers to a variety of highly-seasoned pounded meat and bulgur dishes. The most widespread form of *kibbeh* is a fried torpedo-shaped croquette encased in a thin starchy shell.

Origin: Near East

Other names: Arabic: *kibbe, kibbi*; Iraq: *kubba, kubbeh*; Turkey: *içli köfte*.

Among the recipes in the Roman cookbook by Apicius (c. 400 CE) are stuffed ground meat patties, revealing that the concept of cooking small orbs of forcemeat goes back at least two millennia. Later, meatballs emerged as a prominent part of medieval Persian and Arabic cuisine. In the Near East, people began pounding pieces of lamb with bulgur to make a smooth mixture that they called *kibbeh*, from the Arabic "form into a ball."

In the Levant, *kibbeh* encompasses a variety of ground meat dishes, including basic free-form meatballs (also called *aqras lahm* and *kefte*); *kibbeh nayeh* (raw lamb or beef mixed with bulgur wheat); *kibbeh bi seniyeh* (the meat and bulgur mixture baked in a pan); *shurbat al kibbeh* (small meatballs cooked in a soup); and the most popular form, *kibbeh mahshi*, also called *kibbeh nabelsieh* and *aqras kibbeh* (stuffed torpedo-shaped meat in a thin starchy shell). The city of Aleppo claims sixty different variations of *kibbeh*.

Kibbeh nayeh is the national appetizer of Syria and Lebanon. The dish originated among medieval peasants as a way to stretch limited resources, but eventually became popular among all levels of society. The texture of the raw meat and bulgur is completely smooth; none of its ingredients are individually identifiable by taste or sight. Consequently, before the food processor, preparing *kibbeh nayeh* was a very time-consuming, strenuous process of repeatedly pounding the ingredients in a mortar. It is usually flavored with a little fresh mint or basil. Since *kibbeh nayeh* is eaten very fresh, it is a traditional dish only on Friday night or other celebrations, never for Sabbath lunch. It is served with fresh tomatoes, chilies, and scallions or onion wedges and frequently accompanied with *arak* (anise liqueur). Syrians also enjoy a vegetarian version (*kibbeh nayeh w'khodrawat*) made from red lentils, tomatoes, and bulgur.

Seniyeh, or *siniyya*, is a round, flat-bottomed, copper or brass Arabic tray, which was typically set on a low stool to act as a table. The tray was also occasionally spread with pounded meat and used for baking. *Kibbeh bil seniyeh*, also known as *kefte bil seniyeh*, in essence "baked *kibbeh*," developed as an easier way to prepare *kibbeh* without all the individual shaping and frying. Although it can be baked plain, the meat mixture is usually sandwiched between bulgur or mashed potatoes to make the Middle Eastern equivalent of shepherd's pie. Casseroles with a potato topping are common Mizrachi Passover dishes.

For millennia, the time before any special occasion in the Levant was preceded by the measured thumping of a pestle (*madaqqa*) repeatedly hitting a mortar (*jurn*), as the *kibbeh* ingredients were pounded into a smooth paste. Today, a food processor makes the task immeasurably easier. In the Middle East, various forms of *kibbeh* became popular Sabbath and holiday dishes.

(See also Kebab, Kibbeh Mahshi, Kubbeh, and Kufta)

KIBBEH MAHSHI

Kibbeh mahshi is a deep-fried torpedo-shaped ground meat croquette with a starchy outer shell (typically made of bulgur, semolina, or rice).

Origin: Levant

Other names: Azeri: *kiufta*; Egypt: *kobeba, kubeba*; India: *kooba, kubba*; Iraq: *kubat halab, kubba, kubbeh*; Israel: *kubbeh*; Lebanon: *aqras kibbeh, kibbeh qrass*; Syria: *kibbeh nabilseeyah, kibbeh nabulsieh*; Turkey: *kofte*; Yemen: *kubi*.

Encasing a filling in a thin shell and deep-frying it is an old Arabic culinary technique. The cookbook *Kitab al-Tabikh* (Baghdad, 1226) included a recipe for "*Aqras Mukarrara*," consisting of a ball of almond paste dipped into a thin batter and fried in sesame oil. Centuries later, the term *aqras kibbeh* was applied to a ball of spicy ground meat encased in a thin shell of semolina, bulgur, or rice, typically shaped into a torpedo, and either fried or grilled. If the torpedoes are fried in a skillet, they are called *kibbeh bi ma'ala* (in the frying pan); when grilled, they are *kibbeh mashwiyya*; and when deep-fried, they are *kibbeh maqliyya*. In Aleppo, these torpedoes were called *kibbeh nabelsieh*, from the town of Nablus. They are also widely known simply as *kibbeh*.

When deep-fried, these *kibbeh* develop a crispy, firm exterior and a moist, flavorful center. The shells and seasonings vary from place to place; bulgur is the most common casing in the Levant and semolina in Iraq. The bulgur casing is made with just the grain, resulting in a crunchier texture, or mashed with meat in the manner of *kibbeh nayeh* (raw kibbeh). There is even a Passover version using matza meal. Lamb, from the leg or shoulder, is the preferred meat. Toasted pine nuts, chopped walnuts, chopped pistachio nuts, or pomegranate seeds are frequently mixed in with the meat. The spice blend varies from place to place: Syrians generally add allspice, cinnamon, cumin, and black pepper, while Lebanese favor sumac, nutmeg,

and pomegranate molasses. The presence of tamarind paste in the filling is characteristic of Jewish *kibbeh*. Lebanese near the coast and Iraqis make a fish adaptation (*samakeyah*) and there are even vegetarian versions filled with mashed potatoes or lentils.

Today, in every Israeli supermarket, *kibbeh mahshi* can be found frozen. However, most Syrians consider these store-bought versions far inferior to the homemade torpedoes. Women in the Levant are typically trained in cooking for many years by their mothers and grandmothers, and the measure of their culinary skills is the quality of their *kibbeh mahshi*. The secret to any *kibbeh* is making an evenly thin shell and a cylindrical shape. Fillings must be completely enclosed in crust or the torpedoes will explode in the hot oil. More recently, a special attachment for an electric mixer was developed for making the *kibbeh* shell.

Kibbeh mahshi are rather time-consuming, even for experienced cooks, and are therefore reserved for special occasions. A very experienced cook working quickly can form a torpedo in one minute. Special *kibbeh* makers earn a nice livelihood by preparing large homemade batches of these cylinders and shipping them, sometimes internationally, to grateful patrons. Plain fried *kibbeh* are commonly served as part of a *mezze* (appetizer assortment), at a *sebit* (Syrian kiddush), and at most celebrations, accompanied with tahini sauce or lemon wedges. The fried torpedoes are also cooked as an entrée with various vegetables or fruits, including apricots, artichokes, cherries, eggplant, peas, potatoes, and quince. They are also served with *hamud* (Syrian sour mint sauce) as *kibbeh hamuda* and in soup as *kibbeh yekhniye*. Fried *kibbeh* became traditional Hanukkah fare.

(See also Kebab, Kibbeh, and Kubbeh)

SYRIAN STUFFED TORPEDOES (*KIBBEH MAHSHI*)

ABOUT 12 BALLS [MEAT]

Kibbeh Bulgur Shells:

1½ cups (9 ounces) fine-grain bulgur (do not use any other type)

4½ cups cold water

1 small yellow onion, minced (½ cup)

¾ cup (3.75 ounces) unbleached all-purpose or whole-wheat flour

About 1¼ teaspoons salt

About ½ teaspoon ground black pepper or ¾ teaspoon paprika

Meat Filling (*Tadbileh*):

2 tablespoons vegetable oil

1 small yellow onion, minced (½ cup)

8 ounces ground lamb or beef chuck, or 4 ounces ground beef and 4 ounces ground chicken breast

About ½ teaspoon *baharat* (Lebanese Spice Mixture, page 37) or ¼ teaspoon allspice and ¼ teaspoon ground cinnamon or ground cumin

About ½ teaspoon salt

About ¼ teaspoon ground black pepper

1 teaspoon pomegranate molasses (*dibs al-rumman*) or tamarind concentrate (optional)

3 to 4 tablespoons chopped fresh flat-leaf parsley (optional)

3 tablespoons lightly toasted pine nuts, chopped walnuts, or chopped pistachio nuts; or ½ cup pomegranate seeds (optional)

Vegetable oil for frying

1. To make the shells: In a large bowl, soak the bulgur in the water for 1 hour. Drain and squeeze out the excess moisture. In a food processor fitted with a metal blade or in a mortar, grind the onion. Add the bulgur and process or pound until smooth. Add the flour, salt, and pepper and process to make a firm dough. (If combining by hand, knead for at least 30 minutes.) If the mixture does not hold together, add a few drops of oil or water. Cover and refrigerate for at least 30 minutes.

2. To make the filling: In a medium skillet, heat the oil over medium heat. Add the onion and sauté until soft and translucent, 5 to 10 minutes. Add the meat and sauté until it loses its red color, about 5 minutes. Remove from the heat and stir in the *baharat*, salt, pepper, and, if using, pomegranate molasses, parsley and/or pine nuts. Let cool.

3. To form each shell, with moistened hands, shape about 2 tablespoons shell mixture into a smooth 1-inch ball. Place the ball in the palm of one hand. Using the index finger of the other hand, push into the middle of the ball to form a hole. Move your finger in the hole while pressing the outside of the ball against your palm (squeezing and turning the ball), hollowing out the ball and elongating it to form an even 3-inch-long cylinder that is as thin as possible. Stuff the cavity of each shell with 2 to 3 teaspoons filling and press the open end to enclose the filling and seal the top.

(Alternatively, for easier forming, press the shell balls into thin, flat 3-inch rounds, spoon about 2 teaspoons filling into the center, bring the edges together over the filling, and press to seal.) Pinch the ends of the *kibbeh* to form points.

4. Place on a baking sheet or a dish lined with parchment paper or wax paper, cover, and place in the refrigerator for at least 1 hour or in the freezer for about 10 minutes. The *kibbeh* may be prepared ahead up to this point and frozen for up to 3 months; do not defrost before frying.

5. In a large pot, heat at least 2 inches oil over medium heat to 375°F.

6. In batches, fry the *kibbeh*, turning occasionally, until evenly browned and crisp on all sides, about 4 minutes. Using a slotted spoon, remove from the oil and drain on a wire rack. Serve warm or at room temperature.

KICHEL

Kichel is the Yiddish word for cookie. The most prominent eastern European *kichel* is a tender, dry, egg cookie or savory cracker that puffs and curls at the edges during baking.

Origin: Germany

Other names: Galicia: *keechel*; Lithuania: *kuchel*.

During the early medieval period, smaller variations of the German kuchen (cake) became known as *kichel* (little cake). (From around 800 until 1200, the English prepared little cakes called kechel.) Eventually, many German Jews began to refer to small cakes by the German term for cookies *plaetzchen* (from *platzchen* "little places"), while Jews in eastern Europe kept the term *kichel* (*kichlach* plural). The most common type of cookie in Poland, Ukraine, and the Baltic States was the *eier kichel* (egg cookie). A classic Yiddish nursery rhyme begins *"patche patche kichlach"* (pat pat cookies), referring to these plain, crisp, airy wafers, which were once an integral cultural component of eastern Ashkenazic life.

Kichel dough can be dropped from a spoon or rolled out and cut with a *yahrzeit* glass or a knife. Americans frequently form them into bow-tie shapes. *Kichlach* can be either slightly sweet or savory, and both versions are served with various *forspeizen* (appetizers), such as chopped liver, chopped eggs, chopped herring, and pickled herring. *Eier kichlach* are always made with oil or another nondairy fat, and never butter, so as to be pareve. Sugar-topped *kichlach* are served after Yom Kippur to break the fast with a taste of sweetness. Some savory variations include minced onion. There is even a Passover version made with matza meal.

Among the most popular forms of *kichlach* in central Europe were those made with poppy seeds (*mohn*). Unlike poppy seed–filled hamentaschen, in *mohn kichlach* the poppy seeds are mixed into the dough. *Mohn kichlach* probably arose in Germany in the eighteenth or early nineteenth century, then spread to eastern Europe. A recipe for "Poppy Seed Cookies (Mohn Plaetzchen)" appeared in the early American cookbook *Aunt Babette's* (Cincinnati, 1889). Poppy seed *kichlach* became traditional Purim fare, the square and triangular shapes symbolizing Haman's pockets or hats, and, in some families, they were enjoyed on Hanukkah as well.

Many Jews literally brought these cookies with them to America, preparing tins of hard cookies to eat because little kosher food was available aboard ship. In America, *mohn* cookies eventually became commonplace at sisterhood meetings and as simple, tasty accompaniments to tea. These treats were sometimes made with butter, but the advent in America of pareve vegetable shortening in 1911 and later commercial margarine led to their common substitution and, consequently, the cookies increasingly appeared on the Sabbath and after meat meals.

Just a few decades ago, *eier kichel* were ubiquitous in eastern European synagogues in America at the kiddush following Sabbath morning services, classically accompanied by slices of pickled herring and a glass of schnapps. They were also commonplace for the Sabbath and were included in the basic fare for a bar mitzvah. Guests in an Ashkenazic home were typically served *kichlach* with a glass of tea or schnapps. However, as American celebration fare grew more elaborate and diverse, many European foods lost favor. As a result, *kichlach* all but disappeared from most kiddushes and homes. They do survive in some Jewish bakeries, while commercial matza *kichlach* are still available for Passover. For some Ashkenazim, *eier kichlach* remain a comfort food.

‰ ASHKENAZIC EGG COOKIES (*EIER KICHLACH*)

ABOUT 36 SMALL COOKIES   [PAREVE]

1½ cups (7.5 ounces) all-purpose flour
½ teaspoon double-acting baking powder
½ teaspoon salt
3 large eggs, lightly beaten
3 tablespoons sugar
½ cup vegetable oil
About 1½ teaspoons additional vegetable oil for brushing
About ¼ cup additional sugar (if desired, mixed with 1½ teaspoons ground cinnamon) for sprinkling

1. Arrange the rack in the middle of the oven. Preheat the oven to 375°F. Line 2 large baking sheets with parchment paper or lightly grease the sheets.

2. Sift together the flour, baking powder, and salt. In a large bowl, beat the eggs and 3 tablespoons sugar until light and creamy, 5 to 10 minutes. Add ½ cup oil and beat for 10 minutes. Stir in the flour mixture.

3. On a lightly floured surface, roll out the dough ¼ inch thick. Brush with the additional oil, sprinkle with the additional sugar, and gently run a rolling pin over the top to embed the crystals. Cut into 2-inch diamonds or squares. Place on the prepared baking sheets.

4. Bake 1 sheet at a time until puffed and lightly browned, 25 to 30 minutes. Transfer the cookies to a wire rack and let cool. Store in a paper or cloth bag at room temperature for up to 1 week.

VARIATIONS

Matza Egg Cookies (Matza Eier Kichlach): Omit the baking powder and substitute 1½ cups matza cake meal for the flour.

Poppy Seed Egg Cookies (Mohn Kichlach): Add 3 to 4 tablespoons poppy seeds.

KIDDUSH

Kiddush, literally "sanctification" in Hebrew, is the benediction recited at the onset of the Sabbath and festivals. The Sages interpreted the biblical injunction "Remember the Sabbath day to keep it holy," as meaning to verbally and physically sanctify the day when it enters and departs (Havdalah), in particular, to "remember it with wine," symbolizing joy and fruitfulness. Kiddush is recited before the Friday night meal, as it is forbidden to eat beforehand, and in the place where the meal will be eaten. Germans ritually wash their hands before Kiddush, while Sephardim and most other Ashkenazim wash afterward. The Kiddush cup is filled to the rim, symbolizing a life overflowing with joy and plenty. The first section of the Kiddush, which is omitted on holidays, recounts the completion of Creation on the first Sabbath. The benediction over wine is then recited, *"borei peri hagafen"* (Who creates the fruit of the vine). The final section of the Kiddush involves the Exodus from Egypt, the archetype of redemption. On all festivals except the last days of Passover, the *Shehecheyanu* prayer ("Who has kept us in life and enabled us to reach this season") is recited at the conclusion of Kiddush. In some households one person recites the Kiddush for all of those present, while in other homes each individual says the Kiddush.

The original custom appears to have been to recite the Kiddush while seated, but a kabbalistic notion of saying the introductory passage while standing (it is considered testimony, which is made in court stand-

An essential part of Sabbath and festival meals is reciting the sanctification benediction and drinking from a filled-to-the-rim Kiddush cup symbolizing a life overflowing with joy and plenty.

ing) led to Chasidim and many Sephardim standing during the entire Kiddush. Rabbi Moses Isserles ruled, "one can stand for Kiddush, but it is preferable to sit." Germans traditionally stand for the introductory passage, then sit for the final section.

The Talmud permits beer as a substitute for wine in the Havdalah ceremony at the conclusion of the Sabbath in countries where it is *chemer hamedinah* (a national beverage), meaning a drink highly regarded enough to serve to an honored guest. However, only some form of grape juice is acceptable for the Friday evening Kiddush. When questioned about using beer for Kiddush, Rabbi Meir of Rothenburg (1220–1293) wrote, "Certainly you know it is proper to recite Kiddush over wine." If wine, grape juice, or even raisin wine is unavailable, which was all too often the case for Ashkenazim living in the northern parts of Europe, Friday evening Kiddush is recited over the two challahs before reciting the Hamotzi. For the Sabbath and festivals, adult Yemenites, when they can, drink a dry red wine. For children, they prepare a raisin and water drink, called *kiddush.*

During a stretch of history in Babylonia, travelers to a town were lodged and served Sabbath meals in rooms adjoining the synagogue. Therefore, a public Kiddush was instituted at the conclusion of the Friday evening prayer service to fulfill the strangers' obligation to sanctify the day. Many scholars objected to this custom, especially when the practice of serving meals in the synagogue fell into disuse. Today only Ashkenazim retain it, except in Israel where Kiddush is no longer recited in synagogues at the conclusion of the Friday evening service.

Although women are usually exempted from positive commandments whose performance is bound in time, they are obliged to fulfill Kiddush because the dual phrases "Remember the Sabbath" and "Observe the Sabbath" include women. Since women are obligated to say Kiddush, some scholars assert that they may recite it for men.

The Talmud attributes the Sabbath evening Kiddush over a cup of wine to the *Anshei Kenesset ha-Gadolah* (Members of the Great Assembly), a legislative body that functioned about 500 to 300 BCE. The rabbis of the Talmudic period instituted the recitation of Kiddush for Sabbath and festival mornings as well. The Kiddush for mornings is of less importance and may be recited over either wine or any drink considered *chemer hamedinah*. On the Sabbath and holidays, Ashkenazim traditionally enjoy a buffet in the synagogue following morning services called a kiddush, named after the benediction. This custom was instituted relatively recently in order to allow people who were unable to recite the benediction because of a lack of Hebrew knowledge to fulfill their obligation, as well as to provide an opportunity to socialize. A synagogue kiddush was originally a simple affair consisting solely of wine or schnapps, a plate of pickled herring, perhaps some egg salad, and *kichlach* (egg cookies) and/or crackers. However, following World War II, as American Jews grew more affluent and less connected to the ways of the "old country," the Sabbath morning kiddush generally grew more elaborate, sometimes even becoming a sit-down affair.

KIMOCHDUN

Kimochdun is a light and fluffy festive bread enriched with a scattering of dried apricots and almonds.

Origin: Afghanistan

Kimochdun was originally cooked as a thin flatbread in a large skillet over and under a covering of hot coals. Today, *kimochdun* is still baked in a skillet, but in an oven. As a result, the contemporary round loaf is much thicker—it is about two to three inches high. Most people prefer the flavor of whole-wheat flour in this loaf. The bread contains a little oil, but never any butter. Some cooks chop the almonds, but many leave them whole.

Kimochdun is traditionally served by Muslims in central Asia at the end of Ramadan, and is also popular among central Asian Jews. The apricots and almonds represent the wealth of the land. It is not used for Hamotzi to start a meal, but rather served warm at breakfast or as a treat with tea. *Kimochdun* is sometimes eaten with apricot preserves.

¶ AFGHAN FRUIT-AND-NUT FLATBREAD (*KIMOCHDUN*)

1 LARGE BREAD   [PAREVE OR DAIRY]

   1 package (2¼ teaspoons) active dry yeast or
      1 (0.6-ounce) cake fresh yeast
   1½ cups warm water (105°F to 115°F for dry yeast;
      80°F to 85°F for fresh yeast), or ¼ cup water
      and 1¼ cups milk
   2 tablespoons honey or sugar
   2 tablespoons vegetable oil
   2 teaspoons table salt or 4 teaspoons kosher salt

   About 4 cups (20 ounces) bread or unbleached all-
      purpose flour, or 2 cups white flour and 2 cups
      whole-wheat flour
   ⅔ cup coarsely chopped dried apricots
   ⅔ cup coarsely chopped almonds

   1. Dissolve the yeast in ¼ cup water. Stir in the sugar and let stand until foamy, 5 to 10 minutes. In a large bowl, combine the yeast mixture, remaining water, oil, salt, and 2 cups flour. Gradually add enough of the remaining flour to make a mixture that holds together.

   2. On a lightly floured surface, knead the dough until smooth and elastic, 10 to 15 minutes. Place in an oiled bowl and turn to coat. Cover loosely with plastic wrap or a kitchen towel and let rise in a warm, draft-free place until doubled in bulk, about 1½ hours.

   3. Punch down the dough, knead briefly, cover, and let rest for about 15 minutes.

   4. Roll out the dough into a 1-inch-thick rectangle. Sprinkle with the apricots and almonds. Roll up jelly-roll style. Form the dough into a ball, then roll out into a 10-inch round. Place in a lightly oiled 10-inch skillet with 3-inch sides or a 10-inch round ovenproof dish. Cover and let rise until almost doubled in bulk, about 40 minutes.

   5. Preheat the oven to 350°F.

   6. Cut a ½-inch-deep X in the top of the bread from one end to the other. Bake until golden brown and hollow sounding when tapped, about 45 minutes. Transfer the bread to a wire rack and let cool slightly.

KINDLI

Kindli are filled pastries made from a yeast dough.

Origin: Hungary

Other names: *baigli, beigli, kindl*.

   This pastry resembles a baby wrapped in a swaddling blanket—thus the whimsical Yiddish name *kindli* (little children). It is akin to *kipfel* and rugelach. *Kindli* are made either into large pastries, each about seven inches long, or smaller individual cookies. When large dough rounds are rolled up into a cylinder like a jelly roll, the pastry is known as *beigli*. Over the course of time, inventive cooks found ways to speed up the assembly by rolling up the pastry jelly-roll style and cutting it into slices, some even substituting a cookie dough to make a treat that retained the name but not the shape. Germans and Austrians prefer a poppy seed filling, while Hungarians favor a walnut mixture. Romanians like all types.

Whatever form they take, *kindli* are traditionally prepared for special occasions, in particular Purim—a poppy seed filling and some wine added to the dough make them appropriate for the tone of the day. In addition, the "little children" represent Haman's large family. On Purim, Hungarian households typically feature *kindli* and *flondi* (layered pastry) rather than hamantaschen. A sour cream dough is used to make this pastry for Shavuot and other celebrations for which a dairy meal is traditional. Some cooks add warm mashed potatoes to the dough for a moister texture. Yeast dough pastries were typically brushed with egg wash using a baster made from feathers (*talu*).

(See also Kipfel, Makosh, and Rugelach)

HUNGARIAN FILLED YEAST PASTRIES (*KINDLI*)

ABOUT 18 SMALL PASTRIES   [DAIRY OR PAREVE]

Dough:
1 package (2¼ teaspoons) active dry yeast or
    1 (0.6-ounce) cake fresh yeast
¼ cup warm water or milk (105°F to 115°F for dry
    yeast; 80°F to 85°F for fresh yeast)
¼ cup granulated sugar or ½ cup confectioners'
    sugar
½ cup semidry white wine, orange juice, or water
    or 1 cup sour cream; or 1 cup warm mashed
    potatoes and 2 tablespoons white wine
¾ cup (1½ sticks) unsalted butter or margarine,
    softened
3 large egg yolks
½ teaspoon table salt or 1 teaspoon kosher salt
About 4 cups (20 ounces) bread or unbleached all-
    purpose flour

Nut Filling (*Diós*):
2 cups (8 ounces) ground walnuts
1 cup sugar or honey
1 tablespoon butter or margarine, melted
1 teaspoon grated lemon zest or ground cinnamon
½ cup golden raisins, coarsely chopped (optional)
Egg wash (1 large egg beaten with 1 teaspoon water)

1. To make the dough: Dissolve the yeast in the water. Stir in 1 teaspoon sugar and let stand until foamy, 5 to 10 minutes. In a large bowl, combine the yeast mixture, wine, remaining sugar, butter, egg yolks, and salt. Blend in 1½ cups flour. Gradually add enough of the remaining flour to make a mixture that holds together.

2. On a lightly floured surface, knead the dough

until smooth and springy, about 10 minutes. Place in an oiled bowl and turn to coat. Cover loosely with plastic wrap or a kitchen towel and let rise in a warm, draft-free place until doubled in bulk, about 1½ hours, or in the refrigerator overnight.

3. To make the filling: In a medium bowl, combine all the filling ingredients.

4. Punch down the dough. Fold over and press together several times. Divide into eighteen 1-inch balls and let stand for 10 minutes. On a lightly floured surface, roll out each ball into a thin 3-inch round. Spoon a heaping tablespoon of the filling into the center of each round. Bring the right side of the dough over the filling and tuck it under the filling on the left side, then pull the left side of the dough over the filling and tuck it in the right side. Tuck the bottom of the dough underneath. Pinch together the dough on the top.

5. Place, several inches apart, on baking sheets lined with parchment paper or lightly greased. Cover loosely with plastic wrap or a kitchen towel and let rise until puffy, about 30 minutes.

6. Preheat the oven to 350°F. Brush the kindli with the egg wash. Bake until golden brown, about 30 minutes. Transfer the kindli to a wire rack and let cool. Wrap and store at room temperature for up to 2 days or in the freezer for up to 2 months.

KIPFEL

Kipfel are flaky, crescent-shaped rolls as well as crescent cookies.

Origin: Austria

Other names: America: butterhorns; southern Austria: *kipferl*; Czech Republic: *kifli*; Hungary: *kifli*; Germany: *kipferln*; Romania and Serbia: *kifla*.

Sigmund Freud, in an 1885 letter from Paris back to his native Vienna, noted: "I did at last manage to say 'croissants,' since I always get Kipfel with my coffee."

The idea of small crescent-shaped breads appears to have emerged in Austria during the late seventeenth century, then spread to France. Many believe that after Marie Antoinette married Louis XVI of France in 1770, she so missed *kipfel* that she arranged for a Viennese baker to travel to Paris to instruct his French counterparts on how to make it, and the roll soon become the croissant. By this point, the *kipfel* was about a century old and indelibly implanted in central European gastronomy. In addition to savory *kipfels*, central Europe-

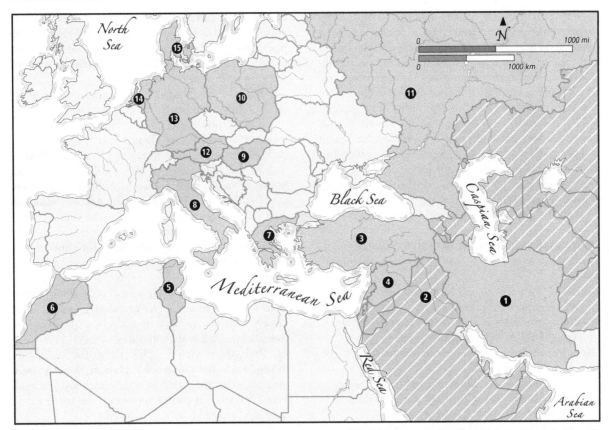

Cookies *The introduction of sugar to Persia led to the emergence there in the seventh century of numerous small pastries and eventually throughout the Arabic world. Then as sugar became more commonplace in Europe, every country adopted cookies.* 1 **Iran**—*hadgi badah, klaitcha, naan-e berenji, naan-e nokhodchi;* 2 **Iraq and Middle East**—*ghraybeh, kourabie, ma'amoul, travados;* 3 **Turkey**—*marunchinos, mustachudos, biscochos de raki, masas de vino, foulares;* 4 **Syria**—*ras-ib-adjway;* 5 **Tunisia**—*makroud;* 6 **Morocco**—*kaab el gh'zal, debla, raricha;* 7 **Greece**—*biscochos, reshicas;* 8 **Italy**—*amaretti, biscotti, impade, sfratti;* 9 **Hungary**—*pogácsa, kindli, kranzli;* 10 **Poland**—*kichel, hamantaschen, reshinke;* 11 **Russia**—*kaletzin;* 12 **Austria**—*kipfel, nusskipferln, polster zipfel;* 13 **Germany**—*geback, lebkuchen, mahltaschen, mandelbrot, plaetzcehn, pfefferneusse, zimstern;* 14 **Netherlands**—*boterkoeke;* 15 **Denmark**—*jodekager*

ans enjoyed a variety of crescent-shaped sweet treats as well.

According to legend, the origins of these crescent-shaped baked goods date back to 1683, when the three hundred thousand–strong Ottoman army laid siege to the walled city of Vienna, Austria. The Turks undertook to secretly dig a tunnel under the barricades in the darkness of night. City bakers, at work in the wee hours of the morning in their underground chambers, heard the noise of the construction, alerted the authorities, and foiled the underground attack. Finally, with the timely military intervention of the Poles, Bavarians, and others, the Turks were repelled.

Purportedly, local Viennese bakers fashioned special small breads and cakes in the shape of a crescent, the symbol displayed on the Turkish flag, to honor the end of the Ottoman siege, in which they had played a role. These pastries proved perfect to serve in a second prominent Austrian institution engendered by the Ottoman invasion, the coffeehouse, which emerged as a result of chests of coffee beans left behind by the Turks. Others suggest that the bakers had actually concluded that the situation was so dire that they baked crescent-shaped breads to curry favor with the Turks, then sold them to a grateful populace afterward. A third group dismisses any connection between the bread and the siege, maintaining that it was a venerable local baked good shaped to represent animal horns, and that the Turkish connection was merely a myth conjured up later.

In any case, Austrian bakers originally called the little pointed loaves of white bread *zipfel* (German meaning "corner/tip"), also spelled *ciphel*. *Zipfel* is still used, in conjunction with *polster* (cushion/padding); *polster-zipfel* refers to a jam-filled Austrian cookie, also known as *Vienna kipfel* and in Germany as *hasenörchen* (little rabbit ears). Meanwhile, the Viennese took to mispronouncing the pointed breads as *kipfel*, and the word soon becoming a synonym for the German *hörnchen* (crescent). Variations of the Austrian pronunciation spread throughout central and eastern Europe.

A crescent-shaped variation of this yeast pastry called *Pressburger kipplach* is named after Pressburg, the German name for Bratislava, one of the oldest and most important European Jewish communities and commonly considered the dividing line between eastern and western Ashkenazim. Today, Bratislava is the capital of Slovakia. To complicate matters further, this pastry is also called *Pozsonyi kifli* after the Hungarian named for Pressburg/Bratislava.

To further confuse the situation, the term *kipfel* was also applied to small crescent cookies (*zuckerkipfel*), including those made from various unleavened doughs and yeast kuchen dough, and one similar to kugelhopf but enriched with *topfen*, a cheese that the Germans call *quark*. The *topfen* type of *kipfel* is traditional on Shavuot and other special dairy meals. In the nineteenth century, Hungarian housewives sometimes substituted mashed potatoes for the butter in the dough.

In Yiddish, the word *kipfel* came to specify crescent cookies, both leavened and unleavened, and not the croissant bread. One form of the cookies, *nusskipferlin* (nut crescents), still ranks among the favorite Ashkenazic cookies. Toward the end of the nineteenth century, Jewish immigrants brought the *kipfel* to America. The American cookbook *Aunt Babette's* (Cincinnati, 1889), includes one of the earliest records in English of the word in a recipe for "Wiener Kipfel," which consists of yeast dough triangles filled with "beaten whites of eggs, raisins, almonds and citron," and with the edges pinched together. The first edition of *The Settlement Cookbook* (Milwaukee, 1901) contains several recipes for *kipfel*, some with yeast and others without, but all made with butter. In the twentieth century, vegetable shortening and margarine were sometimes substituted for the *topfen* and butter in *kipfel*, expanding its usage in kosher households. In Procter & Gamble's 1933 booklet *Crisco Recipes for the Jewish Housewife*, written in Yiddish and English, a *kipfel* is made, of course, with vegetable shortening. In late twentieth century America, *kipfel*, particularly with an unleavened cream cheese dough, became better known as rugelach.

(See also Rugelach)

KIRSCH

Kirsch, short for *kirschwasser* (German for "cherry water"), is a colorless liqueur distilled from crushed cherries, common to Alsace and Germany. As kirsch does not contain any grape products, it is suitable for kosher kitchens without special supervision. Kirsh is an element in Jewish cuisine in Alsace and western Germany, as an aperitif or in baked goods and fruit dishes.

KISHKE

Kishke is stuffed derma.
Origin: Eastern Europe
Other names: *kishka*.

" 'There is a place for stuffed miltz,' Meyer Lansky says, 'but here I advise kishke.' " (From *Read All About It* by Sidney Zion, a 1982 collection of some of his work as a reporter.)

Kishke is a classic example of Jewish soul food, in which kosher odds and ends are scraped together and, by sheer ingenuity, transformed into a luscious treat—in this case, the otherwise useless (and hopefully well-cleaned) beef intestines, flour or matza meal, and a few inexpensive flavorings. Like many now-standard Jewish dishes, *kishke* was adapted from local non-Jewish fare, in particular, a Slavic blood sausage (very unkosher) made with barley or buckwheat, called *kiszka* by Poles and *kyshka* by Ukrainians. This sausage was the inspiration for the 1950s American tune "Who Stole the Keeshka?" by Walt Solek, "the Clown Prince of Polka." Eastern European Jews omitted the unacceptable blood, substituted flour or matza meal for the grains, and added their ubiquitous onion and sometimes garlic, resulting in *kishke*.

Most dictionaries and cookbooks state that the word *kishke* means "intestines," which has led to the common misconception that the dish received its name from the lower part of the alimentary canal. However, the dish is actually named after the stuffing, not the body part. Derived from the Middle High German *darm* (intestines), the original Yiddish word for intestines was *gederem*. The word *darm* was also the source of the English derma. *Kishke* is frequently called stuffed derma, a less unsettlingly term for Westerners than intestines or bowels. The Slavic term was itself adopted from the Persian *kashk*.

In eastern Yiddish, the dish of stuffed intestines is the singular *kishke*, while the body part intestines is usually the plural *kishkes*. The term *kishkes* has not only the literal connotation of guts, but also the figurative implication of profound emotion. Thus, when you know something *"in di kishkes,"* you have a "gut feeling." *Kishke gelt* refers to funds obtained by denying oneself food in order to save money, or denotes self-sacrifice, both of which are felt in the gut.

Much of the *kishke's* flavor comes from cooking it for an extended period in another dish. A favorite way is to simmer it for hours in a tzimmes for Friday dinner or overnight in a cholent (Sabbath stew) for lunch, all the while allowing it to absorb flavor from the cooking liquid. Additional flavor, as well as moistness, comes from a little goose or chicken schmaltz and the predominant (and frequently the only) Ashkenazic seasoning, onion. Some cooks add garlic for extra savor as well as paprika for color; without paprika, the insides can turn out gray.

Middle Easterners devised their own forms of stuffed casings—including the Syrian *gheh*, Moroccan *osbana*, Tunisian *merguez*, and Yemenite *nakahoris*—commonly utilizing sheep innards and, unlike the makers of *kishke*, using plenty of meat and seasonings in the stuffing. However, in the impoverished communities of eastern Europe, meat was particulary expensive and chopped meat, before the advent of the mechanical meat grinder in the 1860s, was extremely labor-intensive and thus even more costly; accordingly, most puddings/sausages consisted primarily or entirely of economical cereals. In families where even flour was costly, mashed potatoes where substituted for some of the grain. When the stuffing was used in the neck skin of a goose or chicken, the dish was called *helzel*.

In the late nineteenth century, eastern European immigrants brought the dish to America. The first edi-tion of *The Settlement Cook Book* (Milwaukee, 1901) included a recipe for "Kischtke, Russian Style." In the twentieth century, intestines grew increasingly difficult to obtain over the counter and, as a result, commercial brands of *kishke* switched to inedible plastic for the casings. Beginning in the 1950s, American housewives, looking for easier dishes, began preparing *falsa kishke* (mock derma). In the most popular version, cooks used Manischewitz's Tam Tam crackers, substituted margarine or oil for the schmaltz, and replaced the casings with aluminum foil. Intestines do impart a distinctive flavor note to the stuffing, which is lacking in versions made with artificial casings.

This former peasant fare, besides being a beloved Sabbath food, was once a common sight at special Ashkenazic celebrations, such as bar mitzvahs and weddings. *Kishke* was still popular enough even in America to be included in subsequent editions of *The Settlement Cook Book*, appearing as late as 1965. However, deemed fatty, heavy, and old-fashioned, *kishke* soon went out of style in many circles. This venerable sausage was getting the *kishkes* kicked out of it. Of late, though, *kishke* has been making something of a comeback. Some cooks view it nostalgically as a flavorful traditional dish and are returning it to its proper place in the Sabbath cholent. *Kishke* remains a standard in Jewish delis. Frozen prepared *kishke* is sold in American kosher markets and in Israel in most supermarkets. It has even occasionally reappeared as respectable wedding fare.

(See also Kashk and Sausage)

ASHKENAZIC STUFFED DERMA (*KISHKE*)

ABOUT 8 SERVINGS   [MEAT]

1 foot large beef casing or 3 feet narrow beef casing

1½ cups all-purpose or whole-wheat flour, or 1 cup flour and ½ cup matza meal, bread crumbs, or fine semolina

1 large onion, grated or finely minced

1 large carrot or 1 stalk celery, grated or finely minced (optional)

1 clove garlic, mashed, or ⅛ teaspoon garlic powder (optional)

½ cup schmaltz or vegetable oil

1 teaspoon sweet paprika or ½ teaspoon hot paprika

About 1 teaspoon salt

About ¼ teaspoon ground black pepper

1. Turn the casing inside out and, using a dull knife, carefully scrape off any fat. If using a narrow casing, cut into 1-foot lengths for easier handling. Wash well, then pat dry. Sew or tie up one end of the casing with sewing thread.

2. In a large bowl, combine all the remaining ingredients.

3. Loosely stuff the flour mixture into the inside out casing, gradually pushing the casing over the stuffing, returning the shiny outer side to the outside. Fill no more then two-thirds full, allowing room for expansion. Sew or tie up the open end.

4. Bring a pot of lightly salted water to a boil, add the *kishke*, and simmer for 10 minutes to shrink the casing. Drain. Prick the kishke in several places to allow the excess fat to seep out.

5. Cook the kishke in a cholent or tzimmes or alongside a chicken or beef roast for at least 1½ hours. Or place it on a bed of onions in a shallow roasting pan, add 1 cup boiling water or chicken soup, and bake in a 350°F oven, basting or turning occasionally, until golden, about 1½ hours. Cut into slices and serve warm.

VARIATIONS

To make kishke without casing: Place the kishke mixture on a large piece of greased aluminum foil, shape into a 2-inch-thick roll, roll up tightly in the foil, prick in several places, and cook as directed in Step 5.

KISSEL

Kissel is a tart fruit puree that is often thickened and served as a pudding, but can also be a soup or sauce.
Origin: Eastern Europe
Other names: Polish: *kisiel*; Scandinavia: *rodgrod*.

Sour is an essential flavor component in northeastern Europe; the flavor appears in foods such as rye breads, sour cream, pickles, and sauerkraut. *Kissel* is the Slavic word meaning "sour," and it is used in particular to refer to an array of tart fruit puree–based puddings, sauces, soups, and beverages, with varying thicknesses. Among Ukrainian, Byelorussian, and Polish Jews, the favorite types of *kissel* were made from berries, which were typically picked wild in the summer through early autumn. A sour prune *kissel* was made during the fall and winter when fresh berries were out of season. Red currants, rhubarb, sour cherries, and cranberries were also common fruits used in the dish.

The consistency of the pudding runs from that of a thick soup to that of a molded custard. The *kissel* was originally thickened with grains, particularly oat flour after its introduction to northeastern Europe in the seventh century. The emergence in the nineteenth century of potato starch and cornstarch led to a more delicate dish. The pudding is traditionally served with whipped cream or sweetened *quark* and slivered almonds. *Kissel* sauce is drizzled over pancakes, ice cream, cookies, and grain puddings. The even-thinner soup is drunk either hot or chilled.

NORTHEASTERN EUROPEAN BERRY PUDDING (*KISSEL*)

6 TO 8 SERVINGS [PAREVE]

24 ounces (4 cups) fresh or 20 ounces frozen raspberries, strawberries, blackberries, or blueberries, or any combination
2 cups water, or 1 cup water and 1 cup dry red wine or orange juice
About ½ cup sugar
⅛ teaspoon table salt or ¼ teaspoon kosher salt
¼ cup potato starch or cornstarch dissolved in ½ cup cold water
1 to 2 tablespoons fresh lemon juice or berry liqueur

1. Puree and strain the berries. There should be about 2⅓ cups puree. Transfer to a medium saucepan, place over medium-high heat, and bring to a boil. Add the water, sugar, and salt and stir until the sugar dissolves, about 3 minutes.

2. Reduce the heat to medium-low, stir in the starch mixture, and simmer, stirring frequently, until the pudding thickens and turns translucent, about 5 minutes. Stir in the lemon juice.

3. Pour into 6 to 8 custard cups. Refrigerate until chilled, at least 2 hours.

KITNIYOT

The Bible is very explicit about what is forbidden for consumption during Passover—*chametz*. The Talmud precisely defines what can become *chametz*—only the Five Species of grains (probably naked wheat varieties, including durum and bread wheat; emmer; einkorn; six-rowed barley; and two-rowed barley) and their subvarieties when exposed to water. Therefore, other grains and legumes were perfectly acceptable on Passover. From the time of Moses and for millennia afterward, this principle remained the standard. The only explicit deviation was the singular opinion of Yochanan ben Nuri in the Talmud that "Rice and millet are near to becoming *chametz*." He therefore forbade these other grains on Passover in addition to the Five Species. This view, however, was roundly rejected by all the other rabbis, who said, "We do not pay attention to the opinion of Yochanan ben Nuri." Some Sages, perhaps to demonstrate their rejection of his assertion, included rice as part of their Seder.

Later Moses Maimonides codified the law according to Sephardim: "Rice [and other items besides the Five Species] cannot become *chametz*." Then an enigmatic custom emerged in late medieval France of forbidding the consumption of *kitniyot* (*kitneet* singular), a Talmudic term, derived from the Hebrew word *katan* (small), originally referring to legumes.

The first recorded reference advocating the practice of not eating *kitniyot* on Passover was in *Sefer Haminhagot* (c. 1210), written in Provence (a separate and distinct cultural community from Ashkenaz) by Rabbi Asher ben Saul of Lunel, an early kabbalist. He wrote, "It is the universal custom not to eat *kitniyot* during Passover because they rise and become *chametz*." This view was supported by Rabbi Isaac ben Joseph (d. 1280) of Corbeil in northern France, who stated, "Concerning *kitniyot*, such as peas, fava beans, rice, lentils, and the like, our Rabbis are accustomed to prohibit eating them at all on Passover, and this seems correct." He contends that this custom was observed since the time of the *kadmonim* ("early ones," denoting the Ashkenazic authorities before the First Crusade in 1096). However, nowhere do any of the early Ashkenazic authorities mention or even hint at the custom of *kitniyot*.

According to many authorities, *kitniyot* did not originate as a specific prohibition on Passover; instead, it originated as a prohibition that some people wanted to impose on the consumption of legumes on all holidays—not in fear of *chametz*, but because legumes were considered "poor person's food" in Persia and parts of Europe. Legumes, especially lentils, were generally avoided by the upper class, except at times of famine and severe need. Lentils were also traditionally a food of mourning and, therefore, in some communities, were not consumed for the entire month of Nisan. This taboo was dismissed by most authorities, including Achai Gaon (eighth century),

the first major rabbinic authority after the closure of the Talmud. He declared, "All types of *kitniyot* may be cooked whether on Passover or on other festivals." There also emerged a medieval European belief that wheat kernels could look like lentils and fava beans. Thus the stringent prohibtion of *kitniyot* probably developed due to mistakes.

The prohibition against *kitniyot* found almost no foothold outside of the Ashkenazic community and also initially faced much opposition within. Rabbi Isaac of Corbeil records that Rabbi Yechiel of Paris (d. 1265), his father-in-law and teacher, ate yellow split peas on Passover. Rabbi Yechiel was the leading Ashkenazic scholar of his time and, therefore, his rejection of the custom was notable. In the thirteenth century, Rav Samuel ben Solomon of Falaise called the prohibition against *kitniyot* "*minhag ta'ut*" (an erroneous custom). Rabbenu Yerucham ben Meshullam (1290–1350), raised in Provence and educated in France and later moving to Toledo, Spain, declared it to be "*minhag shtut*" (a foolish custom).

Nevertheless, the custom not to eat *kitniyot* continued to garner adherence within the widespread Ashkenazic community and, further complicating matters, additional items were gradually included among those considered *kitniyot*, including carob, anise, caraway, cardamom, coriander, cumin, mustard, and poppy seeds. Some American foods—corn, green beans, sunflower seeds, and peanuts—were also later added to the category. Some authorities expanded the ban even to items that are not edible as seeds, but can be processed for edible derivatives, such as cottonseeds, which are not ground into flour or piled like grains, and can in no way be mistaken for grains. Interestingly, the Ashkenazic rabbinic establishment included buckwheat in the taboo category, while Chasidim in the eighteenth century accepted its consumption during Passover and used it instead of matza for making dumplings and pancakes, although not for the Seder. Eventually, Chasidim too rejected the use of buckwheat for Passover. Certain families, primarily Chasidim, forbade garlic under the presumption that it was planted between rows of grain to act as a natural insect repellent. Some Chasidim would not eat anything without a peel, as the item might have been touched by someone in contact with *chametz*, thereby rejecting such foods as strawberries and tomatoes (even though tomato skins can be peeled off). There was even a nineteenth century attempt to include potatoes as *kitniyot*, but this was duly rejected by the populace.

There is a disagreement among authorities as to whether derivatives of *kitniyot* (*mei kitniyot*), such as oils and extracts produced from *kitniyot*, are permissible for consumption on Passover. Before the 1960s, these were generally permitted and kosher-for-Passover peanut oil and cottonseed oil were common. Cottonseed oil has only been used for food since the end of the nineteenth century and was once accepted by most people on Passover and permitted by many authorities. Although the soybean is a legume, it was not initially included by the ban and is processed as well. However, the forces of stringency pressured the supervising agencies, and today, Ashkenazic kashrut organizations do not permit peanut, corn, cottonseed, or soy derivatives. Most canola plants grow in Canada, where, some people claim, they are planted in too close proximity to wheat fields, rendering them problematic. The Israeli rabbinate ruled that canola oil is a *kitniyot* derivative and now most American supervising agencies advise, "Canola oil is not recommended."

All the same, *kitniyot* does not have the same status as *chametz*. Indeed, in periods of severe famine and trouble, Ashkenazic authorities temporarily permitted the consumption of *kitniyot* on Passover, because health and survival outweigh a custom.

Non-Ashkenazic communities differ over which foods are permissible on Passover. Today, some Sephardim, as a rule, eat only fresh legumes, such as fresh green peas, fresh fava beans, and green beans, and not dried legumes, while others enjoyed fresh and dried ones. Generally, Jews from Arabic-speaking countries, except some Moroccans, eat rice, while many of those from European countries do not. Thus the Sephardic list of acceptable Passover foods commonly includes rice cereals and corn flakes (those that are under rabbinic supervision). Even the families who eat rice have the practice of carefully examining the kernels, some repeating their inspection three or seven times, to ascertain that no wheat or barley grains are mixed in. Italian Jews eat *kitniyot*, but eschew all dairy products for the entire holiday, since the animals were usually fed forbidden grains which can fall into the milk. Many Moroccans also abstain from dairy during Passover.

The restriction of *kitniyot* on Passover remains one of the major differences between Ashkenazim and other Jewish communities. In Israel, with its large number of Sephardim and Mizrachim, many of the Israeli products labeled "kosher for Passover" contain *kitniyot*.

(See also Chametz and Passover)

KLAICHA
Klaicha is a small, filled pastry.
Origin: Northern Iraq
Other names: Calcutta: *sambusak*; Iran: *kulcha*, *kullech*; Iraq: *baba bi tamir, kaleecha, kleicha*; Kurdistan: *kasmay.*

In ancient Sumeria, bakers made special small moon-shaped cakes filled with dates or raisins, known as *qullupu* (from the Semitic *kall,* "whole," and *kll,* "to complete"), which were used in temple rituals. Pottery molds for forming similar cakes were discovered in excavations at the Sumerian city of Mari (now in southeast Syria), dating from shortly before the city was sacked by Hammurabi in 1759 BCE. Descendants of those pastries were adopted by ancient Persians and medieval Arabs and their Jewish neighbors, and recipes for baked filled pastries were included in several medieval Arabic cookbooks. Similar cookies are still widely enjoyed today throughout the Middle East.

Klaicha mhashshaya (stuffed *klaicha*) are beloved in Iraqi, Afghan, and Iranian communities. Some are savory but others contain a sweet filling, notably date, walnut, or coconut. The original pastry was made with a yeast dough, but today many people substitute an easier semolina dough. In the Levant, semolina versions are known as *maamoul.* Unlike European yeast pastries, the dough is not sweetened, but contains butter or oil and, for sweet fillings, sometimes spices, notably cardamom or the local spice mixture, *hawayij.* Much of the flavor derives from the filling. *Klaicha* can be formed as small rounds, half-moons, and crescents; a three- to four-inch round disk with little holes cut in the top is a *khfefiyyat,* and triangle-shaped pastries are called *fatayar.* Round cookies are commonly formed in a special wooden mold called *qalab al-klaicha.*

Klaicha are enjoyed for special occasions, served with coffee or tea. Sweet *klaicha* are considered the national cookie of Iraq and no Iraqi celebration would be considered complete without them. *Baba bi tamir* (literally "wad with date"), the Jewish name for *klai-*

chat tamir (date-filled *klaichas*), is a Purim favorite among Iraqis. It can now be found in many Israeli bakeries, especially those in areas with a sizable Iraqi or Persian population.

IRAQI FILLED YEAST PASTRIES (*KLAICHA*)
ABOUT 36 MEDIUM PASTRIES   [DAIRY OR PAREVE]

1 package (2¼ teaspoons) active dry yeast or
   1 (0.6-ounce) cake fresh yeast
1¼ cups warm water (105°F to 115°F for dry yeast;
   80°F to 85°F for fresh yeast), or ¼ cup water
   and 1 cup milk
1 teaspoon sugar
½ cup (1 stick) unsalted butter or margarine,
   melted
½ teaspoon salt
4 cups (20 ounces) bread or unbleached all-purpose
   flour
1 recipe Date Filling or Nut Filling (recipes follow)
Egg wash (1 large egg beaten with 1 teaspoon water)
¼ cup sesame seeds for sprinkling

1. Dissolve the yeast in ¼ cup water. Stir in the sugar and let stand until foamy, 5 to 10 minutes. In a large bowl, combine the yeast mixture, remaining water, butter, salt, and 2 cups flour. Add enough of the remaining flour, ½ cup at a time, to make a mixture that holds together. On a lightly floured surface or in an electric mixer with a dough hook, knead the dough until smooth and springy, about 5 minutes. Place on a flat surface, cover with a large bowl or pot, and let rise in a warm, draft-free place until doubled in bulk, about 1½ hours.

2. Preheat the oven to 375°F. Line 2 large baking sheets with parchment paper or lightly grease the sheets.

3. Punch down the dough. Fold over and press together several times. Let rest for 10 minutes. Divide the dough into 1-inch balls and roll out each ball into a thin 3-inch round. Or roll out the dough ⅛ inch thick and cut out 3-inch rounds, rerolling the scraps. Spoon 1 teaspoon filling into the center of each round. Gather the dough around the filling to meet in the center, pinch the edges to seal, and form into a ball. Using a rolling pin, flatten into a 2-inch round. Alternatively, fold over an edge to form a half-moon and press the edges to seal. Place 2 inches apart on the prepared baking sheets. Cover and let stand for 10 minutes.

4. Brush the tops with the egg wash and lightly sprinkle with the sesame seeds. Prick several times with the tines of a fork to form a flower pattern.

5. Bake until golden brown, about 15 minutes. Transfer the *klaicha* to a wire rack and let cool. Wrap and store at room temperature for up to 2 days or in the freezer for up to 2 months.

Klaicha Fillings
DATE FILLING
ABOUT 2 CUPS   [DAIRY OR PAREVE]

1 pound (about 3 cups) pitted dates, finely
   chopped
½ cup water
2 to 3 tablespoons unsalted butter or margarine

In a medium saucepan, cook the dates and water over low heat, stirring frequently, for 10 minutes. Add the butter and cook until the mixture forms an almost uniform mass, about 5 minutes. Let cool.

NUT FILLING
ABOUT 2 CUPS   [PAREVE]

8 ounces (2 cups) almonds, pistachios, or walnuts,
   ground
About ⅔ cup sugar
1 tablespoon rose water, orange-blossom water, or
   plain water
1 tablespoon vegetable oil or lightly beaten egg
½ teaspoon ground cinnamon (optional)

In a food processor fitted with a metal blade, process all the ingredients until smooth.

KLOP
Klop is a meatball.
Origin: Germany
Other names: Yiddish: *kahklehten, koklaten.*

Until the advent of the hand-cranked mechanical meat grinder in the 1860s, forcemeat, whether prepared at homes or in butcher shops, had to be chopped by hand with a *hackmeiser* (curved blade) in a large wooden bowl, making it very time-consuming and work-extensive. Consequently, chopped meat was generally reserved for special occasions and was usually incorporated into a larger dish; for example, it was stuffed into cabbage leaves and peppers, or provided the filling for the medieval *pastida* (meat pie). Occasionally, the chopped meat was featured as *klops* (meatballs), a shortened form of *fleischklops*, from a northeastern German name for dumplings (*klopse*).

Sweet-and-sour meatballs are sometimes called *kulen* or *kuln* (the name of a Croatian sausage). *Karnatzlach* are Romanian grilled ground meat and garlic patties.

Originally, the Ashkenazic *klops* contained much more bread than meat—it was actually a dumpling with meat. It also included plenty of the favorite Ashkenazic flavoring, onion. In the late nineteenth-century, following the arrival of the meat grinder and expanded beef production, meatballs, now featuring much more meat than filler, became even more commonplace on the Ashkenazic table. On the Sabbath and holidays, they were added to chicken fricassee, soups, or braised cabbage or cooked alone in a sauce. The term *klops* is also at times used in Yiddish to denote meat loaf, which is made from the same ingredients but larger in mass. Indeed, in modern Israel, *klops* frequently refers both to a meat loaf filled with hard-boiled eggs, and to large meatballs with an egg in the center.

Unlike the smooth texture of Middle Eastern ground meat, European ground meat is relatively coarse. Germans and Hungarians favor savory meatballs, while *Galitzianers* (from southern Poland) prefer sweet-and-sour sauces. In America, some cooks add nontraditional ingredients to the sauce, ranging from grape jelly to chili sauce. *Klops* are usually served with bread to sop up the sauce.

(See also Kufta and Meatball)

KNAIDEL/KNEYDL

Knaidel is a dumpling. The most common type is now made with matza meal and is commonly known as a matza ball.

Origin: Germany

Other names: Yiddish: *matza kloese, matza knaidel*; Alsace: *matza knepfle*.

Ashkenazim, more than any other Jewish community, loved and relied on dumplings—in soups and stews or solo—as a major part of their diet. By the twelfth century, the concept of the dumpling, originally made from bread, had spread from Italy to Bohemia, where it was called *knödel* (knot). From there, the name traveled, with variations in pronounciation, to southern Germany, Austria, and France. The term also traveled eastward to the Slavic regions. The most widespread Ashkenazic name for dumpling became *knaidel* or *kneydl*, which is better known by the diminutive plural *knaidlach* or *kneydlakh*. As the medieval

period waned, flour began to replace bread as the base in many dumplings. During the eight days of Passover, creative housewives had to find ways to feed their family using the limited ingredients available due to the dietary restrictions of the holiday. Germans discovered that they could substitute matza for the bread or flour, creating the most widely known type of Ashkenazic dumpling, *matza knaidel*, which is often simply called *knaidel*. Soup with matza dumplings became the star of the Ashkenazic Seder meal.

Until relatively recently, *matza knaidlach* were almost exclusively a Passover food. Dumplings of bread, flour, semolina, or cheese were enjoyed throughout the rest of the year. In addition, until the twentieth century, dumplings made from crumbled matza were more prevalent than those made with the ground form, as pulverizing matza by hand required much more effort before the mechanical grinder and food processor. It was only in the early twentieth century, after Manischewitz introduced packaged matza meal, that this dumpling achieved mass popularization and its current status as an iconic Jewish food. Importantly, the presence of a uniform and inexpensive matza meal, as well as its promotion by its producers, led to matza meal dumplings becoming a Jewish food during the rest of the year—not only on Passover.

The first recorded recipe for ground matza dumplings was in the first Jewish cookbook in English, *The Jewish Manual* (London, 1846). The recipe for "Matso Soup," a beef and vegetable soup, directs: "Take half a pound of matso flour, two ounces of chopped suet, season with a little pepper, salt, ginger, and nutmeg; mix with this, four beaten eggs, and make into a paste, a small onion shredded and browned in a desert spoonful of oil is sometimes added; the paste should be made into rather large balls, and care should be taken to make them very light."

The first Jewish cookbook published in America, *Jewish Cookery,* by Esther Levy (Philadelphia, 1871), contained only "Matzo Cleis Soup," in which the dumplings were made of soaked whole matza and matza meal. It would take a while for the dumpling to garner its current English name, matza ball, reflecting the acculturation of eastern European Jews in America.

Perhaps the first record of the term was in *Mrs. Rorer's New Cook Book* (Philadelphia, 1902), by the food editor of *Ladies' Home Journal* and principal of the Philadelphia Cooking School, in a section called "A Group of Jewish Recipes," which included "Matzoth Balls for Soup." The first edition of *The Settlement Cook Book* (Milwaukee, 1901) contained two recipes for "Matzos Kloese," one made with soaked whole matzas and matza meal and the other calling for "Matzos or cracker meal," as well a recipe for "Matzos-Marrow Balls," made with matza meal. The 1903 edition omitted the previous recipes and included only "Cracker and Matzos Balls," which called for "butter size of walnut," butter being something generally unacceptable in a matza ball.

Abraham Cahan's novel *The Rise of David Levinsky* (New York, 1917) contains the line: "That there was not a trace of leavened bread in the house, its place being taken by thin, flat unleavened 'matzos,' and the repast included 'matzo balls,' wine, mead, and other accessories of a Passover meal, is a matter of course." Shortly thereafter, the term matza ball came into widespread usage.

Jewish comics helped popularize the matza ball in the American mainstream, making it one of the most famous of Jewish foods. Matza ball soup, typically featuring massive dumplings, frequently accompanied with noodles, became a staple of the Jewish deli. In 1939, black jazz musician Slim Galliard composed and recorded the song "Matzoh Balls," which was soon covered by Cab Calloway and included these opening lines: "Matzoh balls, gefilte fish, best ol' dish I ever had, now matzoh balls and gefilte fish makes you order up an extra dish." For Passover 1943, at the Farragut Naval Training Station in Idaho, Chaplain Shulman, along with Cook's Mate Third Class Irving Cohen and his three non-Jewish helpers, planned and prepared a Seder for six thousand boot camp trainees, both Jewish and interested non-Jews, burning out an electric grinder processing matzas into meal for the matza balls. The 1946 edition of *Roget's International Thesaurus* included "matzo ball soup" in its list of soups alongside gumbo, minestrone, and mulligatawny. In a 1979 episode of *Archie Bunker's Place*, Edith Bunker prepared matza ball soup for her Jewish niece, Stephanie. The contemporary popularity of matza balls even among many non-Jews demonstrates the success of those medieval cooks.

Matza balls consist of only a few ingredients—matza meal, eggs, a little fat, a liquid, salt, and pepper. Using matza meal in place of flour and adding eggs results in a lighter dumpling. Adding fat—some cooks use the fat skimmed from the top of the chicken soup or beef marrow—produces a more flavorful dumpling. Some eastern European variations included a little ground almonds or bitter almonds, the latter an item unavailable in America. Some people favor a very peppery *knaidel*, while others only want at best a hint of pepper or prefer a touch of ground ginger (or even ginger ale) and/or nutmeg. Like other Ashkenazic dumplings, matza balls can be plain or filled with a savory or sweet mixture.

Some people prefer firmer *knaidlach* (sinkers), while others favor lighter ones (floaters); the preference is almost always based upon childhood memories of one's mother's or *bubbe's* cooking. As a rule of thumb, the firmer the batter and the more fat, the heavier the matza ball. Use a little less matza meal and fat or add some beaten egg whites for lighter balls.

Knaidlach are most frequently served in chicken soup. This pairing is one of the crowning glories of Ashkenazic cuisine, as the texture and flavor of the matza balls are an ideal foil for the rich, salty broth. Alsatians sometimes serve it in beef broth rather than chicken. Although *knaidlach* can be cooked directly in the soup, they leave the liquid cloudy and are therefore usually prepared in a separate pot of lightly salted water, then transferred to either the soup pot or the soup bowl to meet up with the steaming translucent broth.

In many Ashkenazic households, matza ball soup is standard at the Passover Seder and sometimes at Sabbath dinner throughout the year. Chasidim, who do not eat matza soaked in liquid during the first seven days of Passover, make pseudo–matza balls from ground chicken or turkey and mashed potatoes. *Knaidlach* are also customarily cooked in tzimmes, pot roasts, and cholent (Sabbath stew); when cooked overnight for Sabbath lunch, the dumplings are sometimes called *cholent kugel* or *Shabbos ganif* (Sabbath thief), a name they earned by stealing flavor from the liquids in which they were cooked. Jews in Louisiana serve matza balls seasoned with chopped scallions and parsley in an unorthodox chicken and sausage gumbo.

(See also Dumpling, Gebrochts, Halke, Knedlíky, Matza, and Passover.)

ASHKENAZIC MATZA BALLS (*KNAIDLACH*)

ABOUT 12 SMALL OR 8 LARGE BALLS　　　[PAREVE OR MEAT]

4 large eggs

2 to 4 tablespoons vegetable oil or schmaltz (use less for fluffier balls)

¼ cup seltzer, club soda, chicken soup, or hot water

About 1 teaspoon salt

About ¼ teaspoon ground white or black pepper

1 to 2 tablespoons chopped fresh flat-leaf parsley or dill, or dash of ground ginger, nutmeg, or garlic powder (optional)

1 cup matza meal

About 2 tablespoons water

1. In a medium bowl, beat together the eggs, oil, seltzer, salt, pepper, and, if using, parsley. Stir in the matza meal. Cover and refrigerate for at least 1 hour and up to 2 days. Shortly before cooking, stir in enough water to make a slightly loose dough, but one that can be formed into balls. The looser the dough, the lighter the matza balls.

2. In a large pot, bring lightly salted water to a rapid boil. Using moistened hands, form the matza mixture into twelve 1-inch balls or eight 1¼-inch balls, remoistening your hands after each ball.

3. Gently drop the *knaidlach* into the boiling water, without overcrowding the pot. Cover, reduce the heat to medium, and simmer until tender, about 30 minutes. Do not open the pot for at least 20 minutes. Remove with a slotted spoon.

KNEDLÍKY

Knedlíky is a dumpling.

Origin: Czech

Czech cuisine was strongly influenced by its neighbors, all countries with a long heritage of dumplings—Austria, Germany, Hungary, and Poland. The Czech name for dumplings, *knedlíky*, comes from the Teutonic *knödel*, meaning "knot." The two most prominent types are bread (*houskové knedlíky*) and potato (*bramborové knedlíky*). Czech dumplings may also be made from matza, cheese (*syrove knedlíky*), liver (*jatrov knedlíky*), and even sweet yeast bread dough (*kynuté knedlíky*). Czech food consists largely of very saucy meat roasts and stews, such as *gulás* (goulash), and dumplings are the ideal accompaniment.

Bread dumplings are the most ancient form, allowing cooks to transform leftover loaves into a tasty way to stretch limited resources. The bread should not be too old or the dumplings will taste stale. Some cooks mix a little semolina into the dough for firmness, but this also produces a heavy dumpling. Bread dumplings—large, doughy, absorbent, and rather bland—are lighter than the dense potato ones, but still heavier than most American dumplings. They are commonly large and served cut into slices with a stew and some form of cabbage (*zelo*), such as sauerkraut, braised cabbage, or sweet-and-sour cabbage.

It is a rare Czech meal that fails to include some sort of dumpling (and some meals even include several types of dumpling), either in soup or as a side dish, and also for dessert. The plum-filled variation of the poached sweet bread dough, *svestkove knedlíky*, called *pflaumen en schlaffrok* (plums in nightgowns) in Germany, is a popular Czech Sukkot and Simchat Torah treat, making use of seasonal produce. At other times, cooks substitute a spoonful of *povidla* (plum preserves) or other fruit preserves for the fresh fruit.

By tradition, no Czech will use a knife to cut a dumpling, as it is said to spoil the flavor.

(See also Dumpling and Halke)

CZECH YEAST DUMPLINGS (*KYNUTÉ KNEDLÍKY*)

12 DUMPLINGS　　　[DAIRY OR PAREVE]

1 package (2¼ teaspoons) active dry yeast or 1 (0.6-ounce) cake fresh yeast

½ cup warm water (105°F to 115°F for dry yeast; 80°F to 85°F for fresh yeast), or ¼ cup warm water and ¼ cup milk

2 to 4 tablespoons sugar

3 large egg yolks or 2 large eggs

½ teaspoon table salt or 1 teaspoon kosher salt

½ teaspoon vanilla extract or grated lemon zest (optional)

About 2 cups (10 ounces) bread or unbleached all-purpose flour

½ cup (1 stick) unsalted butter or margarine, melted

Confectioners' sugar, cinnamon-sugar, or poppy seeds for sprinkling (optional)

1. Dissolve the yeast in ¼ cup water. Stir in 1 teaspoon sugar and let stand until foamy, 5 to 10 minutes. In a large bowl, combine the yeast mixture, remaining water, remaining sugar, eggs, salt, and, if using, vanilla. Stir in the flour, ½ cup at a time, to make a mixture that holds together. On a lightly floured surface, knead until smooth and springy, about 5 minutes. Place in an oiled bowl and turn to coat. Cover loosely with plastic wrap or a kitchen towel and let rise in a warm, draft-free place until doubled in bulk, about 1 hour.

2. Punch down the dough. Fold over and press together several times. Let stand for 10 minutes. Divide the dough into 12 equal pieces, form into balls, cover, and let rise until nearly doubled, about 30 minutes.

3. In a large pot, bring lightly salted water to a rapid boil. In batches, carefully lower the dumplings into the water, cover, reduce the heat, and simmer, shaking the pot occasionally, until dry and spongy on the inside, about 15 minutes. Remove with a slotted spoon. Repeat with the remaining dumplings. Drizzle the *knedlíky* with the melted butter and sprinkle with the sugar. Serve warm.

KNISH

Knish is a filled pastry, either baked or fried.
Origin: Probably Ukraine
Other names: Poland: *knysz*; Slovakia: *dolken*;
  Ukraine: *knysh*.

"What do you care about unfamiliar weddings and unfamiliar circumcisions? I tell my wife. Better see to it that we get something to eat. As it is written, Let all who are hungry come and eat. Nobody likes to dance on an empty stomach. If you give us borscht, fine. If not, I'll take knishes or kreplach, kugel, or dumplings. Blintzes with cheese will suit me too. Make anything you like and the more the better, but do it quickly." (From "The Bubble Bursts" [1899], a short story about Tevye the Dairyman by Sholem Aleichem.)

The knish is a classic example of peasant food evolving into comfort food and even sophisticated fare. The origins of the knish lay in a medieval Slavic fried patty called *knysz* in Poland, a peasant dish made from a cooked vegetable, most notably mashed turnips, or kasha; leftovers were typically used. These small cakes commonly accompanied a soup, and frequently the two dishes were the entire meal. Slavic cooks began stuffing the patties with a little sautéed mushrooms, onions, or chopped meat and eventually began adding bread crumbs or flour to the outer portion. In Ukraine, the *knysz* evolved into a filled yeast bread, such as a poppy seed jelly roll (*makovyi knysh*).

Eastern European Jews adapted the *knysz* to the dictates of kosher laws and to their tastes, transforming it into the knish, a small, round, fried filled pastry; this was a tasty way to enhance and stretch staples, notably kasha, cabbage, and curd cheese. Eventually, professional bakers and housewives began making a baked form of knish in which the outer wrapping became more tender and pastry-like. In the mid-nineteenth century, with the popularization of the home oven, the baked knish became the most prevalent type and emerged as the preeminent eastern Ashkenazic filled pastry.

The baked knish's rise coincided with the popularization of the potato in eastern Europe, and potato became the most common knish filling. Potato was frequently also used to make the pastry.

Knishes were sometimes everyday fare, but were more often offered at special occasions. For a Sabbath

Yonah Schimmel began selling his wife's knishes in Coney Island in 1890 and their legacy ("Always baked, never fried") continues on Manhattan's Lower East Side.

meal, they served as an appetizer, filled with chopped liver or chopped meat, or more often, as a side dish, containing kasha or potatoes, to a roast chicken or brisket. Knishes and other stuffed foods, symbolic of the bounty of the harvest, are traditional on Sukkot. Cheese and fruit knishes are customary for Shavuot and a flourless version is made for Passover. They are also popular on Purim.

Immigrants brought the knish to America toward the end of the nineteenth century, where it remained primarily Jewish fare before becoming a New York culinary favorite. As with many American gastronomic icons, such as hot dogs and hamburgers, the knish got its start in the New World by being peddled from carts by street vendors in New York and other large cities. In New York City, many hot dog or pretzel carts kept a separate compartment for knishes. Workers, students, and even businessmen commonly turned to the numerous knish vendors for a warm, hearty, inexpensive snack or meal. Knishes also became commonplace at Jewish delis, specialty stores, and Catskills resorts.

Some of the vendors expanded into larger enterprises. Yonah Schimmel, a Romanian rabbi, began selling his wife's round "always baked" potato and kasha knishes to immigrants, initially in 1890 in Coney Island. In partnership with his cousin, Joseph Berger, Schimmel relocated to the Lower East Side, first peddling knishes by pushcart and then opening a very small shop, where the partners were able to offer a larger variety. Schimmel left the business, although it retained his name, and Berger subsequently opened a still-extant store on Houston Street in 1910.

The word knish was first recorded in English in the January 17, 1916, issue of the *New York Times*, in a headline announcing, "Rivington Street Sees War, Rival Restaurant Men Cut Prices on Succulent Knish." The article explained, "Rivington Street is the latest scene of war. It is a knish war. In the event that there are any persons in the city who don't know what a knish is, it may be explained that it is a dish that was peculiar to Max Green's eating house at 150 Rivington Street until it became popular in the vicinity and competitors sent their chefs to taste it and discover its ingredients. It was made of mashed potatoes with onions and a sprinkling of cheese, all wrapped up in baked dough, like an apple dumpling, and its inventor was doing a land office business sell-

ing knishes—or knishi, or whatever the plural is—at 5 cents a knish."

In 1919, a Sephardic shoemaker from Yugoslavia, Elias Gabay, and his wife, Bella, arrived in New York City. After finding sporadic employment in shoe factories, in 1921, the couple began selling fried square potato knishes in Coney Island, before opening the first mechanized production facility, Gabila's Knishes. In 1988, New York City began to regulate the temperatures at which street food could be sold, practically eliminating the city's once-pervasive knish street vendors and much of Gabila's market. Around 1990, the company introduced frozen knishes, both precooked and uncooked, for sale in groceries. At the turn of the twenty-first century, Gabila's and Sons' plant in the Williamsburg section of Brooklyn was producing more than fifteen million knishes a year, which were sold in groceries and delis; the knishes were shipped as far away as Puerto Rico. In 2005, at around the time Gabila's claimed to have sold its one billionth knish, the company relocated its factory to Long Island.

A rule of thumb in comedy is that *k* is a funny-sounding letter, and thus the knish, along with kasha, *kishke, knaidel,* and kreplach, found its way into various vaudeville routines. Among the compositions of comedian and musician Mickey Katz was the 1959 parody "Knish Doctor." As a result, the knish entered the American consciousness and mainstream, emerging among the favorite noshes of New York City. The knish man was a common sight at New York beaches, including Coney Island. The lower stretch of Second Avenue, once dotted with Yiddish theaters and Jewish delis, was nicknamed Knish Alley. After World War II, there were even knish trucks in parts of Brooklyn and, in the summer, at the bungalows of the Catskills. Yankee Stadium vendors peddled knishes, alongside hot dogs, peanuts, and beer. In 2000, Gabila's estimated that at a typical football game at Giants Stadium, between five thousand and eight thousand knishes were sold. During New York City political campaigns, eating a knish became a common way for candidates to identify with the Jewish voter. Susan Isaacs, in her novel *Close Relations* (New York, 1980), sets such a scene as Governor James d'Avonne Gresham gushes, " 'This is why I like campaigning in Queens. A knish, real food!' " The scene continues: "The crowd beamed as the Ultimate Wasp, their Beloved Non-ethnic, smiled and inhaled, seeming to savor the greatness of the knish." The candidate then chokes on his knish.

In America, the knish continued to change. Knishes were always relatively small in the Old World, but in typical American fashion, they grew to mammoth proportions and also shrank to miniature hors d'oeuvre versions. Standard European fillings consisted of savory potato, kasha, chopped meat, liver, cabbage, and curd cheese. Modern variations include beans, broccoli, mushroom, pumpkin, spinach, sweet potato, pizza, and even tofu. Sweet cheese, cheese and fruit, and chocolate cheese fillings have become commonplace. Although the filling can be sweet, knish pastry is always savory. Many New York knish shops have become more Hispanic or Russian than Yiddish.

Since the knish was something of an undertaking to prepare, homemade knishes practically disappeared in America in the years following World War II and were replaced by knishes conveniently purchased from carts, knisheries, and appetizing stores, and, in frozen form, from grocery stores. By the end of the century, however, as the flavor of commercial knishes declined and prices soared, more people returned to homemade knishes. The knish even gained inroads outside of New York among non-Jews. In some areas of the country, knishes appear at markets and cafeterias alongside *empanadas* and *piroshki*. Knishes have also become a prominent snack in Israel. The knish remains evocative of Ashkenazic cooking.

❦ ASHKENAZIC FILLED PASTRIES (*KNISHES*)

ABOUT 8 LARGE OR 36 SMALL KNISHES   [PAREVE OR DAIRY]

Pastry:

2 cups mashed potatoes
2 large eggs, lightly beaten
2 tablespoons shortening or margarine
1 teaspoon salt
About 3 cups (15 ounces) all-purpose flour

2½ to 3 cups Ashkenazic pastry filling, such as potato, kasha, or cheese (pages 197–198)
Egg wash (1 large egg beaten with 1 tablespoon water)

1. In a large bowl, combine the potatoes, eggs, shortening, and salt. Stir in enough flour to make a soft dough. On a lightly floured surface, knead lightly until soft. Divide into fourths, shape each into a disc, cover with plastic wrap, and refrigerate for at least 2 hours or overnight.

2. Preheat the oven to 375°F. Line a large baking sheet with parchment paper or lightly grease the sheet.

3. On a lightly floured surface, roll out the pastry dough ⅛ inch thick. For large knishes: Cut into 5-by-4-inch rectangles. Place ¼ cup filling in the center of each rectangle, draw the edges together, and pinch to seal. Or fold an edge over the filling and press the edges to seal. For small knishes: Cut the dough into 3-inch rounds or squares and fill with about 1 tablespoon filling.

4. Place on the prepared baking sheet and brush with the egg wash. Bake until lightly browned, 20 to 25 minutes. Serve warm or at room temperature.

VARIATIONS

Substitute Ashkenazic Flaky Pastry or Oil Pastry (see Teig, page 582) for the potato pastry.

KOLACH

Kolach is a round coffee cake with a sweet topping.
Origin: Czech Republic
Other names: *kolac.*

Round breads are some of the most ancient of ritual foods. The ancient Slavonic word for wheel (*kolo*) gave rise to a medieval central European round bread loaf and then to an array of round breads and cakes enjoyed from the Balkans to Poland. Unquestionably, the most famous of these is the Czech *kolach* (*kolache* or *kolacky* plural). The original version was a large round made from sweet yeast dough, but smaller individual cakes have recently become widespread. Some modern cookie versions use cream cheese or sour cream pastry dough.

Some speculate that originally people simply spread *povidla* (prune butter) on slices of baked sweet bread, but eventually bakers began adding it before cooking. Other favorite toppings include apricot, cherry, sweetened farmer cheese (*tvaroh*), poppy seed, raisin, orange marmalade, and pineapple preserves. Czechs enjoy *kolache* on Purim and for other celebrations. In America, small *kolache* have become common at many morning celebrations, such as *brits*.

❦ CZECH FILLED SMALL YEAST CAKES (*KOLACHE*)

ABOUT 24 SMALL PASTRIES   [DAIRY OR PAREVE]

1 recipe Ashkenazic Yeast Pastry (page 582)

These Czech sweet, topped coffee cakes are enjoyed for Purim and smaller versions at morning celebrations such as brits.

About 3 cups various Ashkenazic sweet pastry
  fillings (page 198)
Egg wash (1 large egg beaten with 1 teaspoon
  cream, milk, or water)

1. On a lightly floured surface, roll out the pastry dough ¼ inch thick. Cut into 2½-inch rounds. Place about 3 inches apart on parchment paper–lined or greased baking sheets. Cover and let rise at room temperature until nearly doubled in bulk, about 1 hour.

2. Preheat the oven to 375°F.

3. Using a flat-bottomed drinking glass or a floured thumb, press 1 large indentation into the center of each round, leaving a ½-inch border. Or using the back of a spoon, press 2 smaller indentations into each round. Brush the edges with the egg wash. Spoon about 1 tablespoon filling into the indentation(s).

4. Bake until the kolache are golden brown or an instant-read thermometer inserted into the center registers about 180°F, about 12 minutes. Transfer the kolache to a wire rack and let cool. Wrap and store at room temperature for up to 2 days or in the freezer for up to 3 months.

KOLICHEL

Kolichel (also *kalichel*) is a Yiddish term denoting a cut from the shoulder of the cow; it is a relatively lean cut and is typically used as a pot roast and in beef borscht.

KORAIK (WRAP)

Koraik, also known as Hillel sandwich, is a combination of matza and maror eaten at the Passover Seder.

The Babylonian Talmud, in regard to the course of the Passover Seder, instructs people to first eat matza solo, then *maror* (bitter herbs) solo, and afterward to eat the matza and *maror* together in a ritual called *koraik* (Hebrew meaning "wrap/bind") "in memory of the Temple, like Hillel." *Koraik* is the tenth step of the Seder, the last before the festival meal.

The word *koraik* reveals that at the time the ritual was named, matza was pliable and flexible, as it still is among Yemenites and some Sephardim and Mizrachim. For originally *koraik* was a wrap in the modern sense, a sort of sandwich made by enveloping some meat from the paschal offering and *maror* within soft matza, akin to the modern Middle Eastern *shawarma* (roast lamb wrap). Matza as a wrap, being convenient and portable, fits into the hasty nature of the first Passover. The Bible states, "And so shall you eat it: with your loins girded, your shoes on your feet, and your staff in your hand; and you shall eat it *b'chipazon* [in haste], it is a Passover-offering to God." Thus the Talmudic matza wrap was a version of fast food. When Ashkenazim introduced hard, unflexible matza a number of centuries ago, *koraik* became a sandwich with bitter herbs.

The *koraik* is dipped into charoset before eating it. Although we do not lean when eating the *maror*, the custom is to lean while eating the *koraik*, even though it contains *maror*, because of the matza component.

The effect produced by Hillel's custom is that participants in the Seder taste all the ingredients at once, experiencing the totality of the rituals, instead of experiencing each separately and distinctly. All of

Jewish history is experienced—the good and the bad, the past and the future—in one bite.

KOSHER

Over the millennia, the dietary laws have helped to shape and define the Jewish people and the Jewish table. Kosher, the English pronunciation of the Hebrew adjective *kasher*, *cocher* in Ladino, means "fit/proper," denoting the fitness of ritual objects in general and the fitness of foods for consumption by Jews in particular. Kosher has nothing to do with being blessed by a rabbi. The modern term "kosher-style" connotes traditional Ashkenazic foods, but does not actually connote ritual "fitness."

The Bible designates which mammals may or may not be consumed—only ruminants (animals that chew their cud) with completely cloven hooves. The pig, because it uniquely has cloven hooves but does not ruminate, embodies nonkosher animals. The Bible also lists the species of kosher fowl; their identification has been handed down from generation to generation. All birds of prey are strictly forbidden. Sea creatures must possess fins and cycloid (round) or ctenoid (comblike) scales in order to be kosher. Insects, except for several species of grasshoppers that are unknown to most communities, are not kosher. Produce, especially leafy greens, must be cleaned and inspected for insects and worms. All unprocessed vegetables, fruits, nuts, grains, and minerals are inherently kosher and pareve.

In order for even a "clean" mammal or fowl to be kosher, it must be ritually slaughtered (*shechitah* in Hebrew) by a trained and skilled slaughterer (*shochet*). An improperly slaughtered animal is classified as a *neveilah*, while the victim of a predator is called *treif* (torn), a term that has come to encompass all nonkosher (nonfit) food. In addition, certain parts of ruminants—the sciatic nerve and certain fats—must be removed. Since these forbidden parts are located in the rear of the animal and since the process to remove them—called *treibern* or *nikkur*—is complicated and time-consuming, Ashkenazim generally avoid the entire hindquarter, while Sephardim and Mizrachim still use it. Nonetheless, various veins, arteries, and membranes must also be skillfully removed from the front section of the animal. Fowl are treated similarly to cattle in terms of slaughtering and removal of blood. They are also not mixed with

Kosher communities have long relied on trustworthy food purveyors like the Rosen Brothers meat store in Manhattan, here shown in 1973.

dairy products. Fish are treated differently than cattle and fowl, so the various laws of slaughter and salting do not apply.

The Bible also strictly forbids consuming the blood of animals and birds. Therefore, the blood must be removed, usually by soaking and salting (*hadacha u'melicha*). Liver is an exception and can only be kashered by broiling. If a period of three days passes following slaughter without washing and salting the meat, the blood is considered to have congealed in the capillaries and can only be removed by broiling. However, to avoid mistakes, meat that is not salted or rinsed within a seventy-two-hour period is not used.

Soaking consists of immersing the meat in cool (about 50°F) water for 30 minutes. The meat is cleansed of any visible blood, then generously covered with a layer of salt on all exposed surfaces. The salt granules must be coarse enough to extract the blood without completely dissolving on the surface, yet not be so thick that they fail to dissolve at all; hence the term kosher salt (actually "kashering salt" would be more apt) denotes salt of a medium coarseness. Kosher salt also tends to be purer than many commercial brands of table salt. The coated meat is placed on a rack or inclined board (*zalts bretl* in Yiddish) in such a manner that the blood can flow off. It stands for one hour, then the meat is rinsed in water three times to remove any external salt and blood. At this point, the meat (or chicken) is finally ready for consumption.

Before the 1950s, most kosher meat and poultry was soaked and salted at home. Today, almost all kosher meat and fowl in America and Israel comes already soaked and salted by the slaughterhouse or butcher. However, this must be confirmed, as must the reliability of the individual butcher. Mistakes, misrepresentation, or outright fraud, unfortunately, are not that uncommon. Caveat emptor applies to kosher.

Even after an animal is properly slaughtered and processed, there are still actions that can render the food unfit. In three separate locations, the Bible forbids the cooking of a newborn kid in its mother's milk. Due to this repetition, the restriction was extended to include any cooking or mixing of meat and dairy products. Therefore, kosher homes maintain separate sets of dishes and utensils for meat and dairy foods. Items that are neither meat (*fleishig* in Yiddish and *besari* in Hebrew) nor dairy (*milchig* in Yiddish and *chalavi* in Hebrew) are known as pareve. Although fish is considered a pareve food, a late medieval tradition emerged of not mixing or eating it with meat or chicken.

Food items are not the only products of concern to kosher households. Throughout history, soap was commonly made with animal fat, rendering it either unfit to use with dairy products or, more likely than not, unkosher. This changed after Israel Rokeach moved from his native Vilkovishitzky, Poland, to Kovno, Lithuania, and, under the counsel of the sage Rabbi Yitzchok Elchonon Spektor, began researching soap production. Rokeach developed a pareve (neutral) version of soap—he was the first person to use technology and chemistry in pursuit of kosher obervance. Rabbi Elchonon, however, was worried that people would confuse this new soap with the old unacceptable one, leading to a serious breach of kosher practice. In addition, people could easily use a soap bar previously used with meat with dairy utensils. After weeks of analyzing the situation, Rokeach contrived

a solution, coloring the center part of the bars—blue to be used with dairy and red for meat—and pressing the word "kosher" in Hebrew letters onto each bar. Rabbi Elchonon enthusiastically endorsed the idea and, to demonstrate his approval, wrote a certification for Rokeach's soap, something he had never done previously and never did afterward with any other product. In 1870, Israel Rokeach opened a small factory in Kovno and eastern Europeans were soon using his kosher soap. In 1890 Russian-sponsored pogroms induced Rokeach to relocate to America, where he opened a new soap factory at 470 Grand Street on Manhattan's Lower East Side. In 1924, I. Rokeach & Sons Manufacturing introduced several other nonedible items for the kosher community, including "Aluminum Cleanser and Scouring Powder," as well as various edible products, including jams, honey, cocoa, borscht, and vegetable oil. For many decades, Rokeach products were a necessity for kosher consumers across the United States.

By the beginning of the twentieth century, items aimed at the growing Jewish market, such as matza, horseradish, gefilte fish, and wine, were being produced in a growing number of Jewish-owned small factories in the United States. The reliability of these products was, as it had been in the past, either assumed or based upon the character of the owners. Then in 1925, America's premier pickle producer, the H. J. Heinz Company, decided to do something totally unprecedented—offer a kosher version of a national brand of food. At the time, it was a revolutionary idea. Nonetheless, America's Jewish community was growing in size and prosperity, and Heinz saw an opportunity to reach this untapped market. The Union of Orthodox Jewish Congregations of America in conjunction with a Jewish advertising agency devised the first and still-most-recognized graphic symbol of kosher supervision, the OU, to place on the Heinz Vegetarian Baked Bean label to alert knowing customers that it was kosher. Thus was born a new industry—kosher certification (*hashgachah* in Hebrew). A kashrut supervisor is known as a *mashgiach* and a kosher certification as *hechsher*.

Some other national companies eventually followed suit and secured supervision. Yet, for a long time, the number of kosher-supervised products remained relatively small. Meanwhile, rapid advances in food technology led to a confounding number of previously unknown ingredients and processes, making kosher supervision even more necessary. In addition, U.S. federal standards do not require the listing of minor ingredients, making it practically impossible to ascertain the kosher status of many items without some form of supervision. This meant that the kosher certification agencies needed expertise not only in Jewish law, but also in food chemistry, factory engineering, and food transport. And at the same time that food production was becoming ever more complicated, kosher standards were growing more stringent in many homes.

The situation was to dramatically change in the early 1980s when Entenmann's, a large eastern U.S. bakery, placed its entire line under kosher supervision. The response went beyond the Jewish demographics in the market area, as well as the company's expectations. Entenmann's success pointed out a previously underappreciated phenomenon: The impact of kosher symbols reaches well beyond the Jewish community. There are millions of non-Jews who purchase kosher products for religious reasons, including Seventh Day Adventists and Muslims. In addition, vegetarians can be certain a kosher product does not contain hidden meat ingredients. People suffering from milk allergies are able to avoid hidden dairy products. Furthermore, the presence of a kosher symbol on a label often provides an added enticement for stores, all of which have limited shelf space, to carry that item or place it in a better position. Many distributors, the vital cog in the American food industry, take into account a kosher symbol when considering a new item. Thus a kosher product will usually have a competitive edge over a nonkosher rival. Once this became known, more of America's major food manufacturers obtained kosher supervision when possible.

Also at this time, manufacturers began to insist on kosher tanker trucks, which hauled most of the essential liquid ingredients in prepared foods, including oils and corn syrup. This meant that suddenly almost any product could be easily converted to kosher. By the turn of the twenty-first century, around half of all national American manufactured foods had kosher supervision, accounting for nearly 70,000 products. Today, the OU, which appears on more than 60 percent of all kosher-certified products in the United States, certifies more than 2,400 corporations with 4,500 plants in 68 countries. Various other agencies, including Organized Kashrut Laboratories (OK), Chaf-K, Star-K, and numerous smaller ones, share the balance.

(See also Bird, Chametz, Cheilev, Fish, Fleishig, Glatt, Kitniyot, Liver, Milchig, Pareve, Plumba, and Passover)

KOUCLAS

Kouclas is a dumpling cooked in Sabbath stews.
Origin: Maghreb
Other names: *boulette, coclo, kora, kouclas.*

When the Sephardic Sabbath stew reached the Maghreb, it took on many new names, including *dafina, frackh,* and *skhina,* and new dimensions, including the addition of various dumplings called *kouclas.* Moroccan Sabbath stews are much more liquidy than the Ashkenazic type; the various components are frequently served separately and the dumpling is cut into slices. Every family and community has its own type of dumpling. The most widespread recipes contain rice or ground beef or a combination of both (*kouclas bi ruz*), which is akin to a sausage. Another type is made from bread crumbs (*kouclas bi khobz*) or, on Passover, matza. In Algeria, the meat dumpling is known as a *bobinet,* while a beef and egg hash dumpling is a *megina.* Historically, the dumpling was wrapped in a piece of cloth, but some cooks today use a large piece of aluminum foil or an empty tin can.

(See also Adafina and Hamin)

MOROCCAN RICE AND MEAT DUMPLING
(*KOUCLAS BI RUZ/RELLENO DE ARROZ*)

I SMALL LOAF   [MEAT]

1 cup long-grain rice
4 ounces ground lamb or beef
½ cup (2 ounces) ground walnuts or 3 tablespoons raisins
½ cup chopped fresh flat-leaf parsley
2 large eggs, lightly beaten
1 teaspoon ground cinnamon
½ teaspoon ground nutmeg or a pinch of ground ginger
About ½ teaspoon salt
Ground black pepper to taste

In a large bowl, combine all the ingredients. Wrap loosely in a piece of cheesecloth and tie securely. Or wrap loosely in a piece of aluminum foil and poke several small holes to vent. Place in the center of a hamin/adafina (Sabbath stew) and add more water to the stew to account for absorption.

KREPLACH/KREPL

Kreplach/krepl is a filled pasta triangle, most often served in soup.

Origin: Eastern Europe

Before the advent of Yiddish around 1250, the common language of the nascent Ashkenazim in northern France was a form of Old French, as evidenced in the names of early Ashkenazic dishes, including cholent (Sabbath stew), *fluden* (layered pastries), *oublies* (waffle wafers), and *krepish*. First recorded in the twelfth century, *krepish* consisted of a small piece of meat wrapped in a thin sheet of pastry and fried; the dish was somewhat similar to the later eastern European knish. The name of this very popular treat came from the Old French word *crespe* (curly/wrinkled), which much later also gave rise to crepe, the word for the thin French pancake, and is related to the English word crisp and the German word *krapfen* (fried). Eastern Europeans innovated with a cheese filling, as Rabbi Isaac ben Moses of Vienna (1180–1260) made a point of noting. He commented, "Jews in the Slavic lands also made *krepish* with cheese." Around the sixteenth century, eastern Europeans, about the same time that they ceased making *krepish*, began making filled pasta; this practice may have been a by-product of Tatar incursions from Asia or may have been introduced from Italy, or both. This was a dramatic innovation in northern Europe, since boiling food in water was far cheaper than frying it in fat. Poles called their filled pasta *pierogi*, while in the Ukraine, they became known as *varenikes*. The predominant eastern Ashkenazic name for filled pasta became *krepl* (or *kreplekh* plural).

Kreplach, like all Ashkenazic noodles, are made from wheat flour bound with eggs, not the semolina conventional in the Mediterranean. Originally, *kreplach* were filled with chopped cooked meat, which was typically a way of stretching and enhancing leftovers or a tight budget. Lung and chopped liver were once particularly widespread. After a meat shortage befell Europe in the sixteenth century, fruit and nut fillings also became popular. For dairy meals, a little soft cheese was substituted. Other standard fillings included cabbage, kasha, mushroom, and, in the mid-nineteenth century, potato, although meat remained the most popular.

Kreplach are rarely eaten plain: Meat types are most commonly served swimming in chicken soup, while cheese or potato are typically bathed in sour cream or, like many dumpings, lightly fried after boiling and paired with sautéed onions.

Kreplach quickly became a much-beloved Ashkenazic delicacy and an integral part of Jewish culture. A popular Yiddish expression for "too much of a good thing" is "*Kreplach esn vert oykh nimes*" (One even gets tired of eating *kreplach*). Isaac Bashevis Singer, in his 1956 short story "Gimpel the Fool," wrote, "One night, when the period of mourning was done, as I lay dreaming on the flour sacks, there came the Spirit of Evil himself and said to me, 'Gimpel, why do you sleep?' I said, 'What should I be doing? Eating kreplach?' "

Making noodles by hand was a *potchke* (bother), so historically Ashkenazic housewives prepared them only once a week or less. Filled pasta required even more effort, meat for the filling was typically expensive and rare, and *kreplach* could not be stored for any length of time. Therefore, *kreplach* were generally reserved for special occasions and for four specific holidays: Yom Kippur eve, Hoshanah Rabbah, Purim, and Shavuot. At the meal before the fast of Yom Kippur (*Seudah Mafseket*), meat *kreplach* are traditional in chicken soup, as the mystics compare the wrapping of dough with the divine envelopment of mercy, kindness, and protection demonstrated on Yom Kippur. Hoshanah Rabbah (the seventh day of Sukkot) is regarded as the day on which the verdicts of judgment delivered on Yom Kippur are sealed and, accordingly, traditional Yom Kippur eve foods are served. Another symbolic meaning of *kreplach* is that the filling is "beaten" (i.e., minced), just as willow branches are beaten on Hoshanah Rabbah, Haman was "beaten" on Purim, and sinners theoretically deserve to be beaten on Yom Kippur. All three of these occasions are also days when work is permitted, and the *kreplach* with their concealed filling have been said to remind us of the days' hidden holiness. Cheese *kreplach*, with either a savory or sweet curd filling, are often customary on Shavuot. Dairy *kreplach* were also once served as an occasional weekday treat during the spring and summer when fresh cheese was plentiful.

By the seventeenth century, *kreplach* were becoming traditional Purim fare among eastern Europeans as well; they were served filled with meat and floating in chicken soup. If featured for dessert, they might contain cherry, plum, or strawberry preserves. *Kreplach* also came to represent the three-cornered hat or ear ascribed to the villainous Haman.

Kreplach, spelled *creplich*, was first mentioned in English in Israel Zangwill's *Children of the Ghetto* (London, 1892). A recipe for "Creplech" appeared in the first edition of *The Settlement Cook Book* (Milwaukee, 1901).

Meat *kreplach*, called "meat balls with sport jackets" and "the eternal triangle" by humorist Sam Levenson, became standard at Jewish delis, while hearty cheese ones were a mainstay of Catskills hotels and Jewish dairy restaurants. As a result, cheese *kreplach* with sour cream was adopted as movie star Jimmy Cagney's favorite nosh, which he enjoyed at various Jewish eateries. Mel Brooks, in one of his 2000-Year-Old Man routines, said about the secret to his longevity: "The major thing is that I never eat fried food. I don't eat it, I wouldn't look at it; I don't touch it. Except maybe once in a while a little schnitzel, a few blintzes, a plate of kreplach." Krepl and kreplach even became geometric terms for a type of triangle. Yet *kreplach* never achieved the prominence in mainstream American gastronomy as ravioli or wontons, remaining primarily an iconic Jewish food.

(See also Lokshen, Pirog, and Varenik/Varenikes)

EASTERN EUROPEAN FILLED PASTA TRIANGLES (*KREPLACH*)

ABOUT THIRTY-TWO 3-INCH DUMPLINGS   [MEAT]

Filling:
2 tablespoon vegetable oil or schmaltz
1 medium onion, chopped
1 pound ground beef chuck
1 to 2 tablespoons chopped fresh flat-leaf parsley
    or dill
About 1 teaspoon salt
About ¼ teaspoon ground black pepper

1 recipe (1 pound) Egg Noodle Dough (page 368),
    prepared according to directions below, or
    32 wonton wrappers

1. To make the filling: In a large skillet, heat the oil over medium heat. Add the onion and sauté until soft and translucent, about 5 minutes. Add the beef and sauté until the meat loses its red coloring, about 5 minutes. Remove from the heat and stir in the parsley, salt, and pepper. Let cool.

2. After kneading the dough in Step 2 of the Egg Noodle Dough recipe, cover and let stand at room temperature for 1 hour. Divide the dough in half. On a lightly floured surface, roll out each piece into a rectangle about ⅛ inch thick. Cut into 2½- to 3-inch squares. Reroll any dough scraps.

3. Place 1 teaspoon filling in the center of each 2½-inch square or a heaping teaspoon in the center of each 3-inch square. Brush the dough edges with a little water to moisten and fold over diagonally to form a triangle, pressing out any air. Pinch the edges or press with the tines of a fork to seal.

4. Place on a lightly floured surface or a kitchen towel, cover with a kitchen towel, and let stand until the dough begins to feel dry but is still supple, about 30 minutes. The pasta may be prepared ahead up to this point and refrigerated for up to 1 week or frozen for up to 3 months until ready to use. Do not thaw before cooking, but increase the cooking time by about 5 minutes.

5. In a large pot, bring lightly salted water to a rapid boil. In several batches, drop the pasta into the pot, reduce the heat to medium, and cook, uncovered, until the kreplach are tender but not mushy, about 15 minutes. With a slotted spoon, remove the pasta and drain.

6. Add the kreplach to hot chicken soup or fry in a little schmaltz or vegetable oil until golden brown, 2 to 3 minutes.

VARIATIONS

For the meat filling, substitute about 2 cups Ashkenazic pastry filling, such as potato or cheese (page 197), or Pirogen filling (pages 465–466).

KRUPNIK

Krupnik is barley soup.
Origin: Poland

The most common modern culinary usage of barley, other than in brewing beer and distilling liquor, is in hearty soups. The Slavic word for hulled grains, *krupa*, gave rise to the name of this fundamental Polish and Baltic soup, *krupnik*. *The Jewish Encyclopedia* (New York, 1903) includes *krupnik* in a list of soups common among both Jews and non-Jews.

Although barley served as its basis, this soup always

contained other hearty ingredients, notably mushrooms and various root vegetables. Some Jewish versions were pareve, but others were made with meat. When made pareve, *krupnik* is frequently served with a dollop of sour cream. The Yiddish expression *"Beser bay zikh krupnik, eyder bay yenem gebrotns"* (Better barley soup at home than a roast at someone else's home) reflects the fact that *krupnik* was an unexciting staple of the diet in Poland and the Baltic States and a regular weekday meal; in some households it was eaten on a daily basis.

POLISH BARLEY SOUP (*KRUPNIK*)

6 TO 8 SERVINGS   [MEAT OR PAREVE]

 3 tablespoons vegetable oil or schmaltz
 2 medium yellow onions, chopped
 2 to 3 cloves garlic, minced
 3 tablespoons chopped fresh flat-leaf parsley
 8 cups chicken broth, beef broth, vegetable broth, or water
 1 cup (6.5 ounces) pearl barley, rinsed
 1 to 2 pounds fresh mushrooms, sliced, or 1 ounce dried Polish or Italian mushrooms, soaked and sliced
 3 medium carrots, chopped
 2 medium parsnips or turnips, peeled and chopped
 1 large boiling potato, peeled and diced
 1 bay leaf
 About 1½ teaspoons table salt or 1 tablespoon kosher salt
 Ground black pepper to taste
 1 tablespoon sweet paprika (optional)

In a large, heavy pot, heat the oil over medium heat. Add the onions and garlic and sauté until softened, 5 to 10 minutes. Add the parsley. Add the broth, barley, mushrooms, carrots, parsnips, potatoes, bay leaf, salt, pepper, and, if using, paprika. Bring to a boil, cover, reduce the heat, and simmer until the barley is tender, about 45 minutes.

KRUSHKA

Krushka is a Jewish eastern European stew made from veal innards; as in numerous other widespread dishes, humble parts of the animal were transformed into a hearty meal. Like many once-traditional rustic dishes, especially those made from offal, it lost favor in America and Israel.

KUBANEH

Kubaneh is a long-cooked pull-apart yeast bread.
Origin: Yemen
Other names: *kubana, kubani, kubneh.*

Bread, in various forms, constituted the mainstay of the Yemenite diet. Most of these were very simple loaves, frequently unleavened pancake breads and basic leavened flatbreads. An exception was *kubaneh*, a yeast bread prepared on Friday afternoon before the onset of the Sabbath, then left to cook overnight. On the Sabbath, following Friday night dinner and sometimes after taking a little nap, many Yemenites had a tradition of going to the synagogue to study or recite psalms with a distinctive melody. Women might also attend, in the women's section, soaking in the music and holy words. It was common for people to bring

This unusual Yemenite yeast bread is cooked covered, which steams and bakes the bread, at low temperatures overnight for the Saturday meal.

along jars of sweetened coffee, providing a boost of energy. After several hours, most people would return home to sleep, before rising early to return to the synagogue at sunrise for the morning service. In the morning in every household, Yemenites would enjoy their *kubaneh*. Some people ate this treat before the morning synagogue service, while others had the custom of taking a break in the middle of services and before the Torah reading and *Musaf* service, going home to enjoy the *kubaneh*. Still others waited till after the services, but before lunch.

The secret to *kubaneh* is not in the dough, but in the cooking. Uniquely, the bread is cooked for a very long time in a tightly covered dish at a low temperature, steaming the bread as well as baking it. Some cooks simply roll balls of dough in fat, while others prepare them like *jachnun*, rolling them out flat, spreading them with *samneh* (clarified butter), then rolling them up. The result is a tall golden loaf divided into large balls, with the top part somewhat airier than the bottom. It is soft, but with a heavy, flaky texture and a rich flavor. Eggs in the shell are usually cooked in the pan alongside the bread; the eggs, which turn brown and creamy, and *kubaneh* are then served together, along with *hilbeh* (fenugreek relish), *rotav ahgfaniyot* (fresh tomato puree), and butter, and sometimes spiced coffee.

Since *kubaneh* was customarily made with *samneh*, it was not eaten at Sabbath lunch, which featured meat dishes. However, pareve versions were also prepared using oil or, in Israel, margarine. If necessary, after removing the pot from the heat, the container is covered with a blanket to keep it warm until serving. As with other breads, Yemenites customarily do not eat directly from a very large piece, but rather tear off bite-sized portions.

Kubaneh requires a special round aluminum pot, about eight inches in diameter with a fitted cover containing a very small hole in the center, called either a "*seer kubaneh*" or "*seer jachnun*." Today, *kubaneh* is very popular in Israel. It is available in some restaurants, as well as sold in some supermarkets.

◈ YEMENITE OVERNIGHT BREAD (*KUBANEH*)

8 TO 10 SERVINGS   [PAREVE OR DAIRY]

1 package (2¼ teaspoons) active dry yeast or
    1 (0.6-ounce) cake fresh yeast

1½ cups warm water (105°F to 115°F for dry yeast;
    80°F to 85°F for fresh yeast)
1 teaspoon sugar or honey
¼ cup vegetable oil or samneh (Middle Eastern
    clarified butter)
2 teaspoons table salt or 4 teaspoons kosher salt
About 4 cups (20 ounces) bread or unbleached all-
    purpose flour, or 3 cups white flour and 1 cup
    whole-wheat flour
Additional flour for rolling
½ cup margarine or samneh, melted, for rolling
8 to 10 eggs in shell (optional)

1. Dissolve the yeast in ¼ cup water. Stir in the sugar and let stand until foamy, 5 to 10 minutes. In a large bowl, combine the yeast mixture, remaining water, oil, salt, and 2 cups flour. Gradually add enough of the remaining flour to make a mixture that holds together.

2. On a lightly floured surface, knead the dough until smooth and elastic, 10 to 15 minutes. Place in an oiled bowl and turn to coat. Cover loosely with plastic wrap or a kitchen towel and let rise in a warm, draft-free place until doubled in bulk, about 1½ hours.

3. Grease a kubaneh pan, deep 3-quart ovenproof dish or saucepan, or 10-inch tube pan. Punch down the dough, knead briefly, and form into 1- to 1½-inch balls. Roll the balls in the flour, then in the melted margarine to coat. Arrange in the prepared pan, placing one ball in the center and the remaining ones around it, until all the dough is used. If using, arrange the eggs in the pan. Cover with a kitchen towel and let rise in a warm, draft-free place until nearly doubled in bulk, about 1 hour.

4. Cover with the flat top of the kubaneh pan or a piece of heavy-duty aluminum foil. Place in a 200°F oven and bake overnight, 9 to 12 hours. Alternatively, without the second rise, cook over medium heat until the dough balls begin to expand, about 15 minutes, invert the kubaneh pot onto a baking sheet or directly onto a blech (a thin sheet of metal placed over the range top and knobs), and cook on the stove top over very low heat overnight. Once you remove the pot from the heat, remove the top to prevent the bread from becoming soggy. Serve warm.

KUBBEH

Kubbeh is a round meat dumpling with an outer grain shell.

Origin: Iraq
Other names: *kubba*; Azerbaijan: *kiufta*; Egypt: *kobeba, kubeba.*

Every Middle Eastern community has its own form of ground meat dumpling and in Iraq and Kudistan it is *kubbeh*, from the Arabic meaning "dome/ball." *Kubbeh* is a large meatball encased in a shell of semolina or rice. Iraqi and Kurdish *kubbeh*, their signature dish, are typically round and simmered in a soup or stew, not fried first like the cylindrical Levantine *kibbeh mahshi*.

A *kubbeh* looks something like a matza ball and similarly swells up as it cooks in a soup or flavored broth; the shell has a soft consistency and the meat beneath has a firm texture. The shell absorbs some of the soup and its flavor during cooking, so the ultimate nature of the *kubbeh* depends on the medium in which it is simmered; the mild *kubbeh* is intended to complement and enhance a flavorful soup.

Lamb is the preferred *kubbeh* filling, but beef, veal, chicken, and even fish are also popular. In Israel, mushroom has become a widespread vegetarian version. Unlike the smooth texture of most Middle Eastern ground meat, which is pounded into a paste with a *madaqqa* (pestle) in a *jurn* (mortar), the filling for *kubbeh* is typically slightly coarse. Pine nuts are commonly added to the filling in the Levant, but are not used in Iraq.

Among Iraqis and Kurds, the quality of a cook's *kubbeh* was once a measure of her culinary skills; the technique was typically passed on from mother or grandmother and perfected through considerable practice. The *kubbeh* shell is made from a grain, typically semolina, rice, or bulgur; bulgur is more common in the Levant, while semolina predominates in central Asia. If the shell is too thick, it becomes heavy and doughlike and overwhelms the juicy filling. If it is too thin, the filling leaks out. The Iraqi city of Mosul is renowned for its rice *kubbeh*. Shells made of rice and of a combination of rice and meat are common for Passover.

Iraqis make two basic types of soups for *kubbeh*, containing various seasonal and favored vegetables: *hamudh* (sour) and *huluo* (literally "sweet," but actually denoting one without citrus juice). In Israel, more sugar is typically added, transforming them into sweet-and-sour soups. Spicer fillings are frequently used in *kubbeh* for *huluo* soups. Some cooks use rounder *kubbeh* in *huluo* soups and slightly flattened ones in *hamudh* soups.

Kubbeh prepared in a broth dominated by lemon or lime juice and celery, and frequently containing slightly bitter greens, are called *chamutzta* or *hamoustah*. If lots of garlic is added to the lemon and greens soup, the dish is known as *kubbeh shel paam*. Iraqi soups tend to be more delicate and elegant than the rustic Kurdish types. Iraqis have a particular penchant for *kubbeh* with okra. Meat chunks are sometimes substituted for the *kubbeh*, but the two are very rarely combined in the same soup. Whether tangy or savory, good soups contain an intriguing balance of elements. These soups are almost always served with white rice.

Kurds also cook *kubbeh* in a tomato-based broth (frequently also containing beets) called *matfuniya* (buried) and, in Israel, *marak adom* (red soup). *Matfun* is a Kurdish, Persian, and Arabic variation of *madfun*, akin to the Sephardic word *dafina* (also meaning "buried"). A nineteenth-century name for Abydos, the burial place of Osiris along the Nile, was Arabat el Matfoon. The name probably refers to the meat "buried/hidden" in the grain shell of the *kubbeh*, although in a large bowl, the *kubbeh* could be buried in the red soup and vegetables.

Since *kubbeh* are labor-intensive to prepare, even for experienced cooks, they are generally reserved for special occasions. Among Iraqis and Kurds, *kubbeh* are ubiquitous as Sabbath and holiday fare. A typical Iraqi and Kurdish Friday night meal typically features a bowl of soup containing two or three *kubbeh*. Today, it is not uncommon for home cooks to prepare a large batch of *kubbeh* and keep some in the freezer for future use.

Iraqis and Kurds brought *kubbeh* to Israel in the 1950s and the dish eventually spread to other Jews; it became the culinary term most identified with Mizrachi cookery, the equivalent of the Ashkenazi gefilte fish. Commercial frozen *kubbeh* are found in Israeli markets and butcher shops, where the flavoring is typically milder in the central Asian manner, rather than spicier in the Levantine style. There are Israeli restaurants specializing in *kubbeh* soups and many grills offer these soups as well. Israelis have begun to spread their passion for *kubbeh* to America, where the dumplings can now be found in some Jewish markets and restaurants.

(See also Kebab, Kefte, Kibbeh, and Kufta)

IRAQI FILLED DUMPLINGS/KURDISH FILLED DUMPLINGS (*KUBBEH*)

ABOUT 32 DUMPLINGS   [MEAT]

Filling:

3 tablespoons olive or vegetable oil

1 large yellow onion, minced

20 ounces ground lamb, beef, veal, or chicken

3 to 4 tablespoons chopped fresh flat-leaf parsley

3 tablespoons chopped celery leaves (optional)

About 1 teaspoon table salt or 2 teaspoons kosher salt

About ½ teaspoon ground black pepper

½ teaspoon ground turmeric or ¼ teaspoon cayenne

Shell:

¾ teaspoon table salt or 1½ teaspoons kosher salt

About 1¾ cups water

Ground black pepper to taste (optional)

2 teaspoons vegetable oil (optional)

2½ cups (15 ounces) fine semolina (not semolina flour)

2 quarts *kubbeh* soup (recipes follow) or any chicken or vegetable soup, boiling

1. To make the filling: In a large skillet, heat the oil over medium heat. Add the onion and sauté until soft and translucent, 5 to 10 minutes. Add the meat and sauté until it loses its red color, about 5 minutes. Drain off any excess fat. Stir in the parsley, salt, pepper, and turmeric. Let cool.

2. To make the shell: In a small bowl, stir the salt into the water. If using, add the pepper and/or oil. Place the semolina in a medium bowl, stir in the salted water, and knead to make a smooth, supple dough. Cover and let stand to firm and hydrate, about 20 minutes.

3. To form each shell, with moistened hands, shape about 2 tablespoons *kubbeh* dough into a smooth 1-inch ball. Place the ball in the palm of one hand. Using the index finger of the other hand, push into the middle of a ball to form a hole, then move your finger in the hole while pressing the outside of the ball against your palm (squeezing and turning the ball), hollowing out the ball. Stuff the cavity of each shell with about 1 tablespoon filling and press the open end

to enclose the filling and seal the top. (Alternatively, for easier forming, press the shell balls into thin, flat 3-inch rounds, spoon about 2 teaspoons filling into the center, bring the edges together over the filling, press to seal, and reroll into a ball with an even shell.)

4. Some cooks leave the balls round, while others, particularly in the north of Iraq, slightly flatten them. Place on a baking sheet or dish lined with parchment paper or wax paper, cover, and refrigerate for at least 1 hour. The *kubbeh* may be prepared ahead up to this point and frozen for up to 3 months; do not defrost before cooking.

5. Add the *kubbeh* to the boiling soup, reduce the heat to medium, and simmer until the *kubbeh* are cooked through, about 30 minutes. If the soup becomes too thick, add a little more water.

IRAQI TANGY DUMPLING SOUP (*MARAK KUBBEH HAMUDH*)

6 TO 8 SERVINGS   [MEAT OR PAREVE]

3 tablespoons vegetable oil

2 medium onions, chopped

½ cup tomato paste or 3 tablespoons tomato paste and 2 cups peeled, seeded, and chopped tomatoes

8 cups chicken broth or water

About ¾ cup fresh lemon juice or 1 teaspoon citric acid

1 to 6 tablespoons sugar

2 teaspoons paprika

About 1 teaspoon table salt or 2 teaspoons kosher salt

About ½ teaspoon ground black pepper

In a large nonreactive pot, heat the oil over medium heat. Add the onions and sauté until soft and translucent, about 10 minutes. Add the tomato paste (but not the chopped tomatoes) and stir for 2 minutes. Add the broth, lemon juice, sugar, paprika, salt, pepper, and, if using, chopped tomatoes. Bring to a boil, reduce the heat to medium-low, and simmer for 20 minutes. The soup can be prepared ahead up to this point, stored in the refrigerator for up to 2 days, and reheated.

VARIATIONS

Iraqi Dumplings in Tangy Beet Soup (Kubbeh Aduma/Kubbeh Shwandar/Khelo Hamudh): With the broth, add 1 pound (3 medium) peeled beets cut into 1-inch cubes and increase the cooking time before adding the kubbeh to about 40 minutes. After simmering the beets for 20 minutes, add any combination of 5 to 6 stalks celery cut into 2-inch pieces, 8 ounces chard cut into pieces, 8 ounces trimmed okra, 8 ounces peeled and cubed pumpkin, and/or 2 thickly sliced zucchini and simmer until tender, about 20 minutes.

KUCHEN

Kuchen is a generic German and Yiddish word for a baked good, although it generally specifies a cake; the term was first applied to cakes around 1650. (In some parts of eastern Europe, *lekekh* was the generic word for cake.) Originally, kuchen were made with a rich yeast dough (*feine heifeteig*). The dough was typically pressed onto a baking sheet or into a large baking pan and the resulting baked goods were subsumed under the category of *blechkuchen* (sheet cakes). Popular varieties included *puterkuchen* (buttery yeast cake, sometimes topped with sliced almonds), *streuselkuchen* (crumb cake), *mohnkuchen* (poppy seed cake), *zimtkuchen* (cinnamon cake), *kaesekuchen* (cheese cake), *rahmkuchen* (cream cake), *apfelkuchen* (apple cake), and *zwetschgenkuchen* (plum cake). The advent of chemical leavenings in the nineteenth century led to easier versions of traditional yeast-raised kuchens. Cakes leavened with baking soda or baking powder were known as *blitz kuchen* (lightening cake), as they could be put together rather quickly. German Jewish women, in particular, took to the new nineteenth-century institution of the *kaffeeklatsch* (coffee chat), an hour or so of coffee drinking and socializing with other women; accordingly, they developed a wide array of kuchen to serve with the coffee, many of which later became standards in the American Jewish repertoire.

Beginning in the 1840s, dire economic and social conditions in Germany spurred a mass immigration to America, including many Jews, who settled in the urban areas of the East, as well as in frontier communities in the West. By sheer numbers, German immigrants were bound to affect their new homeland; in particular, they transformed American baking and language. Nevertheless, as with other immigrant groups, it took many decades for the newcomers to become accepted by the general population, and for demographic changes to spark changes in American culture. Among the German dishes appreciated by Americans as well as eastern European immigrants were kuchen, the term first recorded in English in 1854. Kuchen became even more popular when cooks began adapting them to the new chemical leavenings and when the home oven became widespread.

Edna Ferber, the German Jewish author of, among other works, *Giant* and *Show Boat*, drew from her upbringing in Wisconsin for *Fanny Herself* (New York, 1917). The author described the spread for the meal to break the fast of Yom Kippur at one house, noting the custom of German Jews "to begin the evening meal, after the twenty-four hours of abstainment, with coffee and freshly-baked coffee cake of every variety."

She continued, "The pantry was fragrant as a garden with spices, and fruit scents, and the melting, delectable perfume of brown, freshly-baked dough, sugar-coated. There was one giant platter devoted wholly to round, plump cakes, with puffy edges, in the center of each a sunken pool that was all plum, bearing on its bosom a snowy sifting of powdered sugar. There were others whose centers were apricot, pure molten gold in the sunlight. There were speckled expanses of cheese kuchen, the golden-brown surface showing rich cracks through which one caught glimpses of the lemon-yellow cheese beneath—cottage cheese that had been beaten up with eggs, and spices, and sugar, and lemon. Flaky crust rose, jaggedly, above this plateau. There were cakes with jelly, and cinnamon kuchen, and cunning cakes with almond slices nestling side by side."

The word kuchen, however, proved too foreign sounding for many Americans and, instead, the anglicized rendering of the Teutonic *kaffeekuchen*, "coffee cake," became the new name in America. The term was first recorded in an 1870 cookbook, where it referred to butter cakes flavored with coffee. However, drinking coffee with coffee-flavored cake proved redundant and, instead, the term came to be applied to yeast kuchen and the easier new chemically leavened butter cakes.

Aunt Babette's (Cincinnati, 1889), a cookbook written by a German Jew, provided a recipe for an "English Coffee Cake," a coffee-flavored butter cake leavened with soda and cream of tartar. There was also a separate section entitled "Coffee Cakes," encompassing an assortment of German yeast-raised kuchen and other pastries. Besides using the term in the section title, the author refers to one of these cakes as "kaffee kuchen" and two as "coffee cake." In the German tradition, the recipes in the "cake" section are leavened with chemicals, while all the baked goods in the "coffee cakes" section are raised with yeast.

As the twentieth century progressed, the easier baking powder coffee cakes became the most common types. Coffee cakes are generally lightly covered with glaze, streusel, or cinnamon-sugar topping—never frosting. Unquestionably, the favorite kuchen topping has long been streusel (from the German *streusen*, "to scatter"), a simple pastry of flour, sugar, butter, and sometimes some spices. Streusel is called crumble in England, a word and food that only appeared in Britain in the twentieth century.

Eastern European Jews in America typically clung to their fare, or to Americanized versions of it. When it came to baked goods, however, they acknowledged the German superiority by readily adopting kuchen and many other German baked goods into their repertoire. Coffee cakes rank among the most popular of comfort foods—they are welcome at breakfast, lunch, afternoon tea, dinner, sisterhood meetings, and, as the name indicates, coffee breaks. Pareve versions containing margarine or oil are sometimes made for meat occasions. However, the best-flavored kuchen, whether made with yeast or baking powder, are dairy versions made with butter and/or sour cream, and Ashkenazim commonly serve these at the meal following Yom Kippur, on Shavuot, at a dairy Sabbath kiddush, and at the *melaveh malcha* (accompanying the queen) party following the Sabbath. For the latter occasion, spices are sometimes added to the batter and topping, reflecting those used during the Havdalah ceremony signaling the end of the Sabbath.

(See also Bialy, Kakosh, Kugelhopf, Makosh/Mákos Beigli, and Zwetschgenkuchen)

ASHKENAZIC SOUR CREAM COFFEE CAKE (SMETENEH KUCHEN)

ONE 9-INCH SQUARE OR BUNDT CAKE/6 TO 9 SERVINGS

[DAIRY]

Streusel Topping:
½ cup (3.5 ounces) granulated or brown sugar, or ¼ cup each
½ cup (2.5 ounces) all-purpose flour
¾ teaspoon ground cinnamon
⅛ teaspoon salt
¼ to ½ teaspoon ground nutmeg or cloves (optional)
¼ cup (½ stick) unsalted butter or margarine, softened
½ cup coarsely chopped walnuts or pecans, grated coconut, golden raisins, or chocolate chips, or 1 cup any combination (optional)

Batter:
2 cups (10 ounces) all-purpose flour
1 teaspoon double-acting baking powder
1 teaspoon baking soda
½ teaspoon salt
½ cup (1 stick) unsalted butter, softened
1 cup (7 ounces) granulated or brown sugar, or ½ cup each
4 large egg yolks or 3 large eggs
1 cup (8 ounces) sour cream or plain yogurt
1½ teaspoons vanilla extract
1 teaspoon finely grated lemon zest (optional)

1. Preheat the oven to 350°F (325°F if using a glass pan). Grease a 9-inch square baking pan, 9-inch Bundt or tube pan, or 9-inch springform pan. Line the bottom with parchment paper or wax paper, grease again, and dust with flour.

2. To make the streusel: In a medium bowl, combine the sugar, flour, cinnamon, salt, and, if using, nutmeg. Cut in the butter to make a mixture that resembles coarse crumbs. If desired, stir in the nuts.

3. To make the batter: Sift together the flour, baking powder, baking soda, and salt. In a large bowl, beat the butter until smooth, about 1 minute. Gradually add the sugar and beat until light and fluffy, about 4 minutes. Beat in the egg yolks, one at a time. Blend in the sour cream, vanilla, and, if using, zest. Stir in the flour mixture.

4. Spread two-thirds of the batter in the prepared pan. Sprinkle with half of the streusel. Carefully cover with the remaining batter and sprinkle with the remaining streusel.

5. Bake until the cake is golden and pulls away from the sides of the pan, about 50 minutes for a 9-inch pan, or 1 hour for a Bundt pan. Set on a wire rack and let cool in the pan for at least 15 minutes. Serve warm or at room temperature. Wrap the kuchen and store at room temperature for up to 2 days or in the freezer for up to 3 months.

VARIATIONS

Cheese Coffee Cake (Kaesekuchen): Combine 8 ounces softened cream cheese, ¼ cup sugar, 1 large egg, and 1 teaspoon vanilla extract. Spread over the top of the batter, leaving a 1-inch border on all sides.

Fruit Coffee Cake (Fruchtkuchen): After adding the middle layer of streusel, top with 1 cup peeled, cored, and thinly sliced apples; 1 cup peeled, pitted, and sliced peaches; 1 cup pitted cherries; or 1 cup blueberries, blackberries, or raspberries.

KUFTA

Kufta is meat, usually lamb, pounded smooth, seasoned with local spice favorites, and formed into football-shaped patties or balls.

Origin: Middle East

Other names: Azerbaijan: *küfte*; Balkans: *kiofte, kjofte*; Bulgaria: *kiufte*; Calcutta: *kofta, koofta*; Georgia: *kufta*; Greece: *keftaidakia, keftike, keiftede*; Morocco: *kefta, kifta*; Persia: *kiufta, kufteh*; Romania: *chiftea*; Serbia: *cufte*; Sephardim: *kefte*; Turkey: *köfte*.

Chopping and pounding are ancient ways of tenderizing tougher cuts of meat. Until the 1860s and the advent of the mechanical meat grinder, this was done by hand and was very labor-intensive. Typically, Middle Easterners pounded meat into a smooth paste in a *jurn* (mortar) with a *madaqqa* (pestle). Most Middle Eastern cooks prefer ground meat with a smooth texture.

The most widespread use of pounded meat was in meatballs. *Kufta*, from the Persian word *kuftan* (to pound/to smash), refers to the original Middle Eastern method of preparing ground beef. The Arabs, in particular, were responsible for disseminating meatballs far and wide, including the Iberian *albondigas*. Variations of the word *kufteh* referring to patties and meatballs can be found in most Middle Eastern and North African cuisines. Early medieval Arabic cookbooks contain recipes for meatballs, typically the size of oranges.

Unlike the Sephardic *kefte*, the Middle Eastern (Syrian, Lebanese, and Iraqi) variations generally do not contain bread crumbs or eggs. Instead, the loose meat disassociates and congeals when subjected to heat. The meat, though, is typically mixed with chopped onions, parsley, and locally favored spices.

It is formed into balls or patties and then prepared by one of several methods: fried in a thin layer of oil, baked, simmered in hot liquid, or wrapped around skewers and grilled; the latter method produces *kufta kebab*, the most widespread version in modern Israel. Azerbaijan is particularly renowned for its many filled meatballs.

Throughout most of history, preparing ground-meat was a time-consuming and strenuous process; accordingly, ground meat dishes were expensive and reserved for special occasions. More recently, they have become everyday fare. In Israel, fried and grilled patties are frequently eaten as a sandwich in pita bread, topped with a little chopped cucumbers and tomatoes and perhaps a drizzle of *techina* (sesame seed sauce) and harissa (chili paste).

In 2000, during the second intifada in Israel, Shimon Ohana, a new border policeman assigned to the Gilo section of Jerusalem, was hit in the chest with a bullet while protecting a young child. Ohana literally died, but was somehow revived and his heart was mended by the doctors at Hadassah-University Hospital in Ein Kerem. After eighteen days in a coma, Ohana woke, but could not or would not eat anything. Finally, his mother hurried home to make his favorite food, spicy Moroccan meatballs, returning with a large pot the following morning. The young private tasted his first mouthful of food since the attack and began to grunt. The sounds were a request for more and he ate four meatballs right then and there, and more in the following days as he recuperated.

(See also Albondiga, Kebab, Kefte, Kibbeh, and Kubbeh)

AZERBAIJANI STUFFED MEATBALLS (*KÜFTE TABRIZI*)

ABOUT 12 MEDIUM MEATBALLS   [MEAT]

1 pound ground lamb, beef, or veal chuck
1 medium yellow onion, minced
1 large egg
½ cup yellow split peas, cooked and mashed, or ¼ cup raw long-grain rice
1 teaspoon lemon juice
½ teaspoon ground cinnamon or ¼ cup chopped fresh mint
¼ teaspoon ground nutmeg
¼ teaspoon saffron strands or ground turmeric
About 1 teaspoon salt

About ⅛ teaspoon ground black pepper
12 pitted dried plums
Chicken broth, beef broth, or water
1 cup cooked chickpeas or green peas

1. In a large bowl, combine the meat, onion, egg, peas, lemon juice, cinnamon, nutmeg, saffron, salt, and pepper. Cover and refrigerate for at least 30 minutes.

2. With moistened hands, form the meat mixture into twelve 2½-inch meatballs. Place a plum in the center of each ball.

3. Place the meatballs in a large saucepan and add broth to cover. Bring to a boil, cover, reduce the heat to medium-low, and simmer for about 45 minutes.

4. Add the chickpeas and heat through.

VARIATIONS

Large Azerbaijani Stuffed Meatballs: Form the meat mixture into 2 to 3 large balls. Place 1 peeled hard-boiled egg in the center of each meatball. Place in a greased pan, add ¼ cup water, and bake in a 350°F oven for about 1 hour.

KUGEL

Kugel is a baked or steamed pudding, either sweet or savory.

Origin: Germany
Other names: *kugl.*

"Kugel, this holy national dish, has done more for the preservation of Judaism than all three issues of your magazine." (From an 1825 letter to the editor of a new German Jewish periodical by German poet and writer Heinrich Heine.)

Kugel (*kuglen* plural) is part of a general category of Ashkenazic grain-based foods called *mehlspeisen* (meals of flour) and belongs to the more specific category of *teigachz* (pudding). From its birthplace eight centuries ago in southern Germany, Ashkenazim brought the kugel with them eastward and the dish gradually evolved and expanded from its humble origins. Whatever its form and content, the common denominators of all true kugels are a starch base, eggs, and fat, without the addition of water or other liquids. If the dish lacks any of the basic ingredients, it is technically a casserole, quiche, or cake rather than a kugel. Most kugels contain only a few ingredients. Whether spelled kugel (by Poles and Lithuanians), koogle (by Germans), or keegal (by *Galitzianers* in southern Poland), this dish certainly ranks high in the pantheon of Jewish foods.

By the twelfth century, dumplings had arrived in Germany, around the same time as the Sabbath stew. Inspired Franco-German cooks began dropping a savory bread batter containing a little egg as a binder into the center of the Sabbath stew, and this dumpling developed a rich flavor and texture as the stew slowly simmered overnight. The following day after morning services, the dumpling was served warm alongside the stew for Sabbath lunch. Emulating an emerging German practice of steaming puddings in a clay pot in place of intestines and other organs, medieval Jewish housewives began cooking the dumpling in a *kugeltopf*—kugel was the Middle High German for "ball" and *topf* meant "jar/pot"—a commonplace small rounded earthenware jar. The *kugeltopf* was placed in the top of the stew and the steamy environment kept the batter moist and prevented burning. This not only transformed the batter into a pudding, but also gave rise to a new name. To differentiate the pudding still in the stew from the stew, people began calling the pudding variously *weckschalet* (*weck* was German for "bread roll"), *semmelkugel* (also "bread roll"), and *schaletkugel*. In Bavaria and parts of southern Germany, kugel came to denote savory puddings and *schalet* referred to sweet ones. In eastern Europe, kugel became the generic term for all these puddings. When cooked in a stew without the *kugeltopf*, the dumpling whimsically became known as a *Shabbos ganif* (Sabbath thief), as it absorbed flavors from the liquid as it cooked.

As the kugel came out of the cholent (Sabbath stew), the rather plain, rudimentary bread dumplings gradually evolved. Onions, ubiquitous in Ashkenazic cookery, were sautéed and added for extra flavor. *Gribenes*, cracklings made while rendering schmaltz, provided another possible flavor element. Cooks who could afford spices, which were very expensive until recently, mixed in some pepper or other spices. (Salt-and-pepper kugels are still popular among some segments of the community.)

Kugel achieved new gastronomic heights when housewives substituted farfel and noodles and, on Passover, matza for the bread batter. It is uncertain whether eastern Europeans learned of noodles from the Tatars (Mongolian tribes), Byzantines, or Italians. Whatever the case, by the fifteenth century, *lokshen* (noodles) had become a mainstay of northern Europe and within a century were popular in kugels.

By the sixteenth century, rice kugels, once rare and typically reserved for special occasions, emerged in eastern Europe, influenced by the Ottoman advances into Europe and the introduction of numerous Middle Eastern foods. The Turks also introduced cornmeal to Europe, which Romanians used in kugels such as *malai*. Potatoes, after their popularization in the mid-nineteenth century, provided cooks with an inexpensive and filling ingredient, and potato kugel subsequently became the predominant version in the impoverished shtetls of eastern Europe. This widespread use of potatoes is reflected in lines from a popular Yiddish folk song: "Sunday potatoes, Monday potatoes, Tuesday and Wednesday potatoes, Thursday and Friday potatoes, but *Shabbos*, for a change, a potato kugel."

Kugel continued to evolve. Among the beliefs of Renaissance Europe was the notion that "warm" foods should be consumed during the winter to combat the cold—"warm" encompassed not only temperature, but also foods that prickle the tongue, most notably certain spices (e.g., cinnamon and nutmeg) and dried fruit. The most common dried fruits in late medieval Europe were raisins and currants. Of course, only the wealthy could afford most of the ingredients of pudding, so the masses only enjoyed it for a holiday, if then. In the medieval period, Germans began flavoring some of their steamed bread puddings variously with honey, cinnamon, rose water, ground nuts, and raisins, and Jews followed suit in kugels.

By the nineteenth century, with the increasing affordability of sugar, sweetened bread, noodle, and rice kugels became increasingly common, particularly among *Galitzianers*. These kugels, frequently containing raisins and sometimes seasoned with cinnamon, were served as both a side dish and a dessert. In general, Lithuanians and Hungarians retained a preference for savory kugels, although they did also develop a liking for sweet noodle kugel. The sweet versions were served alongside savory dishes, such as cholent, a pairing that endures. For dairy meals, pot cheese and milk or sour cream were added to noodles, producing a custard-like consistency. Mixing in some inexpensive carrots with a sweetened batter yielded the carrot kugel. Hungarians took the dessert concept even further, layering the sweetened noodles with various fillings, including poppy seeds, jam, and apples.

Beginning in the late 1700s, groups of Chasidim as well as adherents of the Vilna Gaon (Rabbi Elijah ben Solomon of Vilna, Lithuania) began moving to Israel in order to live a more fully religious life. They brought with them the traditions of eastern Europe, including their clothing and foods. In the nineteenth century, descendants of those early Ashkenazic arrivals living in Jerusalem developed a distinctive noodle kugel called *kugel yerushalmi*. This hybrid of traditional salt-and-pepper noodle kugel and sweet noodle kugel featured a tantalizing contrast of ground black pepper and caramelized sugar. Subsequently and until today, some families in the neighborhood of Mea Shearim in Jerusalem earned their livelihoods making it for food stores. *Kugel yerushalmi* remains extremely popular in Israel.

During the Middle Ages, few families in Europe other than the nobility owned a home oven. Thus, for most of history, cooking was usually performed directly over a fire (roasting, braising, boiling, steaming, and poaching); accordingly, puddings and kugels were commonly steamed. Baked foods had to be lugged to the town bakery or to the occasional private home oven, and cooks typically had to pay a fee to use these facilities. In addition, temperatures were difficult to regulate in those wood-burning medieval brick or clay ovens, so baked goods had to be carefully watched during the entire baking time. Consequently, except for bread and an occasional cake, baked dishes were rare.

The first Jewish cookbook in English, *The Jewish Manual* (London, 1846), by Judith Montefiore, contained the first record of the word kugel in English and offered a recipe for "Kugel and Commean" (commean refers to *hamin,* "Sabbath stew"). The dish consisted of a sweetened and spiced bread mixture that was placed in a covered "quart basin" and steamed in a meat and bean stew. Similarly, the first American Jewish cookbook, *Jewish Cookery* (Philadephia, 1871), included a recipe for "Coogle, Or Pudding, and Peas and Beans," consisting of a sweetened noodle mixture steamed in a covered basin that was set in a meat and bean stew resembling a soupy cholent.

When the word kugel first appeared in *Webster's Dictionary* in the early twentieth century, it was originally defined as "a suet pudding," a characterization derived from certain similarities between some German kugels and British steamed puddings. By the time the book's name became *Merriam-Webster*

Dictionary in 1983, it had updated the definition to "a baked pudding."

With the popularization of the home oven in the mid-nineteenth century, kugels suddenly shifted from being steamed in the stew pot to being baked in a separate vessel outside the pot. The kugel as we now know it—a baked pudding—had finally arrived. Baking the kugel in an oven had another consequence; the kugel was transformed from being primarily a Sabbath lunch dish and accompaniment for the cholent to a dish that could be served as a side dish for Friday night dinner and even during the weekday. German Jewish cookbooks throughout most of the nineteenth century called for cooking cholents and kugels (inside the stew) for sixteen to twenty-four hours, but by the end of the century, the cooking time had suddenly shrunk to a few hours or much less.

Around the same time that the home oven spread through America, the kugel traveled westward across the Atlantic. *Aunt Babette's* (Cincinnati, 1889) provided a handful of kugel recipes, all baked. These included "Fleisch Kugel (Meat Balls)," basically a meatloaf; a "Noodle Pudding" consisting of cooked egg noodles layered with sugar, pounded almonds, lemon zest, raisins, and goose fat, noting "Bake two hours . . . You ought to have a kugeltopf for this noodelockschen"; "Kraut Kugel" entailing chopped cabbage braised in fat, mixed with soaked bread, sugar, raisins, chopped citron, almonds, cinnamon, allspice, lemon juice and zest, and eggs, then baked; and a sugarless "Matzo Kugel" as well as a sweetened "Matzo Pudding, or Schalet."

Well until the mid-twentieth century, bread, matza, and noodles remained the base for most German kugels. In the original edition of *The Settlement Cook Book* (Milwaukee, 1901), the recipe entitled "Kugel" directed cooks to "soak five wheat rolls in water, then press the bread quite dry." The author also included recipes for a sweetened "Rice Kugel," as well as a savory "Noodle Kugel." Potato kugel became popular in the early twentieth century with the arrival of eastern Europeans. Subsequently, Americans began to tinker with kugels, including adding canned pineapple, fruit cocktail, or maraschino cherries, or crumbling corn flakes over the top. In the second half of the twentieth century, innovative cooks transformed the kugel further with new and sometimes healthier (and yes, even low-fat) kinds of ingredients, most unheard of in east-

ern Europe, including broccoli, cauliflower, spinach, zucchini, and tofu. Traditional kugels, as well as innovative new forms, remain popular Ashkenazic dishes.

The LeeVees, two Jewish boys and indie-rock stalwarts (Adam Gardner and Dave Schneider), wrote a 2005 ode to the iconic Ashkenazic dish, bemoaning, "But kugel/You're not like you used to be/You were once sweet and creamy/Now you're low fat." The venerable dish serves as a metaphor for societal and cultural influences on Jewish tradition, as the song continues, "So don't try to tell me things haven't changed/The way you're made these days you should have another name/I just wished things stayed the same."

Tasty, inexpensive, filling, versatile, kugels proved ideal for the Sabbath, festivals, and life-cycle events, serving as a side dish or, among the very poor, the main course. In most homes, no Sabbath meal or life-cycle event would be considered complete without at least one type of kugel, usually pareve for meat meals. Noodle kugels with cheese are widespread at dairy occasions, such as Hanukkah, Shavuot, and the meal following Yom Kippur. In many synagogues, kugel is common at the Sabbath kiddush. Sweetened noodle or rice kugels with apples are popular on Rosh Hashanah, contributing a sweet note to the new year. There is a custom in some Polish households of serving four specific kugels—*epl* (apple), *mehl* (flour), *lokshen* (noodle), and *kartoffel* (potato)—on *Parshat Zachor* (portion of remembrance), the Sabbath before Purim, as their initials spell Amalek, the ancient enemy of the Israelites and ancestor of Haman. Matza and potato kugels are mainstays during Passover. Leftover kugel is all too commonly snuck out of the refrigerator as a late night snack.

(See also Cholent, Dumpling, Fluden, Pastida, Schalet, and Tish)

ASHKENAZIC SWEET NOODLE PUDDING
(*ZEESIH LOKSHEN KUGEL*)

9 TO 12 SERVINGS   [DAIRY OR PAREVE]

- 1 pound medium or fine egg noodles
- ½ cup (1 stick) unsalted butter or margarine
- 5 large eggs, lightly beaten
- ⅔ to 1 cup sugar
- 2 teaspoons vanilla extract
- 1 teaspoon ground cinnamon or 1 tablespoon orange marmalade

About 1 teaspoon table salt or 2 teaspoons kosher
salt

¾ to 1 cup raisins, chopped dried apricots, dried
cherries, or chopped mixed dried fruit (optional)

About ¾ cup chopped almonds, hazelnuts, or
walnuts (optional)

Additional ground cinnamon for sprinkling

1. Preheat the oven to 350°F. Grease a 13-by-9-inch
baking pan.

2. In a large pot, bring lightly salted water to a rapid
boil. Add the noodles and stir to prevent sticking.
Cook, stirring occasionally, until al dente (tender but
still firm), 7 to 10 minutes for medium noodles, or 3
to 5 minutes for fine noodles. Drain. Add the butter
and toss to melt.

3. In a large bowl, beat together the eggs, sugar,
vanilla, cinnamon, and salt. Stir in the noodles and, if
using, raisins and/or nuts. Pour into the prepared pan,
leveling the top. Sprinkle with the cinnamon.

4. Bake until golden brown, about 1 hour. Serve
warm or at room temperature. Kugel freezes well.

VARIATIONS

*Sweet Noodle-Cheese Kugel (Zeesih Lokshen un
Kaese Kugel): Increase the eggs to 8. Add 1 pound
(2 cups) farmer cheese or small-curd cottage cheese,
and 1 pound (2 cups) sour cream, gevina levana (Israeli
white cheese), or softened cream cheese.*

KUGELHOPF

Kugelhopf is a rich yeast cake baked in a tall fluted
pan with a center hole.

Origin: Austria or Alsace, France

Other names: Austria and southern Germany:
gugelhopf, gugelhupf; Czech Republic and Slovakia: *bábovka;* Hungary: *kuglóf;* Poland: *babka.*

During the Renaissance, Italian chefs, influenced
by Arabic baked goods like the Iberian *bola,* began creating lighter cakes, basically sweetened yeast breads,
called *torta* (Latin for "a round bread"). The dough of
these breads could only be mildly sweet, as too much
honey or sugar hampers or kills yeast. Additional sweetening could be achieved by adding dried fruits. On the
other hand, yeast breads can handle plenty of fat and,
accordingly, bakers sometimes did not skimp when it
came to adding butter. During the sixteenth and seventeenth century, the Italian *torta* spread throughout
Europe, taking on various forms, including the Italian
panettone (baked in an earthenware flowerpot), French

brioche, and Slavic babka (Jewish babka is somewhat
different and pareve). The version of this light cake
in the Teutonic region from Alsace through Austria,
claimed by both Vienna and Alsace as the cake's place
of origin, is known as kugelhopf. Since cake and pastry
baking in Austria became an overwhelmingly Jewish
profession, kugelhopf and other baked goods, many
created by Jews, became part of the Jewish repertoire.

Because the buttery dough was looser than bread
dough, it could not be baked in the usual manner,
directly on the floor of the large wood-burning ovens.
Consequently, the dough was placed in small earthenware pots, such as the Teutonic *kugeltopf (kugel*
was the Middle High German for "ball" and *topf*
meant "jar/pot"); this round container produced a
ball-shaped cake and gave the cake its name. However, because kugelhopf are so dense and the sugar
in the dough quickens browning, the center typically
remained underdone. Eventually, this problem was
resolved with the shift to baking the dough in a rudimentary tube pan known as a Turk's Cap or Turk's
Head, a large, glazed, bowl-shaped terra-cotta mold
with a central tube, similar to a Bundt pan. Potters
added a scalloped surface to the pan, exposing more
of the batter to the heat and giving a cake or bread
baked in it the appearance of a wound turban. In the
mid-nineteenth century, craftsmen began producing a metal version of the Turk's Cap, the first tube
pan. Central European home bakers typically owned
at least one and frequently a variety of metal and
ceramic kugelhopf pans

Jews from Alsace to Vienna, who did not have
the rich eastern European egg challah, adopted the
kugelhopf as their favorite cake. Alsatians typically
use less sweetening, while Austrians tend to make
kugelhopf more cakelike by adding more sugar. In
southern Germany, it was a popular coffee cake. In
the nineteenth century, German immigrants brought
kugelhopf to America and German Jews referred to
various rich yeast cakes with a variation of the name.
The first Jewish cookbook in America, *Jewish Cookery*
(Philadelphia, 1871) by Esther Levy, offered a recipe
for "German Kouglauff," the first record of the term in
America. The cake consisted of a loose, high-butter,
low-sugar yeast batter that was poured into "a mould"
and baked; the recipe and name were adapted from
The Modern Cook (London, 1845), a popular book by
Charles Elmé Francatelli. *Aunt Babette's* (Cincinnati,

1889) included a recipe for "Abgeruerter Gugelhopf," a high-sugar, high-butter yeast cake with raisins and citron baked in a "cake form." The first edition of *The Settlement Cook Book* (Milwaukee, 1901) provided a recipe for "Kuchen Roll or Kugelhopf," akin to the Jewish version of babka, calling for a basic kuchen dough to be rolled out, brushed with melted butter, sprinkled with raisins and cinnamon-sugar, rolled up, and baked in either a "long pan or round form with tube in center." In the 1965 edition, the same recipe was entitled "Kuchen Roll or Kugelhopf."

German Jews adopted various yeast cakes for the Sabbath and other special occasions, notably apple *schalet* and various kuchen. But among Alsatians, kugelhopf became the predominant cake. Many Alsatian households could not imagine a Sabbath without this dessert, which was also traditional on Hanukkah and Purim. Before an Alsatian wedding, guests were offered slices of kugelhopf with coffee and wine. In Alsace, leftover kugelhopf, more of a bread than cake, is commonly served as a breakfast loaf; it is frequently sliced and accompanied with apricot jam and orange marmalade. Stale or even fresh kugelhopf is sometimes moistened with kirsch or rum syrup.

(See also Babka and Kuchen)

❧ ALSATIAN YEAST CAKE (*KUGELHOPF*)

10 TO 16 SERVINGS   [DAIRY]

½ cup golden raisins
½ cup dark raisins
¼ cup kirsch or light rum
2 packages (4½ teaspoons) active dry yeast or
    1 (1-ounce) cake fresh yeast
1 cup warm milk (105°F to 115°F for dry yeast; 80°F
    to 85°F for fresh yeast)
½ to ¾ cup sugar
4 cups (20 ounces) bread or unbleached all-purpose
    flour
4 large eggs, lightly beaten
2 teaspoons vanilla extract
1 teaspoon table salt or 2 teaspoons kosher salt
2 teaspoons grated orange zest or 1 teaspoon grated
    lemon zest (optional)
1 cup (2 sticks) unsalted butter, softened and cut
    into 1-tablespoon pieces
Confectioners' sugar for dusting

1. Soak the raisins in the kirsch until softened, at least 30 minutes.

2. In a small bowl, dissolve the yeast in ⅓ cup milk. Add 1 teaspoon sugar and let stand until foamy, 5 to 10 minutes. Place the flour in the bowl of an electric mixer and make a crater in the center. (Do not use a food processor.) Add the yeast mixture, remaining milk, remaining sugar, eggs, vanilla, salt, if using, zest, and any excess kirsch from the raisins (but not the raisins) and beat until the dough clears the sides of the bowl, about 5 minutes.

3. Lift the dough out of the bowl, then return. With the mixer on low speed, gradually beat in the butter, about 2 minutes. Stir in the raisins. Cover loosely with plastic wrap or a kitchen towel and let rise in a warm, draft-free place until nearly doubled in bulk, about 1½ hours.

4. Grease a 12-cup kugelhopf pan or 10-inch Bundt pan. Stir down the dough and pour into the prepared pan—the dough should reach halfway up the sides. Cover and let rise until nearly doubled in bulk, about 1 hour.

5. Preheat the oven to 350°F.

6. Bake until the kugelhopf is golden brown and a knife inserted in the center comes out clean, 50 to 60 minutes. If the kugelhopf browns too quickly, cover loosely with aluminum foil. Let cool in the pan for 10 minutes, then unmold while still warm and transfer to a wire rack. Just before serving, sprinkle with the confectioners' sugar.

KUKU

Kuku is a vegetable-packed omelet.
Origin: Persia
Other names: *kookoo*.

Persian cuisine is marked by a subtle blend of vegetables and herbs that enhances but does not overwhelm the primary ingredient of a dish. Exemplifying this is *kuku*, a popular Persian egg "pie" that is usually packed with vegetables, cut into wedges, and served warm or at room temperature, accompanied with flatbread. The term *kuku* resembles a Farsi word for fowl, perhaps derived from the sound of its call and also connecting it to the fundamental part of the dish, eggs. In addition to using the original method of cooking the omelet in a skillet, today's cooks also bake *kuku* in the oven as a casserole.

The most popular variation is the bright green *kuku-e sabzi* or *kukuye sabzi* (*sabz* means "green" in Farsi; *sabzi* denotes mixed fresh herbs), a genuine Persian comfort food reflecting the complex seasonings of Persian cuisine; the miscellaneous ingredients mellow when combined and mixed with the eggs. Since *kuku-e sabzi* can be served warm or at room temperature, it often graces the Persian Sabbath table as a side dish or as part of a *mezze* (appetizer assortment), not as a main course. *Kuku-e sabzi* is found at diverse occasions such as a Purim feast or a meal at a house of mourning, because the eggs and greens represent the life cycle and renewal. As a fried food, it is also a traditional Hanukkah dish, typically served with rice and stews or yogurt.

·🐚· PERSIAN OMELET (*KUKU*)

4 TO 6 SERVINGS   [PAREVE]

¼ cup vegetable oil

1 large yellow onion or 2 medium leeks, chopped

⅛ teaspoon ground turmeric

6 large eggs, lightly beaten

About ¾ teaspoon table salt or 1½ teaspoons kosher salt

Ground black pepper to taste

1. In a 9- to 10-inch skillet, heat 2 tablespoons oil over medium heat. Add the onion and sauté until soft and translucent, 5 to 10 minutes. Stir in the turmeric. Remove the onions from the skillet and let cool slightly. In a medium bowl, combine the onions, eggs, salt, and pepper.

2. In the same skillet, heat 1 tablespoon oil over medium heat. Pour in the egg mixture, cover, and simmer over low heat until the bottom is set, about 10 minutes. Loosen the edges and slide the omelet onto a large plate.

3. Add the remaining 1 tablespoon oil to the skillet and invert the omelet, uncooked side down, into the skillet. Cover and continue cooking until set and golden brown, about 5 minutes. To serve, cut into wedges. Serve warm or at room temperature, with yogurt and flatbread, if desired.

VARIATIONS

Persian Spinach Omelet (Kuku-e Esfinadge): After adding the turmeric to the sautéed onion, stir in 1 cup cooked, chopped, and squeezed spinach.

Persian Vegetable Omelet (Kuku-e Sabzi): After adding the turmeric to the sautéed onion, add 1 bunch minced celery, 2 cups minced spinach or chard, 1 cup minced fresh flat-leaf parsley, ½ to 1 cup minced scallions, and, if desired, ½ cup chopped fresh dill or ¼ cup ground walnuts. Sauté until softened, about 5 minutes. Stir in 4 teaspoons all-purpose flour.

L

LABANEH

Labaneh is yogurt cheese.

Origin: Middle East

Other names: Arabic: *labna, labane, labneh, labni*;
India: *dahi, dehin*.

Labaneh (from the Arabic *laban* "milk/white") is
the common Israeli name for a soft, white semisolid
dairy product made by draining the whey from goat's,
sheep's, or cow's milk yogurt. Depending on the degree
of draining, *labaneh* can have the texture of sour cream
or be nearly as thick as cream cheese. *Labaneh* developed
as a method of expanding yogurt's shelf life and
utility. In the Levant, for even longer storage over the
winter, *labaneh* was made in a mass quantity, rolled
into balls, dried, and stored in olive oil.

Labaneh is used as a spread or dip or as a low-fat
substitute for cream cheese and sour cream in many
recipes. For extra flavor, it is blended with garlic and,
sometimes, minced cucumbers (*khyar labni*), roasted
red bell peppers (*mahammara labni*), or spinach
(*sabanigh labni*), or sprinkled with chopped fresh dill,
mint, or thyme. *Labaneh* is also spread over a serving
platter or rolled into balls (*zanakeel labni*), drizzled
with olive oil, and sprinkled with sumac, za'atar, or
crushed spearmint (*labni b'tum w'naanaa*). In Israel,
containers of *labaneh*, plain, as well as balls soaked in
olive oil, are available in groceries.

(See also Cheese, Leben, and Yogurt)

LABLABI

Lablabi is a vegetarian soup originally made from
dried hyacinth beans, but more recently from chickpeas
or sometimes fava beans.

Origin: Tunisia

Other names: *leblebi*.

The hyacinth bean, also called Indian bean and
Egyptian bean, is an Indian native and longtime resident
of the Mediterranean. It has white, yellowish, or
black pea-shaped seeds. Its Arabic name is *lablab*, connoting
the rattling sound of its seeds in a dried pod.
When young, the pods are harvested as vegetables.

Hyacinth beans have a major drawback—the dried
mature beans contain toxic levels of cyanogenic glucosides
that require boiling several times in water to
extract. In some places and times, cooks went through
the trouble of repeatedly boiling the beans in order to
use them as a basis for a soup named *lablabi*. However,
the more popular, widespread, and safer chickpea, as
well as occasionally the fava bean, is commonly substituted
for hyacinth in this popular garlicky Maghrebi
soup. *Lablabi* is the unofficial national dish of Tunisia.

Lablabi was regular fare among many in the
Maghreb; the poor scrimped on or omitted the vegetables
and relied only on chickpeas or fava beans for
a filling dish. The soup gets a little kick from harissa
(chili paste) and an earthiness from cumin. A creamier
version is made by adding yogurt. Spooning the
soup over bread cubes transforms it into a vegetarian
meal. It is typically made in a large batch, especially
in the wintertime, then heated up for breakfast or,
just before siesta time, lunch. Tunisians like to garnish
lablabi with various savories, including capers,
a soft-cooked egg or chopped hard-boiled eggs, and
flaked tuna fish. It is also sometimes enlivened with a
drizzle of lemon juice and olive oil. Once in the soup
bowl, Tunisians lightly or completely mash the ingredients
together using two spoons to produce a thick
stew, but the soup can also be pureed in a blender or
food processor for a smooth texture.

In Turkey, *lablabi* became a snack made from
roasted chickpeas flavored with spices or sugar.

LAFFA

Laffa is a flatbread—larger, fluffier, and chewier than
pita, used to make rolled or wrapped sandwiches.

Origin: Iraq

Other names: *aish tanur, khubz el-taboon, lafa,
laffah, taboon bread*.

In Iraq, the standard flatbread is known as *aish
tanur* (clay-oven bread), but when used for a sandwich
it becomes *laffa* from the Arabic meaning "wrap/
roll." In Iraq, a common lunch or snack, typically pur-

chased from small shops or pushcarts, is *laffa amba*, a piece of bread enwrapping curried mango condiment (*amba*) and, sometimes, hard-boiled egg and tomatoes. Iraqis brought the bread to Israel, where it became a staple and is called *laffa* whether part of a sandwich or not. *Laffa* is larger than a standard pita (it is about a foot in diameter), the texture is fluffier and chewier, and it does not have a pocket. Consequently, food is placed on top and then rolled up in it. One advantage of *laffa* is that it is less likely to crumble or sprout a leak than the flimsier pita. Very thin versions of *laffa* are known as *sajj*, named after the convex metal griddle on which it is cooked.

In Israel, *laffa* follows only pita in popularity for fast-food fare. Israelis use *laffa* for the Iraqi *sabich* sandwich, as well as to enclose falafel, *shawarma*, kebabs, grilled chicken, and almost anything the imagination can pile in a sandwich. It is also served at home as the backbone of a light meal with various spreads and dips, such as *baba ghanouj*, hummus, *labaneh* (yogurt cheese), and *muhammara* (red pepper relish), or for mopping up a sauce.

Laffa has become engrained in the Israeli cuisine and culture. In 1995, the underground Israeli band Tipex released the album "Your Life in a *Laffa*," a witty and edgy look by Mizrachim at Israeli society. The album's title is from the Israeli slang expression, *"v'kol zeh b'laffa"* (and all of that in a *laffa*). This refers to a person who is overly precise and demanding in their instructions, such as someone who orders a falafel with very exacting directions as to which ingredients are wanted and how they are to be arranged, ending with the instruction "and all that in a *laffa*."

LAG B'OMER

Lag b'Omer (thirty-third in the Omer), or among Sephardim, Lag l'Omer (thirty-third to the Omer"), is a minor holiday marking the thirty-third day of the counting of the Omer.

The biblical word *omer*, from the root "to heap together," variously refers to a sheaf of grain, a specific measurement (the volume of 43.2 eggs—approximately 9⅛ cups), and a communal flour offering from the newly harvested barley brought on the second day of Passover.

No grains from the current year could be consumed until after the Omer offering was brought. Upon offering the Omer, Jews would then verbally count for forty-nine days, corresponding to the amount of time from the Exodus until the revelation on Mount Sinai. On the evening following the forty-ninth day of counting, they celebrated the festival of Shavuot. Although grain offerings can no longer be brought, Jews continue the practice of "counting the Omer" each day from the second day of Passover.

The months following Passover were once a time of great happiness—the pantry was stocked with the abundance of the barley crop and expectations ran high for the upcoming wheat harvest. Then a series of national tragedies transformed this span into a very somber one. The Talmud relates that during one of the rebellions against Rome, twenty-four thousand students of Rabbi Akiva died from a plague—some scholars speculate that this plague was actually the Roman army—during the Omer period. (Rabbi Akiva rose from being an illiterate shepherd to become one of the most important Jewish scholars; due to his support of the Bar Kokhba Rebellion, he was killed by the Romans around 135 CE). The Bar Kokhba rebellion against Rome (132–135 CE), ended disastrously with much of the land of Israel decimated. Cassius recorded that 585 Jewish villages were leveled. This was when the real Diaspora began. Furthermore, most of the devastation on the Ashkenazic communities brought by the Crusades, beginning in 1096, occurred in the spring, after the European rivers melted from the winter ice. Subsequently, the Omer became a time of prolonged mourning.

There is an exception to the melancholy nature of the Omer period, a minor holiday of uncertain origin on the eighteenth day of the month of Iyar on the thirty-third (*lag* in Hebrew numerology) day after the Omer. The Talmud records that on this day the plague devastating Rabbi Akiva's students abated. In essence, Lag b'Omer recognizes and unofficially commemorated the Bar Kokhba rebellion.

Rabbi Moshe Schreiber (1762–1839) known as Chatam Sofer, indicated that this was the day on which the manna, which fed the Jews during their 40-year stay in the wilderness, first appeared, contributing to the celebratory nature of the day. Around the same time, the Chasidim also recognized Lag b'Omer as a festive holiday.

One Talmudic figure in particular became associated with Lag b'Omer—Rabbi Shimon bar Yochai, an important student of Rabbi Akiva. Rabbi Shimon and his son spent thirteen years in hiding from the

Romans before the Bar Kokhba revolt. After the Zohar, the essential book of Kabbalah, appeared in the 1290s, Rabbi Shimon was considered by some to be its author. Rabbi Shimon's students disguised clandestine visits to their teacher as outings or hunting expeditions. Therefore, bows and arrows became the symbol of Lag b'Omer. Carob is a traditional food, as legend has it that Rabbi Shimon and his son were sustained by a carob tree during their years of hiding.

Lag b'Omer is a public holiday in modern Israel. Thousands make an annual pilgrimage on the day to Rabbi Shimon's grave in Meron, (in the Upper Galilee near Safed), where they honor his memory with song and dance. Others visit the tomb of Simon ha'Tzadik in Jerusalem. The day is customarily celebrated with picnics and bonfires. Israelis typically enjoy various cookout foods, and wrap whole potatoes and onions in aluminum foil and roast them in bonfires. Hard-boiled eggs are another traditional item—they are associated with mourning and rebirth, but are also convenient to schlep on picnics. Moroccans typically serve *pastilla/bisteeya* ("pigeon" pie) and *kaab el ghazal* (almond-filled crescent cookies). Many American Jews eat Middle Eastern fare on this holiday.

LAGMAN

Lagman is a thick meat and vegetable soup, traditionally served with hand-pulled noodles.

Origin: Uzbekistan

Bukharans take advantage of seasonal fresh produce to make an array of soups, which are served in deep ceramic bowls. A mainstay during the fall and winter are stewlike soups called *vadzha*, which make a hearty main course for lunch or dinner. The favorite *vadzha* is a meat, vegetable, and noodle version known as *shurpa lagman* (noodle soup) or simply *lagman*.

Lagman, the Bukharan word for noodles, is derived from the Chinese *liang mian* (cold noodle). The term is related to the more well-known *lo mein* (pulled/separated noodles). Less than two millennia ago, the concept of noodles and some of the soups in which they were served traveled from China along the Silk Road to central Asia, perhaps brought westward by the nomadic Uyghur. In Uzbekistan and Kazakhstan, the noodles tend to be thicker than those in China and the soups thicker and spicier.

There is no exact recipe for *shurpa lagman*. The amount and types of vegetables and seasonings dif-

A traditional Bukharan soup features handmade noodles similar to Chinese lo mein, from which they were inspired. The traditional way to make these noodles is to continuously stretch the dough into thinner threads, while occasionally slapping the long strands onto a surface to break down the gluten, resulting in pliant, chewy noodles.

fer depending on personal preference and availability. Most Bukharans use a tomato-based broth. Carrot is the most common vegetable used. Cooks from Tashkent typically add black radish. Generally, this chunky soup consists of small pieces of meat (usually mutton) and assorted vegetables served over long, thick homemade noodles (hand-pulled ones are preferred). Few Bukharans would use store-bought dry pasta. When served without the noodles and with a slightly more liquid broth, the soup is called *shurpa*.

BUKHARAN LAMB, VEGETABLE, AND NOODLE SOUP (*LAGMAN*)

6 TO 8 SERVINGS   [MEAT]

¼ cup vegetable oil

1½ pounds boneless lamb or beef shoulder, cut into 1-inch cubes

2 medium yellow onions, thinly sliced

3 to 5 cloves garlic, minced

1 tablespoon sweet paprika, ½ teaspoon red chili flakes, or 1 teaspoon paprika and ¼ teaspoon cayenne

1 to 1½ teaspoons ground cumin

½ teaspoon ground coriander

About 1 teaspoon table salt or 2 teaspoons kosher salt

Ground black pepper to taste

¼ cup tomato paste (optional)

2 cups (1 pound) peeled, seeded, and chopped
   tomatoes

2 large carrots, cut into ½-inch cubes

2 medium boiling potatoes, peeled and cut into
   ½-inch cubes

2 medium Italian frying peppers or red bell
   peppers, seeded and sliced

1 cup (7 ounces) ½-inch-diced black radish or
   daikon (Asian radish)

1 to 2 medium turnips, peeled and cut into ½-inch
   cubes

1 cup cooked chickpeas (optional)

2 quarts lamb broth, beef broth, or water

About 1 tablespoon cider, rice, or wine vinegar
   (optional)

1 recipe (1 pound) Egg Noodle Dough (page 368),
   cut into ¼-inch-thick strips, freshly boiled about
   2 minutes, and drained

¼ cup chopped fresh flat-leaf parsley, cilantro, or
   mint (optional)

1. In a large pot, heat the oil over medium heat. Add the meat and brown on all sides, about 10 minutes. Remove the meat.

2. Add the onions and sauté until light gold, about 15 minutes. Stir in the garlic, paprika, cumin, coriander, salt, pepper, and, if using, tomato paste. Add the tomatoes, carrots, potatoes, peppers, radishes, and turnips and cook, stirring frequently, until slightly softened, about 10 minutes. Return the meat and, if using, add the chickpeas.

3. Add the broth. Bring to a boil, cover, reduce the heat to low, and simmer until the meat is tender, about 1½ hours. The soup may be cooled, stored for up to 3 days ahead, and reheated, adding a little more broth if necessary. If the flavors are flat, stir in the optional vinegar.

4. For each serving, place a heaping handful of noodles in a large bowl. Ladle the thick soup over the top and, if using, sprinkle with a little parsley. Serve hot with *non* (flatbread) or pita bread.

LAHMAJIN

Lahmajin is a small pizza-like flatbread topped with spiced, ground meat.

Origin: Levant

Other names: Lebanon and Syria: *lahamagine, laham b'ajin*; Turkey: *lahmacun, lahmajoun*.

In the Near East for many millennia, very thin flatbreads could be baked at home on the top of a *sajj*, a convex metal dome set over a squat chimney. Slightly thicker ones were baked vertically on the inner walls of a *tanur*, a cylindrical clay oven with openings on the top for inserting the food and at the bottom for the fuel. It was the popularization in the medieval Arab world of the *furn*, "baker's oven" (called *purni* in the Talmud), that led to the proliferation of topped and filled dough. In the *furn*, a large stationary stone-lined oven with a bottom for baking, wood is burned inside, the ashes are raked out or to the side, then the dough or baking sheet is set on the heated floor of the oven or on the walls, and the bread is baked. This oven gave rise to the development of an array of savory pastries made from basic bread dough in different sizes and shapes; these pastries were prominent in the countries once constituting the Ottoman Empire, notably Turkey, Armenia, Syria, Lebanon, and Iraq. Few households had a *furn*, so topped and filled breads were generally prepared at home, then carried to the community *furn* for baking.

The most common form of these simple bread pastries were open-faced pies known variously as *sfeeha/sfiha*, and *manaesh/manakish*. The dough rounds were typically sprinkled before baking with za'atar or other herbs or cheese and afterward enjoyed for breakfast. For lunch, the dough rounds were sometimes spread with meat, then baked. When topped with spiced ground meat, the pastry is called *laham b'ajin* (meat with dough), typically shortened to *lahmajin*.

The dough for *lahmajin* is generally rolled out thinner than for most flatbreads. Lamb is the favorite meat for *lahmajin*, but beef is also used. If there is too much fat in the ground meat, the topping shrinks away from the sides during baking. However, it must have a little fat, for moistness. Although ground meat in the Middle East typically has a smooth consistency, which is produced by pounding it in a mortar, the texture of *lahmajin* is a bit coarser. Some finicky cooks still insist on chopping the raw meat with a knife rather than a machine to ensure the proper texture. The meat is enhanced with onions and tomatoes. Syrians also add pine nuts, allspice, and a souring agent to the meat to produce a fruity tang, while Turks season it with parsley, red bell pepper paste, and a hint of red chili or cinnamon. After baking, some people tear the breads into large pieces, top them with a little fresh mint and/or chopped cucumbers, and roll them up. Syrians Jews who immigrated to Brooklyn, New York, demonstrating the typical American knack for aggrandizing or miniaturizing foods, developed a smaller version of *lahmajin* and in the process transformed it into a beloved party food. Among Syrians, miniature *lahmajin* are now ubiquitous at most celebrations—knowing guests situate themselves by the kitchen door so that they can snare the warm pies before they quickly disappear. Syrians love this treat so much that they developed a version using matza meal in the dough for Passover and a vegetarian adaptation using lentils for dairy occasions.

MIDDLE EASTERN OPEN-FACED MEAT PIES (*LAHMAJIN*)

MAKES EIGHT 6-INCH, SIX 7-INCH, THIRTY 4-INCH,
OR FORTY-EIGHT 3-INCH PIES   [MEAT]

Dough:
  1 package (2¼ teaspoons) active dry yeast or
    1 (0.6-ounce) cake fresh yeast
  1½ cups warm water (105°F to 115°F for dry yeast;
    80°F to 85°F for fresh yeast)
  1 teaspoon sugar
  2 teaspoons table salt or 4 teaspoons kosher salt
  2 tablespoons olive or vegetable oil
  About 4 cups (20 ounces) bread or unbleached all-
    purpose flour

Meat Topping:
  2 pounds ground lamb or beef
  2 medium onions, minced, squeezed, and drained
  ¼ cup vegetable oil
  ¼ cup tomato paste
  About 1½ teaspoons table salt or 1 tablespoon
    kosher salt
  Ground black pepper to taste
  ½ teaspoon ground cinnamon (optional)
  ⅔ cup toasted pine nuts (optional)

1. Dissolve the yeast in ¼ cup water. Stir in the sugar and let stand until foamy, 5 to 10 minutes. In a large bowl, combine the yeast mixture, remaining water, salt, oil, and 2 cups flour. Gradually add enough of the remaining flour to make a mixture that holds together.

2. On a lightly floured surface, knead the dough until smooth and elastic, 10 to 15 minutes. Place in an oiled bowl and turn to coat. Cover loosely with plastic wrap or a kitchen towel and let rise in a warm, draft-free place until doubled in bulk, about 2 hours.

3. Punch down the dough, knead briefly, cover, and let rest for about 15 minutes.

4. Preheat the oven to 400°F. Line several large bak-

ing sheets with parchment paper or lightly sprinkle with fine semolina or flour.

5. To make the topping: In a large bowl, combine all the topping ingredients.

6. Divide the dough into 8 equal pieces. On a lightly floured surface, roll out into ¼-inch-thick rounds, about 6 inches in diameter. Or divide the dough into 6 equal pieces and roll into ¼-inch-thick rounds, about 7 inches in diameter. Or roll out the dough into a ⅛-inch thickness, and cut into 3- or 4-inch rounds; reroll the scraps. Place the dough rounds on the prepared sheets, cover, and let stand for 5 minutes. Press your fingertips all over the top to dimple. Spread with a thin, even layer of topping to the edge.

7. Bake the pies until golden brown on the bottom and around the edges but not crisp, about 20 minutes for medium, or 12 minutes for miniature ones. Serve warm.

VARIATIONS

Syrian Meat Topping: To the topping, add ½ cup tamarhindi (tamarind sauce) or apple butter, 5 to 6 tablespoons fresh lemon juice, 1 to 3 teaspoons ground allspice, and ½ teaspoon ground cinnamon.

LAHM LHALOU

Lahm lhalou is a sweet stew of meat and dried fruit.
Origin: Algeria
Other names: Morocco: *l'ghenmi bil barquq.*

  Lahm lhalou means "sweet meat" in Arabic. Besides the usual dried plums and raisins, some cooks add dried jujubes, which are rare in the West. Also called Chinese dates, jujubes are small yellowish green fruits with large seeds; when the fruits are dried, they taste like dates. The stew is slowly cooked in a tagine (an earthenware pot), producing meat that is meltingly tender. The fruit instills its natural sweetness into the stew, but sugar is also added. Some people like the stew even sweeter, so they adjust the sugar according to personal preferences. The stew is typically served with couscous. Algerian Jews brought the dish to Israel, where it has become popular.

ALGERIAN LAMB WITH DRIED PLUMS (*LAHM LHALOU*)

6 TO 8 SERVINGS   [MEAT]

  3 pounds boneless lamb shoulder or beef chuck,
    cut into 1½-inch pieces
  ¾ teaspoon ground cinnamon
  ¾ teaspoon ground ginger

¾ teaspoon ground turmeric

3 tablespoons vegetable oil

2 medium yellow onions, chopped

About 3 cups water

About 1 teaspoon table salt or 2 teaspoons kosher salt

½ teaspoon ground black pepper

Several saffron strands (optional)

1½ to 2 cups dried plums or dried apricots

⅓ cup raisins

About 6 tablespoons sugar

2 to 3 tablespoons orange-blossom water or ¼ cup orange juice

¾ cup blanched sliced almonds, toasted

1. Pat the meat dry with paper towels. In a large bowl, combine the cinnamon, ginger, and turmeric. Add the lamb and toss to coat. Let stand for at least 30 minutes at room temperature or in the refrigerator overnight.

2. In a large pot, heat the oil over medium-high heat. In several batches, add the lamb and brown on all sides, about 10 minutes per batch. Remove the lamb.

3. Add the onions and sauté until soft and translucent, about 10 minutes. Add 1 cup water and stir to loosen any browned particles from the bottom. Return the lamb. Add the salt, pepper, if using, saffron, and enough water to nearly cover the lamb. Bring to a boil, cover, reduce the heat to medium-low, and simmer, stirring occasionally, until the meat is nearly tender, about 1 hour for lamb, or 1½ hours for beef.

4. Meanwhile, soak the plums and raisins in hot water to cover for at least 30 minutes. Add the fruit to the lamb along with the sugar and orange-blossom water, cover, and simmer until the meat is tender, about 15 minutes. The stew can be stored in the refrigerator for up to 3 days and reheated in a covered pot. Garnish with the almonds.

LAHUH

Lahuh is a spongy flatbread cooked on a griddle or in a skillet.

Origin: Yemen

Other names: *lachuch, lahuhua, lahukh.*

Yemen, a small country in the southwest corner of the Arabian Peninsula, has long been a remote, primitive, and impoverished land. This rusticity is reflected in the region's breads, which are similar in form to those of ancient times. Originally, these breads consisted of a loose batter cooked in the embers of campfires, then the cooking method progressed to heated rocks. Eventually, simple utensils were used for the cooking. These flatbreads include *salufe*, a loaf baked on the walls of a clay oven (*tabun*); *khobiz tawwa*, fried dough; and *lahuh*, a pancake cooked on a griddle or a skillet.

Bread, baked fresh daily except on the Sabbath, was the mainstay of the Yemenite diet. Typically, wives would cook a batch of bread fresh every morning, then use the loaves for all the household's meals for the day. After breakfast, a new batch of dough was made, usually adding a little of the remainder of a previous batch, covered with a cloth, and left in the corner of the house to ferment for the next day. The *lahuh* batter was made from wheat, millet, or sorghum and cooked on a *shula*, a rectangular terra-cotta or metal griddle set over coals. Until recently, *lahuh* were naturally fermented by standing for a day or several, resulting in a sour flavor. Today, *lahuh* is generally raised with yeast and frequently has added sugar, transforming the taste. In addition, the batter is now sometimes cooked in a nonstick skillet.

Yemenite breads are usually some form of spongy flatbread made like a thin round bread baked on the sides of a clay oven or a pancake as "Mr. Lahuh" does here in Safed, Israel.

These flexible, spongy, bubbly loaves are served with a *saltah* (stewlike soup) and spicy condiments, such as *s'chug* (chili paste) and *hilbeh* (fenugreek relish). Or they can be enjoyed drizzled with a little butter and/or honey. Some people wrap a piece of *lahuh*, instead of pita, around falafel balls or kebabs. Yemenite Jews do not have a special bread for Friday night dinner but use either *salufe* (round flatbread) or *lahuh*.

·𝄞·YEMENITE PANCAKE BREAD (*LAHUH*)

ABOUT TWENTY 5-INCH AND TWELVE 6-INCH
BREADS   [PAREVE]

1 package (2¼ teaspoons) active dry yeast or
    1 (0.6-ounce) cake fresh yeast
3 cups warm water (105°F to 115°F for dry yeast;
    80°F to 85°F for fresh yeast)
1 to 2 tablespoons sugar
5 tablespoons vegetable oil
1½ teaspoons table salt or 1 tablespoon kosher salt
3½ cups (17.5 ounces) bread or unbleached all-
    purpose flour

1. Dissolve the yeast in ¼ cup water. Stir in 1 teaspoon sugar and let stand until foamy, 5 to 10 minutes. In a large bowl, combine the yeast mixture, remaining water, remaining sugar, oil, and salt. Stir in the flour to make a smooth batter with the consistency of a thin pancake batter.

2. Cover loosely with plastic wrap or a kitchen towel and let rise in a warm, draft-free place for 1 hour. The batter will be frothy. Stir down, cover, and let rise in a warm place for 1 hour more. Stir again.

3. Into an unheated small nonstick or seasoned cast-iron skillet, pour about ¼ cup batter for a 5-inch pancake. Use ½ cup batter in a 7-inch skillet for a 6-inch pancake. Place over medium heat for 2 minutes, then reduce the heat to low and cook until the bottom is golden and the top is bubbly and dry, about 4 minutes. Do not turn. *Lahuh* is only cooked on one side.

4. After each bread is cooked, cool the skillet in cold water, dry, and repeat until the batter is used up. If you do not have a nonstick skillet, heat a heavy skillet over medium-low heat and cover the bottom with a little oil, then pour in the batter and cook until the bottom is golden and the top is bubbly and dry. *Lahuh* can be stored between sheets of parchment paper or wax paper at room temperature for up to 1 day.

LAMB

In relating the development of very early humanity, the Bible evokes the initial domestication of animals in the phrase "and Abel became a shepherd of *tzon* [flocks]." The term *tzon* encompassed both sheep and goats. Sheep—docile, small, and easily herded—were among the first domesticated animals, subsequent to only dogs and the sheeps' close relative, goats. Ever since sheep were first domesticated in Mesopotamia, these productive ruminants have flourished in the dry climate and mountainous terrain of the Middle East, central Asia, and the Mediterranean, providing milk (used for cheese, butter, and yogurt), wool, leather, parchment, and meat. When cattle were later domesticated, they were primarily used for plowing and hauling, and much less commonly consumed.

The word lamb refers to any sheep below one year of age; older animals are called sheep and their meat is known as mutton. The younger the animal, the more tender the meat and delicate the flavor. Lamb was once a seasonal item—lambs were born in early spring, available as suckling (hothouse) lamb (between six weeks to two months old and raised only on mother's milk) in March and April, and then as spring lamb (three to five months). But because of the diversity of climates, modern animal husbandry, and imports, lamb at any stage can now be found year-round.

Sheep hold a special place in Jewish life and lore. The Bible often uses them as a symbol for Israel and refers to both God and the leaders of Israel as shepherds. A host of biblical figures—including all three patriarchs as well as Moses and King David—were actual shepherds. Rachel, the Hebrew word for ewe, provided the name of one of the matriarchs and the name of her sister, Leah, may very well be a play on *ayil* (ram). Sheep, not surprisingly, play an important role in Jewish ritual. Sounding the shofar (ram's horn) serves as the central Rosh Hashanah rite. As an element in the Exodus story, lamb plays an important role in Passover festivities and is a traditional main course at many Sephardic and Mizrachi Passover Seders. Torah scrolls and mezuzot are written on sheepskin parchment.

When the Bible described the choicest products of the Promised Land as "curd of kine, and milk of sheep, with fat of lamb, and rams of the breed of Bashan," it was referring to the predominant strain of sheep in ancient Israel, the aptly named fat-tailed sheep. Awassi is a modern improved Israeli breed. The male's tail can weigh more than twenty pounds and, like a camel's hump, serves as a source of nourishment under desert conditions. The "fat of lamb" was a delicacy among Middle Easterners. The Talmud recounts that many owners attached a tiny cart under the precious tail of adult sheep to protect it from damage. Since only the choicest animals were presented as sacrifices in the Temple, the fat-tailed sheep was the type offered. During the Geonic period, the tail fat became a major point of contention between the Karaites, who forbade it for consumption, and the rabbis, who permitted it in nonsacrificial animals.

Fat-tailed sheep provided much more than just adipose tissue. The coarse wool—primarily white but also with brown or black spots and rings—was also valuable and considered the best for making carpets than other types of wool. In ancient Mesopotamia, wool production was second only to food manufacture in the economy. Fat-tailed sheep yielded more milk than most breeds, and the milk was generally transformed into tasty cheeses. The meat of the fat-tail sheep was the type preferred by Middle Easterners—mutton for stewing and lamb for roasting. Ashkenazim do not consume the rear of the sheep, while Sephardim and Mizrachim do.

Sheep did not fare well in much of the northern part of Europe, which was once heavily forested, and, therefore were a rarity among Ashkenazim, who overwhelmingly favored beef. The exceptions among Ashkenazim were in the geographic fringes of Alsace and Romania, where sheep were occasionally enjoyed. On the other hand, before Columbus, sheep provided the preponderance of Spain's foreign commerce, especially during the Hundred Years' War between England and France (1337–1453). Much of the wool was exported, while the meat and milk went into the country's larders. Not surprisingly, lamb or sheep's cheese was featured in many Sephardic recipes and consumed on a regular basis. Following the expulsion from Spain in 1492, the number and variety of Sephardic dishes in the Mediterranean incorporating lamb only increased. Sephardim and Mizrachim use lamb in a wide array of dishes, including *albondigas* (meatballs), *keftes* (patties), *kibbeh nayeh* (raw ground lamb), *kubbeh* (filled dumplings), succulent roasts, and tasty stews. Roasted

lamb shoulder is a favorite holiday dish in many Sephardic households, particularly on Passover. Similarly, Italians enjoy *agnello ripieno* (rice-stuffed lamb) for Passover.

(See also Shank)

LÁNGOS

Lángos is a fried flatbread.
Origin: Hungary
Other names: *langosh.*

During the century and a half of Ottoman control of Hungary in the sixteenth and seventeenth centuries, the Turks introduced flatbreads. Throughout most of history, few Hungarians had a home oven. Instead, when housewives wanted to bake something, they would carry the dough to the town bakery and wait for an opportunity to use the facilities, paying the going rate. With the advent of flatbreads, housewives limited the number of trips to the bakery by preparing what they called *lángos*, from the Hungarian word *láng* (flame), on a heated stone on the hearth, quickly baking very thin loaves. In addition, cooks would deep-fry thin loaves of bread at home in a skillet or pot set over an open fire. When the potato became popular in Hungary in the nineteenth century, it was added to the dough and the resulting bread, called *krumplislángos*, quickly became the favorite type. In particular, *lángos* served as a standard cold-weather bread. The warm loaves provided sustenance through the long winter, frequently accompanying a bowl of lentil or bean soup or *gulyás* as a complete meal.

Lángos also became popular in surrounding areas, including Austria, the Czech Republic, Romania, and Serbia. Today, fewer people make them at home, but commercial bakeries throughout Hungary specialize in *lángos* and vendors peddle them on the street.

Lángos are commonly accented with garlic—drizzled with garlic oil, topped with garlic butter, or rubbed with a cut clove of garlic—and sprinkled with kosher salt. No self-respecting Hungarian would use garlic powder for this. Loaves are also served with sour cream, yogurt, creamy feta cheese, or grated Edam or Gruyère cheese. *Lángos*, without the garlic, are sometimes used as a dessert—topped with whipped cream or pastry cream and berries or jam, or simply sprinkled with cinnamon-sugar.

LATKE

Latke, meaning "little oily," is a pancake. The predominate type is made from grated potatoes.

Origin: Eastern Europe

"Can you guess, children, which is the best of all holidays? Why Hanukkah, of course. You don't go to school for eight days in a row, you eat latkes every day . . ." (From "Hanukkah Money," an 1899 short story by Sholem Aleichem.)

Before there were pans and long before ovens, ancient cooks dropped a little gruel on a hot rock of a campfire, resulting in thin cakes that were tastier than plain gruel or cakes cooked directly in the embers of the fire. From these rudimentary beginnings sprang a vast array of breads and pancakes, but the two were originally the same. After the advent of pottery, flatbreads like the Ethiopian *injera* and Yemenite *lahuh*, as well as legume patties, were commonly cooked on terra-cotta griddles and later on metal griddles or skillets. To prevent sticking, these pan breads were often cooked in a thin layer of fat or deep-fried in a lot of fat, producing fritters with added flavor and texture. Over the course of time, people tinkered with the basic concoction, differentiating pancakes from breads and fritters. The ancient Greeks used griddles to cook a flat loaf drizzled with honey called *kreion* and cakes of soft cheese. The Romans, as revealed in the cookbook by Apicius, made dishes similar to modern pancakes; one recipe directed cooks to blend flour, eggs, and milk and drizzle the cakes with honey and pepper. After the collapse of Rome, however, these lighter pancakes with eggs disappeared from Europe and cooks reverted to plain forms of breads and fritters, typically made from rye or barley.

In the wake of the First Crusade and the subsequent improvement in Italian cooking due to Arabic influences, Italian cooks once again began to differentiate some of their pan breads by adding eggs and white wine or milk, then frying the loose batter in a thin layer of oil (rather than deep-frying or baking), creating a dish closer to the modern pancake. Medieval pancakes, frequently made from barley or rye and lacking leavening, were relatively heavy affairs. They were quite different from contemporary fluffy or tender versions. Gradually, Italian pancakes spread north through Europe, becoming a beloved treat. The English term pancakes—the dish is also known as griddle cakes, hotcakes, flapjacks, and by numerous other names—denoting thin cakes

Latkes derive originally from Italian ricotta pancakes. Being fried and made with dairy made them suitable for Hanukkah. The Germans began using potatoes for pancakes in the late 18th century, after which it evolved into the classic recipe of eastern Europe.

made from a starchy batter fried in a thin layer of fat, first appeared in England in 1430.

As with many medieval Ashkenazic foods, pancakes first appeared among Italian Jews, who fried them in olive oil; then the concept spread north, reaching Ashkenazim around the fourteenth century. Pancakes, not yet containing any sugar, were frequently accompanied with honey or fruit preserves. Around the same time that pancakes were experiencing a revival in medieval Europe, two forms of food emerged as traditional Hanukkah fare—fried foods and dairy foods. The first association between Hanukkah and pancakes was by Rabbi Kalonymus ben Kalonymus (c. 1286–1328), who spent his career in Italy. He included pancakes in a list of dishes to serve at an idealized Purim feast, as well as in a poem about Hanukkah. After the Spanish expelled the Jews from Sicily in 1492, the exiles introduced their ricotta cheese pancakes, which were called *cassola* in Rome, to the Jews of northern Italy. Consequently, cheese pancakes, because they combined the two traditional types of foods—fried and dairy—became a natural Hanukkah dish.

Yiddish contains numerous words for pancakes, mostly interchangeable, including *chremslach*, *bubeleh* (a term of endearment equivalent to "dear/sweetie"), *fasputshes*, *grimsel*, *placki*, *pontshkes*, *razelach*, and *pfannkuchen*. A biblical term for pancakes, as well as the modern Hebrew word, is *levivot* (possibly from *lev*, "heart"). But the most prominent Ashkenazic term for pancake is the eastern European latke, derived from the Ukrainian word for pancake and fritter, *oladka*, by the way of the Greek *eladia* (little "oilies") ultimately from the Greek *elaion* (olive oil). *Elaia* (olive), by way of Latin, is also the source of the English word oil. For most of history—until in the mid-nineteenth century, high-quality milled flour became prevalent, baking powder was invented, and less expensive cooking oils became available—pancakes were a limited, seasonal treat, not an everday food. Since pancakes were still a seasonal food, *chremsel* and *bubeleh* were frequently specified to mean matza pancakes, while the word latke became attached to Hanukkah.

Hanukkah pancakes in southern and central Europe were made from soft cheese and fried in olive oil, butter, or any available and relatively inexpensive oil, such as oil from poppy seeds or, after their arrival from America, pumpkin or sunflower seeds. Sour cream was a popular accompaniment. During the winter months in northeastern Europe, however, soft cheese and butter were luxury items and, at all times, oil was scarce and expensive. The principal fat available for frying was schmaltz, but animal fat was unacceptable for cooking with cheese. Therefore, people began substituting rye batter (*roshtshine latkes*) and batter made with the recently arrived buckwheat flour (buckwheat reached Europe around the fourteenth century) making pancakes akin to blini (but without the caviar). Turnips and other vegetables were also used to make patties, including the Slavic *knysz*, which gave rise to the knish. And then the potato arrived.

Although the potato latke has become the iconic Ashkenazic Hanukkah food, it is actually a relatively new innovation. The Maccabees never saw a potato, much less a potato pancake. When the Spanish first brought the potato to Europe from its native South America, it was considered poisonous and many centuries passed before it gradually gained acceptance as food. The first Europeans to fully embrace the potato were the French in the late eighteenth century, made desperate due to the famine in the wake of the Revolution. The Germans joined the potato bandwagon and by the end of the century they were producing potato flour and a variety of dishes, such as dumplings, salads, soups, and pancakes, variously called *kartoffelpfannkuchen* ("potato pancakes" in southern Germany), *reibekuchen* ("grated cakes," made from coarsely grated potatoes and frequently omitting any flour and egg), *rievkooche* (in the Rhine-

land), and *kartoffelpuffer* (in Berlin, made with finely grated potatoes).

German Jews also began making potato pancakes, although not for Hanukkah per se. Pancakes were made from mashed cooked potatoes, potato flour, or, the most popular form, grated raw potatoes. Since geese were the source of much of the schmaltz in central and western Europe, potato pancakes were generally fried in it and frequently were served with *gribenes* (cracklings) as an accompaniment to roast goose for Hanukkah. This new positive attitude toward the potato, however, was initially limited to the common folk, as upper-class Germans viewed the potato as "poor person's food." Most Germans opted for the other popular form of pancake, made from wheat flour.

The potato took longer to gain acceptance in eastern Europe. It was not until a series of crop failures in Ukraine and Poland in 1839 and 1840 that potatoes were planted for the first time in large numbers in that part of the world. Within a short period, potatoes—which can grow in abundance relatively quickly, even in poor soil, and can be stored through the winter—emerged as the staple of the eastern European Jewish diet, providing a cheap way to fill the hungry stomachs of the exploding Jewish population. Eastern European Jews adopted potato dishes prepared by their coreligionists from Germany, notably kugels, dumplings, and pancakes; they also invented their own dishes, including knishes, kreplach, *potatonick* (potato bread), and *bondes* (Lithuanian baked grated potatoes).

After some initial resistance, the potato pancake gained respectability and took its place in the pantheon of Jewish foods, becoming in eastern Europe the *kartofel latke* or simply latke. Since potatoes were much cheaper than wheat flour or cheese, potato latkes became the most widespread eastern European Hanukkah pancake. The inevitable scraped knuckles from a metal grater—some cooks still insist that this is the only way to achieve the proper texture—became an all-too-common feature of Hanukkah. Braised brisket supplanted roast goose as the predominant eastern European Hanukkah dish, typically accompanied with potato latkes. Applesauce (epl tzimmes) became the most popular topping, replacing sour cream, which was forbidden with meat dishes.

The potato pancake came to America in the mid-nineteenth century along with German immigrants; recipes for it are included in both *Aunt Babette's* (Cincinnati, 1889) and the first edition of *The Settlement Cook Book* (Milwaukee, 1901), both composed by German Jewish authors. The term latke arrived later, toward the end of the century, with eastern Europeans and was first recorded in America in the December 22, 1916, issue of the weekly publication *The Jewish Child.* In 1919, Aunt Jemima, which in 1869 was the first national prepackaged pancake mix, began running an advertisement in Yiddish newspapers for "the best flour for latkes." Soon thereafter, Crisco, the vegetable shortening introduced in 1911, advertised itself for frying "Hanukkah latkes." Vegetable oil later became a common frying medium. Sour cream once again became acceptable with a latke.

In 1927, the latke received wider exposure in America in an article entitled "The Jewish Cuisine" by Nettie Zimmerman in *The American Mercury Magazine,* published by H. L. Mencken. The article stated, "Similarly, *Hanukkah,* to the Jewish *bocher,* meant not only yellow candles in a glistening *menorah,* but luscious potato latkes—pancakes made of grated, raw potatoes, mixed with flour and shortening and fried in *schmaltz* (rendered chicken fat). Dozens of these were eaten by after-supper guests who came to participate in the *Hanukkah* revelry." Beginning in 1931 and continuing through the early 1950s, the radio and, later, television program *The Goldbergs* introduced mainstream America to the latke, with lines such as, "Vhen de latkes get cold, dey ain't got no taste."

Although potato latkes remained primarily a Hanukkah treat, they did begin appearing at other times of the year and became a standard in Jewish delis. Latkes, a common subject among Jewish comics and literati, emerged as one of those iconic dishes associated with Judaism. The featured bird of Isaac Bashevis Singer's story set in Brooklyn, "A Parakeet Named Dreidel," had a passion for eating latkes. In a 1996 episode of Seinfeld, in which Kramer runs a Jewish singles night, Kramer tells the caterer, "Ya know these latkes are going like hotcakes." Beginning in 1997, the James Beard House in New York City, the epitome of American gastronomy, conducted an annual Latke Lover's Cook-Off featuring some of America's top chefs.

In the 1950s, packaged dehydrated potato pancake mix appeared (it was even used by many restaurants and some grandmothers, to replace hand peeling and grating), later followed by commercial frozen latkes.

But nothing compares to fresh. As the twentieth century progressed, cooks began using ingredients in latkes unheard of in eastern Europe, such as cauliflower, spinach, and zucchini. Others added unorthodox seasonings, such as Cajun spices and jalapeño chilies. Miniature potato latkes, topped with sour cream and caviar, even became chic fare at cocktail parties.

Some people continue to prepare the original latke made from cheese, which is soft and creamy, like a New York cheesecake or a blintz without the crepe. Nevertheless, potato—crisp on the outside and tender on the inside, alone or smothered with the contrast of a cool topping—remains the favorite type of Ashkenazic Hanukkah pancake. Some cooks insist on coarsely grated spuds, producing a delicate lattice of crispy, golden brown shreds, while others prefer minced. There are also those who like a combination of the two, yielding a softer, more cakelike latke. Latkes are typically complemented with the characteristic Ashkenazic seasoning, onion. Most latkes also contain eggs and a little matza meal or flour to bind, the amount varying. The secret to making crispy potato latkes without absorbing a lot of fat is to fry the batter in enough hot oil or schmaltz (about ¼ inch), enough so that the latkes glide in the pan.

(See also Blini, Hanukkah, Pannekoek, Potato, and Sufganiyah)

ASHKENAZIC CHEESE PANCAKES
(*KAESE LATKES/LEVIVOT GEVINAH*)

ABOUT TWENTY-SIX 3-INCH PANCAKES   [DAIRY]

2 cups (16 ounces) farmer cheese, pot cheese, or drained ricotta cheese

4 large eggs

About ¾ cup all-purpose flour

2 tablespoons sugar or honey

½ teaspoon vanilla extract

About ½ teaspoon table salt or 1 teaspoon kosher salt

Vegetable oil or butter for frying

1. In a large bowl, beat together the cheese, eggs, flour, sugar, vanilla, and salt until well combined.

2. In a large skillet or griddle, heat a thin layer of oil over medium heat.

3. In batches, drop the batter by heaping tablespoonfuls and fry until the top is set and the bottom is lightly browned, about 3 minutes. Turn and fry until golden, about 2 minutes. Serve with sour cream, yogurt, maple syrup, jam, cinnamon-sugar, or fresh fruit.

LAVASH
Lavash is a very thin bread often used as a wrap.
Origin: Middle East
Other names: cracker bread, mountain bread; Arabic: *khobiz sajj*; Farsi: *nan-e lavash*; Lebanon: *markouk*; Turkey: *lavas*.

After humans discovered bread, which was originally cooked as slender cakes in the embers of campfires, the next phase was baking the batter on heated rocks; then, after the invention of pottery, it was baked on terra-cotta griddles. In order to cook the batter in this manner without burning it, the bread had to be rather thin, as it was in the biblical bread *rakik* (literally "thin"). With the advent of rudimentary ovens, slightly thicker loaves, known today as pita and flatbread, became possible. Cooks could roll out the same simple yeast dough to various thicknesses to create an array of peasant breads. Unleavened doughs called *yufka* in Turkish and phyllo in Greek were stretched to extremely thin dimensions that were ideal for pastries but too flimsy for bread.

Despite their antiquity, leavened loaves similar to those early, very thin, rock-cooked breads are still popular today throughout the Middle East and Caucasus. Lavash became the most well-known term for this bread in America. The thin breads were adopted throughout much of central and western Asia and the name *lavash* became ubiquitous on Armenian, Azerbaijani, and Georgian tables. Lavash was the bread of the common man, made at home on a sajj, a convex metal oven, or on the interior wall of a vertical clay oven without the need of a professional baker or advanced oven. A Persian way to eat lavash is to crush the crispy loaves, mash them with clarified butter, and form the mixture into small balls to pop in the mouth.

To keep the bread soft, the loaf is baked only until it begins to color on the bottom, then lightly sprinkled with water, stacked or folded into quarters, and, soon after baking, wrapped in cloth or plastic. If cooked a bit longer and left uncovered, the dough becomes crisp like a cracker. Soft lavash is used to scoop up stews and to enclose a variety of fillings, notably grilled kebabs, *kufta*, and pieces of cheese. Today, wraps made from lavash, providing an easy way to make handheld

meals, are suddenly stylish and can be found in a variety of different restaurants and cafés.

LEBEN
Leben is a coagulated milk product fermented with a different microbial culture than yogurt.
Origin: Israel
Other names: *zivdah*.

In the beginning of the twentieth century, small Ashkenazic-run dairies in Israel, then part of the Ottoman Empire, began producing a variation of a Turkish cultured milk product, which the Israelis called *leben* (from the Arabic meaning "white"). Israeli *leben* is made from partly skimmed pasteurized cow's milk to which a lactate ferment culture is added; the milk in a liquid state is then poured into individual containers and allowed to ferment and thicken, a process that takes four to six hours. Israeli regulations forbid the use of artificial thickeners in leben. A version containing 4.5 percent fat is known as *lebenia* or *eshel*. *Leben* is tarter, thinner, and less smooth than yogurt, and the live cultures are absent. Undisturbed *leben* is eaten with a spoon, but with a little shaking, it can be drunk from the container like buttermilk.

The importance of *leben* to Israelis during the British Mandate and especially during the early years of the new country cannot be overemphasized. Almost every Israeli dairy, large or small, produced a line of *leben*. At first, it was sold in glass bottles, but the tart fermented milk was soon typically packaged in small transparent plastic containers. During the decade of *tzena* (austerity) following the founding of the state in 1948, the small containers of *leben* qualified for the rationing system as "small quantities of milk"; as a result, they became even more indelibly engrained in the Israeli culture. Due to government price setting and subsidies, milk and leben remained rather inexpensive. For many decades, an Israeli breakfast and dinner typically consisted of white bread or rolls, a few simple jellies, Israeli salad, perhaps a bowl of Shalva (slightly sweetened puffed wheat), and any or all of a trio of *leben* in plain, strawberry, and chocolate flavors. Leben made a refreshing part of a meal or snack.

In 1977, Strauss—one of Israel's largest dairies—went into partnership with Danone of France to produce a line of yogurt that was creamier and thicker than *leben*, with more vibrant flavors. By 2002, yogurt sales in Israel surpassed those of *leben* and continue to expand with each passing year. The flavored *leben* has disappeared from Israeli stores, while the plain version is now packaged in containers similar to those of yogurt. As a result, Israelis under twenty have never seen the once-ubiquitous strawberry and chocolate *leben* and generally consider the surviving plain *leben* to be "old people's" food.

Meanwhile, in the late 1980s, a kosher dairy in New York began producing its own American version of Israeli *leben*, which was similar in appearance to the products now extinct in Israel and came in the Israeli flavors of plain, strawberry, and chocolate. However, these products, which are still available today, are only replications of the Israeli version, not actual old-fashioned fermented *leben*—American *leben* contains various artificial stabilizers.

LEBKUCHEN
Lebkuchen is a soft cakelike cookie containing honey and spices.
Origin: Germany
Other names: *braune kuchen, lebkukhes, lebzelt, lezelt, zelten.*

Gingerbread had its origins in honey confections of ancient Egypt, Greece, and Rome. After the collapse of the Roman Empire, European baking regressed. Meanwhile, medieval Arabs sought to produce a harmony of flavors in their food, incorporating a mix of spices, both those native to the Middle East as well as imported from the Orient. Following the First Crusade, international trade grew and, sparked by contact with Arabic culture, European cuisine gradually revived.

For centuries, most European baking advances originated in Italy, including dense rudimentary honey cakes. These early cakes were commonly made from bread crumbs, which were often from rye bread rather than breads made with wheat flour. Eventually, through trade, monastic communities, and Jewish connections, these baked goods made their way north to Germany. Among non-Jews, much of medieval baking was for religious occasions and bore religious motifs, such as *Osterlamm* (Easter lamb). In the thirteenth century, the Italian *panforte* became a rudimentary Teutonic fruit-studded honey cake, called lebkuchen in southern and western Germany and Austria, probably from the Middle High German *laib* (loaf) or *lebbe* (sweet) and *kuchen* (cake); the term was first recorded in 1296.

Many monasteries maintained not only baking ovens, but also apiaries and orchards, which provided honey and walnuts for the baked goods. When these baked goods became widespread and monasteries were no longer capable of meeting demand, the cakes became the province of a guild, from which Jews were excluded. In 1473, the Lebzelter Guild was established in Munich, producing an assortment of cookies—including *gebildegebäck, honiglebkuchen* (honey cake), and *springerle*—as well as mead. Also at this time, Nuremberg in particular became noted for its honey production and the art of its lebkuchen, including the *Elisenlebkuchen*, containing ground hazelnuts and almonds and very little crumbs.

In the sixteenth century, a different version of this Teutonic confection emerged that was based on almonds instead of bread crumbs; the dish was called "white gingerbread" to distinguish it from "dark gingerbread." By the end of the seventeenth century, bakers of gingerbread increasingly began to substitute wheat flour for the bread crumbs that had been used since medieval times, resulting in lighter cakes and cookies. The advent of chemical leavenings in the eighteenth century led to even lighter lebkuchen. One of lebkuchen's attributes was that it could be stored for many weeks and actually improve in flavor as it stood.

There are numerous recipes for lebkuchen, but today all genuine versions contain honey and spices. Initially, Asian spices were rare and expensive and not part of German baking, but gradually they began to arrive by way of Venice, becoming an essential element of lebkuchen. Some bakers insist on adding ground ginger to lebkuchen, while others find it heretical.

By the fifteenth century, German Jews were enjoying homemade lebkuchen (avoiding the guilds). Rabbi Joseph ben Moses of Hoechstaedt, in his tome *Leket Yosher* (c. 1450), recorded that his teacher, Israel Isserlein, the foremost sage of fifteenth-century Germany, considered *lezelt* to be bread in regard to ritual hand washing and the benediction, unless spices were added, rendering it a cake. Lebkuchen, its pareve nature made it ideal for meat occasions, became traditional on Sukkot, because of the presence of fruits and nuts; on Rosh Hashanah, because of the honey; and on Hanukkah, because it was popular among non-Jews at that time of year. Alsatians used a firm version to make gingerbread men or other shapes for Purim. Lebkuchen crumbs were stirred into the cooking liquids of pot roasts, tongue, poached fish, and other dishes to thicken and flavor the gravy.

Lebkuchen was included in early American Jewish cookbooks, all written by German Jews, notably *Aunt Babette's* (Cincinnati, 1889); the first edition of *The Settlement Cook Book* (Milwaukee, 1901), which had two recipes for it; and *The Neighborhood Cook Book* by the Council of Jewish Women (Portland, Oregon, 1912).

Innovations in baking in the nineteenth and twentieth centuries engendered a host of new cakes and cookies, and also led to the disappearance of many of the old-fashioned German bakeries in America. The result was a dramatic decline in the popularity of medieval fare, in particular lebkuchen. Nevertheless, a small number of Ashkenazim retain a passion for this basic gingerbread.

(See also Kuchen and Lekach)

GERMAN HONEY SPICE COOKIES (*LEBKUCHEN*)

ABOUT 25 LARGE OR 42 SMALL BARS   [PAREVE]

1 cup (12 ounces) honey, or ½ cup honey and ½ cup molasses
¾ cup (5.75 ounces) brown sugar
About 3 cups (15 ounces) all-purpose flour
½ teaspoon baking soda
¼ teaspoon salt
1 teaspoon ground cinnamon
½ teaspoon ground cloves
½ teaspoon ground ginger (optional)
¼ teaspoon ground nutmeg, mace, or cardamom
2 small eggs, lightly beaten (about ⅓ cup)
1 tablespoon lemon juice, brandy, or whiskey
2 teaspoons grated lemon or orange zest (optional)
1½ cups (8 ounces) blanched almonds or hazelnuts, or ¾ cup each, finely chopped but not ground
½ to ¾ cup (3 to 4 ounces) finely diced candied citron, orange peel, or pineapple, or any combination

Icing:
1¼ cups confectioners' sugar
½ teaspoon vanilla extract, 1 tablespoon lemon juice, or ½ teaspoon anise extract
1 to 2 tablespoons warm water

1. In a small saucepan, stir the honey and sugar over low heat until the sugar dissolves, about 5 minutes. Transfer to a large bowl and let cool. Sift together the flour, baking soda, salt, cinnamon, cloves, optional ginger, and nutmeg. To the honey mixture, add the eggs, lemon juice, and, if using, zest and stir to combine. Mix in the nuts and fruit. Using a large wooden spoon, stir in the flour mixture to make a stiff dough. Cover and refrigerate for at least 8 hours or for up to 3 days. Let stand at room temperature until malleable, about 40 minutes.

2. Preheat the oven to 325°F. Line 2 large baking sheets with parchment paper, or line with aluminum foil and lightly grease and dust with flour.

3. On a lightly floured surface, roll the dough into a ¼-inch-thick rectangle. Using a large knife and dipping it in water occasionally when it gets sticky, or a pastry wheel, cut into about twenty-five 3-by-2-inch bars or about forty-two 2- by-1½-inch pieces. Place on the prepared baking sheets about ½ inch apart.

4. Bake the cookies until firm and lightly colored, about 25 minutes. Transfer the cookies a wire rack and let cool completely.

5. To make the icing: Stir together the sugar, vanilla, and enough water to make a spreadable icing. Spread over the cookies and let stand until firm.

6. Store in an airtight container at room temperature for up to 2 months or in the freezer for up to 6 months. For softer cookies, place in an airtight container at room temperature with several apple slices.

LECSÓ

Lecsó is a pepper and tomato ragout seasoned with paprika.

Origin: Hungary

Other names: Israel and Russia: *lecho*; Serbia: *djuvece*; Turkey: *guvecs*.

When the upscale Jewish family of Dr. Lajos Engel was deported from the small northern Hungarian town of Abaújszántó to a concentration camp in May 1944, among the items inventoried in their home and confiscated by the Hungarian government were "five bars of soap; one Persian mink coat; one lady's seal mink coat; one man's mink coat, one man's short mink coat; six Persian carpets; three Persian carpet runners; six oil paintings; two jars of *lecsó*."

After peppers and tomatoes arrived in the Old World, they were disregarded by most Europeans, but found quick culinary acceptance among Turks, Arabs, and Sephardim, who commonly cooked the two vegetables together into a simple but flavorful ragout. The

Ottomans introduced the idea to the Balkans during its occupation. The dish spread to its neighbors, in particular the Hungarians to the north, who naturally added some paprika.

Hungarians love peppers not only in the ground form of paprika, but also both fresh and cooked, in dishes subsumed under the category of *paprikás egytálak* (pepper dishes). *Lecsó* is among the most popular of Hungarian foods. It is made with sweet peppers, tomatoes, onions, and paprika, but from there on, the proportions differ from family to family. Some recipes call for only one variety of pepper, while others require two or three. The Hungarian sweet yellow pepper is the favorite.

Hungarians insist that *lecsó* must not be cooked in a hurry, but instead requires slow simmering to meld and develop the flavors. August through October is when peppers and tomatoes are at their best in Hungary and at that time families traditionally cooked up a large kettle of *lecsó* and canned it to last through the winter and spring. *Lecsó* is served, hot or cold, as a dip for bread or as a side dish with steaks, breaded veal, and noodles. *Lecsó* is mixed into scrambled eggs or used as an accompaniment to omelets, transforming the egg dishes—with the addition of potatoes or rice—into a complete light meal.

HUNGARIAN PEPPER RAGOUT (*LECSÓ*)

8 TO 10 SERVINGS AS A SIDE DISH [PAREVE]

3 tablespoons vegetable oil

2 medium onions, chopped

2 pounds Hungarian sweet yellow peppers, sweet yellow banana peppers, Italian frying peppers, or any combination yellow and red bell peppers, seeded and cut into ½-inch-thick slices

2 to 3 teaspoons sweet paprika

⅛ teaspoon hot paprika or cayenne (optional)

4 cups (24 ounces) peeled, seeded, and chopped plum tomatoes

1 teaspoon sugar

About 1 teaspoon table salt or 2 teaspoons kosher salt

Ground black pepper to taste

About ¼ cup tomato puree or water (optional)

1. In a large pot, heat the oil over medium heat. Add the onions and sauté until soft and translucent, 5 to 10 minutes. Add the peppers and sauté until softened but not browned, about 10 minutes.

2. Remove from the heat and stir in the paprika(s). Add the tomatoes, sugar, salt, and pepper. Place over medium heat, cover, and cook for 10 minutes. If the vegetables have not released sufficient liquid, add the tomato puree.

3. Cover, reduce the heat to low, and cook, stirring occasionally and adding more liquid if necessary, until the peppers are very tender and the mixture is thickened, about 20 minutes. Serve warm or at room temperature.

LEEK

Leeks, a mild member of the onion family that resembles a large scallion, have oblong white bulbs and long, flattish, dark green leaves. This native of the eastern Mediterranean was among the most common of plants depicted in ancient Egypt, and their remains, dating back to the early Bronze Age, were found in Jericho. Leeks, one of the foods that the Israelites yearned for after leaving Egypt, have been a part of Jewish cooking from the onset. When cooked, they have a silky texture and subtle flavor.

The Romans loved leeks and sowed them throughout Europe. Charlemagne so cherished leeks that he ordered them planted throughout his realm, and, as a result, they held a prominent place in early Ashkenazic cooking, a position that later waned in eastern Europe. Among Sephardim, on the other hand, the leek was consistently the single most important vegetable; it was used solo or combined with other vegetables in soups, stews, casseroles, patties, and savory pastries. In the area encompassed by the Ottoman Empire, where this vegetable is associated with Sephardic cooking, leeks were also commonly paired with beans or rice. During occasional periods of severe poverty, the leek was the only regular vegetable on the Sephardic table.

Leeks have two growing seasons: Summer leeks, the milder type, come into maturity in early autumn, in time for Rosh Hashanah, while winter leeks, the more intensely flavored variety, are planted before the winter to be ready in the spring, in time for Passover. Consequently, leeks became traditional Sephardic Rosh Hashanah and Passover food. Leeks were among the items that the Talmud suggested eating on Rosh Hashanah, because their Aramaic name *karti* is the same as the Hebrew word "cut off," signifying the removal of all enemies.

(See also Albondiga, Fritada, Kefte, Mina, Quajado, and Sfongato)

LEKACH/HONIG LEKACH

Lekach is a honey cake.

Origin: Germany

Other names: *lekekh, leykekh*; Switzerland: *laeckerli, leckerli*; Ukraine: *medianyk*.

The earliest cakes probably consisted of cooked patties of mashed legumes and honey. The ancient Egyptians were the first people known to add honey to yeast dough to create a light cake. The Romans enjoyed baked loaves of barley gruel mixed with honey, raisins, pine nuts, and pomegranate seeds, as well as various cheesecakes with honey. Absorbing Roman and Middle Eastern culinary techniques, the Arabs spread these cakes west into Sicily and Moorish Spain. By the tenth century, sugar had replaced honey in baking in the Arab world, an evolutionary step that would not occur in Europe for many centuries. Meanwhile, the medieval European masses relied on barley, millet, and rye as the source for gruels and breads. Around the beginning of the eleventh century, Italians began making cakes from bread crumbs and honey and, as imports became available, spices, creating heavy loaves similar to *panforte* ("strong bread," referring to a rudimentary honey cake, the adjective strong denoting its intense amount of spices). These dense cakes were generally formed into the shape of bread and the rounds were baked directly on the floor of the oven or on a piece of parchment paper.

Taking on the typical Jewish role as a conduit for transmitting foods within different parts of medieval Europe and between the Arab and Christian worlds, Italian Jews brought rudimentary honey cakes made from bread crumbs to central and western Europe. *Machzor Vitry*, a late eleventh-century prayer book compiled by Simcha ben Samuel of Vitry, France (d. 1105), mentions "challot of fine flour with honey" an early honey cake. The first record of *lekach* (from the Middle High German *lecke*—"lick") appeared in *Sefer ha-Rokeach* (c. 1200) by Eleazar ben Judah of Worms, a city in southwest Germany. It was 1320 when honey cake was first mentioned in a non-Jewish Franco-German source, the records of a monastery. Honey cakes, including those pervaded with spices, which were known by the English as gingerbread, became the primary festive treat of medieval Europe.

Early Ashkenazic references to *lekach* were in conjunction with a popular medieval Ashkenazic ceremony, later called *Aleph-Bazyn* (from the first two letters of the Hebrew alphabet). Ashkenazim found special significance in the Yiddish name for honey cake because of a verse in Proverbs: "For I give you good *lekach* [instruction/doctrine], do not forsake my teaching." At the initiatory appearance of a child at *cheder* (elementary school), usually on Shavuot (the day on which the Torah was given) or the first day of the month of Nisan (the first day of the Jewish calendar), he was escorted to the schoolhouse, covered by a tallith (prayer shawl). Honey was smeared on a slate containing the letters of the alphabet and the child licked them off so that the "words of the Torah may be sweet as honey." Afterwards, the aspiring scholar was presented with an apple, hard-boiled egg, and round honey cake inscribed on top with an appropriate biblical verse. Although by the eighteenth century, the formal and elaborate ceremony on Shavuot had disappeared, the custom of smearing honey on the letters of the alphabet endures among some groups until this day.

The current form of *lekach* or *honig lekach* is a product of centuries of evolution; the cake that finally emerged in the late nineteenth century was unrecognizable from its early ancestors. When *lekach* first appeared, spices in Europe were incredibly expensive. However, Europeans who could afford these luxury imports tended to make prodigal use of them in ostentatious rather than harmonious displays in all sorts of dishes. Medieval cakes of the upper class typically contained a combination of Asian spices (anise, cardamom, cinnamon, cloves, and pepper), but at that point, rarely ginger. Beginning in the fifteenth century, spurred on by the Renaissance and the importation of Middle Eastern knowledge, European agricultural techniques underwent major improvements and eating habits began to change. Gradually, wheat emerged as the predominant grain in much of Europe, although until the sixteenth century, most European wheat was still imported, notably from Sicily and Egypt. Even after Europeans began cultivating their own wheat in larger amounts, the primary flour consisted of maslin, a natural mixture of wheat and rye grains, which was not conducive to refined baking. Meanwhile Spain,

Portugal, France, Holland, and England were establishing colonies in the Americas and planting sugarcane in the Caribbean and Brazil. As a result, sugar and white flour became increasingly accessible and affordable in Europe.

By the end of the seventeenth century, bakers increasingly began to update the medieval recipe for honey cakes by adding eggs and oil and substituting wheat flour for the bread crumbs, resulting in lighter, more tender loaves. Sugar began to supplement or supplant the honey. By 1573, some English bakers were already replacing the honey or sugar in gingerbread with treacle (a by-product of sugar refinement like molasses, but lighter in color). The advent of alkaline chemical leavenings in the eighteenth century led to even lighter *lekach*. In the mid-nineteenth century, baking soda and, later, baking powder emerged as the principal chemical leavenings. The loose batter of these newfangled honey cakes could no longer be baked free-form, but required metal or wooden cake hoops (round rings, similar to the sides of springform pans, which were placed on flat pans) and metal baking tins, transforming the cakes into rectangles and rounds. In some parts of Eastern Europe (especially Bessarabia and Podolio), *lekach* was used as the generic word for cake or for sponge cake, while honey cake was donoted as *honig lekach* or *honik leykekh*.

There are numerous variations of honey cake recipes, the loaves ranging from dense, dark brown, and intense with honey and spice to light and airy with only a subtle hint of honey and a note of spice. The flavor of a cake varies depending on the type of honey—the stronger the honey (such as buckwheat), the more intense the cake. A little coffee or tea draws out a pleasant bitter note in the cake. Traditional *lekach* is always pareve and never frosted.

The first recipe for "Lekach" in English was in *The International Jewish Cook Book* by Florence Kreisler Greenbaum (New York, 1918). The author noted, "This recipe is one that is used in Palestine."

Beginning in the seventeenth century, the use of honey in Europe markedly declined, and, correspondingly, honey cakes lost favor, surpassed by sponge and butter cakes. Still, for more than a thousand years, *lekach* has remained a common sight at various Ashkenazic rituals, such as kiddushes, *brit milahs*, bar mitzvahs, and weddings. Generations of holiday meals have ended with *lekach*. It is enjoyed on the Sabbath, on Purim, on Hanukkah, and at the meal following Yom Kippur, and flourless versions are even served for Passover. In Germany, honey cakes shaped like a ladder were prepared for Shavuot (honey was compared to the Torah, which was given to the Jewish people on that day and a ladder, from Jacob's dream, a symbol of reaching heaven), although today the custom is to prepare dairy foods. On the eve of Yom Kippur, many Chasidim have a custom that each person should specifically ask for a piece of *lekach* from someone else—accordingly, the Lubavitcher Rebbe in Brooklyn once gave out pieces of honey cake to around ten thousand people. Most notably, honey cake serves as a traditional Ashkenazic Rosh Hashanah treat, allowing people to start the new year off on a sweet note.

(See also Honey and Lebkuchen)

❧ ASHKENAZIC HONEY CAKE (*LEKACH*)

MAKES ONE 10-INCH TUBE CAKE, ONE 13-BY-9-INCH
CAKE, OR TWO LARGE LOAVES   [PAREVE]

3 cups (15 ounces) all-purpose flour, or 1½ cups white flour and 1½ cups rye flour

2 teaspoons baking powder

2 teaspoons baking soda

½ teaspoon salt

2 teaspoons ground cinnamon or 1 teaspoon ground ginger, or 1 teaspoon cinnamon and ½ teaspoon ginger

½ teaspoon ground cardamom, nutmeg, or allspice

¼ teaspoon ground cloves

4 large eggs, lightly beaten

1 cup vegetable oil

1 cup (11.75 ounces) honey

1 cup (7 ounces) granulated sugar

1 cup (8.5 ounces) dark brown sugar, packed

1 cup strong liquid coffee (from about 1 tablespoon instant coffee) or tea (from 2 tea bags)

1 to 1½ cups raisins, diced candied citron, mixed candied fruit, or chopped toasted walnuts or pecans; or ½ cup raisins, ½ cup chopped dried apricots, and ½ cup chopped nuts (optional)

1. Preheat the oven to 325°F. Grease one 10-inch Bundt or tube pan, one 13-by-9-inch baking pan, or two 9-inch loaf pans, line the bottom and sides with parchment paper, and regrease.

2. Sift together the flour, baking powder, baking soda, salt, cinnamon, cardamom, and cloves. In a large bowl, combine the eggs, oil, honey, and sugars.

Add the coffee. Stir in the flour mixture until smooth. If using, add the fruit.

3. Pour into the prepared pan and place on a baking sheet. Bake until a tester inserted in the center comes out clean and the top springs back when lightly touched, about 1 hour for a Bundt or tube pan, 40 to 45 minutes for a 13-by-9-inch pan, or 45 to 55 minutes for loaf pans. Do not overbake or the outside will burn and the interior will dry out. Let cool in the pan for 15 minutes, then transfer the cake(s) to a wire rack and let cool completely. Wrap in plastic wrap or aluminum foil and let stand for at least 24 hours. The flavor improves as the cake matures for a day or two.

LEKVAR

Lekvar is a fruit butter, particularly those made from prunes, but also commonly encompassing those based on apricots, apples and peaches.

Origin: Slovakia

Other names: Czech: *povidla*; Germany/Austria: *powidl*; Hungary: *lekveir*.

Unlike jams and jellies, fruit butters do not obtain their sweetness from added sugar, which for most of history was rare and expensive in Europe. Sugar also detracts from the natural flavor of the fruit. Rather, the sweetness in lekvar comes from the ripe fruit itself and is produced by the concentration of the natural sugar during the long hours of cooking.

Frenchmen from the Fifth Crusade (1217–1221) returned from the Middle East with the European plum tree, which requires a long period of winter chilling to bear fruit, and it gradually spread across central Europe. Plums grow prolifically in this region, coming into season in late August and September, around Rosh Hashanah. During other parts of the year, reductions from dried plums could, as needed, be prepared. These reductions could be cooked more quickly than fresh plums and had a more intense flavor.

In much of the continent, the preferred plum variety to dry was the Italian (Lombard) plum, which produced a tart-sweet dried plum with a winy flavor.

For centuries, the pitted fruit was boiled outdoors in large kettles for three to four hours until it was quite thick, with people taking turns constantly stirring with large wooden utensils to prevent scorching. The fruit reduction was then stored in crocks to last at least through the winter. Today, a slightly sweeter fruit butter is preferred, in which sugar is added not only as a sweetener, but also as a preservative and thickener.

In northern Europe, the prevalent term for fruit reductions was the Czech *povidla* (from *povidat*, "to tell stories"), the same term used in Poland, Ukraine, and Moldavia. In Germany and Austria, plum reductions became known as *powidl*, as well as *pflaumenmus* and *zwetschgenkonfitüre*. Plum butter in Yiddish was generally *povidl*. Nobel Prize–winning writer Shmuel Yosef Agnon, in his 1939 book *A Guest for the Night*, depicting Jewish life in Galicia (southern Poland) before World War II, wrote, "The smell of warm povidl, which had been put away in the oven, sweetened the air of the house. For many years I had not felt its taste or come across its smell—that smell of ripe plums in the oven, which brings back the memory of days gone by, when Mother, may she rest in peace, would spread the sweet povidl on my bread."

Farther south, a different terminology emerged from one of the hallmarks of medieval European medicine, the *latwerge*; known in English as an electuary or a lincture, this paste was made by mixing medicinal powders with honey, sugar syrup, or fruit paste. Among the Czechs, medicinal pastes became known as *lektvar*, and even farther south, around the seventeenth century, the Slovaks transformed this term to lekvar and used it to refer to various fruit butters. Hungarians followed suit, calling fruit reductions *lekvár*.

In the areas where it became known as lekvar, dried plum paste was for centuries the jam of the masses, who spread it on peasant bread or used it in various treats. Because it is so thick, lekvar's quintessential role is as a filling for central and eastern European pastries (such as Danish, *fluden*, hamantaschen, *kipfel*, *kolache*, and *piroshki*) and crepes (the Slovac and Czech *palacinka*), kugels, doughnuts, and dumplings.

After commercial canning became practical in the 1860s, central Europeans began to produce canned fruit butters. In the 1920s, Sokol & Company of Chicago, whose founder was from a Bohemian background, introduced under the Solo brand a line of central European–style fillings, including prune, although at the time the prune filling was not designated as lekvar. From 1926 until it closed near the turn of the twenty-first century, H. Roth & Sons, also later known as Lekvar-by-the-Barrel, on the Upper East Side of Manhattan sold bulk prune and apricot butters in addition to other Hungarian favorites. The availability of commercial fruit butters led to a further emphasis on dried rather than fresh plums in baking, as dried fruit was more accessible and less seasonal. Commercial lekvars also contained added sugar to facilitate the canning process. Consequently, some bakers continued to make their own fruit butters, as commercial lekvar was not as flavorful as homemade.

When *Time* magazine first mentioned lekvar in 1940, it was described as "gluey layers of candied noodles," and not fruit butter. In both Yiddish and English, the term lekvar to denote fruit butter was widely adopted relatively late; in the 1950s, when Hungarian and Slovak immigrants in America brought the term into general usage. Hungarians have long ranked among the best home bakers in Europe and many of their pastries incorporate lekvar. After World War II, various Hungarian baked goods and techniques were adopted by the wider Ashkenazic community, as well as the term lekvar. It soon became the common Yiddish name for fruit butters. Jews, in turn, helped to popularize the use of lekvar, the word and the food, in America.

(See also Plum)

LEMON, PRESERVED

Preserved lemon is actually a pickled lemon.
Origin: Maghreb
Other names: Arabic: *hamid m'syiar, hamid muraqqad*; French: *citron confit*; Hebrew: *limonim hamoutzi*.

Preserved lemons are a staple of Moroccan cuisine, as well as important in Algeria and Tunisia, providing an exotic touch to any dish. Moroccans traditionally prepared a year's supply of preserved lemons every spring, when the fruit was juiciest, preferring *boussera* (bergamot), a tart variety that tends to have more juice, or the very small, thin-skinned *doqq* variety. However, any lemon works well, including Meyer lemons (a cross between a lemon and a mandarin). The lemons are cut and salted, then left to pickle in additional lemon juice, producing a distinctive pungent flavor and silken texture. Moroccan Jews sometimes pickle the lemons in oil instead of lemon juice, which causes the lemons to develop a somewhat different flavor. Another Jewish touch is to add cinnamon sticks to lemons to be used with sweet dishes, and peppercorns and bay leaves to those meant for savory dishes.

Preserved lemons are frequently added to tagines, chicken and fish stews, and vegetable salads. They marry well with olives, cilantro, and ginger. Cooks primarily use the rind, which softens in texture and mellows in flavor as it pickles. Some cooks also include the pulp, while others discard it. The thick brine is used as the souring agent in various dishes.

MOROCCAN PRESERVED LEMONS (*HAMID M'SYIAR*)
6 LEMONS   [PAREVE]

6 medium unblemished lemons, preferably organic
About 7 tablespoons kosher salt
About 1 cup fresh lemon juice or vegetable oil

1. Cover the lemons with warm water and let soak, changing the water every day, for 3 days. Drain and pat dry.

2. Starting from the top of the lemons, cut lengthwise to within ½ inch of the bottom, then turn halfway and cut the same way into quarters—do not cut apart, but leave the lemons attached at the base. Stuff the gashes with the salt, about 1 tablespoon per lemon, and reshape the fruit.

3. Sprinkle the remaining 1 tablespoon salt over the bottom of a sterilized 1-quart jar. Pack in the lemons, squishing them down. Add enough lemon juice to cover. Seal the jar and let stand in a cool, dark place, shaking the jar each day, until soft, about 4 weeks.

4. Refrigerate after opening. Store the lemons in the pickling liquid. Using tongs, and not your fingers, remove the lemons. Preserved lemons will keep in the refrigerator for up to 1 year.

LENTIL

The lentil, the seed of a small annual shrub, was probably the first domesticated legume; its cultivation stretches well back before recorded history. Lentils, together with barley, einkorn, emmer, and millet, constituted the bulk of early agriculture and the human diet.

The low bushy lentil plant bears pods containing two thin biconvex seeds. Immature pods are occasionally eaten as a vegetable, but most are dried and threshed. All lentils of various colors—brown, dark green, orange, pinkish, and red—are members of the same species. The brown variety, which actually ranges in color from olive green to light brown, is the most prevalent in the West. Brown lentils, which come unhulled, have a rather bland flavor and hold their shape well in cooking, making them best for salads and stews. Green lentils, also unhulled, are firmer and take a little longer to cook than brown. Several varieties of very small, dark green lentils, called French lentils or *verte du Puy*, are renowned for their firm texture and are considered a delicacy. Red-brown lentils are unhulled red lentils; they have an earthier flavor than the hulled version and keep their shape better during cooking. Red lentils—also called orange lentils, Egyptian lentils, Persian lentils, and, in India, *massor dal/masur dal*—are hulled, revealing their bright reddish orange interiors. Red lentils—their bright color fades as they cook—become tender more quickly than green varieties. Because they break down while cooking, red lentils are commonly used in pureed dishes or where a smooth texture is desired.

Lentils have been a part of Jewish cookery from the onset, including the most famous lentil dish of all time, Jacob's red pottage, for which his twin, Esau, sold his birthright. Lentils were also used to make *ashishim*, pressed cakes made from ground roasted lentils and honey and fried in oil, such as those King David gave to all the people upon bringing the ark to Jerusalem. Because lentils have a spherical shape with "no mouth" (no opening), they are symbolic of mourners who are required to be silent. Lentils are traditionally served, along with hard-boiled eggs, at a *Seudat Havra'ah* (meal of consolation) following a burial and before fasts. At the same time, lentils are a symbol of fertility and so are sometimes served on joyous occasions as well.

The Romans, however, viewed lentils with disdain and even as harmful, a sentiment adopted by many Jews of the empire. For Ashkenazim, lentils had the standing of poor person's food and were considered something to be avoided except at times of famine. This disparagement of lentils may have, by mistake, led to the Ashkenazic prohibition against consuming *kitniyot* (legumes) on Passover. Arabs, on the other hand, viewed lentils as an energizer and mood brightener, and the legume flourished in Muslim cultures. Accordingly, Mizrachim typically consume lentils on a regular basis, although generally not for the Sabbath and festivals.

By themselves, lentils are rather bland with an earthy flavor, so they are good companions for garlic, tomato, and many assertive herbs. Lentil soup became a common breakfast in parts of the Middle East. Lentils are frequently teamed with grains for complementary nutrition in dishes such as the widespread Middle Eastern rice and lentil *mujaddara*. Sephardim generally use red lentils for soups and brown lentils for most other recipes, including dishes in which lentils are combined with rice, bulgur, or noodles. Syrians use red lentils as a vegetarian substitute in dishes such as *lahmajin* (meat pizzas) and *kibbeh neyeh* (raw ground meat). For the Bene Israel of India, hulled red lentils, along with rice, form the basis of most meals

(See also Dal, Mujaddara, and Wot)

LIBATOPORTYU PASTETOM

Libatoportyu pastetom is a Transylvanian spread, a substitute for chopped liver, made from poultry cracklings. *Pástétom* is Hungarian for "pâté," while *liba* means "goose" and *töpörtyû* denotes "cracklings," which are called *gribenes* in Yiddish. This was a favorite Sabbath lunch dish in the Transylvanian town of Szatmar, now located in eastern Hungary.

LIVER

"I am sorry, but we are all out of pickled fish. You can have some chopped liver instead, and you can have some fine cabbage soup after that."

(From the November 28, 1914, edition of the *Fort Wayne* [Indiana] *Sentinel*, recording one of the first U.S. mentions of chopped liver.)

Food was, until relatively recently, a precious and frequently scarce resource and, therefore, no part of an animal was wasted, including the sometimes less-than-desirable offal. Liver was generally viewed unfavorably by Sephardim and Mizrachim, so it received little attention in their recipes and was rarely, if ever, served on the Sabbath or festivals.

The lack of interest by in liver many Jews was not only attributable to its mineral flavor, which is an acquired taste, but also partially due to its unique status in the Jewish dietary laws. Liver, the largest internal organ (its Hebrew name *kaved* derives from the root "heavy"), fulfills numerous functions in metabolism and the elimination of toxins, including cleansing the blood. Due to the large quantity of blood saturating this complex organ, it cannot be kashered in the same manner as other parts of the animal, by merely soaking and salting, but instead must be broiled under or grilled over a flame. Not only is kosher liver a bit of a bother to prepare, but the organ's distinctive flavor becomes more pronounced the longer it is cooked.

While much of the world tended to disparage liver, among medieval Ashkenazim goose liver emerged as a much-beloved delicacy. The liver's rise to prominence in northern France and Alsace was not initially caused by people's preference for the organ or even for the bird's flesh, but rather by their desire to render the goose's indispensable fat, as goose schmaltz was the predominant cooking medium for Jews in the region.

The liver and skin are the principal repositories of the fat of geese and ducks. For about a month before migrating, these birds gorge on excess food in preparation, eating as much as possible. As explained in the book *Foie Gras: A Passion* by Michael Ginor (Wiley, 1999), force-feeding waterfowl is an ancient practice. Egyptians, who were the first known to domesticate waterfowl, were also, in at least 2500 BCE, the first to force-feed them—with roasted barley and other grains soaked in water—to produce fatter birds, a process probably originating as a means of rendering them too heavy to fly. Subsequently, the techniques were adopted by the Greeks and then the Romans, who were the first to specifically note the resultant fattened goose liver as a desired delicacy. After the fall of the Roman Empire, the practice of force-feeding disappeared from Europe along with many other gastronomic techniques, except among Italian Jews, who retained the venerable methods. Around the eleventh century, Italian Jews introduced this practice to their counterparts in Alsace. Even centuries later, in 1782, Pierre Jean Baptiste, known as Legrand d'Aussy, in a lengthy study of French cuisine, wrote, "The Jews of Metz and Strasbourg possess the same secrets [of the ancient Romans], though their precise methods we do not know. And the secret is one of the branches of commerce that made them rich. As is well known, Strasbourg makes these livers into pâtés whose reputation is renowned."

As early as the eleventh century, in the first medieval records of force-feeding, some rabbinic authorities noted that the geese suffered during the fattening process and that the practice could be considered animal cruelty. However, in general, the practice was accepted by religious authorities, who believed that, due to the hardness of the birds' gullets, they did not actually feel discomfort. Shortly after its founding in 1948, foie gras became one of Israel's first export products. In 2006, however, the Israeli government outlawed the practice of force-feeding, ending the country's foie gras industry, which at the time was producing four hundred tons yearly, and for most intents and purposes, terminating this venerable European Jewish tradition there.

Ashkenazim sometimes accompanied the plain broiled goose liver with sautéed onions. They also mixed the liver with chopped goose meat or veal and stuffed it into the goose neck, making *helzel*. The favorite Ashkenazic way to enjoy liver, which had originated in Alsace by the fourteenth century, was *foie haché*—broiled and chopped.

It was in the Slavic areas of eastern Europe— Poland, Ukraine, and Lithuania—that chopped liver (*gehakte leber*), typically from chicken livers, not goose livers, found its greatest popularity. In eastern Europe, chopped liver was mixed with the two most important medieval Ashkenazic staples—onions and hard-boiled eggs. The additions, besides adding flavor and stretching the meat, helped to counter the heaviness of the broiled liver. By the sixteenth century, chickens could be slaughtered on a weekly or monthly basis, transforming chopped liver into more regular fare; it became a standard Friday night or Sabbath lunch appetizer and a popular filling for various savory pastries, such as strudel and knishes. Since it contained no grain products, chopped liver became a favorite dish during Passover alongside the matza.

Chicken, goose, duck, calf, and beef liver can all be used to make chopped liver. In eastern Europe, chicken or beef liver, both less creamy than goose liver (and beef liver is less creamy than chicken liver), were commonly used and, since the small chicken livers typically failed to yield enough meat, they were frequently supplemented with some beef liver or other organs, such as the lung, heart, and spleen (*milts*). Beef liver is a dark reddish brown and intensely flavored, while calf liver is a paler color and has a more delicate flavor. There is a good deal of disagreement as to the nature of the onions added to the liver—whether they should be raw or sautéed or a combination of both. Sautéed onions contribute a sweet note while raw impart pungency. A once popular practice was to add *gribenes* (cracklings) to the liver. Some eastern Europeans mixed in grated black radishes or apples.

Whatever type of liver is used, the texture of the eastern European version is rustic and slightly coarse. Historically, *gehakte leber* was prepared by chopping the ingredients by hand in a large wooden bowl using a *hackmeister* (curved metal blade) or on a flat board using a cleaver. The resulting dense dish should be a sublime blend of chunky and smooth, sweet and bitter. The name of the dish gave rise to an old Yiddish play on words, *"Gehakte leber is besser vi gehakte tsuris"* (Chopped liver is better than terrible troubles)."

Eastern European immigrants brought chopped liver to America in the late nineteenth century. It became a favorite Ashkenazic appetizer for the Sabbath and festivals, as well as for buffets at other special occasions. In delicatessens, it was slathered on sandwiches solo or layered in conjunction with sliced meats. By the 1950s, chopped liver smeared on a cracker emerged as popular American cocktail fare. In the movie *Godfather II*, an old time mobster exclaims, "A kid comes up to me in a white jacket, gives me a Ritz cracker and chopped liver, he says 'Canapes.' I said, 'Can-o-peas, my ass, that's a Ritz cracker and chopped liver.'"

Catskill resorts molded individual servings of chopped liver into swans, chickens, or other whimsical shapes. Some housewives began to fashion the liver into the form of a pineapple, covering it with rows of sliced olives, or to mold tablespoons of liver into the shape of strawberries and coat the "berries" with paprika. This led to extravagant buffets featuring sculptured chopped liver busts of bar mitzvah boys and brides.

As with most traditional foods, Americans frequently adapted chopped liver. The first edition of *The Settlement Cook Book* (Milwaukee, 1901) included "French Dressing"—made from vinegar, onion, sugar, salt, pepper, a little mustard, and a lot of water—instead of schmaltz in its "Liver and Egg Salad." Later, some cooks used mayonnaise instead of schmaltz for moistness. Toward the end of the twentieth century, as Americans became worried about fat and cholesterol, mock chopped liver made from various pareve substitutes proliferated. Health-conscious Americans frequently began omitting the schmaltz. Chopped liver aficionados responded, "It can be eaten without the fat, but who would want to?"

Then the term "chopped liver" became showbiz lingo for something inferior or trivial used in a comparison, perhaps because the dish is always served as an appetizer or part of another dish and never a main course. The phrase became widespread in 1954 when Jimmy Durante on his television show exclaimed, "Now that ain't chopped liver." Subsequently, the phrase "What am I, chopped liver?" sadly became a common metaphor of derision and insignificance. Generations of Jews, however, know better—properly

prepared chopped liver is a delicacy and an important part of the Ashkenazic cultural heritage.

(See also Goose, Radish, and Schmaltz)

ASHKENAZIC CHOPPED LIVER (*GEHAKTE LEBER*)

ABOUT 5 CUPS/8 TO 10 SERVINGS   [MEAT]

    2 pounds chicken livers (about 24) or beef liver, or 1 pound chicken livers and 1 pound calf or beef liver

About 1 teaspoon kosher salt for sprinkling

½ to 1 cup schmaltz, vegetable oil, or shortening

2 pounds (4 cups) yellow onions, coarsely chopped

4 hard-boiled eggs, peeled

About 2 teaspoons salt

Ground black pepper to taste

Additional schmaltz or oil if needed

1. Cut away any membranes and veins from the livers. If using beef liver, cut several deep crisscross slits in several places or cut into 1-inch pieces. Rinse the liver in cold water. Lightly sprinkle both sides with the kosher salt. Place on an unheated rack on grill or a broiler pan and grill or broil about 4 inches from the heat source, turning once, until the surface no longer appears deep brown and the outer juices cease flowing, about 5 minutes per side for beef liver, or 3 minutes per side for chicken liver. Rinse under cold running water. Let cool.

2. In a large skillet, heat ¼ cup schmaltz over medium heat. Add the onions and cook, stirring occasionally, until golden but not burnt, about 30 minutes. Let cool.

3. Using a knife, finely chop the liver, onions, and eggs. Or using a food grinder or food processor fitted with a metal blade, roughly or finely chop the liver, onions, and eggs.

4. Stir in the salt, pepper, and, remaining schmaltz to moisten. The liver should be moist enough to hold together. Store in an airtight container in the refrigerator for up to 3 days. Serve chilled.

LOBIO

Haricot beans, including fresh green and dried white, black, and red, were brought to Europe from South America by the Spanish and Portuguese, and eventually reached Georgia, where they became the staple of the diet and appear at almost every meal. Georgians took a particular fondness to a small red variety of beans, which they used in numerous dishes, especially salads, spreads, and soups, and as a filling for breads.

Lobio, the Georgian word for beans, from the Farsi *loobia*, refers to both a mushy red bean salad (*lobios salati*) and a soup (*lobios chorba*) made from similar ingredients. *Lobiani khachapuri*, commonly referred to simply as *lobiani*, is a bread filled with red bean paste. *Lobiani nigvsit* is a cold salad similar to the bread filling, consisting of roughly mashed red beans dressed with *bazha* (walnut sauce). *Lobio tkemali* is a dish of red beans with a sour plum sauce.

These bean dishes should never be bland, but should leave a spicy sensation in the mouth. Georgians have a penchant for rather sour flavors, eschewing sugar in their cooking. Traditionally, dishes made with red beans are garnished with red onion rings and crumbled feta. They are served with *deda's puri* (flatbread), *khachapuri* (cheese bread), and *mchadi* (corn cakes).

(See also Beans and Pkhali)

LOKMA

Lokma is a fritter often from a yeast-raised batter and soaked in sugar syrup.

Origin: Middle East

Other names: Arabic: *awamee, luqma, sfingis, zengoula*; Farsi: *bamieh, zengol, zúngol*; Greece: *loukoumas, zvingous*; Italy: *crispella*; Ladino: *bimuelos*; North Africa: *sfenj*.

Deep-frying strips of unleavened dough is an ancient practice, dating back at least as far as the Roman *vermiculous*. The concept traveled throughout the Mediterranean and Middle East, areas where oil for deep-frying was generally abundant and relatively inexpensive. Medieval Arabs or Persians may have been the first to deep-fry blobs of yeast dough; the earliest record of such a dish is a recipe for *luqmat al-qadi* (judge's mouthful) in the 1226 Iraqi cookbook *Kitab al Tabikh* (Book of Dishes) by Muhammad ibn al-Hasan Al-Baghdadi. The medieval Persian name *zengol*, derived from the Farsi *zan* "lady" and *gulé* "ball." The Arabs and Turks spread these irregularly shaped deep-fried yeast batter balls from India to the Maghreb to the Balkans.

The loose dough is made with common wheat flour or, in some areas, fine semolina. What particularly differentiates these ancient Middle Eastern fritters—which are prepared in much the same way today as they were a millennium ago—from European doughnuts is the absence of eggs or dairy products in the batter, although some modern versions do include eggs, making the texture firmer. Moroccans commonly flavor the batter with a little orange zest. There is also a modern version leavened with baking powder. Since the batter is rather plain, the fritters themselves are not particularly interesting. However, drenched in sugar syrup, the Middle Eastern practice, or covered with sugar, the European preference, they became a delectable treat. For a fancier presentation, the *lokma* are mounded on a platter and sprinkled with chopped pistachio nuts. The same batter is used to make a medieval type of funnel cake, *zalabia*, which is popular from the Maghreb to India.

Historically, these light fritters were much beloved throughout the Middle East and were typically accompanied with Turkish coffee. Professional fritter makers, called *lokmaci* in Turkey and *lokmatzi* in Greece, sold them from small stores, and the Ottoman sultans employed fritter chefs in their kitchens. In his seventeenth-century journal, the Ottoman traveler Evliya Celebi noted, "In the shops of the *lokmaci* and *gozlemehci* (sweet cake makers), a Jew is appointed as inspector, because Jews only eat cakes and fritters cooked in oil, while Muslims eat those cooked in butter." Homemade fritters were generally only prepared for special occasions, specifically as a beloved Hanukkah and Purim treat. An unleavened batter made from matza meal is used for Passover versions.

(See also Doughnut, Fritter, Sufganiyah, Zalabia, and Zvingous)

TURKISH FRITTERS (*LOKMA*)

ABOUT 24 FRITTERS [PAREVE]

3 cups (15 ounces) all-purpose flour
1 tablespoon baking powder, or 2 teaspoons active dry yeast
½ teaspoon salt
1 cup water
¼ cup ouzo or *raki* (anise liqueur), or 1 tablespoon orange-blossom water and 2 tablespoons grated orange zest
1 large egg, lightly beaten
2 tablespoons sugar
2 tablespoons olive or vegetable oil
½ teaspoon vanilla extract
Vegetable, sesame, peanut, or sunflower oil for deep-frying

Confectioners' sugar for dusting or cooled *atar* (Middle Eastern Sugar Syrup, page ooo) for dipping

1. In a large bowl, sift together the flour, baking powder, and salt. In a medium bowl, combine the water, ouzo, egg, sugar, oil, and vanilla. Stir into the flour mixture to make a loose batter. Cover and let stand at room temperature for 30 minutes.

2. In a large pot, heat at least 1 inch oil over medium heat to 375°F.

3. Dip a tablespoon into cold water and use the spoon to drop the batter into the hot oil. In batches, fry the fritters, turning, until golden brown on all sides, about 3 minutes. Remove with a wire mesh-skimmer or tongs and drain on a wire rack. Sprinkle with confectioners' sugar or dip the warm fritters into the *atar*.

LOKSHEN

Lokshen (*loksh* singular) are egg noodles.
Origin: China
Other names: *lukshen*; German: *nudel*; Hebrew: *itriyot*; Hungarian: *metelt, nudli*; Western Yiddish: *frimsel*.

"Love is grand, but love with *lokshen* is even better." (A Yiddish proverb.)

Boiling strips of dough in water may seem in hindsight obvious, but the concept only reached Europe sometime during the medieval period. Previously, European dough dishes, except for Moorish Spain, were all fried or baked, not cooked in water.

Noodles and filled dumplings traveled along the Silk Road from China to central Asia and were present in Persia around the fourth or fifth century CE, where they were originally called *lakhsha* (Farsi for "slippery"; *lakhshidan* means "to slide"), a word found in Arabic sources in the tenth century. Subsequently, *reshteh* (string) emerged as the generic Persian term for pasta and *lakhsha* was relegated to the name of a specific Persian noodle dish. Meanwhile, Arabs took to calling noodles *itriya* and, even later, *shayreeye*, and spread the food westward to Spain and Sicily; from Sicily, noodles entered mainland Italy sometime after the tenth century. The first mention of boiled doughs in a European Jewish source outside of Moorish Spain was in the parody *Masekhet Purim* by Kalonymus ben Kalonymus (c. 1286–1328), a native of Provence who spent much of his career in Rome. He included macaroni (then a generic term for pasta strips) and *tortelli* (filled pasta) in a list of twenty-seven dishes served at a fantasy Purim feast. Considering the regular interaction between the Jewish communities of Franco-Germany and Italy, noodles probably reached the western Ashkenazim, who called it *frimsels*, around the fifteenth century.

However, it was still several centuries before the food became popular among non-Jewish Germans, who variously called it *spätzle* (in southern Germany), *knöpfle*, and *eierteigwaren*. The word noodle derived around the sixteenth century from the German *nudel*, which referred to an enriched grain mixture that was shaped into long rolls and force-fed to geese.

By the sixteenth century, pasta reached northeastern Europe from the East. The Persian *lakhsha* gave rise to the Slavic name for noodles: the Polish *lokszyn*, Ukrainian *lokschina*, and Yiddish *lokshen*. The Polish sage Rabbi Moses Isserles (d. 1572) explained in his glosses on the *Shulchan Arukh* that "*verimselish* are *lokshen*"; by then the two terms were used exclusively for pasta. Remnants of the name *lakhsha* did not appear in the two southern routes into eastern Europe: Italy, where noodles were called tagliatelle, and the Balkans, where Romanians referred to noodles as *taitei*, Greek Jews knew them as *hilopites*, and Sephardim called them *fideós*. Although some contend that eastern Europeans learned of noodles from Byzantines or other Europeans, the name *lokshen* reveals the ultimate Persian connection and indicates a direct Asian flow from the east, possibly via the Tatars, Mongolian tribes who overran the area.

Egg noodles became an important component of central European cooking, although they were never more significant than dumplings in the diet. In eastern Europe, on the contrary, noodles soon surpassed dumplings in importance; by the fifteenth century, they had become a mainstay of the Sabbath and holiday table. By this point, chicken soup with noodles had replaced fried dough in honey as the first course for the Ashkenazic Friday evening dinner. As refined wheat flour became more prevalent and less expensive in Europe in the eighteenth and nineteenth centuries, noodles emerged as a beloved staple of the diet.

For several centuries, noodle making was a weekly or biweekly ritual in many Jewish households. The dough was mixed by hand on a large wooden cutting board (*lokshen bretl*). On Passover, the *lokshen bretl*, which was embedded with *chametz* and could not be cleaned, was customarily left outside the house and reclaimed after the holiday. To roll the noodles, a little flour was sprinkled over the board and, typically using a broom handle (*bezemshtecken*), the dough was rolled as thinly as desired. The pasta sheet was then rolled up and sliced—the predominant all-purpose Ashkenazic cutting instrument was a curved *hackmeister* (called a *mezzaluna* by Italians) or a straight-edged cleaver— into the desired width. The strips were hung over the broomstick set over chairs or scattered over the floured noodle board or a white cloth to dry for at least an hour.

Ashkenazim also commonly grated the fresh dough into small pellets called farfel or cut it into various shapes, most notably *fingerhuetchen* (thimbles) or *oofhalaifers*, small rounds cut out with a thimble; *plaetschen* (little place/spot), small squares; and the relatively late *shpaetzlen* (from the German *spätzle*), pasta squares pinched in the middle. On Passover, some cooks make *eier lokshen* from matza meal and eggs, which were basically rolled up blintzes cut into strips. Filled pasta, such as kreplach and pirogen, were reserved for special occasions, most notably the meal before Yom Kippur, Hoshanah Rabbah, Purim, and Shavuot.

Ashkenazim never developed the faculty of shaping and saucing their pasta like Italians and Sephardim. In most cases, Ashkenazic pasta dishes were basic, homey, and filling. The favorite Ashkenazic way to use noodles was in a soup—perhaps indicating a central Asian origin. In America, after matza balls became popular at times other than Passover, they were frequently combined with noodles in chicken soup, especially in delicatessens. At dairy meals, noodles were commonly flavored with a little butter or soft cheese. Hungarians and Germans extended the noodles by adding them to cabbage or other vegetables, while Hungarians also transformed it into a simple dessert with sugar and ground nuts or poppy seeds. Eastern Europeans mixed noodles with the predominant Slavic food, buckwheat, to create the still classic *kasha varnishkes*. Around the sixteenth century, noodles were synthesized with an old Ashkenazic favorite, resulting in what would become the most popular Ashkenazic side dish, *lokshen kugel* (noodle pudding).

The first Jewish cookbook in English, *The Jewish Manual* (London, 1846), mentions a dish called "A Luction, or a Rachael," which certainly shares many similarities with the Ashkenazic noodle kugel. Immigrants brought their noodle dishes with them to America. The first American Jewish cookbook, the German-based *Jewish Cookery* (Philadelphia, 1871), refers to noodles as "frimsels" in a recipe for a sweet noodle-raisin pudding she entitled "A Luxion," which must be an alternate spelling of *lokshen*. Due to the early predominance of German Jews in America, *frimsel* remained the most widespread American Jewish term for noodles into the twentieth century. Israel Zangwill, in his tale of Jewish life in late nineteenth-century London, *Children of the Ghetto* (1892), provides the first verifiable record in English of the term denoting noodles. He mentions "lockshen, which are the apotheosis of vermicelli." With the massive wave of eastern European immigrants, the word *lokshen* emerged in America to supplant *frimsel*.

The word *lokshen* meant more to eastern European Jews than simply another food. *Lokshen* permeated Yiddish life. The Yiddish phrase *langer loksh* (long noodle) connotes a tall, thin person. Calling a person simply a *lokshen*, however, is no compliment, as it connotes a limp, bland personality. This inspired the modern Hebrew expression "*hu chataf loksh*," literally meaning "he caught a noodle," but figuratively meaning "he caught hell." *Lokshen* has seeped into the culture in modern Israel, where noodles are usually called *itriyot*. In Hebrew, a *loksh* means a "pay slip," because until recently this consisted of a thin strip torn off the bottom of a large sheet of paper. Also in modern Hebrew, *lokshim* developed the sense of "lies," as in "*al taachli oti lokshim*" (literally "don't feed me noodles," but meaning "don't tell me lies") and "stop eating *lokshen*" (meaning "stop believing the lies").

(See also Chremsel, Dumpling, Farfel, Frimsel, Kasha Varnishkes, Kreplach, Kugel, Pasta, Pirog, Quadrucci, and Varenik)

❧ EGG NOODLE DOUGH

ABOUT I POUND DOUGH   [PAREVE]

> About 2¼ cups (11.25 ounces) unbleached all-purpose flour
>
> 3 large eggs, at room temperature
>
> ½ teaspoon table salt or 1 teaspoon kosher salt (optional)

1. Onto a pasta board or another flat surface, sift the flour and make a well in the center. Place the eggs and, if using, salt into the well. Using the tips of your fingers or tines of a fork, lightly beat the eggs. Gradually work the flour into the eggs, always working from the sides of the flour, until the mixture holds together, about 3 minutes.

2. Bring any remaining flour over the dough to cover it and form the dough into a ball. Lightly flour the surface and knead until smooth and elastic, about 10 minutes by hand, or 2 minutes if using a food processor. Wrap in plastic wrap and let rest at room temperature for 1 hour.

3. To roll the dough: Divide the dough into 2 to 4 pieces and dust lightly with flour. Cover the other pieces with plastic wrap and set aside. Flatten 1 piece of dough into a ¼-inch-thick square. Place on a lightly floured surface and press with the palm of your hand to flatten. Roll out the dough by using a rolling pin to push it away from you, rather than pressing it down, until it is as thin as possible. Repeat with the remaining dough.

4. To shape the noodles: Let the dough sheets stand until they begin to feel dry but are still supple, about 5 minutes. Lightly dust the sheets with flour. Starting from a short side, roll up jelly-roll style. Cut crosswise into ⅛-inch (thin) to ½-inch (wide) strips. Unroll the dough strips and let stand until dry, at least 1 hour. Store in an airtight container or plastic bag in the refrigerator for up to 4 days or in the freezer for up to 3 months.

5. To cook: Bring a large pot of lightly salted water to a rapid boil. Add the noodles and stir with a fork to separate the pasta. Cook until al dente (tender but still firm), 5 to 10 minutes. Drain.

VARIATIONS

Ashkenazic Fried Thimble Noodles (Oofhalaifers/ Fingerhuetchen): On a lightly floured surface, roll out the dough to a ⅛-inch thickness, fold the dough sheets in half, and using a floured thimble, cut the dough into rounds. Arrange in a single layer, cover, and let dry for about 30 minutes. In a large pot, heat at least 1 inch vegetable oil over medium heat. In batches, deep-fry the pasta until golden brown, about 1 minute. Remove with a slotted spoon and drain on paper towels. Serve these pasta puffs as a soup garnish.

LOOF

In the late 1940s, the Israeli Defense Forces developed a kosher form of the British "bully beef" named Loof (shortened from meat loaf), which was packaged in round cans. Loof constituted part of the soldier's battle food ration (*manot krav*), along with chocolate spread, halva, canned corn, and canned *pilchei* (grapefruit slices). Many Israeli soldiers insist that Loof utilizes all the parts of the cow that the hot dog manufacturers will not accept, but no one outside of the manufacturer and kosher supervisors actually know what is inside. The most common way of consuming this canned processed meat is the "Loof field sandwich." First, both the top and bottom of the can are removed, and the very solid pink "meat" is gradually pressed through one open end. Then, using the bottom of the can, slices are cut directly onto a slice of bread, then sandwiched between a second slice. Loof is also fried like schnitzel and scrambled with eggs.

(See also Corned Beef)

LOQUAT

Loquat, also called Japanese medlar, is native to southeastern China. The average loquat tree bears small, elongated apricot-like fruit with pale orange skin, which, depending on the variety, can be smooth or slightly fuzzy like a peach. The soft, somewhat succulent, orange-colored flesh surrounds three to five large, shiny seeds. The mildly astringent fruit has a combination mango-peach flavor; the degree of acidity and sweetness differs with the variety and degree of ripeness.

The loquat first arrived in Europe in 1784 and gradually spread to parts of the Mediterranean. In 1960, the loquat (called *shesek* in Hebrew) arrived in Israel and subsequently became widespread. It is now grown commercially and is also very popular in home gardens. Today, Israel follows only Japan, which has been cultivating the fruit for more than a millennium, in loquat production. Because of the time of year that it ripens, it has become a popular Passover fruit. In Israel, the fruit is overwhelmingly consumed fresh, but is also used in pies, jams, chutneys, and ice cream, and poached in light syrup.

LOX

A northern European method of preserving salmon was to coat fillets of the fish with salt and let it stand for a few days; the fish could then be stored for an extended period. Initially, Americans called this cured salmon. However, in many places, in order to conserve the scarce resource of salt, the fish was smoked, which is not as effective in warding off harmful bacteria. Later, techniques were developed in which the fish was smoked in conjunction with a light brining, combining the best properties of both methods.

Throughout the nineteenth century, Germans and Scandinavians brought their curing traditions and predilections with them to America. Beginning in 1835, some opened smokehouses in the Northeast, concentrating on the more available salmon from Nova Scotia. Some also brined and smoked species of fish from the Great Lakes, including whitefish and chub, both of which turn golden in color during curing. Within decades of the emergence of German smokehouses in eastern America, the advent of the transcontinental railroad in 1869 opened new vistas of trade, including massive amounts of Pacific Northwest salmon, which was always packed into barrels and layered with salt to preserve it for the long journey.

During the early 1930s, cured salmon fillet became known as lox, which is the Americanized spelling of the Yiddish *laks* (salmon), itself from the German *lachs* (salmon), which is similar to the Swedish gravlax (cured salmon). Originally, lox was a geographic term, emerging to distinguish salmon from the Pacific Northwest, which was at the time always salted, from the Atlantic salmon, which was called Nova. Although Nova referred to Nova Scotia, Canada, a primary supplier of salmon to New York, it came to mean Atlantic salmon from the entire Eastern Seaboard and northern Europe. Initially, Nova could be either smoked or salted. Later, as less salmon came from the Atlantic and shipping and refrigeration methods changed, these geographic terms took on different meanings.

In the twentieth century, the spread of refrigeration and later refrigerated railroad cars eventually removed the need to preserve salmon in an intense brine. Instead, it could be lightly salted, producing a smoother, milder fish. At the beginning of the twentieth century, Jews in America developed their own form of smoked salmon, soaking it in light brine or occasionally dry curing it with salt and sometimes brown sugar, then cold-smoking it. Cold-smoked fillets are smoked over wood chips at a temperature of 72°F to 80°F, which does not cook the fish and results in a delicate, silky, yet dense texture and mild smoke

flavor. In the Pacific Northwest, salmon is typically hot-smoked at a higher temperature, which actually cooks the flesh as well as producing a more pronounced smoke flavor.

Jewish immigrants in England developed the "London cure," dry-salting salmon fillets for a day (dry-curing produces a drier, more flavorful fish than brining), then cold-smoking it for another day. "Scottish salmon" refers to fillets dry-cured in a mixture of salt and spice, then cold-smoked.

Subsequently, the terms lox and Nova applied to the two predominant forms of curing: Lox, also called belly lox, is wet-brined with no additional smoking or cooking. Nova, also known as Nova lox and smoked salmon, is cured in a mild brine of salt, water, and sometimes brown sugar, then lightly cold-smoked for six to twenty-four hours. Lox, the saltier of the two, is usually less expensive because it is easier to prepare.

After World War II, the older generation tended to retain a preference for the saltier flavor of the unsmoked lox, which holds up better when placed between a bagel and schmear of cream cheese, while younger Americans increasingly began to favor the less salty cold-smoked Nova. In response, the large New York smokehouses began to increasingly produce Nova and, consequently, today the terms are often used interchangeably and most of the "lox" sold in America is actually Nova-style smoked salmon.

Another major change was, beginning in the 1980s, the widespread substitution of farm-raised salmon, identifiable by wide stripes of whitish fat, for wild fish. Today, there is no longer any appreciable Atlantic wild salmon in the market and the amount of Pacific wild salmon is greatly reduced and expensive. Farm-raised salmon grow to be gray in color, but they are typically fed a special feed with dyes to achieve a reddish hue. However, one thing that cannot be masked is the weaker flavor of farmed-raised salmon, which has dramatically altered the taste of much of the contemporary lox and Nova. The label "organic" does not indicate whether the fish is wild or farm-raised.

At the beginning of the twentieth century, eastern European immigrants in America preferred the familiar pickled herring to the brined salmon, but since the latter was rather inexpensive at the time, Jews began to increasingly add it to their diet. The discarded belly flaps and other trimmings, called *fliegel* or *figgle* (Yiddish for "wings")—the thin sections of the fillets inappropriate for lox—were cooked by frying, poaching, or grilling. As American Jews, initially Germans and later eastern Europeans, moved into the fish business, Brooklyn became the fish-smoking capital of the United States and factory owners brought in salmon from both the Atlantic and Pacific. After Harry Brownstein arrived on the Lower East Side of Manhattan from Russia in the early 1900s, he took a job in a smoked fish factory, before eventually opening his own company in Brooklyn, Acme Smoked Fish Corporation. His business became the largest producer of Nova-style lox and smoked fish in the country, and today it is run by the fourth generation of the family. At the turn of the twenty-first century, besides Acme, Brooklyn was home to five other major smokehouses, which produced an estimated ten tons of smoked fish a year. In addition, a few specialty stores procured smoke boxes to prepare their own Nova; most, however, order from one of the large smokehouses.

Cured fish has long maintained a prominent place in the Ashkenazic pantry; besides being pareve and convenient, it requires no cooking. Initially, Jews in America ate lox in the manner of salted fish in the Old Country, thinly sliced and served with dark bread, or cut into chunks and mixed with sour cream. Sometimes it was accompanied with iced vodka. Adding lox to an already widespread dish, scrambled eggs with onions, produced the very popular *eier mit laks*.

Lox's main and enduring claim to fame, however, came when partnered with bagels and cream cheese, the mildness of the cheese idyllically countering the saltiness of the fish. Slices of another Ashkenazic staple, onion, are also frequently added, contributing a pleasing pungency. Yet despite the current celebrity of this classic combination, in Europe, cured salmon never touched a bagel or cream cheese. This practice actually began in New York during the 1930s, when many Jews abstained from eating the then-stylish but decidedly unkosher American Sunday brunch classic eggs Benedict. Instead, they substituted a bagel for the English muffin, a schmear of cream cheese for the hollandaise sauce, and lox slices for the ham. Thus was born an American classic. Today, in America and Israel, lox remains a common sight at most life-cycle events featuring dairy meals, such as *brits* and baby namings, as well as Sunday brunches.

(See also Bagel and Fish)

LUNGEN

Lungen, from the German meaning "the light organ," is the German and Yiddish word for lung, which is sometimes called lights in England. In most societies, lung and other offal were held in low esteem. On the contrary, among the impoverished masses in the shtetlach of the Russian Pale, this organ was a favorite. In accordance with the Jewish dietary laws, the lungs, which are the organs most susceptible to disease, were always carefully inspected immediately after slaughter, and any serious defect or sign of illness rendered the entire animal unkosher.

Beef or calf lung, alone or with chopped chicken liver, was also enjoyed as a pastry filling. For a more elaborate dish, *lungen* was mixed with chopped broiled beef liver, about two parts lung for one part liver, spread between lower and upper layers of unfilled blintzes, and baked for about an hour and served in the manner of a kugel. Frequently to stretch the dish, the lungs were cooked with the *miltz* (spleen) or some cubed beef. North Africans make a similar stew from lamb lung. The predominant Ashkenazic way to prepare this was in a simple rustic stew, with plenty of onions sautéed in schmaltz, which helped to flavor and thicken the *gravy*. In Europe, *lungen* was generally reserved for special occasions, but in America it was prepared when someone wanted a taste of the Old Country. The stew was typically served with mashed or boiled potatoes.

Immigrants brought *lungen* stew to America, where it was quite common through the first half of the twentieth century and recalled by many with nostalgic fondness and others with less enthusiasm. In his masterpiece "Howl," the Beat poet Allen Ginsberg, remembering his mother's *lungen*, included the line, "who cooked rotten animals lung heart feet tail borscht & tortillas dreaming of the pure vegetable kingdom." In any case, lung is currently impossible to obtain in many places. In 1971, the U.S. Department of Agriculture (USDA) outlawed it in America for human consumption, and the organs instead primarily end up in pet food. Consequently, few people today are able to make up their own minds about it.

M

MA'AMOUL
Ma'amoul is a small shortbread cookie filled with chopped nuts or dried fruit.

Origin: Levant

Other names: Egypt: *menenas*; Iran: *ghotab*, *klaitcha*; Iraq: *klaicha*; Kurdistan: *kasmay*.

Ma'amoul, which means "filled" in Arabic, is the Levantine version of one of the most ancient pastries. Syrian *ras-ib-adjway* are *ma'amoul* filled with a date and walnut mixture. Syrian *krabeej* are *ma'amoul* topped with *naatiffe* (a white fluff made from eggs whites, sugar, and soapwort), but today commercially prepared marshmallow cream is usually substituted.

As is typical of Middle Eastern baked goods, the original type of *ma'amoul* dough contains no eggs or sugar, but rather depends on the butter in the dough for richness and relies on the filling and dusting of sugar for sweetness and extra flavor. The dough most commonly consists of part semolina and part flour, but there are many different ratios and some cooks use all flour. Semolina makes a crunchier, crumblier, and more flavorful pastry. Sometimes a little yeast or baking powder is added to the dough for a lighter cookie, but many prefer the firmness of unleavened shortbread. Nut is the most common filling, particularly walnut. Pistachio is generally reserved for holidays and other special occasions. The nuts for the fillings are crushed—they are generally not ground into a paste, but left with a little texture—and seasoned with orange-blossom or rose water and spices. Dates are also traditional, alone or mixed with nuts. Modern cooks sometimes use apricots, quince jam, and figs.

Middle Easterners consider the preparation of *ma'amoul* to be a fine art and serious cooks use a *tabi* (a special hand-carved concave wooden mold with handles) to impress ornate designs on the surface of the cookies. The mold is then slammed against a flat surface to firmly imprint the design on top, while releasing the cookie. *Ma'amoul* can also be formed by hand without a mold. A light dusting of confectioners' sugar helps to accentuate the cookie's designs. North Africans like to simmer the cookies in a sugar syrup for a few minutes. *Ma'amoul* are extremely popular in Israel and the molds are sold in many markets.

Making *ma'amoul* was once a time-consuming process of making the firm semolina dough, rolling out little balls of dough, encasing the filling, impressing a design on top, and carrying the cookies on large copper trays to the large public oven for baking. So most home cooks generally prepared it only a few times a year, usually in large batches. Many families prepared three large trays, one for each of the three types of fillings. On the day before many holidays, the streets would be filled with adults and children schlepping their copper trays to the bakery. Quick, proficient *ma'amoul* making requires years of practice under the supervision of mothers and grandmothers. Today, there are machines to mass-produce *ma'amoul*, which can be found even in certain American bakeries and markets, but some cooks insist that these products are not as good as homemade and continue to bake their own. Some modern versions roll out the dough, spread it with filling, roll it up jelly-roll style, then cut the rolls into slices.

Middle Easterners typically kept a box of *ma'amoul* handy for expected and unexpected guests. In the Middle East, *halawiyyat* (sweets) were not typically served as dessert at the end of the meal, but rather with coffee or tea (and today, also Asti Spumante) as a treat during the afternoon or late evening. Therefore, Middle Eastern Jews tended to use butter, an ingredient Ashkenazim rarely used in their cookies. However, oil was substituted for meat occasions. *Ma'amoul* are traditionally present, usually in a large selection, at Middle Eastern celebrations, including weddings and bar mitzvahs. Nut fillings are traditional on Purim (the nuts are a reminder that Esther kept kosher in the king's palace by eating seeds and nuts) and date fillings on Rosh Hashanah and Hanukkah.

(See also Klaicha and Makroud)

Ma'amoul are ornately designed Middle Eastern filled shortbread cookies served at many holidays, such as Rosh Hashanah and Purim, as well as at weddings and bar mitzvahs.

MIDDLE EASTERN FILLED COOKIES (*MA'AMOUL*)

ABOUT 26 COOKIES   [DAIRY OR PAREVE]

Dough:

2 cups (10 ounces) all-purpose flour

1 cup (6 ounces) fine semolina (not semolina flour)

¼ teaspoon salt

1 cup *samneh* (Middle Eastern clarified butter), unsalted butter, or margarine

1 tablespoon orange-blossom water or rose water or 1½ teaspoons each

About ½ cup lukewarm water (80°F to 90°F)

Filling:

2 cups (8 ounces) walnuts, blanched almonds, or shelled pistachios, finely chopped

About ¾ cup sugar

1 to 2 tablespoons rose water or orange-blossom water

1 to 2 teaspoons ground cinnamon (optional)

About ½ cup confectioners' sugar for dusting

1. To make the dough: In a large bowl, combine the flour, semolina, and salt. Cut in the butter until the mixture resembles small crumbs. Drizzle with the orange-blossom water. Gradually stir in enough water to make a mixture that holds together. Briefly knead to form a soft, pliable dough. Wrap in plastic wrap and let stand at room temperature for at least 2 hours or overnight.

2. To make the filling: In a medium bowl, combine all the filling ingredients.

3. Preheat the oven to 350°F. Line 2 large baking sheets with parchment paper.

4. Form the dough into 1-inch balls and, using a thumb or index finger, hollow out the balls to form thin walls. Or roll out each ball into a ⅛-inch-thick round about 3 inches in diameter. Fill with a heaping teaspoon of the filling and press the sides of the dough together to encase the filling. Place the cookies, 1 inch apart, on the baking sheets, flatten slightly, and make designs in the dough with a fork or knife.

5. Bake until the cookies are just starting to turn golden but not browned, about 20 minutes. Let stand for 1 minute, then carefully transfer the cookies to a wire rack.

6. When cooled, roll in confectioners' sugar to lightly coat. Store in an airtight container at room temperature for up to 3 weeks.

MACAROON

Macaroon is a light baked cookie made of almond paste, sugar, and egg whites.

Origin: Spain, Italy

Other names: Italian: *maccarone, ricciarelli*; Ladino: *maronchino*; Yiddish: *makarondelach.*

Before the advent of chemical leavenings, the best way to create light baked goods was with beaten eggs, a technique developed in the Muslim world, possibly in Moorish Spain. Additionally, cooks in the medieval Islamic world created confections and cookies based on ground nuts and sugar: in Moorish Spain, the *amarguillos* (made from a paste of bitter almonds) and *alhagues/alfajores* (made from a paste of almonds, walnuts, and honey); in Iraq, the *hadgi badam* (made from almond paste spiced with cardamom); and in Tunisia, the *guizadas* (made from ground pistachios). Around the late thirteenth or fourteenth century, cookies made from almond-sugar paste and beaten egg whites spread to mainland Italy, probably by way of Sicily; the practice seems to have first appeared in

Venice, the center of trade between Europe and Asia. Jewish exiles from Spain brought their almond cookies to Italy, introducing the concept to various ghettos.

Many names for almond cookies arose throughout Italy, but the most common one that emerged was amaretti (little bitter ones). Some date the term to the court of Saxony in the mid-seventeenth century, others to the early sixteenth century. The name indicates that the original amaretti, like most contemporary Italian versions, were made primarily or totally from flavorful bitter almonds and/or apricot kernels.

There is no single authentic amaretti recipe, as almost every Italian region, as well as many families, has a slightly different version, varying the amount of sugar and nuts, type of egg (whites, yolks, or whole), added flavoring (citrus zest, cocoa, and spices), crispness, and size. Standard amaretti are crisp cookies made from finely ground almonds folded into a meringue (a mixture of stiffly beaten egg whites and sugar, which was named for the German town of Mehringen), then baked. Versions made from almond paste (*pasta di mandorle*) and unbeaten egg whites, called *amaretti morbidi* (delicate/soft) by Italians, are softer and chewier due to a higher proportion of almonds. Flour or starch is sometimes added to meringue amaretti but never to the softer *amaretti morbidi*. The traditional way to present amaretti is to wrap a pair bottom to bottom in pastel-colored tissue paper.

The almond cookie was probably introduced to France in 1533, when Catherine de Médicis of Florence married the future Henry II of France, bringing with her a retinue of Italian chefs and Renaissance recipes. The word macaroon was first used in 1552 by the French satirist Rabelais (who may very well have coined the term, which derived from the Italian *maccare* "to crush") in a list of non-Jewish foods in his parody *Gargantua and Pantagruel*.

By 1660, recipes for macaroons had appeared in England. Subsequently, as Caribbean sugar became increasingly available, macaroons emerged throughout much of western Europe as the preeminent cookie.

Macaroons certainly became a Jewish food; almond paste cookies were mentioned in Italian Jewish sources beginning in the mid-sixteenth century and were possibly popularized among Italian refugees by Sephardic refugees. Because these cookies were flourless, they proved to be ideal Passover fare and were soon adopted by Italian Jews for the holiday

and, following the typical pattern, eventually spread to Ashkenazim. *The Jewish Manual*, the first Jewish cookbook in English (London, 1846), mentioned, but did not provide recipes for, macaroons as well as ratafia, a small English macaroon made from peach pits or bitter almonds and flavored with ratafia liqueur, which was commonly used in trifles. A few decades later, the first American Jewish cookbook, *Jewish Cookery* (Philadelphia, 1871), included recipes for both almond and "cocoanut" macaroons.

Another early American Jewish cookbook, *Aunt Babette's* (Cincinnati, 1889), contained a recipe for "Chocolate Macaroons," which incorporated grated chocolate into a typical amond macaroon. At the time the book was published, chocolate was only initially being used in American baked goods.

In the twentieth century, as numerous new cookies and treats emerged, macaroons gradually became less prominent. Their popularity during Passover, however, not only remained, but also increased as manufacturers began to mass-produce them, initially in three flavors—almond, coconut, and chocolate. Coconut macaroons, which are much softer than almond meringues, eventually emerged as the most widespread type in America for Passover. Sephardim also make coconut macaroons, based on a crisper meringue, called *biscochitos de coco*. Today, commercial Passover versions come in cappuccino, maple-pecan, cinnamon-raisin, and rocky road. Generations grew up equating Passover dessert with macaroons. Although in America, Passover macaroons became associated with the cloying, chewy canned variety, the fresh baked ones make delicious treats.

(See also Almond, Almond Paste, and Coconut)

SEPHARDIC ALMOND MACAROONS (*MARONCHINOS*)

ABOUT THIRTY-SIX 2-INCH COOKIES [PAREVE]

1 pound (about 3¼ cups) blanched whole almonds
About 1½ cups sugar
Pinch of salt
3 large egg whites (6 tablespoons)
1 teaspoon almond extract or 3 drops bitter almond oil
About 36 whole or slivered almonds (optional)

1. Preheat the oven to 325°F. Line 2 large baking sheets with parchment paper or lightly grease the sheets and dust with potato starch or flour.

2. In a food processor fitted with a metal blade, process the almonds, sugar, and salt until finely ground, then add the egg whites and almond extract and process until smooth. Or in a nut grinder, grind the almonds, transfer to a bowl, mix in the sugar and salt, add the egg whites and almond extract, and knead to form a paste.

3. With moistened hands, for each cookie, form about 2 tablespoons of the nut mixture into a 1-inch ball. Arrange on the prepared baking sheets, leaving 1½ inches between the cookies. If using, press an almond into the center of each cookie. Flatten slightly.

4. Bake, switching the baking sheets halfway through, until lightly browned, about 20 minutes. Let cool on the baking sheets. Store in an airtight container at room temperature for up to 2 weeks.

MAFRUM

Mafrum is a slice of a vegetable that is slit, stuffed, fried, and simmered in a sauce.

Origin: Libya

Other names: *mafroum.*

Mafrum is shortened from the Arabic *lahma mafruma* (minced meat). It connotes a Libyan style of stuffed vegetables in which a meat mixture is sandwiched between layers of eggplant, potatoes, or large artichoke hearts. The mafrum are fried in oil, then simmered in a tomato sauce. During the long cooking time, the eggplant develops a velvety texture and the potatoes become airy. *Mafrum* have become very popular in Israel, where they are featured in various restaurants and even prepared by many non-Libyans at home. Eggplant was the more common vegetable in Libya, while potato has become widespread in Israel. Some families prepare half the dish of eggplant and the other half of potato. For dairy meals, a cheese mixture is substituted for the meat, but then it is technically no longer a *mafrum*, but rather a *beitinajn mi'ili* (filled eggplant). Tunisians make the "sandwich" in reverse, with the potato on the inside surrounded by ground beef.

Libyans serve *mafrum* on special occasions, typically accompanied with couscous, as an appetizer, side dish, or sometimes the main course. *Mafrum*, representing the biblical manna that fell between lower and upper layers of dew, is served by Libyan Jews on Friday night and holidays. In Libya, it was typically started over a fire on Friday before the onset of the Sabbath, then set in the coals of a *kanoun* (bra-zier), covered with special bulky blankets, and served warm for Friday dinner. In Israel, it is typically placed on a large hot plate called a *platta* to keep warm for the Sabbath.

LIBYAN MEAT-STUFFED EGGPLANT (*MAFRUM*)

5 TO 6 SERVINGS   [MEAT]

2 medium (about 1¼ pounds each) globe eggplants, peeled and cut crosswise into ½- to ¾-inch-thick slices

About 2 tablespoons kosher salt

Filling:

1 pound ground beef or lamb

1 medium yellow onion, chopped

2 to 4 cloves garlic, minced

2 large eggs

¼ cup matza meal or ½ cup mashed potatoes

2 to 3 tablespoons chopped fresh flat-leaf parsley or cilantro

½ teaspoon ground cinnamon or cumin

About ½ teaspoon table salt or 1 teaspoon kosher salt

Ground black pepper to taste

All-purpose flour for dredging

2 large eggs, lightly beaten

Matza meal or bread crumbs for dredging (optional)

Vegetable oil for frying

Sauce:

2 tablespoons vegetable oil

1 medium yellow onion, chopped

¼ cup tomato paste

3 cups water

Pinch of sugar

Salt to taste

1 teaspoon ground cinnamon (optional)

2 large tomatoes, sliced (optional)

1. Place the eggplant slices in a colander or on a wire rack, lightly sprinkle with the kosher salt, and let stand for about 1 hour. Rinse the eggplant under cold water, then press repeatedly between several layers of paper towels until it feels firm and dry. The eggplant can be stored in the refrigerator for up to 4 hours.

2. Cut a lengthwise pocket three-quarters of the way through the eggplant slices, leaving one end connected.

3. To make the filling: In a large bowl, combine the filling ingredients.

4. Stuff the filling into the pockets, making about a ½-inch-thick layer. Dredge the sandwiches in flour, then dip in the egg. If using, dredge in the matza meal.

5. In a large skillet, heat 3 tablespoons oil over medium heat. Add the sandwiches and fry, turning once, until golden brown on both sides, about 5 minutes. Drain on paper towels.

6. To make the sauce: In a large pot, heat the oil over medium heat. Add the onion and sauté until soft and translucent, 5 to 10 minutes. Add the tomato paste and sauté until darkened, about 2 minutes. Stir in the water, sugar, salt, and, if using, cinnamon. Bring to a boil.

7. If using, arrange the tomato slices and any extra eggplant on the bottom of the pot in the sauce. Add the eggplant sandwiches, cover, reduce the heat to low, and simmer until tender, about 1 hour. If the sauce looks like it is drying out, add a little more water. Serve warm.

MAHLAB

Mahlab, alternately spelled mahleb and mahaleb, is a yellowish western Asian spice, made by grinding the soft seed kernels of a wild cherry, sometimes called the St. Lucie cherry, a member of the rose family. The cherry's name, related to the Hebrew and Arabic words for milk (*halev*), is that of a town in Lebanon mentioned twice in the Bible, which was probably the primary source of the spice. Mahlab has a sour-sweet, almond-cherry-like flavor akin to that of bitter almonds. It is primarily used in Iranian, Turkish, Syrian and Lebanese baked goods, most notably a bread ring called *kaak*. The essential oils dissipate soon after grinding and, therefore, the dried whole kernels are best crushed as needed. Ground mahlab should be sifted before it is used, as it tends to clump. Mahlab is sold in Middle Eastern specialty stores.

MAHMOOSA

Mahmoosa is a dish of stir-fried vegetables bound in scrambled eggs.
Origin: India
Other names: *Mamoosa.*

In her 2004 play, *Calcutta Kosher*, Calcutta-born English writer Shelley Silas examined family and cultural identity, mentioning several classic Indian Jewish dishes, including *aloo makalla, chiturney,* and *mahmoosa*. The author noted, "The food I eat forms part of my cultural identity." *Mahmoosa* is an Indian Jewish adaptation of a Middle Eastern dish. Potato is the most popular vegetable, but variations are also commonly made with spinach and eggplant. A version containing beet greens or spinach is traditional on Rosh Hashanah. *Mahmoosa* is served both as a light meal, accompanied with warm bread, or as a side dish with chicken.

CALCUTTA SCRAMBLED EGGS WITH POTATOES (*MAHMOOSA*)

4 TO 6 SERVINGS [PAREVE]

3 tablespoons vegetable oil or peanut oil
1 medium yellow onion, chopped
2 to 3 teaspoons minced fresh ginger (optional)
1 green chili, minced (optional)
1 teaspoon ground turmeric
1 pound (3 large) potatoes, peeled and cut into ¼-inch cubes
½ cup fresh green peas (optional)
4 large eggs, lightly beaten
About ½ teaspoon table salt or 1 teaspoon kosher salt
Ground black pepper to taste
Lemon slices or chopped fresh cilantro for garnish

1. In a large skillet, heat the oil over medium heat. Add the onion and, if using, ginger and/or chili and sauté until softened, 5 to 10 minutes. Stir in the turmeric.

2. Add the potatoes and sauté until golden brown, about 5 minutes. If using, add the peas. Cover and cook, stirring occasionally, until the potatoes are tender, about 5 minutes. If the potatoes start to stick, add a little water and continue cooking.

3. Add the eggs, salt, and pepper and stir until dry, about 5 minutes. Serve warm or cooled. Garnish with lemon slices.

MAKAGIGI

Makagigi are candied almonds or walnuts.
Origin: Poland
Other names: *gebrennte mandlen.*

In her 1877 novella "Mighty Samson," non-Jewish Polish writer Eliza Orzeszkowa vividly describes Purim in the Polish town of Ongród. Shymshel, a poor, pious, and provincial Jew, performs the role of Samson in a Purim play and recites this line: "In the

dark and misty depths of this corridor, a buffet, illuminated by a tallow candle, had been set up bearing an impressive abundance of sticky and mildly alluring sweets, *makagigi*, slightly spoiled apples, and so on."

These treats from Poland are reminiscent of the pecan pralines of the American South. The proportions of honey and sugar vary among recipes. *Makagigi* can also be made with poppy seeds as well as nuts.

MAKOSH/MÁKOS BEIGLI

Makosh is a cakelike yeast roll with a poppy seed filling.

Origin: Central Europe
Other names: Germany: *mohn kuchen*; Hungary: *mákos beigli*; Poland: *makowiec*.

Kuchen rolls are very popular in central and eastern Europe; they probably originated as a means of transforming some extra bread dough into a special treat for the family. The yeast dough was rolled into a thin rectangle, spread with a sweet filling, and rolled into a cylinder jelly-roll style. The original cake rolls were commonly filled with the most popular medieval central European spice, poppy seeds (*mohn* in German and *mák* in Hungarian), and the name of the rolls became simply *makosh* in Hungary. Hungarians also made a filling from ground walnuts (*diós*). Poles and Germans generally spread the dough with a thicker layer of filling and let the shaped roll rise to produce thicker cake layers. Hungarians tended to roll out the dough very thin and to not allow it to rise, instead rushing it directly into the oven; the resulting pastry had very thin cake layers alternating with thin layers of filling, akin to the layers in a yeast strudel.

In the early American cookbook *Aunt Babette's* (Cincinnati, 1889), the German Jewish author included a recipe for "Mohn Kuchen (Poppy Seed)." The first edition of *The Settlement Cook Book* (Milwaukee, 1901), also by a German Jewish author, included a recipe for "Poppy Seed Roll or Mohn Kuchen."

Enterprising cooks experimented with flavors to produce a host of varieties, in particular cinnamon, almond paste, apricot lekvar, and raspberry. In the late nineteenth century, after chocolate (*kahkahaw* in Yiddish and *kakaó* in Hungarian) was introduced from America, it soon became the most popular filling and appropriately the name of this variation of the pastry evolved into *kakosh*; this pastry is still one of the favorite desserts of Hungarian Jews.

Although central and eastern European Jews have a long tradition of yeast cake rolls, including the Polish babka, none embraced them as enthusiastically as the Hungarians. Many Hungarians serve *makosh, kakosh, diós beigli* (walnut roll), or one or more of the other variations on every Sabbath and at life-cycle events. In the late twentieth century, some Hungarian Jewish commercial bakeries in America began introducing these rolls to the wider public and chocolate and poppy seed rolls became commonplace at American gourmet shops. From a land renowned for its pastry, *makosh* and *kakosh* rank with the best of Hungarian specialties.

❧ HUNGARIAN POPPY SEED ROLL (*MAKOSH*)
2 LARGE, 3 MEDIUM, OR 4 SMALL CAKE ROLLS

[DAIRY OR PAREVE]

Dough:
2 packages (4½ teaspoons) active dry yeast or
    1 (1-ounce) cake fresh yeast
½ cup warm water or milk (105°F to 115°F for dry
    yeast; 80°F to 85°F for fresh yeast), or ¼ cup
    water and add ½ cup sour cream
½ cup sugar
2 large eggs or 3 large egg yolks
¾ cup (1½ sticks) unsalted butter or margarine,
    softened
1 teaspoon table salt or 2 teaspoons kosher salt
1 to 2 teaspoons grated lemon zest (optional)
About 4¼ cups (22 ounces) bread or unbleached
    all-purpose flour

Poppy Seed Filling:
3 cups (15 ounces) poppy seeds
1½ cups water
1½ cups honey, or 1¼ cups sugar and ¼ cup honey,
    or 1 cup honey and ⅓ cup light corn syrup
2 tablespoons fresh lemon juice
1 to 2 teaspoons grated lemon zest (optional)
Pinch of salt

Egg wash (1 large egg or egg yolk beaten with 1
    teaspoon water)

1. To make the dough: Dissolve the yeast in the water. Stir in 1 teaspoon sugar and let stand until foamy, 5 to 10 minutes. In a large bowl, combine the yeast mixture, remaining sugar, eggs, butter, salt, and, if using, zest. Gradually add enough flour to make a soft, sticky dough. (Do not knead.) Cover with plastic wrap and refrigerate for at least 8 hours or up to 2 days.

2. To make the filling: In a nut grinder, food processor fitted with a metal blade, or blender, grind the poppy seeds. In a medium saucepan, combine the poppy seeds, water, honey, lemon juice, optional zest, and salt. Simmer over medium-low heat, stirring frequently, until the mixture thickens, about 12 minutes. Let cool. Store in the refrigerator for up to 1 week.

3. Preheat the oven to 350°F. Line a large baking sheet with parchment paper or lightly grease the sheet.

4. Punch down the dough. Fold over and press together several times. Divide the dough in half, thirds, or quarters. Roll out each piece into a thin ⅛-inch-thick rectangle; each half will be about 24-by-14 inches; thirds will be about 18- by 14-inches; quarters will be about 14-by-12 inches. Spread with the filling, leaving a ½-inch border. Brush the edges with a little egg wash to help seal the cakes. Starting from a long end, roll up jelly-roll style. Place on the prepared baking sheet.

5. Brush the cakes with the egg wash. Prick in several places on the top and sides with the tines of a fork to prevent splitting during baking. Bake without rising until golden brown, 30 to 45 minutes. Place the baking sheet on a wire rack and let the cakes cool on the sheet.

VARIATIONS

Kakosh (Hungarian Chocolate Roll): For the filling, combine 1 cup granulated sugar, ½ cup confectioners' sugar, ⅔ cup unsweetened cocoa powder, 2 tablespoons melted butter or vegetable oil, 1 teaspoon vanilla extract, and enough water to produce a spreading consistency.

MAKOUD

Makoud is an egg casserole with potatoes and/or meat.

Origin: Tunisia

Other names: *minina.*

Makoud was originally an omelet cooked in a skillet and inverted partway through cooking. Modern versions usually contain mashed potatoes and ground meat and are baked as a casserole. The mixture is also thickened with extra potatoes and fried as patties. *Makoud* is a main course for both weekday lunches and special occasions. As a casserole, it is easy to serve in the sukkah, so *makoud* is traditional Tunisian Sukkot fare. *Makoud* with potatoes is a popular Passover dish. Chopped cooked meat or poultry may

be substituted for ground beef; the version made with poultry is called *makoud bil djadj.*

TUNISIAN POTATO AND MEAT CASSEROLE (*MAKOUD*)

6 TO 8 SERVINGS [MEAT]

> 6 large eggs, lightly beaten
> 2 cups mashed potatoes, or 6 slices white bread, soaked and squeezed
> 3 hard-boiled eggs, chopped
> ¼ to ½ cup chopped fresh flat-leaf parsley
> About 1 teaspoon table salt or 2 teaspoons kosher salt
> Ground black pepper to taste
> ½ teaspoon ground turmeric (optional)
> 3 tablespoons vegetable or olive oil
> 1 large yellow onion, chopped
> 1 to 2 cloves garlic, minced
> 1 pound ground beef or lamb chuck or 8 ounces chopped roast beef

1. Preheat the oven to 350°F. Grease a 13-by-9-inch or 11- by 7-inch baking pan.

2. In a large bowl, combine the eggs, potatoes, hard-boiled eggs, parsley, salt, pepper, and, if using, turmeric. In a large skillet, heat the oil over medium heat. Add the onion and garlic and sauté until soft and translucent, 5 to 10 minutes. Add the meat and cook, stirring, until it loses its red color, about 5 minutes. Remove from the heat and stir into the potato mixture.

3. Spoon into the prepared pan. Bake until golden brown, about 30 minutes.

MAKROUD

Makroud is a semolina pastry often made with a date filling.

Origin: Maghreb

Other names: *macroude, macrud, makhroud, makrout.*

Makroud, which means "wound [like a turban]" in Arabic, are popular in many parts of the Maghreb; this pastry is the Berber form of the Middle Eastern *ma'amoul* (small filled shortbread cookies). Moroccans also use the term *makroud* for semolina fritters, which are customary for Hanukkah.

For most of history, these were homemade treats and numerous variations emerged. Since home ovens were rare in the Maghreb, the pastries were originally deep-fried. Today, there are both fried and baked ver-

Makroud *is the Berber form of filled cookies. These sticky treats usually have a date filling and are simmered in syrup or honey.*

poultry bones and the starch from the rice thicken the cooking liquid when the dish is cooled. From this, medieval Arabs developed a milky white pudding made from almond milk, sugar, rose water, and rice flour, which they named, *muhallabia,* from the Arabic for "milk." Jews sometimes substituted white grape juice for the almond milk.

When the Arabs conquered Sicily in the tenth century, they introduced the almond milk and rice-flour pudding, which later, during Spanish rule, was renamed *biancomangiare* (white thing to eat). By the thirteenth century, the pudding had arrived in France, where it was known as *blancmangier* (white eating), which ultimately became the English blancmange.

Unlike custard or contemporary Western soft puddings, *muhallabia* are made without eggs, producing a texture that is a cross between gelatin and pudding. Two families of this pudding emerged: rice flour and cornstarch. Both are sometimes still made with almond milk, but they increasingly use cow's milk. The Turks call rice-flour pudding *sutlach* and cornstarch pudding *muhallebi.* Syrians call rice-flour pudding *suttlage* and cornstarch pudding *al massia.* Israelis learned of the cornstarch pudding from the Turks and, although in Hebrew blancmange is technically *raferfet-karish* (jelly custard), in the common parlance the name became *malabi.*

The basic cornstarch pudding is rather bland in nature, requiring some flavoring. Rose water remains the most widespread addition, although it is an acquired taste. Other flavorings are almond, orange, chocolate, and mastic. Cardamom, sometimes plenty of it, is characteristic of Persian tastes.

In Israel, *malabi* became much more popular than *muhallebi* ever was in Turkey—what falafel is to Israeli street meals, *malabi* is to Israeli summertime street desserts. *Malabi* is sold from innumerable

sions, which are made by housewives as well as commonly sold in Tunisian bakeries. Dates (*dattes*) are the traditional and most widespread filling, but Algerians also fill the pastries with almond paste (*makroud el looz*) or leave them unfilled. Some versions include only semolina in the dough, while others combine semolina and flour; in a more recent version, some Moroccans have substituted cornmeal. Non-Jews generally use clarified butter, which produces a hard dough, while Jews favor oil for a pareve treat. After cooking, *makroud* are simmered in sugar syrup or honey.

These cookies are popular throughout the year, but are traditional for Hanukkah and Purim. *Makroud* are typically served with Turkish coffee or mint tea (*naa-naa*).

MALABI
Malabi is a white pudding generally made of almond milk or cow's milk and thickened with rice flour or cornstarch.
Origin: Middle East
Other names: Cyprus: *mahalepi*; Egypt: *mahalabiya, muhalabiya*; Persia: *masghati*; Turkey: *muhallebi.*

Persians concocted a dish of poached chicken, almonds, rice, and sugar, in which the gelatin from the

kiosks across the country and is even offered as a dessert in many upscale restaurants.

In Israel, *malabi* is typically topped with a sweet syrup, either a date syrup or a neon-pink-colored, rose-flavored raspberry syrup, and commonly garnished with toasted coconut or strands of *kanafeh* (shredded wheat pastry) and/or chopped toasted pistachios or peanuts. Instead of the syrup, some people spoon a little cherry sauce into the serving dish then add the *malabi*—the bright red fruit provides a dramatic contrast to the white pudding. Another trend has been to omit the syrup and top the pudding with bright red slices of rose-flavored Turkish delight (*rahat lokum*).

This light rose water–flavored pudding is traditional in some families for Rosh Hashanah dinner. For Passover, it is made with potato starch. Almond milk versions are ideal for meat meals. For a fancy presentation, the entire *malabi* is cooled in a large bowl, inverted onto a serving platter, and drizzled with syrup. (See also Almond Milk and Sutlach)

ISRAELI CORNSTARCH PUDDING (*MALABI*)

ABOUT 5 CUPS/5 TO 7 SERVINGS   [DAIRY OR PAREVE]

5 cups milk or almond milk, or 4 cups milk and
   1 cup heavy cream
About ½ cup sugar
Pinch of salt
10 tablespoons (3 ounces) cornstarch or potato
   starch
1 to 4 tablespoons rose water, 2 tablespoons almond
   extract, 1 tablespoon orange-blossom water, or
   1 tablespoon vanilla extract

Rose Syrup (Optional):

⅔ cup sugar
½ cup water
1 teaspoon rose water
1 teaspoon red food coloring

½ cup toasted and coarsely chopped pistachios,
   almonds, or peanuts for garnish (optional)
½ cup toasted flaked coconut for garnish
   (optional)

1. In a medium saucepan, combine 4 cups milk, sugar, and salt. Gradually bring to a low boil over medium heat, stirring frequently with a wooden spoon until the sugar dissolves.

2. Dissolve the cornstarch in the remaining 1 cup milk and add to the milk in the saucepan. Reduce the heat to medium-low and simmer, stirring frequently, until the mixture begins to thicken and coats the back of a spoon, about 10 minutes. Add the rose water and cook, stirring constantly, until thickened, about 2 minutes.

3. Divide the pudding between 5 to 7 goblets or other serving dishes—it's best to use glass to show off the bright white color—and press a piece of plastic wrap against the surface. Let cool, then refrigerate until chilled, at least 3 hours.

4. To make the rose syrup: In a small saucepan, combine all the syrup ingredients, bring to a boil, boil until slightly syrupy, and let cool.

5. Just before serving, remove the plastic from the *malabi*, drizzle a little syrup over the puddings, and, if using, sprinkle with the nuts and/or coconut.

MALAI

Malai is corn bread as well as the Romanian word for cornmeal.

Origin: Romania

Other names: *painea de malai, pita de malaior, turta de malai.*

The peasants of southern Europe long subsisted on gruels—and, less frequently, unleavened breads—made primarily from barley or millet. Shortly after Columbus's first voyage, Spanish explorers introduced corn to the Old World and it was spread by the Turks to the Balkans. Although corn did not fare very well in the climes of northern Europe, the milder conditions in the center of the continent proved ideal for growing the new American grain. In the late seventeenth century, the poor found cornmeal a cheaper and more practical replacement for millet, semolina, and other grains in their traditional dishes. In those areas, corn, when served along with large amounts of legumes, provided complementary nutrition and soon emerged as the most important component of the diet, much as potatoes—another American import—did in northeastern Europe and Ireland. The favorite method of preparing cornmeal was to make a mush called *mamaliga* in Romania, and polenta in Italy. Another popular Romanian way of cooking cornmeal was to bake it as a casserole or bread to make a dish called *malai*, which is also the word for cornmeal. Every Romanian meal featured either *mamaliga* or *malai*.

Romanian Jews make numerous versions of *malai*, most containing various dairy products, resulting in a moister texture and tangier flavor than American corn breads. In general, *malai* is crumbly and slightly tart or, when plenty of sugar is added, sweet-tart. The traditional types of *malai* were raised with yeast, but recently baking powder has become more common. In some variations, a curd cheese is mixed into the batter; in others, it is layered in the bread. Dairy *malai* is often accompanied with sour cream or butter; pareve versions are served with schmaltz. Traditionally, after baking their challahs on Friday, some Romanian housewives stuck a *malai* in the oven to serve cold for Sabbath breakfast or lunch. Others preferred it warm from the oven.

(See also Corn/Cornmeal and Mamaliga)

ROMANIAN CHEESE CORN BREAD (*MALAI*)

6 TO 8 SERVINGS   [DAIRY]

Double the recipe and bake in a 13- by 9-inch pan. For a more cake-like malai (*budinca de malai dulce*), increase the sugar to ¾ cup and add ½ teaspoon vanilla extract; for a more savory bread, reduce the sugar to 2 to 3 tablespoons.

    1 cup (5 ounces) unbleached all-purpose flour
    1 cup (4.75 ounces) medium-grind cornmeal,
        preferably stone-ground
    2 teaspoons double-acting baking powder
    ½ teaspoon salt
    2 large eggs, lightly beaten
    1 cup milk
    ½ cup sour cream or plain yogurt
    ½ cup *gevina levana* (Israeli white cheese), creamy
        brinza (Romanian feta), or cream cheese
    ⅓ cup unsalted butter, melted
    ⅓ to ½ cup sugar or honey

1. Preheat the oven to 350°F (325°F if using a glass dish). Grease one 8-inch square baking pan, one 9-inch cast-iron skillet, or two 9-inch pie plates.

2. Combine the flour, cornmeal, baking powder, and salt. In a large bowl, combine the eggs, milk, sour cream, cheese, butter, and sugar. Stir in the cornmeal mixture.

3. Pour into the prepared pan and tap to remove any air bubbles. Bake until the bread is golden brown and pulls away from the sides of the pan, about 50 minutes. Malai is best served warm.

MALIDA

Malida is a mixture of flaked rice, shredded coconut, raisins, nuts, spices, and sugar.

Origin: India
Other names: *maleeda.*

One biblical figure dominates the lore of the Bene Israel of India: Elijah the Prophet, or *Eliyahoo Hannabi,* as they pronounce his name. According to legend, he twice visited their community. The first occurrence followed their ancestors' initial arrival via shipwreck on the Konkan coast. As the nearly drowned survivors struggled to shore, Elijah suddenly arrived and breathed life back into them. Much later, on the fifteenth of the month of Shevat, the prophet appeared nearby the landing point in the hilly village of Khandala, which is in the western part of the western state of Maharashtra. Close to Khandala is a black rock embedded with marks (*Eliyahoo Hannabi*

A confection featuring flaked rice, coconut, raisins, and spices is a signature dish of the Bene Israel of India, which is served at celebrations as an offering of thanks.

cha Tapa), said to have been made by the wheels of Elijah's chariot of fire as he soared heavenward.

The Bene Israel developed a unique ceremony of thanksgiving called *Eliyahoo Hannabi*. Among the auspicious occasions meriting an *Eliyahoo Hannabi* are recuperation from an illness, the purchase of a house or other important item, the return from a long trip, the fulfillment or annulment of a vow, graduation, and the start of a new job. An *Eliyahoo Hannabi* is also held after celebratory life-cycle events; for example, it is held before a wedding, following a birth, and on the evening after a *brit milah*. In addition, the holiday of Tu b'Shevat, the anniversary (*urus*) of Elijah's second appearance, is a customary occasion for the ceremony for all Bene Israel.

The central feature of the ceremony is the *malida* (sweet foods), a sort of confection based on a special form of rice, variously called flaked, flattened, beaten, pounded, or pressed rice, and called *poha* in Hindi. *Poha* consists of husked rice kernels that are soaked in water for eight to ten hours, then roasted and flattened by rollers. *Poha* is a common item in the typical Indian pantry, especially in Maharashtra.

After saying prayers to God and giving thanks to the prophet Elijah, the *malida* is displayed on a special round platter. Also on the platter are five or seven different fresh whole fruits and, in the center, flowers or myrtle branches (for reciting the *besamim* benediction), symbolizing the meal offering of the Temple. In addition, many people accompany the *malida* with a platter of roasted cubes or livers of goat, lamb, or chicken, symbolizing the Temple offerings. The woman preparing the *malida* is sometimes blindfolded, connoting that the ceremony is performed in blind faith. At the end of the ceremony, the *malida* is passed around for all the participants to enjoy and each recites the appropriate benedictions over the *malida* and fruits. In the *malida* preceding a wedding, the fruits are placed near the bride's stomach, symbolizing fertility, and only she eats them. The Bene Israel generally prefer *malida* to be very sweet.

Because of the central role of the sweet foods in the *Eliyahoo Hannabi*, *malida* is commonly used as a synonym for the entire ceremony. It is typically performed at home in private, although some synagogues stage communal ceremonies and many Bene Israel annually trek to Khandala, the site of the prophet's second visit, for a community *malida*, especially on Tu b'Shevat. Some Bene Israel, even those traveling from across the globe, make a pilgrimage once a year or more for a communal *malida* at the Beth-El Synagogue, built in 1849, in Panvel, outside of Mumbai. In Israel, Bene Israel substitute Elijah's Cave on Mount Carmel as the site of pilgrimage for the *malida*. Although the Bene Israel adopted various Western Jewish practices and the majority now reside outside of India, *malida* still constitutes their most distinctive and defining food and custom—it is an enduring and cherished marker of their identity.

MUMBAI SWEET RICE FLAKES (*MALIDA*)

4 TO 6 SERVINGS [PAREVE]

Reduce the amount of sugar by about one-fourth, if using sweetened coconut.

   3⅓ cups (about 20 ounces) thick flaked rice (*poha*)
   1 medium coconut, grated (about 3 cups/ 20 ounces)
   About 1 cup (6 ounces) ground jaggery (raw sugar crystals) or 2 to 4 cups confectioners' sugar
   12 to 16 cardamom pods, crushed, or 1 teaspoon ground cardamom
   1 cup golden raisins
   1 cup almonds, blanched and sliced lengthwise
   1 cup pistachios, blanched and sliced lengthwise

1. Soak the flaked rice in cold water to cover until softened, about 15 minutes. Drain.

2. In a large bowl, combine the coconut, jaggery, and cardamom. Stir in the rice. Add the raisins and nuts. Let stand at room temperature for 30 minutes.

MALPUA

Malpua is a sweet fritter or pancake.

Origin: northern India

Other names: *maal pua*, *malpuah*.

   Plain pancakes are favorite Indian breakfast fare. More elaborate pancakes are made by adding mashed banana for flavor and sweetness. When the pancake or fritter (*pua*) is served with a syrup it becomes a *malpua*. A favorite *malpua* of the Bene Israel of Mumbai consists of banana chunks, pineapple pieces, or other fruit slices, that are dipped into a batter and deep-fried. In many households, *malpua* is served on Hanukkah and Purim and during the monsoon season (*Sawan*), frequently with *kheer* (creamy rice or cornstarch pudding).

✤ MUMBAI FRITTERS (*MALPUA*)

ABOUT 24 SMALL FRITTERS   [DAIRY OR PAREVE]

> 2 cups (10 ounces) unbleached all-purpose flour,
> or 1¼ cups all-purpose flour (*maida*) and ¾ cup
> fine semolina (*sooji*)
> ½ cup sugar
> ¾ teaspoon salt
> 1 teaspoon ground cardamom or 1 tablespoon
> fennel seeds (optional)
> A few strands of saffron (optional)
> 1 cup milk, coconut milk, or water
> 2 large eggs
> 1 teaspoon vanilla extract
> Peanut or vegetable oil or ghee (clarified butter) for
> deep-frying
> 6 medium bananas, cut crosswise into 1½- to
> 2-inch-long pieces, or 8 slices pineapple, cut
> into quarters
> Confectioners' sugar for dusting or *chinir ros* (sugar
> syrup) or *radbi* (Indian milk syrup) for drizzling

1. In a large bowl, combine the flour, sugar, salt, and, if using, cardamom and/or saffron. In a medium bowl, blend together the milk, eggs, and vanilla. Stir into the flour mixture to make a thick batter. Cover and let stand at room temperature for at least 1 hour.

2. In a large pot, heat at least 1 inch oil over medium heat to 375°F.

3. Dip the banana pieces into the batter. In batches, fry the banana pieces, turning occasionally, until puffed and golden brown on all sides, about 1½ minutes per side. Remove with tongs or a wire-mesh skimmer and drain on a wire rack. Sprinkle with confectioners' sugar or drizzle with the syrup. Serve warm or cooled. You can keep the fritters warm in a 250°F oven while preparing the remaining fritters.

MALSOUKA

Malsouka, also called *dioune* and *malsuqa*, is a Tunisian variation of phyllo dough. It is traditionally composed of semolina flour and water and, unlike phyllo, dried by heat. *Malsouka* is used to make *brik* and other flaky pastries.

Tajine malsouka is the Tunisian version of the Moroccan *pastilla* (pigeon pie); the filling is sandwiched between layers of *malsouka* in a terra-cotta tagine and cooked over a fire. This festive dish is prepared for Friday night dinner or holidays.

(See also Phyllo and Warka)

MAMALIGA

Mamaliga is cornmeal mush.

Origin: Romania

Other names: Bulgaria: *kachamak*; Georgia: *gomi*; Hungary: *puliszka*; Italy: polenta; Romania: *terci de malai*; Serbia: *kachamak*; Ukraine: *kulesha*, *mamalyga*.

Mamaliga is the quintessential nostalgia food for any Romanian, the one and perhaps only common denominator uniting people from all classes, regions, and religions. It is memorialized in one of the most famous songs of the Yiddish theater, "Roumania, Roumania."—"A *Mamaliga*, a pastrami, a *Karnatzele*, and a glass of wine!"

From the time of the Etruscans until the middle of the seventeenth century, the peasants of the Italian Peninsula and the Balkans subsisted on starch porridges known as *puls* or *pulmentum*. These porridges were usually made of millet, barley, or chestnut flour, and were cheaper and easier to make than bread. Romanians called the yellowish millet porridge *mamaliga* (food of gold) to differentiate it from the darker barley porridge. In 1650, the Ottoman Turks brought cornmeal to the Balkans with the express intention that the peasants would use it in porridges, leaving the preferred wheat for the Turks. At the time, much of eastern Europe was ravaged and enduring famine because of the Ottoman advances, which culminated in the siege of Vienna in 1683. It is probable that, due to the Turkish control of the Balkans, cornmeal mush first became widespread in Romania before northern Italy. Indeed, Italians called corn *grano turco* (Turkish grain). Whichever country it reached first, this hearty porridge became the staple of the impoverished masses of this stretch of land of the Roman Empire. Due to the traditionally high consumption of both legumes and dairy products in those countries, the population was able to make the transition to cornmeal without incurring nutritional deficits.

No nation so wholeheartedly embraced cornmeal mush as Romania, and the subsequent demographic expansion of both its Jewish and non-Jewish population corresponded to cornmeal's popularization. By the end of the seventeenth century, the masses of Romania had replaced the traditional grains in their gruel with the cheaper and more versatile cornmeal (*farina de malai*).

Preparing *mamaliga* became a daily morning ritual, replete with its own equipment and traditions, in most Romanian and northern Italian households. A special concave copper or cast-iron cauldron called a *ceaun* (*paiolo* in Italy) typically sat in the hearth on a *pirostrii* (iron tripod) or hung from a chain in the center of the main room. There housewives, having risen early, boiled water over an open wood fire, added the right amount of salt, then very gradually dribbled in a calculated measure of cornmeal, frantically stirring, in only one direction, with a *melesteu* (*bastoni* in Italy), a special long-handled wooden stick. If the cornmeal was added too quickly or cooked at too high a temperature, it would seize up, resulting in a gummy texture and raw flavor. Constant stirring was necessary for even cooking and to prevent the dreaded lumps, whimsically called in Yiddish *shikshalach*. With her free hand, the housewife might nurse a baby or help dress an older child. After all the cornmeal was successfully doled into the pot, the *mamaliga* was continuously stirred over a low flame until thickened, producing a smooth, creamy texture and sweet flavor. Romanian *mamaliga* tended to be denser—it was firm enough to be cut into slices—than the softer polenta preferred in the Veneto. The traditional test to determine if the *mamaliga* was done was to moisten the handle of a wooden spoon with cold water and dip the tip into the *mamaliga*—if the handle came out clean, the *mamaliga* was done. When the *mamaliga* had achieved the desired consistency, it was poured onto a special wooden board called a *madia*, then cut using a string or wire. This traditional method of making *mamaliga* required more than an hour and proved so exhausting that the very word became a popular Romanian term for a person lacking energy.

For generations of Romanians, *mamaliga* was served for breakfast, lunch, and dinner, and used as a porridge, casserole, croquette, and bread substitute. Since *mamaliga* could be served with either dairy or meat dishes, it was ideal for any meal, and became a beloved feature of Romanian Jewish cuisine. There were numerous variations of the basic *mamaliga*. Some cooks enhanced it with cheese or buttermilk, while many preferred the pure corn flavor. For breakfast, it was usually served fresh, soft, and warm with butter, sour cream, *brinza* or kashkaval cheese, honey, or fruit preserves. Pickles or other sours almost always accompanied *mamaliga*. Sometimes leftover *mamaliga* from the previous day was cut into slices and fried. School children and workmen frequently carried balls of firm

mamaliga in their pocket to satisfy their hunger during the day. For lunch, slices of fresh *mamaliga* were served with a stew, such as *guvetch* (vegetable stew), *toscana* (meat stew), or *fasole* (cooked beans). Dinner frequently consisted of slices of *mamaliga* served with a selection of raw or fried onions or scallions, cheese, and sour cream, the firm pieces of mush performing like bread. Wheat bread was rare in Romania, except for the Sabbath and festivals.

In the early nineteenth century, a few Romanian Jews immigrated to America, and beginning in 1880, they began arriving in both America and Israel in large numbers, bringing with them a love of *mamaliga*. It was most certainly these early Romanian Jews who introduced the word *mamaliga* to America, although the term was subsequently supplanted by polenta. For the next half century, *mamaliga* was a staple of many impoverished tenement residents on Manhattan's Lower East Side. However, as their descendants became acculturated and more affluent, they generally rejected the stodgy, time-consuming fare. Fewer housewives made it and only a very few Jewish restaurants continued to offer it. *Mamaliga* retained a bit more of its popularity in Israel and can still be found in eateries with a Balkan menu. Ironically, this peasant dish has more recently become popular fare as polenta in chic restaurants in the United States, as it melds with many flavors both delicate and robust.

In Romania, *mamaliga* was almost always made from yellow cornmeal, except on very important occasions; *mamaliga* made from white cornmeal was served on Shavuot, as the white color symbolized purity. A dish of creamy, piping-hot *mamaliga* fresh from the stove is enough to bring a tear of joy to a Romanian's eye.

(See also Corn/Cornmeal and Malai)

ROMANIAN CORNMEAL MUSH (*MAMALIGA*)

ABOUT 7 CUPS/6 TO 8 SERVINGS   [PAREVE OR DAIRY]

7 cups water

About 2½ teaspoons table salt or 5 teaspoons kosher salt

2 cups (9.25 ounces) medium-grind cornmeal, preferably stone-ground

¼ to ½ cup (½ to 1 stick) unsalted butter or margarine (optional)

1. In a large pot, bring the water to a boil over medium heat. Add the salt. For thicker mamaliga intended

for solidifying, use the 7 cups water; for softer porridge similar to polenta, increase the water to 8 cups. Using a long wooden spoon or whisk, in a slow, steady stream, stir in the cornmeal, stirring constantly to prevent lumps. It can take up to 10 minutes to add all the cornmeal. Cook, stirring constantly, until bubbly and slightly thickened, about 5 minutes.

2. Reduce the heat to low and simmer, stirring frequently, until the mixture is creamy and thick and begins to pull away from sides of the pan, about 20 minutes.

3. For softer mamaliga, stir in the butter and serve warm. For firm mamaliga, remove from the heat, dip a wooden spoon into cold water, and use it to scrape the mamaliga from the sides and toward the center of the pot. Place the pot over medium heat and let stand without stirring until the steam loosens the *mamaliga* from the bottom, 1 to 3 minutes.

4. Pour the hot mamaliga onto a large wooden board, at least 18 inches in diameter, an inverted large baking sheet, or a large serving platter. Spread into a rectangle ½ to 1 inch thick and let stand until set.

5. Using thin twine or dental floss, cut into rectangles or squares. Use the slices like bread or as a bed for a stew or sauce.

MANDELBROT

Mandelbrot is a twice-baked cookie, originally made with almonds.

Origin: Germany

Other names: Ukraine: *kamish brot, komish brot*; Yiddish: *mandelbroit.*

In the early Middle Ages, Italians began preparing thin individual crisp breads called biscotti (twice cooked) by partially baking the dough in loaf form, then cutting it in half (later into slices) and briefly returning the pieces to a cooler oven to crisp. The second cooking extracts most of the moisture and greatly lengthens the shelf life. Around the thirteenth century, following the introduction of sugar in Europe in nonmedicinal roles, Tuscans (purportedly initially in the city of Prato or perhaps in the ghetto of Venice) began adding it to some biscotti doughs. Sweetened biscotti—commonly flavored with anise, almond, or hazelnut—soon became the most widespread type. The original hard, dense biscotti contained no fat and, therefore, were typically eaten dipped into sweet wine, brandy, or, later, coffee.

The cookies spread to central Europeans, who primarily flavored them with bitter almonds and eventually called them mandelbrot. *Brot* is German and Yiddish for "bread" and *mandel* is German and Yiddish meaning "almond."

When and how these cookies were adopted by Ashkenazim is unknown. By at least the early nineteenth century, the cookie was certainly well-known in central Europe among Jews and non-Jews. Mandelbrot, like many Jewish baked goods, may have arisen in Germany and traveled eastward. The first record of mandelbrot in Jewish circles was its use as a Polish and Lithuanian surname. Jews bearing this name include Szolem Mandelbrojt (1899–1983), a Polish-born mathematician from a Lithuanian background, and his nephew, Benoît Mandelbrot (b. 1924), who is considered the "father of fractal geometry." (Thus the Mandelbrot Competition is in mathematics, not baking.)

Twice-baked cookies became a favorite Ashkenazic cookie. Its relatively easy preparation and long shelf life made it ideal for the Sabbath; and it could also be served to unexpected company during the week, typically with hot tea. The first edition of *The Settlement Cook Book* (Milwaukee, 1901) contained a recipe for "Koumiss Bread." This Ukrainian version consisted of flour, eggs, sugar, almonds, and a little lemon juice and zest.

The modern form of mandelbrot emerged in the early twentieth century when inexpensive oils from various seeds became available. Baking powder was also commonly added at that time. At this point, mandelbrot became lighter and fluffier than biscotti. Cooks also began to sometimes replace the original almonds with new items—including dried fruit, other nuts, and chocolate chips—although the name of the cookie was retained even when almonds were absent. A Passover variation emerged in which matza cake meal was substituted for the flour. By the 1940s, mandelbrot had become a standard of sisterhood cookbooks and Jewish bakeries. It was typically made with oil or shortening—there was never butter in true mandelbrot. Some cooks used mandelbrot crumbs in strudel in place of bread crumbs.

In the 1980s, mandelbrot were largely eclipsed by biscotti, which suddenly had a greater cachet, although they had previously been unknown in America outside of Italian circles. This phenomenon occurred even though many brands of "biscotti" added fat to the cookies for tenderness, making them in essence mandelbrot. American gourmet shops readily stocked biscotti, but not products labeled "mandelbrot." At least two small American mandelbrot manufacturers switched the name of their products to biscotti, but not the ingredients, to increase sales. Still other companies have held steady to the *haimish* name and some homes still feature a tin of these cookies for a snack or guests, whether they are called mandelbrot, *komishbrot* (Yiddish meaning "funny bread"), or biscotti.

ASHKENAZIC ALMOND COOKIES (*MANDELBROT*)

ABOUT FORTY ½-INCH-THICK SLICES [PAREVE]

- 2¼ cups (11.25 ounces) all-purpose flour
- 1½ teaspoons double-acting baking powder
- ⅛ teaspoon salt
- ¾ cup sugar
- ½ cup vegetable oil
- 2 large eggs
- 1 teaspoon vanilla extract, or ¾ teaspoon vanilla and ½ teaspoon almond extract
- 1 cup coarsely chopped almonds, preferably lightly toasted, or 6 ounces semisweet chocolate chips and ½ cup almonds

1. Preheat the oven to 350°F. Line a large baking sheet with parchment paper or lightly grease the sheet and dust with flour.

2. Sift together the flour, baking powder, and salt. In a large bowl, beat together the sugar and oil. Beat in the eggs, one at a time. Add the vanilla. Stir in the flour mixture to make a soft and only slightly sticky dough. Stir in the nuts.

3. With floured hands, place the dough on the prepared baking sheet, and form into a loaf 2½ inches wide, 1 inch thick, and about 12 inches long. Smooth the top.

4. Bake until firm and lightly browned, about 20 minutes. Let cool slightly on the baking sheet, about 10 minutes.

5. Reduce the heat to 300°F.

6. Transfer the loaf to a flat surface. Using a serrated knife, cut the log into ½-inch-thick slices. Place the slices, cut side down, on the baking sheet. Bake until lightly golden and crisp, about 10 minutes. Transfer the slices to a wire rack and let cool completely. Store in an airtight container at room temperature for up to 2 weeks or in a freezer for up to 3 months.

MANDLEN

Mandlen are deep-fried or baked pasta puffs that are served in soup.

Origin: Eastern Europe
Other names: Hebrew: *shkedim, shkedei marak.*

"Who says that Jews can only be traders, and eat fat soup with *mandlen*, but cannot be workingmen?" (Line from the twentieth-century Yiddish socialist folk song "Hey Zhankoye.")

In Yiddish and German the word *mandlen* means "almonds," but there are no nuts in these pasta pieces—the name refers to its nut-like shape. The dough is rolled into ropes, cut into small pieces, and originally deep-fried, an ancient technique. The eggs in the dough cause the balls to puff up and hollow out during frying, which results in small, crisp, airy puffs. Today *mandlen* are more commonly baked. *Mandlen* are akin to *teiglach*, except the latter, after frying, are boiled in honey. *Mandlen* are among the classic eastern European starch garnishes for chicken soup, along with *lokhshen* (noodles), kreplach (filled pasta), and *knaidlach* (matza balls). In soup, they absorb some of the flavor and soften, while offering an interesting textural contrast to the hot liquid.

Historically, *mandlen* were primarily prepared for the Sabbath, festivals, and weddings. They have a particular significance for the Sabbath as a symbol of the manna, a connection based on the similarity in both the names and shapes. In the 1940s, the advent in America and Israel of packaged commercial "soup nuts," sometimes made from matza meal for Passover, led to the adoption of *mandlen* beyond the Ashkenazic community. Today in Israel, small crispy versions are still extremely popular, although they are rarely made at home.

ASHKENAZIC SOUP NUTS (*MANDLEN*)

ABOUT 50 SOUP NUTS [MEAT OR PAREVE]

- 2 large eggs, lightly beaten
- 2 tablespoons schmaltz or vegetable oil
- ½ teaspoon table salt or 1 teaspoon kosher salt
- About 1 cup (5 ounces) all-purpose flour, or ⅔ cup matza cake meal and 1 teaspoon potato starch
- Vegetable oil for deep-frying

1. In a large bowl, combine the eggs, schmaltz, and salt. Stir in ½ cup flour. Gradually stir in enough of the remaining flour to make a soft dough that is not sticky. Knead until smooth, about 10 minutes. Cover and let stand for at least 20 minutes.

2. Shape the dough into ¼- to ½-inch-thick ropes and cut the ropes into ¼- to ½-inch pieces.

3. In a large pot, heat at least 1 inch oil over medium heat to 375°F.

4. In batches, fry the *mandlen*, turning, until puffed and golden brown on all sides. Remove with a slotted spoon and drain on paper towels. Let cool. Store in an airtight container at room temperature for up to 1 week. Serve as a soup garnish.

MANTI

Manti is a filled dumpling.

Origin: Uzbekistan

Other names: Afghanistan: *mandu*; Turkey: *tabak börek*.

Around the third century BCE, the Mongols of northern China received the grindstone by way of central Asia and mastered wheat flour doughs. They then developed a number of steamed and boiled dough dishes, including a steamed bun filled with chopped boiled mutton called *man tou* (head of a southern savage); its name possibly referred to its crimped edges. This dish eventually evolved into a dumpling similar to the modern wonton.

The Turks, who originated in Mongolia, adopted the filled dumpling and called it *manti*. In the tenth century, a group of Turks led by Seljuk moved into the area of Bukhara, then gradually advanced into western Asia, bringing with them many Chinese and central Asian foods, including *manti*. Considering that the appearance of the Turkish *manti* predates any other

Filled meat dumplings–originally from China, but also beloved in Turkey and Uzbekistan (here they are seen in a Samarkand kitchen)—predate filled pastas from the Mediterranean.

filled pasta in the Mediterranean region, it may have been the inspiration for comparable European pastas. Similarly, it was probably the Tatars (Mongolian tribes) who introduced noodles, including *manti*, to eastern Europe, leading to the Polish *pierogi*, Ukrainian *vareniki*, and Ashkenazic kreplach. Turkish *manti* are smaller than Uzbeki versions and are baked in a liquid.

In Uzbekistan, *manti*, generally eaten in prodigious amounts, are cooked in special multilevel steamers, another gift of the Chinese. The somewhat rustic Bukharan *manti* are larger and less delicate than Chinese wontons. Unlike Turkish and Tatar dumplings, which always contain a meat filling. Bukharans also developed various cheese and vegetarian fillings, such as squash and potato; for dairy meals these dumplings are typically served swimming in yogurt. Meat *manti* are customarily eaten warm, sprinkled with a little chopped fresh parsley or dill, but are also accompanied by a dipping sauce or added to chicken soup, in the Chinese manner.

Since the arrival in the late twentieth century of large numbers of Bukharans in Queens, New York, many restaurants in the area and some in Midtown Manhattan have begun to feature *manti*. Bukharans serve these dumplings on Purim and other festive occasions.

❦ BUKHARAN STEAMED FILLED PASTA (*MANTI*)

ABOUT THIRTY 3-INCH OR TWENTY-FOUR 4-INCH DUMPLINGS
[MEAT]

Filling:

1 pound ground lamb or beef chuck

1 medium yellow onion, finely chopped

About ½ teaspoon salt or 1 teaspoon kosher salt

½ teaspoon ground cinnamon (optional)

1 recipe (1 pound) Egg Noodle Dough (page 368) or 24 to 28 (about 6 ounces) wonton or gyoza wrappers

1. In a medium bowl, combine the meat, onion, salt, and, if using, cinnamon.

2. On a lightly floured surface, roll out the dough ¹⁄₁₆ inch thick and cut into 3-inch rounds. Or divide the dough into 30 or 24 pieces, form into balls, and, on a lightly floured surface, roll out to thin 3- or 4-inch rounds.

3. Place a heaping teaspoon of the filling in the center of each round. Wet the edges of the dough with water. Bring up the sides of the dough around the filling, pinch together at the top, and twist to form a small pouch. The dumplings may be prepared ahead up to this point and refrigerated for up to 3 days or frozen for up to 3 months. Do not thaw before cooking, but increase the cooking time by about 2 minutes.

4. Place an oiled bamboo steamer in a wok and add water to reach about 1 inch from the bottom of the steamer. Or place an oiled colander in a large kettle and add water to reach about 1 inch from the bottom. Arrange the dumplings on the steamer rack in a single layer without touching, cover tightly, and steam until the dough is tender and the filling is cooked through, about 20 minutes. If using a multilevel steamer, reverse the compartments halfway through cooking. Transfer the *manti* to a warm plate, cover, and keep warm until ready to serve.

MARBLE CAKE
Marble cake is made of two different colored batters that are swirled in the pan to create a marble-like effect.
Origin: Central Europe
Other names: *marmorgugelhupf, marmorkuchen.*

Marmor is the German and Yiddish word for marble. The idea of lightly mingling two different batters in one cake seems to have originated in early nineteenth-century Germany. The earliest version of marble cake consisted of a *kugelhupf* (sweet yeast bread), one half of which was colored with molasses and spices. Bakers next began to do the same thing with sponge cake batter.

The cake was brought to America by immigrants shortly before the Civil War and the term marble cake was first recorded in English in the September 29, 1859, issue of the *Illinois State Chronicle* (Decatur). When this novelty initially appeared in American cookbooks—perhaps the earliest recipe was in *Tit-Bits: Or, How to Prepare a Nice Dish at a Moderate Expense* by Mrs. S. G. Knight (Boston, 1864)—spices and molasses were still being used, but the technique was applied to butter cakes. The molasses-spice marble cake remained predominant through the nineteenth century, then, as chocolate gained a greater hold on the American public, it generally replaced spices in this classic treat.

The first Jewish source, and among the earliest anywhere, for a chocolate marble cake was *Aunt Babette's* (Cincinnati, 1889), in which a recipe instructed cooks to "stir into [half the batter] about two heaping table-spoons of grated chocolate (which you must grate before you begin to mix the cake)." Some bakers compromised between the two and created chocolate-spice marble cakes, such as the "Marble Cake" recipe in the first edition of *The Settlement Cook Book* (Milwaukee, 1901), which was flavored with grated chocolate, cinnamon, and cloves and baked in a tube pan.

Initially, the sponge variety of marble cake, which was pareve and was prepared as both loaves and sheet cakes, was adopted by Ashkenazim for use on the Sabbath, festivals, and Jewish celebrations. A few Jewish bakeries still produce the old-fashioned sponge-spice type and it occasionally makes an appearance at a Sabbath morning Kiddush or various life-cycle events. Chocolate generally supplanted spices in most commercial and homemade Jewish versions, in both airy sponge cakes and dense butter cakes. Jewish homemakers generally concentrated on variations of the marbled butter cake, which was easier to make and sturdier than the sponge types. Marble butter cake was rich enough and interesting enough without the need for frosting, so it was often brought to a shiva call (visit to a house of mourning) or when paying a call to a family after the birth of a baby.

Many Jewish bakeries in the New York area in the 1950s through the 1970s would distinctively add a small amount of almond extract to the chocolate marble cake, creating a version sometimes referred to as a "German marble cake" that had a characteristic almond aroma. A relative of marble cake that was particularly popular in New York Jewish bakeries from the end of World War II through the 1960s was the Wonder Cake, a loaf in which melted semisweet chocolate was drizzled into a yellow cake batter; some of the chocolate was absorbed into the batter and marbleized and some of it firmed into hard streaks. The concept of marbling was eventually applied to cheesecakes as well. Manufacturers even turned out packaged marble cake mix made from matza meal for Passover.

Toward the end of the twentieth century, many people began taking marble cake for granted and it lost some of its appeal. Yet there is still something endearing about this classic cake, the contrast in colors and flavors reflecting a yin and yang in every bite. In 2008, the large Israeli manufacturer Osem noted that the best-selling style of the various cakes it exports to Britain is the marble cake. After all, there is a good reason it has endured for so long.

GERMAN SPICE MARBLE CAKE (*MARMORKUCHEN*)

ONE 9-BY-5-INCH LOAF OR 8-INCH SQUARE CAKE/8 TO
10 SERVINGS   [DAIRY OR PAREVE]

2 cups (7 ounces) sifted cake flour, or 1½ cups all-
purpose flour, sifted after measuring
2 teaspoons double-acting baking powder
½ teaspoon salt
3 tablespoons unsulfured molasses
1 teaspoon ground cinnamon
½ teaspoon ground cloves
½ teaspoon ground nutmeg
½ cup (1 stick) unsalted butter or margarine,
softened
1 cup (7 ounces) sugar
3 large eggs
1½ teaspoons vanilla extract
⅔ cup milk, buttermilk, soy milk, or water

1. Preheat the oven to 350°F. Grease a 9-by-5-inch
loaf pan or 8-inch square baking pan, line the bottom
and sides with parchment paper, grease again, and
dust with flour.

2. Sift together the flour, baking powder, and salt. In
a small bowl, beat together the molasses, cinnamon,
cloves, and nutmeg until smooth. In a large bowl, beat
the butter until smooth, about 30 seconds. Gradually
add the sugar and beat until light and fluffy, about 4
minutes. Add the eggs, one at a time, beating well
after each addition. Add the flour mixture alternately
with the milk (4 portions for the flour, 3 portions for
the milk), beginning and ending with the flour.

3. Transfer about one-third of the batter to a
medium bowl and stir in the molasses mixture until
smooth. Drop alternate spoonfuls of the plain and
molasses batter into the prepared pan, filling it about
two-thirds full. For a swirled effect, briefly run a knife
or skewer through the batters to marbleize.

4. Bake until the cake begins to come away from
the sides of the pan, about 50 to 60 minutes. Let cool
in the pan for 10 minutes, then transfer the cake to
a wire rack and let cool completely. Wrap tightly in
plastic, then foil, and store at room temperature for
up to 4 days or in the freezer for up to 2 months.

VARIATIONS

*Chocolate Marble Cake: Substitute 1 ounce melted and
cooled unsweetened chocolate for the molasses and spices.
Or substitute 5 tablespoons nonalkalized (Dutch-processed)
cocoa powder and, if desired, 1 teaspoon espresso powder
dissolved in ¼ cup boiling water and cooled.*

MAROR

The biblical account of the original Passover meal on
which the Seder is based, directs, "And they shall eat
the meat [lamb or goat] in this night, roast with fire,
and matzas; with *marrorim* [bitter herbs] they shall
eat it." Pointedly, matza is distinguished as a separate
entity in the Seder from the lamb, while *marrorim* is
listed as an adjunct to the meat. Thus, unlike matza,
maror is always implicitly tied to the paschal offering
and, since the destruction of the Temple, its observance has been by dint of rabbinic ordinance.

The key to the accompaniment to the paschal
offering is in its name—it must have a bitter flavor.
The text's usage of the plural form *marrorim* reflects
that more than one item is acceptable for the commandment and that the term does not simply refer
to a single plant called *maror*. The Talmud reveals
that *marrorim* must be a vegetable and enumerated
the characteristic features—any bitter herbage that
possesses *seraf* (white sap) and "has a pale [grayish]

Horehound is believed to be tamcha, *one of the original
types of bitter herbs approved for use as maror at the Passover Seder. More recently, some Ashkenazim have thought
that* tamcha *meant "horseradish".*

green appearance." Only the stalk and leaves, but not the root, are valid for the *maror*. Rabbi David Frankel in his commentary on the Jerusalem Talmud (c. 1743) noted, "If you cut it in a thick place there exudes from it a white liquid like milk; all these are the signs of maror." In addition, all the possibilities for *maror* share a similar pattern—after the winter rains cease in Israel, these plants push upwards from the ground in time for Passover, sporting relatively mild-flavored leaves, which when mature form a hard central stalk as the leaves become tough and more bitter. The Talmud notes, "Why are the Egyptians compared to *maror*? To teach that just as this *maror* is at the first soft but at its end is hard, so too the Egyptians at the beginning were soft but at the end were hard [harsh]." The Talmud also stressed that the bitter herb cannot be pickled or cooked for use at the Seder, but must be raw.

The Mishnah lists five items that, having met the qualifications, could be used use for the bitter herb: "*chazeret, ulshin, tamcha, charchavina,* and *maror.*" The Talmud concludes that the five were listed in order of preference and that *chazeret* was the preferable vegetable.

There is unanimity that *chazeret* refers to lettuce, an annual herb native to the eastern Mediterranean region. Egyptian hieroglyphics reveal that lettuce, then a wild plant, was being consumed at least forty-five hundred years ago. The current version of this vegetable, however, has changed dramatically. Wild lettuce is still occasionally found along the eastern Mediterranean. It has an elongated central stalk and prickly, red-tinged, light green leaves. It is extremely bitter, especially as it matures. The ribs of wild lettuce contain a considerable amount of white latex sap; from this characteristic comes its Latin name, *lactuca* (milky). The plant was finally cultivated around 800 BCE and eventually became more like modern lettuce. It was the Romans who developed the now-common head lettuce and also gradually reduced or entirely bred out much of the crimson color, latex, and bitterness from most varieties. The Moors brought the vegetable to Spain and are credited with developing the modern form of romaine lettuce. Romaine has long been the standard *maror* in many Sephardic homes, a role it has recently gained among an increasing number of Ashkenazim. Iceberg lettuce, bland and pale, was only introduced in 1894 and lacks any of the traditional attributes of *maror*.

Ulshin is either endive or chicory or both, since the two close relatives have long been confused with each other. Considering the kinship and confusion of chicory, endive, and escarole, it is hardly surprising that each is used as *maror* in various Sephardic and Mizrachi households.

Tamcha seems to be a leafy, dull green herb. The leading candidate for *tamcha* (according to Rashi) is horehound—also called white horehound and, in Arabic, *hashishat al kalib*—a plant whose primary usage today is in cough medicine and liqueurs. Horehound has crinkled, wooly, grayish green leaves and contains a latex sap; the leaves are indeed bitter. This identification of *tamcha* generally comes as a surprise to the many contemporary Ashkenazim who currently mistranslate it as horseradish. Horseradish lacks all of the characteristics prescribed by the Talmud.

The fourth item, *charchavina*, seems to be either field eryngo or sea eryngo. Field eryngo is a perennial herb thistle that grows in the dry soils of fields and rocky places around the Mediterranean. The plant bears bitter, toothed, heart-shaped gray-green leaves that, when young, are soft and edible. The smaller sea eryngo, also called sea holly, grows in the maritime areas along the Mediterranean and Atlantic. Sea eryngo has spiny evergreen leaves, shaped like holly leaves, which, when young, are generally eaten boiled, but can be eaten raw.

The fifth plant, *maror*, was the least preferable type. It may be wormwood, a European perennial herb with extremely bitter gray-green leaves. More probably it is sow thistle, called *murar* in Arabic, which bears gray-green spiny leaves with a bitter flavor and, notably, the stems secrete a milky sap.

(See also Charoset, Chicory, Horseradish, Koraik, and Seder)

MASA (SEPHARDIC DOUGH)

Until well into the seventeenth century, most European baking remained rather medieval and was characterized by pies with inedible crusts and very heavy honey cakes made from bread crumbs instead of flour. Sephardim, on the other hand, early on began developing a sophisticated repertoire of cakes and pastries encompassing various *bolas* (Ladino for "balls," spheres of yeast dough), *pan dulce* (sweet breads), *biscochos* (cookies), and egg-foam cakes. At the heart of Sephardic pastries are a variety of doughs, called *masa* in Ladino, that are used to make an array of savory and sweet treats for the Sabbath, every holiday, and most other special occasions. The Spanish expulsion in 1492 spread Iberian culinary refinements to many parts of the Middle East and Europe, including to some Ashkenazim. Masas are used to make crisp, flaky savory pies, such as *pastels, pastelitos, pastidas,* and *tapadas;* turnovers, such as *borekas,* empanadas, and *sambusaks* and pastries, such as *kezasdas* (mini cheese cups).

In a different vein, *masa* or *massa* is the Greek pronunciation of matza.

(See Ajin for Middle Eastern Semolina Dough)

SEPHARDIC OIL PASTRY DOUGH (*MASA ACEITE*)

ABOUT 18 OUNCES; ENOUGH FOR ABOUT THIRTY-TWO
3-INCH TURNOVERS OR ONE LARGE TWO-CRUST PIE [PAREVE]

½ cup vegetable or olive oil
½ cup lukewarm water (80°F to 90°F)
¾ teaspoon salt
About 2½ cups (12.5 ounces) unbleached all-purpose flour

In a medium bowl, combine the oil, water, and salt. Stir in 1 cup of the flour. Gradually stir in enough of the remaining flour to make a soft dough that comes away from the sides of the bowl. Form into a ball, flatten slightly, wrap in plastic wrap, and let rest at room temperature for 30 minutes. Do not refrigerate.

VARIATIONS

Sephardic Cheese Pastry (Masa kon kezo): With the flour, add ⅓ to ½ cup grated kefalotiri, kashkaval, Kasseri, Parmesan, or Swiss cheese. Sephardim use it to make cheese turnovers called borekitas *and other dairy pastries.*

SEPHARDIC OIL-BUTTER PASTRY DOUGH (*MASA FINA*)

ABOUT 18 OUNCES; ENOUGH FOR ABOUT THIRTY-TWO
3-INCH TURNOVERS OR ONE LARGE TWO-CRUST PIE [DAIRY]

½ cup (1 stick) unsalted butter, melted
¼ cup vegetable oil
¼ cup lukewarm water (80°F to 90°F)
2½ teaspoons white vinegar
¾ teaspoon salt
About 2½ cups (12.5 ounces) unbleached all-purpose flour

In a medium bowl, beat together the butter, oil, water, vinegar, and salt. Gradually work in enough flour to make a soft dough that pulls away from the sides of the bowl. Do not overwork the dough. Wrap in plastic wrap and refrigerate for 1 hour.

SEPHARDIC SOUR CREAM PASTRY DOUGH (*OTRA MASA AFRIJALDADA*)

ABOUT 22 OUNCES; ENOUGH FOR ABOUT THIRTY-TWO
3-INCH PASTRY TURNOVERS OR TWO 9-INCH PIE SHELLS [DAIRY]

¾ cup (1½ sticks) unsalted butter, softened
¼ cup sour cream or plain yogurt
1 large egg, lightly beaten
½ teaspoon salt
About 2½ cups (12.5 ounces) unbleached all-purpose flour

In a medium bowl, combine the butter, sour cream, egg, and salt. Gradually stir in enough flour to make a soft dough. Form into a ball, cover with plastic wrap, and let stand in a cool place for at least 1 hour or in the refrigerator for up to 2 days.

MASCONOD

Masconod is a pasta roll filled with Parmesan cheese.
Origin: Italy
Other names: *lasagna alla cannella.*

This ancient Italian Jewish dish shares an obvious similarity to the better-known cannelloni (little channels). The pasta squares are spread with grated Parmesan cheese, then rolled up jelly-roll style and baked. There is both a savory version with pepper and a sweeter one one with sugar and cinnamon. In Italian households, *masconod* is a common festival dish, especially on Sukkot (*le Feste*).

ITALIAN PASTA ROLLS (*MASCONOD*)

6 TO 8 SERVINGS [DAIRY]

1 recipe (1 pound) Egg Noodle Dough (page 368)
2⅔ cups (8 ounces) grated Parmesan cheese
1 teaspoon ground black pepper, or 6 tablespoons sugar and 2 teaspoons ground cinnamon

1. On a lightly floured surface, roll out the dough into a ⅛-inch thickness. Cut into 5-inch squares (about 20). Cover and let dry for about 30 minutes.

2. Bring a large pot of lightly salted water to a rapid boil. In several batches, add the pasta and cook until al dente (tender but still firm), about 5 minutes. Drain, rinse the pasta with cold water, then drain again.

3. Preheat the oven to 350°F. Butter a 9-inch square baking pan.

4. In a medium bowl, combine the Parmesan and pepper (or Parmesan, sugar, and cinnamon). Place the pasta squares on a flat surface. Spread 2 tablespoonfuls of the cheese mixture over the pasta, then roll up jelly-roll style. Place, seam side down, in the prepared dish. Sprinkle with any excess cheese. Alternatively, layer the pasta squares with the Parmesan mixture like lasagna.

5. Bake until golden brown, about 30 minutes.

MASHGIACH

Mashgiach (Hebrew meaning "supervisor") is a person qualified to supervise the production of kosher foods, whether in a factory, restaurant, or store, in accordance with the Jewish dietary laws. A *mashgiach* does not need to be a rabbi or male but, when dealing with meat, must be specially trained. The *rav hamachshir* supervising rabbi) is the head rabbi who supervises a *mashgiach*. Kosher supervision is called *hashgachah* and a guarantee of kashrut given by a *mashgiach* is a *hechsher* (*hechsherim* plural).

(See also Kosher)

MASTIC

Mastic (*aza* in Arabic) is the aromatic resin of a small evergreen member of the pistachio family. The liquid, produced by making small cuts into the bark of the trunk and large branches, dries into a hard, pale yellowish, translucent resin, which softens and turns bright white when chewed. The typical mastic plant yields about ten pounds of resin each summer. Mastic may be the biblical spice *loht*, borne by the caravan taking Joseph to Egypt and later sent by Jacob to the Egyptian prime minister, while the mastic shrub may be the biblical *bakha* (meaning "crying," denoting the pea-sized tearlike drops of resin).

Mastic was once widely valued as a protective dressing for wounds and a material for filling cavities in teeth. Accordingly, the *Tosefta* (early rabbinic rulings omitted from the Mishnah) instructs that on the Sabbath mastic may not be chewed as a medicine, but may be chewed to counter bad breath. In the eastern Mediterranean, mastic is also pulverized into a powdery spice used in small amounts to impart a piney-licorice flavor to sweet baked goods, puddings, jams, liqueurs, and confections (such as the Turkish *rahat locum* and Greek *gliko tou koutaliou*). In modern Hebrew, *mastik* means "chewing gum."

MATBUCHA

Matbucha is a tomato and pepper-based cooked salad.
Origin: Morocco

Other names: Morocco: *matbocha*, *salada matbucha*; Tunisia: *makbuba*, *mecbouba*.

Matbucha means "cooked stuff"; the name is derived from the Arabic infinitive *tabukh* (cook). The ingredients are simmered together to meld the flavors and reduce the liquid, but not long enough to transform it into a smooth sauce. There are numerous versions, but all are based on tomatoes. The most widespread type is made simply with tomatoes, roasted red bell peppers, olive oil, and plenty of garlic. Moroccans always peel the tomatoes and peppers before cooking. Some people add mushrooms, carrots, olives, or onions. Like American salsa, *matbucha* comes in plain, mild, and hot versions; the spiciness is controlled by adding varying amounts of chilies or hot paprika. A similar Maghrebi dish, topped with eggs and frequently without the peppers, is called *shakshouka*. Although some people mistakenly refer to *matbucha* as Turkish salad (*salade Turkiye*), the latter is a fresh tomato and pepper salsa.

In the 1950s, Moroccan immigrants brought this Maghrebi-inspired dish to Israel, where it became one of the predominant foods. *Matbucha* is now available in every Israeli grocery and is a staple in *mezzes* (appetizer assortments) and meals. Many Israeli families always keep some handy in the refrigerator, along with hummus and *baba ghanouj*. Still some Israelis insist on making their own *matbucha*, particularly for special occasions.

Although commonly classified as a "salad," *matbucha* is enjoyed as a dip and bread spread rather than eaten straight. It is usually served as an accompaniment to bread or crackers, but is also used as a filling for miniature tarts and omelets and a topping for potatoes and rice. *Matbucha* is beloved on the Sabbath as well as during the week. The widespread Israeli street food called a "Tunisian sandwich" consists of oil-packed tuna, cooked potatoes, preserved lemon, capers, olives, and *matbucha* on a French bread roll. Today, Israeli-inspired versions of *matbucha* are available in American grocery stores, but the dish has yet to catch on in the United States in the manner of hummus.

MOROCCAN COOKED TOMATO AND PEPPER SALAD (*MATBUCHA*)

ABOUT 7 CUPS [PAREVE]

½ cup olive or vegetable oil
1 tablespoon minced garlic

5 pounds (about 20) ripe plum tomatoes, peeled, seeded, and chopped

About ½ teaspoon table salt or 1 teaspoon kosher salt

2½ pounds (5 to 6 large) red or green bell peppers, roasted, peeled, seeded, and cut into thin strips or coarsely chopped

2 to 3 small red or green chilies, seeded and minced, or 1 tablespoon sweet or hot paprika

1. In a large pot, heat the oil over medium heat. Add the garlic and sauté until softened, about 2 minutes. Add the tomatoes and salt and cook, stirring occasionally, until the tomatoes begin to break down, about 5 minutes.

2. Add the bell peppers and chilies. Cook, stirring frequently to prevent burning, until most of the liquid has evaporated, about 1 hour. Serve warm or at room temperature. Store in the refrigerator for up to 2 weeks.

MATZA

Matza (also commonly spelled matzah, matzo, and matzoh), an unleavened bread, is one of the three biblical culinary components of the Passover Seder, along with *pesach* (the paschal offering) and *maror* (bitter herb); it is also the only type of bread eaten throughout the festival. Indeed, the biblical name for the seven-day spring celebration of the redemption from Egypt is actually *Chag ha-Matzot* (Holiday of the Matzas), not Passover; the word Passover originally pertained only to the paschal offering made on the afternoon before Passover and the Seder. The last shared act that every Israelite performed before being freed from slavery in Egypt, as well as the very first act that the entire nation shared as free people at their first stop, was eating matza.

The word matza is derived from the root *mootz* (to press/squeeze). Thus the literal meaning of matza is "pressed bread," and is analogous to the English term flatbread. Matza was actually a rather standard loaf of the ancient Middle East and had been prepared by nomads since time immemorial. The word was first recorded in English in the *Jewish Manual* (London, 1846), in which it was spelled matso (probably from the Hebrew plural form, *matzot*).

What differentiates flatbreads eaten or owned during Passover from those consumed during the rest of the year was not thickness or richness but the mandate for a complete absence of any *chametz* or *se'or* (starter dough) in the loaves. To qualify as matza for the Seder, the loaf must contain no ingredients other than flour and water, and it must be mixed, formed, and baked within a prescribed eighteen-minute period.

Throughout most of history, the making of bread, including matza, was women's work. It was customary for each household to bake their own matza. Typically, this task was performed in groups of two or three women: one to mix and knead, and one or two to add the water, roll or spread the dough, and bake.

The Bible directs, *"u'shemartem* [and you shall guard] the matzas, for on this day I took you out of Egypt," denoting the necessity of supervising and preparing the grain used for matza so that it does not become *chametz*. There are two types of flour for matza: flour from grain that is guarded from the time of harvesting (*shemirah mishaat ketzirah*), yielding *shemurah matza* (guarded matza); and flour that is guarded from the time of milling (*shemirah m'techinah v'ailakh*), yielding *matza peshutah* (regular matza). In addition, there exists a secondary objective to the biblical directive: ensuring that the making of the matza be for the sake of the commandment. Thus, at the beginning of each of the eleven steps of the matza-making process, from harvesting the wheat to placing the matza in the oven, the person involved must declare, *"l'shem matza mitzvah"* (in the name of the commandment of matza).

The wheat for matza is harvested in the early afternoon of a sunny day, after the moisture level in the kernels has decreased to less than 13 percent. After threshing, the kernels are stored in bins and watched over until ready for grinding into flour, around Hanukkah. Milling takes place in thoroughly cleaned and supervised mills. The kernels are not rinsed with water, but kept dry. Split and sprouted kernels, signs of the presence of external moisture, are rejected. The bran and germ are generally removed before milling, yielding a finer flour with a longer shelf life. Some authorities favor white flour, considering it of higher quality, while others insist whole wheat is preferable, since there is less processing and, therefore, less chance of heat affecting the kernels. Matza flour is never bleached or chemically treated. After milling, the matza flour is sacked and stored in a cool, dry place and kept away from heat and moisture.

Although matza is arguably the best-known biblical food, it is today perhaps the least understood; it is equated by most Westerners with a thin, unleavened, cracker-like product that is frequently square. This, however, was not the original bread. For most of its history, matza was relatively thick, dense, and soft—akin to a firm pita bread—and, like most free-form flatbreads, round. Matza does not even have to be thin, as the Talmud and Sephardic authorities allow matza for Passover to be up to the thickness of a *tefach* ("handbreadth," from three to four inches), the size of the *lechem ha'panim* (showbread), an unleavened bread of the Temple. Cracker-like matza was actually a relatively late development, emerging perhaps around the fifteenth century in Ashkenazic communities. The original style of soft matza is still made by many Mizrachi and some Sephardim. Similarly, Ethiopian Jews make a soft matza called *kita* for *Fassikah* (Passover). Sephardim call thick matzas by the name *boyos* (from the Spanish *bollo*, meaning "bun/small cake") and thinner ones *maniuo*; the latter were generally used for cooking.

A softer, more pliable form of matza sheds a different light on several aspects of Seder rituals. Soft matza explains the name and nature of the *koraik* (wrap), the "Hillel sandwich." Soft matza accounts for the kabbalistic custom of placing the heavy Seder plate directly on top of the matzas, for the soft ones could absorb the weight, while brittle, hard loaves would crack or shatter.

Soft matzas do have one major drawback—they tend to become stale rather quickly. Accordingly, they were generally made fresh on a daily basis throughout the festival, except for the Sabbath. Hence the *Arukh Hashulchan* recounts, "In previous times, matzas were not baked before Passover, but instead they would bake on each day of Passover bread for that day." Even today, many Yemenites prepare fresh matzas regularly throughout the holiday, preferring it warm as well as soft.

To avoid even the possibility of creating *chametz* on Passover, during the medieval period, Ashkenazim developed the stringent practice of baking their matza only before the onset of and never during the festival. In addition, in order to make a bread with less capacity to puff up, Ashkenazim reduced the amount of water in the dough to the bare minimum, resulting in an extraordinarily firm dough that was extremely difficult to knead and roll. Consequently, mixing the matza dough and baking the loaves shifted from a female activity to a male; women generally did continue to roll out the individual matzas. These modifications were not acceptable in many non-Ashkenazic communities.

Sephardim living in areas dominated by Ashkenazim were forced by necessity or persuaded to use hard matza. However, many have recently begun returning to the traditional soft style of matza at the Seder. Sephardic frozen soft matzas are widely available in America on the Internet. In Israel, Bukharans and other groups now sell in their markets frozen soft matza prepared before Passover. Consequently, Yemenites, many Sephardim, Italians, and various Mizrachi communities insist on retaining the traditional soft matza.

Hand Matza

By the onset of the eighteenth century, as an increasing number of Jews began living in the large urban centers of Europe, and as many became incapable of making their own matza, the concept of the commercial matza bakery emerged. These bakeries sold their wares to the masses and allowed rabbis and yeshiva students to come and make their own. Because Ashkenazim substituted the hard cracker-like matza for the original soft type, the incredibly firm dough, as well as the strenuous nature of loading and removing the loaves from commercial ovens, required more muscle power. To speed up production and avoid *chametz*, production lines consisting of teams became prevalent. In a process totaling no more than eighteen minutes, the matza dough was mixed, divided, rolled very thin, perforated all over, and baked in an extremely hot oven until dry and very crisp. In the nineteenth century, with the advent of matzas made by machines, the old-fashioned type became known as hand matzas.

Eventually, every Jewish community throughout Europe, large and small, maintained its own commercial matza bakery, many operating six days a week and commonly eighteen hours a day, starting around Hanukkah; these bakeries thus provided workers with months of temporary employment in the period leading up to Passover. A hand matza bakery is an assembly line; traditionally, the workers are efficiently separated into very distinct roles, with most of the labor being performed by men. Illustrations from the mid-1500s depict one man working the dough using a large wooden oar-like paddle, assisted by a second man pushing the dough toward the center of a small table.

Hand matza bakeries only use matza from grain guarded from the time of harvesting. Most machine matza companies use flour guarded from the time of milling, although some, especially in Israel, also only use flour from grain that was guarded from the time of harvesting.

Today, there are hand matza facilities in Israel and the New York metropolitan area. In a modern hand matza bakery, first a large, smooth metal (preferably aluminum) bowl is placed on a stand; frequently there are six bowls used in rotation for six batches in an eighteen-minute session. The task of ensuring that the bowl is immaculately clean and dry is entrusted only to extremely diligent individuals. On cue, the *mehl mester* ("flour master" in Yiddish), secluded in another room or a closed booth, measures the precise amount of flour, scurries to the bowl, dumps in the flour, and retreats to his isolation (or closes his window), all to ensure that no water comes in contact with himself or the flour until the desired time. The maximum amount of wheat flour for one batch of hand matza is the biblical measurement *issaron*; this equals 43⅓ eggs or approximately 9⅛ cups or 2 pounds 11 ounces.

With the flour safely in the metal bowl, the *vassergiesser* (water "boy") then emerges from his own separate room or booth, carefully pours in a measured amount of cool well water (from rain or surface water, not the tap), and returns to his space. Since dough reacts best and more quickly in a warm environment, the Sages strove to keep the matza dough as cool as possible to hinder the formation of *chametz*. The room in which the dough is kneaded must be kept cool and the dough and its ingredients must be kept away from the ovens and direct sunlight. In case the well water or outside temperature is too warm, water used to make matza dough must be held in a vessel in a cool place overnight or for at least twelve hours; this water is called *mayim shelanu* (water that has stayed). Letting the water stand probably also helps to keep out sediments and minerals that could affect the dough. Most machine matza factories use water from reservoirs, not wells.

As soon as the water comes into contact with the flour, the *kneter* (kneader), making sure his hands are initially dry, combines the two ingredients and presses the mixture to form a stiff ball of dough; this

procedure is typically completed in about thirty seconds. An efficient mixer can prepare up to six batches in an eighteen-minute session. An assistant moves the bowl to a long brown paper–lined or aluminum table, quickly pinches off appropriate-sized pieces of dough (*teiglach*), no larger than the palm of a hand, and tosses them to the awaiting *orten* (rollers), generally women. Each batch yields ten balls. The rollers quickly knead the dough pieces, never allowing them to rest, even momentarily, until they are of a uniform consistency; this step takes less than a minute. Without stopping, the dough is efficiently flattened, using long wooden or, increasingly today, metal rolling pins without handles into thin rounds; the most common size is about ten inches in diameter. Upon finishing, the roller typically shouts "matza, matza," informing others of the dough's status, then taps the table with a roller to request the next piece of dough.

The dough for making hard matzas, although very firm, contains water, which expands upon contact with sufficient heat in the form of bubbles. Because the air in a large globule can insulate the dough at the bottom of the bubble, the dough can potentially dry rather than cook during the very short baking time, resulting in chametz. A bubble in a baked matza larger than a hazelnut in the shell is unacceptable (*matza nefucha*). Therefore, after rolling out the very dry dough, it is perforated all over to prevent bubbles. Various medieval etchings and manuscripts reveal matza bakers in the fifteenth century poking the holes one at a time using a spike. Today, the *derlanger* (kicker) drapes five dough rounds on a twelve-foot wooden pole and spreads them on a table, where workers rapidly perforate the rounds all over with a *reddeler* (sharp-toothed metal docker).

The *derlanger* then arranges the perforated disks on the pole and hands it to the *schieber* (slider), sometimes called the *zetser* (setter), who quickly inspects each loaf and hurries to the adjoining room containing an extremely hot wood-burning oven set at about 1000°F. He deftly rolls the disks flat on the floor of the oven, an operation requiring much coordination and practice to prefect. Matzas are fully baked within fifteen to twenty seconds, whereupon the *schieber* removes the charred disks using a long-handled peel and transfers them to a cooling table, sometimes cooled by fans, where they will be sorted. The *treger* (carrier/porter) moves the matzas to the packing area. Any matza that is too thick, is swollen (*nefuchot*), or has folded over (*kefulot*) in the oven is rejected as *chametz*.

At the end of eighteen minutes, the *baker* (head baker) halts the proceedings. Any unbaked dough is disposed of and all the equipment, and hands and fingernails, are meticulously cleaned and inspected. New brown butcher paper is laid over the wooden tables or, if metal, the tables are cleaned anew. The metal *reddeler* and bowls are also cleaned to perfection. The wooden poles are either covered with fresh baking paper or scoured, like the rollers, commonly with sandpaper. The entire procedure is then repeated. The Bible describes matza as *lechem oni*, which the Talmud explains connotes "poor man's" bread; ironically hand matza has become quite expensive to purchase.

Machine Matza

In the wake of the Industrial Revolution, the venerable process of hand baking would face competition, as machines were developed to facilitate matza making. In 1838, Isaac Singer, an Alsatian Jew from Ribeauville, created a machine to roll out matza dough, although the kneading and perforating were still performed by hand. The device consisted of two parallel cylindrical metal drums that were manually rotated by a wheel. The dough was pressed between the drums and flowed out in sheets onto a long table, where workers cut out dough rounds using sharp metal rings, then perforated the dough. The entire process, from mixing to baked matza, took about two minutes. Initially, this modernization inspired little objection and, instead, received letters of approval from the rabbis of France and renowned sages of central Europe. Within a few years, these machines spread throughout much of western and central Europe.

Machines led to an unprecedented physical change—the square matza. Initially, the machine matzas, like the handmade type, were round; when they were cut out, the corners were removed. These edges, for economic reasons, were rerolled and cut, threatening the eighteen-minute time frame. To eliminate trimmings, saving time and money, machine matza makers early on opted for cutting the dough sheets into contiguous squares, altering the traditional shape. In addition to altering the shape, the machine eventually transformed Ashkenazic hard matza from a product generally eaten exclusively during the festival of Passover to a widely available and inexpensive item enjoyed year-round by non-Jews as well as Jews.

In due course, a group of businessmen in Kraków, Poland, announced plans to import the first matza-rolling machine in the area, a proposal met with heated resistance in some circles. One of the primary points of contention was the loss of jobs by the poor women and widows who relied on the yearly work of dough rolling, no small matter in the impoverished and restrictive climate of eastern Europe. The majority of Polish and Ukrainian rabbis, especially Chasidim, followed suit, denouncing the machines. Most rejections were issued on principle by people who had never actually set eyes on a matza machine and did not understand how they worked. In general, Lithuanian rabbis were much less critical of the new technology than their Chasidic brethren.

Unlike the detractors, those who viewed these machines in operation recognized that dough would not stick to the smooth metal drums. Others considered mass production preferable to making matza by hand, as it eliminated the possibility of errors being made by amateur workers, particularly with the contemporary firm, dry dough that was difficult for even the strongest people to knead.

The first matza-rolling machine in Israel arrived in 1863 in Jerusalem, where it generally found acceptance among the non-Chasidim, but, as in Europe, was vehemently denounced by Chasidim. After 1948, several automated matza factories sprung up in Israel, following the example of American firms. In 2010, Israeli machine matza, totaling more than nine million dollars in sales, was exported to forty countries; the United States constituted 52 percent of the total Israeli matza exports.

Large commercial handmade matza bakeries were never established in nineteenth-century America and mass immigration of Chasidim only occurred following World War II. Consequently, machine matza factories found acceptance more easily in the New World.

In 1886, Rabbi Abramson (d. 1914) from the Lithuanian town of Salant purchased the passport of a dead man to escape from Germany or to avoid being drafted into the Russian army for twenty years. The name on the document was Dov Behr Manischewitz. Using his new name, Manischewitz immigrated to Cincinnati, Ohio, and subsequently served as a ritual slaughterer and peddler. Two years later, because matzas were difficult to obtain in his new hometown, Manische-witz started a small matza bakery in his basement for

MATZA BREI ❧ 397

family and friends. Demand grew, as matzas became particularly popular for their keeping ability with pioneers heading west by wagons and Cincinnati was the starting point for many pioneers. By 1900, he opened a large factory and revolutionized the business by switching from coal to gas ovens, allowing for better control. Instead of merely using machines to roll out the dough, Manischewitz established a fully automated factory with machines also mixing, perforating, and cutting, and introducing a patented belt to transfer the dough through the oven. The company built a new oven, at the time the largest on earth. Machine matza is baked at around 900°F for about one minute and twenty seconds. In order to prevent the dough from coming into contact with heat before entering the oven, the machines were insulated, an innovation welcomed by the workers. The factory was soon turning out seventy-five thousand pounds of matza daily, the vast majority of which was purchased by non-Jews heading west.

Through aggressive marketing and advertising, Manischewitz transformed the matza bearing his name from a local product to a high-volume commodity shipped throughout the country as well as to many other parts of the world. The company's introduction and marketing of packaged matza meal also revolutionized the culinary world, transforming the matza ball from a dish eaten solely on Passover to a food enjoyed year-round. In the 1940s, Manischewitz, which had been a public company since 1923, expanded its line to include crackers, soups, and other products. Today, Manischewitz, after acquiring several rival companies, produces more than half the matza consumed in America on Passover.

A few other American machine matza factories followed, most located in the New York metropolitan area and catering to the stricter demands of eastern Europeans arriving after World War I. Around 1890, Aron Streit (d. 1937), a hand matza baker, and his wife, Nettie, emigrated from their native Austria, ending up on the Lower East Side of Manhattan. In 1916, Streit and his partner, Rabbi Weinberger, opened a hand matza bakery on Pitt Street. Then in 1925, Streit, along with his oldest son, Irving, opened a modern machine matza factory on the corner of Rivington and Stanton streets. As the company expanded, Streit's purchased the three adjoining buildings and began to sell its products nationwide. Streit's, which is still owned and operated by Aron's descendents, remains in the same location, as the last of the Lower East Side matza bakeries. Unlike many other machine matza bakeries, Streit's, which now holds about 40 percent of the American matza market, only produces matza in eighteen-minute runs, with rabbis checking the timing with stopwatches. By 2005, however, the company did offer some unorthodox flavors, including sun-dried tomatoes and garlic matza and olive oil matza.

Besides serving as bread, matzas—whole, crumbled, and ground—are used during Passover to create various dishes. Whole and crumbled matzas are typically first softened in liquid, then added to a dish. Crumbled matzas, also called matza farfel, are added to *fritadas*, kugels, stuffings, pancakes, *matza brei*, confections, and even custard. Hard matza is ground to produce matza meal and finely ground for matza cake meal, and these products are the basis of many Passover dumplings and baked goods. Since matza meal has an intriguing nutty flavor, it is often used for binding and breading throughout the year, as well as on Passover.

(See also Bread, Chametz, Chremsel, Farfel, Gebrochts, Knaidel, Kugel, Leche, Mina, and Seor)

MATZA BREI

Matza brei is a dish of soaked pieces of matza mixed with beaten eggs and fried as a pancake or omelet.
Origin: North America
Other names: Hebrew: *matza metugehnet*; Yiddish: *bubbeleh, matza breit, matza pletzl*.

Soaked whole matza fried in butter or schmaltz is a venerable Jewish dish and was included, without the addition of eggs, in the first English-language cookbook, *The Jewish Manual* (London, 1846), as "Fried Matsos."

Ashkenazim, however, generally add another touch, eggs. *Aunt Babette's* (Cincinatti, 1889), in a recipe entitled "Ueberschlagene Matzos or Matzos Dipped in Eggs," called for coating the soaked whole matzas in beaten eggs before frying. The first edition of *The Settlement Cook Book* (Milwaukee, 1901) contained a recipe for "Matzos Pancakes." The recipe directed, "Beat eggs very light, add salt. Heat the fat in a spider [a skillet with feet]. Break matzos into large, equal pieces. Dip each piece in the egg mixture and fry a light brown on both sides. Serve hot, sprinkled with sugar, cinnamon and a little grated lemon rind."

Shortly thereafter, Eastern European Jews in America began to bind crumbled and soaked matza with eggs and fry the mixture in a skillet, which was named *matza brei* (Yiddish meaning "matza pulp/mash"). *Matza brei*, a cross between a pancake and an omelet, is a relatively late innovation, developed from square machine matza. The automated production of matza not only led to greatly reduced prices and increased availability, making dishes like *matza brei* more practical and economical, but also resulted in a slightly thicker and flakier matza than that made by hand. Hand matza, or even machine egg matza, does not yield the same result in *matza brei* as plain machine matza.

Over the years, this dish has provided many an Ashkenazic Passover breakfast and, sometimes, also lunch and dinner. In many families, the husband, who otherwise rarely set foot in the kitchen, somehow became responsible for churning out skillets of *matza brei* for his hungry brood. Some people tire of *matza brei* after a few days and seek alternatives, while others enjoy it for a week straight and beyond. *Matza brei* can now be found on the menu of some delis and even Jewish cafeterias at American universities even when it is not Passover—it is another Jewish comfort food.

There is, to put it mildly, no set recipe for *matza brei*. It can be dry or moist depending on the soaking time and amount of eggs. Some stir it in the pan like scrambled eggs for a fluffier texture; others fry it undisturbed as a pancake for a firmer texture and a contrasting crisp exterior. Much disagreement persists over which style of matza brei is superior. It may be prepared as one large pancake or numerous smaller ones. Cooks have developed many variations of the basic *matza brei* recipe, adding milk, sweeteners, cheese, lox, onions, sliced mushrooms, fruit, and other ingredients. Although *matza brei* purists feel that these variations smack of heresy, nonconformists enjoy the diversity. *Matza brei* is frequently accompanied with jam, honey, cinnamon-sugar, applesauce, sour cream, or yogurt.

ASHKENAZIC FRIED MATZA WITH EGG (*MATZA BREI*)

3 TO 4 SERVINGS [DAIRY, PAREVE, OR MEAT]

3 to 4 large eggs, lightly beaten

4 (6-inch square) matzas

About ¼ teaspoon table salt or ½ teaspoon kosher salt

Ground black pepper to taste

3 tablespoons butter, margarine, or schmaltz (not oil)

1. Place the eggs in a large bowl. One at a time, move the matza under cold running water until softened but not mushy, about 1 minute. Drain the matza and crumble it into coarse pieces, dropping the pieces into the eggs. Alternatively, crumble the hard matza in a colander, pour 3 cups boiling water over the top, squeeze out the excess moisture, and add to the eggs. Season with the salt and pepper.

2. In a large skillet, melt the butter over medium heat. Add the matza mixture and fry, pressing down the center occasionally and turning once, until golden on both sides, about 5 minutes per side. Some people leave the matza brei whole, while others cut it into quarters for easier turning and serving. For scrambled *matza brei*, stir the mixture constantly while frying. To make matza brei pancakes, fry the mixture by heaping tablespoonfuls. Serve warm.

MCHADI

Mchadi is a dense, unleavened skillet corn cake.
Origin: Georgia

The Ottoman Turks introduced corn to Georgia in the seventeenth century and the grain had an overwhelming effect on the western part of the country. Georgia's hot and humid climate proved ideal for growing the American grain, so cornmeal became inexpensive and accessible. While Georgians from the east of the country continued to rely on wheat flatbreads, those in the west came to prefer cornmeal, in the form of porridges and pancakes.

Dense, unleavened skillet corn cakes, known as *mchadi*, were more versatile and much easier to make than porridge, so they became a regular sight at most meals. These pareve, unleavened cornmeal pancakes are crisp on the outside and soft on the inside like American johnnycakes and hoecakes. However, unlike American johnnycakes, which are made from a relatively thin batter poured onto a hot flat surface, *mchadi* are thick, made from coarse cornmeal, and formed by hand. *Mchadi* are generally made with white cornmeal, but yellow is acceptable. *Mchadi* are traditionally cooked on an earthenware plate (*ketsi*) set over hot coals in a fireplace, but a cast-iron skillet on a stove makes a handy substitute, although the flavor will be slightly different.

Mchadi are intended to be firm and relatively dry,

not light and fluffy; their texture allows them to serve as a base for other foods and to sop up liquids. The relatively bland corn cakes perfectly complement spicy foods and are served as an accompaniment to a large variety of dishes, including meat stews and boiled red beans. At dairy meals, *mchadi* are commonly topped with cheese and, sometimes, tomato slices.

(See also Corn/Cornmeal and Mamaliga)

GEORGIAN CORN CAKES (*MCHADI*)

4 MEDIUM OR 8 SMALL CORN CAKES   [PAREVE]

2 cups (9.5 ounces) coarse-grind cornmeal, preferably stone-ground

About ½ teaspoon table salt or 1 teaspoon kosher salt

About 1½ cups water

Vegetable oil for frying (optional)

1. In a large bowl, combine the cornmeal and salt. Gradually stir in enough water to form a firm but pliable batter. Let stand at room temperature for 30 minutes, adding a little more water if necessary. With moistened hands, divide the batter in fourths or eighths and shape into ½-inch-thick ovals.

2. Heat a large, heavy skillet over low heat. If using a seasoned skillet, such as a cast-iron one, no oil is necessary; otherwise add a thin layer of oil to prevent sticking. Place the ovals in the skillet, cover, and cook until golden brown and crusty on the bottom, 5 to 8 minutes. Turn, cover, and cook until golden brown, 8 to 10 minutes. Serve warm.

MECHOUIYA

Mechouiya is a salad or mixture of grilled vegetables, most often including eggplant, peppers, and tomatoes.

Origin: Maghreb

Other names: Arabic: *salata mechouiya, salata mishweeye, shlata filfel*; French: *salade de poivrons grilles.*

Mechouiya means "roasted" or "grilled" in Arabic, as all the vegetable components of this dish are grilled, imparting a smoky flavor and caramelizing the sugars. The dish originated in the Maghreb and is particularly popular in Tunisia, where *mechouiya* is frequently featured at lunch and dinner, garnished with quartered hard-boiled eggs. For a spread, it is mashed and sprinkled with capers. Sephardim also mix it with yogurt for a breakfast dish.

Although the practice of grilling vegetables in the Maghreb dates back thousands of years, all the major ingredients of *mechouiya* are imports—eggplants from India, bell peppers and tomatoes from South America, and garlic from western Asia. A combination of bell peppers and chilies creates an interesting contrast of sweet and pungent.

MELAVEH MALKAH

The Talmud states, "A person should always set his table following the Sabbath." It became customary following the Havdalah ceremony on Saturday evening to enjoy a light repast.

The Sabbath is metaphorically viewed as a queen. A party and meal following the Sabbath was a symbolic way to escort the queen and, in the process, prolong the special feelings of the day. Kabbalists, in particular Isaac Luria, promoted the idea of the Melaveh Malkah as an extension of the Sabbath. This meal is called a Melaveh Malkah (literally "escorting the queen") by Ashkenazim and noche de Alhad (night of Sunday) by Sephardim.

Another source was attached to King David, the ancestor of the messiah. As tradition holds that the messiah will not arrive on the Sabbath, Jews were inspired that he might arrive at days end. King David requested that God tell him the exact date on which he would die, and he was informed on the Sabbath. Subsequently, every Saturday evening following nightfall, he would acknowledge his survival for another week by holding a meal for the members of his household. Consequently, some communities, especially Moroccans, call their Saturday evening meal *Seudat David Hamelek* (Feast of King David).

Whatever the name, cold dishes prepared before the Sabbath and leftovers from the *desayuno* (brunch), often dairy, are integral parts of the event.

MELAWAH

Melawah is a flaky skillet flatbread.

Origin: Yemen

Other names: *malawah, melawach, miloach, tawa.*

The Yemenite *ajin* (dough), a rudimentary form of puff pastry made from white flour and butter (which are atypical in the traditional Yemenite diet), can be transformed into an array of beloved pastries, including *melawah*, a flatbread cooked in a hot skillet.

In Yemen, *melawah* was reserved for special occasions, including Sabbath dinner and lunch, and meals to break a fast. Today among Yemenites, *melawah* are a sign of fine eating and are present at any Yemenite celebration meal. In Israel, *melawah* grew more common, initially as a breakfast bread. The flavor and texture are captivating. *Melawah* are best fresh and hot from the skillet—the golden and crispy exterior contrasts with the spirals of soft, flaky interior. Pareve versions in which the traditional clarified butter is replaced with margarine have become common. Traditional *melawah* have a slightly salty flavor, but in Israel they tend to be slightly sweet (and sometimes very sweet) due to the addition of untraditional sugar.

Melawah are generally accompanied with *s'chug* (chili paste), *hilbeh* (fenugreek relish), *rotav ahgvani-yot* (fresh tomato puree), and hard-boiled eggs. Israelis began serving it topped with a spicy tomato puree, in a manner similar to pizza, and introduced versions sprinkled with za'atar and oil, sautéed mushrooms, and even ground beef. In Israel, *melawah* are also served for dessert, a practice unknown in Yemen; dessert *melawah* are drizzled with a little honey and sometimes also sprinkled with cinnamon and walnuts.

Yemenites popularized melawah in Israel and, more recently, America. In Israel, the uncooked breads can be found frozen in every grocery, large and small. Today in America, commercial imports from Israel now appear in many markets catering to Jews and in restaurants offering Middle Eastern fare.

(See also Ajin Taimani and Jachnun)

⚜ YEMENITE FLAKY BREAD (*MELAWAH*)

MAKES 6 FLATBREADS [DAIRY OR PAREVE]

1 recipe Yemenite Flaky Pastry (page 8)

1. Divide the pastry dough into 6 pieces. On a lightly floured surface, roll out into 8-inch squares. Roll up the dough jelly-roll style into tight cylinders. Place the cylinders, spiral side up, on a lightly greased or oiled surface and flatten into 1-inch thick rounds. Cover with plastic wrap and refrigerate for at least 4 hours or up to 3 days. If very hard, let stand at room temperature until pliable but not soft, about 20 minutes.

2. Place the pastry disks on a lightly greased or oiled surface and with lightly oiled hands press each into a ⅛- to ¼-inch-thick round, about 7 inches in diameter and no bigger than your skillet. At this point, the *melawah* can be placed between sheets of wax paper and frozen for up to 3 months, then thawed before cooking.

3. Heat a large cast-iron or heavy nonstick skillet over medium-high heat. Place a dough round into the skillet and cook for 30 seconds. Reduce the heat to medium-low and cook until the bottom is golden brown, about 3 minutes. Turn and cook until golden, about 5 minutes. If the *melawah* threatens to burn before the interior cooks, remove from the skillet and place in a 375°F oven for a few minutes until cooked through. Serve warm or at room temperature.

MELICHA

Melicha ("salting" in Hebrew) refers to the practice of salting freshly slaughtered raw meat and poultry to extract the blood.

(See also Kosher)

MELOKHIA

Melokhia is an ancient green and a gelatinous soup made from it.

Origin: Egypt

Other names: *milookhiyya, miloukhia, molokhia, mulukhiya, mulukiya.*

Jew's mallow, also known as *tossa jute, nalta jute,* and bush okra, is grown worldwide primarily for the fibers in its stems, which are used to make burlap; the plant is second only to cotton as the most important natural fiber. Its leaves have long been considered a medicinal vegetable and are used to treat aches, fever, and dysentery. In northeastern Africa and the Levant, the leaves are also used to make a venerable gelatinous Egyptian peasant soup known by the Arabic name of the plant, *melokhia*, probably a cognate of the Hebrew *meluach* (salty).

The ancient plant, still grown from North Africa to India, was pictured on the walls of pyramids and may be the *meluach* mentioned in the Book of Job. It is not inconceivable that three millennia ago the Hebrew slaves subsisted off of *melokhia* soup as did the peasants of medieval Egypt, except for a period around 1000 CE when it was banned for absurd political reasons. Historically, *melokhia* (as well as other green vegetables) was particularly popular with Egyptian Jews; accordingly, a common name for this plant is Jew's mallow.

Melokhia soup remains a staple of the Egyptian masses. It is considered, along with *ful medames* (stewed dried fava beans), the Egyptian national dish and the ultimate comfort food. The soup, however, is considered a *baladi* (home-style dish) and, therefore, rarely found on the menus of restaurants or at fancy parties. It is an acquired taste for most non-Egyptians. The dark green leaves, which resemble those of the common mallow, have a mild earthy flavor and viscous nature; when cooked, they produce a soup akin to the gumbo of the American South. Despite the name and appearance, *melokhia* should not be confused with plain mallow leaves, known as malva (*hubeza/khobeiza* in Arabic and *chalamit* in Hebrew), which are also used in peasant cooking. Fresh *melokhia* leaves are harvested after they reach slightly more than two inches in length and are used throughout the summer; dried or frozen leaves (the latter come cleaned and chopped) are served during the winter and spring. The leaves have to be carefully plucked from the stalk so as not to release the substance at the pithy joint responsible for its distinctive mucilaginous quality. The fresh leaves are generally very finely chopped or thinly julienned using a *makhrata* (a curved half-moon blade with two handles).

The *melokhia's* characteristic mucilaginous quality is much beloved in Egypt. In the Levant, on the other hand, this gooiness is not appreciated, and most cooks prepare a more brothy soup. A distinctive flavoring of the bright green soup is *ta'liya*—a mixture of fried garlic (and plenty of it), coriander, and salt, which is commonly prepared using three to four teaspoons of coriander per thirty cloves of garlic. Most Egyptians contend that too little garlic ruins the soup. Other common seasonings include cumin or cardamom and fresh lemon juice. When made from chicken or duck broth, a piece of poultry is frequently added to each soup bowl. *Melokhia* is typically served over white rice.

❦ EGYPTIAN GREEN MALLOW SOUP (*MELOKHIA*)

6 TO 8 SERVINGS [MEAT OR PAREVE]

  8 cups chicken, duck, beef, or vegetable broth
  Ground black pepper to taste
  2 bay leaves
  1 whole small fresh chili or pinch of cayenne
    (optional)
  2 pounds fresh melokhia, washed, stemmed, and
    finely chopped or thinly julienned; 2 pounds
    frozen chopped melokhia; or 1½ cups (1 pound)
    ground dried melokhia
  10 to 18 cloves garlic, minced

  About 1 tablespoon ground coriander
  About 1 teaspoon table salt or 2 teaspoons kosher
    salt
  3 tablespoons vegetable oil
  Juice of 2 to 3 lemons

1. In a large pot, bring the broth, pepper, bay leaves, and, if using, chili to a boil over medium-high heat. Add the melokhia, return to a boil, reduce the heat to medium-low, and simmer until thickened, about 5 minutes, or 15 minutes if frozen.

2. Meanwhile, mash the garlic, coriander, and salt into a paste. In a large skillet, heat the oil over medium heat. Add the garlic mixture and sauté until fragrant and golden, about 2 minutes.

3. Stir the garlic mixture into the broth, then spoon a cup of soup into the skillet to absorb any remaining garlic. Return the contents of the skillet to the soup pot and simmer for 2 minutes. Do not overcook or the melokhia will lose its buoyancy and sink to the bottom of the pot.

4. Add the lemon juice. Serve immediately.

MELON

According to the Bible, shortly after leaving Egypt, the Israelites yearned for five common Egyptian vegetables, all members of two families. They said, "We remember the fish that we did eat in Egypt for free; the *kishuim* [chate melons] and the *avatichim* [watermelons] and the leeks and the onions and the garlic."

There were two basic groups of melons in the ancient world: watermelons and muskmelons/net melons. The muskmelon (*melafefon* in Talmudic Hebrew), a close relative of the chate melon, has a thin sandy-colored rind, usually with a web netting, and a flesh ranging from pale to bright orange. Archeological evidence that muskmelons were already being cultivated in Sumeria more than three thousand years ago reflects a very early domestication for both types of melon. However, references to *melopepo*, as well as a lack of interest in them by Romans, connote that they at best had a mild sweetness at maturity. Modern sweet net melons appear to have emerged in the early fourteenth century, perhaps in Persia or the Levant, and were only introduced to Europe in the late fifteenth century.

The cantaloupe (*dinkeh* in Yiddish and *maylon matok* in Modern Hebrew), named for Cantalupo, a papal villa near Rome, is the most popular net melon. Most American net melons called cantaloupes are actually muskmelons, which are larger, paler, and sweeter than cantaloupes. Persian melons are larger but less sweet than cantaloupes. Galia, named after the daughter of its Israeli developer, is a net melon with a light green flesh. Another Israeli melon is Ogen, named for the kibbutz in Israel where they were first grown.

Throughout the literature and culture of the ancient Middle East, melons, due to their seeds and shape, had symbolic associations with sexuality and fertility. Melons are still considered an aphrodisiac in many areas. Cucurbits remain traditional Rosh Hashanah fare, the seeds a symbol of fertility.

(See also Cucumber and Watermelon)

ME'ORAV YERUSHALMI

Me'orav yerushalmi is an assortment of grilled skewered offal and some chunks of meat.

Origin: Jerusalem
Other names: Jerusalem mix, mixed grill.

Chunks of meat grilled on skewers have been popular fare in the Middle East for many generations. In the early twentieth century, Middle Eastern Jews in Israel opened small eateries throughout the country, often nothing more than an improvised *mangal* (grill) and a table or two, featuring these grilled meats and other foods that could easily be stuffed into a pita. The standard item on the menu is *shipudim* (skewers)—chunks of beef, lamb, or chicken or ground meat wrapped around the skewer and grilled. In the 1960s, these "joints" became known as *steakiyot* (steak houses) or, less commonly, *shipudaia*.

A variation of *shipudim* became one of the classic foods of modern Israel—*me'orav yerushalmi*, consisting of several types of grilled offal (what Israelis sum up as *dvarim pnimi'im*, "inner things") and a little actual meat, with a strong emphasis on chicken spleens, livers, gizzards, and hearts. Chopped and wrapped in a *laffa* or pita and typically topped with some grilled onions and Israeli salad, *me'orav yerushalmi* emerged as Jerusalem's signature fast food. This Israeli dish may have been inspired by the Maghrebi *mechouiya d'abats* (grilled offal), an assortment of lamb offal—liver, heart, kidney, sweetbreads, and testicles—and *merguez* (sausages) that is chopped into cubes, marinated in a lemon juice vinaigrette, strung on skewers, and grilled.

Legend has it that *me'orav yerushalmi* was invented late one night in the early 1960s when the owner of a grill wanted to close, so he chopped up the remaining organs and a little meat, heavily spiced them, fried them all together, stuffed some into pitas, and offered the sandwiches at a very low price just to be done with it. Soon people returned, seeking more of the spicy mystery-meat sandwiches. As the lines of patrons grew longer, nearby grills quickly began offering their own versions. In the 1960s, *me'orav yerushalmi*, because it used less expensive parts of animals, emerged as a cheap and popular staple of small grill restaurants throughout the city and became more prevalent than the more expensive *shipudim*. Various small restaurants competing on Agrippas Street in Jerusalem near the Machaneh Yehudah open market claim to have invented the concept of *me'orav yerushalmi* and coined the term. They all claim to make the best.

The spices vary from restaurant to restaurant and

On November 30, 2009, Jerusalem chefs made the largest me'orav yerushalmi on record—70 pounds of filling topped a six-foot pita.

are zealously guarded secrets, while packaged mixed spices for *me'orav yerushalmi*, heavily accented on the cumin, are sold in supermarkets. Toward the end of the twentieth century, Israeli-style restaurants in America and Europe were also offering "mixed grill," but these tend to be *shipudim* with actual meat or chicken and perhaps an occasional chicken liver.

In Israel, *Me'orav Yerushalmi* has been co-opted as the title of a Klezmer song and a 1990 Israeli book of poetry. Beginning in 2003, *Me'orav Yerushalmi* was the title of a widely acclaimed Israeli television show about a traditional family in Jerusalem. In 2009, eight of Jerusalem's top chefs garnered a Guinness World Record for the world's largest *me'orav yerushalmi*.

MESHWI

Meshwi is slow-roasted lamb.
Origin: Middle East
Other names: *mishui*.

Meshwi, which means "roasted" in Arabic, is popular throughout the Arab world. Similarly roasted vegetables are commonly called *mishwiya*. In the Maghreb, *meshwi* is usually prepared Berber-style from a whole lamb (*kharuf meshwi*) and roasted on a spit in a brick and mud oven. This, however, is impractical for most home kitchens, where a leg of lamb with the thigh or lamb shoulder is substituted. *Meshwi* is a favorite holiday dish in many Sephardic households, particularly on Passover. The well-cooked meat should be very tender and fall off the bone, so traditionally diners simply pull the lamb apart and eat it by hand. The Moroccan version is typically served on a bed of couscous (not on Passover) with dried fruit (apricots, figs, plums, and raisins). Others cook the lamb with white truffles (*terfass*).

MEZZE

The wealthy in ancient Persia would throw lavish parties, such as those recorded in the Scroll of Esther, with copious quantities of wine. To encourage imbibing, and to counterbalance any sour or astringent tastes in the wine, an all-too-frequent occurrence back then, hosts offered various tidbits to eat, such as nuts, dried fruit, roasted grains, and small pieces of roasted meat. Eventually, the food at these parties grew more varied and offerings included dips, pickles, and salads, collectively called *mezze, meze*, or *mazza*. The word probably derived from the Persian noun *mazze*, mean-

ing "taste/flavor," akin to the verb *mazzidan*, "to taste." Although Islam subsequently prohibited alcohol, the appetizer assortment endured and the number of dishes grew over the centuries. The Ottomans spread the concept and its name throughout their empire and, as a result, variations of the word *mezze* are found from the Balkans—Romanians call it *mezzeluri*—to North Africa. Turkish *mezze* tend to be more elegant and filling, while Syrian-Lebanese versions include lighter, more rustic street fare. In Israel, home entertaining, restaurant dining, and Sabbath morning or afternoon lunches commonly feature a *mezze*.

Mezze is more than simply appetizers on a table, but rather an array of dishes—a medley of tastes, textures, aromas, and colors. It can be the start of a meal or the entire dinner. The intent is to delight the palate and foster conversation. A modest *mezze* may feature a mere half-dozen offerings; for special occasions, a *mezze* will abound with forty, fifty, or more different hors d'oeuvres. The dishes are typically arranged on a table in an attractive display of shapes and colors. A *mezze* is not bound by any set measure. Dishes may be cooked or uncooked, simple or elaborate, served at room temperature or chilled. They are usually savory and occasionally sweet-and-sour, and are almost always offered in small portions. Most of the dishes, primarily salads and dips, are relatively simple; hosts rely on the balance of the assortment and the freshness of the ingredients.

A typical Israeli *mezze* selection, reflecting a pronounced Syrian-Lebanese influence with a touch of Moroccan as well, may include a variety of spreads/dips, notably hummus (chickpea puree), *baba ghanouj* (eggplant salad), *matbucha* (cooked tomato and pepper salad), and *muhammara* (red pepper relish). It might also feature assorted salads (Israeli, beet, cooked carrot, raw carrot, cauliflower, tabbouleh, etc.), as well as crudités, olives, *turshi* (pickles), stuffed vegetables, stuffed grape leaves, roasted peppers, fresh fruit, falafel, *kibbeh mahshi* (fried stuffed croquettes), *mortadel* (filled meatballs), and delicate savory pastries. Sweets are rarities. At dairy affairs, foods like *labaneh* (yogurt cheese) sprinkled with za'atar and goat cheeses might also be featured. Unlike westerners who look askance at any repetition of ingredients at a cocktail party or buffet, a *mezze* usually features many of the same ingredients prepared in enticingly different ways. Eggplant, for example, may be served fried, stewed with other vegetables, grilled and pureed to creaminess, bathed in spices and herbs, smothered in yogurt, and enwrapped in phyllo. Due to the hot climate, Middle Easterners favor cool salads and fiery condiments, such as two popular chili sauces, *s'chug* and *harisa*. The foods are generally accompanied with warm flatbreads and chilled *ouzo* or *raki* (anise liqueur) as well as cold nonalcoholic drinks.

Whether the *mezze* constitutes an entire meal or just a starter course, it is always a deeply social ritual, offering the opportunity to share food and converse about food in particular and life in general. The Middle Eastern signal that the *mezze* or party is over and it is about time to leave is when the host offers hot coffee and tea.

MILCHIG

The Yiddish adjective milchig or milchik refers to dairy foods and utensils. Since the late nineteenth century, the colors blue and white have typically been used to designate *milchig* soap, utensils, and sometimes dish towels.

The identical Hebrew prohibition of *"lo tevashel gedi ba'chalav emo"* (you shall not cook a kid in its mother's milk) appears three times in the Pentateuch, closing important sections. The first of these directives follows the institution of the three pilgrimage festivals, all invoking an agricultural and seasonal origin— Passover "in the month of the *aviv* [ripening grains]"; Shavuot, "the festival of the harvest"; and Sukkot, "the festival of the ingathering." The section concludes with the sentence, *"Reisheet* ["choicest," i.e., first "fruits" of your land] you shall bring to the house of the Lord your God; you shall not cook a kid in its mother's milk."

Brevity and precision are hallmarks of Torah legislation, generally explanations and elucidations are left up to the Written Law and exegesis. Therefore, this threefold repetition was certainly intended to impart something. The Talmud records, "The school of Rabbi Ishmael taught: 'You shall not cook a kid in its mother's milk' is stated three times: one is a prohibition against eating it, one a prohibition against deriving benefit from it, and one a prohibition against cooking it." The rabbis extended the ban to include any kind of cooking or mixing, whether with or without a liquid, of meat with a dairy product. The Sages also expanded the prohibition to include fowl as well. From the various

Talmudic rulings on meat and milk evolved much of the distinctiveness of the kosher home—limiting the types of permissible foods, dividing the Jewish kitchen into two sections, and establishing waiting periods between consuming meat and dairy.

According to the Talmud, in order to ensure the separation between consuming meat and dairy, it is necessary to wait at least "until the next meal" to eat dairy after having eaten meat. What constitutes "the next meal" became a matter of dispute; rabbis disagreed as to whether there was a minimum time period between eating meat and dairy, or merely a prohibition against serving both items at the same time. Sephardim, following the ruling of Maimonides, adopted the practice "one must wait about six hours." On the other hand, Ashkenazim initially merely recited the concluding benedictions, changed the table, cleaned their mouths, and could immediately begin a dairy meal. Consequently, the traditional Rosh Hashanah dessert among early Ashkenazim was cheese *fluden*, which they happily enjoyed shortly after their meat meal. Other Ashkenazim began to wait one hour, which was believed to be the amount of time before digestion begins. These lenient practices were generally maintained up to the time of Rabbi Moses Isserles (d. 1572), whose annotations on Joseph Caro's *Shulchan Arukh* were accepted throughout eastern Europe and, thereafter, constituted the codification of Ashkenazic practice. Afterwards, eastern Europeans generally followed Isserles' opinion that it was necessary to wait six hours. Germans never adopted this stringent practice and generally wait only three hours. Dutch and Italian Jews, however, maintain the custom of waiting one hour between eating meat and dairy.

The Sages considered the prohibition of meat and milk to be a *chiddush* (sui generis), distinct and without the rationales attributed to other dietary laws. Ibn Ezra maintained that "the reason of this prohibition is concealed from the eyes of even the wise," although he then proceeded to suggest a reason, as did most commentators.

A widespread viewpoint—first recorded by Philo of Alexandria (20 BCE–50 CE) and subsequently voiced by Nachmanides, Abravanel, Rashbam, and Kimchi—is that the purpose of this prohibition is to avoid the manifest insensitivity of cooking a baby goat in its mother's milk. The third repetition follows a prohibition against pagan mourning rites and precedes the commandment of *ma'aser* (tithes); the adjoining texts connote charity as being the opposite of cruelty and infliction of pain. Part and parcel of the commandments is the building of empathy, which is not innate in humans. Similar prohibitions in this category include the requirement of chasing away a mother bird when taking eggs from the nest and not slaughtering an animal and its offspring on the same day. All these cases involve a mother and her youngster, a relationship that overcomes an animal's innate egocentric nature.

There is also a philosophical explanation for this taboo, involving a reverence for life—meat being death, while milk represents existence. The contrast of this particular yin and yang of life and death is echoed in many biblical laws, most notably those involving *tumah* and *taharha* (impurity and purity) and *kodesh* (holy) and *kadesh* (profane). Indeed, the third instance of the meat and milk passage follows "you shall not eat of *neveilah* [anything that dies of itself]." This passage involves death, while the earlier passage pertaining to first fruits involves life. The laws of cooking meat and milk, as well as *tumah* and *taharha* (impurity and purity), apply only to Jews as a matter of *kedusha* (holiness).

Maimonides advanced the theory that the taboo sprang from a revulsion to an idolatrous Canaanite practice.

Abarbanel rejected a health reason for any of the dietary laws, viewing them as a spiritual and moral matter.

MILK

Milk, *chalav* in Hebrew, the word being a construct of *chalev* (fat), is the fluid secreted by the mammary glands of female mammals for the nourishment of their young. It is a natural emulsion consisting of proteins, fats, carbohydrates, salts, and water; the amounts vary among different species. Goat's milk lacks the carotenoid pigments characteristic of bovine milk and, as a result, goat's milk is stark white in color as is goat cream, cheese, and butter. Cow's milk, on the other hand, yields butter and cheeses of varying shades of yellow.

Goat's and cow's milk have nearly identical levels of protein, but their composition is somewhat different, resulting in distinctions in the characteristics of the curd and in digestibility by humans.

Goat's milk is not normally more strongly flavored than cow's milk, although the fatty acids account for the distinctive flavor of goat's milk products. Goat's milk products are more digestible than those from cows. Hence the Talmud reflected a belief that goat's milk was better for people than that of other animals.

The *chalav* served in biblical times was certainly not the same as that found in cartons on modern grocery store shelves, as there was no pasteurization or homogenization. Nomads, who did not grow produce and were frequently out of reach of safe drinking water, relied heavily on milk, taken directly from the animal, as an integral part of their diet. However, most people settled in urban areas had no direct access to animals and fresh milk, which spoils rather quickly without refrigeration. Indeed, the Greeks, although they loved cheese, considered drinking fresh milk to be the exemplification of barbarian behavior. Turks called fresh milk *saba sut* (morning milk), meaning that it came directly from the cow. Milk would generally sour in a matter of hours, unless exposed to specific enzymes or bacteria that transformed its nature. Early in history, people learned to extend the life of milk by allowing it to become fermented by acid-producing bacteria, resulting in some of our favorite foods, including buttermilk, cheese, sour cream, yogurt, and kefir.

Buttermilk (*rivion* in modern Hebrew) was originally a by-product of churning sweet cream—the motion caused the butterfat to separate from the liquid. When the liquid was contaminated by airborne bacteria, it was transformed into a tangy, creamy drink. Today, this type of buttermilk is rare. Most groceries offer only cultured buttermilk—pasteurized milk to which a bacterial culture (usually *streptococcus lactis*) similar to those in yogurt has been added to produce acid and a tart flavor. Among Algerians, buttermilk customarily accompanies *couscous au beurre*, couscous topped with butter, sugar, cinnamon, raisins, and blanched almonds, a popular Purim dish.

Pasteurization destroys the natural bacteria that produce fermentation. In the 1890s, pasteurization gradually emerged as a common practice in the United States, and Americans began to consume a larger amount of milk, much of it fresh. Hanky-panky by some dairymen and retailers necessitated the adoption of laws regulating dairy sanitation, which only further spurred milk consumption. The milk bottle was patented in 1894 and it soon became a ubiquitous sight in American homes until the advent of the milk carton in the 1930s. America became the world's leading producer and consumer of dairy products. As fresh milk grew more accessible, canned milk lost much of its market and today is only occasionally utilized in American cooking.

In 1966, Israel shifted from glass bottles for milk to one-liter plastic bags; the milk was initially not homogenized and required intense shaking before using. More recently, waxed cardboard, plastic, and aseptic containers have become available as well.

(See also Almond Milk, Butter, Cheese, and Coconut)

MILLET

Millet is a collective term for a group of similar small-seeded grasses; they are among the world's oldest cultivated grains, with only barley and einkorn rivaling them in terms of possible antiquity. There are four major types of millet, of which pearl (also called bulrush and spiked millet) is the most commonly consumed by humans, followed by foxtail, proso (common millet), and finger (African millet). All of these have been cultivated since before the dawn of history. Some authorities categorize sorghum and teff as types of millet, while others consider them relatives.

Today, unhulled millet is most commonly used in the West as birdseed, but for much of history it was one of the most important grains (and in some times and places it was the most important grain). Millet has the shortest growing season of any grain, as little as sixty-five days. It also thrives in deficient soils and harsh climates and stores well. Consequently, it has long served as the grain of the poor and remains to this day a staple for nearly a third of humankind, in impoverished areas of Africa and India. While millet (*dochan* in Hebrew) was a mainstay of ancient Egypt, it was a lesser crop in ancient Israel, superseded by barley and wheat. The Bible, at the most, mentions it only once, as one of the ingredients of the prophet Ezekiel's bread. (Other scholars contend that biblical *dochan* refers to sorghum and millet is the Talmudic *peragim*.) Beginning in the Roman period, millet was largely supplanted by wheat in Europe. It regained its importance following the collapse of the empire, but then, in the seventeenth century, it was replaced by cornmeal. In the West, millet is available today primarily in health food and Asian stores.

Millet is not only a highly nutritious food, but also the least allergenic grain. It is boiled, steamed, or ground into flour. Since millet contains no gluten, it makes poor breads. A venerable steaming method for cooking millet gave rise to the Maghrebi couscous. Millet is frequently soaked or toasted before cooking to remove a slightly bitter taste and reduce what would otherwise be a long cooking time. Millet can also first be ground into a powder, then used as a porridge (*congee*); the porridge can be eaten plain, flavored, or it can be cooled, cut, and fried like *mamaliga*. *Bajray ki roti* is an Indian bread made from ground millet.

(See also Injera and Mamaliga)

MILTZ

The spleen, *miltz* in Yiddish, is part of a vertebrate's lymphatic system. This organ is responsible for removing old and damaged red blood cells and producing lymphocytes. The medieval European theory of humors considered ill temper to be the result of too much bile from the spleen, the seat of passions. Some people believed that eating the long, narrow beef spleen could enhance potency. Nonetheless, the spleen, as with many other organs, was typically neglected or outright scorned by most people when it came to food. Among eastern European Jews, on the contrary, it was roasted or braised, usually after being stuffing with bread crumbs, and transformed into a beloved appetizer for the Sabbath or festival meal. Generations of Ashkenazim viewed roasted cow's *miltz* as a delicacy, a dish that evoked childhood memories of a mother or grandmother's love and culinary skills. Italians preferred veal or lamb spleen.

Spleen has a texture akin to that of liver, though it is more fibrous, and a beefy flavor that is more delicate than that of liver. The otherwise chewy veins should be removed. Today, *miltz* is difficult to come by in America; it is a rarity and is only treasured by the few who remember it and can obtain it. On the other hand, the spleen (*tchol* in Hebrew) is occasionally available stuffed in the Ashkenazic tradition in certain restaurants in Israel and is typically part of *me'orav yerushalmi* (Jerusalem mixed grill).

The spleen is not the same as milt (milch), sometimes also called *miltz* (as in *miltz* herring), a long pinkish gray organ in fish filled with sperm and seminal fluid.

MIMOUNA

"Sweet gateau, La Mimouna." (From *The First Man*, published posthumously in 1995, an unfinished autobiographical novel by Nobel Prize–winning writer Albert Camus; Camus is referring to a cake made by his Sephardic Algerian grandmother.)

In the face of incessant Arab hostility toward the state of Israel and Jews, it is often rather difficult to remember that relations between Jews and some Arabs were not always so tragically strained. Nothing better exemplifies the potential amiability of human beings than Mimouna, a unique Moroccan holiday of brotherhood and peace celebrated at the conclusion of Passover. The holiday and its customs were first recorded in 1787 by an Italian Jewish poet and traveler, Samuel Romanelli. A variation of La Mimouna is celebrated by some Algerians.

There are several suggested sources for the name of this distinctive holiday. The day following Passover is traditionally considered the anniversary of the death of Moses Maimonides' father, Rav Maimon. Mimouna, an Arabic variation of the Hebrew word *emunah* (faith), means "good fortune," an appropriate notion for the onset of spring. Some scholars contend that Mimouna was also the name of a medieval North African female demon or goddess, who was considered Lady Luck and was married to another demon, Mimoun. Whatever the origin of its name, Mimouna offers Moroccan Jews, who have just celebrated the deliverance from bondage in Egypt, an opportunity to express their faith in the ultimate redemption.

Following the afternoon service on the last day of Passover, Moroccans would go to an orchard or vineyard to recite the yearly Benediction of the Trees. Upon returning, they conducted the evening service followed by a number of verses from Proverbs and Psalms reflecting the spirit of the Mimouna. Soon after sunset, the men returned home singing in Arabic, "Oh Lady Mimouna, the blessed and happy, oh may you merit success." The Jews would visit a Muslim neighbor, offering a basket of favorite Passover foods, including a meat pie, hard-boiled egg, salads, and matza, whereupon the Muslim offered a basket of fruit, milk (most Moroccans do not eat dairy products on Passover), butter, flour, and starter dough. The Jews traditionally dressed in their holiday finest, threw open their doors, and held a community-wide open house—without the need for invitations—throughout the evening, their Jewish and Arab neighbors joining in.

The color white appeared in foods and table settings (e.g., milk, wheat flour, tablecloths, and candles) because it represented purity. The numbers five and seven, considered good omens, predominated the dishes and symbols. In addition to the edible treats, a variety of symbolic foods signifying renewal, fertility, abundance, blessings, and prosperity were displayed on the table, including a large fish on a bed of lettuce or, if possible, a live small fish in a bowl of water; a plate (*taifur del Mimouna*) filled with flour and topped with five or seven pea pods or green beans, dates, and coins; and green stalks of wheat. Since Mimouna was a celebration of spring and hope, only sweet, light, nonspicy foods and drinks were served—fresh and dried fruits, nuts, dates stuffed with nuts, candied citrus peels, jams, honey, *almendra* (almond paste), *raricha del kokous* (flourless coconut cookies), *zaban/jabane* (nougat with almonds), meringue cookies, pitchers of milk, and *naa-naa* (mint tea). Housewives would then use their gift of flour and starter dough to prepare their first post-Passover *chametz* in the form of freshly cooked yeast pancakes called *mufleta*. With the exception of *mufleta* and Arab cakes, the foods contain no *chametz* due to its proximity to Passover. Jews from Marrakesh had a unique custom of saving the wine from Elijah's cup at the Seder to make some dishes for Mimouna.

Crowds of men, both Jews and Arabs, then roamed from house to house wishing each other the Arabic blessing "*terb'hou u'tsa'adu*" (may you be successful and have good luck) and sampling from the tables laden with goodies. There was an unofficial order to the visitations: first the rabbi, then parents, then important figures of the community, and finally, ordinary neighbors. Well into the night, Moroccan homes remained open to all. The evening was also considered an auspicious time to set up matches between young men and prospective brides.

The next day was celebrated with family picnics. Tents were pitched in recognition of the biblical phrase, "How goodly are thy tents O Jacob." Those near the ocean went to the beach, as this was the day after the anniversary (on the last day of Passover) of the splitting of the sea when the Israelites left Egypt. Strangers were invited to join families in eating and drinking. Special *piyutim* (poems of prayer and redemption) called *shirei yedidut* (songs of unity) were sung.

In 1948, more than 250,000 Jews lived in Morocco, most of whom were forced to flee their homeland during the following few years. The majority went to Israel, where the secular Ashkenazic authorities of the time discouraged religious and ethnic traditions and, consequently, Mimouna experienced a dramatic decline. Then following the 1967 war, various Jewish ethnic communities in Israel began to reconsider their traditions and find pride in their heritage and cultural pluralism. In 1971, a small group of politically active Moroccans saw Mimouna in particular as a valuable symbol and spearheaded festivities in Jerusalem and other areas with large Moroccan populations. North Africans responded in large numbers, as did politicians seeking their support. Mimouna celebrations in Israel became an annual event, including crowds of picnickers and performances in Sachar Park, situated near the Knesset. Mimouna festivities became increasingly popular in other Jewish communities, and more and more people took part in the evening events as well as the daytime picnics.

Responding to the success of Mimouna, other ethnic groups developed their own communal ethnic holidays with cultural and political overtones, including the Kurdish *serrana*, held during the festival of Sukkot, and the Persian *Ruz-e-bagh*, also held on the day following Passover, in the city of Ramat Gan. Traditional ethnic foods, of course, are part of these celebrations.

(See also Mufleta, Naa-naa, Raricha, and Zaban)

MINA

Mina is a savory pie made with a matza crust and filled with meat or vegetables.

Origin: Spain, Turkey
Other names: Algeria: *méguena*; Egypt: *maiena*, *mayena*; Greece: *megina*; Italy: *scacchi*.

Among the distinctive features of Sephardic cuisine are savory pies—notably the venerable *pastel*, sometimes known as *pastelli*. For more than a thousand years, these pies traditionally served as an appetizer and side dish on the Sabbath and festivals. During Passover, not wanting to let even a week pass without a *pastel*, Sephardim substituted *matzot ablandadas* (softened matzas), moistened with water or broth, for the pastry. Versions of *pastel* using matza for the crust are found in every Sephardic community. Sephardim from Turkey, the Balkans, and Rhodes,

began referring to these Passover casserole pies made from matza as *mina* (Ladino for "mine," as in an excavation for minerals). Some even use the term for large phyllo pies.

For the past several centuries, *mina de carne* (meat-filled matza pie), dense and moist, has been ubiquitous at the Sephardic Seder. It is typically served following the fish and soup, and before the main course. The meat pies are made from lamb or beef that is either ground or cut into chunks, and have a pronounced flavor of spices and herbs. The seasonings and additions (such as mashed potatoes or spinach) vary. Turkish versions tend to be less spicy than those from the Levant and North Africa. Meat pies, as well as vegetarian and dairy versions, are also enjoyed as a side dish for dinner throughout Passover. Vegetable *minas*, usually containing cheese, are a part of the *desayuno* (brunch) served Passover morning with *huevos haminados* (long-cooked eggs) and lemon wedges. Spring produce, most notably spinach and leeks, is popular for vegetable fillings. In the same dish, onions are sometimes prepared in several ways—for example, both caramelized and raw—to produce flavor and textural contrasts. In many Sephardic households, it is impossible to conceive of Passover without a *mina*.

(See also Pastida, Pastelito, Pastilla, and Phyllo)

SEPHARDIC MATZA PIE
(*MINA DE MAZA/PASTEL DE PESACH*)

6 SERVINGS AS A SIDE DISH OR 4 AS A MAIN COURSE

[DAIRY, PAREVE, OR MEAT]

Double the recipe and bake in a 13- by 9-inch baking pan.

4 whole (6-inch square) matzas
1 tablespoon vegetable or olive oil
3 to 4 cups Sephardic meat or vegetable pastry filling, such as cheese, leek, meat, onion, or spinach (pages 230–232)
1 egg, lightly beaten, for brushing

1. Soak the unbroken matzas, 1 or 2 at a time, in warm water until semisoft but not mushy, 30 to 60 seconds. Remove the matzas and place on paper towels to drain.

2. Preheat the oven to 350°F. Spread the oil over an 8- or 9-inch square baking pan, deep-dish pie plate, or ovenproof skillet and place the pan in the oven to heat.

3. Carefully cover the bottom and sides of the prepared pan with 2 matzas, breaking one apart to fill in the spaces. Spread with the filling, then cover with the remaining matzas. Spread the egg over the top. Alternatively, for layered *mina*, cover the bottom of the prepared pan with 2 matzas, spread with half of the filling, top with 1 additional matza, spread with the remaining filling, cover with the remaining 2 matzas, and spread the egg over the top.

4. Bake until golden brown, about 45 minutes. Let stand about 5 minutes before serving. Serve warm.

MINESTRA
Minestra is a medium-thick, chunky soup with rice, pasta, or vegetable pieces.
Origin: Italy

Throughout much of the medieval period, meals for the masses of Italians consisted of a thick stew. When a first course was occasionally served, it was called *minestra* (from the Italian *minestare*, "to administer"), as the dishes were ministered out. Eventually Italian dining grew more diverse and that word came to mean a chunky soup, typically the first course of a modern Italian meal. *Minestrina* refers to a thin soup, while *zuppa* generally denotes a very thick soup made by adding bread or pureeing the ingredients. Thus a *minestra* tends to be a little more delicate and complex than a *zuppa*.

Italians generally do not like their soups too hot, as the heat diminishes the flavor. Most every Italian Sabbath and festival meal commences with a soup. Artichoke soup (*minestra di carciofi*) is popular on Purim, making use of the new crop of artichokes, and is also served on Rosh Hashanah, utilizing the large mature ones at the end of the season. Chicken and rice soup (*minestra de riso*) is a traditional dish at many Italian Passover Seders.

MINT
Mint has been a part of Jewish cooking since biblical times. There are many mint varieties, but spearmint, which may be indigenous to Israel, with its smooth pointed leaves and sweet, mellow flavor, is the most common in the kitchen. Apple mint and pineapple mint are also treasured in cooking. Peppermint, a hybrid that originated in England, has fuzzy, slightly rounded leaves and a more intense flavor, and is preferred for drying and mint liqueurs. Mint, available fresh and dried (dried mint leaves should be gray-green, not brown, with a pronounced minty smell), can best be described as refreshing with a pungent, burning taste.

Although in the West, mint is generally associated with lamb as well as gum and toothpaste, it plays many culinary roles in other parts of the word, such as in Balkan, Syrian, and, especially, Persian cooking. It is used in both savory and sweet dishes to complement delicate flavors and provide a contrast to fiery and piquant foods. Dried mint adds a refreshing touch to dishes, a trait appreciated in the hot climate of the Middle East. In Morocco, green mint is used to make the national beverage, *naa-naa* (mint tea).

MISHLOACH MANOT
The *Megillat Ester* (Scroll of Esther), in reference to the celebration of Purim, declared: "They should make them days of feasting and gladness, of *mishloach manot* [sending portions] one to another, and gifts to the poor." There are four central Purim rituals: reading the Megillah, giving money to the poor, eating a *seudah* (feast), and *mishloach manot*. The obligation of *mishloach manot*, more commonly pronounced by Ashkenazim as *shalachmones*, entails sending on the day of Purim gifts of at least two different ready-to-eat foods, including beverages, to at least one person. This ritual, following the theme of Purim, is intended to demonstrate and increase love, unity, and caring among all Jews. Also, it ensures that everyone has special fare for the day, and counteracts Haman's accusations that the Jews are "a scattered and divided nation." The most common Purim foods are sweets, so distributing them is a symbolic way of wishing others a "good lot" or, in other words, a sweet future. Muslims refer to Purim as *Id-al-Sukkar* (the Sugar Holiday).

Sephardim traditionally arrange the *mishloach manot* on fish-shaped platters, fish being the astrological symbol of the month of Adar. Among the Sephardic pastries are *huevos de Haman* (long-cooked eggs wrapped in pastry, also called *foulares*) and *orejas de Haman* (fried pastry in the shape of Haman's ears). Persians might offer *malfuf* (phyllo tubes), *masafan* (star-shaped baked almond paste), and *sambusak* (turnovers). Among Ashkenazim, *shalachmones* might include a bottle of wine, a kugel, fruit, candies, and various pastries, especially hamantaschen.

MUFLETA

Mufleta is a yeast-raised pancake bread.

Origin: Morocco

Other names: *mofleta, moufleta.*

Following the expulsion of the Jews from Spain in 1492, those exiles that settled across the Straits of Gibraltar brought with them the Ladino language and traditional foods, among them a pancake bread called *mufleta*, which was related to the medieval Provençal soft griddle bread *pan mouflet.* The word *mufleta* may have derived from *muffula,* the Late Latin word for a fur mitten, which the bread resembled. The term *mofletas* became a medieval Spanish expression meaning "puffy cheeks" (referring to the trait Americans call "chubby cheeks").

Moroccans prepare these breads, made from a basic flour and yeast dough, after sunset at the end of Passover for the holiday of Mimouna; the breads thus constitute their first *chametz* since the onset of the festival. After the dough is pressed into thin rounds, the loaves look remarkably like unbaked matza, but contain yeast and, therefore, rise a little and lighten as they cook. Originally, the breads were cooked on earthenware griddles or an inverted tagine, but more recently a metal skillet has become predominant. The plain pancakes are always served with butter—most Moroccans also abstain from dairy products during Passover—and honey. After eight days of matza, the hot, light, sticky breads are most welcome and are considered a true delicacy. *Beghrir*, a spongier, richer

Moroccan Jews mark the end of Passover and beginning of spring with the Mimouna celebration. Family, friends, and neighbors are welcomed with lavish spreads, including spongy yeast pancake breads called mufleta.

version, also served with melted butter and honey, is popular Moroccan breakfast fare.

Beginning in 1948, most Moroccan Jews fled their homeland. Most went to Israel, where religious and cultural traditions were discouraged. As a result, Mimouna declined. Then in the late 1960s, Moroccans in Israel began to reembrace their heritage and in particular the holiday Mimouna returned to prominence in 1971 and the *mufleta* gained fame and popularity outside of the Moroccan community. Israeli politicians, from presidents to mayors of small cities, visit Moroccan homes on Mimouna and make sure to be photographed eating *mufleta.* For these officials, partaking of these breads has become a now-necessary sign of their identification with people from non-Ashkenazic backgrounds. For Moroccans, however, these honey-topped flatbreads are simply a favorite post-Passover treat and a beloved dish that characterizes their religious and culinary traditions.

(See also Mimouna)

MOROCCAN PANCAKE BREADS (*MUFLETA*)

ABOUT 20 MEDIUM OR 40 SMALL BREADS   [PAREVE OR DAIRY]

1 package (2¼ teaspoons) active dry yeast or 1 (0.6-ounce) cake fresh yeast

1½ cups warm water (105°F to 115°F for dry yeast; 80°F to 85°F for fresh yeast)

1 teaspoon sugar or honey

2 teaspoons table salt or 4 teaspoons kosher salt

About 3¾ cups (18 ounces) unbleached all-purpose flour, or 2 cups (10 ounces) unbleached flour and 2 cups (12 ounces) fine semolina

About ½ cup vegetable oil for dipping

Melted butter for drizzling

Honey for drizzling

1. Dissolve the yeast in ¼ cup water. Stir in the sugar and let stand until foamy, 5 to 10 minutes. In a large bowl, combine the yeast mixture, remaining water, salt, and 2 cups flour. Gradually add enough remaining flour to make a supple dough slightly softer than regular bread dough. On a lightly floured surface, knead until smooth and elastic, about 10 minutes.

2. Divide the dough into 20 egg-sized balls or 40 small balls (half-eggs). The traditional way is to grab the mass of dough and squeeze the desired amount between a forefinger and thumb, then twist and pinch off the protruding ball. Dip and roll the balls in the oil to coat, place on a flat surface, and let stand for 30 minutes.

3. Heat an ungreased large cast-iron or nonstick skillet or griddle over medium heat.

4. On an oiled flat surface and using oiled hands, flatten the balls into ⅛-inch-thick rounds. Cook the dough rounds until golden brown on the bottom, about 2 minutes. Turn and cook until golden and cooked through, about 1 minute. Cover the *mufletas* with a kitchen towel until serving to keep soft. Eat warm, drizzled with butter and honey, before the breads toughen.

MUHAMMARA
Muhammara is a red pepper relish.
Origin: Aleppo, Syria
Other names: *mahammara, mouhammara.*

Muhammara is popular throughout the Levant and Turkey. The name derives from the Arabic *hamra* (red)—the prefix *mu* denotes something or someone that is that color. Consequently, *muhammara* means "something that is red"; in terms of this dish, it refers to the hue from the dominant ingredient, roasted red peppers. The relish actually turns out a bit orange-red, so some cooks sneak in a few tablespoons of unorthodox tomato paste for a brighter red color. Roasting the peppers imparts a smoky undertone to the dish. Some cooks use imported Turkish roasted red peppers from jars, which have a slightly different flavor and shape from American varieties.

There are variations of this appetizer favorite, but most contain walnuts and bread for thickening and flavor. A Damascus version includes tahini (sesame seed paste). The sweetness of the peppers is countered by the walnuts' bitterness and the sour-sweet taste of the pomegranate molasses. Quantities and proportions vary; some like more walnuts, others more bread crumbs. Varying amounts of heat come from red chilies. The original Syrian version calls for Aleppo pepper, which is available in specialty stores. There are also hints of cumin, garlic, and lemon juice, all flavors redolent of the region. Plenty of olive oil is necessary for the proper succulent texture. This unusual combination of ingredients, popular in Syria, Turkey, and Lebanon, produces an intriguingly pungent and exotic spread. Originally, the mixture was pounded in a mortar with a pestle; a food processor now makes the task much easier.

Muhammara is a common sight at a *mezze* for the Sabbath and festivals. It is served as an appetizer with pita bread, crackers, or crudités; as a condiment accompanying roasted or grilled meat, chicken, or fish and fried eggplant slices.

🍴 SYRIAN RED PEPPER RELISH (*MUHAMMARA*)
ABOUT 3 CUPS/6 TO 8 SERVINGS   [PAREVE]

1½ cups (6 ounces) walnuts, lightly toasted, cooled, and chopped
½ cup fine dried bread crumbs, fine dried whole-wheat pita crumbs, or wheat cracker crumbs
2½ pounds (about 5 large) red bell peppers, roasted, peeled, and seeded
2 to 3 tablespoons pomegranate concentrate (*hamoud er ruman* or *dibs ruman*)
1 to 2 tablespoons fresh lemon or lime juice
2 to 4 cloves garlic, minced
1 to 3 small hot red chilies, minced (include the seeds and membranes if you prefer the heat), or ¼ to ½ teaspoon red chili flakes (preferably Aleppo pepper)
½ to 1 teaspoon ground cumin
1 teaspoon sugar
About 1 teaspoon table salt or 2 teaspoons kosher salt
About ½ cup extra-virgin olive oil

In a food processor fitted with a metal blade or in a mortar, grind the nuts and bread crumbs until smooth. Add the peppers, pomegranate concentrate, lemon juice, garlic, chilies, cumin, sugar, and salt and puree. With the machine on, gradually add the oil to form a thick, creamy paste. If it is too thin, stir in a little more bread crumbs or walnuts; if too thick, add a little more oil. Cover and refrigerate overnight to allow the flavors to meld. The relish can be stored in the refrigerator for up to 1 week or in the freezer for up to 3 months. Serve at room temperature.

MUJADDARA
Mujaddara is a rice and lentil dish.
Origin: Persia or India
Other names: Egypt: *megadara*; Greece: *mejedra*; India: *khichri*; the Levant: *majadarah, mejadara, mengedarrah, mujeddra*; Yemen: *enjadara.*

After the Persians brought rice from India to central and western Asia, people began cooking this grain with other Middle Eastern favorites, including various meats, vegetables, bulgur, noodles, and, especially, legumes, the latter providing complementary nutrition. Some of these dishes served as filling and healthy everyday fare, while others were intended only for special occasions. It is unknown whether the Persians borrowed the concept for rice with lentils from India or created it.

Mujaddara is the most widespread and beloved rice and legume dish in the Muslim world. Its name literally means "having smallpox" in Arabic, referring to the dots of lentils in the white grain. The cookbook *Kitab al-Tabikh* (Book of Dishes) by Muhammad ibn al-Hasan Al-Baghdadi, written in Iraq in 1226 but based on a collection of ninth-century Persian-inspired recipes, contains the first recorded recipe for *mujaddara*, made with rice, lentils, and pieces of meat. It was served both for celebrations and, without the meat, as working-class meals. Since rice was generally expensive in most of the medieval Muslim world and lentils were cheap, poorer people tended to cook with a much larger proportion of legumes.

Mujaddara can also contain chickpeas or noodles, while in a variation sometimes referred to as "poor man's *mujaddara*," bulgur is substituted for the rice. Iraqis make it with red lentils, cumin, and turmeric and top the servings with fried eggs. The Persian version is prepared with a crispy rice bottom. Bukharans substitute split mung beans for the lentils, a practice common in India as well. More recently, some Middle Eastern restaurants have begun serving bulgur *mujaddara* as a sandwich in a pita along with fried onion, tahini (sesame seed paste), lettuce, tomato, and sour pickles.

As symbols of fertility as well as mortality (life, like a lentil, is round like a wheel), *mujaddara* is traditionally eaten during the Nine Days before the fast of Tisha b'Av and in a house of mourning. The dish is also popular on many happy occasions, such as Shavout, when it is topped with yogurt and served with *huevos haminados* (long-cooked eggs). Middle Eastern Jewish housewives, preoccupied with preparations for the Sabbath, commonly served *mujaddara* as an easy and filling vegetarian Thursday night dinner. In some households, it was also made for Sunday night dinner because exhausted housewives wanted to serve an easy meal—on the day following the Sabbath, it was customary in many Middle Eastern Jewish households to wash clothes, a wearing and time-consuming task involving schlepping everything to a body of water and beating it with rocks. (Saturday was the Arabs' washing day and their day for *mujaddara*.) For many Middle Eastern Jews, *mujaddara* is the ultimate comfort food.

❦ MIDDLE EASTERN RICE AND LENTILS (*MUJADDARA*)

5 TO 6 SERVINGS [PAREVE OR DAIRY]

¼ cup vegetable oil or *samneh* (Middle Eastern clarified butter), or 2 tablespoons each

2 large onions, halved and sliced

About 3¼ cups water

1½ cups brown or green lentils, picked over, rinsed, soaked in warm water to cover for at least 2 hours or overnight, and drained

1½ cups long-grain rice, such as basmati, soaked in cold water to cover for 20 minutes and drained

About 1 teaspoon table salt or 2 teaspoons kosher salt

About ¼ teaspoon ground black pepper

2 to 4 tablespoons unsalted butter or 3 tablespoons chopped fresh flat-leaf parsley (optional)

1. In a medium saucepan, heat the oil over medium heat. Add the onions and sauté until golden brown, about 20 minutes. Remove half of the onions and let cool. Alternatively, you can remove all the onions and use them all for the topping, or leave all the fried onions in the saucepan to mix into the *mujaddara*.

2. Add 3 cups water to the saucepan containing the remaining onions and bring to a boil. Add the lentils, reduce the heat to low, and simmer, uncovered and stirring occasionally, until just tender but still firm, about 20 minutes. Drain the cooking liquid into a measuring cup and add additional water to equal 3 cups, while leaving the lentils in the saucepan.

3. Add the 3 cups liquid, salt, and pepper to the lentils in the saucepan and bring to a boil. Stir in the rice, return to a boil, and cover. Reduce the heat to very low and simmer, without uncovering, until the water is absorbed and the rice is tender, about 18 minutes. Remove from the heat and let stand, covered, for 10 minutes. Fluff with a fork. Transfer to a serving platter and, if using, dot with the butter or sprinkle with the parsley. Top with the reserved fried onions. Serve warm or at room temperature, accompanied with yogurt and/or pita bread, if desired.

VARIATIONS

Indian Lentils and Rice (Khichri/Kitchree): In Step 1, to the fried onions, add 2 to 3 teaspoons cumin seeds, 1 tablespoon minced fresh small green chilies, and 2 teaspoons minced fresh ginger. Sauté for about 2 minutes, then stir in 1 teaspoon ground turmeric and 1 (3-inch) cinnamon stick.

MULBERRY

Mulberries are small deciduous trees, held in high esteem by most ancient Mediterranean civilizations and prominent in biblical Israel. There are more than a dozen species subsumed under the genus *Morus* (mulberry), with three standing out from the others: The black variety (*Morus nigra*) probably originated in Persia and was among the earliest cultivated trees, the white (*Morus alba*) is probably indigenous to China, and the red mulberry (*Morus rubra*) is native to the United States.

Today, the mulberry is probably best known for its leaves, which provide food for silkworms, but for millennia the easily cultivated black mulberry was the predominant berry of the Middle East. Mature black mulberry trees reach thirty-two to fifty feet in height and bear clusters of small drupes, called *toot* in Persian and Hebrew; the trees are capable of bearing fruit for many centuries. The drupes start off as white and dry, but as they mature turn juicy and reddish, then black. Although mulberries resemble fruits from the *Rubus* genus (blackberries), they are a totally different species more closely related to the fig. The mulberry tree does not have thorns like the bush-growing blackberry and raspberry. Mulberries are much drier and less flavorful than the juicy blackberry. Still, they can be substituted for blackberries.

Black mulberries, actually closer to a dark purple, are flavorful when ripe, with a balance of sweetness and tartness. Mulberries, soft and highly perishable, do not fare well during shipping and storage and, therefore, are rarely available fresh commercially. Historically, the predominant Middle Eastern ways of using mulberries were picking the fruit in season in late spring and boiling them into a thick syrup (*sharbet*) or jam. Sephardim use the juice to make a version of fruit paste (*dulce de moras*).

MUSHROOM

A mushroom is not a vegetable, but a fungus, an organism that feeds directly off of organic material. Mushrooms have fed and mystified humans since time immemorial. The French became the first to commercially cultivate mushrooms in 1650. Today, there is a widening range of cultivated mushrooms, including many of the exotic species. The most common cultivated mushroom, accounting for nearly 40 percent of these fungi grown worldwide, is the button mushroom, which is picked when still quite young. Before World War II, brown buttons were the most prevalent cultivated mushrooms, but white buttons later supplanted them in the United States.

In ancient Israel, mushrooms, especially those belonging to the genus *Boletus*, were gathered by the masses, particularly after a major rainfall. Ever since, mushrooms have been an important part of most Jewish cuisines. Many areas in Israel are abundant with mushrooms, which the Talmud noted are exempt from tithes "because they do not grow by being sown nor does the earth extrude them." The Talmud also mentions a predilection of certain Babylonian rabbis for mushrooms, which they enjoyed for dessert at the Passover Seder.

In certain parts of North Africa and the Middle East, mushrooms are sautéed to make salads and added to omelets, rice dishes, and vegetable stews. Turks and Greeks feature sautéed mushroom salads and pickled mushrooms in *mezzes* (appetizer assortments). Georgians serve them in walnut and sour cream sauces. However, mushrooms (*shveml* in Yiddish) were particularly important in Ashkenazic cookery—they were among the few flavoring agents available to the poor in eastern Europe and could be picked free from the fields and dried (*getrukente*) for future use. Many Jews from Poland would only eat a single variety of mushroom, considering the rest unkosher or unhealthy. Ashkenazim sautéed mushrooms with onions, pickled them, stuffed them, and added them to soups, stews, kasha dishes, and pasta and pastry fillings. Romanians served them with *mamaliga*.

The standard mushroom of Europe is the boletus, called *borowik* in Poland, *steinpilz* (stone mushroom) in German, *cèpes* ("trunk," referring to the stubby stem) in French, and *porcini* (piglet) in Italian. This brown mushroom is shaped similarly to button mushrooms, but has a round cap and a fat stem that flares at the base. Rather than gills, the boletus has a pale spongy underlayer consisting of tiny tubes and pores. The size ranges from tiny to up to more than five pounds. When cooked, they have a silky texture and a rich, beefy, winy flavor with a hint of nuts. Drying intensifies the flavor. Due to the widespread substitution of button mushrooms for Boletus, many contemporary dishes fail to taste like those that grandmother prepared.

MUSTARD

Maimonides recommends, "In summer, one should eat cooling foods without excessive amounts of spices, and one should also eat vinegar. In the winter, one should eat warming foods with lots of spices, and small quantities of mustard and asafetida as well."

Early in history, mustard plants spread throughout much of Asia, Africa, and Europe, where they were valued for their medicinal properties, as well as in cooking. Mustard is a relative of cabbage, watercress, and turnip—all contain a volatile oil with a peppery flavor. Young and tender mustard leaves, similar in taste to cress, can be added to salads. More mature, sharper greens are cooked. The main value of the plant lies in its tiny seeds, which contain valuable enzymes and volatile oils.

There are three major species of mustard, each possessing its own characteristics: white, black, and brown. White mustard seed (actually yellowish brown in color), a native of the Middle East, is the largest and mildest. Black, from somewhere around the southern or eastern Mediterranean, is the smallest, yet most pungent. Brown, also called Indian or Oriental, a hybrid, is smaller but more pungent than white varieties and is the most aromatic. Today, most mustards are made chiefly from a mixture of brown and white seeds, with mustard manufacturers combining various types to produce desired qualities and flavors.

Mustard, the most processed of all spices, is available whole, powdered (dry), as oil, or prepared. Whole brown mustard seeds are common in curries and other Indian dishes; the seeds are typically fried in oil until they pop. They are also widely used in European pickles and marinades. However, in order for the oil in the mustard seed to release its distinctive pungency, it must be ground and mixed with a liquid—such as cold water, wine, beer, or vinegar—to activate an enzyme. The ancient Romans used must (unfermented grape juice), which imparted a fruity sweetness and also gave *mustum ardens* (burning must) its English name, mustard.

Black mustard (*chardal* in Hebrew) was used by the ancient Egyptians, Hebrews, Greeks, and Romans, although the first record of using prepared mustard was by the Romans. This spice is not mentioned in the Bible, but is common in the Talmud, including references to the use of both its leaves and seeds. The Midrash, in establishing Abraham's hospitality toward his three visitors, notes that he fed them tongue with mustard. The Talmud employs mustard seeds to represent the smallest measure of size. After the fall of Rome, prepared mustard disappeared from Europe and subsequently the seeds were crushed on dinner plates. By the thirteenth century, the practice of using prepared mustard had begun to revive, particularly in France and Germany.

The mustard plant thrives in most climates and soils and requires very little tending and, therefore, was generally available and affordable. The plant was important in crop rotation, substantially enhancing the yield of wheat and barley. Consequently, during the medieval period, pepper imported from India was the spice of royalty, while mustard served as the spice of the common man. As peppercorns became more widely available and less expensive in the early 1700s, mustard experienced a decline in popularity in Europe. Nevertheless, the small, potent seed of the mustard plant remains among the world's most popular spices.

Among Ashkenazim in particular, mustard (*zeneft* in Yiddish, primarily black mustard, *shvatzser zeneft*) was an important condiment long before its ubiquitous presence in Jewish delis. Mustard, commonly served daily if not at every meal, not only provided much needed flavor, but also helped to lubricate dry foods for easier consumption. Ashkenazim subsumed mustard with many other seeds under the category of *kitniyot* and prohibited it on Passover. There is now artificial mustard for Passover, but it is best avoided.

NAAN

Naan is the Farsi word for bread.

Origin: Persia

Other names: *nân, non*.

Among the culinary innovations of the Persians nearly two millenia ago was a revolutionary cylindrical clay *tanur* (oven). This vertical clay structure capable of heating up to 900°F was frequently mentioned in the Talmud. Previously, bread had been typically cooked on the outer wall of a jar oven, on griddles, or on a concave clay-lined pit oven heated with embers necessitating very thin loaves. With the new Persian oven, food was cooked on the inner wall above the fuel; both sides were exposed to heat, allowing for thicker flatbreads, and the coals below imparted to the food a characteristic smoky flavor. To bake bread, cooks heated the *tanur* to a medium-hot temperature (around 475°F). Using a protective pad or mitt, they slapped thin rounds of dough against the inner walls, producing incredibly flavorful flatbreads that cooked in a matter of minutes. The first record of the term *naan* for flatbread—possibly from the Old Persian *nagna*, "naked," distinguishing the newer loaves baked on the inner oven walls from the original loaves cooked covered in the ashes of a fire—was during the early Sassanid Empire (224 to 651 CE), a successor to the old Persian Empire. The Arab part of the Islamic world to the west generally adopted the Arabic word for bread, *khubz*.

During the medieval period Persians spread their *tanur* and the Farsi word for bread, *naan*, throughout central Asia. By the thirteenth century, the Moguls had brought these inventions to medieval India, where the oven become the tandoor and the bread became the Indian form of *naan*.

There are four predominant types of traditional Persian *naan*, all flatbreads: *sangak, barbari, lavash,* and *taftoon*. The most popular bread in Iran is *naan-e sangak* (from the Farsi *sang*, "small stone"), a large, thin, pliable, rectangular loaf about two feet long and one foot wide, capable of feeding an entire family. *Naan-e sangak* is baked over heated river gravel, which gives the bread

its traditional name, shape, and flavor. For generations this was the standard bread of the Persian army; each soldier carried a bag of flour and a small bag of pebbles, which could be heated alone or merged with those of other soldiers, on which to cook his dough.

Originally a barley bread, *naan-e sangak* is now customarily made with three parts whole-wheat flour to one part white flour, yielding a chewy texture and nutty flavor. The bread is still baked on top of tiny stones, but they are arranged in large ovens fueled with wood or coal. When the bread is done, the pebbles are shaken off, leaving their imprint in the bottom, and the mottled loaves are hung on a stick or nail to await purchase. Occasionally, an errant pebble remains stuck in the loaf, resulting in a burnt lip or broken molar. To serve, *sangak* is commonly cut into strips with scissors.

Naan-e barbari (bread of the Barbars) is named after a people from Afghanistan who introduced the recipe to Tehran around the eighteenth century. Made from white flour, it is thicker than *sangak* with a crisp outside and soft interior; the texture is similar to that of focaccia. *Naan-e barbari* is baked on the floor of a stone or brick oven, which imparts a characteristic charcoal flavor. *Barbari* with goat cheese and fresh herbs is breakfast for many Iranians.

Naan-e lavash, baked in a wide, flat shape, is the thinnest and among the most ancient of Persian breads. When fresh and hot, it is soft and pliable; after cooling, lavash becomes hard and brittle.

Naan-e taftoon (a *taftoon* is a variation of the *tanur*), second in popularity to *sangak*, are basic large round flatbreads—akin to the Arabic *khubz adi*, Turkish *pida*, and Indian *naan*—and are considered lunch bread in Iran. *Taftoon* are made from white flour or part whole-wheat flour and are cooked on the inner walls of a vertical clay oven. Authentic *naan-e taftoon* are medium soft-textured rounds or ovals with a golden bottom crust and a rippled, spotted upper surface. *Komaj* is a slightly thicker Turkish-style version. The *naan* dough is also formed into thin rectangles about two feet long and one foot wide and baked on the inner oven walls.

Bread is the staple of the Iranian diet. The term for hospitality is *naan u namak*, meaning "bread and salt." Iranians rarely bake bread at home, as it is subsidized by the government and readily available at small local bakeries (*naanvayi*), each specializing in one of the four types of bread. Most bakers (*naan-paz*) still use the old-fashioned clay ovens, but some modern versions of the *tanur* feature an electric metal oven with an inner clay pot for baking.

Persian bread is traditionally leavened with a starter dough and not yeast, contributing a mild tang, and is available plain or sprinkled with sesame, poppy, or nigella seeds. Most Middle Eastern bread is lean, without milk or oil, but occasionally these ingredients are used in some loaves; bread made with milk is called *naan-e shirmal* and with sugar *naan shirin*. The lean bread stales quickly, so it's purchased daily and in many households, shortly before each meal. The hot loaves are commonly wrapped in newspaper for transport. Often, the majority of a loaf is consumed on the way home from the bakery, necessitating the purchase of at least two.

A simple meal typically includes a single type of bread, while a formal affair may offer several kinds. Traditionally, Persians used either *taftoon* or *sangak* for their Sabbath and festival bread. Many Persian expatriates in Israel and America contend that they have not tasted real bread since leaving their birthplace.

(See also Bread, Lavash, Nan, and Non)

NAA-NAA
Naa-naa is brewed green tea with mint.
Origin: Morocco
Other names: *atay b'naa-naa.*

In the 1850s during the Crimean War, a British merchant, unable to sell his wares of Chinese gunpowder green tea in the Baltic region, stumbled upon Morocco as an alternative destination. Moroccans, to put it mildly, fell in love with the flavorful leaves, especially in conjunction with mint. Sweetened *atay b'naa-naa* (Arabic for "tea with mint") or simply *naa-naa* quickly became the national drink, a sign of friendship and hospitality. Chinese gunpowder tea (the leaves are rolled into small pellets to retain flavor during shipping) is the favored form of green tea. Some pour a little extra boiling water over the tea for about ten seconds, then strain out the water to wash the leaves and remove any bitterness. Spearmint, noted for its mellow characteristics, is the preferred variety of herb,

but in any case the leaves must always be fresh. Many Moroccans are adamant that the stems be removed, insisting that they make the tea bitter.

The amount of tea and mint varies from person to person and place to place. In the north of the country, the tea tends to be mild and highly sweetened. As one travels south, the tea gets stronger and less sugar is used. Some add a touch of orange-blossom water, lemongrass, or saffron.

Tea making and drinking has become a social ritual in Morocco. Almost every Moroccan family, regardless of its status, has some sort of tea set. It is a rite typically performed by males. Every host and businessman offers his guests mint tea, which is always prepared in front of the guests. It is considered a great offense not to accept. *Naa-naa* is usually served in small, dainty crystal glasses arranged on a *sinya* (three-legged brass tray). The ingredients—tea, mint, and sugar—are set on a separate smaller tray. The tea is prepared in special metal pots, made from brass, tin, stainless steel, or silver, which have a long, slender curved spout. The tea is customarily poured one to four feet above the glasses; the aeration is said to improve the flavor and allow the host to demonstrate his flair. The glasses, many with elegant designs, are generally filled about halfway so the top can be held without burning one's hands. It is understood that the glass will be refilled at least several more times.

Hot tea, sweet and soothing, is drunk many times throughout the day and throughout the year. *Naa-naa* follows most meals to aid digestion. It also complements rich dishes, such as lamb stews. Jews serve *naa-naa* at special occasions, such as Mimouna. Moroccans brought their love of *naa-naa* to Israel, where it is now common in homes and restaurants, and even available in tea bags.

(See also Mint and Tea)

NAN
Nan is the Afghan word for bread, but it also means meal and food.
Origin: Afghanistan
Other names: *naan, noni.*

Beginning in the sixth century BCE, Persians have influenced and frequently ruled the landlocked, mountainous region of Afghanistan to the east. From Persia came the *tanur* (oven) and *naan* (bread)—probably during the Sassanid Empire (224 to 651 CE)—

however in Afghanistan, the *tandoor* was generally built into the ground and frequently manned by a *nanwaee* (bread baker).

In Afghanistan, bread is a standard complement to meals. Silverware historically was not used, but rather bread was employed, always with the right hand, to lift or sop up various stews, soups, kebabs, and rice. Bread is also the main part of breakfast and is served with tea later in the day. Bread is always carried and served top side up.

In Afghan cities, bread is rarely made at home, but purchased from small local bakeries (*nan-e wayis*) once or several times a day. In the countryside, however, it is still frequently made at home. Those without access to an oven use a *tava* (griddle) to cook thin breads known as *nan-e tawagi*. Most commercial bakeries are staffed by males, while home bread baking is done by females. Professional bakers (*nan-e way*) typically work in teams of three: A young boy rolls out balls of dough and passes them to an adult to roll and shape, who in turn flips the loaves to another nearby. This man slaps them onto the sides of the oven, then pulls the golden loaves from the oven walls using a hooked metal rod.

Afghans prepare three principle types of tandoori (clay oven) breads of varying thickness: *nan-e Afghani*, *obi nan*, and lavash. The *nan* may be lean like most Asian flatbreads, but many versions, known as *nan-e roghani*, contain a little oil for a bit of richness; this type is particularly popular for breakfast. Loaves made with milk and sugar are called *kulchi-e tandoori*. *Obi nan*, also called *nan-e gird*, were introduced from nearby Uzbekistan and are shaped as rounds. They are thicker and softer than standard *nan*. Lavash is a very thin bread, as it is throughout the region.

The most common type is *nan-e Afghani*, or simply *nan* or *noni*. These flat oblong loaves are made from white flour or a blend of white and whole-wheat flours, or whatever grains are available, and lightly sprinkled with nigella seeds (*shirini tar*), poppy seeds (*khash khash*), or sesame seeds (*shumshum*). Loaves run in size from less than a foot long to nearly five feet in length and a foot wide; the elongated type is called *nan-e panja kashi*. Authentic Afghan bread is leavened with a starter dough, producing a slight tang, and baked in a barrel-shaped tandoor, also called a *nanwaee* (*nan* maker), resulting in a characteristic smokiness. Loaves containing whole wheat have a slight nutty flavor too.

The loaves are rolled out into thin ovals (they become more oval after being pressed on the walls of the oven) and not raised after shaping and, therefore, are thinner than most flatbreads of the region. What in particular differentiates Afghan *nan* from other flatbreads are rows of indentations (dimples), similar to a tire track, in the thin loaf, which the baker makes by dragging and pressing his fingertips in the dough. The loaves are also frequently poked or slashed to eliminate air bubbles. The result is bread that is crisp on the outside and spongy and chewy in parts of the interior.

Like all lean Middle Eastern flatbreads, *nan* is best when fresh from the oven and gets stale rather quickly. Afghans use the same weekday loaves for the Sabbath and festivals.

(See also Bread and Naan)

AFGHAN FLATBREAD (NAN/NAN-E AFGHANI)

6 BREADS [PAREVE]

1 package (2¼ teaspoons) active dry yeast or 1 (0.6-ounce) cake fresh yeast
1½ cups warm water (105°F to 115°F for dry yeast; 80°F to 85°F for fresh yeast)
1 teaspoon sugar or honey
3 tablespoons vegetable oil (optional)
2 teaspoons table salt or 4 teaspoons kosher salt
About 4 cups (20 ounces) bread or unbleached all-purpose flour, or 3 cups all-purpose flour and 1 cup whole-wheat flour
About 2 tablespoons nigella seeds, poppy seeds, or sesame seeds for sprinkling

1. Dissolve the yeast in ¼ cup water. Stir in the sugar and let stand until foamy, 5 to 10 minutes. In a large bowl, combine the yeast mixture, remaining water, optional oil, salt, and 2 cups flour. Gradually add enough of the remaining flour to make a mixture that holds together.

2. On a lightly floured surface, knead the dough until smooth and elastic, 10 to 15 minutes. Place in an oiled bowl and turn to coat. Cover loosely with plastic wrap or a kitchen towel and let rise in a warm, draft-free place until doubled in bulk, about 2 hours.

3. Preheat the oven to 475°F. Line 2 large baking sheets with parchment paper or lightly grease the sheets. Or use baking stones.

4. Punch down the dough, knead briefly, cover, and let rest for about 15 minutes. Divide the dough into 6 equal pieces. Roll out each piece into a thin oval about ⅓ inch thick. Dip your fingertips in water, spreading your fingers apart, then drag and press them lengthwise through the ovals to produce deep grooves, leaving a ½-inch border on all sides. Sprinkle with about ¾ teaspoon seeds and press them gently into the dough. Place on the prepared baking sheets, cover, and let stand for about 10 minutes.

5. Baking one sheet of bread at a time, place each on the lower oven rack and bake until the bottom of the breads begins to brown, 5 to 10 minutes.

NARGESI

Nargesi is an omelet made with herbs or green vegetables.

Origin: Persia

Other names: India: *nargisi.*

Nargesi is the Farsi word for the narcissus flower, which has white petals and a bright yellow center, reminiscent of the whites and yolks of an egg. It is also the name of a popular variation of the Persian *kuku* (omelet); in this version, some yellow egg is cooked in the center of cooked green herbs or vegetables, reminding Persians of the narcissus. An alternative to scrambling the eggs is to carefully drop one unbeaten egg into the center of the cooked vegetable base, then, one by one, drop the remaining whole eggs around the outside. Mixed herbs and spinach are the most popular vegetable combinations. At dairy meals, each serving is sometimes topped with a dollop of yogurt and served as an appetizer. For meat meals, *nargesi* sometimes contains tiny meatballs. Indians make a dish of the same name, spelled *nargisi*, substituting *paneer* (fresh cheese) for the eggs and tinting some of the *paneer* yellow with saffron to emulate the yolks.

◄ PERSIAN BRAISED HERBS WITH EGGS (*NARGESI*)

4 SERVINGS [PAREVE]

¼ cup olive or vegetable oil
1 large yellow onion, thinly sliced
1 to 3 cloves garlic, minced
2 pounds (6 bunches) chopped fresh flat-leaf parsley
1 pound (3 bunches) chopped fresh cilantro
1½ cups (½ bunch) chopped fresh dill
About ½ cup water
About ¼ teaspoon table salt or ½ teaspoon kosher salt
Ground black pepper to taste

4 large eggs
⅛ teaspoon ground turmeric (optional)

1. In a large skillet, heat the oil over medium heat. Add the onion and sauté until soft and translucent, 5 to 10 minutes. Add the garlic and sauté for 1 minute. Add the parsley, cilantro, and dill and sauté for about 5 minutes. Add the water, salt, and pepper and simmer until most of the liquid evaporates, 10 to 15 minutes.

2. Lightly beat the eggs. Mix in the turmeric, if using. Remove about 3 tablespoons of the eggs. Drizzle the remaining eggs over top of the herb mixture, flatten (do not stir in), and cook until nearly set, about 3 minutes. Using the back of a large spoon, make a slight indentation in the center of the herbs, pour the reserved egg into the indentation, and cook until set, about 3 minutes. Alternatively, do not beat the eggs, but carefully drop one unbeaten egg into the indentation, then drop the remaining unbeaten eggs around the outside of the herb base, cover the pan, and cook until the eggs are set but the yolks are still soft, about 2½ minutes. Cut into wedges. Serve warm.

NIGELLA

Nigella sativa is a member of the Ranunculceae (buttercup) family. The intensely black, sharp-edged seeds are used as both a spice and medicine. It is often confused with black cumin seeds (*kala jeera*), black sesame seeds, and black onion seeds, none of which it is. Although little known in the West, nigella is actually quite ancient; it has been found in Egyptian tombs and many scholars believe it to be the *ketzach* of Isaiah, making it the earliest written record of this spice and showing it was cultivated in Israel more than 2700 years ago. Nigella is used in Indian cooking, including in the spice mixture garam masala, and in Middle Eastern cooking. It is also a familiar topping for Jewish rye bread. In modern Israel, *ketzach* or *ketzach haginah* (garden nigella), has become popular. The Talmud mentions adding them to bread dough, and Israelis today still add the seeds or oil to breads, crackers, and cookies.

NON

Non is the Bukharan word for bread.

Origin: Uzbekistan

Other names: *lepyoshka, nan.*

Along the silk road—caravans brought riches from the Orient to the west, including to central Asian towns including Samarkand, Tashkent, and Bukhara—in modern day Uzbekistan and Tajikistan.

Bukharan food, from the heart of the Silk Road, is a blend of Turkish, Chinese, Russian, and Persian influences. It was from the Persians that the Bukharans adopted the *tanur* (cylindrical clay oven), which they called *tandir* and, probably during the Sassian period (224 to 651 CE), *non* (flatbread). Due to the protracted Russian dominance of the region in the twentieth century *non* is also called *lepyoshka*. Long before the arrival of the Russians, the mainstay of the Uzbeki diet had been bread, which was typically served at every meal. In general, people on the east side of the Caspian Sea (Turkmenistan, Kazakhstan, and Uzbekistan), an area rich in wheat and barley, eat much more bread and pasta than those on the west side (Azerbaijan and western Georgia).

Tandir non, made today as it was centuries ago, is considered the best bread—the ovens contribute a special flavor and texture. Nearly every family in the countryside and even some in the city have a *tandir* in an inner courtyard or backyard in which to prepare fresh bread daily. Loaves are also widely sold by small local bakeries and in marketplaces. The basic lean dough used for most breads is leavened with special starter doughs—some carefully guarded and handed down from generation to generation—that impart a unique flavor. The air of an established Uzbek bakery is saturated with special varieties of yeast from the previous bakings. For a slightly richer bread, some bakers add several tablespoons of oil to the dough.

The most common Bukharan form of bread is a round loaf that is distinguished by an indentation in the center. It is called *parakh non,* or *issik non* (flatbread), or simply *non*. After the first rise, the dough is rolled out using a small wooden pin, covered with a cloth, and either baked immediately for a flatter bread or left to briefly rise a second time. The center indentation was originally made using large bird quills and later with a *parakh* or *chekish,* a nail-studded wooden device about three inches in diameter whose tiny holes restrict the amount of rising in the center and imprint a distinctive design. A single imprint is used for smaller loaves, while for larger loaves the *parakh* is pressed once in the center then five to six times around the central indentation to make a rosette pattern.

In some areas, bakers make the imprint before the dough rises, but most press it in afterward. If the center is perforated beforehand, the bread puffs up; if the center is imprinted after the dough rises, the loaves are flatter, and crisper in the center. Before placing the bread in the oven, the baker lightly rubs the dough round with water, then frequently sprinkles it with nigella or sesame seeds (black, white, or a combination). Using a *rapida* (a round, padded cotton mitten), the baker then slaps the dough onto the vertical sides of the oven and presses it against the walls; the round shape of the *rapida* helps to maintain the shape of the *non*. The outer portion is golden brown on the outside and soft inside, while the center is low, pale, and hard. *Parakh non* are thicker than typical Middle Eastern flatbreads.

Several other widespread Bukharan breads are made from the same or similar dough. *Obi non* is similar to regular *non,* except the dough is a little stiffer and it is imprinted and baked without a second rise, yielding a thinner bread. *Randa* is a large rectangular flatbread; its sides are higher than its center and it is covered with nigella or sesame seeds. When the dough is cooked on the outside of a *sajj* (a cooking vessel akin to an inverted wok atop a fire), the resulting large, thick, concave cracker is called *noni toki* (dome bread).

Visitors to a Bukharan home are typically offered *non* and *choy* (green tea); the two in themselves sometimes constitute a meal, but at other times they are accompanied by salads, soups, or fresh fruit, especially grapes and peaches. It is considered extremely disrespectful to decline food or to start eating before being invited to by the host. In the Asian manner, bread is never cut with a knife, but rather broken into pieces by hand and set, flat side down, next to each place setting. Smaller pieces are torn from these to scoop up food. Throughout the meal, teacups are refilled. Bukharans use the same loaves during the week and on the Sabbath and holidays.

Due to the early presence, beginning in 1868, of Bukharans in Israel, *non* and other Uzbekistani baked goods have long been familiar in Jerusalem and certain other parts of the country. However, as late as the mid-1990s, traditional Bukharan bread was unobtainable in the United States. Now, however, *non* is available in parts of America such as Brooklyn, where Bukharan-owned bakeries churn out time-honored loaves from the vertical walls of traditional *tandirs.*

(See also Bread and Naan)

NOSH

The Yinglish (Yiddish English) word nosh, now entrenched in both American and British English, comes from the Yiddish *nashn*, itself derived from the Middle High German *naschen* (to nibble/gnaw). It first appeared in English in 1892 in *Children of the Ghetto* by Israel Zangwill (London). By the 1930s, it had become nosh (and noshing and nosher), and widespread in the 1950s, popularized by Jewish comedians. Nosh is used as both a noun and a verb, and means "a snack" or "to snack." A nosher is the person who eats the snack. The related noun nosheri/nosherei, from the Yiddish *nasheray* (tidbit), means "food for snacking," "a number of snacks," or "junk food." In England, a nosh is more substantial—to eat a meal—and a noshery is a "snack bar" or "restaurant."

NUSSTORTE

Nusstorte is a cake, sometimes flourless, made with finely ground nuts and leavened with beaten eggs.
Origin: Germany
Other names: nut cake; Hebrew: *oogat egozim*;
  Hungarian: *diós torta*.

"Nu, Fraulein? You gotta tell her whether your heart says plum-kuchen oder Nusstorte, or both, see? Just like that. Now make up your mind. I'd hate t' have you blunder. Have you decided?" (From *Dawn O'Hara, the Girl Who Laughed* [New York, 1911], an early novel by Edna Ferber. The author describes a scene inside a German bakery in the American Midwest in the early 1900s).

Nut cakes are among the earliest of cakes. The first light nut cakes appeared in Moorish Spain, and were made by beating eggs with sugar—a branch and twigs tied together originally served as the agitating utensil. This technique trapped air bubbles in the eggs, providing leaven for the batter. These cakes evolved into *pan d' Espanna* (sponge cake) and various Sephardic almond cakes, such as *torta de almendras* and *torta de las reyes* (orange-almond cake). It was the arrival in the rest of Europe of the sponge cake that would transform European nut cakes into luscious and light treats called *tortas* or tortes.

During the Renaissance, Italians occasionally added ground almonds to their *tortas*, but nuts had to be finely pounded by hand and Italians generally preferred the lighter cakes without the nuts. The English, meanwhile, preferred butter-laden pound cakes

and steamed puddings. However the Hungarians, Austrians, and Germans, probably beginning in the late seventeenth century, did not mind the work of grinding nuts as much, and took these *nuss torten* to their full height.

Some of these central European cakes, typically made from walnuts or hazelnuts, contain flour, while many others are completely flourless. Besides being readily adaptable to Passover, *nusstortes* are also inherently pareve, a major advantage in a kosher kitchen, and relatively low in fat (other than the fat in the nuts and egg yolks). Consequently, central European Jews and eventually other Ashkenazim began making *nusstortes*, not only for Passover, but also for special occasions throughout the year. In many Hungarian families, a nut torte layered with frosting is the customary birthday and anniversary cake.

A basic nut cake can be served plain or, in the central European manner, topped with a dollop of whipped cream (*schlagsahne*) or layered with it. Early American Jewish cookbooks generally called for various fruit mixtures, also pareve, as well as cream concoctions to hold the layers together and provide extra moistness and flavor to the cake. When buttercream frostings became popular during the early twentieth century, they were soon a favorite nut cake filling and topping.

Aunt Babette's (Cincinnati, 1889) offered recipes for an array of tortes, including two types of "Almond Cake, or Mandel Torte," plus a third for Passover made with potato flour; three examples of "Brod Torte" made from rye bread crumbs, along with a fourth brod torte made with matza meal; a pair of "Mohntorte," with poppy seeds; and a "Walnut Cake (Torte)."

The first edition of *The Settlement Cook Book* (Milwaukee, 1901) included recipes for about forty different *torten* incorporating everything from almonds, chestnuts, chocolate, filberts, poppy seeds, rye bread crumbs, and walnuts to matza. The author explained, "Tortes are cakes that contain no butter, but are made rich with nuts and light with eggs, while bread or cracker crumbs usually take the place of flour. The nuts are chopped, rolled or ground fine, mixed with crumbs and spices."

These two works, both by authors from German Jewish backgrounds, contained some of the earliest references to tortes in American cookbooks, reflecting once again the role Jews played in transforming and transmitting foods from one area to another. Note that *Aunt Babette's* directed that the nuts be pounded in a mortar, while *The Settlement Cook Book* explained, "the nuts are chopped, rolled or ground fine." The invention in Europe toward the end of the nineteenth century of the manual mechanical nut grinder made the task of grinding nuts much easier and, consequently, the popularity of nut tortes grew in central Europe and then America. Subsequently, the advent of packaged commercial ground nuts, as well as electric grinders and food processors, took much of the work out of this cake. As the twentieth century progressed, manufacturers of matza meal and potato starch, as well as any cookbook and culinary magazine (even non-Jewish ones) touching on Passover, offered recipes for flourless nut cakes, further increasing their popularity.

Nut tortes remain a favorite in Europe and Israel, both on Passover and during the rest of the year. A staple of Ashkenazic Passover baking everywhere, these cakes are an annual tradition and comfort food for many families.

(See also Sponge Cake)

HUNGARIAN FLOURLESS NUT TORTE (*DIÓS TORTA*)

10 TO 12 SERVINGS   [PAREVE]

8 large eggs, separated (1 cup whites; 9 tablespoons plus 1 teaspoon yolks)
⅔ cup (4.5 ounces) sugar
¼ teaspoon table salt or ½ teaspoon kosher salt
¼ cup orange juice, lemon juice, nut liqueur, or sweet wine
1 cup (2.6 ounces) finely chopped walnuts, hazelnuts, or pecans; or ¾ cup chopped nuts and ¼ cup dry bread crumbs or matza cake meal
1½ teaspoons grated lemon or orange zest or 1 teaspoon vanilla extract
Buttercream, whipped cream, or fruit preserves

1. Preheat the oven to 350°F. Grease one 9-inch springform pan or three 9-inch round cake pans, line with parchment paper, and regrease.

2. In a large bowl, beat the egg yolks until light, about 5 minutes with an electric mixer. Gradually add the sugar and continue beating until thick and creamy, about 5 minutes. Add the salt. Gently stir in the orange juice, nuts, and zest.

3. In a clean large bowl, beat the egg whites until stiff but not dry, 5 to 8 minutes. Fold one-fourth of the whites into the nut mixture, then gently fold in the remaining whites.

4. Pour into the prepared pan(s). Bake until the top of the cake springs bake when lightly touched and a tester inserted in the center comes out clean, about 25 minutes for the 3 cake pans, or 35 to 40 minutes for a springform pan.

5. Place the pans on a wet kitchen towel for 2 minutes, then invert onto a wire rack and let cool completely in the pans, at least 1 hour. Run a thin knife along the sides of the pan(s), and invert the cake onto a flat plate. Carefully remove the paper from the bottom.

6. If using one cake from a springform pan, cut the cake horizontally into 2 to 3 layers. Frost the layers with buttercream. Cover with a large bowl and store in the refrigerator for up to 3 days.

NUT

A nut, among the most ancient of foods, in the botanical sense, denotes any dry one-seeded fruit developed from a compound ovary surrounded by a hard shell. Although there are hundreds of types of nuts, only a few are used to any extent, notably chestnuts, hazelnuts, pecans, and walnuts. Most items we call nuts are botanically actually drupes (e.g., almonds, coconuts, and pistachios) and seeds (e.g., Brazil nuts, candlenuts, cashews, peanuts, and pine nuts). In the culinary sense, these are all nuts.

The Bible mentioned three nuts—almonds (*shekad*), walnuts (*egoz*), and pistachios (*botnim*)—and ever since, they have been essential to Jewish cooking, especially in baked goods, particularly those for Passover. Nuts are also an ingredient in the Passover charoset and are among the items consumed at a Tu b'Shevat Seder. Georgian cuisine, such as the staple sauce *bazha*, would be impossible to imagine without walnuts. The pairing of pine nuts and raisins is characteristic of Roman Jewish cooking. The combination of raisins and almonds is a venerable Ashkenazic Sabbath snack. For special occasions, Moroccans mix fruit and nuts into sweetened couscous. On Purim, Mizrachim and Sephardim enjoy pastries filled with almonds, walnuts, and pistachios. Traditional Sephardic Rosh Hashanah desserts include a nut *tish pishti* (honey-soaked semolina cake) and baklava. For Rosh Hashanah, Indian Jews prepare a coconut milk halva garnished with nuts and raisins. However, Ashkenazim developed a tradition of not eating nuts on Rosh Hashanah and at the meal before Yom Kippur.

(See also Almond, Chestnut, Hazelnut, Pine Nut, Pistachio, and Walnut)

O

OFFAL

"Mr. Leopold Bloom ate with relish the inner organs of beasts and fowls. He liked thick giblet soup, nutty gizzards, a stuffed roast heart, liver slices fried with crustcrumbs, fried hencods' roes." (From *Ulysses* by James Joyce, 1922). The author's revealing introduction to the half-Jewish protagonist of his novel provides insights into Bloom's unorthodox eating habits, as well as the attitudes of non-Jews to these practices.)

Offal—the English term derived in the late fourteenth century from the Middle Dutch *afval* (off-fall), connoting parts of the animal that "fall off" the butcher's table—consists of the internal organs, entrails, and glands of an animal, not including muscles and bones, which consists of about 40 percent (by weight) of an adult cow. To some, tails and feet are also offal. The taste and texture of any particular type of offal is based on the species and age of an animal. In most cultures throughout most of history, waste was considered a sin and people used every part of the animal, including the innards. Since organs contain little or no fat, there is almost no waste. Yemenites, in particular, have a long-standing tradition of using every part of an animal to the maximum effect. Sephardim had a particular fondness for brains; Maghrebis for lamb's tongue and tripe (the lining of the first and second stomachs of a ruminant); and Ashkenazim for almost any of the innards, especially liver, sweetbreads, and tongue. Sephardim and Mizrachim primarily used lamb offal, while Ashkenazim generally only had access to cows. It was not uncommon for Jewish butchers to give a little of the less sought-after types of offal to the poor for use in making a soup for the Sabbath.

However, in some locales, the offal, at least most types of it, was considered undesirable. Medieval English nobles developed a strong objection to offal, then called umbles, considering it poor person's fare. In this vein, the term for performing a humiliating act, "eating humble pie," arose from a fourteenth-century English practice: After a venison hunt, the undesirable internal organs and glands (the umbles) were given to the servants for filling their pies, while the upper class dined on the tender cuts of meat.

This English aversion was absorbed by many modern societies and, as a result, countless traditional dishes have disappeared or became rarities. In animal-rich America and the English-speaking world in general, offal is basically ignored; most people react squeamishly to the very thought of these parts and some are designated as unlawful for human consumption. Many Jews now look askance at once-popular dishes made from offal.

Still, the attachment for offal perseveres in some communities and for some dishes. France and Italy retain a strong history of using organ meats as a feature of gastronomy and creativity—one of the most well-known of these dishes is foie gras. Romans love to cook all types of offal with artichokes. Many cuisines include tripe stews, such as the Italian *busecca*, Turkish *iskembe corbasi*, and Maghrebi *kirsa*. The Tunisian stew *aakode* consists of a mixture of stomach, intestines, penis, and testicles simmered in tomato paste, garlic, harissa (chili paste), and cumin. Liver, especially chopped chicken liver, remains a standard of the Jewish deli. A modern classic of Israel is *me'orav yerushalmi* (Jerusalem mixed grill), a mixture of chopped chicken innards and umble parts generally indiscernible to diners.

(See also Brain, Heart, Kishke, Liver, Lungen, Me'orav Yerushalmi, Miltz, Pupik, Sweetbread, Tongue, and Udder)

OIL

A discussion in the Mishnah revolves around the items that are appropriate for the Sabbath lights. The rabbis allowed "all kinds of *shemanim* [oils]: sesame oil, nut oil, radish oil, fish oil, gourd oil, resin, and naphtha." (The mention of naphtha [*neft*] is the first record in history of a refined petroleum oil product.) Societies once squeezed oil from numerous sources; many are now obscure, while others are still used today.

Oils are fats from various seeds, nuts, and fruits that remain liquid at room temperature. A few, such as olive and sesame, are the result of simply pressing the liquid from the source, while many others require chemical processing. These viscous substances are used for frying and baking, and in salads. Some oils contribute their own flavor to foods; others are completely tasteless. Cold-pressed oils retain their flavor and nutrients better than those extracted by heat or chemicals. Many heat-treated oils are processed to remove unpleasant flavors; as the result of this processing, any vitamins are also removed.

Olive oil was the predominant type in ancient Israel and remains widespread throughout much of the modern Mediterranean. Today, however, sunflower oil, native to the Americas and first popularized in Europe in the eighteenth century, has also become accepted. Sunflower became the preferred oil of Georgia, where the plant covers large swaths of the countryside. Sesame oil has long been the primary oil of central Asia and northern India. The Bene Israel of Mumbai were called Shanwar Teli (Saturday Oilmen) by their Hindu neighbors due to their role in preparing and selling sesame oil and their refusal to work on the Sabbath. Oils are pressed from almonds, hazelnuts, and walnuts and some other nuts. The inhabitants of southern India have long relied on coconut oil and, the most widely produced tropical oil, palm oil. Grapeseed oil, a rare and expensive product until the twentieth century, is a mild, slightly nutty-flavored oil pressed from the seeds of vinifera grapes. Argan oil from the argan nut is a specialty of Morocco.

Since few of the items from which oil could be made were common in northern Europe, oil there was a rarity and people had to rely on animal fats. For a millennium, the principle oil of Germany was pressed from poppy seeds. Around 1870, the Germans discovered a process of extracting a liquid fat from various vegetables and seeds through the use of chemical solvents. In 1887, the Southern Oil Company of Philadelphia began crushing cottonseeds for their oil, but found resistance to the malodorous product. Twelve years later, David Wesson, a Southern Oil chemist, developed a mechanical method for deodorizing cottonseed oil, resulting in the first practical nonanimal-derived fat in America. In 1911, E. T. Bedford's Corn Products Refining Company of Pekin, Illinois, introduced corn oil under the Mazola label;

corn oil was for the ensuing decades the most popular cooking oil in America.

Safflower oil, a light, flavorless, colorless oil extracted from the seeds of a thistle-like plant native to the Mediterranean. In biblical times, the seeds and reddish yellow safflower leaves were both used as spices. Today, the oil is most important in India, Kazakhstan, Ethiopia, and the United States.

Rapeseed—a member of the cabbage family and therefore a relative of mustard—has been cultivated since the thirteenth century in Europe, where the herbage was used for animal fodder and the inedible oil from its seeds pressed to fuel lamps. In 1968, genetically modified rapeseed plants were developed with low levels of erucic acid. These cultivars were renamed canola (*liftit* in modern Hebrew) and emerged as a food crop grown for their oil.

Few legumes except peanuts are rich in easily extractable oil. Soybeans were first cultivated in China in the eleventh century BCE and, as a by-product of soybean meal production, a small amount of beans were soon being pressed to extract the oil. In the early twentieth century, Japan and China and then Europe began extracting large amounts of oil, primarily to make soap from the fat and using the meal to fed livestock. Soybeans were first recorded in America in 1765 in the state of Georgia. By 1940, America had emerged as the world's leading producer of soybean oil. Subsequent advances in processing technology resulted in a light-colored, higher-quality oil suitable for cooking. Since 1966, soybean oil has been the world's leading edible oil in both production and consumption, replacing cottonseed oil, well ahead of second-place palm, third-place canola, and fourth-place corn. Most oils labeled "vegetable" or "cooking" are comprised of soy oil or cottonseed oil or a combination.

In America, since the early 1970s, most oils have been under kosher supervision. The industry decision at that time to maintain kosher tanker trucks for oil would completely transform the kosher supervising industry, leading to an explosion of kosher products throughout the country.

There is disagreement among authorities as to whether derivatives of *kitniyot* (*mei kitniyot*), such as oils and extracts, are permissible for consumption on Passover. Also debated is the question of whether derivatives from plants unknown at the time of the original custom of *kitniyot*, such as peanut oil and soy oil, are permitted. In any case, Ashkenazim proscribe corn and soybean oils and some also abstain from peanut, sesame, and canola oils.

(See also Argan Oil, Olive Oil, and Sesame)

OJALDRE

Ojaldre is an ancient Iberian form of puff pastry, as well as an Eastern Mediterranean filled phyllo triangle.
Origin: Spain, Ottoman Empire
Other names: *hojaldre*.

Among the dishes in the Sephardic culinary repertoire before the expulsion from Spain in 1492 was a pastry called *ojaldre* (little leaf), derived from the Ladino *oja* (leaf). (The Spanish word for leaf is *hoja*.) The original *ojaldre* was made from a rich unleavened dough containing eggs and oil. The dough was rolled out and spread with fat, then rolled into a cylinder. Slices were cut off the cylinder and rolled out to make pies and turnovers. Sometimes the pastry was basted with melted fat during baking, all the better to separate the layers. This rudimentary puff pastry yielded relatively thin layers, although it was less flaky than either phyllo or *pâte feuilletée* (modern puff pastry).

In modern Spanish, *hojaldre* refers to puff pastry, but not in Ladino. After Sephardim arrived in the Ottoman Empire, they eventually adopted phyllo into their repertoire, while generally forgetting about puff pastry, which involved techniques better suited for cooler climates. Subsequently, the term *ojaldres* was applied to filled phyllo pastries, especially the triangles known throughout the Middle East and Mediterranean region. *Ojaldres* joined the extensive Sephardic repertoire of small, savory, filled pastries, including *borekas*, *boyos*, *bulemas*, *empanadas*, and *tapadas*. *Ojaldres* were a particular specialty of Rhodes. In Greece, the two most popular types are cheese-filled triangles known as *tiropites* and spinach-filled ones called spanakopitas. In addition, phyllo triangles are commonly filled with mashed potatoes, eggplant, or meat.

Since *ojaldres* are a labor intensive, they are typically reserved for special occasions. In Salonika, Friday night dinner frequently consisted of *avicas* (white bean and meat soup) accompanied in the spring through early fall with spinach *ojaldres*. Cheese *ojaldres* are especially popular on Hanukkah and to break the fast of Yom Kippur, while fried ones might be served on Hanukkah. Meat-filled versions are popular on Sukkot and at weddings, as either an appetizer or a side dish.

(See also Ajin Taimani, Boreka, and Phyllo)

❧ SEPHARDIC PHYLLO TRIANGLES (*OJALDRES*)

ABOUT 36 TO 48 SMALL APPETIZERS   [DAIRY OR PAREVE]

    1 pound (24 sheets) phyllo dough
    About 1½ cups melted butter or vegetable oil
    About 3 cups Sephardic pastry filling
      (pages 230–232)

1. Preheat the oven to 375°F. Grease a large baking sheet.

2. Lay the phyllo sheets on a flat surface with the shortest end nearest you. Cut lengthwise into 3- to 4-inch-wide, equal-sized strips. Cover the strips with plastic wrap or a damp kitchen towel when not in use. Lightly brush one strip with butter, top with a second strip, and brush with butter.

3. Place a heaping teaspoon of the filling in the center of the strip, about 1 inch from the closest end. Fold a corner diagonally over the filling, forming a triangle. Brush the corner flap with butter and continue folding, maintaining the triangle shape, until the end of the strip.

4. Place the triangles on the prepared baking sheet and brush with butter. Bake until crisp and golden, about 18 minutes.

OKRA

Okra, a member of the mallow family and a relative of cotton, is a native of Ethiopia. Okra plants produce tapered capsules growing as long as eight inches. Larger, mature pods require a longer cooking time; smaller pods have the best flavor.

The Ladino name for okra, *bamia*, and the Arabic name, *bamiya*, are derived from the Bantu *kingombo*, indicating the plant's African origin. There is no specific mention of this plant in the ancient world, though some scholars claim that a few ambiguous Egyptian pyramid drawings are of okra. Its first verified appearance was in twelfth-century CE Egypt. Shortly thereafter, the Moors introduced okra to Spain, where, as with other vegetables, it gained wide acceptance among Sephardim. The few other areas where okra accrued some degree of popularity were the Levant, the Balkans, India, and the American South. In India, it is also called ladies' fingers. After tomatoes arrived from South

America, they became the favorite Sephardic partner for okra; the two vegetables were cooked together without any additions, or with many other vegetables in a stew. In the Middle East, okra pods are sometimes pickled along with other vegetables in *turshi*. Dried okra is enjoyed throughout the winter.

Okra's mucilaginous nature—which is very noticeable when it is overcooked—makes it unappetizing to many. However, blanching it in hot water or pairing it with an acid—such as soaking it in vinegar water or cooking it with tomatoes or lemon juice—lessens this attribute. Some cooks fry okra in a little oil until browned before further cooking, to prevent mushiness and enhance the flavor. On the other hand, okra's primary characteristic can be desirable in stews as a thickener.

Okra and chicken stews are popular summer Sabbath fare from India to Tunisia. Persians cook okra in a lamb stew called *yakhnat*. Among Sephardim from Turkey and the Balkans, okra in tomato sauce, typically accompanied with rice or flatbread, was both everyday fare and a Sabbath dish from late spring through Sukkot. In some households, okra is also common at the meal following the fast of Yom Kippur. Syrians feature okra flavored with tamarind on Rosh Hashanah and festive occasions.

SEPHARDIC OKRA WITH TOMATOES
(*BAMIA KON DOMATES*)

6 TO 8 SERVINGS   [PAREVE]

- 2 pounds (7 cups) whole small okra, caps removed, or 20 ounces frozen okra
- 2 quarts water mixed with ½ cup white or cider vinegar
- 5 tablespoons olive oil
- 2 medium onions, chopped
- 2 to 3 cloves garlic, minced
- 4 cups (24 ounces) peeled, seeded, and chopped plum tomatoes; or 6 ounces tomato paste dissolved in 2 cups water
- About 1 teaspoon table salt or 2 teaspoons kosher salt
- 2 to 4 tablespoons fresh lemon juice
- 1 to 2 tablespoons granulated or brown sugar
- Ground black pepper to taste

1. Soak the okra in the vinegar water for 1 hour. Drain and pat dry.

2. In a large skillet or saucepan, heat 3 tablespoon

oil over medium heat. Add the okra and sauté until golden, about 15 minutes. Remove the okra.

3. Add the remaining 2 tablespoons oil, onions, and garlic and sauté until soft and translucent, 5 to 10 minutes. Add the tomatoes and salt and cook, stirring occasionally, until softened, about 15 minutes.

4. Add the lemon juice, sugar, and pepper. Return the okra, cover, and simmer over low heat until tender, about 30 minutes, or bake in a 375°F oven until tender, about 1 hour. Serve warm or at room temperature.

OLIVE

There are about forty species in the Oleaceae family of evergreen trees, but only one is of importance to humans—the olive, which bears a small drupe, a fruit with a single large pit. Wild olives grow throughout northern Israel and southern Syria, which is considered the probable site of its origin. Although it takes at least five years for an olive tree to bear fruit, it lives for an incredibly long time, thriving even in poor soil and resisting long periods of drought. The Garden of Gethsemane (Hebrew for "olive press"), lying at the base of the Mount of Olives in Jerusalem, contains viable olive trees dating back more than two thousand years and there are a few others in the country that are even older.

Olives, among the Seven Species with which the land of Israel was praised in the Bible, have played a long and important role in Jewish life and lore as a symbol of beauty, endurance, light, and sanctity. After an olive tree is cut down, the roots sprout suckers that grow into a new tree; accordingly, the olive tree also represents renewal and fertility. In addition, the story of Noah and the dove led to the tree's association with peace. Today, olive branches can be seen on both the official emblem of Israel (two olive branches flanking a menorah) and the Great Seal of the United States (an eagle holding an olive branch in its right talon). Some scholars believe that the olive's hard, gnarled root served as the original plow. The Temple doors were also made from olive wood. One of the standard units of measurement used by Biblical and Talmudic authorities was the *kezayit* (like an olive); this was the amount of matza each person was required to eat at the Passover Seder.

The olive tree was first cultivated nearly six thousand years ago. It was initially grown for its oil and the fruit itself was not consumed. Green olives, picked around September, are extremely hard unripe fruit; black olives, ranging in flavor from mild to pungent and in color from reddish brown to purple to deep black, are fruit allowed to fully ripen on the tree until late November or December. All olives contain oleuropein. This bitter substance must be leached out of whole olives in order to make the fruit edible, although the substance separates naturally from the oil. It is possible that thousands of years ago, a traveler walking along the Mediterranean Sea stumbled upon the olives from an abutting tree that had fallen into the salty water and, sufficiently hungry, tasted one, found it palatable, and subsequently figured out how to prepare them by soaking in brine. The Romans seem to have originated lye curing. The hard flesh of most green olives withstands brine and is, therefore, first soaked in a lye solution for about two weeks, removing most of the bitterness and breaking down the flesh. After being immersed in lye, olives are then wet-cured in brine or, occasionally, dry-cured in rock salt. Brine-curing without soaking in lye or cracking can take up to two years. Brine-cured green olives are sometimes cracked to allow the brine to penetrate, thereby cutting the curing time to less than a year. Inhabitants of the Mediterranean tend to favor shriveled brine-cured ripe black olives, sometimes called Greek-style olives, which possess a smoky flavor. Most canned American black olives are actually lye-cured green olives whose color derives from aeration and exposure to ferrous gluconate. They tend to be sweet and juicy, but bereft of any genuine olive flavor.

There are hundreds of types of olives, which may be classified by a number of categories including variety, size, color, place of origin, or type of cure. Olives range from bland to strong, simple to complex. The fruit's texture and flavor is determined by the variety, growing conditions (climate and soil), degree of ripeness, subsequent processing, and storage. Olives are a ubiquitous sight at Middle Eastern tables; they are served as a side dish at breakfast, lunch, and dinner, as well as cooked in a myriad of dishes, such as stews and casseroles, and added to salads. Residents of the Mediterranean believe that brine hides the true flavor of olives and, therefore, generally rinse and sometimes soak them in water before adding to a dish. Cured olives are frequently marinated in various aromatics to create new layers of flavor. The older the olive, the more porous it becomes and the more flavors it absorbs.

Archeological excavations at Masada and other sites reveal that the most common olive varieties in biblical and Talmudic times were the Nabali (indigenous to Israel), followed far behind by Souri (Syrian). In addition, during Roman times, two varieties that do not grow in Israel were occasionally imported: the Shami from Syria and the Toffahi from Egypt. The most important varieties in modern Israel include Barnea, Maalot, Manzanillo, Nabali, and Souri.

OLIVE OIL

Olives, depending on the variety and maturity, are anywhere from 8 percent to a staggering 40 percent oil by weight. As olives ripen on the tree, they darken and develop more oil and sugar. Olives destined for use on the table are generally picked green in September or October, while those for making oil are left on the tree until late November through December. Even long before the advent of Hanukkah in 165 BCE, the twenty-fifth day of Kislev was the traditional date for the end of the harvest of olives for oil, as well as the last day on which the *bikkurim* (first fruits) of that year could be brought to the Temple. A single tree can produce up to twenty gallons of oil every year.

Olive oil was one of the world's first oils; it was first made in the Levant six thousand years ago and eventually became the primary fat of most of the Mediterranean region. The English word oil is derived from the Latin word for olive, *olea*. Neolithic pottery containing olive pits and remnants of olives found near Mount Carmel in Israel reflect the earliest method of oil production—pounding the ripe fruit in small pots. Eventually, a rudimentary form of mass production developed—the olives were pounded by foot in large rock-hewn tubs and the oil was channeled into collection vats, where, over the course of several days, the oil separated from the heavier water and sediments. This process, however, resulted in a great waste of precious resources, with much oil remaining in the pulp, as well as sore feet.

In order to extract the sizable amount of remaining oil, people began to grind the pulp with a millstone and then press it. By the early Iron Age (tenth century BCE), the lever press had developed; it was followed, about three centuries later, by the crushing wheel. In the latter device, the olives, pits and all, were ground in an open tub by a rotating vertical stone wheel attached to a long horizontal wooden beam, which was turned around a large vertical wooden beam by a donkey or ox that had been blindfolded to prevent dizziness. The paste was then transferred to woven fiber baskets, about three inches thick and two feet in diameter; stacked atop several other baskets; and squeezed in a lever press. This process took several hours or even days to complete. The released dark liquid flowed into massive collection basins or pots. Many ancient crushing wheels in Israel have been found in caves—the cooler air and absence of direct sunlight made these locations ideal for preserving the oil. By the Talmudic period, a method had been introduced by which the olives could be crushed without breaking the pits, and the wooden screw had been employed to more effectively press the pulp. Virtually every Israeli village, as well as many homes, possessed at least a small press.

Olive oil formed part of the trio, along with grain (wheat and barley) and wine, that served as the basis of the diet and economy of ancient Israel; it was used not only as a food, but also as a fuel, a medicine, and an ingredient in cosmetics and ointments. Many small pottery lamps made over the course of thousands of

Olives are one of the Seven Species of Israel noted in the Bible. Grindstones, here found in Capernaum, Israel, were used to separate the meat from the oil—a more efficient innovation over the earlier method of pounding olives by foot.

years have been excavated throughout Israel, attesting to oil's once-essential role in interior illumination.

Not surprisingly, olive oil played a central role in the rituals and culture of ancient Israel, serving as a symbol of holiness, wisdom, abundance, and blessing. Olive oil is among the seven agricultural items with which the land of Israel was praised—"a land of wheat and barley, and vines and fig-trees and pomegranates; a land of oil-olives and honey." The Talmud reveals a traditional view in which the oil is preferred over the olives: "Olives produce forgetfulness of what one has learned, while olive oil makes a clear head." The grain offerings of the Temple were kneaded with olive oil. Even the word messiah (anointed) refers to olive oil; Jewish kings were anointed with olive oil, as were Aaron and his sons as priests. In honor of the role of olive oil in the land of Israel, the Sages mandated the kindling of lights (*nayrot*) for the inauguration of the Sabbath and festivals. Wine is represented by the Kiddush and grains by the Hamotzi. The holiday of Hanukkah is associated with the olive oil of the Temple, where a very pure form was used to light the menorah (candelabra) every day. Lights are still used in Jewish tradition to express transition. They are kindled to usher in the Sabbath and the festivals, and to close the Sabbath during the Havdalah ceremony; they are frequently carried by members of a wedding party, and are lit during shiva (mourning) and for a *yahrtzeit* (anniversary of a death).

Today, Israel produces about five thousand tons of olive oil annually, primarily from Barnea, Nabali, and Souri cultivars grown in the Jezreel Valley in the Galilee. Olive oil is generally classified by three grades, based upon the amount of acidity: extra-virgin, virgin, and pure. Extra-virgin oil is cold-pressed from the first pressing. Virgin oil is generally produced from the second or third pressing. Pure, the lowest grade, is a misleading term indicating that it is made only from olives. However, pure olive oil is chemically refined and deodorized to reduce acidity and impurities. If the label contains the word pomace, the oil has been extracted by adding solvents to the pulp.

Olive oil has long been essential to Italian and Sephardic cuisines. Among the Spanish Inquisition's signs of Jewish cooking was the use of olive oil for frying. Ashkenazim in Europe, on the other hand, living far from the Mediterranean home of the olive, rarely if ever saw or tasted its oil. Jews from central

Asia relied on other oils, such as sesame, and rarely enjoyed olive oil. Today in modern Israel, olive oil is commonly used by the entire population.

(See also Hanukkah, Oil, and Olive)

ONION

The onion, a name derived from the Latin *unio* (large pearl), is a member of the lily family. There are three predominant onion bulb colors: yellow, white, and red (purple). Green onions are the shoots of immature onions that have formed a 1- to 2-inch bulb, but the bulb has not yet developed its papery covering. Pearl onions are white onions that are harvested while still small, resulting in a mild flavor.

This native of Afghanistan or central Asia was already used as food by the Stone Age and, for much of history, raw onions, together with bread, beer, and legumes, served as the mainstay of the common person's diet in western and central Asia and north Africa. Today, onions are the world's sixth largest vegetable crop, not only because these bulbs serve as the base flavor of many dishes, but also because they are able to make other foods more flavorful. The earliest Sumerian inscriptions, dating back nearly forty-five hundred years, mentioned onions and later Hammurabi's Code mandated that a ration of bread and onions be given monthly to the poor. The Greek historian Herodotus noted that the workers who built the pyramids, in which pictures of these bulbs were common, subsisted on "[black] radishes, onions, and leeks," all purported to build stamina.

The Bible relates that the Israelites after leaving Egypt yearned for six items, including *betzalim* (onions). From the onset, onions have been an essential and enduring element of Jewish cooking and no contemporary form of Jewish cuisine would be complete without this pungent bulb. Onions were commonly mentioned in rabbinic literature. A Talmudic sage recommended, "Eat *betzal* [onion] and dwell in the *ba'tzel* [shade], and do not eat geese and fowl lest your heart pursue you; reduce your food and drink and increase [expenditure] on your house." In other words, spending too much on rich foods causes debt and diverts money from household expenses; onions were recommended because they were in line with the general Jewish philosophy of moderation and health.

By the eleventh century, salted raw onions were a common Sabbath dish in Franco-Germany. Soon chopped onions were mixed with other favorite foods, including hard-boiled eggs, fish, and chopped liver, creating classic Ashkenazic dishes. Onions remained the principal seasoning for Ashkenazim for a millennium; they were sometimes used both raw and cooked in the same dish for different tastes and textures. In some instances, onions were a major or even sole component of Ashkenazic dishes. Yiddish is replete with onion idioms, including "*tzibeleh trern*" (akin to crocodile tears) and "*s'iz nisht vert tzibeleh*" (it isn't worth an onion).

Browned onions and fried onions are among the elements that define Ashkenazic cuisine. Ashkenazic cooks knew that golden brown fried onions enlivened their otherwise basic and bland food. They mixed browned onions into a host of dishes, such as scrambled eggs, salads (especially egg salad), soups, mashed potatoes, kasha, pasta, savory noodle kugel, pirogen, and sandwiches. Onions lie at the heart of a Hungarian *paprikás*, in which the onions are not sautéed with fat in the typical manner, but rather cooked, covered and with the addition of a little liquid to prevent burning, for an extended time.

Onions were also beloved, if less vital, in the Mediterranean area and central Asia. The Spanish Inquisition considered a sign of being a practicing Jew as "making their meat dishes with onions and garlic and cooking them in oil [instead of lard]." Sephardic dishes include *sevoyas reyenadas* (stuffed onions) and *sevoyas agras dulces* (sweet and sour onions). Raw onion salads remain widespread in central Asia and the Caucasus. Onions lie at the base of Ethiopian stews (*wots*), in which they are uniquely first cooked in a dry pan before being adding to the fat. Lithuanians call browned onions or other fillings in the heart of a dumpling *neshomelekh* (little souls), elevating a simple dish to another level.

ORANGE

The orange, the world's most popular citrus, is the fruit (technically a large berry), of a subtropical tree probably originating in northeastern India and thought to by a hybrid of the pomelo and mandarin. The Sanskrit word *narunga* (fruit like an elephant) is the source of the Persian *narang*. Around 1380, the French word *orenge* made its way into Middle English, and it was eventually spelled orange. From the fruit later came the English name of the color.

The orange, both fruit and tree, was depicted in mosaics from Pompeii (destroyed in 79 CE). Ceiling mosaics for the mausoleum in Rome built by the Emperor Constantine for his daughter around 330 CE clearly depict oranges and lemons. But oranges and other citrus disappeared from Europe following the Lombard invasion in 568 and the fall of the Roman Empire, and did not reappear in Italy until at least the eleventh century.

The Arabs had brought oranges, along with revolutionary agricultural and irrigation techniques, west from Persia through North Africa to Spain by the end of the ninth century, and to Sicily by 1002. Besides the Arabs, the history of oranges in the West is intrinsically intertwined with the Jews who cultivated citrons (etrogim) for Sukkot and also grew new species when they became available. It was by no coincidence that the centers of medieval citrus cultivation directly corresponded to the centers of Jewish population.

Not only did Jews play a historic role in Mediterranean citrus production, but Sephardim were the early citrus distributors and wholesalers. In addition, they actively cultivated and traded oranges and lemons in the Caribbean and South America. In the nineteenth century, Ashkenazic peddlers began selling oranges in many parts of Europe. Scottish clergyman William Brown, in his two-volume *Antiquities of the Jews* (Edinburgh, 1823), recounted, "At present, they carry these branches [palm] into the synagogue, and provide themselves with oranges and citrons in countries where they do not grow." The book *London Labour and the London Poor* by Henry Mayhew (London, 1851) included a chapter entitled "How the Street-Irish Displanted the Street-Jews in the Orange Trade" in which he explained that "the trade was, not many years ago, confined almost entirely to the Jew boys who kept aloof from the vagrant lads of the streets," until Jews found it more profitable to peddle other wares. But although Jewish street peddlers selling oranges disappeared, the Jews maintained for a while a monopoly of the wholesale end of the orange business in England. In many eastern European households, an orange was considered a special Hanukkah present.

The original oranges were bitter oranges, also called sour oranges and Seville oranges. By the thirteenth century, groves of bitter oranges covered the region from Seville to Granada as well as parts of Portugal.

Bitter orange trees tend to be more decorative and fragrant than other orange trees. Bitter oranges were initially used in marinades for meat and fish or merely as an ornamental crop. It was only after Arabs spread sugarcane westward to Syria, North Africa, and Spain that bitter oranges began to make an impact on cooking. Today, these varieties, rarely available fresh in the United States, are processed into preserves, confections, orange-blossom water, perfumes, and liqueurs. About 90 percent of Spain's bitter orange crop is still shipped to England to make marmalade.

The earliest verifiable record of a sweet orange dates from the early twelfth century CE in China, and these fruits were mentioned in India by the early fourteenth century. Sweet oranges were first introduced to Europe in 1529 by Portuguese traders, who found them in China. In 1635, an even sweeter variety of orange reached Lisbon from China and sweet oranges quickly supplanted the bitter ones. Consequently, in many languages, sweet oranges are named after Portugal, such as the Ladino *portokal* and Arabic *bortugal*.

Blood oranges, or pigmented oranges, are small, generally seedless oranges with a deeper flavor and redder color than other sweet oranges. Full blood oranges have red skin and red flesh; semi-blood oranges have orange skin and red flesh. The degree of redness depends on the variety and climate; with hotter climates producing deeper colors and sweeter flavor. Blood oranges have long been sought after in the Mediterranean, where they comprise one-third of all oranges grown and consumed. However, they have not developed a similar popularity among American growers due to their uneven bearing abilities and the unpredictability of the pulp's coloration.

Early on, oranges emerged as a distinctive feature of Sephardic cuisine, particularly in baked goods, such as *torta de los reyes* (orange-almond cake) and *torta de portokal*. Oranges are also boiled to make preserves, poached in sugar syrup, cooked with chicken and cinnamon, and used to make custard. Some Sephardim chop up a whole orange in their Passover charoset.

In the seventh century, the Arabs introduced the bitter orange to Israel and much later the sweet orange arrived; the common variety of the latter is called *baladi* in Arabic and Hebrew. Around 1844, a mutation of a *baladi* occurred somewhere near the city of Jaffa. The new type of orange, called the Shamouti, was a medium-large, oval, aromatic variety that became renowned for its juiciness, sweetness, and extraordinary shipping abilities. Within a few decades, this newcomer had become the predominant orange of the Levant and had become better known as the Jaffa orange, named after the main port through which it passed for export. The first to use the brand name "Jaffa orange" was Sarona, a Christian agricultural colony founded by the German-based Temple Society in 1871. Around 1880, a small shipment of Jaffa oranges was first sent to England by Jewish businessmen as a commercial proposition, and citriculture subsequently became the main source of income for Jewish settlers and, for much of the twentieth century, for Israel. Jaffa became synonymous with the fruit.

In 1855, Sir Moses Montefiore purchased about twenty-five acres of orange trees near Jaffa from the Ottoman sultan and selected thirty-five families from Safed to operate it. This was the first Jewish orange orchard in the country. In 1878, a small group of Orthodox Jews from Jerusalem, desiring to escape the city's cramped conditions, purchased 767 acres of mostly swampland northeast of Jaffa along the Yarkon River, founding the first modern Jewish agricultural settlement, Petach Tikvah (Gateway of Hope). Due to the ravages of malaria, the project was abandoned, but in 1883, with financial backing from Baron Edmond de Rothschild, a few of the founders, along with a new group of religious immigrants, cleared the swamps and planted vines and orange trees. Petach Tikvah is now a city of some one hundred seventy thousand and the second-largest industrial center in Israel.

Following the departure of the Ottomans at the end of World War I, agriculture in the Holy Land flourished, led by orange production. Orange groves covered the dunes and plains around Jaffa and along the ancient Via Maris road leading north from Egypt to Syria. The Jaffa orange became a symbol of the accomplishments of the new state of Israel. At their peak in the early 1970s, orange orchards expanded to 105,000 acres. Then toward the end of the twentieth century, due to trade agreements among European Union members (they do not pay tariffs) and competition from other countries with cheaper labor, Israeli oranges experienced a decline. In their place, some farmers turned to various exotics, such as Sharon fruit, *pitaya* (a juicy cactus fruit, also called "dragon fruit"), kumquats, and other new citrus hybrids. Still,

in 2008, Israel devoted sixty-two thousand acres to oranges, yielding one million tons of fruit, and the orange continues to be immensely popular among the Israeli people.

(See also Citrus and Etrog)

ORANGE-BLOSSOM WATER

In 800 CE, the Arab scholar Jabir ibn Hayyan invented an improved still. About two centuries later, the Bukharan-born physician ibn Sina (980–1037), latinized as Avicenna, discovered how to use the still to extract essential oils from flower petals to produce distilled floral waters, particularly rose water (*ma wared*) and orange-blossom water (*ma zaher*). Initially developed as a means of administering drugs, the distilled waters were soon appropriated for perfumes and cooking. The distillation process for making orange-blossom water, also called orange-flower water, has changed little over the centuries, and some families continue to make their own in basements and garages throughout the Middle East. Kilos of petals from bitter oranges, also called Seville oranges, are placed in a large copper still and covered with plain water. After the lid is secured, the still is placed over a fire and left to boil. The vapor passes through a tube, where it condenses at the other end and drips into bottles.

Middle Easterners frequently use these aromatic distilled waters to flavor and perfume baked goods, confections, puddings, salads, fruit dishes, rice dishes, and poultry and lamb dishes. A popular use is as a flavoring for sugar syrups that are drizzled over pastries and fruit. Several drops of orange-blossom water are added to cups of hot water to create *cahve blanco* (white coffee). Orange-blossom water is very concentrated, so it is used sparingly, adding just a hint of fragrance and an intriguing flavor.

OUBLIE

Oublie is a round wafer cooked between two heated pieces of metal.

Origin: France

From the early twelfth century through the succeeding five hundred years, the most popular treat of France was the *oublie*, a thin, crisp, wafer-like pastry made on iron molds heated over a flame.

The concept of wafers dates back to antiquity. Ancient Egyptians, upon the annual decrease in the water level of the Nile, offered emmer wafers as well as large bread loaves to Osiris, originally the god of grains and later of the dead. The Bible described the manna as "*tzeepeechat* [a loose batter dropped on a hot griddle, from the root "to spread out"] made with honey." Both the words wafer and waffle derive from the same source, the Middle Dutch *wafel* (honeycomb). The difference is that waffles, containing a leavening agent, are lighter.

According to *Larousse Gastronomique*, the ancient Greeks made thin wafer cakes—called *obleios,* probably because they were sold for an *obol* (a Greek coin)—by pressing some thick batter between two heated metal plates. This Greek innovation of cooking both sides of the batter was the next step in the culinary evolution from the earlier practice of cooking very thin breads on one side on a heated earthenware griddle. Others contend that the name derived from the Eucharist, called *oblate* in German and *oublie* in French, from the medieval Latin *oblatus* (offered). In any case, the wafer technique was not invented solely for the Eucharist, but was adopted by the church from existing technology.

Basic medieval European wafers, which consisted of unleavened disks made from flour and water, were prepared in the same manner as the *obleios*—cooked on heated irons. Also like the Greek wafers, the early medieval ones were unsweetened, although they were sometimes served with honey. The wafer batter, like that of early medieval cakes, was generally made from bread crumbs rather than flour.

Toward the end of the eleventh century, Crusaders returning from the Levant brought back with them numerous culinary concepts, one of which resulted in a variation of the *oublie* in which honey and sometimes orange-blossom water were added to the crumb-based batter. Subsequently, the residents of northern and central France had two forms of *oublie*: the plain ones used by the church and the sweetened nonsectarian ones. Both types were cooked in the same manner:

between two flat iron paddles. Many paddles had an imprinted ornamentation, such as a landscape, coat of arms, or, the most common, honeycomb. When the paddles were opened, the thin wafer was peeled off. The *oublie* could be left flat or, while still warm, could be rolled into a cylinder or cone shape. Some wafers were enjoyed as thin cookies, while others were used as a base for various bar cookies, such as lebkuchen. The wafer protected the upper portion from the ashes of the oven during baking. Only a very wealthy home or professional *oublie* maker (*oubloyeur*) possessed a set of the expensive metal wafer irons, so *oublie* was not a homemade treat. *Oubloyeurs* or *oublieurs*, who formed their own guild in 1270 and controlled the quality of wafers, peddled their wares at markets, at fairs, and along the street. Also in the thirteenth century, craftsmen fashioned a metal mold to produce a thicker pastry, called *gaufre* (Old French for "honeycomb"), which became the waffle. Dutch Jews adopted waffles as a holiday treat and later introduced them to English Jews.

In the thirteenth century, metal workers began fashioning the wafer irons as a pair of hinged metal plates embossed with crisscross patterns called *waufres/gaufres*. The iron plates were attached to long wooden handles, allowing the "baker" to easily and safely heat and manipulate the irons. Toward the end of the medieval period, flour replaced bread crumbs and, as sugar became more prominent in Europe, it was increasingly added to wafer batter.

Early Ashkenazic rabbinic literature contains numerous mentions of the term *oublie* and *obleit*, as this wafer was also the most popular early western Ashkenazic treat. Many Jews enjoyed the wafers on a weekly basis. German, and later Polish, Jews never shared their French brethren's affection for *oublies*. By the end of the seventeenth century, French pastry had begun to evolve and the *oublie* declined in popularity, although various wafers and waffles endure.

P

PADHAR
Padhar is a coconut-filled crepe.
Origin: India
Other names: *petar*, sweet puri.

Among the Bene Israel of India, every holiday was associated with at least one sweet. Two or three days before Yom Kippur, the women gathered in groups to prepare *padhar* to be enjoyed after the fast. Actually, the fast was broken with a drink of *sherbet*, a raisin beverage made by boiling black raisins in water, then squashing them and straining the liquid; this drink was followed by fruit, in particular bananas, and then the *padhar*. Plenty were made in order to also give them as gifts to friends, both Jews and non-Jews. Originally, *padhar* were made from deep-fried unleavened flatbreads called puris, but more recently cooks have substituted crepes made with coconut milk. The crepes are spread with a sweetened coconut mixture—the coconut may be either raw or toasted—then rolled up like a cigar. Sometimes the crepes and filling are stacked in seven layers to make a version called *saath padhar* (Hindi meaning "together").

INDIAN COCONUT CREPES (*PADHAR*)
ABOUT TWENTY 5-INCH OR SIXTEEN 6-INCH CIGARS
[DAIRY OR PAREVE]

1½ cups coconut milk
1 large egg, lightly beaten
2 tablespoons ghee (clarified butter), melted butter, or coconut oil
1 tablespoon jaggery or sugar
1 teaspoon vanilla extract
⅛ teaspoon table salt or ¼ teaspoon kosher salt
1½ cups (7.5 ounces) unbleached all-purpose flour

Ghee, butter, or vegetable oil for cooking the crepes
Filling:
1 cup plus 2 tablespoons (8 ounces) jaggery or sugar
¾ cup plus 2 tablespoons water

3¾ cups (10 ounces) grated coconut, fresh or frozen
Pinch of ground cardamom (optional)

1. In a medium bowl, whisk together the coconut milk, egg, butter, sugar, vanilla, and salt. Gradually whisk in the flour to make a smooth, thin batter with the consistency of heavy cream. Strain if there are any lumps. Or process all the ingredients in a blender until smooth. Cover and refrigerate for at least 2 hours or up to 2 days.

2. Heat a 5-, 6-, or 8-inch heavy skillet (cast-iron or nonstick is best) over medium heat. Brush lightly with the ghee.

3. Pour in about 2 tablespoons batter for a 5- to 6-inch pan or 3 tablespoons for an 8-inch pan, tilting the pan until the batter just coats the bottom. Cook until the edges begin to brown, about 45 seconds. Turn the crepe over and cook until golden, about 30 seconds. Flip onto a plate lined with wax paper. Repeat with the remaining batter. Stack the crepes between pieces of wax paper, foil, or dampened paper towels.

4. To make the filling: In a medium saucepan, stir the sugar and water over medium heat until the sugar dissolves. Remove from the heat and stir in the coconut and, if using, cardamom. Let cool.

5. Spread 2 to 3 tablespoons filling over each crepe, leaving a ½-inch border. Roll up jelly-roll style.

PALACSINTA
Palacsinta is a crepe as well as a filled crepe.
Origin: Romania, Hungary
Other names: Austria and eastern Europe: *palatschinke*; Czech: *palačinka*; French: *crêpe*; German: *krepp, palatschinke, pfannkuchen*; Polish: *nalesnik*; Romania: *clatita*; Slovakia: *palacinka*; Ukranian; *blyntsi, mlynets, nalysnyky*; Yiddish: *blintze*.

Pancakes are among humankind's earliest foods. For much of history, they were rather crude, consisting of porridges cooked on heated flat rocks (the early French word for pancake, *galette*, comes from the word meaning "flat stone") and later on clay and then metal griddles. The ancient Roman *placenta* (from the Greek thin bread cooked on a griddle, *plakous*) was a flat rudimentary cake made of soft cheese, flour, and honey and cooked in a pan over the embers of a fire. Medieval Romanians called tarts filled with cheese and sometimes other savory fillings (including cabbage, meat, and spinach) by the name *placinta*.

Beginning in the fourteenth century, the Turks, who had absorbed both Persian and Byzantine cuisines, conquered the Balkans, introducing numerous culinary advances, including phyllo dough, and very thin pancakes made from semolina flour and eggs that were cooked in a shallow skillet, then topped with feta cheese or other fillings, and rolled up. A favorite Romanian way to use phyllo was in a strudel-like *borek*, which was somewhat similar in appearance to the thicker, filled, new-style pancakes. Consequently, both the cheese-filled phyllo and the thin pancakes were initially called *placinta*. The pancakes eventually traveled to Hungary and, since the Hungarian language does not have initial consonant clusters, the *pla* was transformed to *pala* and the word for the thin pancakes became *palacsinta*. (Afterwards in Romania, to differentiate the thin pancake from the popular strudel and the tart, most Romanians referred to it by the generic word for pancake and fritter, *clatita*, while both the strudel and tart retained the name *placinta*.) Gradually, the thin pancakes spread throughout central and eastern Europe. In the middle of the nineteenth century, when fine wheat flour became increasingly available in Europe, the various crepes became widespread. The primary difference between *palacsinta* and the modern French crepe and the blintz is that the latter two typically contain some fat and more eggs in the batter.

For generations, most Hungarian have kept a well-seasoned heavy pan—many Jewish housewives had one for dairy and one for meat—for making *palacsinta*. Many Hungarians insist on only frying the *palacsinta* in butter, contending that the melding of the browning butter with the browning batter is necessary to create the characteristic flavor. For meat meals, however, schmaltz or oil is substituted. Some Hungarians prefer their *palacsinta* very eggy, while others feel that a little carbonated water, a nineteenth-century innovation, makes them lighter and more tender. The pancakes should be moist and slightly pale yellow—the color is a sign that sufficient eggs have been used. Some Romanians and Hungarians still make the batter using semolina, but most opt for regular flour. A few recipes, particularly those from the nineteenth century, include a little yeast, yielding a slightly fluffier *palacsinta* without the need for carbonated beverages; crepes leavened with yeast are called *erjed palacsinta*.

In particular, the characteristic Hungarian fillings and toppings, many adopted by neighbors in Romania and Austria, are what make *palacsinta* distinctive from the crepes of western Europe and the blintzes of eastern Europe. For appetizers and side dishes, Hungarians fill *palacsinta* with savory mixtures, such as ground beef, but their favorites are those with sweet fillings. The most common way of enjoying *palacsinta* is to spread the warm crepes with apricot lekvar that has been slightly thinned with a little wine, liqueur, or water; roll up the crepes; and sprinkle them with confectioners' sugar—in Romania, this dish is called *clatite cu dulceata*. *Palacsinta* with sweetened cheese (*túró*) is a popular Hungarian Shavuot dish. The *gundel palacsinta* is particularly beloved all over Hungary; in this version, introduced around 1910 by Budapest restaurateur Károly Gundel, crepes are spread with a ground walnut, raisin, and lemon zest filling; folded; flambéed in rum; and topped with a warm chocolate sauce (*csokoládé öntettel*). Chocolate sauce is also a favorite topping for other types of *palacsinta* besides those filled with ground walnuts, including sweetened chestnut cream, almond paste, chocolate-hazelnut spread, cheese, pastry cream, or cinnamon-sugar.

Palacsinta remains a favorite Hungarian dessert, rivaled in popularity perhaps only by strudel. However, since good strudel is much more difficult to make, *palacsinta* is more frequently seen in homes. Hostesses generally serve them after a special meal or to make an ordinary meal special, and any Hungarian restaurant worth its paprika offers at least one *palacsinta* dish for dessert. For generations, Hungarian children have typically begged their mother or grandmother to prepare *palacsinta* when the craving strikes, and they are frequently indulged. For Hungarians all over the world, *palacsinta* is the comfort food that conjures up nostalgic memories of childhood and significant occasions.

HUNGARIAN CREPES (*PALACSINTA*)

ABOUT TWELVE 7- OR 8-INCH PANCAKES   [DAIRY OR PAREVE]

3 large eggs, lightly beaten
1 cup milk, almond milk, or water
2 teaspoons sugar

1 teaspoon vanilla extract or grated lemon zest

¼ teaspoon table salt or ½ teaspoon kosher salt

1¼ cups (6.25 ounces) all-purpose flour

½ cup seltzer or cold water

About 2 tablespoons butter or vegetable oil for frying

About 2 cups Ashkenazic Poppy Seed Filling (page 198), apricot lekvar, prune lekvar, jam, almond paste, pastry cream, or sweetened whipped cream (optional)

1. In a medium bowl, whisk together the eggs, milk, sugar, vanilla, and salt. Gradually whisk in the flour. Strain if there are any lumps. Or process all the ingredients in a blender until smooth. Cover and refrigerate for at least 1 hour or overnight.

2. Just before frying, stir in the seltzer to make a smooth, thin batter with the consistency of heavy cream or syrup.

3. Heat a 7- or 8-inch heavy skillet (cast-iron or nonstick is best) over medium heat and add about ¼ tablespoon butter.

4. Pour in 2½ to 3 tablespoons batter, tilting the pan until the batter just coats the bottom. Fry until the edges begin to brown, about 1 minute. Turn the crepe over and fry until set, about 15 seconds. Flip onto a plate lined with wax paper. Repeat with the remaining batter. Stack the crepes between pieces of wax paper, foil, or dampened paper towels.

5. To make töltött palacsinta (filled crepes), place the crepes, speckled side up, on a flat surface. Spread with about 2 tablespoons filling. Roll up jelly-roll style. Or fold in half to form a half-moon shape, then fold in half again to form a triangle. Or fold in half, then roll the ends toward the center to form a triangular cone.

PALAU

Palau is a rice pilaf with meat.

Origin: Afghanistan

Other names: *palow, pulaw.*

In Afghanistan, as in the rest of central Asia, the favorite grain is rice. The overwhelmingly favorite Afghan rice dish is *palau*. It may have traveled from India along the Silk Road or arrived in the other direction from Persia, but the current Afghan version has clearly been affected over the centuries by both regions. Historically, *palau* was cooked in a *dayg* (a large pot similar to a Dutch oven), which was covered and set over an open fire, with extra coals on the lid for more even heating. This remains the standard practice today in many rural areas. More recently, however, many Afghans have adopted the Persian two-stage method for cooking the rice.

The most common method for the initial stage of cooking the rice for *palau* is *dampokht*, in which the grains are simmered for about twenty minutes in just enough liquid (usually a meat broth) to produce dry grains, then steamed. The other method, *sof*, which is the Persian style, calls for the rice to be washed, soaked, and parboiled in a large amount of salted water for about 3 minutes; it is then drained and steamed with a broth and/or meat and spices. Although the *sof* method requires extra work, many cooks prefer it as it is more likely to produce the desired results. Traditionally, the second stage of preparation, the steaming, was performed over a fire, but today many Afghans, particularly those in the cities who own a home oven, bake the *palau* in the oven. Before baking, some cooks mix the meat and rice together, while others separate them into layers. In any case, Afghans insist that their cooking methods reveal the true delicacy of rice like no other. If the rice sticks together—a scandal for a proper *palau*—it is dismissively referred to as *shola* (short-grain rice), a great insult to any cook.

For most dishes, Afghans prefer a fine long-grain rice grown in the south of the country or imported basmati; when cooked, these varieties yield grains that are dry, fluffy, and separate. Several locally grown short-grain varieties have extra starch, which results in sticky cooked rice. They are generally reserved for desserts. The living standard of the average Afghan has long been lower than that of people in many of the surrounding countries. Therefore, even the wealthier Afghans typically eat rice only once a day, while the average family reserves it for special occasions, frequently for making a *palau*.

The usual *palau* features a large amount of rice and just a taste of meat—most of the flavor comes from the cooking liquid. Typically, the *palau* is accented with a combination of cardamom, cinnamon, cloves, and cumin; the Indian-inspired spicing provides a rich aroma and, along with the meat and browned onions, transforms the rice into a brown color. Versions made with chicken broth sometimes include a little saffron or turmeric for a yellowish hue. There is also a popular version in which the rice is cooked in water instead of broth, and caramelized sugar is added for a golden brown color. When cooked in spinach cooking water and/or with chopped spinach, the dish becomes a *zamarud palau* (emerald pilaf). There are also vegetarian versions, such as *narenj palou* (pilaf with orange zest, almonds, and pistachios) and *badenjan palou* (pilaf with eggplant). When the rice is served with kebabs, usually lamb or chicken, the dish is called *palau kabob*. The crust on the bottom of the pan is known as *tie daygi* and is considered a delicacy. To remove the rice from the pot and keep the *tie daygi* intact, Afghans use a *kafgeer*, a large, slotted, flat spatula. Afghans historically did not use silverware; instead the diners ate the *palau* using their right hand or a piece of *nan* (bread).

The *palau*, typically the center of every Afghan *dastarkhan* (literally "tablecloth," but meaning "feast"), is served on a large communal platter, which along with other special dishes—such as *dolmas* (stuffed grape leaves), *kufta* (meatballs), and *bichak* (filled turnovers)—is customarily placed closest to the guests. It is assumed that there will be *palau* at a wedding and other notable occasions. At such affairs and in Afghan restaurants, sautéed carrots, raisins, and nuts are used to garnish the *palou* or mixed in for flavor and textural contrasts, creating a dish known in the West as *kabli palau/qabuli palau*, after the country's capital, Kabul. The carrots of Afghanistan, probably the home of this vegetable, are typically purple, and cooks preparing Western versions must usually make do with sweeter orange varieties. Afghan Jews even make a *palau* for Sabbath lunch, leaving it to slowly bake in a very low oven overnight.

(See also Chelow, Pilau, and Plov)

AFGHAN MEAT AND RICE PILAF/BROWN RICE (*PALAU*)

3 TO 4 SERVINGS AS A MAIN COURSE   [MEAT]

2½ cups (1 pound) long-grain rice, such as basmati
2 pounds boneless lamb shoulder or beef chuck,
    cut into 1-inch cubes; 3 pounds lamb shanks,
    cut in half; or 1 (3- to 4-pound) chicken, cut up
¼ cup vegetable oil
2 medium yellow onions, chopped
1 to 2 cloves garlic, minced
1 teaspoon ground cardamom
1 teaspoon ground cinnamon
1 teaspoon ground cloves
1 teaspoon ground cumin
4 cups water

About ½ teaspoon ground black pepper
About 2½ teaspoons table salt or 5 teaspoons
    kosher salt

1. Rinse the rice in cold water several times until clear. Place the rice in a large bowl, add water to cover, and let soak for at least 30 minutes and up to 3 hours. Drain and set aside.

2. Pat the meat dry with paper towels. In a large, heavy pot, heat 2 tablespoons oil over medium-high heat. Add the meat, if necessary in batches so as not to overcrowd the pan, and brown on all sides, about 8 minutes per batch. Transfer the meat to a warm platter.

3. Reduce the heat to medium and add the remaining 2 tablespoons oil. Add the onions and sauté until golden brown, about 20 minutes. Add the garlic, cardamom, cinnamon, cloves, and cumin and sauté for 1 minute. Add 1 cup water, scrape the pan to loosen any browned bits, and slightly mash the onions. Add the remaining 3 cups water, pepper, and 1 teaspoon salt. Return the meat, cover, and bring to a simmer.

4. Continue to simmer over medium-low heat or bake in a 300°F oven, stirring occasionally, until tender, about 1 hour for lamb, 2 hours for beef or mutton, or 40 minutes for chicken. At this point, the stew can be cooled and stored in the refrigerator for up to 3 days and reheated before cooking the rice.

5. Remove the meat and keep warm, leaving the cooking liquid in the pot. Bring the cooking liquid to a boil, stir in the rice and remaining 1½ teaspoons salt. Cover and simmer until the liquid is absorbed, about 18 minutes.

6. Transfer the rice to an ovenproof dish and top with the meat. Or layer half of the rice in the dish, add all the meat, and top with the remaining rice. Or for *qorma palau*, combine all the ingredients in the dish. Cover and bake in a 300°F oven for at least 30 minutes or up to 1 hour. Serve warm.

VARIATIONS

Afghan Sabbath Pilaf (Palau Shabati): Cut 2 large baking (russet) potatoes into ¼-inch-thick slices and arrange over the bottom of a large ovenproof casserole dish or pan. Add half of the cooked rice, sprinkle with ½ to ¾ cup raisins and the cooked meat, top with the remaining rice, then drizzle with 1 cup hot water and ¼ cup vegetable oil. Cover tightly and bake at 300°F for 30 minutes, then reduce the temperature to 200°F, and cook overnight.

PÁLENKA/PÁLINKA

In Slovakia and the Czech Republic, *pálenka* (from the Slavic *pálit*, "to distill"), called *palinca* in Romania, denotes any distilled spirit, but particularly those made from fruit. Most popular are those made from plum (*slivovica*), but also notable are those distilled from apricot (*marhulovica*), cherry (*ceresnovica*), and pear (*hruskovica*). The concept was also borrowed by the Hungarians, who called these spirits *pálinka*, but in Hungary the word refers only to a strong double-distilled spirit made from various fruits, notably apricot (*barackpálinka*), cherry (*cseresznyepálinka*), pear (*körtepálinka*), and plum (*szilvapálinka*). In Hungary, *pálinka* are produced commercially as well as made at home. Nearly 70 percent of all plums grown in the Slavic region of the Balkans go into the production of plum *pálenka*, commonly referred as slivovitz. Slivovitz became extremely popular among eastern European Jews, especially for Passover, as it is generally not made from grains.

PANDERICAS

Pandericas is a sweet bread or roll.

Origin: Iberia

Other names: *panderas, pan dulce, panisico dulce, reshas.*

Sephardim, unlike Ashkenazim, did not use sweetened breads to make the Hamotzi (benediction before eating bread), as these baked goods were viewed as cakes. They did, however, on special occasions include them in their holiday repertoire as accompaniments for the meal or as a snack. As the cuisine evolved, Sephardic fritters called *bolo/boyo* (from the Ladino for "ball" and now generally translated as "bun") became an array of small sweet and savory fried and then baked goods. A related larger bread, dating back to well before the expulsion from Spain in 1492, is *pandericas* (rich bread), which was typically accented with orange zest, the characteristic Sephardic flavor, or sometimes lemon zest or anise. Bread knots are called *pan de kaza* (home bread). In the first Jewish cookbook in English, *The Jewish Manual* (London, 1846), the author, Judith Montefiore—reflecting the Portuguese background of her husband—included recipes for a "A Plain Bola," "Bola Toliedo," and "A Bola D'Hispaniola." The latter two breads were made from dough similar to that of *pandericas* and were layered with various fillings.

Pandericas, in rolls or large loaves, is served for Sabbath *desayuno* (brunch), on Rosh Hashanah, and before and after the fast of Yom Kippur. In the Maghreb, the loaves are known as *mouna* (Arabic meaning "food") and the rolls, which are frequently shaped into the initials of family and guests, are called *mounettes* and *petit pains*. The texture of bread made from the slightly rich dough is light and moist, yet the bread is firm enough to be sliced when fresh. For dairy meals, such as *desayuno*, the dough is sometimes made with milk.

The many Conversos (forcibly converted Iberian Jews, also called Marrano-Anusim and Crypto-Jews) in the New World in the sixteenth century were probably the source of the contemporary Mexican equivalent, a sweet egg bread known as *pan dulce*, as well as various other local pastries, including *cuernos* (horn-shaped pastries) and *trenzas* (braided pastries). Some of these pastries are shaped like pigs, such as the gingerbread *marronito*, an ironic food allusion as well as a reference to the other term for Conversos, Marranos (pigs). Many non-Jewish Mexican families, as they have for generations, still bake or purchase a sweet bread on Fridays to eat for *meriendas* (afternoon snack) or dinner.

(See also Biscocho, Bolo, Kaak, and Rosca)

SEPHARDIC SWEET BREAD ROLLS
(*PANDERICAS/PANISICO DULCES*)

12 TO 15 ROLLS [PAREVE OR DAIRY]

1 package (2¼ teaspoons) active dry yeast or
    1 (0.6-ounce) cake fresh yeast
1 cup warm water (105°F to 115°F for dry yeast;
    80°F to 85°F for fresh yeast), or ¼ cup water
    and ¾ cup milk
⅓ cup sugar
⅓ cup vegetable or peanut oil
2 large eggs
2 to 3 teaspoons grated orange zest
1 teaspoon table salt or 2 teaspoons kosher salt
About 4 cups (20 ounces) unbleached all-purpose
    flour
Egg wash (1 large egg beaten with 1 teaspoon water)
Sesame seeds for sprinkling (optional)

1. Dissolve the yeast in ¼ cup water. Stir in 1 teaspoon sugar and let stand until foamy, 5 to 10 minutes. In a large bowl, combine the yeast mixture, remaining water, remaining sugar, oil, eggs, zest, and salt. Blend in 1½ cups flour. Gradually add enough of the remaining flour to make a mixture that holds together.

2. On a lightly floured surface or in an electric mixer with a dough hook, knead the dough until smooth and springy, about 5 minutes. Place in an oiled bowl and turn to coat. Cover with plastic wrap or a kitchen towel and let rise in a warm, draft-free place until nearly doubled in bulk, about 2 hours.

3. Punch down the dough. Fold over and press together several times. Divide the dough into 12 to 15 equal pieces. Form into smooth balls, or roll each piece into a rope 6 inches long and ½ inch thick, then tie each rope into a loose knot. Place 1 inch apart on a parchment paper–lined or lightly greased baking sheet, cover, and let rise until nearly doubled in bulk, about 1¼ hours.

4. Preheat the oven to 375°F.

5. Brush the tops of the rolls with the egg wash and, if using, sprinkle with the sesame seeds. Bake until golden brown and hollow sounding when tapped on the bottom, about 20 minutes. Transfer the rolls to a wire rack and let cool.

PANIR

Many Persian words and foods, including *panir/paneer* (Farsi for "cheese"), were spread by the advancing Persian-inspired Mughal Empire throughout much of Asia, *panir* arriving in India in the sixteenth century. Whereas Persians subsumed a number of types of cheese under the term *panir*, including feta-type brined cheeses, Indians use *panir* only to denote a bland, soft, crumbly unripened cheese made by curdling milk with an acid. The Spanish queso blanco (white cheese) and Arabic *jiben beida* (white cheese) are similar, but contain salt. Indians tend to use cow's milk, while goat's and sheep's milk was historically more prominent in western and central Asia.

In India, *panir* is rarely eaten by itself, but rather incorporated into various dishes, absorbing the flavors. For dairy meals, Bene Israel of Mumbai might enjoy *palok panir* (spinach with cheese) or *matar panir* (peas with cheese). In Afghanistan, the soft cheese is served with raisins (*kishmish panir*).

(See also Cheese)

PANNEKOEK

Pannekoek is a pancake.
Origin: the Netherlands
Other names: Dutch baby, *pannenkoek*.

Around the fifteenth century, buckwheat arrived in the Netherlands by way of eastern Europe and, in the Russian manner, the Dutch made buckwheat pancakes, called *pannekoeken*. Recipes for them were recorded in the earliest Dutch cookbook in 1514. By the seventeenth century, cooks began substituting wheat flour for the buckwheat and adding milk and eggs, although these refined pancakes were reserved for special occasions. Wheat pancakes only became commonplace fare in the nineteenth century, when inexpensive high-quality white flour and chemical leavenings became available. As the home oven spread, cooks also began to bake the *pannekoeken*. Dutch *pannekoeken* tend to be larger and thinner than their American counterparts and frequently contain fruit, such as currants, apple slices, and bananas; there are also savory versions.

Sweet *pannekoeken* are a common Dutch breakfast. They are enjoyed with a light sprinkling of confectioners' sugar or *stroop* (syrup), which is thicker than American-style syrup and has the consistency of molasses. Dutch Jews frequently serve *pannekoeken* at the meal to break the fast of Yom Kippur.

PAPANASH

Papanash is a cornmeal and cheese dumpling.
Origin: Romania
Other names: *papanasi*, *papanush*.

Cheese dumplings—called *papanash* by Romanian, Transylvanian, and Bulgarian Jews—are popular throughout central and eastern Europe. *Papanash* are prepared with *brinza de vaci* (a farmer cheese made from cow's milk) and cornmeal, and are a bit different from the Hungarian *gombóc* and other cheese dumplings made in neighboring regions, which are typically made with the creamier *túrós* cheese and semolina or flour. The batter is usually slightly sweetened, but some versions are savory and are served as appetizers. The dumpling mixture is formed into balls (described by cooks as "the size of apricots") and cooked in lightly salted boiling water, yielding soft and creamy dumplings (*papanasi fierti*); the balls may also be deep-fried, or flattened and fried in a little butter (*papanasi prajiti*). The fried version is more prominent in Romanian restaurants, while the boiled version generally predominates at home. Sweet *papanash* are typically served for dessert or a snack; they may be sprinkled with confectioners' sugar or cinnamon-sugar, or served with unsweetened sour cream or yogurt (*cu smantana*) and jam (*dulceata*) or chocolate sauce. They may also be coated with browned bread crumbs and sugar. *Papanash* are traditional on Shavuot and provide a most welcome way of using up leftover soft cheese at other times of the year.

◄ ROMANIAN CHEESE-CORNMEAL DUMPLINGS (*PAPANASH*)

ABOUT 20 DUMPLINGS   [DAIRY]

16 ounces (2 cups) farmer or pot cheese
1 to 3 tablespoons sugar (optional)
1 teaspoon grated lemon zest (optional)
½ teaspoon table salt or 1 teaspoon kosher salt
2 large eggs, lightly beaten
2 tablespoons softened butter or olive oil
About ½ cup fine cornmeal

1. In a food processor fitted with a metal blade, blender, or electric mixer, combine the cheese, sugar, zest, and salt. Add the eggs and beat until smooth. Beat in the butter, 1 tablespoon at a time. Stir in enough cornmeal to produce a firm but soft dough. Cover and refrigerate for at least 2 hours or overnight.

2. Bring a large pot of lightly salted water to a low boil. With moistened hands, form heaping tablespoons of batter into 1½-inch balls.

3. Drop the dumplings in the water. Reduce the heat to medium-low and simmer, uncovered, until cooked through, 10 to 15 minutes (they are done about 5 minutes after they rise to the surface). Remove the dumplings with a slotted spoon. If not serving immediately, keep warm in a 200°F oven.

PAPRIKA

The Turks introduced chilies to the Balkans during their occupation of the region, but how they spread to Hungary remains a matter of contention. In 1526, the Turks began their bid to conquer Hungary, taking the capital Buda in 1529 and remaining in control until 1687, following the Ottoman defeat. Chilies had certainly reached central Europe by then, as the Bavarian botanist Leonhard Fuchs included three varieties in his *Primi de Stirpium* (Basel, 1545), a botanical collection with woodcuts. The plant was first recorded in Hungary in 1569, as "*vörös törökbors*" (red Turkish pepper), in a list written by a noblewoman of the foreign seeds she was planting in her garden. But the chilies were a decorative plant, not a food. Even at that early date, Hungarians associated chilies with the Turks. However, some posit that chilies were brought north by Bulgarians fleeing the Turks or by *Ragusan* (Croatian) spice merchants, many of whom were Sephardim; both of these sources are plausible, especially since the centers of Hungarian paprika, the towns of Szeged and Kalocsa, are in the south of the country near the border.

Originally, Hungarians called chilies either *bors* (black pepper) or the Teutonic *pfeffer*. By the early eighteenth century, these terms were supplanted in the country with the Slavic name for peppercorns, paprika (derived from the Bulgarian *piperka*). In Hungary, the term paprika means both the fresh pods as well as the powder made from grinding dried ones.

The Ottoman army did not share the chilies it brought or grew with the natives of the conquered lands, using the pods for their own food and medicine. Following the departure of the Turks, the plants were left behind, and the popularity of paprika quickly spread among Hungarian peasants. The original paprika chilies were hot—the degree of heat was determined by the variety and the presence of the placenta (the flesh that houses the seeds, located below the stem), which had to be removed by hand, a grueling task, then crumbled by hand or coarsely crushed in a mortar. Since paprika was locally grown and much less expensive than peppercorns, it emerged as the predominant plebeian seasoning and became an essential part of Magyar cuisine, used in classics such as *gulyás* (goulash). On the other hand, paprika was for a long time held in contempt by the Hungarian upper class, who could afford imported peppercorns and ginger. It was finally accepted by the elite in the nineteenth century, when Napoleon's campaigns and blockades prevented imported spices from reaching the region.

At the same time that paprika was gaining the approval of the Hungarian upper class, industrial advances led to improvements in its quality. Paprika first appeared as an ingredient in a cookbook in 1817 in Vienna, in a recipe for "Chicken Fricassee in Indian Style," and it was not until 1829 that it showed up in a Hungarian cookbook, which included the first recipe for *paprikás csirke* (chicken paprikash). Among the first American cookbooks to mention the spice was *Aunt Babette's* (Cincinnati, 1889), the spice cited only once, in a recipe for "Paprica (Hungarian Hash)."

In 1859, the Palfy family in Szeged developed a

machine to both separate the veins and seeds of chilies and finely grind the pods, allowing for the mass production of milder paprika. Only in the 1920s did horticulturalist Ferenc Horváth of Kalocsa develop a sweet red pepper that contained very small amounts of capsaicin and was appropriate for drying and grinding into a spice—this pepper soon emerged as the predominant type in Hungary. The Hungarian red pepper, as well as its many hybrids, is a thick-skinned variety that does not lend itself to being eaten raw. Ground alone, even with the placenta and seeds, it produces a mild, flavorful spice, and when mixed with other varieties, the resulting blends range from mild to hot.

At the turn of the twenty-first century, more than thirteen thousand acres in Hungary, most of them on small farms, were planted with red peppers and the average Hungarian consumed a pound of paprika a year. The peppers ripen on the plant through the summer and are traditionally harvested by hand. The pods are then strung into long garlands and hung to sun-dry for three to four weeks—Hungarians insist that this produces a far superior flavor to oven-drying. The best-quality paprikas are stone-ground, preserving the color and flavor.

The government of Hungary currently recognizes twenty-two varieties of paprika and most brands are made from eight sweet varieties and two hot ones. Hungarians value both the flavor of mild paprika and the piquancy of the fiery ones. When the paprika contains the placenta, stems, and stalks, it is classified as *koenigspaprika* (king's paprika), while the milder paprika made only from the pod is classified as *rosenpaprika*. The mildest in heat is *különleges* (special quality), which has the sweetest, most delicate flavor, finest grind, and deepest red color. The standard Hungarian cooking paprika and the one most exported, designated in recipes as "sweet Hungarian paprika," is *édesnemes* (noble sweet), which has a bright red color, medium grind, complex flavor, and very slight pungency. *Félédes* (semisweet) is a mixture of sweet and hot paprika and has a red-orange color and slightly piquant, bitter flavor. Another major export is *rózsa* (rose), made from the placenta and seeds as well as the pods, resulting in a light red-orange color, relatively coarse grind, and a very mild pungency. The only Hungarian paprika with a real kick, made from hot varieties with the placenta and seeds, such as the two-inch, round *almapaprika* (apple pepper), is called *erős* (fiery).

Hungarians remain the foremost proponents of paprika's attributes, and some of their zeal has seeped into Ashkenazic cooking. In addition to being used as a garnish for egg salad and potato salad, sweet paprika (but not the hot types) is now a common ingredient in cholent (Sabbath stew), stew, pot roast, and chicken fricassee. It is used to season *helzel* (stuffed neck), *kishke* (stuffed derma), and poultry stuffing.

(See also Chili and Pepper, Sweet)

PAPRIKÁS

Paprikás is a meat stew that is slow-cooked in its own juices and seasoned with paprika.
Origin: Hungary
Other names: paprikash, *pörkölt*.

The most distinguishing feature of Hungarian cuisine is the liberal use of paprika. Eventually, the spice was generously added to the classic Hungarian *gulyás* (a soupy stew), called goulash in America, which was a peasant dish until the nineteenth century. The advent of paprika eventually gave rise to two entirely new types of stew: *pörkölt* (literally meaning "roasted"), which is little known in the West, and *paprikás*, which is called paprikash in America and is the same as *pörkölt*, but with sour cream added.

Most Hungarian households kept at least a few chickens for eggs and, for special occasions, an older bird would go into the *paprikás*, making it *paprikás csirke*. The cooking method can also be used for veal (*borjú*), beef (*marha*), or most other meats. The type of meat is relatively unimportant, as onions and paprika lie at the heart of a *paprikás*. The onions are not sautéed or browned in the typical manner, but rather are cooked, covered, with a little liquid to prevent burning, for an unusually long time. Many Hungarians insist that chicken or goose fat is preferable for a *paprikás*, but vegetable oil makes a respectable substitute. Hungarian sweet paprika provides a bold, balanced flavor that does not overpower the few other ingredients. Aficionados and purists argue over whether it is appropriate to add tomatoes and/or peppers or whether *paprikás* should be seasoned with a little caraway seeds or marjoram; these additions are heresies to some, interesting variations to others.

The first recipe in any cookbook for *paprikás csirke* appeared in 1829 in Hungary, after the upper class had already come to realize the spice's virtues. Immigrants brought the dish to America toward the end of the nineteenth century. *The Neighborhood Cook Book* by the Council of Jewish Women (Portland, Oregon, 1912), in addition to including three recipes for "Hungarian Goulash," included one for "Chicken Paprika."

As with most Jewish cookbooks, the recipe for chicken paprika in *The Neighborhood Cook Book* omitted any sour cream, a substance cooks in a kosher kitchen would not add to a chicken or meat stew. Instead, Jews substituted the term *paprikás* for *pörkölt*—the latter name was not particularly popular in an English-speaking kosher kitchen anyway, because it was suggestive of a pig. As with many other Hungarian foods in America, paprikash made its way into the general Ashkenazic kitchen and then into the American mainstream. Many Jewish delis and Catskill hotels featured chicken paprikash (Jewish-style without sour cream), although usually an Americanized version, which omitted the traditional cooking method and used mild American paprika in place of the Hungarian sweet version. Today, quite a few European-style restaurants in Israel offer chicken *paprikás* on their menus—some versions are kosher, while some contain sour cream. Among American Jews, the dish came to be considered fare that while not elegant was special enough to offer to company, particularly as it was an easy dish to prepare. In the movie *When Harry Met Sally*, Billy Crystal, drawing on his Jewish humor, improvised a line during lunch in a restaurant: "Waiter, there is too much pepper on my paprikash."

For many Hungarians, chicken *paprikás* remains a great comfort food as well as festive fare. *Paprikás* is traditionally served with cucumber salad (*kovászos uborka*) and Hungarian dumplings, such as *galuska* or *nokedli*, or noodles, such as *tarhonya* and *tészta*.

◖ **HUNGARIAN CHICKEN PAPRIKASH (*PAPRIKÁS CSIRKE*)**

4 TO 6 SERVINGS   [MEAT]

¼ cup schmaltz or vegetable oil

2 large yellow onions, chopped

About ¾ cup chicken broth or water

2 to 3 teaspoons sweet paprika

1 (3- to 4-pound) chicken, cut into 8 pieces, or 8 (about 3½ pounds total) chicken thighs, bone-in and with the skin on

About 1 teaspoon table salt or 2 teaspoons kosher salt

Dash of ground black pepper

2 medium (1 cup) tomatoes, peeled, seeded and chopped (optional)

1 sweet banana pepper, seeded and chopped (optional)

1. In a large skillet or pot, heat the schmaltz over medium heat. Add the onions and sauté until slightly softened, 2 to 3 minutes. Stir in ¼ cup broth, cover, reduce the heat to medium-low, and simmer for 1 hour. Check the onions occasionally to see if they are in danger of burning. If so, add a little more broth.

2. Remove the skillet from the heat, add the paprika, and stir for 1 minute. Place over low heat, add the chicken, and toss to coat and seal in the juices. Add ¼ cup broth, salt, and pepper. If using, scatter the tomatoes and banana pepper over the top. Cover and simmer for 20 minutes. Check occasionally to see if a little more liquid is needed.

3. Invert the chicken pieces and, if the stew seems as if it might burn, add the remaining ¼ cup broth. Cover and simmer until fork-tender and an instant-read thermometer inserted in the thighs registers 175°F, 15 to 25 minutes.

4. Transfer the chicken to a heated platter and keep warm. The cooking liquid should be a very thick, intensely red gravy. If it is too watery, increase the heat to high, boil until thickened, return the chicken, and toss to coat. Serve warm.

PAREVE

The Yiddish adjective *pareve*—also commonly spelled parev, parve, and parveh—means "neutral," referring to foods and utensils that are neither meat (*fleishig*) nor dairy (*milchig*). These include fruits, vegetables, grains, fish, eggs, honey, water, and minerals.

The term *pareve* probably derived from the Old Czech *párový* (pair/dual), as pareve food can be paired with either meat or milk and has dual usage. The word pareve appeared centuries after the Yiddish *fleishig* and *milchig,* the latter terms dating from around the late fourteenth century. Today, the word pareve is widespread, but that is a relatively recent development due to its adoption by Polish Jews around the early nineteenth century. Previously, in rabbinic literature a paradigmatic case (e.g., "like fish") was used to express the intent of pareve, while Sephardim conveyed the concept with "neither *keso* [cheese] nor *karne* [meat]." The equivalent term was *minikh* in Western Yiddish, *minnich* in Holland, and *bur* in Lithuania. Although *stami* (derived from Aramaic by way of Yiddish) is the official term in modern Hebrew, *paravi* or *parve* is more commonly used on the street and also on food labels. The first printed record of the word in English was in the promotional cookbook *The Story of Crisco* by Marion Neil (Cincinnati, 1913), which explained, "It is what is known in the Hebrew language as a 'parava,' or neutral fat." In a nonculinary usage, pareve also came to designate a milquetoast personality.

PARSLEY

Parsley, from the Greek *petroselinon* (growing among the rocks), is a native of the eastern Mediterranean. It is the world's most popular herb, long valued for its mildly bitter, grassy flavor as well as its healthful properties. In much of Asia and Europe, it is added to salads, soups, stews, and casseroles. In the Levant, parsley is the star of tabbouleh salad. Parsley is one of the items commonly used as *karpas* at the Passover Seder.

(See also Karpas and Seder)

PARSNIP

Parsnip is a native of northeastern Europe. Its English name, as well as the Yiddish name *pasternak* (from the Middle High German), is derived from the Latin term for the plant, *pastinaca*. The surname of author Boris Pasternak was imposed on his grandfather, who was purportedly descended from the Sephardic scholar Isaac Abravanel, by the Russian authorities in Odessa.

Wild parsnips are too bitter and woody to eat, but parsnips were cultivated to produce a sweet, tapered, white root. Since it was first improved more than two thousand years ago, the parsnip has served as one of the primary vegetables of northeastern Europe, where the root is treasured for its sweet, nutty flavor as well as its storage abilities. The Roman writer Apicius recorded several recipes featuring this vegetable, including parsnips simmered in white wine and olive oil with cilantro, and parsnips mixed into a vegetable sausage. With the increased popularization of its relative the carrot in the fifteenth century, and then the potato in the mid-nineteenth century, the usage of the parsnip dramatically decreased.

Cooking intensifies the parsnip's sweetness and flavor; therefore, it is usually added to stews and soups, especially Ashkenazic chicken soup. It is also typically mashed or pureed in pancakes, timbales, or ravioli filling. The sweetness of parsnips is complemented by salty and bitter foods, such as dark leafy greens. The parsnip holds its own as the base for a soup, as well as in latkes and as part of a tzimmes.

PASSOVER (PESACH)

Passover, called *Chag ha'Matzot* (Festival of the Matzas) in the Bible, is a seven-day holiday (eight outside Israel). The first and last days (the first two and last two outside Israel) have restrictions against creative work, although unlike the Sabbath, cooking is allowed. As with Shavuot and Sukkot, Passover has both a historical and an agricultural connection. Passover commemorates the Exodus from Egypt following centuries of oppression and slavery. It also falls at the onset of spring and the barley harvest and coincides with the time when the shepherds and goat herders brought their flocks in from winter pasturing for the birth of their babies.

The Haggadah has offered guidance during Passover for more than a thousand years; here, an example from 1350 Barcelona, before the expulsion of the Jews from Spain.

Hand matza is made today by Ashkenazim in the same way as it has for centuries. Here the schieber (slider) transfers four freshly baked matzas from the oven to the cooling rack. Unbaked matza hang on the pole in the rear left awaiting their turn in the oven.

Today, Passover is the most widely observed of all the Jewish holidays and the Passover Seder ("order" in Aramaic) is the most practiced of all the Jewish rituals. During the Seder, the Passover story is recounted and relived through a progression of symbols and ceremonies as recorded in the Haggadah (literally "retelling"). The story of the Exodus has appealing universal themes—hope and freedom, redemption and justice, family and community—and is told in a uniquely Jewish way. It is a holiday celebrating ancient national events that centers on the family. The Seder provides one of the increasingly rare opportunities for several generations of a family to gather together.

Due to the various dietary regulations resulting from the proscription of *chametz*, Passover fare differs from that of the rest of the year. Among Ashkenazim, a prohibition emerged against eating legumes (*kitniyot*) on Passover, as well as rice, corn, and some seeds. On the other hand, Sephardim, prolific rice and legume consumers, not only reject these prohibitions, but frequently feature these foods at the Seder. Over the centuries, creative cooks have found ways to adapt some of their everyday foods, as well as create new ones to meet the special requirements of Passover. Traditional Ashkenazic Passover fare includes borscht, schav (sorrel soup), gefilte fish with *chrain* (horseradish), *gebratener hindle mit matzafullung* (roast chicken with matza stuffing), carrot tzimmes, matza kugel, potato kugel,

matza brei (fried matza), blintzes, compote, *ingberlach* (ginger candies), and *eingemachts* (preserves).

Eggs are essential in both Ashkenazic and Sephardic Passover fare, binding ingredients in dishes such as Ashkenazic *knaidlach, matza brei, chremslach*, and kugels and Sephardic *minas* (layered pies), *keftes* (patties), and *bimuelos* (pancakes)—and contributing lightness to baked goods. Hard-boiled eggs are common at a Seder. Both Ashkenazim and Sephardim enjoy meringue cookies, known in America as kisses and called *ashuplados* by Sephardim. To increase matza's utility, it is also ground to make matza meal or finely ground to make matza cake meal. Crumbled and ground matza is used to create an imaginative array of Passover dishes, including stuffings, puddings, casseroles, pancakes, fritters, dumplings, pastries, and cakes.

(See also Afikomen, Chametz, Charoset, Gebrochts, Karpas, Kitniyot, Maror, Matza, and Seder)

PASTA/NOODLE

An archaeological dig at Lajia near the Yellow River in northwestern China uncovered a bowl containing thin strips of boiled millet dough that were four thousand years old, the earliest evidence of pasta. The Chinese later began making pasta from buckwheat and mung bean flours and even later from rice. Around the beginning of the Han Dynasty in 206 BCE, the grindstone traveled east along the Silk Road and the northern Chinese learned how to pound wheat berries and barley into flour. Initially, they boiled strips of wheat dough, which the Chinese called *mein* (in Cantonese) or *mian* (in Mandarin); these were the first known wheat noodles. Shortly thereafter, the Chinese were steaming wheat dumplings filled with chopped meat, similar to the modern *zheng jiao*. Originally, pasta was used in China as an extender for soup, a role it would later initially fill in the West as well. Early Chinese noodles were always made fresh and not dried.

Noodles probably spread from China along the Silk Road to central Asia and Persia, where they were initially called *lakhsha* (slippery). Subsequently, *lakhsha* was relegated to the name of a specific Persian noodle dish. The term, however, remains in other languages for pasta, such as the Eastern Yiddish *lokshen*. In any case, in Persia, noodles have always played a minor role, subordinate to that of rice.

The first mention of boiling dough in a non-Chinese source was in the Jerusalem Talmud (c. 350 CE),

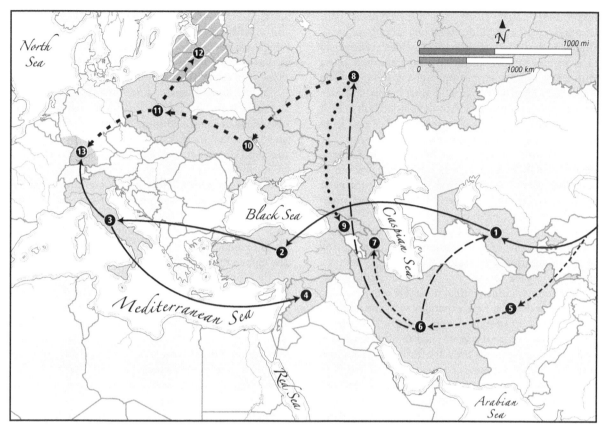

Filled Pasta *The Mongols of northern China developed a steamed filled bun called* man tou *(savage's head), which evolved into a filled pasta. Filled pasta spread through east Asia then along the Silk Road to western Asia, then into Europe.* **1 Uzbekistan**—*manti, chuchvara;* **2 Turkey**—*manti;* **3 Italy**—*cappelletti, ravioli, tortelli;* **4 Syria**—*kelsonnes;* **5 Afghanistan**—*mantu;* **6 Iran**—*gush-e barreh;* **7 Azerbaijan**—*dushbara;* **8 Russia**—*pelmeni;* **9 Georgia**—*khinkali;* **10 Ukraine**—*pelmeni, varenikes;* **11 Poland**—*pirogen, kreplach;* **12 Baltic States**—*kreplach;* **13 Southwestern Germany**—*maultaschen*

where pasta was called *itriya* and *iytree*. Some scholars contend that the words derive from the Greek *itrion*, meaning a sesame-and-honey wafer used in religious rites, while others say it comes from *itriyah* a Farsi word for string. The Babylonian Talmud (c. 500) mentioned a dish of boiled dough called *rihata*; the word is related to the modern Persian term for noodles, *reshteh*.

When medieval Middle Eastern cooks began adding eggs to soft wheat dough, they produced noodles that not only held their shape when dried, but also tasted better and did not become soggy after cooling. They also discovered that noodles made from very high-protein durum flour could be dried (*pasta secca*) without the addition of eggs. In addition, durum wheat (semolina) pasta was easier to manipulate into

shapes, an attribute that would eventually lead to the development of an art form in Italy. The Jerusalem Talmud discussed drying *itriya* for frying, as drying was an activity forbidden on certain holy days—this was the first record anywhere of dried pasta. The Talmud failed to mention whether Jews or Persians dried pasta during the rest of the year, although this seems likely.

The Arabs discovered pasta after conquering Persia and were the first group known to dry pasta on a regular basis, making use of the plentiful crops of durum wheat in the Middle East. Traders and soldiers carried supplies of dried pasta on their journeys. *Itriya* and *tria* became the Arabic names for dried pasta. Prevalent medieval Middle Eastern forms of pasta included *rishta* (thick strips), *shaghria* (thin strips), *lissan* (birds' tongues), and the most common, *kes-kasune/maghribiyya* (little semolina dough pellets), similar to Italian acini de pepe. Besides using pasta as a soup extender, medieval Arabs flavored pasta with sugar, cinnamon, saffron, and almond milk. The Arabs also liked to cook pasta with lentils and fava beans, which eventually led to the classic Italian dish *pasta e fagioli,* (colloquially pronounced *fasool,* from the Arabic for bean stew, *fasoolia*).

By the tenth century, the Arabs had introduced pasta to Sicily and Spain, where the vast amount of semolina grown allowed for the production of *pasta secca.* In 1154, the Arab geographer Al-Idrisi mentioned the mass production of *tria* near Palermo, where Sicilian Jews, unlike the local non-Jewish population, were regularly eating *pasta secca,* as well as manufacturing it for export. Pasta quickly found a prominent place in the Sephardic and Sicilian Jewish kitchen. Its culinary uses, no longer simply a soup extender or dessert, were expanded with the addition of cheese or a variety of savory sauces. The generic Ladino term *macaron* was applied to all dried pasta, while *fila* was generally used for fresh egg pasta. Traditional types of Sephardic pasta included *alatria* (vermicelli), *escolacha* (pasta pressed through a strainer), and especially *fideos* (very thin noodles).

Pasta, both the concept of boiled dough strips and filled packets, first appeared in mainland Italy sometime after the tenth century, probably in the late twelfth. The Medieval Latin word "pasta" derived from the name of a barley gruel sprinkled with salt, itself from the Greek *pastos* (sprinkled); it was initially recorded in 1244 in a prescription of a Genovese doctor not to eat *"pasta lissa"* (slippery noodles). An anonymous Italian cookbook manuscript written between 1260 and 1290 included recipes for vermicelli (little worms), the term used by Apicius (c. 400 CE) in reference to fried strips of dough. The earliest Italian mentions of "macaroni" in the thirteenth century referred not to pasta but rather to dumplings made from "bread paste" and boiled in stews and soups. Eventually, macaroni became a synonym for pasta. Pasta was certainly being eaten in Italy well before the birth of Marco Polo, who is erroneously credited with bringing the dish back to Venice from China in 1295. In his journal, Marco Polo refers to the pasta he saw in China as "lasagne" and "vermicelli."

The first mention of a boiled dough in a European Jewish source outside of Spain appeared around 1300 in the writings of Kalonymus ben Kalonymus, a Provençal native who spent most of his life in Rome and included macaroni and *tortelli* (filled pasta) in a list of dishes served at a fantasy Purim feast.

At first, Italians flavored their macaroni in the Arabic style with almond milk, saffron, and sugar, but eventually began substituting cheese, primarily ricotta and Parmesan, for the almond milk. According to the medieval Galenic theory of humors, ricotta was appropriate for people with energetic dispositions. Italian Jews, when adding cheese, used water instead of the then-prevalent meat broth to cook the pasta, producing a daintier dish. In other instances, bread crumbs were substituted for Parmesan cheese for meat meals. Pasta in tomato sauce would not become popular until the eighteenth century.

By 1400, commercial pasta production, controlled by guilds, was widespread in Italy. The firm dough was mixed for many hours in large troughs by foot, then rolled out by hand or extruded through brass dies. Pasta was so valuable that full-time watchmen were required for protection. The advent of *pasta secca* and a related product, hardtack, enabled Europeans to make longer sea voyages, leading to the successes of Vasco da Gama, Columbus, and others. The concept of pasta did not arrive in England until the late fourteenth century—it became known there as "paste"—leaving the English, for a time, at a distinct disadvantage at sea.

In Naples in the seventeenth century, a pasta-kneading machine and the first mechanical pasta press were invented. *Pasta secca* became cheap and plentiful and, by the eighteenth century, it had become a mainstay of the diet of the common folk. Venice licensed the first pasta factory in 1740.

Exiled southern Italian Jews, Conversos who had managed to escape from Spain, and Sephardim introduced to northern Italy their pasta dishes as well as tomatoes. Italians even made a type of pasta for Passover from matza flour and eggs that was baked before boiling—it was called *sfoglietti* or *foglietti.* Until relatively recently, Italians did not eat cold pasta. When Jews, however, wanted pasta on the Sabbath, it was necessary to find versions that would taste good at room temperature—thus emerged the first pasta salads, such as *tagliolini con brodo brusca* (thin linguine in egg-lemon sauce) and *tagliolini col pomadori* (thin linguine in tomato sauce), which were served cold for Sabbath lunch.

Considering the frequent interaction between the Jewish communities of Italy and Franco-Germany, pasta probably reached the Rhineland around the fifteenth century. Earlier Franco-German dough dishes—such as *vermesel* (fritters and pancakes) and *krepish* (meat filled dough)—were fried or baked.

(See also Calsones, Couscous, Dumplings, Fidellos, Frimsel, Keskasune, Kreplach, Lokshen, Manti, Mascono, Pastitsio, Pirog, Quadrucci, Semolina, Tortelli, and Varenik)

PASTELITO

Pastelito is a small pie.

Origin: Spain

Other names: Greek: *pastelico, pasteliko*; Ladino: *pastele, pastille*; Turkish: *borekita*.

"We make out of it *pastelicos*, they shine on the plates waiting to be served with *huevos haminados*." (From the Ladino folk song "Seven Ways to Cook an Eggplant.")

Pastel is a venerable Sephardic pie made from a short crust (a soft pastry containing a high proportion of fat and no raising agent) dating back to well before the expulsion from Spain. It is different from another traditional pie, the *pastida*, which is baked in a covered dish and left over the heat for an extended period. Cooks also developed small, straight-sided, cuplike versions called *pastelitos*. Both the large pies and small pastries were originally made with a meat filling, but cooks also created versions filled with fish, seasonal vegetables (especially spinach), or cheese. *Pastelitos* may be both open-topped and covered. After the expulsion from Spain, Sephardim brought these pies with them to North Africa, the Ottoman Empire, and Central America and the Caribbean. In Greece, triangular and cigar-shaped phyllo pastries were also sometimes called *pastelicos*.

Large pies are much easier and quicker to prepare than the smaller ones, and are more common during the week. Smaller pies are enjoyed for the Sabbath, holidays, and special occasions, such as weddings and bar mitzvahs. *Pastelitos* served for Sabbath *desayuno* (brunch) and Hanukkah, usually contain cheese; these pastries are also called *quesadas, kezadas,* or *guizadas* (derived from the Ladino word for "cheese") and are frequently made with a sour cream or cheese

crust. Since *quesada* sounds like *casada* (Ladino for "married"), some Sephardim have the custom of holding one of the pastries over the head of the prospective bride when the she goes to the *mikveh* (ritual bath) the night before her wedding. Meat fillings are common for Sabbath dinner. For many Greek Jews, eggplant-and-cheese-filled *pastelitos* are the essence of Sephardic gastronomy.

(See also Boreka, Empanada, Pastida, and Sambusak)

SEPHARDIC SMALL PIES (*PASTELITOS*)

ABOUT 18 SMALL PIES WITH LIDS   [DAIRY, MEAT, OR PAREVE]

1 recipe Sephardic Oil Pastry Dough, Sephardic Oil-Butter Pastry Dough, or Sephardic Sour Cream Pastry Dough (page 391)

About 4 cups Sephardic pastry filling (see Gomo, pages 230–232)

Egg wash (1 large egg beaten with 1 teaspoon water)

3 to 4 tablespoons sesame seeds for sprinkling (optional)

1. Preheat the oven to 375°F. Lightly grease a large baking pan.

2. Form three-quarters of the dough into about eighteen 1-inch balls and the remaining dough into about eighteen smaller balls.

3. On a lightly floured surface, roll out the larger balls into ⅛-inch-thick rounds, then form into 2-inch deep cups with straight sides and 2-inch-wide mouths. The dough can also be pressed into greased muffin tins. Fill the cups to the top with the filling.

4. Roll out the small balls into 2-inch rounds, place the rounds on top of the cups, and crimp or flute the edges to seal. Place the cups in the prepared baking pan. Brush the tops with the egg wash and, if using, sprinkle with the sesame seeds.

5. Bake until golden brown, about 30 minutes. Serve warm or at room temperature.

PASTICCIO

Pasticcio is a savory pie containing pasta, and a top and bottom crust.

Origin: Italy

Other names: *timballo*.

There are three basic types of Italian pies, usually double-crusted: *crostata* (a tart, usually sweet), *torta*, (a pie, either sweet or savory, or cake), and *pastic-*

cio. When the concept of boiled dough traveled from China to Italy, probably in the early thirteenth century, the new dough made from semolina and cut into thin strips was dubbed pasta and eventually emerged as a staple of the Mediterranean diet. Soon a pie containing pasta, based on an Arabic practice of baking pasta with meat, became *pasticcio.* In Italian slang, *pasticcio* also came to mean "hodgepodge" and, in the eighteenth century, it referred to a form of musical theater that borrowed songs from numerous composers and popular melodies.

The distinctiveness of *pasticcio* from other pies lies in the filling consisting of a number of components being assembled in layers; the most widespread variation is *pasticcio di maccheroni* (meat and macaroni pie). *Pasticcio* is often made from a harder dough than other pies in order to maintain its long straight sides, but many modern variations omit the bottom crust or the pastry completely. Some versions of this dish have a sweet crust (*crosta dolce*) with a savory filling, which might sound odd but actually works.

Italian Jews adapted *pasticcio* to kosher regulations, and meat-filled versions (*pasticcio di carne*) or fish-filled versions (*pasticcio di pesce*) became popular Friday night fare. In the pastry for a meat pie, Jewish cooks use olive oil and/or schmaltz for the butter.

Pastitsio, the name derived from the Italian *pasticcio,* are baked pasta dishes from Greece. The pasta is frequently layered with cheese or meat, producing a sort of pasta pie. Since Jews could not combine meat and milk, they developed a variety of separate meat and cheese variations, allowing the main elements to shine. There are numerous versions, some simple and others rather complex. *Pastitsios* are served as an entrée, along with a salad, or as a side dish.

ITALIAN PASTA PIE (*PASTICCIO DI MACCHERONI*)

6 TO 8 SERVINGS [MEAT]

6 ounces (4 to 5) chicken livers
Sauce (*Ragu*):
    3 tablespoons olive oil
    1 medium onion, chopped
    2 cloves garlic, minced
    20 ounces ground beef or veal
    3 ounces mushrooms, sliced

¼ cup dry red or white wine
Pinch of ground nutmeg
About ¾ teaspoon table salt or 1½ teaspoons kosher salt
Ground black pepper to taste
1 large egg

12 ounces penne, ziti, or elbow macaroni
¼ cup olive oil
Salt to taste
1 recipe flaky pastry (see Teig, page 582)
Egg wash (1 large egg beaten with 1 teaspoon water)

1. Cut away any membranes and veins from the liver. Lightly sprinkle both sides with kosher salt. Place on an unheated rack on a broiler pan and broil about 4 inches from the heat source on both sides until light brown and the blood has dripped off, about 3 minutes per side. Rinse and pat dry.

2. To make the sauce: In a large skillet, heat the oil over medium heat. Add the onion and garlic and sauté until soft and translucent, 5 to 10 minutes. Add the meat and sauté until it loses its red color, about 5 minutes. Add the mushrooms and sauté until softened, about 5 minutes. Add the livers and wine and cook until the liquid evaporates. Season with the nutmeg, salt, and pepper. Let cool. Stir in the egg.

3. Bring a large pot of lightly salted water to a rapid boil. Stir in the pasta. Cook until tender but still firm, about 10 minutes. Drain and toss with the oil and salt.

4. Preheat the oven to 375°F. Lightly grease a 9-inch springform pan or round ovenproof dish.

5. On a lightly floured surface, roll out three-quarters of the pastry into a 14-inch round. Place in the prepared pan, letting the excess reach up the sides and hang over. Spread one-third of the pasta in the pastry shell, top with half the sauce, half the remaining pasta, the remaining sauce, and then the remaining pasta. Alternatively, instead of layering, simply mix the pasta and sauce and spoon into the pastry shell.

6. Roll out the remaining pastry into a 9-inch round. Place over the filling and press the edges to seal. Prick four times in the center to vent the steam. Brush the top with the egg wash.

7. Bake until golden brown, 40 to 50 minutes. Let stand for at least 10 minutes before cutting.

PASTIDA

Pastida is a meat or vegetable pie.

Origin: Spain

Other names: Austria: *brietling*; Italy: *pasticcio, pizza Ebraica, torta*; Ladino: *pashtida, pastilla, pastille*.

Double-crusted meat pies became beloved Sabbath fare in medieval European Jewish communities. The upper and lower pastry layers were construed to represent the double portion of manna that the Israelites collected for the Sabbath during their forty years of wandering in the wilderness. The pastry layers were symbolic of the dew that protected the manna.

The lexicon *Arukh* (1101) by Rabbi Nathan ben Yehiel of Rome mentioned meat pies, which remained a timeless part of Italian cuisine. The Jews of early medieval Spain also enjoyed large, baked savory pies called *pastida* (the Latin feminine form of *pastillus*, "little loaf"). Unlike the pies of non-Jewish medieval Europe, whose hard crusts were discarded or fed to animals, tender Sephardic *pastida* were consumed crust and all.

Every Friday morning, Sephardic housewives assembled a *pastida*, consisting of two layers of a rudimentary puff pastry or flaky pastry baked in a special large earthenware dish with a lid. Meat fillings were almost always lamb, but fish was also widespread. During the spring and summer, seasonal vegetable fillings, commonly mixed with cheese, were frequently substituted for the meat. After arranging the ingredients in the dish, the lid was secured and the *pastida* was placed in the family oven or taken to the communal bakery to partially cook. Before the onset of the Sabbath, the pie was retrieved, while the family's *hamin/adafina* (Sabbath stew) was placed in the oven to cook overnight. The *pastida* was set on a metal rack hung over the family's hearth to stay warm for Sabbath dinner.

By at least the twelfth century, the Sabbath double-crusted pie had made its way to the Ashkenazim of France, where it too was called *pastida* and became an integral component of their Friday night dinner. Rashi mentioned *pastida* a number of times, not only in his Talmud commentary, but also in his Responsa, in which he briefly explained how his wife made the dish. With a unique meat surplus in that region of Europe beginning around 1350, in the wake of the Black Plague, meat pies emerged as the primary form of the Ashkenazic *pastida*. The Frankfort rabbi Joseph

Yuspa Hahn (1570–1637), in a book of collected local customs, related the tale of a local Jewish boy who was kidnapped by robbers and cried so pitifully on Friday night for his *pastida* that his location was discovered and he was ransomed.

Each Friday morning, medieval Ashkenazic housewives, similar to their Sephardic counterparts, prepared a dough of flour, water, goose schmaltz, and eggs. The 1553 German cookbook *Das Kochbuch der Sabina Welserin* contained instructions "to make a *pastetentaig* [pastry dough] for all *auffgesetzten pasteten* [shaped pies]," providing a recipe comparable to the dough and techniques used by Ashkenazim for their pies, a form of flaky pastry. Ashkenazic cooks greased a special earthenware casserole dish with schmaltz; pressed a layer of dough over the bottom and sides; spooned in a mixture of ground meat or fish seasoned with onions, garlic, and spices; and topped the filling with another layer of dough. Udder was a particularly popular filling. Alsatian Jews also baked chopped goose liver in pastry as a variation of *pastida*, not unlike the later Alsatian *pâté en croute*. The lid of the casserole dish was secured and the *pastida* was baked in the family oven or, more likely, taken to the communal bakery and baked alongside the pies of neighbors. Before the onset of the Sabbath, the pie was placed on a metal rack hanging over the family's hearth. The embers of the fire kept the pie warm until it was eagerly devoured for the Sabbath dinner.

Around 1550, the Sephardic scholar Rabbi Joseph Caro, in his *Shulchan Arukh,* stated, "It is permitted to kasher with fire a metal pan in which a cheese *fluden* [double-crusted pie] was baked and afterward bake in that pan a *pastida* of meat." He also ruled that although usually the benediction over a dish like *pastida* would be *mezonot*, since it was a special food typically eaten at meals and not as a snack, the benediction of Hamotzi was necessary. Rabbi Moses Isserles of Kraków, Poland, in his glosses on the *Shulchan Arukh*, stated, "Some have written that in a few places [among Ashkenazim] they have the custom on Friday night of eating a dish called *pastida* in commemoration of the manna which was covered above and below," reflecting the absence of *pastida* in at least Galicia (southern Poland) at that time. In the seventeenth century, Rabbi Hayim Benveniste (1603–1673) of Salonika and Izmir, a scion of a prominent

Sephardic family, in his comments on the *Shulchan Arukh*, declared, "In our country we do eat it."

Indeed, Sabbath pies soon waned in the Ashkenazic repertoire, partially due to a meat shortage striking Europe around 1550, as well as to the culinary patterns of eastern Europe that were quite different than that in the west. Some Ashkenazic places and families retained the dish. Hayim Nahman Bialik, one of the pioneers of modern Hebrew literature, mentioned it in his 1915 short story "The Shamed Trumpet." He wrote, "For such a Sabbath, when a full minyan permitted the reading of the Torah from the Scroll, mother would prepare an extra pastida in advance." For most Ashkenazim, however, kugel supplanted the venerable *pastida* on the Sabbath table.

After the concept of the turnover reached Iberia and entered the Sephardic consciousness, large pies lost some, but hardly all, of their prominence, as the smaller *empanadas* and later *borekas* emerged. Today, Sephardim still enjoy a variety of savory pies—large, small, and miniature. Double-crusted pastries are popular as Sephardic Sabbath appetizers, as well as at many celebrations.

Although for nearly half a millennium, the *pastida* was absent from most Ashkenazic kitchens, in modern Israel it underwent a major and unexpected revival. The letter at the end of the word became *hey* instead of *aleph*, the pronunciation changed from *pastida* to *pashtida*, and the term came to denote a baked casserole akin to a quiche and kugel. A modern *pashtida* filling must contain eggs, and many variations include cheese and various vegetables. In some pareve adaptations, mashed potatoes are substituted for cheese; other versions, harking back to the original dish, even contain meat. Many Israeli cooks, to avoid the extra work and/or calories, even omit the pastry, although the resulting dish is technically a *fritada*. The typical Israeli hotel breakfast features a sweet cheese *pashtida*, while dinner might include a savory vegetable version. Many Israeli restaurants offer *pashtida*, sometimes crustless, as a side dish. *Pashtidas* are sold in many bakeries and shops. Homemakers, Sephardic and Ashkenazic, whip one up for a Sabbath side dish, as well as for a light entrée for a weekday meal. A *pashtida* with cheese is commonplace on Shavuot. Even some Americans who spent a little time in Israel have taken to preparing *pashtidas* back home.

Many Israelis now use the term *pashtida* instead of kugel, the name of the dish that had so long ago replaced it. After more than a millennium and many ups and downs, *pashtida* remains an important and beloved Jewish food.

(See also Boreka, Crostata, Fluden, Inchusa, Mina, Pastelito, and Pastilla)

PASTILLA
Pastilla is a rich phyllo-dough pie, once filled with pigeon, but today generally features chicken.
Origin: Morocco
Other names: *bastal, basteela, bastilla, basteya, bisteeya, pastel, pastille.*

Among the variations in spelling of the Sephardi *pastel*, a savory pie made with a short pastry, was *pastilla* (the Latin feminine form of *pastillus*, "little loaf"). Sephardim brought *pastilla* to Morocco and, after the Ottoman version of phyllo, called *warka* ("leaf"), reached the Maghreb, cooks substituted it for the Spanish pastry. Sephardim continued to pronounce the name with a *p*, while Arabic speakers substituted a *b*. The pie was baked or, for those without access to an oven, adapted to be fried in a large skillet. With the advent of the home oven, baking has become the predominant means of cooking *pastilla*. In America and Israel, phyllo sheets are generally substituted for the thicker *warka*.

Since *pastillas* are labor-intensive, they are reserved for special occasions and, in Morocco, no *diffa* (feast) or celebration—especially Sukkot, representing the bounty of the harvest, Hanukkah, and weddings—would be considered complete without this elaborate pastry. Squab—a young pigeon—is the traditional meat filling, although chicken is a more available modern substitute. The poultry is cooked, shredded, seasoned with the traditional Maghrebi spice mixture, *ras-el-hanout*, mixed with a thick egg sauce, and layered with ground almonds. It is traditionally baked in a *t'bseel* (round tin-lined copper pan), but a large baking dish or paella pan can be substituted. Like many Moroccan meat dishes, *pastillas* tend to be a little sweet. In Fez, cooks add more sugar to the filling and sprinkle the finished pie with confectioners' sugar and a lacework of cinnamon. *Pastilla* takes a little work to create, but the end result—a delicious filling sandwiched between delicate layers of crisp, flaky pastry—is well worth the effort.

(See also Pastelito and Warka)

❧ MOROCCAN "PIGEON" PIE (*PASTILLA/BASTILLA*)

Chicken Layer:

¼ cup vegetable oil

2 large onions, chopped

2 to 3 cloves garlic, minced

1 teaspoon ground ginger

1 teaspoon ground black pepper or 12 whole black peppercorns

1 teaspoon ground coriander

½ teaspoon ground turmeric

½ teaspoon saffron strands, crumbled

1 (3-inch) cinnamon stick or ½ teaspoon ground cinnamon

About 5 pounds chicken parts (breasts, thighs, and legs)

4 cups chicken broth or water

½ to 1 cup chopped fresh flat-leaf parsley or cilantro, or ½ cup each

6 large eggs, well beaten

Almond Layer:

1⅔ cups (8 ounces) blanched almonds, toasted (or deep-fried in peanut oil) and cooled

¼ cup sugar

1 teaspoon ground cinnamon

1 tablespoon vegetable oil

1½ teaspoons orange-blossom water or 1 tablespoon rose water (optional)

10 sheets phyllo dough or *warka*

About ¾ cup vegetable oil or melted margarine

About 3 tablespoons confectioners' sugar for sprinkling

1 to 2 tablespoons ground cinnamon for sprinkling

1. To make the chicken layer: In a large pot, heat the oil over medium heat. Add the onions and garlic and sauté until soft and translucent, 5 to 10 minutes. Stir in the ginger, pepper, coriander, turmeric, saffron, and cinnamon and sauté for 1 minute. Add the chicken and toss to coat. Add the broth and parsley. Bring to a boil, cover, reduce the heat to low, and simmer until tender, about 40 minutes.

2. Remove the chicken. Strain the cooking liquid. You can reserve the solids and add to the reduced liquid or discard the solids. Place the cooking liquid over high heat and reduce to about 1 cup, about 20 minutes. Meanwhile, remove the meat from the bones and shred; you should have about 5 cups.

3. Whisk the reduced liquid into the eggs. If desired, add the strained cooking solids. Cook, stirring constantly, over low heat until the mixture thickens, about 5 minutes. Pour into a bowl and let cool.

4. To make the almond layer: In a food processor fitted with a metal blade, finely grind the almonds, sugar, and cinnamon. Add the oil and, if using, orange-blossom water. Set aside.

5. Preheat the oven to 425°F. Lightly grease a 10- or 11-inch round baking dish, springform pan, or oven-proof skillet.

6. Line the prepared dish with a sheet of phyllo, draping the excess over the edge. Brush lightly with oil. Repeat layering and brushing with 5 more sheets, draping each in a different direction. Spread one-third of the egg mixture over the pastry in the pan. Mix another one-third of the egg mixture with the shredded chicken and pack into the pie. Spread the remaining egg mixture over top, then sprinkle with the almond mixture. Fold the pastry edges toward the center of the pie. Top with the remaining 4 sheets of phyllo, brushing each with oil, and tuck in the edges.

7. Bake until golden brown, about 20 minutes. Lightly sprinkle with confectioners' sugar, then sprinkle lines of cinnamon to form a diamond pattern. Let stand at least 10 minutes and up to 30 minutes before cutting into wedges.

PASTRAMI

Drying slices of meat is an ancient means of preservation. The Ottomans pressed slices of meat or fish to extract moisture and either salted or rubbed them with a paste called *çemen* (the Turkish word for "fenugreek") made from a mixture of spices, including fenugreek, cumin, garlic, and salt; they then air-dried the slices. The cured meat, called *basturma* (from the Turkish "to press"), was eaten with further cooking, like the American jerky, or added to various dishes. *Basturma* was introduced to the Balkans by the Ottoman Jannissari troops. As in Arabic, Romanian words are often spelled with a *h* but pronounced with a *p*; thus these cured dishes were called *pastramă* in Romanian. As with those earlier Turkish *basturma*, the Romanian meats were hard and chewy. Romanian Jews, in need of kosher dishes that could be taken on long trips and eaten during periods when fresh meat was unavailable, adapted this technique to various items ranging from beef to geese, adding more spices than their Turkish predecessors and calling the dish *pastrama* and *pastirma* in Yiddish.

Modern pastrami is a relatively recent American innovation—to be precise, it emerged in New York City. As with corned beef, in the late nineteenth century, the advent of artificial refrigeration allowed for the use of a weaker salt brine for curing, leading to the development of a softer form of pastrami. Modern pastrami is usually made from beef plate—also called deckle, belly, and navel—or a fatty part of a brisket. There is always more brisket because each cow yields two briskets, one from each side, but only one plate. Technically, the meat should be cured in a brine in barrels, although today it rarely is. Unlike corned beef, pastrami, after soaking in brine, is subsequently rubbed well with wine vinegar and a heady mix of spices—including allspice, bay leaves, cinnamon, cloves, coriander, ginger, juniper berries, paprika, pepper, and garlic. It is dry-cured for one to two weeks, then smoked at about 320°F for six or seven hours, and finally steamed or braised. The timing and temperature of the steaming translates into major differences in the quality of the finished pastrami; too little and the meat is chewy, too long and it falls apart. When properly cured and steamed, the result is soft, succulent, smoky, and spicy meat with a deep crimson color.

According to his family, a Lithuanian Jewish immigrant by the name of Sussman (née Zusman) Volk (d.1909) was responsible for popularizing pastrami in America. In 1887, Volk, a miller by profession, brought his wife and seven children to New York City and, after failing to find appropriate work, opened a tiny kosher butcher shop on Delancey Street on the Lower East Side. A Romanian acquaintance asked Volk if he could store a trunk in his basement for a few years while he traveled back to the Old Country. Volk agreed and in return, the Romanian gave his family recipe for *pastirma* to Volk. Volk began making and selling *pastirma* from his store and by 1888 was able to move to larger quarters nearby and open a store with tables and chairs, becoming the first deli to sell *pastirma*. In America, the Yiddish name evolved into pastrami (this change was probably influenced by the name of the better-known Italian salami). The earliest record of the word pastrami was in a kvetch about the high price of living in Syracuse, New York, in the January 16, 1916, *Syracuse Herald*. The writer complained, "They stick two cents a pound on pastrami or Frankfurters." The tone indicated that the term had been around for at least a little while.

Pastrami quickly became a staple of delicatessens and, stacked between slices of rye bread and spread with hearty mustard, an eminent sandwich filling. Pastrami remains far and away the best seller in any Jewish deli, well ahead of corned beef. According to aficionados, the true quality of pastrami depends on how it is sliced—proper handling yields juicy slices. However, because of the labor and time involved in producing true pastrami, few delis still make their own or properly carve it. Today, a handful of large purveyors along with some smaller ones make most of America's pastrami, typically injecting the meat with a syringe of brine rather than soaking it. Some also inject it with liquid smoke. Other companies, however, are willing to prepare batches according to an individual deli's recipe.

Beginning in the 1920s, because of the numerous Jewish delis in the vicinity of Times Square, pastrami along with other deli foods became identified with show business in New York and soon entered the mainstream of American culture. In March 1979, food critic Mimi Sheraton published in the *New York Times* the results of her taste test of 104 pastrami and corn beef sandwiches from the area's delis, reflecting pastrami's transition to gourmet status, or at least to that of foodie fare. As with many other ethnic foods they embraced, Americans sometimes adapted pastrami. The "Pastrami Dip," also called a "French Dip," was created in Los Angeles in the 1950s and consists of a slit French roll or hoagie bun that is dipped into gravy and then piled with pastrami; if both the upper and lower buns are moistened, it is a double dip. L.A. even has the pastrami burrito, wrapped in a flour tortilla, while grilled pastrami panini have also emerged.

(See also Corned Beef and Delicatessen)

PATSAS

Patsas is a soup made from the feet (trotters) of a lamb, sheep, or calf.

Origin: Turkey

Other names: Bulgaria: *pacha*; Greece: *sopa de patsas, soupa patsas*; Romania: *ciorba de burta*; Yemen: *marak regal, regale*.

Peasants in medieval Turkey relied on a simple, very murky, glutinous, and flavorful soup made from lamb's feet, also referred to as trotters, called *paca corbasi*, from the Turkish word *paca* (foot). Variations of the basic soup also include *kell-paca corbasi* (head and foot soup) and *iskembe corbasi* ("tripe soup"; tripe is the rubbery lining of the stomach of ruminants). The modern world generally finds the very idea of foot soup unappetizing or outright repulsive. Yet the dish was once considered a healthy and hearty poor person's meal. Indeed, the modern term for a dining establishment was coined in 1765 by a Parisian vendor who sold sheep's foot soup as a *"restaurant"* (restorative).

Foot soup eventually spread throughout the Caucasus, central Asia, and eastern Europe. The Persians picked up the dish, which they called *kaleh pacheh* (head and foot), from the Turks, and typically used the sheep's head (minus the brain) and tongue as well as the feet, and flavored the soup with fresh herbs and a squeeze of lemon juice. In the Levant and Egypt, the soup is typically cooked with chickpeas and known as *kawareh bi hummus*. Among the relics of the Ottomans' centuries-long control of the Balkans is foot soup. In eastern Europe, it gave rise to the jellied dish *p'tcha*. Non-Jewish Greek versions, although mistakenly referred to as *patsas*, are actually tripe soups, which sometimes include trotters as well. On the other hand, Greek Jews tend to include only or primarily feet in their *patsas*.

The popularity of Jewish *patsas* was strongest in the area around Salonika and, in particular, was a favorite of the dock workers of the once-vital port city in northeastern Greece, then part of the Ottoman Empire, who for several centuries had been overwhelmingly Jewish. *Patsas* is considered working person's food; it is consumed at any time of the day, and is especially popular as a cold-weather breakfast. It is often accompanied with flatbread and pickles, providing a filling meal before a long day of strenuous labor. The soup is usually enlivened with lemon juice or white wine vinegar and plenty of garlic. *Patsas* was not only weekday fare. The Jewish masses of Salonika added chickpeas and unshelled eggs to the soup, slow-cooked it overnight, and served it for Sabbath lunch.

GREEK FOOT SOUP (*PATSAS/SOPA DE PATSAS*)

6 TO 8 SERVINGS   [MEAT]

   5 pounds (6 lamb's, 4 sheep's, or 2 calf's) feet

(trotters), cleaned and cut into 2-inch pieces (have your butcher cut the bones for you)

¼ cup olive or vegetable oil

2 large yellow onions, sliced

4 to 7 cloves garlic, sliced

10 cups water

2 bay leaves

Salt to taste

¼ to ½ cup fresh lemon juice or white wine vinegar

3 to 4 tablespoons olive oil

1. Place the feet in a large pot, cover with cold water, and bring to a boil. Boil until scum rises to the surface, about 10 minutes. Drain off and discard the water. Rinse the feet and pat dry.

2. In a clean large pot, heat ¼ cup oil over medium heat. Add the onions and sauté until soft and translucent, 5 to 10 minutes. Add the feet and brown on all sides. Stir in the garlic. Add the water, bay leaves, and salt. Cover, reduce the heat, and simmer over low heat or bake in a 180°F oven until the meat falls away from the bones, 4 to 5 hours, or overnight.

3. Remove the feet from the soup. Shred any meat from the bones and pick out any marrow and add to the soup. Discard the bones. Add the lemon juice and 3 to 4 tablespoons olive oil.

PEPITADA

Pepitada is a drink made of melon seeds.

Origin: Middle East

Other names: Arabic: *soubia, soubiya, subiya*.

For centuries, toward the end of the summer, as musk melons reached their peak in September, many Sephardim from Turkey, Rhodes, Crete, and the Balkans saved the seeds for making a drink known as *pepitada*—*pepita* in Ladino means the "pip/little seed" and the suffix *ada* is the equivalent of the English suffix "ade." The melon seeds can be raw or toasted; toasted seeds produce a flavor akin to that of toasted sesame seeds. *Pepitada* is lightly sweetened with a little sugar and perfumed with rose water or orange-blossom water. A similar Greek beverage made from bitter and sweet almonds is known as *soumada* or *soumatha*.

This milk-like drink, its whiteness symbolizing purity, is traditionally served in small glasses after Yom Kippur to break the fast and sometimes also after Tisha b'Av. Sephardim believe that the *pepitada* coats the stomach, making food more digestible. Unlike Ashkenazim, who typically break their fasts with dairy foods. Sephardim historically began with pareve items, like *pepitada* followed by a light repast of *panisicos dulces* (sweet rolls), *reshicas* (pretzel-like cookies), or other pastries and cookies and fresh fruit—and then frequently a meat meal or fried fish. Today, as melons are available year round, some families make *pepitada* throughout the summer as a refreshing drink.

GREEK MELON SEED "MILK" (*PEPITADA*)

ABOUT I QUART [PAREVE]

2 cups melon seeds (seeds from about 4 cantaloupes, 2 to 3 honeydews, or 2 Persian melons)

4 cups cold water

1 to 6 tablespoons sugar or honey

Several drops rose water, orange-blossom water, or almond extract (optional)

1. Clean all the flesh and filaments from the melon seeds. Spread on a large baking sheet and let dry for 1 week. If desired, toast the seeds in a 350°F oven, shaking the pan occasionally, until golden brown, about 45 minutes, or stir the seeds in a dry skillet over medium heat until they are lightly browned and begin to crackle, 6 to 8 minutes. Let cool.

2. Place the water in a pitcher, large bowl, or other large container. In a blender, mortar, or food processor fitted with a metal blade, finely grind the seeds. Place the seeds in several layers of cheesecloth, bring the corners together, and tie to form a little bag (*sakito*). Place the bag in the water and let soak at room temperature, squeezing the cheesecloth occasionally (the water will begin to turn murky), for 24 to 36 hours.

3. Squeeze any moisture from the cheesecloth into the soaking liquid and discard the seeds. Transfer the liquid to a medium saucepan. Add the sugar, adjusting the amount as desired. Simmer, stirring, over low heat until the sugar dissolves. If using, add 1 to 2 drops of rose water for every 1 cup liquid. Serve chilled.

PEPPER, SWEET

In 1493, Spaniards brought to the Old World the fruits of a member of the nightshade family known as capsicum peppers. (Peppers, like tomatoes, contain seeds meant for dispersal, making them at least botanically a berry.) At this point, these were all chilies, containing stinging amounts of the chemical compound capsaicin, and they were virtually ignored in most of Europe—their fiery charms were more warmly appreciated in areas with hot climates. Capsicum, however, interbreed with relative ease, producing an ever-increasing array of varieties. In the eighteenth century, European horticulturists cultivated milder forms of capsicum, such as the tomato pepper, which has only a hint of a bite, and then those without any fire, called sweet peppers. In America, the predominant sweet pepper is the bell, named for its squarish shape with two to four lobes. Another popular sweet pepper, favored in the Mediterranean and Middle East, is the Italian pepper—also known as pepperoni, Turkish pepper, and frying pepper—a long, tapered variety that is paler green than bell peppers when immature and ripens into a yellowish green or red color. Varieties of Italian peppers include Corno di Toro (bull's horn), Italia, and Sweet Banana.

Small chilies tend to be fiery and are primarily used as a spice, while sweet peppers are larger and are usually employed as a vegetable. All capsicum peppers start out green. As they mature on the vine, they generally grow sweeter and turn into an array of colors, including red, yellow, orange, brown, purple, and black. Green peppers have an herbal flavor and are more bitter and slightly firmer than ripe ones.

Sweet peppers became an important part of cooking, particularly in the moderate climes of the Mediterranean, the Balkans, and Hungary. Bell peppers are routinely added to salads, casseroles, and stews. Sweet peppers are also marinated and used in relishes, such as the Turkish *muhammura*. Middle Easterners commonly cook them with tomatoes. Roasted sweet peppers—roasting brings out a smoky flavor—are popular throughout the Mediterranean area in various salads and stews.

After the advent of the bell pepper, people throughout eastern Europe and the Middle East discovered its boxlike structure made them ideal for stuffing. Cooks eventually began stuffing them with ground meat, grains, and other mixtures and simmering or baking them. Hungarians also enjoyed peppers stuffed with sauerkraut. Cheese-stuffed peppers are particularly popular in Italy, Hungary, and the Balkans. In Romania and the Balkans, Italian frying peppers are used for this dish.

Stuffed peppers became one of the few pepper dishes widely adopted by the general Ashkenazic community. Stuffed peppers seem to have reached America toward the end of the nineteenth century.

The first edition of *The Settlement Cook Book* (Milwaukee, 1901) contained four recipes for them. Most of the few earlier American references to stuffed peppers entailed various pickled peppers.

Initially, stuffed peppers were confined to the pepper season from August through October. Since tomatoes also came into maturity at the same time, the peppers were frequently paired with a tomato sauce—savory among Sephardim and Hungarians, and sweet-and-sour in southern Poland and northern Ukraine. In the twentieth century, as most vegetables became available all year, so did stuffed peppers.

As a rule of thumb, Middle Easterners serve meat-stuffed and cheese-stuffed peppers hot, while rice-stuffed versions are offered both hot and cold. The cold version is perfect for a buffet or *mezze* (appetizer assortment). Some families serve stuffed peppers on Sukkot as a symbol of a plentiful harvest, but in many homes it is a beloved everyday dish, either as a hearty appetizer or a flavorful main course.

(See also Ajvar, Chili, Lecsó, Matbucha, Mechouiya, Muhammara, and Paprika)

PEPPERCORN

Pepper, from the Sanskrit *pippali* (berry), was trafficked by traders from its home on the Malabar Coast of southwest India to the far corners of the ancient world. The majority of the recipes in the Roman cookbook of Apicius (c. 400 CE) called for pepper. For much of history, pepper was incredibly costly. In medieval Europe, pepper—used as a preservative, a flavoring agent, and a mask for rancid meat and off-tasting foods—was affordable only to royalty. Commoners made do primarily with mustard.

As far back as the ancient Roman sea voyages across the Indian Ocean to the Malabar Coast beginning in the first century CE, most of the spice merchants there were Cochini Jews. For four centuries during the early Middle Ages, until around 1000 CE, Jewish merchants known as Radhanites imported all the spices from the Far East into the Middle East and Europe. After the collapse of the Radhanites, Venice acquired the monopoly on the European spice trade. It is not an exaggeration to claim that the modern world emerged as a result of Europe's pursuit of this spice. The Venetian monopoly led Portugal's Prince Henry the Navigator to concoct an unprecedented plan to circumnavigate Africa and bring pepper directly from India. In 1497, Vasco da Gama realized Henry's dream, passing the Cape of Good Hope and reaching India. In 1503, the Portuguese broke the Venetian monopoly by returning from India by ship with thirteen hundred tons of peppercorns. Another source of competition in the pepper trade during the fifteenth and sixteenth century was the Ragusans, who lived in the maritime republic of Dubrovnik, a city-state in southern Croatia. Many of that region's spice merchants were Sephardic Jews. The Dutch also began to ship spices from the Far East. In the meantime, Spain attempted to follow a different course to find the Spice Islands, and Christopher Columbus sailed westward, discovering America in the process.

Throughout this time, most of the spice merchants within Europe were Jews. Many Jewish communities were required to pay an annual tribute of peppercorns and other gifts to the local nobles and the church. Pepper was also commonly used as payment for using land for synagogues and Jewish cemeteries or leasing lakes for farming fish.

Subsequently, the pepper trade became an important form of commerce in Europe and the return of each voyage was awaited with anticipation. However, pepper costs fluctuated greatly depending on the cost of the voyage and whether the ship returned at all. Merchants in Amsterdam and then London solved this dilemma by the creation of stocks, engendering the concept of and coining the term capitalism. The wealth accumulated through the spice trade, as well as the abundance of spices, led to the development of modern European cuisine.

Eventually, spice importers grew more successful at maintaining a large, steady influx of peppercorns. Pepper became accessible to everyone and grew progressively less expensive, quickly emerging as the world's most widely used spice.

True pepper is the small fruit of a climbing vine that grows only in tropical climates, generally within fifteen degrees of the equator. The plant produces long spikes, each of which bears twenty to thirty small berries. There are three types of peppercorns—black, white, and green—all derived from the same vine. Szechuan pepper, sansho (Japanese pepper), and pink peppercorns are from different plants and are not true pepper.

Black peppercorns (*pilpel* in Hebrew, from the Sanskrit name, *pippali*) are berries picked when mature and then sun-dried. They are the most pungent of the three types, with a spicy-fruity aroma and flavor, as well as the most widely used. The longer the berries mature before harvesting—size is an indication of maturity—the richer the flavor.

White peppercorns (*pilpel lavan* in Hebrew) begin life as black peppercorns, but are left on the vine longer to mature more fully. After the peppercorns are harvested, they are soaked in water to soften the outer husks, the husks are removed, and the inside kernels are dried. White pepper has a creamy color and an earthy aroma.

Whole peppercorns are renowned for heat and flavor complexity. Pepper's spicy-fruity aroma and flavor, including citrus and pine, derive from volatile chemical compounds that are released upon cracking. As soon as the peppercorns are cracked, the compounds begin to disperse, which is why commercial ground pepper lacks the subtle nuances of freshly ground pepper. Pepper's pungency comes from piperine, a nonvolatile chemical irritant that activates neurons of the somatosensory system, making the tongue feel warm. The aroma of whole peppercorns is not a guarantee of quality, as the aroma is not fully released until they are cracked. Black pepper varieties, each possessing their own individual attributes, are named for the various places in which they are grown. There are five areas that mass-produce peppercorns: India, Malaysia, Indonesia, Vietnam, and Brazil. The world's best pepper still comes from the Malabar Coast. The largest and most mature Malabar peppercorns, considered to be the most complex and rich, are called Tellicherry. Other Indian peppercorns are called Malabar and remain the most widespread peppers. Malabar is very robust, but lacks the balance of Tellicherry.

By the first and second centuries CE, pepper had become an important seasoning in the Mediterranean region. The spice subsequently found its way into an array of Jewish dishes, although used quite sparingly by most. Beginning around the eighteenth century, as the supply of pepper increased and its price declined in Europe, pepper became the most important and widespread spice in Jewish cookery, although the amount required a matter of heated debate. Pepper is usually a flavor accent in dishes, but can take a starring role, such as the Lithuanian *zalts-un-feffer* kugel, German *pfefferkuchen* and Israeli *kugel yerushalmi*. The plural of its Arabic name, *filfil*, gave rise to the name for fried chickpea croquettes, falafel.

PERSIMMON

There are two kinds of persimmons: American and Japanese. The Japanese persimmon was introduced to the United States by Commodore Matthew Perry in 1855 on his return from Japan. Eventually, the more commercially viable Japanese variety took over the marketplace. Immature Japanese persimmons are firm, encased in edible skin, and mouth-puckeringly astringent. Ripe ones, which tend to fall apart, are red-orange in color and mushy in texture, with a sweet and tangy flavor.

An Israeli hybrid of the Japanese persimmon, the Sharon fruit, named after the valley between Tel Aviv and Haifa where it was first grown, has no seeds, no core, and, even more importantly, no bitter taste even when unripe. Its season runs from October through February. Sharon fruit, a trademark name used exclusively in Israel, is now a major Israeli export—seven thousand tons were exported in 2009—and is also being grown throughout the world under the name Kaki or Fuyu (although commonly called Sharon fruit). The popularity of Sharon fruit, primarily eaten raw, also led to increased usage in Jewish cooking, including in salads, smoothies, chutneys, latkes, and kugels.

PESHKADO FRITO

Peshkado frito is a fish fillet coated in egg and flour, then fried in oil.

Origin: Spain

Other names: *peixe frito, pescado frito.*

Israel Zangwill included a description of Jewish cooking in his tale of Jewish life in late nineteenth-century London, *Children of the Ghetto* (1892). He wrote, "Fish was indeed the staple of the meal. Fried fish, and such fried fish! With the audacity of true culinary genius, Jewish fried fish is always served cold. The skin is a beautiful brown, the substance firm and succulent . . . fried fish reigns above all in cold, unquestioned superiority."

Any Sephardi would instantly recognize this dish as the favorite and most celebrated of the numerous Sephardic fish dishes—*peshkado frito*, fish fillets coated in egg and flour and fried. The first record of coating and frying fish fillets was a recipe for "Hout Mu'affar" (dusted fish) in an anonymous thirteenth-century Andalusian cookbook. The author directed, "Then take ground bread crumbs or wheat flour and add eggs, pepper, coriander, cinnamon, and spikenard [a rhizome from the Himalayas crushed for its aromatic oil with a spicy, piney flavor, probably the *nard* of Song of Songs], beating them all together. Roll the pieces of fish in it over and over, then fry in fresh oil until browned." Well before the expulsion from Spain, Sephardim had developed their fried fish along the same lines.

Following the expulsion in 1492, Sephardic refugees brought their fried fish to their new locales, including Italy, where the dish became a standard of the Roman ghetto. In the sixteenth century, the Portuguese brought deep-fried battered fish and vegetables to Japan, where it became tempura.

Jews were expelled from England in 1290 by Edward I, and only openly readmitted in 1656 under Oliver Cromwell. However, during the sixteenth century, Conversos, particularly from Portugal, made their way to England by way of Holland and introduced to the British their way of frying fish in oil, rather than lard or butter. By the mid-eighteenth century, fried fish was entrenched in British cooking. Thus Hannah Glasse, in the 1781 edition of her extremely popular book, *The Art of Cookery Made Plain and Easy*, included a recipe for "The Jews Way of preserving Salmon, and all Sorts of Fish," and began a recipe for marinated fish by explaining the frying process. Significantly, in her earlier editions, Glasse had provided several other dishes made "the Jews way," but the 1781 edition was the first to include fried fish.

In the first Jewish cookbook in English, *The Jewish Manual* (London, 1846), Judith Montefiore, drawing on her husband's Portuguese roots, included the standard Sephardic oil-fried fish and its marinated version, as well as the non-Jewish butter-fried fish.

Alexis Soyer, a Frenchman who spent most of his career in London and became one of the first celebrity chefs, was a proponent of Sephardic fish. He included a recipe for "Fried Fish, Jewish Fashion" in his book *A Shilling Cookery for the People* (London, 1855), along with this note: "This is another excellent way of frying fish, which is constantly in use by the children of Israel, and I cannot recommend it too highly; so much so, that various kinds of fish which many people despise, are excellent cooked by this process; in eating them many persons are deceived, and would suppose them to be the most expensive of fish. The process is at once simple, effective, and economical."

Thomas Jefferson discovered the dish during his tenure as ambassador to France (1785–1789), shortly after it achieved wider popularity in England, and subsequently Jewish fried fish was served at Monticello and probably in his Washington, D.C. residence as well. Jefferson's granddaughter, Virginia Randolph, copied the recipes he brought from Europe, as well as those prepared at Monticello and the White House, in a handwritten copy of the manuscript passed down through the generations until published in 1949 by Marie Kimball as *Thomas Jefferson's Cook Book*. Jewish fried fish never achieved widespread popularity in America, although another recipe Jefferson brought back from his tenure in France eventually did—deep-fried potatoes.

Meanwhile, French fries also spread across the English Channel to Britain, where they became known as chips, and, in the early nineteenth century, were being sold from small shops. A Jewish fishmonger, Joseph Malin, is credited with combining the Jewish-style fried fish from his store on Old Ford Road in London's East End with the fried potatoes of a neighboring Irish shop, creating the classic British combination of fish and chips. This innovation occurred around 1865 and by the end of that decade, fish-and-chip shops had become a British institution, providing a fast, inexpensive, and filling meal for the working class.

Cod is the most common variety used in *peshkado frito*, but other favored fish are red snapper, sea bass, and halibut. There are two ways of preparing and attaching the coating: dipping the fillets into beaten eggs, then into flour or bread crumbs; or combining the eggs and flour (or bread crumbs) to make a batter, then dipping the fish into the batter. In either case, the coating prevents the fish from sticking to the pan, protects the fish from the heat, holds the tender flesh together, and gives the fried fish a darker color. Frying crisps the flour, seals in the juices, and cooks the fillets quickly. The result is a firm, moist, flavorful fish.

Jewish-styled fried fish, which was typically fried in oil, was historically different from that of non-Jews, who used lard or butter. When they lived in Iberia, Sephardim used olive oil, but once they migrated to the eastern Mediterranean, where the price was typically higher, they frequently substituted sesame or sunflower oil. When fried fish is done right, the flavor and sweetness of the fish are accentuated, and the fish is not greasy or heavy. Some cooks deep-fry the fish, thereby avoiding the delicate task of turning the fillet, while others fry the fish on one side at a time in a smaller amount of oil. *Peshkado frito* is served simply with lemon wedges or with one of two sauces: *agristada* (egg-lemon sauce) or *ajada* (garlic mayonnaise).

Peshkado frito became a part of almost every Friday dinner, and the leftovers were enjoyed cold the following day at *shalosh seudot* (the afternoon meal) and even for several days thereafter. As a way of keeping the fish safe for a day or more—a requirement before the advent of artificial refrigeration—cooks would marinate the cold fried fish in a vinegar dressing.

SEPHARDIC PAN-FRIED FISH FILLETS
(*PESHKADO FRITO*)

4 TO 6 SERVINGS   [PAREVE]

2¼ pounds firm-fleshed fish fillets, such as sea bass, cod, flounder, grouper, haddock, halibut, perch, salmon, snapper, sole, tilapia, or trout, cut into 4-inch pieces

About 1½ teaspoons kosher salt

Olive or vegetable oil for frying

About ⅔ cup unbleached all-purpose flour or matza meal

About ½ teaspoon table salt

⅛ to ¼ teaspoon ground black pepper or paprika

2 large eggs lightly beaten with 2 tablespoons water

1. Arrange the fish in a large, shallow dish, sprinkle with the kosher salt, and add enough water to just cover the fish. Cover and refrigerate for 1 hour. Rinse, then pat dry.

2. In a large, heavy skillet, heat ¼ inch oil over medium heat to 370°F.

3. In a shallow dish, combine the flour, table salt, and pepper. Place the eggs in a second shallow dish. Just before frying, dip the fillets into the eggs, then into the flour to coat. Or stir together the flour, eggs, ⅓ cup water, and table salt and dip the fillets into this batter.

4. Working in batches, immediately place the fillets in a single layer in the skillet, leaving space between each fillet. Cook, without moving the fish, until golden brown on the bottom, about 2 minutes for ¼-inch-thick fillets, 3 minutes for ½-inch-thick, or 3 to 4 minutes for ¾- to 1-inch-thick.

5. Using a spatula, carefully turn the fillets. Reduce the heat to medium and fry until the crust is golden brown and the fish is firm to the touch and opaque, about 1 minute for ¼-inch-thick fillets, 2 minutes

for ½-inch-thick, or 3 minutes for ¾- to 1-inch-thick. Drain on a wire rack. Serve warm or at room temperature.

PFEFFERKUCHEN
Pfefferkuchen is a savory cookie.
Origin: Germany
Other names: *feferkuchen*.

This pastry dates back to around the sixteenth century. Although *pfeffer* means "pepper" in German, the word also connoted any new foreign spice, and various spices were used in these cookies. Like most central European baked goods before sugar became an accessible and inexpensive item, *pfefferkuchen* was not sweet. However, the addition of schmaltz, which Ashkenazim tended to use in baked goods instead of butter or lard, and a hint of spice elevated the long, thin, rich cookies into a dessert or an appetizer for special occasions. *Pfefferkuchen* became a Jewish surname; it was used by Fyodor Dostoyevsky in *The Insulted and Injured* (1861) for a German idealist.

PHYLLO/FILA
There are two predominant ways of creating flaky layered pastries: Puff pastry and phyllo. Puff pastry is made by incorporating pockets of fat, which melt during baking, into a dough. Versatile puff pastry dough can yield crisp and brittle pastries like Napoleons, or soft and fluffy ones like Danishes. Its use is concentrated in an area roughly corresponding to the region of the former Holy Roman Empire.

In the kitchens of the royal palace in Istanbul, cooks perfected a method for stretching plain dough called *yufka* very thin and used it to make an array of baked goods. The Turks introduced their paper-thin dough throughout the Ottoman Empire, including the Balkans, where it became known as phyllo ("leaf" in Greek), and called *fila* in Arabic. The Turks also occupied Hungary and brought the concept of *yufka* into the heart of central Europe, where puff pastry overlaps with phyllo; there it became a dough called *blätterteig*, which was used for strudel. Whatever the name, phyllo is a basic unleavened dough—made from a mixture of flour, water, salt, and a little oil—that is stretched paper-thin.

These delicate sheets of dough are brushed with melted fat, then baked or fried, producing crisp, flaky pastry used in a wide variety of savory and sweet treats. Beginning in the 1960s, Greek immigrants began to popularize hand-made phyllo in parts of America. With the invention of a practical phyllo machine in 1971, commercial phyllo dough was suddenly available frozen in American supermarkets, making it accessible to everyone.

Mizrachim and Sephardim use phyllo in an array of large pies and small pastries, which appear at most celebrations. Among the most popular of phyllo pastries are rolls variously called *dedos* ("fingers" in Spanish), *asabia* ("fingers" in Arabic), and *sigares/cigares/garros* ("cigars"). *Floyera*, a Greek shepherd's flute about twelve inches long, provided the name for long thin phyllo rolls. Small, triangular-shaped phyllo

Phyllo is used to make an array of beloved pastries. Front to back: bulemas/rodanches *(coiled tubes),* farareer/bulbul yuvasi *(bird's nests), and* kanafeh/kadayif.

turnovers are known as *samsada* or *borekas* in Turkey, *pastel* in Morocco, *shamiziko* in the Balkans, *tyropita/tiropetes* in Greece, and *ojaldres* in Ladino.

(See also Baklava, Boreka, Bougatsa, Bulema, Galaktoboureko, Khachapuri, Mina, Ojaldre, Pastilla, Strudel, and Warka)

PICKLE

Today, the produce departments of grocery stores are laden with fresh fruits and vegetables, most available any time of the year. In addition, numerous types of produce are sold in jars and cans, as well as frozen. Consequently, it is difficult to conceive that before the recent advances of modern technology—the appearance of refrigeration and canning, improved agriculture, high-speed transportation, and dinner reservations—food had to be scratched out of the soil and the availability of most seasonal produce was limited to rather short growing periods. To be sure, grains, dried legumes, a handful of dried sugar-rich fruits, and, in cooler climates, a few root vegetables could be stored for an extended period. Most other items, however, had to be consumed rather quickly or be lost to spoilage. Malnutrition and boring diets were all too prevalent, especially during the winter and periods of famine. Thus it was vital for people to find ways to conserve limited resources. The two most effective preservatives of the ancient world were acid and salt, used individually and in conjunction with each other.

One of the most popular and widespread of the ancient keeping methods was pickling. (The English term pickle first appeared around 1400, derived from *pokel*, a northern German word for "salt" and "brine," by way of the Dutch *pekel*.) Vegetables were mixed or cooked with a little salt, resulting in a limited durability of a few days, or brined with vinegar for a lengthier period—the acid was necessary to forestall the growth of bacteria. Salting involves changing the nature of the produce, which in some instances was tolerated, and in others was most welcomed. Salt plays many roles in pickling: It enhances taste, including removing raw flavors; deters bacteria; and extracts water from the vegetables, which not only keeps the produce crisp, but also prevents the water from seeping out later and diluting the preservative effect of the vinegar. Vegetables brined in salt are edible within a day or so, while those preserved with vinegar, which is rather sharp tasting, are generally left to mellow for at least one and sometimes several weeks. Brined vegetables are crunchy for the initial few days unless first blanched. Relishes are similar to pickles, except the ingredients, which are sometimes a combination of vegetables, are chopped into small pieces, producing a mixture that is usable as a dip, bread spread, or condiment. Larger pickle pieces are served as an appetizer or side dish.

Throughout most of history, not only the elite, but even more so the impoverished masses, relied on pickles and relishes, roles fulfilled by kimchi in Korean cuisine, *zuke* in Japan, and chutneys in India. In ancient Egypt, food as well as people (mummies) were pickled. The workers who built the Great Wall of China subsisted on a diet consisting primarily of pickled cabbage. Pickles were also an intrinsic part of dining throughout the medieval Middle East, where pickled vegetables called *turshi* were a favorite dish. Second-century Rome imported pickled vegetables from Spain, and Iberian pickles were later adapted into Sephardic cuisine. To our ancestors, pickles were no trifling matter, but rather a fundamental part of the diet—an essential, not a luxury.

Besides contributing valuable nutrition, relishes and pickles made people's meals palatable and enlivened their diets, which primarily consisted of coarse, hard breads and other starches. The Talmud states, "One who is about to recite the Hamotzi [benediction over bread] is not permitted to do so before salt and *leaftan* [relish] is placed before him." The Hebrew term *leaftan* was derived from the word *lefet* (turnip), which itself came from *lahfaht* (to twist/turn), connoting the way of harvesting a root vegetable like a turnip by twisting it from the ground. During the Talmudic period, the word *lefet* was sometimes used generically to mean vegetables, since the turnip was then the most common one. Accordingly, the turnip (*leaftan*) was the most prevalent form of pickled vegetable in the Middle East; *leaftan* was also the term used for all relishes, the common accompaniment to bread. Pickled turnips are still a ubiquitous sight on many contemporary Middle Eastern tables.

More than twenty-four hundred years ago, the Chinese discovered a better, more long-lasting way of pickling vegetables without vinegar—a process today known as lacto-fermentation. In this technique, acidifying bacteria found naturally in raw vegetables, notably cabbage, feed off the sugar in the vegetables.

The bacteria produce lactic and acetic acids, which give the vegetables a tangy yet mellow taste, slightly soften them, and produce natural compounds that kill harmful bacteria. These acidifying bacteria also transform milk into cheese and yogurt, and are active in bread dough. Lacto-fermentation involves no cooking or vinegar. Instead it requires warmth, and, for most vegetables, sufficient salt to prevent the growth of undesirable bacteria and to extract juice and sugar, while allowing the survival of naturally occurring acid-producing species of bacteria. If there is too little salt, the produce will spoil; if there is too much salt, it will not ferment.

Cooks preparing medieval Middle Eastern pickles relied on vinegar, which was primarily made from wine, an item rare and expensive in northern Europe, where people depended on salt instead. Then around the middle of the sixteenth century, nomadic Tatars and Turks brought the more advanced Chinese technique of lacto-fermentation to eastern Europe, where it was adopted by the Slavs and eastern European Jews from the Baltic to Romania. This technique traveled westward through northern Europe—in many cases spread by Jews—engendering dishes such as sauerkraut, which became the principal vegetable dish in central Europe and a staple of the Ashkenazic diet. In addition to cabbage, produce commonly preserved with lacto-fermentation are beets, carrots, cauliflower, cucumbers, green beans, olives, peppers, green tomatoes, and turnips.

The cucumber itself had only reached eastern Europe from India by way of Spain a little more than a century before the arrival of lacto-fermentation. Once the cucumber was treated with lacto-fermentation, it emerged as a mainstay of eastern European Jewish food. For many generations, Ashkenazim in the autumn prepared crocks or barrels of cucumbers, typically along with one of beets and one of shredded cabbage, and left them to ferment for several weeks in a warm location. (If the temperature gets too high, yeasts begin to ferment, resulting in mushy vegetables and poor flavor.) After reaching the proper degree of sourness, the crocks were moved to a root cellar or other cool place to last through at least the spring and the arrival of new produce. True "kosher dills," short for kosher-style or Jewish-style, never contain vinegar, but rather rely solely on lactic acid fermentation, which, like the fermentation of sauerkraut, produces a distinctive acidity and flavor. The addition of whole garlic also marks cucumbers as "kosher dills." It has become popular in America to use vinegar to prevent the growth of bacteria, although this addition comes at the expense of the pickle's distinguishing bite. Characteristic of the eastern Ashkenazic pantry were *zoyers* (sours), especially pickles.

There are three basic types of pickled cucumbers: sour, half sour, and sweet. Sour pickles are fully fermented cucumbers, while half sours are partially fermented in a salt brine for two to four weeks. Sweet pickles, a relatively new innovation, contain a sizable amount of sugar, which is also a preservative. In Yiddish, sour pickles are *zoyere ugerkehs*, while sweet and sours are *zeesih un zoyere ugerkehs*.

Eastern Ashkenazim brought their love of pickles with them to America, where pickles were frequently associated with Jews. Sarah Rorer, in *Mrs. Rorer's New Cook Book* (Philadelphia, 1902), in a section entitled "A Group of Jewish Recipes," called pickles "Salt Water Cucumbers."

Within a short time, a myriad of small stores appeared in Jewish areas, notably Manhattan's Lower East Side, offering an assortment of Jewish pickles sold from large barrels. Today, very few of these mom-and-pop pickle shops remain; most became casualties of the large corporate brands. In America, the name most associated with pickles is Henry J. Heinz, who in 1869 began offering his now-famous fifty-seven varieties of pickles to stores in the Sharpsburg, Pennsylvania, area. The H. J. Heinz Company would greatly impact America's Jewish community about fifty-five years later, when, in a totally unprecedented move, they introduced the then-revolutionary concept of a national brand of food that was under kosher supervision. Kosher-supervised pickles soon followed. Today, Heinz serves as America's main producer of pickles and relishes, including "kosher dills."

Although we now live in an era when fresh produce is available year-round, pickles still maintain their popularity. One reason is the rise of the delicatessen. After all, what would a pastrami or corn beef sandwich be without a pickle? Yet even more important is something that ancient cultures understood—the pickle's attribute for clearing the palate. The first mouthful of a dish is very flavorful. Then, with each successive bite, the flavors begin to dull and eventually we hardly taste anything as the taste buds get coated with fat or zapped with spices and subsequently the food just glides off the tongue. A pickle cuts through the residue in the mouth, restoring the taste buds and allowing the flavor of the food to emerge.

(See also Choucroute Garnie; Cucumber; Delicatessen; Lemon, Preserved; Rosl; Salt; Sauerkraut; and Turshi)

PIDYON HABEN

During the Tenth Plague in Egypt, all the firstborn Egyptians died, while the Jews were spared. Consequently, the Bible intended that all the future firstborn sons of the Israelites were to be devoted to the service of God. After the incident of the golden calf, which some Israelites worshipped when Moses was on Mount Sinai for forty days, the tribe of Levi was substituted for the firstborn. Henceforth, even though the Temple is no longer in existence, firstborn sons are redeemed through a symbolic ceremony called *Pidyon HaBen* (literally "redemption of the son"). A redemption is not required if the father or the mother is a Levi, including *Kohanim* (priests).

Because of the limited number of first-born sons, a *Pidyon HaBen* is one of the most rarely performed life-cycle ceremonies. It is held on the thirty-first day after the birth. However, since a money transaction is at the heart of this ceremony, it is not held on the Sabbath or a holiday when such business deals are forbidden, but postponed until the following weekday. Sephardim traditionally hold the *Pidyon HaBen* on the evening of the thirty-first day, while Ashkenazim prefer the following morning. Some Moroccans hold the ceremony at the same time of day that the child is born.

The *Pidyon HaBen* is typically performed in the presence of a minyan (quorum). At the ceremony, the father presents his son, frequently on a silver tray, accompanied with the payment of five shekalim or its equivalent in silver coins (the custom in America is to use silver dollars, while the Bank of Israel mints special *Pidyon HaBen* coins) to a *Kohain*. In the tenth century, a symbolic dialogue was established in which the *Kohain* asks the father whether he wants to give up his son for priestly service. Of course, the father responds that he would prefer to keep him. At this point, the father pays the *Kohain*, who repeats the phrase *"bencha pahdoy"* (your son is redeemed) three times. The money is commonly returned to the father, who donates it or its equivalence to charity. Following the *Pidyon HaBen*, the *Kohain* recites a blessing over a cup of wine, blesses the child, and then joins the relatives and friends in a *Seudat Mitzvah* (celebratory meal). Fare at morning ceremonies are generally dairy; Ashkenazim typically serve bagels, lox, and perhaps noodle kugel. Meals at midday and evening ceremonies may be either meat or dairy and, although there are no specific *Pidyon HaBen* foods, most communities tend to feature their standard celebration fare, including a large challah. Some Ashkenazim give all the celebrants sugar cubes (or today, packets), and garlic cloves to share with others not in attendance, as these items give flavor to other foods just as the Pidyon Haben bestows God's blessing to all who celebrate this rite.

PIGEON

Technically, the English terms dove and pigeon can be used interchangeably for any of the roughly three hundred members of the Columbidae family. However, the word dove is generally applied to smaller and sleeker species with graceful necks and pointed tails, while the word pigeon more specifically refers to larger and stockier birds with rounded tails. In any case, doves and pigeons are very close relatives with dramatically contrasting reputations: The dove is esteemed as a symbol of peace and beauty, while today the pigeon is currently considered at best a pest.

The turtledove is the most common dove species in Israel, as well as the most melodious. Like the ancient Israelites, modern Israelis treasure the annual arrival of the turtledove in April through mid-May to begin the mating season, which is initiated with a period of courtship and nest building in scattered trees and shrubs, primarily in the northern and central parts of the country. For a time, the land fills with the male's distinctive mating call, "tirrr, tirrr," the source of this bird's onomatopoeic Hebrew name *tur*. Thus Song of Songs included this natural phenomenon among the welcomed heralds of spring: "The flowers appear on the earth; the time of singing is come; and the voice of the *tur* [turtledove] is heard in our land." Breeding season ends in mid-September and by October the flocks, having molted, return south for the winter.

Unlike the migratory turtledove, its close relative the rock pigeon, also called the rock dove, became a permanent resident of many parts of the Mediterranean region, including Israel. As its name indicates,

rock pigeons in the wild make their nests in rock clefts and caves. Various biblical references reflected this proclivity, including Song of Songs: "O my pigeon, you are in the clefts of the rock, in the hidden places of the cliff." The rock pigeon's Hebrew name, *yonah*, also the name of a prophet (Jonah), probably derives from the word *anah* (mourn), referring to its plaintive, mournful cooing.

The Columbidae family serves as the prototype for kosher birds, exhibiting all four of the signs of kosher fowl developed by the Sages—it is not *dorais* (a bird of prey), while it has an *etzbah yetairah* (extra toe), *zefek* (crop), and *korkebano neeklaf* (peelable gizzard). Pigeons and doves were the only birds sanctioned for use as offerings in the Temple.

Turtledoves remain devoted to each other for life and mourn when their partner disappears. Rock pigeons mate for life too, but may take a new partner if one dies. The rock pigeon, whose fixed habits allowed them to readily adapt to captivity, became the first domesticated avian species. The domestication of the turtledove eventually followed, although the bird was never as useful or prevalent as its cousin. The dependable *yonah* was the bird utilized by Noah after the Flood. Significantly, the raven, the first bird sent out of the ark by Noah, is a scavenger and carrion eater in marked contrast to the vegetarian pigeon.

Egyptians, who were possibly the first to domesticate pigeons, appreciated them not only for their meat but also for their beauty and utility. By the Fourth Dynasty, in at least 2500 BCE, dovecotes ("*arubbah*" in Isaiah) appeared throughout Egypt on the rooftops of many homes or sometimes as separate structures, providing pigeons a solid surface reminiscent of a cliff. Even the pharaoh maintained dovecotes for his prized royal birds. The Great Harris Papyrus, a record of donations to the temples by Ramses III (reigned c. 1182–1151 BCE), included a mention of 57,810 pigeons as well as 25,020 waterfowl. Meanwhile, pigeons appear to have been simultaneously domesticated in several other locations, including Sumeria and Canaan, becoming an integral part of each area's culture. In the Fertile Crescent, the dove became the symbol of beauty and fertility. Pigeons remained the predominant fowl in ancient Israel until the end of the Second Commonwealth.

Nevertheless, those who raised poultry faced the problem that birds living in close proximity to each other in large flocks tend to contract and spread various diseases, which can wipe out most of or all of the animals. A large space is required for raising pigeons in any number, to allow each pair plenty of room. Thus in biblical times even rock pigeons, although cleaner and easier to domesticate and raise than other birds, were still relatively expensive and certainly not a regular part of the diet.

As feral pigeons increasingly occupied the sprawling urban areas of Europe and America, most westerners began to consider them more of a nuisance than a delicacy. Other birds, most notably chicken, geese, and later turkey, gradually supplanted them. For all intents and purposes, pigeon disappeared from the Ashkenazic culinary repertoire, and chicken became the principal fowl. Pigeon remained one of the primary birds of Sephardim and Mizrachim, who enjoyed it stuffed and roasted or featured it in favorite dishes, including the original Moroccan *pastilla/basteya* (pigeon pie), based on an Iberian pigeon pie. Turkish and Moroccan Jews traditionally featured pigeon as the final part of the wedding feast, served only to the couple. Yemenites retained a particular fondness for roasted pigeon, although it was served infrequently. The English substituted the word squab so that more people would eat one of these birds. Today, most American and European domesticated pigeons are bred for show and racing, not food.

(See also Bird)

PILAU/PILAF
Pilau is a dish of rice and meat cooked together.
Origin: Southern India
Other names: Afghanistan: *palau*; Azerbaijan: *p'lav, plov*; Britain: pilau; Iran: *polo, polow*; India: *pilau, pulaw, pulav*; Iraq: *plaaw, timman*; Kurdistan: *pilaw, polaw*; Turkey: *pilav*; United States: pilaf, pilau; Uzbekistan: *palov, plov*.

The vast majority of Asian, African, and European countries have a dish of rice and meat cooked together. This is not a natural pairing, as rice and meat have very different cooking times and techniques. Considering the similarity in the names of this widespread phenomenon, a single source appears to be the inspiration for all these dishes. Many people believe the dish originated in Persia or possibly Mongolia. Etymological, literary, and cultural evidence, however, point to a southern Indian origin.

Rice has served as the mainstay of the diet of southern India since around 2000 BCE. In Tamil, a language from southern India, the word *pulai* means "meat/raw flesh," which gave rise to the term *pulavu*, meaning "smell of meat" as well as "meat with rice." Sangam writings, the earliest Tamil literature, dating between 300 BCE and 200 CE contain several mentions of *pulavu*, centuries before any variation of the term appeared elsewhere.

When *pulavu* spread north in India, the name became shortened in Hindi to *pulav*, a one-pot meal probably prepared by simmering cubes of meat in water with spices until nearly tender, then adding the rice to finish cooking. Later, in India in the fifth century BCE, two religions emphasizing vegetarianism were founded. Buddhism and Jainism, and gradually over the centuries the practice of vegetarianism spread throughout most of the country. Rice-with-meat dishes were forgotten by a sizable segment of the population.

In 515 BCE, Darius, emperor of the expanding Persian Empire, established a sea route to India and consolidated control over the Indus River valley, now northwestern India and Pakistan. The Persians also discovered and brought back rice and, by the fourth century BCE, had already introduced large-scale rice cultivation to central Asia. At this point, rice entered Mizrachi cooking, remaining a staple for the ensuing two and a half millennia. Rice reached Israel shortly thereafter, during the early Second Temple period, but there is no mention of a pilaf-type dish in early rabbinic literature.

The dish then traveled westward along the Silk Road to central Asia, where a form of it was adopted in every country. In Uzbekistan, it was called *plov*. The various forms of *pulav* in central Asia reflect their usefulness among nomads, shepherds, warriors, and travelers on the Silk Road; they could stop to cook a pot of *pulav* over an open fire, using some easily transportable ingredients, including rice, onions, various root vegetables, and whatever meat was available. According to legend, Alexander the Great was served *plov* after capturing the city of Maracanda (now called Samarkand) and in the eastern Persian province of Bactrin (in modern Afghanistan), which would date the dish in the region to at least 329 BCE.

By the time of the Arab conquest of Persia in 656 CE, rice was well established as a basic of Persian and central Asian cuisine. By the fifteenth century,

Persians had developed a more refined form of the dish, called *polow*, in which meats and/or vegetables were mixed into the rice, or more frequently, layered with the rice and then steamed. *Polow* is an art form in Iran—cooks strive to produce light, fluffy grains while retaining the natural flavor.

The Mughals, a Mongol-Turkic group from central Asia, were Sunni Muslims who favored the Persian culture and loved eating meat. Although their Indian subjects practiced different religions and spoke different languages, the official state religion became Islam and the official language became Urdu, which drew much of its vocabulary from Persian. Subsequently *pulaw*, with its chunks of mutton, was viewed in India as a Muslim dish.

The Ottoman Turks, at some point during their passage through central Asia, probably encountered the rice and meat dish there, which they pronounced *pilav*. In any case, *pilav* subsequently became a basic of the Turkish kitchen, part of everyday cooking as well as a ubiquitous dish at special occasions. A *pilav* can star as the main course of a meal or appear as a side dish for kebabs, *sulu yemek* ("foods with water," denoting various stews), and other meat dishes. At a feast, the *pilav* is traditionally served last, piled on a large platter, from which everyone is expected to partake. Turkish cooks' culinary skills are reflected in the quality of their *pilavs*.

The predominant varieties of rice in Turkey are medium-grain and short-grain. For *pilav*, Turks prefer medium-grain rice varieties, notably Baldo (longer and flatter than most medium-grain varieties, and originally from Italy) and the native Osmancik. They also import a rice from Egypt called *"pilav rice"* or "Egyptian rice." Because of the extra starch in medium-grain rice, the grains normally stick together when cooked, a state undesirable for *pilavs*. Consequently, a slightly different cooking technique evolved—no one knows who developed it—of first briefly sautéing (*kavurma* "roasted") the grain in hot fat before adding the liquid, a process that helps to keep the kernels separate and also gives them more flavor. Frying the rice in oil is a Jewish practice, as it allows the dish to be served at a meat meal; the Turks and Arabs typically use clarified butter (*suzme yag*). After cooking, *pilav* is always left to steam (*demlemek*), covered, for at least ten minutes—some cooks steam it for up to one hour—to achieve the desired

consistency: The rice should be moist, tender, and separate (*tane tane*, "grain by grain"); it should never be dry, sticky, or mushy (*lapa*).

The Turks developed a myriad of variations of the dish, including *sade pilav* (plain rice), *nohutlu pilav* (rice with chickpeas), *patlicanli pilav* (rice with eggplant), *dereotlu ve naneli pilav* (rice with dill and mint), and the venerable *etli pilav* (rice with meat). Vegetables, dried fruit, and nuts, along with herbs and seasonings, provide both textural and flavor contrast. A *pilav* made with chicken broth will have more flavor than one made with water. Saffron and turmeric impart a yellow color; the version with these spices is popular for the Sabbath. *Ic pilav* (rice with pine nuts or almonds, dried currants, and cinnamon or allspice) is the most common type in America. Turks use it, sometimes with ground meat mixed in, to stuff dolma (various vegetables, such as eggplants, peppers, and grape leaves) and poultry.

The Turks passed *pilav* on to their former territories in the Balkans and North Africa. In Italy, it gave rise to risotto. It probably was the inspiration for the Spanish paella.

When Sephardim, whose favorite grain already was rice, arrived in western Asia following the expulsion from Spain in 1492, they readily adopted the Turkish-style of *pilav*. However, following the Arabic manner, many Sephardim simply call it *riz*, or in the Spanish manner, *arroz*, rather than *pilav*. Syrian and Egyptian Jews emulate the Turkish style of first frying the rice in oil before adding the liquid, although Syrians simmer it covered like the Turks, while Egyptians cook the rice uncovered. *Pilav* became daily as well as festive fare among Jews from the Maghreb to the Balkans. Each Middle Eastern and Mediterranean Jewish community adopted the local rice varieties as well as the local methods of preparing it.

The dish continued to spread, moving into Europe. In southeastern Europe, the dish generally retained the name *pilav*. The French, like many Europeans, learned of it from the Ottomans; the French word for it, pilaf, was first recorded in 1654, although the dish may have arrived there several centuries earlier. Another French term for these rice dishes is *riz à la turque*.

The first record of the word in English appeared in 1609 in *Travels of Certaine Englishmen into Africa, Asia, etc.* by William Biddulph (London). He wrote,

"The most common [Turkish] dish is Pilaw . . . made of Rice and small morsels of Mutton boiled therein." Meanwhile, the British East India Company arrived in 1600, gradually wrenching control of the subcontinent from the Mughals. The British initially called the dish palow and, by the time they annexed the country in 1858, it was pilau. In due course, the British increasingly tended to think of their pilau back home as Indian rather than Turkish. By the time of Charles Dickens's *All the Year Round* (London, 1872), the British spelling had been more or less standardized as pilau.

In 1787, Thomas Jefferson smuggled rice seed out of Italy to propagate rice paddies in North America. This was thought to be a Patna variety. South Carolina proceeded to lead the country in rice production for the ensuing century. It was there that the rice and meat dish called pilau first arrived, possibly brought by African slaves (who learned of it from the Arabs) or perhaps the original Huguenots who settled the South Carolina Coast, some of whom were Conversos brought the Sephardic pilau. Marjorie Kinnan Rawlings, author of *The Yearling*, included her observations about the dish in *Cross Creek Cookery* (1942), her pioneering book with a gastronomical/historical/cultural approach to cooking. She wrote, "We pronounce the word 'pur-loo.' It is any dish of meat and rice cooked together. No Florida church supper, no large rural gathering, is without it. It is blessed among dishes for such a purpose, or for a large family, for meat goes farther in a pilau than prepared in any other way." Europeans brought the French Turkish-inspired dish called pilaf to the United States as well, although in America it was typically made without meat.

Middle Eastern Jews who immigrated to Calcutta following the British takeover brought with them their rice dishes and adopted the local name, pilau. The Jewish-style pilau, possibly influenced by the early Syrian immigrants, is prepared following the Turkish method of first frying the rice in fat before simmering it in a liquid, rather than the Moghul stewing method or the Persian steaming technique. In Jewish households in Calcutta, *pilau*, garnished with raisins and nuts, is ubiquitous Friday night fare as well as common on various special occasions. A variation made with fried fish is popular for Sabbath and weekday dining.

(See also Chelow, Palau, Plov, and Rice)

❧ CALCUTTA RICE PILAF (*PILAU*)

6 TO 8 SERVINGS [PAREVE OR DAIRY]

¼ cup vegetable oil or ghee (clarified butter)
3 to 4 green cardamom pods, crushed
1 (3-inch) stick cinnamon
3 to 4 whole cloves
1½ teaspoons cumin seeds
1 large onion or 10 scallions (white part only), chopped
1 tablespoon grated fresh ginger
1 to 3 small green chilies, seeded and minced
1 to 2 cloves garlic, minced
1 teaspoon ground turmeric
2 cups basmati, Patna, or other long-grain rice (not converted)
1 cup (4 ounces) green peas, green beans, cauliflower florets, or chopped carrots, or any combination (optional)
3½ cups vegetable broth or water
About 1½ teaspoons table salt or 2½ teaspoons kosher salt
About ¼ teaspoon ground black pepper
¼ cup chopped fresh flat-leaf parsley
½ cup toasted almonds for garnish (optional)
½ cup raisins for garnish (optional)

1. In a large saucepan, heat the oil over medium heat. Add the cardamom, cinnamon, cloves, and cumin seeds and sauté until the cinnamon opens and the cloves begin to pop, about 1 minute. Add the onion, ginger, chilies, garlic, and turmeric and sauté until softened, 5 to 10 minutes. Add the rice and stir until opaque, about 3 minutes. For a vegetable pilau, stir in the optional vegetables.

2. Add the broth, salt, and pepper. Bring to a boil, cover, reduce the heat to low, and simmer until the rice is tender, about 18 minutes. Do not uncover during cooking. Remove from the heat and let stand, covered, for about 10 minutes. Fluff with a fork. Stir in the parsley. If using, garnish with the almonds and/or raisins. Serve warm.

PINE NUT

Of the more than one hundred species of pine trees in the world, only about a dozen produce edible seeds in their cones—many others have a turpentine taste, while most are too small to be useful. The three most prevalent seeds are the stone pine/umbrella pine from the Mediterranean, the Chinese pine, and a native American variety, rarely available outside of the American Southwest, called Indian nut or piñon. The cones are harvested by hand from November to February, dried in the sun, and cracked and sometimes heated to release the nuts; the external hard cover of the seeds is then removed. The labor-intensive nature of this process accounts for the high price of commercial pine nuts.

The small, oily kernels have a soft texture, a delicate flavor, and a high protein value. However, pine nuts, even from the same source, fluctuate greatly in quality—ranging from rich, sweet, and buttery to insipid and plastic-like. The Mediterranean pine nut, called pignoli in Italian, *tznovar* in Hebrew, *snobar* in Arabic, and *camfistigi* in Turkish, has a slightly sweet, piney taste, an oblong shape, a uniform off-white color, and a thinner shell than the squat, beige, and pungent piñon. Chinese pine nuts, the most inexpensive and widespread in the United States, are slightly triangular and have an uneven color. Pignoli, which are more expensive than the other types, are preferred, especially for baking, as they have a more delicate flavor.

The stone pine, a native of the Mediterranean, was introduced to the Levant before the start of recorded history; it has been used as food and traded for thousands of years. Some scholars believe it was the "evergreen fir tree" of Hosea. The Greeks, Romans, and Arabs considered it an aphrodisiac. The Moors introduced organized pine nut cultivation to Spain, still the world's leading producer, and these seeds became an important component of Sephardic cookery. Pine nuts are also an important ingredient in Mediterranean, Middle Eastern, and Far Eastern cuisine; they are added to numerous dishes, including pilafs, meatballs, salads, stuffed vegetables, grape leaves, chicken dishes, omelets, sauces, and pastry fillings. The addition of pine nuts and raisins is a signature of Roman Jewish Sabbath and holiday fare, such as *sogliola di rolatine* (fillet of sole with raisins and pine nuts) and *pizzarelle* con *miele* (matza fritters drizzled with honey, pine nuts, and raisins.)

PINZETTE

Pinzette is a pan-fried meat or chicken patty.
Origin: Italy
Other names: *pizzette ebraiche*.

Among the unique foods of the Italian Jews is a pan-fried meat patty called *pinzette*. The name means "pincers" in Italian, perhaps reflecting the way the patties are plucked from the frying pan using tongs without piercing them, which would release the juices. *Pinzette* are made from various meats, but lighter ones like veal and chicken are the most prominent. Unlike patties from Austria and Germany, these Italian patties do not include bread or eggs. They are, however, dredged in flour before frying. The patties can be served plain, but are usually enhanced with a light flavoring, such as nutmeg and lemon juice. As *pinzette* are light, filling, and nutritious, they are traditionally served on the meal before the fast of Yom Kippur.

ITALIAN VEAL PATTIES (*PINZETTE*)
6 PATTIES   [MEAT]

1½ pounds veal chuck, finely ground
About ½ teaspoon salt
Ground black pepper to taste
Unbleached all-purpose flour for dredging
Olive oil for frying
¼ cup fresh lemon juice or ½ cup dry Marsala (optional)

1. Combine the veal, salt, and pepper. With moistened hands, shape the meat into 6 patties about ½ inch thick. Dredge the patties in the flour.

2. In a large skillet, heat a thin layer of oil over medium heat. Add the patties and fry, turning once, until the patties are golden brown and the center registers 148°F on an instant-read thermometer, about 5 minutes per side.

3. If using, drizzle with the lemon juice and cook until the liquid evaporates, about 1 minute. Serve warm.

PIROG

Pirog is a filled, boiled pasta dumping.
Origin: Poland
Other names: Poland: *pierog*; Russia: *vareniki*; Slovakia: *pirohi*, *pirohy*; Ukraine: *perohy*, *pyroh*.

There exists some confusion over a variety of Russian, Polish, and Ukrainian foods, all of whose names come from the Slavic word *pir* (ritual feast) and the related *pyro* (ritual wheat bread), both from the Greek *pyros* (wheat). *Pirog* (pirogen/*pirogn* plural) is the Yiddish variation of the filled half-moon-shaped boiled pasta. Jewish fruit-filled versions are sometimes called *varenikes*.

Pirogen differ from the similar kreplach, which are triangular and typically filled with meat; the half-moon pirogen usually feature a potato or other vegetable filling. Kreplach were generally reserved for festivals or sporadically offered on the Sabbath, almost always floating in a bowl of soup, while pirogen were everyday fare, occasionally served in soup, but more often adorned with sour cream, fried onions, or even mixed with kasha. In general, pirogen were considered peasant food, while kreplach held a more elevated status.

The original Polish *pierogi* were large turnovers filled with meat or fish; these dishes were common in medieval Slavic countries, where they were either deep-fried or baked in the oven after the bread was finished. The advent of boiled doughs in eastern Europe around the late thirteenth or fourteenth century led to the modern boiled pasta form of the dish, while a smaller baked version became popular with the spread of home ovens in the nineteenth century. The idea of filled pasta may have been brought to Poland from the east by Tatars (Mongols), who made *man tou*, filled pasta with crimped edges, and invaded Ukraine and Poland in the sixteenth century, or it may have arrived later from Persia by the way of Russia or south from Italy. *Pierogi* and pirogen reflect similarities to both the Italian ravioli and the northern Chinese *jiaozi*; the latter is made from dough rounds and typically served with a dipping sauce.

In the early twentieth century, pirogen became a favorite dish at Catskills resorts and various Jewish cafeterias and luncheonettes in New York City, from Ratner's on the Lower East Side to Famous Dairy Restaurant on the Upper West Side and, in between in the garment district, Dubrow's Cafeteria, all of which closed toward the end of the twentieth century in the face of rising real estate prices and changing tastes in food. Pirogen experienced a sharp decline in popularity, supplanted by wontons and ravioli. Cynthia Ozick, in her 1989 short story *Rosa*, conveyed a sense of nostalgia and melancholy when she mentioned this dish. She wrote, "But the women only recited meals they used to cook in their old lives—kugel, pirogen, latkes, blintzes, herring salad."

(See also Kreplach, Lokshen, Pasta, and Varenik)

PIROSHKE
Piroshke is a small baked or fried half-moon turnover.
Origins: Russia
Other names: Russian: *pirozhok*; Ukraine: *pirishke*, *pyrizhky*.

Besides the boiled pirogen, another food derived from the Slavic *pir* (ritual feast) is a baked or fried turnover, called in Yiddish *piroshke*. Jewish cooks prefer sour cream pastry or, for nondairy meals, oil pastry for their *piroshkes*. Most Russians make their *pirozhki* (Russian plural) with the original yeast dough. *Piroshkes* make delicious *zakouski* (appetizers) as well as a tasty accompaniment to borscht and other soups; the duo commonly constitutes a Russian lunch. Many cooks employ two or more fillings for each batch, typically including the classic potato filling. Cabbage and carrot are other popular fillings. Sweet fillings, such as apple and prune, and cookie variations are more common in Ukrainian *pirishkes*.

(See also Pirog)

🖋 RUSSIAN TURNOVERS (*PIROSHKE*)
ABOUT FORTY-EIGHT 3-INCH TURNOVERS   [PAREVE OR DAIRY]
Potato filling:
  3 tablespoons vegetable oil
  1 large onion, chopped
  2½ cups mashed potatoes
  1 large egg, lightly beaten
  Salt and ground black pepper to taste

  1½ pounds Ashkenazic Flaky Pastry, Oil Pastry, Egg Pastry, Potato Pastry, or Sour Cream Pastry (see Teig, page 582)
  1 large egg white, lightly beaten, for brushing
  Egg wash (1 large egg yolk beaten with 1 teaspoon water)

1. To make the filling: In a large skillet, heat the oil over medium heat. Add the onion and sauté until golden brown, about 20 minutes. Stir into the potatoes. Add the egg, salt, and pepper.

2. Preheat the oven to 375°F. Line 2 baking sheets with parchment paper or lightly grease the sheets.

3. On a lightly floured surface, roll out the pastry dough ⅛ inch thick. Using a floured biscuit cutter or drinking glass, cut into 3-inch rounds.

4. Place a heaping teaspoon of the filling in the center of each round. Brush the edges with the egg white and fold over to form a half-circle. Pinch the edges or press with the tines of a fork to seal. Reroll any excess dough.

5. Place on the prepared baking sheet and brush the tops with the egg wash. Bake until golden brown, about 20 minutes. Serve warm or at room temperature.

PISTACHIO

These pale green nuts covered with a papery skin grow on a small deciduous tree native to Persia, the area that still produces the best pistachios. The pistachio, which has been found in some of the earliest dated archaeological sites in Iraq, is one of the first cultivated nuts. It is also one of the few nuts mentioned in the Bible by name (*botnim*); it was among the choice items of Canaan sent by Jacob to the prime minister of Egypt. Today, pistachios remain a favorite in the Middle East.

After the nuts are harvested, they are dried, a process that splits the shells. The traditional method of processing also stains the shell and, therefore, some merchants dye the nuts red.

Cultivated pistachios have a subtle flavor. Most Americans associate the flavor of pistachios with that of salt, since most of these nuts are sold heavily salted, or with that of almonds, since almond extract is used to flavor pistachio ice cream. In the Middle East, pistachios are utilized like almonds in pilafs, sauces, and desserts, such as baklava, *ma'amoul* (filled cookies), and various puddings. In most of the rest of the world, the high price generally limits its use to a decorative effect or a snack.

PITA

Pita is a round leavened flatbread, sometimes with a pocket.

Origin: Middle East

Other names: pitta, pocket bread, Syrian bread;
    Arabic: *khobiz, khubz adi*; Egypt: *aish, baladi*;
    Farsi: *naan*; Turkish: *pida*; Yemen: *salufe*.

Round flatbreads, such as the biblical *kikkar*, are among the most ancient and basic of foods and have been baked throughout the Middle East since before the dawn of history. Middle Easterners did not use silverware for dining, so pieces of these thin, firm breads proved ideal for grasping food. Or the loaves were torn into bite-sized pieces, the chunks were spread over a platter, a stew was poured over the top, and diners popped chunks into their mouth. Pieces were also dipped into soups. Warm flatbread with honey and *samneh* (clarified butter) was a special treat.

Today in America, the name most associated with flatbread is pita, a word commonly attributed to the Greek language. Yet pita was not an ancient Greek term for bread, and there is no related ancient Greek

(Top) A baker in the Old City of Jerusalem uses a domed sajj cital to make old-fashioned thin flatbreads called khubz sajj cital *but better known in the west as* lavash. *Israeli pita bread (below) called* kmaj *or* khobiz *in Arabic is thicker and contains a pocket.*

terminology from which it could reasonably derive. The Turkish equivalent *pida*, borrowed from the Greek, appeared rather late. On the other hand, the Hebrew word *paht*, meaning "piece of bread," and its Aramaic equivalent pita, have been used for many millennia. Already in the book of Genesis, Abraham employed the term *paht lechem* (piece of bread) and in the book of Ruth, Boaz tells her to "dip *pitaik* [your piece of bread] in vinegar."

When Sephardim arrived in Salonika in large numbers after 1492, the word pita had not yet appeared in the Greek language. Perhaps to differentiate the small, round flatbreads they found in the eastern Mediterranean from the thicker types of loaves they were accustomed to making in Spain, Sephardim began calling them pita. Greek Sephardim also use the word pita to denote various savory pies, especially those made from crusts of matza or phyllo, the equivalent of the Ladino *pastel* and *mina*. In Salonika, where from 1519 until the early twentieth century Jews constituted the overwhelming majority of the population, it was only natural that the word spread to non-Jews and then throughout Greece. (The sixteenth-century Neapolitan word pizza probably also came from this source.)

At some more recent point, bakers in the Levant or Egypt developed a variation of flatbread, creating a round loaf with a natural pocket. The distinctive compartment is produced by baking a lean, moist, yeast-leavened dough in an extremely hot oven; the heat turns the water inside into steam, which then puffs up and separates the interior of the bread into two layers. The Middle Eastern method is to form the loaves on a *machbazi*, a round wicker basket covered with a cotton cloth, then slap the dough round onto the side or floor of the hot oven. The bread is not turned during baking, so only the bottom of the loaf touches the oven's surface, while the top is cooked by indirect heat.

In Greece, the term pita is not limited to pocket bread, but more commonly connotes standard pocketless flatbreads. The Greek pita is primarily used to enwrap souvlaki (gyros are an American innovation). Before the 1970s, Greek and Turkish restaurants in America only served the pocketless type of pita. Yet since then, most Americans have come to associate pita with pocket bread. Jews were responsible for this change of meaning.

In the Levant, round flatbread is known as *khubz adi* (ordinary bread), simply *khubz*, or *taboon*, which is the Arabic name of the traditional small domed brick and/or clay oven in which it is baked. At the beginning of the twentieth century, as Jews began arriving in large numbers in Israel, they adopted some of the local foods. Sometimes they kept the names, like hummus and falafel. However, to differentiate pocket bread from standard round flatbreads, Jews began using the term pita.

In modern Israel, the term pita (*pitot* plural) only applies to pocket bread. In the early days of the state, the simple, relatively inexpensive bread provided a filling food in a time of *tzena* (austerity). It is still commonly found at most meals, whether at home or in restaurants. Many households keep a bag in the freezer for emergencies. As it lent itself to inexpensive fillings, hot or cold, pita emerged as the basis of Israeli fast food, such as falafel, *shawarma*, Tunisian sandwiches, kebabs, schnitzel, hamburgers, omelets, salads, and innumerable other foods. It is included in every *mezze* (appetizer assortment), typically warm, as pieces of bread are ideal for scooping up various dips and salads, such as hummus and *baba ghanouj*. Before the 1970s, Israeli pizza consisted of pita rounds topped with tomato sauce and cheese. *Manaeesh* is a Lebanese flatbread topped with za'atar and olive oil.

Pita became a staple of the Israeli diet, but is rarely homemade. In practically every Israeli supermarket, pita bread is the most purchased item—it is typically procured on a daily basis. In 2010, Israel's largest bakery, the Angel Bakery in Jerusalem, produced ten thousand machine-made pitas daily for the city, while many smaller specialized pita bakeries turned out numerous more, some still handmade.

Israelis and visitors to Israel helped popularize the term pita in America, where it generally denotes pocket bread and not generic flatbread. The term first appeared in an American source in the December 16, 1949 issue of the Pittsburgh newspaper, *The Jewish Criterion*. In the article "A Guide for Tourists," the paper recounts, "the bland succulence of "tehina" and "chumus," eaten with hunks of the platter-shaped bread, peeta." There was an attempt to introduce it more widely to America at the 1964 World's Fair in New York City, where the loaves were featured in the General Foods pavilion as "Israeli bread." It would be another decade, however, before pita moved out of the ethnic enclaves to become mainstream fare. It is now sold in every grocery store and the name has been adopted as common American parlance.

(See also Bread and Khobz)

◄ MIDDLE EASTERN POCKET BREAD (*PITA/KHUBZ ADI*)

EIGHT 6-INCH OR TWELVE 5-INCH BREADS   [PAREVE]

1 package (2¼ teaspoons) active dry yeast or
   1 (0.6-ounce) cake fresh yeast
1½ cups warm water (105°F to 115°F for dry yeast;
   80°F to 85°F for fresh yeast)
1 teaspoon sugar or honey
2 teaspoons table salt or 4 teaspoons kosher
   salt
About 4 cups (20 ounces) bread or unbleached all-
   purpose flour, or 3 cups flour and 1 cup whole-
   wheat flour

1. Dissolve the yeast in ¼ cup water. Stir in the sugar and let stand until foamy, 5 to 10 minutes. In a large bowl, combine the yeast mixture, remaining water, salt, and 2 cups flour. Gradually add enough of the remaining flour to make a very soft dough.

2. On a lightly floured surface, knead the dough until smooth and elastic, 10 to 15 minutes. Cover with a large bowl or pot and let rise in a warm, draft-free place until doubled in bulk, about 2 hours.

3. Line 3 large baking sheets with parchment paper or sprinkle the ungreased sheets with cornmeal. Punch down the dough and knead briefly. Divide the dough into 8 equal pieces (4 ounces each) or 12 equal pieces (2.5 ounces each). Shape each piece into a ball, cover, and let stand for about 15 minutes.

4. Flatten each ball. Roll the 4-ounce pieces into ¼-inch-thick rounds, 6 inches in diameter; or the 2.5-ounce pieces into ¼-inch-thick rounds, 5 inches in diameter. Place on the prepared baking sheets, making sure they do not touch, cover with a kitchen towel, and let stand until puffy, about 30 minutes.

5. Position a rack in the center of the oven. Preheat the oven to 475°F.

6. Baking one sheet at a time, place a baking sheet on the middle rack and bake—do not open the oven during the first 5 minutes—until the pitas are puffed and the bottoms begin to brown, about 6 minutes. To keep the breads soft and warm, stack on top of each other and wrap in a kitchen towel.

PITE
Pite is a tart-like cake, most often filled with apples.
Origin: Hungary

Pite, probably from the Greek Sephardic pie called pita, is commonly referred to as a cake, but it is actually more of a tart, with bottom and top pastry layers. Those made without the top crust are sometimes called *lepény*. The most popular crust contains sour cream and egg yolks, making it very tender. Cooks also use a yeast dough for the crust, which is appropriate for meat meals.

Hungarians love filling this dough with various types of fruit, but apple (*almás*) is far and away the most popular. Soft cheese (*túró*), walnuts (*diós*), and poppy seeds (*mákos*) are also common. Apple is a favorite Sabbath and Sukkot treat, while cheese is traditional for Shavuot. *Pites* are customarily cut into squares to serve and are frequently accompanied with another foodstuff the Turks introduced, coffee (*kávé*).

◄ HUNGARIAN APPLE TART (*ALMÁS PITE*)

ABOUT 24 SERVINGS   [DAIRY]
Pastry:
   3 cups (15 ounces) all-purpose flour, sifted
   ½ cup (3.5 ounces) sugar
   ½ teaspoon salt
   1 cup unsalted butter or shortening, chilled
   4 large egg yolks
   3 tablespoons sour cream
   2 tablespoons lemon or orange juice
Filling (*Toltelek*):
   3¼ pounds (10 medium) cooking apples, peeled,
      cored, and diced
   1 tablespoon fresh lemon juice
   ¾ cup (3 ounces) chopped walnuts, hazelnuts, or
      almonds
   ½ cup sugar
   3 tablespoons all-purpose flour
   1 teaspoon grated lemon zest
   1 teaspoon ground cinnamon

   ¼ cup fresh bread crumbs
   Egg wash (1 large egg beaten with 1 tablespoon
      water)

1. To make the pastry: In a medium bowl, combine the flour, sugar, and salt. Cut in the butter to make a mixture that resembles coarse crumbs. In a small bowl, combine the egg yolks, sour cream, and lemon juice. Stir into the flour mixture to make a soft dough. Divide the dough, with one part slightly larger than the other. Cover and refrigerate for at least 1 hour and up to 2 days.

2. Preheat the oven to 350°F. Grease a 15½-by-10½-inch jelly roll pan.

3. On a lightly floured surface, roll out the larger dough piece to fit the prepared pan and arrange in the bottom and up the sides of the pan.

4. To make the filling: In a large bowl, toss the apples with the lemon juice. Stir in the nuts, sugar, flour, zest, and cinnamon.

5. Sprinkle the bread crumbs over the bottom pastry and spread with the apple mixture.

6. Roll out the remaining dough. Cut into strips and arrange in a lattice pattern over the filling. Or simply cut into a second dough rectangle, place over the top, and cut several slits to vent the steam. Brush the pastry with the egg wash.

7. Bake for 30 minutes. Reduce the heat to 300°F and bake until the crust is golden and the liquid in the filling bubbles, about 30 additional minutes. Place the pan on a wire rack and let cool for at least 15 minutes. Serve warm or at room temperature. Store at room temperature for up to 1 day.

PIZZARELLE
Pizzarelle is a fritter, primarily made during Passover.
Origin: Italy

Roman Jews enjoy a number of fritters, all fried in olive oil, including *pizzarelle*. They are most commonly made from rice (*pizzarelle di riso*), chestnut flour (*pizzarelle di farina castagna*), and matza (*pizzarelle di azzima*), all items used by Italians on Passover. There is also a variation incorporating cheese (*pizzarelle di ricotta*), which many Italians refrain from eating during Passover. Matza fritters are a traditional dessert at *la festa di Pèsach* (the Passover Seder), typically following chicken soup with rice and peas, artichokes, and a main course of roasted lamb or goat. Many cooks mix any leftover charoset into the matza batter for extra flavor. Some modern versions include a little chopped chocolate. Nuts can be added to the batter or sprinkled over the warm fritters. Versions without matza are ideal for Hanukkah. When served with a sugar syrup, it is called *pizzarelle con giulebbe* and when drizzled with honey, *pizzarelle con miele*. *Pizzarelle* can also be accompanied with whipped cream or simply sprinkled with cinnamon-sugar or confectioners' sugar.

ROMAN MATZA FRITTERS (*PIZZARELLE DI AZZIMA*)
ABOUT 20 FRITTERS   [PAREVE]

4 (6-inch square) matzas, crumbled (3 cups)
2 cups boiling water
3 large eggs, separated
About ¼ cup sugar
About ½ cup raisins or leftover charoset
About ½ cup slivered almonds or pine nuts
   (Romans tend to use pine nuts)
2 teaspoons grated lemon or orange zest, or
   1 teaspoon grated lemon zest and 1 teaspoon
   ground cinnamon

Matza fritters, called pizzarelli, have long been a Passover specialty in Italy. Chestnut flour and rice are also used in place of the matza.

About ¼ teaspoon table salt or ½ teaspoon kosher salt

Olive or vegetable oil for deep-frying

1. Soak the matza pieces in the water until softened but not mushy, 1 to 2 minutes. Drain and squeeze out the excess moisture. Transfer to a large bowl and add the egg yolks, sugar, raisins, nuts, zest, and salt.

2. In a medium bowl, beat the egg whites until stiff but not dry. Fold one-quarter of the whites into the matza mixture, then fold in the remaining whites.

3. In a large, heavy pot, heat at least 2 inches oil over medium heat to 365°F.

4. In batches, without crowding the pan, drop heaping tablespoonfuls of the batter and deep-fry, turning, until golden brown on all sides, 3 to 5 minutes. Drain on paper towels. Serve warm or at room temperature.

VARIATIONS

Italian Rice Fritters (Pizzarelle di Riso): Substitute 3 cups cooked and cooled rice, preferably arborio, for the matzas and boiling water.

PKHALI

Pkhali is a finely chopped cooked vegetable mixed with a spicy walnut sauce.

Origin: Georgia

Other names: *mkhali.*

Pkhali, which can now be found throughout the former Soviet Union, is a cross between a salad and a dip made from a single type of vegetable. There is a wide variety of produce that can be used to make this dish, but all *pkhali* have the common denominator of a pureed walnut sauce (*bazha*), which imparts a creamy consistency without dairy and without a walnut flavor. Vinegar adds a tart element; spices and garlic contribute a piquant touch. Spinach (*isanakhi*) and beet (*charkhalis*) are the favorite types of *pkhali*, but eggplant (*badrijani*), cabbage (*kombosta*), red bean (*lobio*), and green bean (*mtsvani lobio*) are common and almost any vegetable works. Georgians insist that *pkhali* should be mixed by hand, literally, and never with a machine or even a spoon. The secret to *pkhali* is allowing it to stand a sufficient amount of time, at least six hours or overnight, for the flavors to meld.

At a special home dinner, such as the Sabbath or a festival, Georgians typically serve one or more *pkhali*. At a *supra* (feast), in addition to *shashlik* (shish kebab) and other hot fare, there are always at least three or four kinds of *pkhali*, a splendor of colors and flavors. They are slightly mounded in a large platter and scored on top in a crisscross fashion, or piled into small bowls, and frequently garnished with pomegranate seeds or red onion slices. *Pkhali* is eaten on its own with a fork, or served with *mchadi* (Georgian corn cakes) or *deda's puri* (flatbread), frequently alongside cheese and fresh herbs.

❦ GEORGIAN VEGETABLE PÂTÉ (*PKHALI*)

4 TO 6 SERVINGS   [PAREVE]

About 3 cups chopped cooked vegetable, such as red beans, green beans, beets, beet greens, cabbage, eggplant, leeks, or spinach

1 cup *bazha* (Georgian Walnut Sauce, page 42)

In a large bowl, combine the vegetable and bazha. Cover and refrigerate for at least 6 hours. To serve, spread the pkhali over a plate.

PLETZL

Pletzl is an onion-topped flatbread.

Origin: Eastern Europe

Other names: *kuchelach, pletsl, pletzel, zemel pampalik.*

"Anshel kept his boots well polished and did not drop his eyes in the presence of the women. Stopping in at Beila the Baker's to buy a pletzl, he joked with them in such a worldly fashion that they marveled." (From "Yentl the Yeshiva Boy," a short story by Isaac Bashevis Singer.)

Pletzl denotes an eastern European candy. *Matza pletzl* is a synonym for *matza brei*, soaked matza mixed with eggs and fried like a pancake. But *pletzl* is also the name of a foccacia-like bread once widespread among Polish, Lithuanian, and Ukrainian Jews; it is linguistically related to the German *plätzchen* (crackers). In English, it is sometimes called a board, as the Yiddish *bretl* (little board) sounds similar to *pletzl* and the flat loaves were formed on a *broit bretl* or *lokshen bretl*. Pletzl (Yiddish meaning "little place/little space") is also the name of the historic Jewish quarter in Paris, located on the right bank.

Until relatively recently, black bread was the predominant loaf of the central and eastern European diet. From the sixteenth until the eighteenth century, rye was the most commonly grown crop in Russia. However, in the nineteenth century, as milling and agricultural techniques improved, flatbreads and other lighter wheat loaves gained popularity. There are at least eighteen or so varieties of *pletzl*. The most famous one is topped with the principal Ashkenazic seasoning, onions (*tzibele*); it is known as *tzibele pletzl*, *tzibele zemmel*, *tzibele pampalik*, and simply *pletzl*.

There is no standard dough for *pletzl*, although some versions are made from an eggless dough with a little oil. However, many eastern European housewives would take part of their Friday egg challah dough to make a few small onion-topped loaves for a special Friday treat for the children. Many versions add poppy seeds to the onion topping. There is also a slightly sweet variety of *pletzl*; it is sometimes sprinkled with poppy seeds, but the onions are omitted. A *pletzl* can be shaped into a long plank, then cut into slices for serving; or it can be formed into smaller individual loaves. In either case, these breads are thinner in the center and thicker on the edges, so the teeth experience the crispness of the crust before reaching the smaller amount of the softer chewy interior. If more onions are placed on top, the crust underneath will be softer; if fewer onions are scattered on top, the crust will be crunchier. Some *pletzls* are so crisp that they resemble their German namesake, the cracker.

Pletzls are not designed to be split for sandwiches; instead, at dairy meals they are schmeared on top, not inside, with plenty of butter, Litvak cheese (a creamy pot cheese), or cream cheese, and at meat meals with schmaltz, chopped liver, or egg salad, or they are served with soups or pot roasts to sop up the gravy. The bialy, with which the *pletzl* is frequently confused, is a smaller, softer relative from the northeastern Polish city of Bialystok.

In Poland and Ukraine, onion *pletzls* were sold not only at bakeries but also from pushcarts on the street. They were a weekday bread, a workman or student's meal. The *pletzl* never made much of an impact in Israel, a land populated with many flavored flatbreads. On the other hand, in America, the onion *pletzl*, also called onion board and onion flat, was once commonplace at Jewish bakeries and dairy cafeterias. However, as most of those old-fashioned establishments disappeared toward the end of the twentieth century, so largely did the *pletzl*, although it is still available at some Jewish bakeries.

ASHKENAZIC ONION FLATBREAD (*TZIBELE PLETZL*)

10 MEDIUM OR 2 LARGE BREADS   [PAREVE]

Dough:
1 package (2¼ teaspoons) active dry yeast or 1 (0.6-ounce) cake fresh yeast
1¼ cups warm water (105°F to 115°F for dry yeast; 80°F to 85°F for fresh yeast), or 1 cup warm water and 1 large egg
2 tablespoons sugar
2 tablespoons vegetable oil
2 teaspoons table salt or 4 teaspoons kosher salt
About 4 cups (20 ounces) bread or unbleached all-purpose flour

Topping:
3 tablespoons vegetable oil
2 cups (2 medium) chopped onions

Egg wash (1 large egg beaten with 1 tablespoon water) or water
2 tablespoons poppy seeds for sprinkling
2 tablespoons kosher salt for sprinkling

1. To make the dough: Dissolve the yeast in ¼ cup water. Stir in 1 teaspoon sugar and let stand until foamy, 5 to 10 minutes. In a large bowl, combine the yeast mixture, remaining water, remaining sugar, oil, salt, and 2 cups flour. Gradually add enough of the remaining flour to make a mixture that holds together.

2. Knead the dough until smooth and elastic, 10 to 15 minutes. Place in an oiled bowl and turn to coat. Cover loosely with plastic wrap or a kitchen towel and let rise in a warm, draft-free place until doubled in bulk, about 1½ hours.

3. To make the topping: In a large skillet, heat the oil over medium heat. Add the onions and sauté until soft and translucent, 5 to 10 minutes. Let cool.

4. Punch down the dough, knead briefly, divide into about 10 equal pieces or in half, cover, and let stand for 15 minutes.

5. Line 2 or 3 large baking sheets with parchment paper or sprinkle with cornmeal. Roll each dough tenth into a ¼- to ½-inch-thick oval or each half into a ¼- to ½-inch thick large oval. The thinner the dough, the crisper the bread. Place on the prepared baking sheets. Press down the center and pierce the center all over with the tines of a fork. Brush the dough with the egg wash. Lightly scatter the onions over the top, leaving a ½-inch border. Sprinkle with the poppy seeds and salt. Let stand, uncovered, until puffy, about 20 minutes.

6. Preheat the oven to 375°F. Bake until golden brown, about 20 minutes for small breads, or 30 minutes for large ones. If the onions are not sufficiently browned, you can place the *pletzl* under a broiler for about 1 minute. Transfer the *pletzl* to a wire rack.

PLETZLACH

Pletzlach are flat honey candies, often with nuts or poppy seeds.

Origin: Eastern Europe

Early medieval Persians and Arabs boiled honey and sugar to create a basic syrup candy, such as the Persian *sohan asali*, a honey-nut brittle. This technique spread to the Turks, who in turn introduced it to the Balkans. Around the early seventeenth century, it reached eastern Europe, where it became the foundation for Ashkenazic candies. Throughout the medieval period, honey was the basis for Ashkenazic baked goods and confections. Even after sugar became accessible and inexpensive in the mid-nineteenth century, with the advent of sugar beet factories, the predominant sweetener in eastern European confections was honey. However, when honey was too expensive or otherwise unavailable, sugar was substituted. Honey candies remained popular among eastern European Jews, especially on Passover, Purim, and Hanukkah, and for weddings. These delicacies were typically served with tea.

Plain candy and candy with a small amount of nuts are technically *pletzlach*, from the Yiddish word meaning "little place/little space," so named because the candy is spread into a thin layer and, when cooled, broken into little pieces. The flavor of this candy varies depending on the floral source of the honey. Lighter-colored honeys, such as clover, acacia, and orange blossom, are milder in flavor than darker-colored ones, such as buckwheat, blueberry, and heather.

This basic candy was commonly enhanced and extended with accessible items, such as nuts, seeds, matza, and even certain vegetables. Candy made from the latter is a relative of *eingemachts* (vegetable preserves), but much firmer. When a large amount of nuts is added, the candy becomes *noent* or *nunt* (from the Latin for "nut"), related to an early form of nougat. Adding poppy seeds, especially for Purim, gave rise to *mohn pletzlach* or *mohnlach*. A recipe for "Mohn Candy" was even included in the best-selling *Molly Goldberg Jew-*

ish Cookbook (New Hope, PA, 1955), an offshoot of the television show, although the author did not mention grinding the poppy seeds, which is necessary to prevent a gritty texture and release the full flavor.

When ground ginger (*ingber* in Yiddish) is added to the *pletzlach*, it becomes an *ingberlach*, sometimes pronounced *imberlach*. *The Jewish Encyclopedia* (New York, 1903) included it among "home-made" candies and explained, "The ingberlach are ginger candies made into either small sticks or rectangles." A basic *ingberlach* was frequently flavored and extended like the *pletzlach*, in particular with carrots. Novelist Zelda Popkin (née Feinberg), in *Open Every Door* (New York, 1956), her autobiography describing her childhood in Wilkes-Barre, Pennsylvania, in the early 1900s, recounted, "Papa went to New York and brought back cones of sugar, wrapped in black paper and hard as a rock. It had to be chipped off and pulverized in our brass mortar and pestle. With it Mama made ingberlach, a concoction of carrots and ginger which burned the tongue and palate."

As commercial candy in general and kosher candy in particular grew more prevalent in the twentieth century, homemade confections like *pletzlach* became a rarity and only a few households able to enjoy this taste of the Ashkenazic past.

ASHKENAZIC HONEY CANDY (*PLETZLACH*)

ABOUT 45 PIECES   [PAREVE]

2 cups (14 ounces) sugar

1⅓ cups (1 pound) honey

1 cup water

2 to 3 teaspoons lemon juice (optional)

1 pound (about 3 cups) ground poppy seeds;
1½ pounds grated raw carrots and 2 teaspoons ground ginger; 1 to 1½ pounds (3 to 4 cups) finely or coarsely chopped almonds, hazelnuts, pecans, or walnuts; or 2 cups (4 ounces) crumbled matza and 1 cup coarsely chopped almonds or walnuts (optional)

1. In a medium, heavy saucepan, stir the sugar, honey, water, and, if using, lemon juice over medium-low heat until the sugar dissolves, about 5 minutes. Stop stirring, increase the heat to high, and bring to a boil. If using the poppy seeds or carrots and ginger, stir them in at this point.

2. Cover and cook for about 30 seconds to dissolve any sugar crystals. Uncover and boil gently, without stirring, over medium-high heat. For chewy candy, cook until the syrup reaches the soft-crack stage or 270°F on a candy thermometer, 10 to 15 minutes. For brittle candy, cook until the syrup reaches the hard-crack stage or 300°F.

3. If using the nuts or matza, stir them in. Pour onto an oiled baking sheet or marble slab, spreading to a ¼- to ½-inch thickness. Let stand for several minutes, then score into 2-by-½-inch bars or 1-inch squares or diamonds. Let cool, then cut along the scores to separate the candies. Wrap pieces in wax paper or plastic wrap and store in a cool, dry place for up to 1 month.

PLOV

Plov is a rice pilaf with meat.

Origin: Uzbekistan and Azerbaijan

Other names: *osh plov oshsabo, osh sabo, oshi sabo, palov, p'lav.*

The Indian *pulav* traveled along the Silk Road to central Asia, where it became *plov.* Special long-cooked versions for the Sabbath are known as *oshi sabo.*

Bukharans are extremely proud of their *plov* and visitors in Uzbekistan are constantly asked, "Have you tried the *plov* yet?" At a special occasion, the *plov,* usually an elaborate version, is offered at the end of the meal. When guests are honored in an Uzbeki home or even for a simple gathering of friends, *plov* is customarily the center of the local hospitality ritual, called *dastarkhan* (literally "tablecloth"), and accompanied by hot green tea, which is sipped from a *piala* (special cup). *Plov* is traditionally eaten using the fingers of the right hand to fully appreciate its sensual nature. To refuse to partake of a *plov,* no matter how full you are from the preceding large meal, is to gravely insult the host.

Bukharans prefer a pinkish medium-grain rice called *devzira* or *barakat,* resulting in a slightly chewy and sticky dish. Unlike Persians and Afghan versions, where the rice and meat are layered, Bukharans commonly steam the rice atop a stew, called the *zirvak.* Uzbeks poke the rice with holes before steaming for more even cooking.

There are numerous variations of *plov,* made by using different types and amounts of meat, vegetables, legumes, and seasonings. Most Uzbeki *plovs* contain carrots, which could be stored along with onions in root cellars. The carrots in Uzbekistan are generally heirloom yellow varieties, not the orange European types, giving the *plov* a yellowish hue. Turnips are sometimes used instead of carrots. The meat, onion, and carrots are first browned in oil, but not the rice as in Turkish *pilav,* before adding spices and water. Bukharans tend to add a lot of fat, yielding a somewhat greasy dish. In central Asia, rendered fat from sheep tails is preferred for sautéing the ingredients, but vegetable oil is now frequently substituted. Lamb is the most widespread meat, but many Jews also have a preference for chicken and quail. Chickpeas and dried fruits, especially raisins and apricots, are also commonly used. Adding quince and apple is a popular Bukharan Jewish variation.

The best *plov* chefs (*oshpaz*), almost always men, are revered. Women prepare the rest of the food, including flatbreads, assorted salads, and pickles. According to many *oshpaz,* a good *plov* can only be cooked over a wood-burning fire; therefore, even some Bukharan restaurants in New York manage a fire out back for special occasions. *Plov* is customarily made in a well-seasoned *kazan,* a round-bottomed oval cast-iron pot that is wider on the top than the bottom and is used only for *plov.* For special events, such as a wedding, the *oshpaz,* assisted by a small army of helpers, will make a batch with more than two hundred pounds of rice to give a taste to hundreds of guests or even a thousand people. The *plov* is traditionally served hot, on a *lyagan,* a large, flat ceramic platter. After the *plov,* dessert might consist of fruit, notably grapes or raisins, with more tea.

On the other side of the Caspian Sea, Azerbaijan shares the name and love of *plov,* the country's most important dish, but with Caucasian twists. Unlike the Uzbeki and Persian styles, the rice and flavorings in Azerbaijan *plov* are usually cooked in separate pots, then combined before serving. Azeris customarily use a tin-lined copper pot. The *kazmag* (bottom crust)—made from mixing eggs with a little rice, sliced potatoes, or lavash—prevents the rice from burning and also serves as a crunchy garnish.

In many parts of Azerbaijan, rice is served on a daily basis, but *plov,* the king of Azeri cuisine, is for special occasions, including weddings, funerals, and various family gatherings. The preferred rice is a long-grain variety, such as basmati. *Plov* is typically prepared at home and is rarely offered in Azeri restaurants. *Plov* is always the grand finale, presented on a large platter, and there are over one hundred kinds. Using lamb produces a *kovurma plov*, chicken a *toyug plov*, and dried fruit a *shirin plov*. Azeri pilafs are distinctive for their subtle tartness, from pomegranate juice, sour plums, dried lemons, sour cherries, and unripe grapes (*abgora*), or their slight sweetness, from fruits such as apples, apricots, quinces, and raisins. For substance, cooks add legumes, potatoes, or chestnuts. At dairy meals, *plov* is accompanied with yogurt and, for a tart flavor, ground sumac. Leftover *plov* is used to make *kuku* (omelets).

(See also Bachsh, Chelow, Palau, Pilau, and Rice)

BUKHARAN LAMB PILAF (*KOVURMA PLOV*)

6 TO 8 SERVINGS AS A MAIN COURSE   [MEAT]

2 cups *devzira* or other medium-grain rice, such as calrose or japonica; or long-grain rice, such as basmati

¼ cup vegetable oil

1 lamb rib bone (optional)

2 to 2½ pounds boneless lamb shoulder or beef chuck, cut into 1½-inch cubes

3 medium yellow onions, halved and sliced

5 to 6 medium carrots, julienned or coarsely grated

1 teaspoon cumin seeds, 2 to 3 teaspoons ground cumin, or 1½ teaspoons ground cinnamon

¼ to ½ teaspoon cayenne or 1 to 2 dried red chilies

¼ teaspoon ground turmeric

1 cup water

About ½ teaspoon table salt or 1 teaspoon kosher salt

About ½ teaspoon ground black pepper or 10 whole black peppercorns

½ to 1 cup raisins, soaked in warm water for 30 minutes and drained, or 1½ cups cooked chickpeas (optional)

1 to 2 teaspoons sugar (optional)

1 head garlic, unpeeled (optional)

2½ cups boiling water

1. Place the rice in a medium bowl, add boiling water to cover, and let soak for 30 minutes while preparing the other ingredients.

2. In a *kazan* or large, heavy pot, heat the oil over medium-high heat. Add the rib bone, fry until darkened, and discard. Add the meat, if necessary in batches to prevent overcrowding, and brown on all sides, about 8 to 10 minutes total per batch. Transfer the meat to a warm platter.

3. Add the onions and sauté until lightly golden,

about 15 minutes. Add the carrots and sauté until softened, about 10 minutes. Stir in the cumin, cayenne, and turmeric. Return the meat and toss to coat. Add 1 cup water and the salt and pepper. Cover, reduce the heat to low, and simmer until the meat is tender, about 30 minutes for lamb, or 2 hours for beef or mutton. If using, add the raisins or sugar.

4. Using a spoon, flatten the meat mixture as much as possible. Drain the rice and sprinkle over the meat mixture. Do not stir in. If using, submerge the garlic in the center of the rice. Flatten the rice without stirring into the meat. Drizzle the boiling water over the rice until it reaches slightly less than 1 inch above the rice. Bring to a boil, cover, reduce the heat to medium, and simmer until most of the liquid has been absorbed, about 15 minutes.

5. Using the handle of a large wooden spoon, poke 7 holes into the rice, reaching to the bottom of the pot. Cover the pot with a cloth or several layers of paper towels, cover with the lid, reduce the heat to very low, and simmer until the rice is tender and the liquid has been absorbed, about 30 minutes. You will hear a "goop goop" sounds as the rice finishes absorbing the water. Remove from the heat and let stand for 10 minutes.

6. Invert the pot onto a large serving platter so the rice is on the bottom and the meat on top. Serve warm.

PLUM

Plums, stone fruits from the *rosaceous* family, come in a wide range of flavors (sweet to tart), sizes, and colors (purple, blue, red, green, and yellow). Only about twenty varieties today are grown commercially in any numbers, all from two species, Japanese or European.

Before the spread of the European plum in the thirteenth century, the predominant plum in western Asia and Europe was the damson, named after the city of Damascus; it is closely related to the European plum and sometimes subsumed under that category. The damson is a small, acidic, flavorful, roundish fruit; it is not widely grown today and is most commonly used, with plenty of sugar, to make jams.

The Babylonian Talmud contains two words for plums: *dormaskin* ("of Damascus," the damson plum) and *pega* (denoting the European plum); plums are included with quince and sorb-apples as fruits permitted to be juiced on the Sabbath as they are not generally used for their juice. The Jerusalem Talmud utilizes the word *achvanayah* (from the Syriac word for damson plum). During the Roman period, damsons did not grow in Israel, as the Talmud specifies it as an imported fruit. The modern Hebrew terms *shazif* (plum) and *shazif meyubash* (dried plum) are recent innovations (and a corruption of the Talmudic word for a jujube).

Japanese plums, which actually originated in China, tend to mature earlier in the year; they are yellowish or reddish in color, rounder, and very juicy and, therefore, not as suitable for drying or most cooking as European plums. Japanese plums, introduced to the United States around 1870, include the Santa Rosa.

The *Prunus domestica*, called the European plum, is a hybrid of the sloe plum and another wild plum and probably originated in the Caucasus Mountains near the Caspian Sea around two thousand years ago. European plums are relatively small, have an elongated shape, and have purplish, dark blue, or greenish skins. They have a yellow flesh, are sweet-tart, and are less juicy than Japanese varieties, making them best for cooking and drying. Whereas the varieties of *Prunus domestica* grown in western and central Europe tend to be sweet, many of the varieties from western and central Asia and eastern Europe yield tart fruit.

Frenchmen from the Fifth Crusade returned to southwest France (c. 1221) with *Prunus domestica* trees from Syria, which, after centuries passed, became a cultivar primarily dried, known in France as *prune d'Ente* and, in English, as French plum and D'Agen plum. This is by far the most common plum grown in California. A related European cultivar is the Italian plum—also called Fellenberg and, in Poland, Hungarian plum. Greengage, another *Prunus domestica*, known in France as the Reine Claude, is an old French variety with green to yellow skin and yellow-green flesh. By the sixteenth century, *Prunus domestica* had become a major crop in France, Germany, and Hungary, which together produce about one-third of the world's plums today.

In the early twentieth century, kibbutzniks planted European plums in Israel, but soon discovered that they require a long period of winter chilling to bear fruit and that the Japanese varieties were better suited to the Israeli climate and market.

Since the plum's season was rather limited, it was primarily consumed and used in cooking in its dried form. In most languages, no distinction was originally made between fresh and dried plums. In Yiddish, both plums and dried plums are known as *flohmen* or *floymen*, from the German *pflaume*, although a prune is technically *gehtrikenthe flohmen* (dried plums). Since fresh plums were rarely available in northern Europe, most references to *flohmen* actually connote dried plums. The French called the fresh fruit prunes and, much later the dried ones, *pruneau*. In English, the term plum originally and through the seventeenth century denoted raisins. Thus plum pudding is a dish containing only raisins and currants—it does not traditionally include dried plums. When the French word prune appeared in England in the fourteenth century, it initially retained the meaning of fresh plum. However, since most dried plums were at the time imported to England from France, the term prune eventually switched to specify a dried plum and plum was utilized for the fresh fruit. Since around 2000, American prune marketers have used the name "dried plums" for prunes.

Persians, Georgians, Bukharans, Indians, eastern Europeans, and people from many other cultures prefer sour dried plums in cooking. Sour dried plums, typically an intense violet-brown color, are made from tart red plums, which have a significant amount of sugar in addition to a large amount of acid, adding a slight tang as well as sweetness to dishes. A most important Georgian sauce (*tkemali*) is made from a tart variety of plum. Bukharans pickle tart plums, which they even add to their Sabbath stew (*oshi sabo*) and to salads like *pakhtakhor*. There are also yellow sour dried plums from Turkey and some other Middle Eastern areas. Old-fashioned Ashkenazic appetizing stores once sold sour dried plums, which were popular in tzimmes, compote, fruit soups, farfel, pot roasts, and other traditional dishes, but as these establishments disappeared, the sour types became harder to find and are now primarily available in Middle Eastern and Indian markets and specialty stores. Sephardim enjoy sour dried plums in salads, fish sauces, and stews. Greeks use them in red lentil soup and *poyo con prounes* (Greek stewed chicken with plums), while Syrians cook them with okra and, in the Maghreb, they are used in tagines. Persians add tart dried plums to many stews, such as *gundi barangi* (meatballs in tomato sauce) and *khoresht carafs* (celery stew). Algerians enjoy *lahm lhalou* (lamb with dried plums), a dish now popular in Israel as well.

In Ashkenazic cuisine, European fresh plums and dried plums are used in preserves, salads, soups, tarts, and cakes as well as to stuff dumplings and fill kreplach, and to make *pálenka*/slivovitz (plum brandy). Dried plums were the most common fruit of eastern Europeans, used in jams (*lekvar*), pastries (hamantaschen), tzimmes, compotes, and liqueurs. European plums come into season relatively late in the summer, typically around Rosh Hashanah, leading to their role in areas like Hungary, Germany, and Austria in traditional holiday dishes. Nevertheless, the vast majority of the European plum crop is used either as preserves or in the dried state.

(See also Lekvar and Pálenka)

PLUMBA

Plumba (from the Late Latin *plumba*, "lead") is a tag affixed to a food, certifying that it is kosher. In 1888, the Association of American Orthodox Hebrew Congregations appointed Rabbi Jacob Joseph of Vilna, Lithuania, as the first (ultimately only) chief rabbi of New York City. He instituted a practice in which a metal *plumba* bearing the name of the kosher supervisor was attached to the wing skin of each properly slaughtered chicken. Today, most kosher chickens in America have a *plumba* attached. It may specify the slaughterhouse, kosher supervising agency, and date of slaughter.

POGACA

Pogaca is a group of sweet and savory breads and buns.
Origin: Turkey
Other names: *bogaca*.

Medieval Ottoman Turks prepared a simple flatbread called *pogaca*; the name comes from the Italian focaccia, which originated in ancient Rome as *panis focacius* (bread of the hearth). During the Ottoman control of the Balkans in the fifteenth and sixteenth centuries, *pogaca* spread to the Balkans. In Serbia, *pogaca* came to mean a large round flatbread, which was made for special occasions, such as weddings, although it was simpler than large raised loaves. The diminutive of the word, *pogacice*, denotes a Serbian puff pastry. In the fifteenth century, Serbs and Croats fleeing the Turks brought *pogaca* to Slovenia, where one version of the flatbread, *bela krajina pogaca*, which is scored with a net pattern and sprinkled with caraway seeds and coarse salt, became a national dish.

Over the centuries, the *pogaca* in Turkey evolved into a large variety of breads and buns, both savory and sweet; they are made from a basic yeast dough (*labne peynirli*) commonly enriched with thick Turkish yogurt and eggs, which gave it a yellowish tint. Mahlab (ground cherry pits) is sometimes added. With the addition of sugar to the dough and filling, the bread evolved into a sweet bun, still called *pogaca*. *Zeytinli pogaca* is a loaf containing olives. Small breads rolled like a croissant are called *kolav pogaca*. The most popular of these is *peynirli pogaca*, which is filled with feta or other white cheese; when dill is added, it becomes a *dereotlu peynirli pogaca*. Sometimes a meat filling was used (*kiymali pogaca*), but Jews obviously could not use the yogurt and butter dough with this version. The classic way of filling a *pogaca* is to fold it like an *empanada*, so the filled bun resembles a half-moon.

In modern Turkey, both savory and sweet versions of *pogaca*, typically sprinkled with sesame and/or nigella seeds, remain popular. There is even a quicker baking powder adaptation. All types are common for breakfast and snacks accompanied with black tea.

(See also Bougatsa and Pogácsa)

TURKISH CHEESE BUNS (*PEYNIRLI POGACA*)

MAKES 28 SMALL ROLLS   [DAIRY]

Sponge:
  1 package (2¼ teaspoons) active dry yeast or
    1 (0.6-ounce) cake fresh yeast
  ½ cup warm water (105°F to 115°F for dry yeast;
    80°F to 85°F for fresh yeast)
  1 teaspoon sugar
  ½ cup (2 ounces) bread or unbleached all-purpose
    flour

Dough:
  3¼ cups (1 pound) bread or unbleached all-purpose
    flour
  1 teaspoon table salt or 2 teaspoons kosher salt
  1¼ cups (2½ sticks) unsalted butter, softened
  2 large eggs

Filling:
  2 cups (10 ounces) crumbled feta cheese
  2 large eggs, lightly beaten
  ⅔ cup chopped fresh flat-leaf parsley or dill

Egg wash (1 large egg beaten with 1 teaspoon water)
Sesame or nigella seeds for sprinkling
  1. To make the sponge: In a medium glass or ceramic bowl, dissolve the yeast in the water. Stir in the sugar

and let stand until foamy, 5 to 10 minutes. Stir in the flour, cover with plastic wrap and let stand in a warm, draft-free place for 30 minutes.

2. To make the dough: In a large bowl, combine the flour and salt. Add the sponge, butter, and eggs and stir to make a soft dough. Knead until smooth and elastic, 10 to 15 minutes. Cover with a large bowl or pot and let stand for 30 minutes.

3. To make the filling: In a medium bowl, combine all the filling ingredients.

4. Punch down the dough. Divide into 28 equal pieces, shape into balls, cover, and let rest for 15 minutes.

5. Line 2 large baking sheets with parchment paper or lightly grease the sheets. On a lightly floured surface, roll out the dough balls into 3½-inch rounds. Spoon 1 tablespoon filling into the center of each round, fold over an edge to form a half-moon, and press the edge to seal. Place the *pogaca* on the prepared baking sheets, leaving 1 inch between, cover, and let stand for 15 minutes.

6. Preheat the oven to 375°F.

7. Brush the pogaca with the egg wash and lightly sprinkle with the seeds. Bake until golden brown, 25 to 30 minutes. Serve warm or at room temperature.

POGÁCSA
Pogácsa is a slightly sweetened, fat-enriched scone.
Origin: Hungary
Other names: *pogacha, pogachel, pogatchke.*

When the Turkish bread *pogaca* reached Hungary in the fifteenth or sixteenth century, it developed into a small, round, savory yeast flatbread made with schmaltz (non-Jews typically used lard). The bread then evolved into an array of round scones, all known as *pogácsa.* Plain ones made from only flour, fat, yeast, and salt are *egyszeru pogácsa.* When goose *gribenes* (cracklings) are rolled into the flaky dough, it becomes a *liba töpörtyus pogácsa.* Many versions are enriched with the addition of *túró,* the Hungarian version of *quark* cheese. A *sajtos pogácsa* contains grated hard cheese and a *juhtúrós pogácsa* includes *brinza.* Adding poppy seeds results in *mákos pogácsa. Mézespogácsa* are sweetened with honey. In the nineteenth century, plebian cooks substituted mashed potatoes for the butter and *túró* for some or all of the eggs, producing a heavier but less expensive *burgonyás pogácsa.*

Unquestionably, the favorite type is a butter scone, *vajas pogácsa,* which is both savory and sweetened (*édes vajas pogácsa*); it is similar in texture to a cookie, but not as sweet. The original versions were made from a yeast dough, but cooks in the early twentieth century developed a modern baking powder version. *Vajas pogácsa* are not a dessert, but rather a treat to eat with coffee or tea. In many Hungarian households, no Sabbath would be complete without at least one type of baked good for family and guests to nosh, and slightly sweetened *pogachel* are the favorite.

In Hungary, *pogácsa* are sold at practically every bakery and are commonly made at home. In America and Israel, unlike various other traditional Hungarian baked goods, *pogácsa* are little known outside the Hungarian community. In America, they can primarily be found in Hungarian bakeries and markets, such as those of the Satmar Chasidim in the Williamsburg section of Brooklyn.

Hungarian Jews enjoy pogácsa—round, lightly sweet, rich scones on the Sabbath—and for a special snack during the week.

HUNGARIAN YEAST BUTTER SCONES
(ÉDES VAJAS POGÁCSA)

ABOUT TWENTY 2-INCH SCONES   [DAIRY]

 1 package (2¼ teaspoons) active dry yeast or
  1 (0.6-ounce) cake fresh yeast
 3 tablespoons warm milk
 1 cup (2 sticks) unsalted butter, softened
 About 3½ cups (18 ounces) unbleached all-purpose
  flour
 ½ teaspoon table salt or 1 teaspoon kosher salt
 1 to 6 tablespoons confectioners' or superfine sugar
 ½ cup *quark, gevina levana* (Israeli white cheese),
  or sour cream
 2 large egg yolks
 Egg wash (1 large egg beaten with 1 teaspoon water)

 1. In a small bowl, dissolve the yeast in the milk and set aside. In a large bowl, beat the butter until smooth, about 5 minutes. Gradually blend in the flour and salt, about 2 minutes. Beat in the sugar, about 2 minutes. Add the yeast mixture, *quark*, and egg yolks and stir until the mixture starts sticking together. If the dough is too thin, add a little more flour; if too thick, add a little milk. Place on a lightly floured surface and knead until smooth, about 2 minutes. Form into a ball, cover with plastic wrap, and let stand in a warm, draft-free place for 1 hour.

 2. On a lightly floured surface, roll out the dough into a 13-by-9-inch rectangle, about ½ inch thick. From the shorter side, fold over the top one-third of the dough, then fold over the bottom one-third. Cover and refrigerate for 20 minutes. Roll out, fold as previously, and refrigerate for another 20 minutes. Roll out into a ¼-inch-thick square. Bring the right and left sides together to meet in the center, then fold the top and bottom to meet in the center. Wrap in plastic wrap and refrigerate for at least 8 hours and up to 2 days.

 3. Preheat the oven to 350°F. Line a large baking sheet with parchment paper or lightly grease the sheet.

 4. On a lightly floured surface, roll the dough into a 10-by-8-inch rectangle, about ¾ inch thick. Using the tip of a sharp knife, score a crisscross pattern on the surface. Using a floured 2- or 2½-inch biscuit cutter or drinking glass, cut out rounds as close to each other as possible. Reroll, score, and cut out the scraps; these will be a little tougher. Place on the prepared baking sheet in rows touching each other.

 5. Brush the tops of the *pogácsa* with the egg wash.

Bake until golden brown, about 20 minutes. Transfer the *pogácsa* to a wire rack and let cool slightly. Serve warm or cooled.

POLPETTA

The Italian word *polpetta*, (*polpette* plural), from the Italian *polpo* (pulp), does not connote any specific ingredient, but rather the shape and nature of the item—a small sphere—made from mashed food. The favorite type, *polpette di carne* (meatballs), is made from mashed meat; *polpettone* is a meatloaf. Non-Jewish Italian meatballs typically contained grated cheese; Jews replaced the cheese with bread crumbs—not only stretching the meat, but also making the balls more tender—which would become the standard practice for European Jewish meatballs. *Polpette alla Giudia* (Jewish-style meatballs) frequently contain vegetables, especially spinach, to both extend and flavor the meat, and there are pareve versions made entirely from vegetables. One Jewish *polpette* from Venice consists of spinach, pine nuts, and raisins, and another includes salt cod.

Polpette are typically served in a soup or after the pasta as a second course, at times with other meats, alongside a vegetable and sometimes accompanied by rice. In Italy, *polpette* and *poplettone* were home dishes prepared for the Sabbath and festivals, in particular, Passover, although at one time they had generally been considered too humble to offer to guests.

POLSTERZIPFEL

Polsterzipfel is a jam-filled pocket cookie.

Origin: Austria

Other names: Austrian jam pockets, Vienna tarts.

Polsterzipfel, meaning "cornered cushions," date back to at least the sixteenth century. To form these cookies, a rich pastry dough is rolled out, cut into squares, a little jam dropped into the center, and two diagonally opposite corners brought together over the jam. When formed into turnovers, they are called *hasenörchen* (little rabbit ears). The use of jam in the center differentiates *polsterzipfel* from similar German versions. Hungarians make a similar half-moon turnover called *baratfule*. The original dough was made with *topfen*, a soft, white cheese called *quark* in Germany and *gevina levana* in Israel. In America, cream cheese is substituted. *Polsterzipfel* were once common at dairy celebrations, such as a brit or baby naming.

⚜ AUSTRIAN JAM POCKETS (*POLSTERZIPFEL*)

ABOUT 48 PASTRIES   [DAIRY]

    1 recipe Cream Cheese Dough (see Rugelach, page 510)

    About 2½ cups apricot lekvar, prune lekvar, or fruit jam

1. On a lightly floured surface, roll out the dough ⅛ inch thick. Cut into 2- to 3-inch squares. Spoon 1 teaspoon jam in the center of each square, bring 2 diagonally opposite corners together over the jam, and press to seal. Place on 2 large baking sheets lined with parchment paper or on ungreased sheets. Cover and refrigerate for at least 1 hour or overnight.

2. Preheat the oven to 350°F.

3. Bake until the edges begin to turn golden, about 20 minutes. Transfer the pastries to a wire rack and let cool completely. Store in the refrigerator for up to 2 days or in the freezer for up to 2 months.

Pomegranates have inspired Jewish cooks and artisans for millennia. Here is a sixth century BCE Israelite vessel with a cluster of pomegranates featured around the base.

POMEGRANATE

The pomegranate, which probably originated in Persia, grows on small deciduous bushy trees that thrive in subtropical and mild areas, including most of Israel. The pomegranate is technically not a fruit, but rather a berry; it consists of a tough, leathery, reddish brown skin covering a mass of small shiny arils (seed casings) and crowned by a distinctive calyx. There are two basic types of pomegranates—sweet (with varying degrees of tannin or tartness) and sour. Most pomegranates are the sweet variety, but the flavor varies depending on the subspecies and ripeness. Since pomegranates tend to split when fully mature, they are frequently picked beforehand. A white membrane divides the interior of the pomegranate into six compartments containing the edible part. Each kernel consists of a pip surrounded by a sweet-acidic juice that ranges in color from red to pink to nearly clear. The thick skin keeps the inner fruit moist for an extended period, a particular benefit in a warm climate and for ancient travelers. The arils are added whole in salads and as a garnish, and are eaten seeds and all.

The pomegranate, *rimon* in Hebrew, plays a significant role in Jewish literature and lore: The Bible includes it among the seven agricultural products representative of the bounty of the land of Israel; it was one of the fruits brought back from Canaan by the spies sent by Moses; it is spoken of in glowing terms six times in "Song of Songs"; adornments shaped like pomegranates were woven onto the hem of the robe of the high priest; brass images of them were part of the Temple's pillars; several towns in ancient Israel bore the name Rimon; ancient Jewish coins as well as modern Israeli ones picture them; and silver *rimmonim* are customarily used to decorate and cover the two upper handles of the Torah scrolls. *Rimon yad* is the contemporary Hebrew word for grenade. According to tradition, each pomegranate contains 613 seeds, corresponding to the number of commandments in the Torah, and thus serves as a symbol of righteousness and fruitfulness. Pomegranates begin ripening around August, yielding a plentiful supply just in time for Rosh Hashanah and Sukkot, making them traditional holiday fare. The Rosh Hashanah simile is "May we be full of merits like the pomegranate [is full of seeds]."

In biblical times, the fruit was eaten fresh, used to make juice, or dried. Like other juicy fruits, historically some of the pomegranate berries were spread out in the sun to dry and shrivel for ten to fifteen days to use when fresh fruit was out of season. Dried pomegranate berries, called *anardana,* are still common in Persian and Indian cuisines; they are added whole or ground to stews, soups, vegetables, legumes, and chutneys. The seeds are also dried and pressed to produce pomegranate oil.

Pomegranates were foreign to Ashkenazim, but were extremely important in central Asia and Sephardic culture from the onset. When the Moors invaded Iberia in 711, they found a Jewish community on a hillside in southern Spain, which they named *Gharnata al Yahud* (literally "pomegranates of the Jews"); this city later became Granada, which is generally referred to as Rimon in Jewish literature. In the Near East, pomegranate seeds (sometimes with slivered almonds) are tossed with a little honey and orange-blossom water to make a simple refreshing dessert.

More important in cooking, however, is the juice, which is used straight or boiled down to a thick syrup. Pomegranate juice is used in central Asia to add tartness to food or to marinate meat; it is also simply enjoyed as a refreshing drink. Before the arrival of lemons and later tomatoes in the Mediterranean and Asia, pomegranate juice served as one of the main souring agents, a role it still plays in many stews, soups, sauces, and purees in Georgia, Iran, Afghanistan, Turkey, and Syria. The juice is also fermented into a wine.

(See also Pomegranate Molasses)

POMEGRANATE MOLASSES

Fresh pomegranates have a relatively short season, lasting only from August through early November. Middle Easterners long ago learned to boil down the juice, thereby greatly extending its availability and versatility. Pomegranate juice can be cooked to the consistency of maple syrup; this liquid is generally known as pomegranate syrup and is called *sharab al-rumman* in Arabic. *Sharab* is most commonly diluted in water, seltzer, or lemonade and served as a beverage, but it is also delicious in marinades and vinaigrettes.

More frequently for cooking, the pomegranate juice is further reduced to a thick, blackish, sweet-sour concentrate with the consistency of molasses. Real pomegranate molasses or pomegranate concentrate— *rob-e anar* in Persian, *dibs rumman* in Arabic, and

nar ekşisi in Turkish—is made without added sugar, resulting in a rather tart concentrate; the sweetness is controlled by varying the amount of sweet and sour pomegranates. Today, however, many brands of pomegranate concentrate include sugar and/or lemon juice to adjust the sweetness and control the consistency. *Narsharab*, the name for the pomegranate molasses widely used in Azerbaijan, Georgia, and Kazakhstan, is typically made in the Turkish style with sour pomegranates. Since the intensity and flavor of pomegranate molasses vary widely from batch to batch and brand to brand, it is impossible to give a precise amount in recipes, so cooks need to adjust it to taste.

Pomegranate molasses, available at Middle Eastern stores, is widely used as a souring agent—often in combination with garlic, cilantro, parsley, and tomato sauce—in stews, sauces, vegetables, and savory fillings. In the Caucuses and the Levant, it is traditionally used only in savory dishes. Most homes in these areas keep a bottle of pomegranate molasses on hand at all times to add a fruity acidity to dishes. Pomegranate molasses is essential for *muhammara* (Turkish red pepper relish), *bazargan* (Syrian bulgur relish), and Georgian marinades and sauce for *shashlik* (shish kebab).

POPPY SEED

Mohn is the German and Yiddish word for the poppy plant and its seeds, the word perhaps deriving from *mond* (German for "moon"). The poet Paul Celan (a pseudonym for Paul Antschel) was born to a Jewish family in what was in 1920 Romania and is now part of Ukraine. His parents perished in Nazi concentration camps; he spent much of the war in labor camps. In 1952, Celan entitled his acclaimed second book *Mohn und Gedächtnis* (Poppy and Remembrance). The title and contents reflect the author's feelings of senselessness at the suffering and death during the Holocaust, as well as the inability to negate or even ameliorate memory. Celan understood that the language, culture, and cuisine of a society, even one tainted and perhaps disqualified by murderers, indelibly remained a part of his life and of the Jewish community. The suggestive word *mohn*, therefore, is symbolic and representative of the situation of both the author and his people. The poppy plant provides opium, a narcotic inducing forgetting, yet its seeds conjure up the lost world of his youth, filled with poppy seed pastries and poppy seed–topped Sabbath challah he could never forget.

Although once considered a native of western Asia, evidence now points to a southwestern European origin for the poppy and a gradual move eastward during the Bronze Age to Asia. The earliest seeds were discovered in caves in Spain, while tellingly no poppy seeds have been discovered in Egyptian tombs or ancient Mesopotamian sites. The earliest proof of the presence of opium in Egypt and the Levant appears in the late Bronze Age (around 1300 BCE), the time of the Judges, in the form of *bilbils*, ceramic storage jars imported from Cyprus. Not only were these containers shaped like the capsules of poppies, but tests on substances inside revealed opium. Claims of the earlier existence of opium in Egypt have been disproved. The *bilbils* and their contents were imported from Crete. The actual poppy plant, called *pereg* in Hebrew and *khash-khash* in Farsi and Arabic, probably arrived in the Near East much later with the Greeks or even Romans.

The poppy sprouts large red flowers bearing tiny seeds—purportedly nine hundred thousand seeds in a pound. The Dutch poppy produces dark blue seeds. The seeds of the Indian poppy have a pale cream color. The alkaloids that produce opium are not found in European varieties. And although the Elaine character in the television show *Seinfeld* tested positive for drugs after eating poppy seed muffins, modern testing can now easily determine the difference between the seeds and the drug.

When roasted or steamed, poppy seeds have a mild, nutty flavor. Grinding them releases the flavor more fully. Many European homes possess a large brass mortar and pestle, frequently handed down for many generations, in which to pound the family's poppy seeds.

Americans tend to relegate poppy seeds to a garnish for breads and rolls, missing the full possibilities. In northern India and Turkey, the seeds are roasted and ground to make various sauces to flavor fish and meat. In Slavic regions, they are used in fish and vegetables dishes. In the Mediterranean, they are mixed into salads, pasta, and tuna fish. In Venice, poppy seeds are added, along with chestnut puree, dates, and nuts, to charoset. Lithuanian Jews once made a pareve milk substitute from the oil-rich poppy seeds and water.

Nevertheless, it was in central Europe that the poppy seed achieved its highest degree of popularity and usefulness, becoming essential in Austrian, Czech, German, and Hungarian cuisines. Many central and eastern Europeans would grow and harvest their own poppy seeds each year. Poppy seed oil was the predominant oil in many parts of the region. Poppy is a popular filling for numerous cakes and pastries, including *makosh* (pastry rolls), *mohn torten* (poppy cakes), *mohn kuchen* (coffee cakes), strudel, *kichlach* (egg cookies), and *mohnplatzen* (cookies representing Haman's pocket or hat), as well as puddings and confections, notably *mohnlach* (poppy seed candies). A favorite Hungarian comfort dessert is *mákos metélt* (noodles with poppy seeds and sugar), called *mohn nudeln* in Austria.

Seeds—particularly sesame and poppy—are a symbol of fruitfulness and are therefore commonly sprinkled on Sabbath and Rosh Hashanah challahs. The similarity of the German word *mohn* to the name Haman led to these seeds' becoming the most common ingredient in Ashkenazic Purim dishes. The most famous poppy seed–filled pastry is the hamantaschen. (See also Filling and Pletzlach)

POTATO

The white potato is now such an intrinsic part of Ashkenazic cooking that it is difficult for many to comprehend that this tuber is actually a relatively recent addition to the European and Jewish pantry. Both the white and sweet potatoes, two unrelated tubers, are indigenous to the Andes Mountains of South America. The Incas cultivated the sweet potato, a member of the morning glory family, more than five thousand years ago and, long before the arrival of Europeans, it had spread as far north as the southwestern United States. Columbus found the sweet potato in the Caribbean during his first voyage and brought it to Spain in 1493, where it was called *batata*, the Taino word for "tuber," and soon planted it in many parts of Iberia. For the following century or so, European references to *batata* were to the sweet potato. Columbus never saw a white potato, which had yet to make its way that far eastward or even to Central America.

The thousands of cultivated varieties of white potatoes are generally classified in North America as russet (baking) and waxy (boiling); these groupings are based on starch content and shape. The white potato, perhaps native to Peru or Chile, is a member of the nightshade family related to tomatoes and peppers. It flourished in the difficult conditions and poor soil of the higher elevations of the Andes, exhibiting a hardiness that would eventually make it the world's predominant vegetable and fourth-largest food crop, following three grains—corn, wheat, and rice. During its initial period in both America and then Europe, however, this knobby tuber ran a distant second to the sweet potato in popularity.

The first mention of the white potato, a misnomer as its color can range from yellow to gray to purple, was by a Spanish expedition to northern Peru in 1537. The Spanish called it *patata*—a corruption of the Indian words *papas* (potato) and *batata*—which led to the English name potato. The French called it *pomme de terre* (apple of the earth). Europeans thought the knobby potato resembled a little truffle (*taratufli* in Latin)—hence its German name, *kartoffel*, and central Yiddish name, *kartofl*. There are nearly a dozen other Yiddish names for potato, including the Slavic *kartoshke*, early German *erdepl* (earth apple), and most notably the Lithuanian and northern Polish *bulbe* or *boulbe*, akin to the English bulb. The Yiddish theater slang for an actor blowing a line, "he has a *bulbe* in his mouth," eventually became shortened to "he made a *bulbe*," which gave rise to the American term for a mistake or blunder, boo-boo.

When the white potato finally reached Spain around 1570, it was regarded as a source of leprosy or poisonous. The potato traveled to England and Italy around 1585, to Germany about two year later, and to France around 1600. In each of these locations, most sixteenth- and seventeenth-century Europeans, having ingrained eating habits, rejected a number of the American imports, especially the potato. Even after the potato spread across western and central Europe in the mid-eighteenth century and was widely planted by the governments in some areas, people rejected it as food, considering it unhealthy at best or even considering it "the devil's plant." There is a logical explanation for this notion: Exposure to light produces a toxin in the potato called solanine, indicated by a green tinge, which results in a bitter taste as well as an allergic reaction in some people. In addition, the first Europeans who tried potatoes ate them raw, which can induce upset stomachs.

Initially, when the white potato was utilized at all, it was for animal feed, and a much-contested act of the British Parliament was required to allow the potato to be used for even that purpose. The French, at one point, outlawed growing it entirely. When Prussia's Frederick the Great sent free potatoes to feed his peasants during the famine of 1774, they refused to eat them, although they were starving. Only in the face of abject poverty, most notably in Ireland after 1780, did potatoes—which grow in abundance relatively quickly, even in poor soil—become an important part of the human diet.

The potato owes its current widespread popularity to Antoine-Auguste Parmentier, who spent time as a German prisoner during the Seven Years' War (1756–1763). Although the Germans themselves steadfastly refused to eat potatoes, they had no qualms about feeding them to livestock or their French captives. After surviving his steady diet of potatoes, Parmentier realized that not only had he failed to develop leprosy or become poisoned, but he had emerged rather sound, considering the circumstances. During the ensuing decades, he championed the potato as a source of sustenance for the masses of France. He finally enlisted the support of Louis XVI and potato cultivation spread. Beginning in 1770, the viability of many traditional food crops in France was reduced by a short cooling period. The potato subsequently proved vital when famine and hunger swept over France in the 1790s in the wake of the Revolution. The Germans soon joined the bandwagon and, by the end of the eighteenth century, were using potatoes to make a variety of dishes, such as *kloese* (dumplings), salads, soups, pancakes, and breads, as well as flour. This new attitude, however, was primarily on the part of the masses as most upper-class Germans viewed potatoes as "poor person's food" and deigned not to eat them. As late as the middle of the nineteenth century, most Americans viewed the potato as animal feed; it was the arrival of German immigrants around this time and the development of the russet Burbank potato that led to the popularization of the potato in the United States. Residents of the Mediterranean and central Asia eventually incorporated the potato into dishes as well. Nevertheless, the center of its popularity lay to the north.

In eastern Europe, the potato took longer to gain widespread acceptance, even among the poor. Due to generally impoverished circumstances, as well as climatic conditions and backward agronomy that precluded the growing of most fresh vegetables, starches were indispensable in eastern Europe. Then, a series of crop failures occurred in Ukraine and Poland in 1839 and 1840, and the government ordered the peasants to plant potatoes; tubers were finally grown for the first time and consumed in large numbers in that part of the world. Within a short period, these hearty tubers emerged as the staple of the northeastern European diet, replacing buckwheat and legumes. Jews consumed potatoes in even greater numbers than their non-Jewish neighbors. Significantly, in the northern Romanian version of the Polish song "Bulbes," the word *beblekh* (beans) was used instead of *bulbes* (potatoes), as legumes constituted the bulk of the diet farther south.

Potatoes provided an inexpensive way to fill the hungry stomachs of the exploding Jewish population. During the century after their popularization, any Polish Jew with even a small plot of land would plant some potatoes to support the family or make arrangements to rent part of a nearby property belonging to a non-Jew. The first potatoes of the year were usually dug up around the seventeenth of the month of Tammuz and then replanted through the holiday of Sukkot. Every Jewish residence maintained at least a small cellar or other cool place in which to store the family's supply of potatoes as well as beets, carrots, onions, and turnips and barrels of various pickles. Properly stored, potatoes are capable of keeping for up to eight months. Poorer families survived the winter on potatoes and sauerkraut. The minimum supply of potatoes for the winter for a family of six was 1,260 pounds, but typically they would use double that amount. Many eastern European families ate potatoes, often seasoned with onions, three times a day. They were used to create new dishes, such as *potatonik* (a cross between a kugel and a bread), as well as incorporated into various traditional dishes, most notably cholent (Sabbath stew), *knaidlach* (dumplings), knishes, pirogen (filled pasta), and kugel (pudding). Hot boiled potatoes in cold beet borscht became a particular favorite. Sometimes boiled potatoes were eaten simply with sour cream, providing complementary nutrition. The potato latke (pancake) emerged as the prototypical Ashkenazic Hanukkah food. The latke also gave rise to the Yiddish saying, *"Fun a proste buble kumt aroys di geshmakste lakte"* (From the lowly potato you get the tastiest pancake).

At the time of the partition of Poland among Austria, Prussia, and Russia in 1815, the Jewish population of Russian Poland numbered about one and a quarter million. By the census of 1897, that number, despite massive emigration to America and Israel beginning in 1881, grew to about five million (15 percent of the total population of Poland). Not coincidentally, this Jewish population explosion—reflecting a growth rate more than twice that of their non-Jewish neighbors—corresponded to the availability and emerging popularity of the potato in eastern Europe. Although a nineteenth-century German rabbi tried to forbid potatoes during Passover, his attempt failed and they became a predominant Ashkenazic Passover food; in many northeastern European households, potatoes even served as the *karpas* for the Seder.

The potato's first use in European kitchens was in stews and then in soups. Potato soups became extremely popular in many areas because they fed a large number of people using very limited resources. At some point, people discovered that the smashed cooked potatoes were tasty apart from the stew and that the bland tuber could be cooked in plain water as well, leading to mashed potatoes. In the sixteenth century, the Spanish made a fritter using dried potatoes, but the first record of fried sliced potatoes, the dish Americans call French fries, was in seventeenth-century Holland. Although the most famous way of frying potatoes is credited to the French, that method is actually seldom used in France, while it is common throughout much of the Mediterranean.

Potato salads also became popular in the nineteenth century. The first description in England of the white potato was in the original 1597 edition of John Gerard's detailed description of plants, *Herball*. The author mistakenly thought it was a native of North America and called it the "Virginia Potato." The earliest record of a potato salad–like dish was in the 1633 re-edition of *Herball*. Similar salads, although then served hot, had appeared in Germany by the 1800s, and by the end of the century, most countries had developed some form of a potato salad in a vinaigrette. German Jews served potato salad cold on the Sabbath, a practice that later became widespread among American Jews and Israelis. *Jewish Cookery* (Philadelphia, 1871) included recipes for "Potato Bread," "Potato Fritters," "Potato Souffle, For Passover," "Potato Soup," "Potato Stew," and "Salad of Potatoes."

In the 1920s, European Jews brought the potato to Israel; following the French example, in Hebrew, they called it *tapuach haadamah* (apple of the earth) or the shortened *tapud*. The early Socialist-Zionists in Israel, who despised European Jewish culture and Yiddish, disparagingly referred to the latter as *kartofl Yidish* (potato tongue). Initially, kibbutzniks found they could grow this vegetable only in the coolness of the winter; then in the 1930s, the introduction of sprinklers for irrigation greatly expanded production. Today, potatoes are grown throughout Israel and are a standard ingredient in Israeli cooking.

(See also Ajada, Aloo Makalla, Dumpling, Knish, Kugel, Latke, Peshkado Frito, and Potatonik)

POTATONIK

Potatonik is a combination of a potato kugel and bread.
Origin: Poland
Other names: Galicia: *kartofelnik*; Poland: *bulbanik, bulbenik.*

Potatonik is the American name for this northeastern European dish, which is less dense than a potato kugel, but still somewhat heavy textured. In Ukraine, *kartofelnik* refers to potato patties with a filling of ground beef or mushrooms and sautéed onions sandwiched in between. In the American Yiddish theater, a *bulbanik* (*bulbes* is a Yiddish word for potatoes), sounding like *bilbul* (mix-up), became slang for someone who talked with a stammer or an actor who blew a line, as that person talked as if he or she had a potato in their mouth.

Potatonik comes in both casserole and loaf forms. Unlike most potato breads, potatonik is made from raw spuds; it has a rough texture and marked potato flavor, along with a pronounced accent of onions and black pepper. Some versions include unpeeled potatoes. Sometimes rye or buckwheat flour is substituted for the wheat flour. Those "potatoniks" made without flour and yeast, some lightened a little with beaten egg whites, are actually potato kugel.

In Europe, the rustic *bulbenik* was always a homemade food; some families prepared it for every Sabbath, while others reserved it for rare occasions, such as Hanukkah, and served only standard potato kugel for the Sabbath. However, in America and Israel most second-generation housewives—perhaps intimidated by the yeast or turned off by the oiliness and old-fashioned nature of the dish—stopped making "spud-nik." A few Jewish bakeries and markets in larger American cities took up the slack. In some American synagogues, potatonik became a traditional food at kiddushes, where it was served alongside pickled herring, *kichlach* (egg cookies), and schnapps. However, by the end of the twentieth century, the dish had become a rarity, although it could occasionally be found in some Brooklyn bakeries. Potatonik is usually served as a side dish with meat or poultry, sometimes accompanied with applesauce or, at a dairy meal, sour cream.

POLISH POTATO KUGEL BREAD (*POTATONIK*)
9 TO 12 SERVINGS   [PAREVE OR MEAT]

- 1 package (2¼ teaspoons) active dry yeast or 1 (0.6-ounce) cake fresh yeast
- ¼ cup warm water (105°F to 115°F for dry yeast; 80°F to 85°F for fresh yeast)
- 1 teaspoon sugar
- 3 large eggs, lightly beaten
- ½ cup vegetable oil or schmaltz
- About 1¼ teaspoons table salt or 2½ teaspoons kosher salt
- About ¼ teaspoon ground white or black pepper
- ½ teaspoon baking powder or ¼ teaspoon cream of tartar
- 3 pounds (6 large) baking (russet) potatoes, unpeeled or peeled, and grated
- 2 medium onions, grated (about 1½ cups)
- 2½ cups (12.5 ounces) unbleached all-purpose flour

1. Dissolve the yeast in the water. Stir in the sugar and let stand until foamy, 5 to 10 minutes. In a large bowl, combine the eggs, oil, salt, pepper, and baking powder. Add the potatoes and onions. Stir in the yeast mixture and flour. Cover with plastic wrap or a kitchen towel and let stand in a warm, draft-free place for 1 hour.

2. Oil one 13-by-9-inch baking pan, two (2-quart) 8-inch square or 11-by-7-inch casserole dishes, or three 8-by-4-inch loaf pans. Pour the potato mixture into the pan(s), cover, and let stand for 20 minutes.

3. Preheat the oven to 400°F.

4. Bake for 30 minutes. At this point, some cooks brush the top of the potatonik with a little oil for a crisper surface. Reduce the heat to 350°F and continue baking until golden brown, about 30 minutes for a 13-by-9-inch pan or loaf pan, or 15 minutes for

2-quart pans. Remove from the oven and turn out of the pan(s) onto a wire rack. Serve warm or cooled.

P'TCHA

P'tcha is jellied calves feet.

Origin: Eastern Europe

Other names: Galicia: *drelies*; Germany: *sulze*: Israel: *regel kerushah*; Lithuania: *fisnoga*; Poland: *fissel, galarita, petcha, pitse, p'tcha, p'tsha*; Romania: *piftie*; Ukraine: *cholodyetz*.

Among the relics of the Ottomans' centuries-long control of the Balkans that began in the fourteenth century was a hearty Turkish peasant soup based on lamb's feet, known as *paca corbasi*, from the Turkish *paca* (foot), and called *soupa patsas* or simply *patsas* by the Greeks. When cooled, the gelatin in the bones firms the liquid into an entirely different dish, an aspic. Foot soup and aspic spread to central and eastern Europe, where it was made from cow's feet instead of sheep's feet and was more typically enjoyed cold and jellied. The dish allowed cooks to transform one of the least expensive parts of the animal into an Ashkenazic delicacy.

The process of preparing foot gelatin was quite time-consuming, so among Ashkenazim it was never an everyday or even weekly dish, but rather an occasional Sabbath lunch treat lovingly prepared by a housewife or grandmother.

A calf's or cow's foot was first rotated over a flame to singe off any hair then thoroughly scraped and cleaned. It was then hacked into pieces and boiled for hours with onions, salt, and pepper until the meat had fallen off of the bone and the bones had imparted all their essence into the cooking liquid. Some people ate the hot soup as a main course for Sabbath lunch, at which it was an occasional winter substitute for cholent. The soup would be left in the oven overnight and served hot with vinegar, sliced hard-boiled eggs, and fresh challah or challah toast rubbed with garlic; diners eagerly sucked the marrow out of the bones. Some enjoyed the cooled version, which was typically studded with sliced hard-boiled eggs and plenty of garlic, as an appetizer for Sabbath lunch; others offered it hot at Sabbath lunch and then served the cooled, gelled leftovers at *shalosh seudot* (the third Sabbath meal). When hot, the meat is meltingly soft and the cooking liquid is a concentrated broth, but as the dish cools, the meat toughens and the liquid con-

geals. Therefore, some cooks leave the meat in larger shreds, while others, as a way to tenderize it when cold, finely chop or mash the meat.

For generations, jellied foot soup and calf's foot gelatin—the names of these varied from region to region—were among the most beloved eastern Ashkenazic dishes, perhaps following only cholent (Sabbath stew) as a Sabbath favorite. In Galicia (now southern Poland), some cooks added sugar for a sweet-and-sour flavor.

In a 1915 short story, "What Kind of Rabbi We Have," Sholem Aleichem described some typical eastern European dishes at a special Sabbath lunch: "And after that the cold fish and the meat from yesterday's tzimmes, and then the jellied calf's foot, or fisnoga as you call it, with thin slices of garlic . . ." The whimsical name *fisnoga* from Lithuania and Latvia actually had a practical origin, as Litvaks from the north of the country had difficulty pronouncing the *sh* sound and thus the word *fishe* (fish) and *fis* (foot) sounded the same; to differentiate the two homophones, the Slavic word for foot (*noga*) was added to the Teutonic word for foot (*fis*), and the term became *fisnoga* (literally "foot foot").

Initially, in Russia and Ukraine, either the term *p'tcha* or *fisnoga* connoted the hot soup, while the cooled dish was called *cholodyetz* (*kholod* means "cold" in Russian) or *farglivert* (Yiddish meaning "coagulated"). Eventually, the cooled jellied form became the principal way of serving the dish and *p'tcha* emerged as the predominant name.

In the nineteenth century, immigrants brought *p'tcha* to America and Israel. The dish was included in the earliest American Jewish cookbooks—all by authors who were initially from a German background—including *Jewish Cookery* (Philadelphia, 1871) and *Aunt Babette's* (Cincinnati, 1889); in the latter book, the dish was entitled "Sulze von Kalbsfuessen (jelly from calf's foot)." *The Jewish Encyclopedia* (New York, 1903) refers to the dish as "petshai in Lithuania, drelies in South Russia, Galicia, and Rumania."

At least through the first half of the twentieth century, *p'tcha* was well received by most of the first generation of American Jews to be brought up on the dish. *P'tcha* was a standard at Catskills resorts, weddings, and other special occasions. The prolific science and science fiction writer, Isaac Asimov, in his autobiography, described *p'tcha* as "the real ambrosia of the gods." That most certainly became a minority opinion, as today probably no other Ashkenazic dish evokes more outright antipathy among Ashkenazim than *p'tcha*. The gelatinous texture, grayish hue, and garlicky flavor of the cooled liquid with the firmer grayish brownish strips of boiled meat, fail to translate to most modern tastes. Still, *p'tcha* does retain popularity among certain groups, especially the Gerer Chasidim, and can occasionally be found today in a few delis and eastern European–style restaurants, and in some *bubbes'* kitchens.

(See also Patsas)

ASHKENAZIC CALF'S FOOT GELATIN (*P'TCHA*)

6 TO 8 SERVINGS   [MEAT]

2 calf's feet (2 to 2½ pounds total), cleaned and cut into 2-inch pieces (have your butcher cut the bones for you)

2 medium yellow onions, sliced

2 whole cloves garlic

About 2 tablespoons white wine vinegar or fresh lemon juice

1 to 1½ teaspoons table salt or 2 to 3 teaspoons kosher salt

1 teaspoon whole black peppercorns or ¼ to ½ teaspoon ground black pepper

About 7 cups water

2 to 8 cloves garlic, minced or sliced

3 hard-boiled eggs, thinly sliced

1. Place the feet in a large pot, cover with cold water, and bring to a boil. Boil until scum rises to the surface, about 10 minutes. Drain off and discard the water. Rinse the feet.

2. Place the feet, onions, garlic cloves, vinegar, salt, and pepper in a clean large pot. Add fresh water to cover by 1 inch. Bring to a boil, cover, reduce the heat, and simmer until the meat falls off the bone, at least 4 hours or overnight. Taste for seasonings.

3. Remove the bones from the pot. Remove any meat from the bones and chop or shred, and discard the bones. Strain the liquid. Stir in the meat and minced garlic. At this point, the dish can be served hot as a soup.

4. Pour into a shallow 2-quart (8-inch square or 11-by 7-inch) pan or a 9-by-5-inch loaf pan. Arrange the egg slices over the liquid. Cover with plastic wrap and refrigerate until firm, at least 8 hours. To serve, cut into pieces.

PUMPERNICKEL

Rye tends to spread wild like a weed, so throughout the Middle Ages, most breads in northern Europe were made from maslin, a natural mixture of rye and wheat. Bread made solely from wheat, the majority of it imported, was much more expensive. Then in 1443, during a particularly devastating wheat famine, bakers in Westphalia, Germany, were forced to make a bread solely from coarse whole-grain rye flour, without wheat; this loaf developed into a distinctive form of dark bread called *schwarzbrot* (black bread) and *grobes brot* (coarse bread). In Bavaria, the bread is commonly formed in a flour-dusted large round woven basket, resulting in a beehive shape. To make genuine *schwarzbrot*, part of the rye flour is soaked in water, forming organic acids and flavor compounds. Crumbs from older loaves are added, which makes the dough easier to handle and imparts extra color and flavor. This dough is naturally leavened, without sourdough starter or added yeast, and baked in extremely large loaves at a low temperature for an extended period, resulting in a dense, coarse, slightly acidic, and very dark bread. However, by the late nineteenth century, some German bakeries were already supplementing the dough with *zuckerruebensyrup* (sugar beet syrup) to impart a sweeter flavor and darker color without the traditional *schwarzbrot*-making process.

Meanwhile, the residents of early seventeenth-century Westphalia merged two words, *pumper* (lumbering) or *pumpen* (flatulent) and *nickel* (dwarf or goblin), to form a term of derision meaning "a fool" or "bumpkin," and around 1663 pumpernickel was applied to the dark peasant bread. The widespread story that Napoleon coined the term when feeding the bread to his horse, saying *"pain pour Nicole,"* is pure folk etymology. The word was recorded in England in 1756 in an account of Germany in Thomas Nugent's *The Grand Tour*. He wrote, "Their bread is of the very coarse kind, ill baked, and as black as coal, for they never sift their flour. The people of the country call it Pompernickel." Pumpernickel made its first appearance in print in America in 1839 in Henry Wadsworth Longfellow's accounts of traveling abroad, *Hyperion*. Around this time, German immigrants brought pumpernickel to America.

Few bakers in the New World, however, were willing to maintain the traditional time-consuming process of preparing German pumpernickel, so they adapted the recipe and cooking method. In the early twentieth century, eastern European Jewish immigrants, accustomed to the dark ryes of their homeland, readily adopted American pumpernickel into their repertoire of breads; subsequently, dark rye loaves have been labeled "Jewish pumpernickel." Most of these versions contain some wheat flour for a lighter texture and porous crumb. To impart a deeper color without the lengthy baking time, they also mix in a little molasses, caramel, cocoa powder, or instant coffee. In essence, American pumpernickel came to mean a dark rye bread with added bran. "Jewish rye," made without the bran, is even lighter.

Traditional German *schwarzbrot* has a thin crust, but Jews typically prefer a thicker, chewy crust, which is achieved by glazing the bread with cornstarch or egg white. German pumpernickel is generally baked in a pan, while Jewish versions are typically free-form. Some bakers add caraway seeds. Raisins, an unheard-of addition in Germany, are common in American pumpernickel, their sweetness offsetting the slight sourness of the bread and the tanginess of a schmear of cream cheese. Pumpernickel was also commonly eaten with pickled herring and egg salad. The dark loaves became staples of Jewish bakeries, delis, and Jewish restaurants. In the 1970s, pumpernickel even became a popular bagel flavor.

A marble rye, immortalized in a 1996 episode of *Seinfeld* in which Jerry steals the last bakery loaf from a little old lady, is a New York loaf of half light rye swirled with half pumpernickel.

(See also Bread and Rye)

PUMPKIN

The pumpkin, a large, orange fruit, has been widely cultivated throughout the Americas for about six thousand years and was among the first New World foods introduced to Europeans by Native Americans. Still, it is a much-neglected plant in much of Europe and North America, where it is primarily relegated to pies. Yet the orange-colored flesh with an earthy overtone offers many culinary possibilities: It can be baked, boiled, steamed, or stuffed. The best varities for cooking are small, pale, and sweet, especially the cheese pumpkin, sugar pumpkin, and peanut pumpkin.

In the beginning of the sixteenth century, Sephardim and Italian Jews began selling pumpkins and adopted them into their pantry earlier and more vigor-

ously than their neighbors. Therefore, the presence of pumpkin in early Mediterranean dishes is usually a sign of Sephardic influence. Sephardim and Italians use it to make soups, stews, puddings, jams, cakes, pancakes, and pastry fillings. Toasted pumpkin seeds (*pivites*) are a popular Sephardic snack.

This autumn vegetable is used for various traditional Rosh Hashanah, Sukkot, and Hanukkah dishes. Sephardim from the eastern Mediterranean enjoy it in pancakes; Syrians tend to prefer their pumpkin pancakes spicy (*kibbet yatkeen*), while Sephardim from Turkey and Greece generally favor them slightly sweet (*bimuelos de kalavasa*). The sweet version is traditional on Rosh Hashanah, as the Arabic word for pumpkin is *qara*, which is a homonym for the Hebrew for "called out," denoting that our good deeds should be called out at this time of judgment. The seeds also symbolize fruitfulness and fertility. It is also used to fill pastries, such as empanadas, and mixed into bread dough for *bollos*. Bukharans enjoy *oshee tos kadoo* (stuffed pumpkin) for the Sabbath and Sukkot. *Sopa de gra y chimra* (pumpkin and chickpea soup) is a traditional Rosh Hashanah and Sukkot dish in Morocco. Libyans make a pumpkin dip (*qara*) popular in *mezzes* (appetizer assortments). The Bene Israel of Mumbai use pumpkin to make a curried stew and a pudding-like confection. Pumpkin fritters (*fritelle di zucca*) are a favorite Italian Hanukkah treat. Pumpkin-filled ravioli (*tortelli de zucca*) is a signature dish of Italian Jews.

PUPIK

Birds, lacking teeth, cannot chew and, instead, many species process their food before it enters the intestines by passing it through organs. From the crop, where food is held, it moves in small portions into the proventriculus (glandular stomach) and then into the ventriculus (gizzard or muscular stomach) on the left side of the ventral abdomen; this organ is called *korkeban* in Hebrew and in Eastern Yiddish, from the word for bellybutton, *pupik* or *pipik*. The Western Yiddish word for bellybutton is *nopl*. Birds, of course, do not have navels.

The gizzard of most seed-eating birds and insectivores is more muscular than those of meat eaters, as grains and insects are harder to disintegrate than flesh. Many birds ingest small stones that make their way to the gizzard to help mash the food. In some birds, including all of the kosher ones, the inside of the gizzard is lined with a tough, thick, yellow keratinoid membrane secreted by the mucosa, which allows the gizzard to withstand the impact of grains and stones. Other birds, including the cuckoo and most birds of prey, have a soft nonkeratinoid inner layer. If this lining (*kis* in Hebrew) cannot be peeled off from the muscular part of the gizzard by hand, it is a sign of a nonkosher bird. Since the *pupik* is a muscular organ, it has to be simmered for an extended period, such as in a fricassee or soup, in order to become edible. A *pupiklech* is a dish of chicken gizzards.

A *Moishe Pupik* is a person who is annoyingly self-important.

PURI

Puri is a flatbread made with wheat flour.

Origin: Georgia

In western Georgia, the predominant grain is cornmeal, while in the eastern part of the country, wheat is the more important grain. Georgians from the east eat prodigious amounts of wheat bread called *puri* (from the Hindi deep-fried flatbread, *puri*, from the Sanskrit *purah*, "cake"). There are three main forms of Georgian *puri*: *dedas puri*, *shotis puri*, and lavash. *Dedas puri*, literally meaning "mother's bread," is a slightly chewy round loaf, with a hole punched in the center to prevent it from ballooning and forming a pocket. These large loaves are ubiquitous at Georgian dinners. The same dough is also shaped into long ovals—similar to a flattened baguette but denser and moister inside—called *shotis puri*, *shoti*, and *tonis puri* (oven bread), which are typically enjoyed for breakfast. The shape was purportedly developed so that the loaves could fit inside the high boots of Georgian warriors as they rode off to battle. Lavash is a widespread, very thin, Eurasian bread. In addition, *puri* dough is formed into a rectangle to make *kutkhani*; for *khachapuri* the dough is filled with cheese or beans.

Georgian wheat breads are primarily cooked on the inner walls of a *toné*, a circular clay oven with a large hole on the top similar to the Persian *tanur*. Usually the outside of the oven is surrounded by wood like a barrel, or by tiles with insulating material in between. In the countryside, bread is typically baked in a small family *toné*, usually in large batches to last several days. In the cities, professional bakers supply the population with fresh loaves daily. Georgian bread dough is a basic soft mixture of flour, water, salt, and starter combined in a *vartsli* (trough). The starter imparts a tang to the loaves. While the dough is rising, a roaring fire is lit inside the oven, which is typically ignited with dried grape vine trimmings. When the black soot on the inner walls of the oven turns white, indicating that the temperature is ready, the fire is covered and a dampened burlap rag is rubbed along the interior to clean it. The baker (*mepuri*) forms pieces of dough into rounds or long strips, pats one side three or four times with salted water, and slaps the moistened side against the interior of the oven until the entire wall is covered—the curved surface of the oven forms curved loaves. Only one side of the loaves touches the oven, so all *puri* loaves are relatively flat.

The intense heat of the *toné* leaves the breads moist on the inside, slightly crisp on the exterior, and distinctively smoky in flavor. At informal meals, the bread is simply pulled apart by the diners, but in formal settings it is cut into two-inch pieces for serving. Bread is commonly accompanied with fresh herbs, including basil, cilantro, and tarragon.

Georgian Jews use the standard puris for their Sabbath and holiday loaves. At a wedding, Georgian Jews feature a *kabaluli*, a special loaf enriched with eggs and sprinkled with sugar; the bread is a symbol of the bride, wishing that she should be sweet and the source of happiness.

(See also Bread and Khachapuri)

This 18th century French Purim plate depicts a scene from the Book of Esther—Mordechai being led on horseback by Haman. The plate was used for mishloach manot (*sending gifts of food*).

PURIM

In 539 BCE, Cyrus conquered Babylon and the Jews suddenly found themselves part of the Persian Empire. It was under one of his successors that the Purim story transpired; the episode is recounted in the *Megillat Ester* (Scroll of Esther), the last of the twenty-four books of the Bible. After King Ahasuerus (Artaxerxes) promoted Haman to the position of vizier, Haman conspired to exterminate the entire Jewish population of the Persian Empire. Haman cast lots to determine the most propitious day, choosing the thirteenth of the month of Adar. The plot backfired when it turned out that the new queen, Esther, was Jewish, and the villain and his allies were roundly routed.

In response to Haman's plot to annihilate the Jews, their descendants commemorate the day after Haman's defeat—the day the Jews "gained relief" and celebrated their survival, the fourteenth of Adar (usually in March)—through physical enjoyment and riotous celebration on the holiday of Purim (lots). Because the fighting continued in the Persian capital of Shushan (Susa) for an additional day, any city that possessed a surrounding wall at the time of Joshua, such as Shushan or Jerusalem, celebrates on the fifteenth of Adar, which is called Shushan Purim. In leap years, when a second month of Adar is added, Purim is celebrated in the second Adar.

There are four central Purim rituals: reading the Scroll of Esther; sending *mishloach manot* (gifts of foods) to friends; giving money to the poor; and eating a *seudah* (feast). Children, as well as many adults, dress up in costumes, a custom that originated in Italy at the end of the fifteenth century, inspired by the masked entertainers of the commedia dell'arte.

Food is essential in fulfilling the two rituals held on Purim day: The Purim *seudah* and *mishloach manot*. In addition, alcohol is liberally enjoyed, a practice most strongly disapproved of during the rest of the year. The Purim *seudah* is traditionally held on Purim afternoon.

Purim is a holiday on which no divine miracle occurred and the Scroll of Esther is the only book of the Bible not containing the name of God; therefore, the sense of the mysterious and hidden extends even to the food. Many Purim dishes in both Sephardic and Ashkenazic communities involve a filling, alluding to the many intrigues, secrets, and surprises unfolding in the Purim story. Both Sephardic and Ashkenazic communities eat chickpeas (*nahit* and *arbes* in Yid-

dish) or fava beans (*bub* in Yiddish), the legumes alluding to a tradition that Esther, in order to keep kosher, ate only vegetarian foods while living in the king's palace. Other Holiday foods, however, often vary widely from community to community. Due to the similarity in the Yiddish word for poppy seeds (*mohn*) and the name of the villain Haman (in Hebrew, *Hamohn*), poppy seeds emerged as traditional Ashkenazic Purim fare. Some people eat turkey (*tarnegol hodu*, "Indian chicken," in Hebrew) as Europeans initially thought the bird came from India—they associated the turkey with Purim because Ahasuerus ruled "from Hodu [India] to Kush." In addition, Purim falls at a time in the year before the spring births, when historically there was not an excess of animals, and most of the early spring vegetables had not emerged, so the focus frequently was on baked goods and dried legumes.

Kabbalists compare Purim to another, seemingly unrelated holiday—Yom Kippur. The similarity in names was seen as no coincidence and a parallel was drawn between the lots of Purim cast by Haman and the lots of Yom Kippur cast in the Temple to decide the scapegoat. Foods served on Yom Kippur eve, especially kreplach, became traditional Ashkenazic Purim fare. In addition, triangular foods, including kreplach and hamantaschen (associating Haman with a three-cornered hat arose in the late seventeenth century), became prevalent.

A Sephardic Purim *seudah* might feature small breads or *foulares* (pastries filled with long-cooked eggs), *sambusak* (meat turnovers), stewed chicken, and rice with chickpeas or nuts. An Ashkenazic Purim feast traditionally begins with a long braided challah called *koyletsh*, symbolizing the rope on which Haman was hung. Traditional Ashkenazic fare includes kreplach in chicken soup, knishes, pirogen, stuffed roast chicken or veal breast, stuffed cabbage, and tzimmes. Persians feature sweet rice (*shirin polo*), *gundi* (meatballs), *kuku* (omelets), and halva. Other Purim specialties include Iraqi chickpea turnovers (*sambusak el tawa*), Venetian spinach pasta roll (*rotolo di pasta con spinaci*), Romanian sweetened chickpeas (*tzimmes nahit*), and Ukrainian buckwheat and noodles (*kasha varnishkes*).

The most common Purim foods are sweets and every community enjoys at least one traditional sugary pastry. This emphasis on sweets is based on the very nature of the holiday; sugary foods are a symbolic way to wish for a "good lot" or, in other words, a sweet future. Muslims refer to Purim as *Id-al-Sukkar* (the Sugar Holiday). Middle Eastern Jews traditionally serve similar items on Purim and Hanukkah "to connect miracle with miracle," linking the physical salvation of the Jews by Mordechai and Esther to the spiritual salvation by the Maccabees. In many Sephardic communities on Hanukkah and Purim, members of wealthier families brought trays of these sweets to less fortunate households.

The underlying theme of most Purim pastries is shape—a person symbolically erases Haman's name by eating a pastry formed to represent part of the villainous prime minister's clothing or anatomy, most notably his pocket, hat, foot, or ear. The most widespread of these Purim pastries are deep-fried strips of dough known by an assortment of local names, most meaning "Haman's ears," including *oznei Haman* in Hebrew, *orejas de Haman* in Ladino, and *orecchi de Aman* in Italy.

Sephardim enjoy syrup-drenched pastries such as baklava, *kanafeh* (shredded wheat pastries), *travados* (pastry horns), and *ma'amoul* (filled cookies). For Purim breakfast, many Sephardic families have a custom of preparing *revanadas de parida* (French toast), for the occasion renamed "Queen Esther's toast." Iraqis bake *hadgi badah* (cardamom-almond cookies) and Italians prepare *buricche* (puff pastry turnovers). Bukharans deep-fry dumplings called *samsa*. Grain halvas are popular throughout central Asia, while Greeks enjoy a similar semolina pudding known as *pyota*. Ashkenazim make hamantaschen (tricornered filled pastries), *mohn kichlach* (poppy seed cookies), *kindli* (filled yeast pastries), *lekach* (honey cake), *teiglach* (honey-cooked balls of dough), and strudel. Alsatians and some Germans make gingerbread men (*lebkuchen Hamohns*) and cut fruit *fluden* into triangles. Romanians prepare a rice kugel with raisins. Poles drizzle an unfilled babka with syrup laced with rum, whiskey, or brandy, creating a cake called *shikkera babka* ("drunken"), which is akin to baba au rhum.

(See also Haman's Ear, Hamantasch, and Mischloach Manot)

PURIM KATAN

The Purim of Persia is not the only one on the Jewish calendar. There has long been a widespread practice that whenever a community or individual was saved from eminent peril, the anniversary of that deliverance was commemorated with a special Purim Katan (literally "small Purim").

Although personal celebrations date back to the Bible, the first known community-wide Purim Katan was instituted in 1039 by Shmuel Hanagid, vizier and military commander of Granada, which was held in commemoration of his escape from an assassination attempt, as well as his victory in a war with the fanatical Almeria. In response, the vizier's family along with the entire city of Granada celebrated a Purim on the first day of the month of Elul. More than a hundred community Purims have subsequently been instituted across the globe. In some instances, the Purim Katan was commemorated only once or for only a few years; in other cases, the observation continued for centuries. In some instances, communities have established multiple Purim Katans, such as the town of Ancona, Italy, which memorialized four such acts of deliverance during a hundred-year period.

Some Purim Katans were established in commemoration of a community's escape from a natural disaster, such as an earthquake or a fire, but more often than not they were in response to man-made tribulations, notably wars, riots, and blood libels (false claims of Jews using blood in religious rituals, frequently resulting in pogroms and expulsions). Many of these near disasters are reminiscent of the original Purim story. Cairo, Egypt, observed a Purim Katan on the twenty-eighth of Adar, the day in 1524 on which the recently appointed governor of Egypt, Ahmed Pasha, planned to massacre the Jews of his realm. Instead, the evil governor was assassinated by forces loyal to Sultan Suleiman. Frankfort, Germany, memorialized the twentieth of Adar with Purim Vintz, the day in 1614 on which a virulent anti-Semite named Vincenz (hence Vintz) Fettmilch, who was preparing to lead a mob against the Jewish quarters, was executed by the Emperor. The Jewish community on the island of Rhodes actually celebrated a double Purim on the fourteenth of Adar because on that day in 1840, the sultan removed the governor of the island, who had instigated a blood libel against its Jewish residents.

The day preceding a Purim Katan is customarily observed with a fast and the day itself is observed by reciting special prayers, giving charity to the poor, holding a festive meal (*seudah*) with many of the dishes traditional on Purim, and, in some instances, holding a public reading of a special megillah and sending *mishloach manot* (gifts of foods).

Q

QUADRUCCI

Quadrucci are small egg-pasta squares.

Origin: northern Italy

Other names: *quadrettini.*

After the concept of pasta reached mainland Italy around the thirteenth century, one of the first shapes was small squares named *quadrucci* after the flat, square tiles used for paving floors. Unlike southern Italy, where semolina pasta was widespread, Italy's north was not favorable for growing durum wheat, so pasta was made from common wheat flour and bound with eggs. Since the egg dough was too soft to shape into forms, it was always flat.

These small squares are primarily added to soups, giving textural contrast and extra body to light broths and bean soups. In the spring, green peas are sometimes featured in the soups. *Quadrucci in brodo*, pasta squares in either chicken or beef broth, is traditional Sabbath and holiday fare. Fresh spinach is sometimes added to the soup to make *quadrucci coi spinaci*, a dish that begins the meal following the fast of Yom Kippur.

(See also Pasta)

QUAIL

At the end of the eleventh century, Rabbi Menachem ben Machir of Ratisbon (Regensburg) in Bavaria, Germany, composed a still-very-popular Sabbath song, "*Mah Yedidut*" (How Beloved), with the refrain "To delight in delicacies, in fatted fowl [goose], and *slav*, and fish." The reference to *slav* is most certainly an allusion to one of the foods eaten by the Israelites in the wilderness of Sinai after leaving Egypt. Unlike many other animals that make a brief appearance in the Bible, practical unanimity exists as to the identity of the *slav*. Jewish tradition, supported by Semitic cognates (*slawi* in Arabic), depictions on ancient Egyptian murals, and other historical accounts, designate the *slav* (from *shalah*, "to be secure" or "tranquil," connoting the sluggishness of its flight) as the quail.

The Talmud relates that there are four kinds of *slav*: "*shichli* [grouse], *kivli* [partridges], *pisyuni* [pheasant], and *slav* [quail], with *sichli* being the most superior and *slav* the most inferior." The Talmud's perception of game birds may have been based upon size rather than the quality of the flesh, as each quail possesses very little meat. Still, many gourmets consider grouse, with its flavorful, dark meat, the choicest of all game birds. Birds belonging to the genus *Galliformes*, which includes the chicken as well as many game birds (partridge, pheasant, and grouse), are distinguished by a stocky body, a small head, and short wings. As a result, their flight is rapid, yet low to the ground. The quail is the smallest member and is also known as the common quail, Mediterranean quail, migratory quail, pharaoh quail, and, in England, "wet-my-lips," a reference to the male's call.

Many ancient Greek and Roman authorities—including Aristotle, Galen, Lucretius, and Philo—mentioned poisoning by quail, a condition now called coturnism, which is possibly produced by a genetic susceptibility. Various medieval Sephardic physicians, including Maimonides, noted similar accounts. Except for quail, no migratory bird exhibits any toxicity, and the only quails that are toxic—and toxicity only occurs occasionally—are those that use the western flyway during the spring northward migration. What transforms a harmless quail into a toxic delicacy is its winter diet, possibly the seeds of *Stachys annua*, a member of the mint family. This could account for the biblical account of some Israelites dying after eating them.

Quails were not indigenous to the lands of the Ashkenazim and, indeed, some groups will not eat them as quail lack an established tradition (*mesorah*) in Europe. Mizrachim and Sephardim, on the other hand, have a long-established tradition of eating quail and enjoy, on occasion, both the birds and eggs. In any case, kosher quail is difficult if not impossible to find commercially in either Israel or the United States, although some slaughterers will prepare it on demand. In addition, a few select kosher restaurants feature quail.

QUAJADO

Quajado is an egg and vegetable casserole.
Origin: Spain
Other names: Greek: *sfoungato*; Ladino: *cuajada, cuazbado, kwazado*; Spanish: *cuajada*.

Among the signature and enduring features of Sephardic cuisine is the combination of eggs and vegetables, frequently with the addition of cheese. Indeed, the Spanish Inquisition considered these dishes a sign of practicing Judaism and preparing them could lead to imprisonment. Initially, the mixture was fried in a skillet atop a fire, the dish known as *fritada*. For those Sephardim with a home oven, the baked *fritada* became known as *quajado*, meaning "coagulated" in Ladino. *Quajados* were a particular favorite among the Sephardim of Rhodes.

These baked casseroles typically contain a smaller amount of egg and larger amount of cheese than a *fritada*, concentrating on the vegetables—especially spinach, eggplant, leek, tomato, and zucchini. In Turkey, the eggplant version is known as *almodrote* or *almodroti*, which also became a Ladino term for hodgepodge. Most versions contain a combination of soft cheese and hard cheese—the soft cheese imparts a custardy texture and the hard cheese provides flavor and saltiness. The addition of bread crumbs or potatoes, which can be omitted, reflects a Turkish influence and results in a firmer-textured dish that holds together better when it is removed from the pan. Soaked crumbled matza is frequently added during Passover. Besides vegetables, *quajado* can contain ground meat (*quajado de carne*) or cooked chicken (*quajado de gayina*).

Quajados are popular for Passover. A version in which ground meat is substituted for the cheese is called *megina* and it is a frequent sight at a Greek or Turkish Seder. A leek or spinach *quajado* appears at some Sephardic Rosh Hashanah dinners as one of the symbolic foods of the *Yehi Ratzones* (May It Be Your Will), a Seder-like ceremony featuring various foods representing a good omen for the ensuing year. Cheese versions, served hot or cold, are popular at a Sabbath *desayuno* (brunch) and for the meal to break the fast after Yom Kippur.

(See also Almodrote, Fritada, and Sfoungato)

SEPHARDIC EGG AND VEGETABLE CASSEROLE (*QUAJADO DE LEGUMBRES*)

6 TO 8 SERVINGS [DAIRY]

¼ cup olive or vegetable oil
1 large onion, chopped
6 large eggs, lightly beaten
1 cup (5 ounces) farmer, pot, or creamy feta cheese; or ½ cup farmer or pot cheese and ½ cup feta
1 cup (4 ounces) grated kashkaval, Cheddar, Gruyère, Muenster, or Parmesan cheese
¼ cup chopped fresh flat-leaf parsley or dill, or ½ teaspoon ground nutmeg
About 1 teaspoon table salt or 2 teaspoons kosher salt
Ground black pepper to taste or about ½ teaspoon cayenne
5 to 6 cups vegetables, such as 3 pounds sliced and cooked leeks, 2 pounds chopped spinach, 3 pounds seeded and chopped tomatoes, or 2 pounds grated and squeezed zucchini
Yogurt (optional)

1. Preheat the oven to 350°F. Oil one 9-inch square baking dish or 11-by-7-inch baking dish.

2. In a large skillet, heat the oil over medium heat. Add the onion and sauté until soft and translucent, 5 to 10 minutes.

3. In a large bowl, combine the eggs, cheeses, parsley, salt, and pepper. Stir in the vegetables and onions.

4. Spoon the mixture into the prepared baking dish. Bake until set in the center and golden brown, about 40 to 50 minutes. Serve warm or at room temperature. If desired, top each wedge with a dollop of yogurt.

QUINCE

Quince is a member of the Rosaceae family; its fruit resembles a combination of two relatives, apples and pears. It is a temperate weather tree, requiring a cold period to yield fruit. In the areas in which it thrives, it is a beloved part of the pantry. Today, there are two primary varieties: the oblong perfumed quince and the pear-shaped pineapple quince, which was developed by Luther Burbank. The exterior of the fruit is lumpy and covered with a grayish fuzz, which is sometimes removed before the fruit arrives on the supermarket shelves. As quinces mature, the greenish skin turns a pale yellow color with blotches and the fruit develops an intense musky aroma. The quince's fragrance is highly regarded—the Talmud prescribed a benediction be recited over the aroma of the quince and the etrog, the only fruits to require such a distinction. Some cultivated quinces, however, lack the characteristic intense aroma.

The quince is a native of the Caucasus and was first cultivated in Mesopotamia, long before the apple. Many scholars believe that quince is the *tapuach* of Song of Songs. Among the quince's names in the Talmud are *asphargal* and *p'rish*. The Jerusalem Talmud discussed these names: "Why are *asarpharlnin* called *p'rishin* [from the Hebrew meaning "set aside/separated"]? Because there is no tree [species of fruit] *parush* [set aside] for the cooking pot [that is only edible when cooked] except that kind." Indeed, quinces have a hard, granular texture and intense astringency, so they are not eaten raw. The pale yellow flesh becomes pink and sweet when cooked; if cooked in an aluminum pan, it becomes deep red.

The peel and core of quinces have a high pectin content; honey and acid, in the form of vinegar or verjuice (unripe grape juice), were added to the quince peel and core, creating a solid gel and thus producing the first jams and jellies. (Later sugar and lemon juice were added instead.) Quince was not only the first fruit preserve—until relatively recently, it was the most common and widespread type of fruit preserve. The word for marmalade comes from the Portuguese word for quince, *marmelo*, because the original marmalade was made from quince. Marmalade reached Britain during the fifteenth century and the British eventually began experimenting with other fruits to substitute for quinces, replacing them with oranges in the seventeenth century. During the early twentieth century, quinces as well as preserves made from them lost favor in the West to the point of disappearing in many places, but both the fruit and the preserves remain very popular in the Middle East.

Some cultures use quinces in cooking without honey or sugar; the quinces are cooked with meat, especially lamb and poultry, to add a touch of sweetness, or quinces are poached and served as a side dish to meats. Unlike most other fruits, quince flesh does not break down during cooking, but rather remains firm, making it ideal for slow-simmering in compotes,

stews, and pilaus. The addition of quinces to stews became popular in the region extending from Spain through Morocco to central Asia.

Quinces were an important part of Sephardic cuisine from the onset. An anonymous Andalusian cookbook of the thirteenth century included a recipe for "Sarafjaliyya," a lamb or veal stew simmered with peeled and quartered quince and verjuice. The same cookbook also recorded "A Dish of Chicken or Partridge with Quince or Apple." A third quince recipe in the book was "Quince Paste," made from peeled, seeded, and chopped quinces simmered with honey or sugar "until it takes the form of a paste." Similar quince dishes remain a part of the Sephardic repertoire today.

A traditional part of many Sephardic homes has been a *cucharera*, a decorated silver bowl with small silver spoons, which would be filled with *dulce de bimbrillo* (quince paste) or another *dulce* (sweet paste) and offered to guests, who would take a spoonful, recite a blessing or wish, sample the preserves, and take a sip of cold water.

Quinces ripen around Rosh Hashanah and are traditional Rosh Hashanah and Sukkot fare among Sephardim and many Mizrachim. Georgians serve poached quinces topped with whipped cream (*kompot iz aivi*). During quince season, Sephardim frequently cook them with chicken for Sabbath dinner or simply poach them in sugar syrup (*bimbriyo* or *membrillo*). Bukharans add quinces to their classic rice dish, *plov*. Persian Jews commonly serve stuffed quinces (*dolma bay*) on the Sabbath and Sukkot. In Greek and Iraqi communities, quince preserves, poached quinces, or candied quinces are enjoyed on Rosh Hashanah instead of apples and honey. Turks poach them in pomegranate juice, combining two traditional Rosh Hashanah foods in one dish (*ayva tatlisi*). Italians poach quinces in wine (*cotogne in giulebbe*) and serve them at the meal to break the fast of Yom Kippur and on special occasions with sponge cake. Candied quince is a beloved Passover treat. Some Mizrachim, especially Kurds, and some Sephardim incorporate grated, peeled raw quince into their Passover charoset.

(See also Charoset, Dulce, and Hilu)

R

RADISH

Radishes are edible roots of the Brassicaceae family with varying amounts of pungency. There are numerous varieties of radishes in three basic categories: table (red) radishes, black radishes, and Asian (white) radishes. Horseradish, despite its name, is not a real radish.

The most familiar radishes in the West today, only developed in the early eighteenth century, are the small globular red-skinned types. They are variously called table radish, European radish, spring radish, and, in Hebrew, *tznonit*.

The most ancient type of radish and the one consumed by people for most of history is the black radish, also known as winter radish and, in Hebrew, *tznon*, from the root "to be sharp/pointed." Although some black radishes actually have a sooty exterior, many are violet, tan, or white in color as well as round, oval, or cylindrical in shape, the latter sometimes stretching up to a foot in length. Whatever the shape or exterior color, the interior is ivory and crisp. Currently, the most popular member of the black radish family is the Round Black Spanish variety, which is shaped like a large beet and has a black or purple-brown exterior. Black radishes are larger and more pungent, and have a much longer shelf life, than the red varieties. Black radishes are predominantly eaten raw; they are sometimes salted, particularly large roots, to mellow their bite and remove excess water.

Black radishes, probably native to the area between the Mediterranean and the Caspian Sea, were one of the earliest cultivated crops; they have been eaten in the Mediterranean area since the dawn of recorded history. Radishes reached Egypt by at least 2800 BCE. The seeds of some varieties subsequently provided the country with its main source of oil until the medieval period. When one Talmudic rabbi wanted to limit the fuel for the Sabbath lights exclusively to olive oil, another sage asked, "What will the inhabitants of Alexandria do who have only radish oil?" According to Herodotus, radishes were one of the primary foods of the workers building the pyramids. Although radishes are not mentioned in the Bible, by biblical times Jews were certainly eating them. Black radishes were generally a seasonal item, available during the autumn and winter; they were unable to withstand the heat of the summer and continued to grow until killed by the ground freezing. The Talmud cited as a sign of the affluence of Rabbi Judah Ha'Nasi that "lettuce [typically spring and summer produce], chate melon [a late-summer and early-autumn plant], and [black] radishes were not absent from his table either in summer or winter." The Talmud continues, "Radish helps the food to dissolve, lettuce helps the food to be digested, chate melon makes the intestines expand." In many cultures, radishes have long been considered beneficial to health.

Following the collapse of the Roman Empire, radishes disappeared from European records until the thirteenth century, except in rabbinic literature. One reason for the constant presence of the radish in Jewish sources is its status as the archetype of a *devar charif* (sharp food)—if one cuts a cold radish with a cold meat knife, the entire root cannot be eaten with dairy because, as the Talmud explains, "the sharpness of the radish assisted with [the friction of] the knife in the meat's absorption into the radish."

Radishes endure in many forms of Jewish cooking. Sephardim typically add them to a mixed salad. Moroccans sometimes mix them into an orange salad. Bukharans add black radishes to stews and soups, such as *lagman* (meat-and-vegetable soup served over noodles). Yemenites cook meat-stuffed radishes and mix grated raw radishes with tahini (sesame seed paste).

It was among northeastern Europeans, who suffered from a dearth of vegetables, that radishes commonly served as the headliner and sometimes, with black bread, constituted "a poor person's dinner." The crisp, sharp, white flesh was used in salads, added to tzimmes, and even cooked with honey and gin-

From the early Talmudic period, the most common radish available and used in Jewish cooking has been the black radish.

ger into preserves for a favorite Passover treat. Since black radishes can be stored through the winter and red ones can be planted in late winter and mature in about twenty-two days, some eastern Europeans used radish leaves or roots for the *karpas* or *chazeret* (a second green different from that used for the *maror*) of the Passover Seder. Raw radishes with sour cream (*retachlich mit smeteneh*) are popular on Shavuot and during the summer.

In particular, a characteristic dish of Lithuania, northern Poland, and Ukraine was grated black radish, schmaltz, onion, salt, and pepper, sometimes raw and sometimes sautéed, known as *schvartze retach mit schmaltz* or simply *retachlich*. A little grated carrot was sometimes added for a touch of sweetness and color. Sholem Aleichem, in his 1909 short story "Tevye Goes to Palestine," included this line recited by Tevye: "Anything could have happened; maybe he has settled all his accounts and left us altogether—moved to the place where black radishes and chicken fat are not eaten?"

In that stretch of eastern Europe, Jews of the nineteenth century could not imagine a world without *retachlich*. According to a legend, radishes were a favorite food of the Maccabees and, therefore, radishes flavored with schmaltz became a traditional eastern European Hanukkah dish. During the winter, *retachlich* was a regular Sabbath lunch appetizer and salad, served with bread, as well as a favorite garnish for chopped liver.

In his biography, *An American in the Making: The Life Story of an Immigrant* (New York, 1917), Marcus

Eli Ravage included a comment on food in America in contrast and comparison to food in his native Romania, marveling that items considered expensive and, in Europe, reserved for the Sabbath were enjoyed by Americans on a daily basis. He recounted, "I remember writing home about it the next day and telling the folks that they might think I was exaggerating, but that it was literally true, all the same, that in New York every night was Friday night and every day was Saturday, as far as food went, anyway. Why, they even had twists of plain rye bread, to say nothing of rice-and-raisins (which is properly a Purim dish) and liver paste and black radish."

The tables of some old-fashioned Jewish restaurants in America were customarily preset with a bowl of sliced black radishes mixed with chicken fat and a plate of bread for the customers to nosh on while waiting for their orders. However, as both the black radish and schmaltz lost favor in the mid-twentieth century, this once-classic dish practically vanished from most Jewish homes. Still, almost the entire American black radish crop is sold immediately before Passover and Rosh Hashanah, to make traditional Ashkenazic dishes.

(See also Eingemacht and Schmaltz)

RAHAT LOKUM

In 1777, a young Turkish confectioner named Ali Muhiddin Bekir moved from his native town of Kastamonu near the Black Sea to Istanbul and established a shop in the center of the city. Not content

Translucent jellied candies commonly referred to as Turkish delight are a staple for Jewish holidays and festive occasions in Turkey and much of the Middle East.

with the standard hard candies and almond pastes, he developed a new, softer, translucent treat based on earlier Persian and Turkish jellied candies. The new confections became known in Turkish as *rahat lokum* (giving rest to the throat), and are commonly called *lokum*, *halkum*, and, in Arabic, *malban* (from the Arabic for "milk"). Syrians refer to them simply as *raha*. The confection quickly became a favorite of the sultan's court and Bekir was appointed chief confectioner. The jellied cubes went on to become one of the most well-known and beloved Middle Eastern confections, and they are typically accompanied with bitter Turkish coffee. Around 1872, an Englishman traveling in Turkey sent several boxes of the confection back home, calling it Turkish Delight, a name that stuck.

The confection seems to have originally included flour as the binding agent and *pezmez* (grape molasses) as the sweetener, but an elderly Bekir, always abreast of new developments, in the mid-nineteenth century substituted the new cornstarch and beet sugar to fill those roles, creating the contemporary form of *lokum*. The candy is enhanced with rose water, and later various other popular flavorings, notably orange, strawberry, vanilla, and mint. It can be plain or with *fistikh* (pistachio), *bademli* (almond), or *cevizli* (walnut). *Lokum* is usually cut into one-inch cubes, but the warm syrup can also be shaped on confectioners' sugar into a log and cut into round slices.

Rahat lokum was adopted by Jews throughout the Ottoman Empire from Morocco to Romania and became a common sight at celebrations. It is enjoyed not only plain, but also in pastries. For Simchat Torah, Romanians used the candy as a filling for strudel and on Purim they used it as a filling for hamantaschen, practices continued today by some Israeli bakers. *Lokum* is widely sold throughout Israel.

RAISIN

From its home somewhere in southern Transcaucasia or in southwest Asia not far from Mount Ararat, the vinifera grape spread early in human history across much of Europe, Asia, and North Africa. Around four thousand years ago, probably somewhere in the Levant, people first discovered a way to preserve perishable seasonal grapes by drying them. Perhaps humans first recognized the possibility after stumbling upon grapes that had dried naturally on the vine. Not willing to sacrifice resources, they sampled the dried fruit and found it to be sweeter and more transportable than fresh fruit. Each year, some of the grape crop was spread over flat wicker baskets in the sun to dry, or the grapes were pressed into clusters and dried as cakes, keeping the interior raisins softer.

The world's three most popular raisins are Muscat, sultana, and currants. Muscat is a large, sweet, smoky-flavored black raisin with seeds, perhaps the oldest domesticated raisin variety. Sultana or sultanieh is a small, amber-colored, rich, pearish-flavored seedless raisin native to Turkey or Iran; the grapes that they are made from are called Thompson seedless grapes in America—about 95 percent of American raisins, both dark and golden, are made from Thompson. Currants are very small raisins made from the tiny Black Corinth grape, also marketed fresh under the name champagne grape, a small seedless variety named after a city in Greece. They are also called Zante currants after Zakynthos (Zante), the third largest of the Ionian islands, where the dried fruit trade shifted in the early 1700s.

Raisins, *tzimukim* in Hebrew (from the root "to shrivel"), have been part of Jewish food from the onset of the Israelite nation; they were already mentioned in the Pentateuch in regard to the Nazerite—a person who made a vow of abstience, including from wine and any grape product. In the Diaspora, raisins became part of every form of Jewish cooking, especially foods connected with festivals. Phoenicians introduced the Muscat grape to Iberia and the Maghreb around 900 BCE and from the onset raisins made from them played a supporting role in Sephardic everyday fare as well. Jews maintained many of the vineyards in many Muslim countries and produced much of the raisins, exporting them to Muslim countries as well as Europe, where many Jewish merchants did the importing. The father of Dutch philosopher Baruch de Spinoza, a descendant of Portuguese Sephardim, was an importer of raisins, figs, and other Mediterranean fruits.

Raisins are commonly used in Sabbath foods to temper the vinegar added as a preservative, and are a popular feature of sweet-and-sour dishes. Raisins and pine nuts are the classic addition to vegetables and sauces of Italian and Levantine cuisines. Raisins are among the ingredients of the ubiquitous Indian ritual dish *malida* (a sweetened rice, coconut, and fruit dish) and the Yemenite Sabbath appetizer and snack *jaaleh*. Some Egyptians, Turks, and Yemenites add black raisins to the Passover charoset. In Turkey and the Balkans, they are used in rice pilaf and semolina puddings. In the Netherlands, they are added to pancakes and apple tarts. Moroccans hold a special ceremony called a *tufera* ("unbraiding" of the bride's hair) in which a bride unveils her trousseau several days before the wedding; before the ceremony, the groom sends her a tray with raisins, almonds, candies, a ribbon, and candles as symbols of sweetness and purity, and the snacks are enjoyed by the guests. Raisins, along with nuts and oil, remain the signature ingredients of baking of the secret Jews, descendants of Conversos, most of whom do not know of their Jewish roots, of the American Southwest.

Raisins were introduced to Christian Europe in the eleventh century by Crusaders returning from the Levant. With the emergence of the raisin trade in Europe from Spain and the Levant in the 1300s, raisins and currants became the most common dried fruit in Europe and a standard part of Ashkenazic cooking and culture; they were called *rozshinke* in Western Yiddish and *vaymperlekh* in Eastern Yiddish. If someone was disrespected, the Yiddish response was "*Iz mayn neshome den a rozshinke?*" (Is my soul a raisin?) Whereas dried plums, the other standard European dried fruit, were frequently made from locally grown fruit and were relatively economical, imported raisins were more expensive and were typically reserved for special occasions, such as the Sabbath and holidays. Germans and Galitzianers added them to tzimmes, kugels, stuffed cabbage, and numerous pastries. Around 1400, Germans began making raisin bread and eventually other Ashkenazim followed suit for Rosh Hashanah and Sukkot, adding raisins to provide extra sweetness to the holiday challah. Raisins paired with rice became a traditional Ashkenazic Purim dish.

In particular, Ashkenazim paired raisins with another biblical food, almonds. On the Sabbath before an Ashkenazic wedding, the groom celebrated with an *aufruf*—after his Torah reading, he was showered with raisins and nuts, a custom inspired by the numerology symbolizing a good marriage and fertility and sweetness. Raisins and nuts, along with a small amount of gelt (money), were the traditional Ashkenazic Hanukkah gifts for children. Arguably the best-known Yiddish folk song is "*Rozhinkess mit Mandlen*" (Raisins with Almonds) by Avrom Goldfaden, which includes

these lines: "Raisins and almonds are very sweet. My baby will grow up healthy and strong."

In northern Europe as well as parts of Asia, such as the Arabian Peninsula and India, grapes were unavailable for making wine. In addition, Conversos, in order to avoid Catholic sacramental wines, commonly made their own raisin wine, especially for Passover. In all these areas, the far-more-accessible raisin was often used instead of fresh fruit for making wine (*yayin tzemukim*). Raisin wine was also prevalent among Jews in America until the late nineteenth century, when kosher wine was first made from indigenous Concord grapes. In *Jewish Cookery* (Philadelphia, 1871), written in a period before kosher grape wine became available in America, Esther Levy noted, "It is usual on Friday for persons of our faith to use raisin wine to say the blessing of the sanctification." Sarah Rorer, in *Mrs. Rorer's New Cook Book* (Philadelphia, 1902), included a recipe for "Passover Raisin Wine" in a section entitled "A Group of Jewish Recipes."

Grape growing led to raisin production in modern Israel, and the majority of raisins in the country are homegrown. In the twentieth century, with the expansion of raisin production in California, Israel, and other locations, raisins became inexpensive items and part of everyday life, while remaining traditional in Sabbath and holiday fare.

(See also Grape and Wine)

RAISIN WINE (*YAYIN TZEMUKIM*)

ABOUT 1 QUART   [PAREVE]

  1 pound (3¼ cups) raisins, chopped
  About 3¼ cups water (an amount equal to the
    raisins)
  ½ cup plus 1 tablespoon (4 ounces) sugar (optional)

In a 2-quart jar or enamel crock, combine all the ingredients, cover with fine cheesecloth, and let stand in a cool place until the raisins rise to the surface, about 3 weeks. Drain, pressing the solids to extract all the moisture. Pour through a coffee filter 2 to 3 times until the liquid is clear.

RARICHA

Raricha is a flourless coconut cookie.
Origin: Morocco
Other names: *friandise á la noix de coco*
Among the delicacies traditional for the Moroccan holiday of Mimouna, held at the conclusion of Passover,

are flourless cookies made from coconut (*raricha del kokous*), and almond paste (*friandises de pate d'amandel amadines*) either baked or unbaked. Most of the treats for Mimouna are prepared during the week of Passover and, therefore, cannot contain flour. Home ovens were rare and the local bakery was unsuitable due to bread baked in it, so unbaked items were common. Today, baked versions are more common. The cookie dough is typically tinted with various food colorings.

MOROCCAN UNBAKED FLOURLESS COCONUT COOKIES (*RARICHA DEL KOKOUS*)

ABOUT 16 CONFECTIONS   [PAREVE]

1 cup (7 ounces) sugar
½ cup water
1 tablespoon fresh lemon juice
2 cups (5 ounces) shredded coconut
1 large egg white, lightly beaten
Any combination of drops of red, green, yellow, blue, or other food coloring
Additional sugar for rolling

1. In a medium saucepan, stir the sugar, water, and lemon juice over low heat until the sugar is dissolved. Stop stirring, increase the heat to medium, and cook until syrupy, about 10 minutes. Remove from the heat. Using a wooden spoon, stir in the coconut and egg white.

2. Work the dough with your hands until malleable. Divide into parts and tint each portion with a different food coloring.

3. Form into 1-inch balls, logs, or other shapes. Roll in the sugar to coat. If desired, transfer to paper liners.

RAS EL HANOUT

Ras el hanout is a complex spice mixture.
Origin: Morocco
Other names: *lacama.*

Ras el hanout (literally "head of the shop" in Arabic), referring to the best ingredients in the store, is a complex blend of spices used in both savory and sweet dishes. It is essential to the Moroccan Jewish kitchen, added to tagines and other stews and in *pastilla* (pigeon pie). It is also used to season a broth served to new mothers (*bouillon d'accoucher*). Because *ras el hanout* is so expensive, it is generally reserved for special occasions and is so strong it is not used in mild foods, such as fish.

Although recipes vary among shops and cooks, the basic formula contains at least ten ingredients including cardamon, cinnamon, ground ginger, nutmeg, black pepper, and turmeric. More elaborate blends may contain more than twenty spices and some a hundred, including allspice, anise, cassia, cloves, coriander, black cumin, fennel, galangal, grains of paradise, juniper, mace, mustard seeds, rosebuds, and sesame seeds. *La kama* is a simpler blend made from only a few spices, usually cinnamon, ground ginger, nutmeg, black pepper, and turmeric. Because some versions of *ras el hanout* made in stores contained the golden Spanish fly (its sale was only banned in Morocco in the 1990s) and to ensure that nothing else unkosher was inside, Jews always blended their own spices at home.

MOROCCAN SPICE MIXTURE (*RAS EL HANOUT*)

ABOUT ½ CUP   [PAREVE]

15 whole black peppercorns
6 to 8 whole allspice berries or ½ to 1 teaspoon ground allspice
6 to 8 cardamom pods or about 1 teaspoon ground cardamom
6 to 8 whole cloves or ½ to 1 teaspoon ground cloves
1 (3-inch) stick cinnamon or 1 teaspoon ground cinnamon
1 tablespoon ground ginger
1 teaspoon ground mace
1 teaspoon ground nutmeg
1 teaspoon ground turmeric
1 teaspoon fennel seeds, toasted
½ teaspoon anise seeds
Pinch of red chili flakes or ½ teaspoon cayenne
½ teaspoon sea salt (optional)

In a spice grinder, finely grind all the ingredients. Store the spice mixture in an airtight container in the refrigerator.

REGEL

Regel is a soup made from the feet (trotters) of lamb, sheep, calf, or cow.
Origin: Yemen
Other names: *marak regel, marak taimani, regale.*

Yemenites usually serve meat only for lunch—it is rarely offered for dinner as that is considered unhealthy. The exception is on the Sabbath and festivals, when meat is featured in stews and soups that were, until recently, left to simmer all day in a copper pot. Among the most popular is this traditional Yemenite Friday night dish made from a foot or shank, called *regel* (from the Hebrew for "foot"). When durum wheat berries are added to the soup and it is cooked overnight for Sabbath lunch, this dish becomes *harisa*. Since Yemenites prefer a spicy soup, they generally stir in a spoonful of *hilbeh* (fenugreek relish) or *s'chug* (chili paste).

Some Yemenites came to Israel beginning in the later nineteenth century and a few eventually set up small primitive shops, such as those in the Kerem Hataimanim (Yemenite Quarter) in Tel Aviv, that offered only one or a few spare Yemenite soups. Yemenite foot soup, commonly called *marak taimani* (Yemenite soup) in Israel, emerged to become a beloved element of Israeli culture.

Regel was historically made from a few very inexpensive ingredients and with a limited range of flavorings, and strongly seasoned with *hawaij* (Yemenite spice mixture). In Israel, vegetables are sometimes added to the basic soup. The principal ingredient, sliced into manageable pieces, is the foot or shank, which comes from the shin section of the leg. The flavor and texture is extracted during the long, slow cooking. As elsewhere in the Middle East, lamb has long been the predominant meat. However, since the Yemenites emigrated to the West, beef has gained popularity. *Regel* is served warm with hard-boiled eggs and *lachuach* (Yemenite skillet bread), *melawah* (Yemenite flaky bread), or *salufe* (round flatbread).

(See also Fatoot and Patsas)

❧ YEMENITE FOOT SOUP (*REGEL*)

6 TO 8 SERVINGS   [MEAT]

- 2 pounds calf's or beef feet or shank bones, cleaned and cut into 2-inch pieces (have your butcher cut the bones for you)
- ¼ cup fresh lemon juice (optional)
- 2 medium yellow onions, chopped
- ½ teaspoon ground turmeric
- 8 to 10 whole black peppercorns
- 8 cups cold water
- About 2 teaspoons table salt or 4 teaspoons kosher salt
- 1 to 3 teaspoons *hawaij* (Yemenite Spice Mixture, page 260)

1. Place the feet in a large pot, cover with cold water and, if using, add the lemon juice, which helps whiten the bones. Bring to a boil and boil until scum rises to the surface, about 10 minutes. Drain off and discard the water. Rinse the feet.

2. In a clean large pot, bring the bones, onions, turmeric, peppercorns, and 8 cups cold water to a boil. Reduce the heat to medium-low, partially cover, and simmer, occasionally skimming the scum from the surface, for at least 4 hours or up to 12 hours.

3. Remove any meat from the bones, shred, and add to the soup. Discard the bones. Add the salt and hawaij and simmer for about 5 minutes. The soup can be prepared ahead to this point and stored in the refrigerator for 2 days, then reheated.

RESHINKE

Reshinke is an Ashkenazic celebration cookie with two coils of dough forming a decorative border.
Origin: Poland
Other names: *chosnbroyt.*

Reshinke is an elaborate cookie prepared for a *brit* or wedding. It most likely derived from the Sephardic twisted cookies *reshicas/reshikas* and *roskitas* (little coils), perhaps traveling by way of Romania into Poland during the Ottoman domination of the Balkans. They were first mentioned in Kraków in 1595, in a community statute concerning weddings. A 1619 letter from Prague in regards to a *brit* reveals their presence in central Europe as well.

A *reshinke* consists of a large flat cookie surface, either circular or rectangular, with two intertwined twists of dough forming a decorative border. Typically, a whole almond was inserted in each section of the twist. Another strip of dough was used to spell out the words "*mazel tov*" in the center of the cookie. More elaborate versions also featured additional dough formed into small flowers and wreaths. Colored sugar (*matshik*) was sprinkled over the entire surface.

After a *brit*, the cookie was offered to the guests as part of the celebratory feast, except the "*mazel tov*" section, which was customarily reserved for the *kimpetorn* ("indulgence" in Yiddish, the term used for a new mother, usually confined to bed). The custom of the *reshinke* faded with the destruction of the European Jewish communities during World War II.

REVANADA DE PARIDA

Revanada de parida is fried egg-and-milk-soaked bread similar to French toast.

Origin: Spain

Other names: French: *pain à la Romain*, *pain perdu*, *tostées dorées*; German: *arme ritter*; Hungarian: *bundás kenyér*; Italian: *fette di pan carré*; Spanish: *sopas doradas*, *torriga*.

The concept of frying slices of milk-soaked bread dates back at least to ancient Rome, where Apicius, in his work *De re Coquinaria Libri Decem* (Cuisine in Ten Books), written around 400 CE, recorded this recipe: "*Aliter dulcia* [another sweet]—break fine white bread, crust removed, into large pieces, which soak in milk. Fry in oil, cover with honey, and serve."

The primary difference between Apicius' *aliter dulcia* and modern French toast is the absence of eggs, which were a rarity in Roman cooking. Egg toast may have originated in medieval Spain, influenced by the Moorish tradition of sweet egg-rich dishes. During the late medieval period, as chickens and eggs became increasingly prevalent in the rest of Europe and sugar arrived from the Middle East, the dish spread throughout western and central Europe and first became popular as dinner fare. However, as in many medieval European dishes, almond milk or juice was initially used instead of cow's milk.

Sephardic Jews, who left Iberia in 1492, called the dish *revanadas de parida* (slices of birth), perhaps because it was considered healthy fare for new mothers and invalids. There is also a Passover version made with fried matzas.

The *Oxford English Dictionary* states that the term French toast initially appeared in 1660 in *The Accomplisht Cook* by Robert May (London), although in that recipe the stale bread was actually soaked in a mixture of wine and orange juice, not eggs or milk, and its name reflected the use of "French bread," rather than a Gaelic origin. The English referred to the egg-soaked version as panperdy and eggy bread. Initially, Americans variously called the dish egg toast, Spanish toast, American toast, and, according to Fannie Farmer in the original edition of *The Boston Cooking-School Cook Book* (Boston, 1896), German toast. Among the foods that Mark Twain yearned for while on a steamer in *A Tramp Abroad* (Hartford, CN, 1880) was "American toast."

The Neighborhood Cook Book by the Council of Jewish Women (Portland, Oregon, 1914) included separate similar recipes for "French toast" and "German Toast." The terms German toast and Spanish toast, however, lost favor during World War I and French toast emerged as the common American name of the dish. In addition, French toast shifted from dinner fare to a breakfast and brunch food.

SEPHARDIC FRENCH TOAST (*REVANADAS DE PARIDA*)

6 PIECES   [DAIRY]

4 large eggs, lightly beaten
1¼ cups half-and-half or whole milk
3 tablespoons sugar
1 teaspoon vanilla extract
¼ teaspoon salt
½ teaspoon ground cinnamon or ¼ teaspoon ground nutmeg (optional)
6 (¾- to 1-inch-thick) slices bread (about 6 ounces total)
¼ cup (½ stick) unsalted butter
Atar (Middle Eastern Sugar Syrup, page 27), *arrope* (Sephardic Raisin Syrup, page 22), or honey, for drizzling

1. In a medium bowl, whisk together the eggs, half-and-half, sugar, vanilla, salt, and, if using, cinnamon. The taste will be improved if the custard is allowed to stand, covered, in the refrigerator overnight.

2. Dip the bread in a single layer in the custard and let stand for about 30 seconds per side. Transfer to a wire rack to let stand for about 3 minutes.

3. In a large skillet or griddle, melt 1 tablespoon butter over medium heat. In several batches, add the bread and fry, turning once, until crisp and golden brown on both sides, about 4 minutes per side. Drizzle the syrup over the toast.

RICE

Rice, a native of Southeast Asia, follows only corn as the most widely cultivated grain in the world. However, whereas much of the corn crop is used for animal feed and to produce industrial chemicals, almost all of the rice is consumed by humans. Rice has numerous attributes—it is nutritious, easily digestible, high-yielding, reliable to grow, easy to process, and, unlike most grains, it does not need to be ground into flour for practical usage. Rice is typically started in seedling beds, then transplanted to flooded fields that are drained before harvest. The more than seven thousand varieties of rice are defined by four basic characteristics: size (long, medium, and short grains), texture, color, and aroma. Long-grain rice expands in length during cooking, while short-grain varieties maintain their shape. Each category possesses distinctive characteristics that make it specially suited for a particular type of cooking. Each Jewish community adopted the local rice varieties as well as the local methods of preparing rice.

Fields in China and India have produced this grain for at least five thousand years and it serves as the primary food of nearly half the human race. Indians eat rice at practically every meal, while wheat products are occasional or even rare. More than twenty-three hundred years ago, rice (*berenj* in Farsi) spread westward to Persia, where it became a beloved food and was incorporated into a wide variety of dishes. The preferred Persian rice is a long-grain variety called *domsiah* (black-tailed), which is rather low yielding. There are also two less desirable but prominent varieties, *Sadri* and *Champa*. No Persian celebration is considered complete without rice and usually two or more dishes made from it are served.

Contact with the Persians brought rice, *orez* in Hebrew, ultimately from the Tamil word for rice, *arisi*, to Israel during the early Second Temple period and, by Roman times, Israeli rice had become an important export of which the Jerusalem Talmud boasted, "There is none like it outside Israel." Suggestions in the Talmud for the blessing over this grain included "Who creates delicacies to delight the soul of every living being." The Talmud noted that several rabbis included rice along with beet greens on the Passover Seder plate. After conquering Persia, Arabs learned how to grow rice (*ar-ruzz* in Arabic, also from the Tamil). As they vanquished swaths of Asia, North Africa, Sicily, and Spain during the ninth and tenth centuries, they introduced rice cultivation and advanced irrigation techniques that made it possible to grow this water-loving grain throughout much of the Mediterranean. In the Arabic world, with the exception of the couscous-loving Maghreb, rice has long been a staple of the diet. By the tenth century, Egypt emerged as the largest producer of rice outside of the Far East. A favorite medieval Arabic way to eat rice was warm with melted butter and sugar or milk. For meat meals, Jews substituted oil for butter and commonly added onions and garlic.

Since its arrival in Spain, most of the rice (*arroz* in Spanish and Ladino from the Arabic) grown in the country has been the nearly round short-grain type, which absorbs flavors easily, unlike the firmer, fluffy long-grain varieties more common in Persia and the Ottoman Empire. Rice quickly became an integral part of Sephardic cuisine and was served practically every day in many households. Following the expulsion from Spain in 1492, each group of exiles adopted additional rice dishes in the region where it had settled, and since most Sephardim continued to speak Ladino at home, the new rice dishes usually had Ladino names. Frequently, however, they had to substitute long-grain rice for their preferred short-grain.

Members of Alexander the Great's Indian campaign made note of rice, but it only reached Europe during the Arab invasions at the beginning of the ninth century and began spreading to non-Muslim areas of the continent in the fourteenth century. Rice became a fundamental part of the cuisine only in Italy and Spain, where it was used to create classic fare such as risotto and paella. In the fifteenth century, rice was widely planted in the Po Valley of Italy and thereafter rivaled wheat as the staple of Lombardy. Around that time, Sephardim fleeing from Spain, as well as Jews exiled by the Spanish from Sicily in 1493, introduced their rice dishes to northern Italy.

Rice became traditional Friday night fare in most Mizrachi and Sephardic communities. Medieval Arabs utilized large amounts of saffron and turmeric to give food a yellow color, their traditional symbol of joy and happiness. This practice influenced not only Jews in the Middle East but also Sephardim and, beginning in the fifteenth century, Italians. For centuries, golden rice, called *ruz bi zaffaran* (rice with saffron) in Arabic, *riso col zafran* in Italian, and *arroz de Sabato* (Sabbath rice) in Ladino, has been a Friday night and holiday tradition in Middle Eastern, Italian, and Sephardic communities. The Bene Israel of Mumbai flavor their yellow rice (*nariel chawal*) with coconut and cardamom.

The practice of adding a little tomato sauce to rice—the dish is called *arroz con tomat* (rice with tomatoes) and often simply *arroz*—developed among Sephardim in the Ottoman Empire after that area embraced the American tomato in the sixteenth century. Syrian Jews call rice and tomato casseroles *riz espanie* (Spanish rice), since it was Sephardim who popularized the concept in the Middle East. Whereas yellow rice was customary for the Sabbath, rice cooked with tomato sauce once served in many households at both lunch and dinner and was far more common than plain white rice (*arroz blanco*). Traditional at Sephardic weddings and other special occasions is *arroz de bodas*, rice mixed with green grapes or golden raisins and pine nuts or slivered almonds.

Most Europeans, however, treated rice with indifference. In general, the farther north in Europe, the less rice was eaten. Rice entered Ashkenazic cooking rather late and even then was only incorporated into a few dishes, primarily dairy puddings, pareve kugel, and meat stuffings. Rice and raisins became a traditional Purim pairing. Medieval Ashkenazim, who rarely if ever saw rice, forbade its consumption on Passover, while Italians, Sephardim, and Mizrachim continued to permit it. Many Italians feature risotto with artichokes as the appetizer for the Passover Seder meal.

Rice remains a fundamental side dish around the Mediterranean and in modern Israel, where it is prepared plain or flavored with herbs, chickpeas, orzo, or pine nuts. It is commonly used to fill dolmas (stuffed vegetables) and to prepare various types of pilafs and puddings; it is also paired with lentils for *mujaddara*. The Bene Israel serve *malida* (a sweetened rice, coconut, and fruit dish) at all festive occasions. Rice proved uneconomical to grow in modern Israel, so supermarkets feature imported Indian long-grain basmati and Patna rice, along with many other types.

Rice is primarily consumed in an unprocessed form, simply husked and cooked, but is also milled to make rice flour, which is available in fine and coarse grinds. Flour from polished white rice is rather bland, while that from brown rice has a slightly nutty flavor. In Persian cuisine, rice flour is used for noodles and *nane berenji* (rice-flour cookies), which are enjoyed after important meals.

(See also Arroz, Bachsh, Biryani, Bomba, Chelow, Malida, Mujaddara, Palau, Pilau, Plov, Risotto, Sutlach, Tabyett, Tachin, and Timman)

RICE PUDDING

Like other grains, probably the earliest way of preparing rice was boiling it in water until it became a thick consistency. Romans added goat's milk to cooked rice, but not sweeteners, and ate it as a savory dish. The Byzantine doctor Anthimus (c. 500 CE) prescribed "*oryza*" (Greek for "rice") made from imported grains for upset stomachs. He directed, "Boil rice in fresh water. When it is properly cooked, drain off the water and add goat's milk. Put the pot on the flame and cook slowly until it becomes a solid mass. It is eaten like this, hot not cold, but without salt and oil."

Perhaps the Chinese were the first to make sweetened rice, although they did not use milk. With the addition of goat's milk or almond milk and honey or sugar, a practice probably originating in Persia, rice porridge was transformed into rice pudding. Rice puddings, first mentioned in medieval Middle Eastern medical texts, have long been recommended for the infirm, infants, and elderly. The rather simple concept of sweetened rice cooked with milk spread to every corner of the globe where this grain was enjoyed, and rice pudding became one of the world's favorite comfort foods, although the rice varieties, cooking methods, and flavorings vary widely. Some puddings are made from whole grains, while others are made from rice flour. Some are relatively plain and others are enhanced with fruits, spices, and various flavorings. Some are watery, while others are thick or custardy. Local forms made their way into Jewish cooking.

An anonymous, untitled Andalusian cookbook of the thirteenth century included a recipe for "Rice Dissolved with Sugar." It directed, "Wash what you want of the rice and cook it as usual. Then take it to the hearthstone and leave it a while and when it is ready and has become mushy, mash it with a spoon until it dissolves and not a trace of the grain remains. Then add ground white Egyptian sugar and stir it vigorously. Add sugar bit by bit until its sweetness dominates and it becomes like dissolved *fanid* [a sugar candy]. Then turn it onto a platter and make a hole in the center and fill with fresh butter or with oil of fresh sweet almonds. If you cook this with fresh milk instead of water, it will be more delicious and better." Sephardim of that time most certainly prepared similar rice dishes.

Medieval Persians cooked several types of rice pudding, including *shir-berenj* (milk-rice), consisting of whole rice kernels cooked for an extended time to produce a creamier texture. In addition, Persians developed a version known as *shola*, consisting of rice flour, almond milk, sugar, and rose water or orange-blossom water. For special occasions, it was tinted yellow with saffron (*shola-e zard*). The Persian-influenced Mughals introduced rice-flour puddings called *firni/phirni* to India, substituting cow's or coconut milk for the almond milk and slow-cooking them in *kulhars* (earthenware cups). In addition, Indians enjoy rice puddings made from whole grains, called *kheer* and, in the south, *payasam*.

With the collapse of Byzantium and arrival of the Turks, rice emerged as a more important part of Greek cuisine and *rizgalo* (rice pudding), typically flavored with citrus zest and cinnamon, became a popular treat. In Italy, rice pudding (*budino di riso*), typically flavored with citrus zest and raisins, was initially considered a health food and was served to invalids. During the Renaissance, primarily due to Arabic culinary influences, European cookery and puddings began evolving. With the advent in Europe of custard, Europeans began adding eggs, producing a firmer, more custardy rice pudding. Rice puddings, made from rice imported primarily from Spain, had appeared in England by the end of the sixteenth century. Baked rice puddings emerged in Europe in the seventeenth century.

Among Ashkenazim, rice was occasional, minor fare. Those from central Europe and Romania enjoyed baked rice puddings and pareve rice kugels for the Sabbath and stovetop dairy rice puddings. *The Jewish Manual* (London, 1846), included the recipe "A Nice Rice Pudding for Children," a baked dish, and "Rice Custard"; neither of the puddings contained eggs. *Jewish Cookery* (Philadelphia, 1871) provided three rice puddings: a stovetop dairy pudding, a pareve variation incorporating eggs and baked in puff pastry, and a baked dairy pudding.

Among Sephardim, rice was both an everyday food and celebration delicacies. Rice pudding was a standard everyday Sephardic dessert, served both hot and cold and at breakfast, lunch, and dinner. The Sephardic *arroz con leche* is typically flavored with citrus zest and cinnamon. Dairy rice pudding is traditional on Shavuot; on this holiday, Middle Easterners customarily decorate the synagogue with an abundance of rose petals (hence the name "the Festival of Roses"), so rose water in the pudding takes on an added significance.

(See also Kheer, Kugel, and Sutlach)

RISOTTO

Risotto is short-grain or sometimes medium-grain rice cooked in a meat or vegetable broth until creamy but the grains are still separate and slightly al dente.

Origin: Italy

In the fifteenth century, rice (*riso*) was widely planted in northern Italy, and people became avid consumers. The three major rice-growing regions in Italy—Lombardy, Veneto, and Piedmonte—primarily produce short-grain rice. A special form of rice cookery, risotto, originated in the center of Italian rice culture, Lombardy, and by the nineteenth century, every northern part of the country had developed its own version. The most famous *risotto* is *risotto alla Milanese*, which contains white wine and saffron. Risotto is prepared similar to the Spanish style of cooking rice, in which the grains are never rinsed, but are first sautéed with onions in fat before liquid is added; this is unlike most forms of Asian cookery, where the raw rice is rinsed to remove the surface starch. The common denominator in every good risotto is that it be *mantecato* (creamy); the texture is produced from the starch and not the addition of cream. To achieve the desired consistency, some recipes require stirring throughout the cooking process, while simpler versions only call for occasional stirring.

Risotto was probably inspired by the rice dishes brought to the region by Sicilian exiles or Sephardim who arrived in Italy at the same time that rice cultivation became widespread in northern Italy and risotto initially appeared. Italian Jews have long prepared risotto, serving it plain (*risotto bianco*) or enhanced with various vegetables (artichokes, celery, eggplant, peas, pumpkin, spinach, and zucchini), meat, sausages, chicken giblets (*con regagli*), or mushrooms. Risotto tinted with saffron (*risotto giallo* or *riso col zafran*) is still prepared on Friday afternoon for Sabbath dinner (*risotto del Sabato*). On Hanukkah, raisins are added. *Risotto coi carciofi* (rice with artichokes), making use of the new crop, is common during Passover. The Jews of the Venetian Ghetto typically made a simple form of the dish, *risotto semplice*.

Many cooks insist on using Arborio, a short-grain rice grown in the Po Valley of northern Italy, which is almost as thick as it is long. Arborio is perfect for making risotto as it can absorb a great deal of liquid while simultaneously releasing its starch, resulting in a creamy sauce and a rice kernel that remains *al dente* (firm to the tooth). Other Italian varieties can be substituted for Arborio; these varieties can be divided into three grades based upon size: *semifino* (the smallest), *fino*, and *superfino*. Arborio is a *superfino*. Vialone Nano (a *semifino*), the most popular variety in Venice, is slightly smaller and rounder than Arborio and quicker cooking. Carnaroli, a *superfino* variety, is more elongated than Arborio, has a slightly firmer texture, and takes longer to cook than other types. Another *superfino* rice is Baldo, which is longer, slimmer, and flatter than Arborio.

Risotto was historically a simple comfort food largely consigned to family dinners, at which it was usually served as a first course (*primo piatto*) following the antipasto or sometimes as an accompaniment to classical veal dishes, such as osso buco, or as a light main course. Toward the end of the twentieth century, risotto became fare at chic American restaurants.

(See also Bomba)

VENETIAN SIMPLE RISOTTO (*RISOTTO SEMPLICE*)

3 TO 4 SERVINGS   [DAIRY OR MEAT]

- 3 tablespoons olive oil
- 1 medium onion, chopped
- 1 large clove garlic, chopped
- 1½ cups (10 ounces) Vialone Nano, Arborio, or Carnaroli rice
- ½ cup dry white wine
- 4 cups vegetable or chicken broth, heated to a simmer
- About ½ teaspoon table salt or 1 teaspoon kosher salt
- About ½ teaspoon ground black pepper
- A pinch (about 18 strands) of saffron (optional)
- 6 tablespoons grated Parmesan cheese (optional)

1. In a large saucepan, heat the oil over medium heat. Add the onion and sauté until soft and translucent, 5 to 10 minutes. Add the garlic and sauté until fragrant, about 1 minute. Add the rice and stir until well coated and opaque, about 3 minutes. Add the wine and cook until the liquid evaporates, about 3 minutes.

2. Add 2 cups broth and the salt, pepper, and, if using, saffron. Cook over low heat, uncovered, stirring occasionally, until the liquid has been absorbed, about 15 minutes. Add the remaining 2 cups broth and simmer, uncovered, stirring occasionally, until the rice is tender but still very moist and not mushy, about 15 minutes.

3. If using the vegetable broth, stir in the Parmesan. Serve immediately on preheated plates or bowls to maintain the creaminess.

ROSCA

Rosca is the name of various ring-shaped breads and cookies.

Origin: Spain

Other names: *biscocho de levadura, roskita, roskita de gueve.*

In Washington Irving's 1832 collection of short stories, *The Alhambra*, derived from his visit to Spain, he noted, "Here live the bakers who furnish Seville with that delicious bread for which it is renowned; here are fabricated those roscas well known by the well-merited appellation of *pan de Dios* (bread of God); for which, by the way, we ordered our man, Sancho, to stock his alforjas for the journey." Irving was referring to hard baked bread rings called *rosca* (Spanish for "coil/spiral").

The original type of *rosca* consisted of rings of yeast bread baked twice, greatly extending its shelf life, like the Italian biscotti. For centuries, Spanish ships carried *roscas* as provisions for the sailors, as they can last for many years. (The term *rosca* gave rise in 1595 to the English term for twice-baked cookies, rusk.) Small hard rings made from bread dough were neither a new nor a Spanish concept, as these breads were an ancient Middle Eastern food, one mentioned in the Talmud as *kaak*. The Spanish developed a cookie version (*roscas dulce*) sweetened with sugar and typically flavored with anise, also known as *biscochos dulces*; those containing eggs are called *biscochos de huevo* (egg cookies). Hard pretzel-shaped versions are *reshi-*

For many centuries, hard baked Spanish bread rings called rosca have served as staples for travelers and soldiers. These breads also gave rise to various ring-shaped Sephardic pastries and softer breads also called rosca.

cas. Hard sweetened *roscas*, shaped into rings and flavored with anise or cinnamon, are found in parts of the American Southwest, where they were introduced by Conversos.

In addition to the various hard pastries, cooks created a softer bread, similar to a coffee cake ring, which is also called *rosca*. In many Sephardic homes, the sweet yeast cake version of *roscas*, in the form of a large bread or more commonly smaller ring-shaped rolls, is served for *desayuno* (brunch) on the Sabbath along with feta and Kasseri cheese, olives, and coffee. In Turkey, the coffee cake is typically accented with cloves. Any leftover rolls are sliced and toasted until hard, like biscotti, for longer storage; the toasted slices are sometimes called *parmaks*. These sweet breads became traditional for holidays and celebrations, in particular for Purim and Shavuot. A ring- or crescent-shaped cookie with a filling is referred to as *roskitas alhashu* or *roscas di alhashu*. This is a popular Purim treat in the Balkans—the crescent-shaped cookie is said to resemble the ear that the villain Haman lost before his execution. In Greece, the bread is also referred to as *tsoureki*, and typically braided, the twisted ring of bread resembling the noose used to hang Haman. *"Roscas de Purim"* is the name of a nineteenth-century Ladino song traditional for that holiday.

(See also Biscocho, Bollo, Kaak, and Pandericas)

⚜ SEPHARDIC SWEET YEAST RINGS (*ROSCAS*)

3 MEDIUM BREADS   [PAREVE]

   1 recipe *bollo* dough (see Sephardic Sweet Anise
       Bread, page 60), flavored with ¾ teaspoon
       ground anise, ½ teaspoon anise liqueur,
       ¾ teaspoon ground cinnamon, or ½ teaspoon
       ground cloves
   Egg wash (1 large egg beaten with 1 teaspoon water)
   Sesame seeds for sprinkling

   1. Divide the dough into thirds and form into balls. Poke a hole in the center of each ball and form into a 2-inch-thick doughnut. Place on a parchment paper–lined or lightly greased baking sheet. If desired, on the outer side of the rings at 2-inch intervals, cut ½-inch-deep slashes, separating the sections. Cover loosely with plastic wrap or a kitchen towel and let rise in a warm, draft-free place until nearly doubled in bulk, about 1 hour.

   2. Preheat the oven to 350°F.

   3. Brush with the egg wash, then sprinkle with the sesame seeds. Bake until golden brown, about 30 minutes. Transfer the breads to a wire rack and let cool.

ROSE WATER

In 800 CE, the Arab scholar Jabir ibn Hayyan invented an improved still. About two centuries later, the Bukharan-born physician ibn Sina (980–1037), whose name was Latinized as Avicenna, discovered how to use the still to extract the essential oil from flower petals. This allowed for the steam distillation of floral waters, particularly rose water—*ma wared* in Arabic, *golab* in Persian, and *gulab-jal* in India. Rose water is distilled from fresh rose petals from the damask variety (*Rosa damascena*), which has small pink and white flowers and leaves that are glossy on the top and hairy on the bottom. Damask roses are also preferred for making rose preserves. The rose petals are placed in a large copper still, covered with water, and simmered over a low heat; the vapor passes through a tube, where it condenses at the other end. Initially developed as a means of administering drugs, the floral waters were soon appropriated for perfumes and cooking. Some Middle Eastern women wash with rose water or use it as a body mist. In many Yemenite homes, a bottle of rose water was kept near the door to sprinkle on arriving guests and it was also sprinkled at celebrations. Although Americans value roses almost exclusively for their aesthetic quality, Middle Easterners and Indians know that they have a beauty in the kitchen, adding flavor and aroma to puddings, pastries, con-

Rose water used in pastries and other dishes throughout the Middle East comes from the Damask rose.

fections (such as Turkish delight), fruit dishes, and beverages (including teas).

The distillation process has changed little over the centuries, and some families throughout the Middle East continue to make their own floral waters in home stills in basements and garages, producing enough to last for a year or more. In Israel and other Middle Eastern countries, commercial bottles of rose water are sold from grocery stores. In the West, rose water is available at Middle Eastern and Indian markets as well as many pharmacies. Some commercial distilled waters are concentrated and others are diluted, the strength varying depending on the amount of dilution. Therefore, cooks must adjust the amount used in cooking according to the individual product and personal preference. Too much rose water results in a soapy taste, so it is used sparingly. For reasons of kashrut, many Jewish cooks avoid distilled waters containing glycerine.

During the medieval period, the use of rose water spread to Europe and later America and it became a prominent flavoring. Hence Rosenwasser (rose water) became a German surname. However, in the nineteenth century, with the advent of vanilla extract and other new flavorings, rose water all but disappeared from Western cookery. On the other hand, it remains a prominent feature of Middle Eastern cuisines. Rose water is a traditional flavoring on Shavuot among Sephardim, who call the holiday "the Feast of Roses."

(See also Orange-Blossom Water)

ROSH HASHANAH

Rosh Hashanah (literally "Head of the Year") is a two-day autumn holiday traditionally marking the creation of the world. Rosh Hashanah begins a ten-day period of transition, concentrated introspection, prayer, and inner transformation leading to Yom Kippur, known as *Yamim Noraim* (Days of Awe). Nevertheless, Rosh Hashanah is an occasion of great joy and feasting. During the holiday, it is considered a *segulah* (good omen) to eat certain foods and perform *simanim* (symbolic acts) that help a person to reflect on the past and ponder the future. Consequently, no other holiday has more symbolic foods than Rosh Hashanah.

The initial source of these symbolic foods is the Talmud, which suggested five items to eat on Rosh Hashanah—*kraa* (gourds), *rubiya* (fenugreek), *karti* (leeks), *silka* (beet greens/chard), and *tamar* (dates).

These particular plants were specified because of a phonological similarity between their names and other words, thereby signifying an aspiration for the new year. The Hebrew word for gourd, *kraa*, is similar to *yikara* (to be called out), suggesting that our good deeds should be called out at this time of judgment. In addition, it is similar to *karah* (to tear up), meaning that any harsh edicts against us should be torn up. The Aramaic word for fenugreek, *rubiya*, is similar to *yirbu* (increase/multiply). However, *rubiya* is commonly mistranslated as black-eyed peas, which is actually *lubiya*—as a result, black-eyed peas became traditional among Sephardim. The Hebrew word for leek, *karti*, is similar to *yikartu* (to be cut off), signifying that our enemies should be cut off. The term for beet greens and chard, *silka*, is reminiscent of the Hebrew *she'yistalqu* (that they will be removed), referring to our enemies. Similarly, the Hebrew word for date, *tamar*, sounds like *yitamu* (to be removed).

Over the course of time, other foods gained their own status. Sephardim serve lung (*re'ah* in Hebrew) while reciting "*Re'ah na bee'onyainu*" (See us in our affliction). During the medieval period, the carrot reached the West; its Hebrew name became *gezer*, which also means "tear," as in "tear up any bad decrees," as well as "decree," signifying "*Shelo yeehyu gezerot ra'ot olainu*" (May there be no evil decrees against us). The carrot has several other attributes: Its Yiddish name, *mehren*, is similar to "multiply/increase"; it is sweet; and when sliced, its shape resembles golden coins. Rabbi David Oppenheim (1664–1736), chief rabbi of Prague, recorded the custom of eating turnips (*rube*) or carrots (*mehren*) on Rosh Hashanah.

An ancient custom is to eat a new fruit—one not yet sampled that season—on the second night of Rosh Hashanah while reciting the blessing "*Shehechiyanu*" (Who has preserved us). In addition, seasonal produce frequently finds its way into favorite Rosh Hashanah fare, such as spinach and leeks among Sephardim, pumpkins among Italians, and apples and plums among Ashkenazim.

The first recorded association of apples with Rosh Hashanah was in *Machzor Vitry* (a *siddur* compiled around 1100), which included this explanation: "The residents of France have the custom to eat on Rosh Hashanah red apples. Every thing new and bright and good for a good sign for all Israel." Future generations of Ashkenazim adopted the French custom of eating apples, leading to the most popular and widespread Ashkenazic Rosh Hashanah tradition. At the beginning of the evening meal, apple slices are dipped in honey and this phrase is recited: "May it be Your will to renew on us a good and sweet year."

Rabbi Jacob ben Asher, who was born in Germany around 1269 and fled with his family to Spain in 1303, was the first to mention the custom of apples dipped in honey in his legal compendium *Arbah Turim* (c. 1310), citing it as a German tradition. Shortly after, the custom was recorded by Rabbi Alexander Susslein of Frankfort, Germany, in his work *Sefer Agudah*, revealing that it had become a widespread practice in Germany.

As with a number of symbolic foods, the custom of apples in honey developed many layers of meaning. In mystical literature, an apple orchard is frequently pictured as a symbol of the divine presence, which the Zohar compares to "an apple orchard." In the Bible, honey is a food associated with the land of Israel. Honey is also an ancient symbol of immortality and truth. The sweetness of both the honey and apple serves as a wish for a sweet year to come.

The custom of dipping apples into honey was connected to the biblical incident of Jonathan, who had not heard the oath of his father, King Saul, cursing anyone eating "*vayehi hayom* (it was that day)," and dipped his staff into and ate honey from a bee hive. According to tradition, in the Bible, the term "*vayehi hayom*" always refers to Rosh Hashanah. The incident of Jonathan serves as an inspiration for dipping an apple slice into honey, appealing to God to pardon us, as Jonathan was pardoned by his father.

The first piece of challah, generally from a round loaf that frequently contains raisins or other dried fruits, is dipped into honey instead of the customary salt, a custom that is continued in many households until after Sukkot. Ashkenazim traditionally serve a honey cake called *lekach*, alluding to the phrase in Proverbs "for a goodly *lekach* [portion] have I given you," signifying the wish that we be given a salutary portion. Honey-cooked balls of dough are called *teiglach*. Sephardim make honey-soaked cakes, such as *tishpishti*. Hungarian Rosh Hashanah desserts generally continue the apple theme—hosts offer apple cakes, pie, or compote.

Those fruits mentioned in the Bible—grapes, figs, dates, melons, and pomegranates—have a special place in Jewish tradition. Date trees are a symbol not only of beauty but of a paradigm for people to stand as straight and tall as a date palm. The many seeds of the pomegranate symbolize both fertility and good deeds: "May our merits multiply like pomegranate seeds." Melons and vegetables containing many seeds, such as pumpkin and squash, represent fertility and plenty. Syrian Jews enjoy date-filled cookies called *ras ib adjweh*. Indian Jews prepare a coconut milk halva garnished with nuts and raisins.

For Mizrachim and Sephardim, the predominant Rosh Hashanah fruit is the quince, which comes into season around the holiday. Many Sephardim poach quinces in a syrup to serve as the first course of the Rosh Hashanah dinner. Greek Jews serve quince or rose preserves at the start of the meal. Persians stew quinces with lamb and onions. Moroccans combine quinces with carrots and prunes, as well as poaching them. And often quinces are the base in different confections and cakes.

In some homes, the head of a fish or lamb is displayed on the table, signifying the hope that in the coming year family members be the "*rosh* [head] and not the tail." Both lamb and fish also hold other meanings. Lamb is a reminder of the ram substituted for Isaac as a sacrifice, which tradition holds occurred on Rosh Hashanah. Fish is a symbol of fruitfulness ("May we be fruitful and multiply like fish"), the Jewish people, and the Leviathan to be served at the feast following the arrival of the messiah.

Many Sephardic hosts feature a cornucopia of symbolic fruits and vegetables, customarily served in a basket called a *trashkal*, while others arrange seven symbolic foods, called *Sheva Berachot* (Seven Blessings), on a plate, creating a display similar to a Seder plate. It is the custom in Jerusalem to serve as many symbolic foods as possible. The head of the family removes one item at a time and recites an appropriate verse and/or a "*Yehi ratztone . . .*" (May it be Your will . . .). The first symbolic food is usually a date, which in some Sephardic homes is dipped into a mixture of ground sesame seeds, anise seeds, and sugar, called *yitamu*. Next is the pomegranate, followed by an apple or quince. These are followed by leeks, spinach or chard, and finally the head of a fish or lamb.

In the Maghreb, the evening is organized into a Seder, an ordered succession of disparate tastes, smells, and colors. As a prelude to the festival meal, those gathered sample one or several vegetables representing the removal of enemies, notably beet greens, spinach, and pumpkin. Next, everyone is given a piece of a cooked lamb's or cow's head "to be like a head," then a piece of calf's heart "to open the heart to the Torah." The next theme is fertility and plenty, represented by beans, seeds (especially sesame), and fish. Afterward, biblical fruits are sampled—pomegranates ("may our merits be plentiful"), dates ("may the righteous flourish"), then figs (for a sweet year). The wish for an easy year is represented by a piece of cooked lung. Next comes the biblical olive. Finally, an apple slice is dipped in honey.

There are also foods traditionally avoided on Rosh Hashanah. Eastern Europeans eschew nuts, as well as any sour food, even sweet-and-sour dishes. In North Africa, black foods, a color associated with mourning—including olives, raisins, eggplant, coffee, and chocolate—are banned, although some permit these items on the second day. Iraqi Jews avoid fish, since its Hebrew name *dag* is similar to the Hebrew *da'ag* (to worry).

ROSL

Nobel laureate Saul Bellow, in a May 18, 1983 *New York Times* interview by Mimi Sheraton reminisced about the dishes made by his mother from Riga, Latvia: "She pickled many foods, and there were always big crocks around with things like pickled beets, from which she made the special borscht called Russell." In fifteenth century Poland, the Slavic term *rosól* first meant salt brine. Eastern European Jews eventually adopted it into Yiddish as *rosl*, also spelled *rosel*, *rossel*, and *russel*; the Yiddish meaning of the word, which varied from place to place, included a gravy and any sour liquid (e.g., pickle juice and herring brine), and in some locales it specifically denoted a fermented beet liquid that was a vibrantly red vinegar due to its high amount of acid.

For most of history, people grew beets for their nutritious leaves, generally ignoring the thin yellowish roots. During the late medieval period, European farmers began breeding beets with larger roots and deeper color; the common red beetroot first appeared in the early sixteenth century in either northern Italy or southern Germany. During the course of the next century, the beet spread to eastern Europe, becoming one of several root vegetables in that area that were easy to grow and could be stored throughout the winter. Shortly before the arrival of the beet, nomadic Tartars and Turks brought the technique of lacto-fermentation from China to eastern Europe, where it was adopted by the Slavs and by eastern European Jews from the Baltic to Romania, engendering sauerkraut, pickled cucumbers, and *rosl* beets. In this process, acidifying bacteria found naturally in raw beets (or cabbage or cucumbers) feed off the sugar in the vegetables producing lactic acid and acetic acid, which gives the vegetables and brining liquid a characteristic tangy yet mellow taste, and slightly softens them. When working properly, the beneficial bacteria prevent deleterious microorganisms from spoiling the beets.

After the fall harvest, beets were stashed in a root cellar throughout the autumn and winter. Around the week after Purim, most of the remaining beets, their flavor faded, were peeled, cut up, placed in a large earthenware crock, topped with water (no salt was added), covered with a tablecloth, and left near the stove or another warm place to ferment for about four weeks. When the liquid had transformed into a clear, bright red, enticingly pungent vinegar with a winy aroma, the crock was moved to a cool, dark cellar to stop the fermentation. Some families cherished *rosl* so much that they made batches both in the autumn around Sukkot, along with barrels of small cucumbers and sauerkraut, and in the early spring before Passover.

Rosl, either the vinegar and/or the beets (*rosl burik*), was added to soups, kugels, horseradish, and other traditional dishes. The fermented beets were frequently substituted for fresh beets in dishes such as *eingemachts* (preserves) and borscht. In Ukraine and southern Poland, *rosl* was used as the cooking liquid for pot roast and other meats; these dishes were called *roslfleisch*.

The first edition of *The Settlement Cook Book* (Milwaukee, 1901) included a recipe for "Rosel, Beet Vinegar," explaining "This is used as a vinegar during Easter or Pesach and to make beet soup, Russian style." The same recipe was still found in the 1976 edition, although the title had changed to "Beet Vinegar (Rosel)." However, by the time of the later edition, *rosl*'s usage in the American Jewish community had seriously declined, although it was still prepared in a few households for Passover.

(See also Beet, Borscht, Eingemacht, and Essig Fleisch)

RUSSIAN FERMENTED BEETS (*ROSL BURIK*)

ABOUT 8 CUPS LIQUID AND 4 CUPS BEETS   [PAREVE]

   5 pounds (1 peck) beets, peeled and cubed

   Cold spring water (do not use chlorinated or hard water)

1. Place the beets in a sterilized 1-gallon earthenware or glass crock and add enough spring water to reach 2 inches above the beets. Tie a layer of cheesecloth over the top to keep out any dust. Cover loosely and leave in a warm, dark place to ferment.

2. A white foam should appear on the surface after about 10 days—skim it off, then stir the beets, repeating every week or so. Make sure the beets are always covered with liquid. If the fermentation process is working properly, each week the cloudy liquid will grow a darker shade of pink and, when the beets are ready in about 3 to 4 weeks, the liquid will have turned a clear, deep wine red. Store in an airtight container in the refrigerator.

RUGELACH

Rugelach is a crescent-shaped, filled sweet pastry.

Origin: Central Europe

Other names: *beyglech, kipfel,* rugala, rugelech, rugelekh.

In the 1994 movie *Quiz Show*, set in 1957, a Harvard Law School graduate working for the Congressional Oversight Committee visits the home of an obviously Jewish character to discuss a corrupt game show, and the Jewish host, upon offering his guest rugelach, starts to explain what it is. The lawyer interjects, "I'm familiar with rugelach," revealing his Jewishness at a time when few outside the Jewish community knew what rugelach were, and when Harvard, like most other American schools, had a quota system that allowed only a small number of Jews to be admitted. Within a few decades, almost every American had heard of rugelach, another Jewish food that became prominent in the American mainstream.

Rugelach, arguably today the best known and most popular of all Ashkenazic baked goods in America, is a cross between a pastry and a cookie; it consists of tender, flaky dough coiled with a sweet filling. Rugelach is actually a mid-twentieth-century American adaptation of one of the hallmarks of central European baking, the crescent-shaped *kipfel*. The original *kipfel* was made from a rich yeast dough; Jewish renderings were typically pareve so they could be served for dessert on the Sabbath and holidays after a meat meal.

The origin of the name rugelach is unknown, but may derive from the Yiddish word *rog* (corner) or the Slavic *rog* (horn) with the diminutive plural *lakh*, hence either "little corners," as they are made from rolled up corners of dough, or "little horns," denoting the pastry's curved shape. The word may even be a Yiddishized contraction of the English term "rolled things."

The first record of the word rugelach was only in 1941 in *The Jewish Home Beautiful* by Betty D. Greenberg and Althea O. Silverman (New York), in a recipe entitled "Crescents or Rugelach." This version consisted of a yeast dough enriched with sour cream and eggs. The authors explained, "Here is a raised dough recipe minus the bogey of countless hours of rising and endless kneading. The method is not traditional; in fact, it is quite modern, but as long as the finished product is just like mother's, does it matter?"

Not only the name, but the nature of the dough changed in twentieth-century America. The first edition of *The Settlement Cook Book* (Milwaukee, 1901) provided a recipe for a traditional European-style yeastless pastry crescent made from flour, butter, sour cream, and egg yolks entitled "Sour Cream Kipfel," as well as a cottage cheese adaptation without eggs called "Vienna Kipfel." In America, Jewish grandmothers and mothers-in-law commonly baked batch after batch of unleavened rugelach—the dough was easier to make and remained fresher longer than yeast pastries—and then taught their techniques to future generations. The first known record of a cream cheese rugelach, a popular American innovation, was in *The Perfect Hostess* by Mildred O. Knopf (New York, 1950), who accredited the recipe to Nela Rubenstein, wife of noted pianist Arthur Rubenstein. Within a decade or so, the name rugelach would almost totally supplant *kipfel* among American Jews and Israelis.

Cream cheese pastry emerged as the underpinning of the great American rugelach; the rich, flavorful pastry balanced the sweet filling. Typical rugelach dough is made from only a few ingredients—flour, cream cheese, butter, and salt—although some versions include a little sugar or egg yolks. American bakers came up with various alternatives to cream cheese, substituting softened ice cream or pareve tofu ice cream and margarine. In addition to the original cinnamon and raisin filling, numerous other flavor variations developed, most notably chocolate, apricot, and raspberry. Also, as rugelach attained popularity in America, many commercial producers replaced the traditional crescent with the square-cut, which was easier to prepare and allowed for a greater concentration of filling in the center. However, whereas cream cheese dough predominates in the United States, Israeli rugelach are still commonly pareve and made with a yeast dough, and sometimes even paired with a savory filling, such as olives. Cream cheese rugelach have only recently begun to appear in England.

Rugelach became a traditional Hanukkah and Shavuot treat; it was also served at various dairy celebrations, such as *brits* and baby namings, and at sisterhood meetings. In the 1980s, rugelach began spreading to the American mainstream and an increasing number of commercial bakeries, some of them not Jewish, began mass production. By the time of *Baking with Julia* (1996), a television show and accompanying book by Julia Child, rugelach were among the treats prepared for her by top American bakers. Also by the end of the twentieth century, rugelach were common in American bakeries, groceries, gourmet stores, and coffee shops.

(See also Cheese, Cream; and Kipfel)

⟅ ASHKENAZIC COOKIE CRESCENTS (*RUGELACH*)

32 LARGE, 48 MEDIUM, OR 64 SMALL COOKIES   [DAIRY]

Cream Cheese Dough:
- 1 cup (2 sticks) unsalted butter or margarine, softened
- 1 cup (8 ounces) cream cheese, softened
- 1 tablespoon sour cream
- ½ teaspoon salt
- 2 tablespoons sugar (optional)
- 1 teaspoon vanilla or almond extract (optional)
- 2 cups (10 ounces) all-purpose flour, sifted

- 1 cup jam, such as apricot or raspberry, or ¼ cup (½ stick) melted butter

- ½ cup sugar mixed with 1½ teaspoons ground cinnamon
- ¾ cup dried currants or raisins (optional)
- Egg wash (1 large egg beaten with 1 teaspoon water or milk)
- About 2 tablespoons sugar, or 2 tablespoons sugar mixed with 1 teaspoon ground cinnamon, for sprinkling

1. To make the dough: In a large bowl, beat together the butter, cream cheese, and sour cream until light and fluffy, about 5 minutes. Add the salt and, if using, sugar and vanilla. Gradually beat in the flour. Divide the dough into 4 equal pieces, form into balls, flatten into 1-inch-thick rounds, wrap in plastic wrap, and refrigerate for at least 6 hours or overnight.

2. Preheat the oven to 375°F. Line 2 baking sheets with parchment paper or use ungreased sheets.

3. Let the dough stand at room temperature until malleable. On a lightly floured surface (or a surface sprinkled with cinnamon-sugar), roll out each dough piece to a ⅛-inch-thick round, about 9 inches in diameter. Brush with jam and sprinkle with cinnamon-sugar, leaving a ½-inch border around the edge. If using, sprinkle with the currants.

4. Cut each round into equal wedges—12 for medium cookies, 8 for large cookies, or 16 for small cookies. Starting from the wide end, roll up the wedges toward the point and gently bend to form a crescent.

5. Place the crescents on the prepared baking sheets, pointed side down, 1 inch apart. Brush with the egg wash and sprinkle lightly with the sugar.

6. Bake until golden, 20 to 25 minutes. Let the cookies stand until firm, about 1 minute, then transfer to a wire rack and let cool completely. Store in an airtight container at room temperature for up to 5 days or in the freezer for up to 3 months.

RYE

"Do not make a stingy sandwich; pile the cold cuts high. Customers should see salami comin' through the rye." (Lyrics from the 1962 song parody, "Don't Buy the Liverwurst," by humorist Alan Sherman.)

Rye probably originated in south central Europe, Armenia, or Turkmenistan, regions where wild species still grow, and was perhaps first domesticated around 1000 BCE in northern Europe. This grain was unknown in ancient Israel, Egypt, and early Rome. For a long time, it was considered an undesirable weed in most areas. The first written record of rye cultivation was by Pliny the Elder (c. 77 CE), who noted that *secale* was grown around the Alps, while also disparaging it as "a very poor food and good only to avert starvation." As late as Talmudic times, rye was not a cultivated crop anywhere in the Middle East.

Despite rye's poor reception in southern Europe and absence in most of the rest of the Old World, its usage proliferated throughout the northern section of the continent and into Russia due to its ability to grow in colder climates and under poor conditions. Another important reason for rye's dissemination in the cooler parts of Europe was its weedlike tendency to spread. In wheat fields, farmers were unable to weed it out. As a result, when wheat was grown in northern Europe, it was typically harvested with rye, then the seeds were planted together or ground into flour together; this combination of flours was called maslin in English and *sitnice* or *shitnitse* in Yiddish. Maslin was the primary form of flour in northern Europe until well into the nineteenth century. Rye was also sometimes ground, on purpose, with barley or split peas. Even in Romania, the most southern stretch of Ashkenazic culture, where corn has long been the predominant grain, rye and maslin still today constitute about 20 percent of the diet. Consequently, rye was unfamiliar to most Sephardim and Mizrachim, while omnipresent for Ashkenazim.

For millennia, the residents of northern Europe subsisted off of breads made from rye leavened with a rye starter called *roshtshine*. For a special treat, the same rye dough, but with more water, was used to make pancakes called *roshtshine latkes*, which were typically topped with a dollop of sour cream or pat of butter. Most Polish towns had at least one Jewish bakery, which sold its own wares to both Jews and non-Jews and also allowed housewives to bake homemade loaves for a small remuneration. Commercial bakers' rye loaves were usually large rounds or ovals weighing fifteen to twenty-five pounds; these were baked for the lengthy time of four to six hours, then sold in pieces by weight. A distinctive Jewish technique was to sift some of the rye flour to remove the bran, then mix this finer, lighter flour with water to make a glaze called *kharmushke*, which was rubbed over the top of the unbaked loaves. The result of this practice was that the crusts of the Jewish loaves were lighter in color than the blackened crusts of

their non-Jewish neighbors. Malted rye grains and rye bread were also fermented to make the most widespread alcoholic beverage in eastern Europe, an acidic, mildly alcoholic beer, *kvas*.

The traditional European way to darken rye bread, as well as enhance the flavor and increase moistness, was to use an altus or *alte brot* (old bread). This was made from soaked, mashed, stale sour rye bread. In America, molasses or caramel color is typically added to most mass-produced rye loaves to darken the color and mask the high wheat content.

Today, rye, the last in rank in production among the world's primary grains, is mainly used for three purposes: whiskey, flour, and livestock feed. There are four basic grades of rye flour—light, dark, medium, and pumpernickel. Light rye contains no bran and is therefore very pale in color. Dark rye contains all the bran, so its flavor and color are more intense. Medium rye is a mixture of light and dark rye flours. Pumpernickel is a dark rye with added bran.

Caraway seeds (*kimmel*) and nigella are commonly added to Jewish rye bread, imparting a bit of spice. In most Jewish bakeries, the generic term "rye bread" refers to a loaf containing seeds, while loaves without caraway are identified as "seedless." The seeds are mixed into the dough and sometimes also sprinkled on top.

For the Sabbath and festivals, Ashkenazim would somehow scrounge up the funds to bake challah from wheat, even if very small loaves. During the rest of the week, most families subsisted on *kornbroyt* (rye containing all the germ and bran along with varying amounts of wheat) or *schwarzbroyt* (black bread), a coarse, dark rye bread with little or no wheat. The eastern Yiddish word for rye is *korn* and, therefore, Jewish rye bread in America is sometimes called "corn bread" or "corn rye." A round, tall rye loaf is called *tzitzl*, from the Yiddish meaning "breast." In eastern Europe, *broyt* ("bread" in Yiddish), without any other description, meant rye bread. Rye bread was among the *zoyers* (sours), such as pickles and sour cream, ubiquitous in eastern Ashkenazic meals, providing essential nutrition as well as enlivening the diet. Classic rye bread was not used in Europe for sandwiches, but rather slices or hunks were simply schmeared with schmaltz or butter or eaten along with other foods, such as herring, cheese, or slices of meat. A favorite Ashkenazic treat was rye bread spread with chopped liver and topped with *retachlich* (black radish salad with onions and schmaltz).

In the United States, from the mid-nineteenth century, German, Polish, and Jewish bakeries always featured rye breads. Sour rye, with a tangy flavor derived from a rye starter, now commonly known in America as Jewish rye, is basically a typical Polish bread made from rye and wheat. Rye became the foundation of the American delicatessen sandwich—it was ideal not only for cold cuts, but also for egg salad and fish salad. A popular deli food in Montreal, Canada, is *karnatzel* (grilled beef sausages, not the garlicky Romanian type) with mustard on rye—a Jewish hamburger.

You don't have to be Jewish

to love Levy's
real Jewish Rye

This memorable ad campaign helped popularize Jewish rye bread across the United States.

Beginning in 1919, the kitchens of Grossinger's Hotel in the Catskill's, under the supervision of matriarch Jennie Grossinger, became famous for classic *haimish* (Jewish comfort) foods, including their signature rye bread. In 1954, the General Baking Company of Brooklyn purchased from the Grossinger family the right to sell bread under its name. On each wrapper was Jennie's smiling face, along with a label declaring the bread had been made using "the authentic formula from the kitchen of Jennie Grossinger." In order to have slices of the same size, more compatible with sandwiches, the shape of prepackaged rye loaves changed—they were made from larger oblong loaves that were split into one-pound sections and presliced. Jennie's rye bread and pumpernickel lived on after her death in 1972 and even after the resort was shut fourteen years later. The popularization of Jennie's bread helped to spread Jewish rye to the American mainstream, as well as perpetuate and reinforce the image of the Jewish mother as the loving, supportive provider of food and encouragement.

Rye bread had evolved from being solely the province of bakeries and delis to being a staple in American grocery stores as well, but was still primarily purchased by Ashkenazim and other northern European communities. Then beginning in 1961, Henry S. Levy & Son, a Jewish bakery in Brooklyn dating back to 1888 that had been mentioned in the 1943 novel *A Tree Grows in Brooklyn*, introduced an endearing ad tagline, "You don't have to be Jewish to love Levy's." A 1967 subway poster campaign, one of the most influential ad promotions of all time, featuring that line along with a series of photographs of individuals from diverse ethnic backgrounds all happily eating a slice of "Levy's Real Jewish Rye" became a cultural phenomenon. It coincided with the visible movement of traditional Ashkenazic culture into the American mainstream. As a result, Levy's emerged as the largest seller of rye bread in the New York City area and rye bread became commonplace in American homes across the country. In 1979, the company was sold to Arnold Bakery of Greenwich, Connecticut, and the Brooklyn facility was shut down. The Levy's name and its impact on American culture endures. Once again, Jews had transformed a food not originally their own and transmitted it from one region to another, and in the process, become associated with it.

(See also Bread and Pumpernickel)

S

SABBATH/SHABBAT

From twilight Friday, until the appearance of the first three stars on Saturday night, observant Jews refrain from creative work. They pray, study, reflect, and, in fulfillment of the commandment of *oneg Shabbat* (enjoyment of the Sabbath), also socialize, sing, and partake of three meals. In the words of Ahad Haam (pen name of Asher Ginsberg, considered the founder of spiritual Zionism as opposed to Theodor Herzl's political Zionism), "It is not so much that Israel has kept the Sabbath, but the Sabbath has kept Israel."

The Sabbath commences with a series of ceremonies—*Hadlakat Nayrot* (kindling of the lamps), Kiddush ("sanctification" of the day), and Hamotzi (benediction over bread). These rites are attributed to the *Anshei Knesset ha-Gadolah* (Members of the Great Assembly), an enigmatic legislative body that functioned from about 500 BCE to 300 BCE. For these rituals, the Sages incorporated a biblical trio of agricultural products that were the mainstays of the diet and economy of ancient Israel and indispensible components of the Temple offerings—grain, wine, and olive oil. As a result, Sabbath dinner possesses a distinctive ambience. The table is set with a cloth and the family's finery. In the room where the Friday meal is eaten, at least two lights cast a glow over the celebrants, as food is best enjoyed when seen. The meal commences with Kiddush over a cup of wine or grape juice.

Two loaves of bread, in remembrance of the double portion of manna that fell on Friday while the Israelites were in the wilderness, dominate the table. Historically, Ashkenazim subsisted on rye breads throughout the week, but for the Sabbath even the poorest attempted to procure white flour for a special braided challah. However, Sephardim and Mizrachim used the same weekday wheat bread for their Sabbath loaves. The bread is covered with a cloth, as the manna was protected by a lower and upper layer of dew. After ritually washing the hands (*netilat yadayim*), the benediction Hamotzi is recited over the loaves. The bread is then sliced or torn, customarily dipped into salt (another mandatory component of the Temple offerings), and given to all the diners.

A repast of favorite and traditional delicacies follows. Sabbath food is traditional or special, intended to enhance, enliven, and differentiate the occasion. In many households, fish is the first course for Friday night, usually followed by a soup. Chicken is the predominant main course, accompanied with various starches and salads. Lively *zemirot* (Sabbath songs) are customarily sung and school children commonly repeat some of the lessons they learned during the previous week. Thus, a profoundly religious activity and enjoyably gastronomic and social experience become one and the same.

The Sabbath is not an ascetic day, but rather one of feasting and enjoyment. Among those foods that promote joy are hot dishes. However, cooking, including heating and reheating liquids, is among the thirty-nine categories of creative work forbidden on the Sabbath. According to Jewish law, the food must be at least half-cooked before the onset of the Sabbath. Therefore, Jewish cooks needed to develop creative ways to serve some dishes warm not only for Friday night, but also for Saturday lunch, without using the usual methods. Thus the Talmud, in a list of the activities that a person must do on Friday afternoon before the onset of the Sabbath, included *tomnin et ha'hamin* (Aramaic meaning "cover/bury the warmed" dish). The content of the ancient *hamin* was not stated, but it probably consisted of some combination of whole grains, meat, and onions, akin to *harisa* (Sabbath porridge). Some Romans, notably the satiric poet Juvenal (early second century CE), derided Jews for preparing *cophinus faenumque* (a large bucket filled with hay), as hay was among the items used to insulate the food to keep it warm.

A dispute between the followers of rabbinic Judaism and the Karaites led to the transformation of hot food on the Sabbath from a mere enjoyment to an imperative. Following the destruction of the First Temple, the Jews of Babylon and subsequently Persia

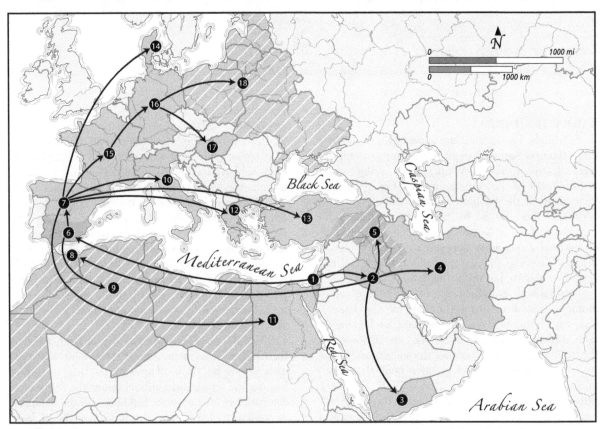

More than two millennia ago, Jews in Israel began preparing stews to cook overnight for Sabbath lunch. By the seventh century, Yemenites were enjoying harisa on the Sabbath. Gradually, Sabbath stews spread through Sephardic and Ashkenazic communities to become a beloved part of their culinary repertoire. *1 Israel to Iraq; 2 Iraq—harisa, tabyeet; 3 from Iraq to Yemen—harisa; 4 from Iraq to Iran—Chalebibi; 5 from Iraq to Kurdistan—Matphoni; 6 from Israel to southern Spain—adafina, harisa; 7 from southern Spain to northern Spain—hamin, harisa; 8 from Iraq to Tangiers—orissa (horisa); 9 from Spain to Maghreb—adafina/dafina, frackh, skhina, t'fina; 10 from Spain to Italy—hamin; 11 from northern Spain to Egypt—hamin; 12 from Spain to Greece—hamin; 13 from Spain to Turkey—hamin; 14 from Spain to Netherlands—Shkanah; 15 from Spain to France—Schalet (shalet); 16 from France to Germany—Schalet (shalet); 17 from Germany to Hungary—Sholet; 18 from Germany to Poland, Baltic States, Ukraine—Cholent (tsholnt)*

enjoyed a substantial amount of autonomy. Without a legislative body, the Jewish community needed a unifying element as well as a way to manage its internal government, including the appointment of judges. At the same time, the Persian authorities required an administrator who could reach the sizable Jewish community, especially to serve as chief tax collector. Therefore, a hereditary exilarchate (secular Jewish authority over the Jews of Babylonia and Persia) was established, headed by a descendant of the house of David. From at least the second century BCE until the thirteenth century CE, the head of the exi-

larchate, the *Resh Galutha* (exilarch) served as the lay head of the Jewish community of Babylon and Persia. Meanwhile, Jews all over the world turned to the heads of the two Babylonian Talmudic academies of Sura and Pumbeditha for religious guidance.

In 761, the exilarch Solomon ben Chisdai died childless and next in the line of succession was his oldest nephew, Anan ben David. However, the heads of the Talmudic academies passed over Anan to select his younger brother. In response, the disgruntled Anan denied the authority of the Talmud and rabbinic interpretation and professed a belief in strict adherence to the Written Law. The caliph imprisoned him as a rebel, but after Anan declared his beliefs a separate religion, he was released and made his way to Israel.

At first, the Ananites proved relatively unsuccessful in attracting adherents. Then in the early tenth century, the group was absorbed into another sect, the *Bnai Mikra* (followers of the Scripture), abbreviated as *Karaim* (Karaites). The term *Karaim* was first recorded in the early seventh century, a century before Anan. However, the Karaites subsequently considered him the founder of their group and his descendants became leaders of the sect. Soon this antirabbinic movement emerged as a major force in some areas, at one point threatening to surpass the orthodox establishments in Egypt and Israel. However, faced with the fierce opposition of rabbinic Judaism, particularly by Saadiah Gaon (882–942), whose intellectual prowess, indefatigable energy, and command of Arabic made him an overwhelming opponent, the Karaite movement waned. The Crusades in 1099 further weakened the movement as did the arrival in Egypt in 1166 of Moses Maimonides. The masses of Sephardic refugees who appeared in the Ottoman Empire after 1492 overwhelmed the remaining Karaites both culturally and numerically. Today, a small remnant of the Karaite community survives, including about twenty thousand living in Israel and perhaps ten thousand living elsewhere, primarily in the Crimea.

In considering the claims of the Karaites, several facts become apparent. Many of the features and rites that practitioners currently prize most about Judaism are rabbinic in origin, including Hanukkah, Purim, Tu b'Shevat, Lag b'Omer, the *siddur*, Kiddush, Havdalah, the Seder (including the four cups of wine, charoset, and the Haggadah), and *nayrot Shabbat* (Sabbath lights). In addition, although some may claim that the written Torah is the only legitimate source of Jewish law, the text itself proves completely inadequate for constructing a way of life, requiring interpretation as well as frequent adaptations. Thus Karaites as well as the earlier sect, Saducees, were quickly forced to establish their own traditions, which were frequently more ascetic than those of rabbinic Judaism.

Anan instructed that the thirty-nine types of work forbidden on Shabbat were extended to include anything not imperative for worship, sustenance, or essential human needs. Based on the biblical verse "Let every man remain where he is, let no man leave

his place on the seventh day," Karaites stayed in their homes on the Sabbath except to go to their synagogue, an institution, which, it should be noted, was rabbinic in origin. One of the Karaites' principal doctrines, which was similar to a belief of the Saducees, involved the admonishment, "You shall not *teva'aru* a fire in all your habitations upon the Sabbath day." Whereas the rabbis interpreted *teva'aru* as a reference to kindling a fire, Karaites forbade the very presence of any fire or even hot food on the Sabbath. To followers of rabbinic Judaism, the Karaite version of the Sabbath was a cold and gloomy experience.

As the dispute with the Karaites intensified, the practice of kindling the Sabbath lights and eating hot food for Sabbath lunch was no longer simply a matter of enjoyment, but an attestation of identification with rabbinic tradition. To emphasize the point, the rabbis instituted the recitation of a blessing for the Shabbat lights, *"asher kidshanu b'mitzvotav v'tzivanu lehadlik ner shel Shabbat"* (Who has made us holy with His commandments and has commanded us to kindle the Sabbath lights). Zerahiah ben Isaac ha-Levi (the late fourteenth-century rabbi of Saragossa and Aragon) in his *Sefer ha-Ma'or* declared, "Whoever does not eat *hamin* [Sabbath stew] on the Sabbath should be investigated on suspicion of being a heretic [a Karaite]." In the fifteenth century, many Karaite authorities began to permit the presence of fire on the Sabbath and many followers emulated the practice of Sabbath lights and even allowed warm foods.

The second Sabbath meal follows the morning prayer service on Saturday. The mood at lunch is similar to that of the first meal, but the foods served are quite different. In order to stay fresh without refrigeration, many Sabbath dishes contain vinegar or other acids as a preservative and often a sweetener or dried fruit to counter the piquancy. Kugel, *kishke* (stuffed

Beginning in the late eighteenth century, samovars and other heating devices were used to keep liquids and foods warm for the Sabbath.

derma), and other dishes were devised that could simmer over a very low fire until Sabbath lunch.

Sholem Aleichem, in his 1915 short story "Tit for Tat," described a special Sabbath lunch consisting of typical eastern European dishes:

"The next day, after services, we sat down at the table. Well, you should have seen the spread. First the appetizers: wafers [*kichlach*] and chopped herring, and onions and schmaltz with [black] radishes and chopped liver and eggs and gribenes. And after that the cold fish and the meat from yesterday's tzimmes, and then the jellied calf's foot, or fisnoga as you call it, with thin slices of garlic, and after that the potato cholent with the kugel that had been in the oven all night—and you know what that smells like when you take it out of the oven and take the cover off the pot. And what it tastes like. Our visitor could not find words to praise it. So I tell him: 'This is still nothing. Wait until you have tasted our borscht tonight, then you'll know what good food is.'"

Late on Saturday afternoon is *shalosh seudot* (third meal). The atmosphere contrasts with that of the rest of the day—the participants are saddened by the imminent departure of the Sabbath. The songs are slow and almost mournful. *Shalosh seudot* fare is generally simpler than that served at the other two Sabbath meals; it consists primarily of bread, cold fish, perhaps a few salads, and some leftover dessert. This meal is often held in the synagogue between the afternoon and evening services.

The Sabbath departs with the Havdalah ritual: the lighting of a candle, a sniff of spice, and a blessing over a cup of wine. In the words of Isaac Bashevis Singer from *In My Father's Court*, (1966): "Our house was filled with the odor of burning wax, blessed spices, and with the atmosphere of wonder and miracles."

On Saturday night following the Sabbath, many families hold a party called *melaveh malkah* (literally "escorting the queen") by Ashkenazim and *noche de Alhad* (night of Sunday) by Sephardim. The Sabbath, metaphorically viewed as a queen, is symbolically escorted away at this gathering. In the process, the special feelings of the Sabbath are prolonged for a while longer. Of course, food, typically cold dishes and dairy, is an integral part of the event.

(See also Adafina, Challah, Cholent, Desayuno, Hamin, Hamotzi, Harisa, Kiddush, Melaveh Malkah, Schalet, Seudah, Shkanah, Tabyett, and T'fina)

SABICH

Sabich is a *laffa* or pita sandwich with a filling of fried eggplant, hard-boiled egg, Israeli salad, and various sauces or pickles.

Origin: Iraq

Other names: *sabeek.*

Among the foods introduced to Israel by Iraqis is *sabich*; the name probably derived from the Arabic *sabah* (morning). The sandwich is a combination of popular items from a traditional Iraqi Sabbath morning *mezze* (appetizer assortment), all wrapped in flatbread. Besides the fried eggplant and Israeli salad, the sandwich can include hummus, tahini (sesame seed paste), pickles, and *amba* (curried mango condiment) and/or *s'chug* or *harissa* (chili sauce). Some also add sliced potatoes. *Sabich* is not a bland sandwich—it is spicy.

Sabich first appeared in Israel in the 1950s in the city of Ramat Gan, which had a large Iraqi population. Ramat Gan remains the area where it is most popular. By the turn of the twentieth century, *sabich* had become commonplace throughout the country and was frequently offered alongside falafel as an alternative sandwich. There exists a great deal of heated debate over which of several shops in Ramat Gan and adjacent Tel Aviv makes the best *sabich*. More recently, *sabich* came to America, where it is now featured in many New York City falafel and hummus restaurants.

SABRA

Sabra is Hebrew for cactus and its fruit (prickly pear). Cacti, a succulent fruit, are indigenous to the Ameri-

Although not grown in Israel until the nineteenth century, the sabra (prickly pear)—tough on the outside and sweet inside—became the symbol of native Israelis.

cas. Upon reaching Israel in the nineteenth century, they soon become a familiar sight throughout the land, where they were frequently planted to serve as natural barriers and fences. In the April 18, 1931, issue of the Israeli newspaper *Do'ar HaYom*, journalist Uri Kesari penned an essay entitled "We Are the Leaves of the *Sabra!*" Subsequently, the word *sabra* became identified with native-born Israelis, who were regarded as this fruit—tough and prickly on the outside but sweet on the inside.

The fruit is usually eaten raw, although the many seeds make this a challenging task. After the fruit is mashed and the seeds are strained out, the pulp is used in sauces, vinaigrettes, sorbets, and ice cream.

In 1963, the Bronfman family, then owners of the Seagram Company, decided to create a uniquely Israeli liqueur and developed one from local *sabras*. This flavor, however, failed to catch on, and by the following year a new version, retaining the same name, was created from chocolate and orange, inspired by the native Jaffa orange. This time the flavor proved very successful and Sabra liqueur joined the list of the world's best liqueurs.

SABZI

Sabzi is the Farsi word for herbs. A distinctive feature of Persian cuisine is the use of mixed of fresh herbs to dishes such as salads (*salada sabzi*), soups (*ash-e sabzi*), stews (*khoreshe sabzi*), meatballs (*kufteh sabzi*), and omelets (*kuku sabzi*). These dishes are featured on Persian Jewish tables for Passover, Rosh Hashanah, and other special occasions.

SACHLAV

Sachlav is a thick hot beverage and a thicker hot pudding made from ground orchid root.
Origin: Eastern Mediterranean
Other names: Arabic: *sahlab*; England: saloop;
   Greece: *salepi*; Turkey: *salep*.

The tubers of orchids grow as a pair of small round globes, giving rise to the ancient Greek name for the plant, *orchis* (testicle), and, in the same vein, its Arabic name, *sahlab*, from the Arabic term *hasyu al-thalab* (fox testicles). Today, the whole dried orchid tubers are sold in some Middle Eastern markets, but they are predominantly found ground into a powder. *Sahlab* or, in Hebrew, *sachlav*, variously refers to the orchid plant itself, its ground bulbs, and several dishes

made from them. When the powder is dissolved in a liquid, it acts as a stabilizer and thickener. *Sachlav* has a distinctive subtle earthy flavor.

It takes about one thousand orchids to produce one kilogram of *sachlav* powder; the best-quality powder is a translucent yellow. For most of the past several millennia, during the spring and summer, people have harvested only one of the tubers of each plant, keeping it alive to produce future generations. However, because demand and cost have recently risen, both tubers are now commonly taken, further decreasing their availability. Consequently, *sachlav* is rather expensive and frequently the ground form is adulterated or is completely replaced with cornstarch and other inferior ingredients. Some of the best tubers grow in Turkey, but today the Turkish government forbids their export.

The ancient Greeks and Romans ground the tubers of various orchids and cooked the powder to make a beverage that was thought to be an aphrodisiac. Medieval Arabs picked up this practice of drinking *sachlav*, as did the Turks. Middle Easterners still consider the beverage an aphrodisiac, and an aid in resisting colds. Maimonides cited the medicinal use of *sachlav* for several ailments, noting its ability to "to revive the spirits and to arouse sexual desire."

Sachlav is a slightly thick, white beverage that is served hot. When larger amounts of powder are added, the mixture becomes thicker and turns into a hot pudding. In the Middle East, the powder is dissolved in milk, flavored with sugar and orange-blossom water or rose water, and sprinkled with a little ground cinnamon. many Middle Easterners eagerly await the first *sachlav* of the season, considering it a favorite comfort food. In Turkey, it is dispensed from large brass or copper urns at pastry shops, kiosks, and carts.

In addition, for the past three centuries, a favorite Turkish usage of the tuber has been in *salepi dondurma*, an orchid ice cream further flavored with mastic. The mixture is uniquely kneaded and stretched into a firm, chewy mass. The orchid powder impedes the melting of the ice cream.

In the seventeenth century, England and Germany adapted the orchid beverage from the Turks, substituting water for the milk and pronouncing the name saloop. Around the same time, two other foreign hot beverages appeared in Europe, coffee and tea. All three soon had their advocates, with saloop initially becoming the most widespread in England. For the ensuing two centuries, saloop was sold from kiosks and street vendors, as well as frequently found in European coffeehouses and tea houses. Saloop even became common in colonial America. Charles Dickens, in his weekly journal, *All the Year Round* (London, 1885), reminisced, "'Saloop—loop-loop!' was formerly a well-known cry in London. The decoction sold under this name seems, however, to have been superseded by coffee when that article became cheap. Saloop seems to have been sold down to modern time at street-stalls, from a late hour at night to early morning, just as coffee is sold now." During the nineteenth century, as coffee and tea emerged as inexpensive everyday fare, the popularity of saloop in Europe and America faded.

Sachlav, *a thick, hot beverage made from the orchid root remains widely popular in the Middle East. Here a man in Jerusalem sells the drink piping hot from the large brass urn on his back.*

Not so in the Levant, Egypt, and India, where the hot orchid beverage remains widespread to this day.

Jews from Turkey, Egypt, and the Levant brought the hot beverage and thicker hot pudding versions to Israel. It has a bright white color and distinctive flowery flavor. The thicker hot, sweet pudding form is served in tall cups and sprinkled with finely shredded coconut, chopped nuts, and cinnamon and, more recently, sometimes dried banana chips and raisins. A spoon is required to eat it. The pudding is also cooled and used to fill semolina pastry. Numerous small vendors on the street and in *souks* (marketplaces) and malls specialize in thick *sachlav cham* (hot), typically served in paper cups. Many coffee shops and even some fancier restaurants offer it as well, but usually in glasses. It is particularly a winter treat and many Israelis look forward to the arrival of cold weather so that they can enjoy their first *sachlav* of the season. Packaged *sachlav* powder and "instant *sachlav*" are sold at local groceries. However, most of these do not include the expensive orchid root, so beverages and puddings made from them do not have quite the same flavor and consistency as those made from high-quality powder.

MIDDLE EASTERN ORCHID ROOT PUDDING (*SACHLAV*)

3 TO 5 SERVINGS   [DAIRY]

- 4 cups whole or low-fat milk (do not use nonfat)
- About 6 tablespoons *sachlav* powder or ½ cup cornstarch or potato starch
- ¼ to ½ cup sugar
- About 2 teaspoons orange-blossom water or rose water, or 1 teaspoon vanilla extract
- About 1 teaspoon ground cinnamon for sprinkling
- About ¼ cup unsweetened dried shredded coconut for sprinkling
- About 3 tablespoons chopped pistachios or almonds for sprinkling

1. In a small bowl, stir ½ cup milk into the *sachlav*. In a medium, heavy saucepan, combine the remaining milk and sugar to taste and cook over medium-low heat until the mixture is heated and the sugar dissolves, about 5 minutes.

2. Add the *sachlav* mixture and cook, stirring constantly, until the pudding boils and thickens, then boil and stir for an additional 2 minutes.

3. Remove from the heat and stir in the orange-blossom water. Divide among 3 to 5 bowls or cups and sprinkle with the cinnamon, coconut, and pistachios.

The pudding is typically eaten hot, but can be eaten cooled as well.

SAFFRON

Saffron, from the Arabic *asfar* (yellow), is the world's most expensive spice. Saffron is made from the red-orange or yellowish stigmas of the fall-flowering purple crocus. Each blossom produces three stigmas (female organs of the flower) and an expert can hand strip up to twelve thousand flowers a day. However, more than eighty thousand blossoms and much manual labor are required to produce a single pound of the spice. An acre of land yields only about six pounds of saffron. In October, pickers gather the flowers just as the plants open in the morning, then remove and sort the stigmas by hand. Historically, the valuable strands were packed in linen bags, then secured in a leather pouch for transport.

Saffron is a native of Asia Minor or perhaps Crete, where it has been cultivated in both places since the Bronze Age. Most of the ancient Mediterranean civilizations, including the Hebrews, Egyptians, Greeks, and Romans, treasured it not only as a spice, but also as an ingredient in medicines and perfumes, and as a dye.

Saffron is mentioned once in the Bible—it is called *karkom* (which is the source of the English word crocus) in Song of Songs and is included among "the chief spices." In modern Hebrew, the spice is *zafran* and the crocus is *karkom*, while *kurkum* became the Arabic and modern Hebrew word for turmeric. Saffron was among the eleven aromatic components of the Temple incense. In the *Midrash Sechel Tov* by Menachem ben Sholomo of Italy (twelfth century), saffron along with cumin spiced the venison stew that Isaac requested of his son Esau. The Talmud used a field sowed with saffron as the paradigm of an expensively planted field. It also mentioned *zetoom hamitzri* (Egyptian beer), made from barley, salt, and saffron. The Talmud used the related word *nitkarkam* to mean "he became embarrassed or angry," denoting that his face became the reddish color of saffron threads.

Persians brought the plant eastward to India around 500 BCE. The Arabs introduced the saffron crocus flowers, as well as the techniques for preparing them, to Spain one thousand years ago. Until recently, Spain was the largest producer of saffron, producing nearly two-thirds of the world's supply. Today, Iran is the world's major producer of saffron, followed by Spain, while Italy, Turkey, Morocco, and Greece grow it on a much smaller scale.

The more intense the red hue of the stigma, the better the quality of the spice. Saffron with a brown color or too many yellow threads should be avoided. It is preferable to purchase saffron threads rather than the ground spice not only because grinding releases some of the volatile oils, but also because commercially prepared powdered "saffron" is often adulterated and may actually contain no genuine saffron. This is hardly a modern phenomenon, as evidenced by the fact that various medieval European governments imposed severe penalties, even death, for adulterating saffron.

During the medieval period, Middle Eastern and European Jews were an integral part of the saffron trade (the original yellow Jew badges decreed by Pope Innocent III in 1215 had to be dyed by saffron). As a result, saffron, with its earthy, slighty bitter, honey-like flavor, became an ingredient in Jewish cooking even in many areas where it did not grow. Some eastern Ashkenazim added a little saffron or the much-less-expensive safflower to the Sabbath challah and other foods to produce a bright yellow color. Medieval Arabic cooking utilized large amounts of *zaffaran* to produce a yellow color, their traditional symbol of joy and happiness, influencing not only Sephardim, but also Persian, Turkish, and Moroccan Jews and, beginning in the fifteenth century, Italians. For centuries, saffron-tinted golden rice, called *roz bi zaffaran* in Arabic, *riso col zafran* in Italian, and *arroz con azafran* or *arroz de Sabato* in Ladino, has been a Friday night and holiday tradition in Sephardic and Middle Eastern communities.

SALADE RUSSE (RUSSIAN SALAD)

Salade Russe is an assortment of diced cooked vegetables and sometimes proteins.

Other names: French: *salade à la Russe*; Iran: *salad-e olivieh*; Russia: Salad Olivier.

Salads were unknown in Russia until the nineteenth century, when nobles began importing French chefs. Among them was Lucien Olivier, who in 1864 in Moscow left the employ of a Russian noble and opened the Hermitage restaurant. There chef Olivier created a fancy potato salad bound with mayonnaise, called Salad Olivier, which became wildly popular in its native Russia. Olivier later opened a restaurant in Wiesbaden, Germany, where he offered the dish as "*salade à la Russe*." Following the Russian Revolution, immigrants spread Olivier's creaion far and wide. In most countries, including Italy, France, Germany, Turkey, and Morocco, it is known as Russian Salad.

The predominant Russian vegetables—potatoes, beets, carrots, and cucumbers, always cooked or pickled—all made their way into this salad. Russians commonly add plenty of meat, poultry, and fish to the dish, but Jews make a vegetarian version because sour cream is sometimes used in the dressing and because it is served at dairy meals. Mediterranean Jewish variations substitute a vinaigrette for the sour cream and mayonnaise. The "Russian Vegetable Salad" in the first edition of *The Settlement Cook Book* (Milwaukee, 1901) called for peas, carrots, string beans, and turnips; the author noted, "Potatoes may be used in place of turnips, or a combination of any two of the vegetables."

Because this salad can be prepared well ahead of time, it was adopted as Sabbath and holiday fare. *Salade Russe* with a vinaigrette became a traditional Passover dish among Moroccans, who did not eat dairy products during the holiday. Italians typically serve it for the third Sabbath meal on Saturday afternoon with cold *zuppa di verdura* (mixed vegetable soup) and crusty bread. Russians in Israel commonly present this salad on a bed of soft lettuce accompanied with dark bread and chilled vodka.

⊰ RUSSIAN COOKED VEGETABLE SALAD
(*SALADE RUSSE*)

6 TO 8 SERVINGS　　　　　　　　　　[PAREVE]

3 to 4 medium beets, peeled and cut into ½-inch cubes
1 tablespoon olive or vegetable oil
4 medium (about 1 pound total) boiling potatoes
8 ounces green beans, cut into ½-inch pieces
4 medium carrots, cut into ½-inch pieces
1 cup shelled green peas
2 medium onions, coarsely chopped
4 medium dill pickles, cut into ½-inch cubes
4 scallions (white and light green parts), sliced

Dressing:
¼ cup red wine vinegar or white wine vinegar
1 teaspoon dry mustard or 1½ teaspoons Dijon mustard

¾ teaspoon sugar
About ¼ teaspoon table salt or ½ teaspoon kosher salt
Ground white or black pepper to taste
½ cup vegetable oil

2 hard-boiled eggs, sliced, for garnish (optional)

1. Preheat the oven to 375°F. Toss the beets with the oil and wrap in aluminum foil. Bake until tender, about 25 minutes.

2. Meanwhile, bring a large pot of lightly salted water to a boil, add the potatoes, reduce the heat to low, cover, and simmer until fork-tender, 20 to 30 minutes. Drain, peel, and cut into ½-inch cubes.

3. Steam or boil the beans, carrots, peas, and onion until crisp-tender, about 2 minutes.

4. In a large bowl, combine the beets, potatoes, beans, carrots, peas, onions, pickles, and scallions.

5. To make the dressing: In a medium bowl, stir together the vinegar, mustard, sugar, salt, and pepper. In a slow, steady stream, whisk in the oil.

6. Pour the dressing over the vegetables and toss to coat. Cover and refrigerate for at least 30 minutes or up to 2 days to let the vegetables absorb the dressing. Serve chilled or at room temperature, if desired, garnished with the eggs.

SALAMI

"As life's pleasures go, food is second only to sex. Except for salami and eggs. Now that's better than sex, but only if the salami is thickly sliced." (From a monologue performed by comedian Alan King.)

In Italy, since the time of the Roman Empire, much of the meat has been preserved by chopping and salting. *Salumi*, from the Latin *sal* (salt), is the generic Italian term for all manner of cured meats—the equivalent of the French *charcuterie*—including those with and without a casing. A specific type of *salumi* is *salame* (salami is the plural), denoting a cured sausage. *Salame* vary according to spicing and the type of meat grinding (fine, medium, or coarse) and can be dry-aged, precooked, or fresh, the latter requiring cooking before consumption. Modena emerged as the center of *salame* production, but the dish eventually spread far and wide.

Although the typical Italian *salumi* contains pork, Jews substituted beef, resulting in *salsicce di manzo* (beef sausage), or poultry, notably creating *salame d'oca* (goose sausage). In northern Italy, where the raising of geese had been widespread among Jews since Roman times, geese were known as "poor person's pig." By using geese, every Jewish household could annually prepare sausages without owning large livestock.

The Italian *salame* has been adapted by many cultures. Hungarians make a version of sausages (*kolbász*) called *salámi*, a coarsely textured firm sausage more heavily smoked than the Italian version. Hungarian *téli salami* is mildly seasoned, while the *csabai salami* is rather spicy and loaded with plenty of paprika.

In America, salami came to mean a cooked or dry-cured garlic sausage. It was in America, living next to Italians on Manhattan's Lower East Side, that Ashkenazim, some familiar with German wursts and Polish kielbasa, became acquainted with Italian salami. Toward the end of the nineteenth century, an increasing number of small kosher meat-processing plants opened in America to produced kosher sausages, especially garlic sausages, which eventually assumed the name salami. The Yiddish writer Sholem Aleichem, who first visited New York in 1906 and would die there in 1916, wrote about early American-Jewish life in the comic novel *Motl, the Cantor's Son*. He mentioned salami in this passage describing a New York eatery: "Maybe you've heard of Hebrew National Delicatessen. It's a company that sells kosher salami, frankfurters, pickled tongues, and corned beef. It has stores all over town. If you're hungry, you step into one and order a hot dog with mustard and horseradish."

The salami emerged in America as a favorite Jewish food and cultural staple. Salami was adopted by Jewish delicatessens, although it never became as prominent as pastrami, corned beef, and chopped liver. In delis, the hanging hard salamis, air-dried for at least three months, were typically wiped daily to remove a chalky white crust of salt and chemicals that formed on the outside. For decades before World War II, many Jewish delicatessens posted a sign, "a nickel a shtickel," indicating that the ends of salamis were on sale for five cents each.

Salami was more commonly consumed in homes, in simple dishes, than in restaurants. In many Jewish families, salami sandwiches became a common school lunch. Southern Jewish families might make red beans and rice with salami instead of pork sausage. In the 1950s, kosher salami on white bread reflected the synthesis and acculturation of American Jews.

Spare and inexpensive ingredients, like eggs and sausage, made a filling dinner for harried American Jewish housewives, hapless bachelors, or for many a father, on the rare occasion when he was forced to cook. Some cooks leave the salami slices whole, while others cut them in halves. Some people prefer to cook the eggs without stirring, creating a sort of pancake, while others scramble the eggs. Some people eat it with mustard, while others place slices of salami and eggs on bread, rendering the dish more filling.

In the days when kosher food was still rare in American stores, Jewish travelers frequently packed a salami or several in their luggage, in case of emergency. During World War II, a whole kosher salami was a common and welcomed present from worried families or the Jewish Welfare Board to their children in the military, and in the years afterward, from parents to their children in college. In 1948, the *New Yorker* magazine mentioned a "Kosher Salami-of-the-Month-Club." In the 1960s and 1970s, when westerners were protesting Soviet repression of Jews, activists smuggled kosher salamis to refuseniks in Russia. The first punk rock group, the Ramones, in the 1977 song "Commando," declared, "Fourth rule is eat kosher salami."

(See also Sausage)

ASHKENAZIC SALAMI AND EGGS (*VURSHT UN EIER*)

2 TO 3 SERVINGS   [MEAT]

1 tablespoon vegetable oil
8 to 12 slices beef salami
6 large eggs, lightly beaten
About ¼ teaspoon table salt or ½ teaspoon kosher salt
About ¼ teaspoon ground black pepper

1. In a large skillet, heat the oil over medium-high heat. Add the salami in a single layer and fry, turning, until browned on both sides, 1 to 2 minutes per side.

2. In a medium bowl, combine the eggs, salt, and pepper. Add to the skillet, making sure to distribute the eggs evenly among the salami slices. Reduce the heat to medium-low and cook until set on the bottom, 1 to 2 minutes. Loosen the edges, then turn the eggs and cook until set, 1 to 2 minutes. Cut into wedges and serve, if desired, with prepared mustard.

SALT

Common salt (sodium chloride) is a crystalline compound produced by the reaction of a base (sodium hydroxide) with an acid (hydrogen chloride). Salt, unlike other foods and spices, is inorganic; it is a mineral component of the oceans that cover three-fourths of the earth's surface.

Salt, an essential part of life on earth, helps in the contraction of muscles and transmission of nerve impulses, and without it living cells would quickly expire from dehydration. This mineral's two components, sodium and chloride, are essential nutrients. In addition to nutritional requirements, salt constitutes one of the four tastes on the human taste buds, reflecting its biological necessity and ensuring humans' positive natural reaction to it. Besides its value as a seasoning, salt also serves as a flavor enhancer and balancer, making other items taste better, and is therefore added to most dishes, both savory and sweet. Salt is of great importance in leavened breads—it enhances the elastic properties of gluten and controls yeast, allowing the bread to rise and making it taste better.

Common salt is obtained by two methods: Mines on land contain the residue of ancient seas that yield a type called halite, and contemporary seawater is evaporated to produce a type called saline. Around the eighth century CE, the advent of pumps and sluices to speed up the evaporation of seawater, producing coarse granules, led to a dramatic increase in the amount of salt available in those ocean areas with no salt mines.

Table salt, like rock salt, is obtained from mine deposits, but it is processed to remove impurities and then ground into small granules. Sea salt is produced from sea water by means of evaporation; it is not refined. All salt is kosher. "Kosher salt," sometimes called coarse salt, is named for its use in kashering, as it is used for drawing blood from meat and poultry. Salt for kashering must be medium grain so it doesn't bounce off or dissolve too quickly.

Salt is also the earliest and still most widely used preservative. Before electricity, vacuum packing, and other advances of modern technology, salt was an imperative for the human food supply. It was used to cure meat and fish for longtime storage, and to discourage the growth of harmful bacteria; it also allowed the survival of flavor-producing bacteria for lacto-fermentation in staple vegetables, such as cabbage, cucumbers, beets, and olives. Salted meat was the forerunner of corned beef and other classic delicatessen meats. The English word pickle is derived

from *pokel*, a Teutonic word for salt. Pickled and cured foods were a way to extend a short growing season. They were portable, so people could travel great distances without having to stop to hunt or forage. The need for salt sparked international commerce, which originally evolved primarily to trade or obtain salt, as well as many wars.

In the ancient world, salt was a limited resource in many regions and was thus an expensive item, more treasured than gold. In Egypt, where depictions of the salt-making process date back to 1450 BCE, salt was obtained from the evaporation of seawater in shallow pans along the Mediterranean coast, as well as from mines in the eastern and western deserts. In Roman times, the army, which was in charge of guarding salt shipments and storehouses, was once paid in salt—salary (literally "salt money" in Latin) thus became the term for fixed compensation. Many of the earliest towns grew up near salt deposits and early trade routes developed in response to the salt trade. The Latin *sal* and English word salt are derived from As-Salt, a town once located several miles east of the Jordan River.

Israel was blessed with an abundance of salt, from both sides. The port of Caesarea served as one of the major sites of salt exports to Rome. Mount Sedom, a ten-mile stretch on the western shore of the southern Dead Sea, offered an abundant supply of salt, as did pools and mounds around the Dead Sea, in Hebrew, *Yam ha'Melach* (Salt Sea). Herod's fortress of Masada served to protect and control the Dead Sea salt supply route. In addition, sea salt came from shallow coastal salt pans along the Mediterranean Sea. Thus salt, although still precious, was never unobtainable or exorbitantly priced in Israel. Medieval Jews were commonly involved in salt production and trade.

The most prominent salt in ancient Israel was *melach sedomit* (Sodom salt), a sea salt possibly extracted from Mount Sedom. The Talmud listed it among the ingredients of the Temple incense. Sodom salt could be particularly caustic, engendering the practice of a ritual washing of the hands after a meal to protect the eyes from potential blindness. The Talmud contrasted Sodom salt with "*istrokanit* salt," which Rashi described as "mined and processed." The origin of the word *istrokanit* was probably *serak* (desert/barren land); *istrokanit* denotes the coarser mined halite, in contrast to the flaky saline from the sea.

The Bible contains numerous references to salt, *melach* in Hebrew, derived from the root "to rub small/to reduce to dust." Lot's wife famously turned into a *netziv melach* (pillar of salt) as the family fled the destruction of Sodom and she stopped to look back. All the offerings in the Temple, both flour and meat, before coming into contact with the altar, had to be salted. In addition, salt was also sprinkled on the ramp to the altar to prevent the barefoot priests from slipping. Thus the Temple required massive amounts of salt on a daily basis, necessitating three chambers on the southern side of the Temple courtyard: one where salt was stored and prepared for the offerings, another where the animal hides were salted and processed, and a third where the animal parts were rinsed and cleaned. Among the provisions of the Persian king Artaxerxes (c. 458 BCE) for the needs of the newly rebuilt Temple was "unlimited salt."

The Talmud noted that as long as the Temple stood, the altar atoned for Israel, but upon its destruction, the home table atones, when the poor are invited as guests. Rabbi Moses Isserles, referring to the custom of dipping the first piece of bread in salt, explained that salt is placed on the table before making the benediction Hamotzi over bread, "because the table is like the altar and eating is like an offering." Many families dip the *karpas* of the Passover Seder into salt water and some also eat hard-boiled eggs in salt water. Salt, the ultimate condiment, and bread, the staff of life, are the customary Jewish housewarming gifts. Thus salt remains not only a condiment, but also part of Jewish life and ritual.

SAMBUSAK

Sambusak is a fried or baked turnover made with pastry or yeast dough.

Origin: Middle East

Other names: Arabic: *fatayar*; Farsi: *sanbusa*, *sanbusaj*, *sambuse*; India: samosa; Syria: *bastel*; Turkey: *börek*.

In the bread-loving Middle East, medieval cooks began enhancing basic bread dough by spreading rounds of dough with spiced ground meat, making dishes such as the medium-sized open-faced pizzas *sfeeha* and *lahmajin* (literally "meat with dough"). Cooks who lacked a horizontal baking surface folded the edges of the dough over the ground beef and deep-fried the pastry in fat, transforming it into a turnover with a distinctive crisp, rich crust that contrasted with the moist filling. Turnovers are flavorful, convenient, and portable. Small pastries make a tasty appetizer and a large one can be a substantial side dish or a meal in itself. Because turnovers could be prepared anywhere by anyone who had a pot, enough fat, and a fire, they emerged as common street food throughout much of the Middle East. Travelers could easily fry up a batch around a campfire at night, reserving the leftovers as provisions for the next day. For the poor, filled pastries provided a tasty way to stretch scarce resources or use up leftovers, while the wealthy loved refined versions for their flavor. Later, the turnovers were also baked.

The earliest known of these Middle Eastern turnovers is *sanbusak* or *sanbusaj*; the name derived from the Farsi *sanbusa* (triangular) with the diminutive ending *ak*, connoting a Persian origin. The most common Sephardic pronunciation is *sambusak*. *Sambusak* is most probably the forerunner of most medieval pastry turnovers, including the northern Iberian *empanada* as well as the Italian calzone.

The first written record of *sanbusak* dates back to early ninth-century Iraq; Arabs subsequently spread the pastry from India to Spain. In India, by at least 1300, fried turnovers filled with meat and onion appeared as the *samosa*; these were still typically triangular. In the opposite direction, the dish reached Spain by at least the thirteenth century. An anonymous Andalusian cookbook of that time contained a Moorish recipe for "Sanbûsak," a turnover fried in oil.

The original *sambusak* consisted of pieces of bread dough folded over a meat filling into a triangular shape and fried in sesame oil, a form that predominated well into the fourteenth century. Eventually, since rolling a ball of dough more naturally and easily forms a round rather than a square, the half-moon emerged as the prevailing version. As newer types of pastry developed, they were frequently substituted for the yeast dough. Yeast dough versions, however, remain extremely popular in Syrian, Lebanese, and Iraqi communities. Although some yeast-dough turnovers continue to be cooked in hot oil, especially those containing meat fillings, in our fat-conscious era, most *sambusak* are now baked. The quality of a housewife's culinary skills was once measured by her preparation of *sambusak* and the crimping and fluting of the edges. Significantly, *sambusak* fell from favor among most non-Jews in its native Iran around the seventeenth century, but retained is popularity among many Persian Jews.

Cheese, typically very salty types, has long been the most common filling for Jews, but vegetables, particularly spinach, chard, and pumpkin, are also popular. Leeks, onions, and potatoes are all used individually or paired with other flavors. Iraqi Jews specialize in chickpea fillings, adding some ground chicken or meat for the festivals and using only chickpeas for pareve occasions. Although most fillings are savory, there are a few popular versions made with sweet fillings, most notably almond (*sambusak bil loz*) and walnut with cardamom (*sambusak b'shikir*). Little date- or nut-filled pies are called *baba bi tamar* or *klaicha* in Iraq and *kasmay* in Kurdistan. The Jews of Calcutta also developed a sweetened coconut filling.

Turnovers—*sambusaks*, *borekas*, and *empanadas*—became a traditional part of the Sephardic Sabbath, as well as ubiquitous at most Middle Eastern celebrations. Meat *sambusak* is traditional on the Sabbath and Sukkot and cheese *sambusak* on Hanukkah and dairy meals. On Shavuot *sambusak* is symbolic of a Torah scroll—it is covered on the outside and the essence is inside. Sweetened almond or walnut filling is popular for holidays, especially Purim. Iraqis and Kurds feature chickpea *sambusak* on special occasions, such as for Purim; the chickpeas are a reminder of Queen Esther, who in order to keep kosher while living in the palace, only ate legumes and other produce.

Middle Easterners brought the *sambusak* to modern Israel where, generally under the name *borekas*, it became a popular snack, street food, school lunch item, and a standard in *mezzes* (appetizer assortments). Most Mizrachi affairs feature them. To share the burden of preparing for a special function, all the women of a family or perhaps a group of friends will spend a day rolling, filling, and crimping large batches of turnovers while socializing.

(See also Boreka, Empanada, Klaicha, and Pastelito)

SAMSA
Samsa is a baked or fried dumpling.
Origin: Uzbekistan
Other names: *somsa*.

The cuisine of central Asia was greatly affected by its two powerful and gastronomically advanced neighbors, Persia and China. An indispensible feature of Bukharan cooking is filled dough dishes from both of those empires, variously deep-fried, pan-fried, steamed, boiled, and baked. Fried and baked filled dumplings are descended from the Persian *sambusak* and are called *samsa*. Today, *samsa* stands can be found all over Uzbekistan and most traditional bakeries sell them along with the local flatbreads, while many home cooks also prepare their own pastries.

Samsa is made in two basic shapes: triangular and round. Frying the dumplings produces a crisp texture, caramelized flavor, and rich color. Fried *samsa* have a simple, thin dumpling skin (called *pi* in Chinese and *gyoza* in Japan) notable for the absence of eggs. Since oil and other frying mediums were at a premium in Uzbekistan, baked versions became the more widespread. Similar to wontons, these dumplings typically include some egg and sometimes baking powder in the dough for tenderness. They are usually baked on the inner wall of a *tandor* (vertical clay oven), a device also introduced by the Persians. Aficionados inspect the shape of the *samsa*, turning them over to scrutinize whether they are golden on the bottom or blackened, the latter indicating inferior culinary skills.

Bukharan *samsa* are very mildly spiced, although a favorite condiment is hot pepper sauce. In Uzbekistan, the filling is typically made with the tail fat of sheep instead of oil. Meat was the original filling, but potatoes emerged as an inexpensive substitute and a sweetened walnut mixture became popular for special occasions. A few types of *samsa* are seasonal—spinach and other young greens are used in fillings in the spring, and *qowoq* (a winter squash) or pumpkin is popular during the autumn. *Kuk samsa* (*kuk* means "green" in Uzbek), contain various fresh herbs.

Samsa are an everyday snack, typically served with tea or soup, as well as at feasts. Fried *samsa* with meat filling are traditional on Hanukkah and Purim.

(See also Sambusak)

SARDINE
There is no such fish as a sardine. The word first appeared around 1430, as a diminutive of the Latin *sarda* from the ancient Greek name for the Mediterranean island of Sardinia, *Sardo*. Sardine has come to refer to the immature members of several varieties of small oily fish, most notably young pilchards, relatives of herring and anchovies. In the eastern Atlantic, pilchards tend to grow larger and live longer than relatives in the Mediterranean. In the Mediterranean

region, where, for thousands of years sardines have been caught in vast numbers, they have long served a role similar to that of the herring farther north, providing protein for the poor.

Sardines are common in the cooking of Mediterranean Jews, primarily as everyday fare. As they are rather small, sardines require three or more per serving as an appetizer. Fresh sardines, simply scaled and gutted, are most popularly grilled, but are also dredged in flour and fried. Greeks grill the fish wrapped in grape leaves (*yaprakites de sardela*). Sephardim marinate them in wine vinegar and lemon juice, then serve them atop a salad with hard-boiled eggs. Italians make a variation by sautéing onions, raisins, and pine nuts, then marinating fried sardines in the mixture. Algerians fry sardines, cover them with a spicy sauce (*scabetch*), and let them marinate for a day.

The sardine catch typically surpassed the amount that could be used fresh and, therefore, for millennia the remaining fish were scaled, gutted, salted, and dried. Before being eaten, the dried fish had to be soaked in water for at least an hour to soften the fish and remove the excess saltiness. Fish were first canned in the 1820s, and sardines were among the initial types used for this purpose; they were typically packed in oil as a preservative and flavor enhancer. In the early twentieth century, a Sabbath meal on the Lower East Side of Manhattan sometimes consisted of a can of sardines and hard-boiled eggs. Later, when economic situations improved, canned sardines emerged as indispensible for Jewish travelers, providing kosher food when little else was available.

SAUERBRATEN
Sauerbraten is a slow-cooked beef pot roast that is marinated in vinegar and sometimes wine before cooking.
Origin: Germany

In the time before the advent of artificial refrigeration, meat tended to spoil relatively quickly. In the Rhineland and southwest Germany, cooks learned how to forestall rotting or salvage minimally spoiled meat by pickling it in vinegar. Meat prepared in this way was called sauerbraten from *sauer*, German for "sour," and *braten*, meaning "to roast," the compound word denoting a tangy pot roast. Modern cooks, relying on refrigeration as well as acid, substitute red wine for some of the vinegar for a milder, more flavorful sauce. The meat is marinated for two to three days

before cooking; the longer it sits in the marinade, the more intensely sour it will be. Whereas many Germans originally used horsemeat or venison, and some still do today, Jews always substituted beef. Jews, in the style of the Rhineland, also tended to add *lebkuchen* (now replaced with gingersnaps) or sugar to create a sweet-and-sour flavor and thicken the broth. The secret to good sauerbraten is the balance of its numerous assertive flavors—the vinegar should not overwhelm the meat. Sauerbraten is related to the eastern European *essig fleisch*, although the latter is not marinated.

German immigrants brought the dish to America in the nineteenth century. The first record of the word in English is a recipe for "Sauerbraten" in the cookbook *Aunt Babette's* (Cincinnati, 1889), reflecting the author's German Jewish heritage.

For many Germans, sauerbraten was a favorite comfort food. In America, some eastern Ashkenazim adopted the Teutonic sauerbraten, which became a popular Hanukkah treat, appeared as occasional Friday night fare, and was common in American Jewish cookbooks of the time. In the 1932 animated film "Minnie the Moocher" by Jewish immigrants from Kraków, Poland, Max and Dave Fleischer, a pair of overweight Germanic parents, chastise the thin Betty Boop for not eating her sauerbraten, reflecting the Fleischers' own feelings of disconnection between the Old World and the New. However, as the twentieth century progressed, sauerbraten's assertive flavors fell out of fashion. Sauerbraten's popularity faded and it was replaced by the milder American pot roast and eastern European brisket.

Sauerbraten is usually served with spaetzle or wide noodles and braised red cabbage.

GERMAN SOUR POT ROAST (*SAUERBRATEN*)
8 TO 10 SERVINGS [MEAT]
Marinade:
2 cups dry red wine, such as Pinot Noir or Burgundy
1½ cups water
½ cup red wine vinegar
2 medium yellow onions, sliced
2 medium carrots, chopped
1 stalk celery, chopped
2 tablespoons sugar
1 tablespoon kosher salt

5 to 7 whole black peppercorns
4 whole cloves
2 bay leaves
3 to 6 whole juniper or allspice berries (optional)
1 teaspoon mustard seeds (optional)

1 (4- to 6-pound) boneless beef chuck roast
3 tablespoons vegetable oil
½ cup (about 5 ounces) finely ground gingersnaps
¼ cup brown sugar (optional)
½ cup raisins (optional)

1. To make the marinade: In a medium saucepan, bring all the marinade ingredients to a simmer and simmer for 10 minutes. Let cool.

2. Place the roast in a large nonreactive container and pour the marinade over the top. Cover and refrigerate, turning the roast every 12 hours, for 1 to 3 days. Remove the roast from the marinade and pat dry. Allow the meat to return to room temperature, about 1 hour. Strain the marinade, reserving the solids and liquid separately.

3. In a large, heavy pot, heat the oil over medium-high heat. Add the roast and brown, turning, on all sides, about 15 minutes total. Remove the roast from the pot. Reduce the heat to medium-low, add the marinade vegetables, and sauté until caramelized, about 15 minutes.

4. Place the roast on top of the vegetables, add the marinade liquid, cover, and bring to a simmer. Place in a 325°F oven or simmer over a low heat, turning occasionally, until fork-tender, about 3½ hours.

5. Transfer the roast to a warm platter. Skim off any fat from the surface of the cooking liquid. Gradually add the gingersnap crumbs and cook over medium-high heat, stirring, until the mixture thickens. Puree and strain the cooking liquid. For a *Rheinischer* sauerbraten, add the sugar and, if desired, raisins. Return to the pot and heat through. Slice the roast across the grain and serve with the gravy.

SAUERKRAUT

The technique of pickling shredded cabbage with naturally occurring bacteria, known as lacto-fermentation, dates back more than twenty-four hundred years to ancient China. In this process, acidifying bacteria found naturally in raw cabbage feed off its sugar, producing lactic and acetic acids, which gives the cabbage a characteristic tangy yet mellow taste, and slightly softens it. The process produces natural bacteriocins that kill harmful bacteria. These bacteria also transform milk into cheese and yogurt, and are active in bread dough. Lacto-fermentation is a natural process, involving no cooking; all that is needed is the vegetable or fruit, enough warmth to allow the bacteria to develop, and, for cabbage, sufficient salt to prevent the growth of undesirable bacteria and to extract juice and sugar from the cabbage, while allowing the survival of naturally occurring acid-producing species of bacteria. If there is too little salt, the cabbage will spoil; if there is too much salt, it will not ferment. Other produce commonly preserved with lacto-fermentation are beets, carrots, cauliflower, cucumbers, olives, peppers, green tomatoes, and turnips. The other vegetables, however, require the addition of water, while cabbage, rather uniquely, ferments only in its own juice. Koreans adapted this process for their kimchi, adding chilies and garlic to the cabbage, and Indians for various chutneys.

Before this technique was introduced to eastern Europe, around the middle of the sixteenth century, medieval European methods for pickling vegetables with salt proved limited. The other major preservative, vinegar, primarily made from wine, was rare and expensive in northern Europe. Lacto-fermentaion was adopted by the Slavs and eastern European Jews from the Baltic to Romania. Poles called the pickled cabbage *kiszona kapusta*, while Jews used the Yiddish *zoyere kroyt* (sour cabbage). It traveled westward—in many cases, it was spread by Jews—to Germany and Austria, then France and the Netherlands. The result is one of the most important northern European dishes, widely known by the German name sauerkraut (sour cabbage); the word first appeared in England in the early seventeenth century and in America in 1776. German sailors of the eighteenth century relied on sauerkraut to prevent scurvy, a practice adopted by the British in 1776.

Each fall as the weather cooled, around the holiday of Sukkot, Ashkenazic households throughout eastern Europe set aside at least two large wooden barrels or ceramic crocks for fermenting vegetables—one for small cucumbers and one for cabbages. Beets for *rosl* (beet vinegar) were typically fermented shortly after Purim, although some families also put up another barrel of beets around Sukkot. Large, mature cabbage heads, which contain more sugar, were preferable for this dish. First the outer leaves and cores were removed. Using a metal grater or knife, the cabbages were shredded or thinly sliced into the barrel. The shreds were sprinkled with coarse salt and pounded with a wooden mallet or clean feet to extract some of the cabbage juice. Layered with the cabbage were the stalks (*katchelkehs*) and frequently grated carrots or apples to enhance the flavor. The vegetables were weighed down with a large stone to ensure their total immersion in the brine.

As the cabbage sat, the salt extracted much of its juices, forming and flavoring the brine. After at least two weeks and up to one month, the sauerkraut was ready and the cured cabbage was moved to a cool place, such as a dirt cellar, to slow the fermentation. In a cool environment, sauerkraut could keep for at least a year, lasting until the next batch in the following autumn.

Sauerkraut quickly became a mainstay of much of northern Europe. Characteristic of the eastern Ashkenazic pantry were *zoyers* (sours), which added zest and complementary nutrition, including in the case of cabbage, vitamin C, to the bland high-starch diet of eastern Europe.

Sauerkraut was eaten plain, either hot or cold, as well as mixed with noodles, browned with potatoes and onions, cooked with brisket or sausages, or simmered with a few bones or perhaps some flanken into a soup (*shchi*). Sauerkraut was also used in more upscale peasant dishes, such as the Alsatian classic *choucroute garni*, made with corned beef and sausages, which is still a Sabbath hot lunch favorite. Sauerkraut complements the richness of goose and duck. Hungarians and Romanians use it as a strudel filling and frequently spread a layer of rinsed sauerkraut over their stuffed cabbage. As the level of sauerkraut dropped in the barrel, the cabbage brine was drunk as a beverage. In many instances, an Ashkenazic winter lunch consisted solely of black bread and sauerkraut. It also became a common sight on the Sabbath, in particular for lunch. Some Chasidim explain that because the Yiddish word *zoyerlach* (little sours) sounds like *azoi erlech* (so honest), sours, such as sauerkraut, are traditional for the Sabbath.

German immigrants began to popularize sauerkraut in America in the eighteenth century. The first American Jewish cookbook, *Jewish Cookery* (Philadelphia, 1871), included a recipe for "How To Make Sauer Krout." The author noted, "It will keep for years." The same note was included in the first edition of *The Settlement Cook Book* (Milwaukee, 1901), although there the word was spelled sauerkraut. Sauerkraut became a standard of delicatessens.

In the twentieth century, as various modern preserving methods developed, sauerkraut lost much of its status and was typically replaced on the table with the easier-to-make coleslaw, whose tangy flavor derived from added vinegar. In addition, most modern mass-produced sauerkraut is not lacto-fermented and therefore lacks the old-fashioned flavor. Today, sauerkraut is primarily used in America as a condiment for hot dogs and sandwiches.

(See also Cabbage, Choucroute Garni, and Pickle)

SAUSAGE

Sausage is an ancient way of transforming limited resources into a substantial meal—it basically consists of salted and seasoned chopped meat and offal stuffed into an intestine, stomach, or other casing. There are two basic types of sausages: fresh and cured. To make either type, for most of history, the meat had to be pounded or chopped by hand, making sausages time-consuming, expensive, and, for most people, reserved for special occasions. The concept of stuffing chopped meat, typically from the less desirable parts of an animal, into intestines and other hollow organs dates back at least five thousand years to Sumeria. Three millennia later, Judeans referred to sausages as *naknik* and *nukanika*; the Aramaic name was borrowed from the *lucanica* sausage from southern Italy. In modern Hebrew, sausage is *naknik* and hot dog *naknikiya*. The generic Roman terms for sausages were the Latin *botulus* (from the Latin "intestines") and the Vulgar Latin *salsicia* (from *salsus,* meaning "salted," salt being an essential element in preserving the meat), the source of the English word sausage.

Historically, many Europeans preferred part or all pork in their sausages, while Ashkenazic variations were always strictly pure beef, Italians favored goose, and Middle Eastern Jews tended to use lamb. Fat (about 22 percent, according to experts) contributes flavor and texture.

Sausages in cooler climates, notably northern Europe, are overwhelmingly fresh and are intended to be cooked and eaten, usually hot, shortly after production. The classic sausage of Germany is bratwurst;

it first appeared in the fifteenth century and the name probably derived from the Old High German *brät* (chopped meat) and *wurst* (sausage). Knackwurst is a smoked German sausage with plenty of garlic and it is therefore also called *knoblauchwurst* (*knoblauch* means garlic in German). Notwithstanding its place in American life and culture, the hot dog is in actuality a mere fresh sausage from Frankfurt, Germany. The Hungarian version, *kolbasz*, contains paprika. The Polish kielbasa, flavored with garlic and sometimes cloves, is smoked. *Kishke* is the classic Jewish sausage of eastern Europe, primarily or entirely made from fillers.

On the other hand, in the warmer climes of the Mediterranean, most of the sausages are cured by smoking or lacto-fermentation, a process in which naturally occurring bacteria in the presence of sufficient (but not too much) salt produce acids that act as a preservative and also impart a tangy flavor. Cured sausages are commonly eaten without cooking. Italian sausages are typically zesty with fennel seeds or crushed red pepper. Kosher salami is an American Jewish adaptation of the Italian classic—for generations, Jewish travelers and peddlers have carried these salamis with them, along with hard-boiled eggs, in order to maintain a kosher diet away from home.

Sausages were a minor food in the medieval Muslim world in contrast to their prominence in Christian Europe, where the pig was favored. The Jewish Manual (London, 1846), reflecting Sephardic influence, explains, "Chorissa, a sausage peculiar to the Jewish kitchen, of delicate and piquante flavor." The very first recipe in an anonymous Moorish Andalusian cookbook of the thirteenth century was "Mirqaz," now commonly called in Arabic *merguez*. The recipe directed, "It is as nutritious as meatballs and quick to digest, since the pounding ripens it." Sephardim of that time made similar sausages, and later in the sixteenth century during the Spanish Inquisition, a sign of Jewish cooking was using lamb or goat to make sausages. Today, Jews from the Maghreb still enjoy *merguez*, which are also very popular in Israel. The Maghrebi *merguez* is a lamb or veal sausage turned red in color and fiery in flavor by the addition of harissa (chili paste) and typically formed into links or patties.

Sausages, *vurst* in Yiddish, became a mainstay among central European Jews. At first, sausages were primarily made by butchers and a few competent housewives. The first American Jewish cookbook, *Jewish Cookery* (Philadelphia, 1871), provided a recipe for "Veal Sausage Meat," which directed "chop it fine."

The advent of the mechanical meat grinder in the 1860s greatly reduced the effort and cost of making sausages, transforming them into everyday foods and even poverty fare. Soon large factories began to churn out inexpensive sausages, although some of these businesses were less than reputable, as described in Upton Sinclair's *The Jungle* (1906). By the end of the nineteenth century, the German Frankfurt sausage, *vurshtlekh* in Yiddish, had become the all-American hot dog. In early twentieth-century New York, Hebrew National Kosher Sausage Factory and Williamsburg Genuine Kosher Meat Products provided sausages for most of the area's delicatessens. In addition, some kosher delicatessens made their own sausages. A few, like Isaac Gellis Delicatessen of New York, distributed products, including hot dogs, throughout the region, advertising itself as "the first and largest kosher sausage factory in the United States." In the 1940s, Waldbaum's Supermarkets began stocking Hebrew National, becoming the first food chain to sell kosher sausages.

In 1886, German Jewish immigrant Isaac Oscherwitz began selling sausages from his small kosher butcher shop in Cincinnati, Ohio, eventually distributing his products throughout the Midwest. In 1909, along with his five sons, Oscherwitz built a large plant for a kosher sausage company. In 1925, following Isaac's death, his two youngest sons moved to Chicago to launch the separate Best's Kosher Sausage Company. Then in 1962, after the Cincinnati plant was sacrificed for a new expressway, the two family-run companies merged, subsequently also acquiring Sinai Kosher Sausage Company. At this point, hot dogs remained their best-selling item, with traditional salami second, but the company also innovated with kosher Italian-style sausages, Polish kielbasa, and later chorizo. As kosher went mainstream in America, the company, America's second-largest kosher meat processor, was acquired by Sara Lee Corporation in 1993. In the same year, the giant ConAgra Inc. acquired America's largest kosher meat processor, Hebrew National. Now backed by heavy marketing, kosher sausages in America began to move out from their traditional urban strongholds across the country.

(See also Aufschnitz, Hot Dog, Offal, and Salami)

SCACCHI

Scacchi is a casserole of matza and fillings.

Origin: Italy

Scacchi is a popular Italian Passover dish. The name, meaning "chess" in Italian, reflects the perforated matza's resemblance to a game board. It is not certain whether *scacchi* evolved as a Passover form of lasagna from the similar Sephardic *mina*, or whether both dishes sprang from some ancient Jewish source. Originally, *scacchi* was cooked in a skillet on top of the stove, but as the home oven became more prevalent, the contemporary baked form emerged. The most widespread version features alternating fillings of leek, spinach, artichoke, and ground beef. However, a less dramatic presentation can be made with simply one or two fillings. In a Venetian variation, cooked fava beans, peas, or lentils are substituted for the fillings, legumes being permissible for Italians during Passover.

ITALIAN VEGETABLE MATZA CASSEROLE (*SCACCHI*)

4 TO 6 SERVINGS   [MEAT]

Leek Filling:

3 pounds (6 to 8) leeks

Salt and ground black pepper to taste

Meat Filling:

2 tablespoons olive oil

1 small onion, chopped

8 ounces ground beef

About ½ teaspoon salt

Ground black pepper to taste

Spinach Filling:

8 ounces fresh or frozen spinach or chard, washed well

2 tablespoons olive oil

1 clove garlic, minced

Salt and ground black pepper to taste

⅛ teaspoon ground nutmeg (optional)

7 whole (6-inch square) square matzas

2 to 3 artichoke hearts, cooked and sliced

3 large eggs, lightly beaten

½ cup chicken or vegetable broth

1. Preheat the oven to 375°F. Oil an 8- or 9-inch pie plate, ovenproof skillet, or baking pan. Or double the recipe and bake in a 13-by-9-inch baking pan.

2. To make the leek filling: Trim the leeks, saving only the white and light green parts. Rinse well. Place in a large pot of lightly salted boiling water and simmer until soft, 10 to 15 minutes. Drain. Season with the salt and pepper.

3. To make the meat filling: In a large skillet, heat the oil over medium-high heat. Add the onion and sauté until soft and translucent, 5 to 10 minutes. Add the beef and sauté until it loses its red color, about 5 minutes. Season with the salt and pepper

4. To make the spinach filling: In a large pot, cook the spinach over medium heat in the water clinging to its leaves until wilted, 3 to 5 minutes. Chop and squeeze dry. In a large skillet, heat the oil over medium heat. Add the spinach and garlic and sauté until dry. Season with the salt, pepper, and, if using, nutmeg.

5. Soak the unbroken matzas in warm water until semisoft but not soggy, 1 to 2 minutes. Drain and place on paper towels.

6. To assemble the scacchi: Cover the bottom of the prepared pan with 2 matzas. Spread with the meat mixture. Top with 1 matza and spread with the leek mixture. Cover with 1 matza and spread with the spinach mixture. Cover with 1 matza and spread with the artichokes. Cover with the remaining 2 matzas. Beat together the eggs and broth and drizzle over the top of the matzas.

7. Bake until golden brown, about 35 minutes. Let stand for 5 minutes before serving.

SCALLION

The terms scallion and green onion are generally used interchangeably, although technically they are different members of the onion family. Scallions, mild varieties of onion that do not form bulbs, are named for the Israeli seaport city of Ashkelon, whose name is derived from the ancient Israeli unit of money, the shekel. It is unknown whether Ashkelon was the home of the scallion or was the port from which it was originally shipped to Europe. The word shallot (*shoom ashkelon* in Hebrew) also comes from the same source. Scallion is *betzaltzul-ashkelon* or *betzalzul* in Hebrew. Green onions (*betzal yarok*), also called spring onions, are the shoots of immature onions, and they have a slightly softer texture.

SCHALET

Schalet is the Western Yiddish word for cholent (Sabbath stew), and is also used as a synonym for sweet kugel, for apple *fluden* (layered pastry), and apple cake.

Origin: France
Other names: charlotte; Germany: *apfelboyeleh, apfelbuwele, apfelschalet, schaleth*; Russian: *sharlotka.*

By at least the twelfth century, early Ashkenazim in northern France and southwestern Germany, had adapted the Sephardic Sabbath stew, calling it *schalet*, later pronounced cholent in Eastern Yiddish, from the Old French *chald* (*chaud* in modern French), meaning "warm." Around the same time, the favorite Ashkenazic Sabbath and holiday dessert was *fluden*, (also from an Old French term), a pastry layered in a large pot with curd cheese, seasonal fruit, or nuts. Later, after dumplings had appeared in Europe and the center of Ashkenazic culture had shifted eastward to Germany, housewives began cooking a large bread dumpling in the Sabbath stew and serving it as a side dish for Sabbath lunch. After a time, the dumplings came out of the stew and evolved into a variety of steamed puddings; at this stage, the puddings were cooked in a rounded pot and maintained at least a partially rounded shape. In Alsace and parts of Germany, *schalet* emerged as the generic term for these baked bread puddings, while in much of eastern Europe the name became kugel.

Besides the original bread pudding, a matza version for Passover was recorded in Austria in the fifteenth century. In the sixteenth and seventeenth centuries, Caribbean plantations led to the wider use of sugar in Europe. Accordingly, in Bavaria, southern Germany, and a few parts of Poland, kugel came to denote savory puddings and *schalet* took on the meaning of sweet ones. *Kartoffel shalet* is an eastern European sweetened potato kugel. To further complicate matters, by at least the seventeenth century, Jews in Alsace and the adjacent parts of southwestern Germany had begun applying the names *schalet* and *apfelschalet* to versions of deep-dish apple-filled *fluden* (perhaps the forerunner of the apple pie) that were kept warm in the hearth for the Sabbath. Consequently, there are numerous types of *schalet*.

The basic apple pie form of *schalet* was made by lining a large iron pot with yeast dough or pastry dough, adding several layers of apples and dough, covering it with a top crust of dough, then baking it until the apples were tender and the pastry golden. Some cooks continued to make *schalet* in the traditional layered manner, while others adapted it into a cake roll, sort of a rudimentary strudel. This method was not only quicker to assemble, but also reduced the amount of filling in proportion to dough, stretching limited resources. In parts of Germany, this rolled treat was called *apfelboyeleh* (apple little boy).

These apple pastries were identified with Jews, as reflected in the classic French encyclopedia of food, *The New Larousse Gastronomique* (Paris and New York, 1977), which recorded a recipe for "*Schaleth à la Juive,*" in which cooks were directed to "line a large metal, well-buttered basin" with "noodle paste," fill it with a type of applesauce, cover it with a top layer of pastry, and "cook in a moderately hot oven for 50 minutes to 1 hour."

When the concept of apple *schalet* reached England in the late eighteenth century, it was alliteratively pronounced Charlotte. The first American Jewish cookbook, *Jewish Cookery* (Philadelphia, 1871), contained a recipe for "Matzas Charlotte," which consisted of soaked matzas baked in a custard, without any fruit. The author also starts the "Puddings" chapter with "A Baked Pudding (Sthephon) of Ripe Fruit or Apples," in essence a typical apple *schalet*. The first edition of *The Settlement Cook Book* (Milwaukee, 1901) included, in sequence, "Apple Charlotte," which was akin to an apple pie; "Matzos Schalet," a sweet matza kugel; and "Matzos Charlotte with Apples," a similar dish with apples.

Whatever the name and shape, *schalet* remains a popular Sabbath dessert among Alsatians and western Germans, served throughout the fall and winter when fresh apples are readily available. In many German homes, it was also a traditional Rosh Hashanah and Sukkot treat, a symbol of a sweet and fruitful year to come.

(See also Cholent, Fluden, and Kugel)

SCHARFE FISH
Scharf refers to a method of serving poached fish in a tangy or spicy egg sauce.
Origin: Eastern Europe

Scharf is German and Yiddish for "sharp" and "spicy," denoting a pungent or biting dish. Some Poles refer to a savory kugel as *scharfe kugel*. Among the variations of Ashkenazic poached fish is *scharfe fish*, served in a thickened sauce warm on Friday night or cold for *seudat shlishit* [third Sabbath meal].

Scharfe fish is similar to the venerable Sephardic dish of fish in *agristada* (a tangy egg-lemon or egg-verjuice sauce). German Jews began to cover poached fish fillets with a sauce made from the cooking liquid that was spiced with a little ginger or lemon juice and thickened with egg yolks and a little flour. The early American Jewish cookbook, *Aunt Babette's* (Cincinnati, 1889), written by an author from a German heritage, included a recipe entitled "Hecht (Pickerel)." The author wrote, "This fish is best prepared 'scharf.'" She ended the recipe with this note: "Give this a fair trial and you will never prepare pickerel any other way." However, some American versions, such as the "'Sharfe' Fish" in the first edition of *The Settlement Cook Book* (Milwaukee, 1901) and the "Scharfe Fish" in *The Neighborhood Cookbook* (Portland, Oregon, 1912), omit the lemon and use the term to denote poached fish in a sauce thickened with egg yolks and flour.

SCHAV

Sorrel (sour grass)—*szczaw* in Polish, *shtshav* or *tshav* in Yiddish, and schav in American Yiddish, referring both to the plant and the soup made from it—is a member of the buckwheat and rhubarb family, a native of Eurasia. Its English name is derived from the Old French for "sour," which is appropriate as the greens have a striking, but pleasantly tart taste due to the presence of oxalic acid. In modern French, sorrel goes by the name *oseille*. The arrow-shaped, dark green sorrel leaves, which look like spinach, are primarily cooked in soups and sauces, but young ones are used raw in salads. In Europe, sorrel was almost always picked wild; wild sorrel is more intensely tart than the cultivated leaves.

Sorrel appears in early spring and is still growing by the onset of the summer, making it ideal for a seasonal peasant soup called schav or schav borscht. Schav was another of the *zoyers* (sours) adding zest and nutrition to an otherwise bland diet of starches. Jews from Galicia (now southern Poland) typically make a sweet-and-sour soup, while Lithuanians generally eschew any sweetening in their schav. Unlike the heavy fare of winter, Ashkenazic spring and particularly summer food was lighter and frequently dairy—thus schav was almost always pareve or *milchig*. Cold schav proved especially refreshing on a hot day. Wealthier people added a few eggs to thicken the soup and create a slightly yellowish cast. The fat and protein in the eggs or sour cream also helped to tame the oxalic acid. Poorer Polish Jews commonly used an inexpensive potato for the thickening agent. As a result of its spring season, schav emerged in eastern Europe as a widespread Passover and Shavuot dish.

Since Jewish immigrants from eastern Europe were the first to commonly prepare sorrel soup in America, it took on the Yiddish name *schav*, becoming one of the few English words to end in *v*. Today in America, where sorrel is difficult to find in the market, many people substitute spinach, which also produces a greener color, and add plenty of lemon juice or citric acid, although without achieving the same distinctive results. Many of the Jewish hotels in the Catskill Mountains opted for the easier spinach, although sorrel grew wild in the area. Bottled commercial *schav* in America is also predominantly spinach. Consequently, many people have had a negative culinary experience with "*schav*."

EASTERN EUROPEAN SORREL SOUP (*SCHAV*)
ABOUT 2 QUARTS/6 TO 8 SERVINGS   [PAREVE OR DAIRY]

8 cups water
1½ pounds (about 9 cups) sorrel, washed, stemmed, and chopped
6 to 8 scallions (white and light green parts), chopped, or 1 large whole onion
1 to 4 tablespoons sugar or honey
About 1¼ teaspoons table salt or 2½ teaspoons kosher salt
About ½ teaspoon ground white or black pepper, or 1 teaspoon paprika
1 to 4 tablespoons fresh lemon juice
2 to 3 large eggs or 4 large egg yolks, lightly beaten (optional)
1 cup sour cream (optional)

1. Place the water, sorrel, scallions, sugar, salt, and pepper in a large pot (do not use aluminum or cast iron). Bring to a boil, reduce the heat to low, and simmer until the sorrel is very tender, about 20 minutes.

2. If using a whole onion, discard it now. Add the lemon juice. Leave the soup with a chunky texture or puree in a blender or a food processor fitted with a metal blade until nearly smooth. Adjust the lemon juice and sugar to make the soup more sour or sweet-and-sour, according to your preference.

3. If using the eggs, gradually whisk 1 cup of the hot soup into the eggs, then stir the egg mixture into the soup. Place over low heat and stir until slightly thickened, about 5 minutes. Do not boil.

4. Serve warm or refrigerate for at least 4 hours until chilled. The soup can be stored in the refrigerator for up to 3 days with the eggs, or up to 1 week without the eggs. If desired, garnish with a dollop of sour cream or stir it into the soup.

SCHMALTZ

The taste and smell of authentic Ashkenazic food is schmaltz. Schmaltz or *schmalts* in Yiddish (from the Middle High German *smalz*, "animal fat") is the generic Yiddish term for animal fat, but more specifically and colloquially, it denotes melted and purified poultry fat. Schmaltz became to Ashkenazic cooking what olive oil was to Mediterranean food, indispensable for frying and cooking, and as a flavoring agent. Because rendering concentrates and enhances the taste of the creamy fat, it is more flavorful than the greasy yellowish mass that rises to the top of chilled chicken soup. Schmaltz is typically rendered with chopped onion, for a note of sweetness, and chicken skin, which imparts meatiness, and there are those who also add a chopped green apple or garlic clove for extra flavor. The slow rendering process, similar to that of ghee (Indian clarified butter), also removes the water and proteins from the fat, and, as a result, properly prepared schmaltz can last for an extended period without spoiling—it stays fresh at room temperature for many months and in the refrigerator for at least a year. Schmaltz is liquid at room temperature and solidifies in the refrigerator.

Jews in ancient Israel and the Mediterranean primarily relied on olive oil. In central Asia, they substituted sesame oil or the tail fat from certain types of sheep. As Jews moved north in Europe, many of the ingredients that had previously been an essential part of their larder became scarce or, more often than not, unobtainable, including most oils. For dairy meals, Ashkenazim used butter, which was relatively plentiful during the late spring and summer. However, butter became less available during the autumn and through the winter, and it could not be used at meat meals anytime of the year. Non-Jews were dependent on lard for cooking, but Jews had to look toward kosher animal fats.

The use of fattened geese as a source for oil was first mentioned in a Jewish source in the Talmud, where a third-century Babylonian rabbi noted, "We were once traveling in the wilderness, and we saw geese whose feathers had fallen out because they were so fat, and streams of fat flowed under them." But it was in northern Europe that poultry fat became ubiquitous. Goose was the bird of choice in western and central Europe, but as the Ashkenazim moved farther east—and in the wake of the revival of European cuisine and agronomy that followed the First Crusade—chickens emerged as the standard in eastern Europe. Many eastern Europeans, however, still raised or annually purchased a goose or two for their winter's supply of schmaltz. In America, where kosher geese were hard to obtain, chicken became the predominant source.

Each year as winter approached and geese were at their fattest, near Hanukkah, any male geese and other unwanted birds, which had previously fed on free grasses, were slaughtered. Fat birds were particularly desirable, as they yielded the most schmaltz. In previous generations, geese and chickens had more fat and were eaten when older, and geese were force-fed, so each bird yielded more schmaltz than today's birds. After the fat was rendered down, a special separate glazed crock was set aside in a cool cellar for Passover, and the remainder was enjoyed throughout the winter. In the frigid winters of northern Europe, energy-rich schmaltz sustained life as well as added flavor to it. Throughout the rest of the year, additional schmaltz awaited the occasional slaughter of the family's chickens or geese or the purchase of one from a farmer.

Schmaltz was essential for frying everything from onions, the most widespread seasoning of Ashkenazim, to schnitzel. The rich flavor infuses a myriad of classic Ashkenazic dishes, including chopped liver, chopped eggs, cholent (Sabbath stew), kugels, *kishke* (stuffed derma), *kasha varnishkes*, matza balls, latkes, and various other potato dishes. It was schmeared over rye bread and toast (*schmaltzbrot*), then sprinkled with kosher salt or perhaps sliced black radish. Schmaltz was once a cornerstone of the Jewish delicatessen—some establishments even offered small pitchers or saucers of it on the tables as a condiment. The fried skin is called *gribenes* and is considered a special treat. Although vegetable oil or margarine can be substituted for schmaltz, it will not replicate the rich flavor and texture. Matza balls made with schmaltz turn out more flavorful and tender than those containing oil, while latkes fried in oil are a pale comparison to those cooked in schmaltz.

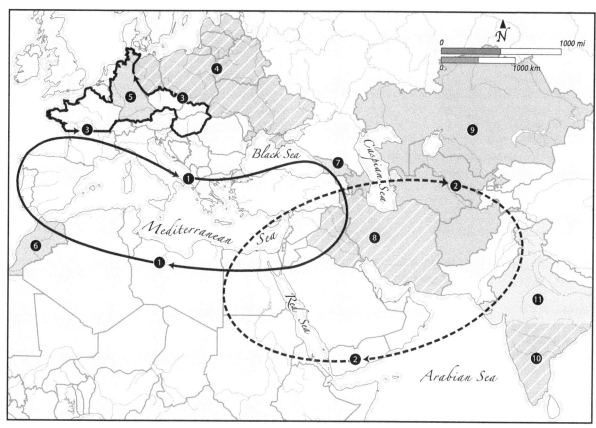

Principal Fats *Before the global economy, various regions of the world relied on a predominant local fat—some from animals and some from plants—greatly influencing local cookery. 1* **Olive oil**—*Mediterranean (Spain, Portugal, southern France, southern Italy, Greece, Turkey, Syria, the Levant, North Africa); 2* **Samneh** *(clarified butter)—Arab world (southern Mediterranean, Middle East, Afghanistan); 3* **Goose fat**—*northern France, western Germany, Hungary, Czech Republic, Slovakia; 4* **Chicken Fat**—*eastern Germany, Poland, Baltic States, Ukraine, Byelorussia, Hungary; 5* **Poppy seed oil**—*Germany; 6* **Argan oil**—*Morocco; 7* **Sunflower oil**—*Georgia; 8* **Sesame oil** *(raw)—Iraq, Iran; 9* **Sheep Tail Fat**—*central Asia (Uzbekistan, Azerbaijan, Afghanistan, Kazakhstan, Turkmenia, Iran); 10* **Coconut oil/ Palm oil**—*southern India; 11* **Ghee** *(clarified butter)—northern and central India*

Because of its importance, schmaltz became entwined in Ashkenazic culture. Thus the Yiddish phrase for "to strike it rich by luck," which refers to situations like inheriting money or marrying a wealthy spouse, is *"araynfaln un a schmaltzgruh"* (to fall into a schmaltz pit).

Early American Jewish cookbooks referred to "chicken fat" and "goose fat," and the word schmaltz did not show up in English until 1932, when it appeared in *Manhattan Oases, New York's 1932 Speak-Easies* by Al Hirschfeld, later known as a caricaturist. He wrote, "Same price and same brew at the rough board tables,

glistening with 'schmaltz' rubbed in by the elbows of two generations."

In America, schmaltz early on in the twentieth century lost some of its importance, due to the availability of kosher oils, margarine, and vegetable shortening, yet remained a staple in many Jewish households. In an article in the November 1935 issue of *Vanity Fair*, the word schmaltz was used as a derogatory term for jazz. Around 1950, due to the prominent Jewish presence in show business, "schmaltz" took on a new, negative connotation in America as a noun meaning cloying sentimentalism, perhaps because schmaltz is mushy, unctuous, and heavy, while "schmaltzy" emerged as an adjective denoting something corny, mawkish, and excessively sentimental, especially music and literature.

In America in the second half of the twentieth century, fat became something it had never been before in all of human history—undesirable. As health and cholesterol concerns rose and Ashkenazim became acculturated in America, the role of schmaltz dramatically diminished. Even many delis cut back on or nearly eliminated the use of schmaltz, much to the detriment of the authenticity and flavor of the food. And in authentic Ashkenazic cuisine, there is no substitute.

(See also Goose, Gribenes, Herring, and Liver)

ASHKENAZIC RENDERED CHICKEN FAT WITH CRACKLINGS (*SCHMALTZ MIT GRIBENES*)

ABOUT 2 CUPS   [MEAT]

1 pound (4 cups) chicken or goose fat
8 ounces chicken or goose skin
½ cup water
1 medium yellow onion, chopped (optional)

1. Cut the fat into small pieces and cut the skin into ¼-inch-wide strips. In a large, heavy saucepan or skillet, cook the fat, skin, and water, uncovered, over medium heat until the water evaporates and the fat is melted, as announced by the stopping of crackling sounds, about 35 minutes.

2. Reduce the heat to low and, if using, add the onion. Cook, stirring occasionally, until the skin turns a deep golden brown, about 1 hour. Do not let the cracklings and onion burn.

3. Pour the liquid through a fine-mesh sieve or coffee filter into a jar, then place the *gribenes* (browned pieces) in a separate container. Store the schmaltz and *gribenes* separately in the refrigerator for several months to a year or in the freezer indefinitely. Schmaltz turns bright white in the freezer. To stretch the schmaltz, combine it in a one-one ratio with peanut oil.

SCHNAPPS

Schnapps or *shnaps*, from the German *schnaps*, derived from the verb *schnappen* ("to snatch/to snap," denoting emptying the glass in one gulp), is the most widespread generic Yiddish term for any strong liquor. This includes whiskey, slivovitz (distilled from plums), brandy (dis-

tilled from grapes), and vodka, which is Russian whiskey, the type most common in northeastern Europe.

Yiddish synonyms for schnapps are *mashke* (from the Hebrew word for beverage, *mashkeh*) and *yash* (a contraction of the Hebrew *yayim* "wine" and *soref* "burning."). In addition, there is *bronfn* (derived from the German *branntwein*, "burned wine"), specifying whiskey. The latter appropriately gave rise to the family name of Samuel Bronfman, a Canadian Jew who founded a distilling empire and purchased Joseph Seagram & Sons during Prohibition. In modern Hebrew, hard liquor is *mashkeh charif*.

Drinking a shot of schnapps is *makhn a shnepsl* (make a bit of liquor). To drink too much is to become *shiker* (used as both an adjective and noun) or *batrinkn*. A drink of schnapps in the synagogue or study hall is a *tikn*, from the Hebrew *tikkun* (repair/improvement), as Chasidim developed a custom of taking a drink (*trinkn tikn*) to celebrate the elevation of the soul of a departed loved one or friend.

In northern Europe, where wine was scarce and expensive, schnapps were of particular importance, as they could be substituted for wine on Sabbath morning for Kiddush and at the end of the Sabbath for Havdalah. Bottles of schnapps remain common at most Ashkenazic life-cycle events, where shots are typically preceded by the salutation *l'chaim* (to life).

(See also Pálenka and Vishniak)

SCHNECKEN

Schnecken is a small, coiled yeast-raised pastry filled with cinnamon-sugar.
Origin: Germany

In sixteenth- and seventeenth-century Europe, yeast rolls sweetened with Caribbean sugar and accented with spice grew in prevalence, but the spice was always mixed into the dough. Eventually, bakers in central Europe devised a different method: They made miniature versions of the large *kaffee kuchen* (coffee cake roll) by rolling out a rich yeast *kuchen* dough, sprinkling it with sugar and cinnamon—a favorite spice of central Europeans—then rolling it up and cutting into spiral slices. A variation substitutes poppy seed filling (*mohn*) for the cinnamon. The original rolls were relatively dainty pastries, intended to fit on a saucer beside a cup of tea or coffee. The shape of these rolls was reminiscent of a coiled mollusk shell and, consequently, they became known as schnecken, German for "snails." Although the singular of the word is schnecke, the plural form is commonly used even for a single pastry. These cinnamon rolls eventually spread through Germany and Austria. Since many of the professional bakers of that area were Jews, schnecken early on was adopted by Jewish communities.

Schnecken arrived in America with German immigrants. As with many German baked goods, they first became popular in Pennsylvania, which was once the site of the country's largest German community. Shortly before the Civil War, these rolls began appearing in bakeries in other areas with large German and German Jewish populations, most notably New York, Chicago, and Cincinnati. This European treat, however, did not remain restricted to Germans for long. By 1886, it could already be found in the *Kansas Home Cookbook*, an early fund-raising work, in which it was called "Snail's House Cake." Among American Jews from Germany, schnecken became a beloved Sabbath morning treat. Some people, particularly in Baltimore, mistakenly call rolled crescents made from a sour cream dough, which are akin to *kipfel* and rugelach, by the name schnecken, but real schnecken is a spiral roll.

By the end of the nineteenth century, the name schnecken had transitioned into "cinnamon rolls" and "sticky buns." In the first edition of *The Settlement Cook Book* (Milwaukee, 1901), by an author from a

German Jewish background, the pastry was entitled "Cinnamon Rolls or Schnecken," while in later editions the name was trimmed to just "Cinnamon Rolls." The book's instructions, which included baking the pastries close together in a large pan, are akin to directions for modern cinnamon buns.

Subsequently, schnecken could be found in almost every cookbook from American Jewish sisterhoods and women's organizations. *The Neighborhood Cook Book* by the Council of Jewish Women (Portland, Oregon, 1912) included a recipe in which raisins, nuts, and a gooey topping were added, and the rolls were baked individually in a gem pan, the forerunner of the muffin pan.

Following World War II, the appearance of tubes of frozen ready-to-bake cinnamon rolls in supermarkets further spurred the popularity of these pastries in mainstream America. As with many other European imports, the American version grew into monstrous, excessively sweet proportions. In the late twentieth century, cinnamon rolls became one of America's favorite treats, with some chain stores focusing exclusively on this delectable, slightly gooey kuchen. Whatever the size or, for that matter, time of the day, few foods are as satisfying or tasty as these small (or massive) coffee cakes.

The schnecken came to America with German immigrants, and served as the inspiration for the widely popular cinnamon roll. The poppy seed variation, however, failed to make a similar impact.

🍀 GERMAN CINNAMON ROLLS (SCHNECKEN)

ABOUT 36 SMALL PASTRIES   [DAIRY]

Dough:
- 1 package (2¼ teaspoons) active dry yeast or 1 (0.6-ounce) cake fresh yeast
- ¼ cup warm water (105°F to 115°F for dry yeast; 80°F to 85°F for fresh yeast)
- ¼ cup sugar
- 1 cup (2 sticks) unsalted butter, softened
- 3 large egg yolks or 2 large eggs
- 1 cup sour cream or plain yogurt
- ¼ cup milk
- ½ teaspoon vanilla extract or ¼ teaspoon lemon extract
- ½ teaspoon table salt or 1 teaspoon kosher salt
- About 4 cups (20 ounces) bread or unbleached all-purpose flour

- 1 cup granulated or brown sugar, or ½ cup each
- 1½ teaspoons ground cinnamon
- ½ cup (1 stick) unsalted butter, melted

1 cup dried currants or chopped raisins
1 cup chopped pecans or walnuts (optional)

1. To make the dough: Dissolve the yeast in the warm water. Stir in 1 teaspoon sugar and let stand until foamy, 5 to 10 minutes. Meanwhile, in a large bowl, beat the butter until light and fluffy. Gradually beat in the remaining sugar. Beat in the egg yolks, one at a time. Blend in the yeast mixture, sour cream, milk, vanilla, salt, and 1½ cups flour. Gradually add enough of the remaining flour to make a smooth, very soft dough. Place in an oiled bowl and turn to coat. Cover loosely with plastic wrap or a kitchen towel and let stand in a warm, draft-free place for 30 minutes, then refrigerate overnight or up to 3 days.

2. Line a baking sheet or 2 large baking pans with parchment paper or lightly grease the sheet or pans. Punch down the dough. Fold over and press together several times. Divide in half; let stand for 15 minutes.

3. Combine the sugar and cinnamon. Roll out each dough piece into a ¼-inch-thick rectangle, about 9 by 5 inches. Brush with the melted butter and sprinkle with the cinnamon-sugar, raisins, and, if using, nuts, leaving a ½-inch border. Starting from a long side, roll up jelly-roll style. Using a sharp knife or dental floss, cut into ½-inch-thick slices.

4. Place the slices, cut side down, on the prepared baking sheet. Cover and let rise until nearly doubled in bulk, about 1 hour.

5. Preheat the oven to 375°F.

6. Bake until golden brown, about 20 minutes. Transfer the schnecken to a wire rack. Serve warm or at room temperature.

SCHNITZEL

Schnitzel is a slice of meat or poultry coated with breading and pan-fried.

Origin: Austria

Other names: Czech Republic: *rizek*; Hungary: *becsi szelet, ranthotus*; Slovakia: *rezen*.

A coating not only protects food from the intense heat of frying, but also provides an interesting contrast in texture and flavor. The technique of coating slices of meat in bread crumbs before frying may have originated around the ninth century in the Byzantine Empire, where it was discovered by Arabs, who had transported it across North Africa to Spain by at least the thirteenth century. Sephardim use similar methods in one of their most famous dishes, *peshkado frito* (pan-fried fish fillets). Perhaps Sephardim brought the concept to Italy in the sixteenth century after the expulsion from Spain. In Milan, around that time, it was adapted specifically for veal, creating the classic *cotoletta alla Milanese*, consisting of pounded bone-in veal chops dipped into beaten eggs, then dredged in bread crumbs and fried.

In 1706, the French yielded their possessions in northern Italy, including Lombardy and its capital, Milan, to the Habsburgs of Austria, and the region finally gained independence from the Austrian Empire only in 1859. During this period, the Austrian court brought the best cooks from all parts of its domains to the capital, and pan-fried breaded meat thus traveled the two hundred miles from Milan to Vienna. There *cotoletta alla Milanese* was transformed by removing the bone from the chops, and dredging the meat first in flour before dipping it into the eggs and finally bread crumbs (*semmelbrösel*), and the dish was renamed schnitzel (German meaning "little cut/cutlet"). A related word is *schnitz*, meaning "dried apple slices," which are used in certain Central European pastries. Schnitzel soon became widespread in Germany as well.

The most famous of all schnitzels is Wiener schnitzel; the term first appeared in Austrian cookbooks around 1880, and the dish is named for the city of Vienna, which is spelled *Wien* in German. Genuine Weiner schnitzel is made from veal (*kalb*), usually from the leg or shoulder. Without a prefix, the word schnitzel in Europe denotes a dish that consists solely of veal and is prepared in the classic manner. However, any boneless meat can be breaded and fried as a schnitzel. Austrians refer to poultry schnitzel as *hausmeisterschnitzel* (poor man's schnitzel), and a variation in which flour is used for both the first dredging and a second coating (instead of the bread crumbs usually used for the second coating), as *Pariser schnitzel* (Parisian schnitzel). *Holsteiner schnitzel* is Wiener schnitzel topped with a sunny-side-up fried egg. An American variation is chicken-fried steak; the term was first recorded in 1949, and despite its name, the dish consists of beef slices fried like schnitzel.

Whatever meat is used, the cutlet is pounded to an even thickness, which slightly tenderizes the meat and, more importantly, allows it to cook evenly. The size of a schnitzel ranges from cutlets the size of a hand to slices that drape over the sides of a large plate. Although European schnitzel is generally fried in clarified butter or lard, in kosher versions schmaltz or oil is substituted. Schnitzel should never be soggy on the outside or dry inside. The meat should be supple and succulent, in contrast to the taste and texture of the thin, crisp, and fluffy breading. Austrians never serve schnitzel with a sauce, which would soften its crispy coating. Many central Europeans began spritzing schnitzel with lemon juice to hide the taste of meat that had spoiled (a common occurrence in the time before refrigeration) and the practice endures—the dish is typically served with lemon wedges to be squeezed over the top. Schnitzel is commonly accompanied with potatoes (fried, roasted, or salad) and cucumber or beet salad.

By the beginning of the twentieth century, central Europeans had brought the concept of schnitzel to Israel, where the kibbutzim and *moshavim* generally raised turkeys and chicken instead of cattle, and Israelis substituted these for veal. Schnitzel was particularly important in a country where few people possessed an oven in their home, as thin cutlets could be easily fried over a flame. Another advantage was that schnitzel fried in oil could be served cold or reheated. For the decade following the establishment of the state of Israel in 1948, the government out of necessity imposed a period of national rationing of many basic food items, known as the *tzena* (austerity). The new Ministry of Absorption taught the diverse housewives from across the globe how to prepare various simple recipes made from readily accessible, inexpensive items; these dishes included chicken and turkey schnitzel, sometimes called *k'tita* (pounding) but more commobly referred to simply as schnitzel.

Schnitzel, not falafel, became to Israelis of all ethnic backgrounds what hamburgers, fried chicken, and pizza are to Americans—it is featured in many restaurants, both fast-food and upscale, as well as offered at home, for either dinner or lunch, both on the Sabbath and during the week. Schnitzel is a common sight at life-cycle events in Israel featuring a meat meal, even some weddings. On Purim, some people add poppy seeds to the breading, while sesame seeds are sometimes mixed in on other occasions. On Passover, matza meal is substituted for the flour and bread crumbs. Leftovers are slipped into a pita along with hummus or ketchup for a favorite sandwich, both as a meal and a popular snack. Israeli food companies even produce commercial vegetarian versions. The Israeli innovation of turkey schnitzel eventually made its way to Austria and became common in the homeland of the schnitzel.

🍃 ISRAELI BREADED CHICKEN CUTLETS (*SCHNITZEL*)

8 SERVINGS   [MEAT]

8 (5- to 6-ounces each) chicken or turkey cutlets
About 1½ cups fine dry bread crumbs or matza meal
About 1 teaspoon salt
About ¾ teaspoon ground black pepper
1 teaspoon paprika (optional)
About ½ cup all-purpose flour or matza cake meal
3 large eggs, lightly beaten
Vegetable oil or schmaltz for frying
Lemon wedges for garnish

1. Rinse the cutlets and pat dry. Using a meat mallet or the bottom of a heavy skillet, pound the chicken between two pieces of plastic wrap to an even ¼-inch thickness. Combine the bread crumbs, salt, pepper, and, if using, paprika and place in a shallow dish or plastic bag. Place the flour in a second shallow dish or plastic bag and the eggs in another shallow dish.

2. In a large, heavy skillet, heat ⅛ inch oil over medium heat to about 355°F. In batches, dredge the cutlets lightly in the flour, shaking to remove the excess. Using one hand or tongs, dip the cutlets in the eggs, then into the bread crumbs to cover.

3. In batches, add the schnitzel to the pan (do not overcrowd) and fry, carefully moving the skillet back and forth to splash oil over the top, until golden brown on the bottom, about 3 to 4 minutes. Turn and fry until browned but not burnt, about 2 to 3 minutes depending on the thickness. The cutlets are done when they fill springy when touched lightly and the insides are no longer pink. Remove the cutlets and add more oil before frying the next batch. Drain on a wire rack. Serve with the lemon wedges.

S'CHUG

S'chug is a paste made from green chilies and cilantro.
Origin: Yemen
Other names: *charief, s'hug, skhug, z'chug.*

Yemenite cuisine is fiery and zesty, dominated by chilies, cumin, and cilantro. Yemenites contend that the fire in their dishes helps to cleanse the body, and it is difficult to argue with the results of their diet because Yemenites are usually free of the afflictions of Western society, such as high blood pressure, high cholesterol levels, and diabetes. The predominant Yemenite condiment is *s'chug*, an herbal, green chili paste with hints of black pepper and other spices. It originated around the seventeenth century, after the arrival of the American chili pepper, as a way of combining several local seasonings that were already being used in most dishes. *S'chug* eventually emerged as an all-purpose relish, topping, and hot sauce.

The name *s'chug* comes from the Arabic *skhuk* (pounded/ground), a cognate of the Hebrew *shachak* (to pound/to beat into powder). Traditionally, the chilies, cilantro, garlic, and spices are pounded, each separately, in a mortar or on a flat stone, then mixed together. Experienced Yemenite cooks can crush the ingredients in a few minutes, producing the exact desired texture and consistency. Today, a blender makes the process easier.

There are no strict rules for making *s'chug*. However, it should be a relatively thick and slightly rough paste, not a puree or a watery mixture. In Yemen, cooks tended to use a combination of the small fiery and larger sweeter Indian varieties of chilies, but in Israel many cooks adopted the larger North African types and the Mexican jalapeño or serrano. When red chilies are used, rendering fruity undertones, the red paste is called *shatta*.

Cumin and black pepper are the most commonly added spices, but other ones, particularly those typical of the Yemenite spice mixture *hawaij*, notably cardamom, cloves, and turmeric, are used or substituted. Many Yemenites insist on grinding the spices just before using or simply stir in a little of the *hawaij* at hand. *S'chug* is sometimes served with *rotav aghtaniyot* (crushed tomatoes) or diluted with a little *hilbeh* (fenugreek relish) or tahini (sesame seed paste) to soften the potency. At dairy meals, yogurt is commonly kept nearby to help douse the heat.

Yemenites use *s'chug* as a condiment, especially with chicken, meats, rice, *lahuh* (pancake bread), *melaweh* (flatbread), and *jachnun* (flaky rolls), and add a little or a lot to hummus, stews, salads, and sauces. *S'chug* appears on a Yemenite dining table for breakfast, lunch, and dinner. It is not atypical for some Yemenites to carry a small jar of *s'chug* with them to add to food eaten outside their homes.

In the early twentieth century, Yemenites were the primary proprietors of falafel stands in Israel, where they offered their favored *s'chug* as one of the condiments and, consequently, today it remains a common and fiery addition to Israeli falafel and *shawarma*. In particular, during the period of rationing in the 1950s, *s'chug* was among the few available seasonings to brighten the rather bland cuisine; thus *s'chug*, or *charief* (fiery), the Hebrew name by which it is generally known, became one of Israel's national condiments. In Israel, *s'chug* can be commonly purchased in groceries, although some insist on making it fresh at home. More recently, companies in the United States selling Israeli salads have also begun offering *s'chug*, both green and red.

YEMENITE CHILI PASTE (S'CHUG)

ABOUT 2 CUPS [PAREVE]

9 ounces green chilies, any combination jalapeño, serrano, and milder New Mexico chiles, stemmed and cut into thirds

1 to 1½ cups chopped fresh cilantro, or ¾ cup cilantro and ¾ cup chopped fresh flat-leaf parsley

4 to 5 cloves garlic, crushed

1 teaspoon ground cumin

3 to 5 green cardamom pods, ¼ to ¾ teaspoon ground cardamom, or 3 whole cloves, ground (optional)

1 to 2 teaspoons ground black pepper

About 1 teaspoon table salt or 2 teaspoons kosher salt

About 2 tablespoons olive oil

Using a mortar and pestle, puree all the ingredients separately, then mix to produce a paste. Or using a blender, gradually grind the chilies, beginning with a few and gradually adding the rest until ground. In 3 or 4 additions, add the cilantro and grind, then add the garlic and process until ground. Add the cardamom, turmeric, pepper, salt, and olive oil and process until mixed. Store in an airtight container in the refrigerator for up to 2 months.

SEBIT

The Sabbath to a Syrian family revolves around the *keneese* ("synagogue") and the dining table. To mark special events, such as birthdays and anniversaries, Syrians host a festive buffet lunch following Sabbath morning services called *sebit* or *sabt* (Arabic meaning

"Saturday"). The buffet is held either at home, if the house is large enough to accommodate all the guests, or in the synagogue or a catering hall. A *sebit* always features plenty of food, both hot and cold. While the Sephardic *desayunos* (brunches) are always dairy, *sebits* tend to feature meat dishes, although some Syrians make vegetarian substitutes of favorites such as *kibbeh nabelsieh* (fried ground meat torpedoes) and miniature *lahamagine* (meat pizzas) for dairy occasions.

SEDER

According to the Bible, the first night of Passover, the fifteenth of the month of Nisan, is a *"lail sheemurim* [night of vigil/protection] for all generations." It is a night established for the redemption from Egypt and subsequently sanctified by future generations through the Seder, a series of rituals centering around a meal. The word *seder*, found in the Bible only in the Book of Job, is actually Aramaic in origin, the equivalent of the Hebrew *arukh* (to arrange/to order). By the time of the Mishnah, the term had become widely used among Jews—not in reference to Passover, but to fast days, benedictions, the daily offering in the Temple, and the sounding of the shofar. The same word also gave rise in the early medieval period to the *siddur*, the Jewish prayer book. During the Geonic period (the time from about 700 to 1000 CE when the *geonim*, the heads of two major Talmudic academies in Babylonia, served as the principal authorities of Jewish law and tradition), the term Seder took on its current usage, denoting an order of ritual on the first night of Passover. Many of these rituals involve food.

During the Seder, the Passover story is recounted and relived through a progression of symbols and ceremonies as recorded in the Haggadah (literally "retelling"). The sights, sounds, tastes, and smells of the Seder—the Four Cups of wine, the Four Questions, the Seder plate, Elijah's cup, the Hillel sandwich ("wrap" of matza and maror), the search for the *afikomen*, and the songs—captivate young and old alike.

The makeup of the Seder did not emerge fully formed at any one point in time, but evolved and changed over the centuries. The Bible mandated four commandments for the evening: to eat the paschal offering, to eat matza, to eat *maror* (bitter herbs) with the paschal offering, and to tell the story of the Exodus from Egypt. Passover night was initially a rather informal affair and each father and mother explained the events of the Exodus in their own words and manner. The ritual of the paschal offering has long since ceased with the destruction of the Temple, and for the past two thousand years, the paramount Passover symbol has been matza, a reminder of bondage and the night the Jews hastily fled Egypt.

The Mishnah reveals that while the Temple existed, the Levites recited specific psalms of praise called *Hallel* while the people slaughtered their paschal offerings, and the Sages directed all Jews to recite them as well at home when the paschal meat was eaten, a practice retained in the Seder. There was also the requirement to recite *Birkhat Hamazon* (Grace after Meals), the only biblically mandated benediction. In addition, other early rabbinic regulations dictated the recitation of three texts in the Seder: the four formalized questions, a section of the *Mikra Bikkurim* (Deuteronomy 26:5–8), and Rabbi Gamaliel's comment, "Anyone who has not explained these three things on Passover has not fulfilled his obligation, and these are: Pesach, matza, and maror." These requirements reveal that by the time of the Mishnah, a ritual liturgy for Passover had developed, but one less extensive than the service used today. During the Geonic period, the Passover night liturgy expanded further and became formalized in its current form.

Two thousand years ago, when the Sages living in Israel, then under Roman occupation, were developing the formalized Passover night liturgy, they incorporated into it not only the various Biblical commandments but also many elements from the Greco-Roman *symposium* (Greek for "drinking together"), a ritualized upper-class banquet and intellectual dialogue. These elements included reclining on couches, eating from private small tables, ritual hand washing, dipping hors d'oeuvres, fruit and nut relishes, a series of ritual wine libations, a sumptuous meal, and a series of questions as a starting point for an intellectual discussion of a designated topic. These aspects of the symposium served as idealized models of freedom and affluence, and reflected the Sages' view of the manner in which Seder participants should view themselves and conduct the Seder.

The Seder, although drawing practices from the symposium, was never intended as a Jewish replica or simulation of that banquet. The stark difference between the Seder and Greco-Roman feasts is most dramatically evidenced in the guest list and finale of the symposium: only adult males and the elite were invited, its rituals were performed exclusively by aristocrats and forbidden to slaves, and the finale of the symposium was an orgy. Instead, the Sages structured the Seder to be an egalitarian, spiritual experience with everyone participating.

The original Seder had a definite Greco-Roman and Middle Eastern flavor; most notably, participants dined in a Greek style by reclining on low couches, pillows, or carpets around a central location. The various Seder items were placed on several low tables, which were carried in and out of the room at designated points in the ceremony and placed in front of the Seder leader, a practice still maintained today by many Yemenites and other Eastern Jews. At a traditional Yemenite Seder, the attendees sit on the floor or cushions around a low table. The edges of the table are decorated with celery, chicory, parsley, radishes, and scallions. Three large platters cover the tables: one with three covered matzas (freshly baked, soft loaves), one with hard-boiled eggs, and one with a cooked lamb shank (*zeroah*) for each person (or whatever number of shanks the host can afford). Smaller containers hold the charoset, sometimes called *dukah*, and salt water. In addition, each place has a wine cup.

However, problems emerged in Europe with the original traditions of participants lying on one side during the Seder and moving small tables containing the Seder items when during the early medieval period, people began to dine around a single large table while seated on chairs. In the rest of the world, until the nineteenth century, the vast majority of people did not use chairs—when eating or at any other time—believing that they weakened the spine. At first, Ashkenazim arranged various Seder items on any large platter, which could be moved at appropriate times. Eventually, craftsmen created special plates (*ke'arah*) to hold the traditional symbols. The original movable small tables actually contained all the items to be consumed at the Seder by the entire assemblage, but this was impractical for the relatively small Seder plate. Therefore, the custom developed of only putting a symbolic amount of food on the Seder plate and serving the bulk of it separately.

The Mishnah prescribed two independent tables for the Seder items and, as a result, there emerged a dispute as to which items would be placed on the single Seder plate. There are three widespread customs regarding the number and arrangement of the items on the Seder plate, but today most Ashkenazim follow Rabbi Isaac Luria, known as the Ari, who directed that people use a plate featuring spaces for six items: *karpas* (a green vegetable), *maror* (a bitter herb), *charoset* (a fruit and nut mixture), *chazeret* (a second bitter herb), *betzah* (a roasted hard-boiled egg, representing the festival offering), and *zeroah* (a roasted shank bone or poultry neck, representing the paschal offering). Some authorities omit the *chazeret*, considering it to be redundant of the *maror*. Rabbi Moses Isserles advised that the items be arranged in a circle, in the order they are used in the Seder. Artisan Seder plates, with six items in a circle, reflect a combination of the customs of the Ari and of Rabbi Isserles.

The Seder commences with Kiddush being recited over a cup of wine, and leads up to the matza. At the Seder, the first dipping (*karpas*), immediately following the first cup of wine, helps to open the evening and announce its incongruity and special nature. Many Ashkenazim start the Seder meal with hard-boiled eggs in salt water, while Sephardim serve *huevos haminados* (long-cooked eggs); both customs are derived from the Roman practice of starting feasts with eggs.

The fondness among German communities for dumplings led to the creation of the most well-known Passover food—*knaidlach* (matza balls). Other traditional Ashkenazic Passover dishes that are featured at many Seders include gefilte fish with *chrain* (horseradish), stuffed veal breast, *gedempte hindle* (stewed chicken), carrot tzimmes, and matza kugel. Historically, Ashkenazim did not serve roasted meat or poultry at the Seder because the paschal offering was roasted. Traditional desserts include compote, nut cakes, honey cake, sponge cake, and *ingberlach* (ginger candies).

Visitors to a Sephardic Seder would notice a number of differences from its Ashkenazic counterpart. Sephardim use escarole, endive, or romaine lettuce, never horseradish, for the bitter herbs. Many Sephardim use vinegar instead of salt water for dipping the *karpas*. Typical Sephardic charoset contains dates and other fruits in addition to apples, nuts and cinnamon. A Sephardic Seder might begin with *sopa de prassa* (leek soup), a fish appetizer, and *mina* (meat-filled matza pie). A main course of lamb—Egyptian Jews often eat roast lamb—or poultry may be accompanied by *mimulim* (meat-stuffed vegetables), and *apio* (sweet and sour celery). Desserts include *pan de spana* (sponge cake), *torta de muez* (nut cake), and *mustachudos* (nut crescents).

The Passover Seder is an event artfully structured by the Sages to serve as a teaching tool. Optimally, various generations are represented. The Seder remains the most beloved and widely kept of all Jewish traditions—its continuing popularity illustrates just how successful the Sages were at obtaining their goal.

(See also Afikomen, Chametz, Charoset, Gebrochts, Karpas, Maror, Matza, and Passover)

SELTZER

Seltzer is plain flavorless carbonated water, which, unlike club soda, contains no salt. The name is derived from Niederselters, Germany, a town near Frankfurt. In the sixteenth century, the town began producing a naturally carbonated tonic called *Selters Wasser*, which was considered to have medicinal value. The German *selterswasser* became *zeltzer* and *seltzer vasser* in Yiddish, which due to the prominence of Jews in the carbonated water business, provided the American word seltzer. The first major development in seltzer making occurred in 1767 when Joseph Priestly invented a process for making carbonated water. Seltzer is made by filtering tap water to remove salt and minerals, then infusing it with carbon dioxide. For the following century and a half, seltzer was primarily dispensed by doctors, spas, and later pharmacies. In the mid-nineteenth century, some English merchants began making a version of this effervescent beverage using baking soda—hence the name soda water. As the word soda became associated with sweetened carbonated drinks, the slightly elegant "club" was added to plain soda water.

The modern seltzer industry traces its origin to 1809, when Joseph Hawkins patented a machine for hermetically sealing seltzer in bottles. Jews in Germany and Russia entered the "zeltzer" business and, in the early twentieth century, brought their experience to America, where seltzer temporarily became an important part of Jewish life. Being pareve, it was ideal for a kosher household. Beginning in the 1920s, blue and green siphon bottles were a common sight on American tables, with seltzer men, most of them Jewish, making regular weekly deliveries. Specifically Jewish seltzer bottles might be embossed with a Star of David or the term "*Shomer Shabbos*" (Sabbath observant). In the early twentieth century, the cost of a glass of seltzer was two pennies, giving rise to the nickname "two cents plain." Seltzer is indispensable for creating another classic, the egg cream, which became a popular part of New York culture beginning in the 1930s. Also in the 1930s, seltzer became known as "Jewish champagne" or, less politely, *grepsvasser* (belch water) in Yiddish.

Seltzer bottles became a standard prop of vaudeville and Jewish comics. In a 1991 episode of *The Simpsons*, Rabbi Krustofski reprimands his son who wants to be a clown: "Seltzer is for drinking, not spraying. Pie is for noshing, not for throwing." Seltzer served a more serious purpose in the 1948 war of independence when Israelis dropped some siphon bottles to fool the Arabs into thinking they had missiles.

In 1807, Dr. Philip Syng Physick of Philadelphia flavored seltzer and added sugar to make it more palatable for his patients, creating the first carbonated soft drink. One of the first bottled flavored seltzers in 1869 was Dr. Brown's Cel-Ray Tonic; it was infused with celery seeds and sugar and was purported to have been invented by a doctor on New York's Lower East Side. In 1832, John Matthews, an English immigrant living in New York, created the soda fountain, a small carbonating machine for stores, which was first used in pharmacies. Seltzer's popularity began eroding after World War II as sweetened carbonated beverages began capturing the market, and was further weakened in the late 1960s by the rising popularity of imported bottled waters.

(See also Celery and Egg Cream)

SEMOLINA

The only flour used in the Temple—with the exception of the Omer offering of new barley on the second day of Passover and the jealousy offering brought in conjunction with the unfaithful wife—was *solet*. Abraham Ibn Ezra explained that *solet* is "wheat flour cleaned of bran," and added, "in Arabic this is called *smeed*." *Smeed* comes from the Aramaic *semida* (the Talmudic equivalent of *solet*), the Greek *semidalis* (fine flour), and the Latin *simila* (fine flour), the source of the English word semolina. *Solet* is not the same all-purpose flour that we currently buy in bags at grocery stores, but a distinct variety—durum wheat.

By the Neolithic period, in Southwestern Turkey wild *Triticum urartu* spontaneously hybridized with the wild grass *Aegilops speltoides*, leading to the most important tetraploid wheat, *Triticum durum* (from the Latin for "hard"). This species, the firmest and most flavorful of all wheat species, is not only higher yielding than emmer, but also free-threshing (naked), which means that the grains are easily released from the glumes and hull, greatly reducing the amount of labor required for its use. In addition, durum contains a larger amount of gluten than emmer, resulting in lighter breads. Unlike other wheat species, the hard endosperm of durum breaks down into granules, called semolina, rather than a powder. When the resulting meal from the inner kernel is further pounded and sieved, it separates into a fine flour, the biblical *solet* (from the root "to sift/to select"). A high level of xanthophyll pigment in the endosperm of durum gives it a bright yellow color.

By the time the Israelites entered the Promised Land, durum had become the preferred species of wheat in Israel, although emmer was initially more commonplace. Durum kernels (wheat berries) were variously parboiled and dried (bulgur), ground into meal (*kemach*), roasted, and boiled. Emmer remained the wheat of ancient Egypt, where durum was unknown.

Today, durum is typically ground into six basic degrees of fineness and purity. The most common type in American markets is coarse grind (*dysat solet* in modern Hebrew)—also called semolina and farina—the type used for porridges, halva, and some cakes. Fine grind—also labeled #1 quality, durum granular, semolina flour, and *suji*—is a slightly granular meal used to make pasta, couscous, and halva, and to add crunch and flavor to pastries and cakes. Durum patent flour (the biblical *solet*) is a powdery product made from the inner portion of the endosperm and used to make pasta and bread. In comparison to common wheat, durum bread has a coarser crumb and heavier texture but is more flavorful (slightly nutty) and does not stale as quickly.

Eventually, durum, emmer, and other types of wheat were surpassed by another subspecies, *Triticum aestivum*, called common wheat and bread wheat. The Romans, in particular, favored *aestivum* and planted it as well as durum in the territories under its dominion. Durum, however, is better for pasta, couscous, and bulgur than other varieties, and retains a large degree of popularity in the Middle East, Mediterranean, and North America.

(See also Couscous, Tishpishti, and Wheat)

SEOR (STARTER DOUGH)

When barley and wheat gruels accidentally spilled into ancient campfires, the first breads emerged from the ashes. Wild yeast occasionally made its way into early wheat doughs, perhaps from naturally fermenting dates, giving rise to the first leavened breads. For millennia thereafter, bread making using wheat flour was a difficult and unpredictable chore. When yeast bread was baked in an area for any significant time, the amount of wild yeast in the air increased, as did the chances of successful leavening and more consistency in flavor. However, even in the best of circumstances, wild yeast proved notoriously unreliable and unpredictable. So until well into the nineteenth century, brewers provided some bakers with the foam (called barm, brewer's yeast, and bitter beer) from the tops of vats of fresh ale to serve as leavening for breads. Barm, however, was all too often of poor quality or even failed to work. Consequently, until the invention of compressed yeast by Dutch distillers in the late eighteenth century, the most efficient way to leaven bread was with a self-perpetuating flour and yeast mixture, known in the Bible as *seor*.

Seor (from the Hebrew "to swell/to lift up") is among the most commonly mistranslated and misunderstood words in the entire Bible. The noun *seor* is almost always rendered in English as "leaven," a generic term meaning an agent that acts to produce a gradual change in another substance, which describes a host of leavening agents. Although *seor* is a leavening agent, not all leavening agents are *seor*. Rather, it refers to a specific leavening agent, known in English as starter, starter dough, or sourdough, and called *biga* in Italian, *sauerteig* in German, and *zeurteig* in Yiddish. (The similarity between the Teutonic *sauer* and the more ancient Hebrew *seor* points to a connection.) A starter is not simply a piece of reserved bread dough, which lacks the strength to adequately raise another batch of dough and spoils relatively quickly. Nor is a starter the same as a sponge, which is a light dough composed of yeast mixed with some of the liquid and some of the flour that will be used in the bread.

A starter is a balancing act, a carefully developed and nurtured flour and water mixture possessing a natural culture of wild yeast and lactobacilli (bacteria). To use a starter, a predetermined amount of starter is mixed into a dough. Dough leavened with a starter requires a lengthy prefermentation process, a much longer time than that needed for modern commercial yeast.

Making a starter can be a long and complicated process—it takes at least five days and commonly up to two weeks. Thus in Morocco, it was traditional on the evening following the last day of Passover, called Mimouna, for Muslim neighbors to bring a piece of starter dough to Jewish friends. Wild yeast are attracted to the sugar in grapes, while the fruit's acid helps to prevent the growth of dangerous organisms, so bakers discovered that inserting a whole bunch into the flour and water mixture for several days helps to create a starter. Flour, especially organic, contains organisms that aid the wild yeast in leavening the bread and also contribute to the flavor. Because the varieties of airborne yeast and bacteria differ from place to place, the flavor of the starter will differ as well. When ready, a starter will be bubbly and yellowish on top; it will sometimes be covered with a liquid because yeast produces carbon dioxide and water when exposed to air. The starter will develop a pleasantly sour, not spoiled, odor. Due primarily to the lactic acid, the starter also imparts a distinctive tangy flavor to bread—hence the term sourdough. Mold or a green or pinkish color is a sign that the yeast and bacteria in the starter are out of balance.

After the starter is ready, if fed and maintained properly, it can last nearly indefinitely. To replenish the starter, bakers simply refresh it with equal amounts of flour and warm water and allow it to stand at room temperature overnight. It is then ready to use again or stored for future use. A specific starter culture can be passed not only from one batch of dough to the next, but also from generation to generation in a family. Certain European bakers zealously guard starters dating back many centuries. Until the twentieth century, professional bakers as well as many housewives commonly maintained their own treasured crock of starter to always be ready to bake bread.

The invention of the starter is generally attributed to the ancient Egyptians, who created and refined many of the bread-baking techniques still used today. The association of raised bread with Egypt, as well as the starter's Egyptian origins, certainly contribute to the inclusion and significance of *chametz* and *seor* as Passover taboos. Due to the high concentration of lactobacilli and yeast, which create an intensely sour and raw flour taste, *seor* is inedible. Hence the Bible never used the word *seor* in reference to eating, but instead prohibited its possession on Passover. *Chametz*, on the other hand, which is an edible grain product, is banned from consumption as well as possession. Thus, according to the Bible, all *seor* had to be destroyed before midday on the fourteenth of Nisan, as was the case with edible *chametz*. Eliminating the *seor* before Passover required not only a thorough cleaning of the house and a genuine personal sacrifice, but also a manifest severing of the past and a faith that bread would again be available in the future.

(See also Bread, Chametz, and Matza)

SESAME

Sesame is the seed of an herb grown in hot climates. It has long been an important part of Asian and African cooking. In India, perhaps its homeland, the plant has been cultivated from at least 2000 BCE.

Sesame is not mentioned in the Bible, but the Mishnah includes *shemen shumshum* among the oils suitable for kindling the Sabbath lights. The Talmud explained, "What would the Babylonians do [if only olive oil was permitted for the Sabbath lights] who have nothing but sesame oil?" The Hebrew name *shumshum*, as well as the English sesame, ultimately derived from the Akkadian *samassammu*, literally meaning "oil plant." The plant bore this name because the seeds, which contain about 50 percent oil, were initially valued for their oil. Sesame oil was once the predominant fat for cooking, as well as fueling lamps, in central Asia and India. The Bene Israel of Mumbai were called *Shanwar Teli* (Saturday oilmen) by their non-Jewish neighbors as they primarily made their livelihoods preparing and selling sesame oil, refusing to work on the Sabbath. Today, the type of sesame oil common in the Middle East is made from raw sesame seeds, while Asian sesame oil, which has a dark brown color and nutty flavor, is frequently made from toasted sesame seeds.

There are two basic varieties of sesame—tan and black. The tan seeds, which are also hulled and sold as white seeds, possess a nutty sweet flavor. Black seeds are more pungent than the lighter ones.

Sesame seeds are greatly valued in Middle Eastern cooking. Whole seeds are used to add flavor and texture to various vegetables, baked goods, candies, and spice mixtures, such as *za'atar*. Tahini (sesame seed paste) is a key component of Middle Eastern foods, including hummus, sauces, eggplants dishes, and confections. Ashkenazim primarily use the seeds as a garnish for breads and, rather recently, in halva.

(See also Halva and Tahini)

SEUDAH

There are two Hebrew words for meal: *arucha* and *seudah*. *Arucha* derives from the root *arak* (to wander). The original meaning of *arucha* was "food for the journey" or "basic food." There are many types of meals, such as an *aruchat boker* (breakfast), *arucha mispachtit* (family meal), *arucha iskit* (business meal), and *arucha meshutaf* (joint meal/meal for everyone). An *arucha* is not the same as an *aracha* (reception/ceremony). On the other hand, *seudah*, from the root *sa'ad* (to support/ to sustain), connotes a substantial amount of food, implying more than simply the intake of sustenance; rather, it means "to strengthen/to refresh" by food, denoting a feast, banquet, or special meal.

Not all *seudah* meals are created equal. The Talmud differentiated between two forms of *seudah*— *seudah shel mitzvah* (a meal associated with a religious purpose), including the Sabbath and festival meals as well as those connected to life-cycle events and rituals, and *seudah shel reshoot*, a feast for a temporal purpose. In Judaism, food, entertaining, and ritual are intertwined. Integral to every holiday and *simcha* (celebration) is a *seudat mitzvah*, establishing and enhancing the spirit of the occasion. The meal before the fast of Tisha B'Av is called a *Seudat Hamafseket* (meal of separation) and consists of only one cooked food and bread—for Ashkenazim, typically a cold hard-boiled egg and a roll. So the intent of *seudah* is not necessarily fancy food, but special food. In the words of Ecclesiastes, there is "a time to weep and a time to laugh; a time to wail and a time to dance." There are occasions when a large amount of fancy fare is appropriate, while other occasions call for merely a hard-boiled egg and a bagel. Some occasions demand extravagant treats, while others require simple, but meaningful fare. A party commemorating a life-cycle event calls for something special like wine, which would be most inappropriate at a meal to break a fast. Knowing when and what to serve is more than a matter of etiquette—it is a mark of understanding and commitment.

In Judaism, enjoying food is not considered wrong. Indeed, in the words of the Chasidic master, Rabbi Nachman of Bratzlav, "One who fails to savor his food

has clearly separated from the God of Blessing." The Talmud contains numerous references to enjoying wine, including, "A person in whose house wine is not poured like water has not attained blessedness." As can be repeatedly seen in the Bible, bread and wine are integral aspects of blessing. Bread and wine, both representative of *Tikkun Olam* (mending the world), serve as the basis of every Jewish feast.

Jewish celebrations are, by design, communal acts accompanied by shared meals. These feasts are much more than an opportunity to eat, although plenty of food is the general rule. Eating together builds relationships and reinforces the bonds of family and community. Among the most important roles of the *seudat mitzvah* is education. The Sages structured the most well-known *seudah*, the Passover Seder, to serve as a teaching tool. Although no other *seudat mitzvah* is as highly ritualized and structured as the Seder, all of them offer unparalleled opportunities for learning in an informal atmosphere. At any seudah, there is an unrivaled opportunity for children to observe and learn how rituals are performed and people interact. Perhaps the most important function of a *seudat mitzvah* is the development of an emotional attachment to Judaism, which has been a key to its continuing survival.

(See also Purim, Seder, Seudat Havra'ah, and Tish)

SEUDAT HAVRA'AH

In Jewish tradition, the sacredness that human beings possess in life does not depart with their demise. This belief is reflected in the various laws and customs concerned with death and mourning. From antiquity until today, a consistency has existed in Jewish mourning practices (*aveilut*) revolving around two principles: *kevod ha'met* (honor of the dead) and *kevod ha'chai* (honor of the living). Jewish law demands that both the deceased and survivors be treated with dignity and respect. Preparation and burial of the body is performed by the local burial society, *Chevra Kadisha* (literally "holy society"). It is the duty of the entire community to see to the needs of the relatives.

The Talmud instructs that the first meal after the burial of a close relative be provided by people other than the mourners. Therefore, it is customary for friends and neighbors of the bereaved to prepare a *Seudat Havra'ah* (meal of consolation) upon returning from the cemetery, beginning the formal mourning process, called shiva, whose name comes from the Hebrew word for the length it lasts, seven days. The act of grieving is actually akin to fear—a grieving person is focused on survival and typically does not have an appetite. The mourner, however, needs nourishment, which is supplied at the *Seudat Havra'ah*. In addition, the mere act of eating acknowledges that a person is alive. The *Seudat Havra'ah* is not the occasion for a fancy catered affair. This simple dairy meal usually consists of bagels or rolls, hard-boiled eggs, and lentils, all circular in shape, symbolizing the cycle of life and death. Eggs obviously represent life and hard-boiled ones denote the ability of people to endure and toughen with the tragedies of life, as eggs do when heated. Lentils also trace back to Jacob and his lentil pottage, which according to tradition was prepared by him for the *Seudat Havra'ah* following the death of his grandfather, Abraham. In Salonika, the meal consisted of bread, eggs, and olives. Iranian Jews, like their Muslim neighbors, serve halva (grain confections) and *kuku* (omelets) at a house of mourning. Other foods served to mourners in the Middle East include round cakes, fish, chickpeas, and coffee.

Throughout the ensuing week of shiva, friends continue to bring food, although more elaborate than the food at the *Seudat Havra'ah*, so that the mourners do not have to worry themselves with everyday concerns.

(See also Seudah and Yahrzeit)

SFENJ

Sfenj is a yeast-raised doughnut.
Origin: Maghreb
Other names: Arabic: *sifanj*; Hebrew: *sefeng*; Tunisia: *yoyo*.

Sfenj, from the Arabic *isfenj* (sponge), is a yeast fritter widespread in Algeria, Libya, Morocco, and Tunisia. It is crisper outside than European-style doughnuts. Unlike European doughnuts, *sfenj* dough does not contain any eggs, fat, or milk. Orange is a favorite flavor.

The predominant shape is a ring, but variations include balls and balls filled with plums. In the souks (marketplaces) of Morocco, professional *sfenj* makers in tiny stalls customarily string fried rings on a palm frond. As with other Middle Eastern treats, they can be dipped in syrup or coated with confectioners' sugar. In Morocco, *sfenj* is typically served with *naa-naa* (hot mint tea).

Sfenj is a traditional Hanukkah indulgence throughout the Maghreb. Moroccans also make these doughnuts as an occasional breakfast treat for their children.

SFOUNGATO

Sfoungato is a baked egg casserole, most often made with spinach and cheese.
Origin: Greece
Other names: *esponga*, *sfougato*; Syria: *sabanigh b'jiben*.

The combination of vegetables, cheese, and eggs in a casserole, such as the venerable *quajado* (coagulated), is a characteristic feature of Sephardic cookery. In Greece and Rhodes, variations of these baked omelets became known as *sfoungato* (from *sfoggos*, the Greek word for "sponge"). Spinach is the predominant vegetable used in this dish. Exacting Old World cooks commonly spread the washed fresh spinach outside in the sun to ensure that it dried sufficiently; too much moisture results in a soggy texture.

Kashkaval and feta cheeses and a sizable amount of fresh herbs mark the Greek version of *sfoungato*. Adding mashed potatoes to the spinach is a Turkish practice. Some versions are baked with a crust like a pie. Popular Greek variations include zucchini and leeks. Cretan Jews made a meat version with spinach and lamb organs and a dairy one with zucchini and tomatoes. A Greek adaptation with the cheese interspersed in the spinach in nests is *sfongo* or *fongos*.

Sfoungato is a popular dish on Passover and Shavuot, when spinach is in season. It is commonly accompanied with yogurt, or yogurt mixed with mint, and flatbreads.

(See also Quajado)

GREEK SPINACH AND CHEESE CASSEROLE (*SFOUNGATO*)

4 TO 6 SERVINGS   [DAIRY]

3 tablespoons olive or vegetable oil
1 medium onion or 4 scallions, chopped
2 pounds fresh spinach, washed, coarsely chopped, and well dried, or 20 ounces frozen spinach, thawed and squeezed dry
½ cup chopped fresh dill, ½ cup chopped fresh flat-leaf parsley, 2 tablespoons chopped fresh mint, or ¼ teaspoon ground nutmeg (optional)
4 large eggs, lightly beaten
1 cup (8 ounces) farmer or cream cheese

1 cup (5 ounces) crumbled feta cheese
½ to 1 cup (2 to 4 ounces) grated kashkaval,
    Muenster, yellow Cheddar, or Swiss cheese
About ½ teaspoon table salt or 1 teaspoon kosher salt
About ¼ teaspoon ground black pepper

About 3 tablespoons grated kashkaval or Parmesan
    cheese for sprinkling
¼ cup (½ stick) unsalted butter or 3 tablespoons
    vegetable oil

1. Preheat the oven to 350°F. Grease a 9-inch square baking pan or other ovenproof dish.

2. In a large skillet, heat the oil over medium heat. Add the onion and sauté until soft and translucent, 5 to 10 minutes. Add the spinach and cook until wilted, about 5 minutes. If using, stir in the dill.

3. In a large bowl, combine the eggs, cheeses, salt, and pepper. Stir in the spinach mixture. Spread in the prepared pan. Sprinkle with the 3 tablespoons kashkaval cheese and dot with the butter.

4. Bake until set and golden brown, about 45 minutes. Let stand for at least 5 minutes before serving. Serve warm or at room temperature.

SFRATTO

Sfratto is a stick-shaped cookie with a honey-nut filling.

Origin: Italy

Sfratti means "sticks" in Italian as well as "evicted," as at one time landlords were allowed to persuade unwanted and delinquent tenants to leave by force of a rod. A similar practice was employed to chase away Jews during all-too-frequent periods of expulsion. These cookies, a popular Italian Rosh Hashanah treat, got their name due to their resemblance to sticks. Thus the Jewish sense of humor transformed an object of persecution into a sweet symbol. *Sfratti* are a particular specialty of the towns of Pitigliano and Sorano in Tuscany and may date to around the establishment of the Pitigliano ghetto in 1622.

TUSCAN HONEY-NUT "STICKS" (*SFRATTI*)

ABOUT FORTY-EIGHT 1½-INCH COOKIES   [DAIRY OR PAREVE]

Pastry:
    3 cups (15 ounces) pastry or all-purpose flour, sifted
    1 cup (7 ounces) sugar
    ¼ teaspoon salt

    ⅓ cup unsalted butter or margarine, chilled
    About ⅔ cup sweet or dry white wine
Filling:
    1 cup (12 ounces) honey
    2½ cups (about 12.5 ounces) walnuts, chopped
    2 teaspoons grated orange zest
    2 teaspoons grated lemon zest (optional)
    ¾ teaspoon ground cinnamon
    ¼ teaspoon ground cloves
    ⅛ to ¼ teaspoon freshly grated black pepper

Egg wash (1 large egg beaten with 1 tablespoon
    water)

1. To make the pastry: In a large bowl, combine the flour, sugar, and salt. Cut in the butter to make a mixture that resembles coarse crumbs. Gradually sprinkle the wine over a section of the flour, then gently mix with a fork to moisten that section. Push the moistened dough aside and continue adding enough wine to make a mixture that just holds together. Divide the dough in half. Using your fingertips, lightly press and knead each half into a ball. Wrap in plastic wrap, flatten into disks, and refrigerate for at least 30 minutes and up to 3 days.

2. To make the filling: In a medium saucepan, bring the honey to a boil over medium heat and cook for 5 minutes. Add the walnuts, zests, cinnamon, cloves, and pepper and cook, stirring constantly, for another 5 minutes. Remove from the heat and let stand, stirring occasionally, until the mixture is cool enough to handle. Pour onto a lightly floured surface, divide into 6 equal portions, and shape the portions into thin 13-inch-long strips.

3. Preheat the oven to 375°F. Line a large baking sheet with parchment paper or grease the sheet.

4. On a lightly floured surface, roll out each piece of dough into a 14- by-12-inch rectangle, then cut lengthwise into three 14-by-4-inch rectangles. Place a nut strip in the center of each rectangle and bring the sides of the dough over the filling, covering it. Pinch the ends to seal.

5. Place the pastries, seam side down, on the prepared baking sheet and brush with the egg wash. Bake until golden, about 20 minutes. Transfer the pastries to a wire rack and let cool. Cut into 1- or 1½-inch pieces. Wrap in aluminum foil until ready to serve. Sfratti can be stored at room temperature for 2 weeks.

SHALOM ZAKHAR/BEN ZAKHAR

On the first Friday night following the birth of a son, relatives and friends gather in the house of the new parents for a party commonly called *Shalom Zakhar* (welcome/peace to the male child) by Ashkenazim. Some Sephardim have adopted a similar ritual known as *Ben Zakhar* (male son), or as *Shasha* among Yemenites. The *Shalom Zakhar*, a party of thanksgiving for the health of the baby, provides an opportunity to offer congratulations to the family on the birth. It also fulfills the commandment of *bikour cholim* (visiting the sick) in regards to the baby's upcoming *brit*; *Shalom Zakhar* is considered to be similar to the visit of God and three travelers to Abraham following his circumcision.

Another possible source of the custom can be found in lines from the Talmud: "While in the womb, an angel comes and teaches a child the entire Torah . . . and just before birth, the angel hits him on the mouth [hence the indentation on the top lip] and he forgets all the Torah." Thus the *Shalom Zakhar* is held as a consolation (*Seudat Havra'ah*) for this lost knowledge. Rabbi Jacob Emden contended that the original name was actually the similar-sounding *Seudat Zakhar* (meal of remembering), as its purpose was to inspire the baby with words of Torah, helping to get him started in relearning what he lost.

There are no set rituals for this occasion, but it is common to recite Jacob's blessing in the Bible to Ephraim and Manasseh as well as assorted psalms. Light food is served, including pastries, fruit, and drinks. One standard food is chickpeas, an ancient symbol of fertility and mourning, in this case a lament for the baby's lost Torah. A Yiddish name for chickpeas is *arbes*, which sounds like the Hebrew *arbeh* (multiply), reminiscent of the biblical promise to Abraham, "I shall *arbeh* [multiply] your seed like the stars of the heavens."

(See also Vakhnacht)

SHAKSHUKA

Shakshuka is a tomato stew with eggs.
Origin: Maghreb
Other names: *beid b'benadora, chakhchoukha.*

Among the favorite stews of the Ottoman Empire was *saksuka* (meaning "goatee" in Turkish), consisting of various cooked vegetables and minced meat or sheep's liver. As *saksuka* evolved, the meat was sometimes eliminated and newcomers from America—tomatoes and peppers—were commonly added. Similar tomato-based stews became a standard throughout the former Ottoman Empire—in Turkey, Syria, Egypt, the Balkans, and the Maghreb, the area where it enjoys the greatest popularity. A related dish is *menemen*, a Turkish tomato and pepper stew that is cooked with lightly beaten eggs and is similar to a thick omelet; the dish is named after a village located near the Turkish city of Smyrna.

When the Ottoman tomato stew reached the Maghreb, it was called *shakshuka*. Jews made a vegetarian version to render it pareve. *Shakshuka* became a popular working person's breakfast when cooked in a skillet with eggs and accompanied with fresh bread. Tunisian Jews, in particular, became recognized for their numerous egg dishes, including *shakshuka*, which they prefer with more fire and spice than Moroccans. In Algeria, the tomato base, called *marqa*, contains numerous vegetables and is served over the top of torn *khobz* (semolina flatbread).

Immigrants from the Maghreb brought *shakshuka* to Israel, where it was widely adopted and variously served as part of breakfast, a light lunch, or dinner. Israeli *shakshuka* features eggs, either poached on top or scrambled in the stew as in the Turkish *menemen*. For Sephardim, both of these methods of cooking eggs with vegetables date back to before the expulsion from Spain. The large-scale egg production of kibbutzim and *moshavim* meant that, even in tough times, eggs in Israel were relatively plentiful and inexpensive. As a result, a can of tomatoes, a few eggs, some bread, and

The Maghrebi tomato stew with eggs, shakshuka, *still provides a healthy and filling breakfast.*

a skillet meant that Israeli families—many of whom in the early days had only a range or burner and no oven—could quickly whip up a tasty and filling meal.

The ingredients beyond tomatoes and eggs and the types of spices vary greatly from cook to cook and place to place. *Shakshuka* runs from mild to particularly fiery. Jewish tomato-based stews typically contain sautéed onion and garlic. Some cooks add various vegetables, notably bell peppers, artichoke hearts, cauliflower, eggplant, fava beans, okra, potatoes, and zucchini. There are even those who fry some *merguez* sausages or chunks of salami or hot dogs in it. A popular Israeli practice is sprinkling the eggs with *za'atar*. Israeli army cooks, to stretch the dish, typically add two handy ingredients, canned corn and baked beans.

For many years, *shakshuka* was an Israeli staple, served several times a week or nearly every day in some households and offered in many restaurants, but more recently, as Israeli culture and food has become more international, it has somewhat declined. Still, kibbutzim, army cafeterias, and upscale Israeli hotels commonly offer *shakshuka* as part of a breakfast buffet. It is widespread during the Nine Days before Tisha' b'Av, when meat is traditionally not eaten. Also in Israel, *shakshuka* has recently become a popular filling for *sambusak* and *borekas* (turnovers). Some families prepare a large pot of the tomato base for the Sabbath to serve with bread, then for Sunday breakfast reheat the remainder with eggs. At a *mezze* (appetizer assortment), *shakshuka* is sometimes accompanied with pita bread, couscous, or rice and a glass of chilled *arak*.

⚜ ISRAELI TOMATO STEW WITH EGGS (SHAKSHUKA)

4 SERVINGS [PAREVE]

3 tablespoons olive or vegetable oil

1 large onion, chopped

2 to 4 cloves garlic, minced

4 medium Anaheim chilies or red bell peppers or any combination, seeded and diced or sliced (optional)

2 pounds (4 cups) plum tomatoes, peeled, seeded, and chopped, or 28 ounces canned plum tomatoes, squished

1 teaspoon paprika, ½ teaspoon ground turmeric, or ½ teaspoon ground cumin

½ teaspoon sugar

About 1 teaspoon table salt or 2 teaspoons kosher salt

Ground black pepper to taste

1 to 2 tablespoons harissa (Northwest African Chili Paste, page 260) or *s'chug* (Yemenite Chili Paste, page 530), 2 to 6 teaspoons hot paprika, or 3 to 5 drops cayenne sauce (optional)

4 large eggs

1. In a large skillet, heat the oil over medium heat. Add the onion and sauté until soft and translucent, 5 to 10 minutes. Add the garlic and sauté for 2 minutes. If using, add the peppers and sauté until tender-crisp, about 5 minutes.

2. Add the tomatoes, paprika, sugar, salt, pepper, and, for a more fiery stew, harissa. Bring to a boil, reduce the heat to medium-low, and cook, stirring occasionally, until the tomatoes soften and thicken, about 20 to 30 minutes. Check the seasonings, as you will not be able to adjust them once you add the eggs.

3. With the back of a spoon, make 4 equidistant indentations in the stew. Carefully break the eggs, one at a time, into a small dish and slide one into each indentation. Cover the pan and cook over low heat until the egg whites are set but the yolks are still soft, about 5 minutes. Or divide the tomato mixture between 4 small baking dishes, make an indentation in the center of each, break in an egg, cover, and bake in a 400°F oven until the eggs are set, about 10 minutes. Serve immediately.

SHANK

A cow or sheep's foreshanks or shins, the portion of the two front legs between the knee and the ankle, contain a large amount of connective tissue and little fat and, therefore, require gentle, slow braising to tenderize and produce a flavorful dish. This method is most commonly used for shanks of lamb or veal. Middle Easterners serve braised lamb and veal shanks with rice, Italians with risotto, Moroccans with couscous, and Romanians with *mamaliga* (cornmeal mush) or garlic mashed potatoes. In many families, braised lamb shanks rank as the favorite holiday dish; they are frequently the main course at a Mizrachi or Sephardic Passover Seder, and a shank bone (*zeroah*) is also included on the Seder plate.

SHARBAT

Sharbat is a fruit syrup.

Origin: Persia

Other names: Israel: *petel*, *tarkiz*; Turkey: *serbet*.

Before the dawn of recorded history, Middle Easterners boiled certain sugar-rich fruits, notably dates and grapes, into a thick honey, known as *dibs* in Arabic and *devash* in the Bible. Then more than two thousand years ago, Persians began boiling lighter fruit juices with bee honey to make a concentrated syrup; they also prepared versions made from flower petals or almonds. The concept of these syrups perhaps originated in China and traveled the Silk Road westward. It appears that ancient versions were thicker, almost jamlike. After sugar arrived in the region from India around the sixth century CE, it was typically substituted for the honey. Until the arrival of the refrigerator, this process remained one of the few ways of preserving many fruits, such as cherries and berries, which have a short season.

Ever since these syrups were developed, Middle Easterners have counteracted the effects of hot weather and thirst with a refreshing drink made by mixing a little fruit syrup concentrate with cold water. Persians stirred the syrup directly into snow and crushed ice to create a frozen treat. Additions appear in fancier variations, such as the Persian *faludeh*, which is made with rice noodles and rose water. In many parts of the Middle East, ice and snow were stored in special icehouses and caves during the winter to last through the summer, and sold in marketplaces to chill drinks and make slushes.

The syrups became known as *sharbat*, from the Arabic *sharba* (a drink), which also gave rise to the English word syrup. With the advent of Islam and its prohibition of alcohol, *sharbat* took on even greater importance and to this day remains popular throughout the Middle East, where it is used as a flavoring agent for water and seltzer, and drinks made with it are still commonly served with meals. Many Middle Eastern Jews rely on beverages made with almond or lemon *sharbat* to break the fast of Yom Kippur. *Sharbat* also became a staple in India.

The Arabs, during their occupation of Sicily, introduced *sharbat* to Europe; the Italians renamed it *sorbetto* and around the early sixteenth century began to make iced versions. This led to the French sorbet, a fruit ice, which was purportedly introduced to France by Catherine de Médicis in 1533; the word sorbet first appeared in English in 1585. In the dairy-rich northern part of Italy, cream and milk were generally added to the fruit syrup, resulting in gelato. In a unique Turkish version, *kariskik komposto*, the syrup is flavored with a combination of apple, apricot, peach, pear, and quince. Around 1600, the Turkish *serbet* led to the English sherbet, which originally denoted a drink of fruit syrup and water, but in the late nineteenth century came to mean a frozen fruit mixture.

Toward the end of the nineteenth century, Turkish and Greek Jews brought their beloved fruit syrups to Israel. The fruit concentrates were among the first processed Israeli foods and they were sold in glass bottles at every *mahkolet* (small market) throughout the country. Raspberry (*petel*) became the most popular and widespread flavor. The official Hebrew word for the syrup was *tarkiz*, although in the Israeli vernacular the generic word for these fruit syrups became *petel*.

In the era before most Israelis owned a refrigerator, *petel*, which keeps at room temperature, was commonly used to make drinks served with meals and snacks, and when entertaining. To Israeli children, *petel* was a cultural icon akin to soda in America. However, in the 1970s, with the popularization of bottled fruit juices and various foreign soft drinks, *gazoz* (*petel* with a squirt of seltzer) and the kiosks peddling it all but disappeared from the country. At the same time, *petel* lost its supremacy in Israeli lives, although it remains an important Israeli food.

SHAVUOT

The one-day (two days outside of Israel) festival of Shavuot (Hebrew for "weeks") falls at the end of the seven-week Omer period after the onset of Passover. The Talmud refers to Shavuot as *Atzeret shel Pesach* (the Conclusion of Passover) and it is analogous to the holiday of Shemini Atzeret, which occurs at the end of Sukkot. Although Shavuot is one of the trio of Pilgrim Festivals mandated in the Bible, it is comparatively little known in America, even among many Jews. This relatively low profile is due partially to the brevity of the festival and partially to a scarcity of holiday rituals and symbols.

Agriculturally, Shavuot marks the end of the barley harvest and the beginning of the wheat harvest. It is also around the time of the first of the two annual fig crops. The Book of Ruth, which describes events occurring at this time of year, is read in the synagogue.

During the time when the Temple stood, two loaves of wheat bread were "waved before the Lord."

This, along with the thanksgiving offering, is the only occasion when leavened bread was used in the Temple. In addition, the holiday is called *Yom ha'Bikkurim* as it is the first day of the year when the first fruits could be brought to the Temple.

After the Temple was destroyed and the Jews moved away from Israel, eventually losing their agricultural lifestyle, Shavuot took on a more pronounced historical meaning—commemorating the giving of the Torah at Mount Sinai seven weeks after the Israelites departed Egypt. Rabbi Isaac Luria, the Ari, instituted the custom of *Tikun Leil Shavuot*, staying awake and studying the entire night of Shavuot.

In recognition of the harvest, as well as the trees that according to tradition flourished on Mount Sinai during the giving of the Torah, synagogues and homes are customarily decorated with flowers and greenery. In the Middle East, the synagogue is bedecked with an abundance of rose petals—hence the nickname "the Festival of Roses." Accordingly, Middle Eastern Shavuot fare is frequently flavored with rose water, and rose-petal preserves are commonly served with the meal.

The preeminent food symbol of the holiday among Ashkenazim is dairy, as Shavuot corresponds to the time of the year when young animals are able to graze and dairy products are in abundance. The Torah is compared in Song of Songs to milk and honey and the Bible refers to Israel as a "land flowing with milk and honey."

In addition to the biblical references, tradition recounts that after receiving the Torah and the laws of kashrut on Shavuot, the Jews could no longer eat the meat foods they had prepared beforehand or use any of the cooking utensils, which were now unkosher. Another legend relates that when the Jews returned to camp after receiving the Torah, they found that their milk had soured and turned into cheese. Therefore, it was necessary to eat dairy dishes and cheese on the first Shavuot. In addition to dairy products, other white foods, such as rice and white cornmeal, are considered symbols of purity and are customary on this holy day.

Since the bread offering is one of the few Biblical rites prescribed for this holiday, a special emphasis is placed on the Shavuot loaves. Ukrainian Jews top their long holiday bread with a five- or seven-rung ladder design, an allusion to Moses' ascent on Mount Sinai to receive the Torah and because the numerical value

of the Hebrew word for ladder is the same as Sinai. Five rungs represent the Five Books of Moses; seven rungs represent the number of weeks from Passover to Shavuot, as well as the seven spheres of heaven. Many Sephardim prepare round seven-layered breads called *siete cielos* (seven heavens). Some communities developed a specially marked dairy bread on Shavuot. Greek communities make a honey and yogurt bread, while some German Jews prepare a cheese challah called *kauletsch*.

Sephardim often serve *borekas* (pastry turnovers), phyllo turnovers, *sfongo/fongos* (spinach-cheese nests), yogurt salads, *sutlach* (rice-flour pudding), and *biscochos Har Sinai* (mounded cookies representing Mount Sinai). Middle Eastern Jews typically make *mengedarrah* (lentils with rice topped with yogurt) and *ruz ib assal* (honey-and-milk rice pudding). Syrians typically enjoy *calsones* (filled pasta) and *sambusak bi jiben* (cheese turnovers).

Ashkenazic fare includes blintzes, noodle or rice kugels, knishes, kreplach, pirogen, vegetable salads with sour cream, *kaesekuchen* (cheesecake), strudel, *schnecken*, rugelach, kuchen, and cheese *fluden* (layered pastry). Two blintzes placed side by side resemble the two tablets that Moses received on Mount Sinai on that day, as well as the two leavened loaves waved in the Temple on Shavuot.

SHAWARMA

Shawarma is thinly sliced roasted seasoned lamb or turkey wrapped in flatbread.

Origin: Turkey

Other names: *chawarma, shaurma, showarma;*
  Turkey: *döner kebab*

Roasted lamb with flatbread is an ancient Middle Eastern combination, dating in Jewish cookery to the biblical paschal lamb of the Passover Seder wrapped in soft matza. The more recent *shawarma* is a similar combination consisting of highly seasoned marinated slices of meat, originally lamb, stacked about two feet tall on a skewer and slowly roasted on a vertical spit in front of a flame. The word *shawarma*, from the Turkish *çevirme* (rotating), is the Arabic name for what the Turks call *döner kebabs* (*döner* means "one that turns"). The dish originated in Anatolia around the 1830s, after the invention of a mechanical vertical rotisserie, also called a cone tower, and soon emerged as the favorite Middle Eastern fast food/street food, prepared fresh to order. As the rotisserie turns, paper-thin slices of caramelized meat are shaved from the roasted surface using a very sharp knife; the falling shards are piled into a pita or *laffa*. Turkish versions tend to be spicier than those from Greece. Turkish immigrants introduced the *döner kebab* to Germany and England, where they eventually emerged as the favorite fast food.

Jews from the Near East brought a love for *shawarma* with them to Israel, and the enjoyment of the dish soon spread to Ashkenazim and Sephardim as well—*shawarma* rivals falafel as Israel's favorite street food. In the early years of the state, when few homes had an oven, small shops and kiosks could purchase or jerry-rig a rotisserie, providing a practical method for roasting meat for a casual but filling meal. Because lamb was relatively expensive, Israelis typically began substituting locally raised turkey, frequently with a little lamb fat added for flavor and moisture. The meat is commonly served with Israeli salad or chopped tomatoes, tahini sauce or *amba* (curried mango condiment), and pickles. Recently, frozen packaged turkey *shawarma* and packets of *shawarma* spice mix have appeared in Israeli groceries.

SHECHITA

According to the Bible, humans had originally been assigned a vegetarian diet, but later Noah and his descendants were granted permission to eat animals. God said to Noah, "Every moving thing that lives shall be for you for food, as the green herb have I given you everything." Later when the Israelites are on the verge of entering the Promised Land, God declares, "According to the desire of your soul, you shall eat meat," which connotes not a commandment to consume meat but rather a concession to human cravings. The Talmud explained the biblical passage, "The Torah here teaches a rule of conduct that a person should not eat meat unless he has a craving for it . . . and even then he should eat it only occasionally and sparingly." Consequently, the Bible permits the killing of permitted animals for food in prescribed ways—through *shechita*, the act of ritual slaughter of animals and fowl. If an animal or fowl is killed otherwise than by *shechita*, it is not kosher. *Shechita* is not applicable to fish. A *shochet* (slaughterer) is a person trained to perform ritual slaughter. This is different from a butcher (*metzger* in Yiddish and *itleez* in Hebrew), although the

two jobs can be performed by the same person if qualified. The Torah decrees a positive commandment to employ *shechita* in slaughtering animals, as well as a negative commandment forbidding the consumption of any meat not obtained through *shechita*.

Shechita is designed to be the most humane method of killing, causing the least possible pain to a live, unimpaired animal. The act of *shechita* in ruminant animals entails cutting, in a single knife stroke, through the majority of both the windpipe (trachea) and gullet (esophagus); fowl can be cut through either of these organs. In addition, the carotid arteries and jugular veins along both sides of these organs are severed at the same time, which is helpful in removing the blood from the animal. The area in which the knife must cut ranges from the large ring (cricoid cartilage) in the windpipe down to the top of the upper lobe of the lungs; in an adult cow this region is generally more than 12 inches. The result of *shechita* is a quick, thorough draining of blood (*dam nefesh*), a substance strictly forbidden for consumption. This intense loss of blood and dramatic drop in blood pressure renders the animal unconsciousness irreversibly and almost instantaneously, in about two seconds.

Some critics—as part of an attempt to eliminate meat eating altogether or sometimes simply as a matter of anti-Semitism—claim other methods of slaughter are more humane than *shechita*, without knowing or acknowledging the reality of the situation. For example, the now-common Western practice of stunning an animal (captive-bolt shot and electric shock) frequently requires numerous repetitions of the shot to the head to produce unconsciousness, commonly causing damage to the skull and brain, which is not only painful but renders it *treifa* (unkosher).

Originally, anyone, man or woman, conversant with the regulations of ritual slaughter could perform this act. However, around 1220, Ashkenazim restricted the performance of slaughter to only an adult male and a designated communal official, the *shochet*. Not just anyone, however, could be a *shochet*—the position required a pious and sensitive person who had been specially trained in both anatomy and Jewish law, and had been tested and regularly retested for the role. Before performing *shechita*, the *shochet* recites a benediction, reminding himself of the divine presence and the gravity of his act. When the *shochet* ages, before his hands begin to shake, he retires.

SHIRINI

Shirini is a Persian cookie.

Origin: Persia

Other names: *naan-e shirini-ye khoshk, naan-e shirini.*

Persians enjoy an assortment of cookies and various firm treats called *shirini khoshk* (dry sweets) and *shirini tar* (moist sweets), which are typically served with tea (*naan-e chai*). Popular cookies include *naan-e shirini* (sugar cookies), *naan-e ardi* (flour cookies), *naan-e keshmeshi* (raisin cookies), and *naan-e gerdooi* (walnut cookies). While many modern versions call for butter or clarified butter, earlier recipes used oil because dairy products were once rare in Middle Eastern Jewish baking.

The favorite Persian cookie is *naan-e berenji*, meaning "rice bread," also known as *shirini berenji*, and called *naan-berenji* by Kurds. These delicate cookies are usually bright white, but are occasionally tinted yellow. Some bakeries extrude the dough into simple flower shapes, while home bakers might press a pattern into the top.

Naan-e nokhodchi, also known as *shirini nokhodchi*, is another important cookie, similar to shortbread, but a little crumbly and less dense. Moist and subtly sweet, they have a slightly nutty flavor from the chickpea flour. *Nokhodchi* are frequently perfumed with rose water and sprinkled with ground pistachios, producing a harmonious blend of flavors. Persians have a special traditional clover-shaped cutter for these.

Naan-e berenji and *naan-e nokhodchi* are traditionally served on Purim and Passover and at weddings. Persians never accepted the Ashkenazic restrictions against eating rice and legumes on Passover. Other *shirini* (sweets) typical at a Persian wedding include *noghl* (Jordan almonds), *sohan asali* (honey almonds), *toot* (mulberry-shaped almond paste), *naan-e badami* (almond cookies), and baklava. More recently, some Ashkenazim in Israel have begun making *berenji* with poppy seeds for Purim, combining the Ashkenazic tradition of *mohn* with a cookie from the location of the Purim story.

❧ PERSIAN RICE FLOUR COOKIES (*NAAN-E BERENJI*)

ABOUT 40 SMALL COOKIES   [DAIRY OR PAREVE]

1 cup unsalted butter or margarine, softened; coconut oil; or vegetable oil (not canola oil)

⅔ cup superfine sugar or 1¼ cups confectioners' sugar

4 large egg yolks or 2 large eggs

1 tablespoon rose water, 2 teaspoons orange-blossom water, or 1½ teaspoons vanilla extract

¼ teaspoon salt

1 to 3 teaspoons ground cardamom (optional)

About 2½ cups (12.5 ounces) rice flour or cream of rice

About ¼ cup poppy seeds or finely chopped pistachios for sprinkling (optional)

1. In a large bowl, beat the butter until smooth, about 1 minute. Gradually add the sugar and beat until light and fluffy, about 4 minutes. Beat in the egg yolks, one at a time. Add the rose water, salt, and, if using, cardamom. Gradually add the rice flour and beat until smooth, soft, and thick. (If using the oil, you can process all the ingredients in a food processor fitted with a metal blade until smooth.) Cover with plastic wrap and refrigerate for at least 8 hours.

2. Preheat the oven to 350°F. Line 2 large baking sheets with parchment paper or lightly grease the sheets.

3. Shape the dough by about 2 teaspoonfuls into 1-inch balls, place 2 inches apart on the prepared baking sheets, and press to flatten to a ¼-inch thickness. If using, lightly sprinkle with the poppy seeds.

4. Bake until set but not browned, 10 to 15 minutes. Do not overbake, because overbaking changes the taste and texture. Let the cookies stand until firm, about 4 minutes, then transfer to a wire rack and let cool completely. Store in an airtight container at room temperature for up to 3 days or in the freezer for up to 6 months.

SHKANAH

Shkanah is a dish of baked beans cooked overnight for Sabbath lunch.

Origin: Spain, Netherlands

Other names: *skhina.*

"After passing Saturday as a Sabbath of rest from our journey, eating with the Jews their hot baked beans, swimming in marrow from the bones of beeves, called *skanah*, with roasted meats and eggs, which had lain in the oven since Friday afternoon, all fat and savory, (the constant Sabbath dinner of all Jews in this country), and taking another night's rest, we were quite refreshed, and concluded to occupy our time to the best advantage." (From an account of Captain James Riley's stay with a Jewish family during a trip to Morocco in *Sequel to Riley's Narrative* [Columbus, 1851].)

In the sixteenth century, Sephardim brought their long-simmered Sabbath stews to the Netherlands, then under Spanish rule, including one made with fava beans, which was known as *shkanah*, from an Arabic word meaning "hot." In the Netherlands, *shkanah* was enriched with honey and goose fat rather than the olive oil of the Mediterranean. Shortly thereafter, the Pilgrims, who did not go directly to Plymouth Rock from England, spent a decade in Leyden in the Netherlands before seeking religious freedom in America in 1620. During their stay in Holland, the expatriates came in contact with the descendants of Sephardim, a new experience for the English as the Jews had been expelled from England in 1290 and would not be officially permitted to return until the mid-seventeenth century. Being members of a fundamentalist sect, the Puritans observed Sunday as a day of rest and, therefore, refrained from cooking. Accustomed to the rather dull fare of their native England, they took a special interest in the exotic Sabbath dishes of the Jews. The British certainly had no previous history of baking beans.

In America, the immigrants substituted native white haricot beans for the fava beans, molasses for the honey, and bacon for the goose fat. The Pilgrims' synthesis of *shkanah* and American produce emerged as New England or Boston baked beans, a traditional Sunday dish placed in the oven on Saturday and left to simmer until after church services the following morning. Thus a descendant of an ancient Jewish Sabbath stew became an American standard. For several centuries, baked beans remained a local Boston specialty. The first recorded American recipe for the dish which contained no mention of sweeteners, appeared as late as 1829 in a cookbook from Boston by Lydia Maria Child, entitled *The American Frugal Housewife*.

SHLISHKES

Shlishkes is a dish of potato dumplings tossed with sautéed bread crumbs.

Origin: Hungary

Other names: *krumplinudli, nokedli*.

   Shlishkes is a Hungarian variation of the *kartoffel kloese*, a central European potato dumpling. It is similar to the Italian *gnocchi di patate*, although *shlishkes* is firmer and does not have ridges. The dish originated as a means of using any leftover mashed potato dough from making the popular *gombotzen* (plum-filled

dumplings), by boiling small dough pieces, then sautéing them. Whereas their non-Jewish neighbors typically coated similar potato dumplings with grated hard cheese, Hungarian Jews, who most commonly served the dumplings at a meat meal, substituted browned bread crumbs. Sautéed onions are also sometimes added. A popular baked or pan-fried version of these dumplings is called *bilkas* or *bilkalekh*; matza cake meal is substituted for the flour during Passover.

   In the nineteenth century, *shlishkes* became a cherished Friday night treat in some Hungarian homes. A recipe for "Shlishkas" was recorded in *The Jewish Examiner Prize Kosher Recipe Book* (Brooklyn, 1937). Around this time, the dish was widely adopted by eastern European Jews in Brooklyn and Queens, becoming a popular Friday night and holiday side dish. *Shlishkes* remain common in New York City's *haimish* kosher take-out stores and at some weddings and bar mitzvah smorgasbords.

   (See also Gombóc)

HUNGARIAN POTATO DUMPLINGS (*SHLISHKES*)

6 TO 8 SERVINGS   [PAREVE OR MEAT]

   2 pounds (4 large) baking (russet) potatoes, peeled and sliced

   1 tablespoon shortening, vegetable oil, or schmaltz

   2 large eggs

   About 1 teaspoon table salt or 2 teaspoons kosher salt

   About 3 cups (15 ounces) all-purpose flour

Topping:

   3 tablespoons vegetable oil or schmaltz

   1 cup fresh bread crumbs

   1. Place the potatoes in a large pot and add water to cover. Bring to a boil and cook until tender, about 20 minutes. Drain. Mash the potatoes with the shortening. Blend in the eggs and salt, then add enough flour to make a soft dough.

   2. On a lightly floured surface, roll the dough into ½-inch-thick ropes. Cut the ropes into 1- to 1½-inch pieces.

   3. Bring a large pot of water to a boil. Add the dough pieces and stir to prevent sticking. Boil until they float to the surface and are firm, about 5 minutes. Drain.

   4. To make the topping: In a large skillet, heat the oil over medium heat. Add the bread crumbs and sauté until golden, about 1 minute.

   5. Stir in the shlishkes. Serve warm.

SIGD

For more than two millennia, the land lying to the west of the Red Sea served as home to a group of black Jews known to the Ethiopians by the derogatory term of *Falasha* ("wanderers" in Geez). They called themselves Beta Israel ("House of Israel").

When the Beta Israel lived in Ethiopia, they expressed their yearning for the land of Israel and devotion to the Torah in a special mass celebration, the festival of *Sigd* (meaning "prostration" in Amharic, related to the word for the Temple, *Mesgid*), held fifty days after Yom Kippur. For thousands of years on the twenty-ninth day of the month of Cheshvan (usually in mid-November), the Beta Israel purified themselves with water, dressed in their finest clothes, traveled from their villages, frequently a three-day trek, and at dawn, began to ascend a grassy hilltop, reminiscent of Mount Sinai as well as the Temple Mount in Jerusalem. The *Kesim* (ritual leaders) would head the assemblage, followed by honored members carrying *Orit*, Torah scrolls written in their language of Geez. The people fasted for the first half of the day. On the mountain, the assemblage prayed and the *Kesim* read from the scrolls and recited Nehemiah, chapters 8 and 9, relating the details of the return to Zion from Babylonia, including the verse, "Go your way, eat the fat, and drink the sweet." In the afternoon, the people would descend from the mountain and break their fast with a joyous communal meal accompanied with much singing and dancing. The fast was typically broken with *misvaot* (from the Hebrew word *miztvot*, "commandments"), breads blessed by a *Kes*.

In the 1980s, Ethiopians in Israel began to celebrate *Sigd*. It was recognized as an official state holiday in 2008. Today, Beta Israel from across Israel, from the total population numbering about eighty thousand, gather in the Armon Hanatziv neighborhood of Jerusalem, overlooking the Temple Mount. The *Kesim*, dressed in simple white robes and prayer shawls, are each accompanied by an assistant holding a brightly colored umbrella over his head. Many of the worshippers fast half of the day, recite Psalms, then listen to the *Kesim* read from the *Orit* scrolls. The current site and size of the crowd no longer supports a communal meal, but many Ethiopian families bring their own food, while vendors nearby sell supplies from stalls. The *Sigd* meal features *injera* (pancake bread), *dabo* (honey buns), or pita along with a vegetable *wot* (stew) and plenty of coffee—drinking three cups is considered lucky.

SIMCHAT TORAH

At the conclusion of the holiday of Sukkot falls a separate series of holidays, Shemini Atzeret and Simchat Torah. In Israel, they occur on the same day, but outside Israel, they are celebrated as two separate days. Shemini Atzeret (The Eighth Day of Assembly) is a Biblical festival concluding the extensive holiday period that begins nearly a month earlier with Rosh Hashanah. In recognition of the approaching winter, a special prayer for rain in Israel is recited, which is continued until Passover.

Simchat Torah (literally "Happiness of the Torah") is a relatively late creation; it emerged only around the ninth century CE. Its source lies in the ancient and enduring Jewish tradition of publicly reading from a Torah scroll in a cycle that begins and ends on Simchat Torah. The tradition in Israel was to read the Torah in a cycle of three and half years, with the conclusion of the seventh year corresponding to the *Hakhel* ceremony at the end of the Sabbatical year. In Babylonia, where the Sabbatical year was not in force, a one-year cycle developed, concluding with the second day of Shemini Atzeret. The name Simchat Torah is not mentioned in the Talmud, but occurs first in the post-Geonic literature (after 1040 CE, the end of the nearly 450-year-period when the heads, called a *gaon*—"pride of" in Hebrew—of the two most important Babylonia academies served as the spiritual leaders of world Jewry). Eventually, the Babylonian custom supplanted the Israeli one. Still, in the thirteenth century, Benjamin of Tudela reported that there were two synagogues in Cairo, one for those following the Babylonian customs and the other for those adhering to the Israeli customs.

Simchat Torah, along with Purim, is one of the two most uninhibitedly joyful occasions on the Jewish calendar, replete with singing, dancing, and feasting. Rabbi Joseph Caro wrote that the inspiration for the Simchat Torah celebration came from King Solomon, who made a large feast after God granted him great wisdom. Simchat Torah feasts should be particularly festive and not simply a nibble and an overabundance of alcohol. Simchat Torah fare, similar to that of Sukkot, is intended to reflect the bounty of the harvest and includes thick soups and stews incorporating seasonal produce and filled foods—such as stuffed chicken, stuffed veal breast, stuffed vegetables, and filled pastries, including knishes and strudel—symbolizing abundance. In addition, filled food is symbolic of a Torah scroll, which is covered on the outside and the essence is inside. Particularly widespread among Ashkenazim is stuffed cabbage, whose shape resembles a Torah scroll. In Israel, Turkish Delight and candied apples have become popular treats.

SINGARA

Singara is a fried filled pastry.

Origin: India

Singara, the Bengali version of a samosa, is a synthesis of southern Indian and Middle Eastern cuisines. The original dish was a triangular turnover, but today it is more commonly formed into a cone shape, which is attractive although more difficult to form. The filling can be savory—including spiced vegetables (*sobj*), mashed or fried potatoes (*aloo*), and lamb (*gost*)—or sweet (*mishti*). The sweet ones are commonly served on Hanukkah as well as at the meal following Yom Kippur. The favorite sweet filling is a form of semolina halva, which Cochinis also use to make fritters called *neyyappam*.

(See also Sambusak)

SIYYUM

Siyyum (Hebrew meaning "finishing/conclusion") denotes the completion by individuals or groups of the study of an entire Jewish work of scholarship, such as the Five Books of Moses (*Siyyum ha-Torah*), a tractate of the Talmud (*Siyyum ha-Sefer*), or the entire six subdivisions of the Talmud (*Siyyum ha-Shas*). An annual public *Siyyum ha-Torah* occurs on Simchat Torah, a time of great joy and celebration. A *siyyum* is also observed for the completion of writing a Torah scroll (*Siyyum Sefer Torah*). These achievements are marked with a communal sharing of food in a home or synagogue, ranging from a simple bottle of schnapps and some cookies to a *seudat mitzvah* consisting of a sit-down repast. There is a tradition for firstborn males to fast on the day before Passover, but they are exempt if they attend a *siyyum*. Therefore, many synagogues commonly hold a *siyyum* on that morning.

SOFRITO

Sofrito is a meat or poultry stew cooked in a small amount of liquid.

Origin: Spain

The term *sofrito*, from the Spanish *sofreir* (to fry lightly), encompasses a variety of subtle savory Hispanic and Italian seasoning bases and sauces built on sautéed vegetables and spices. In Latin America, it means an onion-based flavoring, which in many countries is enhanced with bell peppers and tomatoes. Among Sephardim, it refers to a method of simmering pieces of chicken, veal, beef, or lamb in a small amount of seasoned liquid, a procedure somewhat different from both stewing and braising and actually more akin to the methods used to prepare Hungarian *paprikás* and Moroccan *tagine*.

Sofrito is slow-simmered so that all the ingredients meld with a minimum of liquid, resulting in very tender meat in a thick, flavorful sauce. After small pieces of meat or poultry are browned in a little oil, some garlic and/or onions are added and sautéed—hence the name *sofrito*. The presence and amount of garlic or onion varies. Some cooks mince the garlic and onion, while others use whole cloves and whole tiny onions. The dish is typically enhanced with lemon juice or vinegar, while turmeric gives it a vibrant yellow hue. For tartness, some Turks substitute sour plum juice for the lemon. Syrians generally favor a zesty rendition made with a spice blend called *baharat*, while Egyptians prefer a milder version, perhaps with a little allspice and/or cardamom. Deep-fried potatoes are frequently added, as they maintain their shape and texture during the extended cooking time.

Since it holds up like a Sabbath stew, *sofrito* became a traditional Friday night entrée in many Sephardic families from the eastern Mediterranean; it was typically made with chicken by wealthier families and perhaps beef brisket by the less well-off. Any leftovers were enjoyed cold on Saturday or Sunday. However, today some families leave the *sofrito* on a hot plate overnight to enjoy warm for Sabbath lunch instead of *hamin/adafina* (Sabbath stew). Syrians serve it, using veal or chicken, with potatoes (*sofrito batatas*) on Sukkot, as it is a warming one-dish meal that is easy to transport outside to the sukkah. *Sofrito* is usually accompanied with rice.

Sephardim brought *sofrito* to Israel, where it became a popular comfort food. Small old-fashioned restaurants in Jerusalem's Machaneh Yehudah market offer it only on Fridays and it is intended to be taken home and left on a *platta* (electric hot plate) for the evening meal.

SEPHARDIC MEAT IN THICK SAUCE (*SOFRITO*)

6 TO 8 SERVINGS   [MEAT]

3 pounds boneless beef, veal, or lamb shoulder,
    beef brisket, or beef shank or veal shin, cut into
    1¼-inch cubes; or 8 to 12 chicken thighs and
    drumsticks

3 tablespoons olive or vegetable oil

2 to 3 cloves garlic, minced, or 1 medium onion,
    sliced, or 8 small whole onions

About ¾ cup boiling chicken broth or water

2 tablespoons fresh lemon juice

1 teaspoon ground turmeric

About ¾ teaspoon table salt or 1½ teaspoons kosher
    salt

About ½ teaspoon ground black pepper

1. Pat the meat dry with paper towels. In a large, heavy pot, heat the oil over medium heat. In batches, add the meat and brown on all sides, 5 to 8 minutes per batch. Remove the meat. Add the garlic and sauté until fragrant, 1 to 2 minutes, or the onion and sauté until soft and translucent, 5 to 10 minutes.

2. Add the broth and scrape the pan to loosen any browned bits. Add the lemon juice, turmeric, salt, and pepper. Return the meat to the pot.

3. Bring to a boil, cover, reduce the heat to very low, and cook, turning the meat about every 20 to 30 minutes and adding a little more water when necessary, until the meat is very tender and the sauce thick, 2 to 2½ hours. Serve hot.

VARIATIONS

Sephardic Meat and Potatoes in Thick Sauce (Sofrito Batatas): Cut 4 to 8 medium potatoes into 1-inch cubes or ½-inch-thick wedges. Heat about 2 inches vegetable oil to 375°F, deep-fry the potatoes until golden brown (but not completely cooked through), about 5 minutes. Drain the potatoes. About 30 minutes before the meat is tender, add the potatoes.

SOHAN ASALI

Sohan asali is a honey-nut brittle.

Origin: Persia

In Farsi, *sohan* means "beautiful" and *asal* means "honey." *Sohan asali* is a specialty of Shiraz, where professional confectioners whip up large batches in copper kettles. This honey treat is similar to and most certainly the source of the Turkish Passover confection *asashoo*, which in turn is probably the source of the very similar Ashkenazic *pletzlach* and *ingberlach*.

However, *sohan asali* is enhanced with saffron and rose water. Contemporary versions are sometimes coated in untraditional chocolate. In Persian culture, candy and the color yellow represent joy, and this treat incorporating both is served at festive occasions, such as Rosh Hashanah, Passover, and weddings.

PERSIAN HONEY-NUT BRITTLE (*SOHAN ASALI*)

ABOUT 50 PIECES   [PAREVE]

2 cups (14 ounces) sugar

½ cup honey

½ cup vegetable oil

¼ cup water

Pinch of salt

¾ teaspoon ground saffron or ½ teaspoon ground
    turmeric

½ teaspoon ground cardamom (optional)

2 tablespoons rose water or hot water

1 pound (about 4 cups) coarsely chopped or
    sliced or slivered toasted almonds, hazelnuts,
    pistachios, or walnuts

1. In a medium, heavy saucepan, stir the sugar, honey, oil, water, and salt over medium-low heat until the sugar dissolves, about 5 minutes. Stop stirring, increase the heat to high, and bring to a boil.

2. Cover and cook for about 30 seconds to dissolve any sugar crystals. Uncover and boil gently, without stirring, until the syrup reaches the soft crack stage or registers 270°F on a candy thermometer, about 10 minutes.

3. Meanwhile, dissolve the saffron and, if using, cardamom in the rose water. Add to the syrup and stir for 3 minutes. Stir in the almonds.

4. Pour onto an oiled large marble slab or large baking sheet and spread evenly to a ½-inch thickness. While still soft, cut into squares. Let cool until firm. Store in an airtight container at room temperature for up to 2 weeks.

SOUR CREAM

In the time before pasteurization and refrigeration, milk spoiled rather quickly and, therefore, the predominant way of consuming dairy was in a fermented form, including cheese, butter, buttermilk, yogurt, kefir, and sour cream. Originally, sour cream consisted of heavy cream left at room temperature until partially fermented; the acid produced by lactobacilli acted as a preservative, coagulated the proteins to a thick consistency, and imparted a slightly tangy flavor. Today, sour cream is made by adding a bacterial culture to unpasteurized cream and heating the cream to achieve the desired level of lactic acid. Then various additives are used, sometimes gelatin and rennet, to prevent separation and extend the shelf life; these additives can pose problems for kosher consumers. There is also a nonfermented version, labeled "acidified sour cream," made by coagulating the cream through the addition of an acid. The original type of sour cream has a mild tart flavor and a consistency somewhat thinner than that of modern commercial brands.

Sour cream—*smeteneh* in Yiddish and *tejföl* in Hungarian—became the primary cultured milk product in Slavic regions, a role played by the similar clotted cream in England, *quark* in Germany, and crème fraîche in France. Sour cream is among the flavors associated with eastern European Jewry. Along with various other *zoyers* (sours), such as pickles and sauerkraut, sour cream enlivened an otherwise bland diet consisting primarily of starches. It also filled a crucial role in balanced nutrition, as it contained the major vitamins (A and D) lacking in the staple of the nineteenth-century eastern European diet, potatoes. During the intervening one hundred years after the popularization of the potato in eastern Europe and until World War II, many Jewish meals from the spring through autumn consisted of boiled potatoes and sour cream. In Ashkenazic baked goods, sour cream adds moisture, richness, and a tang. It tops blintzes, blinis, potato latkes, and pirogen and is mixed with pickled herring, salads, and chopped radishes. Sour cream is essential for Ashkenazic Passover and Shavuot meals and is served with potatoes, borscht, *schav* (sorrel soup), and vegetables.

In the nineteenth century, eastern Europeans brought sour cream to America. In 1888, Lithuanian Jewish immigrants Isaac (1864–1945) and Joseph (1859–1930) Breakstone (originally Bregstein) opened a small shop on Manhattan's Lower East Side to sell traditional eastern European dairy products, most notably sour cream, for which the cream was incubated in ten-gallon containers. In 1896, Wolf Axelrod began selling sour cream and pot cheese from a store on Madison Street in New York's Lower East Side, then relocated to a larger facility in Brooklyn. He primarily sold his products wholesale and they were delivered by horse and wagon and cooled by blocks of ice. In those days before prepackaged foods, the products were spooned out of large barrels into various receptacles. The introduction of homogenization in 1919 led to a much more uniform texture. Eventually, manufacturers began packaging their sour cream in reusable glass jars. When innovations led to sour cream being prepackaged in small plastic containers and supermarkets introduced refrigerated cases, this Old World necessity became a standard of the mainstream American kitchen as well. Kraft purchased Breakstone's in 1928 and Axelrod's in 1932, becoming one of the largest sour cream producers in the world.

SOUR SALT

Sour salt, *melach limon* in Hebrew, is not related to table salt and does not possess a salty flavor, but rather is crystallized citric acid obtained from citrus fruits and fermented molasses. Citric acid was first isolated in crystalline form in 1784. Before fresh lemons were readily available, beginning in the nineteenth century, northern European cooks and immigrants to America used these crystals, balanced with sugar, to create a sweet-and-sour flavor in their dishes, such as meatballs, stuffed cabbage, cabbage soups, and borsch. Unlike vinegar and lemon juice, which have their own distinctive flavor and odor, sour salt produces only a pure sour flavor and no odor. It also inhibits the browning affects of enzymes and oxidation in fruits. Sour salt is stronger than either vinegar or lemon juice, so cooks use it sparingly and add it to foods gradually until the desired level of sourness is reached. The large white crystals dissolve readily in liquids. Sour salt is available in most Jewish groceries, as well as in the Jewish section of many American supermarkets.

SPAETZLE

Spaetzle is a small flour and egg dumpling.
Origin: Southwestern Germany
Other names: *knöpfle, spatzen, spätzle.*

Spaetzle (meaning "little sparrow") originated in southwest Germany around the eighteenth century and soon spread to neighboring regions of Alsace and Austria. Spaetzle is traditionally made with a special spaetzle maker that looks like a grater with large holes, although the dough may also simply be pushed through a large-holed colander. Spaetzle can also be prepared in the same manner as the Hungarian *galuska* by cutting the dough and sliding it off of a board. Spaetzle is served with soups, stews, gravies, brisket, or sauerbraten.

◄ GERMAN DUMPLINGS (*SPAETZLE*)

ABOUT 4 CUPS   [PAREVE]

   2 cups (10 ounces) all-purpose flour
   ⅔ cup water
   3 large eggs
   ½ teaspoon table salt or 1 teaspoon kosher salt
   ⅛ teaspoon ground nutmeg
   Dash of ground white pepper (optional)

   1. In a large bowl, beat together all the ingredients until smooth. Let stand at room temperature for about 30 minutes.

   2. Bring a large pot of lightly salted water to a boil over high heat. Reduce the heat to medium.

   3. Place about ⅓ cup batter in a large colander with ¼-inch holes and press through the holes into the water. Stir gently and cook until the spaetzle rise to the top, 2 to 5 minutes. Remove with a slotted spoon and arrange on a baking sheet in a single layer. Repeat with the remaining batter.

SPICE

Spices are aromatic seeds, barks, roots, and berries. Long before the first permanent settlements, people discovered that parts of some plants make food taste and smell better. Certain spices contain chemicals that activate neurons of the somatosensory system. Archeological digs point to either cumin or poppy seeds as possibly the first spice.

Spices were no small matter in the ancient world, but considered among the most valued of possessions. A passage from the Book of Kings reflects their regard: "Hezekiah listened to them, and showed them all his treasure-house, the silver and the gold, and the spices, and the precious oil [resin oil], and the house of his armor, and all that was found in his treasures." Medieval European aristocrats secured their spices and other valuables in the towers of castles. Consequently, Ashkenazic spice boxes for Havdalah were traditionally shaped like the towers.

In the ancient world, spices were utilized to flavor foods and wines and as medicines, perfumes, and mood enhancers. In the Temple, they were used in the *ketoret hasamim* (incense) and *shemen hamischa* (anointing oil). In Temple times, during the days preceding the Passover holiday, merchants could be heard throughout Jerusalem calling out, "Come and buy your spices for the commandment [of charoset]."

Spices store well and are relatively light, so they were easily transported. Nonetheless, scarcity and long-distance transport meant that many spices were expensive and fought over. Spice trading was one of the primary movers of history, engendering wealth, exploration, and wars, particularly after the thirteenth century. As recorded in the Bible, donkey caravans and, then around 1000 BCE, camels, carried these goods from Arabia through Petra to the Levant and then to Egypt, and North Africa. In the middle of the first century CE, the Romans learned of the cycle of the monsoons. This enabled them to sail their ships from the Red Sea around the time of the summer solstice, reach the Malabar Coast of southwest India, and return in less than a year with large amounts of peppercorns, thus bypassing Arab traders. Around the same time, the Han dynasty of China imposed peace in central Asia, allowing the Chinese to control and secure the three-hundred-year-old land route from the Orient to the Mediterranean known as the Silk Road, on which Eastern goods were transported. Around the second century CE, Arabia became a major conduit of the spice trade between East and West, passing along routes through Syria or Egypt, and accruing great wealth in the process.

After the fall of Rome, the European spice trade initially ceased and was further complicated by the Arab conquest of the vital port of Alexandria in 641, which left the spice trade in Muslim hands. In 973 CE, Ibrahim ibn Yaacub, a Moorish merchant visiting Mainz (a city along the Rhine River and a center of early Ashkenazic life), noted the presence of cloves, ginger, and pepper in the marketplace. He learned that these spices were supplied by Jewish merchants called Radhanites, who maintained international trade routes between the Christian and Islamic worlds. In the eighth and ninth centuries, "Jewish merchants" were rather recurrent figures at the courts of Charlemagne and Louis the Pious. The Radhanites were first mentioned by name, and not simply as Jewish merchants, in the mid-ninth-century work *The Book of Routes and Kingdoms* by the postmaster of the caliph of Baghdad. From around 700 to 1000 CE, they completely controlled the East-West spice trade and were the only group accepted by both Christians and Mus-

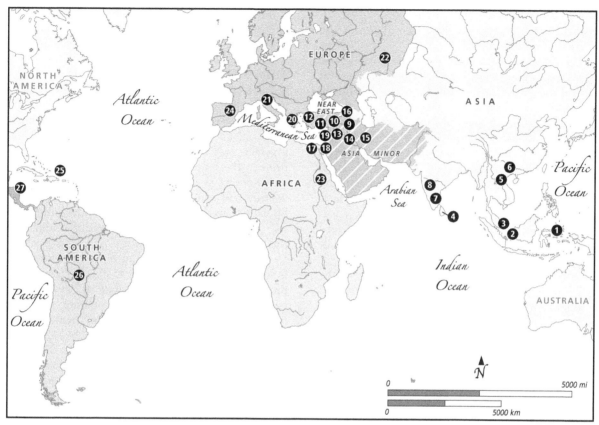

The World of Spices *Many of the world's favorite spices come from a few plant families and a few locations, particularly southeast Asia and members of the Apiaceae family from the eastern Mediterranean and western Asia. Here are where many spices originated. 1* **Cloves**—*Moluccas in the East Indies; 2* **Mace**—*Moluccas (Indonesia); 3* **Nutmeg**—*Moluccas (Indonesia); 4* **Cinnamon**—*Sri Lanka; 5* **Ginger**—*southeast Asia; 6* **Turmeric**—*southeast Asia; 7* **Cardamom**—*southern India; 8* **Pepper**—*southern India; 9* **Anise**—*Near East; 10* **Asafetida**—*Near East; 11* **Sesame**—*Near East; 12* **Mahlab**—*western Asia; 13* **Nigella**—*western Asia; 14* **Sumac**—*western Asia; 15* **Saffron**—*Asia Minor; 16* **Caraway**—*western Asia and eastern Europe; 17* **Coriander**—*Levant; 18* **Cumin**—*Levant or northeast Africa; 19* **Fenugreek**—*eastern Mediterranean; 20* **Fennel**—*northeastern Mediterranean; 21* **Mustard**—*southern Europe; 22* **Dill seed**—*southern Russia; 23* **Ajwain**—*northeast Africa; 24* **Poppy seeds**—*southwest Europe; 25* **Allspice**—*West Indies; 26* **Chilies**—*South America; 27* **Vanilla**—*Central America*

lims. All four of the Radhanite trade routes, by both land and sea, began in the West, either in Iberia or France, and ended in China or India. They brought swords, furs, and cloth from Europe to eastern Asia and returned westward with the luxurious items craved by Christians and Muslims, such as silk, perfumes, oils, gems, musk, aloe wood, camphor, cloves, ginger, and pepper. (They also brought westward what became known as Arabic numerals, as well as possibly the science of making paper.) It was by no coincidence that all the Radhanite trade routes passed through a series of Jewish communities. The shared language of Hebrew allowed communication, while religious contacts and a code of law provided essential access to cooperation and credit.

As a result of Radhanite trade, Asian spices were a part of upper-class European and Jewish cookery in the early medieval period. It was also probably the wealth generated by the Radhanites that helped spark the initial flourishing of the nascent Ashkenazic communities along the Rhine River toward the end of the tenth century. The Radhanites' monopoly of international trade continued until around 1000, when following the fall of the Tang dynasty, traffic along the Silk Road was interrupted.

Following the disappearance of the Radhanites, Asian spices temporarily vanished from Europe until around the First Crusade and the rise of the Italian mercantile states, especially Venice, in the tenth and eleventh centuries. Meanwhile, medieval Arabs made liberal use of spices brought across the Arabian Sea. Marco Polo's accounts of Asian spices in the thirteenth century and then the appearance of the first European cookbooks since the one written by Apicius around 400 CE further enticed Europeans to foreign spices. For the ensuing several centuries, the European aristocracy and emerging bourgeoisie zealously indulged in spices. The masses made do with a few locally grown plants, notably mustard and poppy seeds.

The desire to break the Venetian monopoly on the spice trade led Vasco da Gama in 1497 to sail around southern Africa and Columbus to venture westward at the exact time that the Jews were being expelled from Spain to find an all-water route to the Spice Islands. Many of these voyages or ships were manned by or sponsored by Conversos, including Rui de Brito Mendes, who backed one of the ships in da Gama's second voyage in 1502. Spice trading then shifted from Venice to Lisbon. The Portuguese monopoly was short-lived, for in the sixteenth century, the Dutch, noted for their sailing and business acuity, gained sway over the spice trade. The majority of Dutch spice importers were Sephardim. In turn, the British achieved dominance over India in 1616 and quickly took control.

Eventually political intrigue led to a dispersal of spices. For example, the French smuggled cloves from their home in the Moluccas and successfully planted them on the islands of Mauritius and Réunion. Soon more cloves were being grown in other lands than in their native East Indies. This widening availability of spices and improved means of transportation caused a decrease in prices and a corresponding increase in general use. However, as spices grew more accessible and affordable, European overindulgence in spices waned and the moderate use of seasonings subsequently became the norm in European cooking.

(See also Ajwain, Allspice, Anise, Asafetida, Baharat, Berbere, Caraway, Cardamom, Chili, Cinnamon, Coriander, Cumin, Dill, Dukkah, Fenugreek, Ginger, Hawaij, Mahlab, Mastic, Mustard, Nigella, Paprika, Peppercorn, Poppy Seed, Ras el Hanout, Saffron, Sesame, Sumac, Tabil, Vanilla and Za'atar)

SPINACH

Spinach appeared rather late on the culinary scene. It was developed and first recorded in Sasanian Persia between 226 and 640 CE. Medieval Arab agronomists improved and spread spinach cultivation, and the vegetable was initially mentioned in the Mediterranean in the tenth century. Spinach was introduced to Europe by way of the Moors in the late eleventh century and quickly became a Sephardic favorite. Spinach arrived in Italy in the thirteenth century and the Italians subsequently popularized it in much of the northern Mediterranean.

Spinach makes its appearance in early spring and is harvested into early summer, so it became a traditional Passover and Shavuot food. It does not fare well in the hot temperatures of summer, but after the nights begin to cool again in late August or early September, farmers plant the fall spinach crop, which matures in time for Rosh Hashanah.

There are a number of different approaches to cooking and seasoning spinach. The French and Hungarians boil it very briefly over high heat to maintain the bright green color, then blend the leaves with butter, perhaps some meltable cheese or a cream sauce, and a few subtle seasonings. Persians cook spinach for a moderate time, then pair it with yogurt to make a smooth, creamy dish. Indians prefer to simmer the leaves slowly for an extended period, then counter the saucelike result with cubes of firm *panir* (fresh cheese), potatoes, or chickpeas, and plenty of spices, especially ginger and chilies. In India and the Middle East, spinach is frequently combined with legumes for complementary nutrition and textures. Arabs began to cook it with pine nuts and raisins (*sabanigh bi snobar wa sbeeb*), creating a dish that Sicilian Jews brought to northern Italy, where it became a specialty of the Roman and Venetian ghettos and was called *spinaci pinoli e passerine*. Sephardim use spinach interchangeably with chard in an extensive variety of recipes, including salads, stews, soups, patties, casseroles, omelets, pies, pastry fillings, and even a Sabbath soup using the spinach stalks.

(See also Borani, Fritada, Kefte, Mina, Pkhali, and Sfoungato)

SPONGE CAKE

Sponge cake is a cake made light and airy with beaten eggs.

Origin: Spain

Other names: Britain: *plava*; Italian: *pan di spagna*; Ladino: *pan de Espana, pan esponjádo*; Morocco: *pallebe*; Tunisia: *biscoutou*; Yiddish: *poshetteh lekach, tawrt*.

Around the year 1000, bakers in Moorish Spain discovered that beating eggs together with sugar granules trapped numerous air bubbles, making possible the leavening of batters without yeast or chemicals. The result, after a little flour was added and the mixture was baked, was a light, airy cake, enjoyed by Sephardim early on. A branch and twigs tied together originally served as the agitating utensil. However, the batter required more than an hour of beating by hand, so sponge cakes were only enjoyed by the rich or reserved for special occasions. Egg-foam cakes rely solely or primarily on beaten eggs for volume and light texture, but today, some contain baking powder for additional leavening.

Sponge cake reached mainland Italy during the Renaissance (c. 1450s), perhaps spreading from Sicily, where the Arabs had introduced this baking technique, or perhaps brought by Sephardic exiles arriving in Italy. One of the ways Italians served sponge cake was to cover slices with a custard, creating a dish called *zuppa Inglese* (English soup), which was the forerunner of the English trifle. Italians bakers created their own versions of the cake, including *genoise* (named after Genoa), which contained butter and much less sugar, and *bocca di dama* (mouth of a lady), called *biscuit de Savoie* in French, which contained no butter and a larger amount of eggs, resulting in a sturdier cake. Both of these drier Italian egg-foam cakes, unlike sponge cake, required a soaking syrup or liqueur to moisten them.

By the early seventeenth century, egg-foam techniques crossed the English Channel, initially as thin, crisp cakes called biscuits, and, in turn, spread to the American colonies. The first known recipe for a classic sponge cake in a European cookbook was in the German *Die Wol Unterwiesene Koechinn* by Maria Schellhammer (Braunschweig, 1692). The cake was called "French Sweet Bread," indicating that this particular dish had reached northern Europe by way of France and not Italy. The first record of the English term "Spunge Cake" was in and a recipe for it, *A New System Domestic Cookery* by Maria Rundell (London 1807), a time when egg foam was largely replacing yeast in England as the raising agent in cakes. It was first mentioned by a Jewish source in the memoirs of Mordecai Manuel Noah, native of Philadelphia and United States consul in Tunis, *Travels in England, France, Spain, and the Barbary States* (New York and London, 1819), in an account of his 1813 visit to a Spanish chocolate house, noting, "The chocolate, rich and thick, is served up in tumblers, accompanied with a spunge cake, and a glass of water."

The advent of the rotary eggbeater around 1870 greatly reduced the tedium and time involved in making egg-foam desserts. Accordingly, the popularity of home-baked sponge cake greatly increased, abetted by the spread of the home oven. Improvements in bakeware led to even greater popularity for the sponge cake. Originally, European sponge cakes were baked in a tin hoop placed on a parchment paper–lined baking sheet. The next step was a Turk's Cap, a large, glazed, bowl-shaped terra-cotta mold with a central tube, akin to a Bundt pan. The scalloped surface gave a cake the appearance of wound turban. In the mid-nineteenth century, craftsmen began producing a metal version of the Turk's Cap, the first tube pan. However, many of the earlier metal tube pans were square, as pans of this shape were easier to fabricate than the now-standard round ones.

Since it contains no butter, sponge cake proved ideal for kosher meals. Most are flavored with lemon or orange. In the nineteenth century, when sugar beet factories opened in sections of eastern Europe and sugar became more readily available, sponge cake became popular among Eastern Ashkenazim. Recipes for "Sponge Cake" were included in the first English Jewish cookbook, *The Jewish Manual* (London, 1846), and the first American Jewish cookbook, *Jewish Cookery* (Philadelphia, 1871). Sponge cake, typically baked in loaves or large rectangular pans, became a mainstay of kosher bakeries and a common sight at Jewish celebrations. A particular eastern European favorite was a sponge cake containing both sugar and honey, which was popular on Rosh Hashanah, at bar mitzvahs, and at the groom's table at weddings.

When bakers discovered that matza meal and potato starch could be substituted for the flour in sponge cake, it emerged as a widespread Passover treat. The earliest known record for what would become a Passover staple appeared in the first edition of *The Settlement Cook Book* (Milwaukee, 1901), which contained three recipes for "Matzos Sponge Cake," variously with six, eight, and twelve eggs. All three recipes directed, "Bake in a moderate oven in loaf or in layers." A year later, Sarah Rorer, in *Mrs. Rorer's New Cook Book* (Philadelphia, 1902), included "Matzoth Sponge Cake" in a section entitled "A Group of Jewish Recipes."

In many subsequent Jewish cookbooks, sponge cakes were named based on the number of eggs in the recipe—titles typically ranged from "Five-Egg Sponge" to "Twelve-Egg Sponge"—as this information was of major importance to frazzled holiday cooks. As a result of the cake's growing popularity, Jewish households commonly purchased copious amounts of eggs for their Passover baking. Jewish cooks did not stop with basic sponge cakes, but flavored them with a profusion of ingredients, including ground nuts, bananas, carrots, chocolate chips, and spices. However, the quality of the cake depended on the skill of the cook, and sponge cakes all too often came out dry or rubbery, or even collapsed.

Following World War II, the popularization of packaged cake mixes and a growing general American predilection for butter cakes, not to mention a fear of eggs due to health concerns, resulted in a marked decline in the popularity of sponge cakes. On the other hand, this style remains popular in Europe, where people are still partial to the lighter egg-foam cakes. Nevertheless, sponge cakes—whether purchased from a bakery, prepared at home from scratch, or baked at home using a packaged Passover mix, often with a disposable aluminum pan in the box—remain the most widespread Passover and Seder desserts.

(See also Nusstorte)

STRUDEL

Strudel is a pastry made of a dough that is stretched very thin, brushed with butter or oil, filled, rolled up, and baked.

Origin: Romania or Hungary

Other names: Czech: *strudl, závin*; Hebrew: *krukhit, strudel*; Hungarian: *rétes*; Romanian: *placinta*; Yiddish: *shtrudel*.

Strudel in German means "vortex" or "eddy," reflecting the swirl of pastry and filling. As with much of modern Western cuisine, strudel's roots lie in Asia.

More than a thousand years ago, nomads of central Asia began to roll unleavened bread dough very thin; the low moisture content of the firm, extremely thin loaves greatly enhanced its storage properties and they were capable of lasting under dry conditions up to two years. When needed, a loaf was spritzed lightly with water, covered with a cloth, and left to refresh and soften for about ten minutes. Women would prepare a large batch of these very thin loaves and stack a bunch together to last the family for many months on their journey. In this way, the Turks brought these breads, which they called *yuvgha*, westward along the Silk Road.

By at least the end of the fifteenth century, Ottoman cooks began adding a little oil to the dough, now pronounced *yufka*, allowing it to be stretched even thinner, and then cut the sheet into pieces, which were layered with clarified butter and fillings. This innovation led to classic pastries, such as *börek* and baklava. The Turks, who occupied the Balkans and Hungary in the fifteenth century, brought the concept of *yufka*, called phyllo in Greek, into the heart of central Europe where, instead of cutting and layering the dough like the Turks and Greeks, cooks filled and rolled up a large sheet of dough. It is unknown whether the Romanians or the Hungarians first began using the rolling technique, but it was the Hungarians who expanded the range of fillings. After the with-

Hungarian women, as in other Jewish communities, often use pastry making tasks for special occasions, such as stretching strudel dough, as an opportunity to socialize and share the work.

drawal of the Turks, Hungary was absorbed into the Austrian sphere of power and the dough roll traveled northward into Austria, where it was renamed strudel, perhaps inspired by a large vortex in the Danube River upriver of Vienna.

The earliest recipe for strudel in Vienna, a handwritten recipe, now held by the Viennese City Library, dates from 1696. Within half a century, strudel had been introduced at the royal court of Empress Maria Theresia and had become a national dish of the Austro-Hungarian Empire. Strudels began commonly appearing in German cookbooks around 1830. As a result, the historical strudel-making region stretches from Germany, particularly Bavaria, south to northern Italy, parts of which were within the Austro-Hungarian Empire until the late nineteenth century, and through much of the Balkans. Since many of the professional bakers of Austria were Jewish, strudel early on became a part of the Ashkenazic repertoire.

Unlike many baked goods of the time, which were enjoyed primarily or exclusively by the wealthy, strudel was a treat that crossed all class barriers. In central Europe, the ultimate quality of a housewife's culinary skills was judged by her ability to make strudel *ausgezogen* (pulled by hand). Old World strudel makers take their pastry very seriously, ritualistically performing each step. Some bakers insist on *glatt* ("smooth," meaning finely ground) flour, while others demand *griffig* ("rough," denoting a slightly coarse grind). Hungarians claim their local hard wheat produces the best strudel, as the flour requires a large amount of protein in order to stretch and not tear. The brand of flour, as well as the baker's skill, will affect the extent to which the dough can be stretched. Many cooks incorporate an egg or egg white into the dough for strength, while others add only a little oil and sometimes acid to produce a more tender pastry. The kitchen table or a long board (in some households these were one and the same) was lined with a tablecloth or clean sheet and the dough, called *strudelblatter*, was gently maneuvered and stretched until it was paper-thin and its edges hung over the four edges of the table or board. Originally, cooks commonly coiled the rolled-up strudel in a circle to fit better on a small pan, but the long strip or horseshoe shape has become more common.

There are numerous variations of strudel, both sweet and savory. Cabbage strudel, long a fixture in Hungarian homes, is made with caramelized onions and shredded cabbage and is served with soup or as a side dish for a roast, while sweetened ones are enjoyed for dessert and treats. Both Hungarians and Austrians claim credit for creating the classic apple strudel. In Germany, apple strudel is typically served with a vanilla custard sauce. The Turks also brought sour cherries to Hungary, where strudel filled with sour cherries became one of the favorite versions, following only apple strudel. Other standard fillings include cheese, mushrooms, nuts, onions, poppy seeds, mashed potatoes, rice, and various vegetables. Meat is a particularly widespread Romanian filling. In a unique Romanian filling, jam is mixed with Turkish delight (*rahat*). Dessert strudels are typically accompanied with another gift from the Turks, coffee.

Since classic strudel making was a demanding process, many housewives limited it to special occasions, sometimes preparing it only once or twice a year—most notably for Rosh Hashanah or Sukkot, making use of the new apple crop. More adept and ambitious cooks made it a regular Sabbath treat, sometimes using poppy seeds or cabbage, either savory and accented with black pepper, or sweet. Poppy seed strudel is traditional for Purim. Cherry filling, making use of the seasonal fruit, and cheese filling appear on Shavuot; sometimes these are combined in one pastry.

Some Romanians and Hungarians began calling a pastry roll made from a cookie dough *haimish strudel* and *gebleterter* (leaf after leaf) *kugel*. Filling variations tend to incorporate jams and dried fruit, allowing for pastry making beyond the time frame of seasonal fresh fruit. A version in which matza cake meal is substituted for flour was developed for Passover. In America, some people called slices of *haimish strudel* by the name "raisin tea biscuits," which became corrupted to "Russian tea biscuits."

Central European immigrants brought strudel to America in the mid-nineteenth century. One of the first records of the word strudel in English was in *Aunt Babette's* (Cincinnati, 1889), a cookbook that reflected the author's German Jewish background. The book contained a separate section for strudels, including apple, cherry, rice, quark, *aus kalbslunge* (lung and heart), and cabbage. By the early twentieth century, strudel was commonplace in Jewish bakeries, restaurants, and Catskills resorts.

The pastry also became widely popular in Israel; although the name is officially *krukhit* in Hebrew, the pastry is commonly referred to as strudel. The word "strudel" is also colloquially used by Israelis for the @ sign, as the symbol sort of resembles a cross-sectional slice of the pastry.

(See also Phyllo)

CLASSIC STRUDEL

ABOUT FORTY EIGHT 2-INCH PIECES   [PAREVE OR DAIRY]

  1 recipe (1 pound) Strudelblatter (Strudel Dough), stretched as below

  Melted butter or margarine or vegetable oil for brushing

  1 cup fine fresh or fried bread crumbs (optional)

  1 recipe (about 5 cups) apple strudel filling (recipe follows) or Ashkenazic filling (pages 197–198)

1. Preheat the oven to 400°F. Grease a large baking sheet.

2. Brush the dough with the butter. If using, sprinkle with the bread crumbs. About 4-inches from one end, mound the desired filling in a 3- to 4-inch wide strip. Lift the cloth by the filling end and allow the edge of the dough to cover the filling. Gradually lift the cloth higher, allowing the dough to roll over itself. Tuck the ends under.

3. Carefully move to the prepared baking sheet, seam side down. If the strudel is too large for your baking sheets, bend into a horseshoe shape. Brush with more butter and score on top in several locations to vent the steam.

4. Place the strudel in the center of the oven and bake for 10 minutes. Reduce the heat to 350 degrees, turn the baking sheet around in the oven, and continue baking until golden and crisp, about 30 minutes.

5. Place the sheet on a rack and let cool slightly or completely. Cut the strudel into 2-inch slices and serve warm, cooled, or reheated.

STRUDEL DOUGH (*STRUDELBLATTER*)

ABOUT 1 POUND; ENOUGH FOR ONE 3- TO
4-FOOT-LONG STRUDEL   [PAREVE]

  2 cups (10 ounces) bread flour or unbleached all-purpose flour, or 1 cup each

  About ¾ cup lukewarm water

  3 tablespoons vegetable oil

  1 teaspoon white vinegar or fresh lemon juice

  ½ teaspoon salt

Additional vegetable oil for brushing
Additional flour for dusting

1. Put the flour in a large bowl and make a well in the center. Combine the water, oil, vinegar, and salt and pour into the well. Stir, then add enough additional warm water, if necessary, to make a sticky dough. On a lightly floured surface, knead until smooth and elastic, about 10 minutes.

2. For one very large strudel, form the dough into a ball, or for two medium pastries, divide in half and form into balls. Lightly cover with about 1 teaspoon oil. Cover with plastic wrap and let rest for at least 30 minutes.

3. Cover a table (5 to 6 feet long and 2½ to 3 feet wide) with a cloth that drapes over the sides. Dust with about 1 cup flour. Place the dough in the center and roll out as thinly as possible. Brush lightly with oil and let rest for several minutes.

4. Remove any rings and lightly flour your hands. Beginning from the center of the dough, place your hands, palms down, under the dough. Using the back of your hands, gently lift and stretch the dough toward you—do not use your fingers, which tend to tear the dough. Stretching can also be done with two or more people working across from each other. Continue stretching the dough, paying particular attention to any thick areas, until it covers the table and is uniformly thin and transparent, about 15 minutes. The dough in this recipe reaches up to 6 feet or, divided in half and separately stretched, 3 to 4 feet.

5. Using scissors, trim off the thick edges. Patch any large tears with a piece of dough trimmed from the sides and stretched. Brush lightly with oil and let dry for 15 minutes.

APPLE STRUDEL FILLING (*APFEL STRUDELFULLE*)

ABOUT 5 CUPS; ENOUGH FOR A 3- TO 4-FOOT-LONG
STRUDEL   [PAREVE]

  ½ cup raisins

  2 tablespoons dark rum, kirsch, or water

  2 pounds (about 6 medium) cooking apples, such as Golden Delicious, Granny Smith, Gravenstein, Greening, Jonathan, Macoun, Pippin, Rome, Starr, Winesap, Yellow Transparent, or any combination, peeled, cored, and thinly sliced

  1 tablespoon fresh lemon juice

  About ½ cup sugar

½ cup finely chopped toasted walnuts, or ¼ cup fine semolina

¾ teaspoon ground cinnamon

Pinch of salt

2 teaspoons grated lemon zest (optional)

¼ teaspoon ground nutmeg (optional)

Soak the raisins in the rum for 30 minutes. Drain. Toss the apples with the lemon juice. Combine the apples, raisins, sugar, walnuts (to help absorb some of the excess liquid and add flavor), cinnamon, salt, and, if using, zest and/or nutmeg. Do not let the apples stand long or they will start to exude their liquid.

SUBYA

Subya is a flaky loaf pastry.

Origin: Yemen

Other names: *ma'asuba, saba'ya.*

As is typical of Yemenite cookery, *subya* is made from only a few basic ingredients. Non-Jews use a standard lean yeast dough layered with *samneh* (clarified butter) to make the loaf, while Jews usually substitute a type of Yemenite puff pastry called *ajin.* The *ajin* is rolled out and layered with beaten eggs or *samneh* and put in the oven before the advent of the Sabbath to slow-cook for Friday night dinner. *Subya* is also commonly served in a meal to break a fast. Traditionally, Yemenite women presented a gift of *subya* as a token of honor or to welcome a new neighbor. *Subya* is served with savory accompaniments such as hearty soup or chopped tomatoes with *s'chug* (chili paste), or drizzled with honey.

❦ YEMENITE PASTRY LOAF (*SUBYA*)

6 TO 8 SERVINGS   [DAIRY OR PAREVE]

1 recipe Yemenite Flaky Pastry (page 8), divided into fourths

3 large eggs, lightly beaten, or 6 tablespoons *samneh* (Middle Eastern clarified butter)

2 to 3 teaspoons nigella for sprinkling

1. Preheat the oven to 250°F. Grease a 9-by-5-inch loaf pan or 8-inch round cake pan.

2. On a lightly floured surface, roll out the 4 pieces of dough into 9-by-5-inch rectangles to fit the loaf pan or 8-inch rounds to fit the round pan. Press a dough rectangle or round into the bottom of the prepared pan and spread with one-third of the eggs (about 3 tablespoons). Repeat the layering, ending with a dough rectangle or round. Sprinkle with the nigella.

3. Bake, uncovered, until golden brown, at least 3 hours. Let cool slightly or completely in the pan before cutting into slices.

SUFGANIYAH

Sufganiyah is a jelly doughnut.

Origin: Germany

Other names: Austria: *krapfen*; France: *boule de Berlin*; Germany: *Berlinerkrapfen, Berlinerpfannkuchen, Berliners, gefüllte krapfen, Pfannkuchen*; Italy: *krafen*; Poland: *paczka, paczki*; Portugal; *sonhos*; Russia: *ponchiki, pyshki*; Yiddish: *ponchik, pontshke.*

In 1485, the cookbook *Kuchenmeisterei* (Mastery of the Kitchen) was published in Nuremberg, Germany, and in 1532 it was translated into Polish as *Kuchmistrzostwo.* Besides serving as a resource for postmedieval central European cooking and being one of the first cookbooks to be run off Johannes Gutenberg's revolutionary printing press, this tome contained what was then a revolutionary recipe, the first record of a jelly doughnut, "Gefüllte Krapfen." This early version consisted of a bit of jam sandwiched between two rounds of yeast bread dough and deep-fried in lard. Whether the anonymous author actually invented the idea or recounted a new practice, the concept of filling a doughnut with jam spread across the globe.

Although most modern versions of doughnuts have a sweet interior, the original filled doughnuts were primarily packed with meat, fish, mushrooms, cheese, or other savory mixtures. At that time, sugar was still very expensive and rare in Germany, so savory dishes were much more practical, even for the middle class. In the sixteenth century, the price of sugar fell with the introduction of Caribbean sugar plantations. Soon sugar and, in turn, fruit preserves proliferated in Europe, all the more so with the introduction of sugar beet factories in the nineteenth century. Within a century of the jelly doughnut's initial appearance in Germany, every northern European country from Denmark to Russia had adopted the pastry, although it was still a rare treat generally associated with specific holidays. Much later, someone in Germany invented a metal pastry syringe with which to inject jelly into already fried doughnuts, making the treat much easier, neater, and diverse. In the twentieth century, machines were developed to inject doughnuts two at a time or in mass production.

Since at least the early 1800s, Germans had called jelly doughnuts and custard-filled doughnuts simply Berliners, except in Berlin and Saxony. According to a German anecdote, in 1756 a patriotic baker from Berlin was turned down as unfit for Prussian military service, but allowed to remain as a field baker for the regiment. Because armies in the field had no access to ovens, he began frying doughnuts over an open fire, which the soldiers began calling after the baker's home, Berliners. The term soon became narrowed to denote only filled *krapfen*. Thus technically John F. Kennedy's famous declaration at the Berlin Wall, "*Ich bin ein Berliner*," means "I am a jelly doughnut." The Dutch also adopted filled doughnuts, commonly using an apple mixture. In Chile and some other South American countries, due to the large number of German immigrants, jelly doughnuts are known as Berlins.

By the end of the century, jelly doughnuts were also called *Bismarcken*, after Chancellor Otto von Bismarck. Due to the large number of central European immigrants, jelly doughnuts are known as bismarcks in parts of the American Upper Midwest, in Alberta and Saskatchewan in Canada, and even in Boston, Massachusetts. However, in Manitoba, they are called jam busters. In Britain, they became jam doughnuts, and in general American parlance, they are jelly doughnuts.

Poles named jelly doughnuts *paczki* (flower buds). When French cooks were enticed to work in the Polish royal court in the mid-eighteenth century, they improved the quality of *paczki* dough—they added eggs and milk, resulting in a lighter, less greasy doughnut. These treats were originally filled with lekvar (prune preserves) and occasionally raspberry jam or rose-petal marmalade. Poles traditionally eat *paczki*, and plenty of them, on Fat Thursday, the Thursday before Ash Wednesday. This occasion, also called *Paczki* Day, is celebrated with dances, balls, and mounds of doughnuts.

Polish Jews fried these doughnuts in schmaltz or oil instead of lard and called them *ponchiks*. In certain areas of Poland, they became the favorite Hanukkah dessert. A doughnut without a filling in Yiddish is a *donat*. Some Australian Jews, many of whom emigrated from Poland, still refer to jelly doughnuts as *ponchiks*. Polish immigrants brought *ponchiks* to Israel, along with the custom of eating them on Hanukkah.

In Israel, however, *ponchiks* soon took the name *sufganiyah* (*sufganiyot* plural), from a "spongy dough"

mentioned in the Talmud, *sofgan* and *sfogga*. The word *sphog*, meaning "sponge," is so ancient that there is a question as to whether it was initially of Semitic or Indo-European origin.

In the late 1920s, the Histadrut, the Israeli labor federation—which was founded in 1920 and seven years later claimed twenty-five thousand members, or 75 percent of all the Jewish workers in Mandatory Palestine—decided to champion the less widespread jelly doughnut as a Hanukkah treat rather than *levivot* (latkes), because latkes were relatively easy and homemade, while *sufganiyot* were rather difficult for most home cooks, thereby providing work (preparing, transporting, and selling the doughnuts) for its members. Companies began turning out the doughnuts days or even weeks before Hanukkah, stretching both the amount of work and the period of enjoyment for eating them, although there are those who insist on waiting to eat one until after lighting the first candle. *Sufganiyot* subsequently emerged as by far the most popular Israeli Hanukkah food. They are sold throughout the eight-day festival at almost every bakery and market, and enjoyed by people in every community and of every religious stripe. In 1995, culinary students at the Hadassah College of Technology in Jerusalem whipped up the world's largest *sufganiyah*, weighing 35 pounds, including 5 pounds of jelly, although it paled in comparison to the jelly doughnut listed in the *Guinness Book of World Records* made in Utica, New York, in 1993 and weighed 1.7 tons.

Today, about 70 percent of all *sufganiyot* consumed are stuffed with jelly, but recently a number of contemporary Israeli fillings have become popular, including halva, crème espresso, chocolate truffle, and numerous exotic flavors. Jelly doughnuts in Brazil are commonly filled with dulce de leche (a milky caramel), which recently also became a popular Israeli filling, known as *ribat chalav* in Hebrew.

In 2009, about eighteen million *sufganiyot* were consumed in the few weeks before and during the eight-day holiday, or about three doughnuts per each Israeli, with the Israeli Defense Force alone purchasing around a half million that year. American Jews by and large adopted the *sufganiyah*. It is now common at most Hanukkah parties, although most Americans tend to stick to the old-fashioned jelly fillings and a confectioners' sugar dusting.

(See also Doughnut and Hanukkah)

SUGAR

Sugarcane is a tropical grass that grows twenty or more feet in length and one to two inches in diameter. Some scholars believe it originated in the South Pacific, perhaps in New Guinea, and made its way to the Indian subcontinent about five thousand years ago. It may have been mentioned twice in the Bible, but only in contexts that reflect its rarity and foreignness. For example, in Jeremiah, God asks, "To what purpose is to Me the frankincense that comes from Sheba and the sweet cane from a far country?" The first mention of sugar by a European can be found in the accounts of Nearchus, a Greek general who was introduced to the "reed that makes honey without bees" during Alexander the Great's campaign in India in 327 BCE. However, ancient Greeks and Romans were generally unfamiliar with this eastern sweetener.

The word sugar is derived from the Sanskrit word *sarkara* (grit/sand), referring to sugarcane crystals. Around the sixth century CE, Persians or Radhanites (Jewish traders) brought sugar from India to Persia, where it was soon planted and called *shakar*. In the seventh century, the Arabs spread what they pronounced *sukkar* farther west to Syria, North Africa, and Sicily, and by 760, it had arrived in southern Spain.

By the tenth century, the Nile River valley was the home of the world's finest *sukkar*. Documents from the Cairo *Genizah* (synagogue archives) indicate that Jewish merchants dominated North African sugar planting and production, a role they maintained until modern times. It was in Egypt that techniques for refining the cane were first developed, transforming sugar production into a large-scale industry. The method for processing sugar remained basically the same for the next thousand years. The juice was squeezed from the cane and boiled with egg white, which trapped the impurities as it coagulated. After the impurities were skimmed off, the remaining mixture was boiled down until most of the moisture evaporated. The residue was poured into cone-shaped molds—with a hole in the tip to drain the molasses—where it was allowed to crystallize. Then wet clay was pressed onto the wide end of the cone and allowed to stand while the moisture from the clay passed through the sugar, drawing out impurities. The molded crystals were called sugarloaf. A special device called a sugar cutter was used to remove pieces of sugar from the loaf. (Sugar cubes are the modern-day equiva-

lent.) The pieces were ground in a mortar for easier incorporation into baked goods.

The introduction of sugar to the Middle East led to a revolution in confections and baking, as sucrose proved far more versatile than other sweeteners in candy making. Soon confectioners in the Middle East were mixing sugar syrups with such items as nuts, seeds, and gum arabic to create a multitude of confections. Many of these, such as almond paste and sesame lozenges, are still widely enjoyed today.

In the eleventh century, sugar continued its move westward as the Crusaders returned from the Middle East with a taste for the then-exotic sweetener. The Venetians quickly gained a monopoly over Europe's sugar trade and developed a method of refining it into uniform crystals, which were still sold in large conical loaves.

Although sugar had arrived in Europe, it would not be until the eighteenth century that it found a place on most Western tables. Sugar's first use in Europe was as a mask for the bitter taste of medicine, a role not unknown today. Initially, apothecaries possessed the exclusive rights to dispense sugar, but the crystals' use gradually expanded in the fifteenth century to confections, baked goods, and various dishes. For centuries, because of its high price, sugar was the sole province of the European upper class. The masses continued to rely on honey for sweetening.

The Portuguese began to break the Venetian monopoly on sugar in the 1420s by growing cane in their Atlantic islands, such as the Azores. Sugar arrived in the New World with Columbus on his second trip. The Portuguese began planting it in Brazil. Europeans colonizing the New World quickly recognized the Caribbean's potential for growing cane and saw a ripe opportunity to break the Venetian stranglehold. The presence of sugar in the New World did have a tragic consequence. The need for cheap labor to work these sugar plantations led to the introduction of slavery.

Not surprisingly, Sephardim and Conversos, with a long history in the sugar business and connections to other Jews in the financial centers of Amsterdam and Antwerp, initiated many of the New World sugar projects, although in many cases they were later forced out by the anti-Semitic European powers. When the Portuguese occupied Dutch Brazil in 1630 and expelled its Jews, many of them spread throughout the Caribbean, bringing along their sugar-growing and sugar-refining techniques.

West Indian sugar became such an important element in world trade that Holland ceded New Amsterdam to England in exchange for its captured sugar colony of Suriname and, in a similar vein, France was willing to yield its claim to Canada for the return of Guadeloupe. The loss of its sugar plantations was one of the key factors in France's decision to actively support the new United States during the American Revolution. In the 1540s, the first sugar refineries in England opened outside London and, as sugar became increasingly available and affordable there, the British quickly developed a passion for sweets. Sugar complemented other new foods that had recently arrived in Europe, including coffee, tea, and especially chocolate. The influx of Caribbean sugarcane meant a marked increase in the availability of sugar, transforming it from a luxury to a commodity, although the price was still too steep for the masses of eastern Europe.

Sugarcane, however, is not the only source of sucrose. Today, about half of the world's supply comes from the long white roots of sugar beets. Many connoisseurs insist that cane sugar is better for boiling than sugar made from sugar beets, yet in terms of taste, cooking properties, and nutrition, they are almost indistinguishable. The sugar beet possesses one major advantage over sugarcane. Sugarcane grows only in tropical and subtropical climates, while sugar beets flourish in temperate climates. Together these two plants supply the world's demand for sugar.

The process of producing sucrose from sugar beets was invented by German chemist Andreas Marggraf in 1747. When the techniques were developed to the point of economic feasibility, the sugar beet industry was launched. The first sugar beet–refining factory was established in Silesia, Germany (now southwestern Poland), in 1802. Others soon followed, many of them Jewish owned, in parts of central and eastern Europe. During Britain's blockade of Napoleonic Europe, the sugar beet gained unprecedented importance as, cut off from all sources of sugarcane, Napoleon was forced to turn to the German sugar beet process for Europe's sugar supply. Sugar beet factories promptly spread to many parts of northern Europe. As the price plummeted, suddenly everyone could afford the sweetener of royalty.

Considering the Jewish domination of much of Middle Eastern sugar production, it is hardly surprising that sugar early on became a standard ingredient in Mizrachi and Sephardic households. Sugar syrups, known in Arabic as *atar* and *shira*, became a widespread way to sweeten treats. In eastern Europe, however, honey remained the primary sweetener until the advent of the sugar beet. Yet even in Europe, differences emerged. Ashkenazim who lived in regions where sugar beets grew, such as Galicia (now Southern Poland) and northern Ukraine, developed a preference for sweeter dishes and added plenty of sugar to their gefilte fish, stuffed cabbage, kugels, and challah. In some areas, such as northern Poland, Lithuania, and much of Hungary, sugar remained an expensive item because local authorities rejected requests to erect sugar beet refineries or the beet failed to thrive. People in these regions generally used much less sugar in their food, reserving it for desserts.

(See also Atar, Beet, and Tea)

SUKKOT

The seven-day holiday (eight outside Israel) of Sukkot begins two weeks after Rosh Hashanah. This festival represents a thanksgiving for the final major harvest of the agricultural year (Festival of the Ingathering), while its historical component commemorates the Lord's protection of the Israelites during the forty-year transitional period in the wilderness (Festival of

This 1734 engraving by Bernard Picart depicts a Portuguese family in Holland dining in the sukkah (booth) during the holiday of Sukkot.

Booths). During the entire festival, the family dines and sometimes sleeps in a sukkah (booth), a structure with a temporary roof made of branches or reeds. The sukkah is customarily decorated with seasonal fruits and vegetables. The other major symbol of the holiday is the Four Species—the etrog (citron), *lulav* (palm branch), *hadas* (myrtle branches), and *aravah* (willow branches). Alone among holidays, Sukkot is regarded as *Z'man Simchateinu* (Season of Our Rejoicing), a time after the introspection of the High Holidays and after collecting the bounty the land has yielded to experience unsurpassed joy.

The harvest theme of Sukkot led to the incorporation of a bounty of fruits and vegetables into the dishes. Pickled vegetables and vegetable salads are also customary in most Jewish communities. In particular, stuffed vegetables and filled pasta, filled pastries, and filled pies, symbolizing plenty, are commonplace on Sukkot tables. In addition, the fare must be easy to shuttle outside to the sukkah and keep hot; accordingly, casseroles and meal-in-one stews are popular fare.

Ashkenazic Sukkot foods include tzimmes, stuffed veal breast or poultry, knishes, filled dumplings, fruit and cabbage strudels, fruit *fludens* (layered pastry), and fruit or vegetable cakes. Romanians make *guvetch* (vegetable stew), while Russians customarily serve a cabbage and meat soup. A favored Polish delicacy was *gebruteheh euter* (roasted cow's udder). Sephardic fare includes eggplant stews, green beans, vegetable salads, and filled phyllo pastries. Greeks and Turks serve eggplant casseroles, such as moussaka/*saku*. Persians enjoy *tachin-e badenjan* (rice and eggplant casserole). Bukharans favor *oshee tos kadoo* (stuffed pumpkin) and *samsa* (turnovers).

Sukkot is a popular time for visiting and entertaining and, after being seated in the sukkah, guests are offered a wide variety of treats. A medieval European tradition, first mentioned in the Zohar, is *Ushpizin* (from the Aramaic *ushpiz*, "guest"). On each of the seven nights of Sukkot, one of seven biblical figures is welcomed in order into the Sukkah—Abraham, Isaac, Jacob, Joseph, Moses, Aaron, and David—emphasizing the importance of inviting guests and, in particular, the poor to share the experience of the sukkah.

The seventh day of Sukkot, called Hoshanah Rabbah, is regarded as the day on which the divine verdicts of judgment decided on Yom Kippur are sealed. Therefore, as an extension of the Day of Atonement, foods traditional for the meal before the fast, such as kreplach, are served.

At the conclusion of Sukkot falls another series of holidays, Shemini Atzeret and Simchat Torah. Shemini Atzeret is a one-day (two outside Israel) Biblical festival ending the nearly month-long holiday period.

(See also Date, Etrog, Simchat Torah, and Water)

SUMAC

Sumac/sumach, from the Aramaic *samaq* (dark red), *og* in the Talmud, is the tart red fruit of a tall Middle Eastern shrub from the Anacardiaceae family. In the late summer, when they turn deep red upon ripening, the clusters of berries are harvested and dried in the sun for several days. Before lemons and tamarinds arrived in the Middle East, sumac was the primary souring agent. Today, sumac is most popular in the Levant, Iran, Georgia, and Azerbaijan. The tart, citrus flavor and light red color adds a pleasant tart, acidic-fruity touch to eggplant spreads, hummus, kebabs, grilled fish and chicken, sauces, rice pilaf, red lentil soup, salads, and—in its most prominent culinary role—the spice blend *za'atar*. Sumac berries are dried and used whole, ground, or soaked. A little salt is generally added to facilitate the grinding of the moist berries, but pure sumac is preferable when using fresh *za'atar*, as salt damages the leaves.

SUTLACH

Sutlach is a rice-flour pudding.
Origin: Middle East
Other names: Afghanistan: *firni*; Arabic: *mahallebi*, *muhalabeeya*, *muhallabiyya*; Farsi: *firni, yakh dar behest*; India: *dodail, firni*; Ladino: *sutlag, sutlage*; Turkish: *sütlaç, sütlaj, süt muhallebisi*.

The cooking of rice into porridge is an ancient story. Romans added goat's milk to cooked rice, but not sweeteners, eating it savory. Perhaps the Chinese were the first to make sweetened rice, although they did not add milk. Medieval Persians cooked rice with almond milk or goat's milk, sugar, and frequently rose water or orange-blossom water, which they called *shir-berenj* and the Arabs referred to as *riz bi haleeb*. In a later variation, short-grain rice kernels were cooked for an extended time to break them down and produce a creamy texture, which was known by the Persians as *shola-e shireen*. A similar version in which mashed cooked rice is cooked with sugar is described in a recipe for "Rice Dissolved with Sugar" in an untitled anonymous thirteenth-century Andalusian cookbook.

Around the thirteenth century, Persians developed a way to achieve a smooth texture from long-grain kernels by first finely grinding the rice into a flour. The texture of rice flour ranges from a fine powder (*chaaval ka atta* in India) produced by sifting out larger particles to a slightly grainy texture like that of fine sand (*idli-rava*). In puddings, the finer the flour, the smoother the texture, while larger granules result in a gritty consistency.

Persians called rice-flour pudding by the name *firni/fereni*. The Persian-influenced Mughals introduced *firni* to northern India, substituting cow's milk or coconut milk for the almond milk. Rice-flour pudding also spread westward through the Ottoman Empire, where the Turks referred to it as *süt muhallebisi* or more commonly *sütlaç* (*süt* means "milk" and *sütlu* "with milk" in Turkish). Sephardim pronounced it *sutlach*.

Unlike Western puddings, *sutlach* does not contain eggs. Rather, it is a balance of the two main ingredients—rice and milk. Rice-flour pudding was originally cooked atop a fire or brazier, but later a variation emerged in which the rice mixture was baked in an oven. Both types remain popular. In either case, the pudding is soft when warm, but firms when cooled or refrigerated. Middle Easterners generally prefer rice-flour pudding cool and often make it the day before it will be served so that it can properly cool and firm; the dish is widespread breakfast fare.

The delicate *sutlach* is considered appropriate for the ill and others who lack an appetite. *Sutlach* is served in many Sephardic households on the Sabbath, on Purim, and at the meal following Yom Kippur. For Shavuot, called the "Feast of Roses," honey is usually substituted for the sugar and many Middle Eastern Jews flavor the pudding with rose water or serve it with rose preserves. Turkish Jews also serve *sutlach* as the first course of a wedding feast. Nondairy versions are made with *pipitada* (melon seed milk), almond milk, or coconut milk. For *desayanu* (brunch), some mothers write young children's names or initials with cinnamon on top of individual puddings.

(See also Asabia, Malabi, and Rice Pudding)

TURKISH RICE-FLOUR PUDDING (*SUTLACH*)

6 TO 8 SERVINGS   [DAIRY]

 ¾ cup rice flour or Cream of Rice, or ¼ cup rice flour and ¼ cup cornstarch)

 ½ cup sugar

 Pinch of salt

 5½ cups milk, or 4½ cups milk and 1 cup heavy cream

 2 tablespoons rose water or orange blossom water, or 1 teaspoon vanilla extract

 Ground cinnamon and/or chopped pistachios for garnish (optional)

1. In a large saucepan, combine the rice flour, sugar, and salt. Gradually stir in about 1 cup milk to make a smooth paste. Gradually stir in the remaining milk. Bring to a boil over medium heat, stirring constantly to prevent lumps, about 10 minutes. Reduce the heat to low and simmer, stirring frequently to prevent the bottom from burning, until bubbly and thickened, about 5 minutes. The pudding thickens more as it cools.

2. Remove from the heat and stir in the rose water. Pour into 6 to 8 bowls and, if desired, sprinkle with the cinnamon and/or pistachios. Press a piece of plastic wrap against the surface. Serve hot, at room temperature, or chilled. Store in the refrigerator, covered with plastic wrap, for up to 4 days.

SWANNE

Among traditional Jews, a bride, shortly before her wedding, immerses herself in a *mikveh* (ritual bath). Ashkenazim generally consider the *mikveh* an extremely private matter. On the other hand, many Sephardic communities hold special parties to celebrate this occasion and enhance the practice of ritual purity. These various prenuptial gatherings for the bride were once generally all-female affairs. In some areas, this event was linked to the henna ceremony.

In the afternoon, anytime up to three days before the wedding, Syrians perform one of their most beloved premarital customs, the *swanne* or *swehnie* (Arabic for "trays," plural of *seniyeh*) or *hamman-il-aros* (Arabic for "the bride's bath"), a lavish party thrown by the groom's parents. The groom sends his bride-to-be three trays, today typically a series of elaborately decorated tables. One tray is covered with perfumes, soaps, robes, jewelry, candlesticks, and other items to be used at the *mikveh* and for the bride to adorn herself with. The guests place their presents on another tray. An elaborate luncheon is served, including pastries, confections, and *sharbat el loz* (almond drink), accompanied with much singing and dancing. Later, the mothers and a few close friends accompany the bride to the *mikveh*. After emerging from the *mikveh*, the bride is presented with a silver tray bearing *lebas* (Jordan almonds), *kaak ib loz* (a special pistachio confection), marzipan, and coffee surrounded by flowers.

In the Balkans and Turkey, the day before the wedding is called *El Dio de Bana* or *Banio* (Day of the Bath). The mother of the groom throws a party for female relatives and friends called *bogo de bana* (bag for the bath). The celebrants bring gifts of soaps, perfumes, lingerie, and other items appropriate for a new bride. After she emerges from the *mikveh*, the mother of the bride holds a smaller party called *cafe de bano* (coffee of the bath) featuring fancy pastries and coffee. The groom, who according to tradition is never left alone the day before his wedding, frequently has his own party or series of parties called *salidura de boda* (delivering to the wedding).

SWEETBREAD

In late medieval English the word bread was also used as a term for morsel; thus the term sweetbread literally means a "sweet morsel." Sweetbread is the thymus gland (thorax sweetbreads) of a calf, lamb, or kid. It is called *grashitze* and *kalbsmilch* in Yiddish and *molejas* in Ladino. The thymus is rather large in young ruminants, but as they age the thymus becomes more fibrous and after about six months shrinks and disappears. The thymus separates into a larger, less fatty, rounder section that is easier to slice (called the "heart sweetbread" or in French *la noi*, "nut") and a less desirable, but similar-tasting, irregularly shaped section (throat sweetbreads). Although they are not true sweetbreads, in some places the term also includes the pancreas (stomach sweetbreads), which are rounder and have fewer membranes than the thymus. In the United States today, sweetbreads are generally from the thymus. In any case, the thymus and pancreas—both of which come in pairs—are prepared the same.

In its discussion of the Passover Seder, the *Tosefta* (early rabbinic rulings omitted from the Mishnah) directed people to serve hors d'oeuvres of *b'nei m'eim* in salt water after the first cup of wine. Although *b'nei*

m'eim is usually translated as "intestines," it probably meant sweetbreads—in either case, this custom is not accepted. Among the ancient dishes from Rome's ghetto are *animelle d'abbacchio* (lamb sweetbreads) and *animelle di vitello* (veal sweetbreads); these entrées were either fried (*fritte*) or served in a white wine sauce. Sephardim have long cherished sweetbreads, which they frequently sauté in olive oil. Middle Easterners tend to grill sweetbreads. Arguably, no community more closely embraced sweetbreads as food than Ashkenazim, for whom they followed only liver in popularity among the organs. Simply fried in schmaltz or enveloped with a sauce, they were frequently served as a Sabbath appetizer, at holiday meals, at wedding banquets, and on other special occasions.

The first Jewish cookbook in English, *The Jewish Manual* (London, 1846) included three recipes for sweetbreads: "Sweetbreads Roasted," "Sweetbreads Stewed White [in béchamel sauce]," and "Sweetbreads Stewed Brown [in beef gravy]." The first American Jewish cookbook, *Jewish Cookery* (Philadelphia, 1871), also offered a recipe for "Sweet Breads." The recipe directed, "Blanch them and let them stand a while in cold water. Then put them in a stewpan, with a ladleful of water, some pepper, salt, onions, and mace. Stew them half and hour. Have ready two or three eggs, well beaten, with a little chopped parsley, and a few grates of nutmeg. Put in some small boiled asparagus to the other ingredients."

Sweetbreads were sometimes mixed with pieces of cooked chicken to stretch the dish. Ashkenazim, in particular, frequently paired sweetbreads with mushrooms. In the nineteenth century, those Ashkenazim who were influenced by the Russians, who in turn imitated the French, served them in vol-au-vents or on the less fancy toasted bread. In the early twentieth century, sweetbreads were ubiquitous at Jewish delis and Catskills Jewish resorts. However, in the face of changing tastes and because they are labor-intensive to prepare, sweetbreads grew much less common. Once a relatively inexpensive item, sweetbreads are now rather costly, even in America, where they are generally unappreciated. In Israel, on the other hand, sweetbreads, *m'taamei tymos* in modern Hebrew, have become standard fare both in old-fashioned Ashkenazic restaurants and Middle Eastern grills, as well as at many new upscale establishments.

TABBOULEH

Tabbouleh is a salad of chopped fresh parsley, bulgur, and other common eastern Mediterranean ingredients.

Origin: Levant

Other names: tabbouli, tabouli.

Fresh herbs have long been an essential component of Middle Eastern cooking. One herb in particular, parsley, is found in numerous dishes, but usually in a supporting role and rarely as the star. Among the exceptions is the classic peasant summer salad of the Levant, tabbouleh; the name, derived from the Arabic *tabbula* (to spice), means "little spicy." The simple salad consists primarily of parsley and many of the region's most common ingredients, including mint, scallions, tomatoes, olive oil, lemon juice, and various seasonings. Arabs in the Levant added a little soaked bulgur to the chopped parsley to absorb some of the juice and impart a nutty accent. Akin to tabbouleh is *kisir*, a related Turkish bulgur salad containing only a little parsley and made bright red with tomato paste or red bell peppers.

The amount of herbs in the traditional version comes as a surprise to many Americans, who are more accustomed to a bulgur salad with a smaller amount of parsley. The version with much more bulgur is actually preferred by Syrian Jews, who introduced it to Israel. In the 1970s, as American Jews increasingly incorporated Israeli foods into their culinary repertoire, the bulgur-heavy Israeli style of tabbouleh was spread through America and not the parsley-heavy Arabic style. Among Arabs, tabbouleh is typically served as part of a *mezze* (appetizer assortment) and eaten with scoops of romaine lettuce leaves, but Israelis more commonly use pita bread, a practice they passed on to Americans as well.

(See also Bulgur)

TABIL

Tabil is a spice mixture, with an emphasis on coriander and caraway.

Origin: Tunisia

When the Jews and some Moors fled Andalusia in 1492, they brought their foods and seasonings to North Africa, including a spice mixture called *tabil*. Although *tabil* in Tunisia means "coriander seeds," it also refers to a particular spice blend containing coriander, caraway, chilies, and garlic. The garlic and spices were traditionally pounded in a mortar then spread out to dry in the sun, but modern cooks toast the spices in a skillet or oven and substitute garlic powder. *Tabil* is used to flavor meat stews, stuffings, and vegetables.

TUNISIAN SPICE MIXTURE (*TABIL*)

ABOUT 3 TABLESPOONS   [PAREVE]

- 2 tablespoons coriander seeds
- 1 tablespoon caraway seeds
- 2 to 3 teaspoons crushed dried chili or red chili flakes, or ½ to 1 teaspoon cayenne
- 4 cloves garlic or ½ teaspoon garlic powder
- 1 teaspoon whole black peppercorns or ½ teaspoon ground black pepper

In a dry large skillet, toast the coriander, caraway, and chili over medium heat until fragrant, 2 to 3 minutes. Let cool. In a mortar or spice grinder, crush together the toasted spices along with the garlic and pepper into a smooth paste. Store in an airtight container in a cool, dry place for up to 2 weeks or, if using garlic powder, up to 3 months.

TABYEET

Tabyeet is a slow-cooked Sabbath chicken and rice dish.

Origin: Iraq

Other names: *hamin, tabit, tebeet*; India: *hameen*.

For much of the past three thousand years, Iraq, Syria, and Lebanon were under the control of the same political and cultural forces. Thus, many similarities exist in the food of the region's Jews, whose cuisine is a blend of Persian, Byzantine, Arabic, Turkish, and Iberian influences. On special occasions, people in this region serve rice and chicken, including a dish called *tabyeet* based on a medieval Middle Eastern technique of stuffing chicken with meat, rice, and Middle Eastern seasonings. A cookbook from Aleppo, Syria, *Kitab al-Wusla* (c. 1260), included recipes for four similar Arabic stewed stuffed chicken dishes.

Tabyeet ("shelter" in Arabic) was designed as a variation of the Sabbath stew—it slow-cooks the chicken for an extended period, while keeping it moist. Whole eggs are typically cooked in the rice in the Sephardic fashion. Chickpeas, beans, winter squash, or whole okra also may be added. The rice is typically seasoned with cardamom and perhaps also a little cumin or cinnamon. The Indian version, introduced to the country in the nineteenth century by Iraqi Jews, is more vibrantly flavored with garam masala and fresh ginger. Some cooks remove the entire skin of the chicken, stuff it with meat, and cook it alongside the chicken.

Housewives traditionally wrapped the pot in insulating blankets, then placed it atop a flame to heat. Today, some people cook *tabyeet* for only a few hours over moderate heat and serve it on Friday night, but most leave it overnight over a very low flame for Sabbath lunch. The result is a chicken that is very tender and rice that, in the Persian style, is deeply flavored and fluffy in the center of the pot and crisp on the bottom. For Sabbath lunch, this style of chicken is customarily served with a *mezze* (appetizer assortment). The eggs are either removed early in the day for Sabbath breakfast or offered with the chicken and rice at lunch.

❦ IRAQI CHICKEN AND RICE (*TABYEET*)

6 TO 8 SERVINGS   [MEAT]

3 tablespoons vegetable oil
1 (3½- to 4-pound) whole chicken
1 large yellow onion, chopped
1 teaspoon ground turmeric
3 cups (20 ounces) basmati or other long-grain or medium-grain rice
¾ teaspoon ground cardamom, 6 whole cardamom pods, or ¾ teaspoon ground cumin
1 teaspoon ground cinnamon or ¼ teaspoon ground ginger
4 cups (2 pounds) chopped tomatoes or 6 tablespoons tomato paste
Salt and ground black pepper to taste
8 cups chicken broth or water
8 ounces (1 cup) dried chickpeas or fava beans, soaked in water to cover for 8 hours and drained
6 to 8 eggs in shell (optional)

1. In a large ovenproof pot, heat the oil over medium-high heat. Add the chicken and brown, turning to brown on all sides, about 15 minutes. Remove the chicken.

2. Reduce the heat to medium, add the onion, and sauté until soft and translucent, 5 to 10 minutes. Stir in the turmeric and the rice and sauté until golden, about 5 minutes. Stir in the cardamom and cinnamon. Add the tomatoes, salt, and pepper. Add 6 cups broth, cover, reduce the heat, and simmer for 15 minutes. Stir in the chickpeas and remaining 2 cups broth.

3. Return the chicken to the pot, breast side up, pressing it into the rice. If using, bury the eggs in the rice. Tightly cover and bake in a 225°F oven for 10 hours. Or bake in a 350°F oven for 2 hours, then reduce the heat to 250°F and cook for an additional 2 to 3 hours.

4. Mound the rice on a large serving platter, then debone the chicken and arrange it and the eggs around the rice. Place the pot in a sink with cold water and let stand for 2 minutes to loosen the crust. Scrape the crispy rice from the bottom of the pot and serve with the chicken.

TACHIN

Tachin is a baked rice casserole.
Origin: Persia
Other names: *tacheen*.

Tachin is the Farsi word for "bottom of the pot," but also refers to a type of Persian rice casserole, which entails less preparation than the more famous Persian method of making rice, *chelow*. There are numerous variations: Some are dairy and made with yogurt, which adds richness and moistness. In others, chicken pieces are buried in the mound of rice (*tachin-e morgh*) for a one-dish meal. As is typical of Persian cookery, *tachin* is not highly spiced. Instead, the focus of the dish is the texture and color of the rice; many people from neighboring countries consider it rather bland. Most *tachin* are layered, sometimes with fried eggplant slices in the center (*tachin-e bademjan*), traditional sukkot fare, with the rice on the bottom becoming crispy. Turmeric or saffron is common; these spices are added to many Persian dishes to mask any unpleasant cooking odors and also to impart a yellow color, a Middle East symbol of joy. Historically, rice was much beloved but expensive in many parts of Persia, and casseroles were considered ideal for entertaining. Accordingly, *tachins* were generally served only on special occasions. *Tachin* is typically accompanied with *turshi* (pickles).

PERSIAN RICE CASSEROLE (*TACHIN*)

6 TO 8 SERVINGS   [PAREVE OR DAIRY]

2½ cups (1 pound) basmati or other long-grain rice
3 large eggs, lightly beaten
¼ cup vegetable oil
½ teaspoon ground turmeric or ground saffron
About 1 teaspoon table salt or 2 teaspoons kosher salt
About ⅛ teaspoon ground white or black pepper
1 cup plain yogurt or 1 tablespoon fresh lemon juice (optional)

1. Fill a large pot halfway with water and bring to a boil. Add the rice and boil on high until the rice is nearly cooked, about 15 minutes. Drain.

2. Preheat the oven to 400°F. Spread a thin layer of olive oil over a 9-inch square ovenproof dish or a round 1½-quart ovenproof dish.

3. In a large bowl, combine the eggs, oil, turmeric, salt, pepper, and, if using, yogurt. Stir in the rice. Spoon into the prepared dish.

4. Cover and bake until heated through and the bottom is crisp, about 50 minutes. Let stand for 10 minutes before slicing. Some cooks like to invert the casserole onto a serving platter.

TAGINE

Tagine is a cooking vessel as well as the stew made in the pot.

Origin: Morocco

Other name: *tajine.*

Cooking in earthenware vessels has long been common in the Mediterranean. The wealthy frequently used metal versions of these vessels, while the masses relied on the more affordable and, for some tasks, more effective clay. Originally, the bottom of these clay skillets was concave, but eventually some evolved into flat-bottomed skillets. The entire base of a flat skillet could then be exposed to the heat and the skillet could also double as a plate. Multiple uses were quite common—in addition to being utilized for cooking, the Roman *olla* served as a receptacle for

money, as well as a funeral urn. The Greeks used the word *teganon*, source of the Italian *tegame* (skillet), for a shallow, round earthenware pan, which was essentially a rudimentary terra-cotta skillet; the pan's round shape made it well suited for shallow frying. The term *teganon* first appeared in a Jewish text in 2 Maccabees, which was possibly written around the end of the second century BCE. The word subsequently emerged in rabbinic literature as a term for "skillet" and in Hebrew as the verb "to fry." Consequently, the modern Hebrew word for "skillet" is *machavat tegon* and the verb "to fry" is *teegain*.

In Spain, the Roman *patella* became *paella*, denoting both a specific shallow, circular, flat-bottomed earthenware dish and a special stew with rice that was cooked in this dish. However, across the Straits of Gibraltar and throughout the Maghreb, the name of these vessels generally derived from the Greek *teganon*, which had been popularized in the area by either Greeks or perhaps Jews. Unique to Marrakesh

The Moroccan tagine serves as both a cooking vessel and serving platter, although in many parts of the country the couscous is usually served separately from the other foods in the tagine.

is the *tangia* or *tajina*, a deep terra-cotta jar traditionally covered with oiled parchment, but more recently with an earthenware lid. Typically, it was set in the ashes of a *hammam* (bathhouse) or hearth and left overnight so that the meat—with very little or no added liquid—could slowly cook; this was the same method that Jews used to cook Sabbath stews. In Tunisia, the word tagine generally refers to a small, round earthenware pan with a lid, as well as to a type of omelet, akin to a *fritada*, that is baked in the pan; originally, the pan was smothered with hot coals to cook the food inside.

From the Moroccan town of Tafraout, high in the Anti-Atlas Mountains, came a unique two-piece cooking vessel made from red clay called a tagine, which is now ubiquitous throughout the country as well as in Algeria. This tagine consists of a shallow, circular, flat-bottomed dish standing about three inches high, with a tall, heavy conical lid that fits in the base. During cooking, the lid seals in the moisture, making the pan ideal for long, slow simmering on a stove or over live coals. The steam accumulates near the top of the cone, then drips back down, keeping the stew moist and intensifying the flavors. When the food is ready, the top is removed and the base then acts as a serving platter. The relatively dry stews cooked in the tagine are referred to by the same name. Tagine and couscous are the two national dishes of Morocco.

In Morocco, the typical stew cooked in these earthenware vessels is a relative of the Persian *geimeh*. It originated as a way of preserving lamb in spices and fat; the meat is slow-cooked until it is very tender. The resulting meat and thick, spicy sauce are served with flatbread or couscous. Tagines can be sweet, savory, or piquant. They often have a combination of sweet spices and various fruits. Preserved lemons, olives, and dried fruit are common flavorings. Lamb tagines are typically served as everyday fare, while chicken tagines are usually reserved for special occasions. Seasonal vegetables are also added, stretching the meat into an economical dish. Although most Arabs use *samneh* (clarified butter) to cook their tagines, Jews substitute oil. Otherwise, there are few differences between Jewish and Berber tagines.

Tagines are not demanding and can be kept on a low heat for a while, making them ideal for Sabbath evening dinner. A tagine is served at most holiday meals, usually preceded by a small, savory phyllo appetizer or *pastilla* (pigeon pie) and accompanied by a number of vibrant salads.

(See also Couscous)

MOROCCAN LAMB STEW (*L'HAAM TAGINE*)

5 TO 6 SERVINGS   [MEAT]

⅓ cup olive oil

⅓ cup vegetable oil

4 medium yellow onions, chopped

½ cup chopped fresh cilantro or flat-leaf parsley, or ¼ cup each

About 1 teaspoon table salt or 2 teaspoons kosher salt

½ teaspoon ground black pepper

1 teaspoon sweet paprika

½ to 1 teaspoon ground cumin or cinnamon

½ teaspoon ground ginger

¼ teaspoon crushed saffron strands or ½ teaspoon ground turmeric

½ teaspoon cayenne (optional)

3 pounds boneless lamb shoulder, neck, or shank, cut into 1¼-inch cubes

About 2 cups chicken broth or water

1. In a large bowl or plastic bag, combine the oils, onions, cilantro, salt, pepper, paprika, cumin, ginger, saffron, and, if using, cayenne. Add the lamb and toss to coat.

2. Place the meat mixture in a tagine, a heavy heat-proof dish, or a large pot. Cover and cook over medium-high heat, stirring occasionally, until the meat has absorbed most of the oil, about 15 minutes. Uncover and stir the meat, browning on all sides.

3. Add the broth, cover, and simmer over low heat or bake in a 325°F oven until very tender, about 1½ hours. The sauce will be very thick; if necessary, add a little more water while cooking. Serve with couscous or rice.

TAHINI

For millennia, the primary oil in many parts of Asia was derived from pressing sesame seeds. Originating as a medieval by-product of sesame oil production, but emerging as a beloved food in its own right, was a thick paste made by grinding hulled and lightly roasted sesame seeds. When the paste is made from unhulled roasted sesame seeds, it has a darker color and somewhat bitter flavor and is called sesame butter. In some areas of the Middle East, especially Iraq, sesame seed paste was called *rashi*. In most places, it became known as *tahina*—from the Arabic *tahn* (ground)—but it is more commonly pronounced in the West with the Greek spelling, tahini. Tahini has become a staple in Israel; the modern Hebrew word for it is *tachina*.

In 1905, twenty-two-year old Nathan Radutzky, a Jewish immigrant from Kiev, arrived in the United States. Two years later, he founded Independent Halvah and Candies on the Lower East Side of Manhattan. The company's featured product was sesame paste halva, which was made by hand from his special recipe. The confection was sold initially through pushcart vendors and later in Jewish delis and appetizing stores. Following World War II, Radutzky's four sons renamed the family-owned company the Joyva Corporation. The company, which had relocated to Williamsburg, Brooklyn, began marketing tahini in vacuum tins, eliminating the need for refrigeration. For decades, Joyva served as the predominant American source of sesame paste. In the United States, initially tahini was generally limited to various Middle Eastern and health food stores. The word tahini first appeared in English toward the end of the nineteenth century, but the actual product did not become commonplace in America until the late 1960s, when Middle Eastern dishes began gaining popularity. Today, tahini can be purchased in small cans or bottles in most Western supermarkets and is available in bulk in many health food and specialty stores.

One of the most common uses of tahini is in a raw sauce, typically made with lemon juice, water, garlic, and sometimes chopped parsley. Sesame seed sauce is officially *taratur bi tahina*, but in actual parlance the name is usually shortened to simply *taratur* in the Arabic part of the Levant and to *techina* in Israel. Unquestionably, tahini sauce's most famous role in Israel is as part of a falafel sandwich, but plain *taratur bi tahina* also serves as a dip and salad dressing, a sauce for cooked vegetables (such as roasted cauliflower), a topping for *shawarma* and other roasted meats, a sauce for *kibbeh* (fried torpedo-shaped meat in a thin starchy shell), and a topping for fish. When made for fish, the sauce tends to be more lemony.

In many areas, tahini is mixed with lemon juice and plenty of chopped parsley for a simple salad, which is served with pita bread. Tahini has a nutty flavor and serves as a key component of Middle Eastern cooking—it appears in hummus; eggplant dishes, such as *baba ghanouj*; and confections, notably halva.

(See also Sesame)

❦ MIDDLE EASTERN SESAME SEED SAUCE
(*TARATUR BI TAHINA/TECHINA*)

ABOUT 1¾ CUPS   [PAREVE]

> 1 cup tahini (sesame seed paste), stirred well before using
> About ¼ cup fresh lemon juice, or 3 tablespoons lemon juice and 1 tablespoon white vinegar
> 1 to 3 cloves garlic, mashed
> About ¾ teaspoon table salt or 1½ teaspoons kosher salt
> ½ to 1 cup cold water

Blend together the tahini, lemon juice, garlic, and salt until smooth. It will become a bit lumpy at first as the oil binds up, until exposed to sufficient liquid to form a smooth emulsion. Add enough water to make a sauce of pouring consistency.

TAMARIND

Tamarind, a name derived from the Arabic *tamir hindi* (date of India), is the fruit of an evergreen tree from the legume family. The Arabic name is a misnomer, as it is not from a palm tree, and is probably indigenous to tropical eastern Africa. Early in history, it was transported to India, where it flourished. When Persians or Radhanites (international Jewish merchants) brought it to central Asia from India around the seventh century CE, everyone assumed it was native to that country. The ancient Egyptians may have culled the plant from Sudan, but it is unmentioned in the Bible or Talmud.

Tamarind fruit consists of brown pods resembling the carob. Inside the pods are a sticky, tart, brown pulp and up to twelve glossy brown seeds. When the fruit matures, the shell turns brown and brittle as the pulp and seeds darken in color. Among fruits, tamarind follows only dates in the amount of sugar. However, tamarind is also the most acidic of fruits, with a flavor similar to a combination of apricots and dried plums. In cooking, neither lemon juice nor pomegranate concentrate is an adequate substitute for tamarind.

Tamarind was first recorded in cooking outside of India during the Middle Ages. Before the popularization of lemons in the Middle East, tamarind served as the primary souring agent in cooking throughout much of Asia, a role it still maintains in India and Syria and to a lesser degree in Iraq, Iran, and Georgia. The pulp is used to make jams, candies, marinades, and sauces (including Worcestershire). Tamarind's acidity acts as a natural meat tenderizer. Tamarind is the basis for a favorite Indian chutney, *imli chanti*. Syrian tamarind sauce, variously known as *tamarhindi*, *temerhindi*, *ourt*, or *ooht*, is tamarind pulp and water boiled down with sugar and lemon juice into a very thick, dark liquid. The sauce is a distinctive flavor of Syrian Jewish cooking; and added to numerous sweet-and-sour dishes, including *lahmajin* (open-faced meat pies), *bazargan* (bulgur relish), stuffed grape leaves, stews, and meatballs. In Egypt and parts of Israel, *tamarhindi* is the name of a drink made from tamarind concentrate and sugar.

Tamarind pods are rarely available in the United States, but tamarind is sold in several other forms: concentrated pulp, dried blocks, pure concentrate (or paste), and syrup. Concentrated pulp or dried blocks, both of which usually contain seeds, must be softened in liquid before using. Pure tamarind concentrate, sometimes called tamarind paste, is made by boiling seedless pulp so that some of the moisture evaporates; today the moisture is sometimes removed under vacuum. Tamarind syrup is a slightly thickened mixture of tamarind pulp, sugar, and water.

TARAMASALATA

Taramasalata is a salted fish roe dip.
Origin: Greece, Turkey
Other names: *taramosalata*; Romania: *salata de icre*.

The foreign influences on Greek cuisine, most notably Ottoman, Persian, and Italian, is clearly demonstrated in the foreign titles of so many of the country's dishes. The name *taramasalata* is derived from *tarama*, Turkish for "soft roe," indicating the Turkish source of the dish. *Taramasalata*, a creamy, slightly briny dip, is made with the roe of various fish, such as lightly smoked gray mullet as well as cod and shad, but ever since Jewish merchants popularized carp in the Balkans in the sixteenth century, it has been primarily made from carp roe, which imparts a now-preferred pinkish orange color. The pink hue of many commercial brands today, however, derives from artificial coloring rather than carp roe. The base was originally made

from bread, but as in Greek *skordalia* (garlic sauce), potatoes have recently become an accepted substitute. Olive oil and fresh lemon juice not only contribute flavor, but also serve to create an emulsion as in mayonnaise. The Greeks tend to add garlic to *taramasalata*, which the Turks generally omit. In Romania, vegetable oil and sometimes vinegar are incorporated instead of olive oil and lemon juice, and a little seltzer is frequently beaten in for a fluffier consistency.

Unprocessed *tarama* can be found in Greek and many Middle Eastern food stores. Red salmon caviar makes a tasty substitute. *Taramasalata* was originally made in a large wooden mortar with a pestle, but today most cooks substitute a food processor, although many aficionados insist that the best texture can only be achieved in a mortar.

Taramasalata is popular among Greek and Turkish Jews, who typically include it as part of a *mezze* ("appetizer assortment," *mezedes* in Greek). Some serve it for Rosh Hashanah dinner, as fish symbolizes fertility and creation. *Ikra* (the term used in parts of the Balkans) and *taramaslalata* can be found on the menus of quite a few Israeli restaurants, especially those focusing on Balkan or Mediterranean fare. *Taramasalata* is served with pita bread, French bread, crackers, or vegetable crudités. It is traditionally accompanied with anise-flavored liquor, such as ouzo or *arak*.

GREEK FISH ROE DIP (*TARAMASALATA*)

ABOUT 2 CUPS/4 TO 5 SERVINGS   [PAREVE]

    4 thick slices semolina or Italian white bread,
        trimmed of crusts, or 1 cup fresh bread crumbs
    ½ cup (4 ounces) *tarama* from carp or shad roe, or
        red caviar
    2 to 4 tablespoons fresh lemon juice
    1 cup extra-virgin olive or vegetable oil, or ¾ cup
        olive oil and ¼ cup vegetable oil

1. Soak the bread in cold water to cover until soggy, about 5 minutes. Squeeze out the excess liquid and crumble the bread.

2. In a blender or food processor fitted with a metal blade, using an electric mixer, or in a large wooden mortar, puree the bread, roe, and lemon juice into a uniform paste. With the machine on, gradually add the oil in a slow, steady stream (or in a mortar grind in and stir), processing until the mixture is smooth and has a mayonnaise-like consistency. Cover and refrigerate for up to 2 days. Remove from the refrigerator about 1 hour before serving.

TARATOR

Tarator is a yogurt and cucumber mixture used as a sauce, salad, and soup.

Origin: Turkey

Other names: Afghanistan: *chaka*; Arabic: *khyar ib leban*; Armenian: *jajik*; Farsi: *mast-o khiar*; Greek: *tzatziki*; Iraq: *jajeek*; Turkish: *cacik, taratuar, toroto*.

Tarator was originally the name of a medieval Turkish sauce made from ground walnuts and vinegar, and various dishes bearing the name can be found throughout the former Ottoman Empire. Among Levantine Arabs, *taratur* denotes a sauce based on tahini (sesame seed paste). Among Sephardim of Turkey and the Balkans, the term *tarator* came to mean a mixture of cucumbers and yogurt, which occasionally also contained chopped walnuts. Each locale has its own flavoring variation. When the yogurt mixture is thick (*gust*) and the cucumbers are finely chopped, *tarator* is used as a dip; when the cucumbers are sliced, it becomes a salad; when the mixture is relatively thin, it is served as a soup. *Tarator* dip is served as part of a *mezze* (appetizer assortment) with pita or toasted pita triangles.

TURKISH YOGURT AND CUCUMBER SALAD (*TARATOR*)

ABOUT 6 CUPS [DAIRY]

2 medium (about 1 pound total) cucumbers, peeled, halved lengthwise, seeded, and coarsely grated, diced, or thinly sliced; or 1 large English cucumber, coarsely grated, diced, or thinly sliced

About 2 teaspoons table salt or 4 teaspoons kosher salt for sprinkling

3 cups thick plain yogurt

1 cup ground toasted walnuts or 3 tablespoons white wine vinegar (optional)

2 to 6 cloves garlic, mashed

About ⅛ teaspoon ground white or black pepper

3 to 4 tablespoons chopped fresh cilantro, dill, or mint; or ½ cup chopped watercress

1. Place the cucumbers in a colander or large strainer, toss with the salt, weigh down with a plate, and let stand at room temperature for at least 30 minutes

and up to 3 hours. Drain and squeeze out the excess moisture.

2. In a large bowl, mix together the remaining ingredients. Add the cucumbers and toss to coat. Cover and refrigerate for at least 6 hours.

TEA

The most widely drunk beverage in the world, following water, is tea, which is made from the dried leaves of an evergreen shrub native to southern China. The tea plant resembles a small orange tree and sprouts odorless, long, leathery, dark green leaves. Originally, the leaves were simply chewed, yielding a mild astringent taste and stimulation. Tea as a beverage probably developed first as a medicine and subsequently as a soup. The first written record of tea occurred only about two thousand years ago in a contract of a Chinese emperor's poet laureate. Drinking tea probably only became common among the Chinese upper class in the Tang dynasty (618–907 CE); during this period, the preparation and consumption of tea developed into a fine art. During the Ming dynasty (1368–1644), the now-common fermentation and brewing (infusing rather than boiling) techniques were developed, around the same time that European powers began taking a stronger interest in Asia.

The flavor of tea depends on the variety, growing conditions, and processing method. There are four basic types: green, white, oolong (brown), and black. Black tea, the world's most popular type, is withered, then lightly crushed to expose its enzymes to the air,

A glezele tey (Yiddish for "glass of tea") with a sugar cube was emblematic of the life of eastern Ashkenazim.

thereby inducing fermentation. As the leaves dry, they turn coppery, then black, resulting in a milder flavor. Tea descriptions and grades are usually named after the variety and size of leaves or region of origin. Today, most teas are made from blends of tea leaves.

Tea spread throughout eastern Asia, where it was often prepared and served in a ritualistic and poetic manner. In the nearby regions of central Asia, Persia, and parts of the Arab world, tea became not merely a beverage, but an important means of social interaction. Although Marco Polo mentioned seeing tea in China in 1285 and the Portuguese noticed it in their port of Macau in 1557, it was only introduced to the West in Amsterdam by the Dutch in 1610. At this time, the Portuguese began transporting the dried leaves as well. Tea appeared in France in 1636 and was subsequently available in England, but was largely ignored until 1662, when Charles II of England married the Portuguese princess Catherine de Braganza, who introduced the practice of drinking tea to English society. Shortly thereafter, the first shops specializing in serving hot tea, as well as those offering coffee and cocoa, opened in London. Soon wealthier Englishmen were brewing these hot drinks at home and London quickly became the tea capital of the world. It was, however, only in the eighteenth century, when cane sugar became increasingly available and less expensive, that tea emerged as the British national drink.

Differences in preparing and serving this beverage developed. Some prefer plain tea, while others add sweeteners or a spot of lemon juice. The British commonly mix in honey and milk. Some eastern Europeans sweeten tea with a spoonful of preserves. Mint tea is especially popular in parts of the Middle East. Russians and Arabs prefer drinking tea from glasses, while Asians and the British favor pottery cups.

In Uzbekistan, hot green tea (*kuk cha*) prepared in a samovar is enjoyed at the end of every meal as well as frequently in between. Visitors to an Uzbeki house are given the royal treatment and presented with green tea and then a *dastarkhan* (literally meaning "tablecloth") featuring an array of treats, including confections, pastries, dried fruit, nuts, and preserves. In the cities, a *chaykhana* (tea house) dots practically every other block. Most *chaykhana* have a roofed pavilion where Uzbeks sit, any time of the day or night, on cushions at low tables sipping green tea, munching

samsas (filled pastries) and sweets, chatting, and playing backgammon.

In the mid-eighteenth century, Russia began importing tea from China; it was initially transported by camel caravans. However, only in the nineteenth century—with the emergence of sugar beet factories, the increasing availability of less expensive and time-consuming means of transportation, and the spread of the samovar—did tea emerge as the predominant social drink in Russia and then much of eastern Europe. A samovar is a large metal urn that keeps liquids hot for an extended period. (The word derived from the Russian *samo*, "self," and *varit*, "to boil," so it literally means "self-boiler.") In the period before Louis Pasteur, people sensed that tea was much safer to drink than plain water and quickly gravitated to it.

While coffee became the hot beverage of preference for those Jews in central Europe, tea became a way of life among eastern Ashkenazim. A *glezele tey* (little glass of tea), an experience of relaxation typically shared with others, became the embodiment of Yiddish informal social interaction (a schmooze) and eastern European culture. Over glasses of tea around a samovar, families laughed and chatted about their day and current events, rabbinic scholars discussed points of law, and socialists spiritedly debated politics. An individual would inevitably sit and read the Bible or perhaps peruse a Yiddish newspaper while sipping a glass. Among the numerous songs of influential Yiddish songwriter Mordechai Gebirtig, killed by the Nazis in the Kraków Ghetto on Bloody Thursday (June 4, 1942), is *"Noch a Glezele Tey"* (Another Little Glass of Tea), about a husband and wife arguing about the name of their unborn baby. A glass of tea with a sugar cube was among the few items allowed by eastern European sages before the morning prayers.

Eastern European tea was typically black and relatively weak. The water was commonly boiled in a samovar or, less preferably, an inexpensive *tcheinik* (teakettle). (The famous Yiddish phrase *"hocken a tcheinik"* means "to nag/chop like a teakettle.") Tea was rarely prepared for an individual cup, but rather loose leaves were brewed in a small teapot into a concentrated tea "essence/sense," from which a little of the concentrated tea liquid was later mixed into hot water. The tea was blended in a glass so the preparer could determine the strength of the tea by the degree of darkness. The sense method proved particularly ideal for enjoying tea on the Sabbath; both the hot water and concentrate were prepared before nightfall on Friday and mixed just before drinking any time during the day.

Eastern Europeans drank their tea, typically five to six cups a day and frequently many more, in a customary way—they took sips from a *glezele* (glass) with a small lump of sugar wedged between the teeth (*v'prikusku*, "with a bite"). This custom was as ingrained for them as the tea ceremony was for the Japanese. Sugar came in large conical loaves, which were chopped into bite-sized pieces using a large wooden board with an attached sharp blade and a second blade on a hinge that was forced down like a paper cutter. When sipping a cup of tea, a lump was placed between the teeth or sometimes nestled in the pocket of the cheek or under the tongue. Perhaps this initially emerged as a more economical method than stirring in granulated sugar, or maybe it was a way for people to demonstrate to others that they could afford sugar, as the lump remained visible for everyone to see, or perhaps it was simply easier to cut out cubes than to pound the sugar in a mortar into small granules. As Leo Tolstoy wrote in *Resurrection* (1899), "An ordinary lump of sugar used so by an expert peasant tea drinker will sweeten over a dozen glasses of tea." In parts of Poland, a *glezele tey* was also drunk with a spoonful of *slivkes* (plum preserves), but in most areas of eastern Europe a sugar lump was de rigueur among non-Jews and Jews. On Hanukkah, the Festival of Lights, sugar lumps were sometimes dipped with a teaspoon into plum brandy and then set on fire before they were dropped into the tea glass. A Yiddish proverb advises, "If you are bitter at heart, sugar in the mouth will not help you."

In Harold Robbins's best-selling novel *The Carpetbaggers* (New York, 1961), one of the characters, a junkman, initiates a typical business transaction with an elderly Jewish woman over a glass of tea in her apartment:

His father picked up a lump of sugar from the bowl and placed it between his lips, then sipped the tea. After he swallowed the first scalding mouthful, he opened his mouth and said, "Ah!" "Good, isn't it?" Mrs. Saperstein was smiling. "That's real tea. Swee-Touch-Nee. Like in the Old Country. Not like the *chazerai* they try to sell you here."

His father nodded and lifted the glass again. When he put it back on the table, it was empty and the polite formalities were over. Now it was time to attend to business. "Nu, Mrs. Saperstein?"

Eastern European Jews, even as immigrants to America, never served tea with granulated sugar and never dissolved the lumps in the tea. The class differences in Russia, where the elite would not comport themselves like common folk, who used sugar cubes, even in the act of drinking tea, led to a famous nineteenth century Yiddish folksong, "*Vi Azoi Trinkt Der Kayser Tey?*" (How Does the Czar Drink Tea?). The lyrics supplied the response to the question: "One takes a loaf of sugar and one makes a hole in it and pours in the tea, and mixes and mixes and mixes. That's how the czar drinks tea." (The song then asks how the czar eats potatoes.) In America, however, as the descendants of eastern Europeans acculturated, the sugar cube between the teeth disappeared and was replaced by granulated crystals, and often the tea was supplanted by coffee.

The British control over the Levant as well as the arrival of tea-loving Jewish immigrants from across the globe led to an early tea industry in Israel as well as the modern Hebrew word for it, *tey*. Consequently, afternoon tea, like the British habit, became a widespread Israeli practice. Also due to the British influence, many Israelis began serving their tea in cups and, appropriately for the land, with milk and honey, frequently accompanied with *biskotim* (simple flat cookies).

In Moscow in 1849, Klonimus Wolf Wissotzky (1824–1904), a young Russian Jew and Torah scholar, dissatisfied with the poor-quality tea being sold, launched a small store selling imported tea from China and quickly found success. The company eventually began opening offices throughout eastern Europe, in New York City in 1904, and, finally in 1907, in London. Wissotzky emerged as the world's largest purveyor of tea, with factories in Russia, Ukraine, and Poland and tea plantations in India and Ceylon. Following the revolution in 1917, the company, then headed by Wissotzky's descendants, relocated to London and Poland. In 1922, the company opened a branch in Tel Aviv and in 1936, one of the Wissotzky's descendents, Shimon Zidler, established a plant in Israel, becoming the company's headquarters. Today

Wissotzky, run by the fifth generation of the family, is by far Israel's largest tea company. Following the collapse of the Soviet Union, after an eighty-year absence, Wissotzky returned to its roots, selling prepackaged tea in Russia.

Meanwhile after the British departed from Israel and other Western areas grew in influence there, coffee soon overshadowed tea. For many years, Israeli tea was often strong and of questionable quality. Sugar cubes by and large became a novelty of the past, although Anwar Sadat, during his 1977 diplomatic meetings with the Israeli prime minster, noted that his fellow inveterate tea drinker Menachem Begin drank his tea Russian-style with a cube of sugar in his mouth. However, between 1998 and 2003, coffee sales dropped by 7 percent, while tea correspondingly increased. Part of this change was due to the influx of nearly a million Russians, as well as an increase in health consciousness. In addition, more recently high-quality teas have become a trend in Israel. As a result, Israeli newspapers began to write articles about "the renaissance of tea in Israel." And suddenly sugar cubes have returned, to a limited degree.

(See also Naa-Naa)

TEIG/TEYG (ASHKENAZIC PASTRY DOUGH)

By the late nineteenth century, Ashkenazim made three basic types of dough (*teig/teyg* in Yiddish) many originating in the kitchens of central Europe: *hefeteig* (yeast dough), *murbeteig* (flaky pastry), and *boymlteig* (oil pastry). These doughs lay at the heart of Ashkenazic baking and were used to make various savory pastries, such as knishes and *piroshkes*, and sweet ones, notably an assortment of *kichlach* (egg cookies) and *kuchen* (cakes).

Hefeteig is simply enriched bread dough. A very rich version, with larger amounts of sugar and butter, is *feine heifeteig*. Yeast doughs also contain varying amounts of eggs. Oil is used for pareve baked goods. For dairy treats, sour cream or *quark* is sometimes added to the dough for flavor and texture. Yeasts doughs are used to make *fluden* (layered pastry), *kuchen* (coffee cakes), *kipfel* (crescents), babka, and hamantaschen.

Boymlteig, actually a variation of strudel dough (*strudelblatter*), is a firm dough made with oil. It was originally unleavened, but many modern variations include baking powder. Some versions are made with egg, while others omit it. In an innovative late nineteenth-century adaptation, some mashed potatoes from the filling are incorporated into the dough. As a result of the oil, the dough remains tender even when rolled out, making it ideal for the thin, crisp crust of knishes and *piroshkes*. The advent in the nineteenth century of various inexpensive vegetable oils led to their widespread use in baking; for Jews, they largely replaced schmaltz and butter until the popularization of margarine and vegetable shortening in the twentieth century.

Muerbeteig or *murbeteig* (*mürbe* is German for "crumbly") refers to the crumbly texture of the baked pastry made from a butter-rich dough. Classic *muerbeteig* contains no other tenderizing ingredients (i.e., no sugar, eggs, or milk) besides fat; the amount of fat must equal at least half the weight of the flour or the pastry will be tough and chewy. A little water is necessary in order to bind the dough and build up enough gluten so that the crust holds its shape. Too much liquid produces a tough, unflaky pastry; too little causes it to fall apart. A little acid (vinegar, lemon juice, or sour cream) is sometimes substituted for an equal amount of water to help keep the gluten relaxed, which makes the dough easier to handle and the pastry more tender. Sour cream also adds flavor. When sour cream is substituted for the water in *muerbeteig*, it becomes *smetenehteig*. Adding a little sugar and sometimes eggs or egg yolks to *muerbeteig* results in what the French call *pâte sucrée*, used for sweet fillings, while increasing the amount of sugar creates a dough for cookies. *Muerbeteig* serves as the basis of Ashkenazic pastries (*geback*), including tarts, turnovers, *fluden*, *apfelschalet*, *apfelboyeleh*, *gebleterter kugels* (cookie strudels), and even cheesecake crust and American pies.

The first edition of *The Settlement Cook Book* (Milwaukee, 1901) included three recipes for "Murberteig," all made with butter. Until the popularization of shortening and margarine at the beginning of the twentieth century, *muerbeteig* was always made with butter. Since solid vegetable shortening contains no water, it melts slowly, producing the flakiest and most tender crusts. Shortening, however, also coats the tongue, thereby smothering the taste buds. Butter, on the other hand, melts in the mouth as well as possesses superior flavor, producing the most flavorful, colorful crusts. Since butter contains water, however, the water in the butter turns to steam before the pastry is able to set, resulting in a less flaky crust. Therefore, some bakers use both shortening and butter. For meat occasions, kosher bakers use shortening or margarine.

Since most Ashkenazic baking was for the Sabbath, festivals, or other occasions with a meat meal, a pareve dough was the most common. More recently, as the healthfulness of margarine and shortening have been questioned, oil pastry has risen again.

(See also Filling, Fluden, Knish, Kuchen, Masa, Pastida, Piroshke, Strudel, and Zwetschgenkuchen.)

ASHKENAZIC FLAKY PASTRY (*MUERBETEIG*)

ABOUT 1½ POUNDS   [DAIRY OR PAREVE]

This makes enough for one double-crust 9-inch deep-dish pie, three single-crust 9-inch pies, one 15½-by-10½-inch baking sheet, two 13-by-9-inch baking pans, twelve 4-inch tartlets, or thirty-six 3-inch turnovers.

3 cups (15 ounces) all-purpose flour
1 teaspoon salt
4 to 6 tablespoons sugar (optional)
1 cup plus 2 tablespoons (9 ounces) unsalted
     butter or shortening, chilled, or ½ cup plus 2
     tablespoons shortening and ½ cup butter
About 7 tablespoons ice water, or about 6
     tablespoons water mixed with 1 tablespoon cider
     vinegar or lemon juice

1. In a medium bowl, combine the flour, salt, and, for a sweet pastry, the sugar. Using the tips of your fingers or a pastry blender, cut in the butter to make a mixture that resembles coarse crumbs.

2. Sprinkle the ice water, 1 tablespoon at a time, over a section of the flour. Gently mix with a fork after each addition, moistening that section. Push the moistened dough aside and gradually add enough of the remaining water to barely moisten the flour and make a mixture that just holds together. Do not overmix.

3. Place on a lightly floured surface and form into a rectangle. Using the heel of your hand, beginning with the end farthest from you, gently push down a little of the dough (about 2 tablespoons at a time), then push and smear it away from you. Flatten into a disk and wrap in plastic wrap. Refrigerate for at least 30 minutes and up to 3 days.

ASHKENAZIC OIL PASTRY (*BOYMLTEIG*)

ABOUT 1½ POUNDS   [PAREVE]

This recipe makes enough for about thirty-six 3-inch turnovers, twelve large knishes, forty-eight small knishes, or ninety-six bite-sized knishes.

About 3 cups (15 ounces) all-purpose flour
1 teaspoon baking powder or 1 package (2¼
     teaspoons) active dry yeast
½ teaspoon table salt or 1 teaspoon kosher salt
6 tablespoons vegetable oil
1 large egg, lightly beaten
½ cup plus 2 tablespoons water
2 teaspoons white vinegar

In a medium bowl, combine the flour, baking powder, and salt and make a well in the center. Blend together the oil and egg, then stir in the water and vinegar. Pour into the well and stir to form a soft, smooth dough, adding more flour if necessary. Cover and let stand at room temperature for at least 1 hour.

ASHKENAZIC YEAST PASTRY (*HEFETEIG*)

ABOUT 2 POUNDS   [DAIRY OR PAREVE]

This dough makes enough for two medium breads or about forty-two turnovers. The sweetened variations are most commonly used in pastries, including *kuchen* (coffee cakes), *zwetschgenkuchen* (plum cake), *kipfel* (crescents), babka, and hamantaschen.

1 package (2¼ teaspoons) active dry yeast or
     1 (0.6-ounce) cake fresh yeast
1 cup warm water (105°F to 115°F for dry yeast;
     80°F to 85°F for fresh yeast), or ¼ cup warm
     water and ¾ cup sour cream or warm milk
1 to 6 tablespoons sugar or honey
2 large eggs or 4 large egg yolks
¼ cup unsalted butter or shortening, softened
1½ teaspoons table salt or 1 tablespoon kosher
     salt
About 3¾ cups (16 ounces) bread or unbleached
     all-purpose flour

1. Dissolve the yeast in ¼ cup water. Stir in 1 teaspoon sugar and let stand until foamy, 5 to 10 minutes. In a large bowl, combine the yeast mixture, remaining water, remaining sugar, eggs, butter, salt, and 2 cups flour. Gradually add enough of the remaining flour to make a dough that holds together.

2. Knead the dough until smooth and elastic, 10 to 15 minutes. Place in an oiled bowl and turn to coat.

Cover loosely with plastic wrap or a kitchen towel and let rise in warm, draft-free place until doubled in bulk, about 1½ hours. Punch down the dough, knead briefly, cover, and refrigerate for 8 hours and up to 24 hours.

TEIGLACH

Teiglach are small pieces of dough cooked in a honey syrup.

Origin: Eastern Europe

Other names: *taiglach, tayglach, teyglekh*; Italy: *ceciarchiata, struffoli*; Ladino: *pinyonati*.

A Middle Eastern culinary practice, still very much in vogue today, consists of soaking pastries and cakes in a honey or sugar syrup as a means of keeping them from drying out or refreshing them once stale. In a Moorish confection called *pinonate* (from the word for "pine nut"), eggs were added to the dough, which was deep-fried as small balls and simmered in honey. *Pinonate* was adopted by Sephardim and called *pinyonati*, although its popularity has faded recently. This dish eventually reached Italy, although it is unknown whether it arrived by way of Sicily or was introduced by Sephardim, or perhaps both; it is called *ceciarchiata* (referring to its resemblance to chickpeas, *ceci* in Italian) in northern Italy, and *struffoli* in the south. Italian Jews typically add toasted chopped hazelnuts for a popular Hanukkah treat.

It was among eastern European Jews, however, that these little pieces of dough in honey syrup gained the widest appeal. The nuggets are called *teiglach* (literally "little dough pieces"). The obvious similarity in texture and taste of *teiglach* to *pinyonati* and *ceciarchiata* suggests an Italian or Sephardic origin.

Since fat for frying was very limited among northern European Jews, they abandoned it, substituting two other basic methods of preparing *teiglach*: The raw dough nuggets can be fully cooked in the honey syrup or they can be baked first and then added to the syrup. The prebaked nuggets tend to be very hard, while the unbaked ones are chewy. Plenty of egg is necessary so that the dough puffs up, although today baking powder is commonly added. A firm dough produces a more tender interior.

In addition to the differences resulting from preparation methods, there are other variations in the pastry. The small dough pieces can be round, cylindrical, tied into knots, braided like a cruller, or even formed into rings like doughnuts. In a Passover version, matza meal is substituted for the flour. In another variation, a raisin or piece of dried plum or date is stuffed in the center of each nugget. Nuts and/or candied fruit can also be added to the syrup. There must be plenty of syrup, so that the dough nuggets can swim in it. As is typical of eastern Ashkenazic cooking, the syrup is usually flavored with ground ginger.

Before commercial catering, the food at most Jewish *simchot* (celebrations) was prepared by the community. In the typical Jewish area, most housewives had one special dish they prepared for these events. Inevitably one was *teiglach*. Thus Ashkenazim, particularly those from Lithuania and Latvia, traditionally enjoyed this treat on most celebrations, such as a *brit milah*, bar mitzvah, and wedding. In a number of households, *teiglach* was traditional on Shavuot and Simchat Torah, symbolizing that Torah was as sweet as honey, as well as on Purim, and in some families it was served on every Sabbath. Today, *teiglach* is primarily and most prominently featured on Rosh Hashanah, to start the new year on a sweet note. In many households, the confection was typically made several days before Rosh Hashanah, then any remaining syrup was used the following day for the New Year's honey cake, getting the baking out of the way before turning to the other holiday dishes.

Eastern Europeans brought *teiglach* to America. The word first appeared in English in *The Jewish Encyclopedia* (New York) in 1903, but *teiglach* was virtually unknown in England at that time and gained only limited popularity in Israel. On the other hand, Lithuanian immigrants brought it to South Africa, where it is a New Year's delicacy and cooks sometimes substitute golden syrup for the honey. *Teiglach* are available in American Jewish bakeries and even some non-Jewish establishments, where they appear each year shortly before Rosh Hashanah. Since eastern European Jews developed the custom of abstaining from nuts on Rosh Hashanah, in the Old Country they were omitted from *teiglach* for this holiday. Many American bakers add nuts, sometimes almonds and/or hazelnuts, and often candied cherries. Consequently, in America the pastry ironically became associated with nuts, which are still a taboo Rosh Hashanah item in Orthodox Ashkenazic circles.

In the mid-twentieth century, after American kosher food producers introduced packaged commercial "soup nuts" (*mandlen* in Yiddish), one-inch puffed balls of matza-egg dough, some cooks began substituting them for the *teiglach* dough balls simmering them in a syrup for a few minutes. Traditionalists, of course, insist on the genuine article, although the disagreement endures over whether chewy or crunchy nuggets are superior.

ASHKENAZIC HONEY DOUGH BALLS
(*TEIGLACH/TEYGLEKH*)

ABOUT 36 PIECES [PAREVE]

Pastry:
- 2½ cups (12.5 ounces) all-purpose flour or 1½ cups matza cake meal
- 1 teaspoon double-acting baking powder
- ¼ teaspoon salt
- 4 large eggs, lightly beaten
- 3 tablespoons vegetable or peanut oil

Syrup:
- 2 cups (1½ pounds) dark honey
- 1 to 3 teaspoons ground ginger, 1 teaspoon grated lemon zest, or 1 tablespoon fresh lemon juice

- 1 cup coarsely chopped blanched almonds, hazelnuts, pecans, or walnuts; or ½ cup nuts and ½ cup raisins (optional)
- ½ cup boiling water

1. To make the pastry: Sift together the flour, baking powder, and salt. In a medium bowl, combine the eggs, and oil. Stir in the flour mixture, adding more flour if necessary, to make a fairly firm, workable dough. On a lightly floured surface, knead until smooth, 2 to 3 minutes.

2. Divide the dough into pieces and roll into ½-inch-thick ropes. Cut into ½-inch pieces. Leave as oblong shapes or roll into balls. Arrange on a flat surface and let dry for at least 30 minutes.

3. To make the syrup: In a large pot, stir the honey and ginger over low heat until the honey melts, about 5 minutes. Increase the heat to medium and bring to a boil.

4. Add the dough pieces, a few at a time to prevent sticking and to keep the syrup boiling. When all the pieces are in the pot, return the syrup to a boil.

5. To cook on the stovetop: Cover, reduce the heat to low, and cook, without uncovering, for 25 minutes.

Stir the teiglach. Increase the heat to medium and cook, uncovered and stirring every 5 minutes, until the teiglach are deep brown and hollow sounding when tapped, about 40 minutes. Alternatively, to cook in the oven: Cover the pot and cook over medium heat on the stove for 10 minutes. Place in a 375°F oven and bake, stirring at 15-minute intervals, until the *teiglach* are deep brown and hollow sounding when tapped, about 35 minutes.

6. If using, stir in the nuts. Carefully stir in the boiling water, remove from the heat, and let stand for 1 minute. Pour the teiglach onto a greased baking sheet or a large wooden board moistened with cold water.

7. Have a bowl of ice water handy. Using hands moistened with ice water, shape the teiglach into a single large mound or several 3-inch mounds. Or spread to a 1½-inch thickness and cut into diamonds or squares. Let cool completely. Store in an airtight container at room temperature for up to 2 weeks.

T'FINA
T'fina is a Sabbath stew.
Origin: Maghreb
Other names: Algeria: *d'fina*; Libya and Tunisia: *tafinah*; Tangiers: *horisa, orissa*.

T'fina, which means "buried" in Arabic, and is a variation of the Iberian *adafina*, the name that Tunisians and Libyans use for their Sabbath stew, of which there are several very colorful and unique varieties. In most Tunisian *t'finas*, the ingredients are mixed together as a stew, unlike the more complicated Moroccan *hamins/adafinas* and *skhinas*, which are traditionally cooked in layers and separated into different dishes for serving. As is typical in the Maghreb, harissa (chili paste) is commonly added for a bit of fire (*t'fina ou harissa*). Tunisian red *t'fina* (*t'fina camounia*) contains harissa and paprika, while green *t'fina* (*t'fina bka-ïla* or *t'fina sfanach*) includes spinach, chard, or beet greens. Algerians commonly add turnips. The version from the island of Djerba includes dried plums, dried apricots, and cinnamon. Many Algerians, Tunisians, and Libyans add a *bobinet* (beef sausage) or *osbana* (a sort of sausage made from the chopped entrails of a sheep mixed with eggs, rice or bread crumbs, and spices—generally cumin, coriander, and chilies—and stuffed into a sheep's stomach). *T'fina* is typically served with couscous.

(See also Adafina, Hamin, Harisa, and Sabbath)

TIGANITE

Tiganite is a small pancake.

Origin: Greece

In Greek, a skillet is a *tigani*; anything fried in it is called *tiganita*, and that term provides the name for these pancakes. Greeks have been enjoying pancakes from at least the sixth century BCE, when they were a common breakfast fried in olive oil, drizzled with honey, and topped with various nuts and fruits. Many people still serve them with honey, while others substitute *petimezi* (a syrup made from boiled grapes) or various other syrups. Some spread them with *anthotyro*, a soft fresh goat or sheep cheese, or top them with Greek yogurt. There are numerous variations of the basic pancake, including some made with whole-wheat flour or rice flour, and others with an anise flavor that comes from a little ouzo. Greek Jews enjoy *tiganites* on Hanukkah. Passover versions are made with matza meal.

(See also Tagine)

❧ GREEK PANCAKES (*TIGANITES*)

ABOUT FIFTEEN 4-INCH PANCAKES   [DAIRY OR PAREVE]

   1¼ cups (6.25 ounces) all-purpose flour, or ¾ cup all-purpose flour and ½ cup whole-wheat or rice flour
   1 teaspoon double-acting baking powder
   1 teaspoon baking soda
   ½ teaspoon table salt or 1 teaspoon kosher salt
   1 large egg, lightly beaten
   1¼ cups buttermilk or sour milk (1¼ cups milk mixed with 1 tablespoon lemon juice or vinegar), or ½ cup milk and ¾ cup plain yogurt, or 1 cup water and ¼ cup ouzo
   3 tablespoons olive or vegetable oil
   3 tablespoons sugar or honey
   Olive or vegetable oil for frying
   Warm honey, *petimezi*, or *atar* (Middle Eastern Sugar Syrup, page 27), for drizzling; or cinnamon-sugar for sprinkling
   Chopped almonds, pistachios, or walnuts; or sesame seeds; for sprinkling

1. In a medium bowl, combine the flour, baking powder, baking soda, and salt. Blend together the egg, milk, oil, and sugar. Add to the flour mixture and stir just to combine. If the batter is too thick, add a little milk; if too thin, stir in a little flour. Cover and let stand in the refrigerator for at least 1 hour.

2. Heat a large skillet or griddle over medium heat until a few drops of water sprinkled on the surface scatter and evaporate. Lightly grease with the oil.

3. In batches, drop the batter by ¼ cupfuls onto the skillet to form 4-inch pancakes. Cook until bubbles appear on the top and the bottom is lightly browned, about 2 minutes. Turn and cook until golden brown, about 1 minute. Drizzle with the honey and sprinkle with the nuts.

TIMMAN

Timman is a rice dish that has a crust on the bottom.

Origin: Iraq

Ruz is the most common Arabic word for rice, but in Iraq it also goes by the name *timman* or *temn*. Rice dishes, many similar to those prepared today, were recorded in thirteenth-century Baghdad cookbooks. In many Iraqi homes, rice is a daily dish and the ability to make perfect rice is the measure of a good cook. The favorite rice variety in modern Iraq is *ambar/anbar*, a yellowish, very aromatic, long-grain rice grown in the provinces of Anbar and Kadisiya. Iraqi rice cooking is based on the method used for Persian *chelow*, a multistepped process intended to produce just-tender, fluffy grains of rice.

A prominent aspect of Iraqi rice cooking is the *hkaka*, a crisp bottom crust. It differs slightly from the Persian *tahdiq*, which is a single thick piece; the *hkaka* contains some loose rice as well. Cooks use a *kifkir*, a special meat spatula, to scrape loose the crust while keeping it intact, then invert the rice onto a *seeniyya* (serving platter). Before serving, the *hkaka* is broken into pieces so that everyone is provided with some along with the fluffy rice.

Besides plain cooked white rice (*timman abyadh*), which is served with a stew or other dishes with a sauce, there are numerous flavored ones. In many Iraqi households, *timman ahmar* (red rice), saffron rice (*timman zaffran*), or turmeric rice (*timman asfar*) were reserved for Friday night.

(See also Chelow and Tabyeet)

❧ IRAQI CRUSTY RICE (*TIMMAN*)

ABOUT 7½ CUPS/6 TO 8 SERVINGS   [PAREVE OR DAIRY]

   2½ cups (1 pound) basmati, jasmine, or other long-grain rice
   4 cups water
   2 teaspoons table salt or 4 teaspoons kosher salt
   3 tablespoons vegetable oil or ghee

1. Place the rice in a bowl, add water to cover, and let soak for 30 minutes. In a fine-mesh sieve or colander, rinse the rice under cold running water until the water runs clear. Drain.

2. In a large pot, bring the 4 cups water to a boil and add the salt. Add the rice and boil, uncovered, on high until the outside is soft, but the inside is still hard, about 8 minutes. Pour the rice into a sieve or colander, rinse with water, and drain. At this point, before the steaming step, the rice can also used as stuffing for chickens before roasting.

3. In a medium, heavy saucepan, heat the oil over medium heat. Add the rice, cover with a kitchen towel, then the lid. Cook over low heat until the rice is fluffy, about 25 minutes. The bottom of the rice should be brown, but not burnt. Dip the bottom of the pot into a sink full of cold water for 30 seconds, then invert onto a serving platter.

VARIATIONS

Iraqi Red Rice (Timman Ahmar): Combine 1 tablespoon tomato paste, 1 tablespoon olive oil, and 2 cardamom pods. Or combine 1 tablespoon tomato paste, 1 tablespoon olive oil, ½ teaspoon ground turmeric, ½ teaspoon ground black pepper, and ¼ to ½ teaspoon cayenne. In Step 3, before adding the parboiled rice to the saucepan, stir the tomato mixture into the rice.

TISH

Tish literally means "table" in Yiddish, and it appears in terms for various meals, including *Shabbos tish* (Sabbath table) and *chason's tish* (groom's table). Among Chasidim, a *tish* has a much more significant connotation: A *rebbe's tish* is a public gathering of adherents of Chasidic rabbis at a communal meal. It began in the eighteenth century as the third meal of the Sabbath, the *seudat shlishit* held before sunset on Saturday. At first, it was an intimate feast shared between a rebbe, seated at the head of the table, and his male devotees scattered around the table. Women observed from the *ezrat nashim* (women's section). Along with food, the *tish* always includes singing in the form of *niggunim* (melodies) and *zemirot* (hymns) and, if enough room, dancing. The *tish* became a form of worship. During the nineteenth century, the *tish* expanded from a Saturday afternoon event to also one held at the end of the Friday night meal as well as holiday meals. A similar communal meal at which the rebbe is not present, but which is typically headed by the rebbe's son or an important rabbi, is called a *botteh*.

As the number of Chasidim dramatically increased, the *tish* grew less intimate and more mystical. The rebbe would now taste a small portion of each dish, then the remainder (*shirayim*), which was considered sanctified and a source of blessing, would be distributed among his followers; the rebbe sometimes personally doled out each portion. Today, in some of the larger Chasidic courts, the attendees sit or stand on bleachers (*parentches*) and the food is passed from person to person.

Challah and fish typically begin these meals. One item in particular emerged as the most prominent food at a *tish*, the kugel, to which the Chasidim attached numerous Kabbalistic meanings.

TISHA B'AV

No date reverberates as large in Jewish history as the ninth of the month of Av (Tisha b'Av), which falls in late July or early August. The first mention of this date was in the Bible, when Moses sent twelve spies to survey the land of Canaan and ten of them, who preferred to remain in the wilderness, returned with a report calculated to provoke fear and resistance in a group only recently emancipated from slavery. The result was forty years of wandering in the wilderness before their children finally were able to enter Canaan. That single date reappears over and over in Jewish history through the subsequent millennia as one of tragedy. Consequently, the most somber span of the Jewish calendar is a three-week period of semi-mourning known as *Shloshet Hashavuot* (Three Weeks) or *Bein Hametzarim* (Between the Troubles). It stretches from the seventeenth day of the month of Tammuz, a minor fast day marking the beginning of the siege of Jerusalem, to the major fast of Tisha b'Av (the ninth day of the month of Av), commemorating a host of national disasters that occurred on this day.

The First Temple was erected around 960 BCE and remained the center of Jewish life for nearly four centuries until, on the ninth day of the month of Av in the year 586 BCE, Babylonian forces entered Jerusalem and torched Solomon's Temple and much of the city. The upper and middle classes of Judea were exiled to Babylonia, inaugurating the Diaspora. Although a small group of Jews returned fifty years later and in 516 BCE constructed the Second Temple, the majority of Jews would subsequently live outside of the land of Israel.

In 63 BCE, Pompey annexed Judea to Rome, setting in motion centuries of conflict due to ongoing Roman misgovernment and affronts to Judaism. Roman procurators, like Pontius Pilate (26–36 CE) and Gessius Florus (64–66 CE), purchased their positions and then used the opportunity to extract as much loot as possible from the subject populations. In addition, emperors who deemed themselves gods and arbiters of morality had a tendency to place statues of themselves in Jewish holy sites and forbid what they considered to be objectionable rituals. According to Josephus, the Jews' frustration bubbled over in 66 CE, triggered by the killing of several Jews by Greeks in the city of Caesarea, along with Florus' appropriation of funds from the Temple. A spontaneous revolt spread through the Galilee and Judea. At this time, Jews constituted fully 10 percent of the entire population of the Empire of approximately fifty million people. In response, Rome dispatched General Vespasian and several legions to suppress the insurrection, first vanquishing the Galilee in 67 and then laying siege to Jerusalem the following year.

Again on the ninth day of the month of Av, in 70 CE, after three years of revolution, Roman forces breached the walls of Jerusalem and burned the wooden parts of the Second Temple. The loss of the First Roman War and capture of Jerusalem resulted in large-scale death or enslavement and deportation from Judea, the first instance of widespread Jewish enslavement since the redemption from Egypt. Josephus reported that 1.1 million people died in Jerusalem alone. There were 97,000 more taken captive, many ending up in the mines of Egypt or in bondage in Italy. The Roman historian Tacitus estimated the number of deaths and captives at 600,000.

On the ninth of Av in 86 CE, the emperor Domitian had the stones of the Temple torn down, effectively ending the hope of salvaging the remnants from which to rebuild.

In 132 CE, a second major insurgency erupted in Judea. Under the leadership of Simon Bar Kokhba, the rebels captured numerous strongholds and towns and defeated the initial Roman forces sent to suppress them. Hadrian then dispatched his best generals and legions. Bar Kokhba's last remaining forces as well as numerous refugees gathered in his headquarters, the fortress of Betar southwest of Jerusalem, and attempted to outlast a lengthy siege.

Sixty-five years after the Roman legions crushed the first revolt, the second met the same fate, as Betar fell on the ninth day of Av in 135, effectively ending military resistance.

For centuries, Jews were forbidden from entering Jerusalem, except once a year on the ninth of Av, to mourn.

Afterward, various other tragedies occurred on the ninth of Av, including the expulsion of the Jews from England in 1290. Notably, the Alhambra Decree issued by Ferdinand and Isabella ordered the Jews of Spain to convert or leave by the end of July 1492, and that day was Tisha b'Av. World War I also broke out on this date. A practice in some German concentration camps during World War II was to starve the prisoners for several days before Tisha b'Av to ensure that they would need to eat on that day.

In the Talmud, Rav Papa predicts that Tisha b'Av and the minor fasts day will be transformed into days of rejoicing "when there is shalom [peace]." In the meantime, as the Mishnah states, "As Av enters, we diminish our joy." Weddings are not held during the entire three weeks. For the nine-day period (*Tishat HaYamim*) commencing with the first of Av, Jews traditionally do not eat meat or drink wine, except on the Sabbath; some abstain during the entire three-week span. Accordingly, cooks prepare an assortment of dairy and vegetarian fare during this time of year.

As a fast day, there are no traditional foods during Tisha b'Av. However, immediately before sunset is the *Seudat Hamafseket* (meal of separation), consisting of only one cooked food in addition to bread. For Ashkenazim, this meal typically consists of a roll or bagel and a hard-boiled egg. Most Sephardim have pita bread and a hard-boiled egg. Some Mizrachim partake of a piece of flatbread and *mengedarrah*, even though consisting of lentils and rice, it is considered one food. There is no *Seudat Hamafseket* when Tisha b'Av falls immediately after the Sabbath, but rather a somewhat regular *seudat shlishit* (third meal of the Sabbath).

Since the *Seudat Hamafseket* is so sparse, a custom emerged to have a sustaining meal beforehand, one also consisting of dairy or vegetarian foods, usually dishes containing lentils and eggs, both ancient Jewish symbols of mourning as well as fertility (life, like a lentil, goes around like a wheel).

Among Ashkenazim, the meal to break the fast is also dairy or vegetarian, as meat and wine are not eaten again until the following day. Many Sephardim, however, serve chicken. Turkish and Greek Jews begin with *pepitada*, a beverage made from melon seeds. In Iraq, a little rose water in cold water was customary. Many Ashkenazim sip tea or juice, perhaps accompanied with cake, before beginning the meal. Syrians and Iraqis serve *kaak*. Sephardim offer almond cookies or almond paste–filled pastries, representing a tradition that when the Messiah, who will be born on Tisha b'Av, arrives, the first to greet him will be an almond tree. Some Sephardim serve a dried fava bean dish called *bessara*, as it sounds like the Hebrew *b'tzara* (in troubles) and Arabic *f'sarra* (in troubles). Many Mizrachim eat watermelon to provide some relief from the heat. Persians serve *polow adas* (rice with brown lentils). Other traditional dishes include Sephardic red lentil soup (*sopa de lentejas*), Alsatian green lentil soup (*soupe de lentille*), Sephardic lentil salad (*salata de lentejas*), Middle Eastern lentils and rice (*mengedarrah*), and Sephardic long-cooked eggs (*huevos haminados*).

TISHPISHTI

Tishpishti is a semolina cake, frequently containing ground nuts, that is soaked in a syrup.

Origin: Turkey

Other names: Algeria: *kalb-el louz*; Crete: *shamali*; Egypt: *basboosah, basboussa*; Ladino: *pispiti, tezpisti, tupishti*; Lebanon: *hareesa, hrisseh*; Morocco: *chamali, chamia, gâteau de semoule*; Syria: *namora, namoura*; Turkey and Greece: *revani*.

In the Middle East, pastries and puddings were typically made from semolina, the predominant form of wheat in much of that region through the medieval period. For more than a millennium, Persians have enjoyed a golden pudding, *halva aurd-e sujee*, made by sautéing fine semolina in butter, then gradually stirring in sugar syrup. Ground nuts and various spices were commonly added. Although semolina halva is typically eaten warm, people began spreading it into a round metal tray, letting it cool, then cutting it into diamond shapes. At some point, cooks began baking the uncooked halva ingredients in a *tifsin* (large round pan) and adding the syrup afterwards; this method

was easier than the time-consuming practice of making halva over a fire and resulted in a favorite Middle Eastern cake.

In the former domains of the Ottoman Empire, there are a myriad of variations and names for semolina cakes. The most common name in Israel and among the Sephardim from Turkey, Greece, and the Balkans is *tishpishti*–probably a nonsense name from the Turkish *tez* (fast/quick) and *pişti* (plane/slope). For centuries in Egypt, men stood on street corners in the morning selling homemade semolina cakes from trays to passersby on their way to work. Today, sweet shops throughout the Middle East sell the semolina diamonds.

The predominant common threads among these cakes are the presence of semolina and a soaking syrup. Greeks call the various syrup-soaked pastries and cakes *siropiasta*. However, these cakes fall into three main categories: denser ones containing all semolina (and nuts) and no egg or baking powder; slightly lighter ones with a few whole eggs; and much lighter ones, particularly from Greece, made with some white flour and beaten egg whites (the contribution of Sephardim), and baking powder (a more modern innovation). The granular semolina imparts a slightly wheaty flavor, crunchy texture, and yellow hue. Fine semolina (called *smeed* in Arabic) is necessary to prevent the cake from being gritty. Sephardim make this cake with oil instead of butter and add a touch of orange. Algerians first toast the semolina, creating a nutty flavor, and typically fill the cake with almond paste.

Drenching the cakes with sugar syrup creates moisture as well as a striking sweetness. The syrup varies depending on the place of origin: It is usually made from sugar, but sometimes honey is added as well, and it can be accented with lemon, rose water, orange-blossom water, or cinnamon, or any combination.

Some semolina cakes are rather thick, while others are relatively thin. Many recipes call for finely ground nuts, which contribute flavor and a pleasant textural contrast. *Tishpishti* and *revani* always incorporate at least a small amount of nuts. Some cooks add grated coconut. Semolina cakes made with plenty of coconut are sometimes called *baseema* and, in India, *bolo de coco*. Some Indian cooks add a little turmeric for a bright yellow color. More than a few Greeks include a shot of ouzo. Some versions contain yogurt or milk, but Jews usually make a nondairy cake to serve in conjunction with meat. Jews typically use oil instead of butter.

Tishpishti is a frequent sight at most special occasions. It is a traditional Rosh Hashanah dessert, served to start the new year on a sweet note. Although any kind of nut may be used, blanched almonds are traditional on Rosh Hashanah to produce a light color so that the year should be *dulce y aclarada* (sweet and bright). At other times, walnuts, creating a darker cake, are more common. Many Mizrachim include semolina cake in the meal to break the fast of Yom Kippur. It is also popular on Purim. All-nut or matza meal versions are enjoyed on Passover. Among Middle Eastern Jews, it is also a favorite Sabbath afternoon indulgence. *Tishpishti* is frequently served topped with dollops of whipped cream, *ushta* (clotted cream), or yogurt and accompanied with, as are most Middle Eastern sweets, Turkish coffee or mint tea.

(See also Semolina)

MIDDLE EASTERN SEMOLINA CAKE (*TISHPISHTI*)

ABOUT TWENTY-FOUR 2-INCH PIECES   [PAREVE]

1 cup (6 ounces) fine semolina (not semolina flour)
1 cup (5 ounces) all-purpose flour
1 cup (3.5 ounces) ground blanched almonds, walnuts, pistachios, or hazelnuts
1 tablespoon baking powder
¼ teaspoon salt
1 teaspoon ground cinnamon or vanilla extract (optional)
6 large eggs, separated
1 cup sugar
½ cup vegetable, olive, or nut oil
2 tablespoons orange-blossom water or orange juice
2 teaspoons grated orange zest, or 1 teaspoon orange zest and 1 teaspoon lemon zest
24 or 48 whole almonds, walnuts, pistachios, or hazelnuts for decoration (optional)
2 cups atar (Middle Eastern Sugar Syrup, page 27), cooled

1. Preheat the oven to 350°F. Grease a 13-by-9-inch baking pan or a 10-inch round cake pan that is at least 2-inches deep.

2. Combine the semolina, flour, nuts, baking powder, salt, and, if using, cinnamon. In a large bowl, beat the egg yolks and sugar until thick and creamy, 5 to 10 minutes. Add the oil, juice, and, if using, zest and/or vanilla. Stir in the semolina mixture.

3. In a large bowl, beat the egg whites until stiff but not dry, 5 to 8 minutes. Fold one-fourth of the egg whites into the semolina mixture, then gently fold in the remaining whites.

4. Pour into the prepared pan. If using, arrange the whole nuts in even rows on top of the batter. Bake until a tester inserted in the center comes out clean, about 45 minutes.

5. Remove from the oven and immediately drizzle the cooled syrup evenly over the hot cake. Let the cake cool and absorb the syrup. Cut into diamond shapes or 2-inch squares. Cover with plastic wrap and store at room temperature for up to 48 hours.

TKEMALI

Tkemali is a cherry plum and a tart sauce made from the plums.

Origin: Georgia

The pride and joy of every Georgian cook is *tkemali*, a tart, slightly spicy plum sauce. The fruit is stewed with various typical Georgian spices and herbs, notably garlic, coriander, fennel, chili, and cilantro. Many people like a hint of mint or dill too. Depending on the ripeness and color of the plums, the sauce is pink, reddish, or green.

In Georgia, this sauce is made from a very tart variety of plum, known as *tkemali* and, in English, called cherry plum or *myrobalan*. Unripe Santa Rosa plums or Golden Gage or Japanese plum varieties may be substituted and a little lemon juice added. In addition, a version can be made with more readily attainable sour prunes. More recently, Georgians have developed a tomato and garlic sauce (*adjika*) used similarly to *tkemali*. Today, several Georgian companies produce bottled *tkemali*, although some cooks still insist on making their own to control the spices. Tkemali or raw sour plums are also boiled into a puree, spread into a thin sheet, and dried to make the fruit leather known as *tklapi/tkhlopi*.

Tkemali is used as a souring agent in the same manner as lemon juice in the West; it adds tartness to dishes such as *lobio tkemali* (red beans with plum sauce) and *kufta* (meatballs). *Tkemali* also serves as a condiment, akin to ketchup and salsa in America, with any number of dishes, including *tapaka* (pressed fried Cornish hens), *shashlik* (grilled skewered meat), and other grilled meat and fish.

TOMATO

Tomatoes are the mildly acidic, pulpy fruit of a South American vine. While botanically it is a fruit, the tomato is generally used as a vegetable; it is almost always found in the vegetable section of stores and is called a vegetable by most people. In an 1893 ruling, the United States Supreme Court classified it as a vegetable for marketing purposes.

Tomatoes first arrived in Spain in 1523 and in Italy about two decades later, and soon traveled to the eastern part of the Mediterranean. Europeans initially believed that this member of the nightshade family, originally called *mala insana* (Greek for "unhealthy fruit"), was poisonous and, for many years, relegated the plant solely to decorative use. The earliest European record of tomatoes used in a sauce appeared in Italy in 1692, and the pairing of tomato sauce with pasta was first recorded nearly a century later.

In contrast, the tomato received an enthusiastic reception in the Middle East, particularly among Jews in the Ottoman Empire, who incorporated it into numerous stews, salads, and vegetable dishes. Much of the tomato crop was cooked into a concentration, known as tomato paste, which was used to add body to dishes such as soups and sauces. People in many regions enjoy fresh tomato salads, including the Bukharan *banadora*, Indian *kuccha*, and Moroccan *shlata bi matesha*. A basic Yemenite sauce, now widespread in Israel, is made from chopped fresh tomatoes (*rotav aghvaniyot*).

No one more completely adopted the tomato early on than the Sephardim of the eastern Mediterranean. Tomato-based sauces (such as *ahilado*), typically with garlic and often with a squeeze of lemon, lie at the heart of the cooking of the Sephardim of Turkey and Greece; vegetables, rice, meat, chicken, and fish are commonly cooked in a tomato sauce. The presence of tomatoes and onions together was frequently a sign of Sephardic influence. Sephardim also added sliced tomatoes to numerous dishes, including *fritadas* (omelets) and *quajados* (casseroles). The northern Ashkenazim had the exact opposite response to the tomato, as reflected in a Yiddish nickname for it—*treyfene epl* (unkosher apple). It was only in

America and Israel, after becoming acculturated, that many Ashkenazim finally accepted the tomato.

By the end of the eighteenth century, the tomato had gained widespread acceptance in Italy, as reflected in a change of name to *pomo dei Moro* (apple of the Moors), connoting its usage in Arab lands, and *pomodoro* (golden apple), connoting the yellow color of the small Mexican variety that originally reached Europe. The rest of the continent eventually followed Italy's lead. Thomas Jefferson credited Dr. John de Sequeyra, a Sephardic physician who settled in Williamsburg in 1745, with first importing the tomato to Virginia, as well as with persuading Jefferson that they were not only edible but also healthful. Nevertheless, it was another half century before the tomato was firmly embedded in American cuisine, and even then, it was only eaten cooked, usually for hours, and not yet eaten raw.

(See also Israeli Salad)

TONGUE

The tongue is a bundle of muscles on the floor of the mouth used to manipulate food for chewing and swallowing, and in humans also for enabling speech. Accordingly, in many languages, the word for tongue is used as a word for language, such as the Hebrew *lashon* (the Hebrew *safa*, "lip," also means language and is more commonly used in modern Hebrew). The Latin *lingua* gave rise to the Italian and Ladino *lingua* as well as the English word language, while the Indo-European *dnghu* evolved into the German *zunge*, Yiddish *tsung*, and English tongue.

Animal tongue is rather tough and requires a slow moist cooking. Its dense and velvety texture, beloved by some but unpleasant to others, is different from that of beef muscle. If tongue is not cooked sufficiently, the texture is rubbery, but if it is overcooked, the meat will break down. Most of the tongue is covered with skin, whose thickness varies from front to back. The skin of the tongue can be peeled off easily when the tongue is still warm. Beef tongue is available fresh, pickled, and smoked. Veal and lamb tongues are found only fresh. Pickled and smoked tongues require soaking before cooking and some cooks add a whole potato to the cooking water to extract even more of the salt. Tongue's flavor is somewhat bland, so piquant and lively accompaniments are common. Consequently, after cooking, it is usually thickly sliced and accompanied with mustard or prepared horserad-ish or baked in a sweet-and-sour sauce.

Since beef or lamb heads are rarely available these days, tongue is often served on Rosh Hashanah to symbolize that the diners should be a "head" and not a tail. Tongue with black-eyed peas is a traditional Persian Rosh Hashanah dish. According to Rashi, in the Bible, Abraham prepared three calves for his three guests in order to give each a veal tongue with mustard, reflecting the enduring Ashkenazic con-ception of tongue as a special delicacy. Many Hun-garians like to add a whole tongue to their Sabbath cholent. Generations of Polish grandmothers made tongue with a sweet-and-sour or raisin sauce for spe-cial occasions.

Tongue can still be found in many Jewish delica-tessens, typically cold in sandwiches or occasionally hot in a raisin sauce. Some Ashkenazic households serve it every Friday night as an appetizer. Neverthe-less, its days of starring in Catskills resorts, or being part of the menu for Jewish caterers, and at grand-mother's Sabbath tables have certainly waned. Once a preferred part of an animal, tongue has generally fallen out of favor among American Jews, who, at best, consider it an exotic by-product. To most, it has gone the way of the neighborhood kosher butcher. Instead, today in America, Asians and Mexicans covet this piece of meat, and it has recently become trendy in hip restaurants.

TORTELLI

Tortelli is filled pasta.

Origin: Italy

Other names: ravioli, *torteleti*.

Basic noodles as well as filled pasta spread from China to the Near East. In the twelfth century, they were probably introduced by the Arabs to Italy by way of Sicily. The first record of filled pasta in an Italian source appeared around 1260, which mentioned *tor-telli* (a diminutive form of the Late Latin *torta*, "round bread"), a term that encompassed various filled pasta, including rounds, squares, rectangles, and crescents. Shortly afterward, *tortelli* first appeared in a Jewish source around 1300 in the writings of Kalonymus ben Kalonymus, a Provençal native who spent many years in Rome and included it along with macaroni in a list of dishes served at a fantasy Purim feast. As with many dumpling dishes, it originated as a way of using up leftovers and stretching limited resources—leftover cooked meats and vegetables could be chopped and wrapped up in pasta.

The word ravioli, derived from either the Ital-ian word *raviolo* (little turnip) or *rabiole* (items of little value), was first recorded in 1233 in Nice, where it referred to a pie. In the fourteenth cen-tury in Naples, the cookbook *Liber de Coquina* (c. 1300), incorporating foods from all parts of the pen-insula, contained a recipe for ravioli (as well as the first recipe for lasagna). This early version of ravioli consisted of a meat filling that was wrapped in caul fat and fried; a pastry dough wrapping, also fried, was offered as an alternative. Soon ravioli became a synonym for *tortelli*, a boiled filled pasta. To fur-ther complicate matters, the terms *tortelli* and ravioli are used to denote both boiled as well as deep-fried filled dough. Ravioli, however, are typically made by enclosing a filling between two sheets of thin pasta, then cutting out squares or rounds. Whether called *tortelli* or ravioli, the dish was historically reserved for special occasions.

Italian Jews filled their pasta with meat or cheese as well as various vegetables, notably spinach and beet greens. In the sixteenth century, Conversos fleeing Spain and Sephardim from other parts of the Mediterranean brought with them to Italy their affinity for pumpkin, giving rise to pumpkin-filled *tortelli*. This dish, called (*tortelli di zucca*), is a par-ticular specialty of Mantua in Lombardy; some cooks prefer them earthy and savory with sometimes a little cheese mixed in for a dairy meal, while others add a hint of sweetness with some crushed amaretti (almond macaroons). Spinach is historically a spring and late-summer ingredient and is, therefore, tradi-tional for Purim and Rosh Hashanah, while pump-kin and winter squash are autumn and winter fillings, and are sometimes used to fill round *tortelli* for Rosh Hashanah, as well as the usual square-shaped pasta for Sukkot. Cheese fillings are traditional for Shavuot and Hanukkah. Meat filled pastas tend to be rela-tively small, while those with cheese and vegetables are typically larger.

Tortelli and ravioli are never served alone: meat-filled pasta is typically enjoyed in a broth, while cheese-filled and vegetable-filled versions are usually topped with a delicate sauce, such as butter or tomato.

(See also Pasta)

TRAVADO

Travado is a small, nut-filled, crescent-shaped cookie that is typically dipped into a sugar syrup.

Origin: Greece, Turkey

Other names: *beurekito con muez, boreka de muez.*

Small cookies called *travados* are a favorite eastern Sephardic pastry, a sweet form of *empanadas* and *borekas*. The word *travado* means "joined" or "twist together" in Ladino; in Portuguese, *travado* also means "tornado." Bulgarian Jews call a similar cookie *rosca di alhasu* (filled coil).

Traditionally, the pastries were submerged in a sugar syrup, so the dough itself was not sweet. More recently, a variation emerged in which the soaking syrup is omitted and the cookies are coated with confectioners' sugar, and, to compensate for the lack of syrup, the amount of sugar in the dough is greatly increased. Greeks favor an almond filling, while Turks tend to like walnut. The nuts are frequently accented with orange-blossom water, orange zest, or marmalade.

Since they are labor intensive, *travados* are usually reserved for special occasions, in particular Purim. For Rosh Hashanah, they are made with an almond filling and dipped into a honey syrup, signifying the wish for a sweet and bright (*dulce y aclarada*) New Year. Some Turkish Jews include them in the meal to break the fast of Yom Kippur, along with *pepitada* (melon seed drink) and grapes. These pastries are commonly served with *naa-naa* (mint tea) or Turkish coffee.

(See also Kaab el Ghazal and Ma'amoul)

◄ MIDDLE EASTERN PASTRY CRESCENTS (*TRAVADOS*)

ABOUT 50 COOKIES   [PAREVE]

Dough:

1 cup vegetable oil

½ cup water and 1 teaspoon orange-blossom water
  or ½ teaspoon almond extract; or ½ cup orange
  juice, sweet red wine, or sweet white wine

2 tablespoons sugar

½ teaspoon baking soda

About 3½ cups (17.5 ounces) all-purpose flour, or
  1½ cups whole-wheat flour and about 2 cups
  all-purpose flour

Filling:

2 cups ground walnuts or blanched almonds, or
  1 cup each

½ cup honey; or ½ cup sugar, ¼ cup honey, and
  ¼ cup water

½ teaspoon ground cinnamon

⅛ teaspoon ground cloves or 1 teaspoon grated
  lemon zest (optional)

Syrup:

¾ cup sugar

¾ cup water

¾ cup (9 ounces) honey

1 tablespoon fresh lemon juice

1. Preheat the oven to 350°F. Line 2 large baking sheets with parchment paper or lightly grease the sheets.

2. To make the dough: In a large bowl, combine the oil, water, and sugar. Gradually add the baking soda and enough flour to form a soft, nonsticky dough.

3. To make the filling: In a medium bowl, combine all the ingredients.

4. Divide the dough into 1½-inch balls. On a lightly floured surface, roll out the balls into ⅛-inch-thick rounds, about 2 inches in diameter. Place 1 teaspoon filling in the center of each round, fold a side over to form a half-moon, and crimp the edges to seal. If desired, run a serrated pastry cutter around the curved side. Bend slightly to form a crescent.

5. Place on the prepared baking sheets. Bake until the cookies begin to turn golden, 15 to 25 minutes. Let stand for 5 minutes, transfer the cookies to wire racks, and let cool completely.

6. To make the syrup: In a medium saucepan, heat the sugar and water over medium-low heat, stirring constantly, until the sugar dissolves, about 5 minutes. Increase the heat to medium-high and bring to a boil. Add the honey and lemon juice, reduce the heat to medium, and boil, without stirring, until syrupy, about 10 minutes.

7. Using tongs, dip the cooled *travados*, one at a time, into the warm syrup, completely submerging them for about 15 seconds, then let the excess syrup drip off into the pan. Place on wire racks or a platter and let cool. Store in an airtight container at room temperature for up to 1 week.

TREIBERN

Treibern (a Yiddish noun from the Slavic *trebiti*, "to cleanse"; *nikkur* in Hebrew) is the process of removing the sciatic nerve (*gid hanosheh*) and forbidden fats (*cheilev*) from ritually slaughtered animals. The verb is *treiber.* Since this process is extremely exacting and tedious, Ashkenazim do not use the hindquarter of animals, after the twelfth rib, where most of the forbidden items are located. Other Jewish communities continue to use the hindquarters.

TREIF

Treif ("torn" in Hebrew) is a biblical term meaning an animal killed by a predator. It is also used colloquially to denote all foods and items that are not kosher.

TU B'SHEVAT

Tu b'Shevat (the fifteenth day of the month of Shevat), the New Year for trees (which falls in mid-January to mid-February) is not a festival like the New Year in Tishrei, but rather a biblically significant day. In agriculture-based ancient Israel, this was an especially meaningful occasion, accompanied with singing and dancing. Sephardim, due to the warm climate and early growing season in their locales, have long manifested a deep devotion to the day—they call it *Las Frutus* (The Fruit)—which they express through a large number of customs and even by providing a vacation from school for children. On the day of Tu b'Shevat, Sephardic families customarily visit the homes of relatives, where they are offered a veritable feast, appropriately containing an abundance of fruits and nuts. The children are encouraged to not only partake of the spread, but to take *bolsas de frutas* (bags of fruit) home with them.

The community of kabbalists who made their home in sixteenth-century Safed maintained a profound regard for this minor holiday and developed a new liturgy and rituals for it. An expanded version of these prayers was collected in an eighteenth-century work appropriately called *Peri Etz Hadar* ("Fruit of the Goodly Tree," the biblical name for citron), which described the kabbalistic Tu b'Shevat "Seder" (ceremonial meal). This ceremony, based on the Passover Seder, includes rituals such as drinking four cups of wine—each wine a different type—and sampling at least twelve fruits and nuts; in other versions of the ritual, the number is increased to fifteen, corresponding to the numerical value of *tu*. Iraqi Jews further expanded on the concept, increasing the number to a minimum of one hundred fruits, nuts, grains, and vegetables.

In the Tu b'Shevat Seder, the first cup of wine is white—symbolizing the snows of winter—and it is followed by fruits that have an inedible covering, including nuts, citrus fruits, pineapples, and pomegranates. The second cup is golden/yellow—symbolizing the sap beginning to flow in the trees—and it precedes fruits that have edible coverings but also contain large pits, including apricots, carob, cherries, dates, peaches, plums, and olives. The third cup is pink—symbolizing the blossoms that are just sprouting on the branches—and it is followed by completely edible fruits or those with very small seeds, including apples, berries, figs, grapes, quinces, and pears. The fourth and final cup is a deep red—symbolizing the fertility of the land. Appropriate psalms and Biblical verses referring to fruit and vegetables are recited during the course of the Seder.

In contrast, Tu b'Shevat was only marginally celebrated among Ashkenazim, probably because it fell in the dead of winter in northern climates. The Magen Avraham noted, "The custom in Ashkenaz is to increase the consumption of different types of fruits on this day." Beginning in the late 1900s, with the establishment of agricultural settlements in Israel as well as the growing need to plant trees to rebuild the land, this holiday took on new significance throughout the Jewish world.

Since Tu b'Shevat is a minor holiday, few specific dishes evolved for its celebration, but rather the practice emerged of serving food containing fruits and nuts. There is a widespread custom of eating the *Shevah Minim* ("Seven Species," the five fruits and two grains for which the Land of Israel is praised), either in the order in which they are mentioned in the biblical verse—wheat, barley, grapes, figs, pomegranates, olives, and dates—or in the order of their importance in ancient Israel—wheat, barley, olives or olive oil, dates, grapes or wine, figs, and pomegranates. In addition, many people eat other fruits mentioned in the Bible or associated with Israel, most notably *bokser* (carob), apples, quinces, walnuts, and pistachios. Since almond trees are traditionally the first to bloom, as well as biblically significant, their nuts have special meaning on Tu b'Shevat. Some families serve jam or candy made from etrogim (citrons) that were used during the festival of Sukkot.

Popular Tu b'Shevat dishes include Hungarian wine soup (*borleves*), Moroccan orange salad (*salata latsheen*), Middle Eastern bulgur-stuffed cabbage (*malfoof mahshee*), Bukharan vegetable and fruit stew (*dimlama*), Bukharan baked rice and fruit (*savo*), Persian sweet rice (*shirin polow*), Ashkenazic barley with mushrooms (*gersht un shveml*), Persian carrot omelets (*havij edjeh*), Middle Eastern wheat berry pudding (*ashure*), and German fried dumplings with fruit (*schnitzelkloese*). Fruit strudels and kugels are popular Ashkenazic treats. Turkish Jews enjoy *prehito*, a dish of sweetened cracked wheat, or *kofyas*, a dish of sweetened wheat berries. Syrians serve fruit and nut pastries, such as *ma'amoul* (nut pastries) and *ras ib adjweh* (date pastries).

The weekly Torah portion read on the Sabbath preceding Tu b'Shevat, *Beshallach*, relates the story of the splitting of the sea and the disastrous consequences that befell the Egyptians, who were drowned while pursuing the Israelites. In commemoration of this event, many communities serve dishes with sauces, symbolizing the sea, or other symbolic foods. Italian Jews prepare a dish of pasta in meat sauce called *ruota di faraone* (Pharaoh's wheel). Alsatians serve small dumplings in chicken soup. Due to its proximity to Tu b'Shevat, many dishes served on this Sabbath also contain fruit.

TURKEY

The Book of Kings reveals, "For the king [Solomon] had at sea a navy of Tarshish with the navy of Hiram [king of Israel's northern neighbor, Phoenicia]; once every three years came the navy of Tarshish, bringing gold, silver, ivory, and monkeys, and *tukiyim* [peacocks]." Solomon's navy sailed from the area of modern day Eliat through the Red Sea, bringing back exotic imports from east Asia, including domesticated peacocks. The biblical Hebrew *tuki* probably derived from the Tamil word for that bird, *tokei*. (In modern Hebrew, *tuki* means "parrot" and *tavas*, related to the Greek *taos*, is used for "peacock.")

The ancient Greeks and Romans also knew peafowl (*pavo* in Latin) and, in addition, raised large colorful birds native to the savannas of sub-Saharan Africa, called *melagris* (now known as the guinea fowl). Both of these birds were then a rarity and delicacy. After the fall of the Roman Empire, these exotic birds mostly disappeared from Europe. Then during the medieval period, merchants from the Ottoman Empire began to import the Blue Peafowl from India to Europe. By the fourteenth century, peafowl (the English term derived from the Latin *pavo*) were widespread and served as food on the tables of the European upper class until the arrival of the fleshier American turkey in the sixteenth century.

In 1446, the Portuguese claimed the area of western Africa now known as Guinea-Bissau. Among the items the colonizers took from the region, besides slaves, was the domesticated helmeted guinea fowl, a large roundish bird with a red and blue head, red waddles, and grayish feathers covered with numerous white spots. The Portuguese named it *pintada* (painted), referring to its spots. The French mistook the bird for a native of east Asia, perhaps confusing it with the peafowl or thinking that these two colorful birds came from the same place, and called it '*poule de l'Inde*' (Indian bird) or *dinde*, although the term was eventually switched to *pintade*. Although much of the rest of Europe confused the guinea fowl with an Indian heritage, the English mistook it for an Ottoman bird. When the guinea fowl arrived in England in the early sixteenth century by way of Ottoman merchants, the British took to calling it a turkey-bird, the term first recorded in 1541.

Part of the confusion over the guinea fowl's origin and identity came from the nature of fourteenth and fifteenth century commerce in the Mediterranean, which involved eastern Asian merchandise passing through the Ottoman Empire on its way to Europe. As a result, "turkey" was commonly attached to the name of exotic items. In the sixteenth century, after European countries began developing their sea trade, Ottoman merchants frequently purchased items from the Portuguese and Spanish and then sold them to various European countries. As a result, Italians called the guinea fowl *faraona*, from the Italian word for pharaoh, as the bird reached Italy by way of Egypt, then part of the Ottoman Empire. Since American corn arrived in Italy by way of the Ottomans, it was originally named *grano turco* (Turkish grain), while Hungarians called chilies *törökbors*" (Turkey pepper). The initial European misnomers of the guinea fowl as both Indian bird and turkey bird may have actually been due to Jewish merchants, typically acting as the middle men, mistaking its origin as Indian and using the biblical word for peacock, *tuki*. In any case, for the following two centuries after its arrival in Europe, the large African bird, commonly called Indian bird (or turkey in English), would be confused with the earlier multihued Indian peacock as well as, shortly thereafter, a newly-arrived large, colorful America bird.

There were two species of wild birds in America that would later become known as turkey. *Agiocharis ocellata*, from the Yucatán and northern Guatemala, is a great flyer, though it was never domesticated and was only known to Europeans through reports. The other, more important, species is *Meleagris gallopavo* of Mexico. More than a thousand years ago, Native Americans domesticated the Mexican species, which to casual observers resembles the helmeted guinea fowl. Besides the domesticated bird, there are five wild subspecies, whose ranges once stretched from Mexico to Canada.

Spaniards found this strange but tasty domesticated bird in Mexico and brought it back to Europe around 1519, and it probably reached England in 1541 or perhaps during the 1530s. When this previously unknown American bird originally entered Europe, it was widely confused by many with the guinea fowl and others confused it with the peafowl. Consequently, the Spanish know it as *pavo* and *gallipavo* (from the Latin *gallus*, "peafowl rooster"). The French, initially thinking that Columbus and the Spaniards were bringing these strange items from India and not an unknown continent, or that these were guinea fowl, called the American bird *dinde* (of India), a similar misnomer made its way into Turkish as *hindi*, Yiddish as *indik* and *hendika*, and modern Hebrew as *tarnagol hodu*, all meaning "Indian chicken." The Yiddish term for guinea fowl (the African bird), *perlahener*, was sometimes mistranslated as turkey (the American bird), further confusing the situation. The British initially used the same name, turkey, for both the African and American birds. During the sixteenth century, in the parlance of the common Englishman, turkey came to denote the increasingly common American birds, while guinea hen, the term first recorded in 1578, shifted to the more rare African one. In 1755, Samuel Johnson described turkey, the American native, as "a large domestick fowl brought from Turkey."

When the English colonists arrived in Virginia in 1607 and Massachusetts in 1620, they brought domesticated turkeys with them and were surprised to find the American woods full of wild turkeys—which were smarter, scrawnier, and livelier than the domesticated Mexican ones. Over the centuries, turkeys have been bred from the gaunt, tough forest dwellers into full-breasted birds capable of reaching a massive sixty-five pounds, a size so large that they can no longer procreate naturally, but must be bred through artificial insemination. Selective breeding and more nutritious and purer feed have produced larger birds and shorter growth cycles.

Until the eighteenth century, there was little discussion in Ashkenazic rabbinic literature about turkey or guinea fowl. Then, after the American turkey had become widespread on Jewish tables across Europe, questions and disagreements broke out over the kosher status of both birds. A kosher home is allowed to use any bird that has a *mesorah* (oral tradition) without further investigation. Although some of the Jewish communities of northwest Africa maintained a *mesorah* for the guinea fowl, Ashkenazim had no such tradition and in Europe the guinea fowl was generally considered unkosher. The guinea fowl, like the peafowl, never became widespread in the Ashkenazic parts of Europe and never became fare for the common man, so its kosher status there was a moot point.

On the contrary, the American turkey relatively quickly spread through much of Europe to all segments of society, and a large majority of common Jews accepted the "Indian" bird as kosher. There were a few European rabbis who forbade both the African and American birds for lack of a *mesorah*. Some misidentified the American turkey as the guinea fowl. On the other hand, most authorities believed that the turkey was a relative of the chicken from India, a misconception that was widespread well through the end of the nineteenth century. Some associated the American turkey—which was assumed to have come to England by way of India—with red chickens mentioned in the Talmud and, therefore, considered it acceptable. Even among most of those who understood that the turkey was an American native (*Americanisha huhn*) and had never previously had a *mesorah*, many rabbis contended that it possessed all the appropriate Talmudic signs of a kosher bird and considered it acceptable with a retroactive *mesorah*. Some relied on the approval of Sephardim, who were generally more lenient with establishing a new *mesorah*, while a few contended that it had a valid *mesorah* among the Jews of India. Consequently, the turkey became accepted as kosher although it did not originally have a *mesorah*. Turkey has since emerged as an important part of Jewish cookery and has been embraced by every facet of the community. On the other hand, the guinea fowl, which did have a *mesorah* among some from the Maghreb, is considered questionable or unkosher by most Ashkenazic authorities, and generally not allowed.

The first American Jewish cookbook, *Jewish Cookery* (Philadelphia, 1871), mentioned turkey first in its list of poultry, followed by chickens, geese, and ducks. The author's recipes all called for whole turkeys, which were prepared either by roasting or boiling.

Despite turkey's New World origins, no American country leads the world in turkey consumption. From almost the time of its inception as a modern state, Israel has consumed more turkey per capita than any other nation, far more than Americans. Part of turkey's success in Israel is due to a lack of grazing land for cattle, which creates a need for alternative sources of animal protein. Turkey provided a less expensive alternative to meat and could be transformed into pastrami, packaged coated strips, ground meat, kebabs, schnitzel, and *shawarma* (in place of lamb). Since the fatty dark meat works best in *shawarma*, Israelis developed a preference for it, and much of the white meat is typically shipped to Europe. Whole turkeys are rarely cooked in homes or restaurants or even sold commercially in Israel. Instead, turkey is usually found in parts or ground.

Israeli turkeys, once raised by small farms, now come from large facilities. Established in 1971, Ramit in Hadera is Israel's preeminent force in turkey, producing 80 percent of the breeding stock in the domestic market; it also produces turkeys for parts of Europe and is Israel's largest egg producer. The Israeli turkey industry suffered a blow in 2006, when a bird flu outbreak forced producers to destroy many birds. However, the country's quick reaction to the disease mitigated the potential damage, while demand was met from birds outside the infection radius. The worldwide economic slump of 2009 lessened export demand, flooding the local market with excess white meat. Still, Israel remains passionate about turkey.

(See also Bird and Schnitzel)

TURMERIC
Turmeric, a member of the ginger family native to southeastern Asia, is the orange-colored rhizome of a perennial herb. After the plant is harvested in the winter, the rhizome is boiled for up to an hour or steamed, then dried and ground. Today, it is grown in China, Japan, Java, and Haiti, but India remains the world's major producer and user.

Ground turmeric is a golden powder that imparts a rich saffron-like color, although it lacks saffron's flavor and aroma. There are two main varieties: Alleppey, which has an orange-yellow color, and Madras, which is a bright yellow. Turmeric imparts a slightly bitter, musky flavor to foods. The color and flavor are more intense and pungent when it is sautéed in oil before being added to other ingredients.

Turmeric is particularly popular in Indian, Persian, Yemenite and Moroccan cuisines. Indians use it in practically every vegetable, legume, and meat dish and it is an essential component of curry powder. Turmeric may be the root mentioned in the Mishnah, *zargun* (Persian for "gold-colored," the Farsi is *zardchub*). By the early medieval period, turmeric was already an essential spice in Persia, where it was common in *ash* (soups) and *khoresht* (meat stews). It also tints the Jewish *gundi* (chickpea and chicken meatballs). The spice was subsequently spread westward by the Arabs, and the name became *kurkum* in Arabic and Hebrew, a confusion with the ancient word for crocus, *karkom*, the source of saffron. In Mizrachi and Sephardic communities, turmeric is added to Sabbath stews, soups, poultry, rice, and eggs. In Morocco, it enhances tagines, stews, and salads. Because of its preservative effects, turmeric became common as a pickling spice. In America, turmeric is commonly used to give a yellow color to prepared mustard.

TURNIP
Among the world's first recorded recipes, all imprinted in cuneiform on a four-thousand-year-old Sumerian tablet, involved the cooking of turnips. The recipe stated, "No meat is needed. Turnips. Boil water. Throw fat in. Add onion, dorsal thorn [an unknown seasoning], coriander, cumin, and *kanasu* [a legume]. Squeeze leek and garlic and spread juice over dish. Add onion and mint." Since the inscribed recipes were intended for the upper class, turnips were obviously considered a choice food at that time.

The turnip, a cool-weather crop that is drought tolerant, was one of the earliest cultivated vegetables. This member of the cabbage family has fleshy tuberous taproots with a sharp flavor and coarse texture. The greens, which have a mustardy flavor that intensifies as the leaves grow larger, were also consumed during the autumn and winter and used for animal fodder. The root, which has a white flesh, comes in numerous shapes, sizes, and exterior colors. Fresh young turnips can be eaten raw and are added to salads, while more mature roots must be cooked or pickled.

Rutabaga, also called yellow turnip and swede, is a round relative of the turnip that was first recorded in 1620. It is probably a hybrid of the turnip and a form of cabbage. It has a tan peel with a violet neck and orange-yellow flesh and contains more vitamins than white turnips.

Turnips, which thrive in temperate climates, soon spread far and wide from their home in western Asia. Cave paintings in France depict prehistoric man boiling these roots in clay pots, and evidence of turnips has been found in Chinese caves from the same period. Well before Roman times, turnips along with barley served as the staple of the European diet. The Roman author Pliny the Elder noted that "turnip prevents the effects of famine." He also pointed out another attribute—it could be left in the ground until the next harvest.

The Hebrew word for turnip is *lefet*, derived from *lahfaht* (to twist/to turn), connoting the action of harvesting a root vegetable, which is twisted from the ground. During the Talmudic period, the word *lefet*, specifically denoting "turnip," was sometimes also used generically to mean "vegetables," since the turnip was then the most common vegetable, while *leaftan* came to mean "relish."

As history progressed and more vegetables became available, however, the turnip was generally disdained by the elite and relegated to poor person's food and animal fodder. This attitude is reflected in the Talmudic statement, "Woe to the house where the turnip is common." In the early nineteenth century, the potato, a native of South America, supplanted the turnip, particularly in Europe and America. As a result, few Westerners today are aware of the turnip's true role throughout much of human history. Nevertheless, turnips remain important in much of Asia, where they are made into pickles (*turshi*) and added to stews. Turnip stews and soups are commonplace in Iran, Afghanistan, and northern India. *Shalgham* (boiled turnips with date honey) is a popular Iraqi treat and is sold by street vendors.

(See also Pickle and Turshi)

TURSHI

Turshi is a vegetable pickled with vinegar and salt, but it also denotes the most common type of Middle Eastern pickle, turnip.

Origin: Middle East

Other names: Arabic: *mekhelal*; Balkans: *turshi*; Farsi: *torshi*; Hebrew: *chamutzim*; Turkish: *tursu*.

Pickles were an essential food throughout the ancient Middle East. Since the time of the earliest records on cuneiform tablets, turnips have been the most common pickles in the region. More than twenty-four hundred years ago, the Chinese mastered the technique of lacto-fermentation, in which only salt is used to pickle vegetables. Ancient and early medieval Middle Easterners were unfamiliar with this technique and, consequently, Middle Eastern vegetables were pickled with vinegar and a little salt, which was added to forestall the growth of bacteria. Therefore, *turshi* (*torsh* means "sour" in Farsi) tend to be more acidic than Ashkenazic pickles. The variation in which salt is used with little or no vinegar, a practice more common in Turkey than Iran, is known as *shoor* ("salty" in Farsi).

The Talmudic term *leaftan* (relish), derived from the Hebrew word for turnip (*lefet*), denotes both pickled turnips and pickled vegetables in general. The Talmud teaches, "One is not permitted to recite the blessing [Hamotzi] and break bread before salt or *leeftan* [relish] is placed before each and every one [of the diners]." In the ancient Middle East, bread was very different from the refined loaves of the modern world—bread was typically coarse and hard, as it was frequently made from barley or emmer that was coarsely ground. Consequently, to make the bread palatable, people ate it with a relish or salt.

Among Ashkenazim, the cucumber is the most popular type of pickle. The turnip still serves that role in much of the Middle East, where it is called *turshi left*. The Iraqi cookbook *Kitab al-Tabikh* (Book of Dishes) by Muhammad ibn al-Hasan Al-Baghdadi, written in 1226 but based on a collection of ninth-century Persian-inspired recipes, included a recipe for turnips pickled in vinegar with honey, saffron, and herbs. The Turks picked up the Farsi term *torshi* and the pickles and variations of the name spread throughout their Empire; *turshi* were enjoyed in the Balkans and by Sephardim in the Mediterranean. The term *turshi* also became common in the region extending east through the Persian sphere of influence, including Afghanistan. In addition to turnips, other common types of *turshi* include beets, cabbage, cauliflower, peppers, green tomatoes, and zucchini. Mixed pickles are *turshi khodar.*

Unlike many other prepared foods, which most people now purchase in stores, *turshi* are still made in a vast number of households and restaurants throughout the Middle East and Balkans. Massive jars of *turshi* are often seen in the windows and at the counters of restaurants. Vegetables are pickled in large glazed-clay vessels and stored, alongside *sharbats* (fruit syrups) and date honey, in cool, dark cellars. A few slices of raw beet are typically added to tint the turnips pink, or occasionally turmeric is used for a yellow hue. A dark red color is usually an indication that red food coloring has been added. Many people prefer pickles with a pronounced garlic flavor, but some also like a little heat from small hot red chilies. In Turkey and the Balkans, cooks generally make a mélange of pickled vegetables.

Pickled turnips, accompanied with ouzo or *raki*, are a mainstay of a *mezze* (appetizer assortment); they are also an essential condiment at most meals. A few slices of pickled turnips are frequently added to falafel sandwiches for a little crunch and zing.

(See also Pickle and Salt)

TZIMMES

Tzimmes is a sweetened root vegetable stew that sometimes includes meat.

Origin: Germany

Other names: *tsimmes.*

Cooking root vegetables, primarily parsnips and turnips, with honey was a common medieval German practice. Cooking meats with vegetables was another venerable medieval practice of central Europe. By the thirteenth century, yellow carrots (originally they were violet) were being planted in France and Germany, but remained a rarity and luxury item through the following century. Around the early fifteenth century, after the flavor of the roots had improved through selection and hybridization over the centuries, cultivation grew widespread and carrots became a significant European food. At this time, the carrot emerged as one of the foremost vegetables in the cookery of central European Jews, a position it would shortly achieve

among the Jews of eastern Europe as well. Also at that time, a soon-to-be-widespread honey-sweetened carrot stew emerged among German Jews as a Sabbath side dish. This dish was initially differentiated from the carrot stews of their non-Jewish neighbors by its lengthy cooking time, which allowed it to be served hot on the Sabbath.

Because of the prohibition of cooking on the Sabbath and the Jewish predilection for hot food on that day, Jews have always had a particular fondness for slow-cooked foods. In addition to mellowing and harmonizing the ingredients, the long, slow cooking time and moist environment break down the connective tissue of tough cuts of meat, transforming them into a tender, flavorful dish. One of the most popular of these dishes among Ashkenazim is tzimmes, a food that was intentionally designed to be heated for a long time for Friday night dinner or even Saturday lunch. The word tzimmes—and a number of its permutations—is probably derived from two Yiddish words, *zum* (a contraction of the preposition *zu* and the article *dem,* meaning "to the") and *essen* (eat), which were combined to form a word meaning "side dish." Others contend that it is derived from the Middle High German word *zuomuose,* denoting a side dish, which in essence is the same idea. In any case, the vegetables were sometimes cooked with meat, transforming tzimmes into a more substantial dish.

As tzimmes spread eastward, it gained even greater popularity, providing a hearty, hot dish to combat the cold weather of northeastern Europe, and emerging as a mainstay of Sabbath cooking and Jewish culture. In a 1970 collection of memoirs about the town of Krynki, Poland, by former residents living "in Israel and the Diaspora," Berl Zakon reminisced about the lifestyle in pre–World War II Krynki:

"Sabbath morning, coming from praying, the men receive a veritable feast for lunch, which they look forward to the entire week. Here in Krinik the Jews knew nothing about dieting and people ate as an appetizer mashed eggs with onions, radish with chicken fat; after that—fatty meat (people would complain that the fattest meats would be sold to the wealthy, not to the poor) and a cholent with noodle kugel (even with two kugels), tzimmes, and so forth. The Krinik revolutionaries were freethinkers. But as for the resurrection of the dead, they believed a sign, they would say. The men lay down for a nap after such a heavy meal, and later got up and were healthy."

Sholem Aleichem wrote of a *shadchan* (marriage broker) who describes how well she was treated at the home of a hopeful bride: "They serve me the best portions of the meat and feed me tzimmes even on weekdays." In another of his tales, a Vilna housewife prepares her *yontefdiker tzimmes* (holiday tzimmes) in the morning and leaves it to cook in the stove of the shared sukkah in a communal courtyard while she visits an ill sister. By the time she returns before dinner, the contents have gradually vanished.

Tzimmes certainly did not remain limited to carrots and turnips, nor was it restricted only to the Sabbath. Over the centuries, various new ingredients, as well as symbolic touches and meanings, were added. Tzimmes emerged as the prototypical Ashkenazic Rosh Hashanah dish. This holiday's fare was traditionally enhanced with honey to symbolically usher in a sweet year; in addition, the Yiddish word for carrot is *mehren*, which is similar to the word "multiply/increase," so tzimmes represented good wishes for the new year. Also, the shape of sliced carrots in the tzimmes resembled golden coins, auguring a prosperous year, and various added fruits represented a sweet and fruitful year. During the harvest festival of Sukkot, tzimmes' vegetables and fruits served as apt reminders of the earth's bounty. Vegetarian versions were sometimes served as a side dish at the meal before Yom Kippur, but generally these were made without spices because it was customary to eat bland dishes before the fast. Cooks began making it for Passover as well, as none of its ingredients were prohibited during the holiday. A *farfel tzimmes* was sometimes served on Shavuot—it was made with pasta nuggets, dried plums, and honey, but no vegetables or meat. *Epl tzimmes* became an Eastern Yiddish term for applesauce.

The vegetables in tzimmes are never left whole, but rather cut into chunks or slices. Beginning in the mid-nineteenth century, inexpensive white potatoes were frequently added as well, as a way of stretching the dish. In America, sweet potatoes, which share many of the carrot's attributes, became a popular ingredient, frequently replacing white potatoes. Ukrainians add chickpeas on Rosh Hashanah, com-bining two traditional holiday symbols in one dish. Lithuanians, in particular, continued to combine only carrots and turnips, while Romanians and Galitzianers began adding a variety of dried fruits, especially plums (*flaumen tzimmes*) and dried or fresh apples, for additional sweetness and flavor. In Europe, large dried sour plums, once available at any Jewish appetizing store, were a standard addition, giving the dish a slight sweet-and-sour accent. To replicate this flavor today, many American cooks add some sweet-tart dried apricots with the sweeter American dried plums. Pineapple is another American contribution. Some people cook a *kishke* (stuffed derma) or *helzel* (stuffed poultry neck) in the tzimmes along with or in place of the meat, while Lithuanians often simmer *knaidlach* (dumplings) atop the stew.

Obviously, there is no one standard way of making tzimmes. Some recipes call for whole cuts of meat, others direct cutting the meat into cubes, and some are vegetarian. In some modern versions chicken is substituted. Many tzimmes are seasoned with cinnamon or a few other spices, while others call simply for salt and pepper. There are even some cooks who use paprika. On the other hand, tzimmes can be as simple as cooked carrots and honey. A tzimmes containing meat, fruit, and any other possibilities is a *gantze tzimmes*, which is also any deluxe version or big production. (*Gantze* is Yiddish for "entire," as in *gantze megilla*, "the whole story.")

Tzimmes should be sweet, but not cloying. The flavor of the autumn vegetables should predominate. Tzimmes was originally simmered over a flame or more likely the embers of a fire, but with the spread of the home oven in the nineteenth century, a baked rendition became quite popular. More recently, slow-cooker versions have emerged, which are simmered all day on a low setting. Tzimmes recipes are typically for a considerable quantity, as they are intended for large, festive meals—using a substantial mass of ingredients actually enhances the ultimate flavor. Whatever the ingredients, tzimmes' main requirement is a long cooking time over a low heat to blend the multifarious flavors.

In Yiddish, "tzimmes" also came to mean "a fuss," or more specifically, to make a fuss over something minor, as in *machan a tzimmes fun* (to make a fuss out of). Perhaps this expression referred not so much to all the peeling, chopping, stirring, and stewing involved, but rather to the Jewish housewife's detailed attention to what ingredients went into her dishes and how they got onto her table, as she took a basically simple procedure and a few simple ingredients and made a tzimmes out of it.

Tzimmes and all of its meanings arrived in America with eastern European immigrants in the late nineteenth century. The word was first mentioned in America in 1882, in reference to an incident at the Ward's Island Shelter for new eastern European Jewish immigrants run by the Hebrew Emigrant Aid Society (HEAS). During a Jewish holiday in October, when tzimmes was being served, one of the waiters refused to serve one of the immigrants due to a previous argument. When the assistant superintendent of the shelter threatened the immigrant, he threw a nearby bowl of tzimmes, which catalyzed a fight, called the Tzimmes Revolt, involving all of the immigrants, whom were already angered by the poor conditions and treatment in the shelter. The immigrants elected a leadership council by the time order was restored. The superintendent and his assistant were fired and the shelter was closed in 1883. HEAS ceased operations the following year. Tzimmes is one of those beloved comfort foods that fail to command the respect it deserves, perhaps because of its funny-sounding name or unpretentious nature. It is among the Ashkenazic dishes that has retained popularity in Israel, where it frequently appears at hotel buffets. In America, significantly more meat, such as an entire brisket, was cooked in the dish. Indicative of its popularity, the word tzimmes has even entered the English language and can be found in most dictionaries. Many non-Jewish vegetarian American and British cookbooks now include recipes for tzimmes, although the authors sometimes forget the most important spice—the long cooking time.

ASHKENAZIC STEWED ROOT VEGETABLES WITH BEEF (*FLEISHIG TZIMMES*)

6 TO 8 SERVINGS AS A MAIN COURSE   [MEAT]

- 3 pounds beef brisket, flanken, or chuck; or 4 pounds short ribs (whole or cut into 6 to 8 pieces)
- 2 tablespoons vegetable oil or schmaltz
- 2 medium onions, halved and sliced
- 1 to 1½ pounds carrots, sliced into rounds
- 2 pounds (6 medium) sweet potatoes, peeled and quartered; or 1 pound sweet potatoes and 1 pound (3 medium) white potatoes, peeled and sliced; or 12 ounces parsnips, peeled and sliced
- 2 to 3 cups pitted prunes, or 1½ cups prunes and 1½ cups dried apricots or peaches (optional)
- ½ to ¾ cup honey, granulated sugar, or brown sugar
- 2 bay leaves
- About 1 teaspoon table salt or 2 teaspoons kosher salt
- Ground black pepper to taste
- ¾ teaspoon ground cinnamon
- 2 whole cloves, pinch of ground cloves, or dash of ground nutmeg
- ½ teaspoon ground ginger (optional)
- About 4 cups water, or 2 cups water and 2 cups orange juice

1. Pat the meat dry with paper towels. In a large pot, roasting pan, or heat-proof dish, heat the oil over medium-high heat. Add the meat, without crowding the pan, and brown on all sides, about 10 minutes. Remove the meat. Add the onions and sauté until soft and translucent, scraping up any browned bits on the bottom, about 10 minutes.

2. Return the meat to the pot. Add the carrots, sweet potatoes, optional prunes, honey, bay leaves, salt, pepper, cinnamon, cloves, and, if using, ginger. Add enough water to cover.

3. Cover and bake in a 325°F oven or simmer over a low heat until the meat is tender, 2½ to 3 hours.

U

UDDER

The udder is the mammary organ of ruminants; it contains both muscle tissue and glandular meat. Throughout history, it was primarily peasant fare. The texture and flavor of cow's udder when cooked is akin to that of another gland, the pancreas.

The udder was commonly mentioned in rabbinic literature, as any milk found inside a slaughtered animal is not included in the biblical prohibition of meat and milk. The Sages of the Sanhedrin, however, decreed that the milky substance in the udder, because of its similarity to real milk, could not be cooked or eaten with meat. To avoid the act, all the milk had to be carefully removed from the udder before it was cooked. To prepare it, cooks cut two deep perpendicular gashes into the udder, squeeze out any milk, then wash it thoroughly. Ashkenazim and Sephardim also require it to be prepared like liver, so it is sprinkled lightly with salt, broiled under an open flame, and finally well rinsed. This type of practical information, once passed from generation to generation through experience in the kitchen, has largely been lost among Ashkenazim,

as few westerners prepare or eat udder and it is at best considered exotic.

The story was quite different until recently. In the past, Ashkenazim and Yemenites prized udder—*eiter* in Yiddish and *kechal* in rabbinic Hebrew—over many other types of offal. Udder was generally reserved for special occasions such as holidays, for which it was roasted with some liquid or stewed for an extended time to soften it. The first American Jewish cookbook, *Jewish Cookery* (Philadelphia, 1871), included this note: "The fillet of the cow-calf is generally preferred for the udder." As late as the early twentieth century, stewed udder remained a common dish among American Jews, even those who managed to make it to the middle class. Thus Regina Frischwasser, food columnist for the *Jewish Daily Forward*, included "Stewed Udder and Vegetables" in her *Jewish American Cook Book* (New York, 1945). America's tastes and butchery, however, were quickly changing, and today udder tends to end up processed into sausages. Consumption of udder does, however, continue in some Mizrachi households and a few restaurants in Israel.

V

VANILLA

Of the more than thirty-five thousand members of the orchid family, the only plants that produce an edible fruit are those belonging to the genus *Vanilla* (from the Spanish for "little sheath"). The flowers of a delicate climbing green-yellow orchid native to Central America form a single long thin pod filled with a black pulp and numerous tiny seeds. After about six weeks, the green pods begin to turn yellow at the tip, a sign of ripeness. After harvesting, producers cure the relatively bland pods by placing them under blankets, which causes them to sweat; this process develops the characteristic vanilla flavor. By the end of the two- to six-month curing process, the pods are shriveled and brown but still supple. Proper processing is vital in achieving vanilla's full flavor. The pods are then graded according to quality and moisture content. Vanilla, due to the labor-intensive process, follows only saffron as the world's most expensive flavoring.

The vanilla pod and seeds contain around four hundred organic flavor components, the primary one being vanillin. Vanilla adds warm undertones and subtle dimensions to a dish. Beyond adding its own flavor, vanilla, like salt, also serves as a flavor enhancer and its absence from a dish can be very noticeable. In particular, vanilla heightens the flavor of chocolate, softens acids, such as lemon and pineapple, and mellows the flavor of eggs.

For much of its history, vanilla has been intertwined with chocolate. Vanilla was originally cultivated by the Totonaco Indians of the eastern coast of Mexico. After the Aztecs conquered the Totonacos, they demanded vanilla as part of their tribute. The Aztecs mixed the vanilla with cacao beans, another Central American gift, to make a drink called *xocolatl* (bitter water). In 1520, the Aztecs and their emperor, Montezuma, were in turn conquered by Hernando Cortés. After tasting chocolate and deeming it to be delicious, Cortés shipped cacao beans and vanilla pods to Europe. Besides its use in cocoa, vanilla was initially considered a "hot" food as a medicinal ingredient in the medieval European theory of humors. In 1602, Hugh Morgan, apothecary to Elizabeth I, suggested the use of vanilla as a flavoring by itself beyond its role in cocoa. Vanilla was on its way to becoming the world's favorite flavoring.

The Native Americans refused to share their secrets for growing and processing vanilla with the Spanish, Dutch, and French, but did so with some Jews. Sephardim and Conversos living in Central America, who frequently served as translators between the Spanish, Dutch, and English and local natives, learned the secrets of vanilla from the Indians whom they befriended. A pair of Jewish brothers, David and Rafael Mercado of Pomeroon (now French Guiana), had developed the machinery and processes for refining sugarcane, but then the local Dutch authorities prohibited them from continuing their sugar business. The brothers turned instead to the production of vanilla and cocoa in Mexico, which they controlled from Pomeroon, until the arrival of the French in 1690. Besides developing positive relations with Native Americans, Sephardim living in French Guiana and the Caribbean islands of Jamaica, Suriname, and Barbados, established commercial routes with Conversos in Central and South America, many of whom were relatives. They also traded with Sephardim in the Old World, notably in the commercial centers of Amsterdam, Bordeaux, Genoa, Leghorn (Livorno), London, Venice, the Ottoman Empire, and eventually Calcutta. In due course, Ashkenazim also entered some of these businesses. Despite occasional economic oppression by the authorities, from the sixteenth through eighteenth centuries, Jewish merchants, by keeping the vanilla process a secret and through their unparalleled contacts, held a virtual monopoly on the production and trade of vanilla, as along with many other New World products, including allspice, cocoa, indigo, and much of the sugarcane. As a result, in the eighteenth century, there were more Jews and synagogues in Jamaica than in the entire Thirteen Colonies and Canada combined.

At the beginning of the nineteenth century, the French smuggled some vanilla vines from Mexico to Réunion, an island in the Indian Ocean once called Ile de Bourbon. The vine flourished in its new home, but since the bean pod could only be produced through pollination by special bees (the tiny melipone), the pod remained unique to Mexico. Then in 1840, Tahitians found a way to artificially pollinate the orchid by using a thin bamboo stick to move a membrane separating the stigma from the anther (male organ), thereby releasing the pollen. Soon the vanilla bean was being grown in the Indian Ocean area—Réunion, Madagascar, the Seychelles, and the Comoros—as well as other places with moist tropical climates, such as Tahiti, Indonesia, and Tonga.

In order to transfer vanilla's mellow flavor and aroma to baked goods, Europeans began to insert a bean into a container of sugar so that the surrounding crystals could absorb the vanilla's essence. Vanilla sugar is still extremely popular in central Europe, where it is used in baking instead of vanilla extract, as well as to flavor other desserts and coffee.

In the mid-nineteenth century, as vanilla became more available, pharmacists began to macerate the pods in alcohol to add a little to medicine syrups to mask off flavors. Soon people realized the value of vanilla extract in baking and cooking, and it quickly supplanted rose water. Vanilla beans possess a sweet tone and rounder flavor lacking in vanilla extract. Beans from various locations, as well as extracts made from them, have subtle differences in flavor based on soil and style of curing.

Imitation vanilla, an inexpensive substitute for vanilla extract, is made from only one flavor component, either USP vanillin, derived from cloves or the pulp of coniferous trees, or ethyl vanillin, derived from coal tar. It lacks vanilla's complexity and rich flavor. In addition, when a food containing vanillin is frozen, it has a bitter aftertaste.

(See also Chocolate)

VARENIK/VARENIKES
Varenik is a stuffed half-moon pasta.
Origin: Ukraine
Other names: Bessarabia and Ukraine: *varenyk*;
  Poland: *pierog, pirog*; Russia: *pelmen*; Slovakia:
  piroh.

Varenikes are a quintessential Ukrainian comfort food, inspiring songs and memories. In 1954, Mark Olf, one of America's most prominent Yiddish singers and composers, recorded the song, *"Die Mame Kacht Varenikes"* (The Mama Cooks the *Varenikes*).

The contemporary Israel-based singer and musician Samson Kemelmakher, who was born in Moldova in the former Soviet Union in 1953, began his Yiddish song, *"Yidishe Maykholim"* (Jewish Foods) with the line *"Varnishkes mit kaese un mit puter* [noodles with cheese and with butter], on Shavuot, my mother gave me." The chorus was, *"Yidishe Maykholim,* you are in my memory, my mother used to cook and bake. I will never forget, *geshmak geven dos esn* [how tasty the food was]."

By the sixteenth century, noodles and filled pasta dumplings reached eastern Europe from central Asia, probably as a result of incursions by the Tatars—(Mongolian tribes) who overran Ukraine beginning in 1240 with the sacking of Kiev—or contacts with central Asian traders. They were a dramatic innovation because boiling strips of dough in water was far cheaper than the previous method of deep-frying them in fat. Ukrainians called noodles *lokshyna*, while eastern Ashkenazim used the similar term *lokshen*, both from a Persian word for noodles. Poles called their filled pasta half-moons *pierogi*, and the Yiddish word became *pirogen*. Meanwhile, the predominant Ashkenazic name for filled pasta triangles became kreplach. In Russia and Ukraine, the half-moon dumplings became known as *vareniki*, from the Slavic adjective *varenyi*, "boiled"; thus the word literally meant "boiled one."

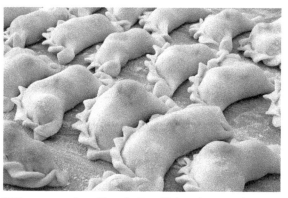

With potatoes and cracklings for Hanukkah or cheese for Shavuot or even with fruit or vegetable fillings, half-moon-shaped pasta called varenikes *are the favorite comfort food for Ukrainian Jews.*

Varenikes filled with mashed potato, the most common filling, were usually mixed with fried onions; for very special occasions, notably Hanukkah, the potatoes were enhanced with *gribenes* (cracklings)—this combination was called *varenikes mit griben*. In the late spring through summer, dumplings were filled with curd cheese (*varenikes mit kaese*); this was a popular Shavuot dish and another special treat for Hanukkah. A beloved indulgence was fillings made from seasonal fruit—most prominently sour cherries, berries, and Italian plums—and fruit preserves; fruit-filled *varenikes* were often accompanied with sour cream. Other fillings included cabbage and mushrooms; these *varenikes* were typically pareve and were served with fried onions, although sometimes they were fried in schmaltz.

In Poland, some people employ the term *varenikes* to specify fruit-filled pirogen and kreplach.

In addition, at some point cooks figured out that it was simpler to mix cooked noodles with fillings, rather than to craft each dumpling; this innovation resulted in unfilled flat pasta squares and rectangles known in Yiddish as *varnishkes*. Later in America, where immigrants were exposed to the Italian pasta farfalle (butterflies), the term *varnishkes* came to denote bowtie pasta. The most famous dish made with pasta squares and bowties is *kashe mit varnishkes*, known in America as *kasha varnishkes*, which is pasta mixed with cooked buckwheat groats. In addition, *varnishkes* are also commonly tossed *mit kaese* (with cheese).

(See also Kasha Varnishkes, Kreplach, Lokshen, and Pirog)

VINEGAR

Vinegar, a word derived from the Old French *vin aigre* (sour wine), is the world's most important condiment—unless salt is counted as one—as well as one of the earliest preservatives. Its discovery was most certainly a fortunate accident, the result of the exposure of wine and beer to naturally occurring bacteria in the air. Not wanting to waste even seemingly spoiled food, the ancients found that the sour yet refreshing liquid was a boon to dishes and food preservation.

Vinegar, a mixture of acetic acid and water, is produced when bacteria metabolize alcohol. Technically, any spirit containing less than 18 percent alcohol can naturally become vinegar when infected by certain airborne bacteria. The results of this method of fermentation, however, are rather inconsistent. Therefore, vinegar is usually made by adding a bacterial culture called a "mother"—it is the slimy film that forms on top of vinegar" and, when it grows heavy, sinks to the bottom—to alcoholic beverages, such as wine, hard cider, and malt.

Red wine vinegar is a tangy, full-bodied type made from red grapes, such as Burgundy and Pinot Noir, and used in salads, marinades, and sauces. White wine vinegar is made from white grapes, such as Sauvignon Blanc and Chardonnay. Cider vinegar is an amber-colored, sharp, fruity vinegar made from fermented apple cider; its bite is ideal for condiments and pickled fruits. White vinegar is made from ethyl alcohol distilled from grain, and is unacceptable for Passover. Malt vinegar is a mild and slightly sweet type made from malted barley, generally in the form of soured ale, and is also unacceptable for Passover.

Before the arrival of lemons, vinegar served as the primary souring agent in much of Europe and western Asia. Vinegar has long held a conspicuous position in the Jewish pantry. In biblical and Talmudic times, vinegar (*chometz* in Hebrew, literally "sour") was an important flavoring, preservative, and medicine. It was essential for various Sabbath salads, as the acid served to preserve the produce even in hot climates. Sephardim typically used wine vinegars (*vinagre* in Ladino), while Ashkenazim rarely had access to anything other than *epl essig* (cider vinegar) or *rosl* (beet vinegar).

VISHNIAK

Vishniak or *wishniak*, from the Polish *wisznia* (cherry tree), is a liqueur made from sour cherries that is very popular in Poland, Ukraine, and Byelorussia. It is rather sweet and syrupy, unlike the Alsatian kirsch. *Vishniak* was usually made at home using seasonal sour cherries in June and left to macerate with sugar and vodka in the cellar for at least three months. It would be ready in time for Rosh Hashanah and would last through Hanukkah or possibly for several years. If there was a celebration in town, such as a wedding, friends and neighbors would donate a bottle from their supply of *vishniak* to enliven the event.

W

WALNUT

In terms of world production, the most important of all nuts today is the walnut, the oily seed of a deciduous temperate-zone tree native to southwest Asia. Exploration of the Shanidar caves in northern Iraq revealed evidence of human consumption of walnuts in prehistoric times. Wild walnuts had a thick shell and small kernel, but due to artificial selection and natural hybridization over the millennia, the cultivated descendants of one variety, now called Persian walnut or English walnut, developed a large kernel with a relatively thin shell. At maturity, the green fleshy fruit splits, revealing the familiar wrinkled tan nut inside. According to Pliny and other Romans, walnuts reached Greece and Rome by way of Persia. The Romans in turn spread the walnut throughout Europe and eventually the nut found its way into nearly every country. Thus when introduced by the Romans to England, it was called *wealhhnutu* in Old English (foreign nut), which was later pronounced walnut.

The walnut, which reached Israel by at least 2000 BCE, is mentioned only once in the Bible, in a line in Song of Songs: "I went down to the *egoz* [walnut] garden." The Hebrew *egoz*, cognate of the Arabic *joz*, derives from "pair," as the kernel grows as two sections. Walnuts only became widespread in Israel during the Second Commonwealth, but became so common that *egoz* emerged as the generic Hebrew word for nut. Rabbinic literature is replete with references to the walnut, in which its characteristics are described in great detail. The Mishnah recognized three varieties of walnuts: hard-shelled, medium-shelled, and soft-shelled, the last being the most important. Walnut branches, along with palm and pine, were preferred for the fire of the altar in the Temple. The Talmud advised giving nuts to children on the eve of Passover to help keep them awake during the Seder. In Talmudic times, walnut shells were tossed in front of a bride and groom as a symbol of fruitfulness and prosperity. This may have evolved into the enduring German custom of *aufruf*, throwing nuts and dried fruits at the groom on the Sabbath before his wedding. The *egoz* became a major symbol of medieval Kabbalah, with both strong sexual and intellectual motifs. In 2006, drawing from these venerable traditions, Canadian composer Moshe Denburg created the musical piece *El Ginat Egoz* (Into the Walnut Garden), evoking vineyards, pomegranates, and love that is sometimes misplaced.

In 1956, the Northern Command of the Israel Defense Forces established a reconnaissance unit of the Golani Brigade to protect the northern frontier, naming it Egoz. Following the 1967 War, Egoz was assigned to prevent terrorist infiltration from Jordan, Syria, and especially Lebanon. Sayeret Egoz was disbanded in 1973, but in 1994, Egoz was the name given to an elite covert Israeli squad charged with dealing with Hezbollah guerillas in southern Lebanon.

Today, California, France, Italy, and Georgia (of the former Soviet Union) are major walnut growers and consumers. Arguably, no culture loves this nut more than the Georgians, who utilize it as a flavoring agent as well as thickener. Sephardim add walnuts to such dishes as *sazan* (Greek carp in walnut sauce), *prehito* (Turkish wheat pudding), *mustachudos* (walnut crescents), baklava, *trigona* (phyllo nut triangles), *tishpishti* (semolina cake), and *torta de muez* (walnut cake). Whereas Mizrachim and Sephardim typically had a choice of nuts, often opting for almonds and pistachios, Ashkenazim generally had only the walnut or occasionally the hazelnut. Not surprisingly, walnuts are common to a host of Ashkenazic baked goods, including those made for Passover. Some Jewish communities, especially eastern Ashkenazim, incorporate walnuts in the Passover charoset. Eastern Ashkenazim, however, have a custom of not eating nuts on Rosh Hashanah.

Walnut has a rich, pronounced flavor. However, the walnut's thin skin (pellicle) contains tannin that produces an astringent aftertaste that some people find off-putting. Toasting brings out the walnut's flavor.

Walnuts are also cold-pressed to produce an oil with a rich nut flavor. Walnut oil is primarily used in salads, as it complements most greens, but occasionally finds its way into baked goods.

(See also Bazha and Nut)

WARKA

By at least the fifteenth century, Turks were making *yufka*, the forerunner of phyllo and strudel, by stretching the dough very thin, cutting it into squares, and allowing it to dry slightly. The uncooked squares were wrapped around savory fillings or layered with butter and fillings and baked. In the farthest western extremes of the Ottoman Empire, the Maghreb, cooks developed their own version of *yufka* from semolina flour; this dough was called *warka* or *ouarka* (leaf) in Morocco, *malsouqa* or *malsouka* (to adhere) in Tunisia, and *diyul* (perhaps from the French *feuille* for "leaf") in Algeria. These Maghrebi dough rounds are cooked on one side, not raw like *yufka*, phyllo, and strudel. The thin sheets, a bit thicker than phyllo and almost

Semolina dough rounds called warka *in Morocco (but also used throughout the Maghreb) are cooked on one side, not used raw like phyllo and strudel dough. The sheets are thicker and more flexible than phyllo and better suited for round shapes and wrapping, such as into thin rolls called "fingers" or "cigars."*

rubbery in texture, are firmer and more flexible than phyllo and are thus better suited for round shapes and wrapping. *Warka* require great skill to prepare and are therefore rarely made by home cooks.

In Morocco, every marketplace has at least one *warka* maker, typically a *dadas* (descendant of Sudanese slaves), who deftly plies her trade. In the past, wealthy families hired a professional *warka* maker to come to their homes. The dough is very moist and springy and is made by kneading fine semolina flour with water and a touch of oil. It is cooked on a *tabsil*—a special large, round, flat-topped, tin-plated, copper dish, like an inverted pan—that is heated over a charcoal brazier. A small handful of dough is placed on top of the *tabsil* and is quickly worked into a very thin round, ten to fourteen inches in diameter. The moist dough initially clings to the surface, then comes away from the pan as it cooks; the entire process takes about twenty seconds. When the sheet is dry, it is piled on top of other sheets and wrapped to keep the dough fresh and soft. Commercial packaged *warka* is widely available in France and is generally labeled *"feuilles d'ouarka"* and *"feuilles de brick"* (from the Tunisian pastry *brik*). However, packaged *warka* in America and England is rare. Chinese spring roll (not egg roll) skins or frozen phyllo dough are often substituted.

The traditional manner of using *warka* was frying, yielding the crispest pastry, but many people now prefer baking it. Among the most popular of *warka* pastries are rolls variously called *dedos* ("fingers" in Spanish), *asabia* ("fingers" in Arabic), and *sigares/cigares* ("cigars"); and the classic Moroccan *pastilla* or *bisteeya* (pigeon pie). Algerians refer to potato-filled *sigares*, now prevalent in Israel, as *beztels*. Tunisians use *warka*, which they call *malsouqa*, for their national snack, *brik* pastries.

(See also Brik, Pastilla, and Phyllo)

WATER

In the beginning there was only water, the substance from which all life flowed. The Hebrew word for water—*mayim*—is in the plural form and thus actually means "waters." *Mayim* is also a palindrome, reading the same backward or forward, reflecting the water cycle of repeated precipitation and evaporation, birth and rebirth. Just as water is an unchanging cycle, so too is life.

For most of history and in many locales, sources

of water were scarce and those extant all too often proved tainted. Drought and famine were common. The limited amount of drinking water available primarily came from springs, collected rain water, or man-made wells, which were zealously guarded and frequently fought over. Cities grew up around limited water sources, such as the Gihon Spring of Jerusalem. The Israeli city of Beersheba means "well of the oath," named after Abraham's well. In many places, alcoholic beverages, notably beer and wine, were commonly consumed throughout the day instead of water. Eventually, people learned how to boil water and invented other forms of purification, such as filtering through sand and charcoal. In 1804, the first municipal water treatment plant was constructed in Scotland and throughout the nineteenth century, many urban areas in the Western world followed suit, transforming water into a safe and regular part of the diet.

Mayim crops up throughout the Bible—the word is mentioned 180 times in the Pentateuch alone. *Mayim* shares the same root as "*mah*," meaning "what," revealing that in contemplation of water or immersing in it, a person feels insignificant and asks, "What am I?" This question appears in the context of water in an episode in Exodus. After three successive water-related incidents—*Kriat haYam* (splitting of the sea), the bitter water of Marah, and the twelve springs of Elim—the "whole congregation" murmured against Moses and Aaron. The two leaders then entreated, "What are we?" What humans are, amongst other things, is about 80 percent water. This seemingly simple combination of two molecules of hydrogen and one of oxygen is the ultimate source and vivifying agent of everything—all existence and all life.

In Jewish tradition, water and bread are considered the essentials of the human diet and are, therefore, sources of blessing. In addition, water represents change, especially spiritual transformation such as the cleansing that occurs in the *mikveh* (ritual bath). In this vein, crossing bodies of water—Noah on the ark, Abraham westward over the Euphrates, Jacob over the brook upon his return to Canaan, the Jews through the splitting sea while leaving Egypt, and the Jews through the Jordan to enter Israel—are all occasions of momentous spiritual flux and development. Water is especially connected to Torah. The Talmud asserted, "Water means nothing but Torah, as it says,

'Ho, everyone that is thirsty come you for water,'" which is interpreted as "come for Torah."

There are several instances of one-time water offerings found in the Bible, such as the offering of Samuel at Mitzpah and with King David. Water per se, however, was seldom employed in the Temple ritual, although a dip in the *mikveh* was necessary before entering. In the Temple, every burnt offering was accompanied with a flour offering (mixed with olive oil) and a wine offering; the latter was poured on the altar. An exception occurred during the seven days of Sukkot, when three *lugim* (around one quart) of pure water were drawn daily from the pool of Siloach and poured by the high priest on the altar at the regular morning offering simultaneously with the wine. Although not specifically mentioned in the Bible, the water libation (ritual pouring of a liquid) is considered in Jewish tradition to be "a law given to Moses at Sinai" and subsequently transmitted orally.

The nature of the water libation was based on the famous verse from Isaiah, "You shall draw water with joy from the wells of salvation." Sukkot is the most joyous of festivals, and the most intense joy centered around the *nisuch ha-mayim* (pouring of the water). On the intermediate days, with the exception of the Sabbath, these festivities, called *Simchat Beit ha-Shoavah* (happiness of the place of water-drawing), were accompanied with great public celebrations, replete with music and song. The Talmud recounts that each evening, the people would gather in the courtyard of the outer Temple and "men of piety and good deeds danced with burning torches in their hands singing." The Mishnah asserted, "Whoever has not seen the *Simchat Beit ha-Shoavah*, has never seen rejoicing in his life."

The timing of the water libation on Sukkot was "in order that the [ensuing] rainy season would be blessed." In Israel in the month of Cheshvan, corresponding to October and November, the extended dry season abruptly comes to an end with a series of intermittent showers that continue to fall for two months, called *yoreh*. The rain intensifies both in strength and duration during December becoming *geshem*, the soaking downpours that replenish the aquafilter and the Sea of Galilee. About 70 percent of the country's rainfall occurs in the three months from December through February. In late winter, the rain pauses, then falls intermittently during the month of Nisan (late

March and April), the *malkosh*. In Jewish thought, the timing and amount of rain each year was a direct result of the divine will, which in turn was a direct consequence of the conduct of the Israelites.

According to Jewish tradition, the biblical episode of Eliezer and Rebecca at the well occurred on the fifteenth of Tishrei, the first day of Sukkot, and the water libations of Sukkot were in recompense for Rebecca's act of kindness in giving water to Eliezer, his men, and his camels. The Torah associates the blessings of water with women. Jacob first encounters and falls in love with Rachel at a well. Moses' mother places the basket holding her son into the Nile. Miriam, in the spirit of her ancestors, waits to see what befalls Moses by the river and exalts God at the splitting of the sea, meriting the well of water that the Israelites in the wilderness enjoyed. Moses meets his wife Tzipporah by a well. It was the proactive nature of the biblical women—Sarah, Milcah, Deborah, Rebecca, Yocheved, and Miriam—that enabled them to shape and direct, frequently behind the scenes, the Jewish community.

Water, like *chesed* (kindness), can be salutary, but in the wrong place and time, it can be dangerous and even deadly. As Jacob noted in his blessing of Reuben, "unstable as water does not allow your preeminence."

WATERCRESS

Watercress, possibly a native of Turkey, is not a true cress, but a close relative of mustard. Watercress early on spread throughout much of Europe and Asia, growing wild near streams and ponds, but was first cultivated on a large scale in 1750. The plant became particularly popular in France. Watercress has small, dark green leaves that give a peppery flavor to salads, sandwiches, and soups.

The Talmud mentioned the domain of King Alexander Yannai (c. 126–76 BCE), including Kefar Shachalayim (Village of Watercress) in Edom (modern-day west Jordan), explaining that the inhabitants made their living from watercress. In Roman times, the residents of Sepphoris would cook pots of fava beans seasoned with wine vinegar in the city's warm springs for the Sabbath—they called the dish *shachalayim* because watercress was also commonly seasoned with vinegar. The Talmud also included watercress among the plants exempt from the tithe, as it was only found wild.

Watercress is believed to be a digestive and stimu-

lant. Cooks predominantly use it fresh in salads and add it to soups. Moroccans enjoy the peppery flavor as a contrast to slices of oranges in a salad.

WATERMELON

Among the six foods the Israelites longed for upon leaving bondage in Egypt were *avatichim* (watermelons), from the root *batach* (to swell/to be thick). More than three millennia later, watermelon is one of the favorite foods of modern Israel, engrained in the culture and cuisine. One of the most popular Israeli pioneer songs was the 1938 "*Avatiach*" by Shmuel Bass and Menashe Rabinowitz and arranged by Ernst Toch, which begins with these lines: "Not on a tree and not on a bush, on the ground it grows, also in the sun, also in the shade, *avatiach*." Among the more than fifty albums of Israel's longest-tenured and most respected singer, Chava Alberstein, is the 1971 gold record album *Isha ba'Avatiach* (A Woman in a Watermelon), featuring the music of young up-and-coming composers of that time.

Watermelons, which probably originated in central Africa, have a dark green and yellow skin, a thick rind, and a pink to deep red flesh, which ranges in flavor from insipid to sweet. The *avatiach* of biblical times was quite different from its modern descendants, and much less flavorful. The original watermelon was probably the *tsamma* melon of the Kalahari Desert. Watermelons were probably already cultivated by the Bronze Age. In Egyptian tombs dating back at least

Unlike the large, oblong American watermelon varieties, Israeli avatiach *are typically small and round; most are now seedless. Loud calls of "A-va-ti-ach, A-va-ti-ach" are common throughout the summer as either the farmers themselves or distributors sell fresh watermelon off their trucks to locals.*

5,000 years, watermelon seeds have been found, as well as wall paintings depicting small, round watermelons. While ripe watermelons provided a refreshing treat, immature ones, both fresh and dried, were cooked as a vegetable. Watermelons, which are relatively drought resistant, proved invaluable in Africa not so much as a food—though even the rinds and seeds were utilized—but rather as an important source of water; they are 90 percent water. Despite its high water and sugar content, it is also nutritious. In addition, the melon's numerous seeds made it a symbol of fertility.

Outside of Egypt, watermelons were first widely cultivated throughout the Middle East and other parts of Asia as early as three thousand years ago. Moors had introduced them to Spain by the thirteenth century. According to some historians, it was medieval Jews who first introduced watermelon cultivation to France. The word watermelon first appeared in English in 1615.

In the early days of the state of Israel, watermelon was a refreshing sign of the arrival of summer—these fruits first appear in late May and the height of the season is in July and August. Unlike the large, oblong American varieties, Israeli *avatiach* are typically small and round and most are now seedless; seedless watermelons were invented by a Japanese scientist in 1939 and subsequently improved by Israeli agricultural scientists. As soon as the year's crop begins to ripen, the beloved green fruits appear in groceries, *souks* (marketplaces), and watermelon stands on nearly every corner throughout the country. Today, the raucous cries of sellers announcing "A-va-ti-ach, A-va-ti-ach" still ring through the land each summer, although trucks have replaced the horse-drawn wagons of yesteryear. People scramble from their houses to make sure of getting the best pick. Israelis really do not need much encouragement, for as the summer progresses and the weather grows more intense, watermelon remains a favorite Israeli way to deal with a sweltering day.

Watermelon has long been ubiquitous at Israeli beaches and picnics. It is a popular flavor for popsicles and ices. The more recent pairing of cubes of salty Bulgarian feta cheese with sweet watermelon, a duo now popular as beach fare as well as at upscale cafes, is possibly the dish most emblematic of modern Israeli gastronomy.

(See also Melon)

ISRAELI WATERMELON AND FETA SALAD
(*AVATIACH SALAT*)

3 TO 4 SERVINGS [DAIRY]

4 cups 1-inch watermelon cubes
¼ to ½ cup crumbled creamy feta cheese
¼ cup chopped red onion
2 tablespoons chopped fresh mint
2 tablespoons chopped fresh flat-leaf parsley or cilantro
¼ cup fresh lime juice

In a large bowl, combine all the ingredients. Serve immediately.

WEDDING

A Jewish wedding, in effect a legal contract, is a two-part process. Before the eleventh century, a Jewish couple, the *chatan* (groom) and *kallah* (bride), were betrothed in one ceremony, called *erusin* (bound) or *kiddushin* (set aside/sanctified). Even though they were not yet living together, in order to separate, they required a divorce. The gap of time allowed the couple to build a house, and to make or accumulate the goods necessary for a life together (in a time before department stores and gift registries). In conjunction with the betrothal, the families agreed on the financial conditions of the marriage and the *ketubah* (marriage contract) was signed. *Erusin* commenced when the

A Yemenite Jewish bride dons an elaborate dress, a large silver necklace, and a jewel-encrusted headdress decorated with red and white carnations. On one side of the headdress is sweet basil, symbolizing a life of joy, and on the other side rue, a malodorous plant used to ward off the evil eye. Weddings also feature traditional foods, symbolizing fertility and a life of beauty.

groom gave the bride something of value, typically a ring, and the woman accepted it. Then, up to a year later, the couple performed the actual marriage ceremony, known as *nissuin* (elevation) or *chupah* (marriage canopy), and then began living together. Each of these occasions was accompanied by a festive meal. However, due to the increasing insecurity of life in medieval times, which all too frequently meant a quick relocation or other unexpected changes, by the eleventh century, the waiting period was abolished and the two ceremonies were adjoined. The change also meant one banquet instead of two, no small matter in economically pressed times. More recently, many of the customs accompanying a wedding, such as the dowry and trousseau, have been abandoned.

After the two parts of the wedding were combined, communities developed other rituals to mark the engagement, commonly accompanied with a party. When a Syrian couple decides to wed, relatives of both families gather for a "coming together party" commonly referred to as a *kinyan* (Hebrew for "acquisition") or *bozra* (Arabic for "negotiating session"). Originally, this meeting provided an opportunity for the two families to agree on the terms and for the rabbi to legalize them by enacting the *tenaim* (conditions) between the fathers. Today, the couple generally uses the occasion to make the engagement official. The bride's family customarily prepares an elaborate repast for the occasion. Guests send white flowers for decorations and the crowd is entertained with a *nobeh* (special musical renderings) played on traditional Middle Eastern instruments, including a *qanoon* (zither), *oud* (lute), and *dirbakkeh* (a small drum).

Sephardim from the Balkans and Turkey have a similar though less elaborate ceremony, sometimes called *espoziria* (engagement), in which the families meet and agree on financial terms. The hosts customarily offer an extensive assortment of treats, including a *tavla de dulce* (tray of sweets) featuring a large assortment of confections, *dulce de kumquat* (preserved whole kumquats), and various fruit preserves served in glass bowls. Also on the ornate tray are silver teaspoons and glasses of water. The guests sample a spoonful of *dulce*, then deposit the spoon in a glass of water. Turkish coffee accompanies the *dulces*.

In Jewish tradition, almonds, which come in both bitter and sweet varieties, are a metaphor for marriage. In addition, Ecclesiastes uses the almond as a symbol of human life, and the numerical value of the Hebrew word for nut, *egoz*, is seventeen, the same value as *tov* (good). Therefore, almonds are common at the various Jewish engagement and wedding rites. Sephardim still offer Jordan almonds and almond paste confections at weddings and other life-cycle events.

Among Ashkenazim, a separate ceremony called *tenaim shidukin* (conditions of engagement) was established for the families to announce the engagement and agree on their legally binding financial obligations. The terms in the *tenaim*, set in writing and enforced through various edicts and bans, included the date and place of the wedding, the dowry, and inheritance rights. Today, the *tenaim*, out of tradition, is usually signed at the wedding at the *chatan's tish* (groom's table), where the groom and various male family and friends gather before the wedding. Honey cake and schnapps are traditional at the *chatan's tish*. After the document is signed, the mothers of the bride and groom customarily break a plate (usually safely enclosed in a napkin), reflecting the severity of breaking this legal document, although no divorce is required, and also as a remembrance, even in a moment of joy, of the destruction of the Temple. The pieces, considered lucky, are customarily distributed to unmarried friends.

When the *tenaim* were also adjoined to the wedding, a vacuum was left as to how to announce the engagement. To meet this need without officially having an "engagement party," the *vort* (verbal agreement) has become an increasingly popular custom in certain religious circles of the Ashkenazic community. Both families gather to meet each other, listen to friends describe the qualities of the bride and groom, and eat. Sometimes, as in a *tenaim*, the mothers break a plate, although nothing is yet legal.

In Talmudic times, weddings were frequently held on Sunday and Wednesday, as the Jewish court met on Monday and Thursday and could deal swiftly with any points of contentions the next day. Rosh Chodesh (the first day of the new month) is considered especially favorable. Jewish weddings are traditionally not held on the Sabbath or festivals, due to the restrictions on work, travel, and making a contract. In addition, since the medieval period, weddings have also not been held during much of the seven-week Omer period between Passover and Shavuot and during the Three Weeks preceding the fast of Tisha b'Av.

The traditional day for a Yemenite wedding was Thursday. The week preceding the nuptials was celebrated with feasting, as was the week afterward. On the Thursday before his wedding, the groom bathed and immersed himself in the *mikvah* (ritual bath). On Monday and Tuesday, henna was applied to the bride and the women in her family, then to the women in the groom's family, and finally to the groom. On Wednesday, the groom sent his gifts to the bride and the *erusin* ceremony was conducted that evening in the bride's home. On the following day, the *nissuin* was held at the groom's house.

Initially, Ashkenazim typically held weddings on Friday afternoon, with the wedding feast simultaneously providing a Sabbath dinner for the family and the poor of the community. However, there was an episode in Kraków in which Rabbi Moses Isserles (1520–1572), the most respected Ashkenazic rabbi of his era, was officiating at the wedding of an orphaned young woman whose brothers had failed to meet the expected dowry. By the time Isserles convinced the prospective groom to proceed with the wedding, the Sabbath had begun and he feared that if he waited until after the Sabbath, the groom's parents might talk him out of it. In order to avoid embarrassing the young woman and inflicting pain on the bride and groom, Isserles himself conducted the wedding on the Sabbath. This provoked an uproar in Europe and, to avoid any future such instances, weddings were subsequently avoided on Fridays.

Thereafter, Tuesday—because in the biblical account of Creation, on the third day, the phrase "and God saw it was good" appears twice—became the auspicious day for Ashkenazic weddings. In America, Sunday emerged as a popular wedding day, simply because most people have the day off from work. In Israel, on the other hand, where Sunday is a typical work day, weddings are held any day of the week, usually in the evening after most people have concluded their workday.

At Jewish weddings, auspicious signs (*segulot*) to protect the couple and to induce fertility are sought and ominous ones avoided. Sephardic brides wear jewelry and Mizrachi brides don plenty of it, while many Ashkenazic couples follow a custom of not wearing any jewelry. Middle Eastern Jewish women reflect their joy at a wedding or other celebration in the traditional Arabic manner, with high-pitched, extended ululations performed with the tongue.

Until relatively recently, Jews did not marry in a synagogue. Ashkenazim held their weddings outdoors, perhaps outside the synagogue or in a courtyard, then moved elsewhere for the wedding feast. Among Sephardim, the wedding was traditionally held at the home of the groom's parents. The bride and her family would be escorted by a large procession accompanied with musicians, who in the eastern Mediterranean played Turkish or Greek music. Following the *chupah*, the couple would depart, as the guests threw almonds and coins as a sign of their wish for prosperity and plenty for the newlyweds. Afterward, the assemblage headed to the wedding feast.

Today at a Jewish wedding, the *erusin* begins with a special blessing over marriage and ends with the groom giving the bride a ring. The *nissuin* consists of the recital of seven marital blessings (*Sheva Berachot/Berachot Nissiun*) and the breaking of a glass. In between, the *ketubah* is publicly read to mark a distinction between the two ceremonies. Both rituals take place under the *chupah*, a symbol of the home to be shared by the couple. As with most Jewish celebrations, wine is present, in fact, there are two cups, one for the *kiddushin* and a second one for the *nissuin*. The couple drinks from each of the two cups as a symbol of their joy and sanctification.

Some Ashkenazic couples fast on the day of their wedding. Some Sephardim consider fasting at this time inappropriate, while others fast as do two male friends of the groom and two female friends of the bride. Some Sephardim break the fast with a light meal of symbolic foods—wine, matza, bitter herbs, apple, and honey. Among Ashkenazim, after the *chupah*, the couple breaks their fast in a formal period of seclusion in a room apart (*yichud*), which today is typically followed by an extended period of picture taking. Sephardim arrange the formal period of seclusion after the entire wedding.

The wedding, as it has been since the onset of the religion, is an occasion for a special feast, accompanied with joyous singing, dancing, and music. Each community developed its own special weddings songs. The wedding *seudah* commences with the Hamotzi (benediction over bread), and wine or schnapps is typically plentiful. Since Talmudic times, chicken dishes have been traditional for weddings, a custom derived from a once common saying at marriage ceremonies, "Be fruitful and multiply like chickens." It was among eastern European Jews that chicken soup, also called *golden yoych* and *goldzup* (the gold refers to the globules of fat floating on top of the soup), was most appreciated. For many generations, bowls of golden chicken soup with noodles appeared at Ashkenazic weddings, and the soup is still often served today. The actual Ashkenazic meal consists of familiar Western fare, including chicken or beef, potatoes, and pickles. Today, it is common to precede the ceremony with a lavish smorgasbord featuring contemporary as well as traditional items, such as chopped liver, gefilte fish, smoked salmon, herring, knishes, and kugel.

At a Sephardic wedding, the bride and groom traditionally eat from the same plate and drink from the same glass. A wedding is also the time for serving traditional Sephardic foods, as this fare is associated with the warmth of home and the bonds of family and community. Lamb is the traditional main dish. Sephardic and Mizrachi weddings, except for those in the couscous-loving Maghreb, always include rice, usually tinted yellow, the Middle Eastern color of happiness, and sometimes sweetened or enhanced with nuts or dried fruit. Among the prized dishes at Sephardic nuptials is *arroz de bodas* (wedding rice), yellow rice with grapes, scallions, and pine nuts, elaborately sculptured. Persians feature a *shirin polow* (sweet rice with cherries and other fruits) served with roast chicken. The Bene Israel of Mumbai accent their wedding rice with turmeric, almonds, raisins, fresh ginger, and notes of cardamom, cinnamon, and cloves. Moroccans present a festive sweetened couscous (*seffa*) mounded in a pyramid shape, decorated with ground cinnamon, and garnished with almond-stuffed pitted dates.

A Turkish Jewish wedding feast—weddings were customarily held on Friday afternoon—traditionally features seven courses. The first dish is *sutlach*, a rich, rose-flavored rice-flour pudding symbolizing a sweet life for the newlyweds. Next comes an ancient symbol of fertility, fish, followed by *siete en boca* (tiny sugar-coated almond pieces), *ojaldres de carne* (meat-filled phyllo triangles), and *albondigas de meyoyo* (calf's brain meatballs). The *meneado* (main course) is left to the discretion of the cook, but always contains almonds. The final dish, served only to the couple, is pigeon. Similarly, a Moroccan couple is served *hamam del aroussa* (the bride's pigeons), a pair of stuffed pigeons in an onion-honey sauce, pigeons being monogamous and prolific birds that, once

mated, share their lives and parental duties. Yemenites typically feature *fatoot*, their special meat soup spiced with *hawaij*. For Sephardim and Mizrachim, sweet pastries and confections are a must, symbolizing a happy and joyous relationship.

In Jewish tradition, *shivat ye'mei hamishteh* (seven days of partying) follow the wedding. During this week-long period when the newlyweds, a *minyan* (quorum of ten), and at least one person who did not attend the wedding are present for a meal, the *Sheva Berachot* are recited after the *Birkhat Hamazon* (Grace after Meals). There are no specific requirements for the food at these meals beyond bread and wine, but, whether homemade or catered, they are typically festive and special.

(See also Aufruf, Seudah, and Swanne)

WHEAT

Well before humankind discovered agriculture, primitive wheat and barley, spread by the wind, grew wild throughout much of the Fertile Crescent and was gathered by our nomadic ancestors. Over the course of time, several wild grasses spontaneously crossbred with various wild and domesticated wheats, yielding newer forms of wheat. All wheat falls into two basic categories: hulled wheat, such as einkorn, emmer, and spelt, in which the husks adhere to the seeds and the only way to remove them is by burning or pounding; and naked wheat or free-threshing wheat, notably durum and common wheat, in which the husks fall easily from the seeds. The earliest wheat but not an ancestor of modern wheat species, was einkorn (one-seed), a type in which the spikelets (flowers) typically produce one grain each. Besides a relatively low yield and a nearly negligible amount of gluten, einkorn is "hulled" wheat.

Although the first farmers planted einkorn, which fares well in poor soil and is disease resistant, this cereal was impractical for wide-scale cultivation. Wheat species, however, crossbreed spontaneously as well as relatively frequently and easily in nature—there are now more than thirty thousand varieties of wheat. Therefore, einkorn's importance waned during the Bronze Age when more preferable wheat varieties became available. Einkorn is probably the *shippon/shifon* of the Talmud—one of the Five Species of grain capable of becoming *chametz*. To further confuse matters, in modern Hebrew, *shifon* is rye.

At some point in prehistory, a close relative of einkorn crossbred with another wild grass, yielding emmer, whose Latin name, *Triticum*, means "two-seed." Like einkorn, emmer is a hulled wheat and therefore difficult to thresh. The numerous biblical references to *goren* (threshing floor), including the site of the Temple itself, and threshing sledges, reflect the widespread use of hulled grains. Among emmer's advantages were its ability to grow in poor soils, its resistance to fungal diseases, and the simultaneous ripening of its spiklets, all of which made it a more practical crop for cultivation than other grains; in addition, it contained a higher level of gluten. Many varieties of wheat contain a large amount of two particular proteins—glutenin and gliadin; when these proteins come into contact with water, they combine with each other to form gluten, the viscid substance that gives flour the elasticity required for it to rise and keep its structure under heat. Thus bread made from emmer turns out lighter than that made from its early competitors, einkorn and barley, although it is less feathery than modern bread.

Emmer, which was already the predominant wheat in predynastic Egypt, was probably the grains purchased in Egypt by Jacob's sons during the famine in Canaan and also used to make the matzas of the Exodus. Emmer is still grown by farmers in a few parts of the world, notably southeastern Europe; it is called *farro* in Italian.

Spelt is another domesticated species of wheat, probably a descendant of emmer and a wild goat grass; like emmer, it is a hulled variety, and it is sometimes confused with emmer. Spelt was unknown in ancient Egypt, Greece, and Israel and therefore, despite many Bible translations, not the grain (*Kussemet*) saved along with free-threshing wheat (*chittah*) from the plague of hail in Egypt. In modern Hebrew, spelt is *kusmin*.

These grains—einkorn, emmer, and two-row barley—along with four legumes—lentils, chickpeas, split peas, and bitter vetch—are considered the founder crops; they provided the protein and nutrition of early civilization. At first, people roasted the grains, as this was the easiest way to remove the kernel from the glumes. Then they discovered that they could pound the grains to loosen the husks. However, pounding not only required much labor, but also in the process broke many of the grains, rendering them less suited for long-term storage. Eventually, cooks began boiling barley, einkorn, and emmer kernels to make gruels, which in some areas would remain the staple of the diet well into modern times. When people accidentally dropped some of the porridge into campfires, they discovered that the flat mishaps—the first rudimentary breads—were tastier and far more portable than the gruel.

During the late Bronze Age, emmer spontaneously hybridized, leading to tetraploid grains. The most important was durum (from the Latin for "hard"), the firmest and most flavorful of all wheat species. This new species was a naked (free-threshing) variety—it easily released the grains from the chaff and therefore could be threshed without first being roasted or pounded, not only reducing the amount of labor involved, but also leaving the grains intact and thus suitable for longer storage. On the other hand, it was extremely difficult for the primitive milling devices to grind the hard durum, particularly the inner portion. The resultant meal had to be repeatedly sifted in sieves with gradually finer mesh to finally accumulate any amount of fine flour (*solet*), the type required in the Temple. Thus durum was primarily used for porridges, except when bakers wanted to exert the extra effort to produce the fine flour. Instead, during the early biblical period, the hardier emmer (probably the biblical kussemet), which was tolerant of environmental extremes and poorer soils and was generally resistant to insect damage, remained the most widely planted form of wheat in the Middle East.

Wheat, which is mentioned twenty-one times in the Pentateuch, thirteen of which are in conjunction with barley, was the preferred grain in biblical times; barley's value was generally half that of wheat. However, wheat was harder to grow and thresh than barley. Barley served as the bulk of the common person's and the army's diet.

Eventually, emmer spontaneously crossbred with a wild goat grass, giving rise to hexaploid wheat. Among the new species, one in particular, called common wheat or bread wheat (*aestivum*), was larger in size, higher yielding, and more adaptable than its predecessors. In addition, *aestivum* contained more starch than durum did and a had high level of gluten; these traits meant that cooks could use it to produce loaves with the light texture and satisfying taste that the modern world associates with bread, and to turn out delicate, flaky pastry. The Romans, in particular, favored *aestivum* and planted it in all the territories under its dominion. Thus *aestivum* gradually spread from its home in the Caspian plains and eventually superseded the other species of wheat, becoming the source of most modern flour and far and away the most important of all the myriad species of wheat. Today, *aestivum* accounts for around 90 percent of the world's wheat crops (and almost all the matza).

Ancient Rome imported much of its wheat, primarily from North Africa and Sicily. After the collapse of the Roman Empire, in most of Europe, wheat—which was still primarily being imported but without the imperial subsidies—grew prohibitively expensive and, subsequently, barley and millet provided the bread and gruels for the masses. Rye and rye-wheat blends were the predominant grains of northern Europe. In the medieval Middle East, wheat remained the most widespread grain. Until a population explosion and Ottoman mismanagement in the late sixteenth century, wheat was grown in abundance in the Levant and Egypt. In the Arab world, wheat was a mainstay of the diet—in the form of bulgur and bread in the Levant, pasta and bread in Egypt, and couscous and bread in the Maghreb. In Iberia, wheat became known as *trigo* (from the Latin *triticu*) and quickly emerged as the predominant form of bread and a staple of the diet. As a result, Sephardim early on developed a large repertoire of sophisticated baked goods and wheat dishes. Wheat breads, pies, and cakes were also associated with Sephardic holidays and celebrations.

In the fifteenth century, spurred on by the importation of Middle Eastern knowledge and by the Renaissance, Europeans greatly improved their agricultural techniques and began to change their eating habits. At this time, another wheat product began to assume an increasingly larger role in the European diet—pasta and noodles. Gradually wheat became the predominant grain in much of Europe. Until the sixteenth century, most European wheat was still imported. However, Spanish mismanagement and overtaxation of Sicily led to a marked decline in wheat production, as well as to an enduring poverty on that island. Eventually, European farmers took up the slack and wheat continued its growth in usage, following only corn and rice among the world's most widely grown grains.

Modern flour is typically made from two types of common wheat—red and white. The Mishnah included in the category of *chittah* (wheat) both *she-chamtis* ("red," the color of the sun in the morning and evening) and *levanah* (white) wheat. Red wheat contains three extra genes, resulting in a darker color and, due to chemical compounds, a slightly bitter, nutty flavor in the bran. The bran of white wheat is actually an amber color. The protein content of wheat varies depending on such factors as soil, rainfall, temperature, maturity, the milling process, and time of planting. Autumn planting, taking advantage of the cold and moisture of winter, yields a lower protein wheat than spring planting, which does not undergo a dormant state. The moderate climates of the American South yield wheat with much lower amounts of gluten than the more severe environment of the North and Canada.

While the vast majority of westerners only know wheat in flour form, in the Middle East it has a wider assortment of uses, including as *farik* ("green wheat" in Arabic, corresponding to the biblical *aviv*, colloquially called *frikeh* or *freekeh*), wheat berries (hulled wheat kernels), cracked wheat (*jareesh* in Arabic), and bulgur.

Since ancient times, there has only been one known product made from immature durum wheat or barley—roasted grains, called *frikeh*. Today, *frikeh* is still prepared the old-fashioned way in parts of the Middle East, where, in some countries, it is sold commercially in stores. Traditionally, Arabs harvest wheat kernels for *frikeh* when the kernels were still ever so slightly green. After the kernels are harvested, they are laid in the late spring sun to dry for at least two hours. At this point, some Arabs traditionally roast the kernels in a pan, while others set them afire to burn the chaff (the kernels' high moisture content protects them from the heat). Today, this is sometimes done for commercial purposes with a flame-thrower. After the chaff has blackened, the kernels are thrashed (or rubbed) to remove the hulls. The result is a smoky flavor. One particular advantage of roasted grains is that they cook more quickly than raw kernels; crushing the kernels reduces the cooking time even further.

Frikeh is most certainly identical with the biblical and Talmudic *kali* (roasted kernels), the type (from barley) mandated for the Omer offering. *Kali* was a common food item and was presented to Ruth by Boaz. *Kali* from barley was produced shortly after Passover and *kali* from durum wheat was prepared around Shavuot, when the grains were green and could only be used for human consumption if roasted.

Wheat berries are unprocessed whole wheat with only the outer husk removed. Hulled wheat berries (also called shelled or peeled wheat) are white in color, lack whole wheat's flavor, and are stickier and softer when cooked. The berry has a nutty flavor and chewy texture and is delicious alone or mixed with other grains. Ancient Middle Easterners cooked wheat berries with meat and mashed the mixture into a smooth consistency, resulted in *harisa*, a type of Sabbath stew. Wheat berries are used in Middle Eastern soups, stews, salads, casseroles, and puddings. Sweetened and mixed with fruits and nuts, they become a holiday dish—called *kofyas* in Turkey, *ashure* or *koliva* in Greece, and *korkoti* in Georgia.

Cracked wheat is uncooked durum wheat berries broken into pieces—fine, medium, or coarse. Unlike bulgur, which is precooked before being sold commercially, cracked wheat must be cooked. Cracked wheat is used to make soups, such as the Middle Eastern *shorobit il-jareesh*, porridges, and salads.

Today, Israel buys 90 percent of its wheat from the American Midwest.

(See also Ashure, Barley, Bread Bulgur, Chametz, Emmer, Grain, Gruenkern, Matza, Rye, and Semolina)

WHITEFISH

Landlocked parts of northeastern Europe relied on freshwater fish species, most notably carp, perch, pike, smelts, and whitefish. The term whitefish, *veisfische* in Yiddish, refers to about thirty species of non-

Whitefish encompasses about thirty species of small fish from Europe and America with dry, white flesh. It is one of three traditional fish, along with carp and pike, used to make gefilte fish. In America, smoked whitefish and a salad made from it are commonly found in delis.

oily fish with dry, white flesh from both Europe and America, such as whiting (also called hake), haddock, and pollack. The Volga River and Caspian Sea yielded whitefish, such as zander (closely related to perch) and other species, in sizable amounts. Considered a trash fish by some, whitefish was relatively inexpensive, but still primarily a Sabbath and festival food. Whitefish, pike, and carp constituted the trio of traditional types of fish used to make gefilte fish. Fresh whitefish were also poached for a Sabbath appetizer.

Smoking is one of the oldest methods of preserving fish; first the fish is salted, then the salt is removed and the fish is set aside to dry before being smoked. Before the advent of refrigeration, the fish were heavily salted and smoked until very dry, enabling them to be stored for an extended period. Then in the early twentieth century, as refrigeration spread, the salting became milder, usually a brine, and the smoked fish thus became softer—the new version is more perishable and must be refrigerated.

Ashkenazim in America found species of whitefish from the Great Lakes nearly identical to those of eastern Europe, and soon golden-colored smoked whitefish—as well as lox and smoked sablefish (also called "black cod")—became standard in Jewish delicatessens and appetizing stores and also emerged as Ashkenazic culinary icons. Before the popularity of canned tuna, smoked whitefish, along with pickled herring, provided the basis for Ashkenazic fish salads; gourmets now call it "smoked whitefish pâté." In America, whole golden whitefish, today mainly Alaskan pollack, as well as a creamy whitefish salad, became a popular sight at morning celebrations, such as *brits*, and Sunday morning brunches. The tiny gold or black roe of whitefish are used to make kosher caviar.

🐟 ASHKENAZIC WHITEFISH SALAD

ABOUT 3 CUPS/6 TO 8 SERVINGS   [PAREVE]

> 3 pounds (1 medium whole) smoked whitefish, skinned, boned, and flaked
> 1 cup mayonnaise
> 1 cup chopped celery
> 2 to 3 tablespoons fresh lemon juice
> Ground black pepper to taste

In a large bowl, combine all the ingredients. Whitefish salad can be stored in the refrigerator for up to 3 days.

WINE

The Talmud noted, "Wine is the greatest of all medicines. Where there is no wine, drugs are necessary."

In the mid-1970s, archeologists digging in northwest Iran excavated potsherds from a large jar capable of containing about 2.5 gallons, dating back to the late Stone Age. Twenty years later, researchers chemically analyzed a yellowish residue clinging to this Neolithic pottery, revealing the earliest evidence of wine. The date of the pottery, which coincides with humankind's first permanent settlements, demonstrates that wine is at least as old as civilization itself. The pottery in which the wine was stored had a narrow neck—this design allowed the jar to be easily stoppered in order to keep out airborne bacteria. Ancient enologists knew not only how to make wine, but how to flavor and preserve it.

From the onset of the Jewish people at Mount Sinai, wine has been intertwined with Jewish culture and life. The Bible records that after surviving mass destruction while being confined in the ark for a year, Noah's second recorded action was to plant a vineyard. The grape was one of the Talmud's candidates for the forbidden fruit of Eden. On sixteen occasions, the Pentateuch paired wine with grain and

Sam Schapiro, originally from Galicia (now southern Poland), started the first kosher wine company in America, operating out of New York's Lower East Side. The thick sweet wine was made from Concord grapes grown in the state.

olive oil, reflecting the trio's role as the staples of the diet and economy of biblical Israel. In the Temple, wine was used as an offering, generally as a concomitant to other offerings. Wine merits a special benediction: *"borei peri hagafen"* (Who creates the fruit of the vine). Symbolizing joy and fruitfulness (in Psalms, "wine that cheers man's heart"), wine is an integral element of many Jewish rituals, including Kiddush, Havdalah, the Passover Seder, *brit milah*, and weddings.

The sun-drenched limestone slopes of the Holy Land were particularly suited for viticulture, as they featured hot, dry summers and moderate winter temperatures. Vineyards flourished on the terraced hillsides of ancient Judea. Some vineyards were mere plots consisting of only a handful of vines, while others were massive. The Israelites learned to train the vines on trellises. Isaiah detailed the time-honored process of tending a vineyard: "He dug it, and cleared it of stones, and planted it with the choicest vines, and built a [watch] tower in the middle of it [to spot trespassers and animals], and also hewed out [from stone] a vat [winepress] there, and he hoped it would yield grapes, and it brought forth stinking grapes."

In ancient Israel, the grape harvest, a time of great festiveness, began in the Jordan Valley in late July and along the coast in August and reached its peak throughout the country in September. When it was time for the harvest, vineyard workers left their homes to camp in temporary booths close to the grapes. Encouraged by song, the pickers performed the arduous task of harvesting the grapes—they cut the clusters with pruning hooks, placed them in special workbaskets, then carrying the accumulated fruit to the nearby winepress.

The harvested grapes were stomped by foot in a vat. The crushing was customarily accompanied with the rhythmic chants of the treaders. Rock vats from the biblical period have been found in nearly every part of the country, generally in great abundance, attesting to the pervasiveness of wine in the land. The crushed grapes were then transferred via clay jars to a fermentation vat or large crocks. The liquid obtained from the initial stomping (without heavy pressure) was stored separately, as it was of much higher quality. The lowest-quality juice was produced by mixing water with the dross; the mixture was not well-regarded and stored separately as well.

Archeological evidence at Gibeon, a city in the tribe of Benjamin about 4.5 miles north of Jerusalem, renowned for its famous biblical battle recorded in Joshua, reflects the magnitude of wine production in ancient Israel. Near the "Pool of Gibeon" were discovered pre-Babylonian underground facilities for a commercial-scale winery, including sixty six rock-cut circular vaults about six feet deep and in diameter, some used as presses and others, safeguarded by waterproof covers and naturally cooled, for fermentation vats. Nearby were numerous stoppers, seals, weights, and, notably, handles of clay wine jugs, neatly inscribed in ancient Hebrew with the names of the city, vineyard owners, and various nearby Judean towns to which wine was to be delivered. The storage capacity of the Gibeon cellar equals about 25,000 gallons, on a par with many modern wineries. Gibeon was destroyed by the Babylonians, bringing to an end this ancient wine center.

Hebrew contains numerous words for various stages and types of vines, grapes, and wine, denoting the importance of the vine and wine in ancient Israel and their effect on the Israelites. The word *yayin*, derived from the root *yvn* (that which bubbles), an obvious reference to the fermentation process, was used in the Bible both as a generic term for wine and, more specifically, a term for wine in its first year. In order for wine to be considered proper for religious uses, it must be at least 40 days old, having undergone secondary fermentation, at which point it passes from the *tirash* (immature/unfinished) stage into *yayin*.

As the grapes were crushed, the clear grape juice was exposed to the naturally occurring yeast adhering to the skins and stems. In the warm climate of Israel, the yeast almost immediately began to convert the sugar into alcohol and carbon dioxide, a process called fermentation. As long as the grape juice was not boiled, thereby killing the yeast, the fungi would continue to feed on the sugar and reproduce. If the juice was boiled before it had been fermented (before alcohol had been produced), the juice would spoil relatively quickly, while fermentation allowed it to be stored for a year or more.

As the level of alcohol rose, the yeast was killed and the bitter dead cells (*shmarim*) sank to the bottom of the container. The bitter dregs are mentioned in Psalms: "There is a cup in God's hand, with strong red wine, full of mixture, and He pours out of the same, surely the dregs thereof, all the wicked of the earth shall drain them, and drink them." Eventually, as more and more of the yeast died, the bubbling subsided. The wine was strained to remove as much of the undesirable dregs as possible. The immature wine was then transferred to airtight fermentation containers, commonly large earthenware jugs with a narrow neck, to mature and develop flavor during the slower secondary fermentation.

After the secondary fermentation of about forty days, the wine was strained to remove any sediment, then transferred to wineskins or amphorae—large ceramic jugs with a pointed bottom and narrow top—for storage or transport. Leather bottles were useful because new ones were pliable enough to stretch as the wine fermented. Israeli amphorae were generally tall with large handles and little or no decoration, unlike the typically ornate versions from Greece and Rome. The amphorae's handles were frequently inscribed with the name of the city where the wine had been produced, the winemaker's stamp, and sometimes the year and particular vintage. The inner surface of the amphorae was frequently coated with a resin, such as terebinth, which acted as a preservative and also imparted a pine flavor and aroma. The jars were filled to the brim and the wine was frequently topped with a thin layer of olive oil to seal out the air; the jars were then capped and sealed with pitch, another attempt to keep out the air. Amphorae made possible longtime storage, especially in caves or cool cellars. Glass bottles were not utilized for wine storage until the first century CE, when the Romans developed mass-production techniques, and wooden casks were not used until a century later.

After the biblical period, the character of Israeli wine changed with the widespread adoption of the Greek style of winemaking, which produced wines that were so concentrated that they needed to be diluted with water in order to be palatable. In the Greek method, fully ripe grapes were spread out on straw mats in the vineyard to dry in the sun for about a week, concentrating the sugar. Evaporation during storage in earthenware amphorae resulted in a thick, sweet, concentrated wine. The Greek style, which was already common in Greece by the time of Homer (c. eighth century BCE), probably developed because high-alcohol, high-sugar wines last much longer than low-alcohol ones, and are also much easier to transport. Before the Greek period, watered-down wine was considered by Jews to be corrupted, but by the time of the Talmud, wine that did not require three parts of water to dilute it was "not considered wine" and was deemed unfit for consumption. In this vein, the Talmud instructed that the Four Cups drunk at the Roman-era Passover Seder had to be mixed with three parts water to one part wine. Subsequently, the advent of the later Roman style of wine led to a return to wine requiring less or no dilution. In Roman times, it is estimated that the average person consumed a quart of wine every day.

At the end of the Second Commonwealth, Roman legions laid waste to the ancient Judean vineyards. The might of Rome, however, could not erase fifteen hundred years of accumulated knowledge, and the Jews brought their viticultural skills with them to the Diaspora. One reason that Jews continued to engage in this form of agriculture was to ensure the continuing availability of kosher wine. According to Jewish law, after the crushing of the grapes, only a Sabbath-observant person may come in contact with the juice, unless it has been heated above a certain point (*yayin mevushal*), rendering it out of the category of wine. This special restriction applies only to grape wine and juice, and not to other alcoholic beverages.

Since Muslim law forbids alcohol, Jews generally ran the vineyards and wine trade—when the authorities permitted these enterprises—in Islamic lands. The frequent mention of wine in Sephardic poetry reveals the Iberian Jews' fondness for it.

Early Ashkenazim also retained their love of wine. Jews in France, who were tilling vineyards there centuries before the arrival of the Franks (the Germanic tribe that conquered Gaul in the sixth century gave the land its name, France), proved to be particularly adept at this ancient craft. However, the restrictions and persecutions of medieval Europe took their toll, and these lands and the ancient viticultural lore were eventually lost. On the other hand, Italian Jews have been making dry wines for thousands of years. Due to the climate in Hungary, Romania, and Slovakia, Jews in these lands had access to high-quality grapes that produced fine wines. Many families made their own supply at home, while some Jewish communities made arrangements with local winemakers to produce special kosher batches under the supervision of a local rabbi. In these areas, wine was not only a ritual object, but also a beverage that was consumed with meals on a regular basis.

While the Jews of western and southern Europe retained a preference for dry wines, the story was very different in the northeast, where most of the Ashkenazim eventually settled. The climate, soil, and culture of Poland, northern Germany, Ukraine, and the Baltic States did not lend itself to viticulture, and high-quality grapes were generally too expensive or nonexistent. Whiskey, such as vodka and rye, and distilled liqueurs were more prevalent in these areas. Wine, made from whatever substandard grapes were occasionally available, generally required a large amount of sugar to be potable. More often, it was made from raisins, berries, or other fruit, which yielded intensely sweet wines. In northern Europe, wine was no longer drunk in place of water or as an integral part of the meal, but merely for rituals. As a result, eastern Europeans developed an affinity for syrupy sweet varieties, called Kiddush wine or sacramental wine. Thus the first wineries established in modern Israel—Schorr in the Old City of Jerusalem in 1848 and Teperberg in 1870—which were backed by Sir Moses Montefiore, devoted themselves solely to sweet wine.

Eastern European immigrants brought their affinity for sweet wines to the New World; as in eastern Europe, in the eastern United States, high-quality grapes were nonexistent. In 1899, Sam Schapiro, an immigrant from Galicia (now southern Poland), opened a small restaurant on Attorney Street on the Lower East Side of Manhattan, where he made his own wine, the sweet type. Schapiro's wine proved more popular than his food and he soon began expanding that business, starting the first kosher wine company in America. The introduction in 1869 of Concord grape juice—which was first commercially sold in bottles in 1893—quickly led to the planting of Concord grape vines in Upstate New York, just in time for Sam Schapiro's new business. In 1907, Schapiro opened a structure on Rivington Street with a block-long cellar, which endured until 2001. Schapiro initially offered only one type of wine, a Kiddush wine made from inexpensive Concord grapes transported down the Hudson River from Upstate New York; these grapes yielded a harsh juice that required the addition of plenty of sugar during the winemaking process. Schapiro soon expanded to Malaga, another sweet wine, although Concord remained the best seller. The company proudly boasted, "The wine you can almost cut with a knife."

In 1935, shortly after the end of Prohibition, Leo Starr and Meyer Robinson, two former employees of the defunct Gafen Industries, a wine company closed due to Prohibition, partnered with the large matza producer Manischewitz to use its brand name for an unconnected wine business. The winery in Bush Terminal in Brooklyn soon became the largest kosher winery in America. Manischewitz's main competitor was Mogen David, founded in Chicago in 1933 by the Cohen and Marcus families. Sweet wines completely dominated the American Jewish wine market and, in the minds of Jewish consumers and non-Jews alike, sweet wine became synonymous with Jewish wine, not to mention the butt of many a joke.

In the 1940s, the Pluczenik brothers opened the Kedem Winery on the Lower East Side to appeal to the Orthodox community and sold typical sweet wine. In 1848, Emanuel Herzog founded a winery in Vrobove, Slovakia. The Herzog's operation eventually became the royal wine supplier to Emperor Franz Josef, who loved the family's off-dry Riesling, and presented the title of baron to Emanuel's great grandson, Philip. At the onset of World War II, the winery was seized by the Nazis. The family survived in hiding and in 1948, following the Communist takeover of Czechoslovakia, Philip's grandson, Eugene Herzog, brought his family to America and went to work for Kedem as a truck driver and eventually winemaker. In 1958, Eugene purchased Kedem and brought his four sons into the business. Against the prevailing wisdom of the elder statesmen of the wine trade and nearly everyone else, Kedem revolutionized the American kosher wine market. In 1972, remembering the drier wines of Slovakia, Eugene's son, David Herzog, in an unprecedented move, imported one thousand cases of three varieties of kosher French dry wines. The company continued importing dry wines and in 1986 introduced its own line. In addition to Herzog, various other kosher wineries opened in California. Today, nearly every wine-growing area of Europe produces high-quality kosher wines. Kosher wineries operate from Chile to Australia.

Meanwhile, the situation in Israel changed in a major way in 1889 when Baron Edmond de Rothschild, owner of Chateau Lafite in Bordeaux and a dedicated supporter of Jewish settlements in Israel, invested a significant sum of money in the effort to establish new vineyards and obtained and planted high-grade varieties of European grapes in local vineyards. He built large wine cellars at Rishon le-Zion in 1889, southeast of Tel Aviv, and a second facility in Zichron Ya'akov in 1892, south of Haifa, both of which produced wines in the French style. In 1906, Rothschild established the Carmel Wine Growers Cooperative to produce the grapes and make and export the wine; the Carmel Mizrachi cooperative is still Israel's largest winery.

In 1976, kibbutzniks in the Golan Heights, who previously had concentrated on apple processing, planted the first vines that had been seen in the Golan in nearly two thousand years. The new enterprise imported vine stock from California and brought in young American winemakers. In 1983, eight kibbutzim and *moshavim* in the Golan joined forces to form the Hazor Wineries cooperative (the enterprise was later incorporated as the Golan Heights Winery), which marketed its wine under three labels—Yarden, Gamla, and Golan. The Golan group's wines set high standards and were consistent in quality. Within a few years, the Golan Winery had grown into Israel's third-largest winery.

In 1950, the Segal family, known in Israel for its distilleries, took over Askalon Wines in Ramle. Influenced by what the Golan Winery had achieved, Askalon went from making two generic wines to producing many varietals. In 1988, Stock, distiller of numerous liquors and brandies, built a new winery in the town of Ariel. Two years later, two of Stock's largest grape growers, Shmuel Boxer and Yair Lerner, acquired the Israeli Stock Company and renamed the winery Barkan Wine Cellars. They then acquired Segal Winery in 2001, making Barkan Israel's second largest winery.

Beginning in the 1980s, Israelis began traveling abroad more, returning home with an increased appetite for fine wines, and thus providing a ready market for the new high-quality Israeli vintages. In 2009, Israel had eight major wineries, ten medium-sized wineries, and more than 180 boutique wineries, which produced around 33 million bottles. From the coastal plain, with its sandy soil and semitropical temperatures, to the Golan Heights, with its ideal volcanic basalt plateau and microclimate of warm days and cool nights, the land of Israel once again abounds with vines.

(See also Grape and Raisin)

WOT

Wot is a spicy and fiery stew.
Origin: Ethiopia
Other names: *watt.*

Wot, the national dish of Ethiopia, is commonly cooked in a clay vessel over an open fire. For large celebrations, men take over the cooking duties, preparing the *wot* outdoors in large kettles. A *wot* may contain *doro* (chicken), *begee* (lamb or goat), *siga* (beef), or *assa* (fish) or be vegetarian with *shirro* (chickpeas), *kik* (split peas), or *misir* (lentils). A *wot* always contains *berbere*, a chili-based combination of spices similar to Indian curry powder but much hotter. The *berbere* is typically added to a *wot* early, in large amounts, so that the longer cooking time develops the full flavor and heat. The result is one of the world's hottest dishes. *Alicha/aleecha* ("mild" in Amharic) is a less fiery version of this stew.

Ethiopian stews include a rather thick sauce with a large amount of onions serving as the base. The unique method of cooking the onions in a dry skillet before adding the fat helps to break them down completely, thereby thickening the sauce. *Wots* also include plenty of garlic and ginger. Tomato sauce or plenty of paprika is used to make a *keiy* (red) *wot*. *Doro wot*, unquestionably the favorite Ethiopian dish, typically contains hard-boiled eggs; traditionally, one piece of chicken and one egg is served per portion. Jews generally reserved meat *wots* for special occasions, such as the Sabbath and festivals.

Wots are daily fare in Ethiopia, making up nearly 10 percent of the diet; *injera* (pancake bread) constitutes much of the remaining 90 percent. Several layers of *injera* are piled in the middle of a *mesob* (woven straw mat that serves as the table) as a common platter and the stew is placed on top, as well as perhaps a few salads and cooked vegetables. Ethiopian stews and side dishes are characteristically eaten with the right hand; the diners tear off pieces of *injera* and use them to scoop up little portions of *wot*. When *injera* is torn into small pieces and stirred into a *wot*, the dish is called *fitfit*. Less common is *enferfer*, made by finely crumbling dried *injera* and stirring it into a *wot* along with fried onions and green peppers. *Wots* made from legumes supplement the lysine deficiency of a diet based on teff *injera*.

The *injera* or other flatbreads also help, somewhat, to mute the fire of the chilies. Vegetarian *wots* may be accompanied with *iab* (Ethiopian cheese), as dairy also helps to cool the heat. Sometimes extra *wot* is rolled up in an *injera*, making a *gursha*, and one to three of them may be presented to an honored guest as a token of respect and affection. Coffee is typically sipped at the end of the meal.

The Sanbat (Sabbath) was and is a very special part of the Ethiopian Jew's week. Beta Israel meals are prepared in advance with everything ready before sundown on Friday and all dishes are served at room temperature. Even those who cannot afford it during the week, make a special effort to have a little chicken or meat in their Sabbath *wots*.

(See also Alicha, Berbere, Iab, and Injera)

ETHIOPIAN SPICY CHICKEN STEW (*DORO WOT*)

4 TO 6 SERVINGS   [MEAT]

- 5 large red or yellow onions, minced
- ½ cup vegetable oil
- 3 to 4 cloves garlic, minced
- 1 teaspoon minced fresh ginger
- 2 to 4 tablespoons *berbere* (Ethiopian chili powder)
- 1 cup water
- 1 cup tomato sauce
- About 1 teaspoon salt
- About ⅛ teaspoon ground black pepper
- 1 (3- to 4-pound) chicken, cut into 12 pieces, or 6 chicken thighs and 6 drumsticks
- 4 to 6 hard-boiled eggs, peeled

1. In a dry large skillet or pot, cook the onions over medium heat, stirring constantly, until they begin to soften, about 5 minutes. Do not burn.

2. Add the oil. When it begins to sputter, add the garlic, ginger, and berbere and sauté until fragrant, about 1 minute. Add ½ cup water. Add the tomato sauce, salt, and pepper. Bring to a boil and cook, stirring constantly, until the liquid is reduced to the consistency of heavy cream, about 8 minutes.

3. Add the chicken and toss until well coated, 2 to 3 minutes. Stir in the remaining ½ cup water. Cover, reduce the heat to low, and simmer, stirring occasionally, until the chicken is tender, about 30 minutes. Add a little more water if the liquid reduces too much.

4. With a toothpick or the tines of a fork, pierce ½-inch-deep holes over the surface of each egg. Add the eggs to the wot, turn gently in the sauce, and heat through, about 5 minutes.

Y

YAHRZEIT

Various Jewish communities hold special ceremonies to recognize the anniversary of a relative's death, practices dating back to the late medieval period. The Talmud mentioned the theoretical case of someone who takes a vow to eschew meat or wine on the anniversary of the death of his father, but not in regard to any fixed or official ritual. Ashkenazim commemorate the anniversary of a close relative's death, according to the Hebrew calendar, with a *yahrzeit* (Yiddish meaning "year time"). The term was first recorded in a Jewish source around 1420 by Rabbi Jacob Mollin of Mainz, Germany. The customs were described in detail shortly thereafter by Rabbi Isaac Tyrnau of Austria in *Sefer Ha-Minhagim*. The observance of *yahrzeit* spread from Germany to most other Jewish communities; Sephardim substituted the Hebrew term *nachalah* (heritage/inheritance) or *petira* (death). In modern Hebrew, it is generally *yom ha'shanah* (day of the year). Originally, a *yahrzeit* was only held for a parent, but the ritual was extended to include a spouse, sibling, and child.

The *yahrzeit* is marked by several customs, which became deeply ingrained among Jews. Based on the line in Proverbs, "The soul of a man is the light of the Lord," a twenty-four-hour memorial candle is lit at sundown on the evening preceding the anniversary of the death. *Yahrzeit* candles are also lit during the week of shiva (seven days) following the burial, as well as at sundown preceding Yom Kippur, and on the last day of Sukkot, Passover, and Shavuot, when Ashkenazim recite the *Yizkor* (memorial prayer) in the synagogue. On the *yahrzeit*, the Mourner's Kaddish prayer is recited in the synagogue. Some people visit the grave of the departed, while many make a special effort to perform extra mitzvot (good deeds) and Torah study to bring merit to the departed. Some relatives commemorate a *yahrzeit* by fasting, but among Chasidim it became common to sponsor a kiddush in the synagogue, saying a "*L'chaim*" over a glass of schnapps. Some hold a *siyyum* (the completion of the study of an entire Jewish work of scholarship) on the occasion in honor of the deceased, including a celebratory meal.

Sephardim, on the anniversary of a death, hold a *meldado* or *meldadura* (from the Ladino *companas de meldar*, "study group") for the deceased with relatives and friends. Candles are burned and various sections of the Mishnah and Zohar are read, including those beginning with letters spelling out the names of the deceased and his or her mother. Afterwards, various foods, including *biscochos de levadura* (bread rings) or *biscochos de huevo* (unsweetened egg pastries), raisins, hard-boiled eggs, chickpeas, and sweetened drinks are served, allowing the participants to recite various benedictions. Extra food is prepared for distribution to the poor. The *meldado* was originally a home ritual, but recently it has largely been shifted to the synagogue.

Syrians hold *ariyat* (readings) at various stages of the mourning process to mark the conclusion of each phase, reciting passages of the Zohar and offering eulogies. An *aryiat* is held after the afternoon prayer service of the final day of shiva. Those present later join the mourners in a dinner. At the conclusion of *sheloshim* (thirty days), another *ariyat* is held, followed by a sweet buffet.

Moroccans conduct a *mishmarah* (Hebrew for "guard/vigil"), to study the Zohar and *Pirkei Avot* (Ethics of the Fathers) and read Hosea 14:2–10 in memory of a man and Samuel 2:1 in memory of a woman. Afterwards, a dinner is served featuring traditional foods of mourning and benedictions are recited in memory of the deceased.

The Talmud also mentions a tradition recalling the anniversary of the death of a revered rabbi. Around the late sixteenth century, this emerged as a Mizrachi custom of *hilula* ("celebration/wedding" in Aramaic) often in the form of a pilgramage. Mizrachim, especially those from North Africa, also celebrate a *hilula* on the anniversary of the death of departed *tzadikim* (righteous persons)—people gather at the gravesite and hold study sessions, celebrating, and feasting in their memory. *Hilulot* served as a strong unifying element in the Maghrebi Jewish communities.

The most significant *hilula* is on the eighteenth of Iyar, coinciding with the minor festival of Lag b'Omer. Held for Rabbi Shimon bar Yochai (died c. 170 CE), one of the most prominent sages of the Mishnah and purportedly the primary author of the Zohar. He left instructions not to commemorate *Yom Sh'met* (day of his death) with sadness, but *Yom Simchato* (day of his happiness). In Israel, since the mid-nineteenth century, large groups numbering in the thousands, including Mizrachim, Sephardim, and Ashkenazim have gathered at Rabbi Shimon's gravesite in Meron in the Galilee, lighting bonfires and torches, dancing, singing, and roasting meat. On Lag b'Omer, three other major but smaller *hilulot* are held in Israel for Rabbi Meir Ba'al haNess in Tiberias, for Rabbi Simeon the Just in Jerusalem, and for Elijah the Prophet near his cave outside Haifa.

(See also Seudat Havra'ah)

YAKHNA

Yakhna is a meat stew usually with vegetables.
Origin: Persia
Other names: *khorak, yakhni;* Turkey and Greece: *yahni.*

In the Middle East, meat is rarely cooked in large pieces; instead, it is cut into small chunks and frequently simmered in stews, such as the simple Persian peasant *yakhna.* It is named after the covered earthenware crock in which it was originally cooked; the name of this vessel came from a Farsi word meaning "store of food." *Yahkna,* akin to the Persian *khoresh,* is the eastern equivalent of the Maghrebi tagine. A *yakhni-polow* is a Persian pilau made in a stew; the broth makes the rice brown and flavorful, qualities that are favored in India and Afghanistan. For more than a millennium, these tasty stews served as the regular fare of Persian Jews.

Arabs and Turks spread similar forms of *yakhna* westward to Syria, Lebanon, Egypt, and Libya as well as eastward to Uzbekistan and northern India, where they became standard fare. Turkish Jews commonly add green beans or fava beans. Yemenite *batata yakhni* is a stew of chicken, potatoes, tomatoes, and cabbage.

In many Middle Eastern homes, a crock of stew hung near the hearth—a single batch along with plenty of bread could feed a family for several days or longer. The meat used for a *yakhna* is usually tough, requiring a long, slow simmer. Originally, cooks added the meat to the stew without browning it, but many cooks today prefer to brown it first and also sauté the onions for added levels of flavor. Lamb, specifically from young fat-tailed sheep, is the predominant meat in Persian cooking. The meat serves as a flavoring agent for various vegetables and legumes; poorer families make do with less meat and more vegetables. Turnip was once the primary ingredient, but more recent arrivals to the area, including eggplant, green beans, and okra, are now preferred. When unexpected guests appeared, a little water and some more vegetables were added.

Besides meat, the other necessity in these stews is onion and plenty of it. Garlic is generally ignored by Persians, but included by their neighbors. The arrival of the South American tomato led to its use in the stew; in a version called *yakhnat al-banadura,* tomatoes frequently replace all of the water, and the meat is simmered in a thick tomato sauce. Whereas olive oil is used near the Mediterranean, in central Asia sheep's tail fat or sesame oil is more common. Typical of Persian cuisine, this dish includes fewer spices and more fresh herbs than stews of other Middle Eastern countries. *Yakhna* is usually served with rice or noodles.

(See also Chelow and Guvetch)

❦ PERSIAN LAMB STEW (*YAKHNA BARHE*)

6 TO 8 SERVINGS   [MEAT]

 ¼ cup vegetable oil
 3 pounds boneless lamb shoulder, cut into ½-inch cubes
 4 medium yellow onions, sliced
 4 cups (2 pounds) peeled, seeded, and chopped tomatoes
 ½ cup chopped fresh cilantro or flat-leaf parsley
 About 1 teaspoon table salt or 2 teaspoons kosher salt
 About ½ teaspoon ground black pepper
 1½ pounds stemmed okra (do not cut the pods), green beans, lima beans, peeled and cubed carrots, or peeled and cubed turnips, or 4 cups cooked chickpeas (optional)

1. In a large pot, heat the oil over medium heat. Add the lamb and onions and sauté until the meat is browned on all sides and the onions are softened, about 10 minutes. Cover and cook over medium heat, stirring frequently, for 30 minutes.

2. Add the tomatoes, cilantro, salt, pepper, and, if using, okra. Cover and simmer over low heat, adding a little water if necessary, until the meat is tender and the sauce is thick, about 1 hour, or longer if using more mature meat.

YEAST

Yeast is a microscopic single-celled plant responsible for turning fruit juice into wine, barley into beer, and wheat flour into leavened bread through a chemical reaction called fermentation. In wine and beer, alcohol is the desired by-product of yeast fermentation, and the carbon dioxide is allowed to bubble off. In bread, it is the carbon dioxide, along with a little assistance from the steam generated during baking from the liquid in the dough, that causes the dough to rise (leaven); the alcohol burns off in the course of baking.

Many home bakers lacked the time, patience, and expertise for making and maintaining starter doughs (*seor* in Hebrew) and, particularly in the ale-brewing areas of northern Europe, began using the foam from the top of ale vats to leaven breads. The English took to calling the ale froth by various names, most now archaic: yest from the Old English gyst (foam/boil); barm from the German *barme* (substance causing boiling); and godesgood, since its mysterious and unpredictable properties came "from the grace of God." Barm is called brewer's yeast in contemporary English.

Among the disadvantages of barm are its unavailability except while brewing and the risk of passing any undesirable or even dangerous species of yeast and bacteria from the fermentation vat to the dough. Barm also varied from batch to batch and, therefore, the quality and flavor of bread made with barm was always unpredictable. Nevertheless, many Europeans preferred barm bread to one made from a starter dough, as it was lighter (when it worked) and lacked the starter's pronounced sourdough flavor.

Barm was used in a liquid form. Then in the late eighteenth century, Dutch distillers discovered how to separate the yeast in the foam that rose to the surface of fermenting ale from most of the water and press it into cakes that could stay fresh for up to a few weeks. Soon distillers began to manufacture yeast for bakers by feeding a small culture of a yeast strain in a liquid medium until it reached the proper stage of development; this product is called "cream yeast"

In 1868, Charles Fleischmann, a Hungarian Jewish immigrant, distressed by the poor quality of American bread, introduced compressed yeast to America. Ads, like this one from 1890, helped to bring yeast to the American mainstream.

and it is still sold to large-scale manufacturers. The process of producing fresh yeast was further refined in Vienna, Austria, and the product was called "German yeast" in England. Many of the central European distillers and bakers were Jews and, as a result, central European Jews began making and using fresh yeast for leavening their breads. As the nineteenth century progressed, the term yeast supplanted the other English synonyms, although no one yet understood the chemical process of fermentation.

In 1836, French physician Charles Cagniard de la Tour became the first person to actually report that yeast was an accumulation of numerous minuscule plants and to demonstrate that the cells were necessary for fermentation. De la Tour and the few other scientists who agreed with him were met with scorn by the scientific establishment, which believed that fermentation was caused by a chemical process. In 1857, Louis Pasteur proved the cell theory.

Charles Louis Fleischmann, a Jewish native of Budapest, Hungary, who was descended from a line of distillers, managed a distillery in Vienna that also produced yeast. In 1865, he traveled to New York to attend the wedding of a sister. While in the United States, he met and married his wife, Henrietta, and decided to remain. Fleischmann was distressed by the poor quality of American bread. Further complicating matters, at this time there was a shift in tastes—Americans began to prefer lighter, German-style lagers over English-style ales, resulting in a drastic shortage of barm. Consequently, many American bakers used fermented potato peelings for leavening their breads. In 1867, Fleischmann briefly visited Austria and then returned to America with a vial of a desirable strain of live yeast.

In 1868, Charles and his brother Maximilian relocated to Cincinnati, Ohio, and garnered the interest of a local distiller, James Gaff, who went into business with the two brothers. In 1870, Fleischmann built his first yeast-manufacturing plant outside of Cincinnati (the factory also distilled the first American gin). In large copper vats, he concocted a mixture of rye, corn, and barley malt in which to feed his imported yeast (later molasses replaced the grain for feeding the yeast). Charles was granted a patent in 1872 for the first commercially produced and standardized yeast, which was in the form of compressed fresh yeast cakes.

Initially, Americans largely ignored Fleischmann's innovation, but central European immigrants accustomed to fresh yeast purchased it. In 1876, at the Philadelphia Centennial Exposition, the brothers introduced their innovation to the American public through a "Vienna Model Bakery" exhibit, demonstrating how the dough was made and the bread and Viennese pastries were baked, and even serving samples. Fleischmann's yeast quickly became a nationwide success, revolutionizing American baking. He soon had fourteen scattered factories to provide his highly perishable product. The advent of refrigerated railroad cars in the 1880s meant that Fleischmann's yeast could be shipped far and wide. By the 1920s, the company had nine hundred distribution centers throughout much of the United States and Fleischmann's yeast was being sold at most groceries.

In 1883, Fleischmann's began the selective breeding of pure yeast cultures, which in the 1930s led to the introduction of active dry yeast, a dehydrated strain that becomes reactivated when combined with moisture. The longer shelf life and handiness of the newcomer quickly made it the type used in most American homes and recipes.

Toward the end of the twentieth century, a new dry yeast variety was developed, made with a gentler drying process from a more potent strain of yeast, leaving almost all the cells alive; this product is known as rapid-rising or instant yeast. It is more porous and granular than the active dry type and, since there are no dead cells encasing the living ones, is not dissolved in liquid first but mixed directly into the flour. Today, Fleischmann's remains the world's leading producer of yeast.

(See also Beer, Bread, Chametz, Seor, and Wine)

YOGURT

Before the dawn of recorded history, people learned to extend the life of highly perishable dairy products by allowing them to ferment with certain beneficial acid-producing bacteria in leather bags and gourds. The biblical Job referred to fermented milk in his lament: "Have You not poured me out like [fermented] milk, and curdled me like cheese?" Today, the most well-known and widespread type of cultured dairy product is yogurt. This was not the case at all just a mere half century ago.

The word yogurt or yoghurt, derived from the Turkish *yogun* (dense/thick), was first recorded in eleventh-century Turkish texts, but is believed to date to the eighth century. Meanwhile, yogurt was known as *laban* in standard Arabic, *zabadi* in Yemen and Egypt (in Egypt, *laban* means "milk"), *kiselo mlyako* in Bulgaria, *oxygala* or *yaourti* in Greece, *mast* in Farsi, *matsoni* in Georgia, and *dahi* in India.

Yogurt is made by mixing warm milk (90°F to 110°F) with a specific starter culture and allowing it to sit in a warm place without being disturbed until it firms in ten to twelve hours. Fresh yogurt contains billions of live cells per milliliter that prevent the growth of harmful bacteria and thereby keep the milk safe for several days without refrigeration. The microbial conversion of the milk-sugar lactose into lactic acid produces the characteristic "sourness" or "tanginess" of these products and also inhibits the growth of bacteria that can cause food poisoning. The growth of lactic acid in yogurt reduces the pH of the milk, resulting in its coagulation and creamy texture.

The direct ancestor of today's yogurt was probably created by accident when two equal amounts of benign bacteria—*Lactobacillus bulgaricus* and *Streptococcus thermophilus*, now the standard bacterial culture—came in contact with and coagulated a batch of milk. This may have happened six thousand years ago among the nomads of central Asia, who learned how to replicate the process. The Arabs have a legend that an angel taught Abraham how to make *laban*. Until very recently, yogurt was a homemade product, prepared with naturally occurring beneficial bacteria saved from the previous batch.

It was the Ottoman Turks who most eagerly embraced yogurt, putting it to many culinary uses and spreading it throughout their domain. While yogurt has long been a staple from the Balkans to India, it was until recently practically unknown to most of Europe. Yogurt was such a rare item in France that it made history when a Turkish Jewish doctor sent by Sultan Suleiman the Magnificent used it to cure King Francis I (1494–1547) of France of his severe intestinal trouble. Centuries later, it was another Sephardic doctor who popularized yogurt, both the item and its Turkish name, in modern Europe and America.

Isaac Karasu (1874–1939), a Sephardic physician from Salonika, left home in 1912 due to the Balkan Wars and relocated his family to Barcelona, Spain. Changing the spelling of his name to Carasso, he opened a medical practice in his new home, and noticed that many of his patients suffered from digestive problems. Importing cultures from Bulgaria, Carasso set about producing yogurt and selling it, at first as medicine. In 1919, Carasso started a yogurt business in Spain, becoming the first industrial manufacturer of this cultured product. He named his company Danone, using the nickname of his young son Daniel, and produced only plain yogurt. Among his innovations was packaging the yogurt in individual glass containers.

In 1929, Daniel Carasso, having studied in France, expanded the company to Paris, eventually taking over the business from his father. Fleeing Europe during World War II, Daniel, along with a family friend from Spain, Joseph Metzger, a Swiss-born Jewish businessman, arrived in the United States in 1942. Together they opened an American branch of the company, spelling the name Dannon, in the Bronx, New York. At the onset, distribution was small—about 648 half-pint jars a day, sold primarily to Greeks and Turks. Soon disposable waxed cups replaced the returnable glass jars. In 1947, Dannon became the first manufacturer to introduce a variety that included strawberry preserves on the bottom of the yogurt. This innovation proved so successful that Dannon soon added blueberry, raspberry, and lemon flavors. In 1951, Carasso returned to France to reclaim his confiscated yogurt plant and eight years later sold his interest in American Dannon to the Beatrice Corporation. Previously, his French operations had been a modest success, but yogurt caught on in France in the 1950s. Danone expanded to 150 countries, including Turkey, turning Groupe Danone into a multinational business and the world's leading producer of cultured dairy products.

Joe Metzger's son, Juan, born in Barcelona, became president of Dannon in 1959 and subsequently spurred the company's unprecedented growth in the United States. Sparked by the success of Dannon's television commercials beginning in 1976 showing centenarians from Soviet Georgia eating yogurt, and further hyped by health writers, dieters, and hippies, yogurt rapidly emerged as a true pop phenomenon. Many contend that Dannon's marketing campaign was the most successful food product campaign of the twentieth century, as it transformed an item practically unknown to most Americans before the 1960s into an integral part of the American diet and culture. Until the 1970s, yogurt was practically unknown in Israel. In 1971, Strauss—one of Israel's largest dairies—partnered with Danone, to produce a line of yogurt. By 2002, yogurt sales in Israel surpassed those of the previous dominant cultured milk product, *Leben*, and continue to expand every year.

Yogurt is ubiquitous at Middle Eastern dairy meals—plain or mixed into chopped vegetables as a salad; as a sauce for cooked vegetables, rice, and lentils; and as a dessert drizzled with jam or honey. In the Levant, yogurt is also strained to produce a cheeselike product known as *labaneh*. *Ayran* is a drink from the Near East and the Balkans consisting of yogurt mixed with water; it is akin to the Indian *lassi*.

(See also Borani, Iab, Kashk, Labaneh, Leben, and Tarator)

YOM HA'ATZMAUT

On the fifth day of the Hebrew month of Iyar (May 14, 1948), Israel declared its independence, ending more than two thousand years of foreign domination. On the anniversary of that historic occasion, Jews celebrate Yom Ha'atzmaut (Israel Independence Day). The day immediately before is observed as Yom Ha'zikkaron (Israeli Memorial Day), the fourth of Iyar, a time to memorialize the soldiers who died defending Israel. At sunset sirens blast throughout the country, signaling the end of solemnity and the commencement of Yom Ha'atzmaut. The streets fill with people—laughing, conversing, and singing. The following day is celebrated with parades, fireworks, picnics, and an international Bible quiz. In Israel, many kibbutzim serve traditional Sabbath and holiday fare. In America, it is customary to serve foods associated with Israel—pita, falafel, hummus, Israeli salad, and baba ghanouj—many of which are perfect for picnics. The décor follows the color of the Israeli flag—blue and white.

YOM KIPPUR

Tradition relates that on the tenth day of the month of Tishri (which falls in September or October), Moses returned from Mount Sinai with the second set of tablets of the Ten Commandments and informed the people that they had been forgiven for the incident with the golden calf. Ever since, that day has been Yom Kippur, the Day of Atonement. This twenty-five-hour fast, the culmination of the ten-day period that begins with Rosh Hashanah, is the most profoundly moving day on the Jewish calendar.

Around the ninth century, a ritual developed, perhaps in central Asia, called *kapparot* ("atonements," *kappores* in Yiddish), which spread among eastern Ashkenazim in the following centuries. On the day before Yom Kippur, people symbolically transfer their sins to any kosher animal not offered in the Temple by swinging (*shlugen*) it three times above their head. A chicken (*kappores-hindel*) in particular was deemed appropriate because the Hebrew word for rooster, *gever*, also means "man." Afterward, the chicken was ritually slaughtered and served as dinner for the family or given to the poor. At the time, Sephardic authori-

ties strongly disparaged this ritual; Rabbi Joseph Caro called it a foolish custom based on paganism.

However, sixteenth century Kabbalists, who viewed the link between men and chickens as mystical, strongly supported the ritual and this sentiment was adopted by some Sephardim and Mizrachim. Some Ashkenazim, especially Germans, object to the entire concept of *kapparot* and refuse to perform the ritual, while others fault the insensitivity to which the animals are subjected and substitute coins wrapped in a cloth for the bird and, after swinging it above their head, donate the money to charity.

As it is a fast day, there are obviously no traditional Yom Kippur foods. However, the meals before and after the fast have both developed their own traditions. The eve prior to the fast has a festive character. Partaking of a lavish meal at that time is elevated to a special status because the Talmud declared, "Everyone who eats and drinks on the ninth of Tishri is considered as having fasted on the ninth and tenth." Thus the merit of eating on the ninth is considered to be on a par with fasting on the following day. The table for the *Seudat Mafseket* (meal of cessation) is set in the same way as for the Sabbath and diners wear white clothes or their usual Sabbath clothing. Ukrainian Jews developed the custom of forming the challahs for the meal before the fast into images of ascension: birds (Isaiah 31:5), symbolizing that all sins should fly away and that our prayers should soar to the heavens; or ladders, reminiscent of Jacob's dream.

For the prefast meal, carbohydrates and proteins predominate. Salty, spicy, and fried foods are avoided—bland is the name of the game—so as not to induce thirst during the fast. Nuts, which supposedly produce throat problems, and legumes and other gas-producing foods are also studiously avoided. Chicken, usually stewed, is the most common entrée. Among Ashkenazim, the inclusion of chicken dates back to the medieval ritual of *kapparot*. Many Sephardim, who generally do not practice *kapparot*, still serve chicken, often in tomato sauce, as it is lighter than meat. Sephardic meals always include a variety of salads. It is customary in Ashkenazic households to serve *goldena yoich* (chicken soup) with kreplach or farfel. Moroccan Jews serve both chicken soup and a chicken stew called *fricassada*. Syrian households might offer roast chicken accompanied with *hallob* (artichokes with stewed meat) or *inferike* (a ground veal mixture served with rice). Sweet desserts, which induce thirst, are avoided. Instead the meal may be ended with fresh fruit or compote or nothing at all.

The common denominator in break-the-fast foods is that cooks must be able to prepare them in advance and store them. Many of the dishes are included for either their purported restorative powers or their symbolic significance. Sephardim traditionally break their fast with a cool drink, the type varying from community to community. Greek and Turkish Jews traditionally sip *pepitada/soubiya*, a melon seed beverage whose whiteness symbolizes purity. Some Greek Jews break their fast with a glass of lemonade. Iraqis drink *hariri* (sweetened almond milk). Many other Sephardic communities serve flavored coffee. The Bene Israel of India make *sherbet*, a beverage prepared by boiling raisins in water, then straining the liquid.

The meal itself can be as simple or elaborate as desired. For Ashkenazim, it is usually a dairy affair, as the whiteness of milk befits Yom Kippur's theme of purity, and dairy foods are relatively simple. An Ashkenazic meal to break the fast might consist of bagels, noodle kugel, blintzes, cottage cheese or farmer cheese, and egg salad. It is a Chasidic custom to serve pickled or smoked fish, purportedly to restore some of the minerals lost during the fast.

A traditional Greek and Turkish meal to break the fast consists of pieces of bread dipped into an olive oil and lemon juice dressing, poached fish seasoned with lemon, *tzatziki* (cucumber and yogurt salad), *salata de pipino* (cucumber salad), cheeses, olives, and the traditional three pastries—*borekas*, *bulemas* and *boyos*. Syrian Jews might serve *koosa ou jiben* (baked zucchini with cheese), fish salad, cheeses, olives, and fresh fruit, as well as *jiben sambusak* (pastry cheese turnovers) and the ubiquitous *kaak* (sesame rings). Many Iraqis eat okra in tomato sauce.

Moroccan Jews follow the custom of their Arab neighbors, who eat *harira*, a meat, chickpea, and lentil soup after the fast of Ramadan, and also serve *m'kuli* (chicken with lemons and olives) for the main course. Some Sephardim serve chicken and a form of chicken soup, *avgolemono* (egg and lemon soup), as both are considered restorative. In Salonika, following the dairy portion of the meal, the dishes were removed and the chicken-based *avgolemono* was served. Some Hungarians offer their favorite dish, chicken *paprikás*.

Although the pre–Yom Kippur meal rarely contains a dessert, it is customary to include some sweet yeast bread or pastry in the meal to break the fast. Jews from central Europe enjoy sweet yeast rolls, such as *bilkes* (usually kneaded with fruits and nuts) or *schnecken* (cinnamon rolls). Sephardim traditionally serve sweet rolls called *panisicos dulces*. Many Italian Jews break their fast with *dictinobis di kipur* (doughnuts). Similarly, Jews from Mumbai break the fast with deep-fried sugar-stuffed semolina puffs called *karanjis*. Some Russians serve cheese-filled pastries called *kaletzin*. Alsatians and Hungarians enjoy kugelhopf. The Dutch prepare an apple cake or tart. Germans serve cookies called *zimtsterne* (cinnamon stars). Italians traditionally offer *dolce Rebecca* (spice cake) or *borriche pitiglianesi* (pastry turnovers). Many Greeks and Turks enjoy *reshicas* (pretzel-like cookies). Moroccans serve *fijuelas* (honey-soaked fried pastries). Iraqis feature *hadgi badah* (cardamom-almond cookies). Many Sephardim offer *tishpishti* or another syrup-drenched semolina cake. The Bene Israel prepare coconut crepes called *padhar*. Many Sephardim from the Levant and the Balkans end this meal with *sutlach* (rice-flour pudding).

Some families begin building their sukkah for Sukkot directly after the meal, thereby performing a mitzvah immediately after Yom Kippur. At this time, some Sephardic communities perform *Jufrah* (Arabic for "reconciliation"), visiting people to show respect and demonstrate camaraderie.

YOYO
Yoyo is an orange doughnut.
Origin: Tunisia

Tunisians love snacking, which they developed into an art form, including *brik* (potato-filled pastry), various sandwiches, and doughnuts. *Yoyo*, sometimes called a beignet, is one of the most popular Tunisian pastries. It is prepared both at home and at specialty stores and kiosks. The name of this dish is probably derived from the Ladino *boyo*, which in turn is derived from *bolo* (ball).

The original fried dough balls evolved into a baking powder doughnut with a hole. The similar Moroccan *sfenj* and Libyan *sfenz* are leavened with yeast. These baking powder–raised doughnuts have a denser texture than the airier yeast-raised versions. The surface is slightly crunchy. In the Middle Eastern manner, *yoyos* are dipped into a honey syrup, producing a sort of glaze, or sprinkled with sugar.

Small doughnuts are made for breakfast, while large versions, called *babalouni* or *shishi*, appear in the afternoon as a snack. *Yoyos* are traditional on Hanukkah and popular on most joyous occasions. They are also common treats taken on a *hilula* (pilgrimage), along with *bollos* (almond-raisin breads), *makroud* (date-filled semolina cookies), date-filled *briks*, Jordan almonds, and *boukha* (fig liqueur). *Yoyos* are commonly accompanied with *naa-naa* (mint tea).

✦ TUNISIAN ORANGE DOUGHNUTS (*YOYO*)
ABOUT TWENTY-FOUR 3-INCH DOUGHNUTS [PAREVE OR DAIRY]

About 3½ cups (17.5 ounces) all-purpose flour
2 teaspoons double-acting baking powder
½ teaspoon table salt
4 large eggs
6 tablespoons orange juice, milk, or water
⅓ cup sugar
3 tablespoons vegetable oil
1 teaspoon orange-blossom water or vanilla extract
1 teaspoon grated orange zest (optional)
2 to 3 tablespoons finely grated fresh or
  unsweetened desiccated coconut (optional)
About 6 cups peanut or safflower oil for deep-frying

About 2 cups cooled *atar* (Middle Eastern Sugar Syrup, page 27), or confectioners' sugar for sprinkling

1. In a medium bowl, sift together the flour, baking powder, and salt. In a large bowl, combine the eggs, juice, sugar, vegetable oil, orange-blossom water, and, if using, zest and/or coconut. Gradually blend in the flour mixture to make a soft dough. Cover and refrigerate until the dough is easy to handle, about 2 hours.

2. Roll the dough into 2-inch balls, flatten into ½-inch thick rounds, and poke a large hole in the center of each one, forming a ring.

3. Place on a lightly floured surface, cover, and let stand for at least 10 minutes. Store at room temperature for up to 2 hours or in the refrigerator for up to 8 hours.

4. In a large pot, heat at least 2 inches peanut oil over medium heat to 365°F.

5. Fry 3 or 4 doughnuts at a time, turning once, until golden on all sides, about 1 minute per side. Remove with tongs, chopsticks, or a wire-mesh skimmer and let drain on a wire rack. Dip the warm doughnuts in the cooled syrup or dust with confectioners' sugar.

Z

ZA'ATAR (HYSSOP)

Za'atar or zahtar, called *eizov* in the Bible and *eizov matzui* (common hyssop) in modern Hebrew, is both the Arabic name of *Origanum syriacum* and a Levantine spice mixture made from this herb. Za'atar, a member of the Labiatae family, is also variously known as Syrian oregano, Lebanese oregano, white oregano, and Bible hyssop. It is a close relative of the common Greek oregano (*oregehno* and *eizovit peshutah* in Hebrew) and sweet marjoram (*eizovit* and *mayoran* in Hebrew). Za'atar and *eizov* are commonly translated into English as hyssop. There is, however, another plant also called by that name. The other hyssop (*Hyssopus officinalis*) is a native of southern Europe and has never grown in Israel. Furthermore, it is so bitter that it is rarely used in cooking.

The bushy perennial za'atar is native to the Levant. It is common in ledges and outcrops on mountains and grows between rocks, thriving where most plants cannot. It reaches about eighteen inches in height and the upright, slender, reddish stems sport a considerable number of fuzzy, heart-shaped leaves. The leaves are bright green when young in the spring, but they turn grayish green and the stems become woody and brown as the plant matures in the summer. The leaves have a pungent fragrance and a slightly minty, mildly bitter flavor; they are a bit spicier and more aromatic than both oregano and marjoram. The oil of *Origanum syriacum* contains at least forty compounds—some with antimicrobial and antioxidant properties—and has long been used in the Middle East to cure stomach aches, alleviate congestion, and for other medicinal purposes. Psalms exclaims, "Cleanse me with *eizov* that I may be pure; wash me that I may be whiter than snow."

Za'atar first appeared in the Bible before the Exodus: "You shall take a bunch of *eizov*, and dip it into the blood that is in the basin, and strike the beam over the door and the two doorposts from the blood in the basin; and none of you shall go out the door of his house until the morning."

Za'atar was subsequently a component of two biblical purification rites. It was part of the ceremony for cleansing lepers and part of the enigmatic red heifer rite (*parah adumah*), there utilized to remove the impurity of contact with a dead body. The Midrash explains, "The *eizov* is a lowly plant and, because of this, God singles it out as necessary for the performance of important duties: for Passover, for the purification of the leper, and for the burning of the red heifer." Another Midrash relates the significance of za'atar to the leper, "You were proud like the cedar, and the Holy One, humbled you like this *eizov* that is crushed by all." The Bible uses incidents and symbols, such as za'atar's modest status (as a lowly plant, crushed by all), for people to contemplate and internalize the attribute of humility.

In ancient Israel, za'atar and two related herbs, summer savory (*seeah*) and thyme (*korahnit*), were the three predominant herbs; they were used in cooking and for various medicinal purposes. Yet za'atar was not a highly valued seasoning in the Levant—those positions were held by coriander and cumin and imported spices like saffron. Za'atar was the spice of the common person, plentiful and useful but rarely found at fancy occasions or in sophisticated fare. Za'atar was generally not purchased in shops and bazaars, but rather gathered by individuals from wild plants or plucked from small home plots. Each spring, before the flowers formed and the plant's flavor was at its peak, families harvested a year's supply, dried the leaves in the sun, and stored the dried herb for future use. A little za'atar helped to enliven a farmer or peasant's diet, which consisted primarily of barley bread and barley gruel and various legumes.

Za'atar, a powerful symbol of the protection of the firstborn sons of the Israelites during the Tenth Plague in Egypt, is memorialized in the contemporary Seder in the form of the *karpas*, generally parsley or celery, which is dipped into salt water or vinegar. Some people, such as Maimonides, added a few za'atar leaves to charoset for its symbolic status rather than as a flavor preference. In his role as a physician, Maimonides, recommended za'atar for its healthful properties.

In the cuisine of modern Israel, drawing from local Arab practices, fresh za'atar leaves are added to salads and marinades. However, this spice's most popular role, and what it is currently best known for in America, is dried as the main ingredient of the Levantine spice mixture bearing its name; the mixture also contains ground sumac (a tart red berry) and toasted sesame seeds to mellow the intense flavor of the za'atar. Some blends include ground chickpeas, nuts, and/or wheat as well. The spice mixture is used to flavor salads and vegetables; sprinkled on *labaneh* (yogurt cheese), hummus, and eggs; spread over flatbreads before baking; used as a dry rub for fish, poultry, and meat; and mixed with olive oil as a spread and dip (*za'atar im zayit*). Arab bread vendors commonly offer small triangular packets of za'atar in which customers can dip their fresh *bagaleh* and bread.

Due to overexploitation, wild za'atar was declared a protected plant in Israel in 1977; picking commercial quantities carries a large fine or six months imprisonment. Each household is permitted up to ten kilograms annually, but most Arab families consume much more than that. Consequently, in the early 1990s, commercial za'atar growing and packaging emerged in the Galilee. Specially developed Israeli varieties of za'atar, as well as advanced irrigation techniques, resulted in superior leaves and large yields. Whereas ancient Israelis picked za'atar with backbreaking hand labor, today mechanical combines are used for harvesting. Official exports of za'atar now go to America and England, and it is unofficially exported to many parts of the Arab world. Nonetheless, the producers of many commercial Israeli products labeled "za'atar" actually substitute thyme, oregano, the spicier Roman hyssop/Persian za'atar (*Satureja thymbra*), or a mixture of cultivated herbs for the preferred *Origanum syriacum*.

◌ MIDDLE EASTERN HYSSOP, SESAME, AND SUMAC BLEND (ZA'ATAR)

ABOUT ⅔ CUP   [PAREVE]

¼ cup sesame seeds

¼ cup dried crushed za'atar leaves (or a mixture of dried marjoram, oregano, and thyme)

2 to 3 tablespoons ground sumac

About 1 tablespoon salt (optional)

1. In a dry skillet, toast the sesame seeds over medium heat, shaking the pan frequently, until lightly browned, 2 to 3 minutes. Transfer to a bowl and let cool.

2. In a spice grinder or blender, grind the sesame seeds with the za'atar, sumac, and, if using, salt. Store in an airtight container at room temperature for up to 2 months.

ZABAN

Zaban is a confection made of egg whites, sugar, and nuts.

Origin: Morocco

Other names: *jaban*, *zabane*.

Zaban is a beloved Moroccan confection that comes in several forms. An easy version of it is made by simply beating egg whites with sugar until the mixture is thick and fluffy. Another soft type involves a type of Italian meringue that is made by beating boiled sugar syrup and lemon juice into egg whites until the mixture has the consistency of marshmallow cream. These mixtures are sprinkled with chopped nuts and eaten with spoons. Another rendition is a taffy-like confection with a firmer consistency, called nougat.

Nougat, derived from the Latin word *nux* (nut) and known as *torrone* in Italy and *turron* in Spain, is a nut-based sweetmeat. Its origin dates back to at least medieval Byzantium and Persia—the name *zaban* appears to derive from the Persian word meaning "tongue"—and probably even further back to Rome, where confections were boiled from honey, eggs, and nuts.

There are two forms of nougat. Brown nougat is a crunchy brittle containing nuts, generally almonds, and sometimes fruit or chocolate. White nougat, akin to divinity and marshmallow, is a softer, chewier variety made by beating sugar syrup into egg whites, then folding in chopped nuts. White nougat emerged in seventeenth-century Montélimar, France, with the introduction of almond trees to Provence. In this confection, honey is beaten into egg whites, mixed with nuts, and dried in the sun. A commercial nougat factory opened in Montélimar in 1770. Cooks in the Maghreb added a little gum Arabic (*meski*) and alum (*chebba*) to flavor and stabilize the meringue, but today corn syrup and liquid glucose have become common. In Iran, white nougat is *gaz* (short for *nougaz*), made with pistachios or almonds, while *shirini zaban* are sugar cookies.

Zaban, frequently sporting a red stripe, was sold from small confection stands in Moroccan bazaars, while more ambitious vendors roamed the streets shouting *"Zaban! Zaban!"* or *"Zaban goul ou ban!"* (Buy or order nougat!)—hence the dish is sometimes called *zaban koulouban* to attract customers. The sticky nougat was wrapped around a long stick of bamboo or wood and the desired amount was cut off. Competitors peddled cotton candy, red candied apples, and other sweets. These entrepreneurs have all but disappeared, replaced by large manufacturers and stores. Only experienced cooks make the nougat type of *zaban* at home.

Zaban, usually the simpler, softer types, is traditional for the post-Passover celebration of Mimouna, as the ingredients are all kosher for Passover and readily available. White nougat is enjoyed by Moroccans on Purim and Hanukkah and is also given to a new bride during the week before her wedding, as its color is a sign of purity. Persians frequently serve white nougat at special occasions, notably Rosh Hashanah. *Zaban* is typically served with sweetened mint tea (*naa-naa*).

ZALABIA

Zalabia is a deep-fried pastry commonly known as funnel cake.

Origin: Middle East

Other names: Arabic: *zalabiya, zelabiya, zelebi*; Farsi: *zoolbia, zoolbiya, zolubiya*; India: *jalebi*; Iraq: *zengoula, zingzoola*; Kurdistan: *zülubiye*; Syria: *zinghol, zingol*; Turkey: *zulbiye*.

Funnel cakes became a mainstay of American fairs, carnivals, and ballparks in the late twentieth century, transforming a localized Pennsylvania Dutch breakfast dish into a national snack. The concept of "funnel cake," however, actually dates back to the early medieval Persian and Arabic worlds, where similar yeast-risen dishes were first prepared and later spread to Europe. German immigrants brought the yeast dish to America, originally called *drechter kuche*, and around 1879 developed the baking powder version along with its new name, funnel cake. Unlike the Pennsylvania Dutch version, the Middle Eastern funnel cake was a special treat, not breakfast fare.

There were two widespread deep-fried yeast-dough dishes in the medieval Muslim lands: one consisted of simple balls of regular loose yeast dough (*lokma*, what Sephardim called *bimuelos*), and the other was a more elaborate version made by drizzling a runny batter into hot oil in an overlapping stream to create lacy cakes. *Zalabia* (from the Farsi *zulab* "water of vitriol")date back more than a millennium. The tenth-century cookbook from Baghdad by Ibn Sayyar al-Warraq contains recipes for both *zalabiya mushabbak* (latticed fritters) and *zalabiya ghayr mushabbaka* (unlatticed fritters). In an anonymous Andulsian cookbook of the thirteenth century, there was a recipe for *"Zulabiya,"* denoting a funnel cake. The recipe directed, "Knead the flour and gradually add water to make a very loose dough." Cooks were then instructed to drop the batter into the oil by means of a "vessel with small holes in the bottom."

Variations of *zalabia* are popular in the swath of land from the Maghreb to India, the flavor and texture varying slightly from place to place based upon the type of leavening and the type of soaking syrup. The batter is not sweet, but in the typical Middle Eastern manner, the fried pastry is enrobed with a honey or sugar syrup, frequently accented with rose water, or, in a more modern manner, the pastry is sprinkled with confectioners' sugar. Some people dye the syrup a bright orange, yellow, or red, and the color then soaks into the pastries. Indians typically use a combination of rose water and saffron.

Persians frequently make these pastries with yogurt and they are crisper than the Arabic style and typically accompanied with another Persian treat, *bamieh*, deep-fried, flattened, ridged dough balls,

A thin, pourable dough makes decorative fried pastries commonly called funnel cakes in the United States, zalabia in the Middle East, and jalebi in India. They are enjoyed for Hanukkah and Purim.

akin to doughnut holes. Among Arabs, *zalabia* is a traditional sweet eaten to break the fasts of Ramadan; they are made in homes and featured at most Middle Eastern sweet shops.

The concept of funnel cakes arrived in medieval Italy, then traveled north. The Harleian Manuscript 279 (c. 1430), a collection in the British Museum, contains an early English recipe for "Cryspey," a yeast-raised form of this dish, which was prepared using the crude method of drizzling the batter into the oil with the fingers. The German work *Practisches Kochbuch fur die gewöhnliche une feinere Küche* by Henriette Davidis (1845) recorded a recipe for "Spritzkuchen," in which cooks were directed to use a syringe to "*spritz*" (squirt) a loose cream puff dough into hot oil. The modern American funnel cake developed in the late nineteenth century after the invention of baking soda and baking powder, which eliminated the need to wait for yeast to rise, a benefit that was particularly helpful for early morning fare. Indians tend to use baking powder rather than yeast to make *jalebis*.

Unlike thick doughnut dough and cream puff pastry, funnel cake batter should be thin enough to pour, but not too thin. For each pastry, the batter must be continuously poured into hot oil to form a single mass. The original Middle Eastern fried yeast cakes did not contain egg, but it is sometimes added to modern versions, contributing richness and helping to prevent the absorption of oil. As the name reflects, an early way to form the cakes was using a funnel. The Pennsylvania Dutch invented a special pitcher with a long spout to drizzle the batter.

Zalabia are traditional Middle Eastern and Indian Hanukkah and Purim treats. Kurds customarily also serve them on Tu b'Shevat. Forms of the Arabic pastry and name were adopted in modern Israel as well.

(See also Bimuelo, Doughnut, Lokma, Sfenj, and Yoyo)

🍗 MIDDLE EASTERN FUNNEL CAKES (*ZALABIA*)

ABOUT TWELVE 4-INCH CAKES   [PAREVE]

1 package (2¼ teaspoons) active dry yeast or
   1 (0.6-ounce) cake fresh yeast
2 cups warm water (105°F to 115°F for dry yeast;
   80°F to 85°F for fresh yeast), or 1¾ cups water
   and 1 large egg, lightly beaten
1 teaspoon sugar

2½ cups (12.5 ounces) unbleached all-purpose flour
¼ teaspoon table salt or ½ teaspoon kosher salt
2 teaspoons grated lemon zest, several drops of
   dissolved saffron, or several drops of orange, red,
   or yellow food coloring (optional)
Peanut or safflower oil for deep-frying
2 cups cooled *atar* (Middle Eastern Sugar Syrup,
   page 27) or ½ cup confectioners' sugar for
   dusting

1. Dissolve the yeast in ¼ cup water. Stir in the sugar and let stand until foamy, 5 to 10 minutes. In a large bowl, combine the flour and salt. Make a well in the center. Pour the yeast mixture, remaining water, and, if using, zest, into the well and beat with a wooden spoon or electric mixer until smooth and elastic, about 5 minutes. The dough will not be very thick. Cover loosely with plastic wrap or a kitchen towel or and let rise in a warm, draft-free place until nearly doubled in bulk, about 1 hour. Stir the batter down to deflate any bubbles, about 2 minutes. Cover and let rise about 30 minutes.

2. In a large, heavy skillet, such as a cast-iron skillet, heat about 1½ inches oil over medium heat to 375°F.

3. Stir the batter down to deflate any bubbles. Place some of the batter in a pastry bag fitted with a ¼- to ½-inch hole or nozzle tip or squeeze bottle with a ¼- to ½-inch nozzle tip. Moving from the center of the pan, continuously swirl the batter in a steady stream in circular motions to produce overlapping circles about 4 inches in diameter; this should take about 20 seconds. The *zalabia* should be a lacy coil. Fry, turning once, until golden brown on both sides, about 1 minute per side. Drain very briefly on a wire rack.

4. Dip the warm pastries into the cooled syrup, turning to coat on all sides, or sprinkle with confectioners' sugar. Serve immediately. Repeat with the remaining batter.

ZEMMEL

Zemmel is a bread roll made from fine wheat flour.
Origin: Germany or Austria
Other names: Austria: *semmel, wecken*; Bavaria: *semmel*; northern Germany: *brötchen*; southern Germany: *wecken*; Hungary: *zsemle*; Poland and Ukraine: *bilke, bilkele, bulke, bulkele, shtengl, weck, zemelekh, zeml*.

"*Mame hot a kreml, oyfn altn mark, beygl, broyt, un zeml, shlept zi oyf ir kark.*" ("Mother has a grocery, in the old market, bagel, bread, and *zeml*, she lugs around her neck." From the Yiddish poem "*Mayn Viglid*" [My Lullaby] by H. H. Leyvik [pseudonym of Leyvik Halpern], a native of Byelorussia.)

The bulk of the diet of eastern Ashkenazim was bread, much of it coarse black bread made from rye. For the Sabbath and as an occasional weekday treat, they enjoyed several types of bread made from white flour, frequently in the smaller bagel or roll size. The name of the roll varied depending on what part of eastern Europe they lived, but the two most common terms were *bulke* (from the Slavic *bulka* "white bread") and *zemmel*.

The Middle High German word *semel* and the Yiddish equivalent *zemmel* or *zeml*, from the Latin *simila* (finest wheat flour), means "fine wheat flour," in contradistinction to the then-more-common European coarse rye flour. Initially, *zemmel* came to mean "fine bread roll." A bread roll sprinkled with poppy seeds is a *mohnsemmel*, with caraway *kummelsemmel*, and with sesame seeds *sesamsemmel*. *Zemmel* was typically a breakfast roll, fresh from the bakery, served with butter, *quark* (*topfen* in Austria), and hot coffee. Among Ashkenazim, Semmel and Zemmel became surnames for bakers and sellers of white rolls.

In Austria, *semmel* developed a more specific denotation—a fine roll, three to four inches in diameter and about two inches high, with a crisp crust and a distinctive cleavage down the center. In parts of New England, these are known by the redundant term bulkie rolls, probably from the Yiddish *bulke*. A famous variation of this is the Kaiser roll, an Austrian hard roll so named because the top is cut to look like the emperor's crown, technically a *kaisersemmel*(*csaszarasemle in Hungary*). However, some authorities date the term *kaisersemmel* to 1487 and the Emperor Friedrich IV. A *semmel knoedle* is an Austrian dumpling made from *semmel* rolls.

In eastern Europe, *zeml* retained its original sense of a roll made from fine wheat flour. In this vein, a Yiddish proverb from Poland advises, "When one has broyt [black bread], one should not look for *zemi*" (other versions substitute *lekakh*, "cake"). To further complicate matters, *tzibele zemmel* and *zemmel pampalik* are synonyms for the eastern European *tzibele pletzlach* (onion flatbread).

ZIMTSTERN

Zimtstern is a star-shaped cinnamon cookie.

Origin: Germany

German Jews adopted a local Teutonic nut meringue known as *zimtsternen* (cinnamon stars). The nut meringue is cut into six-pointed stars, which happens to also be a Star of David (Magen David in Hebrew), a symbol that only first became widely used by Jews beginning in the seventeenth century in central Europe. Toward the end of baking, the cookie is covered with a thin layer of plain, slightly creamy meringue that contrasts in color and texture to the chewy brown bottom. The delicate dough is somewhat difficult to work with, so most housewives limited making these cookies to a few special occasions. These flourless cookies are also called *erstesternen* (first stars), an intimation of the heavenly signs indicating the end of a Jewish fast day. *Zimtsternen* are traditionally served at the meal following Yom Kippur.

🍂 GERMAN CINNAMON STARS (*ZIMTSTERNEN*)

ABOUT FIFTY 2-INCH COOKIES   [PAREVE]

3 cups (12 ounces) finely ground blanched almonds or hazelnuts

4½ teaspoons ground cinnamon

1½ teaspoons grated lemon zest or kirsch

6 tablespoons egg whites (about 3 large)

Pinch of salt

2¼ cups (9 ounces) confectioners' sugar, plus about 1 cup additional for rolling

1. Preheat the oven to 300°F. Line 2 large baking sheets with parchment paper.

2. Combine the nuts, cinnamon, and zest. In a medium bowl, beat the egg whites until foamy, about 30 seconds. Add the salt and beat until soft peaks form, 1 to 2 minutes. Gradually add the confectioners' sugar and beat until stiff and glossy, 5 to 8 minutes. Reserve one-third of the meringue in a covered container and fold the nut mixture into the remaining meringue. Cover the nut mixture with greased plastic wrap or aluminum foil and refrigerate for 1 hour.

3. Place a large piece of parchment paper or wax paper on a flat surface and sprinkle with additional confectioners' sugar. Place the nut mixture on the sugar, lightly sprinkle with more confectioners' sugar, top with a second piece of paper, and pat and roll out ¼ inch thick. Remove the top piece of wax paper. Using a cookie cutter dipped in confectioners' sugar, cut into 2-inch star shapes or use a sharp knife to cut into diamonds. Reroll any scraps and cut. Using a thin spatula, place on the prepared baking sheets about ½-inch apart.

4. Bake until set and lightly browned, about 20 minutes.

5. Spread the reserved meringue over the tops of the cookies and bake until the tops are lightly colored, about 5 minutes. Transfer the cookies to a wire rack and let cool. The *zimtsternen* taste best if allowed to stand, covered, for 24 hours. Store in an airtight container at room temperature for up to 3 weeks.

ZVINGOUS

Zvingous is a deep-fried ball of *masa escaldada* (boiled dough).

Origin: Spain

Other names: France and Maghreb: beignet; Greece: *loukoumades, zvingoi*; Italy: *frittelle di pasta soffiata, zeppole*; Ladino: *bimuelo, bola de miel, burmuelo*; Syria: *zengol*; Turkey: *tulumba tatlisi*.

The practice of frying pastries made from cooked flour (*panada*) dates back to at least Roman times, but was forgotten in Europe with the collapse of the Roman empire. Beginning in the early medieval period, the Moors and Sephardim deep-fried balls of lean yeast dough and a rudimentary cooked dough, which was the forerunner of the Spanish *masa escaldada* (boiled dough). This simple mixture of flour, salt, boiling water, and olive oil was used to make fried pastries, such as *churros* (long, ridged fritters). Sephardic immigrants may have brought the concept of cooked dough to Italy. In turn, in 1533, Catherine de Médicis of Florence arrived in France to marry Prince Henri, accompanied by her Italian chefs, who introduced their culinary advances, including what the French called *pâte à chaud* (hot paste). Around the same time, chickens were becoming more widespread in Europe, and the increasing supply of eggs led to the transformation of this simple flour paste into a more versatile batter.

The leavening agent in cooked pastry dough is steam. As the balls of dough are heated, steam forms and pushes the batter upward and outward, producing a puffed, hollow shell, as in a cream puff. According to legend, Catherine's Italian head chef, Panterelli, was the first person to make the leap of adding eggs in 1540

and he named the resulting pastry *pâte à Panterelli*. French chefs refined the original recipe and the name eventually changed to the current *pâte à choux* (*choux* is French for "cabbage," a reference to the appearance of the puffs). Italians refer to it as *pasta soffiata* (blown batter) and Americans call it "cream puff dough" after the pastry most commonly made from it.

Since at the time, few homes except those of the upper class possessed an oven, the easiest way for most housewives to cook this dough was by frying and the best way to fry the dough was as small balls. Most Sephardim in Turkey and Greece adopted a term used by Romaniotes (Jews whose ancestors lived in Greece before the arrival of the Sephardim), *zvingous*, derived from the Arabic *isfenj* (sponge); the term probably originally referred to a Byzantine fried pastry and is sometimes used to denote deep-fried yeast-raised balls (*lokma*).

To make the most popular Turkish variation of this pastry, cooks pipe two- to three-inch-long logs of dough through a ridged tip, forming a shape reminiscent of a *tulumba* (kettledrum). Today, Turks even manufacture a dessert machine to mass-produce *tulumba*. Greeks prefer small globes made by dropping the batter from a spoon.

In the Middle Eastern manner, the fried balls are dipped into a honey or sugar syrup, while the French serve them with warm jam or filled with pastry cream. Cooks add a little more flour to *zvingous* dough than is typical for cream puff dough, producing a sturdier pastry that will not dissolve in the syrup. The dough is not made with much sugar, as too much sugar results in overbrowning.

These pastries are a traditional Hanukkah treat, also known in Ladino as *zvingous de januca* (of Hanukkah), and, in honey syrup, popular for Rosh Hashanah. A Passover version is made by substituting matza cake meal for the flour. After a baked version of *zvingous* was mentioned in a 1999 *New York Times* Hanukkah article, the pastry suddenly earned attention among Americans.

(See also Bimuelo, Doughnut, and Lokma)

᚛ SEPHARDIC BEIGNETS (*ZVINGOUS*)

ABOUT 24 MEDIUM OR 36 SMALL FRITTERS [PAREVE OR DAIRY]

    1 cup water

    3 tablespoons olive oil or unsalted butter

    1 teaspoon sugar

½ teaspoon table salt or 1 teaspoon kosher salt

1½ cups (7.5 ounces) high-gluten flour, sifted; or 1¼ cups unbleached all-purpose flour and ¼ cup fine semolina; or 1½ cups matza cake meal

1 teaspoon grated orange and/or lemon zest (optional)

4 large eggs, at room temperature (¾ cup)

Vegetable, sunflower, or peanut oil for deep-frying

½ cup confectioners' sugar, cinnamon-sugar (⅔ cup sugar mixed with 2 teaspoons ground cinnamon), or 1 cup *atar* (Middle Eastern Sugar Syrup, page 27)

1. In a medium saucepan, bring the water, oil, sugar, and salt to a rapid boil over medium heat. Remove from the heat, add the flour all at once, and stir with a wooden spoon until the mixture leaves the sides of the pan and forms a ball, about 1 minute. Return to the heat and cook on low heat, stirring, until the dough dries slightly, about 1 minute. Let cool slightly, about 10 minutes. If using, add the zest.

2. Beat in the eggs, one at a time, beating well after each addition. The batter should be soft yet stiff enough to retain its shape. It is ready when it drops with difficulty from a spoon. Let cool completely, at least 30 minutes.

3. In a large pot, heat at least 1½ inches oil over medium heat to 375°F.

4. Dip a tablespoon or teaspoon into the hot oil. In batches, drop the batter by spoonfuls from the oiled spoon into the oil, using a second spoon to scrape it off, and fry, turning, until puffed and golden, 2 to 4 minutes. Remove with a wire-mesh skimmer or tongs and drain on a wire rack.

5. Sprinkle the beignets with confectioners' sugar or dip hot ones into the cooled syrup or cooled puffs into hot syrup. Serve warm.

ZWETSCHGENKUCHEN

Zwetschgenkuchen is a cross between a cake and a tart made with Italian prune plums.

Origin: central Europe

Other names: *pflaumenkuchen*; Bavaria: *zwetsch-gendatschi*; Hungary: *szilvaslepeny*; Rhineland-Palatinate: *Quetschekuche.*

Humphrey Bogart personified cool and there was no question that he was a star; the American Film Institute named him the top male star of the twentieth century. Ironically, the New York–born actor, married to Lauren Bacall (née Betty Perske and first cousin of Israeli president Shimon Peres), owed part of his unforgettable mannerisms to an unusual source, plum kuchen. During his career, Bogie starred in numerous classic movies, most notably *The African Queen, To Have and Have Not, The Caine Mutiny, The Maltese Falcon*, and *Casablanca*. During breaks in the filming of the latter, released in 1942, he frequently enjoyed his favorite food, plum cake. There was one problem—tiny pieces of plum got stuck in his teeth. Naturally, this was particularly perturbing to his costar, Ingrid Bergman, during the kissing scenes. The dark dots of plum were also conspicuously showing up on camera. Finally, the exasperated director, Michael Curtiz, yelled out, "Cut! Cut! For Christ's sake Humphrey, you got bits of plum cake stuck in your teeth again. It simply ain't romantic!" Bogart reluctantly reduced his plum cake consumption for the remainder of the shoot, but began to frequently pull his upper lip over his teeth, in the habit of covering up any seeds in his teeth. After a while, the director, running behind schedule, despaired of curing Bogart of his twitches and left them in the film. The audience actually favored the new idiosyncrasy and it became one of the actor's trademarks. And plum cake remained his favorite.

At the end of the summer, tarts and cakes made from fresh seasonal Italian plums are widespread in bakeries and homes throughout central Europe; most popular of all is a combination of *blechkuchen* (sheet cake) and *obstkuchen* (fruit topped cake) called *zwetschgenkuchen*. *Zwetschge* is the German word for "Italian plum," equivalent to the French *quetsche*, while *pflaume* is the generic German for "plum." Some of the best European plums come from Baden in southwest Germany and Alsace. This dish could just as easily have been entitled "Alsatian plum cake" or "Viennese plum cake," as it enjoys great popularity in southern Germany, Alsace, Austria, the Czech Republic, Hungary, and northern Switzerland.

The original and still most widespread version of *zwetschgenkuchen* is a rectangular *blechkuchen* made with a relatively thin layer of rich yeast dough (*feine hefeteig*) pressed into a large baking sheet. A more recent tart version substitutes *mürbeteig*, a moist, crumbly, buttery pastry, and baked in a round pan, for the yeast dough. Although Americans overwhelmingly prefer sloped-sided pies, Europeans favor the more versatile pastry made in straight-sided, flat-bottomed pans. Whether made from yeast dough or short pastry, the plums densely cover the surface of the kuchen. Italian prune plums, also called Fellenberg, release less liquid and hold their shape better than other varieties during baking. The tart-sweet fruit with just hint of cinnamon (many modern versions sprinkle the fruit with streusel) provides an intriguing contrast to the rich, pastry.

In many Alsatian and central European families, *zwetschgenkuchen* is a popular Rosh Hashanah and Sukkot dessert, making use of the seasonal Italian plums. But it is also enjoyed for a gratifying seasonal snack. Fresh apricots are substituted for the plums earlier in the summer and apples during the fall and winter, but plum is by far the favorite *obstkuchen*. These fruit cakes are among the beloved comfort foods of central European Jews, like *oma* (grandma) used to make.

(See also Kuchen)

❧ GERMAN PLUM CAKE (*ZWETSCHGENKUCHEN*)

ONE 15½ BY 10½-INCH CAKE   [DAIRY OR PAREVE]

Dough:

- 1 package (2 ¼ teaspoons) active dry yeast or 1 (0.6-ounce) cake fresh yeast
- 1 cup warm milk or water (105°F to 115°F for dry yeast; 80°F for fresh yeast)
- ½ cup (1 stick) unsalted butter or margarine, softened
- ½ cup (3.5 ounces) sugar
- ¾ teaspoon salt
- 1 large egg, lightly beaten
- About 4 cups (20 ounces) all-purpose flour

Topping:

- 3 to 3½ pounds plums, preferably Italian prune plums, quartered and pitted
- ½ cup turbinado or granulated sugar
- 1½ tablespoons all-purpose flour
- ½ teaspoon ground cinnamon

1. To make the dough: Dissolve the yeast in ¼ cup milk. Stir in 1 teaspoon sugar and let stand until foamy, 5 to 10 minutes. In a large bowl, combine the yeast mixture, remaining milk, remaining sugar, butter, egg, and salt. Blend in 2 cups flour. Gradually add enough of the remaining flour to make a mixture that holds together.

2. On a lightly floured surface or in an electric mixer with a dough hook, knead the dough until smooth and springy, about 5 minutes. Place in an oiled bowl and turn to coat. Cover with plastic wrap or a kitchen towel and let rise in a warm, draft-free place until nearly doubled in bulk, about 1½ hours.

3. Preheat the oven to 375°F. Grease a 15½-by 10½-inch jelly roll pan.

4. On a lightly floured surface, roll out the dough slightly larger than the pan, then place the dough in the bottom of the pan and reaching about 1 inch up the sides.

5. To make the topping: Arrange the plums, cut side up, in rows on top of the dough, pressing slightly into the dough and slightly overlapping. Combine the sugar, flour, and cinnamon and sprinkle over the plums Let stand for 15 minutes

6. Bake until the fruit is tender and the pastry is golden brown, 25 to 35 minutes. Place the pan on a wire rack and let the cake cool for at least 10 minutes. Serve warm or at room temperature. *Zwetschgenkuchen* is best the day it is made.

BIBLIOGRAPHY

The Encyclopedia of Jewish Food is a compilation of knowledge I have accrued throughout my life, and I owe much debt and gratitude to the teachers and students who have shared their erudition and wisdom with me. During the course of the past three decades, I created a database of information on Judaism and food; in the process I read numerous books and publications, as well as interviewed a vast array of individuals, who shared their recipes, ideas, and insights.

Among the tomes I consulted were ancient and medieval Jewish texts, including the Talmud (both Babylonian c. fifth century CE and Jerusalem c. 368 CE), *Seder Rav Amram Gaon* (written in 857; the first comprehensive and systematic compilation of Jewish liturgy), and the *Shulchan Arukh* of Rabbi Joseph Caro (published in 1564 the authoritative code of law of Sephardim and, when accompanied with the glosses of Rabbi Moses Isserles, of Ashkenazim); these and various other rabbinic works provided valuable details and insights into generic and Jewish foods and culinary habits over the centuries. Many of these works are cited in specific entries in the *Encyclopedia of Jewish Food*.

This bibliography includes the most significant nonrabbinic sources, as well as the sources that will be of the most benefit to general readers, who wish to increase their understanding of Jewish history and culture.

GENERAL REFERENCES

Abrahams, Israel. *Jewish Life in the Middle Ages*. Philadelphia: Jewish Publication Society, 1961.

Adler, Elkan Nathan. *Jewish Travelers in the Middle Ages*. New York: Dover Publications, 1987.

Adler, Marcus.N. *The Itinerary of Benjamin of Tudela*. New York: Philipp Feldheim, 1907.

Alon, Gedaliah. *The Jews in Their Land in the Talmudic Age*. Cambridge, MA: Harvard University Press, 1989.

Ashtor, Eliyahu. *The Jews of Moslem Spain*. Translated by Aaron Klein and Jenny Machlowitz Klein. 3 vols. Philadelphia: Jewish Publication Society, 1979.

Baer, Yitzhak. *A History of the Jews in Christian Spain*. Philadelphia: Jewish Publication Society, 1992.

Baron, Salo Wittmayer. *The Jewish Community: Its History and Structure to the American Revolution*. 3 vols. Philadelphia: Jewish Publication Society, 1942.

Baron, Salo Wittmayer. *A Social and Religious History of the Jews*. 27 vols. New York: Columbia University Press, 1952.

Ben-Sasson, Haim H., ed. *A History of the Jewish People*. Cambridge, MA: Harvard University Press, 1969.

Bernardini, Paaolo and Norman Fiering, eds. *The Jews and the Expansion of Europe to the West 1450–1800*. Oxford: Berghahn Books, 2001.

Birmingham, Stephen. *The Grandees*. New York: Harper and Row, 1971.

Cooper, John. *Eat and Be Satisfied: A Social History of Jewish Food*. London: Jason Aronson, 1993.

Daly, Charles P., *The Settlement of Jews in North America*. New York: Phillip Crown, 1893.

Davidson, Alan. *The Oxford Companion to Food*. New York: Oxford University Press, 2006.

Dawidowicz, Lucy S. *The Golden Tradition: Jewish Life and Thought in Eastern Europe*. New York: Holt, Rinehart, and Winston, 1967.

Dobrinsky, Herbert. *A Treasury of Sephardic Laws and Customs*. New York: Ktav Publishing, 1986.

Dubnow, Simon. *History of the Jews*. 5 vols. New Jersey: A.S. Barnes, 1967.

Encyclopedia Judaica. 16 vols. Jerusalem, Israel: Keter Publishing, 1972.

Encyclopedia Talmudit (Talmudic Encyclopedia). Currently in 29 vols. Founding editor, Sholmo Yosef Zevin. Jerusalem: Yad Harav Herzog, 1942-.

Finkelstein, Louis, ed. *The Jews: Their History, Culture and Religion*. New York: Harper and Brothers, 1949.

Gerber, Jane S. *The Jews of Spain: A History of the Sephardic Experience*. New York: The Free Press, 1992.

Glückel of Hameln. Glückel of Hameln. 1646–1724. Written by Herself. Translated by Beth-Zion Abrahams. New York: T. Yoseloff, 1962.

Goitein, S.D. *Jews and Arabs: Their Contact through the Ages*, New York: Schoken, 1955.

Goitein, S.D. *A Mediterranean Society*. 6 vols. Berkley: University of California Press, 1967–1993.

Goldish, Josette. *Once Jews: Stories of Caribbean Sephardim*. Princeton: Markus Wiener, 2009.

The Jewish Encyclopedia. 12 vols. New York: Funk and Wagnalls Company, 1901–1906).

Josephus, Flavius. *The Works of Josephus, Complete and Unabridged New Updated Edition*. Translated by William Whiston. Peabody, MA: Hendrickson Publishers Inc, 1987.

Marcus, Jacob Rader. *The American Jew, 1585–1990*. Brooklyn, NY: Carlson Publishing, 1995.

Marcus, Jacob Rader. *Colonial American Jews*. Detroit: Wayne State University Press, 1970.

Marcus, Jacob Rader. *The Jew in the Medieval World: A Source Book*. Cincinnati: Sinai Press, 1938.

Margolis, Max and Alexander Marx. *History of the Jewish People*. Philadelphia: Jewish Publication Society, 1927.

Pedersen, Johannes. *Israel: Its Life and Culture*. 4 vols. in 2 books. Reprint of 1926 edition. London: Oxford University Press, 1947.

Pollack, Herman. *Jewish Folkways in Germanic Lands (1648–1806)*. Cambridge, MA: M.I.T. Press, 1971.

Robinson, Edward. *Biblical Researches in Palestine and in the Adjacent Region*. 3 vols. Boston: Crocker and Brewster, 1856.

Root, Waverly. *Food*. New York: Simon and Schuster, 1980.

Rosten, Leo. *The Joys of Yiddish*. New York: McGraw Hill, 1960.

Roth, Cecil. *The Jews in the Renaissance*. Philadelphia: Jewish Publication Society, 1959.

Sachar, Howard M. *The Course of Modern Jewish History*. New York: Dell, 1977.

Schwartz, Oded. *In Search of Plenty: A History of Jewish Food*. London: Kyle Cathie, 1992.

Shosteck, Patti. *A Lexicon of Jewish Cooking*. Chicago: Contemporary Books, 1979.

Stillman, Norman. *The Jews of Arab Lands: A History and Source Book*. Philadelphia: Jewish Publication Society, 1979

Tannahill, Reay. *Food in History*. Briarcliff Manor, NY: Stein and Day,1973.

Trachenberg, Joshua. *Jewish Magic and Superstition: A Study in Folk Religion*. New York: Antheneum, 1979.

Trager, James. *Food Chronology*. New York: Henry Holt, 1995.

Wright, Clifford A. *A Mediterranean Feast*. New York: Morrow, 1999.

Zborowski, Mark and Elizabeth Herzog. *Life Is with People: The Culture of the Shtetl*. New York: International Universities Press, 1952

Zevin, Shlomo Yosef. *The Festivals in Halacha*. New York: Mesorah Publications, 1981

Zohary, Daniel and Maria Hopf, *Domestication of Plants in the Old World*, 3rd edition. New York: Oxford University Press, 2000.

COOKBOOKS

These historical or ethnic cookbooks shed light on the cookery of various Jewish communities.

Abadi, Jennifer. *A Fistful of Lentils: Syrian-Jewish Recipes from Grandma Fritzie's Kitchen*. Boston: Harvard Common Press, 2002.

Amchanitzki, Hinde. *Lehrbukh vi azoy tsu kokhen un baken* (Textbook on How to Cook and Bake). New York: S. Druckerman, 1901. The first Yiddish cookbook published in America.

Angel, Gilda. *Sephardic Holiday Cooking*. Mount Vernon, NY: Decalogue Books, 1986.

Apicius. *Apicius de re Coquinaria*. Translated by Barbara Flower and Elisabeth Rosenbaum, Reprinted as *The Roman Cookery Book: A critical Translation of the Art of Cooking by Apicius for Use in the Study and the Kitchen*. New York: British Book Center, 1958.

Bar-David, Molly Lyons. *Jewish Cooking for Pleasure*. London: Hamlyn Publishing Group, 1967.

Bene-Israel Cookbook. Anonymous. Bombay: self-published, 1986.

Berg, Gertrude, and Myra Waldo. *The Molly Goldberg Jewish Cookbook*. New York: Doubleday, 1955.

David, Suzy. *The Sephardic Kosher Kitchen*. Middle Village, NY: Jonathan David, 1984.

de Pomiane, Edouard. *The Jews of Poland: Recollections and Recipes*. 1929. Translated by Josephine Bacon. Garden Grove, CA: Philiota Press, 1985.

Dweck, Poopa. *Aromas of Aleppo*. New York: Ecco, 2007.

Engle, Fannie, and Gertrude Blair. *The Jewish Festival Cookbook*. New York: D. McKay, 1954.

Ferris, Marcie Cohen. *Matzoh Ball Gumbo: Culinary Tales of the Jewish South*. Chapel Hill, NC: University of North Carolina Press, 2005.

Ganor, Avi, and Ron Maiberg. *A Taste of Israel: A Mediterranean Feast*. New York: Rizzoli, 1990.

Gitlitz, David M., and Linda Kay Davidson. *A Drizzle of Honey: The Lives and Recipes of Spain's Secret Jews*. New York: St. Martin's Press, 1999.

Glezer, Maggie. *A Blessing of Bread*. New York: Artisan, 2004.

Goldman, Rivka. *Mama Nazima's Jewish-Iraqi Cuisine*. New York: Hippocrene, 2006.

Goldstein, Joyce. *Cucina Ebraica: Flavors of the Italian Jewish Kitchen*. San Francisco: Chronicle Books, 1998.

Goldstein, Joyce. *Saffron Shores: Jewish Cooking of the Southern Mediterranean*. San Francisco: Chronicle Books, 2002.

Greene, Gloria Kaufer. *The Jewish Holiday Cookbook*. New York: Times Books, 1985.

Grossinger, Jennie. *The Art of Jewish Cooking*. New York: Random House, 1958.

Gur, Janna. *The Book of New Israeli Food*. Tel Aviv: Al Hashulchan, 2007.

Hyman, Mavis. *Indian-Jewish Cooking*. London: self-published, 1992.

Kander, Lizzie Black. *The Settlement Cook Book*. Milwaukee: [S.N.] 1901.

Kasdan, Sara. *Love and Knishes: An Irrepressible Guide to Jewish Cooking*. New York: Vanguard Press, 1956.

Kaufman, Sheilah. *Sephardic Israeli Cuisine: A Mediterranean Mosaic*. New York: Hippocrene, 2002.

Koerner, András. *A Taste of the Past: The Daily Life and Cooking of a Nineteenth-Century Hungarian Jewish Homemaker*. Lebanon, NH: University Press of New England, 2004.

Levi, Zion, and Hani Agabria. *The Yemenite Cookbook*. New York: Seaver Books, 1988.

Levy, Emilie de Vidas. *Sephardic Cookery*. New York: Central Sephardic Jewish Community of America, 1983.

Levy, Esther Jacobs. *Jewish Cookery Book, On Principles of Economy*. New York: Arno Press, 1975. First published in Philadelphia in 1871; the first Jewish cookbook published in America.

Levy, Faye. *Faye Levy's International Jewish Cookbook*. New York: Warner Books, 1991.

Levy, Faye. *1,000 Jewish Recipes*. Hoboken, NJ: John Wiley and Sons, 2000.

Machlin, Edda Servi. *The Classic Cuisine of Italian Jews*. New York: Dodd, Mead, 1981).

Marks, Copeland. *Sephardic Cooking*. New York: Donald I. Fine, 1992.

Montefiore, Lady Judith Cohen. *The Jewish Manual, or Practical Information in Jewish and Modern Cookery with a Collection of Valuable Recipes and Hints Relating to the Toilette, Edited by a Lady*. London, 1846.

Nash, Helen. *Kosher Cuisine*. New York: Random House, 1979.

Nasrallah, Nawal. *Annals of the Caliph's Kitchens: Ibn Sayyar al-Warraq's Tenth-century Baghdadhi Cookbook*. Leiden, The Netherlands: Brill, 2007.

Perry, Charles, trans. *An Anonymous Andalusian Cookbook of the 13th Century*. In *A Collection of Medieval and Renaissance Cookery Books*. Vol. 2. Edited by David Friedman (Sir Cariadoc of the Bow). Published privately, 1992.

Perry, Charles. *A Baghdad Cookery Book*. Devon, UK: Prospect Books, 2006. This is a translation of *Kitab al-Tabikh* by Al-Baghdadi, Muhammad ibn al-Hasan. Baghdad, 1226. An earlier translation of was work was by A. J. Arberry. Reprinted as *A Baghdad Cookery Book*. *Islamic Culture* 13 (1939): 21–47, 189–214.

Roden, Claudia. *The Book of Jewish Food*. New York: Alfred A. Knopf, 1997.

Sasson, Grace. *Kosher Syrian Cooking*. Self-published, 1958.

Shenker, Israel. *Noshing Is Sacred*. Indianapolis: Bobbs-Merrill, 1979.

Sheraton, Mimi. *From My Mother's Kitchen*. New York: Harper Collins, 1991.

Sirkis, Ruth. *A Taste of Tradition: The How and Why of Jewish Cooking*. Lynbrook, NY: Gefen Books, 1996.

Sisterhood of Mikve Israel-Emanuel, comp. *Recipes from the Jewish Kitchens of Curaçao*. Netherlands Antilles: Sisterhood of Mikve Israel-Emanuel, 1982.

Stavroulakis, Nicholas. *Cookbook of the Jews of Greece*. New York: Cadmus Press, 1986.

Stolz, Josef. *Kochbuch für Israeliten, oder prakt. Unweisung, wie man nach den juedischen Religionsgruenden alle Gattungen der feinsten Speisen kauscher bereitet*, Carlsruhe: 1815. The first known Jewish cookbook.

Twena, Pamela Grau. *The Sephardic Table: The Vibrant Cooking of the Mediterranean Jews*. New York: Houghton Mifflin Harcourt, 1998.

Wolfert, Paula. *Mediterranean Cooking*. Rev. ed. New York: William Morrow, 1994.

INDEX